A Companion to Ancient Philosophy

32.83
Phil

D0731751

San Diego Christian College
2100 Greenfield Drive
El Cajon, CA 92019

Blackwell Companions to Philosophy

This outstanding student reference series offers a comprehensive and authoritative survey of philosophy as a whole. Written by today's leading philosophers, each volume provides lucid and engaging coverage of the key figures, terms, topics, and problems of the field. Taken together, the volumes provide the ideal basis for course use, representing an unparalleled work of reference for students and specialists alike.

Already published in the series:

1. The Blackwell Companion to Philosophy, Second Edition
   Edited by Nicholas Bunnin and Eric Tsui-James

2. A Companion to Ethics
   Edited by Peter Singer

3. A Companion to Aesthetics
   Edited by David Cooper

4. A Companion to Epistemology
   Edited by Jonathan Dancy and Ernest Sosa

5. A Companion to Contemporary Political Philosophy (two-volume set), Second Edition
   Edited by Robert E. Goodin and Philip Pettit

6. A Companion to Philosophy of Mind
   Edited by Samuel Guttenplan

7. A Companion to Metaphysics
   Edited by Jaegwon Kim and Ernest Sosa

8. A Companion to Philosophy of Law and Legal Theory
   Edited by Dennis Patterson

9. A Companion to Philosophy of Religion
   Edited by Philip L. Quinn and Charles Taliaferro

10. A Companion to the Philosophy of Language
    Edited by Bob Hale and Crispin Wright

11. A Companion to World Philosophies
    Edited by Eliot Deutsch and Ron Bontekoe

12. A Companion to Continental Philosophy
    Edited by Simon Critchley and William Schroeder

13. A Companion to Feminist Philosophy
    Edited by Alison M. Jaggar and Iris Marion Young

14. A Companion to Cognitive Science
    Edited by William Bechtel and George Graham

15. A Companion to Bioethics
    Edited by Helga Kuhse and Peter Singer

16. A Companion to the Philosophers
    Edited by Robert L. Arrington

17. A Companion to Business Ethics
    Edited by Robert E. Frederick

18. A Companion to the Philosophy of Science
    Edited by W. H. Newton-Smith

19. A Companion to Environmental Philosophy
    Edited by Dale Jamieson

20. A Companion to Analytic Philosophy
    Edited by A. P. Martinich and David Sosa

21. A Companion to Genethics
    Edited by Justine Burley and John Harris

22. A Companion to Philosophical Logic
    Edited by Dale Jacquette

23. A Companion to Early Modern Philosophy
    Edited by Steven Nadler

24. A Companion to Philosophy in the Middle Ages
    Edited by Jorge J. E. Gracia and Timothy B. Noone

25. A Companion to African-American Philosophy
    Edited by Tommy L. Lott and John P. Pittman

26. A Companion to Applied Ethics
    Edited by R. G. Frey and Christopher Heath Wellman

27. A Companion to the Philosophy of Education
    Edited by Randall Curren

28. A Companion to African Philosophy
    Edited by Kwasi Wiredu

29. A Companion to Heidegger
    Edited by Hubert L. Dreyfus and Mark A. Wrathall

30. A Companion to Rationalism
    Edited by Alan Nelson

31. A Companion to Ancient Philosophy
    Edited by Mary Louise Gill and Pierre Pellegrin

32. A Companion to Pragmatism
    Edited by John R. Shook and Joseph Margolis

33. A Companion to Nietzsche
    Edited by Keith Ansell Pearson

34. A Companion to Socrates
    Edited by Sara Ahbel-Rappe and Rachana Kamtekar

35. A Companion to Phenomenology and Existentialism
    Edited by Hubert L. Dreyfus and Mark A. Wrathall

36. A Companion to Kant
    Edited by Graham Bird

37. A Companion to Plato
    Edited by Hugh H. Benson

38. A Companion to Descartes
    Edited by Janet Broughton and John Carriero

39. A Companion to the Philosophy of Biology
    Edited by Sahotra Sarkar and Anya Plutynski

40. A Companion to Hume
    Edited by Elizabeth S. Radcliffe

41. A Companion to the Philosophy of History and Historiography
    Edited by Aviezer Tucker

Forthcoming

42. A Companion to Aristotle
    Edited by Georgios Anagnostopoulos

43. A Companion to Philosophy of Literature
    Edited by Jost and Hagberg

44. A Companion to Schopenhauer
    Edited by Bart Vandenabeele

45. A Companion to the Philosophy of Technology
    Edited by Jan-Kyrre Berg Olsen, Stig Andur Pedersen and Vincent F. Hendricks

46. A Companion to Relativism
    Edited by Steven D. Hales

180
C737a

*Blackwell Companions
to Philosophy*

A Companion to
Ancient Philosophy

Edited by

Mary Louise Gill and Pierre Pellegrin

WILEY-BLACKWELL

A John Wiley & Sons, Ltd., Publication

This paperback edition first published 2009
© 2009 Blackwell Publishing Ltd
Edition history: Blackwell Publishing Ltd (hardback, 2006)

Blackwell Publishing was acquired by John Wiley & Sons in February 2007. Blackwell's publishing program has been merged with Wiley's global Scientific, Technical, and Medical business to form Wiley-Blackwell.

Registered Office
John Wiley & Sons Ltd, The Atrium, Southern Gate, Chichester, West Sussex, PO19 8SQ, United Kingdom

Editorial Offices
350 Main Street, Malden, MA 02148-5020, USA
9600 Garsington Road, Oxford, OX4 2DQ, UK
The Atrium, Southern Gate, Chichester, West Sussex, PO19 8SQ, UK

For details of our global editorial offices, for customer services, and for information about how to apply for permission to reuse the copyright material in this book please see our website at www.wiley.com/wiley-blackwell.

The right of Mary Louise Gill and Pierre Pellegrin to be identified as the authors of the editorial material in this work has been asserted in accordance with the Copyright, Designs and Patents Act 1988.

All rights reserved. No part of this publication may be reproduced, stored in a retrieval system, or transmitted, in any form or by any means, electronic, mechanical, photocopying, recording or otherwise, except as permitted by the UK Copyright, Designs and Patents Act 1988, without the prior permission of the publisher.

Wiley also publishes its books in a variety of electronic formats. Some content that appears in print may not be available in electronic books.

Designations used by companies to distinguish their products are often claimed as trademarks. All brand names and product names used in this book are trade names, service marks, trademarks or registered trademarks of their respective owners. The publisher is not associated with any product or vendor mentioned in this book. This publication is designed to provide accurate and authoritative information in regard to the subject matter covered. It is sold on the understanding that the publisher is not engaged in rendering professional services. If professional advice or other expert assistance is required, the services of a competent professional should be sought.

Library of Congress Cataloging-in-Publication Data

A companion to ancient philosophy / edited by Mary Louise Gill and Pierre Pellegrin.
  p. cm. — (Blackwell companions to philosophy)
  Includes bibliographical references and indexes.
  ISBN: 978-0-631-21061-0 (hardcover : alk. paper), ISBN: 978-1-4051-8834-0 (paperback : alk. paper) 1. Philosophy, Ancient. I. Gill, Mary Louise, 1950– II. Pellegrin, Pierre, 1944– III. Series.

  B111.C66 2005
  180—dc22

                                                                                            2005014100

A catalogue record for this book is available from the British Library.

Set in 10/12.5pt Photina by Graphicraft Limited, Hong Kong
Printed in Singapore by Markono Print Media Pte Ltd

01 2009

Contents

Notes on Contributors

Rachel Barney is Canada Research Chair in Classical Philosophy at the University of Toronto, and Director of its Collaborative Program in Ancient and Medieval Philosophy. She has published essays on Plato and Hellenistic epistemology and ethics, and a book on Plato's *Cratylus, Names and Nature in Plato's Cratylus* (Routledge, 2001). Her current research is focused on Plato's ethics.

Thomas Bénatouïl is Maître de conférences in Philosophy at the University of Nancy II (France). He is the author of an anthology with commentary, *Le Scepticisme* (Paris: Flammarion, 1997), and of *La Pratique du stoïcisme* (Paris: Vrin, 2006), a work on the concept of use (*chresis*) in Hellenistic Stoicism.

Gábor Betegh is Associate Professor of Philosophy at the Central European University, Budapest (Hungary). He is the author of *The Derveni Papyrus. Cosmology, Theology and Interpretation* (Cambridge, 2004) and articles on ancient cosmology, metaphysics, and theology.

Richard Bett is Professor of Philosophy and Classics at Johns Hopkins University. He is the author of *Pyrrho, His Antecedents and His Legacy* (Oxford, 2000), and of translations of Sextus Empiricus' *Against the Ethicists* (with introduction and commentary: Oxford, 1997) and *Against the Logicians* (with introduction, notes and other supporting materials: Cambridge, 2005). He has published extensively on Greek skepticism, including comparisons between ancient and modern approaches to skepticism; he has also published articles on other aspects of Hellenistic philosophy, as well as on Plato, Socrates, the Sophists, and Nietzsche.

István Bodnár is Associate Professor at the Institute of Philosophy of Eötvös University, Budapest (Hungary), and Visiting Professor at the Department of Philosophy of Central European University, Budapest. He has published essays on the Presocratics, Aristotle, and the Peripatetic tradition. Recently he edited, with William W. Fortenbaugh, a collection of articles about Eudemus of Rhodes (New Brunswick, NJ/London: Transaction Books, 2002).

Luc Brisson is Researcher at the National Center for Scientific Research (Paris), and has published widely on both Plato and Plotinus, including bibliographies, translations, and commentaries. He has also published numerous works on the history of philosophy and religion in Antiquity. He is co-editor (with J.-F. Pradeau) of an ongoing French translation of Plotinus' treatises in the Flammarion series (4 volumes have so far been published, 2001–5).

Eric Brown, Associate Professor of Philosophy at Washington University, is the author of *Stoic Cosmopolitanism* (Cambridge University Press, 2005) and several articles on various topics in ancient philosophy.

Jacques Brunschwig is Professor Emeritus of Ancient Philosophy at the University of Paris I – Panthéon – Sorbonne. He edited and translated into French Aristotle's *Topics* (vol. I, Budé series 1967; vol. II currently in progress). His main publications in English are *Papers in Hellenistic Philosophy* (Cambridge University Press, 1994) and (co-edited with G. E. R. Lloyd) *Greek Thought: A Guide to Classical Knowledge* (Harvard University Press, 2000). His main fields of interest are Aristotle and the Hellenistic schools.

Victor Caston is Professor of Philosophy at the University of Michigan. He has published on the Presocratics, Aristotle, the Stoics, and Augustine, on issues concerning the philosophy of mind. He is presently at work on a book for Cambridge University Press entitled *The Problem of Intentionality in Ancient Philosophy*.

Patricia Curd is Professor of Philosophy at Purdue University. She is the author of *The Legacy of Parmenides: Eleatic Monism and Later Presocratic Thought* (Princeton, 1998; revised edition Parmenides Publishing, 2004). Her recent work has concentrated on the Presocratics, including Anaxagoras, Empedocles, Heraclitus, Parmenides, and Gorgias. At present she is completing *Anaxagoras of Clazomenae: Fragments. Text and Translation with Testimonia, Notes, and Essays*.

Fernanda Decleva Caizzi is Professor of Ancient Philosophy at the Università degli Studi in Milan (Italy). She is the author of *Antisthenis Fragmenta, Antiphontis Tetralogiae, Pirrone: Testimonianze*. Since 1984 she has been a member of the editorial Committee of the *Corpus dei Papiri Filosofici* and currently coordinates the research group involved in the program. She has edited, and published research on, many philosophical texts by known and unknown authors preserved on papyrus.

Wolfgang Detel is Professor of Philosophy (Chair for ancient philosophy and philosophy of science) at the University of Frankfurt/Main, Germany, and has taught at Hamburg, Bielefeld, Reykjavik, Princeton, Rutgers, Pittsburgh, and Columbia/New York. He is the author of books on Plato's theory of false statements and on Pierre Gassendi's physics. In 1993, he published an introduction, German translation, and commentary on Aristotle's *Posterior Analytics* (in 2 volumes). His latest book is on Foucault's *History and Sexuality* vol. 2 (1998) (English trans.: *Foucault and Classical Antiquity*, Cambridge, 2004). He has published numerous articles on different topics, mainly on ancient philosophy, on the history and philosophy of science, and on modern semantics.

Christopher Gill is Professor of Ancient Thought at the University of Exeter. He has written *Personality in Greek Epic, Tragedy, and Philosophy: The Self in Dialogue* (1996) and *The Structured Self in Hellenistic and Roman Thought* (forthcoming) (both with Oxford University Press). He has written many papers on ancient philosophy and edited seven volumes of new essays, including (with M. M. McCabe), *Form and Argument in Late Plato* (1996). He is co-editor of the journal, *Phronesis*.

Mary Louise Gill is Professor of Philosophy and Classics at Brown University. She is the author of *Aristotle on Substance: The Paradox of Unity* (Princeton, 1989), *Plato: Parmenides*, Introduction and co-translation (with P. Ryan) (Hackett, 1996), and co-editor (with J. G. Lennox) of *Self-Motion: From Aristotle to Newton* (Princeton, 1994), and (with T. Scaltsas and D. Charles) of *Unity, Identity, and Explanation in Aristotle's Metaphysics* (Oxford, 1994).

Philippe Hoffmann is Director of Studies and Chair of Religious Studies at the École Pratique des Hautes Études (Paris). His research focuses on the Neoplatonic comment-aries of late Antiquity (the manuscript tradition and the history of doctrine). He is the author of studies on the general principles of exegesis and pedagogical thought of the Neoplatonists, on doctrinal aspects of Simplicius' commentaries on the *Categories* and *De Caelo*, and he currently directs research on reason and faith in Neoplatonism (Proclus, Simplicius).

Edward Hussey is a Fellow of All Souls College Oxford. His publications include *The Presocratics* (Duckworth, 1972), *Aristotle Physics III–IV* (Oxford, 1983) and essays on many aspects of early Greek philosophy and of Aristotle.

Katerina Ierodiakonou is Assistant Professor in the Department of Humanities at the National Technical University of Athens. She has edited two collections of articles: *Topics in Stoic Philosophy* (Oxford, 1999) and *Byzantine Philosophy and its Ancient Sources* (Oxford, 2002). Her recent articles include: "Aristotle's Use of Examples in the *Prior Analytics*," *Phronesis* (2002), and "Ancient Thought Experiments: A First Approach," *Ancient Philosophy* (2005). She is currently writing a book on ancient theories of color and color-perception.

David Keyt has for many years been a professor of philosophy at the University of Washington in Seattle. While on leave from that post he has also taught at Cornell University, the University of Hong Kong, Princeton University, and the Los Angeles and Irvine campuses of the University of California, and held research appointments at the Institute for Research in the Humanities at the University of Wisconsin, the Center for Hellenic Studies in Washington, DC, the Institute for Advanced Study at Princeton, and the Social Philosophy and Policy Center at Bowling Green State University. He is the author of *Aristotle Politics Books V and VI* (Clarendon Press, 1999) and co-editor with Fred D. Miller, Jr. of *A Companion to Aristotle's Politics* (Blackwell, 1991).

Melissa Lane is University Lecturer in History and a Fellow of King's College at Cam-bridge University, where she received her PhD in philosophy. Her books include *Method and Politics in Plato's Statesman* (Cambridge, 1998) and *Plato's Progeny: How Socrates and Plato Still Captivate the Modern Mind* (Duckworth, 2001). She is an Associate Editor of the *Cambridge History of Greek and Roman Political Thought* (2000) as well as a contributor to the *Cambridge History of Twentieth Century Political Thought* (2003) and a Syndic of Cambridge University Press.

James G. Lennox is Professor of History and Philosophy of Science and Director, Center for Philosophy of Science at the University of Pittsburgh. His research specialties include Ancient Greek philosophy, science and medicine and Charles Darwin and Darwinism, with a focus on philosophical issues related to the life sciences. He is author of *Aristotle's Philosophy of Biology* (Cambridge, 2001) and *Aristotle on the Parts of Animals I–IV* (Oxford, 2001); and co-editor of *Philosophical Issues in Aristotle's Biology* (Cambridge, 1987); *Self-Motion From Aristotle to Newton* (Princeton, 1994); and *Concepts, Theories, and Rationality in the Biological Sciences* (Pittsburgh and Konstanz, 1995).

Carlos Lévy is a specialist in Hellenistic and Roman philosophy. He is the author of *Cicero Academicus* (Rome: 1992) and *Les philosophies hellénistiques* (Paris: 1998). He has edited many collective works on the thought of this period. In 1993 he created the Center for the Study of Hellenistic and Roman Philosophy at the University of Paris XII and he is currently Professor at the University of Paris IV – Sorbonne.

Jørgen Mejer has taught classics at the University of Copenhagen since the early 1970s and has been a guest professor at various American universities and at Nankai University, China. He was Director of the Danish Institute at Athens 2001–3. He has published books on Presocratic philosophy and history of philosophy in antiquity, and written extensively on Greek and Latin literature. He has also translated Greek tragedies for The Royal Danish Theatre in Copenhagen.

Deborah K. W. Modrak is a Professor of Philosophy at the University of Rochester. Her publications include: *Aristotle. The Power of Perception* (1987) and *Aristotle's Theory of Language and Meaning* (2001).

Pierre-Marie Morel is Maître de conférences in Philosophy at the University of Paris I – Panthéon – Sorbonne. His specialties include ancient atomism and Epicureanism and the natural philosophy and psychology of Aristotle. His books include *Démocrite et la recherche des causes* (Paris, 1996), *Atome et nécessité: Démocrite, Épicure, Lucrèce* (Paris, 2000), a translation with notes on Aristotle's *Parva naturalia* (Paris, 2000), and a general book, *Aristote. Une philosophie de l'activité* (Paris, 2003).

Donald R. Morrison is Professor of Philosophy and Classical Studies at Rice University. His current research interests include Socrates, ancient political philosophy, and late ancient conceptions of philosophical method. Recent publications on Socrates include: "Tyrannie et royauté selon le Socrate de Xenophon," *Études philosophiques* (2004); "Some Central Elements of Socratic Political Theory," *Polis* (2001); and "On the Alleged Historical Reliability of Plato's *Apology*," *Archiv für Geschichte der Philosophie* (2000).

Alexander P. D. Mourelatos, is Professor of Philosophy and Classics at The University of Texas at Austin, where he founded and for 25 years directed the Joint

Classics-Philosophy Graduate Program in Ancient Philosophy. He is the author of *The Route of Parmenides* (1970) and editor of *The Pre-Socratics: A Collection of Critical Essays* (Princeton University Press, 1993). Articles of his have appeared in journals and in essay collections in the fields of classics, philosophy, history and philosophy of science, linguistics, and in major encyclopedias and dictionaries.

Ian Mueller is Professor of Philosophy Emeritus at the University of Chicago. He is the author of *Philosophy of Mathematics and Deductive Structure in Euclid's "Elements"* (MIT, 1981), and the translator (with Josiah Gould) of the commentary on Aristotle's *Prior Analytics* i.8–22 written by Alexander of Aphrodisias (Cornell, 1999), and of Simplicius' commentary on Book II of Aristotle's *De Caelo* (Cornell, 2004, 2005).

Noburu Notomi is Associate Professor of Philosophy, Keio University, Japan, having received his MA in Philosophy from Tokyo University and his PhD in Classics from Cambridge University. He is the author of *The Unity of Plato's Sophist: Between the Sophist and the Philosopher* (Cambridge, 1999; Japanese translation, Nagoya University Press, 2002). He is the author of a number of articles on Plato, and is currently working on the Sophists and the Socratics.

Michael Pakaluk is Associate Professor of Philosophy at Clark University in Worcester, Massachusetts. The author of the Clarendon Aristotle commentary on *Nicomachean Ethics* VIII and IX (Oxford, 1998), and of *Aristotle's Nicomachean Ethics: An Introduction* (Cambridge, 2005), he has published numerous articles in ancient philosophy, political philosophy, and the history of philosophy generally. He is currently Director of the Boston Area Colloquium in Ancient Philosophy.

Pierre Pellegrin is Researcher at the National Center for Scientific Research (Paris), and has had visiting teaching positions in the US and Canada, at Princeton, Rutgers, and Montreal. He has published mainly on Aristotle's natural philosophy (and in particular Aristotelian biology), Aristotle's politics, history of ancient medicine and ancient Skepticism. He is the author of *La Classification des animaux chez Aristote* (1982, English trans.: *Classification of Animals*, University of California Press, 1986). His works also include translations of Aristotle, Galen, and Sextus Empiricus.

Terry Penner did his apprenticeship as an analytical philosopher studying Plato and Aristotle at Oxford with Ryle, Owen, and Ackrill and at Princeton, where he was Gregory Vlastos's junior colleague. He taught Philosophy for 34 years (and, later on, Greek) at the University of Wisconsin-Madison. His main interests are Socratic Ethics, Platonic metaphysics, Frege, and modern analytical philosophy. In the winter term of 2005, he was Visiting Leventis Research Professor of Greek at the University of Edinburgh.

Jean-François Pradeau teaches the history of ancient philosophy at the University of Nanterre (Paris X – Nanterre) and is a member of the Institut Universitaire de France. His research and publications mainly concern Plato's philosophy and the Platonic tradition. He is the founder and present editor of *Études Platoniciennes* (Paris, Les Belles

Lettres) and author of a study of Plotinus' philosophy: *L'imitation du principe. Plotin et la procession* (Paris: Vrin, 2003). He is co-editor (with L. Brisson) of an ongoing French translation of Plotinus' treatises in the Flammarion series (4 volumes have so far been published, 2001–5).

Robert W. Sharples is Professor of Classics at University College London. He is the author of a general book on Hellenistic philosophy (*Stoics, Epicureans and Sceptics*, London: Routledge, 1996). His research interests are especially in the Aristotelian tradition; he has published commentaries on the physical and biological fragments of Theophrastus, and several volumes of translations of works by Alexander of Aphrodisias, most recently of the *Supplement to the Book on the Soul*, based on a new edition of the Greek text which is currently being prepared for publication. His other major current projects are a collaborative edition of part of the *Problems* variously attributed to Alexander or to Aristotle, and a new edition of the fragments of Strato.

Marco Zambon is Researcher at the History Department of the University of Padua (Italy); in addition to several articles and essays on the Platonic philosophy of the Imperial age, he published in 2002 a volume entitled *Porphyre et le moyen-platonisme* (Paris: Vrin).

Acknowledgments

This project has been long in the making, and many people have helped along the way. Michael Frede gave us sage advice about the contents early on in the project. Andrea Falcon and David Sedley contributed to the translation of Fernanda Decleva Caizzi's paper from Italian. Mark Possanza answered queries about chronology and the study of ancient books. Kurt Raaflaub and Alan Boegehold gave us advice about maps. We are grateful to all these people and especially to David Yates, who carefully checked the Chronology and saved us from many errors.

For more technical help, we thank Eleanor Thum and Carol O'Malley for vital assistance in the final preparation of the manuscript. We also thank the Blackwell editors, and particularly Jeff Dean and Danielle Descoteaux, for their advice and patience in seeing the project through its various stages. We are very grateful to Mervyn Thomas for his expert work in the homestretch. We both appreciated his efficient copy-editing, his kindness, and wit.

Two people, Adam Rachlis and Paul Coppock, deserve special thanks. Adam Rachlis was a Research Assistant on this project at Brown University in the spring and summer, 2003. In that role he read and wrote detailed comments on drafts of many of the papers. We hope that our book will be useful to a number of audiences. The book aims to make a contribution to scholarship in ancient philosophy, but it also aims to enable non-specialists and newcomers to the field to learn about the subject generally or to find their way into areas they have not previously explored. Adam was in many ways an ideal reader – an upper level undergraduate Philosophy concentrator, not specializing in ancient philosophy but with a keen interest in learning about the subject. He wrote comments on the papers from that perspective, and authors found them very useful in revising their papers. Paul Coppock translated seven of the papers in this volume from French into English (chapters 13, 21, 23, 24, 25, 31, and 34). He also contributed his editorial and philosophical expertise throughout the final editing stages of the volume. He is responsible for the general index. We are very grateful to them.

M. L. G. and P. P.

Abbreviations

Modern Works and Editions

ANRW   Haase, W. (ed.). (1972–). *Aufstieg und Niedergang der römischen Welt*. Berlin: de Gruyter.

CAG   Commentaria in Aristotelem Graeca. (1882–1909). (23 vols.). Berlin: Reimer.

DK   Diels, H. (1951–2). *Die Fragmente der Vorsokratiker*. (3 vols.). 6th edn., revised by W. Kranz and often reprinted. Berlin: Weidmann. (Original work published 1903.)

EK   Edelstein, L. and Kidd, I. G. (eds). (1988–99). *Posidonius: The Fragments*. (3 vols.). 2nd edn. Cambridge: Cambridge University Press.

K   Kühn, K. G. (ed.). (1821–33). Galen. *Opera omnia*. Medicorum Graecorum opera quae exstant. (20 vols.) Leipzig: Cnobloch. Repr. Hildesheim: Olms, 1964–5.

KRS   Kirk, G. S., Raven, J. E., and Schofield, M. (1983). *The Presocratic Philosophers*. 2nd edn. Cambridge: Cambridge University Press.

LS   Long, A. A. and Sedley, D. N. (1987). *The Hellenistic Philosophers*. (2 vols.). Cambridge: Cambridge University Press.

SVF   von Arnim, J. (1903–24). *Stoicorum Veterum Fragmenta*. (3 vols.). vol. 4: indexes by M. Adler. Leipzig: Teubner.

Abbreviations for Ancient Authors and Texts can be found in the Index Locorum.

Chronology

History	Philosophy	Sciences, Arts, Religion
776–490 BCE: Archaic Period		776 BCE: First celebration of the Olympic games
753 BCE: Traditional founding of Rome		c. 750–725 BCE?: Homeric poems fl. c. 700 BCE: Hesiod
		Early or mid 7th century BCE: Archilochus (poet) Mid to late 7th century: Alcman (poet) b. 630 BCE: Sappho (poet)
594/3 BCE: Solon, chief archon in Athens	fl. 600–550 BCE: Thales of Miletus d. 547+ BCE: Anaximander of Miletus fl. 546–525 BCE: Anaximenes of Miletus	585 BCE: eclipse predicted by Thales fl. 544 BCE: Pherecydes of Syros
561/0–556/5; 550/49; 540/39–528/7 BCE: 3 periods of Peisistratus' rule in Athens	c. 570–478 BCE: Xenophanes of Colophon c. 570–490 BCE: Pythagoras of Samos (migrated to Croton c. 530 BCE).	560–480 BCE: Hecataeus of Miletus (made map of the world; participated in Ionian Revolt 499 BCE)
c. 524–459 BCE: Themistocles (statesman) 521–486 BCE: Darius king of Persia 508/7 BCE: Cleisthenes' political reforms in Athens	fl. c. 490 BCE: Heraclitus of Ephesus *515–440s BCE: Parmenides of Elea	525/4–456/5 BCE: Aeschylus (tragic poet) 518–446+ BCE: Pindar (poet)

499 BCE: Ionian Revolt
*495–429 BCE: Pericles (statesman)

500–428 BCE: Anaxagoras
c. 492–432 BCE: Empedocles
5th century BCE: Zeno of Elea
5th century BCE: Melissus of Samos (Eleatic; participated in Samian defeat over Athens 441 BCE)

Early 5th century BCE: Hippasus of Metapontum (Pythagorean, mathematician, music theory)
*496–406 BCE: Sophocles (tragic poet)

490–323 BCE: Classical Period
490–479 BCE: Persian Wars
490 BCE: Battle of Marathon

c. 490–420 BCE: Protagoras (sophist)
c. 485–380 BCE: Gorgias (sophist)
5th century BCE: Hippias (sophist)

*485–420s BCE: Herodotus (historian)
480s–406 BCE: Euripides (tragic poet)

480 BCE: Battle of Salamis
478 BCE. Delian League established (Athenian alliance against the Persians)

c. 470–390 BCE: Philolaus (Pythagorean)
fl. 440–430 BCE: Diogenes of Apollonia

465–425 BCE: Phidias active (sculptor)

*460–403 BCE: Critias (poet, associate of Socrates and leader of the Thirty)

469–399 BCE: Socrates
fl. late 5th century BCE: Antiphon (sophist)
5th century BCE: Leucippus (atomist)
c. 460–370 BCE: Democritus of Abdera (atomist)

c. 469–399 BCE: Hippocrates of Chios (mathematician)
460s–399+ BCE: Theodorus of Cyrene (mathematician)
c. 460–370 BCE?: Hippocrates of Cos (medicine)
460/55–400 BCE: Thucydides (historian)

451/0–404/3 BCE: Alcibiades

c. 450–380 or early 360s BCE: Euclides (Socratic/Megarian)

459/8–*380 BCE: Lysias (orator)
*450–386 BCE: Aristophanes (comic poet)
2nd half 5th century BCE: Oinipides of Chios (mathematician)

443–429 BCE: Pericles general of Athens

*445–365 BCE: Antisthenes (Socratic/Cynic)

447–432 BCE: Construction of Parthenon
438 BCE: Statue of Athena Parthenos by Phidias

431–404 BCE: Peloponnesian War

c. 430–355 BCE: Aristippus (Socratic/Cyrenaic)
429–347 BCE: Plato

436–338 BCE: Isocrates (orator, teacher)
*430–355+ BCE: Xenophon (historian)

420s BCE?: Treatise contained in Derveni Papyrus (Orphic)

411–410 BCE: Rule of Four Hundred in Athens
404–403 BCE: Rule of Thirty Tyrants in Athens

412/03–324/21 BCE: Diogenes of Sinope (the Cynic)

*415–369 BCE: Theaetetus (mathematician)

399 BCE: Trial and execution of Socrates

fl. c. 400–350 BCE: Archytus (Pythagorian)
400/380 BCE?: Anonymous *Dissoi Logoi*

391/0–*340 BCE: Eudoxus (mathematician, astronomer)
c. 397–322 BCE: Aeschines (orator)

387/6 BCE: Foundation of the Academy
384–322 BCE: Aristotle

384–322 BCE: Demosthenes (orator)
c. 384–322 BCE: Diocles of Carystus (medicine)

372/70–288/86 BCE: Theophrastus (Peripatetic)

*370–?300 BCE: Aristoxenus (music)

367–357 BCE: Dionysius II tyrant of Syracuse (in exile 357–344, retired 344 BCE)

c. 365–275 BCE: Pyrrho

359–336 BCE: Philip II king of Macedon

347–339/8 BCE: Speusippus head of Academy
341–270 BCE: Epicurus

344/3–292/1 BCE: Menander (comic poet)

338 BCE: Defeat of Athens by Philip at Chaeronea

339/8–314 BCE: Xenocrates head of Academy
335 BCE: Foundation of the Lyceum

fl. 330 BCE: Callippus (mathematician, astronomer) Athenian calendar reform on basis of Callippus' astronomical theory

336–323 BCE: Alexander the Great, king of Macedon

2nd half 4th century BCE: Eudemus of Rhodes (Peripatetic, student of Aristotle)

2nd half 4th–early 3rd century BCE: Stilpo (Megarian)

4th–3rd century BCE: Diodorus Cronus and Philo of Megara (Megarians)

331 BCE: Foundation of Alexandria

334/3–262/1 BCE: Zeno of Citium (founder of Stoicism; arrival in Athens 313 BCE)
331/0–230/29 BCE: Cleanthes (Stoic)
c. 331–278 BCE: Metrodorus of Lampsacus (Epicurean)

c. 330–300 BCE: Derveni Papyrus
c. 330–260 BCE?: Herophilus (medicine) in Alexandria

323–31 BCE: Hellenistic Period
323 BCE: Alexander's death followed by warfare among his generals and their successors

c. 325–235 BCE: Timon (student of Pyrrho)
322/1–288/86 BCE: Theophrastus head of Lyceum
fl. c. 320–300 BCE: Dicaearchus (Peripatetic)

c. 325–250 BCE: Euclid (mathematician)

317–307 BCE: Demetrius of Phaleron (student of Theophrastus) governs Athens

316/15–241/0 BCE: Arcesilaus (Academic)
314/13–270/69 BCE: Polemo head of the Academy

307/6 or 305/4 BCE: Foundation of the Epicurean school (the Garden)

c. 315–240 BCE?: Erasistratus (medicine) in Alexandria

301 BCE: "Battle of the kings" at Ipsus
Kingdoms of the successors:
Antigonids in Macedonia
Seleucids in Syria and Babylonia
Ptolemies in Egypt

c. 300 BCE: Foundation of the Stoa

Early 3rd century BCE: Foundation of the Museum and Library at Alexandria

288/86–270/68 BCE: Strato head of Lyceum
280/76–208/4 BCE: Chrysippus (Stoic)

First half 3rd century BCE: Aristarchus of Samos (astronomer)
*287–212/11 BCE: Archimedes (mathematician)
c. 276 BCE: *Phaenomena* by Aratus

270/69–268/64 BCE: Crates head of Academy
270/68–226/24 BCE: Lyco head of Lyceum for 44 years

275/73–*194 BCE: Eratosthenes (scholar and head of Library in Alexandria)

264–241 BCE: First Punic War
247–183/2 BCE: Hannibal (Carthaginian general)

268/64–241/0 BCE: Arcesilaus head of Academy
Mid 3rd century BCE: Aristo of Chios (Stoic)

236–183 BCE: Scipio Africanus, poltician and conqueror of Spain

*230–140s BCE: Diogenes of Seleucia/Babylon (Stoic)

fl. c. 205–184 BCE: Plautus (comic poet)
239–169 BCE: Ennius (comic poet)

218–201 BCE: Second Punic War

214/13–130/29 BCE: Carneades the Elder of Cyrene (Academic)

fl. 200 BCE: Apollonius of Perge (mathematician), author of *Conics*

2nd century BCE: Antipater of Tarsus (Stoic)
185/80–110/9 BCE: Panaetius of Rhodes (Stoic)
2nd century BCE: Critolaus head of Lyceum

c. 200/170 BCE: *Successions* by Sotion of Alexandria
c. 200–118 BCE: Polybius (historian)
185–*159 BCE: Terence (comic poet)

167/6–137/6 BCE: Carneades head of Academy
155 BCE: Carneades, Diogenes of Babylon, and Critolaus' embassy from Athens to Rome (bringing philosophy to Rome for the first time)

149–146 BCE: Third Punic War
146 BCE: Destruction of Carthage
146 BCE: Greece becomes a Roman Province

147–127 BCE: Recorded observations of Hipparchus (astronomer)

133 BCE: Tiberius Gracchus, tribune of the people

137/6–131/0 BCE: Carneades the Younger head of Academy
c. 135–51 BCE: Posidonius (Stoic)
c. 130–68 BCE: Antiochus of Ascalon (Platonist)

123 and 122 BCE: Gaius Gracchus, tribune of the people

127/6–110/9 BCE: Clitomachus head of Academy

	Late 2nd century BCE: Metrodorus of Stratonica (Academic)	
106–43 BCE: Cicero (orator, statesman, and philosopher) 100–44 BCE: Julius Caesar	110/9–84/3 BCE: Philo of Larissa last head of Academy *110–40/35 BCE: Philodemus (Epicurean) *94–50s BCE: Lucretius (poet, Epicurean)	
86 BCE: Sulla conquers Athens	Before 88 BCE?: Antiochus of Ascalon (Platonist) sets up his own Academy in Athens c. 70–50 BCE: Andronicus of Rhodes head of Peripatetic school	c. 86–35 BCE: Sallust (historian) c. 84–54 BCE: Catullus (poet) 70–19 BCE: Virgil (poet)
63 BCE–14 CE: Octavian (later Augustus)	1st century BCE?: Andronicus' publication of Aristotle's works 1st century BCE: Aenesidemus (Pyrrhonist) 1st century BCE?: Agrippa (Pyrrhonist)	65–8 BCE: Horace (poet) *64 BCE–21+ CE: Strabo (geographer and historian) 59 BCE–17 CE: Livy (historian) 48 BCE: First fire in library of Alexandria
31 BCE: Battle of Actium: Egypt becomes a Roman Province 27 BCE: End of the Roman Republic	1st century BCE: Arius Didymus (doxographer) fl. c. 25 BCE: Eudorus of Alexandia (Platonist)	1st century BCE–early 1st century CE: Vitruvius (architect)
27 BCE–476 CE Imperial Rome 27 BCE–14 CE: Augustus emperor 14–37 CE: Tiberius emperor	c. 20 BCE–45 CE: Philo of Alexandria (Judaeus) (philosopher/theologian) 4 BCE/1 CE–65 CE: Seneca (poet and Stoic)	*8/4 BCE: birth of Jesus fl. 14–37 CE?: Celsus (Roman encyclopedist; medicine) d. 36 CE: Thrasyllus (editor of Plato and Democritus)

41–54 CE: Claudius emperor

c. 40/50–110+ CE: Dio Chrysostom (orator and Cynic philosopher)
c. 45–125 CE: Plutarch of Chaeronea (Platonist, biographer, essayist)

*35–90s CE: Quintillian (orator)

54–68 CE: Nero emperor
69–79 CE: Vespasian emperor
70 CE: Titus takes Jerusalem
79 CE: Eruption of Mt. Vesuvius
79–81 CE: Titus emperor

50/60–*135 CE: Epictetus (Stoic)
c. 50–100 CE: Moderatus (Platonist)
Late 1st century CE?: Aëtius (doxographer)

fl. 62 CE: Heron of Alexandria (mathematician), author of *Mechanica*
*56–118+ CE: Tacitus (historian)

81–96 CE: Domitian emperor
95 CE: Domitian expels philosophers from Rome, including Epictetus

fl. c. 100 CE: Nicomachus of Gerasa (mathematician and neo-Pythagorean)

117–138 CE: Hadrian emperor

fl. c. 120 CE: Hierocles (Stoic philosopher), author of *Elements of Ethics*
*125–170+ CE: Apuleius (author and philosopher)

115/25–late 180s/early 190s CE: Lucian (satirist)
129–?199/216 CE: Galen (medicine)

138–161 CE: Antoninus Pius emperor

2nd century CE: Numenius (Platonist)
2nd century CE?: Alcinous (Platonist)
c. 150–200 CE: Atticus (Platonist)

fl. 146–*170 CE: Ptolemy (mathematician, astronomer)
*150–211/16 CE: Clement of Alexandria (Christian theologian)
2nd century CE?: *Chaldaean Oracles* edited or composed by Julian (the sacred text of middle and late Platonists)

161–180 CE: Marcus Aurelius emperor

176 CE: Marcus Aurelius founds four chairs of philosophy in Athens

c. 170–236 CE: Bishop Hippolytus (Christian theologian)
175/81 CE: *True Doctrine* by Celsus (anti-Christian)
c. 180 CE: *Attic Nights* by Aulus Gellius

193–211 CE: Septimius Severus emperor

fl. late 2nd century CE: Sextus Empiricus (Pyrrhonist)
198/209 CE: Alexander of Aphrodisias (commentator

c. 185–254 CE: Origen of Alexandria (Christian philosopher and exegete)

	on Aristotle) appointed public teacher, probably in Athens	
222–235 CE: Alexander Severus emperor	First half 3rd century CE: Diogenes Laertius, author of *Lives of Philosophers* 3rd century CE: Ammonius Saccas (Platonist in Alexandria, teacher of Plotinus, Origen, and Longinus)	
	205–270 CE: Plotinus (inaugurates Neoplatonism) c. 213–273 CE: Longinus (rhetorician and philosopher)	
	234–*305 CE: Porphyry (Neoplatonist) 3rd century CE: Amelius (Platonist) c. 245–325 CE: Iamblichus (founded a Neoplatonic school in Syria at Apamea)	fl. 250 CE: Diophantus, author of *Arithmetics*
	273 CE: Longinus executed by the Romans	c. 260–339 CE: Eusebius of Caesarea (theologian and historian)
284–305 CE: Diocletian emperor of Eastern empire 286–305 CE: Maximian rules West	c. 300 CE: Porphyry publishes Plotinus' *Enneads*	
306–337 CE: Constantine the Great emperor (converts to Christianity) 313 CE: Edict of Milan (toleration of Christianity)	c. 317–388 CE: Themistius (commentator on Aristotle)	fl. 320 CE: Pappus of Alexandria (mathematician)
	fl. c. 350 CE: Calcidius (Christian translator and commentator on Plato's *Timaeus*)	c. 328–373 CE: Athanasius bishop of Alexandria 329–389 CE: Gregory of Nazianz (theologian)

c. 330–379 CE: Basil of
Caesarea (theologian)
c. 330–395 CE: Gregory of
Nyssa (theologian)

361–363 CE: Reign of Julian
(the Apostate), restoration
of paganism

379–395 CE: Reign of
Theodosius
391 CE: Paganism outlawed

354–430 CE: Augustine,
author of *Confessions* (c.
397–400 CE) and *City of God*
(c. 413–426 CE)

374–397 CE: Ambrose
bishop of Milan
398–403 CE: John
Chrysostom bishop of
Constantinople

411 CE: Alaric, king of the
Visigoths, sacks Rome

After 400 CE: Neoplatonic
schools in Athens and
Alexandria
415 CE: Hypatia
(mathematician and
philosopher) murdered by
Christians in Alexandria
d. 432 CE (at a great age):
Plutarch of Athens
(Neoplatonist)
d. c. 437 CE: Syrianus
(Neoplatonist)
412–485 CE: Proclus
(Neoplatonist)

fl. early 5th century CE:
Stobaeus (anthologist)

455 CE: Rome sacked by
Gaiseric, king of the
Vandals

*440–517+ CE: Ammonius
(Alexandria, teacher of
Damascius, Philoponus, and
Simplicius)
5th century CE: Hierocles of
Alexandria (Neoplatonist)

**476 CE: Fall of the
Western Empire**
Romulus Augustulus
deposed by Odoacer, king of
the Heruli

c. 480–524 CE: Boethius
(commentator and author
of *Consolation of Philosophy*)

493–526 CE: Theodoric
Ostrogothic king of Italy

c. 490–560 CE: Simplicius
(Neoplatonist)
c. 490–570s CE: Philoponus
(Christianized school in
Alexandria)
495/505–565+ CE:
Olympiodorus (Platonist)

527–565 CE: Justinian emperor in Constantinople
529 CE: Justinian closes the Neoplatonic school in Athens

529 CE: Neoplatonists in Athens, including Damascius, Simplicius, and Priscian, flee to Persia (Ctesiphon)
532 CE: Simplicius' commentaries on Aristotle probably all written after this date

6th century CE: David and Elias (Alexandria)
2nd half 6th century CE: Anonymous *Introduction to Philosophy of Plato*

570?–632 CE: Muhammad, prophet of Islam

c. 580–662 CE: Maximus the Confessor (theologian)

7th century CE: Arab conquest of Syria, Jerusalem, Egypt, and elsewhere

c. 640 CE: Destruction of library at Alexandria

c.   circa: around this/these date(s)
*   date approximate
?   date(s) uncertain or disputed
+   sometime after date listed
s   decade of
/   sometime within dates listed
fl. floruit: date(s) when person was active

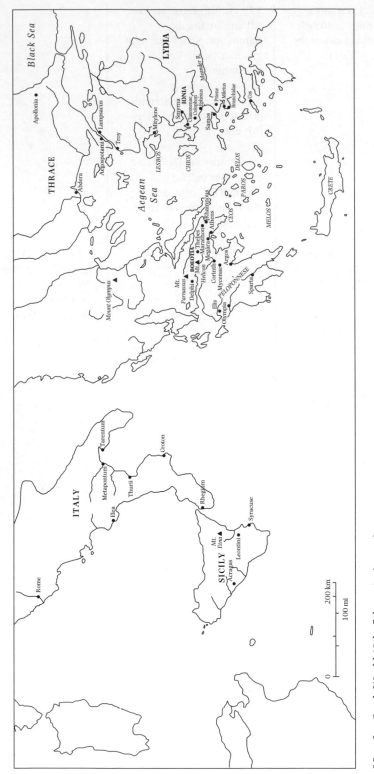

Map 1 Greek World (6th–5th centuries BCE)

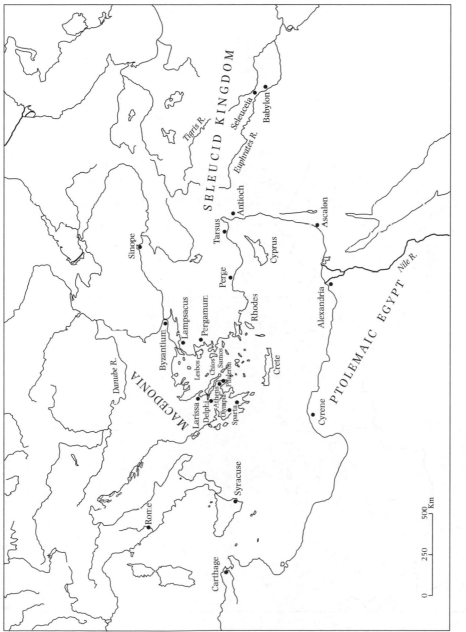

Map 2 The Hellenistic Period (323–31 BCE)

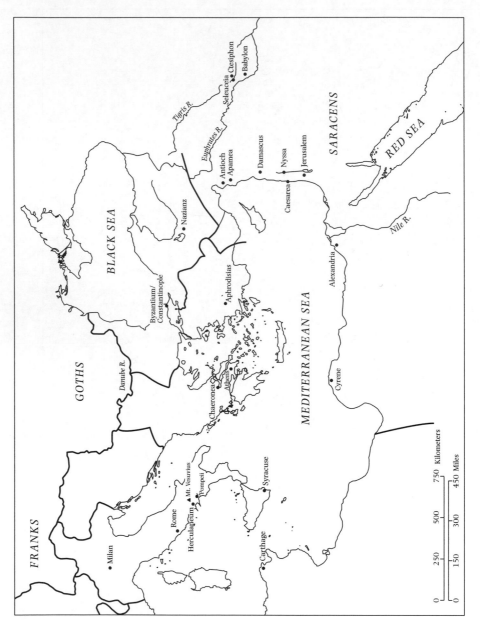

Map 3 The Late Roman Empire

Introduction

Our aim as editors of *A Companion to Ancient Philosophy* is to show how specialists today read the texts of the Greek and Roman philosophers. To indicate the range of work in this field, we have solicited contributors from the United States and Canada, from numerous European countries (Denmark, England, France, Germany, Greece, Hungary, Italy) and from Japan. In addition to senior scholars, we have also invited a number of younger specialists in the history of ancient philosophy, who are destined, in the near future, not only to continue the work of their predecessors, but also to revise their approaches, methods, and results. We want to demonstrate, in a general way, that it is *philosophically* important to do the history of philosophy, and especially the history of ancient philosophy. The need to justify this enterprise is not as long-standing as one might think, since the idea that it is philosophically important to do the history of philosophy and even, quite simply, that "doing the history of philosophy" has a meaning, are not very old claims but date back at most to the end of the eighteenth century. Even if one admits the importance of the history of philosophy in philosophical activity, one might ask more particularly: Why is a work like ours useful, given that since the second half of the nineteenth century at least, histories of ancient philosophy have been written according to "scientific" criteria that are still roughly ours? In answering the particular question, we will make some remarks about the more general question.

Ancient Philosophy is defined as the group of philosophical works written in the Greek and Roman world from the beginning of philosophy in the sixth century BCE in the Greek colony of Miletus on the coast of Asia Minor to the end of antiquity, some 50 years after the fall of the Roman Empire in the West. In 529 CE Justinian, the Christian ruler of the Eastern Empire in Constantinople, closed the Neoplatonic (pagan) school in Athens, and the philosophers fled to Ctesiphon (in modern Iraq). Later a lively Arabic philosophical and scientific tradition developed in the region, which had deep roots in Greek and Roman thought. The 1,200 years to which our volume is devoted, from the sixth century BCE to the sixth century CE (see CHRONOLOGY) is a period full of noise and passion, but the philosophers took part in one and the same drama, a drama that makes sense and that lasted until Christianity, after engulfing political power, was imposed as the only permissible thought. The last fires of ancient thought were set by Neoplatonists of the sixth century CE, by individuals like Simplicius and Philoponus, but were then quenched. Between the moment of its birth and the moment of its disappearance, however, ancient philosophy had its own dynamic and logic, which the chapters in this volume explore.

The vast majority of philosophical texts from antiquity have been lost, many of them already in antiquity (see Mejer, ANCIENT PHILOSOPHY AND THE DOXOGRAPHICAL TRADITION). Of important philosophers, we are fortunate to have the complete or relatively complete works in Greek of Plato, Aristotle (his school treatises but not his published works), Epictetus, Marcus Aurelius, Sextus Empiricus, and Plotinus; and in Latin of Lucretius, Cicero, and Seneca. We owe a tremendous debt to the commentary tradition of late antiquity for preserving much of what has come down to us, and especially the works of Plato and Aristotle (see Mejer's paper on the preservation of fragments of pre-Socratic philosophy; see Hoffmann, WHAT WAS COMMENTARY IN LATE ANTIQUITY? THE EXAMPLE OF THE NEOPLATONIC COMMENTATORS, on the commentary tradition more generally).

Different historical periods have had different conceptions about the relationship between their own philosophical practice and that of their philosophical predecessors. Aristotle, for example, who was perhaps the first philosopher to take seriously the history of philosophy, famously represented his predecessors in the first book of the *Metaphysics* as taking important but stumbling steps toward his own theory of the four causes. This approach to the history of philosophy, which is sometimes called "Whig history" and which we will call the "teleological" approach, takes as the culmination or "end" of philosophy the current and/or preferred philosophical theory, and interprets earlier thinkers as contributing in one way or another to the development of that theory (see Hussey, THE BEGINNINGS OF SCIENCE AND PHILOSOPHY IN ARCHAIC GREECE, pp. 7–8). Hegel adopted a similar approach in his *Lectures on the History of Philosophy* in the early nineteenth century. The attitude can be found even in a philosopher as modern as Heidegger, who thought that Plato and Aristotle opened a chapter in the history of being ("the forgetting of being") which Heidegger himself intended to close.

The history of science is often interpreted in a similar way. Earlier scientific achievements are understood from the perspective of the current "correct" theory. Newton's Laws are often considered a special case of Relativity Theory (for bodies moving at slow speeds). Such an approach to the history of both philosophy and science risks anachronism, because the earlier thinkers were quite probably not working in the same conceptual framework as their descendants, using some vaguely articulated conception of a much later goal, and developing theories in light of that goal. On the contrary, they were asking questions that seemed pressing at the time and in response to their own predecessors. As Thomas Kuhn points out in the case of Newton, the later theory has to reinterpret the concepts of the earlier theory to make it a special case of its own.[1] Thus the teleological approach tends to distort the earlier theory. It also tends to marginalize figures whose views, from a later perspective, appear to be false starts.

There has always been an interest in the ancient philosophers as the source of views that are currently in fashion. In the second half of the twentieth century, for example, Oxford ordinary language philosophers in the 1950s and 1960s found that Aristotle, too, was engaged in their project of conceptual analysis. Metaphysicians have looked to Aristotle for insight into the notion of essence. Philosophers interested in functionalism

---

1. Thomas Kuhn (1970). *The Structure of Scienctific Revolutions*. 2nd edn. (ch. 9). Chicago: University of Chicago Press.

in the philosophy of mind and the philosophy of biology trace various versions of the theory back to Aristotle. Modern virtue ethics owes its inspiration to him. In turn, contemporary epistemologists look to Sextus Empiricus' account of Pyrrhonism for an early version of skepticism. This is not the history of philosophy, but the use of earlier views in the service of contemporary philosophical concerns. The ancients, too, regularly made philosophical use of their predecessors in arguing for their own agenda, as our previous example of Aristotle shows (and see Sharples, THE PROBLEM OF SOURCES, for examples from the Hellenistic era).

This productive use of earlier philosophy suggests that philosophy and science have quite different relationships to their own earlier traditions. A good physicist needs no special knowledge of the history of his science more than 20 years old. A doctor need not read Hippocrates. Indeed, in not reading Hippocrates, he may well become a better doctor, because he has more time to devote to mastering his art (reading Hippocrates is a lot of work). This observation does not rule out the history of the sciences, but it does decouple the history of the sciences from effective scientific practice. Philosophy is different. To be sure, one need not know the historical background of concepts at play in the works of contemporary philosophers in order to understand their discourse, especially when they make no reference to that background. One can in fact understand any philosopher this way. But the situation is different from that of the physician who is ignorant of the history of his field. The physician ignorant of history practices *without theoretical damage* to his theoretical research in medicine. This is not the case for the philosophical reader and even less for the philosophical "professional." Our philosophical concepts have evolved from the ancient concepts, and are thus *historically constituted.* For many centuries people *understood* Descartes as a thinker without intellectual ties. But we undoubtedly understand him better since the efforts of the twentieth century have revealed his debt to medieval and pre-modern thought. The revolutionary concepts of Descartes gain in philosophical richness when one sees in the image of what and in opposition to what they were conceived and put to work. The same is true of our contemporary philosophical concepts, which have evolved from those of the ancients. The knowledge of the historical roots of concepts and of traditions is far from being a simple matter of curiosity.[2]

In some historical periods, and sometimes even concurrently with the teleological approach, one can find an apparently opposite attitude, that there is nothing new under the sun, because everything thinkable has already been thought by the Great Ancients. In the history of thought this attitude is quite often linked with some kind of fundamentalism, which urges a return to the original doctrine of the Founding Fathers of philosophy. We see this sort of approach, for example, among the Platonists of Imperial Rome and late Antiquity (on this topic, see Zambon, MIDDLE PLATONISM, and Hoffmann's chapter, cited above, on the Neoplatonic commentators). Very often, despite the profession of orthodoxy, the later work differs substantially from its source, since it interprets the source in light of other philosophical and cultural currents of

---

2.   For an excellent discussion of the special relations philosophy has to history, see Bernard Williams, "Philosophy as a Humanistic Discipline," The Royal Institute of Philosophy Annual Lecture 2000, online at: http://royalinstitutephilosophy.org.

its own time (such as Christianity). Philosophers in the Middle and Late Platonic traditions also thought that Plato and Aristotle (and others) shared the same doctrine – the one true doctrine. So a large part of the philososophical project was to reconcile positions that appeared from a literal reading of the texts to conflict with one another (for instance, the creation of the world in Plato's *Timaeus* and its eternity in Aristotle).

Connected with this second attitude is the idea that philosophy has certain "styles" of thinking that cross the borders of historical periods. From this perspective, when Coleridge claims that each of us is a Platonist or an Aristotelian, he may sin by simplification since there are perhaps more than two paradigms of this genre, but he is nonetheless profoundly right. Since the end of antiquity until the modern era one can effectively read the history of philosophy as a sort of struggle between an approach that places true reality in some Ideal and an approach that attempts as far as possible to combine thought with perception. Likewise, and this is especially true for epistemology and the philosophy of science, one notices an uninterrupted oscillation between a reductionist position that tends to make all sorts of knowledge subdivisions of a single knowledge and a position that affirms the irreducibility of distinct domains of knowledge. When one speaks, correctly, of the "rediscovery" of Aristotle in the thirteenth century, of Plato in the fifteenth century, of the Skeptics in the sixteenth century, of Epicurus by Gassendi or of Platonism by the philosophical logicians in the early twentieth century, the issue is not – or not only – the rediscovery of texts that had been, in different ways, rendered inaccessible to philosophers. The issue is simply the active and effective rediscovery of *philosophical postures* which one does not fully understand unless one understands the original version. (See further, Pellegrin, THE ARISTOTELIAN WAY.)

A third attitude turns up sometimes in the Humanities, concerned as they are to understand the human condition and human constructions. This is the view that there are certain perennial questions about the human condition – questions about human happiness, suffering, weakness, mortality. Our human nature, our aspirations, and vulnerablilities have remained the same across the millenia, even if our external circumstances have changed. On this view we turn to the greatest of the ancients, whether poets, historians, or philosophers, because they answered these questions particularly well and have much to teach us for our own lives.

These various approaches certainly have value in supporting current philosophical positions or in generating new ones, but none is a *historical* approach to the ancient texts. They are not historical, precisely because they assume that the ancient authors were answering (or trying to answer) our current questions. So they are liable to distort the evidence to fit expectations. Of course, all interpreters bring to the text their own expectations, shaped by their own experience and education. We cannot avoid this. The danger is a failure to recognize what we are doing. If we want to understand the ideas of an ancient author, and to interpret those ideas historically, we have to become aware of our own perspective and take care not to be unduly influenced by it. As Heraclitus said: "Unless one expects the unexpected, one will not find it" (DK 22B18, part). We must be prepared to be surprised.

Up to the end of the nineteenth century, modern philosophers rarely detected a significant historical discrepancy between ancient ways of thinking and their own, and, consequently, they considered Greek and Roman philosophers as their direct interlocutors. But with the development of a rigorously historical approach to the classical texts (known in German as *Wissenschaft*), particularly in the German historical school (which includes people like F. Ast, I. Bekker, J. Bernays, H. Bonitz, C. A. Brandis, C. Prantl, L. Preller, H. Ritter, F. Susemihl, E. Zeller, and many others), philosophy became a historical object. This is quite a radical change in western philosophy and, in a way, the real beginning of the history of philosophy in the sense we understand it. For there cannot be any history of philosophy before its object has become a historical object. The most immediate benefit of such a transformation in the approach to philosophical texts is the enormous philological and historical work accomplished by modern scholars – continuing, to be sure, the efforts of their forerunners from the Renaissance onwards – work that made those texts available in reliable editions that we still use today. As examples, we mention the multi-volume edition of the ancient Greek commentators on Aristotle and others, Commentaria in Aristotelem Graeca (cited as CAG), published in Berlin between 1882 and 1909; Herman Diels' three-volume edition of the fragments of the pre-Socratic philosophers, *Die Fragmente der Vorsokratiker*, published in 1903, revised by Walter Kranz in 1951–2, which remains our principal source for early Greek philosophy (cited as DK) (on Diels and the doxographical tradition, see Mejer's chapter in this volume). We also owe to this period the edition of Plato's works by John Burnet, *Platonis opera* (5 vols., Oxford Classical Texts, 1900–7), which is only now being revised (by E. A. Duke and others, vol. 1: 1995).

In part because of that meticulous scholarly work, which included the careful study and editing of classical texts of many kinds, historians of ancient philosophy have competed with philologists in the study of the works of ancient philosophy. Philologists sometimes consider their scholarly tools sufficient for the interpretation of ancient philosophical texts without recognizing that ancient philosophical texts need some specific interpretative procedures. Treating philosophical texts as on a par with oratorical prose or epic verse – differing only in subject matter and genre – on the assumption that all the texts were written in the same languages during the same period, is to miss what is exceptional about philosophical texts no matter when they were composed. Certainly, everyone would agree that a good historian of ancient philosophy must be able to read the languages in which the texts were written. Furthermore, having a sound basis in philological techniques is a most valuable aid in the study of the ancient philosophical texts. But philology is only part of what those who study ancient philosophy need to know.

The interpretation of ancient philosophical texts requires philosophical expertise, as well as philological. Just as philosophers today must undertake to make sense of the arguments of their opponents before they can evaluate and criticize them, so the student of ancient philosophy must do the same, though in this case the main task is the initial step of making sense, a task made more difficult by our temporal distance. But like any philosopher reading the work of another philosopher, our task is to understand what the philosophical text is trying to show and how it demonstrates its conclusions. When an argument is missing or fragmentary, as is often the case with the ancient philosophers whose works have come down to us in fragmentary form, we must try to reconstruct what the argument was, given the evidence we have. This undertaking demands *philosophical* tools, including those of logic and conceptual analysis. The questions the ancients were asking may in some cases differ considerably from those that philosophers are asking today, but uncovering and clarifying the issues requires sound philosophical judgment on our part.

The 1950s, 1960s, and 1970s were exhilarating times for the study of ancient philosophy. In the first half of the twentieth century philosophers like Gilbert Ryle, Ludwig Wittgenstein, and Martin Heidegger had discovered, especially in Plato, what they took to be the seeds of their own philosophical positions. The development of various analytical tools, especially logic, provided new means for interpreting the ancient texts. A legendary six-week NEH seminar in Colorado Springs in 1970, organized by the leaders in ancient philosophy in the English-speaking world at the time – Gregory Vlastos, G. E. L. Owen, and John Ackrill – stimulated talented young philosophers to study and reevaluate the ancient texts.

At the same time, among "continental" scholars, the most remarkable event in the field of ancient philosophy was Aristotle's return to favor in the Academic world, from which he had been ostracized for religious reasons. For before and after the Second World War a new interest in Aristotle originated in the Thomistic revival, which took place around Jacques Maritain and Etienne Gilson. Among the most prominent figures of this trend were members of the Belgian school of Louvain, led by Mgr. Augustin Mansion. This movement produced some important works, such as the translation of Aristotle's *Nicomachean Ethics* with commentary by R. A. Gauthier and J. Y. Jolif. The main witness of the reintroduction of Aristotle in French Academic circles is probably the book by Pierre Aubenque, *Le Problème de l'être chez Aristote*, published in 1962 – a book that displays a strong Heideggerian influence.

The mid twentieth century thus demonstrated a renewed interest in ancient philosophy in its own right, but the attraction was what ancient philosophy could contribute to modern philosophical debate. The late 1970s and 1980s witnessed a significant shift in scholarly interest, which may be considered, in a way, an aftershock of the nineteenth-century historical earthquake mentioned above. This shift was led by a group of young scholars, who are now leaders in the field. Julia Annas, in her opening editorial in *Oxford Studies in Ancient Philosophy* (1983), characterized the time as an exciting moment in ancient philosophy, with "horizons expanding and interests shifting." She encouraged contributors to venture into less familiar territory, especially in post-Aristotelian philosophy. Michael Frede, in the manifesto introducing his collection of papers, published in 1987, spoke of the enormous increase in interest in Hellenistic philosophy in the past ten years, and exhorted others to devote similar attention to late antiquity. He characterized different approaches to the history of philosophy, and advocated the examination of ancient philosophers, not as exemplars who fit into the history of philosophy because they answered philosophical questions especially well or poorly (that would be to assume there are perennial philosophical questions or that today's philosophical framework is "correct"), but instead to study them within all the various histories in which they occur. Our task as interpreters, on this view, is to uncover the philosophers' questions and to discover or reconstruct their reasons for answering them as they did. Although the methods of philosophical reconstruction are philosophical, the overall approach is vigorously *historical*.

In a similar spirit, scholars of ancient philosophy in the 1980s began seriously to question the use of Aristotle and other historical figures to support contemporary philosophical theories. Myles Burnyeat, in an influential paper presented in the mid 1980s, which was widely circulated thereafter and published (as a draft) some years later, "Is Aristotle's Philosophy of Mind Still Credible?" argued strenuously against functionalist interpretations of Aristotle's psychology, concluding that "new function-alist minds do not fit into old Aristotelian bodies." The paper has stimulated much thoughtful response (on this debate, see Caston, ARISTOTLE'S PSYCHOLOGY).

While questions were being raised about the relevance of ancient philosophy to contemporary philosophical problems and about the appropriateness of interpreting them as answering our modern questions, extensive scholarly work was being done in a variety of areas of ancient philosophy, which allowed texts to be reevaluated philosophically from a number of new perspectives. Particularly important was the work on Hellenistic philosophy and the later stages of ancient philosophy. For instance, the "rediscovery" of the library at Herculaneum (buried together with Pompeii by the eruption of Mt. Vesuvius in 79 CE), which contains many works by the hitherto obscure Epicurean philosopher Philodemus, and the development of techniques enabling the fragmentary papyri to be read and edited have allowed for a critical reassessment of Epicureanism (see Sharples's chapter in this volume, and Morel, EPICUREANISM). Similarly, the recent "rediscovery" of a fragment of Empedocles identified in the early 1990s and published in 1999 has enabled scholars to reassess the thought of that pre-Socratic philosopher (see Curd, PARMENIDES AND AFTER: UNITY AND PLURALITY, pp. 36–42). Richard Sorabji's massive translation project, The Ancient Commentators on Aristotle, which saw its first publication in the late 1980s, has made those works of late antiquity (edited a century ago as Commentaria in Aristotelem Graeca, mentioned above) more accessible to philosophical scholars.

In the late 1970s and 1980s, scholars in significant numbers began to explore a relatively neglected area of Aristotelian studies, his research in biology (which constitutes one-quarter of Aristotle's surviving works) and the relation between his philosophy of science in the *Posterior Analytics* and his practice in the biological works (see Detel, ARISTOTLE'S LOGIC AND PHILOSOPHY OF SCIENCE, and Lennox, ARISTOTLE'S BIOLOGY AND ARISTOTLE'S PHILOSOPHY). This enormously productive movement also gave scholars a new perspective from which to investigate his metaphysics, psychology, and political philosophy. The access to new information and attention to neglected texts has affected our understanding of more familiar texts.

In addition, ancient philosophy has profited from the application of a number of new or previously unheeded methods of interpretation. Many historians of ancient philosophy in the analytic tradition have come to recognize (what literary interpreters appreciated all along) that it is not enough to analyze particular arguments, especially in Plato, without serious attention to the narrative or dramatic context, which may well affect the meaning (see C. Gill, THE PLATONIC DIALOGUE). Some of the most fruitful recent work on Plato combines careful analysis of the arguments with attention to the dialogue form and nuances of the drama. Furthermore, especially in continental Europe but increasingly in the English-speaking world as well, students of ancient philosophy are looking outside their own discipline – especially to the history of ancient science, religion, politics, institutions, literature, law, and so on – for insight into the ancient philosophical texts. The theoretical tools used by historians of philosophy in interpreting the texts have also been influenced by recent developments in social science and psychology. Philosophy has come to be recognized as a cultural production, if not in the same way as other disciplines, at least alongside them, that has arisen, like other cultural productions, from a complex of historical factors. This is the profound meaning of the veritable revolution in ancient studies initiated by Jean-Pierre Vernant in the 1960s. He regarded philosophy mainly as an *effect* of that new organization of power which was called then and is still called "democracy."

Our collection takes account of these various developments. For instance, we have undertaken to display the interconnections between ancient philosophy and other disciplines and domains by devoting several chapters to the relationship between philosophy and mathematics (Mueller, GREEK MATHEMATICS TO THE TIME OF EUCLID), medicine (Pellegrin, ANCIENT MEDICINE AND ITS CONTRIBUTION TO THE PHILOSOPHICAL TRADITION), and religion (Betegh, GREEK PHILOSOPHY AND RELIGION). The aim of this collection, which emphasizes a number of different approaches, is to present our most current understanding of ancient philosophy. This is the justification for the present collection. We hope that our collection will give not only an overview of the history of ancient philosophy as presently understood and debated, but will also stimulate readers to reflect on how the study of ancient philosophy may best proceed from here, combining insights from different approaches. Not only that: We believe that the history of ancient philosophy, properly understood *historically* in its own cultural and intellectual context, has much to contribute to our present understanding of philosophical problems. That is not because Ancient Philosophy is answering the very same questions modern philosophers are asking. On the contrary, it is because the questions and answers we find in ancient philosophy may stimulate us to think again or to reconsider a well-worn issue from a new perspective. Thus we hope that our readers will also have much to gain *philosophically* from the chapters in this volume.

M. L. G. and P. P.

Part I

Early Greek Philosophy

1

The Beginnings of Science and Philosophy in Archaic Greece

EDWARD HUSSEY

Homer and Hesiod: A Pre-scientific Conception of the World

Ancient Greek science and philosophy were radical innovations, but they did not emerge from a void.[1] This chapter will first look at the way in which the world was conceived and understood, around 800 BCE, in the poems of Homer and Hesiod. These poems soon came to be taken as canonical: in archaic Greece, and right down to the end of the fifth century, to know and understand Homer and Hesiod was the accepted test of an educated person. This canonical status was not created or enforced by political or economic power. Apart from their poetic achievement, the conception of the world and of human life that they provided was one that was found convincing, authoritative, and comprehensive by successive generations.

Their way of representing the world, and the god-given authority they claimed for their statements, constituted the established view, against which the Ionian proto-scientists of the sixth century were sharply reacting, but to which (not surprisingly) they were also indebted. There are no discontinuities in this kind of history, without accompanying partial continuities, which are also part of the story.

It makes sense to focus, at the outset, exclusively on Homer and Hesiod, but the reader should remember that they were not the products of a static or self-contained society. Archaic Greece was, on the contrary, constantly receiving and reacting to all kinds of stimuli from the older civilizations of the "Ancient Near East" (to use a convenient, though Eurocentric, and now almost unintelligible term).

There are two characteristic features of the Homeric-Hesiodic world-view that are of leading significance for a study of the "origins of science." These two features are connected, though one of them is very obvious and one rather less so. The obvious feature, overwhelmingly so to a modern reader, is the *centrality of anthropomorphic gods* (especially the Olympian gods) in the world. The less obvious feature is the *finitude* and the *vagueness about the limits* (spatial, temporal, and of other kinds) of the world. These characteristic features must now be examined.

The gods of Homer and Hesiod (many of whom were gods of actual Greek religious cults) were conceived of anthropomorphically. Though they were immortal, and had

---

1. I am much indebted to Hywel Clifford for his helpful comments on an earlier draft of this chapter.

superhuman powers, their nature was physically and psychologically like that of human beings. Hence the world of Homer and Hesiod is, in its essence and its details, a familiar one, closely related to ordinary human experience.

The centrality of the gods in the world is such that it can almost be said that the gods *are* the world. The principal and defining constituents of the body of the world are themselves ancient gods in Hesiod (Sky, Earth, Erebus, Tartarus, Sea: *Theog.* 117–132). Within this cosmic framework, other gods are active, of which the ruling dynasty is that of the Olympian gods under the leadership of Zeus. The rule of Zeus and the Olympians seems not guaranteed to be inevitable, and in theory could be challenged; but in practice Zeus' unequalled combination of power and wisdom means that he is *de facto* king of the world. (The difficulties Zeus encounters in Homer in putting his plans into effect are mostly due to the need to carry the rest of his family with him and to circumvent opposition from some of them on some particular matters.) Human beings, even when favored by the gods, are transient and marginal beings, subject to the will of the gods.

The gods are, therefore, central to the intelligibility of the world in a straightforward way: they are in fact the source and the explanation of any intelligibility it may have, both as a whole and as to particular objects or events. To understand anything is to know which god or gods are responsible for it; and that is usually the most that can be done. The gods themselves are not to be understood in terms of anything else, though some of them may be partly intelligible in terms of *other* gods.

The world as a whole, then, may be seen and partly understood as something shaped by the choices of various gods acting in an earlier stage of the world. The choices of gods may be understood in so far as they have motivations that make sense in human terms.

Hesiod offers the most ambitious attempt at providing, systematically, an intelligible world along these lines. His *Theogony* contains a vast genealogical scheme, which enables one to determine the exact kin-relationship of any god to any other. The knowledge of the gods' pedigrees and their interrelations is just as important for understanding their actions and wishes as the corresponding knowledge about human kings and princes is in Homer's epics.

Hesiod's *Theogony* is instructive because it so clearly aims to be an account of the world in terms of anthropomorphic gods that was as complete and coherent as its author could devise. The characteristic limitations of this way of thinking appear all the more clearly.

There is first of all the point that the world is essentially *finite* in all respects, because the gods are finite. Spatially, it does not extend further than the sky above and the murky region of Tartarus below, while the earth is encompassed by the circularly flowing Ocean. In time, it does not go back before the appearance of Chaos, the first god, of whom it is expressly said that it "came to be first of all" (*Theog.* 116). Nothing is said about the other end of time, but the stock epithet of the gods, "living always" (*aien eontes*), certainly need not imply an unending future. The power and knowledge of the gods themselves, though it is superhuman, is also finite, being intelligible only after the human pattern. Even within the finite world, there are things that are beyond the power of any gods to change or to prevent: not only the general nature of the world and the gods including himself, but certain matters that are impersonally "fated to be," whether conditionally or absolutely (examples in Hesiod: *Theog.* 463–465, 475–476, 891–894). Nor do any of the gods appear to know anything about what may lie beyond the spatial and temporal boundaries mentioned. In this sense it may be said that the gods themselves have only a limited understanding of themselves and their own situation.

Finitude is not in itself a hindrance to intelligibility; rather the reverse. But it is a feature of the Homeric-Hesiodic world that though it is finite its limits are not only vaguely expressed, but are in themselves, apparently, indefinite; in any case, not to be precisely known. As a result, even the finitude of the world remains indefinite, and conceivably revisable.

This point is difficult to establish with certainty, because the attention of Hesiod or Homer is, naturally, mostly focused on the center of the world, the Olympian gods, and the events in recent history in the central region, in heaven and on earth. But, just because the gods are finite and central to the world, the limits of the world, and anything that might lie beyond, are beyond the gods' powers to affect, and beyond their knowledge. To say this, for Homer and Hesiod, is as good as to say that anything that is beyond the limits is unknowable, and cannot be considered as having any relevance to human life or divine beings.

This holds not only for the spatial and temporal limits; the same indefiniteness attaches to the limits of the gods' power, to the limits of intelligibility of the gods themselves, and to that of the world as a whole. For, as has been said, the gods are conceived of as "super-humans," who are not to be understood otherwise than by analogy with human nature as it is known in common experience. While this makes it easy to understand, in a general way, many aspects of their nature and their acts, it leaves it impossible to state with any precision how or why any one god will act in any one particular case. And intelligibility of the world as a whole depends directly, as has been said, on that of the gods.

To take a case directly affecting the observable regular order of the world: at *Odyssey* 12.377–388, the Sun, angered at the slaughter of his sacred cattle by Odysseus' men, threatens to go down into the underworld and shine among the dead. This threat is parried by Zeus with a promise to kill those responsible. So even the continuance of the Sun in his regular course, on which so much depends, is never absolutely guaranteed. In general it seems that the prevention of cosmic anarchy is entirely dependent on the continuing but finite watchfulness and resourcefulness of Zeus; so that there can be no absolute guarantee.

So far as can be seen, the Homeric-Hesiodic account of the world was the generally accepted one in archaic Greece. This is not to say that it was regarded as wholly unchallengeable, or was left wholly unchallenged. According to the Homeric-Hesiodic world-view itself, any *human* claim to know the truth about important matters concerning the gods, was in principle open to challenge. So Homer and Hesiod themselves had to explain how it was that they had better access to the truth than other human beings.

Their claim was that they were "inspired," that their stories were told them by the Muses, the goddesses who presided over memory and song; hence the source of their knowledge was, as it had to be, the gods themselves. But what supported the claim by any one particular poet to be so inspired? It could only be the public success of that

5

poet in poetically reproducing and enhancing traditional materials, in a way that was manifestly pleasing and convincing to most listeners.

At this point, then, there was necessarily an appeal to traditional beliefs and stories about the gods. The Homeric-Hesiodic reworking of these beliefs and stories imposed itself because it was found to be, ultimately, the most satisfying. If this is right, it follows that it was open to anyone (even to a character within the Homeric narrative itself) to doubt or to challenge the Homeric-Hesiodic account of things, on any one particular point, even a very important one. Thus, at *Odyssey* 24.351–352, it appears that Laertes, in his despair at Odysseus' failure to return, has been doubting whether the Olympian gods are still dispensing justice on Olympus. And there is evidence for myths discrepant from those of Homer and Hesiod being asserted by other poets, sometimes in what seems to be more or less free allegory; for example, Alcman's story of Poros and Tekmor (Alcman fr. 5 Davies).

But what it was not possible to do, was to doubt or to challenge the supporting substratum of traditional belief: above all, the belief that the beings central to the understanding of the world were the anthropomorphic gods of traditional Greek religion. When the whole Homeric-Hesiodic view finally came under systematic attack, the first serious critic of whom we know, Xenophanes of Colophon, centered his polemic precisely on the anthropomorphic gods.

It is clear then that the Homeric-Hesiodic view of the world was not and could not be a "free-standing" one, appealing to some intrinsic authority of its own. It was dependent on the tacit support of the "traditional substratum" of assumptions.

Thus this view of the world was clearly "pre-scientific." To say this, is not to deny that it represents the result of a great deal of intense reflection on the problems of understanding the world. Moreover, some of this reflection is recognizably concerned with questions that are typically philosophical. Thus, Aristotle (*Phys.* IV.1, 208b29–33) plausibly interprets Hesiod's introduction of Chaos as the temporally first god, as drawn from a recognition that some concept of *place* is necessary and antecedent to any account of material existence.

But, in spite of such interesting suggestions of proto-philosophical reflection, it has to be said that the Homeric-Hesiodic view was even in a certain sense "anti-scientific" (and "anti-philosophical"). This is meant as follows: it positively made impossible the development of any scientific thinking about the world as a whole, so long as it (or rather the "substratum" of supporting beliefs) retained any authority. It was recognition of this incompatibility that underlay what Plato later called "the ancient quarrel between philosophy and poetry" (*Rep.* X, 607b5–c4; the poets, Homer and Hesiod above all, being the principal exponents of the pre-scientific view).

What constitutes the division between "scientific" and "pre-scientific" is not the use of "gods" in explanations of the world. It all depends on the nature of the gods. As will be seen, the Milesian theorists also postulated intelligent "gods;" but these were *not* the traditional anthropomorphic ones.

The gods of Homer and Hesiod, and generally those of the traditional Greek belief, were too humanly credible, too straightforwardly similar to common human experience, to serve as elements of a scientific theory. They leave no room for any effort to rise above vagueness and ambiguity in understanding, and to develop a more detached and precise style of describing and understanding. As has been seen, the very

6

notion and limits of the "world" have to be left indeterminate, and not determinable even in principle. They therefore make a scientific effort to understand the world impossible, so long as they are taken to be indispensable.

Innovation at Miletus: Aristotle on Thales and His New Style of Cosmology

There is all too much we do not know about how people were thinking in the Greek world between 800 and 600 BCE. A few fragments of poets throw only an uncertain and indirect light here. While traditional political structures were crumbling and new ones appearing, it seems that nevertheless the Homeric-Hesiodic world-view, and the traditional religious beliefs and practices that underlay it, remained dominant. After 600 BCE, though, the picture becomes fuller, and other forms of religious belief and practice (particularly mystery-cults and occult beliefs) come into view.

One innovation that was surely of more than incidental significance was the introduction of Greek alphabetic writing. This made it possible, for one thing, to stabilize the texts of Homer and other poets in "canonical" versions. It made it possible also to reduce customary law to a standard, publicly available, and revisable written form. More than that, the ease of alphabetic writing, and the growth of literacy among the richer citizens, meant that any thinking involving more than the simplest kind of argumentation could now, for the first time, be exactly recorded and preserved by anyone literate, for consideration by anyone else who was literate and interested. It was no longer necessary to write metrically and to be dependent on surviving in enough memories. The mere possibility of committing one's thoughts to writing (not to mention the sheer pleasure of doing so) was itself an encouragement to any kind of speculation that went beyond the bounds of everyday experience.

An archaeological point is perhaps of interest here. Very little Greek writing, apart from inscriptions and graffiti, has been materially preserved from the archaic and classical centuries. Outstanding among the scanty finds are certain enigmatic texts dealing with occult religious matters: the gold plates found in Southern Italy, the Olbia bone-fragments, the Derveni papyrus.

Aristotle, whose testimony is our natural starting-point, ascribes to Thales of Miletus (active c. 600–550 BCE) the distinction of being the "founding father" (archēgos) of "natural science," or of a kind of "philosophy" (Met. A.3, 983a24–b27). It is clear enough what, in Aristotle's view, separated Thales and his successors from anything whatever that had preceded. For Aristotle, Thales was the first of those who "undertook proper examination of things that are" (eis episkepsin tōn ontōn elthontas), who "philosophized about reality" (philosophēsantes peri tēs alētheias), and was therefore trying to construct a science (epistēmē).

Aristotle is not here supposing that Thales produced anything like his (Aristotle's) own ideal of a science of nature. On the contrary, he forthrightly points out the defects, as he sees them, in the assumptions and methods of all the earlier theorists that he recognizes as forerunners. But his central point in Metaphysics A is that though they were fumbling beginners, they have an incontestable claim to be recognized as predecessors, as at least would-be scientists, because of the kind of explanations that they gave.

Thales apparently said that everything came out of, and was made of, water. This statement, taken on its own, could well be part of a creation myth of the kind familiar from some Ancient Near Eastern texts. But Aristotle interprets it (no doubt partly in the light of the better-attested theorizing of Thales' successors) as the provision of a "material cause." That is, he sees Thales as claiming that everything there is, its nature and behavior, can and must be understood exclusively in terms of the properties of water.

It is clear that this sort of general and abstract claim is not the kind of thing that one meets with, either expressed or latent, in Homer or Hesiod. It is characteristic of a theoretical enterprise. Aristotle elsewhere (e.g., *Met.* B.4, 1000a9–19; *Meteor.* II.1, 353a34–b5) contrasts with scientific explanations the explanations of those he calls "writers about gods" (*theologoi*), those who speak "in myths" (*muthikōs*), implying that they are incomplete, unsatisfactory and not worth wasting time on.

Whether or not we accept the Aristotelian account, it is important at least to understand what it does and what it does not imply. (The points made here apply also, and more clearly, to the better-documented successors of Thales.)

Above all, it does not imply that Thales was scientific because his theory was a "materialist" theory, or because it avoided explanations in terms of "gods." (Here I bypass questions about what was for Aristotle a "material" cause;[2] it is clear at least that Aristotle does not mean to attribute any well-developed concept of "matter" or "corporeality" to Thales.) Aristotle elsewhere (*Phys.* III.4, 203b3–15) implies that Thales' "water" was not just the water of ordinary everyday experience, as nowadays conceived, but a theoretically loaded version of the same, which was alive and intelligent, and could reasonably be entitled "the divine."

Aristotle himself disapproves of this sort of explanation, and finds it perhaps almost as archaic and bizarre as do most moderns. But that does not deter him from seeing it as being, at least in intention, a genuinely "scientific" explanation. The point, for Aristotle, is that, even if Thales' water is a "god," this is a very different kind of god from any of Homer and Hesiod's gods. It is an exceptionally well-defined god, of which the properties and powers could in principle be stated precisely in a finite list. Because of this theoretical precision, it can without absurdity be suggested as capable of giving a complete theoretical explanation of the universe.

The Theoretical Enterprise Unfolds: A Post-Aristotelian Interpretation

Aristotle's account of the beginnings of Greek science and philosophy is the unavoidable starting-point for any investigation. This is so for obvious reasons: Aristotle is by far the fullest, most coherent, most expert, and most intelligent witness we have. His conception of what happened is naturally hard to challenge; it has been accepted often enough, often without being very precisely understood.

But our dependence on Aristotle is not absolute. A certain amount of independent evidence survives, particularly in the shape of brief or longer quotations from original

2. See Bodnár and Pellegrin, ARISTOTLE'S PHYSICS AND COSMOLOGY, in this volume.

works of the sixth and fifth centuries. This other evidence can often suggest ways in which Aristotle, like any other historian of science and philosophy, has oversimplified and distorted. Inevitably Aristotle, like everyone else, sometimes cannot free himself sufficiently from his own temporal and philosophical standpoint.

From the discussion of the "flagship" case of Thales, above, it seems that the core of Aristotle's view about the nature of his innovation can be accepted, even if we do not accept Aristotle's whole philosophy of science and scientific explanation. We can understand that the new cosmology was new, and was proto-scientific, because it was a self-consciously *theoretical* enterprise.

Against this view, it can be argued that the non-Aristotelian evidence does not support such an understanding. (Here I draw on Frede, 2000.) The argument is partly linguistic: before Plato, the word "philosophy" and its derived verb (*philosophia*, *philosophein*) are rarely attested and have no specialized sense. Nor are there any other words that are obviously used to designate the new approach to cosmology and its practitioners as something separate and distinct. In parallel to these linguistic points, it can be pointed out that in the surviving remarks of the "pre-Socratic philosophers," we find them comparing themselves with, and attacking or praising, not only others of the same narrow group but also a whole range of poets and sages.

Much must be conceded to these arguments. It is certainly probable that, right down to the end of the fifth century, there was no one word or phrase in use to denote, exclusively, those we now separate off as "pre-Socratics." It is also highly likely that both their admirers and their detractors made use of the general terms "sage" (*sophos*: usually approving) and "clever person" (*sophistēs*: ambiguous as between approval and disapproval). These terms covered a multitude of activities, but their import was a person of real or pretended general intelligence, applied to all sorts of matters, whose insights might well not endorse traditional views. It is Herodotus who provides, in his portraits of such men as Solon and Amasis and his vignettes of Thales and others, the clearest view of what a "sage" was expected to be. It was characteristic of the sage to present himself as confidently in opposition to the general mass of received opinion; and this is certainly the attitude and the tone we find, to give an outstanding instance, in the opening of Heraclitus' book:

> While this *logos* is always men always prove to have no understanding, both before they have heard it and when once they have heard it. For though all things come about according to this *logos* they are like people of no experience when they experience words and deeds such as I set forth, dividing each thing according to nature (*phusin*) and pointing out how it is. (Heraclitus DK 22B1, part)

Corresponding to the inclusivity of these terms, it is also highly likely that at least the earliest theoretical cosmologists did not see themselves *exclusively* as such. Thales even won a place among the "Seven Sages," and it is his practical wisdom, as well as his "prediction" of a solar eclipse, that is illustrated by Herodotus. Xenophanes and Heraclitus mingle moral, political, and religious exhortation, and social criticism with their cosmologies.

Yet, even when all this is conceded, it by no means follows that Aristotle was wrong, that there were no new theoretical enterprises or new methods in cosmology, or that

9

they were not seen as something new. Here one must take account of a certain linguistic conservatism, which can be seen in other instances too. The evidence suggests strongly that Greek geometry and arithmetic were already developing as theoretical sciences before the end of the fifth century BCE. And yet the terms always used to denote these theoretical activities were ones that did not distinguish them at all from the corresponding practical ones: "geometry" (*geōmetria*) means "land-measurement," i.e. land-surveying; and the words for number theory (*arithmētikē, logismoi*) mean "the art of counting" and "reckonings."[3]

One important mark of such an enterprise is that it deals primarily in what may, loosely and untechnically, be called "abstract" entities. More precisely, its explanatory terms refer to entities which are theoretically postulated, and which, though related to the objects of experience, are at some remove from them. Most importantly, they are "sanitized" to enable them to be handled with precision in general theoretical reasonings.

The abstractness of even the earliest theorists, the Milesians, can be seen even in the case of Thales, if we accept on Aristotle's testimony that his "water" was not just the "water" of the modern physicist; but it appears more clearly with his successor Anaximander. For Anaximander the ultimate theoretical entity was "the infinite" (*to apeiron*): a self-confessed abstract entity, but one that sustains the same central role assigned by Thales to "water." With later theories of the same sort it is equally clear, and by no means exclusively on Aristotle's evidence, that even when "water" or "air" or "fire" figure as ultimate theoretical terms, the meaning of these words is only partly to be understood from our ordinary experience of the corresponding everyday things.

Corresponding to the new abstractness of the explanations is a new precision about what is to be explained. We saw that an impenetrable vagueness hangs over all the limits of Hesiod's or Homer's world. There is no plausible way, within the Homeric-Hesiodic world-view, in which even the gods could have more precise knowledge about these limits and what might or might not lie beyond them. This being so, it may be meaningless and it is certainly pointless to ask for such knowledge.

By contrast, the new-style cosmology has questions of limits, or their absence, at the forefront; and the subject for theoretical inquiry is not just the observable world-system (*kosmos*), but the universe, all that there is (*to pan, to holon, ta onta*). The Milesians, and many others later in the same tradition, opted for what was then the easiest solution, a spatially and temporally infinite universe. Hence one of their central theoretical tasks was to account for the existence of one or more finite world-systems (*kosmoi*) within the basically uniform universe. (In this connection, it is regrettable that so little is known about the early development of mathematics as an exact science in Greece. It is hard to believe that the advent of theoretical cosmology and that of theoretical arithmetic and geometry were not causally connected.)

Part of the point of this new kind of theoretical entity is that it lends itself to unrestricted general reasonings. This raises the question of the relevance of the concepts of *reason* and *rationality* to the innovations of the sixth century.

---

3.   On the development of Greek mathematics, see Mueller, GREEK MATHEMATICS TO THE TIME OF EUCLID, in this volume.

It would be a mistake to assume that the Homeric-Hesiodic world-view did not allow the application of reasoned argument to large questions about the nature of the world. Apart from the intrinsic implausibility of supposing that before around 600 BCE people were somehow "not rational" (at least on non-practical matters), but that thereafter they became so, there is actually no need to suppose any such thing. What we should say is, rather, that the Homeric-Hesiodic account of the world represents a favorable example of what human reason could produce, when working under the restrictive condition of not having yet discovered the possibility of a purely theoretical enterprise.

The problem (from a post-Milesian point of view) is that if one starts, not from theoretical entities specially postulated, but simply from things one takes to be directly and wholly given in experience, then, however rational one is, the possible power and reach of one's reasonings is severely limited. First, no Milesian-style reductions are possible: for example, stones, animals, and water are all given in experience as different things, so none of them can be theoretically "reduced" to anything else. All must stand side-by-side, equally primary, in any catalog of the contents of the world. Nor will counter-factual reasoning, that great weapon in the theoretical armory, be possible; for it will have no Archimedean point from which to exert leverage. To ask, about some feature of the world, "what if X were not as it in fact is?" is meaningless, if X is something that is wholly given by experience alone. For, in that case, one can have no grasp whatever of what it might mean for X *not* to be as it is. In short, while the theoretical enterprise is not to be identified with rationality *per se*, it is characteristic of the theoretical approach that it is needed to release the full power of which reasoned argument is capable.

Conversely, it is characteristic of the pre-theoretical approach that it is *necessarily* at the mercy of some generally accepted assumptions. We may see Homer and Hesiod as trying to make the best sense they could out of certain universally accepted assumptions of their time: above all, that the world was dominated by a group of anthropomorphic gods who were, by and large, friendly towards humankind and gave them information. (The fact that these particular assumptions have few adherents nowadays, and are indeed widely considered absurd and irrational, is not relevant to the point being made here, though it may have contributed to the confusions about the relevance of "rationality.")

It is only a purely theoretical approach that can give the necessary leverage to reveal generally accepted assumptions as what they are, namely mere assumptions. For generally accepted assumptions, a theoretical approach substitutes as its postulates other assumptions, which are claimed to be both intrinsically more acceptable and more successful at giving explanations of the experienced world.

Aristotle rightly saw the giving of certain types of explanation as an essential part of a science. The new style of cosmology was characterized and almost constituted by a new style of explanations. As Aristotle suggests, pre-theoretical explanations in the style of Homer and Hesiod are always essentially incomplete. At best they present an outline of a possible way of *understanding* the explanandum in outline, within a context of generally accepted assumptions; they do not and cannot show that it follows of necessity from the nature of things. By contrast, the new-style cosmology based its claim to attention precisely on its supposed ability to deliver an account of the

11

universe that not only agreed with experience but also followed of necessity from the stated principles.

Thus the postulates from which the whole enterprise started had to be not only true without exception, but also capable in principle of delivering a theory covering the whole of the universe in a coherent and unified way. Any suggestion of anything introduced *ad hoc*, to meet a particular difficulty, would be fatal to their plausibility. Everything about the universe had to be seen to flow of necessity from what it essentially *was*. Around this time the term *phusis*, usually translated "nature," began to become current to indicate the object of the new-style theorizing. As has been shown by Holwerda (1951), in archaic and early classical Greek *phusis* served as the noun corresponding to the verb *einai* "be" in most senses.

These theoretical demands naturally lead to a particular style of theorizing. Observable things have to be *reduced* to combinations of primary constituents; and their powers and interactions have to be *subsumed* as special cases under more general truths about the powers and interactions of the primary constituents. In particular, apparently abnormal and paradoxical phenomena must be shown to be naturally and convincingly explicable in the terms of the theory.

Instead of the chaos of accepted opinions, the new aesthetic of theoretical explanation requires structural unity and the maximum of symmetry and essential uniformity to be displayed in the universe. The principle later formulated as the "Principle of Sufficient Reason" seems to be implicit in this approach, and there are already signs of its conscious use in Anaximander's explanation of why the earth remains at rest (it is symmetrically placed with regard to the rest of the *kosmos*).

Theoretical Reflections on the Limits and Presuppositions of Cosmology: The Origins of Greek Philosophy

Like every other real revolution, the revolution in cosmology was irreversible. This was not because the new theoretical approach was self-evidently or provably truer in its results, and still less because of any impact on practical life (it had none), but because it was in itself obviously and incontestably an advance in the technology of reasoning. As with every revolution, there were those who tried to ignore or resist it ("they pluck the fruit of wisdom when it is unripe" complained Pindar (fr. 209 Snell) about the new style of cosmology); and those who fruitlessly attempted compromise between the old ways and the new, such as Pherecydes of Syros (on whom see Schibli, 1990).

But, also like every other real revolution, the revolution in cosmology tended in some sense to devour its own children. For it quickly became apparent that the shared program of theoretical investigation of the universe might lead equally intelligent theorists in different directions. This awkward fact is already evident within the Milesian group. All were monists, but each chose a different fundamental constituent and gave different mechanisms for the production of *kosmoi*.

Any one theorist, therefore, was likely to be in conflict not only with traditional ideas but with all other theorists as well. How was the new paradise of theoretical reasoning to be secured from internal disagreements? And what universally accept-able reasons could be found for preferring one theory to another?

Once these questions had been raised, they too could not be erased from the general awareness. They can be seen as the founding questions of Greek philosophy. The sup-porters of the theoretical approach in cosmology were forced henceforward to apply that same approach to higher-order questions, about knowledge, about reasoning and reasonableness, about the epistemic status of the theoretical approach itself.

The first person whom our evidence shows unambiguously to have been concerned with these problems, is Xenophanes of Colophon (active before and around 500 BCE). It is Xenophanes, then, who has the best claim to the title of "the first Greek philosopher."

Xenophanes raises the question of human knowledge directly and explicitly, and makes the fundamental point that truth is not a sufficient condition for knowledge. He concludes that on the central questions (the general nature of the universe as a whole, and the nature of the gods) no knowledge is to be had, for human beings at least: "And as for the certain truth, no man has known or ever will know that, concerning the gods and all the other things I speak of; for even if one should chance to say what is fully correct, still one does not *know*; it is *opinion* that is constructed about all these matters" (DK 21B34).

The natural supposition is that for Xenophanes knowledge is gained from first-hand experience only. Yet he himself went beyond that limit, as he indicates in these lines. And another remark (DK 21B18) expresses optimism about the possibility of human beings to "find out something better" without the help of the gods. How better "opinion" should be constructed on the basis of limited experience is indicated directly: "let these things be taken as opinions that resemble the truth" (DK 21B35). Indirectly, the pre-scription to be followed is indicated by the reports about Xenophanes' own ontologically parsimonious cosmology. Here his guiding principle is to assume that the parts of the universe inaccessible to direct human experience are essentially similar to the accessible parts. No unobserved constituents or forces are postulated.

In offering this cosmology, Xenophanes seems, at first sight, to have jettisoned one of the principal aims of the theoretical enterprise: that of giving a convincingly *unified* overall explanation of the universe. Xenophanes' universe, as revealed by his cosmology, hardly has much unity. But it turns out that Xenophanes has a second branch to his theorizing; the universe that is a subject for empirical cosmology, is *not* the whole universe. Beyond and behind it, there is a supreme god.[4]

Though our knowledge of this theology is tantalizingly incomplete (and Aristotle, who had read it entire, found it "unclear" at certain vital points), it seems that it was based on the principle that a god, or at least a supreme god, must be in every possible respect complete and perfect. It must therefore be a unity in some strong sense, and must also in some sense contain the rest of the universe. The desired overall unity of explanation, denied by the cosmology, is therefore restored by the theology. The prin-ciple of "perfection" on which it was based can hardly have been seen as something given in human experience; Xenophanes therefore must have taken it as something like an *a priori* truth.

---

4. On Xenophanes' theology, see also Betegh, GREEK PHILOSOPHY AND RELIGION, in this volume.

This conclusion is borne out to some extent by the evidence. First, Xenophanes made bitter attacks on the traditional, Homeric-Hesiodic religious opinions. These he lampooned as showing all traditional supposed "gods" to be theoretically unfit to be considered gods: they were morally vicious, limited by contingent circumstances, and were conceived of anthropomorphically, and according to the prevailing human physical type of each society. The implicit appeal is to some unvarying and absolute standard of divinity, implying (at least) moral and other kinds of superhuman perfection, in opposition to the various and confused conceptions of imperfect, "human" gods current in the tradition.

Also, Xenophanes' positive statements show the results of this appeal, and contain some statements directly indicating the standard being appealed to. "One god is greatest among gods and humankind, not like mortals either in bodily form or in thought." "It is as a whole that he sees, as a whole that he thinks, as a whole that he hears." "Always he stays still in the same place, not stirring at all; nor is it fitting for him to move about hither and thither (DK 21B23, B24, B26).

The most obscure part of Xenophanes' theology is the question of this god's relation to the observable universe. It is here that Aristotle (*Met.* A.5, 986b21–25) complains of "unclarity," but tells us at least that in some sense the supreme god *is* the whole universe, or the unity of the whole universe. The most natural way to make sense of this may be to take the supreme god as containing the rest of the universe in much the same way that a mind contains its contents. That at least would explain how the god "without effort, sways all things by the thought of his mind" (DK 21B25).

It is striking that Xenophanes, the first recognizable philosopher, thus stands at the beginning of two Greek philosophical traditions which are usually thought of as naturally opposed, and frequently were: the empiricist tradition and the tradition of *a priori* metaphysics.

In its process of development, philosophy gradually separated itself from the purely cosmological enterprise and the more specialized areas of study (astronomy, mathematics, medicine, biology) that had developed their own theoretical impetus partly in interaction with cosmology. But for both of the two great philosophers of the pre-Socratic period, Heraclitus of Ephesus (active c. 490 BCE) and Parmenides of Elea (active c. 470 BCE; not discussed in this chapter),[5] cosmology was still an integral part of their enterprise.

In his theory of the observable *kosmos*, Heraclitus maintained a Xenophanean empiricism, and a similar ontological parsimony, not postulating any unobserved but in principle observable entities (or forces or mechanisms). The observed and observable forces at work are therefore just the hot and the cold, the wet and the dry, engaged as forces in unending struggle among themselves, and embodying themselves in fire, water, and other manifest constituents of the *kosmos*.

But this cosmic struggle, warlike and yet also lawlike in its regular changes, is for Heraclitus only one particular example of an abstract schematism ("unity-in-opposites") which he found in all aspects of pre-theoretical human experience, and postulated as fundamental in all the underlying structures of the universe:

---

5. On Parmenides, see Curd, PARMENIDES AND AFTER, in this volume.

A road: uphill downhill one and the same. (DK 22B59)

Sea: water purest and most impure, for fishes drinkable and life-saving, for people undrinkable and deadly. (DK 22B61)

On those who step into the same rivers, other and other waters flow. (DK 22B12)

From these particular examples Heraclitus proceeded to a first attempt to conceptualize the notion of "structure" (*harmoniē*), and the assertion that "latent structure is master of visible" (DK 22B54).

So the understanding of the universe requires the uncovering of non-obvious "structures" which are determinative of everything else. This is a thought that would seem to have been implicit in the theoretical enterprise all along; in formulating it explicitly, Heraclitus comes to stand at the beginnings of the philosophy of science.

Rather less easy to decipher is another key concept of Heraclitus, "the *logos*" (or "this *logos*"), the introduction of which has already been cited. No even approximate equivalent of "*logos*", as used by Heraclitus, exists in English (or in any other modern language, so far as I know). The many uses of this word in ordinary Greek ("word", "story", "account", "reckoning", "selection", "proportion", "reasoning" are the most usual) are systematically exploited and theoretically united by Heraclitus. The details, and the upshot, are controversial; it is at least arguable that here we have, among other things, the beginnings of philosophical engagement with the concept of *reason*. "Though the *logos* is public, the many live their lives as though they had a private source of understanding" (DK 22B2).

But the *logos* is certainly not only the shared reason that enables human beings to understand the universe. Heraclitus sees it also as the reason that controls that same universe, on the principle that what reason can grasp must also be produced by reason. This active reason is traceable in the patterns of "unity-in-opposites" embedded in the observable universe: "When one listens not to me but to the *logos* it is wise to agree (*homologein*) that all things are one" (DK 22B50).

How the direction of the universe by the *logos* is to be conceived of, is perhaps the obscurest question in interpreting Heraclitus; but it seems that like Xenophanes he postulated a supreme and unifying deity, whose mind served as the carrier of the cosmic *logos*.

Xenophanes and Heraclitus can be seen as seeking, through philosophical reflection, to locate the cause and the cure of the troubles besetting the new theoretical cosmology. A rather different reaction, perhaps, was that of Pythagoras of Samos (active before and around 500 BCE), another personage of this period, and one mentioned with some contempt by both Xenophanes and Heraclitus.

Pythagoras, so far as one can penetrate the fog of legend that surrounds his life, presented himself to his contemporaries primarily as a magician, a wonder-worker, a mystagogue of charismatic personality. But he clearly also laid some claim to the all-round knowledge and the revealing insights of the "sage." It seems fairly certain that the "Pythagorean way of life" he imposed upon his followers included the study of mathematics and of music and astronomy, seen as exhibiting mathematical structures. At least this was a central point in the intellectual activity of many who saw themselves as "Pythagoreans" in the fifth century. A "Pythagorean" program of "reducing everything to numbers" was current then; and may possibly go back to

Pythagoras himself. If so, it is yet another example of the emergence in this period of thoughts that were to have a long subsequent history in the practice and philosophy of science.

Questions and Disputes

The previous part of this chapter has outlined an interpretation of certain texts from the archaic and classical periods of ancient Greece. It will already be obvious that the evidence for many points is fragmentary and miscellaneous; and that, even though some complete texts survive (notably the poems of Homer and Hesiod), these texts never tell us unambiguously and fully all that we want to know. Interpretations on such matters are always open to dispute.

It is also clear that any interpreter must necessarily, knowingly or not, take up positions on some fundamental matters of method and approach. It cannot be said that there is a great deal of agreement on any of these matters in recent scholarship; nor is that a fact to be regretted. In this final section I offer a brief survey of some of the more fundamental disputes, in the light of some recent scholarly works.

One question that causes trouble is that of "teleology" in the understanding of the history of science and philosophy. In this chapter I have been professedly concerned with the "beginnings of science and philosophy," and have therefore been taking as a starting-point and a guide some *modern* notions of what constitutes "science" and "philosophy" respectively. Such a procedure is exposed to obvious dangers: one must constantly be aware of the all the ways in which the archaic Greek "beginnings" were significantly *unlike* modern science and philosophy, as well as all the ways in which they were significantly *like* them. But that is just one way of formulating all the central questions about the subject-matter.

Some would, perhaps, reject any such procedure at the outset, as irredeemably "teleological." In this context the word "teleology" is often used as a convenient term of abuse, and like many such terms it serves to cover a multitude of different things, which need to be distinguished.

"Teleology", in the broadest sense of studying the ancient world in the light of a modern understanding of things, may be not wholly desirable (because of the dangers already mentioned), but is in any case completely inevitable. It is absurd to suppose that the ancient texts alone could generate for us a purely "ancient" way of understanding them.

More properly "teleology" implies the understanding of historical developments by seeing them as moving towards some, supposedly somehow pre-ordained, goal. Here we must distinguish different suppositions about the goal involved. Science and philosophy are of their very nature directed towards goals: the better knowing and understanding of human experience, and of the world as given in experience. Hence *if* any progress towards these goals is in fact possible, and *if* human minds collectively are capable of learning from the results of repeated trial and error, then there will be a kind of "teleology" inherent in the history of science and philosophy, without which no sort of understanding of it is possible. But to say this is not to say that such progress is always possible, still less that progress will always be made.

Above all, to say this is not at all to discount the importance, both historical and philosophical, of what appear from a modern point of view as "dead-ends" and "failures." To take a striking example from this period: in the development of archaic Greek theorizing, the "cosmo-theology" of the Milesians, described above, is such a "dead-end," an evolutionary curiosity having no living descendants. Yet it was, of course, of the greatest possible importance in the development of both science and philosophy.

Even if it is admitted that we may reasonably look for "the beginnings of science and philosophy" in the archaic period of ancient Greece, there is still room for disputes about the nature of the developments in that period. For a start, the value of Aristotle's evidence may be questioned. The attempt by Cherniss (1964) at a root-and-branch destruction of Aristotle's credibility as a witness, no longer commands much assent. Yet one may still reasonably suspect that Aristotle does not always avoid, or even notice, the dangers inherent in his way of seeing things. And it would certainly be wholly unjustified to assume that Aristotle always tells us all that we wish to know about the earlier theorists. In any particular case, the question is a complex one, and there is no room for sweeping generalizations. (For an example of moderate and well-based skepticism about Aristotle's evidence on one important point, and how it might be answered, see page 9.)

There are always those who emphasize continuity in human history, at the expense of discontinuity; and conversely those who emphasize discontinuity at the expense of continuity. It is better to admit at once that in any line of development there are always both continuities and discontinuities to be found. That does not help us to answer any specific questions: for example, was Hesiod already "scientific?" were the Milesians still "pre-scientific?" Reasons for saying "no" to both questions have been given above. They depend essentially on a particular view about which aspects of science (as at present understood) are essential and which are not. In general, any particular understanding of "early Greek science and philosophy" inevitably involves some general conception of *science* and of *philosophy*. It is hardly surprising, given the contestability of any such conceptions, that many different kinds of answer to these two questions are to be found in recent scholarship.

There are those who seek to show that, for example, the cosmology of Hesiod is of essentially the same kind as that of the earliest "pre-Socratics." The strong cultural influence of the "Ancient Near East" on archaic Greece is often invoked in this connection. One notable representative of this view is Martin West, whose book *Early Greek philosophy and the Orient* (West, 1971) goes further than most in claiming the essential dependence of early Greek science and philosophy on the "Ancient Near East;" while claims along the same lines are made, for example, by Burkert (1999) and Hölscher (1968).

If one accepts that there is indeed a qualitative difference between the Homeric-Hesiodic world view and that of the Milesian cosmologists, there is still scope for disagreement about the ultimate nature of this difference. The most favored view, until recently, was that Hesiod's and similar cosmologies were not "rational" but "mythical;" whereas the new theoretical enterprise was "rational" (see, for example, Barnes, 1979; Kirk, Raven, and Schofield, 1983; Vernant, 1983). This view has lost popularity recently, perhaps because it is now generally perceived that, at best, without further explanation of what is meant by "rationality," it merely rephrases the problem rather than giving any insight into it. As argued above, there is *no* obvious sense in which Hesiod's cosmogony was not the result of rational thought; yet there is something important that is half-concealed in this view, and needs to be brought out.

Another type of view places the emphasis on changing conceptions of "truth;" but here it is doubtful whether we can make sense of a conception of truth that is as flexible as seems to be required. (See Detienne, 1996; and Williams, 2002.) As argued above, there is certainly a most important difference between the *sources* of authoritative truth, as conceived of by the Homeric-Hesiodic view and by the sixth-century theorists. But whether this was the cause or the consequence of the different conceptions of reality, is another question.

There are also questions, hardly touched on in this chapter, about the circumstances (political, economic, social, and cultural) in which Greek science and philosophy began, and which may have helped or hindered their development. Some have pointed to political changes: the decay of the traditional political authority of kings and princes, and the development of new political structures with more widespread participation of citizens in the political process. (On all this, see Lloyd, 1987; Vernant, 1983.) Here I have suggested, following many others, that the spread of an alphabetic script and hence of a degree of literacy in Greece may well have been important, at least as a catalyst. (For other views on this question, see, for example, Lloyd, 1979; Osborne, 1997.)

Bibliography

Presocratics: Texts and Translations

Diels, H. (1951–2). (Cited as DK). *Die Fragmente der Vorsokratiker* (3 vols., 6th edn., revised by W. Kranz and often reprinted). Berlin: Weidmann. (Original work published 1903.)

Kirk, G. S., Raven, J. E. and Schofield, M. (1983). *The Presocratic Philosophers* (2nd edn.). Cambridge: Cambridge University Press.

McKirahan, R. D., Jr. (1994). *Philosophy before Socrates: An Introduction with Texts and Commentary*. Indianapolis: Hackett.

Works Cited

Barnes, J. (1979). *The Presocratic Philosophers*. London: Routledge and Kegan Paul.

Burkert, W. (1999). "The Logic of Cosmogony." In R. Buxton (ed.), *From Myth to Reason? Studies in the Development of Greek Thought* (pp. 87–106). Oxford: Oxford University Press.

Cherniss, H. (1964). *Aristotle's Criticism of Presocratic Philosophy*. New York: Octagon Books Inc.

Davies, M. (1991). *Poetarum Melicorum Graecorum Fragmenta*. vol 1. Oxford: Oxford University Press.

Detienne, M. (1996). *The Masters of Truth in Archaic Greece*. New York: Zone Books.

Frede, M. (2000). "The Philosopher." In J. Brunschwig and G. E. R. Lloyd (eds.), *The Greek Pursuit of Knowledge* (pp. 1–17). Cambridge, Mass. and London: Belknap Press of Harvard University Press.

Hölscher, U. (1968). *Anfängliches Fragen*. Göttingen: Vandenhoeck and Ruprecht.

Holwerda, D. (1951). *Commentatio de vocis quae est FUSIS vi atque usu praesertim in Graecitate Aristotele anteriore*. Groningen: J. B. Walters.

Kirk, G. S., Raven, J. E. and Schofield, M. (1983). *The Presocratic Philosophers* (2nd edn.). Cambridge: Cambridge University Press.

Lloyd, G. E. R. (1979). *Magic, Reason and Experience: Studies in the Origins and Development of Greek Science*. Cambridge: Cambridge University Press.

——. (1987). *The Revolutions of Wisdom: Studies in the Claims and Practices of Ancient Greek Science*. Berkeley: University of California Press.

Osborne, R. (1997). "The Polis and its Culture." In C. C. W. Taylor (ed.). *Routledge History of Philosophy*. vol. 1: *From the Beginning to Plato* (pp. 9–46). London and New York: Routledge.

Schibli, H. S. (1990). *Pherekydes of Syros*. Oxford: Clarendon Press.

Snell, B. (1964). *Pindarus*. Lipsiae [Leipzig]: B. G. Teubner.

Vernant, J.-P. (1983). *Myth and Thought Among the Greeks*. London: Routledge and Kegan Paul.

West, M. L. (1971). *Early Greek Philosophy and the Orient*. Oxford: Oxford University Press.

Williams, B. (2002). *Truth and Truthfulness: An Essay in Genealogy*. Princeton and Oxford: Princeton University Press.

Further Readings

Frede, M. (1996). "Introduction." In M. Frede and G. Striker (eds.), *Rationality in Greek Thought* (pp. 1–28). Oxford: Clarendon Press.

Hussey, E. (1990). "The Beginnings of Epistemology." In S. Everson (ed.), *Epistemology* (pp. 11–38). Cambridge: Cambridge University Press.

——. (1995). "Ionian Inquiries." In A. Powell (ed.), *The Greek World* (pp. 530–49). London and New York: Routledge.

——. (2000). "Heraclitus." In A. A. Long (ed.), *The Cambridge Companion to Early Greek Philosophy* (pp. 88–112). Cambridge: Cambridge University Press.

Jordan, W. (1990). *Ancient Concepts of Philosophy*. London: Routledge.

Kahn, C. H. (1979). *The Art and Thought of Heraclitus*. Cambridge: Cambridge University Press.

Lloyd, G. E. R. (1966). *Polarity and Analogy: Two Types of Argumentation in early Greek Thought*. Cambridge: Cambridge University Press.

——. (1990). *Demystifying Mentalities*. Cambridge: Cambridge University Press.

——. (1991). *Methods and Problems in Greek Science*. Cambridge: Cambridge University Press.

Vlastos, G. (1995). *Studies in Greek Philosophy*. (vol. 1): *The Presocratics* (ed. D. W. Graham). Princeton: Princeton University Press.

West, M. L. (1966). *Hesiod Theogony*. Oxford: Oxford University Press.

2

Ancient Philosophy and the Doxographical Tradition

JØRGEN MEJER

It is an unfortunate fact that by far most of the texts written by ancient philosophers have been lost. We are lucky to have the more or less complete works of important philosophers like Plato, Aristotle, Epictetus (as reported by Arrian), Sextus Empiricus, Plotinus, Lucretius, Cicero and Seneca; we have many late commentators on Plato and Aristotle, and we have some important texts by Epicurus, preserved in Diogenes Laertius (cf. below). In addition to these texts transmitted through medieval manuscripts, a few philosophical texts have been preserved on papyrus: a long section from Empedocles' poem, a couple of sections from the Sophist Antiphon's *On Truth*, longer and shorter passages in the Herculanean papyri from Epicurus' *On Nature* and from Philodemus' treatises, and the second century CE Stoic Hierocles' *Elements of Ethics* (Sider, 2005). But most of the philosophical texts written by the pre-Socratic, the Socratic and the Hellenistic philosophers have not survived even though many passages were quoted by other ancient authors.

This is not surprising. In fact, most ancient texts disappeared before the end of antiquity, and the study of philosophical texts had an even smaller public in Greco-Roman antiquity than has been the case since the Renaissance. It demanded a public interest like the dramatic tradition in Athens, or a dedicated group of people like the members of an established philosophical school to secure the transmission and survival of texts. The situation as we find it first described in Plato's dialogues did not change significantly in Greek and Roman antiquity: philosophy was practiced in gymnasia, stoas, and other public places, or in private homes, not in institutions of teaching or learning. The Platonic Academy, the Aristotelian Peripatos and Epicurus' Garden were the only institutions that provided space for continuous philosophical activity and for collections of philosophical texts, and even these locations were not able to survive Sulla's attack on Athens in 86 BCE.[1] The famous Villa of the Papyri in Herculaneum from shortly after that date was an Epicurean establishment, and the library found there was beyond doubt the library of the Epicurean scholar Philodemus, but apart from Epicurean philosophical texts it has so far not provided other original works by philosophers (Gigante, 1995). In general, the study of texts does not seem to have played a significant role in philosophical activity, at least down to the Roman Empire.

---

1.   See Bénatouïl, PHILOSOPHIC SCHOOLS IN HELLENISTIC AND ROMAN TIMES.

There are numerous testimonies that philosophical texts became very difficult to get hold of and even disappeared before the end of antiquity. In fact, in the second century BCE the Athenian scholar Apollodorus "happened to find" (D.L. 2.2) a copy of the pre-Socratic philosopher Anaximander's one and only book – which is otherwise lost except for one possible sentence. The Platonic dialogues were not readily available one hundred years after his death (D.L. 3.66), and though some of the Aristotelian treatises were known during the Hellenistic period, the main body of his works only became available to the public after the editorial work done by Andronicus and others in the first century BCE (Barnes, 1997; Gottschalk, 1987; Moraux, 1973) when the scholarly tradition of commenting upon his works began. A commentary in antiquity was usually a separate volume and the commentaries followed the order of the statements of the original work, citing a few words to indicate from where the comment took off, the so-called *lemma*. Hence a commentary presupposes the presence of the book with which it deals.

Even if it was possible to find a copy of a philosophical text, it was difficult to be certain what was a genuine work, to find a good copy of a genuine work by an earlier philosopher, and to get hold of the complete œuvre of an author. Hence the work of Andronicus who had to put together various Aristotelian treatises and determine the authorship of some of the texts; hence the work of Thrasyllus on the works of Plato and of Democritus in the first half of the first century CE – the Corpus Platonicum as it has been transmitted to us in the medieval manuscripts (and as it is still printed in the Oxford Classical Library) goes back to Thrasyllus (Tarrant, 1993). It is no coincidence that many quotations from Democritus come from authors living between 50 and 230 CE, and that the tradition of making commentaries on the texts of Plato and Aristotle gained ground in the same period. In the middle of the fourth century CE Emperor Julian complains that most of the Epicurean and Skeptic texts had disappeared (Julian fr. *Ep.* 89, p. 141 Bidez), and the commentator Simplicius in the sixth century CE specifically states that he will quote from Parmenides' poem and other pre-Socratic texts because they were hard to find (e.g., *In Phys.* 39.20–21 or 144.28 Diels). The fact that philological questions play such a significant role in the late Platonic commentators proves that it was always hard to study philosophical texts, not only because of the scarcity of texts, but also because it was, then as now, difficult to read texts that were hundreds of years old.

It is only when we reach the Neoplatonic school in the third century CE, that we find direct evidence for the use of philosophical texts in the daily routine of a philosophical school, and it is no coincidence that we have not only a substantial body of texts by Plato and Aristotle, but also numerous commentaries on these texts.[2] A vivid account of the reading of philosophical texts in a "class," accompanied by written or oral commentaries, was given by Plotinus' student Porphyry in his *Life of Plotinus* as follows:

> In the meetings of the school he [Plotinus] used to have the commentaries read, perhaps of Severus, perhaps of Cronius or Numenius, or Gaius or Atticus, and among the

2. On the composition and production of these commentaries, see Hoffmann, WHAT WAS COMMENTARY IN LATE ANTIQUITY?

Peripatetics of Aspasius, Alexander, Adrastus, and others that were available. But he did not just speak straight out of these books but took a distinctive personal line in his consideration, and brought the mind of Ammonius to bear on the investigation at hand. He quickly absorbed what was read, and would give the sense of some profound subject of study in a few words and pass on. When Longinus' work *On Principles* and his *Lover of Antiquity* were read to him, he said, "Longinus is a scholar, but certainly not a philosopher" . . . The rhetorician Diophanes read a defense of Alcibiades in Plato's *Symposium* in which he asserted that a pupil for the sake of advancing in the study of virtue should submit himself to carnal intercourse with his master if the master desired it. Plotinus repeatedly started up to leave the meeting, but restrained himself, and after the end of the lecture gave me, Porphyry, the task of writing a refutation. Diophanes refused to lend me his manuscript, and I depended in writing my refutation on my memory of his arguments. When I read it before the assembled hearers . . . (Porphyry *Plot.* 14–15 Armstrong)

Towards the end of antiquity, the period in which most of our commentaries on Aristotelian texts were written, the teaching of philosophy had become a very systematic enterprise in which texts and commentaries played a central role, including the study of philosophical predecessors whose views had bearing on the texts of Plato and Aristotle. Already Seneca had complained that philosophy had become philology (*Ep.* 108.23ff.), and in the Neoplatonic school after Plotinus there was a more or less fixed curriculum of texts to be studied and explained according to a prescribed method. The reading of Aristotelian texts preceded the reading of a selection of Platonic dialogues, and in each case the curriculum began with a series of topics that we also find in modern courses on Plato and Aristotle. Thus, when reading Plato, the lecturer would begin his teaching by discussing the following topics (cf., Anon. *Prolegomena in Philosophiam Platonis*; cf., Sorabji, 1990):

1. The nature of Platonic philosophy; Plato compared to other philosophical schools
2. Why has Plato, but not Pythagoras and Socrates, written philosophical books?
3. Why did Plato write dialogues?
4. The main elements of a dialogue, in particular the dramatic setting, the style, and the arguments.
5. The title of the dialogues.
6. How are the philosophical topics of the dialogues to be distinguished from one another?
7. The style of presentation.
8. How many rules are there for determining the purpose of the dialogue?
9. The order of the dialogues.
10. Plato's way of teaching philosophy.

While this approach may seem natural to us, there is little evidence that this or any other systematic approach was common before the Neoplatonic school. A similar, systematic approach was given in connection with the study of Aristotle's *Categories*. But the fact that philosophy now had become mainly the study of texts by Aristotle and Plato is the reason why so many of the fragments of the pre-Socratic philosophers come from the commentaries of the Neoplatonic commentators, especially Simplicius:

in order to understand the Aristotelian text it was necessary to know the many names and views of previous philosophers to whom Aristotle refers.

The modern concept of "history of philosophy" did not exist in the Greco-Roman antiquity. Philosophers turned to their predecessors in order to throw light on the problems they themselves were dealing with or in order to reject competing views, not because they were interested in the historical development of human thinking. It is important to keep this in mind because the reason for quoting a philosophical text is almost always to find confirmation or to express criticism. Thus, the modern scholar is obliged always to take the context into consideration before evaluating the significance of a quotation or "fragment," the more so since the concept "fragment" is nowhere clearly defined in modern scholarship. Many so-called fragments appear in different sources with different variations, and it is often difficult to determine whether a reference to an earlier philosopher is a direct quotation (fragment), a paraphrase, or an individual interpretation of a text.

No ancient text pretends to offer an account of the development of philosophy as a sequence of conceptual thinking. It may have been Sophists like Gorgias and Hippias who began to collect excerpts from philosophical and other texts in the fifth century BCE, but this is not the beginning of history of philosophy. It is, however, one important characteristic of early Greek philosophy that philosophers seem to have been aware of their predecessors and contemporaries (see e.g., DK 31B1 and B112 Empedocles, DK 47B1 Archytas, or DK 64B1 Diogenes of Apollonia), but a real interest in the philosophy of the past was at first closely connected with Aristotle's view of philosophy and the acquisition of knowledge. Plato may have known many of the pre-Socratics, but since reality for him was the world of Forms and this reality came to the philosopher as a direct experience, as, for example, described in the *Symposium*, history as such was never central to his philosophical project.

For Aristotle, the reality of the world as described by earlier philosophers was too strong to be neglected even if his predecessors only had discovered part of the truth: "Let us remember that we should not disregard the experience of the ages; in the multitude of years these things, if they were good, would certainly not have been unknown; for almost everything has been found out, although sometimes they are not put together; in other cases men do not use the knowledge which they have (Arist. *Pol.* II.5, 1264a1–4, cf. also *Met.* α.1, 993a31–b19 and M.1, 1076a12–16). Aristotle always stressed the significance of the beginning (*archē* meaning both beginning and principle) of thoughts and things and hence he always tried to lead up to his own views by reviewing those of his predecessors. This was part of the dialectical process, cf. *Top.* II.2 and II.14. Needless to say, he was never writing history of philosophy as such, but always reviewed the past in the light of his own philosophical problems and solutions. Some of the most influential passages of this kind are in the first book of the *Metaphysics* and in the early books of his *Physics*. In addition to the numerous passages that deal with earlier and contemporary philosophy in his preserved works, he also wrote a fair number of (now lost) books on individual pre-Socratics. His work was in particular carried on by his pupil and successor, Theophrastus, and a significant part of the so-called doxographical tradition must have been derived ultimately from their books even though there were also other kinds of works on philosophical ideas, in particular of Hellenistic philosophy (see below). There can be little doubt that it was far more common for intellectuals to have learnt about earlier philosophy from such reports than from reading the original philosophical works themselves, except for the Platonic dialogues which were known throughout antiquity, and for those Aristotelian texts which were studied by members of the Peripatos and especially the Platonic Academy in the Roman Empire.

It is, however, wrong to think of doxographical works as constituting a literary genre in classical antiquity. Doxography is a nineteenth-century term, made famous by Hermann Diels' *Doxographi Graeci* (Berlin, 1879), in which he collected a number of texts that all report the views of Greek philosophers from Thales to the mid first century BCE. In the long Latin preface to this collection Diels discussed the characteristics of these texts, which exhibit so many similarities that they can be considered with some justification as belonging to a particular tradition. Diels' establishment of this so-called doxographical tradition has dominated the discussion of the sources for early Greek philosophy for more than 100 years, but has recently come under decisive criticism (see Mansfeld and Runia, 1996). It is important to notice that the term "doxography" is modern, created as an analogy to the term *logographos* (= speech-writer for litigants in courts, writer of prose), and based on the title of a number of Hellenistic books called *On the Opinions of . . .* (Greek *doxa*, *dogma*; other terms are used, and in particular the Latin word *placita* has been used to designate these texts).

The two texts that constitute the main specimens of doxography are Pseudo-Plutarch's *Epitome of the Opinions of the Philosophers* (often called *Placita Philosophorum*) from the second century CE, also copied out by Eusebius in his *Praeparatio Evangelica* Books 14–15 in the fourth century and translated into Arabic shortly before 900 CE, and the very similar anonymous excerpts in Stobaeus' *Anthology* (1.1–46; 4.36–37; and 4.50a30). The texts of these two sources were printed in parallel columns by Diels (*Doxographi Graeci*, pp. 273–444; for an example, see Table 2.1); they consist of entries, or questions, on philosophical and other matters, according to Ps.-Plutarch arranged in five books dealing with cosmology and (meta)physics (I), the heavenly bodies (II), meteorology (III), psychology and perception (IV), and human physiology and embryonics (V). Under each entry are listed the views of a number of philosophers, from the pre-Socratics to the first century BCE (and even in a few cases later), views that purport to give answers to topics like: On the void, On time, How did the world originate? What is the nature of the heavenly bodies? Are sense impressions true? How does conception take place? The selection of philosophers is far from systematic, and their views are presented as simple statements of fact, without any context or arguments. The different views are organized in such a way that similar views are put together, without regard for the chronological sequence, and then contrasted with a different view. As an example, in Table 2.1 we take two chapters on time as presented in Diels p. 318, labeled Aëtius 1.21–22.

In fact, Diels' presentation is deceptive unless the reader takes his critical apparatus into consideration, for the chapter headings are not in Stobaeus, and the three sections on Plato (21.2; 22.1 and 9) are not listed here by Stobaeus but in a later chapter (1.8.45), and 22.7–8 follow the section on Eratosthenes. Furthermore, Stobaeus has an extra section on the Stoic Chrysippus following Xenocrates, obviously taken from a later chapter on Chrysippus (1.8.42).

24

Table 2.1   Sample from *Doxographi Graeci*

Ps.-Plutarch *Epitome* 1.21 *On Time*		Stobaeus *Ecl.* 1.8.40b *On Time*
Pythagoras says that time is the sphere of the surrounding.	1	Pythagoras says that it is the sphere of the surrounding.
Plato, that it is a moving image or the distance of the movement of the world.	2	Plato that it is a moving image or the distance of the movement of the world.
Eratosthenes, that it is the path of the sun.	3	Eratosthenes that it is the path of the sun.

Ps.-Plutarch *Epitome* 1.22 *On the Nature of Time*		Stobaeus *Ecl.* 1.8.40b *On the Nature of Time*
Plato says that the movement of the universe is the nature of time.	1	[Plato] says that the movement of the universe is the nature of time.
	2	Xenocrates says that the nature of time is what measures things created, and eternal movement.
	3	Hestiaeus from Perinthus, the physicist, says that it is the movement of the stars relative to one another.
	4	Strato says that it is the size of the things in movement and at rest.
	5	Epicurus says that it is an attribute [of attributes], i.e. an attendant circumstance of movements.
	6	Antiphon and Critolaus say that time is a thought or a measure, not a substance.
Most of the Stoics say that it is movement in itself.	7	The Stoics say that time is movement in itself.
Most people say that time is ungenerated.	8	Most people say that time is ungenerated.
Plato says that it is generated in thinking.	9	[Plato] says that it is generated in thinking.

These two chapters demonstrate some of the problems that make it difficult to reconstruct a common source, and the recent analysis in Mansfeld and Runia (1996, 226–8), suggests a different arrangement of the original text than that given by Diels. While there is good reason to assume that Ps.-Plutarch has preserved the structure of the lost sources, it is not always certain that all the views presented by Stobaeus belong to the original text, and it is obvious that it is far more important to study the later doxographical texts as transmitted than Diels did. They may have had different purposes in shaping their presentations than the sources which they used, and this may affect the reliability of their reports. What matters, obviously, is the variety of opinions, not the connection between notions nor the argumentation of individual philosophers as such: the order follows neither chronology nor connections to philosophical schools, and the presence or absence of any individual philosopher is no indication of the significance of the information. If we follow Ps.-Plutarch, *Epit.* 1.22 begins with two opposing views (Plato vs. the Stoics) while sections 2–4 give the views of philosophers who gave time a place in the physical world, 5 and 6 the views of those who seem to deny the reality of time. Sections 8–9 deal with a separate issue, viz. whether or not time is generated.

Both Ps.-Plutarch's and Stobaeus' accounts must, despite variations, have been based on the same source, who according to Diels and most other scholars was an otherwise unknown writer of a doxographical work by the name of Aëtius, to be dated c. 100 CE. This work, in its turn, seems to be based on similar works from the first century BCE and even the earlier Hellenistic period since the earliest trace of it is found in Chrysippus in the third century BCE. One or more of these works were extremely popular both in the Hellenistic period and in the Roman Empire, and we can recognize their influence in, for example, Cicero, Varro, Athenagoras, Soranus, and the *Historia Philosopha*, which is falsely attributed to Galen, but in fact dates from late antiquity. But it is obvious from the example given above that there are major variations in the doxographical texts: It is important that the modern scholar look not only at what is claimed to be the reconstructed text of Aëtius but also at the transmitted text of the numerous doxographical sources from the second to the sixth centuries CE (see further Mansfeld and Runia, 1996).

A different kind of doxography is found in (primarily) the church father Hippolytus, Diogenes Laertius, and Ps.-Plutarch's *Stromateis* (= *Patchwork*, *Miscellanies*), (see Mansfeld, 1992, and Mejer, 1992). These doxographies differ from the first kind in that they present the views of each philosopher in a separate chapter, but they are similar to it in that they report on the same five areas, often in the same order and with the same wording. As an example we may take Diogenes Laertius' summary of Democritus' philosophy (D.L. 9.44–45):

> Democritus' opinions are as follows:
> (44) The principles of everything are atoms and void, and everything else is conventional. There are infinitely many worlds which come into being and pass away. The atoms are infinite in size and number, and they are carried about in the whole in a swirl, and in that way they generate all the compounds, fire, water, air, earth. For these things too are complexes of atoms, which are incapable of being affected and changeless because of their solidity. The sun and the moon are compounded of smooth, round bodies of that kind, as is the soul, which is the same as the mind. We see through the impact of images. (45) Everything comes to be by necessity, the swirl, which he calls necessity, being the cause of the coming to be of everything. The goal in life is to be in a good state of mind (*euthumia*), but this state is not, as some erroneously have interpreted it, the same as pleasure, but the state in which the soul is quiet and well balanced, undisturbed by any fear or superstition or any other emotion. Democritus calls this state of mind "well-being" (*euestō*) and uses many other terms. Conventions are artificial; in reality only atoms and the void exist. – These are the opinions of Democritus. (Taylor, 1999, with some changes)

In §44 the information follows the order of the presentation in Ps.-Plutarch's *Epitome*, and once again, there are no arguments or reasons offered. This report does not, like so many other doxographical sources, add to what we know from other sources, mainly Aristotle and Theophrastus, though in some instances it is possible to draw conclusions that we could not obtain from other sources. Thus, the cosmological information about Anaximander in Hippolytus' *Refutatio* 1.6.1–7 (= DK 12A11) is important, and the otherwise questionable interpretation of Heraclitus' cosmology in D.L. 9.7–11 is indicative of some definite structure of Heraclitus' book, which must have been more than just a collection of sayings (cf. D.L. 9.5).

The second paragraph of the Democritean doxography is, however, unique and deserves further scrutiny. It confirms the important principle stated in the beginning of §44 that only atoms and void are real, thus denying the possibility of primary and secondary qualities, a distinction which is sometimes attributed to Democritus, and it proves that there must have been a discussion of Democritus' ethics, a subject which is otherwise neglected in the ancient sources, though Thrasyllus placed Democritus' ethical works first in his catalog of his writings (cf. D.L. 9.46). It is also noteworthy that a reference to ethics can be combined with the usual five areas of doxographical reports, thus demonstrating that the individual doxographer can add to or subtract from what he found in his sources.

While some of these doxographical reports thus contain important information, others demonstrate that the knowledge about earlier Greek philosophy in late antiquity can be confused and misleading. It is important to notice that both kinds of doxography basically abstain from criticizing or discussing the views presented, as is also clear from some remarks quoted by St. Augustine in his preface to *De haeresibus* (*Patr. Lat.* vol. 42, p. 23):

> A certain Celsus [otherwise unknown] has presented the views of all philosophers who founded philosophical schools down to his own period . . . in six rather large volumes. He did not refute any of them, he just explained what they thought, with such brevity that both style and content gave room, not for praising and criticizing, nor for confirming or defending, but only for explaining and presenting their ideas. For Celsus mentioned more than one hundred philosophers, not all of whom even founded their own schools, since he was of the opinion that he ought not to neglect those philosophers who followed their teachers without dissent.

Quotations from Aristotle's student Theophrastus in the Aristotelian commentator Simplicius in the sixth century CE demonstrate that the sections on the Greek philosophers from Thales to Plato in the doxographical sources must ultimately go back to Theophrastus who both in independent treatises (on Democritus, Anaxagoras, etc.) and in his philosophical works discussed his predecessors. It is not certain that all this information is derived from his *Peri phusikōn doxōn* (= *Physical Opinions*, as the likely meaning is), though this has often been assumed, since Theophrastus like Aristotle used to discuss the historical development of ideas as a preliminary step to his own philosophy: many of the fragments which Diels attributed to his *Peri phusikōn doxōn* in fact come from Theophrastus' *Physics*. We cannot be sure from which book the fragment of his *De Sensibus* comes (Balthussen, 2000), but it seems likely that this fragment in any case gives a fair impression of the way Theophrastus presented the views of his predecessors.

It is not known who changed the Aristotelian-Theophrastean way of discussing their predecessors according to the affiliation of their views into the less problem-oriented system we find in the so-called doxographers. It is important to notice that each doxographer seems to have changed and added to his immediate predecessor, but the fact that several sources attribute the same view to a particular philosopher does not by itself increase the likelihood that it reflects the original ideas of that philosopher. All it means is that this was a standard item within the doxographical tradition.

Though doxography in a strict sense originally applied only to those sources that were thought to derive from Theophrastus, it has later come to be used about any ancient source which reports the views of earlier philosophers. It has even been suggested (Giusta, 1964–8) that, corresponding to the doxographies on physics and metaphysics, there must have been another doxographical tradition dealing with ethics. There seems, however, to be general agreement that such a parallel tradition cannot be proven to have existed. The similarity between various texts, e.g. in Cicero and Seneca, is no greater than can be explained as a result of a common way of dealing with particular ethical problems.

There is another type of philosophical historiography which may be called doxographical, viz. a series of works called *Peri haireseōn* (= *On Sects*), written in the second and first centuries BCE. These works are all lost and only known from references and quotations in, especially, Diogenes Laertius; only one substantial excerpt on Peripatetic and Stoic ethics, from Arius Didymus preserved by Stobaeus, can possibly be attributed to this type of work (*Ecl.* 2.7 = 2.37, 14–152, 25 Wachsmuth; the identity of Arius Didymus, commonly assumed to be Augustus' Stoic court philosopher, is uncertain, cf. Göransson, 1995). Eusebius and Stobaeus also preserve sections on the physical theories of these two schools which may come from the same work; since we can compare the Peripatetic material with Aristotle's own works, it is of less importance than the sections on the Stoics whose writings are all lost (cf. Pomeroy, 1999). It appears that this type of doxography dealt with only the post-Socratic schools of philosophy, and mainly with ethics, and that they offered systematic accounts of the philosophical doctrines, so that the views of each school on a particular philosophical topic were presented in separate sections.

In late antiquity, for instance, in the church fathers, there can be little doubt that doxographical works of one type or another were the sources consulted by most students of philosophy. Few of the original works by pre-Socratic and Hellenistic philosophers were available outside Alexandria and other centers of scholarship. Hence the study of doxography and of the transmission of philosophical texts in antiquity is important for a proper evaluation of the significance of late testimonies and of their interpretations *vis-à-vis* the original statements by philosophers who are now lost.

Biography

The ancient Greeks and Romans were just as fascinated by the lives of philosophers and other famous men as the modern world is, though it is obvious that they were more interested in the personalities than in the social and educational aspects of biography. Thus, we know next to nothing about the early development and the philosophical studies of young philosophers. In fact, it is important to understand that it was always difficult to find information about men of the past because the documentary evidence was virtually nonexistent: the biographer had to cull whatever evidence he could from the writings of the individual personality, something which was difficult in the case of both ancient dramatists and philosophers, the dramatists because they do not speak in propria persona – the philosophers because they concentrate on argument and do not describe their own lives. Even when philosophers seem to have spoken about themselves, it is often hard to connect this information with their external life. When we are told that Democritus in a book stated that he wrote it 730 years after the fall of Troy, we are completely at a loss as to which date he assigned to this event (D.L. 9.41), and thus the information does not help us date Democritus.

This lack of information did not prevent ancient writers from producing a large number of biographies of philosophers, but it is important to realize that they necessarily had to rely on very scattered evidence. The main element in ancient biography was anecdotes and characteristic sayings (gnomic statements, *apophthegmata*), but unless the author had a personal relationship with his subject, there is little chance that the information provided is correct in a historical sense. This can, for instance, be gathered from the fact that the same anecdote can be told about more than one philosopher: the anecdotes say more about which characteristics the ancients attributed to a philosopher than about the actual life of that individual.

One of the basic problems in biography is of course to determine the life span of the subject in question. Since the ancients had no absolute chronology, it was necessary to establish dates by means of synchronisms with known events like Olympiads or with names of office holders; thus the Athenians dated years by referring to one of the nine archons. Sometimes a well-known event took place during a philosopher's life, e.g. the foundation of the Athenian colony Thurii in 444 BCE with which Protagoras was associated since he was said to have written the laws for that city. Consequently, he was assumed to have been at the height of his career at that date, and it was said to be his *acme* (Gr.) or *floruit* (Lat.), usually identified with his fortieth year of age. The fortieth year was also used to fix the date of two philosophers when one of them was supposed to be the student of the other. Democritus had said something about being young when Anaxagoras was old, and as their relationship was supposed to be that of teacher/student, Democritus' birth was dated to 460 BC, which was Anaxagoras' *floruit*. It is very unlikely that this interval of 40 years reflects any actual difference in age between the two philosophers, not to mention the fact that we cannot be sure that Democritus ever studied with Anaxagoras. But the Hellenistic biographers had a tendency to link philosophers in successions so that any relationship between two philosophers would be interpreted as that of teacher to student. In some cases it was known how old a philosopher was when he died – for example, Socrates was 70 years old when he was executed in Olympiad 95.1 (= 399 BCE), hence he must have been born Ol. 77.4 (= 469 BCE). Contrary to modern practice, it is in fact of great interest to contemplate those pieces of information that do not fit in with the usual dating systems. Thus, when we are told by Thrasyllus that Democritus was born one year before Socrates (i.e., 470 BCE), this deserves to be taken into serious consideration

29

since it is hard to see why Thrasyllus should have contradicted the usual date unless he had good reasons to do so.

The first biographies of philosophers seem to have been written by Plato's students shortly after his death, but philosophical biographies were popular throughout the Hellenistic period. Around 200 BCE Sotion from Alexandria wrote a book called *Successions of Philosophers*, in which he made one philosopher succeed another as head of a particular philosophical school and similarly connected various schools with one another. This system of "successions" were generally followed by all later writers; the two main successions were a) the Ionic line from Thales via Archelaus and Socrates, Plato and Aristotle to Clitomachus as head of the Academy and Chrysippus as head of the Stoa, and b) an Italic line from Pythagoras over Democritus to the Epicurean and Skeptic schools. Sometimes a separate line of Eleatics was added. There can be little doubt that this way of organizing the history of philosophy was modeled on the Hellenistic schools and that the notion that philosophers were organized in schools prior to Plato's Academy is anachronistic. All of these historical works have been lost, but neither from the bits and pieces quoted by Diogenes Laertius and other sources nor from the two partly preserved books of the Epicurean Philodemus' *Survey of Philosophers* (*Suntaxis tōn philosophōn*) on the Academy and the Stoa (Dorandi 1991, 1993) from the middle of the first century BCE, does it appear that they were much concerned with the philosophical contributions of the various schools covered: the emphasis was on the life of the individual philosopher and of the institution to which he belonged, and philosophical topics seem mostly to have been introduced when the innovations ("inventions") of a philosopher were listed.

The most important specimen of historiography of philosophy from antiquity follows the structure of the *Successions*, viz. Diogenes Laertius' *Compendium of the Lives and Opinions of Philosophers*. The author is not otherwise known and his work can only be dated from a combination of the latest personalities he mentions, and the fact that he was not yet influenced by Neoplatonism, i.e., it must have been written around 200 CE. His work is divided into ten books: introduction and various wise men (including Thales) (1); The Ionian Tradition (Books 2–7): Ionian physicists, Socrates and the minor Socratics (2), Plato (3), the Academy down to Clitomachus (4), Aristotle and the Peripatetics down to Lyco (5), Antisthenes and the Cynics (6), Zeno of Citium and the Stoics – possibly down to the first century CE; the end of Book 7 is lost (7); the Italic Tradition (Books 8–10): Pythagoras and his early successors, and Empedocles (8), Heraclitus, the Eleatics, the Atomists, Protagoras, Diogenes of Apollonia, and Pyrrho (9), and finally Epicurus (10).

Diogenes' book is basically a compilation of excerpts from a large number of sources and often provides us with the main evidence for the Hellenistic tradition. The qualities and the structure are very uneven: some lives are nothing but anecdotes and aphorism while others are primarily doxographies. Some Lives have important sections on philosophy (e.g., the Lives of Zeno in Book 7 and Pyrrho in Book 9) while others are of no help in reconstructing the philosophy of a thinker (e.g., Plato in Book 3 and Aristotle in Book 5; in both cases, however, they exemplify how later generations interpreted their predecessors). For the pre-Socratics, Diogenes has used a doxographical source of the type described above, pp. 24–8. However, in Book 10 Diogenes has chosen to quote four long texts by Epicurus himself that constitute the most important evidence for Epicurus' philosophy prior to the first century BCE (viz., Cicero and the papyri from Herculaneum). Diogenes ends his book with Epicurus' 40 "Principal Doctrines" because he considers them a culmination of philosophical wisdom.

Most of Diogenes' biographies included a number of items like birth, parents, name, appearance, relations to other philosophers, travels, life style, and manner of death; many Lives also contain bibliographies and some pieces of documentary evidence. There is no fixed order in which these items are presented, some Lives are much more comprehensive than others, but in most cases the comprehensiveness of a Life depends on the number of anecdotes available. The factual information must always be viewed with skepticism and there are many obvious mistakes. Though it is clear that Diogenes is no philosopher, he has preserved much of philosophical interest.

Most of the other philosophical Lives from late antiquity are written in the context of the Platonic philosophy: Apuleius wrote a book on Plato and his philosophy in the second century CE, and a hundred years later both Porphyry and Iamblichus wrote biographies of Pythagoras, but they are all three more of value as a source to the times of their authors than as a source to the subject of their biographies. Porphyry's life of Pythagoras was part of his *Historia Philosopha*, on the history of philosophy in four books up to and culminating in Plato. More important is the fact that we have biographies of some Neoplatonic philosophers written by their students: Porphyry not only collected and edited Plotinus' writings at the end of the third century CE, he also wrote a vivid description of Plotinus' life as he knew it from his own time with the Neoplatonic philosopher in Rome.[3] Two hundred years later Marinus wrote a life of Proclus who was head of the Academy in Athens in the fifth century CE, and early in the sixth century Damascius wrote a *Historia Philosopha* (previously called *Life of Isidorus*), which covers the last couple of generations of Platonic philosophers in Athens. Since we have so many writings by the Neoplatonic philosophers themselves, the significance of these biographies is not what they have to tell us about the thoughts of these Neoplatonists, but their description of the philosophical activities in Athens. Taken together with the numerous commentaries on works of Plato and Aristotle, they offer important information about the institutional aspects of doing philosophy in late antiquity, and much remains to be done in this area.[4] It is no coincidence that Simplicius and many others in this period were capable of composing commentaries that are still important both for our understanding of the texts they comment on and for our knowledge of Greek philosophy.

Bibliography

Works Cited

Balthussen, H. (2000). *Theophrastus Against the Presocratics and Plato. Peripatetic Dialectic in the* De sensibus. Leiden: Brill.

Barnes, J. (1997). "Roman Aristotle." In J. Barnes and M. Griffin (eds.), *Philosophia Togata 2.* Oxford: Oxford University Press.

3. On Porphyry's biography, see further Brisson and Pradeau, PLOTINUS.
4. On this topic, see Hoffmann WHAT WAS COMMENTARY IN LATE ANTIQUITY?

31

Bidez, J. (ed.). (1924). L'empereur Julien Oeuvres complètes I.2 Lettres et fragments. Paris: Les Belles Lettres.

Diels, H. (1879). *Doxographi Graeci*. Berlin: G. Reimer.

Dorandi, T. (1991). *Filodemo. Storia dei filosofi [.] Platone e l'Academia (PHerc. 164 e 1021)*. Naples: Bibliopolis.

——. (1993). *Filodemo. Storia dei filosofi: La stoa da Zenone a Panezio (PHerc. 1018)*. Leiden: Brill.

Gigante, M. (1995). *Philodemus in Italy. The Books from Herculaneum*. Ann Arbor: University of Michigan Press.

Giusta, M. (1964–8). *I dossografi di etica 1–2*. Torino: Universita di Torino.

Göransson, T. (1995). *Albinus, Alcinous, Arius Didymus*. Gothenburg: University of Gotherburg Press.

Gottschalk, H. B. (1987). "Aristotelian Philosophy in the Roman World From the Time of Cicero to the End of the Second Century AD." *ANRW* II 36.2, 1079–174.

Mansfeld, J. (1992). "Physikai doxai and Problemata Physika from Aristotle to Aetius." In W. W. Fortenbaugh and D. Gutas (eds.), *Theophrastus, his Psychological, Doxographical and Scientific Writings* (pp. 63–111). New Brunswick: Transaction.

Mansfeld J. and Runia, D. T. (1996). *Aëtiana. The Method and Intellectual Context of a Doxographer* (vol. 1): *The Sources*. Leiden: Brill.

Mejer, J. (1992). "Diogenes Laertius and the Transmission of Greek Philosophy." *ANRW* II 36.5, 3556–602.

Moraux, P. (1973). *Der Aristotelismus bei den Griechen. Von Andronikos bis Alexander von Aphrodisias* (vol. 1): *Die Renaissance des Aristotelismus im 1. Jh. v. Chr.* Berlin: de Gruyter.

Pomeroy, A. (1999). *Areios Didymos. Epitome of Stoic Ethics. English and Greek*. Atlanta: Society of Biblical Literature.

Sider, D. (2005). *The Library of the Villa Dei Papyri at Herculaneum*. Los Angeles: Getty Museum.

Sorabji, R. (ed.). (1990). *Aristotle Transformed. The Ancient Commentators and their Influence*. London: Routledge.

Tarrant, H. (1993). *Thrasyllan Platonism*. Ithaca: Cornell University Press.

Taylor, C. C. W. (1999). *The Atomists. Leucippus and Democritus: Fragments: A Text and Translation*. Toronto: University of Toronto Press.

Further Editions of Texts

Full bibliography of both texts editions and modern studies 1926–1996

Mejer, J. (2000). *Überlieferung der Philosophie im Altertum. Eine Einführung*. Copenhagen: Reitzel.

Doxographical and biographical texts

Andria, R. G. (1989). *I frammenti delle "Successioni dei filosofi."* Naples: Arte Tipigrafica.

Athanassiadi, P. (1999). *Damascius, The Philosophical History: Text with Translation and Notes*. Athens: Apamea Cultural Association.

Bollansée, J. (1999). *Hermippus of Smyrna, Die Fragmente der griechischen Historiker Part Four Biography and Antiquarian Literature IVA* Fasc. 3. Leiden: Brill.

Brisson, L., Goulet-Cazé, M.-O., Goulet, R., and O'Brien, D. (1982). *Porphyre, La Vie de Plotin I*. Paris: Vrin.

Daiber, H. (ed.). (1980). *Aetius Arabus. Die Vorsokratiker in arabischer Überlieferung*. Wiesbaden: Steiner.

Düring, I. (1957). *Aristotle in the Ancient Biographical Tradition*. Gothenburg: University of Gothenburg Press.

Fortenbaugh, W. W., Huby, P. M., Sharples, R. W., and Gutas, D. (1992). *Theophrastus of Eresus. Sources for his Life, Writings, Thought and Influence*. Leiden: Brill.

Lachenaud, G. (ed.). (1993). *Plutarque Œuvres morales*. (vol. 12, part 2): *Opinions des philosophes*. Paris: Les Belles Lettres.

Marcovich, M. (ed.). (1999). *Diogenes Laertius Vitae Philosophorum*. Leipzig: Teubner.

Riginos, A. S. (1976). *Platonica. The Anecdotes Concerning the Life and Writings of Plato*. Leiden: Brill.

Saffrey, H. D. and Segonds, A.-P. (eds.). (2001). *Marinus, Proclus ou Sur le bonheur*. Paris: Les Belles Lettres.

Schorn, S. (2005). *Satyros aus Kallatis. Sammlung der Fragmente mit Kommentar*. Basel: Schwabe.

Wehrli, F. (1978). *Sotion, Die Schule des Aristoteles*. Suppl. vol 2. Basel: Schwabe.

Further Reading

ANRW II 36.5–6 has numerous papers on Diogenes Laertius in various languages.

Burkert, W., Gemelli Marciano, L., Matelli, E., and Orelli, L. (eds.). (1998). *Fragmentsammlungen philosophischer Text der Antike*. Gottingen: Vanderhoeck and Ruprecht.

Cherniss, H. (1977). "Ancient Forms of Philosophical Discourse." *Selected Papers*. Leiden: Brill.

Döring, K. (1987). *Historia Philosopha. Grundzüge der antiken Philosophiegeschichtsschreibung*. Freiburg i. Br.: Ploetz.

Fortenbaugh, W. W. and Steinmetz, P. (eds.). (1989). *Cicero's Knowledge of the Peripatos*. New Brunswick: Transaction.

Gigon, O. (1959). *Grundprobleme der antiken Philosophie*. Bern: Francke.

Glucker, J. (1978). *Antiochus and the Late Academy*, Göttingen: Vanderhoeck and Ruprecht.

Goulet, R. (2001). *Études sur les vies de philosophes dans l'antiquité tardive. Diogène Laërce, Porphyre de Tyr, Eunape de Sardes*. Paris: Vrin.

Hadot, I. (1984). *Arts liberaux et philosophie dans la pensée antique*. Paris: Études augustiniennes.

Makin, S. (1988). "How Can We Find Out What Ancient Philosophers Said?" *Phronesis*, 33, 121–32.

Mansfeld, J. (1990). *Studies in the Historiography of Ancient Philosophy*. Leiden: Brill.

——. (1992). "Doxography and Dialectic. The Sitz im Leben of the 'Placita.' " In *ANRW* II 36.4, 3056–229.

——. (1994). *Prolegomena. Questions to be Settled Before the Study of an Author or a Text*. Leiden: Brill.

Mejer, J. (1978). *Diogenes Laertius and his Hellenstic Background*. Wiesbaden: Steiner.

Momigliano, A. (1971). *The Development of Greek Biography*. Cambridge, Mass.: Harvard University Press.

Snell, B. (1976). "Die Nachrichtenüber die Lehre des Thales und die Anfänge der griechschen Philosophie- und Literaturgeschichte." In C. J. Classen *Sophistik* (pp. 478–90). Darmstadt: Wissenschaftliches Buchgesellschaft.

Whittaker, J. (1987). "The Value of Indirect Tradition in the Establishment of Greek Philosophical Texts or the Art of Misquotation." In J. N. Grant (ed.), *Editing Greek and Latin texts*. New York: AMS.

Wycherley, R. E. (1961, 1962). "Peripatos: The Athenian Philosophical Scene 1–2." *Greece and Rome* 8, 152–63 & 9, 2–21.

3

Parmenides and After: Unity and Plurality[1]

PATRICIA CURD

The early Greek philosophers, usually called the pre-Socratics (because they were not influenced by Socrates) were above all moved by a desire to understand the world around them. They developed theories of the world that sought to discover its first principles (its fundamental building blocks), and to show how knowledge of these principles is possible. In the history of this period, Parmenides occupies a special place, for it was he who first inquired into the nature of explanation, and argued for criteria that must be satisfied by any adequate theory of what there is and our knowledge of it. Before Parmenides, the early Greek thinkers had proposed several accounts of the world, but had paid little attention to the nature of explanation or criteria for an appropriate object of knowledge. After Parmenides, the pre-Socratics strove to work within the limits set by his arguments.

A helpful way to approach the question of Parmenides' importance for Greek philosophy is to examine questions of unity and plurality in pre-Socratic thought, seeing how these questions dovetail with those about the possibility of genuine knowledge and its object.[2] In this chapter, I shall argue that Parmenides' criticisms of his predecessors rest on the principle that what can be genuinely known must be a unity of a particular sort, which I call a predicational unity. On this view, anything that genuinely is (that truly can be said to be), and so can be known, must be of a single, wholly unified kind. Parmenides drew conclusions from this that later philosophers took very seriously. One consequence is that what is genuinely real cannot come to be, pass away, or alter, thus posing the problems of change and knowledge: How can we account for the appearance of change that we see in the world around us? And how can we have knowledge of such a changing world? An advantage of viewing Parmenides in this way is that it makes sense of the cosmological theorizing of post-Parmenidean figures such as Anaxagoras, Empedocles, and Democritus. All these philosophers were (in their different ways) pluralists, holding that there is a numerical plurality of metaphysically basic entities; and yet, I shall argue, all were working in the Parmenidean tradition because they all accepted Parmenides' criteria for what is genuinely real.

1. References to the pre-Socratics are made using the standard numbering system of Diels and Kranz (cited as DK), 1951–2. Unless otherwise indicated, translations are my own. Many thanks to Mary Louise Gill and to Martin Curd for helpful suggestions and comments.
2. Stokes (1971) provides a comprehensive treatment of unity and plurality in early Greek thought in English.

Before Parmenides

Aristotle describes many of the early Greek thinkers as *phusiologoi*, because they sought to give an account of nature (or *phusis*). Although Aristotle has been accused of misunderstanding and oversimplifying the thought of the pre-Socratics, his account has much to recommend it. As far as we can tell from the very skimpy evidence (much of which comes from Aristotle himself and the Aristotelian tradition), the earliest philosophers, the Milesians, sought to explain the sensible world in terms of what might be called a generating substance, a single basic stuff that undergoes a series of transformations and generates the sensible world as we perceive it: for Thales this was most probably water, for Anaximander it is some characterless stuff called the *apeiron* (the indefinite), for Anaximenes, it is air (Graham, 1997). (For modern disputes about the best way to understand the Milesians see Algra, 1999; Barnes, 1979b; and in this volume Hussey, THE BEGINNINGS OF SCIENCE AND PHILOSOPHY IN ARCHAIC GREECE, esp. pp. 7–12.)

Because our evidence for the Milesians is so meager, it is difficult to draw any firm conclusion about their views or their reasoning. For Heraclitus we have more evidence, and it reveals him arguing not only about the real constitution of the world, but also about the character of our knowledge of that world. Although the surviving fragments present formidable interpretive challenges, it is clear that Heraclitus regards what he calls the *logos* (which can be translated as "account") as the single governing principle of the universe and the proper object of genuine knowledge (DK 22B1 and B2). In B1, after indicating that the account (*logos*) that he gives "holds forever," Heraclitus says that he will distinguish "each thing in accordance with its nature (*phusis*), saying how it is." It is understanding the *logos* that allows him to do this. At B50 he specifically links the *logos* with a special kind of unity: "Listening not to me but to the *logos*, it is wise to agree that all things are one." How all things are one is suggested (but not spelled out) in some of the fragments. In the case of certain opposites, Heraclitus claims that they are really one and the same (a doctrine that has received much attention in Heraclitus studies). Day and night (B57), the road up and down (B60), and the healthiness and noxiousness of sea water (B61) are but particularly vivid and paradoxical manifestations of this unity of opposites. Yet there is a more basic unity underlying that of the opposites, namely the interconnectedness and susceptibility to a single explanation of all that there is, and it is this that the *logos* explains (MacKenzie, 1988). This unity is exemplified primarily by fire, a part of the natural world and, for Heraclitus, an important symbol of the *logos*. At B30 Heraclitus says: "this cosmos, the same for all, no god or man made, but it always was and is and will be, fire everliving, kindling in measures and going out in measures." Heraclitus is not claiming that the world is literally made out of fire (in the sense of an Aristotelian material first principle) but, through the reference to measure, that it is a system of perpetual but ordered change. Just like fire, the cosmos is always changing its appearance yet remains one and the same in its nature; indeed it is tempting to see Heraclitus as saying that the real constitution or nature of a thing just is the ordered series of changes that it undergoes (Graham, 1997; MacKenzie, 1988). Real knowledge is the grasping of this point and thus understanding the underlying unity of all that there is (Curd, 1991; Lesher, 1983; MacKenzie, 1988).

35

In Heraclitus we have claims about both knowledge and its object: to know is to grasp the real nature of a thing, and that nature must itself be unified in a certain way. Although the content of the *logos* can be grasped by the human mind (B2), most people fail to hear or understand it (even after Heraclitus himself has told his story; B2, B1, B17, B34). In B40, Heraclitus condemns certain of predecessors for having much learning (*polumathiē*) but no understanding or comprehension (*noos*). B41 spells out in what that understanding consists: "the wise is one thing: to know the plan by which all things are steered." The polymaths of B40 have collected much information, but there is no unifying understanding of the nature of things that brings all the bits and pieces together into a comprehensive grasping of the single system that is the cosmos. Wisdom consists in knowing that which governs and controls the workings of the whole, and that is the *logos*. Truly to know the *logos* would be to know its content, knowing not only the grand scheme of changes that constitutes the cosmos but also to know the real nature of each thing and to be able to say how it is (as B1 puts it). It is only through the latter that we can know the former: an understanding of the cosmos is grounded in the knowledge of the nature of each thing. The *logos* itself is the unifying principle that guides and steers all things, a single account of how things are, and the object of genuine knowledge.

Parmenides

The surviving fragments of Parmenides' writings are contained in a poem that has two main sections: the *Alētheia* ("Truth") and the *Doxa* ("Opinion").[3] Parmenides' argument begins with an introduction (DK 28B1, "the Proem") telling of a journey by a young man (the *kouros*) to an unnamed goddess who both reveals an important truth and teaches that the truth must be accepted only after her arguments have been evaluated, and not because it comes from a goddess. Meeting the *kouros*, the goddess tells him that it is right that he learn "all things" (*panta*), "both the unshaking heart of well-persuasive truth and the beliefs of mortals, in which there is no true trust" (DK 28B1.28–30).[4] The task of learning *all* things cannot be achieved through learning by rote and then rejecting whatever is not on the approved list. Given the goddess's frequent demands that the *kouros* take control of his *noos* or thought (Lesher, 1984), to learn "all things" would seem to be to learn to judge correctly about things that present themselves as being the case, or concerning claims about what is the case made by others. This is reinforced by the words at B7.5–6 where the *kouros* is exhorted to judge

---

3. The *Doxa* describes a cosmological theory similar in many respects to the theories that Parmenides criticizes in the *Alētheia*. Even ancient commentators were unsure what Parmenides' intentions were in the *Doxa*. Parmenides might have meant it as a genuine cosmology, as an illustration of the sorts of errors mortals make, or as a test for the sorts of mistakes he had diagnosed in the *Alētheia* as a kind of training tool. (For a range of accounts of the *Doxa*, see Curd (2004), Long (1963), Mourelatos (1971), and Nehamas (2002).) The arguments I give here are based on those of the *Alētheia*, and do not depend on an interpretation of the *Doxa*.

4. Reading *eupeitheos* (well-persuasive) rather than *eukukleos* (well-rounded) in B1.29.

(*krinai*) by *logos*, at B8.15 where the test is a judgment or decision (*krisis*), and at B8.62, where the goddess tells the *kouros* that she gives the account of mortal thought in the *Doxa* so that "no mortal thought will ever drive past you" (Lesher, 1984). A sign that the goddess intends to teach the *kouros* (and Parmenides' readers and hearers) to judge correctly comes in B2–3 when she begins her lesson:

> Come now, and I will tell you, and you, hearing, preserve the story,
> the only routes of inquiry there are for thinking;
> the one that it is (*estin*) and that it cannot not be
> is the path of Persuasion (for it attends on truth)
> the other, that it is not (*ouk estin*) and that it is right that it not be,
> this I point out to you is a path wholly inscrutable
> for you could not know what is not (for it is not to be accomplished)
> nor could you point it out . . . (DK 28B2)
>
> . . . for the same thing is for thinking and for being. (DK 28B3)

Although the fragments do not explicitly state the object of the inquiry (there is no subject provided for the verbs in lines 3 and 5), the content of the *Alētheia* and the *Doxa* point to it as being the fundamental nature of things – the ultimate entity or entities in an account of what there is. When the goddess promises that the *kouros* will learn all things, she is saying that she will teach a method of inquiry that will result in truth about the way things really are. Parmenides criticizes his predecessors because they have taken the wrong route in their attempts to explain the world. From Parmenides' point of view, they were unsuccessful because they accepted as basic certain entities that were not genuinely real insofar as they admitted change or incorporated opposites, and so embraced both what-is and what-is-not. To take what-is-not as the starting point is to set out on a route that can never be completed. As B2.7–8 says, to know or point out what-is-not "is not to be accomplished." Such an endeavor is doomed to fail because what-is-not is inherently vague (Mourelatos, 1976, 1979); it cannot be grasped or understood. In B6 and B7 Parmenides castigates those who rely on sense experience as a source of understanding and thus conflate what-is and what-is-not.

Many philosophers read the bare "is" in B2 and the other Parmenidean fragments as primarily existential, and regard Parmenides' arguments as dealing with what can exist as a subject of inquiry or discourse, and so as about anything that can be spoken of and thought. Thus, his subject could be grasshoppers or unicorns, as well as the basic entities like air or the *apeiron* of earlier philosophical theories (Barnes, 1979b; Coxon, 1986; Furth, 1974; Gallop, 1979, 1984; McKirahan, 1994; Owen, 1960). Despite its popularity, there are difficulties in reconciling the existential interpretation with the wording and context of Parmenides' arguments. For example, the target of the goddess's scorn seems to be less those who try to think about what does not exist, than those who conflate what-is and what-is-not in their inquiries and subsequent explanations of what is fundamental. In B1.31–32, the *kouros* is *warned* against mortal beliefs, not because they try to study or talk about what does not exist, but because they conflate things that merely seem to be with those that really are. (For further arguments against the existential interpretation, see Curd, 2004; Kahn, 1978, 1988, 2002; and Mourelatos, 1979.)

An alternate account of the bare "is," and the one I adopt in this chapter, interprets it not as existential, but as predicative in a particularly strong and fundamental sense. On this view, the subject of Parmenides' inquiry is the proper way to give an account of the nature or reality of things. Parmenides is concerned with the character of entities that can provide this sort of ultimate explanation (Curd, 2004; Mourelatos, 1971, 1989). What-is, in this sense, is what is metaphysically basic, the starting point in an explanation. Thus, to be, for Parmenides, is to be the nature or, as we would say, the essence of something: to be F, is to be what being F is, or what it is to be F. Only such entities are the appropriate basis for explanation. When we give an explanation, saying that thus and so is the ultimate nature of X, or that X is really Y, we are using Parmenides' "is" of ultimate explanation.[5] Such a subject is the object of legitimate knowledge or understanding (we have seen this link between knowledge and the nature of things in the work of Heraclitus). This is why Parmenides stresses the connection between what-is and genuine thought or understanding (see B3 and B8.34–38). To be sure, there is an existential aspect to such a claim, for anything that is a genuine nature or essence must exist, but the claim of existence is not primary: it follows from the truth that something indeed is a nature or essence. Thus, Parmenides' subject is not just anything that can be a subject of discourse; rather he is concerned with what can serve as the legitimate object of inquiry into the way things really are.

Parmenides gives the positive arguments about the nature of what-is in the long fragment B8. He opens his account this way:

> ... a single story still
> remains of the route that it is; and on this route there are
> very many signs, that what-is is ungenerable and imperishable,
> a whole of a single kind, and unshaking and complete;
> nor was it nor will it be, since it is now all together
> one, cohesive. (DK 28B8.1–6, reading *oulon mounogenes* and *teleion* in B8.4)

These opening lines of B8 give formal requirements for a metaphysically basic entity; they tell us, not *what* what-is is, but *how* what-is is what it is. Reading "ungenerable and imperishable," and "unshaking and complete" as adverbial claims about the way that a basic entity holds (or is) its essential nature, we see that Parmenides claims that genuinely to be, to be F, say, is to be so ungenerably and imperishably, as a whole of a single kind, unalterably and completely F. Only what is in such a strong way is a possible nature and so an object of thought and understanding, because only such an entity can be grasped as a whole by *noos*, the capacity of thought in us. Parmenides does not tell us how many entities of differing kinds can satisfy those requirements, nor does he identify those that do. Rather, he gives us the criteria and tells us how to go about looking for these natures. These requirements can be discovered by applying the "decision" (*krisis*) stated in B8.15–16:

5. For a fused "is" involving both predicative and existential aspects, see Furth (1974), although Furth stresses the existential component. Mourelatos (1971) discusses alternative interpretations of the subjectless "is" of B2 and defends a notion of "speculative predication." For fuller discussion of the claim "X is really Y" see Mourelatos (1989) and Curd (2004).

> And the decision (*krisis*) concerning these things is in this:
> is or is not; and it has been decided, just as is necessary,
> to leave the one unthinkable and unnamed (for it is not a true
> path), the other to be and to be genuine.

The arguments of B2 and B3 and the opening lines of B6 spell out the basis of the *krisis*: "It is right that what is for saying and thinking be; for it can be, but nothing (*mēden*) cannot; this I bid you ponder." (For a discussion of this controversial text, see Cordero, 1979, 1987; and Coxon, 1986.) There is no way for thought or discourse to fasten on what-is-not; its vagueness frustrates any attempt to know or say what it is. Applied repeatedly in B8, the decision between is and is not shows that if being a certain way opens what-is to what-is-not, then what-is cannot be that way. Any attribute that entails the reality of what-is-not (or depends on its reality) is denied to what-is.

The arguments in B8 unfold the consequences of the claim that only what-is can be, and they reveal that Parmenides is committed to some sort of monism. Taken together, the cluster of signs along the route of inquiry (B8.1–6, above) point to an object of that inquiry that is unified, an indivisible whole of a single kind. So, what-is must be one. Plato and later thinkers describe Parmenides' position as something like "the all is one" (the *Sophist*) or report him as holding a view about "the One" (the *Parmenides*). Unity is a crucial notion for Parmenides, but in what sense is he a monist? Many histories of Greek philosophy portray Parmenides as a numerical monist committed to the existence of only one thing that is genuinely real (Guthrie, 1965; KRS, 1983; McKirahan, 1994), but this view has been challenged (Barnes, 1979a; Curd, 2004; Jones, 1973; Mourelatos, 1971; Solmsen, 1969). One early hint that Parmenides was not a numerical monist can be found in Book I of Aristotle's *Metaphysics*, where Aristotle contrasts Parmenides and Melissus. Recognizing certain affinities among the Eleatics, "those who spoke of the universe as having a single nature," he also notes differences: "Parmenides seems to fasten on what is one in account (*logos*), Melissus on that which is one in matter" (*Met.* A.5, 986b10–11, b19–20).[6] Although Aristotle seems to think that numerical monism (of the type advocated by Melissus) is a consequence of Parmenides' arguments, he sees that Parmenides is primarily concerned with the unity of the nature or essence of a thing. Once we abandon the notion that Parmenides' primary concern is with what can exist (and so give up thinking that the denial of what-is-not is to be equated with a fundamental rejection of what does not exist), it is less obvious that we are forced to understand Parmenides as asserting that only one thing exists.[7] Whatever is genuinely real is one, but that does not entail that there can be only one genuinely real thing. In the remainder of this section, I examine Parmenides' claims about what-is and his monism, and then, in the following sections, I explore the importance of his views about knowledge and unity for later pre-Socratic thinkers.

6. In *Met.* Δ.6 Aristotle explores the various senses of "one," and says that things are one in *logos* when statements of their essences are indivisible (1016a32–5).
7. Nevertheless, it is possible to accept both the existential interpretation and deny that Parmenides is a numerical monist, as in Barnes (1979a).

In considering Parmenides' arguments about what-is, it is crucial to remember that, for him, any genuine or legitimate predication of the form "X is Y" is the description of a knowable essence (Y), revealing the very nature of X. It is this understanding of predication that accounts for the peculiarly strong requirements that he places on what-is. The goddess begins her account of what-is by denying that it can come to be or pass away. Such changes, equivalent to birth and death, require that what-is come from or become what-is-not, and that it impossible. This prohibition against substantial change is then expanded into a general argument against any kind of change for what-is. The nature of a thing that is (a basic entity) is stable, subject to no alteration or modification. Thus, once we grasp it, we can hold it with confidence, for that nature can neither grow, alter, nor pass away. Whatever genuinely is will be always just what it is.

After denying the reality of coming-to-be, passing-away, and alteration, the arguments take up the claim that what-is is all alike and hence indivisible. At B8.4 we learned that what-is is a "whole of a single kind:" *oulon mounogenes*. The character or nature of what-is is uniform all the way through as we might say. Because it is the same all the way through, what-is is not divisible: anything that is genuinely real must be all and only just the one thing that it is. The only way to mark a division in an entity, E, would be to find some difference in E. But any predicate that E holds, it holds essentially; so to suppose that E had differences would be to suppose that it is essentially f and essentially g, and thus had two different natures. Thus, to know E or grasp it with the understanding would entail that we would have to know two things. But if E were essentially both f and g (and what it is to be f is different from what it is to be g), then E would then turn out to be essentially not-f (insofar as it is g) and essentially not-g (insofar as it is f).[8] Because it is impossible for what-is-not to be, what-is cannot be divisible. The argument against the divisibility of what-is is not an argument for numerical monism, but rather an exploration of the claim that each thing that is can have only one essence or nature. Parmenides' view of the connection between the immunity to change of what-is and its unified nature can be seen in the signs at the opening of B8. Lines 4 to 6 assert that what-is is "a whole of a single kind, and unshaking and complete; nor was it nor will it be, since it is now all together one, cohesive." In these claims the unity of what-is and its stability are linked by necessity: because what-is cannot change, it must be one, and because it is a whole of a single kind, it cannot change.

The continuation of the argument at lines B8.26–31 presents an image of what-is as held changeless, firm, and stable "within great bonds" by the force of "mighty Necessity;" thus what-is "lies by itself" and is steadfast. If we think of this as the reality of a thing, we can see that such a thing lacks nothing – it is completed and perfected, as lines B8.32–33 and 42–49 assert. Nothing can be taken away and nothing needs

8.   If being f is what it is to be E (i.e. E is f), then there cannot be any other essence different from f that is also what it is to be E. For, to grasp the essence g would be to grasp a thing that is different from the thing whose essence or nature is f. The apparent peculiarity of the argument depends on the nature of Parmenidean predication and the strong distinction between is and is not.

40

to be added: "for it is not in need; for if it were, it would lack everything." Because what-is, as an essence or nature, is whole and perfect, it can be grasped directly and completely with the understanding. Such a thing is the natural home of thinking, the natural target for *noos*, the power of understanding for Parmenides:

> And the same thing is for thinking and wherefore there is thought;
> for not without what-is, in which it is expressed,
> will you find thinking; for nothing either is or will be
> except what-is, since fate shackled just this
> to be whole and unchanging. (DK 28B8.34–38)

A controlled *noos*, taking the path of what-is, engages in inquiry that ends (both completes its journey and perfects itself) in what-is. The internal unity and stability of what-is makes this possible. An inquiry that misunderstands its appropriate object and fastens on the wrong kind of entity (one that seems genuine but is not) can never be completed, for a *noos* that attempts to grasp what-is-not will be caught in a loop of negations that lead it nowhere. This putative object of thought is too vague to be grasped, and so one traveling that path of inquiry can never complete the journey. (Think of trying to understand or intellectually grasp Anaximander's *apeiron*.) In contrast, the unified, bounded, completed, homogenous nature of a genuinely basic entity is the goal of controlled thought. Testing as he goes, judging by *logos*, as instructed in B7, and in sharp contrast to the uncritical hordes of B6 who rely on experience rather than thinking, a traveler on the route of what-is could reach the "unshaking heart of well-persuasive truth" about how things are. The tests have both a negative and positive role to play. Negatively, they can be used to rule out certain accounts of how things are, and so protect the inquirer from falling into the error of beginning with the wrong sort of entity. Positively, the tests tell us what is acceptable as a basic entity in a theory that explains the world as we perceive it. Such an entity could be a building block in an explanation of the world that human beings perceive, but it will not itself be subject to change. Only what is so strongly unified that it meets the requirements of Parmenides' arguments can be such a genuine entity. What and how many the basic entities are, and how they give rise to the perceptible world and the appearance of change, is left open by Parmenides – there may be one or many. Thus, the way is left open for a pluralism that is consistent with the monistic requirements of Parmenidean metaphysics. There are hints of such a view in the story told by the *Doxa*; if we take that story as a suggestion of how to provide a rational cosmology, then mixture and separation would be acceptable mechanisms, allowing a plurality of basic ingredients to maintain their character throughout the processes that produce the phenomenal world (see note 3).

The three major philosophical theories after Parmenides and before Plato were those of Anaxagoras, Empedocles, and the Atomists, Leucippus and Democritus (I follow the tradition, going back at least to Aristotle, that Leucippus and Democritus held the same version of atomism). The three theories differ in important ways, but they all share one important feature: all three adopt "Eleatic pluralism" (Wardy (1988), who concentrates on atomism). The surviving fragments indicate that this consistency with Parmenidean criteria is not accidental. In all three, there are passages that deny genuine coming-to-be and passing-away, that affirm the internal consistency and hence internal unity of the basic entities of the theories, and that ground knowledge in those entities. Similarly, in all three, the numerical plurality of the basic entities is simply assumed or asserted, and mechanisms strikingly like the mixture and separation of the *Doxa* appear. None felt the need to refute numerical monism or argue for a plurality of basic entities, while all seem aware of the requirements of predicational monism. I now turn to a consideration of these three Eleatic Pluralists.[9]

Empedocles

In his account of the nature of things, Empedocles follows Parmenides in emphasizing the unreality of coming-to-be and passing-away:

> For it is impossible that there should be coming-to-be from what-is-not,
> and that what-is should be destroyed is not to be fulfilled and is unheard of;[10]
> for wherever one may set it, there is truth it will always be. (Empedocles, DK 31B12)[11]

Empedocles postulates six fundamental entities as the basis of his theory: four roots (earth, water, air, and fire) and two forces, Love and Strife.[12] The roots, through the motives forces of Love and Strife (Love is a power that pulls apart likes and brings together unlikes; Strife breaks up mixtures of unlikes and pulls together likes), are the source of the cosmos with its heavenly bodies, the earth, and the living beings – plants, animals, human beings – that inhabit it. The alternating ascendancies of Love and Strife produce and break up the cosmos as we perceive it. When Love absolutely dominates, there is a motionless Sphere, in which the roots are so thoroughly mixed that none can be discerned. Strife then gathers force and breaks up the Sphere; under its growing power, there is increasing separation until the roots are utterly segregated from one another. Love then increases her power and mixtures of unlikes begin to form. Although the details of the cosmic cycles are controversial, it is clear from B17, B21, and B26 that the only genuinely real entities are the roots, and Love and Strife. B26 makes the point clearly:

---

9. On later Presocratic thinkers, see also Mourelatos, THE CONCEPT OF THE UNIVERSAL IN SOME LATER PRE-PLATONIC COSMOLOGISTS, in this volume.

10. Compare Parmenides DK 28B2.7 "it is not to be fulfilled" that one could know what-is-not, and B8.21, where destruction is "unheard of."

11. There are difficulties in the text of line 1. I follow Wright (1981) (fragment 9 in her numbering), and Inwood (1992) (fragment 18 in his ordering) (ἐκ γὰρ τοῦ μὴ ἐόντος), rather than Diels's version as given in DK (ἔκ τε γὰρ οὐδάμ᾽ ἐόντος). As Wright notes (p. 173), this gives a better parallel with Parmenidean usage.

12. Here, I concentrate on physics and metaphysics in Empedocles. These are intimately connected with his views about the best way for human beings to live. On the religious aspects of Empedocles' poem, see Betegh, GREEK PHILOSOPHY AND RELIGION, in this volume.

For these very things are, and running through each other they
become humans and the kinds of other beasts. (DK 31B26.3–4)[13]

Here, through the use of forms of the verbs "to be" and "to become," there is a clear distinction between the things that are real (the roots), and the temporary phenomena that result from the mixing (running through one another) of the roots. Empedocles shows how this is possible in B23:

Just as when painters adorn votive offerings –
men well taught by cunning in their craft –
who when they take the many colored paints in their hands,
mixing in harmony more of these but less of those,
out of them make shapes resembling all things,
crafting trees and men and women
and beasts and birds and water-nourished fish
and long-lived gods best in honors.
So in this way do not let deception overcome your mind
[to think] there is any other source for mortal things, as many as are
seen, countless, perishable,
but know these things clearly, having heard the story from a god. (DK 31B23)

Certain fragments (B96 and B98) actually give recipes for the proportions and degrees of mixture that will produce bone, flesh, and blood. Other fragments indicate the roles of different roots in accounting for phenomenal properties: for instance, in creatures with hard shells or horns, Empedocles attributes their hardness to the earth that makes up the surfaces of these animals.[14] In his commentary on Aristotle's *De Anima* (Simpl. *In De An.* 68.10–13, part of the context for fragment 96), Simplicius suggests that fire predominates in the recipe for bone "because of their dryness and pale color;" presumably, the heat and brightness of fire is responsible for both these properties. One could presumably know this both by perception of the (relatively) purer states of the roots, and by analysis of other perceptions, so working to the explanation. Thus, knowledge of the roots and the forces can lead to a principled understanding of the phenomenal world.

As metaphysically basic entities that conform to the Eleatic model, the roots and Love and Strife are each unified essences or natures, and each is knowable. In a passage at B17.27–35, Empedocles emphasizes that the roots constitute what is real, stressing that each has its own nature. We can come to understand the contents and

13. The line "For these very things are, and running through each other . . ." occurs three times in the extant fragments: here in B26, and also at B17.34 and at B21.13–14. In each case we are given an example of the result of running through one another of the roots.
14. This claim occurs in ensemble *b* from the reconstruction of the exciting new fragments of Empedocles that were discovered on a papyrus in the library at the University of Strasbourg. The texts and the remarkable story behind the rediscovery and reconstruction of the fragments can be found in Martin and Primavesi (1999). Other discussions of the Strasbourg material, which is still being evaluated, can be found in Curd (2001), Laks (2002), and Osborne (2000).

processes of the sensible world through knowledge of these basic things. For Empedocles this knowledge has great importance, for it is understanding, not just of the processes of the world, but also of the best way to live (Kingsley, 2002). Great care must be taken to understand things properly; the hearer of Empedocles' poem is exhorted in B3 to "consider, by every art, the way each thing is clear," spurning none of the senses, to "think in the way each is clear;" this clarity is possible because, as B110 says, "all have thought and a share of mind." The claim in B110 may refer to all things or to all human beings (the contexts in which the fragment is found suggest the former). In either case, the suggestion is that human inquiry can be conducted well or badly (see Wright, 1981, pp. 236, 259–61). Sense perception can be a means to knowledge of the roots and the forces, but perception alone is apparently insufficient. There must be thought grounded in perception to reach the truth about the characters of the roots. Empedocles agrees with Parmenides that one can control one's thought and thus increase one's wisdom. Because there is a settled nature for each of the roots, we can in each case extrapolate from perceptual evidence to those characters. B21 refers to phenomenal sun, rain, air (indirectly), and earth as "witnesses" to the character of the roots (Simplicius quotes B21 twice as evidence for this). I take it that the perceived occurrences are not pure instances of the roots (which would occur only in complete separation under Strife), but the closest to that pure state available to human experience. Although Empedocles' theory embraces a plurality of basic entities; it is compatible with Parmenides' requirements for an acceptable and rational cosmology insofar as each of its constituents is a knowable, unified, metaphysically basic entity.

Anaxagoras

As with Empedocles, Anaxagoras' commitment to the Parmenidean framework (Curd, forthcoming; Furley, 1989, 1992, 2002) is clearly revealed by his emphatic denial that coming-to-be and passing-away are genuinely real:

> The Greeks do not think correctly about coming-to-be and perishing; for nothing comes to be or perishes. But they are mixed together and separated from the things that are. And thus they would rightly call coming-to-be being mixed and perishing being separated. (DK 59B17)

The changing things of the world of experience are conceived as temporary, local mixtures of the enduring and permanent things that are, the basic ingredients. Anaxagoras begins with an all-pervasive cosmic mix from which the cosmos evolved, as it is set rotating by Mind (or *Nous*). Through the force of the rotation, ingredients emerge from the original mixture, and they are mixed and separated again and again. It is these mixtures and separations that Anaxagoras calls coming-to-be and passing-away, and it is these that result in the world as we perceive it.

The ingredients in the original mix are characterized in DK 59B1: "all things were together, unlimited in extent (*plēthos*) and in smallness, for the small, too, was unlimited." Although there have been suggestions that the ingredients are restricted to the opposites (Schofield, 1980; Tannery, 1930; Vlastos, 1950), many passages (e.g., B10, B1, B2, and B4a) indicate that the original mix includes more than the opposites (Graham, 1994). The unlimited extent and number of kinds of original ingredients show Anaxagoras' strategy for dealing with the Eleatic prohibition on coming-to-be for what is genuinely real. He agrees (in B17) that some objects can come to be (by mixture and separation), but these are not genuinely real since they depend for their existence on the basic (unchanging) entities of which they are composed. This is obviously true for what we would call artifacts, items produced by human agency. Anaxagoras acknowledges this in B4a, where he speaks of the works made by human beings; but Anaxagoras also regards plants and animals as complicated "natural artifacts" that result from the compounding of ingredients under the "direction" of a seed, rather than viewing seeds simply as microscopic versions of plants and animals that grow by expansion (Furley, 1989).

Everything was together in the original mix (B1); the original state is a completely blended cosmic soup. Moreover, Anaxagoras says that "everything is in everything" (B11, B12), so there is a sense in which the original well-mixed state of all things together is maintained at all places and times (B6: "just as in the beginning so too now all things are together"). Even after the rotation of the mix results in the formation of stars, planets, and animals, the separation out of things is only relative. Anaxagoras claims that everything remains in everything, although some things are larger or smaller in different areas. This means that the densities of the ingredients may differ in such a way that what looks like a discrete entity may appear, but this is only a temporary emergence from the background mixture. Just as in the original mix, the densities of air and aether are so overwhelming that air and aether appear to cover and pervade all things (Furth, 1991; Inwood, 1986). If we suppose that there are pure or unmixed stuffs, then there must have been (at least locally) a complete separation from the original state of all things together. That means that the things in the original mix could have reached the state of being "smallest" (no matter how we interpret "large" and "small" here). For suppose we start with a mix that, unlike Anaxagoras' own (which has an indefinite (*apeiron*) number of ingredients), contains only three ingredients, *xyz*. We then extract all of the *y* and the *z* to end up with a pure state consisting solely of *x*. If such a complete separation were possible, that would imply that there was a least amount (*plēthos*) of *y* and of *z*, such that, once it is removed from our hypothetical mixture, no more *y* or *z* would remain. Thus, complete separation implies that there is a least or smallest; but Anaxagoras denies that there can be a smallest (as well as a largest):

> Nor of the small is there a smallest, but only a smaller (for [*gar*] it is not possible for what-is not to be)[15] – but also of the large there is always a larger. And it is equal to the

15. There is a problem with the manuscript text at this point, since it makes no real sense, either on its own or as part of the claims of B3. One suggestion (Sider, 1981) is *to gar eon ouk esti tomēi [mē] ouk einai*, translated as, "For that which is cannot be cut away to nothing." Schofield (1980), whose text I follow here, rejects both the MSS reading and the suggestion adopted by Sider, arguing that the simplest emendation is the following: *to gar eon ouk esti [to] mē ouk einai*. He translates: for what is cannot not be (i.e., it is not possible that what-is not be).

small in extent (*plēthos*), but in relation to itself each is both large and small. (Anaxagoras fr. 3, text following Schofield, 1980)

Despite its obscurity, one thing in this passage is plain. The denial of a smallest is linked to the assertion that what-is cannot not be. This is a good Parmenidean claim, and Anaxagoras thinks that it entails the denial of a smallest. If we understand small and large as degrees of manifestation of an ingredient or thing, then Anaxagoras is asserting that even when a stuff or quality is not apparent, it must still be present, just as in the original state.

The explanatory clause in B3 (introduced by *gar*) suggests that Anaxagoras supposes that if an object were genuinely to lose a quality (by alteration, for instance), then that quality would cease to be. But there can be no passing-away; so there must be some way of explaining the apparent disappearance of the quality. Anaxagoras does this by placing no lower limit on smallness. Rather than ceasing to be, the quality becomes smaller (in the sense of less manifest), perhaps by being swamped by the larger extent (greater manifestation) of some other property. Thus in the case of illness, pallor may swamp the ruddiness of a normal healthy complexion, but that ruddiness has not ceased to be in the mixture, but has only become smaller in comparison with the greater extent of the pallor. Thus, the everything in everything claim can be maintained even as, speaking loosely, what we might call coming-to-be, passing-away, and altera-tion take place. Generation (as approved in B17) and alteration or growth (by mixture and separation) will continue. Anaxagoras respects Parmenides' principle that genuine change, generation, and destruction (that is, alteration, generation, and destruction of what is genuinely real) is impossible, while embracing an indefinite plurality of basic entities.

The denial of the reality of change alone does not make the Anaxagorean system consistent with Parmenidean requirements. As we have seen, Parmenides rejects change as part of his analysis of what it means for something to be real, or genuinely to be, but that analysis also requires that each thing that is must be a unity and must be knowable. Anaxagoras' position seems to be that although human beings probably will not be able to fathom all that there was in the original mix and so what there is in each perceptible object (for everything is in everything and remains so), they may nonetheless have real (although limited) knowledge. B21 claims that we are unable to judge the truth because of the feebleness of the senses; but B21a suggests that the senses can be a clue to what is real: "phenomena are a glimpse of the unseen." Moreover there is evidence that Anaxagoras thought that the ingredients are in principle knowable. For after quoting our B7, Simplicius adds "That he supposed them (the ingredients) to be limited in form, he makes clear by saying that mind (*Nous*) knows them all," and there are claims in B12 that support his attribution of complete knowledge to cosmic *Nous*.

The question of the Eleatic knowability of the Anaxagorean basic ingredients is connected to the issue of the nature of their characters, but we have only indirect discussion of this. In B12 Anaxagoras claims that *Nous* not only initiates the rotation that ultimately results in the physical world as we perceive it, it also rules and controls all things, "maintains complete understanding (*gnōmē*) . . . and wields the greatest power." B12 also says that "*Nous* knew (*egnō*) all things, the things mixing together and separating out and breaking up, and as many as were going to be and as many were and are not now and as many as are now, and as many as will be" (DK 59B12). In order for *Nous* to perform these tasks of initiating, controlling, and ruling the rotation, it must know or understand all things (just as Anaxagoras says), and this is possible only if those things (the *chrēmata*) each have a genuine or settled character that *Nous* knows and understands. (Different views of *Nous* and the nature of its cosmic understanding can be found in Laks (1993) and Lesher (1995).) If each ingredient is something that *Nous* can indeed know, each is separable and pure in analysis, even though it can never be so in actuality. This seems to be what Simplicius meant in saying that Anaxagoras thought the ingredients "limited in form." As such, each will have the requisite Parmenidean character for serving as a basic entity, thus guaranteeing that Anaxagoras' theory is a rational cosmology, consistent with Eleatic pluralism.

Atomism

Atomism follows the pattern we have seen in both Anaxagoras and Empedocles: a plurality (here an infinite number) of basic entities that neither come to be nor pass away, and which mix and separate to account for the phenomena of the sensible world. That atoms are genuinely real in the appropriate Parmenidean sense is indicated by their being called "what is" or "being."

One of the clearest statements of atomic principles is contained in a fragment of Aristotle's *On Democritus*, quoted by Simplicius in his commentary on Aristotle's *De Caelo* (DK 68A37); there Aristotle discusses the nature and characteristics of atoms, contrasts them with the void, and explains the apparent coming-to-be and passing-away of sensibles through the action of atoms and void. The basic components of the theory are atoms, infinite in number, indivisible, all made of the same stuff, having differing shapes, sizes, and (perhaps) weights, but having no other characteristics, called the full or what-is; and void, called the empty or what-is-not.[16] Each atom is internally unified, being a simple mass of atomic stuff, and in being what it is, every atom is like every other: atoms belong to a single kind and each is itself a Parmenidean unity.

These two types of things, atoms and void, are the only things that are real and basic; anything else is simply a collection of atoms and void: "By convention sweet, and by convention bitter, by convention hot, by convention cold, by convention color:

---

16.   Although some surviving fragments assert the reality of atoms and void (DK 68B125), none discuss their natures in detail. We must rely on testimony from Aristotle and later writers, and Aristotle's own separate treatment of Democritus is largely lost (as are those of other ancient writers to whom books on Democritus are attributed). Atomic indivisibility is a vexed question; modern commentators disagree about whether atoms are theoretically as well as physically indivisible. There is also no consensus about whether Democritean atoms have weight. (See Bodnár, 2001; Makin, 1989; O'Brien, 1981; and Taylor, 1999a, 1999b.)

in reality atoms and void" (DK 68B9 = B125). Galen, one of the sources for this fragment, explains that such things as color, sweetness, and so on are what we would call secondary qualities: when Democritus says something is "by convention," he means (according to Galen), what is relative to us, and "not what is in the nature of the things themselves" (DK 68A49). But not only are colors and flavors like this, so are the ordinary physical objects that we perceive, and indeed our cosmos itself (as well as other universes that can form in the infinite void). These have no independent reality themselves, but are the result of the arrangements and rearrangements of atoms and void that occur as atoms move and intermingle. Atoms are in motion, and when they collide (or come very close to one another) some of them intermingle and these collections or clouds of atoms, when large enough, constitute the perceptible objects of our world. Their perceptible characters (the things that are "by convention") are determined by the characters of the atoms and by the amount and arrangement of void in the mixtures. (Theophrastus' *De Sensibus* is our source for these claims; see DK 68A135.62, 65–67.)

The atomists' picture is complicated by their insistence on the reality of void. Void must be just as real (and just as knowable) as atoms in order for the theory to succeed; but there is good ancient evidence that the atomists called the void "not-being" or "what-is-not." To the Eleatic ear this sounds heretical. How can what-is-not be, much less be a fundamental and knowable part of a theory that explains what there is? This aspect of atomism apparently conflicts with Parmenides' assertion: "for never shall this be forced through: that things that are not are" (DK 28B7.1). So the question is, how can an atomist say that void both is what-is-not and that it is "in reality"? I suggest that the atomists regard void as a kind of thing that is (i.e., as meeting Parmenidean requirements that it have a genuine and unchanging nature), thus explaining why they say that what-is is no more than what-is-not. (A different view of the relation between the atomist view of void and Parmenidean requirements, that the atomists simply deny that what-is-not cannot be, can be found in Taylor, 1999a.)

A passage in Plutarch gives a clue to the nature of void. In his *Against Colotes*, Plutarch quotes B156, saying Colotes has been misled by the statement of Democritus: "in which he [Democritus] declares that thing (*den*) is no more than nothing (*mēden*), calling body *thing* and void *nothing*, since it too has a nature (*phusis*) and existence (*hupostasis*) of its own." Plutarch's attribution to void of a nature and existence supports what is already evident from DK 68B9/125, namely that void is "in reality," and is a genuine being. The problem is to determine what that essence or nature is, and why the atomists chose to call it "nothing" or "what is not." One obvious reason for this appears in Plutarch's comment. Atoms are bodies: they are hard, impenetrable, take up space, and so on. Although void has no bodily characteristics, it nonetheless plays an indispensable role in the theory. If there were no void, there could not be a plurality of atoms, for void is what separates atoms from one another; moreover, void has a further role to play in explaining both the characters and the movements of complex macroscopic bodies. We know from Theophrastus that the atomists appealed to the arrangement of atoms and void in metals such as iron and lead to explain their heaviness or lightness, and their hardness or softness. There is also evidence that Democritus thought that macroscopic bodies (collections of atoms) tend to move or drift in a direction that contains more void (since those regions will offer less resistance). Thus, although void does not cause the motion of atoms, it helps to explain it at the level of compound bodies (Berryman, 2002; Sedley, 1982). So void has a nature as an atomic separator and is a necessary part of the atomic theory; this accounts for its reality. Nevertheless, void is not a body, and so it might reasonably be called what-is-not.

Atoms are not perceptible. Democritus recognizes the difficulty in coming to know atoms and void, saying that we are separated from reality (DK 68B6) and that "truth is in the depths" (B117), but he is nevertheless committed to the knowability of both atoms and void. All knowledge of atoms and void must be grounded in reasoning rather than perception. Sextus Empiricus acknowledges that there are, for Democritus, "two kinds of knowing, one through the senses and the other through the understanding; the one through the understanding he calls genuine, witnessing to its trustworthiness in deciding truth; the one through the senses he names bastard, denying it steadfastness in the discernment of what is true" (context of DK 68B11). Sextus continues, and quotes Democritus:

> He says in these words, "there are two forms of knowing: one genuine, the other bastard. To the bastard belong all these: sight, hearing, smell, taste, touch. The other, the genuine, has been separated from this." Then, preferring the genuine to the bastard, he continues, saying, "Whenever the bastard is no longer able to see more finely nor hear nor smell nor taste nor perceive by touch, but something finer" (DK 68B11)

Sense perception is an illegitimate form of knowing because it does not connect with what is real (atoms and void) but only what is apparent (the temporary collections of atoms and void that are "by convention" and that we call physical objects and their properties). To get beyond those objects to what is real we must examine smaller and smaller things – all the way down to the atoms themselves. But they cannot be perceived directly and so we must extrapolate, use our understanding (which indeed connects with the genuine – what is in reality) to achieve non-sensory knowledge of atoms and void. Just how this process works, Democritus either did not say or the evidence has not survived (Sextus' quotation breaks off at a crucial point), but it seems to involve beginning with perception and then moving to understanding (Lee, forthcoming).

Eleaticism after Parmenides: Melissus

The post-Parmenidean theories examined so far share a confidence that the unity required by Parmenidean arguments is consistent with a numerical plurality of entities, each of which individually satisfies the requirements for what-is given in Parmenides B8. I have suggested that Parmenides himself leaves open the question of how many entities there are (or might be) that satisfy his requirements. Melissus, exploring implications of certain aspects of the Eleatic position, and rejecting Parmenides' requirement that what-is be limited, advocates numerical monism. Thus, on my view,

49

Melissus is an innovator, not a mere imitator of Parmenides, as he is often represented. (Barnes (1979a, 1979b) is an outspoken advocate of Melissus' originality.)[17]

Beginning with the claim that nothing can come from nothing, Melissus argues that what-is never came to be, but "it is and always was and always will be"; moreover, as such it has no beginning, and no end, and is unlimited. Melissus tries to derive the unlimited character of what-is from its lack of coming-to-be: "just as it always is, in this way too it is necessary that it is always unlimited in magnitude (DK 30B3); nothing having both beginning and end is either eternal or unlimited" (B4). Because what-is must be unlimited, it must be one: "for if they were two, they could not be unlimited, but would have limits against each other" (B6). Thus, Melissus concludes in B7, "it is eternal and unlimited, and one and all alike." Here then indeed is the One (as he will call it in B8); post-Parmenidean pluralism is rejected. Melissus' crucial move is the requirement that what-is be unlimited. Parmenides had argued that what-is neither comes to be nor passes away; yet he had also declared that what-is is limited, "changeless in the limits of great bonds" (DK 28B8.26), "mighty Necessity holds in the limits of a bond" (DK 28B8.30–31). The difference may be that Parmenides, more than Melissus, emphasizes the epistemological aspects of what-is: the limited nature of what-is makes it complete and perfect, and thus entirely thinkable and knowable; indeed if it were unlimited it could not be grasped by understanding. Melissus, perhaps responding to the physical theories of Anaxagoras, Empedocles, and the Atomists, argues that something that has no beginning and no end must lack all limits, not only temporal but also spatial. Once that move is made, he thinks that uniqueness follows. (For a clear analysis and discussion of the argument, see Sedley, 1999.)

Melissus marshals other arguments against the mechanisms invoked by Eleatic pluralism and against the reliability of perception (or even its usefulness as a glimpse of the unseen). In B7 he argues that rearrangement is impossible (thus attacking mixture and separation as an acceptable method of explaining apparent change), and rejects both void and motion (thus attacking the foundations of atomism). In B8 he takes on sense perception. The pluralists can only argue that perception is a guide to what is genuinely real if there is some connection between what is real and what appears to the senses – only, that is, if there is a physical projection of basic entities into the sensible world. Thus, for example, Empedocles asserts that "mortal things" (i.e., the temporary mixtures of the roots that constitute sensible objects) have the characters they do because of the underlying natures of the roots that constitute them, and the Atomists say that qualities of perceptible objects are determined by the shapes and sizes of the atoms that constitute them. Melissus argues against this kind of

17. Because of limitations of space, I omit a discussion of Zeno. He is best known for the paradoxes of motion that have come down to us from Aristotle's discussions of them. The literature on these paradoxes, in both their ancient and modern interpretations, is vast. For texts, see Lee (1936); clear introductory discussions can be found in McKirahan (1994) and (1999); and in this volume, see Bodnár and Pellegrin, ARISTOTLE'S PHYSICS AND COSMOLOGY. Zeno's paradoxes of motion can be read as concerned with plurality (for they deal with a plurality of places and times) and the general paradoxes of plurality (as given in Plato's *Parmenides* = DK 29A11, and in the paradox of the millet seed, DK 29A29) can be read as supporting the predicational monism that I have attributed to Parmenides (see Curd, 1993, 1998).

rational cosmology by offering a destructive dilemma. If sense perception is reliable, and shows (as it seems to) that things come to be and pass away and alter, then the underlying entities must also come to be, pass away and alter; but that is impossible. Thus, if sense perception is reliable, then no account of the perceived world that begins with underlying entities is possible. If sense perception is not reliable, we cannot use its evidence in the construction or testing of theories. Conclusion: rational cosmology is a hopeless project. If Melissus is right, then numerical monism is inconsistent with inquiry into nature (just as Aristotle claims in the *Physics*).

Aftermath

As we have seen, for Parmenides and most of the thinkers who came after him, the real question about unity and plurality is not how many beings there are but the nature of the beings that there are. The concern with the unity of what is metaphysically and epistemologically basic continues into later Greek thought, but an important shift occurs in Plato's late dialogues and in Aristotle. While Plato appears in the early and middle dialogues to accept Parmenides' claims, his critical examination of them in the *Parmenides* leads to a rejection of his assumption that there is only one kind of predication. Aristotle follows Plato in this, and argues that "being is said in many ways" (*Met.* Γ.2; Z.1).[18]

Plato's forms in the period of the *Phaedo*, *Symposium*, and *Republic*, are Parmenidean entities; one need look no further than the account of the Beautiful itself in the *Symposium* to find linguistic echoes and metaphysical parallels (see Nehamas, 1979; Solmsen, 1982; there are also Parmenidean echoes in the arguments of Book V of the *Republic*). But in the *Parmenides* Plato takes up the question of the coherence of the very idea of a unified Parmenidean entity. Using the characters Zeno and Parmenides, he questions whether a plurality of Eleatic ones, such as are required for his theory and for the Eleatic pluralisms that we have examined here, is possible. In Part I of the dialogue, he argues that the requirement that a form be a predicational unity undermines the participation relation between forms and particulars. In Part II, examining the internal unified structure of a selected form (the One), Plato shows that the Eleatic conceptions of unity and being are too strong to allow the attribution of such attributes as sameness and difference to forms (see Gill's introduction in Gill and Ryan, 1996). He begins the task of rethinking the relations among forms that culminates in the arguments of the *Sophist*, with its claim (put in the mouth of a Stranger from Elea) that there is a way that what-is is not and that what-is-not is. He begins to argue that not all uses of "to be" are the attribution of an essence or nature (in the *Phaedo* he had argued that only Forms can be said to be what they are, other things merely have their attributes through participation in the form).[19] Aristotle, too, rejects Parmenides' insistence that anything that genuinely is must be an essence or a nature. Nevertheless, even in Aristotle we can see traces of Parmenides' views, for Aristotle agrees with Parmenides that what absolutely is not cannot be (*Phys.* I), and he is much concerned

---

18. On this topic, see M. L. Gill, FIRST PHILOSOPHY IN ARISTOTLE, in this volume.
19. See Notomi, PLATO'S METAPHYSICS AND DIALECTIC, in this volume.

to show that a statement or definition of an essence must be a unity of a particularly strong sort, and to demonstrate how such a requirement can be met (*Met.* Z.10–12).

Bibliography

Works Cited

Algra, K. (1999). "The Beginnings of Cosmology." In A. A. Long (ed.), *The Cambridge Companion to Early Greek Philosophy* (pp. 45–65). Cambridge: Cambridge University Press.

Barnes, J. (1979a). "Parmenides and the Eleatic One." *Archiv für Geschichte der Philosophie*, 61, 1–21.

——. (1979b). *The Presocratic Philosophers.* (2 vols.). London: Routledge and Kegan Paul.

Berryman, S. (2002). "Democritus and the Explanatory Power of the Void." In V. Caston and D. Graham (eds.), *Presocratic Philosophy* (Festschrift for A. P. D. Mourelatos) (pp. 183–91). Aldershot: Ashgate.

Bodnár, I. (2001). "Atomic Independence and Divisibilty." In A. Preus (ed.), *Before Plato* (pp. 123–47). Albany, NY: SUNY Press.

Caston, V. and Graham, D. (eds.). (2002). *Presocratic Philosophy* (Festschrift for A. P. D. Mourelatos). Aldershot: Ashgate.

Cordero, N.-L. (1979). "Les deux chemins de Parménide dans les fragments 6 et 7." *Phronesis*, 24, 1–32.

——. (1987). "L'histoire du Texte de Parménide." In P. Aubenque (ed.), *Études sur Parménide* (vol. 2, pp. 3–24). Paris: Vrin.

Coxon, A. H. (1986). *The Fragments of Parmenides.* Assen: Van Gorcum.

Curd, P. (1991). "Knowledge and Unity in Heraclitus." *The Monist*, 74, 531–49.

——. (1993). "Eleatic Monism in Zeno and Melissus." *Ancient Philosophy*, 13, 1–22.

——. (2001). "A New Empedocles? The Implications of the Strasbourg Fragments for Presocratic Philosophy." In *Proceedings of the Boston Area Colloquium in Ancient Philosophy*, 17, 27–49.

——. (2004). *The Legacy of Parmenides: Eleatic Monism and Later Presocratic Thought.* Revised paperback edition; Las Vegas: Parmenides Publishing. (1st edn., Princeton: Princeton University Press, 1998.).

——. (forthcoming). *Anaxagoras of Clazomenae. A Text and Translation with Introduction and Commentary.*

Diels, H. (1951–2). (Cited as DK). *Die Fragmente der Vorsokratiker.* (3 vols.). 6th edn. revised by W. Kranz and often reprinted. Berlin: Weidmann. (Original work published 1903).

Furley, D. J. (1989). "Anaxagoras in Response to Parmenides." In D. J. Furley, *Cosmic Problems* (pp. 47–65). Cambridge: Cambridge University Press.

——. (1992). "From Anaxagoras to Socrates." In K. Boudouris (ed.), *The Philosophy of Socrates* (Vol. 2): *Elenchus, Ethics, and Truth* (pp. 74–80). Athens: International Center for Greek Philosophy and Culture.

——. (2002). "Anaxagoras, Plato, and the Naming of Parts." In V. Caston and D. Graham, (eds.), *Presocratic Philosophy* (Festschrift for A. P. D. Mourelatos) (pp. 119–26). Aldershot: Ashgate.

Furth, M. (1974). "Elements of Eleatic Ontology." In A. P. D. Mourelatos (ed.), *The Pre-Socratics* (pp. 241–70). Garden City, NJ: Anchor.

——. (1991). "'A Philosophical Hero?' Anaxagoras and the Eleatics." *Oxford Studies in Ancient Philosophy*, 9, 95–129.

Gallop, D. (1979). "'Is Or Is Not'?" *The Monist*, 62, 61–80.

——. (1984). *Parmenides of Elea: Fragments.* Toronto: University of Toronto Press.

52

Gill, M. L. and Ryan, P. (1996). *Plato: Parmenides*. Indianapolis: Hackett.

Graham, D. W. (1994). "The Postulates of Anaxagoras." *Apeiron*, 27, 77–121.

——. (1997). "Heraclitus' Criticism of Ionian Philosophy." *Oxford Studies in Ancient Philosophy*, 15, 1–50.

Guthrie, W. K. C. (1965). *A History of Greek Philosophy*. (vol. 2): *The Presocratic Tradition from Parmenides to Democritus*. Cambridge: Cambridge University Press.

Inwood, B. (1986). "Anaxagoras and Infinite Divisibility." *Illinois Classical Studies*, 11, 17–33.

——. (1992). *The Poem of Empedocles: A Text and Translation with an Introduction*. Toronto: The University of Toronto Press. (Revised edn. 2001.)

Jones, B. (1973). "Parmenides' 'Way of Truth'." *Journal of the History of Philosophy*, 11, 287–98.

Kahn, C. H. (1978). "Why Existence does not Emerge as a Distinct Concept in Greek Philosophy." *Archiv für Geschichte der Philosophie*, 58, 323–34.

——. (1988). "Being in Parmenides and Plato." *La Parola del Passato*, 43, 237–61.

——. (2002). "Parmenides and Plato." In V. Caston and D. Graham (eds.), *Presocratic Philosophy* (Festschrift for A. P. D. Mourelatos) (pp. 81–93). Aldershot: Ashgate.

Kingsley, P. (2002). "Empedocles for the New Millennium." *Ancient Philosophy*, 22, 333–413.

Kirk, G. S., Raven, J. E., and Schofield, M. (eds.). (1983). (Cited as KRS). *The Presocratic Philosophers*. 2nd edn. Cambridge: Cambridge University Press.

Laks, A. (1993). "Mind's Crisis: On Anaxagoras' NOUS." *The Southern Journal of Philosophy*, 31 (Suppl. Vol.), 19–38.

——. (2002). "Reading the Readings: On the First Person Plurals in the Strasbourg Empedocles." In V. Caston and D. Graham (eds.), *Presocratic Philosophy* (Festschrift for A. P. D. Mourelatos) (pp. 127–37). Aldershot: Ashgate.

Lee, H. D. P. (1936). *Zeno of Elea*. Cambridge: Cambridge University Press.

Lee, M. (forthcoming). *Epistemology after Protagoras: Responses to Relativism in Plato, Aristotle and Democritus*. Oxford: Oxford University Press.

Lesher, J. H. (1983). "Heraclitus' Epistemological Vocabulary." *Hermes*, 111, 155–70.

——. (1984). "Parmenides' Critique of Thinking: The *poludēris elenchos* of Fragment 7." *Oxford Studies in Ancient Philosophy*, 2, 1–30.

——. (1995). "Mind's Knowledge and Powers of Control in Anaxagoras DK B12." *Phronesis*, 40, 125–42.

Long, A. A. (1963). "The Principles of Parmenides' Cosmogony." *Phronesis*, 8, 90–107.

——. (ed.). (1999). *The Cambridge Companion to Early Greek Philosophy*. Cambridge: Cambridge University Press.

MacKenzie, M. M. (1988). "Heraclitus and the Art of Paradox." *Oxford Studies in Ancient Philosophy*, 6, 1–37.

Makin, S. (1989). "The Indivisibility of the Atom." *Archiv für Geschichte der Philosophie*, 71, 125–49.

Martin, A. and O. Primavesi. (1999). *L'Empédocle de Strasbourg*. Berlin: Walter de Gruyter.

McKirahan, R. (1994). *Philosophy before Socrates*. Indianapolis: Hackett.

——. (1999). "Zeno." In A. A. Long (ed.), *The Cambridge Companion to Early Greek Philosophy* (pp. 134–58). Cambridge: Cambridge University Press.

Mourelatos, A. P. D. (1971). *The Route of Parmenides*. New Haven: Yale University Press.

——. (1976). "Determinacy and Indeterminacy, Being and Non-Being in the Fragments of Parmenides." *Canadian Journal of Philosophy*, suppl. vol. 2, 45–60.

——. (1979). " 'Nothing' as 'Not-Being': Some Literary Contexts that Bear on Plato." In G. W. Bowersock, W. Burkert, and M. C. J. Putnam (eds.), *Arkturos: Hellenic Studies* (Festschrift for Bernard M. W. Knox). Berlin: Walter de Gruyter. Repr. in J. P. Anton and T. Preus (eds.), *Essays in Ancient Greek Philosophy* (vol. 2: pp. 59–69). Albany, NY: SUNY Press, 1983. (References are to the latter version.)

——. (1989). "'X is Really Y:' Ionian Origins of a Thought Pattern." In K. Boudouris (ed.), *Ionian Philosophy* (pp. 280–90). Athens: International Center for Greek Philosophy and Culture.

Nehamas, A. (1979). "Self-Predication and Plato's Theory of Forms." *American Philosophical Quarterly*, 16, 93–103.

——. (2002). "Parmenidean Being/Heraclitean Fire." In V. Caston and D. Graham (eds.), *Presocratic Philosophy* (Festschrift for A. P. D. Mourelatos) (pp. 45–64). Aldershot: Ashgate.

O'Brien, D. (1981). *Theories of Weight in the Ancient World* (vol. 1): *Democritus, Weight and Size*. Philosophia Antiqua 37. Paris: Les Belles Lettres / Leiden: Brill.

Osborne, C. (2000). "Rummaging in the Recycling Bins of Upper Egypt: A Discussion of A. Martin and O. Primavesi, *L'Empédocle de Strasbourg*." *Oxford Studies in Ancient Philosophy*, 18, 329–56.

Owen, G. E. L. (1960). "Eleatic Questions." *Classical Quarterly*, 10, 84–102. Revised edition in G. E. L. Owen, *Logic, Science, and Dialectic: Collected Papers in Greek Philosophy* (pp. 3–26). Ithaca: Cornell University Press. (References are to the latter version.)

Sedley, D. (1982). "Two Conceptions of Vacuum." *Phronesis*, 27, 175–93.

——. (1999). "Parmenides and Melissus." In A. A. Long (ed.), *The Cambridge Companion to Early Greek Philosophy* (pp. 113–33). Cambridge: Cambridge University Press.

Schofield, M. (1980). *An Essay on Anaxagoras*. Cambridge: Cambridge University Press.

Sider, D. (1981). *The Fragments of Anaxagoras: Edited with an Introduction and Commentary*. Meisenheim am Glan: Anton Hain. (2nd edn., Sankt Augustin: Academia Verlag, 2005.)

Solmsen, F. (1969). "The 'Eleatic One' in Melissus." *Mededelingen der Koninklijke Nederlandse Akademie van Wetenschappen*, Afd. Letterkunds, Nieuwe Reeks 32/8, 221–33.

——. (1982). "Parmenides and the Description of Perfect Beauty in Plato's *Symposium*." In F. Solmsen (ed.), *Kleine Schriften* (vol. 3, pp. 202–10). Hildesheim: Olms.

Stokes, M. C. (1971). *One and Many in Presocratic Philosophy*. Washington, DC: The Center for Hellenic Studies.

Tannery, P. (1930). *Pour l'histoire de la science hellène*. (2nd edn., Paris: Gauthier-Villars.)

Taylor, C. C. W. (1999a). *The Atomists: Leucippus and Democritus: Fragments*. Toronto: University of Toronto Press.

——. (1999b). "The Atomists." In A. A. Long (ed.), *The Cambridge Companion to Early Greek Philosophy* (pp. 181–204). Cambridge: Cambridge University Press.

Vlastos, G. (1950). "The Physical Theory of Anaxagoras." *Philosophical Review*, 59, 31–57.

Wardy, R. B. B. (1988). "Eleatic Pluralism." *Archiv für Geschichte der Philosophie*, 70, 125–46.

Wright, M. R. (1981). *Empedocles: The Extant Fragments*. New Haven: Yale University Press.

Further Reading

Good general discussions of pre-Socratic philosophy: Barnes (1979b); Kirk, Raven and Schofield (1983); McKirahan (1994). See also Guthrie (1965) (vol. 2).

In addition:

Lloyd, G. E. R. (1992). *Polarity and Analogy: Two Types of Argumentation in Early Greek Thought*. Indianapolis: Hackett. (Original work published 1966.)

Osborne, C. (2004). *Presocratic Philosophy: A Very Short Introduction*. Oxford: Oxford University Press.

An excellent study of Parmenides: Mourelatos (1971).

On Parmenides and later thinkers: Curd (2004).

See also:

Stokes, M. C. (1971). *One and Many in Presocratic Philosophy*. Washington, DC: The Center for Hellenic Studies.

Collections of essays on pre-Socratic philosophy: Caston and Graham (2002); Long (1999).

See also:

Curd, P. and Graham, D. W. (eds.). (forthcoming). *The Oxford Handbook of Presocratic Philosophy*. New York: Oxford University Press.

Furley, D. and Allen, R. E. (eds.). (1970 and 1975). *Studies in Presocratic Philosophy*. (2 vols.). London: Routledge and Kegan Paul / New York: Humanities Press.

Mourelatos, A. P. D. (ed.). (1993). *The Presocratics*. 2nd edn., Princeton: Princeton University Press. (Original work published 1974.)

Vlastos, G. (1995). *Studies in Greek Philosophy* (vol. 1): *The Presocratics*. Princeton: Princeton University Press.

4

The Concept of the Universal in Some Later Pre-Platonic Cosmologists

ALEXANDER P. D. MOURELATOS

The history proper of the concept of the universal has an obvious and familiar start: the philosophies of Plato and of Aristotle. Both of these classical philosophers recognized – indeed they made it the central part of their metaphysical teaching – that we grasp reality in two significantly different modes: in terms of concrete individuals or particulars (e.g., Socrates, the Parthenon, Miltiades' sword, the jury's verdict in Socrates' trial); and in terms of types or kinds (e.g., man or animal, temple or building, sword or weapon, justice, wisdom).[1] The term used by both philosophers with reference to the second of the two modes is, of course, *eidos* or *idea*, "form," "kind"; and Aristotle also employs the ancestor to the modern term "universal," viz., *to/ta katholou* (in contrast to *to/ta kath' hekaston*), as well as the term *to koinon*, "the common," and other terms as well.[2] Within and beyond classical ancient philosophy, and down to the present day, the concept of the universal undergoes many transformations; and the so-called "problem of universals," i.e., the long-standing debate between realists and nominalists, plays a major role in these transformations. Accordingly, modern scholars who write on Plato or Aristotle have often questioned whether either Plato's or Aristotle's "forms" may qualify as "universals" under one or another of variously restrictive definitions of the concept of the universal.[3] In this chapter, I seek to rely on a reasonably minimalist specification of the content of the claim that the two classical philosophers have grasped the concept. By the qualification "minimalist" I signal my intention to assume a low-level, intuitively accessible, conception of the universal; and by the qualification "reasonably," my concern that the specification should not be so broad as to allow any act of attending to the distinction between referring expressions and predicates (common nouns, adjectives, verbs) to count as recognition of the universal.

---

1. There is an excellent concise account of the development of the concept, and of related metaphysical debates, beginning with Plato and Aristotle, in the most recent lexicon for ancient philosophy, Bächli and Graeser (2000, s.v. "*Allgemeines*," pp. 18–24).
2. The *locus classicus* for the introduction of the distinction between universals and particulars in Aristotle is *Int.* 7, 17a38–b1.
3. For a comprehensive recent comparison of how the concept of the universal is introduced and how it functions in the two philosophies, respectively, of Aristotle and of Plato, see Segalerba (2003, esp. pp. 67–70, 82–3); cf. Segalerba (2001, pp. 95–106, 223–7).

56

But before I attempt such a specification, let me confirm what may be perceived as implied in the title of this chapter: my account is not one about the history proper of the concept but about its pre-history. D. M. Armstrong's elegant modern philosophical introduction to our subject opens with this remark: "The topic of universals is a very old one. It goes back to Plato at least, perhaps to Socrates, perhaps to even earlier times" (1989, p. 1). My interest is precisely in those "earlier times." I seek to identify and to discuss contributions to the grasp of the universal that were made by the earliest philosophers in the Western tradition, the pre-Socratics.[4] Socrates himself, no doubt, made major contributions to the development of the concept; that is Aristotle's explicit testimony (*Met.* A.6, 987b1–4; M.4, 1078b17–19 and b27–31; M.9, 1086b1–5), and that is what Plato, in his portrait of Socrates, would have us believe. But the Socratic problem is a scholarly issue I need to skirt. For our purposes here, Plato (including Plato's Socrates) will serve as the *terminus ante quem*.

Still, before proceeding, some thought is in order concerning the level of understanding of the distinction between particulars and universals we may assume for the Socratic-Sophistic circles of the fifth century that form the context and background of many of Plato's early and middle dialogues. For it has been widely supposed by modern scholars that in this group of dialogues, fifth-century characters other than Socrates (his interlocutors), are presented as inept in handling the concept of the universal. The alleged ineptness is that of confusing – at least initially in the conversation – universals and particulars. But Alexander Nehamas (1975, 1999) has shown that this interpretive diagnosis has little support in the relevant texts (1999, pp. 159–76). Typically the initial error is rather one of offering too narrow a characterization of the universal at issue, not the error of citing merely an instance or example. More significant is the fact that Socrates often asks, "Is there such a thing as the F (e.g., 'the pious/piety,' or 'the beautiful/beauty')?" or "Do we say that the F is something?" and his interlocutors unhesitatingly answer, "Yes, there is," or "Yes, it is." Plato and Plato's Socrates seem to regard it a prerequisite – indeed one they typically assume as having been fulfilled before the conversation starts – that the two sides in dialogue have an understanding of the difference between "Which thing is/things are F" and "What it is to be F." It is not unreasonable to imagine, therefore, that issues concerning either the distinction between a universal and its instances or the distinction between universals of different scope (ones at different levels of generality, genus-species distinctions) would have been broached in the course of Sophistic instruction and Sophistic debates. Strongly suggestive evidence of this is in the reports concerning Prodicus' practice of *onomatōn orthotēs*, "correct use of words," which entailed both the formulation of definitions and the canvassing of issues of sameness and difference between abstract concepts (typically expressed by infinitives, articulate adjectives, or nouns; see DK 84A9, A11, A13–A19).[5] Also

---

4.   As it has often been pointed out, more than half of the "pre-Socratics" are contemporaries or near-contemporaries of Socrates. The term is best understood as referring to fifth-century philosophers who were not *influenced* by Socrates.

5.   References to fragments from the works of the pre-Socratics or to testimonia (reports) concerning their doctrines, is, as usual, by the chapter number and section ("A" for testimonia, "B" for fragments) in the edition by Hermann Diels (revised by Walther Kranz), referred to as "DK": see Works Cited, below.

relevant and suggestive is the evidence implied in Plato's testimony that Gorgias would admit only special kinds of *aretē*, "excellence," but no single encompassing type (*Meno* 71b–73c). And it is worth noting that the theme of sameness/difference involving abstract concepts is conspicuous in the Sophistic treatise *Dissoi logoi* (DK 90). The internal dating of this treatise, however, places its composition some time after the end of the Peloponnesian war (DK 90.1.8); so, the *Dissoi logoi* is rather too late to qualify as pre-Platonic. (For a discussion of this interesting text, see in this volume Barney, THE SOPHISTIC MOVEMENT, pp. 87–90.)

But what about the main line of the pre-Socratics, the cosmologists or natural philosophers of the tradition (Aristotle's *phusiologoi*)? What thematically significant uses of the concept of the universal are found in their sayings and doctrines? What evidence of antecedents, anticipations, or pre-formations of the concept might be found in what we know of the philosophical writings and projects of these philosophical pioneers? The question has been raised before. Aristotle, as one may well expect, was first to raise it. The answers he offered have been cited by modern scholars and historians of philosophy, who have also made additional independent proposals. The results of my own investigation differ in some significant respects from the answers traditionally offered. In a larger study it would be of interest to trace the full pre-history of the universal, from the early Ionians down to the pluralist cosmologies of the late fifth century – and I hope and aim to undertake such a broader study in the future. In this chapter, however, I shall concentrate on contributions made by the later pre-Socratics. I trust this limited scope is reasonable, inasmuch as this is also the scope of the traditional answers.

Criteria Used for the Concept of the Universal

Let me now offer what was promised at the start, a "reasonably minimalist" specification of the concept of the universal. Using the philosophies of Plato and of Aristotle as our benchmark, we can safely claim that the concept is recognizably present in the thinking of the two classical philosophers on the basis of three criteria. The criteria are not disjunctive; all three must be met if we are to claim that the concept has been grasped by a particular philosopher or in a certain period. I give the criteria first in a bald statement, and then I append needed explications and comments. In both the two classical philosophers we find:

1. the type–token distinction in thematically significant contexts;
2. uses, in thematically significant contexts, of a distinction between two types, a type$_1$ (subordinate) and a type$_2$ (superordinate); and
3. some awareness, explicit or implicit, of the distinction between
   a. the type–token relation, or the type$_1$–type$_2$ relation, and
   b. the mereological relation that connects the whole of any mass-entity (partitive entity) with the component parts or portions of that whole.

The first and most famous formulation of the first criterion is, of course, in Aristotle's distinction between *hen arithmōi* and *hen eidei/logōi/genei*, "one in number/numerically one" vs. "one in form/definition/genus/species." In Plato this helpful terminology has not yet been established, though it is often implied in context. I shall need to dwell some on the first criterion, not only so as to justify my seemingly anachronistic preference for C. S. Peirce's now familiar terminology of "type" vs. "token" (see Armstrong, 1989, pp. 1–2; cf. Audi, 1995, s.v.) but also because ultimately this criterion will emerge as especially apt for the purpose of assaying contributions to the concept of the universal by fifth-century cosmologists. Three texts merit our attention: first, the passage in Peirce which introduces the terminology and explains its rationale; and then – most interestingly – two ancient texts in which Peirce's distinction is pre-figured. Here is the key passage in the Peirce corpus:

> A common mode of estimating the amount of matter in a MS. or printed book is to count the number of words. There will ordinarily be about twenty "the"s on a page, and of course they count as twenty words. In another sense of the word "word," however, there is but one word "the" in the English language; and it is impossible that this word should lie visibly on a page or be heard in any voice. . . . Such a definitely significant Form, I propose to term a Type. A Single event, which happens once and whose identity is limited to that one happening, or a Single object or thing which is in some single place at any one instant of time, . . . I will venture to call a Token.[6]

Armstrong notes that Peirce's distinction is one "that practically all contemporary philosophers accept" (1989, p. 1). This is ostensibly because of its "minimalist" character, which permits capture of the essentials of the distinction between universals and particulars with the lightest burden of metaphysical interpretation or question-begging. Often the distinction is illustrated not with Peirce's example of individual words but with that of individual letters. Amazingly, in this version the distinction had already been formulated in antiquity. For it occurs unmistakably in Galen:

> When an utterance signifies a single thing (tēs men phōnēs hen sēmainousēs), necessarily the type of the thing at issue is one. Nonetheless, a given letter can be many in number (arithmōi polla), as in the case of the letter alpha. And for this reason when we say that there are seven vowels in our language, and twenty-four elements of the alphabet in all, clearly we are considering the common form underlying them all (to koinon hapantōn eidos), and not the particulars of them (ta kata meros) written on papyrus, wood, parchment, and stone. . . . [W]hen we say that they number twenty-four in all, we canvass (procheirizomenoi) not the particulars but rather just the types (ou ta kata meros . . . ta d' eidē monon), to which, in my view, we attach the names. (Meth. med. 2.7–8 = X, 131–132 Kühn)[7]

---

6. Peirce (1931–60, vol. 4, pp. 423–4 [= section 537]). I thank my colleague Fred Kronz for pointing me to this passage. Later in his career, Peirce changed his terminology, calling *type* a "famisign" and *token* an "actisign." But eventually (in 1908), he conceded that the "former names are better than the ones I now use" (Peirce, 1998, vol. 2, p. 488).

7. Cf. Hankinson (1991, pp. 66, 213–14). I have modified Hankinson's translation. He very perceptively gives the translation "tokens" for *ta kata meros*; but this might well seem tendentious in the context of my own argument.

The full context in Galen's treatise shows that use of the alphabet example is motivated by Galen's acceptance of the Aristotelian doctrine of universals as inherent in things, *universalia in rebus*. Nonetheless, as with Peirce's use of the example of words, Galen's alphabet example seeks to make the concept accessible and intuitive, metaphysical baggage being kept to a minimum.[8]

Even more remarkable – and perhaps sufficient for abating any lingering concern that my use of the type–token terminology may be anachronistic – is the fact that Galen's use of the alphabet example has its precedent in Aristotle. In *Metaphysics* M Aristotle uses this very example in order to distance himself from the Platonic tenet that the distinction between universals and particulars requires a separately existing Form, a transcendent "the F itself." The relevant text is intricately dialectical, but the rationale in the use of the alphabet example comes through clearly enough:

> [T]here is nothing to stop there being many alphas and betas, as with the elements (*stoicheiōn*) of speech (*tēs phōnēs*), without there also being over and above the many (*para ta polla*) a certain "alpha itself" and "beta itself" (*auto alpha kai auto bēta*). (*Met.* M.10, 1087a7–10)[9]

It is telling that the Neoplatonist commentator Syrianus, in his discussion of this passage, resists Aristotle's deflationary exploitation of the alphabet example.[10] And it is likewise telling that a modern commentator adopts Peirce's terminology of types and tokens in paraphrasing the same text of Aristotle's:

> There can be many elements or letters of the same kind, e.g., many As, without this implying either that there is a Form of A or a mysterious universal A. Tokens can be tokens of the same type without this leading to the manufacture of an exalted status for the type over and above its tokens and separate and independent of them.[11]

The fact that Platonists may find the type–token distinction unacceptably deflationary is not surprising. The important fact in the present context is that, no matter how Plato and his followers would have ultimately conceptualized the distinction between

---

8. "And it is so evident, and it so naturally belongs to everything, be it man or beast, to recognize ... the unitary form (*hōs eidos hen*), that even donkeys, ... the stupidest creatures of all, manage to distinguish between things which are one in form and those which are one numerically": *Meth. med.* 2.7 = X, 133 Kühn; trans. from Hankinson (1991, p. 67).

9. My translation, drawing on Annas (1976, p. 115). I am grateful to Dr. Segalerba for calling my attention to this important passage.

10. I translate from Syrianus, *In Met.* pp. 163–164: "He [Aristotle] claims that just as the elements (*stoicheia*) of speech (*phōnēs*) make for infinitely many utterances, even though they are not separate from utterances (*tōn phōnōn*), in like fashion the principles of things are inseparable from individuals. ... [But] we would not be able to produce an infinite number of utterances out of the twenty-four specific elements of the alphabet if we did not have within ourselves both the form (*eidos*) of each and also the patterns for combining them all (*logous syntheseōs*)." I thank Dr. Gerald Bechtle for calling my attention to this passage.

11. Annas (1976, p. 190). And, without using Peirce's terminology, but, in effect, applying the same distinction to the passage from *Met.* M.10: Segalerba (2001, pp. 210–12).

the F-itself and F-things, that distinction involves *at a minimum* the distinction between the F-type and F-tokens.

Turning now to both the first and the second of the three criteria for the universal listed above, let me explain the qualification "thematically significant." I call a distinction "thematically significant" not only if, in the context at issue, the distinction itself becomes a topic of discussion, but also if major philosophical claims are being put forward by virtue of deploying the distinction. Examples of thematically significant uses of either the type–token or the type$_1$–type$_2$ distinction in Plato and Aristotle are far too numerous to list. It may suffice just to allude here to two famous passages in Platonic dialogues. In *Phaedo* 74a–c Socrates prompts Simmias' agreement that we ought to distinguish between "the equal" as it applies concretely to sticks or stones and *auto to ison*, "the equal itself," or *auto ho estin ison*, "what it is to be equal," or *isotēs*, "equality." In *Meno* 71d–e Socrates calls on his interlocutor to specify the encompassing type referred to as *aretē*, "virtue, human excellence" (type$_2$); but Meno (adhering to the teachings of Gorgias) responds by citing plural subordinate or special types, such as "virtue for a man," "virtue for a woman," "virtue for a slave," etc. (type$_1$). Briefly after this exchange, Socrates distinguishes between *schēma*, "shape" (type$_2$) and *schēma ti*, "*a* shape," e.g., *strongulon*, "curvilinear," or *euthu*, "rectilinear" (type$_1$).

The third criterion may seem at first blush too technical to qualify as part of a "minimalist" specification; and yet it is absolutely essential and elementary. For, without it, the type–token distinction (and thus the distinction between a universal and its particulars) might be confused with the distinction between a partitive whole and its parts. Though there is a certain one–many relation between, say, scoopfuls, or even stretches, of water in a lake and the lake water taken as a whole, that relation is "mereological," it is not one between either a token and a type or between a subordinate type$_1$ and a superordinate type$_2$. A thinker who grasps the mereological relation may not necessarily be en route to grasping the universal. Plato took pains to distinguish the relation that holds between a Platonic Form and its instances from the one that holds between a mass-entity and its portions. The so-called "Sail" (*istion*) argument (perhaps better translated the "Awning argument") at *Parmenides* 131b–c is directly aimed at an assimilation of the universal to a mass-entity.[12]

Some Conceptual Barriers to Early Grasp of the Universal

One of the reasons why the pre-history of the universal is an engaging topic is that there are certain thematic barriers that may have served to block or to delay recognition

---

12.   The text, in translation as in Allen (1983, p. 8), slightly revised: [Parmenides to Socrates] "You make one and the same thing be in many different places at once, as if you'd spread an awning (*istion*) over a number of men and then claimed that one thing as a whole was over many. . . . But would the whole awning be over each man, or part of it over one and part over another? – [Socr.] Part of it. – [Parm.] Therefore, Socrates, the Forms (*eidē*) are divisible, and things that have a share of them have a share of parts of them; whole would no longer be in each, but part of each in each."

or significant deployment of the concept. In cosmologies that advocate some version of material monism, the concept of the universal inevitably lacks prominence, or indeed relevance. We today, as students of Anaximander, might distinguish between (a) his *apeiron* as a massive individual and (b) such properties as are attributed to it in our sources, viz., "eternal," "unaging," "deathless," "indestructible," "encompassing." That is, we are free to envisage these properties as in principle or potentially detachable, applicable also to individuals other than the *apeiron*. But that is precisely what Anaximander's monism precludes. These properties are possessed uniquely and exclusively by the *apeiron*. For him, the cosmic individual and its properties form an inseparable whole. The cosmology gives us no encouragement or stimulus to detach the properties, to begin to view them as universals.

What is said here about Anaximander's *apeiron* applies correspondingly to the cosmic air of Anaximenes, which is likewise the subject of such attributes as "infinite," and "divine" (DK 13A5, A6, A9, A10). But it also applies with reference to the various states of rarefaction-condensation of cosmic air. For, however natural it might be for us to view like states of rarefaction (or of condensation) in different regions or at different times as distinct tokens of the same type, for Anaximenes these manifestations in different regions or different times are integral parts of a global individual.

Pursuing this line of thought, one might suppose that the one God of Xenophanes, the unitary what-is of Parmenides, and the One of Melissus should also be judged barren as conceptual soil for the universal. There are, however, some noteworthy complexities in these cases, and discussion of these must be deferred to another occasion.

Interestingly, pluralism may also be inhospitable to the concept of the universal. As W. A. Heidel pointed out a century ago (1906), a thought-structure that holds sway in philosophical and scientific thought before Plato is that of composition/re-composition of partitive entities, or mass-entities, of stuffs. The "opposites" in Anaximander and in Alcmaeon, the intermingling earth and water of Xenophanes, the opposite *morphai* in Parmenides' "Doxa," the four elements of Empedocles, the infinite *chrēmata* of Anaxagoras' cosmology, and (in parallel to these more properly philosophical contexts) the *dunamies*, "powers," of the medical treatises – all these entities represent a hybrid category of thing-stuff-power-quality (Mourelatos, 1973, pp. 17–30). Even the four that became the canonical "contraries" in Aristotle's scheme – the hot, the cold, the dry, the moist – are conceptualized by many of the pre-Socratics not as qualities or properties but as "the-hot-burning-stuff" or "the-dry-desiccating-stuff," fully on a par ontologically with those stuffs that bear familiar mass-noun designations, such as air, soil, bone, or sap. Accordingly, the hot in the oven and the hot in the kiln are not two tokens of the type *hot* but rather two portions of a single mass-entity that have been parceled out to different regions. There is good reason to believe that this dominantly mereological thought structure is a hold-over from a characteristically pre-philosophical conceptual scheme (Mourelatos, 1973, pp. 21–2). For the reasons that have already been suggested above (when I specified criteria with respect to Plato's and Aristotle's grasp of the universal), the hybrid category that is at issue here may have served more as a block or deviation and less as a proper stage in the development of the universal.

Interference from this hybrid category may also render moot the contribution to our account that could have been made by two noteworthy conceptual devices that are well-attested in pre-Socratic thought: the principle Like to Like; and the so-called Synonymy Principle of Causation, which stipulates that the presence of a certain property F in an effect must be traced to the presence of F in the cause (Barnes, 1979, vol. 1, pp. 88, 119). Clearly, the Like to Like principle can be applied to entities of the hybrid category – and this, almost certainly, is the original version of the principle. So applied, if the-hot-burning-stuff consorts with its like, the assimilation may be understood in concrete, physical, and mereological terms as attraction or agglutination between different portions of the same stuff. As for the Synonymy Principle, there are famously special versions of it in Plato and in Aristotle that point straight to form as an abstract entity and a universal: the Platonic formula, F-things are F because of the form F-ness; the Aristotelian metaphysical slogan, *anthrōpos anthrōpon gennāi*, "a human being begets a human being." Applied, however, to entities of the hybrid category, the Synonymy Principle envisages a mere physical transfer (imparting, invading, encroachment, spillage, contamination) from cause to effect: when the hot brick is put in the water, the-hot spills out of the brick and heats (invades) the water. The community of the F-character is not one involving different tokens of the same type but rather one of redistribution of portions of the same individual.

Another factor that may blunt awareness of the type–token relation is attention to cyclically recurring phenomena. A modern student of philosophy would not require much prompting to realize that such recurring events as nightfall, dusk, daybreak, dawn, new moon, or – for that matter and more broadly – each of the four seasons, are all properly types, and that under each type there are distinct tokens distributed over more or less regular intervals in time. But early students of the cosmos, who were indeed pre-occupied with such recurrences, are likely to have perceived in them successive reappearances or returns *of the same token individuals*. Winter and summer would have been conceived as individuals of that hybrid category: they periodically make their advent, and then recede – even today, we speak of the coming of dawn, or the coming of winter. Other cyclically recurring events would have been perceived as temporal parts of such conspicuous individuals as the sun or the moon, no more detachable from either luminary than the traits and behavior of Achilles are detachable from the person of that unique individual in Homer.

Those modern scholars who have looked for anticipations of the Platonic concept of Form independently of Aristotle's suggestions on the topic have focused their investigations on that hybrid category of thing-stuff-power-quality,[13] the category I have specifically set outside the scope of the present account. This focus in scholarship is understandable, in view of the extensive overlap, both lexical and syntactic, between the early mereological scheme and that of Plato's theory. In both schemes we have substantives formed from the articulate neuter (*to thermon*, "the hot"/*to hosion*, "the pious"); in both we have the language of "sharing," "partaking," "participating," "communion" (*metechein, koinōnein*), as well as language for the converse relation of "inherence" or "presence in" (*pareinai* or *eneinai* with dative); and in both schemes the "sharing," etc., admit of degrees ("more" and "less"). But it has generally been recognized that the mereological model can be applied, at best, only to a limited range

13. See, e.g., Furley (1976, pp. 81–2); Furley (1987, pp. 69–70, 171–3); Meinwald (1992, p. 375); Moline (1981, pp. 84–97).

of Platonic Forms.[14] It obviously fails in the case of arithmetical and geometric Forms – structure Forms, generally – also in the case of biological Forms, and in other cases. Given that the focus of the present account is on the universal as an abstract type (the paradigm being the type–token and the $type_1$–$type_2$ distinctions) "anticipations" that draw on the mereological scheme are simply off our topic.

Empedocles: Formulae for Compounds; Biological Forms; Type-Identities Across Cycles

Aristotle recognizes three pre-Socratic antecedents for his concept of *to katholou*, "the universal": numbers and proportions in Pythagoreanism;[15] the formulae of composition for compounds in Empedocles;[16] and Democritus' attention to issues of "form" and "essence."[17] Aristotle is characteristically chary in all three cases, which may to some extent be justified by his narrow focus on "defining essence." We, however, can be more generous.

I shall take up Empedocles first. We find in the Empedocles fragments arithmetical formulae not only for bone (DK 31B96), which is the only case cited by Aristotle, but also for "the forms (*eidea*) of other tissue (*allēs sarkos*)" (B98). Blood requires exactly equal parts of the four elements (*isē malista*, B98.1), whereas other tissues and body fluids involve specific variations from the norm of equality: slightly more of earth, or slightly more of the other three (B98.4). The numerical formula for bone envisages transparently a universal, as Aristotle noted. Moreover, the principle of variation of proportion allows Empedocles to construct an entire domain of types of biological tissue.

The term *eidos* and its cognate *idea* are prominent in yet another context in Empedocles. The plurals (*eidē, eidea, ideai*) are employed along with the plural of *ethnos*, "tribe, kind" (*ethnea*) in reference to kinds of living beings, including gods (who for Empedocles are *dolichaiōnes*, "long-lived," but not immortal).[18] Emphasizing the

---

14. See, e.g., Brentlinger (1972). I am not convinced by the argument in Moline (1981, pp. 143–55), that the mereological model persists into Plato's middle and late periods.

15. *Met.* M.4, 1078b17–23: Socrates was first to seek *katholou horizesthai*, "universal definitions"; Democritus "touched on it" (see below); the Pythagoreans, asked "what is opportunity (*kairos*) or the just or marriage" and reduced these to numbers (*eis tous arithmous anēpton*). Cf. *Met.* A.5, 985b23–31, 987a13–22. For an explanation of such reductions of abstract entities to numbers, see McKirahan (1994, pp. 91–111).

16. *Phys.* II.2, 194a20–21: "Empedocles and Democritus touched in small part on form (*eidous*) and essence (*tou ti ēn einai*)." Cf. *PA* I.1, 642a17–24: Empedocles "driven by truth itself is compelled to say that constitutive nature (*phusis*) is the ratio, as when he explains what bone is"; *Met.* A.10, 993a17–18: "even Empedocles says that bone is what it is by virtue of a ratio, which is the essence and reality (*to ti ēn einai kai hē ousia*)."

17. See *Phys.* text in preceding note. Cf. *Met.* M.4, 1078b17–21: "Democritus just touched on it slightly (the *katholou*), and roughly (*pōs*) defined the hot and the cold." Also *PA* I.1, 642a17–24: "Democritus was the first to touch on *to ti ēn einai*, 'essence,' and on *to horisasthai tēn ousian*, 'working out definitions of the reality at issue.'"

18. In addition to the citations from DK 31B98 (above in the text), plural forms *eidē/eidea* also appear in B22.7, B23.5, B71.3, B73.2, B115.7, and B125.1.

immense variety of these forms and kinds, Empedocles describes their evolutionary advent in these words: "countless tribes (*ethnea muria*) of mortal beings poured forth, structured in all sorts of forms (*pantoiais ideesin arērota*), a marvel to behold (*thauma idesthai*)" (DK 31B35.16–17; cf. B35.7).

Not limiting himself to this global characterization, he frequently sorts out the "mortal beings" into sub-genera: "human beings" (further subdivided into "men" and "women"), "beasts," "birds," "fish," "trees," "shrubs."[19]

Of course, the fact that we have in Empedocles classificatory uses of *eidos* and related terms does not by itself satisfy the demand for thematic significance I have stipulated. If, however, we follow the majority of interpreters in assuming that in Empedocles' cosmology we have a cosmic cycle, the distinct phases of which are indefinitely or eternally repeated, then the issue of *eidea* and *ethnea* becomes philosophically momentous. We saw earlier how cyclical phenomena may serve to block awareness of types by allowing that different tokens of the same type should be conceptualized as recurring advents of the same token (e.g., last year's and this year's summer). In Empedocles' scheme, there is no possibility of such blockage. For, with the possible exception of transmigrating *daimones*, the vast majority of individuals (the tokens corresponding to the types) do not survive through the phase of maximum Love (the *sphairos*), and probably also not through that of maximum Strife. What recurs are unmistakably types. Theoretically scrutinizing any two complete cycles M and N, out of the entirety of elapsed cycles, any hearer or reader of Empedocles' verses would have been prompted – as today any reader is likewise prompted – to wonder, "Are the *eidea* of cycle M the same as those in the corresponding phase of cycle N?" Even within one given cycle, the question arises, "Are the *eidea* that are temporally separated either by the period of total Love or by the period of total Strife the same or different?"

Philolaus: Genus, Species, and the Relation to Particulars

With respect to my second of the three antecedents acknowledged by Aristotle, it is important to stress that Aristotle speaks of "Pythagoreans," or even of "ones who call themselves Pythagoreans," not of Pythagoras. It is certainly not clear whether the reference is to Pythagoreans of the early fifth or the late fifth century, or, for that matter, of the fourth century. Indeed, the most penetrating and critically balanced account of the subject of Pythagoras and Pythagoreanism in modern scholarship, Walter Burkert's magisterial book of 1962 (original German edition), would lead one to surmise that Pythagoras' contribution to the development of the concept of the universal would have been, at most, a proclamation of mystical faith in universal affinity. Even the much-discussed discovery of the arithmetical ratios for the musical concords was probably not, according to Burkert (1972, esp. chs. 5 and 6), one made exclusively by Pythagoras' successors – let alone by the founder of the school.

If we limit our purview to this later period, we may appreciate with some confidence the contributions made by Philolaus of Croton, certain important fragments of whose writings are now securely acknowledged as authentic. It is especially significant

---

19.   See these fragments (all in DK 31B): 9, 20, 21, 23, 26, 76, 77–80, 117, 127, and 130.

that Philolaus names his cosmological principles not *apeiron* and *peras* but (using the plural) *apeira* and *perainonta*, "unlimited and limited things" (DK 44B1, B2, B6), thus openly proclaiming his purpose to classify *ta eonta panta*, "all existing things," under these two broad types (see Huffman, 1993, pp. 37–53, 93, 101). A conceptually more articulate typology, together with some notably sophisticated distinctions, is implied in a context of narrower scope, the domain of numbers. The viewpoint, nonetheless, is equally abstract as in Philolaus' statement of cosmological principles, and the implied metaphysical bearing is no less fundamental:

> Number, indeed, has two proper kinds (*idia eidē*), odd and even, and a third from both mixed together, the even-odd. Of each of the two kinds there are many forms (*morphai*), of which [scil., the forms] each thing, in and of itself, provides a sign (*hekaston auto sēmainei*). (DK 44B5)[20]

We need not be side-tracked by the vexed question of the nature and scope of the derivative "third" type, the "even-odd";[21] for it is clear from the second sentence that the focus is on the two kinds that were just denominated "proper" or "intrinsic" (*idia*). So read, the fragment offers a statement of major importance, as has rightly been emphasized by Carl Huffman: Philolaus here speaks not only of a relation between numbers as individual species and their two genera, even and odd, but also of "the relation between numbers and things" (1993, p. 178). In the terminology used in the present chapter, Philolaus takes note both of a type$_1$–type$_2$ relation and also of the relation between individual tokens and their appropriate type. He is contrasting the *mediated* relation that obtains between, say, four pebbles and the type picked out by the expression "even" with the more immediate relation of *signification* that holds between the tetrad of pebbles and the type picked out by "four." In the latter case, the physical tetrad "in and of itself" (*hekaston auto*) is a token of the type – indeed, "betokens" would be an excellent alternative translation for *sēmainei*. By contrast, in the former case, the relation of the particular to the *eidos* referred to as "even" is mediated by the *morphē* referred to as "four."

So explicated, Philolaus B5 gains even more in significance. Its phrasing shows Philolaus groping for a metaphor that may convey the relation between a particular and a universal. Unmistakably it is in this text, not in Plato, that we have the first recorded attempt in the history of metaphysics at coining a term for this relation. Philolaus opts not for "participates in" or "shares in" or "imitates" or "exemplifies" but rather for *sēmainei*, "provides a sign of," "betokens" – remarkably, an expression that

20. Except for slight variation in the translation of the final three words, text and translation is as in Huffman (1993, p. 178; see also pp. 184–93). I agree with Huffman that the reading αὐταυτό (Doric reflexive pronoun) of the MSS needs to be emended to simply αὐτό. Huffman has pointed out to me, however (in private correspondence), that αὐταυτό could be retained, provided we insert δι (ά) to read δι' αὐταυτό, and this might help explain the origin of the nonsensical δημαίνει (emended by Huffman and other editors into σημαίνει).
21. The solution in Huffman (1993, p. 190), is plausible enough: "[T]he even-odd is a derived class of numbers whose first member is, as the ancient tradition indicates, the one, but which also includes . . . even and odd numbers combined in ratios (e.g., 2:1, 4:3, and 3:2)."

is a close semantic congener of the modern term "instantiates." One is naturally led to wonder how differently the history proper of the universal may have unfolded had it started with philosophical reflection on the relation conveyed by Philolaus' *sēmainein* rather than with the other metaphors cited above – the ones introduced and favored by Plato.

Democritus: An Infinity of Atomic Types, Atomic Tokens

I turn now to the third case of anticipation Aristotle recognizes. The philosophy of Democritus[22] was the subject of a lost treatise by Aristotle;[23] and it is clear from the preserved treatises of the Aristotelian corpus that Aristotle viewed Democritus as a major philosophical rival. Aristotle's own testimony belies his grudging comments on the topic of the universal ("Democritus just touched on it slightly . . . roughly defined the hot and the cold": see above n. 15). For it is Aristotle himself who tells us that Democritean atoms are "infinite in multitude . . . and have all sorts of forms (*pantoias morphas*) and all sorts of shapes (*schēmata pantoia*) and differences in size" (Arist. fr. 208 Rose, cf. DK 68A37). And it is Aristotle who, in other passages, leaves no doubt that "all sorts" must be given the strongest possible reading, in other words, that Democritus envisaged infinity in both the relevant respects:

> The indivisible bodies are infinite both in multitude and in the shapes. (GC I.1, 314a22, cf. DK 67A9)

> Since [ordinary] bodies differ in shape, and the shapes are infinite, then the simple bodies as well are infinite. (*Cael.* III.4, 303a11; cf. DK 67A15)

Especially striking is the inference from the infinity of types of shape to the infinity of atoms: the range of shapes is intrinsically infinite; there must be at least one specimen for each type (Democritus was no believer in purely ideal possibilities); therefore the number of atoms bearing shape must be infinite. The inference here could not have been drawn without a firm grasp of the type–token distinction. The degree of insight into that distinction these reports assign to Democritus compares favorably with what may be assigned not only to corresponding passages in Epicurus and Lucretius[24] but also to the many similar contexts in Plato and in Aristotle.

22.   It is, by and large, not possible to distinguish between the contributions to the original philosophy of Atomism made by the founder of the theory, Leucippus, and those made by his successor Democritus: see McKirahan (1994, p. 304); Taylor (1999, pp. 157–8). I adhere to the widely adopted practice of using the name "Democritus" in synecdoche for the sayings and doctrines of both Leucippus and Democritus.

23.   Perhaps two treatises, "On Democritus" and "Problems from Democritus." See DK 68A34.

24.   Cf. Epic. *Hdt.* 42–3; Lucr. 2.478–531. The Epicureans' doctrine of minimal parts dictated adjusting Democritean doctrine: the token atoms are infinite; but the types of atomic shape are finite, though vastly numerous, *aperilēpta*, "unencompassable." See Morel, EPICUREANISM, in this volume.

Moreover, it is likely that Democritus went further: he posited an infinity of token atoms for each of the infinite types of shape. This is implied by testimony that presents the early Atomists as having recourse to a version of the Principle of Sufficient Reason, the so-called argument from *ou mallon*, "no more this than that":

> They [Leucippus and Democritus] say that the multitude of shapes in the atoms is infinite since there is no more reason (*dia to mēden mallon*) that [a given atom] should have this shape rather than another (*toiouton ē toiouton einai*). (Simpl. *In Phys.* 28.15ff. = DK 68A38)

As in the *De Caelo* text cited earlier, the inference does not go beyond establishing the infinity of types of shape. But if the *ou mallon* argument works to produce this inference, it should also work to establish that the number of token atoms for any one of the infinity of types of atomic shape is infinite.[25] Furthermore, relying on the same argument, it may well seem reasonable to strengthen Aristotle's "all sorts of sizes" into "an infinity of atomic sizes," and then proceed to the corollary, that with respect also to any one size-type there is an infinite supply of token atoms.[26] In any event, just as there is an infinity of types with respect to at least one of the two properties possessed by the atoms intrinsically (shape, size), there is a corresponding immense multitude (perhaps infinity) of types for what might be called extrinsic or relational properties, those acquired by atoms after collision and rebound, or in the course of aggregation into compounds: motion (including the *differentiae* of speed and direction); *taxis*, "array, order, position" (the difference between AN and NA); and *thesis*, "posture, tilt, orientation" (the difference between N and Z).[27] Finally, at the widest compass, in the infinite

25. The inference is indeed drawn by the Epicureans for each of the types of shape – in this respect probably in adherence to Democritean doctrine – even though the number of atomic shapes is finite: see preceding note.
26. The evidence is, admittedly, ambiguous. See Taylor (1999, pp. 173–5). But the emphasis placed by the Epicureans on limiting the variety of atomic sizes does perhaps indicate that Democritus, by contrast, had envisaged such an infinity. It is sometimes assumed – and I have so been inclined to assume myself – that any infinite variation of size would have to obtain between a lower and an upper bound (smallest and largest atomic size). The positing of any such bounds would be unfortunate; for it would significantly qualify Democritus' adherence to the *ou mallon* principle. But as Victor Caston and others pointed out to me (in a discussion of Mourelatos, 2005), the unqualified infinity of the Democritean universe could perhaps allow for finite atomic sizes that recede or proceed *ad infinitum* to smaller-and-smaller and to larger-and-larger, respectively. The Like to Like principle would guarantee that *kosmoi*, "worlds" (which in all ancient atomist cosmologies are large-scale regional clusterings of atomic compounds) would involve only compatible atomic sizes – ones that fall within a range appropriate for the dimensions of the *kosmos* at issue. To be sure, if atoms are to be thought of as indivisible magnitudes in a strong sense (metaphysically or mathematically, not just physically), then there would have to be a lower bound atomic size. But I strongly doubt that Democritus would have entertained the contradictory concept of *ideai*, "shapes," that are indivisible.
27. Aristotle *Met.* A.4, 985b4–21; DK 67A6. I deliberately select the Aristotelian terms over the Democritean *diathigē* and *tropē* which refer, I believe, to the dispositions that correspond, respectively, to the two occurrent and acquired properties of *taxis* and *thesis*. See Mourelatos (2005, pp. 56–8).

expanse of the void there is an infinity of *kosmoi*, "world structures" (DK 67A1, A21, 68A1[44]).

Democritus may well appear intoxicated by the theme of infinity, obsessed with it. In the overall ramified scheme, we have five superordinate types (the five distinct intrinsic or extrinsic properties of atoms cited above: shape, size, motion, array, posture); for at least the first of these there is an infinity of subordinate types of that property; and for each of the subordinate types (be they infinite or finite) there is an infinity of token atoms. One of our ancient sources comments, with evident irritation, that "it is a consequence of their [Leucippus' and Democritus'] theories that there is something more infinite than the infinite."[28] What drives this exuberant proliferation of entities – here is the crucial point for the present account – are the two distinctions: type–token and type$_1$–type$_2$.

Given the important work these distinctions accomplish within Democritus' system, it would not have required too difficult an act of abstraction for him to focus on the infinite domain of any one of the five super-ordinate types cited here. Certainly in the case of atomic shape, we have evidence that he did approach the subject abstractly and typologically. For he spoke not only globally of an infinity of shapes; he took note also of such sub-genera as "convex," "concave," "lop-sided," "curviform," "spherical," "angular," "polygonal," "hook-like";[29] and he wrote treatises titled *Peri diapherontōn rhysmōn*, "On Different Shapes," and *Peri ameipsirhysmiōn*, "On Changes of Shape" (DK 68A33), as well as several treatises on topics of geometry (DK 68A33).

Comments by Democritus on the Universal

My argument so far has been that the uses of the type–token and type$_1$–type$_2$ distinctions by Democritus have enough thematic significance to justify the claim that this philosopher has a well-articulated grasp of the concept of the universal. But I believe an even stronger case can be made: there is good evidence that Democritus not only made use of the concept of the universal but that he "thematized" it, that he made the concept itself a topic for explanation and comment. The evidence is in two seldom discussed fragments. In a separate study, I have analyzed the two ostensible quotations in these two fragments, together with the contexts in the source in which the quotations have been preserved (2003). Here I must limit myself to a précis of the interpretive issues involved and to reporting of my conclusions. For details of the supporting evidence and interpretive argument, I refer the reader to this other study.

The first of these fragments is B124. The part in which Democritus is quoted reads:

> Democritus, inasmuch as he says, "one will be [*estai*, singular] men and [they] all [will be] man" (*anthrōpoi heis estai kai anthrōpos pantes*). Hippocrates, however, says. . . .

---

28. John Philoponus *In GC* 12.4–5 (commenting on Arist. *GC* I.1, 314a15). Cf. Taylor (1999, p. 73).

29. See DK 68A37, A101–102, A132, A135. Cf. Stückelberger (1979, pp. 319–20).

The source is pseudo-Galen *Medical Definitions* (439 = XIX, 449–450 Kühn), and the theme in the paragraph in which the quotation occurs is history of the embryological doctrine of pangenesis, the doctrine that seed is drawn from the whole of the body of the father or (whole of the body of each) of the parents. As would only seem reasonable for a start, embryological readings of the quoted sentence have been tried; but they appear forced. Moreover, other passages of *Medical Definitions* show pseudo-Galen quoting from philosophers or using their terminology more for the purpose of displaying erudition, exploiting the quoted sayings or terms on the basis of utterly tenuous and merely verbal connections with the medical subject at issue. We are not compelled, therefore, to assume that the original context, in Democritus' own work, was embryological.

My proposal is that the original context was metaphysical. Let me first briefly resolve syntactical issues. The future form *estai* does not envisage embryological development; it is a *futurum consequentiae* (cf. "Given what was said, this will be the case. . . ."). Moreover, the fact that *estai* is grammatically singular need not dictate taking "one" as the subject of the sentence. For it is quite possible and plausible that the copula logically represents an identity relation: "men = one; i.e., men will be identical with single (man)." In that case, the grammatical subject is *anthrōpoi*, "men," and this construal is – after all – the more natural one, given the word order.[30]

My metaphysical reading of B124 can, accordingly, be conveyed in this paraphrase:

> If one adopts the synoptic view, the many men will be (may be viewed as) a single man – the type Man. Nonetheless, the many men, severally, taken as separate individuals (tokens), will count as (or simply are) *a* man.

If this interpretation is correct, Democritus did not only conform to the third of the criteria listed above (p. 58), he stated that criterion. In effect, he intuitively anticipates Plato's *istion* argument in the *Parmenides*: the "one" that is collected in a universal is not a "one over many" in the way an awning extends over many spectators (see above, p. 61). Discernible in the Democritean saying are two points: (a) As we look for the universal, the plural individual human beings will come to be viewed as one, the type Man. (b) This, however, does not mean that Man is a partitive entity, one that can be distributed mereologically; rather, each and every human being is in himself or herself sufficiently and exhaustively "*a* man."

But why, one may wonder, should Democritus have been concerned to make this point? I can think of two good reasons: one is that he sought to differentiate his ontology sharply from that of such rivals as Empedocles, Anaxagoras, or Diogenes of Apollonia, in all of whose theories the fundamental realities, belonging as they do to what I earlier called the "hybrid" category, are indeed partitive. Moreover, by drawing attention to the dual use (both for the type and for tokens) of the familiar expression *anthrōpos*, he could provide an intelligible analogue for his own technical dual use of the term *idea*, "shape." For he uses the latter in referring both to the type – the property of shape all atoms inherently possess – and also to the tokens, which he distributively calls not only *atomoi* or *atoma* but also simply *ideai*.

30. Cf. Kahn (1973, p. 427): "There seems to be no doubt that the statistically favored order, both in Homer and in classic prose, is . . . *N* [subject] φ [predicate] *is*."

70

The other Democritean saying that shows, I believe, our philosopher attending to the concept of the universal is in B165, which in DK is printed as a fragment in two parts, joined by a dash. In the source text, in Sextus Empiricus, the two parts are separated by two intervening sentences of Sextus' own comments. It is not even certain that the first part is a quotation rather than a summarizing remark by Sextus; nor is there much support in the full context for Diels' conjecture that the two parts originally constituted a single statement. So, my interest, like that of other scholars who have discussed this fragment, is only in the second part:

anthrōpos esti ho pantes idmen.

Man is what we all know. (DK 68B165)

Perhaps – so goes the traditional interpretation – this was a reductive remark, something of this force: it is theoretical entities, atoms and the void, that challenge our reflection; no need to concern ourselves with a commonplace topic, the nature of man. But such an interpretation would run directly against the evidence that Democritus wrote an entire treatise on *The Nature of Man* (DK 68B5d); and it also goes against Democritus' professed avid and global yearning for finding *aitiologiai*, "explanations" (DK 68B118).

My proposal is that the saying combines epistemological and metaphysical import. It introduces and explains the universal implied in Man by pointing out a disparity between our knowledge of universals and our knowledge of particulars. There is no way that all human beings, certainly not across all the ages, but not even (assuming ancient modes of transport) over some limited stretch of time, should know one single individual – say, Democritus, or Leucippus, or Protagoras, or the present king of Persia. And yet we all know what it is to be human, we know the universal *anthrōpos*.

It is not at all difficult to imagine what circumstances might have prompted Democritus to make this comment. Other fragments show him contrasting the clarity and security with which we know general and fundamental truths about atoms and the void against the obscurity of knowledge of *hekasta*, "things in particular":

Even so (*kaitoi*), it will become evident that it is not possible to know what each particular thing is (*hoion hekaston*) in reality (*eteēi*). (DK 68B8)

Surely, on the one hand (*men*), it has been shown in many ways that, in terms of reality (*eteēi*), we do not grasp what each particular thing is or is not (*hoion hekaston estin ē ouk estin*), ... (DK 68B10)

But the example of "man" in B165 may also have served the same purpose the example of the alphabet had served in Galen (see above, pp. 59–60). If a critic had objected that concrete particulars are more easily knowable than types, B165 would have provided an effective rejoinder.

Democritus and Aristotle: Origins of the Type–Token Distinction

Emerging from the preceding two sections is a historical diagnosis that is absent in standard accounts of the pre-Socratics. It would appear that in Democritus we have an anticipation of the Aristotelian solution to the metaphysical problem of the status of universals: *universalia in rebus.*[31] But if this is right, then Aristotle's use of the alphabet example in *Met.* M.10 (cited above, p. 60) gains enormously in significance. For it is also in Aristotle, at *Met.* A.4, 985b4–21, that we find the suggestion that Democritus had used the alphabet example in order to illustrate the basic differences in the fundamental properties of the atoms – *schēma,* "shape," *taxis,* "array, order," and *thesis,* "posture, tilt." Since the Greek word for letter, *stoicheion,* is the one that is ultimately adopted (clearly by Plato's time) as the term for metaphysical elements, and Democritus pre-eminently and famously has a metaphysics of elements, there is no reason to doubt that the example Aristotle used came from Democritus himself.

And once this connection is made, it is difficult to resist the further inference that Democritus' choice of the alphabet example made it possible for him also to illustrate the distinction which, as I argued above (pp. 67–9), is absolutely essential for formulating the doctrine of dual pluralities and infinities: the distinction between types and tokens. Just as the letter alpha can refer either to a token or to a type, so too "cube" can refer either to a particular atom or to a type of atomic shape. And, more broadly, *ideai* may be either types of atomic shape or atoms viewed individually, token atoms (see above, p. 70).

One may wonder whether there is a historical chain that binds Galen's use of the type–token distinction with its counterpart in Peirce. In the case of the ancients, at any rate, there is good reason to suppose that we do have such a chain. Its later links show up in Galen and Syrianus; it certainly runs through Aristotle; and its start and mooring is in Democritus.

Democritus and Plato

The domain of infinitely various types of shape posited by Democritus could well be envisaged as an enormous upside down typological tree, with prodigious branchings and sub-branchings – in effect, a hierarchical inventory of all possible shapes, the entirety of the conceptual matrix of shape. Naturally, one is drawn to a comparison with the Platonic universe of *ideai,* "forms." That universe is vastly greater in compass than Democritus' inventory of the totality of *ideai,* "shapes." Nonetheless, the special region of Plato's ideal universe which is allocated to shape has exactly the same content and logical structure as Democritus' hierarchical inventory.

Plato's grand metaphor in the *Sophist* of a battle between "the Gods and the Giants" (the idealist friends of the Forms and the materialists, 246a–c), has given rise to simplistic, almost hackneyed, contrasting of Democritus and Plato in histories of philosophy. And yet, as is suggested by the remarkable fact that the term *idea* plays a key role in the system of both philosophers, there are also striking affinities, both on

---

31.   The alternative, that he might have intuitively assumed some version of nominalism, is quite unlikely. For there would have been little point in Democritus' insistence on the actual infinity of shape-types if all he posited as present in reality were gross resemblances between atom-tokens.

the theme of the importance of form as structure or shape (Mourelatos, 1984) and – as the present study has sought to demonstrate – in their respective approaches to the concept of the universal.[32]

To be sure, there are also radical and stark differences. What for Plato is a universe of ideal possibilities (e.g., all the possible shapes) is for Democritus an actual universe of realized atomic shapes. For it would be remiss of us not to notice that the exuberant application of the *ou mallon* argument has the effect of making Democritus an adherent not only to the Principle of Sufficient Reason but also to Lovejoy's aptly named Principle of Plenitude (1936, p. 52, and generally ch. 2). Other adherents to this second principle would find it sufficient to posit that all possibilities should be realized eventually, in infinite time. Democritus, by contrast, would have to insist that all possibilities are realized at every moment – if the whole of the spatially infinite universe is taken into consideration. Any of the types of atomic shapes which at some particular time are represented by no tokens at all in some particular *kosmos*, "world structure" (e.g., our world, here and now) are so represented at that same time in other *kosmoi* – elsewhere in the infinite expanse of the void.[33]

Since Democritus not only outlived Socrates but may have still been active philosophically into the first ten or twenty years of Plato's philosophical career, the trenchant saying in B165 ("Man is what we all know") may have also served as a vehicle for conveying the difference Democritus himself perceived between his concept of type – and, more pointedly, of *idea*, "shape," as a type – and the more exalted concept of the Platonic *idea* as a sublime exemplar.

The crucial point in the present account is that, so far as the logic of the concept of the universal is concerned, Plato would not have had to teach Democritus much – certainly not what he presents Socrates as explaining to Meno about the logic of shape.[34]

32. For affinities on topics other than the ones taken up in the present study, see Paneris (1984, esp. pp. 80–1); also Nikolaou (1998, esp. pp. 140–52).

33. See Taylor (1999, pp. 94, 96, 197). For the distinction between *kosmos* and universe (*to pan*), see Furley (1987, p. 136).

34. An early version of this chapter was presented in November 2000 in Modern Greek to the Academy of Athens, and later as a lecture at the University of Crete (Rethimno), and at the University of Patras. The Greek text was published in 2002 in the *Proceedings of the Academy of Athens*: Mourelatos (2000). English versions earlier than the present one were read at: the University of Aarhus, Denmark; the University of Edinburgh; the Twenty-Fourth Annual Ancient Philosophy Workshop, Florida State University; Texas A & M University; Central European University, Hungary; the University of Utrecht; the Center for Hellenic Studies, Washington, DC; and Marquette University. I am deeply grateful to Dr. Johanna Seibt of Aarhus University for her elegant translation of the penultimate English version, under the title "Vorplatonische Zugänge zum Universalienbegriff," which made it possible for me also to present the work in October 2003 at the University of Bern, Switzerland, and at the Freie Universität Berlin. – I sincerely thank the sponsors of the events listed above, and I am indebted to the respective audiences for comments and suggestions that have resulted in significant improvements in the text published here. I wish to acknowledge in particular suggestions by Dr. Gianluigi Segalerba and Dr. Gerald Bechtle, both of the University of Bern.

Bibliography

Works Cited

Allen, R. E. (1983). *Plato's* Parmenides: *Translation and Analysis.* Minneapolis: University of Minnesota Press.

Annas, J. (1976). *Aristotle's* Metaphysics: *Books M and N.* Oxford: Clarendon Press.

Armstrong, D. M. (1989). *Universals: An Opinionated Introduction.* Boulder/London: Westview Press.

Audi, R. (ed.). (1995). *The Cambridge Dictionary of Philosophy.* Cambridge: Cambridge University Press.

Bächli, A. and Graeser, A. (2000). *Grundbegriffe der antiken Philosophie: ein Lexikon.* Stuttgart: Philipp Reclam.

Barnes, J. (1979). *The Presocratic Philosophers.* (2 vols.). London: Routledge & Kegan Paul.

Brentlinger, J. (1972). "Incomplete Predicates and the Two-World Theory of the *Phaedo.*" *Phronesis,* 17, 61–79.

Burkert, W. (1972). *Lore and Science in Ancient Pythagoreanism* (trans. E. L. Minar, Jr.). Cambridge, Mass.: Harvard University Press. Original work (1962) *Weisheit und Wissenschaft: Studien zu Pythagoras, Philolaos und Platon.* Nürnberg: Verlag Hans Carl.

Diels, H. (1951–2). (Cited as DK). *Die Fragmente der Vorsokratiker.* (3 vols.). 6th edn. Revised by W. Kranz, with several subsequent reprintings. Berlin: Weidmann. Original work, by Diels alone, published 1903.

Furley, D. J. (1976). "Anaxagoras in Response to Parmenides." In R. A. Shiner and J. King-Farlow (eds.), *New Essays on Plato and the Pre-Socratics* [= *Canadian Journal of Philosophy,* suppl. vol. 2] (pp. 61–85). Guelph, Ontario: Canadian Association for Publishing in Philosophy.

——. (1987). *The Greek Cosmologists: The Formation of the Atomic Theory and Its Earliest Critics.* Cambridge: Cambridge University Press.

Galen. *Claudii Galeni Opera omnia.* Medicorum Graecorum opera quae extant, C. G. Kühn (ed.) (20 vols.). Leipzig 1821–33. Repr. Hildesheim: Olms, 1964–5 – *De methodo medendi* in vol. X (1825), repr. 1965; pseudo-Galen *Definitiones medicae* in vol. XIX (1830), repr. 1965.

Hankinson, R. J. (1991). *Galen, On the Therapeutic Method, Books I and II: Translated with an Introduction and Commentary.* Oxford: Clarendon Press.

Heidel, W. A. (1906). "Qualitative Change in Pre-Socratic Philosophy." *Archiv für Geschichte der Philosophie,* 19, 333–79. Repr. with the original pagination in W. A. Heidel, *Selected Papers,* ed. Leonardo Tarán. New York/London: Garland, 1980. In abridged version repr. in Mourelatos (1974), pp. 86–95.

Huffman, C. (1993). *Philolaus of Croton, Pythagorean and Presocratic: A Commentary on the Fragments and Testimonia with Interpretive Essays.* Cambridge: Cambridge University Press.

Kahn, C. H. (1973). *The Verb 'be' in Ancient Greek. Foundations of Language,* suppl. series, 16. Dordrecht: D. Reidel. Repr. with a new introductory essay, Indianapolis: Hackett, 2003.

Kraut, R. (ed.). (1992). *The Cambridge Companion to Plato.* Cambridge: Cambridge University Press.

Lovejoy, A. O. (1936). *The Great Chain of Being.* Cambridge, Mass.: Harvard University Press. (Repr. 1964).

McKirahan, R. D., Jr. (1994). *Philosophy before Socrates: An Introduction with Texts and Commentary.* Indianapolis: Hackett.

Meinwald, C. C. (1992). "Good-bye to the Third Man." In R. Kraut (ed.), *The Cambridge Companion to Plato* (pp. 365–96). Cambridge: Cambridge University Press.

Moline, J. (1981). *Plato's Theory of Understanding.* Madison, Wisc.: University of Wisconsin Press.

Mourelatos, A. P. D. (1973). "Heraclitus, Parmenides, and the Naïve Metaphysics of Things." In E. N. Lee, A. P. D. Mourelatos, and R. M. Rorty (eds.), *Exegesis and Argument: Studies in Greek*

Philosophy Presented to Gregory Vlastos. [= *Phronesis*, suppl. vol. 1] (pp. 16–48). Assen: Royal van Gorcum/New York: Humanities Press.

——. (ed.). (1974). *The Pre-Socratics: A Collection of Critical Essays.* Garden City, NY: Anchor Press/Doubleday. Repr. with new introduction, Princeton, NJ: Princeton University Press, 1993.

——. (1984). "*Dhimókritos: filósofos tis morfis*" [Democritus: Philosopher of Form]. In *Proceedings of the First International Congress on Democritus.* (2 vols.) (vol. 1: pp. 109–19, English summary, pp. 118–19). Xanthi: International Democritean Foundation.

——. (2000). "*I aparkhyés tis filosofikyís énias tou katholou*" [Beginnings of the Philosophical Concept of the Universal]. *Praktiká tis Akadhimías Athinón* [Proceedings of the Academy of Athens], 75, 509–25 [issued in 2002; English summary, p. 526].

——. (2003). "Democritus on the Distinction between Universals and Particulars." In A. Bächli and K. Peter (eds.), *Monism* (Festschrift for Andreas Graeser) (pp. 43–56). Philosophische Analyse, 9. Frankfurt: Ontos Verlag.

——. (2005). "Intrinsic and Relational Properties in the Democritean Ontology." In R. Salles (ed.), *Metaphysics, Soul and Ethics: Themes from the Work of Richard Sorabji* (pp. 39–63). Oxford: Clarendon Press.

Nehamas, A. (1975). "Confusing Universals and Particulars in Plato's Early Dialogues." *Review of Metaphysics,* 29, 287–306 [quoted here from its reprinting as ch. 8 in Nehamas (1999), pp. 159–75].

——. (1999). *Virtues of Authenticity: Essays on Plato and Socrates.* Princeton, NJ: Princeton University Press.

Nikolaou, S.-M. (1998). *Die Atomlehre Demokrits und Platons Timaios: eine vergleichende Untersuchung.* Beiträge zur Altertumskunde, 112. Stuttgart: Teubner.

Paneris, I. P. (1984). *I kosmologhyía tou Plátona se schyési me tin atomikyí theoría tou Dhimókritou* [Plato's Cosmology in Relation to the Atomic Theory of Democritus]. Xanthi: International Democritean Foundation.

Peirce, C. S. (1931–60). *Collected Papers.* Edited by C. Hartshorne and P. Weiss (8 vols. in 5). Cambridge, Mass.: Harvard University Press.

——. (1998). *The Essential Peirce.* Edited by the Peirce Project (2 vols.). Bloomington: Indiana University Press.

Prauss, G. (1966). *Platon und der logische Eleatismus.* Berlin: de Gruyter.

Segalerba, G. (2001). *Note su Ousia: volume primo.* Florence: Edizioni ETS.

——. (2003). "Numerische Einheit als ontologisches Kriterium: zur Unterscheidung der Entitäten bei Aristoteles." *Wiener Jahrbuch für Philosophie,* 35, 59–96.

Stückelberger, A. (1979). *Antike Atomphysik.* Munich: Heimeran.

Syrianus. *Syriani in Metaphysica Commentaria.* G. Kroll (ed.) (1902). CAG, 6. Berlin: Reimer.

Taylor, C. C. W. (1999). *The Atomists, Leucippus and Democritus: Fragments, a Text and Translation with a Commentary. Phoenix* suppl. vol. 36 (= Phoenix Presocratics, 5). Toronto: University of Toronto Press.

Further Reading

Clear, concise, and philosophically engaged general introduction to the topic of universals: Armstrong (1989).

Excellent survey of all of pre-Socratic philosophy: McKirahan (1994).

Accounts of pre-Aristotelian and pre-Platonic conceptions of quality and of change (cf. "hybrid category," above): Heidel (1906); Mourelatos (1973).

An important alternative account of the pre-Aristotelian background: Mann, W.-R. (2000). *The Discovery of Things: Aristotle's* Categories *and Their Context.* Princeton, NJ: Princeton University Press.

The concept of the universal in Plato's Socratic dialogues: Nehamas (1975, 1999).

Fuller general studies of the three pre-Socratics discussed above:

- Philolaus and the Pythagoreans: Huffman (1993).
- Empedocles: Inwood, B. (1992). *The Poem of Empedocles: A Text and Translation with an Introduction. Phoenix* suppl. vol. 29 (= Phoenix Presocratics, 3). Toronto: University of Toronto Press. Revised edition 2001.
- Democritus: Taylor (1999).

Details on the textual evidence for the interpretation of Democritus offered here: Mourelatos (2003).

5

The Sophistic Movement

RACHEL BARNEY

Introduction

"I know few characters in history who have been so hardly dealt with as these so-called Sophists", says an indignant George Grote in his monumental *History of Greece* (Grote, 1872, p. 43). The sophists he refers to are an influential group of teachers, intellectuals, and authors of fifth-century (BCE) Greece; the "so-called" registers a protest against what Grote argues is an unfairly pejorative label. Though associated with the words for wisdom (*sophia*) and wise man (*sophos*), and originally meaning simply an expert or teacher, *sophistēs* had begun to take on connotations of intellectual deviousness already in the fifth century – a trend powerfully reinforced by Plato's largely unsympathetic portrayal (cf. Guthrie, 1969, pp. 27–34). For our purposes, "the sophists" will simply pick out a group of fifth-century teachers and thinkers who were so labeled in antiquity, and whose practices and ideas seem to overlap in important ways; they include Protagoras, Gorgias, Hippias, Prodicus, and Antiphon, and, in some respects, Socrates.[1] Since our concern is with their ideas, the group will also include the unidentifiable authors of some kindred anonymous texts (the *Dissoi Logoi*, the *Anonymus Iamblichi*); and light can also be shed on sophistic ideas by passages in other contemporary authors such as Democritus, Euripides and Thucydides. In fact, there may be little point in trying to separate off sophistic ideas from the broader intellectual currents of their era – the "Fifth-Century Enlightenment", as it has suggestively been called. Perhaps that is the hallmark of a successful intellectual movement.

---

1. Besides Socrates, of whom more later, the most questionable name here is Gorgias, who was first and foremost a *rhētorikos*, a rhetorician or teacher of public speaking. I here assume that "rhetorician" and "sophist" are overlapping categories (cf. Plato, *Grg.* 465c, 520a–b). Both professed public speaking: the difference would perhaps be that a sophist taught rhetorical skills not simply as such, but in the context of theorizing about language, ethics, and politics. The division of labor might be epitomized by the fact that Gorgias served as an ambassador to Athens from his home city of Leontini (DK 82A4), while Protagoras drafted laws for the colony of Thurii (DK 80A1). On the other hand, it would be wrong to assume that Gorgias as a rhetorician lacked theoretical interests, in light of his *On Not Being* (discussed below). The strongest argument for excluding Gorgias is that in Plato's *Meno*, he is said *not* to undertake to make men virtuous, a standard feature of sophistic teaching, and to scoff at those who do (95c; but cf. DK 82A8b).

That the sophists have been deprived of their due is a truism oddly undisturbed by scholarly progress and the passage of time: it can be found in Hegel's *Lectures on the History of Philosophy* (1840) and in George Kerferd's *The Sophistic Movement* (1981a), which begins by asking why the significance of the sophists "has been so underrated up to now" (p. 3). The reason is perhaps that every defender of the sophists has sought to rehabilitate something different. For Grote, they are above all professional teachers, adding progressive insights to the mainstream morality of the day. Nietzsche, denouncing Grote's reading as a whitewash, presents them as subversive moral critics after his own heart: "they postulate the first truth that a 'morality-in-itself', a 'good-in-itself' do not exist, that it is a swindle to talk of 'truth' in this field" (Nietzsche, 1968, p. 233). If there is any consensus to be found among their defenders (and their enemies as well), it is the constantly mutating view that *the sophists are our contemporaries* – whether that makes them Enlightenment rationalists, eminent Victorians, cynical *fin de siècle* perspectivists, analytic moral philosophers, or, most recently of all, postmodernists.[2]

This Rorschach quality is unlikely ever to disappear, for there are special barriers to an authentically historical grasp of the sophistic movement. One is the looming shadow of Plato. Plato depicts sophists memorably in a number of dialogues, including the *Protagoras*, *Gorgias*, *Hippias Major* and *Minor*, *Republic* and *Euthydemus*, and he devotes the *Sophist* to defining the beast. But all of this testimony is problematic – not only because of Plato's notorious hostility to the sophists, which has sometimes been overstated by scholars (cf. Grote, 1872 and 1865; and Irwin, 1995), but because his evidence is inconsistent. For instance, the sophists of the *Sophist* and *Euthydemus* are specialists in question-and-answer refutation, those of the *Protagoras* in long speeches. Moreover, the dialogue form, with its reliance on individual characters, makes the extrapolation of general claims problematic in any case: if Hippias is consistently represented by Plato as a nitwit, does that tell us something about the sophistic movement, or just about Hippias? Is Callicles in the *Gorgias* a canonical representative of sophistic thought, as Nietzsche clearly assumed; or is he just a feral (and quite possibly fictional) politician who happens to be friends with Gorgias?

Our other evidence for sophistic thought is scattered and uneven. A few brief but complete sophistic texts have survived – though alas nothing by Protagoras, the senior and most celebrated member of the profession – including several by Gorgias. So have a number of informative "fragments": the term is standardly used for any reliable-looking quotation found in a later author, but we also have some actual scraps of papyrus containing substantial passages from Antiphon's book *On Truth*. However, much of this direct evidence is obscure or hard to interpret; and taken as a whole, our evidence raises two central puzzles. One is what I will call the problem of *theory*: to what extent were the sophists engaged in offering what would later be termed *dogmata*, i.e., doctrines or theories? Scholars have often spoken of "sophistic ethics", taking the sophists to have offered overlapping if not identical positions on questions such as relativism, the nature of justice and whether virtue can be taught. But the

2. The first three are somewhat caricatured references to the readings of Hegel, Grote, and Nietzsche respectively. For the sophists as (again to oversimplify) analytic moral philosophers, see Barnes (1982); for postmodernists, Fish (1989) and Jarratt (1991).

attribution of *dogmata* to the sophists can be a slippery business. For instance, when Thrasymachus in Plato's *Republic* claims that "Justice is the advantage of the stronger" (339a), is he giving a revisionist definition of justice, or merely debunking justice as commonly understood? And in any case, does he mean what he says? Pressed by Socrates, he responds, "What difference does it make to you, whether I believe it or not? Aren't you refuting my account?" (*Rep.* I, 349a).[3] The sophist's claims are, it seems, offered not to express conviction, but for the sake of professional display – and for money (337d). Of our surviving texts, Gorgias' *On Not Being* presents a deadpan systematic argument that nothing exists; the anonymous *Dissoi Logoi* argues on both sides of various topics. One way or another, a startlingly high proportion of sophistic texts elude confident interpretation as *dogmata*: I will consider later on what we might make of this fact.

A second puzzle raised by our evidence is the question of *unity*. Did the sophists really share a common intellectual project, with distinctive projects and positions? The shared label "sophist" is no guarantee of a common nature. Recent scholarship has largely followed Grote in insisting on the diversity of sophistic thought; and Richard Bett has argued that the commonality revealed by our texts is really just one of attitude: "What unites the Sophists in the area of ethics, I suggest, is not so much any particular views they hold . . . but rather a certain type of attitude or approach. . . . This attitude or approach we might call 'naturalistic', or perhaps, more ambitiously, 'social scientific' " (2002, pp. 254–5; cf. Guthrie's "empiricism," 1969, pp. 8–9, 47). The sophists were collectively interested in the human and social realm; their ideas were supported by observation of the phenomena and by rational argument, rather than tradition, inspiration or authority; but in content those ideas were enormously diverse.

I will try to make the case for two somewhat stronger kinds of unity. First, sophistic thought is marked not merely by a common intellectual approach but by a shared agenda or set of problems. Whether the topic is justice, religion, or grammar, the sophists are concerned to disentangle the contribution of the subjective and the socially constructed from the natural or objective, and to work out the implications of that analysis. At the same time – and this is the second point – this shared project does not entail shared *dogmata*; if anything, sophistic philosophizing tends to mean philosophizing in a critical, self-undermining, or otherwise less than dogmatic way.

After a brief sketch of sophistic interests and methods, I will discuss three central and overlapping themes: the distinction between nature and convention, particularly as applied to justice; variability, relativity, and qualified truth in ethics; and the relation of language to reality. This will not add up to a comprehensive overview of sophistic thought, and readers are referred to the longer treatments of Kerferd (1981a, b) and Guthrie (1969) for fuller and more historically detailed accounts. Readers are also warned that few if any general claims about the sophists, or readings of particular sophistic texts, are uncontroversial, and I cannot here document all the points at which scholarly opinion differs. My aim is merely to bring out the range and liveliness of sophistic debate, and the complexities of some still-underappreciated texts.

---

3. Quotations from Plato are from the versions by various translators in Cooper (1997), often with some revisions.

Sophistic Thought: Scope and Methods

A standard definition of a sophist, both in antiquity and among modern scholars, is as a professional teacher of virtue or excellence (*aretē*) (cf. Plato, *Ap.* 19d–20c); but just what this involves is not so obvious. In Plato's *Protagoras*, Protagoras claims to teach "good judgment" and the successful management of both domestic and public affairs (318e–319a). Meno, apparently following Gorgias, says in Plato's *Meno* that a man's virtue is to manage public affairs so as to benefit his friends and harm his enemies (71e); or, in sum, "to rule over people" (73c–d). And Meno insists that the virtue of a woman is different, as is that of a boy or slave. So *aretē* evidently consists in the skills and aptitudes that enable someone to fulfill his or her social role. This "functional" conception of virtue is a deeply traditional one: the *aretē* of the Homeric warrior consisted in traits such as strength, courage, and intelligence, which made a man excel in deliberations and on the battlefield. In the later world of democratic Athens, where the primary arena of competition for ambitious gentlemen is not war but politics, *aretē* functionally understood comes to consist above all in the art of public speaking. For it is the ability to persuade one's fellow citizens, gathered *en masse* in the Assembly or courts, that enables a man to successfully wield political power.

But this is only one strand of the complex moral tradition which the sophists inherit. Even in Homer's world, self-restraint, reverence, and an acceptance of one's limitations are important norms of character; and Hesiod's *Works and Days*, the other pillar of early Greek moral thought, centers on the virtue of justice, understood in terms of honesty, fair dealing, and refraining from what belongs to others. Much of the liveliness of fifth- and fourth-century moral thought comes from the attempts of various Greek thinkers to reconcile or negotiate between the functional and the Hesiodic conceptions of virtue (cf. Adkins, 1960). The elite political skills taught by the sophists generally sound much more like the former; but whether the claims of the Hesiodic virtues could be denied or reinterpreted was a question they could not afford to ignore.

The other ingredients of a sophistic education were variable. Traditionally, the sophists have been seen as specialists in ethics and politics, contrasted with the "pre-Socratic" philosophers who investigated the nature and origins of the cosmos. But the evidence against this stereotyped contrast is strong. Sophists like Antiphon and Hippias had views on mathematics and natural science, while "pre-Socratics" like Democritus wrote works of ethics and literary criticism (cf. Kerferd, 1981a, pp. 38–41). Plato's *Protagoras* snipes at competitors like Hippias for dragging young men "into subjects the likes of which they have escaped from at school," including arithmetic, astronomy, geometry, and music (*Prt.* 318e). So sophistic interests were broad, and curriculum design a matter of debate. Diversity was also characteristic of sophistic intellectual practices, and breadth itself was highly valued. Hippias was a famous polymath (Plato, *Hp. Ma.* 285b–286b, *Hp. Mi.* 368b–d), and Gorgias boasted of being able to answer any question impromptu (Plato, *Grg.* 447d–448a). Plato's dialogues present vivid depictions of the sophists as traveling polymaths and pundits, earning their keep not only with private lessons but through public displays of memorization and moralistic oratory, brilliant flights of literary interpretation, and combative refutations at house parties.

Three terms recur in our sources in relation to sophistic discourse: eristic, *makrologia*, and *antilogikē*.[4] Eristic (from *erizein*, "strive" or "quarrel") is a pejorative term for what we might more neutrally call sophistic refutation. Its practice is depicted in Plato's *Euthydemus*, and is central to his definition of the profession in the *Sophist* (268b–d); it is also analyzed by Aristotle in his *Sophistical Refutations*. It is a sort of intellectual martial art for two players, who take on well-defined roles of questioner and respondent. The respondent affirms some thesis; the questioner attempts to lead him into affirming its contradictory. Fallacious inferences (or at any rate what we, and Aristotle, would regard as such) run rampant, and the questioner sometimes uses tactics to which the respondent objects (*Euthd.* 295bff., *Prt.* 331c–e, 334e–335a) – eristic seems to have been one of those games in which wrangling about the rules is part of the fun. For Plato, the orientation of eristic to victory at all costs, rather than the truth, is morally repellent, and represents a deep division between Socrates and the sophists: but as a practice of question-and-answer refutation through contradiction, eristic is formally indistinguishable from the *elenchus*, Socrates' standard mode of argument in Plato's early dialogues. According to Diogenes Laertius, Protagoras was the first to introduce "Socratic-style" argument (DK 80A1); and Plato's *Protagoras* shows Protagoras producing an elegant *elenchus* of the younger Socrates (339b–e). So Socrates' *elenchus* was likely an adaptation of sophistic, and perhaps specifically Protagorean practice. To modern readers, ancient references to Socrates as a sophist seem bizarre, given Plato's insistence on his distinctive moral mission, his commitment to the truth, and his refusal to teach for money.[5] But like Protagoras and the others, Socrates occupied himself by discoursing on virtue and practising the art of refutation; his distinctive features might well have been less visible to his fellow citizens. The extent to which the sophists might, like Socrates, have used their techniques of refutation for serious philosophical purposes is now impossible to gauge.

Makrologia, which simply means speaking at length, is said by Socrates in the *Protagoras* to be distinctive of Protagoras and beyond his own capacities (334d–336b). In fact the *Protagoras* itself shows Socrates making a long speech on Simonides, but certainly the set-piece speech is a characteristic sophistic mode. Examples which have survived would include Prodicus' *Choice of Heracles* (DK 84B2), Protagoras' "Great Speech" in the *Protagoras*, and Gorgias' *Helen*, *Defense of Palamedes*, *On Not Being* and *Funeral Oration*. Gorgias' texts are usually classed as rhetorical *epideixeis* or display pieces; whether and how we should distinguish between sophistic *makrologia* and rhetorical *epideixis* is unclear.

The third genre, *antilogikē*, "opposed argument," is one with deep roots in Greek culture. Antithetical arguments can be found in the *Iliad* and in Greek tragedy; they were of course standard in the Assembly and law courts, and are satirized by Aristophanes – most notably in his *Clouds*, in the combat of the Just and the Unjust Speech. As a sophistic speciality, *antilogikē* is particularly associated with Protagoras,

---

4.   The meanings of these terms are all contested; I carve up the sophistic genres somewhat differently from either Kerferd (1981a, pp. 59–67) or Nehamas (1990).

5.   Socrates is of course depicted as sophist (and *phusikos*) *par excellence* in Aristophanes' *Clouds* (see Morrison, SOCRATES, in this volume); cf. the orator Aeschines (*In Tim.* 173) and Kerferd (1981a, pp. 55–7).

who was said to have written books of *Antilogiai* (DK 80A1) and to have been the first to claim that on every question there are two arguments opposed to each other (DK 80B6; cf. *Sph.* 232d–e). The *Dissoi Logoi* ("Double Arguments") puts into practice this Protagorean principle; so do the *Tetralogies* of Antiphon, which argue both sides of three hypothetical legal cases. As with eristic, much remains to be understood about how "antilogic" is supposed to function: in particular, whether it should be seen as purely a gymnastic exercise or something more, and whether it depends on particular views about the nature of truth. A further question is whether we should view *antilogikē* as a genre in itself or as something which might take a number of forms. Eristic refutation performed on both sides of a question would presumably count as *antilogikē*; so perhaps should *epideixeis* such as Gorgias' *Helen* and *On Not Being*, defenses of the patently indefensible for which the obvious other side of the case can be left unspoken.

These different sophistic practices have some common features. All are verbal in nature, and involve prose rather than verse; most (and most obviously eristic) seem to have been originally and primarily oral rather than written genres. All are explicitly or implicitly agonistic or competitive. Scholars since Burckhardt and Nietzsche have noted the pervasively agonistic style of ancient Greek culture: the sophists belonged to a world in which intellectuals, poets, and politicians were as much competitive public performers as the Olympic athletes (cf. Guthrie, 1969, pp. 41–4). Finally, and in part as a result of this agonistic stance, the characteristic sophistic genres all have an uneasy relation to truth and belief. *Antilogikē* and eristic are both indifferent to the content of the thesis under discussion. Long speeches *can* express conviction, of course, but the recognition of *makrologia* or *epideixis* as a mode of competitive display should warn us against any assumption that sophistic speeches will do so. This is one of the reasons it will be easier to extract themes and arguments than *dogmata* from sophistic texts.

Justice, Nature, and Convention

Our most important surviving text for understanding sophistic moral thought is probably Antiphon's *On Truth*. Three substantial papyrus fragments have come down to us, each making an important argument; their order, unfortunately, cannot be known.[6]

One brief fragment claims that ethnocentric bias misleads us: "[the laws of nearby communities] we know and respect, but those of communities far away we neither know nor respect. In this we have become barbarous to each other, when by nature (*phusis*) we are all at birth in all respects equally adapted to being either barbarians or Greeks" (F44(b), II.1–15). Greek and barbarian (i.e., literally, non-Greek speaker,

---

6.   See Pendrick (2002, pp. 315–18). Antiphon's fragments are cited by Pendrick's numeration. Translations are based on both Pendrick and Gagarin and Woodruff (1995), with revisions; translations of other sophistic texts are from the latter, with revisions, unless otherwise noted. There has been much scholarly debate over how many Antiphons there were, and in particular whether the sophist who wrote *On Truth* is to be identified with the oligarchic Athenian politician Antiphon of Rhamnus: see Pendrick (2002, pp. 1–26).

though the term is often pejorative) share a universal nature: "For we all breathe the air through our mouth and nostrils, and we laugh when we are pleased and weep when we are pained" (II.27–III.3). Note the apparently self-undermining form of the argument: the accusation that "we have become barbarous" relies on the pejorative connotations of "barbarian" which the argument itself undermines. Presumably the point is to startle us into reflection on how, if at all, the term "barbarian" *should* be used.

This contrast between the given and the artificial receives fuller development in the longest fragment of *On Truth* (F44(a)), which applies it to justice. The passage begins with an affirmation of conventionalism about justice (not itself an uncommon or threatening view, cf. Socrates in Xenophon *Mem.* 4.4.12). "Thus justice (*dikaiosunē*) is not violating the rules (*nomima*) of the city in which one is a citizen" (F44(a), I.5–11). The upshot immediately follows: "Thus a person would best use justice to his own advantage if he considered the laws (*nomoi*) important when witnesses are present, but the consequences of nature (*phusis*) important in the absence of witnesses" (I.12–23). For, Antiphon explains, legal requirements are merely a matter of agreement, and violations of them may go unpunished; "but the requirements of nature are necessary" (I.25–27), and actions against them are self-defeating. And the two are not just distinct but opposed: "most things that are just according to law are inimical to nature" (II.26–30). The things advantageous to nature turn out to include life itself and pleasure; the natural, equated as in F44(b) with the physiologically and psychologically given, points us towards a simple hedonism.

The conception of human nature here assumed can plausibly be filled out from some kindred sources, including Callicles, Thrasymachus, and Glaucon in Plato, and certain speeches in Thucydides.[7] Human nature is egoistic and *pleonectic*: we by nature strive to have more (*pleon echein*) of the good, understood as wealth and power and the pleasures they can provide. Natural human behavior is thus red in tooth and claw; but since unbridled *pleonexia* would do most of us more harm than good, each community has adopted *nomoi*, laws and moral conventions, to restrain and punish it. (*Nomos* means both "law" and social and moral "convention"; indeed, as we will see, in some texts it extends more widely, to the whole realm of human subjectivity.) This social contract is construed in various ways: as a self-interested compact by all parties (Glaucon), a conspiracy of the many against the naturally dominant few (Callicles), and a self-serving imposition by the regime in power (Thrasymachus). In any case the upshot is often an "immoralist" stance: the demands of *nomos* and conventional justice are something to be seen through, and anyone who can violate them with impunity has no reason not to. As the Unjust Speech says in Aristophanes' *Clouds*: "Keeping company with me, use [your] nature, leap, laugh, consider nothing shameful!" (1077–1078).

However, Antiphon's discussion of justice does not end here; and in F44(c), he argues *against* the conventionalist understanding of justice so far assumed. Suppose, Antiphon says, that I am called as a witness in a legal dispute; according to convention, for me to give true testimony is just. But suppose that by testifying truly I will

7. Plato, *Grg.* 483a–484c, *Rep.* I, 338c–348d and II, 357b–362c, Thucydides I.75–77, V.84–114.

harm someone who has not harmed me. Conventional justice also includes the notion that for me to harm someone who has never done me harm is *unjust*, which results in a contradiction: these two things "cannot both be just" (II.17–21). This is a classic *elenchus*, and, as when used by Socrates, it effectively refutes a claim to authority: the conventional understanding of justice cannot be right. This apparent inconsistency between the two fragments is puzzling,[8] and perhaps we should simply read Antiphon's discussion of justice as an exercise in *antilogikē*; but it seems more plausible to read both fragments as objections to conventionalism. In that case the point of F44(a) too must be, implicitly, that conventional justice does not deserve the name of justice at all – perhaps because it is essential to the concept of justice that it is worth pursuing.

On this reading, all three arguments have some resemblance to another important fragment of Antiphon (also from *On Truth*), reported by Aristotle in his *Physics*. This is a bizarre scientific thought-experiment: "if one were to bury a bed and the putrefaction were to get the power to send up a shoot, it would not be a bed but wood, since the one – the arrangement in accordance with convention (*kata nomon*) and the artistic form – exists accidentally, whereas the essence is that which persists, continuously undergoing these modifications" (*Phys.* II.1, 193a12–17 = F15(b), Pendrick trans.). The Greek word "nature" (*phusis*) is closely connected to the verb "grow" (*phuō*): the sophists and pre-Socratic natural scientists share a deep assumption, rooted in the Greek language itself, that the nature of something is revealed in its origins and generative powers. That nature consists, Antiphon claims, not in the superficial identity established by human agency and represented in the names we use for things, but in the underlying material on which we act.[9] As this odd argument brings out, the nature/convention dichotomy has its origins in the search of pre-Socratic natural scientists for the basic principles of the cosmos.[10] In particular, it presses on a contrast which pervades pre-Socratic thought from Parmenides onward, between a misleading, mind-dependent realm of appearance and enduring, underlying realities.

So it is perhaps no surprise that the contrast between nature and convention comes to be applied in a wide range of contexts. Democritus, for instance, is said to have argued that names are a matter of convention rather than nature (DK 68B26: cf. the section on "Names and things" below); and his atomism was summed up in the slogan that perceptual qualities are merely by convention (*nomōi*: i.e., presumably, subjective or mind-dependent), while only atoms and the void are real (DK 68B9, B125 etc.).[11] But the principal arena of the contrast was in ethics and politics. Indeed, the appeal to nature as a source for ethical norms is undoubtedly the sophistic movement's most powerful legacy to philosophy. That appeal took various forms. For Antiphon, "nature" seems to mean human nature, represented by our common physiology. In the *Gorgias*

8.   Cf. Furley (1981); Pendrick is agnostic (2002, pp. 368–9), and Bett relegates F44(c) to a footnote (2002, p. 250 n. 28).
9.   Cf. Morrison (1963, pp. 40–6).
10.   Indeed, in his attack on irreligion in Book X of the *Laws*, Plato treats atheism, the *nomos/phusis* distinction as applied to values, and pre-Socratic-style naturalistic explanations of the origins of the cosmos as a single, threatening intellectual position (885c–907d).
11.   Quotations from "pre-Socratic" philosophers are by Richard McKirahan in Curd (1996), with revisions.

Callicles draws on animal behavior and the aggression of states to argue that there is a "natural justice" according to which the strong should have more than the weak (*Grg.* 483a–484c; cf. Aristophanes, *Clouds* 1427–1429). Socrates' response is not to reject the appeal to nature but to redefine it: what really characterizes the natural world, and invites our emulation, is "partnership and friendship, orderliness, self-control, and justice," particularly as displayed in the orderly motions of the heavenly bodies (*Grg.* 508a, cf. *Ti.* 47a–e). So Callicles errs not because there is anything invalid about deriving ethical norms from the observation of nature (as David Hume would later argue), but because he has got nature wrong; and later philosophers such as the Stoics and Epicureans also find fuel for their conceptions of the good in competing appeals to the observation of nature.

The question raised by these analyses is how the diagnosis of something as conventional should affect our attitude to it. When Democritus says that color is a matter of convention, his agenda seems to be eliminativist: no such thing really exists, and color-phenomena can be reduced to the interactions of colorless atoms and void. At the other end of the spectrum, that language is conventional hardly seems to make it unreal or invalid. An interesting case study is provided by two surviving sophistic texts on the origins of religion.[12] According to a fragment of the play *Sisyphus*, belief in the gods originated as a clever device to reinforce the social order.[13] At first, human life, like that of animals, was ruled by force; then men enacted laws and punishments, establishing justice "as a tyrant (*tyrannos*)" (DK 88B25.6). But this could not prevent wrongdoing in secret: so "some shrewd, intelligent man invented fear of the gods for mortals, so that the wicked would have something to fear even if their deeds or words or thoughts were secret" (B25.12–15). By contrast, a fragment of Prodicus asserts a different relation between worship and social utility: "The sun and the moon and rivers and springs and in general all things that benefit our lives were recognized as (*enomisan*) gods by the ancients because of their benefits. . . . for this reason bread was worshipped as (*nomisthēnai*) Demeter, wine as Dionysus, water as Poseidon, fire as Hephaestus, and so on with everything of service to us" (DK 84B5).[14]

It is easy to see from these texts both why some sophists came to be accused of atheism (as did the pre-Socratic natural scientists, cf. Aristophanes, *Clouds* 365ff. and Plato, *Ap.* 18b–d), and why some at least might have disputed the charge.[15] Prodicus

---

12. Sophistic analysis of conventions often takes the form of storytelling about the origins of society, following the traditional Greek genre of "anthropology": see Cole (1990), and still, Lovejoy and Boas (1935).

13. The *Sisyphus* fragment is attributed to both Critias and Euripides: see Bett (2002, p. 251 n. 30).

14. Cf. also Philodemus *de Pietate*, which adds a second stage in which human inventors of beneficial arts were deified (DK 84B5 = Philod. *De Piet.* PHerc. 1428 col. 3.12–13 Henrichs).

15. Protagoras, interestingly, was evidently a thoroughgoing agnostic: "Concerning the gods, I am not in a position to know either that they exist or that they do not, nor can I know what they look like, for many things prevent our knowing – the subject is obscure and human life is short" (DK 80B4). Just how this relates to his thesis that "Man is the measure of all things," and how if at all it should inform our reading of the myth in the "Great Speech," are difficult questions.

could argue that his explanation presents a legitimate basis for an enlightened worship, freed from primitive anthropomorphism. On the other hand, this might be seen by traditionalists as little better than atheism; and Prodicus' account could also be read as, like the *Sisyphus*, explaining how men came to worship non-existent beings. As for the *Sisyphus*, its import is paradoxical, for it points out the social utility of religion in a way which must nullify the hold of religion on its audience.

So the revelation that something is a matter of convention can support a wide range of responses. Returning to the central case of justice, Antiphon's diagnosis of justice contrasts with that of an anonymous but almost certainly contemporary text, the *Anonymus Iamblichi*. The *Anon. Iamb.* argues that human beings are by nature less than self-sufficient, and we cannot live together without law: "because of all these constraints law and justice are made king (*ton te nomon kai to dikaion embasileuein*) among human beings, and will never be displaced; for their strength is ingrained by nature (*phusei*)" (6.1). So, paradoxically, nothing is more natural to us than the moral conventions which make possible civil society. A similar response is expressed, as I read it, in the "Great Speech" of Protagoras in the *Protagoras* (320c–328d).[16] The "Great Speech" depicts in mythic terms the claim, presented as the key assumption behind Athenian participatory democracy, that all human beings in society possess some measure of justice. At first, as per the *Sisyphus*, human life was lawless: humans "wronged each other, because they did not possess the craft of politics (*politikē technē*)" (322b7–8), and so were unable to form sustainable societies. So Zeus and Hermes bestowed justice and shame upon mankind. This notion that the virtues are crafts, *technai*, or something like them, may be an important sophistic contribution to moral thought, though it is usually associated with Plato's Socrates. Protagoras' point here, however, is that while the virtues are craft-like, they are unlike the specialized crafts in being open to achievement by all; indeed they are continually taught by all of us to each other. The mythic genre does not allow for explicit use of the contrast between nature and convention; and Protagoras' emphasis on the original feral condition of humanity, and on the importance of social conditioning, can be read as implying that justice is conventional. On the other hand, to say that justice is a divine gift, universally shared, sounds like the mythic way of saying that it is a part of human nature. In that case, Protagoras' position is the same as that of the *Anon. Iamb.*, and restates that of Hesiod in the *Works and Days*: "This was the *nomos* Zeus established for human beings: for fish and beasts and flying birds he allowed that one may eat another, since

---

16. How close the "Great Speech" comes to an accurate representation of Protagoras' views is impossible to say; and it is philosophically incompatible with the relativism attributed to Protagoras in Plato's *Theaetetus*. Still, both can be seen as developments of a position which, by triangulation, we might suspect to have been that of the historical Protagoras, viz. a simple endorsement of all existing moral conventions. (As Kahn drily notes, this is "an extraordinarily convenient view for a moral philosopher who earns his living by travelling on a lecture circuit from one city to another" (1981, p. 106).) The *Protagoras* grounds that endorsement of *nomos* in functionalist anthropology: all societies are just because without justice (assumed to be a real and independently specifiable virtue, along "Hesiodic" lines) they could not survive. The *Theaetetus* takes the alternative route of relativism: all communities' *nomoi* count as just because they *determine* what justice is.

there is no justice among them; but to human beings he gave justice, which turns out to be much better" (276–280, Gagarin and Woodruff, 1995, trans.).

This debate about justice suggests a general division of sophistic thinkers into two wings: call them subversives and reaffirmers. For the subversives (Antiphon, the *Sisyphus*, Callicles), our norms and institutions conflict with our pleonectic human nature, and so cannot withstand transparency. For the reaffirmer, conventions are legitimately authoritative and even natural to us. Some sophistic texts fall into an ambiguous middle ground: we might count Prodicus on religion as neither a reaffirmer nor a subversive but a reinterpreter of tradition. To complete the taxonomy, a fourth stance would be one of selective reform or critique: some conventions conform to nature better than others, and those which do not should be corrected (cf. Protagoras on language in the section on "Names and things").[17]

Among other enduring issues, this sophistic debate raises a puzzle about where authentic human nature is to be observed. Look, says the subversive, to behavior *freed from constraint*: study animals, tyrants or empires, or imagine an agent endowed with superpowers (*Anon. Iamb.* 6.2–4; Plato *Rep.* II, 359c–360d), and you will see us as we really are. The reaffirmer turns instead to what is *distinctive* about human beings. For Aristotle, the reaffirmer *par excellence*, that will turn out to be rationality itself (cf. the "function argument" of *EN* I.7); for the rhetorician Isocrates, it is the discursive capacity which makes persuasion and with it civil society possible (*Antidosis* 253–257); for Protagoras, it seems to be sociability and the rule of law itself.

Relativity, Variability, and Qualified Truth

The sophists have often been collectively labeled "relativists"; but the evidence for this is surprisingly thin (cf. Bett, 1989). The principal text is the theory attributed to Protagoras in Plato's *Theaetetus*; but the interpretation of this is enormously controversial, and how much of it is authentically Protagorean cannot be known. We can be fairly sure that its starting-point, the famous "Measure Thesis," is a quotation from Protagoras: "A human being is the measure of all things, of those things that are, that they are, and of those things that are not, that they are not" (DK 80B1).[18] This is

17. Many scholars have seen a generational progression in sophistic thought towards increasing radicalism, from reaffirmers like Protagoras to subversives like Antiphon and Critias; the evidence for this seems to me inconclusive. Cf. Kahn (1981, pp. 106–8) and Wallace (1998, pp. 214–22).

18. It has been much debated how we are to understand such early philosophical uses of the verb "to be" (*einai*: note that there is no distinct Greek verb for "exist"), in terms of modern distinctions between existential, predicative, and other uses. Does Protagoras mean that we are each the measure of *whether* each thing exists, or of *how* each thing "is", i.e., what properties should be predicated of it? The short answer, I take it, is both. The standard (and perfectly reasonable) Greek tendency is to view existential uses of "to be" as short for predicative ones: to say that something exists implies that we can predicate some properties of it, and to predicate properties of something is to imply or presuppose some sort of existential claim about it. Cf. DK 80B4, *Dissoi Logoi* 5.15, the Hippocratic *On the Art* (2), and Kerferd (1981a, pp. 94–5).

glossed by Plato as a validation of conflicting perceptions: if the wind seems cold to me and warm to you, it *is* cold for me and warm for you. Our opinions or "appearances" are all true – for ourselves (*Tht.* 152a–c). But does that mean that the wind itself is really both warm and cold (so that the world is, as Heraclitus argued, a contradictory place); or that it is neither; or perhaps even that there is no "wind itself" at all? (These are only a few of our interpretive options.)[19] Moreover, rather late in Plato's discussion the thesis is complicated by two important addenda. First, though all opinions are equally true, some are still *better* than others, by being more subjectively satisfying and functional for those who hold them. So there is still a role for the expert or wise man, such as Protagoras himself, namely replacing dysfunctional opinions with better ones (*Tht.* 166a–167d). (So Protagoras here would belong to the "reformer" camp in the typology above.) Second, on ethical matters at least, Protagoras' validation of opinion extends to communities as well as individuals: "Whatever in any city is regarded as just and admirable *is* just and admirable, in that city and for so long as that convention maintains itself" (*Tht.* 167c, cf. 168b, 177dff.). One can imagine the historical Protagoras taking this endorsement of *nomos* as his starting point and developing an epistemology to suit; but it is hard to see how both cities *and* individuals can be ethically infallible, and harder still to reconcile all this with the politics of the "Great Speech" (cf. n. 16).

The only other sophistic text which discusses relativity at length is the *Dissoi Logoi*. This anonymous, undatable and enigmatic work is often dismissed as philosophically crude and confused: this is, I think, a serious underestimation.[20] The *DL* is a rare surviving exercise in Protagorean *antilogikē*, "opposed argument," arguing successively on both sides of five parallel theses (and then, in a concluding section I will not discuss, unraveling into miscellaneous reflections on a variety of topics). It argues that the good and the bad are the same and that they are different; and likewise with the fine and the shameful, the just and the unjust, the true and the false, and whether the mad and the wise say the same things or different ones. The text begins: "Concerning the good and bad, contrasting arguments are put forward in Greece by intellectuals (*tōn philosophoutōn*)" (*DL* 1.1);[21] there is no reason to attribute either side of any of the arguments to the author *in propria persona*.

Cultural relativity enters the picture in support of the claim that the fine (*kalon*) and shameful (*aischron*) are the same: "The Spartans think it fine for girls to do athletics and go around with bare arms and without tunics, but Ionians think it shameful. . . . The Massagetai cut up their parents and eat them, and they think the finest tomb is to be buried inside one's children, but in Greece if someone did these things, he would be driven out of Greece" (*DL* 2.9–14). And the same goes for pre-marital sex, tattoos,

19. For explanation of the issues here, cf. Woodruff (1999, pp. 302–4), Gibert (2003, pp. 39–44), Kerferd (1981a, pp. 85–93), and Barnes (1982, pp. 541–53).
20. See Robinson (1979, 2001). Gratuitous abuse of the author goes back to Diels' "talentlose" (1951–2, vol. 2, p. 405); cf. Burnyeat "feeble" (1998, p. 106) and Barnes "the more interesting in that it reflects a feeble layman's apprehension of things" (1982, p. 517).
21. Translations from the *DL* are based on Robinson (1979) and Gagarin and Woodruff (1995) with revisions.

incest, scalping, and moistening flour with one's feet. This survey of diversity follows a series of arguments appealing to "relativity" of other kinds: "to have intercourse with one's husband in private is fine . . . but outside is shameful, where someone will see them . . . to adorn oneself and put on makeup and wear gold jewelry is shameful for a man but fine for a woman," and so on (*DL* 2.5–6). The *DL*'s arguments for the "Same" position on the other theses also invoke relativity or contextual variation. Death is bad for those who die but good for the gravediggers; and there are situations in which the use of force or fraud may be just.

Thus the *DL*'s relativity arguments are just a subset of arguments from *variability* (cf. Bett, 2002, pp. 238–44). A preoccupation with ethical variability recurs in other sophistic texts: Bett cites Protagoras in Plato's *Protagoras* (some things are good for humans and others for horses, 334a–c) and Meno's enumeration of different virtues in his *Meno* (71e–72a). We might also note the position of the unnamed "lovers of sights and sounds" against whom Socrates argues in *Republic* V. They deny the unity of each Form, refusing to allow "that the fine itself is one or that the just is one or any of the rest" (479a, cf. 475e–476a), but agree that any particular fine thing is also shameful, and anything just also unjust (479a). In sum, our evidence suggests that a number of sophists held what we might call *the variability thesis*: whatever is good in some qualified way is also bad in some other way, and so on for some central range of contrary predicates.

The *DL*'s arguments for the "Same" position, with their wearisome enumeration of opposed predications, look like arguments by induction for the variability thesis. But that thesis does nothing to support the "Same" position without two further assumptions. One is that we can legitimately infer an unqualified thesis from a qualified one: if death is good for the gravediggers or shameful to the Persians, then death is good or shameful *tout court*. (This would follow from the reasonable-sounding assumption that, as Socrates puts it in Plato's *Cratylus* (385c), a true statement or account must be composed of true parts.) The other assumption is that the meaning of a concept is its extension: if "fine" and "shameful" denote the same set of things, the fine and the shameful *are* the same thing. The "Different" arguments then proceed by *reductio*, relying on the further assumption that terms which are "the same" can be substituted for each other: for instance, if the proponents of the "Same" thesis claim to have done anything fine, they must agree that it was also shameful (*DL* 2.21). The effect is to show that the assumptions relied upon by the "Same" arguments, taken together with the variability thesis, lead to absurd results. And this paradoxical dialectic could, incidentally, be put in terms of our familiar contrast. The *Dissoi Logoi* shows that by *nomos* – including all our habitual evaluations of particular things as good and bad – the good and bad turn out to be the same thing; but surely by *phusis* they are different?

The author's solution to this puzzle emerges only rather shyly at the end of the opposed arguments – it is rather as if the ostension of puzzles is assumed to be more interesting than their solution. In the course of arguing that the mad and the wise do *not* say the same things, the author notes that proponents of the "Same" thesis will admit "that the two groups say the same things, only the wise say them at the right moment and the mad at moments when it is not proper" (*DL* 5.9). But this qualification, he notes, makes all the difference: "they seem to me to have added the small phrases 'when it is proper' and 'when it is not proper', with the result that it is no longer the same thing" (*DL* 5.10). In other words, where the "Same" arguments went wrong was in fallaciously assuming qualification-dropping to preserve truth (a diagnosis repeated by Aristotle, *SE* 5, 166b37–167a21).

The legitimacy of qualification-dropping may look like a minor question of logical procedure; in fact, it is bound up with some of the deepest and most urgently debated philosophical puzzles of the age – ones often discussed by scholars under other headings, such as the "unity of opposites" and "conflicting appearances." These puzzles can all be seen as offspring of the variability thesis, combined with a dilemma about qualification. If some x is both good and bad – or hot and cold, or large and small, or existent and non-existent – in different qualified ways, what are we to say of x as such? Does it follow that x is also good *simpliciter* and bad *simpliciter*, or neither? To allow qualification-dropping across the board leads immediately to contradictions, absurdities, and a world of indeterminacy in which nothing is by nature any more good than bad. But prohibiting all such inferences leads, paradoxically, to much the same result, for it entails that for the same range of cases x as such is once again no more the one thing than the other.

The *DL* leaves that problem standing, and with it the question of how meaning relates to denotation. If everything fine is also shameful in some way, in what sense are "fine" and "shameful" opposites that exclude each other? For any opposition to be left, it seems there must be something more to "the fine" than the set of particular fine things: but what? This is, strikingly, one of the central problems that Plato's theory of Forms is engineered to solve. Plato accepts the variability thesis; but he denies, in spectacular fashion, the assumption that their denotation of sensible particular individuals is what gives our words their meanings. The names of things refer in the first instance not to the particular things around us, which are indeed susceptible only of qualified truth, but to essences or natures – the Forms – which are "separate" from them, and unmixed with their opposites, and which can therefore serve as subjects of unqualified truth and knowledge (Plato, *Phd.* 74a–75a, *Hp. Ma.* 288d–292e, *Symp.* 211a–212a, *Rep.* V, 479a–e, *Prm.* 129a–130a).

So the problems over which the *DL* puzzles are also those that motivate Plato. And the *DL* shows that for the sophists, as for Plato, arguments about ethics are simultaneously vehicles for exploring important problems about language and reality – problems about what we might call the gap between names and things. In the next section I turn to texts that confront this gap directly.

Names and Things

Many texts testify to sophistic fascination with the workings of language: they range from discussions of rhetoric and literary criticism to what would nowadays count as linguistics, grammar, and the philosophy of language. In Plato's *Protagoras*, Protagoras declares that "the greatest part of education" is to be able to analyze and evaluate the words of the poets (339a). Protagoras goes on to subject Socrates to an *elenchus* by getting him to endorse an ode of Simonides, which is then shown to contain a contradiction (339b–e). As a mode of education, such sparring would have involved at once a lesson in the art of eristic, the honing of literary and critical skills, and reflection on a serious ethical question (here, the relation of "becoming good" to "being good") about which the poet might have something valuable to say.

Protagoras evidently adopted a similarly critical stance towards the Greek language itself, claiming that the words "wrath" and "helmet" (both grammatically feminine) are masculine (DK 80A28; cf. the parody by Aristophanes at *Clouds* 659–691).[22] We have no evidence that Protagoras was a serious campaigner for linguistic reform, but he clearly counts, on this front at least, as a "reformer" in terms of the typology suggested above, holding conventions up for correction in the light of nature. Other sophistic texts show a similar mix of analysis and prescription. Prodicus is portrayed by Plato as a specialist in the "correctness of names, " and in particular the drawing of fine distinctions between words of similar meaning (*Prt.* 337a–b, 358a–b, *Chrm.* 163d, *Cra.* 384b, *La.* 197d, *Meno* 75e, cf. Classen, 1981, pp. 230–8). Plato's attitude seems to be one of half-respectful amusement: Prodicus is wrong to think that any wisdom is to be gained by such exercises in lexicography, but it *is* the job of the philosopher to distinguish meanings correctly, through dialectic. Like eristic and *antilogikē*, Prodican linguistic analysis is a simulacrum of, and perhaps a prolegomenon to, real philosophical method. Plato's *Cratylus* discusses the "correctness of names" rather differently, in terms of the dichotomy of nature and convention. Names bear the twin hallmarks of social construction, since they vary from place to place and are subject to change at will (cf. Democritus DK 68B26). At the same time, their functioning somehow outruns convention: different languages can say the same thing, and the truth or falsity of what we say depends not only on our conventions but on how things are. For Plato, a natural correctness of names would mean that names could be judged according to whether they correspond to the natures of the things they name (*Cra.* 391d–427d) – another version of a "reformist" stance towards language. This idea of "natural correctness," which the *Cratylus* spells out in terms of etymology and phonetic "likeness," is very alien to modern thought about language; it becomes more intelligible if we reflect that for Plato, and for the sophists as well, concerns about language were also driven by high ethical and political stakes. Thucydides famously discusses the ways in which moral terminology comes to be abused and corrupted in times of civil war (Thuc. III.82–83), and Plato's early dialogues testify to the sharply different ways in which terms like "virtue" and "justice" might be applied. It is not so easy to determine where linguistic conventions end and ethical and political ones begin.

The *Cratylus* also testifies to intense contemporary puzzlement over truth and reference.[23] Our evidence on this topic is rather confusing, much of it consisting of paradoxical slogans and unattributed arguments.[24] The most notorious pair of slogans assert the impossibility of contradiction and false statement.[25] Just who is likely to

---

22.   Cf. also the criticism of Homer at DK 80A2. Protagoras' analyses of gender (DK 80A27), the tenses of verbs (DK 80A1) and modes of speech (DK 80A1) were presumably used to provide ammunition for such criticisms of the poets.

23.   On the treatment of language in the *Cratylus*, see also Modrak's PHILOSOPHY OF LANGUAGE in this volume.

24.   See Guthrie (1969, pp. 204–19), Classen (1981), and Denyer (1991) for discussion.

25.   Plato, *Euthd.* 283e–286d, *Cra.* 429c–430a; cf. D.L. 10.53, Isoc. *Helen* 1; Kerferd (1981a, pp. 88–90), and Guthrie (1969, pp. 218–19).

RACHEL BARNEY

have asserted either is uncertain (the Socratic Antisthenes is a leading candidate), and a sophistic origin would be puzzling given that both *antilogikē* and eristic seem to *require* contradiction. Still, the paradoxes might have been generated by two sophistic ideas. One is the "Measure" thesis. If the wind can be at once warm for you and cold for me, then our descriptions of it do not exclude each other after all; so there is a lot less contradiction about than we might think – perhaps, if Protagoras can give an intelligible relativization of *all* our claims, none at all. The other source of the paradoxes is a set of puzzles about truth and reference. Parmenides had already argued that one cannot say or think what is not: for it is not there to be picked out by language (DK 28B2, B6, B7). A true statement says "what is "; a false one "what is not." But "what is not" is *nothing*, so speech which says "what is not" says nothing at all (Plato, *Cra.* 429c–430a). (Or, in slightly different terms: to be meaningful a statement must be "of" or "about" something. But a falsehood would have to say something other than that thing, and so would really be "of" something else; and for two statements to contradict each other, by saying different things about the same thing, is impossible (Plato, *Euthd.* 283e–284a, 285d–286b).) Plato struggles with these puzzles in several dialogues; his eventual solution in the *Sophist* depends on a long and complex excursus into the metaphysics of what is and is not. I cannot discuss his solution fully, but its central strategic move is, roughly, to distinguish between reference and assertion: false statement says "what is, but not *as* it is" (*Sph.* 262e–263d).

Our most important sophistic text on language, Gorgias' *On Not Being*, argues for the still more unnerving thesis that we cannot communicate what is *true*. In fact, this enigmatic *tour de force* argues for three startling conclusions. First, nothing "is" or exists; second, even if something did exist, we could not think or comprehend it; and third, even if we could think it, we could not communicate it.[26] Interpreters have long debated in what spirit these arguments should be read (cf. Caston, 2002, pp. 205–8). The *ONB* is certainly an exercise in rhetorical technique: it is, after all, hard to think of a more convincing test case for the ability to "make the weaker argument the stronger." But it is also plausibly a parody, at once playful and seriously critical, of contemporary philosophy, and Parmenides in particular. The first part of the argument looks like a *reductio* of Parmenides' proof that only Being exists; and as Kerferd notes, the argument taken as a whole amounts to "pulling apart and separating three things which Parmenides had identified," namely being, thought, and speech (1981a, p. 99; cf. DK 28B2, B3, B6, B8.34–36).

The oddly recessive structure of the *ONB* means that it can also be taken as collectively arguing, through a series of fall-back positions, for its final conclusion: *even if* there were things (which there aren't), and *even if* they could be known (which they can't), we could not communicate them.[27] And these latter stages of the argument have the look of a non-parodic philosophical agenda. In the second part of the *ONB*,

26. Two quite different versions of the *ONB*, neither of which can be taken as Gorgias' *ipsissima verba*, have come down to us (S.E. *M* 7.65–87 and [Aristotle], *De Melisso, Xenophane, Gorgia* (79a11–80b21). I will be free in extracting and amalgamating what seem to me the main points.
27. This *recessive* strategy also structures Gorgias' *Defense of Palamedes* (DK 82B11(a)).

92

Gorgias argues for a chasm between objects and our thoughts about them. "For if things that are thought of, says Gorgias, are not things that are, then what is is not thought of" (S.E. *M* 7.77).[28] And indeed things that are thought of are *not* things that are. After all, "if someone thinks of a person flying or chariots racing in the sea, it is not the case that forthwith a person is flying or chariots racing in the sea" (S.E. *M* 7.79). Of course, the fact that a sea-chariot is not both thought of and existent hardly proves that nothing can be both; but it does show that intentional entities such as mental representations constitute an order of being quite distinct from ordinary "things that are," including any which we might claim to be thinking of. It is unclear whether Gorgias takes himself to have established only this reasonable claim, or also the outrageous one that nothing can be both existent and an object to which thought refers: perhaps we should read the text as systematically ambiguous, between a strong thesis which offends common sense and a weaker one which controverts only Parmenidean philosophers. (The first part of the *ONB* could perhaps also be read this way, as denying existence either to the everyday things of common sense or only to Parmenidean Being.) The third part of the argument, on the impossibility of communication, largely follows the model of the second. Another "categorial gulf" (Mourelatos, 1987, p. 139) separates speech (*logos*) from the objects we might hope to signify: "it is not the case that we communicate things that are to our neighbours, but *logos*, which is different from the objects" (*S.E. M* 7.84). Just as sight has the visible as its object, and not the audible, so too when a speaker speaks, what he says is *logos* rather than a colour or a thing or a thought. Moreover, it is impossible for the same thought to exist in two people; and there is no reason even to expect their thoughts to be qualitatively similar.[29]

Whatever we make of his intentions, these arguments display Gorgias at work on real and intractable philosophical puzzles: how is it possible to refer to non-existent objects? If a thought is a different kind of thing from an object in world, how can it communicate that object? A reading of his conclusions as both radical and seriously intended gains some confirmation from Gorgias' *Encomium of Helen* (DK 82B11). In this epideictic speech, Gorgias argues that Helen's decision to go with Paris to Troy must have been caused by one of four factors: fate and divine will, force, persuasive speech (*logos*), or love. Whichever it is, he argues, she is not to blame; for each of these causes really counts as a kind of force, rendering her action involuntary. The general intent of Gorgias' work is once again opaque;[30] but the agenda of the *Helen* does seem to come clear in its extended praise of *logos*, described as a "mighty master" (DK 82B11.8) which works on the soul as drugs do on the body (14). The power of *logos*

---

28. Translations from the *ONB* are from Richard McKirahan in Curd (1996), with revisions.
29. Cf. also the cryptic Antiphon DK 87B1.
30. The *Helen* is often read as a "paradigm case" argument that no one is responsible for any action. But at the close of the *Helen* Gorgias refers to it as a "plaything for myself" (DK 82B11.21), effectively calling into question any reading of it as ethical dogma. This self-undermining should, I think, be read as a tease and a challenge: We must decide for ourselves whether the *Helen* should count as serious moral philosophy, and what it proves if so.

derives from its sway over fallible human opinion (*doxa*): "For if all men on all subjects had memory of the past, [understanding] of the present, and foresight into the future, speech would not be the same in the same way . . . but as it is . . . most men on most subjects make opinion an adviser to their minds" (11).[31] As Mourelatos has argued, the arguments of the *Helen* and the *ONB* on language are complementary (1987). The *ONB* shows what language *cannot* be: either a means of communicating the objective natures of things or of representing our ideas of them. The *Helen* expounds the alternative which remains, namely that language is simply a tool for manipulating behavior.

It is difficult to ascribe a full and coherent metaphysics and epistemology to Gorgias – or, all the more obviously, to the sophists as a group. Scholars have sometimes spoken in a general way of the sophists as collectively "empiricists," "skeptics," and "relativists" without adequately noting that these are distinct theories with little if anything in common (e.g., Guthrie, 1969, pp. 9–11, 49–51). Sophistic thought on reality and our epistemic access to it only forms a genuine unity to the extent that it is seen as fundamentally negative and critical, exploring various strategies for denying the pretensions to knowledge of a Parmenides, Empedocles, or, proleptically, Plato. From that angle, Gorgias and Protagoras can plausibly be seen as forming a united front of deflationary anti-realism: against metaphysicians like Parmenides, they argue that there is no point in speculating about, or even any intelligible way of thinking and talking about, a Being which transcends our experience. There is no reality beyond appearance, and no hope for any knowledge which would be different in kind from our fallible opinions. If this is a fair reading, then sophistic discussion of language and thought revolves even more closely around the question we saw raised by their ethical inquiries: how far our customary ways of thinking and talking are grounded in anything beyond themselves.

Conclusions

At the start I noted two questions we face in interpreting the sophists: did they expound philosophical *dogmata*, and were they engaged in a common project at all? Unsurprisingly, the texts we have examined provide no snappy answers. On the question of unity, we have encountered a few shared positions, but much more common ground in the sophists' conceptual framework and modes of argument. The sophistic movement has what we might call *dialectical* unity: the unity of a debate or tradition, with both the commonality and the diversity, indeed conflict, it implies. More controversially, I have argued that we can see much if not all of sophistic thought as driven by a single (albeit broad) philosophical agenda. The decomposition of institutions and values into natural and conventional; the fascination with variability and

---

31. Cf. another important, but puzzling dictum attributed to Gorgias: "Being (*to einai*) is obscure when it does not encounter opinion (*tou dokein*); opinion is weak when it does not encounter being" (DK 82B26).

qualified truth in ethics; the subversion of easy assumptions about meaning and communication: all make manifest a preoccupation with measuring the gap between our words and the realities – if any – to which they may or may not conform.

This project had a profound influence on later thought, and it is hard to see any grounds for denying the sophists a place in books on "pre-Socratic Philosophy." On the other hand, much sophistic argument is not like philosophical argument as we usually understand it – that is, I take it, as involving the best arguments one can muster for conclusions in which one believes. The sophists are more interested in fallacies and puzzles than in proofs and solutions, more comfortable with paradox and satire than with dogmatic assertion. This may in part express a subversive relation to their philosophical rivals, as in the case of the *On Not Being* and Parmenides. So arguably the sophists are less the ancestors of philosophy in general than of subsequent attempts to cure or debunk it; and it is no accident that deflationary movements such as ancient skepticism, modern pragmatism, and postmodernism have looked back to them for inspiration.[32] Yet, paradoxically, the sophists' methodological slipperiness can also be seen as a crucial first step towards later philosophical norms of objective rationality. Pre-Socratics such as Parmenides and Empedocles combine appeals to the reader's rationality with claims to supernatural authority (DK 28B1, B7; DK 31B23, B110, B112), but the arguments of a text like the *Dissoi Logoi* or Antiphon's *On Truth* are detached from any authority at all; in sophistic writings, the authorial first person is either absent or is a strikingly unhelpful and unreliable narrator. If we could ask Gorgias, "But do you really *mean* that nothing exists?" he might well shrug his shoulders and answer, deadpan, "Can you refute me?" Sophistic texts are challenges, inviting us to judge their arguments for ourselves.

This should sound familiar; for the same can be said of Plato, who is notoriously absent from his works and whose Socrates emphasizes that *logoi* must be judged on their own merits. And the other commonalities between the sophists and Plato are striking. Socratic *elenchus* is formally indistinguishable from Protagorean eristic; and a number of Plato's dialogues are, in whole or part, exercises in *antilogikē*, including the *Meno, Protagoras, Phaedrus, Cratylus,* arguably the *Parmenides* and rather lopsidedly the *Republic* (on which cf. the disquieting DK 80B5: according to some ancient historians of philosophy, the *Republic* was largely a rip-off of Protagorean arguments). On questions like the correctness of names (the *Cratylus*) and the normative standing of justice (*Gorgias, Republic*), Plato can be seen as concerned with the analysis of nature and convention, and as fitting into a "reformer-reaffirmer" niche. Above all, we can see the theory of Forms as Plato's solution to sophistic puzzles about variability and qualified truth. Given the state of our evidence, the sophists are likely to continue to resist confident interpretation; but we may come to understand them better if we can learn to read Plato as the flowering of the sophistic tradition rather than – or as well as – its nemesis.

---

32. The *Dissoi Logoi* has come down to us attached to MSS of Sextus Empiricus, presumably because *Antilogikē* was seen as the ancestor of skeptical "equipollent argument." For pragmatism, cf. Mailloux (1995, pp. 8–14), for postmodernism, Fish (1989) and Jarratt (1991).

Bibliography

Works Cited

Adkins, A. W. H. (1960). *Merit and Responsibility*. Oxford: Clarendon Press.

Barnes, J. (1982). *The Presocratic Philosophers*. London: Routledge and Kegan Paul.

Bett, R. (1989). "The Sophists and Relativism." *Phronesis*, 34, 139–69.

——. (2002). "Is There a Sophistic Ethics?" *Ancient Philosophy*, 22, 235–62.

Burnyeat, M. F. (1998). "*Dissoi Logoi*." In E. Craig (ed.), *The Routledge Encyclopedia of Philosophy* (vol 3, pp. 106–7). London: Routledge.

Caston, V. (2002). "Gorgias on Thought and its Objects." In V. Caston and D. W. Graham (eds.), *Presocratic Philosophy*. (Festschrift for A. P. D. Mourelatos) (pp. 205–32). Aldershot: Ashgate.

Classen, C. J. (1981). "The Study of Language amongst Socrates' Contemporaries." In G. B. Kerferd (ed.), *The Sophists and their Legacy* (pp. 215–47). Wiesbaden: Steiner. (Original work published 1959.)

Cole, T. (1990). *Democritus and the Sources of Greek Anthropology*. Atlanta: Scholars Press. (Original work published 1967.)

Cooper, J. M. (ed.) and Hutchinson, D. S. (assoc. ed.). (1997). *Plato: Complete Works*. Indianapolis: Hackett.

Curd, P. (ed.). (1996). *A Presocratics Reader*. (Translations by R. McKirahan.) Indianapolis: Hackett.

Denyer, N. (1991). *Language, Thought and Falsehood in Ancient Greek Philosophy*. London: Routledge.

Diels, H. (1951–2). (Cited as DK). *Die Fragmente der Vorsokratiker*. (3 vols.). 6th edn. revised by W. Kranz and often reprinted. Berlin: Weidmann. (Original work published 1903.)

Fish, S. (1989). "Rhetoric." In S. Fish, *Doing What Comes Naturally* (pp. 471–502). Durham, NC: Duke University Press.

Furley, D. J. (1981). "Antiphon's Case against Justice." In G. B. Kerferd (ed.), *The Sophists and their Legacy* (pp. 81–91). Wiesbaden: Steiner.

Gagarin, M. and Woodruff, P. (eds.). (1995). *Early Greek Political Thought from Homer to the Sophists*. Cambridge: Cambridge University Press.

Gibert, J. (2003). "The Sophists." In C. Shields (ed.), *The Blackwell Guide to Ancient Philosophy* (pp. 27–50). Oxford: Blackwell.

Grote, G. (1865). *Plato and the Other Companions of Sokrates*. (3 vols.). London: John Murray.

——. (1872). *A History of Greece*. (10 vols., vol. 7). 4th edn. London: Murray.

Guthrie, W. K. C. (1969). *A History of Greek Philosophy* (vol. 3): *The Fifth-Century Enlightenment*. Cambridge: Cambridge University Press.

Hegel, G. W. F. (1995). *Lectures on the History of Philosophy* (trans. E. S. Haldane). Lincoln: University of Nebraska Press. (Original work published 1840.)

Irwin, T. H. (1995). "Plato's Objections to the Sophists." In C. A. Powell (ed.), *The Greek World* (pp. 568–87). London: Routledge.

Jarratt, S. (1991). *Rereading the Sophists*. Carbondale: Southern Illinois University Press.

Kahn, C. (1981). "The Origins of Social Contract Theory in the Fifth Century B.C." In G. B. Kerferd (ed.), *The Sophists and their Legacy* (pp. 92–108). Wiesbaden: Steiner.

Kerferd, G. B. (1981a). *The Sophistic Movement*. Cambridge: Cambridge University Press.

Kerferd, G. B. (ed.). (1981b). *The Sophists and their Legacy*. Wiesbaden: Steiner.

Long, A. A. (ed.). (1999). *The Cambridge Companion to Early Greek Philosophy*. Cambridge: Cambridge University Press.

Lovejoy, A. O. and Boas, G. (1935). *Primitivism and Related Ideas in Greek Antiquity*. Baltimore: Johns Hopkins University Press.

Mailloux, S. (ed.). (1995). *Rhetoric, Sophistry, Pragmatism*. Cambridge: Cambridge University Press.

Morrison, J. S. (1963). "The Truth of Antiphon." *Phronesis*, 8, 35–49.

Mourelatos, A. P. D. (1987). "Gorgias on the Function of Language." *Philosophical Topics*, 15, 135–70.

Nehamas, A. (1990). "Eristic, Antilogic, Sophistic, Dialectic: Plato's Demarcation of Philosophy from Sophistry." *History of Philosophy Quarterly*, 7, 3–16.

Nietzsche, F. (1968). *The Will to Power* (trans. W. Kaufman). New York: Random House. (Original work published 1901.)

Pendrick, G. (ed.). (2002). *Antiphon the Sophist: The Fragments*. Cambridge: Cambridge University Press.

Preus, A. (ed.). (2001). *Before Plato: Essays in Ancient Greek Philosophy VI*. Albany, NY: SUNY Press.

Robinson, T. M. (ed.). (1979). *Contrasting Arguments: An Edition of the* Dissoi Logoi. New York: Arno Press.

——. (2001). "The *Dissoi Logoi* and early Greek Scepticism." In A. Preus (ed.), *Before Plato: Essays in Ancient Greek Philosophy VI* (pp. 187–197). Albany, NY: SUNY Press.

Wallace, R. W. (1998). "The Sophists in Athens." In D. Boedeker and K. Raaflaub (eds.), *Democracy, Empire, and the Arts in Fifth-Century Athens* (pp. 203–22). Cambridge, Mass.: Harvard University Press.

Woodruff, P. (1999). "Rhetoric and Relativism: Protagoras and Gorgias." In A. A. Long (ed.), *The Cambridge Companion to Early Greek Philosophy* (pp. 290–310). Cambridge: Cambridge University Press.

Further Readings

Detienne, M. (1996). *The Masters of Truth in Archaic Greece* (trans. J. Lloyd,) New York: Zone Books. (Original work published 1967.)

Dover, K. (1974). *Greek Popular Morality in the Time of Plato and Aristotle*. Oxford: Blackwell.

Lee, M. (2000). "The Secret Doctrine: Plato's Defence of Protagoras in the *Theaetetus*." *Oxford Studies in Ancient Philosophy*, 19, 47–86.

Pfeiffer, R. (1968). *History of Classical Scholarship: From the Beginnings to the End of the Hellenistic Age*. Oxford: Clarendon Press.

Schiappa, E. (1991). *Protagoras and Logos*. New York: Columbia University Press.

Striker, G. (1996). "Methods of Sophistry." In G. Striker, *Essays on Hellenistic Epistemology and Ethics* (pp. 3–21). Cambridge: Cambridge University Press.

Part II

Socrates, the Socratics, and Plato

6

Socrates

DONALD R. MORRISON

Socrates is the mythic father and patron saint of philosophy. One answer to the question, "What is philosophy?" is: Philosophy is what Socrates did and what he started. Socrates remains mythic because he himself wrote nothing. Our earliest images of Socrates come from ancient, complex literary works whose aim and values are not easy to assess, and they partly diverge and disagree. Socrates had the great good fortune that one of his followers, Plato, was one of the greatest geniuses and most brilliant writers of all time. The character "Socrates" in Plato's dialogues is one of the most fascinating in world literature. Yet it is hard to know in this portrait where the historical Socrates leaves off and Plato begins.

Life and Character

A few facts are clear. Socrates was born about 469 BCE in Athens. He belonged to the middle class: he is said to have been the son of a stonemason, and he may himself have practiced that craft. Socrates lived in Athens until he was sentenced to death by an Athenian jury and was executed by hemlock poisoning in 399 BCE.

Socrates' courage and endurance while serving as an infantryman in the Peloponnesian War became legendary (Plato, *Ap.* 28e; *Symp.* 219e–221b). Socrates twice risked danger by opposing authorities, once in 406 when he tried to prevent an unconstitutional trial (*Ap.* 32b–c; Xen. *Hell.* 1.7.14–15; *Mem.* 1.1.18; 4.4.2), and later under the junta of the Thirty Tyrants, when he refused to co-operate in the arrest of Leon of Salamis (*Ap.* 32d; Xen. *Mem.* 4.4.3). These stories of Socrates' unusual physical and moral courage show him as a person of extraordinary integrity. If he believed something to be right, he would do it; and if he believed it to be wrong, he would refuse, regardless of social pressure or physical danger. Socrates' consistency of thought and action is central to his greatness.

Socrates says in Plato's *Apology* that he has had a "divine sign" since childhood, a voice that warns him when he is about to do something he should not. In Xenophon, the voice not only warns Socrates away from actions, but also gives positive advice (*Mem.* 4.3.12, 4.8.1; *Ap.* 12). Socrates' divine sign or "daimonion" creates a magnificent paradox. Socrates the rationalist philosopher goes about Athens asking people to account for their lives and actions. Irrefutable reason and argument are the standard for knowledge, one almost impossible to meet. According to Plato's portrait, Socrates cannot meet it either. He is wise only in knowing his own ignorance. This puts both

Socrates and the Athenians in a deep hole. But Socrates – uniquely – has a divine voice, a "little bird" that whispers into his ear and gives him infallible advice. The paradox is inescapable: a philosopher committed to public reason, who has a private pipeline to the truth.

Socrates spent much of his adult life conversing with others about such questions as "What is justice?" and "What is law?" He discussed these matters daily with a close circle of friends and admirers, but also with whoever happened by, and with famous men like Pericles and Gorgias. Socrates' philosophical refutations of the prominent and the powerful annoyed many, and his questioning of traditional Athenian values and religious beliefs offended conservatives. Certainly for these reasons, along with others, Socrates was brought to trial in 399 BCE and sentenced to death by hemlock poisoning.

The most important ancient evidence regarding Socrates comes from four sources: Aristophanes' *Clouds*, the Socratic writings of Plato, the Socratic writings of Xenophon, and some scattered remarks in Aristotle. The sources paint rather different portraits. "The problem of the historical Socrates" is the difficult and perhaps insoluble problem of sifting and distilling these sources into a historically accurate picture of Socrates. No consensus exists today on how, or whether, this problem can be solved (Patzer, 1987).

One traditional view is that Xenophon's account is trustworthy, whereas Plato's is not. This view has hardly any adherents today.

Many scholars believe that a reasonably faithful portrait of the historical Socrates and his philosophical views can be found in certain early works of Plato. On this view, Plato first began writing remembrances of his beloved master, but as he matured he began to put his own philosophical views into the mouth of Socrates. The dialogues regarded as "Socratic" rather than "mature Platonic" typically include: *Apology, Charmides, Crito, Euthydemus, Euthyphro, Gorgias, Hippias Major, Hippias Minor, Ion, Laches, Lysis, Menexenus, Protagoras, Republic* (Book I). The most prominent defender of this approach was Gregory Vlastos (1991). Many scholars believe that if anything in Plato is meant to give a faithful picture of the historical Socrates, it is Socrates' dramatic defense of himself and his way of life in Plato's *Apology* (Döring, 1998; Vlastos, 1971, Introduction; cf. Morrison, 2000).

Many other scholars hold the skeptical view that the problem of the historical Socrates is insoluble. Certain facts about his life and features of his character are consistently enough portrayed that we can be reasonably sure about them. But all of our sources were, in large part, using Socrates for ends of their own (Kahn, 1996). To disentangle from their writings what originated with the historical Socrates and what did not may be a hopeless task. But our inability to solve the historical problem need not be disheartening. For there remains the possibility of giving up on the *noumenon* Socrates – Socrates as he actually historically was – while retaining a vivid interest in the *phenomenon* Socrates – that is, Socrates as he is manifested through his influence on his followers, and more generally on the culture around him. Think of each of the Socratics as a facet through which Socrates may be viewed. The view through each facet is different. The views are of the same object, yet they are not reducible to any simple unity. Socrates-as-seen-through-the-many-facets-of-the-Socratic-movement – that is a Socrates that is available to us, and one that is endlessly fascinating (Van der Waerdt, 1994).

Some aspects of the phenomenon Socrates are covered elsewhere in this volume. The Socratics other than Plato and Xenophon have a chapter to themselves (MINOR SOCRATICS). Some scholars distinguish a "Socratic period" within Plato's dialogues. On this view, the character "Socrates" in certain dialogues written early in Plato's career has a coherent philosophical outlook different from the outlook of "Socrates" in dialogues like the *Republic*. The earlier dialogues present "Socratic" views, in contrast to the "mature Platonic" views of the *Republic* and later dialogues. The difference between the "Socratic" and "Platonic" views on ethics and moral psychology is covered in PLATO'S ETHICS: EARLY AND MIDDLE DIALOGUES. On the other hand, all Platonic writings in which the character "Socrates" appears present an image of Socrates. Thus the subject matters of THE SOPHISTIC MOVEMENT, THE PLATONIC DIALOGUE, PLATO'S META-PHYSICS, and PLATO'S POLITICAL PHILOSOPHY all overlap with this chapter.

Socrates in Aristophanes' *Clouds*

Our only portrait of Socrates from his own lifetime is found in Aristophanes' comic play *Clouds*, produced in 423 when Socrates was about 50 years old. Socrates in *Clouds* is head of a school, the "Thinkery." He and his students are pale, unwashed, and poor. They spend all their time thinking, and care not for food or wine or exercise. A principal activity of the school is scientific research into such subjects as astronomy, meteorology, natural history, geometry, and grammar. But what drives the plot is the desire of a chronic debtor, Strepsiades, to learn another subject: forensic rhetoric, or the art of making an unjust cause appear just. When Strepsiades flunks out of Socrates' Thinkery, he sends his son Pheidippides instead, who masters this art and returns home to punish his father with a beating.

Socrates investigates heaven and earth. He teaches natural philosophy, on topics ranging from the physiology of the gnat (*Nub.* 156–165) to the courses and revolutions of the moon (171–172). Aristophanes' Socrates rejects the traditional gods of Greece, substituting the Clouds, or other personifications of nature such as Breath and Air and Chaos. Socrates explains natural phenomena by material necessity rather than by divine intervention: thunder is caused by the collision of water-filled clouds, instead of Zeus. In fact, the natural philosophy of Aristophanes' Socrates closely resembles that of Diogenes of Apollonia, a "materialist" philosopher who had probably visited Athens (see Van der Waerdt 1994, ch. 2). Aristophanes' portrait of Socrates as a natural philosopher contrasts sharply with our other sources. Xenophon's Socrates claims that knowledge of heavenly phenomena is impossible, and that those who try to acquire it are mad. Xenophon's Socrates, like Plato's, devotes himself to human affairs. What is justice? What is law? What is most valuable in human life? How can Socrates and those he speaks with learn to lead good lives and do the right thing?

In an autobiographical interlude in Plato's *Phaedo*, Socrates tells a story that might reconcile these portraits (*Phd.* 96aff.) Socrates says that in his youth he was marvelously eager for natural philosophy. But he grew dissatisfied when he could not find the sort of answer that would satisfy him, so he abandoned natural philosophy. Aristophanes' early portrait of Socrates as a natural philosopher may be correct (though exaggerated for comic effect), and consistent with the later accounts of Plato and Xenophon, which

103

reflect a later phase in Socrates' life. Even if Socrates did go through this earlier phase, Socrates' importance in the history of thought is not due to the physical doctrines attributed to him in the *Clouds*.

The centerpiece of the *Clouds* is a debate between personifications of two modes of reasoning: Just and Unjust Argument. This debate is won by Unjust Argument, who cleverly advocates the use of speech to further crass self-interest at the expense of traditional morality.

The art of persuasion, including the ability to make the weaker argument appear the stronger, was taught during the second half of the fifth century by "sophists" like Protagoras and Gorgias, who charged hefty fees. An influential interpretation of the character Socrates in the *Clouds* is that it does not really portray Socrates himself, but rather a typical member of the Greek Enlightenment, a sophist (see Barney, THE SOPHISTIC MOVEMENT).

Yet we must be careful. Strepsiades says that Socrates charges fees; but in the play we do not see Socrates charging fees, and Socrates – unlike, for example, Protagoras – is utterly poor. Socrates does not himself teach Unjust Argument, and he leaves the stage when Unjust Argument appears. The point is a subtle one, and not all scholars will agree, but Aristophanes may be saying that one can learn how to turn clever argument to immoral purposes from Socrates' associates, but not from Socrates himself.

Plato's *Apology of Socrates*

The charge that Aristophanes unfairly presents Socrates as a sophist begins with Plato. In Plato's *Apology* Socrates credits Aristophanes with malign influence:

> There have been many who have accused me for many years now, and none of their accusations are true. . . . [They] persuaded you and accused me quite falsely, saying that there is a man called Socrates, a wise man, a student of all things in the sky and below the earth, who makes the worse argument appear the stronger. . . . What is most absurd in all this is that one cannot even know or mention their names unless one of them is a writer of comedies. (*Ap.* 18b–c)

The *Apology of Socrates* presents Socrates' defense speech at his trial. How accurate an image is it of the speech Socrates actually gave? We cannot know. What is clear is that Plato's *Apology of Socrates* is one of the greatest speeches in history. The most vivid, inspiring, and psychologically convincing image we have of Socrates comes from this speech.

Socrates defends himself against the three Aristophanic charges by arguing that he is not wise, but ignorant; that he does not study physics, but rather ethics and politics; and that his sole concern is not to win the argument, but to discover the truth. These three traits help make Socrates the founder of philosophy. The commitment to truth rather than persuasion is what distinguishes (true) philosophy from (false) rhetoric. Plato has Socrates hammer this point home at length in the *Gorgias*. The "pre-Socratic philosophers," such as Anaxagoras and Xenophanes, did inquire into "things in the sky and below the earth": they were primarily cosmologists and physicists. Socrates re-directed inquiry from the world of nature to the affairs of human beings.

"Philo-sophia" means "love of wisdom". One can love wisdom – and strive for it with love-struck obsessiveness – without oneself being wise. "Pre-Socratic" philosophers like Parmenides and Heraclitus claimed to be already wise. Socrates, by contrast, insisted both that wisdom is the most important thing to have, and that he himself did not have it. Devoting his life to the search for the wisdom that he lacked, Socrates was "philo-sophos" in a special sense.

Socrates explains his life's mission with a story (*Ap.* 21–22). His lifelong friend Chaerephon went to the Delphic Oracle and asked if anyone was wiser than Socrates. The oracle replied that no one is. Socrates took this as a riddle: Socrates knew that he was not wise, yet the oracle does not lie. To test the riddle, Socrates went to those with a reputation for great wisdom – poets, politicians, and such – and questioned them to see if they were really wise. Upon examination, no one turned out to have the wisdom that he claimed or people thought he had. When Socrates approached ordinary craftsmen, he discovered that these artisans were indeed wise in their particular crafts, for example, carpentry and shoemaking. But out of pride in their craft, these people also thought that they were wise in the most important matters – ethics and politics. But the craftsmen could no better explain and defend their views on these topics than the politicians and the poets. Socrates concluded about all these people: "I am wiser than this man; It is likely that neither of us knows anything worthwhile, but he thinks he knows something when he does not, whereas when I do not know, neither do I think I know; so I am likely to be wiser than he is to this small extent, that I do not think I know what I do not know" (*Ap.* 21d).

One might think that after proving the oracle right in this way, Socrates would stop. But Socrates interprets the testing of the oracle as a lifelong mission: "So even now I continue this investigation as the god bade me – and I go around seeking out anyone, citizen or stranger, whom I think wise. Then if I do not think he is, I come to the assistance of the god and show him that he is not wise" (*Ap.* 23b).

Why does Socrates keep on, year after year, exposing as false people's pretensions to wisdom? According to some scholars, the oracle from Delphi is a pivotal event in Socrates' life. The activity we think of as characteristic of Socrates – examining others and exposing their pretensions to wisdom – began as a response to the oracle, and Socrates' reason for continuing this activity is fundamentally a religious reason: he has been commanded to do so by Apollo. Other scholars believe that Socrates behaved in this way long before Chaerephon visited Delphi (if indeed Chaerephon did visit Delphi, and Plato did not simply invent this story as he did so many others in the dialogues). On this view, Socrates' talk of "a mission from Apollo" provides the cover of a religious sanction for an activity that Socrates had a deeper, and more fundamentally philosophical, reason to pursue. This reason is benevolence: a desire to benefit his fellow Athenians. Socrates' inquiries have convinced him that people generally lead thoughtless lives, acting on the basis of unexamined values they cannot justify. Everyone – not just politicians and poets, but also ordinary people – needs the medicine that philosophy provides. Socrates says, "An unexamined life is not worth living" (*Ap.* 38a).

Socrates' powerful critique risks nihilism. If no one's opinions about value can be justified, who is to say what is right or wrong? If I find that I have no good reason to do one thing rather than another, perhaps I can do whatever I want!

This brings us to the official charges against which Socrates defended himself at his trial. Socrates' official accuser was Meletus, backed by Anytus and Lycon. The charges were (1) that Socrates is guilty of corrupting the young and (2) of not believing in the gods of the city, but in other new divinities.[1] The defense Socrates gives in the *Apology* against these charges is surprisingly weak. What Socrates does is to show that Meletus is thoughtless and not a credible accuser, while avoiding the substance of the charges.

Socrates responds to the religious charge by getting Meletus to restate "not believing in the gods of the city" as a charge that Socrates is an atheist, that he believes in no gods. Socrates then points out that he cannot *both* be an atheist *and* believe in other new divinities! This does not address the substance of the charge. Meletus was foolish to revise the charge to atheism. Plato elsewhere has Socrates strongly criticize the traditional Homeric stories about the gods (*Republic*). Socrates' criticism of traditional Greek religion is simple and brilliant. The gods are good; it would be impious to suggest otherwise. But the traditional stories show the gods misbehaving in all the ways that humans behave: for example, Zeus tells lies and rapes women and kills his father. So these stories must be untrue.

Socrates' critique of Greek religion had a dramatic impact on Western culture. It gave rise to philosophical theology, the "god or gods of the philosophers" as opposed to the myth or the story. The task of Socratic philosophical theology can be stated thus: assuming that divinity exists, and is good, and (being more powerful than mortals) is their ultimate cause, what must divinity be like? Plato, Aristotle, the Stoics, and the Christian fathers all constructed their theologies on this basis. The revolutionary implications of Socrates' arguments, however, make them profoundly threatening to traditional Greek religion. If Socrates teaches the young to believe that what Homer and Hesiod teach about the gods is false, a reasonable Athenian citizen might well regard this as "corrupting the young."

Two other issues raised by Meletus' impiety charge should be mentioned. "Introducing new divinities" presumably alludes to Socrates' personal daimonion. This "divinity" is odd and mysterious, but introducing new divinities was not so unusual in Athens. For example, foreigners in the harbor town brought their divinities with them (see Parker, 1996). More importantly, Greek religion – like Judaism and unlike Christianity – was primarily a matter of practice and not belief. The entire community had an interest in seeing to it that every citizen carried out the proper rites and sacrifices, and did nothing offensive to the gods. A single person's offense might lead an angry god to bring down a plague or military defeat upon the whole city. Plato's Socrates casts doubt on Athenian religious belief, but Plato never shows him neglecting his everyday religious duty. Xenophon goes further, and explicitly answers the impiety charge with the argument that Socrates was openly faithful in the performance of his religious duty (*Mem.* 1.1.11, 1.2.1–2; cf. 4.3.16).

Socrates responds to the corruption charge in the *Apology* by arguing that bad people harm those who are close to them. Since Socrates, like all men, would rather be benefited than harmed by his associates, he would never intentionally worsen his

---

1. For discussion of the charge of impiety, see Betegh, GREEK PHILOSOPHY AND RELIGION, in this volume.

young companions' character. So either Socrates does not corrupt the young, and is innocent of the charge, or he does so unintentionally, and deserves instruction and advice rather than punishment (*Ap.* 25b–26a).

This is a poor argument. Its most important flaw is that Socrates has persisted in his way of life for many years in the face of criticism. If Socrates does corrupt the young, there is every reason to think that he is incorrigible.

Did Socrates corrupt the young? Or (what is a different question) was it reasonable for a typical Athenian juror to believe that Socrates corrupted the young? These are not easy questions to answer. Prominent in the Athenians' minds were the cases of Critias and Alcibiades, two associates of Socrates who became notorious for evil deeds – and in Alcibiades' case, for impiety (*Mem.* 1.2.12–34; Plato, *Alc.* I; cf. Thuc. V–VIII; Plut. *Alc.*). But the issue goes beyond particular individuals, or even particular beliefs. Socrates' withering critique of his interlocutors' statements undermines more than just Homeric religion. His critique of mere opinion threatens all existing values. The mere fact that most people believe something, or our ancestors believed it, does not give us reason to think that the belief is true. Behind the official charge that Socrates "corrupted the youth" is surely the correct perception that Socrates undermined traditional values.

Even so, Socrates was no nihilist. Socrates had strong and distinctive views about how to act and what is valuable in life. After claiming that his mission from Apollo is a blessing to the city, Socrates continues, "For I go around doing nothing but persuading both young and old among you not to care for your body or your wealth in preference to or as strongly as for the best possible state of the soul" (30a). Socrates held that what matters most in life is not (what most people in his society thought it is) wealth, or fame, or power, or even bodily health. What matters most is the excellence of one's soul, or virtue. This point of view is familiar enough to us today, but it was absolutely new and revolutionary in the fifth century BCE.

Socrates expresses other strong moral views in the *Apology*. Immediately before making his famous remark about the unexamined life, Socrates says: "it is the greatest good for a man to discuss virtue every day and those other things about which you hear me conversing and testing myself and others" (*Ap.* 38a). This is a strong statement. The benefit Socrates claimed earlier for his philosophical activity is that it punctures complacency: it is better to be aware of one's own ignorance than to think one knows what one does not. But one powerful encounter with Socrates, taken to heart, may suffice to accomplish that. Here Socrates insists that philosophy, as a way of life, is superior to bricklaying or generalship or managing a shipyard. In this passage Socrates is no nihilist or skeptic. He seems to know, or believe with confidence, that the most valuable thing for a human being is virtue, and philosophy is the best activity.

Socrates' distinctive moral views are further revealed in the *Crito*. This dialogue takes place while Socrates is in prison. Crito and his friends have arranged to bribe the jailers and transport Socrates into exile. Crito argues that Socrates owes it to himself, his friends, and his family to escape. Socrates argues that he has a duty to Athens to remain in jail and accept his punishment, even though the sentence is unjust.

Socrates begins his argument by reminding Crito of certain moral principles he and Crito share. Among these are: The soul is more important than the body. Life is not worth living with a ruined or unhealthy body or soul. Unjust action harms the soul, and just action helps it (*Cri.* 47e–48a, cf. *Grg.* 469c–522c). One must never do wrong willingly (49a) or even injure another willingly (49c). This prohibition is absolute: even if one is oneself wronged or injured, it is not right to inflict an injury in return (49c).

Socrates is well aware that these principles contradict traditional values. The traditional Greek conception of a virtuous person is one who "helps his friends and harms his enemies." Socrates held, and influenced his followers to hold, moral beliefs contrary to traditional values. If Socrates is right about morality, he does not corrupt his followers, but saves them. If traditional Greek morality is right, on the other hand, Socrates corrupts the young.

This shows that there is no shortcut answer to the question, "Does Socrates corrupt the young?" The only way to know whether Socrates corrupts the young or not is through moral knowledge itself. To know whether or not Socrates is guilty of the charges at his trial, one must know what goodness is and what badness is, which actions are right and which ones wrong. Socrates makes plain in the *Crito* that he thinks most jurors were not competent to judge his guilt. By the standard we have just laid out, Socrates is surely correct in his condemnation. The problem is that, by his own admission, Socrates also lacks moral knowledge. This entails that he also is not in a position to know whether or not he corrupts the young! Socrates' confidence in his own innocence is unjustified.

How Socrates' avowal of ignorance is compatible with confidence in his own innocence is a paradox. Perhaps the reason why Socrates in the *Apology* does not give a substantive refutation of the corruption charge is that he cannot.

Late in his speech Socrates attempts to escape the corruption charge on a technicality that has become renowned. Socrates insists that he has never been anyone's teacher (33a). The reason he gives is that, unlike the professional sophists, he does not charge a fee for his conversation. "And I cannot justly be held responsible for the good or bad conduct of these people, as I never promised to teach them anything and have not done so" (33b).

The noble image of impoverished Socrates has made it harder for philosophers to justify a decent living ever since! Socrates' refusal to charge a fee did have the important effect of keeping him free to choose his own company. The professional sophists, like university teachers today, were obliged to converse with whoever paid their fees. But it is not really plausible for Socrates to imply that unless he charged his followers a fee he is not responsible for his influence upon them.

Socratic Method

According to Plato's *Apology*, the purpose and value of Socratic refutation is negative and existential: the interlocutor's claim to wisdom is exposed as false. Platonic dialogues often show Socrates engaged in this sort of refutation. He will ask a general, "What is courage?" (*Laches*) or a politician, "What is justice?" (*Republic*), or a self-described religious expert, "What is piety?" (*Euthyphro*). Plato's Socrates is almost never shown discussing immediately relevant practical questions, such as whether *this* statue is beautiful or whether *this* man's leaving the battlefield was cowardly. Confronted with questions of this sort, Plato's Socrates will make the issue abstract again: We cannot judge whether this statue is beautiful unless we know what beauty is. I myself do not know what beauty is. So tell me, what do *you* say beauty is?

After the interlocutor offers a definition, Socrates will ask a series of further questions, which reveal that the definition is inadequate. Typically, either Socrates or the interlocutor will suggest a revised definition, and Socrates proceeds through a series of questions to show that this definition will not do, either.

Socratic refutation is often referred to by its Greek name, *elenchus*. Socrates regards the elenchus as a touchstone for wisdom or knowledge. If you are a religious expert, you can explain what piety is, and defend your definition against objections. To be politically wise, you must understand justice, and thus be able to define it and defend your definition.

Socrates seems to think that experts in ordinary crafts satisfy this requirement. But we may doubt that a typical Athenian carpenter could successfully defend a definition of "bed" against Socratic attack! Socrates does not distinguish technical verbal skill – either logical argument or rhetorical persuasion – from substantive knowledge of a subject matter. Socrates' interlocutors sometimes feel they have been refuted, not because they lack expertise in the subject, but by verbal trickery. Socrates would deny the distinction.

Plato shows vividly in his dialogues how being refuted by Socrates could be deeply annoying. Socrates implies that one factor in his trial and conviction was widespread built-up annoyance at the way Socrates punctured pretensions to wisdom. But there is another reason why Socratic refutation could "get under your skin." One rule of Socratic discussion was sincerity: participants in the discussion should say or assent only to what they really believe. Since Socrates converses about the most important issues in human life, when he refutes a person, he shows that the person's basic beliefs about good and bad and how to live are unfounded. This experience can be shattering.

This effect of Socratic refutation is especially important, because Socrates did not merely converse with the prominent and powerful. Socrates spent time in the marketplace, willing to converse with whoever happened by. Even if you are a modest person and do not claim wisdom, a conversation with Socrates can reveal that your opinions about good and bad and how to live have no basis. In conversation with Socrates, your basic values, your whole way of life, your very *self*, are on trial.

This aspect of Socratic refutation is highlighted by Nicias in the *Laches*:

> [W]hoever comes into close contact with Socrates and associates with him in conversation must necessarily, even if he began by conversing about something quite different in the first place, keep on being led about by the man's arguments until he submits to answering questions about himself concerning both his present manner of life and the life he has lived hitherto. (*Laches* 187e)

Yet the process by which Socrates refutes his interlocutor has value that goes beyond the merely negative and existential. If all we learned from the dialogues bearing their names were that Laches, Lysis, Hippias, and Meno lack wisdom, these dialogues would not have survived the ages. But these dialogues do more. Even when his conversation partner is an unpromising dolt like Euthyphro, Socrates steers the conversation in such a way as to make it a rich and profound philosophical exploration of its topic (see C. Gill, THE PLATONIC DIALOGUE).

Socrates steers the conversation by searching for a "definition." Socrates asks his conversation partner to give a definition, to "say what courage is" or "what justice is." What Socrates wants is not (what we would call) a dictionary definition, telling how the word is typically used, but (what philosophers have come to call) a "real definition," an account displaying the essential nature of, for example, courage or justice. In fact our concept "essence" goes back historically to Socrates' quest for definitions: "the essence of F" is whatever is given by a correct answer to the Socratic question, "What is F?"

For any attribute F, Socrates wants to know the "one thing" common to all F things that makes them F. This definition must be general.[2] Socrates' interlocutors often err by giving examples in place of a general account. "Justice" is not an acceptable definition of "virtue," because there are other virtues besides justice, e.g., temperance and courage. The successful definition is neither too wide nor too narrow. The definition must be true of everything that is F, but not hold true of anything that that is not F. In addition, the definition must explain *why* F things are F. In many Platonic dialogues, Socrates' attempts to arrive at a definition fail. But in the *Meno* – where Socrates tries and fails to define "virtue" – Socrates gives a model definition using this example: "shape" is "the limit of a solid" (*Meno* 76). And in the *Republic* Socrates defines civic justice as "each one doing its own job well" (*Rep.* IV, 443d–444a).

After eliciting a definition, Socrates continues to quiz, obtaining from his interlocutor answers to a string of questions concerning the definition and related issues. Eventually Socrates is able to show that one of the responses contradicts the original thesis. The interlocutor is refuted. The enduring value of these discussions is mostly due to the brilliance and depth of their ideas and arguments. Socrates does not aim simply for a quick and easy refutation. He steers the discussion through profound territory along the way.

But Socrates often claims to have accomplished more than "an interesting exploration." He claims the refutation shows that the initial definition is false. As a matter of logic, this claim is mistaken. If the theses D, A, B, and C are inconsistent, at least one of them must be false, but the inconsistency alone does not tell us whether the falsehood lies with the original definition D, or with one the other claims A, B, or C. How Socrates can claim to have proved that the initial definition is false, when all he has shown is that the interlocutor's beliefs are internally inconsistent, is a notorious "problem of the elenchus" which many scholars have tried to solve.

We have seen that Socrates is not a skeptic. He and his companions share a set of moral principles sharply at odds with their society. Another problem of the elenchus is how and whether this negative procedure can produce constructive results. Is Socrates' confidence in his own moral principles somehow justified through the elenchus?

Socrates' famous comparison of his activity with that of a midwife suggests a way:

---

2. Aristotle testifies that a search for general definitions was characteristic of Socrates (*Met.* M.4, 1078b). Aristotle here also confirms that one method Socrates used in his search for definitions was generalizing from examples, a method Aristotle calls "induction." Xenophon's depiction of Socrates' search for definitions agrees with Plato and Aristotle on both these points (*Mem.* 1.1.16, 4.3–6).

110

> Now my activity is just like [midwives'] in most respects. The difference is that I attend men and not women, and that I watch over the labor of their souls, not of their bodies. And the most important thing about my art is the ability to apply all possible tests to the offspring, to determine whether the young mind is being delivered of a phantom, that is, an error, or a fertile truth. For one thing which I have in common with ordinary midwives is that I myself am barren of wisdom. (*Tht.* 150b–c)

Socrates here suggests that attempts at refutation are a test for truth as well as falsity. If a philosophical thesis withstands Socratic examination, it has been shown to be a "fertile truth." Notice a changed perspective from the *Apology*: what is being tested here is no longer a person or his claim to wisdom, but a philosophical thesis or idea.

If the distinctive moral principles that Socrates and his associates share have withstood many attempts to refute them, perhaps over many years, then by the *Theaetetus* standard they have been shown to be true. Although (according to the midwife metaphor) Socrates was not the source of these ideas, as their examiner he is optimally placed to judge their truth. If the elenchus is a test for truth, perhaps it can produce knowledge after all, and Socrates is not as ignorant as he pretends.

Moral Psychology

One powerful and widespread interpretation of the ethics and moral psychology of the Platonic Socrates holds that Socrates is a psychological egoist: he believes that the ultimate end of all our actions is our own good. This makes him also an intellectualist: everyone always does what seems (to him) best (for himself). Socrates' intellectualism leads him to deny weakness of will: no one ever "does wrong willingly" (*Prt.* 345e). Virtue is the art of living a good life, i.e., promoting and securing one's own good. Since no one acts against his better judgment, the ability to reliably recognize what is good and what is bad suffices to be able to choose the good and reject the bad. Call the ability to reliably recognize good and bad "knowledge of good and bad." Socratic intellectualism about human action thus leads to Socratic intellectualism about virtue. Virtue is knowledge. What kind of knowledge? Not carpentry or mathematics, but expertise concerning what is good or bad.[3]

But this interpretation of Plato's Socrates faces difficulties. The evidence for Socratic psychological egoism is thin. (In fact the most explicit expression of Socratic egoism is found not in Plato, but in Xenophon: *Mem.* 3.9.4.) The passages most often cited (*Euthd.* 278e, *Meno* 77–78, *Grg.* 468, 486, 507) support a weaker doctrine, Universal Self-Interest. Socrates holds the plausible thesis that everyone desires, and intensely desires, his own well-being. Socrates assumes that virtually everyone is aware of having this desire. This makes egoistic motives a natural starting point for ethical discussion. Some interlocutors, like Callicles in Plato's *Gorgias*, have no non-egoistic desires. With them, discussion must proceed from narrowly egoistic assumptions. But many people care, ultimately and intrinsically, about goods beyond themselves: their

3. For an excellent presentation of this approach to Socrates, see Penner, PLATO'S ETHICS: EARLY AND MIDDLE DIALOGUES, in this volume.

friends, their families, the city. With these people, Socrates' philosophical inquiries can build on a broader base.

Throughout Plato's dialogues (and not just the so-called "Socratic" ones) Socrates assumes Universal Self-Interest. Socrates also holds that all rational desire is for the good, but "the good" can be filled out in different ways. Some rational desires are for one's own good. Other rational desires are for the good of one's city, or for the goodness of the cosmos (the Demiurge in Plato's *Timaeus*). Different people will have different shapes and ranges of desires for the good. But Socrates (throughout Plato) does seem to think that all rational desire is for the good.

Drawing upon Plato's *Protagoras*, Aristotle reports: "It would be strange – so Socrates thought – if when knowledge was in a man something else could master it and drag it about like a slave. For Socrates was entirely opposed to the view in question, holding that there is no such thing as weakness of will" (*EN* VII.2, 1145b23–26). The thesis that knowledge is such a powerful state that it cannot be overcome by passions is not distinctly Socratic. When Socrates suggests it, Protagoras readily agrees (352b–d). The knowledge that Socrates thinks cannot be overcome by passion is not just any sort of knowledge (like the knowledge that today is Tuesday), but knowledge of good and bad. Another name for this knowledge is practical wisdom. Socrates in the *Republic* also gives practical wisdom this strength. Even Aristotle agrees that a person who has practical wisdom is not subject to weakness of will (*EN* VII, X). The reason that the knowledge which is wisdom cannot be overcome by the passions is that wisdom is so very, very strong. An ordinary person's beliefs do not have that strength. So, as Aristotle recognized (VII.2, 1145b31–1146a9), the two claims "No wise man does wrong willingly", and "No one does wrong willingly" are philosophically very different.

Moreover, the evidence for attributing "no one does wrong willingly" to Socrates comes from a very different context in the *Protagoras*. Socrates makes this claim as part of a convoluted interpretation of a poem by Simonides: "For I am pretty much of this opinion, that no intelligent man believes that anyone does wrong freely or acts shamefully and badly of his own free will, but they well know that all who do shameful and bad things do so other than freely" (*Prt.* 345d–e). Socrates does not here say that no one acts against his better judgment, or does what he believes to be wrong. What he says is that no one does wrong freely or willingly (*hekōn*). A person who does something unwillingly does it because of some constraint. You remain in jail because the cell door is locked. You hand your wallet to a thief because of his gun. This constraint can be either external or internal. A recovering alcoholic takes a drink, relapsing against his will, because of the power of his addiction.

Looking at an earlier philosopher through the lens of his own philosophical views, Aristotle misinterprets Socrates' remarks in the *Protagoras*. Socrates does not mean to say that no one does what he believes to be wrong or acts against his better judgment, but rather that when a person does that, he acts unwillingly.

Education and Politics

The Socratic principle that virtue is knowledge need not imply that all education is narrowly cognitive, or that the only means of moral improvement is philosophical dialectic. For dialectic to be useful, certain character traits must already be in place: patience, humility, and a strong desire to learn. In both Plato and Xenophon, Socrates appeals to emotions as well as reason; above all, Socrates makes use of *shame*. Socrates believes that the characters of some immoral and unjust people can be improved by punishments such flogging, prison, and fines (*Grg.* 472–480). The beneficial effects of the Laws of Athens upon the character of its citizens are acknowledged by Socrates in the *Crito*.

In the *Apology* Socrates denies that he practices politics (on the grounds that he would surely fail) (*Ap.* 31), while in the *Gorgias* he claims that he is the only Athenian who truly practices politics (*Grg.* 521d). These apparently contradictory statements are reconcilable. Socrates denies that he is able to benefit the city "in the public space" of the Assembly or city government, yet claims to be able to benefit the city privately, by making certain of its members better one-on-one by dialectic.

Less easily reconcilable are Socrates' love of Athens and his contempt for Athenian democracy. Socrates believes that the Laws of Athens are worthy of respect and beneficial, and that only in Athens can philosophy flourish. Yet he also believes that none of the Athenian political actors "truly practice politics," and that putting political power in the hands of the many is like practicing medicine by majority vote.

Irony

Plato's Socrates is not always honest. He claims a barren ignorance that his moral self-confidence belies. Socrates insincerely flatters his interlocutors by attributing to them a wisdom he does not for a moment believe in. In Aristophanes and Plato, *eirōneia* and its cognates mean "dissimulation, deception." This is a different notion from our concept of irony, although it is related. Ironical speech does not intend to deceive the hearer, but to successfully communicate a message that is different from the literal meaning of what is said. Quintilian's definition of irony fits our concept well: speech "in which something contrary to what is said is to be understood" (*Inst. orat.* 9.2.44).

In the *Symposium* Alcibiades says that, when it comes to Socrates, appearances are misleading. Socrates claims to be completely ignorant and know nothing, while inside he is completely different. "His whole life is spent dissembling (*eirōneuomenos*) and toying with his fellow men" (*Symp.* 216e). Thrasymachus in the *Republic* charges that Socrates is deceitful in pretending not to have an answer for the questions he asks: "Heracles! This is Socrates' habitual deception (*eirōneia*)" (*Rep.* I, 337a). In the *Gorgias*, Socrates says to Callicles, "O wonderful one, teach me more gently, so that I don't give up attending to you." Callicles replies: "You are mocking me (*eirōneue*) Socrates" (*Grg.* 489d–e). These charges are fair. But Socrates' disingenuousness and mockery may involve more than simple dishonesty. If Socrates intends Callicles to recognize the mockery, then Socrates' remark is not deceptive, but ironical.

Socrates was the first great philosopher, and also the first great ironist in history. His irony has been celebrated, scorned, and puzzled over from his time to ours (Kierkegaard, 1989; Nehamas, 1998, pt. 1; Vlastos, 1991, ch. 1). When Socrates praises Euthyphro, he engages in *eirōneia*, but not irony. His words are deceptive and mocking, but they are not intended "to communicate something other than what is said," because Socrates realizes that Euthyphro is too stolid to catch on.

The example from the *Gorgias* is more complicated. Callicles accuses Socrates of *eirōneia*, of intending to deceive with his praise. By this accusation, Callicles means to signal that the *eirōneia* has failed: he, Callicles, has seen through the deception. But what if Callicles is wrong? What if Socrates did not intend to deceive Callicles, but – aware of Callicles' sharpness – expected him to see through the deception and realize that Socrates thinks little of him? In that case, Socrates' remark is an insulting irony.

The situation in Plato's dialogues is even more complicated. There is another character whose intentions matter: the author (see Nehamas 1998, and in this volume the chapter by C. Gill). When Plato has Socrates praise Euthyphro, he expects the reader to "get" the insincerity of the praise. So although Socrates deceives Euthyphro, Plato enlightens the reader, through the use of irony.

Literally deceptive speech – saying something other than what you mean or believe – has an enormous variety of uses, many of them relevant to Socrates (Nehamas, 1998; Vlastos, 1991). I have discussed some of these uses. Here is one more: Suppose one of Socrates' close companions was present while Socrates was talking with Euthyphro. Then when Socrates praises Euthyphro, he will expect that Euthyphro will be deceived, but his friend will recognize the irony and understand it as an expression of contempt. Ironical speech can thus be used to separate out "insiders" who get the joke from "outsiders" who do not. The distinction between insiders and outsiders was crucial to Socrates, who saw himself and his companions as united by a commitment to a way of life and a set of values dramatically different from those of the rest of society. When discussing in public, Socrates may often have spoken with this double intention, deliberately misleading outsiders while ironically communicating his real thoughts to his friends.

Xenophon

The distinction between insiders and outsiders helps to explain a characteristic difference between Plato's Socrates and Xenophon's. Plato's Socrates appears more savage and ironical, and Xenophon's Socrates more kindly and straightforward, because Plato mainly shows Socrates in conversation with professional sophists and other "outsiders," while Xenophon mainly shows him in conversation with his friends. But when Xenophon's Socrates converses with sophists and tyrants, he can display a similar irony (*Mem.* 1.2.30–34, 4.4.5; Morrison, 1987).

Xenophon wrote four Socratic works: *Apology of Socrates to the Jury, Memorabilia, Oeconomicus,* and *Symposium*. He wrote three other works of political philosophy in which Socrates does not appear: *Hiero, Agesilaus,* and *Cyropaedia*. These other works are important for understanding Xenophon's contribution to the Socratic movement, but do not contribute directly to his image of Socrates.

Unlike Plato's *Apology*, Xenophon's *Apology* does not pretend to present Socrates' entire speech. Xenophon focuses instead on a single question: why did Socrates speak so arrogantly as almost to ensure conviction? Plato's implied answer to this question is that only thus could Socrates be true to himself. Socrates understood that he was wise (with a human wisdom, through awareness of his own ignorance), in a way that most Athenians are not, and that his philosophical mission makes him Athens' greatest benefactor. If making these facts clear appears arrogant, so be it. Xenophon thinks, plausibly, that this explanation is insufficient. Socrates could have presented the same basic defense in a much more conciliatory manner. Xenophon is surely right about this, although his explanation of Socrates' arrogant presentation is less noble than Plato's. Xenophon claims that the reason Socrates speaks so arrogantly is that he preferred death to the infirmities of old age.

The *Memorabilia* or *Recollections of Socrates* is Xenophon's own "apology," or defense of Socrates. Most of the book is devoted to defending Socrates against the charge of corrupting the youth: "In my opinion [Socrates] actually benefited his associates, partly by practical example and partly by conversation. I shall record as many instances as I can recall" (*Mem.* 1.3.1). Thus Xenophon directly confronts the corruption charge that Plato's *Apology* evades.

Socrates benefited his young associates by argument and advice; but above all, by his example (*Mem.* 1.2.2–3). Socrates "made his associates desire virtue and gave them hope that if they took care for themselves, they would become good. And though he never professed to be a teacher, he made his associates hope by imitating him to become so, since he himself was manifestly of this sort" (*Mem.* 1.2.2–3).

Xenophon's Socrates is avuncular. He gives his young associates practical advice. His philosophical conversations are often (though not always) more concrete than Plato's, and lead to positive conclusions. Consonant with his apologetic purpose, Xenophon de-emphasizes what is controversial about Socrates. Consider the traditional Greek maxim: "Help your friends and harm your enemies." Plato in the *Crito* has Socrates deny this, insisting that you should not harm anyone, not even your enemies. By contrast, Xenophon's Socrates does advocate helping friends and harming enemies (*Mem.* 2.3.14; 2.6.35; 3.1.6; 4.2.14–16). But his Socrates transforms the meaning of this traditional maxim through a radical new understanding of friendship. Socrates argues that bad men cannot be friends to anyone (*Mem.* 2.6.1–7, 14–16). On his view of friendship, good men are naturally friends with each other, and enemies of the bad. Since truly bad people cannot be improved, good people cannot either benefit or harm them.

Socrates is a master of erotics. In Plato's *Symposium*, Socrates says that erotics is the one thing he knows (177d, cf. *Lysis* 211e and *Theages* 128b). In Xenophon's *Symposium*, Socrates says that he prides himself on being a "procurer," where that word has sexual connotation. (*Symp.* 4.57). Socrates does not employ his erotic power for the purposes of physical seduction. In Plato, Alcibiades bemoans Socrates' sexual continence in the face of Alcibiades' desire (*Symp.* 219b–d). When Socrates and his companions visit a prostitute in Xenophon's *Memorabilia*, she falls in love with him while he remains immune to her charms (*Mem.* 3.11).[4] Socrates' seduction is aimed at the souls of his young admirers. The most brilliant and vivid image of Socratic spiritual seduction is Alcibiades' speech in Plato's *Symposium*. But the most detailed and informative account of Socrates' selection and intellectual seduction of a gifted young man is the story of

4. Socratic eros is also a major theme in Aeschines. See Kahn (1994) and Decleva Caizzi, MINOR SOCRATICS, in this volume.

Euthydemus in Xenophon's *Memorabilia* (4.2). This account shows that Socrates was very choosy. To be admitted as one of Socrates' close associates, a young man needed to be intelligent, desirous of all forms of learning, persistent in the face of shame and discouragement, and inclined toward virtue.

Socrates' religious outlook is somewhat different in Xenophon's treatment than Plato's. Xenophon defends against the impiety charge by stressing Socrates' faithful observance of religious rituals and sacrifices (*Mem.* 1.1.2). Xenophon's Socrates believes in divination: the ability of ominous birds or sheep entrails, properly interpreted, to foretell the future. One might think that this makes Xenophon's Socrates more conventional and less philosophical than Plato's. But this would be wrong: Xenophon's Socrates gives a philosophical argument in favor of divination. In both Plato and Xenophon, Socrates holds the anti-Homeric view that the gods are good. Whereas in Plato Socrates merely assumes that the gods exist and are good, Xenophon's Socrates gives a philosophical argument for the existence of benevolent and beneficent deities. This is what has become known as an "argument from design": the world around us reveals so much marvelously functional design that it must have been produced by intelligent and powerful beneficent designers (*Mem.* 1.4.2–8). Xenophon's Socrates takes another step beyond Plato's when he argues that the gods are not only good, but also omniscient (*Mem.* 1.2.19). It stands to reason that all-knowing and benevolent gods will assist human beings, with their limited intelligence, by sending them signs.

Conclusion

Socrates, the founder of philosophy, is a paradox, a mystery, and an inspiration. He is a historical figure, and a myth. He is profoundly rational, and profoundly devout. He raises the standards for ethical and practical knowledge so high that no one can meet them; but at crucial moments he is relieved of this inconvenience by the private revelation of an infallible divinity. Socrates' most outstanding personal characteristics were a devotion to rational inquiry about values, and an unflinching consistency of thought and action. Together these traits lead to condemnation and execution at the hands of his native city Athens.

What is philosophy? What is a philosophical life? What are the ties of loyalty that bind, and the divergences of outlook and purpose that divide, the Philosopher and the City, the realm of ethics and the world of politics? For those interested in such questions, throughout history and today, the ancient images of Socrates provide an inexhaustible source of inspiration.

Bibliography

Sources

Aristophanes

Dover, K. J. (ed.). (1968). *Aristophanes: Clouds*. Oxford: Clarendon Press.
Sommerstein, A. (trans.) (1981). *Aristophanes: The Acharnians; The Clouds; Lysistrata*. Harmondsworth: Penguin.

Plato

The works of Plato are cited by Stephanus numbers, indicating page and section on that page of the edition of Plato's works by Henri Estienne (Paris, 1578). Modern editions of the Greek text and translations commonly use these standard numbers in the margins of the text.

Greek text of Plato: Burnet, J. (ed.). (1900–7). *Platonis opera*. (5 vols.). Oxford: Clarendon Press.

The Oxford Classical Text is currently being revised: Duke, E. A., Hicken, W. F., Nicoll, W. S. M., Robinson, D. B., and Strachan, J. C. G. (eds.). (1995). *Platonis opera*. (vol. 1): *Euthyphro, Apology, Crito, Phaedo, Cratylus, Theaetetus, Sophist, Politicus*. Oxford: Clarendon Press.

Euthyphro, Apology, Crito: Burnet, J. (1924). *Plato's "Euthyphro", "Apology of Socrates", and "Crito"*. Oxford: Oxford University Press.

Concordance of Plato: Ast, D. F. (1835–8). *Lexicon Platonicum; sive, Vocum Platonicarum index*. (3 vols.). Leipzig: Weidman. Repr. New York: Burt Franklin, 1969.

Translation of Plato: Cooper, J. M. (ed.). (1997). *Plato: Complete Works*. (D. S. Hutchinson, assoc. ed.). Indianapolis: Hackett.

Xenophon

Bandini, M. (ed.) and L.-A. Dorion (trans.). (2000). *Xénophon: Mémorables*. (vol. 1). Paris: Les Belles Lettres.

Marchant, E. C. and Todd, O. J. (eds.). (1979). *Xenophon* (vol. 4): *Memorabilia, Oeconomicus, Symposium, Apology*. Loeb Classical Library. Cambridge, Mass.: Harvard University Press/ London: Heinemann.

Tredennick, H. and Waterfield, R. (trans.). (1990). *Xenophon: Conversations of Socrates*. London: Penguin.

Works Cited

Döring, K. (1998). *Grundriss der Geschichte der Philosophie*. (vol. 2/1): *Sokrates, die Sokratiker und die von ihnen begründeten Traditionen*. Basel: Schwabe.

Kahn, C. (1994). "Aeschines on Socratic Eros." In P. Van der Waerdt (ed.) *The Socratic Movement* (pp. 87–106). Ithaca, NY: Cornell University Press.

——. (1996). *Plato and the Socratic Dialogue*. Cambridge: Cambridge University Press.

Kierkegaard, S. (1989). The *Concept of Irony with Constant Reference to Socrates*. (trans. H. Hong and E. Hong). Princeton: Princeton University Press.

Morrison, D. (1987). "On Professor Vlastos' Xenophon." *Ancient Philosophy*, 7, 9–22.

——. (2000). "On the Alleged Historical Reliability of Plato's *Apology*." *Archiv für Geschichte der Philosophie*, 82, 235–65.

Nehamas, A. (1998). *The Art of Living: Socratic Reflections from Plato to Foucault*. Berkeley: University of California Press.

Parker, R. (1996). *Athenian Religion: A History*. Oxford: Clarendon Press.

Patzer, A. (1987). *Der Historische Sokrates*. Darmstadt: Wissenschaftliche Buchgesellschaft.

Van der Waerdt, P. (ed.). (1994). *The Socratic Movement*. Ithaca, NY: Cornell University Press.

Vlastos, G. (ed.). (1971). *The Philosophy of Socrates*. New York: Doubleday.

——. (1991). *Socrates: Ironist and Moral Philosopher*. Cambridge: Cambridge University Press/ Ithaca, NY: Cornell University Press.

Further Reading

Benson, H. H. (ed.). (1992). *Essays on the Philosophy of Socrates.* New York: Oxford University Press.

Brickhouse, T. and Smith, N. (2000). *The Philosophy of Socrates.* Boulder: Westview.

Edmunds, L. (1985). "Aristophanes' Socrates." *Proceedings of the Boston Area Colloquium in Ancient Philosophy*, 1, 209–30.

Field, G. C. (1930). *Plato and his Contemporaries: A Study in Fourth-century Life and Thought.* London: Methuen.

Gomez-Lobo, A. (1994). *Foundations of Socratic Ethics.* Indianapolis: Hackett.

Grote, George. (1865). *Plato and the Other Companions of Socrates.* (3 vols.). London: Murray.

Guthrie, W. K. C. (1971). *The Philosophy of Socrates.* Cambridge: Cambridge University Press.

Hadot, P. (1995). *Philosophy as a Way of Life: Spiritual Exercises from Socrates to Foucault.* Oxford: Blackwell.

Irwin, T. (1995). *Plato's Ethics.* Oxford: Oxford University Press.

McPherran, M. (1996). *The Religion of Socrates.* University Park: Pennsylvania State University Press.

Nussbaum, M. C. (1980). "Aristophanes and Socrates on Learning Practical Wisdom." *Yale Classical Studies*, 26, 43–97.

Prior, W. (ed.). (1996). *Socrates: Critical Examinations.* (4 vols.). London: Routledge.

Slings, S. R. (1994). *Plato's Apology of Socrates. A Literary and Philosophical Study with Running Commentary.* Edited and completed from the papers of the late É. de Strycker, S.J. Leiden: Brill.

Strauss, L. (1989). "The Problem of Socrates: Five Lectures." In T. Pangle (ed.). *The Rebirth of Classical Political Rationalism* (pp. 103–83). Chicago: University of Chicago Press.

Vlastos, G. (ed.). (1971). *The Philosophy of Socrates.* Garden City, NY: Anchor.

——. (1994). *Socratic Studies.* Cambridge: Cambridge University Press.

de Vogel, C. J. (1963). "Who was Socrates?" *Journal of the History of Philosophy*, 1, 143–61.

Zeller, E. (1885). *Socrates and the Socratic Schools.* (trans. O. J. Reichel.). New York: Russell & Russell.

7

Minor Socratics

FERNANDA DECLEVA CAIZZI

Introduction

Although everyone wanted to be called a Socratic, and thought that they were, the followers of Socrates actually gave rise to diverse and conflicting traditions (Cicero, *De Or.* 3.16.61; Aristocles of Messene, *ap.* Eus. *Praep. Evang.* 11.3.4). The vagaries of textual transmission and the cultural preferences of late antiquity combined to preserve the entire *Corpus Platonicum*, but not so for the other figures, major or minor, of the Socratic circle – not even for Antisthenes, whose output was varied, impressive in quantity, and important enough to earn the praise of the ancients, who read and valued his works for many centuries. This situation, whose repercussions on the development of philosophical thought in modern times are well known, has favored the separation of Plato from the other Socratics. This separation is not merely due to the enormous difference between the amount we know about Plato and about the others; it is often accompanied by more partisan philosophical justifications and value judgments.

Socrates, Plato, and the Socratics are three pawns in a complex game, a game that has never ceased to challenge and to fascinate all those who have worked in the field of philosophy. On the table, one might say, are two large interconnected problems. On the one hand, there is the enigmatic and elusive figure of Socrates, who, although he wrote nothing, gave his name to a genre of literature, the *logos Sokratikos*, a genre practiced by many authors who in various ways invoked him. On the other hand, there is the interpretation of Plato's philosophy and of its relationship to Socrates' thought, on which our positive or negative valuation of the other Socratics depends in many cases.

The modern labels 'Minor Socratics', 'Socratici minori' and 'Demi-Socratiques' that today are retained mostly for reasons of convenience, owe their success to the seminal history of Greek philosophy by Eduard Zeller, *Die Philosophie der Griechen* (1844–6, cited from fifth edition 1922). The great German scholar opened the second part of his work with a section entitled "Sokrates und die unvollkommenen Sokratiker" ("Socrates and the incomplete Socratics"). Here we find the thesis that the Socratics who, besides Plato, founded philosophical schools – Euclides (with Phaedo), Antisthenes and Aristippus – all invoked Socrates. They did so, however, in a one-sided way, reflecting the spirit of their master's doctrine only incompletely. Some kept to the general content of the Socratic principle, the abstract idea of the Good. Others started out from a eudaemonistic construal of this idea and made the Good into something relative.

Within the first group, the theoretical perspective was fundamental for Euclides, the practical perspective for Antisthenes. Thus the Socratics were divided into three schools: the Megarian, the Antisthenean and Cynic, and finally the Cyrenaic. Each one of these schools, while developing a single aspect of Socrates' thought, also reconnected to earlier doctrinal positions. The Megarians and the Cynics linked themselves to the Eleatic tradition and to the sophistic movement as represented by Gorgias, the Cyrenaics to Protagorean skepticism and to its Heraclitean foundations (Zeller, 1922, 2.1, p. 244).

Zeller's historical construction and the authority of his work contributed not only to the establishment of the label "Minor Socratics," but also to the influence of the philosophical judgment that justified it, that the Socratics should be considered "minor" relative to Plato because "Plato alone achieved a deeper understanding of Socrates' philosophy and brought it to perfection in every aspect" (p. 388), while their philosophical doctrines revealed a contamination of Socratic by pre-Socratic thought.

In 1865 George Grote published *Plato and the Other Companions of Sokrates* (cited below from the second edition, London 1885), in which he extolled – not without polemical digs at Zeller – the critical openness and focus on dialectical refutation characteristic of Socrates and inherited by all the Socratics, Plato included. "He [Sokrates] was the generator, indirectly and through others, of a new and abundant crop of compositions – the 'Sokratic dialogues': composed by many different authors, among whom Plato stands out as unquestionable coryphaeus, yet amidst other names well deserving respectful mention as seconds, companions, or opponents" (vol. 1, p. vi). As in the case of Zeller's section, even the title that Grote chose for his book reveals his way of conceiving the relationship among Socrates, Plato, and the "Socratics."

Of course, the exegetical line proposed by Zeller, and largely accepted after him, is not without support in the ancient sources. It is precisely the nature and the reliability of these sources that need to be assessed with particular care, in the light of the enormous progress achieved, after the publication of *Philosophie der Griechen*, by studies of ancient philosophical historiography, studies that have received impetus and inspiration from Hermann Diels' magisterial *Doxographi Graeci* (1879) (see Calder and Mansfeld, 1999).

The Followers of Socrates

Speaking of "so-called Socratics," Diogenes Laertius (2.47) makes it clear that the label "Socratics" had already assumed a peculiar character, one that differentiated it from other labels also derived from a founding master (*apo tou didaskalou*), such as "Epicureans" (for the names of the philosophical schools see e.g. D.L. 1.17). For a number of reasons the label "Socratics" could not be easily adapted to the schema of scholastic and doctrinal "successions" (*diadochai*) propagated from the Hellenistic age onwards. This was due to the profound divergences between those that called themselves, or were called, Socratics. According to the ancients (aside from a few hostile sources), Socrates had not taught in the manner of the Sophists, nor had he founded an authentic school. At all events, correctly or incorrectly, the notion of "schools" first entered general discourse only in reference to his followers. (On the schools in the later tradition, see Bénatouïl, PHILOSOPHIC SCHOOLS IN HELLENISTIC AND ROMAN TIMES, in this volume.)

Socrates' entourage constituted a rather variegated group. Some of them associated with him only occasionally or irregularly; others were distinguished by their assiduity, and still others by assiduity combined with a high level of philosophical ability. We know that several of them made the practice of philosophy what we would today call their "profession." However, we must not forget that what we call philosophy, with its familiar list of figures starting with Thales, is the product of the reflection and activity of the heirs of Socrates, notably Plato and his disciple Aristotle. In other words, those who formed Socrates' audience, a few of whom also became faithful companions, were not motivated by the desire to become "philosophers," but rather by the conviction that Socrates had something of importance to offer them for their own life.

Ancient philosophical historiography, such as the manual that has come down to us under the name of Galen (*Hist. philos.* 3), felt the need to justify the selection it made within this multiplicity of figures. In this pseudo-Galenic work we read that, of the numerous Socratics, only those that left a succession need be mentioned: that is (apart from Plato) Antisthenes and the Cynics, Aristippus and the Cyrenaics, Euclides and the Megarians. As in antiquity, we still find in modern histories of philosophy, alongside a major chapter on Plato, a section dedicated to Antisthenes, Aristippus, Euclides and their successors, with brief mentions of other figures associated with Socrates by the ancient tradition. This historiographic choice privileges doctrinal continuity and the capacity for transmitting relatively stable philosophical thought. In antiquity, it emerged out of a series of factors that we should keep in mind to avoid viewing the post-Socratic period (and therefore Socrates himself) with inadequate tools and anachronistic categories of analysis.

In the early Hellenistic age, two fundamental factors reached maturity. First of all, the Aristotelian idea that philosophy constitutes a discrete discipline gained acceptance, with the parallel practice, encouraged by Aristotle himself, of doxography – (i.e., the collection of philosophical opinions). The work of Theophrastus on the philosophers of nature is the earliest example of this kind of literature. Second, several schools of the Hellenistic age, in strong competition with one another, endeavored to enhance their own authority and that of their leaders by establishing a prestigious pedigree – a role which fell to none other than Socrates. The Stoics, for instance, contended with the Academics for the Socratic heritage, tying themselves to one or more representatives of what would become the sequence Antisthenes – Diogenes of Sinope – Crates of Thebes – Zeno of Citium. Epicurean polemics against Socrates all but confirm that Socrates was still a very significant presence in the Hellenistic age (cf. Long, 1996, and Alesse, 2000).

Hence rivalry among the schools and continuity over time were important ingredients in the nascent philosophical historiography. The latter ingredient gave rise to the creation, wherever even remotely plausible, of a network of master–disciple relationships. In the case of the Socratics the theme of rivalry thus won ample coverage in the biographical and anecdotal tradition, and doctrinal disagreement (*diaphonia*), later a flagship in the Skeptical critique of dogmatic philosophies, proved useful to an erudite historical tradition interested mainly in establishing classifications, oppositions, and relations among the schools.

Socrates' popularity during the entire century following his death had attracted attention to the "Socratics," who were the natural link between Socrates and the

Hellenistic schools, to their role in relation to their master, and to their interrelationships. In the later fourth and the third centuries BCE there appeared, besides monographs on Socrates such as that of Demetrius of Phaleron, at least two works entitled *On the Socratics*: one by the Peripatetic Phaenias of Eresus (frr. 30–31 Wehrli), a contemporary of Theophrastus, and one by Idomeneus of Lampsacus (cf. D.L. 2.20). We know very little about either of these works. However, it is likely that, together with others that are also lost to us, they were used by Sotion of Alexandria around the end of the third century BCE when composing a multi-volume biographical work, *Successions of the Philosophers*. A distant heir to this is the *Lives of the Philosophers* by Diogenes Laertius, and it is to this work that we must now turn to begin to get an idea of the ancient tradition about the Socratics.[1]

At the end of the "Life of Socrates," Diogenes (2.47) offers a list of figures who fall into two groups: Plato, Xenophon, and Antisthenes (jointly "the greatest of the so-called Socratics"); and Aeschines, Phaedo, Euclides, Aristippus (jointly "the most illustrious of the traditional ten"). The "Life of Plato" takes up Book 3, followed by those of the Academics in Book 4 and those of Aristotle and the Peripatetics in Book 5. Antisthenes and the Cynics are found in Book 6, which is followed by the Stoics in Book 7. In Book 2, the "Life of Socrates" is followed by the *Lives* of Xenophon, Aeschines, Aristippus and the Cyrenaics, Euclides and the Megarians, and Stilpo. Very brief chapters are dedicated also to Phaedo (before the one on Euclides), Crito, Simon, Glaucon, Simmias, and Cebes. Diogenes Laertius sought, as much as possible, to maintain an order in his *Lives* that respected the structure of the successions. It is also very important to note that what loosely unites all the first-generation Socratics selected by Diogenes Laertius is not so much that they had known Socrates personally and had spent time with him (if this had been the criterion, we would also expect other names well known to readers of Plato and Xenophon), but rather that the ancient tradition attributes to all of them the composition of dialogues, whose titles are always mentioned, in a few cases in the form of a proper catalog. In confirmation of the great importance of this fact, suffice it to add that from the information scattered throughout Diogenes' biographies emerge the traces of a centuries-long erudite discussion of the authenticity of such works. In this discussion, Panaetius of Rhodes (*circa* mid second century BCE) undoubtedly played a significant role. In the light of this observation, one better understands the fact, surprising to us, that in D.L. 2. 47 Xenophon appears between two professional "philosophers": Plato and Antisthenes.

A Literary Genre

In the light of these facts, the following hypothesis appears quite plausible. When the ancients began to speak of "Socratics," they were referring primarily to authors who had something to do with Socrates. Only later does the label indicate philosophers in the strict sense. It then became problematic for ancient historiography, primarily, as

1. On the value of Diogenes Laertius as a source, see Mejer, ANCIENT PHILOSOPHY AND THE DOXOGRAPHICAL TRADITION, in this volume.

we have seen, because of the doctrinal differences separating those who got dubbed Socratics.

The oldest occurrences of the adjective "Socratic" appear in Aristotle. He uses it twice to indicate Socrates' theories or aspects of his method (*EE* VIII.1, 1246b34; *Rh*. II.20, 1393b4), twice in application to *logoi* (*Rh*. III.16, 1417a21; *Poet*. 1, 1447b11), and once with *dialogoi* (fr. 61 Rose = 15 Gigon, from the *de poetis*). Aristotle also informs us that the first to write "Socratic dialogues" was Alexamenus of Teos, of whom unfortunately we know nothing; that, unlike mathematical *logoi*, Socratic *logoi* have a moral character; and that verse mimes by Sophron of Syracuse and Socratic dialogues in prose are both part of a single genre, the genre which through language alone imitates character (*ethos*), the things that happen to people (*pathe*), and their actions (*praxeis*). It is no wonder that ancient scholars of rhetoric devoted much attention to the stylistic characteristics of the Socratic dialogue as a literary genre. Naturally, however, what interests modern scholars of philosophy most about this type of literature is the question of its content's purpose and historicity (an issue that exercised the ancients too). Granting that the mimetic character of the Socratic dialogues focused primarily on Socrates, what was the aim of those who composed them? Where, if at all, can one draw the line between the "philosophy" of Socrates and that of the author of the work? And furthermore, returning to Aristotle's statement, what does it mean, in the case of the *logoi Sokratikoi*, to imitate *ethos*, *pathe*, and *praxeis*? Does it mean to reproduce what Socrates did and said, or rather to reproduce his method, or, even more vaguely, to stay in the same thematic area in which Socratic conversation had operated? Where does the literary work end and the philosophical work begin? Where do we look for the thought of the dialogue's author, assuming that he really does intend to expound it? Can a dialogue be called Socratic even without having Socrates as its main character? The answers to these and to other questions familiar to scholars of Plato's dialogues encounter the difficulty caused by the fact that, apart from Plato and the rather special case of Xenophon (see Döring, 1998, pp. 182–200, and in this volume Morrison, SOCRATES), no other intact examples of Socratic dialogues have come down to us. The lack of terms of comparison has its negative effects, unfortunately, even when one concentrates on Plato alone.

For reasons of space, I will pass over the stimulus that the debate about Socrates and his condemnation (for example, the circulation of Polycrates' *Accusation against Socrates* in 393 BCE) brought to the composition of works by the Socratics. The most attentive modern interpreters of this body of literature, which must have been very vast and spread over at least half a century, rightly emphasize the importance of intertextuality and the part played by emulation and internal competition. All such elements, while inviting us to pay attention to the complex motivations that underlie the origin of a literary composition, also seem bound to distance us from the historical Socrates; for they warn us not to view these works as chronicles or to use them as authentic historical sources (Blank, 1985, p. 24). That said, we must not forget that, in the case of the *logoi Sokratikoi*, competition between works of the same genre (not to mention polemics against adversaries outside the Socratic circle) assumed a character that was rather different from that of a contest between men of letters. The subject-matter of this literature – the figure of Socrates, and the significance of his life and death

– concerned the "most important things": human nature, the foundations and purposes of action, good and bad, and happiness and unhappiness.

By deciding to write about Socrates (who himself had chosen not to write), the Socratics took the field on Greek *paideia*'s very own territory, in order to save from oblivion not so much themselves as the man who was their inspiration, along with his message. One of the more significant results of this decision, albeit one not always given due consideration by modern scholars, was the construction of an image of Socrates and the philosophical life capable of evoking, and at the same time re-interpreting or questioning, the great educational models and the moral values trans-mitted by the literary tradition. Hence a significant part of Socrates' heritage – the heritage by embracing which one could, in the eyes of the ancients, legitimately call oneself "Socratic" – lay, more than in living a philosopher's life, in conveying by way of the written word the path to whatever it was that only such a life seemed able to provide, using as a model the figure of Socrates, the virtuous and happy man *par excellence* (see Clay, 1994, p. 23). At the same time, this choice permitted the Socratics to present themselves as educators, and to compete with other figures (such as Isocrates) who, in the first half of the fourth century BCE, aspired to the same role.

The figure of Antisthenes appears particularly significant from this viewpoint. What we know of him, which is very little compared with his literary output and the role he must have played in Athens in the first half of the fourth century BCE, allows us nevertheless to grasp his precise intention. This was to re-read, from the Socratic viewpoint, the Greek cultural tradition, as represented by Homer, the mythological heritage (Heracles), and the history of far-off epochs and places (Cyrus the Great).

Antisthenes' exegetical, philosophical and educational activity was culturally effective. A significant example of this is offered by the similarity between the image of Odysseus transformed into a beggar by Athena upon his return to Ithaca (*Od.* 18.429–438) and the type of Cynic philosopher found in the Greco-Roman world until late antiquity. There are many indications making it plausible that Odysseus became a model for the Cynic tradition because of Antisthenes' interpretation, which in turn was closely connected with his personal image of Socrates. But not all of the many reinterpretations of the poetic heritage conducted under Socrates' banner of which we have traces go back to Antisthenes, even if he worked with particular authority in this area. Let me mention only one example: the theme of nakedness. This theme, well-known to readers of the final myth of Plato's *Gorgias* (523aff.), appears in an elegant remark attributed to Aristippus (*ap.* D.L. 2.73: "To the person who asked him the difference between the wise and the unwise, he said: 'send both of them naked among strangers and you will know'"). The response alludes to themes from the *Odyssey*, primarily from the account of the arrival of the shipwrecked Odysseus on the island of the Phaeacians (*Od.* 6.127ff.). Nakedness (which in the *Iliad* is associated rather with shame and humiliation) in the case of Odysseus is a way of allowing the hero to demonstrate his real nature, and allowing the Phaeacians to demonstrate their virtue of hospitality. The contrast between appearance and reality, exterior and interior, physical and psychic beauty (recall, too, the famous description in the third book of the *Iliad* of Odysseus as ambassador to Troy with Menelaus, especially 3.216–224), are all motifs that take us back to Socrates, and from Socrates they can be traced back to the Homeric poems.

124

More generally, reflection on wisdom/ignorance, virtue/vice (with the necessary connection between virtue and happiness), soul/body and freedom/slavery constitutes the common Socratic legacy (the "most important things"). His heirs elaborated in different ways on this legacy in their own writings, but always in relation – positive or negative – to the preceding tradition. They believed firmly that they were thus adhering to Socrates' message and faithfully perpetuating his image. They believed that linking him to illustrious precursors and to models well known to their readers guaranteed their writing both force and persuasive impact. In this way, the philosopher condemned by the Athenians was transformed into a figure powerful enough to be compared to the great heroes of the Greek tradition and to emerge victorious. He was at any rate destined, like them, to remain alive in the centuries to come.

Virtue and Happiness

Their contemporary and rival Isocrates also confirms the centrality of the theme of "virtue and happiness" in the Socratic tradition. In his *Against the Sophists* (ca. 390 BCE; see also the *Helen*, ca. 385 BCE), Isocrates argues against those who concern themselves with education and promise more than they can deliver. Again, taking up the epithet that in Aristophanes' *Clouds* (e.g., *Nub.* 102; *alazonas*) had been used for Socrates and his companions, Isocrates also speaks of *alazoneuesthai*, "bragging," and attacks those who spend their time in disputes (*hoi peri tas eridas diatribontes*, cf. *Sph.* 10), who make a show of seeking the truth and instead lie from the outset (*Sph.* 3–4):

> They have gone so far in their lack of scruple that they seek to persuade the youth that, should they choose to follow them, they will learn what must be done in life and through this knowledge they will become happy. And presenting themselves as teachers and dispensers of goods so precious, they are not ashamed of asking in exchange three or four minas. But if they were to sell one of the other goods at a price so much less than its value, they would not deny their folly. Instead, by valuing all virtue and happiness so little, they expect to become the teachers of others as if they had a mind. Furthermore, they claim to have no need of money, calling wealth filthy lucre and gold worth nothing, and they hold their hands out for a trifling gain and promise to make their disciples all but immortal. (Norlin's translation, slightly modified)

Later Isocrates again emphasizes that these people claim to teach wisdom and happiness (*Sph.* 7) without being able to provide genuinely useful rules of behavior either for the present or for the future. Admittedly, among those that Isocrates calls "sophists" there are diverse individuals and groups, who are also mutual rivals. Still, the connection made between knowledge, virtue, and happiness, and the motif of one's relationships to external goods (essentially, in this context, wealth) allow us to identify the Socratics, and above all Antisthenes, as the principal target of this passage. Granted that the moral use of poverty, which we will find later on in Zeno the Stoic (cf. Decleva Caizzi, 1993), dates back to Socrates, it was certainly Antisthenes who made it central.

From one who speaks of virtue, knowledge, good, and happiness, in short, of how to live (remember too the Socrates of Plato's *Gorgias*), one expects behavior consistent with the main thrust of his teaching. Every contradiction, whether real or invented, provides a welcome argument for adversaries. The theme of consistency (*akolouthia*), which will become a *topos* of Hellenistic biography, has ancient origins, as the passage in Isocrates attests. The confrontation between the "sophist" Antiphon and Socrates in Xenophon (*Mem.* 1.6) exhibits this theme in the debate over the meaning of happiness. Anecdotes about the Socratics, plentifully transmitted by the biographical tradition, confirm that in the eyes of the ancients any claimant to the legacy of Socrates (whose own consistency between thought and action lent much persuasive impact to arguments leading to conclusions radically opposed to the received wisdom) was, and was felt to be, expected to provide by his own conduct living proof of the truth of his convictions – that is, of his conception of happiness, good, and virtue.

In reviewing briefly what we know about the three Socratics the ancients considered to be founders of "schools," we will return to these important themes.

Antisthenes

Antisthenes (ca. 445–365 BCE), son of an Athenian citizen and a female slave, is described by the ancients as utterly loyal to Socrates, a rival of Plato and a source of philosophical inspiration for the Stoics. A prolific and refined writer, he was much appreciated for the literary quality of his style, which the ancients attributed to the rhetorical teaching of Gorgias. However, the historical thesis which separates two phases of his formation, namely a sophistical and a Socratic one, and so makes him an incomplete Socratic, a sort of sophist "converted" to Socratic philosophy, is a late construction and cannot be accepted without reservation. Isocrates' polemic testifies to Antisthenes' activity in Athens in the two decades following the condemnation of Socrates. The catalog of his works contains about 60 titles, ordered according to subject, in ten volumes. The titles in the first volume reveal his interest in rhetoric. The declamations *Ajax* and *Odysseus*, his only writings to come down to us intact, are found alongside polemical works against Isocrates and Lysias. The sixth and seventh volumes contained his linguistic and logical writings, in which he argued mostly against Plato regarding the method of acquiring and transmitting knowledge: *Truth, Sathon or On Contradiction, On Education or On Names, On the Use of Names, On Question and Answer*, and *On Opinion and Knowledge*. In these works, Antisthenes identified linguistic analysis as the tool for bringing into focus the network of predications that are proper to a subject and eliminating the non-proper ones, so as to arrive at the type of predication that he called "the proper account (*logos oikeios*), one for each thing" (Arist. *Met.* Δ.29, 1024b26ff. = *SSR* V A 152 = 47A Caizzi). From this was inferred the impossibility of contradiction, another thesis attributed to Antisthenes (D.L. 9.53 = *SSR* V Λ 154 = 48 Caizzi). The "proper account" must be identified, in all probability, with the "*logos* that shows what a thing was or is" (D.L. 6.3 = *SSR* V A 151 = 45 Caizzi). For Antisthenes this account replaced the unattainable definition of the thing's essence (*ti esti*) which his rival Plato had sought. He may have believed that the Platonic theory of Forms, which postulated as a condition for knowledge a reality that humans cannot apprehend (at least in this earthly life), carried with it the risk of skepticism ("I see a horse, not horseness," *SSR* V A 149 = 50 Caizzi). Aristotle informs us that Antisthenes denied

126

that the *ti esti* can be defined, inasmuch as the definition is only a "long account," but allowed that the quality (*poion*) can be stated and taught (*Met.* H.3, 1043b4ff. = *SSR* V A 150 = 44A Caizzi). From this, and from other evidence which is hard to interpret, one can hypothesize that Antisthenes' precise aim was to seek the qualities appropriate to a specific subject (mainly, it seems likely, of a moral nature) and that he suggested recourse to the cognitive tool of analogy (which Euclides, on the other hand, criticized: see below). In the case of moral concepts (such as courage, freedom, slavery, injustice, and impiety), the analysis of names ("the beginning of education is the investigation of names", Epict. *Diss.* 1.17.10–12 = *SSR* V A 160 = 38 Caizzi) included the testing of their use, with a clarification of contradictions and of abuses (one thinks of the celebrated page by Thucydides III.82, on the distortion of the meanings of words caused by war). In so doing, one would arrive finally at the name's unambiguous content, with a clear distinction between positive and negative, good and bad, truth and error. This faith in language as a cognitive and pedagogical instrument is probably criticized in Plato's *Cratylus*.[2]

A rather disordered list (D.L. 6.10–11) reports a few of the principal theses held by Antisthenes (many later taken up by the Stoics): virtue can be taught; nobility belongs to none other than the virtuous; virtue is sufficient for happiness; virtue needs nothing else except the strength of a Socrates; virtue is a matter of deeds and does not need a store of words and learning; virtue is the same for men and women; virtue is a weapon that cannot be taken away; wisdom (*phronēsis*) is an indestructible wall; walls of defense must be constructed with our own incontrovertible arguments; disrepute (*adoxia*) is a good thing, as is exertion or strain (*ponos*); the wise man is self-sufficient because others' goods belong to him. The references to *phronēsis*, to incontrovertible arguments, and to the fact that virtue cannot be lost, and the antithesis between the person who knows and the person who does not, confirm that for Antisthenes too virtue is identified with knowledge (cf. the work of Antisthenes already cited, *On Opinion and Knowledge*). In all probability these *doxai* were obtained from the second and third volumes of the catalog (which grouped together works that dealt with themes of ethics and politics), and from the fourth and fifth volumes (*Cyrus, The Greater Heracles or On Strength; Cyrus or On Kingship*).

In the same philosophical context (and not as a product of a separate "sophistic" phase) must be included his numerous works of Homeric exegesis (volumes eight and nine). Characters and episodes of the *Iliad* and the *Odyssey*, read in the light of Socratic principles, provided means of confirmation that were pedagogically effective because they linked these principles to the very source of the cultural tradition. So Socrates' morality, far from having the subversive character that had led to his condemnation in 399, turned out to be, on the contrary, the genuine heir to the values present in the tradition but distorted by vulgar thinking incapable of grasping the significance of the texts.

Antisthenes found in Odysseus the mythical antecedent of Socrates, interpreting him as a paradigm of the capacity for endurance and self-control ("have endurance, my heart: you have suffered worse pain," *Od.* 20.18, was to become a sort of motto of

---

2. See Modrak, PHILOSOPHY OF LANGUAGE, in this volume.

Cynic-Antisthenean Socraticism) in pursuit of true goodness. Of course Homer did not relate Odysseus' attitude explicitly to the achievement of happiness. However, on closer inspection, Odysseus' sufferings aim at the recovery of his social role and all those goods that, for the archaic culture, constituted the happiness of the individual. The hero's situation is re-interpreted as the struggle of an individual to overcome the adversities of fate, as an affirmation of worth and of interior strength through renunciation, albeit temporary, of his own rank. Read in the light of the Socratic message, the story of Odysseus becomes an opportunity for a more general reflection: not only are reputation, honors, and riches of little importance, but in fact adverse circumstances and an inferior social role facilitate the emergence of the person's true qualities. It is no accident that Antisthenes held *adoxia* (disrepute), as well as *ponos* (exertion or strain), to be a good thing. This is not because they are goods in and of themselves, but because they facilitate the achievement of the true goodness for which everyone strives. Material and physical goods hinder the recognition of the good, making the achievement of virtue difficult. That is why it is necessary to practice self-control (*enkrateia*), which requires the strength which, according to Antisthenes, Socrates had manifested in the highest degree.

In the fictitious speeches of Odysseus and Ajax competing for the arms of Achilles (the only surviving writings by Antisthenes), as in other fragments of Homeric exegesis (*SSR* V A 185–197 = 51–62 Caizzi), Antisthenes sides with Odysseus, emphasizing the hero's adaptability to circumstances. This becomes the mark of the individual's freedom from the restrictions imposed by conventions, from empty opinions, and from appearances. Antisthenes' Odysseus is a conqueror who challenges events, intervening in them actively and dominating them thanks to his intelligence and capacity for self-control. In him we find certain aspects of the Cynic philosopher, with the characteristic trait that the comic poets had already noticed in Socrates (for example, Ar. *Nub.* 362–363; Ameipsias, ap. D.L. 2.28 = fr. 9 Kassel and Austin): the contrast between exterior and interior, between a humble appearance and internal strength. This strength is expressed in behavior and language calculated to assert the personality of the philosopher, to attract the attention of and provoke reactions from those around him and, we could say, to create an effective image.

Alongside his works of Homeric exegesis, Antisthenes' writings on Heracles and on Cyrus the Great were of great importance. Like Odysseus, the Persian Cyrus was also depicted as the paradigm of the "true king" because of all he had managed to endure and to do. In this way the philosopher, the person who behaves like Odysseus for the sake of virtue – that is, in order to attain the good, which coincides with the fulfillment of human nature and human capacities – is the only one to earn the title of true king. In his soul reside all the good things that belong to a king: riches, honor, power. They depend only on him, and so no one can take them away. In this sense, the person who possesses virtue is happy, and virtue suffices for happiness. In this sense, again, only the "philosopher" is a king. This thought (which finds a large following in the Stoic tradition: see Bett, STOIC ETHICS, in this volume) seems in Antisthenes to leave very little room for external goods, which appear less as indifferent factors, capable of being transformed in either a positive or negative way depending on how they are used, than as morally negative obstacles on the path to virtue, and as alien once a person has achieved virtue. This position is consistent with the Socratic tenet that identifies virtue and happiness, but the notion of the sage it presupposes emphasizes detachment from the traditional goods, rather than a change, guided by reason, in the way one uses them.

The theme of *adoxia* and *ponos* was also confronted in one of Antisthenes' most famous works, the *Heracles*. Like Odysseus, Heracles offered a model of an exceptional personality, but unlike Odysseus he was, as the son of Zeus and a mortal, a demigod. In the moralizing version of the myth, he is adrift from society, wandering from place to place to perform arduous labors. If in the case of Odysseus the dominant theme is the contrast between appearance and reality, in Heracles' case it is rather the co-existence of the human and the divine and the manifestation of the divine nature in the actions of the human component. In this sense, the actions of Heracles express the struggle of the superior against the inferior: they can be seen as anticipating the hierarchical distinction between soul and body attributed to Socrates. In Antisthenes, however, this theme appears in a naturalistic setting far removed from Platonic metaphysical dualism. The contrast between "earthly" and "celestial" elements seems to be applied to Heracles in a fragment which is difficult to interpret because it is preserved only in the Syriac translation of Themistius (*SSR* V A 96 = 27 Caizzi). The sense of the passage seems to be that the outward manifestation of one's own interior forces coincides with the realization of true human nature, without any need for a transcendent order. The above-mentioned polemic against Plato on the existence of Forms ("I see a horse, not horseness") is linked to the probable rejection by Antisthenes of an other-worldly dimension radically separated from the sensible world: the divine coincides with nature, and it is nature that, through *phronēsis*, guides people toward the good.

The polemic against pleasure, expressed in the celebrated dictum "I would rather go mad than feel pleasure" (*SSR* V A 122 = 108 Caizzi), is prominent in Antisthenes. Yielding to pleasures implies an obscuring of reason and excludes the virtuous life; so one must train oneself to renounce them. How much importance Antisthenes attributed to reason can be inferred from D.L. 6.13 (*SSR* V A 134 = 63 Caizzi), where indestructible arguments are compared to the walls of the city, or from the report (Plut. *St. rep.* 1039E = *SSR* V A 105 = 67 Caizzi) that Chrysippus admired the statement of Antisthenes that one must possess either an intellect or a rope (to hang oneself). However, the anti-hedonistic component of Antisthenes' thought should not be exaggerated. His polemic did not rail against every type of pleasure, but rather advocated the substitution of a true pleasure for a false one. Xenophon attributes a similar notion to both Socrates (*Mem.* 1.6) and Antisthenes (*ap.* Xen. *Symp.* 4.34–45). In Stobaeus (*Anth.* 4.39.18 = *SSR* I C 313) we read: "To those who asked him what happiness is, Socrates answered: 'a pleasure which one should not regret'." The fact that Athenaeus (12.513A = *SSR* V A 127 = 110 Caizzi) explicitly attributes the same concept to Antisthenes shows that, in all probability, the source of the Socratic sentence was a work by the latter. In the following sentence we can also find a positive appreciation of certain pleasures (Stob. *Anth.* 3.29.65 = *SSR* V A 126 = 113 Caizzi): "One must seek out pleasures that follow exertion, not those that precede it." Compare also (Stob. *Anth.* 3.1.28 = *SSR* V A 125 = 93 Caizzi): "Neither a banquet without harmony nor wealth without virtue brings pleasure." These texts are a warning against the temptation to exaggerate the contrasts between Socrates' various disciples and in particular between Antisthenes and Aristippus, who was considered a pleasure-theorist by the ancient tradition.

Aristippus

Aristippus of Cyrene was attracted to Athens by the fame of Socrates. He was the first Socratic to earn a living by charging for his teaching. Numerous anecdotes refer to his sojourn at the court of Dionysius in Syracuse, linking him to Plato as well as to Diogenes of Sinope. Because he became in antiquity the representative *par excellence* of a life devoted to pleasure, his biography is full of stories and jokes based on this characteristic. Nevertheless, if the fictional encrustations are stripped away to reveal the historical core beneath, a "Socratic" figure emerges who is not so heterodox with respect to the master as he might seem. Unlike the case of Antisthenes, information on Aristippus' writings offered by Diogenes Laertius reveals an uncertain tradition (a volume that contained 25 dialogues, six books of diatribes, 12 titles identified by Sotion and Panaetius). In the unanimous opinion of scholars, the important doctrinal contributions attributed to the Cyrenaics (reported in D.L. 2.86ff.; S.E. *M* 7.191ff.) derive from his grandson, Aristippus the Younger, son of his daughter and disciple Arete.

Of Aristippus, we are told (D.L. 2.66–67) that:

> He was able to adapt himself to places, times, and persons and played his role appropriately in every circumstance. That is why he, more than others, enjoyed the favor of Dionysius, in that he always managed to make every situation acceptable. He enjoyed the pleasure of what was present, but declined to make an effort to enjoy what was not present. . . . Once Dionysius gave him his choice of one of three courtesans. He carried off all three, saying: "Paris paid dearly for giving the preference to one out of three." But when he had brought them as far as the porch, he let them go. To such extremes did he go both in choosing and in disdaining. Hence the saying [. . .]: "You alone are endowed with the gift to flaunt in robes or go in rags." (Hicks's translation, slightly modified)

The reference to Odysseus, and to the themes mentioned above, emerges clearly from [Plut.] *De vita et poesi Homeri* 2.150 (*SSR* IV A 55 = 30 Mannebach):

> And as Odysseus sometimes wore a furry and soft cloak and sometimes rags and knapsacks, sometimes he rested near Calypso and sometimes suffered the vexations of Irus and Melanthius, so Aristippus assuming such an image of life endured poverty and toil with a strength of spirit, and gave into pleasure without restraint.

Interestingly enough, these are all themes that appear in a fragment of Epictetus on Socrates (*ap.* Stob. *Anth.* 4.33.28):

> When Archelaus sent for Socrates with the intention of making him rich, Socrates ordered that he be told: "In Athens four quarters of flour can be bought for one obol and water flows from the springs for free. So if what I have is not enough for me, I will be enough for it, and so in this way it will be enough for me. And do you not see that Polus was accustomed to play the parts of Oedipus at Colonus, the outcast and the beggar, and

of Oedipus the King equally well? And then shall the man of noble nature be inferior to Polus and not play well any part assigned to him by the daimon? And will he not follow the example of Odysseus who even in rags did not have lesser dignity than in the rich and purple cloak?" (*Od.* 18.67; 19.225). (Oldfather's translation, slightly modified)

We cannot certainly identify the work from which this is quoted, but it confirms the moral use of the figure of Odysseus in the ancient Socratic tradition and its importance in the Socratics' creation of the image of Socrates.

In Aristippus, it seems central that the philosopher manifests his superiority through his control of the external world, with regard to which he keeps his own freedom to "choose" or to "reject." This motif appears also in Antisthenes, but in Aristippus the bitter attack on pleasure as an obstacle to virtue is absent. On the contrary, Aristippus maintained, perhaps not without reason, that the radical rejection of pleasure limits true liberty (see also Xen. *Mem.* 2.1.17 and *SSR* IV A 19): to experience pleasure without becoming enslaved to it is just as much a manifestation of virtue as the acceptance of the most drastic denials.

Two centuries later, Horace (*Ep.* 1.17.23ff. = *SSR* IV A 45 = 32A Mannebach) would sketch a fine portrait of Aristippus, contrasting him with the *Cynicum mordacem*:

Every aspect, every condition and every thing suited Aristippus. He could suit himself to any situation, though given the choice he would always choose the better. On the other hand, I wonder if the man clothed in the rags that Cynics always wear would be able to deal with a better circumstance. Aristippus would not require a purple robe; he would make his elegant way through the crowded streets wearing whatever there happened to be at hand, and would play one or the other role without ever cutting a poor figure. The other man would look at a nice cloak made out of beautiful cloth from Miletus as if he thought it was much worse than a dog or a snake. You would have to give him back his beggar's rags or he would die of the cold. So, give him back his rags and leave him alone to lead his foolish life. (Trans. by Ferry)[3]

Readers of Plato will think of Alcibiades' encomium of Socrates in the *Symposium* (220a; cf. 214a):

When we were cut off from our supplies, as often happens in the field, no one else stood up to hunger as well as he did. And yet he was the one man who could really enjoy a feast; and though he didn't much want to drink, when he had to, he could drink the best of us under the table. Still, and most amazingly, no one ever saw him drunk (as we'll straightaway put to test). (Trans. by Nehamas and Woodruff)

We can add that Socrates' sociability as described by Plato in the dialogue, the way in which he does not withdraw from his environment yet remains indefinably detached

---

3.   See also Sen. *Ep.* 5.6. Arguing against the ostentatious difference between the philosopher and the ruggedness of the Cynic way of life, Seneca writes: "He is a great man who uses earthenware dishes as if they were silver; but he is equally great who uses silver as if it were earthenware. It is a sign of an unstable mind not to be able to endure riches" (trans. by Gummere).

from others, is certainly closer to the image of Aristippus than to the more rugged one of Antisthenes. Some scholars have noted that Xenophon, although hostile to Aristippus, relies not on Socrates but on an exposition of Prodicus' written text in order to refute him (*Mem.* 2.1.21ff.). In that conversation Aristippus defended his ideal of freedom, presented as that which more than any other thing leads to happiness (2.1.11). In the name of this freedom he rejected the "city" and proclaimed himself "a stranger everywhere" (2.1.13). In Xenophon this choice appears tied to the theme of political power and manifests itself as a form of egoism. However, the remark assumes a more profound meaning if, yet again, one keeps in mind the literary theme of the beggar hero, wandering and stateless, and its philosophical interpretation (compare the remark on nakedness cited above, D.L. 2.73).

Aristippus' aim, to live an easy and pleasant life (Xen. *Mem.* 2.1.9–10: *rhasta te kai hedista bioteuein*), recalls the ancient model of the gods' happiness in the Homeric world, and his view of the means to that end does not presuppose the possession of many external goods, nor the exclusive enjoyment of physical pleasures. For everything external to be transformed into a good, what is needed is internal strength, wisdom, and the freedom and independence that prevent enslavement to anything external. Thus even Aristippus is, in his way, a devotee of *enkrateia*. At all events, even for him, as a true Socratic, it is *phronēsis* (wisdom), that allows a person to redirect the whole life toward the good (cf. also his attack on useless sciences, such as mathematics, for not having the good as their object, *SSR* IV A 170, 171).

Euclides

In the case of Euclides of Megara, the third of the Minor Socratics who according to the ancients created a school, the biographical and anecdotal tradition is singularly impoverished. The brief chapter by Diogenes Laertius (2.106–113) mentions numerous figures, along with varied kinds of information: Eubulides of Miletus, Alexinus of Elis, Euphantus of Olynthus, Apollonius Cronus, Diodorus Cronus, Ichthyas, and Clinomachus of Thurii. All these are connected, directly or indirectly, to Euclides. The last one named in this group is Stilpo of Megara, whose Life is much richer in information and takes up all of sections 113–120. The place of the life of Stilpo in this tradition is justified by personal relations among philosophers, relations whose variability by itself indicates their fictional character. For instance, in Cic. *Acad.* II. (*Lucullus*) 42.129 (*SSR* II A 31 = 26A Döring) Euclides is inserted into a succession that starts from Xenophanes and includes Parmenides and Zeno of Elea. The same succession, but with, significantly, Stilpo of Megara in place of Euclides, is repeated by Aristocles, *On Philosophy* (fr. 27 Döring). In D.L. 2.106 (*SSR* II A 30 = fr. 31 Döring) we read that Euclides "applied himself to the writings of Parmenides" (*kai ta Parmenideia metecheirizeto*).

The so-called Megarian school was never a genuine institution nor did it consist in a unified philosophical position. Alongside the label "Megarians," we find also "Dialecticians" and "Eristics." It is difficult to say whether these terms are used to characterize distinct groups. Besides Euclides' and Stilpo's common origin from Megara, the aim of tracing the tradition of Pyrrhonist Skepticism back to Socrates probably also played a determining role in the Hellenistic construction of the Megarian succession and "school" (cf. D.L. 9.61). In light of these data and of what we know of the orientations of Hellenistic historiography, the evaluation of possibly Eleatic themes ought to follow investigation of Euclides' primary cultural relationship with Socrates, not be a point of departure for the reconstruction of Euclides' philosophy in its entirety.

Diogenes Laertius (2.108) reports the titles of six dialogues, from which it appears that Euclides engaged fully in the writing of Socratic literature: *Lamprias, Aeschines, Phoenix, Crito, Alcibiades, Eroticus*. Three of these titles deal with characters in the Socratic circle. Even the *Eroticus* recalls a Socratic theme which, as well as in Plato, was present in the *Alcibiades* of Aeschines (*SSR* VI A 53 = 12 Dittmar) and probably also in the *Heracles* by Antisthenes (*SSR* V A 92 = 24 Caizzi). We can say nothing for certain about *Lamprias* and *Phoenix*. The only verbatim fragment we possess (reported by Stob. *Anth.* 3.6.63 = *SSR* II A 11 = 19 Döring), contrasting sleep and death (cf. Hom. *Il.* 14.231; Hes. *Theog.* 212; 756–759) which are represented as two daemons, is most probably taken from one of these works, but it is impossible to reconstruct its context. One of the few interesting anecdotes, reported by the Platonist philosopher Taurus (*ap.* Gell. *NA* 7.10.1–4 = *SSR* II A 2 = 1 Döring), tells how, in order to listen to Socrates even after the Athenians had forbidden the Megarians entrance into the city, Euclides would arrive in Athens at sunset, dressed as a woman, leaving again at dawn, still disguised, and traveling on foot between the two cities. The recourse to disguise (like Odysseus on his arrival at Ithaca) certainly indicates indifference toward appearances.

Plato mentions Euclides as present at Socrates' death along with the other Socratics (*Phd.* 59b–c). Furthermore, in the surviving version of the preface to the *Theaetetus*, he is the person made responsible for composing the written version of the conversation that took place many years earlier between Socrates and the young Theaetetus.[4] Finally, taking into account that Plato and others took refuge in Megara after Socrates' death (Hermodorus *ap.* D.L. 2.106), and the absence of anecdotes alluding to polemics between Euclides and Plato, it appears plausible that their relations were friendly. It is much more difficult to determine how far they agreed or disagreed philosophically, and whether – and if so, to what extent – Plato's dialogues contain allusions to Euclides. Modern attempts to identify such references (for instance behind the "friends of the Forms" in Plato's *Sophist*) have not led to secure results. No mention of discussion between Euclides and Antisthenes has reached us.

Regarding his thought, the principal testimony is in Diogenes Laertius (2.106 = *SSR* II A 30 = 24 Döring): "He held the good to be one (*hen to agathon*), called by many names: sometimes wisdom, sometimes god, sometimes intelligence, and so on. All that is contradictory to the good he used to reject, maintaining that it has no existence." To this we may add D.L. 2.161 (*SSR* II A 32 = 25 Döring), from which we learn that, for the Megarians, virtue is one thing, called by many names. Cicero (*Acad.* II. [*Lucullus*] 42.129, cited above) writes that the Megarians said "the sole good is that which is

---

4. From the *Theaetetus* one infers that Euclides was still alive in 369, yet he is not cited by Diodorus as being among those who were alive in 366. His date of birth can be no later than 450.

always one and alike and the same. These authors also took much from Plato" (trans. Rackham).

Euclides' concepts and terminology, but above all his insertion into the Eleatic succession by ancient doxography, underlie the dominant interpretation of his philosophy as the product of contamination between Eleatic and Socratic thought, with greater emphasis placed sometimes on the former component, sometimes on the latter. The most determined reaction against this exegetical line came from Kurt von Fritz (1931), followed more recently by Klaus Döring (1972 and 1998) and Gabriele Giannantoni (1990). Von Fritz has shown that the emphasis is not on being but rather on the good, and that the idea that what is opposite to the good is non-existent derives from the recognition of the good's unity and identity in all its manifestations. Even in the scant testimony on Euclides we can glimpse the themes we tend to consider typically Socratic: what really matters is the moral good; the person who knows the good will do it; the person who does something bad acts in the mistaken belief that it is good. Along the same lines, Giannantoni (*SSR* 1990 vol. 4, n. 5, pp. 51–60) has observed that the thesis of Euclides is the one held by the Socrates of Plato's *Protagoras* and operative in Plato's "Socratic" dialogues, that the virtues form a unity, understood as *epistēmē* of what is good and bad.

That Euclides attacked proofs not from their premises but from their conclusion (D.L. 2.107 = *SSR* II A 34 = 29 Döring) may be likened to the Socratic method of refutation. Apparently, he also criticized argument from analogy, maintaining that it must be drawn either from similar or from dissimilar elements: if from similar elements, one should concern oneself with the things themselves rather than with those which are similar to them; if from dissimilar elements, the comparison fails.

Timon of Phlius (D.L. 2.107 = *PPF* fr. 28), who attacks all the Socratics, calling them chatterers, speaks of the "wrangling (*eridantēs*) Euclides, who infused the Megarians with a frenzied love of strife (*erismou*)." This judgment makes Euclides responsible for an argumentative method that other sources attribute to his compatriot Stilpo (cf. D.L. 2.113, 119). However, the dialectical method developed and refined by Socrates and his followers was considered eristic, and was popularly confused with the practices of persons who had nothing to do with Socrates, as is clear from the polemic by Isocrates cited above. And the care with which Plato sets out in the *Euthydemus* to show how Socratic dialectic differs from Eleatic or Protagorean eristic points in the same direction. One must not forget that the qualification "eristic" refers to the intention of the person propounding the argument, not to the argument itself. The *logos* can present either a fallacy or a serious linguistic *aporia*. An anecdote reported in D.L. 2.30, where Socrates deplores Euclides' commitment to eristic *logoi*, very likely reflects, as do other anecdotes of the kind, polemics internal to the Socratic circle. It is certain, however, that the philosophers' tradition associated with the "Megarian school" concentrated their efforts in the logical-linguistic area. And by employing celebrated paradoxes such as the Veiled Man and the Liar, they cast light on problems and *aporiai* that still constitute a challenge for philosophy.[5]

5. For the treatment of these puzzles by the Stoics, see Ierodiakonou, STOIC LOGIC, in this volume.

Bibliography

Principal Editions of Fragments

Decleva Caizzi, F. (1966). *Antisthenis Fragmenta.* Milan and Varese: Cisalpino.

Döring, K. (1972). *Die Megariker. Kommentierte Sammlung der Testimonien.* Amsterdam: Grüner.

Giannantoni, G. (1990). (Cited as *SSR*). *Socratis et Socraticorum Reliquiae.* (4 vols.) Naples: Bibliopolis. (Contains very extensive bibliography and a volume of notes).

Mannebach, E. (1961). *Aristippi et Cyrenaicorum Fragmenta.* Leiden: Brill.

Works Cited

Alesse, F. (2000). *La Stoa e la tradizione socratica.* Naples: Bibliopolis.

Blank, D. (1985). "Socratics Versus Sophists on Payment for Teachings." *Classical Antiquity,* 4, 1–49.

Calder III, W. F. and Mansfeld, J. (eds.). (1999). *Hermann Diels (1848–1922) et la science de l'antiquité.* Entretiens sur l'Antiquité Classique 45. Vandoeuvres-Genève: Fondation Hardt.

Clay, D. (1994). "The Origins of the Socratic Dialogue." In P. A. Van der Waerdt (ed.), *The Socratic Movement* (pp. 23–47). Ithaca, NY: Cornell University Press.

Decleva Caizzi, F. (1993). "The Porch and the Garden: Early Hellenistic Images of the Philosophical Life." In A. W. Bulloch, E. Gruen, A. A. Long, and A. Stewart (eds.), *Images & Ideologies: Self-Definition in the Hellenistic World* (pp. 303–29). Berkeley, Ca.: University of California Press.

Diels, H. (1901). (Cited as *PPF*). *Poetarum philosophorum fragmenta.* Berlin: Weidmann.

——. (1965). *Doxographi Graeci,* 4th edn. Berlin: de Gruyter. (Original work published 1879.)

Döring, K. (1998). "Sokrates, die Sokratiker und die von ihnen begründeten Traditionen." In *Die Philosophie der Antike,* 2.1 (pp. 139–364). Basel: Schwabe. (Contains complete bibliography from 1926 down to 1994, with additions up to 1996.)

Ferry, D. (trans.). (2001). *The Epistles of Horace.* New York: Farrar, Straus and Giroux.

Grote, G. (1885). *Plato and the Other Companions of Sokrates.* (4 vols.). 2nd edn. London: Murray. (Original work published 1865.)

Gummere, R. M. (1989). *Seneca: Ad Lucilium, Epistulae Morales.* Loeb Classical Library. Cambridge, Mass.: Harvard University Press and London: Heinemann. (Original work published 1917.)

Hicks, R. D. (1970). *Diogenes Laertius. Lives of Eminent Philosophers.* Loeb Classical Library. Cambridge, Mass.: Harvard University Press/London: Heinemann. (Original work published 1923.)

Kassel, R. and Austin, C. (eds.). (1991). *Poetae comici Graeci.* Berlin/New York: de Gruyter.

Long, A. A. (1996). "Socrates in Hellenistic Philosophy." In A. A. Long, *Stoic Studies* (pp. 1–34). Cambridge: Cambridge University Press.

Nehamas, A. and Woodruff, P. (trans.). (1989). *Plato, Symposium.* Indianapolis: Hackett.

Norlin, G. (1980). *Isocrates.* (3 vols.). Loeb Classical Library. Cambridge, Mass.: Harvard University Press/London: Heinemann.

Rackham, H. (1972). *Cicero. De Natura Deorum, Academica.* Loeb Classical Library. Cambridge, Mass.: Harvard University Press/London: Heinemann.

von Fritz, K. (1931). *Megariker, Realencyclopädie der classischen Altertumswisseschaft.* Suppl. 5, 702–24. An abbreviated version appears in K. von Fritz, (1978). *Schriften zur griechischen Logik.* (vol. 2, pp. 75–92). Stuttgart-Bad Cannstatt: Frommann-Holzboog.

Zeller, E. (1922). *Die Philosophie der Griechen in ihrer geschichtlichen Entwicklung.* 5th edn. Leipzig: Reisland. (Original work published 1844–6.)

8

The Platonic Dialogue

CHRISTOPHER GILL

Introduction

The idea that the Platonic dialogue is a distinctive literary form, which is in some special way the vehicle of Plato's philosophical objectives, goes back to antiquity. In origin, the Platonic form belongs to the genre of writing (the "Socratic dialogue") used by his followers to perpetuate the character and style of argument of Socrates after his trial and execution in 399 BCE (Kahn, 1996, ch. 1). But, although most of the other Socratic dialogues are now lost, it seems clear that the Platonic version of this genre has distinctive qualities which scholars, ancient and modern, have tried to define. Two comments from antiquity exemplify this attempt, by Diogenes Laertius (early third century CE) and Proclus (fifth century CE):

> A dialogue is a discourse in question-and-answer form on some philosophical or political topic, with appropriate characterization of the figures presented and appropriate style of language. Dialectic is a technique of discourse by which we either refute or establish some assertion through question-and-answer between those engaging in dialogue. (D.L. 3.48)

> The preludes of the Platonic dialogues fit in with their overall objectives and are not devised for dramatic impact . . . nor do they just aim to tell a story . . . but are linked with the overall project of the dialogues. (Procl. *In Alc.* 308.11.24ff. Westerink)

Diogenes identifies features which were, to some extent, shared with other Socratic dialogues but were developed in an exceptional way by Plato: the representation of "dialectic," that is, creative philosophy conducted through one-to-one, directed, question-and-answer, presented in a literary form that deploys dramatic characterization. Proclus' view is more complex: it is that a Platonic dialogue constitutes a unified literary-philosophical medium in which all aspects, including the scene-setting preludes, are subordinated to an overall conceptual message. These are just two strands in a rich tradition of interpretative responses to the Platonic dialogue form, which we can partly reconstruct from antiquity and which forms an increasingly important part of the modern reception of Plato's works.

This chapter explores this tradition in three ways. First, I outline three broad types of interpretative reading of the Platonic dialogues, illustrated by representative ancient and modern examples. In some cases, I also indicate how the style of reading is linked with a specific conception of what is central to the project of philosophy. Second, I

136

consider how modern scholarship on the dialogue form is interconnected with the division of Platonic works into chronologically distinct groups and with the question how far and in what sense Plato's thought develops – two highly controversial topics. Third, I offer more extended treatment of one of the three styles of reading outlined here (the "maieutic" approach), which I combine with an attempt to define Plato's thinking on dialectic and to characterize Plato's overall philosophical outlook.

Styles of Reading and Conceptions of Philosophy

The first style of reading is so widespread and unself-conscious that it may escape notice as a distinct mode of interpretation at all (though it is one). This approach, while recognizing that the dialogues constitute a distinctive literary form, treats them as, in effect, a wholly explicit vehicle of Socratic-Platonic philosophy. The assumption is that the main speaker, who in each case dominates the discussion (Socrates in most of the dialogues, various figures in the late dialogues) is the mouthpiece of the philo-sophical project. The focus of this project is variously interpreted by those who read the dialogues in this way. For most interpreters, ancient and modern, the main con-cern is ideas or theories, often understood as teachings or doctrines. These ideas are sometimes taken to form a connected system of doctrines, which are explicated in a certain sub-group of dialogues or in the dialogues as a whole. Versions of this reading can be found in Aristotle and in the school of Plato in its various phases from the late fourth century BCE until the end of antiquity.[1] This way of reading has also been common among modern Platonic scholars; "unitarianism" (reading all the dialogues as expressing a single set of ideas) has been adopted notably by Paul Shorey (1904) and Harold Cherniss (1936) and is widely assumed in much recent French scholar-ship, for instance by Luc Brisson (1998) and Jean-François Pradeau (2002).

A second focus for this way of reading has been on methods of argument and on quality of argumentation. This concern also goes back to Aristotle (see further Vlastos, 1991, pp. 91–8) and later thinkers in the Platonic tradition. The Platonic dialogues were sometimes categorized in antiquity by reference to the kind of argumentative method being applied (D.L. 3.49–62; Tarrant, 1993). In modern times, this has been the central concern of the "analytic" school of interpretation, originally Anglo-American but now more widespread. A powerful influence on this group was the preoccupation with philosophical method, especially logical and conceptual analysis, among early twentieth-century thinkers such as Frege, Russell, and Wittgenstein. For leading figures of this group, especially G.E.L. Owen and Gregory Vlastos, modern methods of analysis served as a model of what counted as "philosophy" and also pro-vided standards by which Plato and other ancient thinkers were judged. The typical form of interpretative discussion is an analysis of a specific stretch of argument in a single Platonic dialogue, taken either as displaying argumentative method or as attempting to establish or undermine a determinate claim. One central concern for this

---

1. See Kahn, 1996, pp. 79–87, on Aristotle; Sedley, 1996, on Platonic approaches; and Hoffmann, WHAT WAS COMMENTARY IN LATE ANTIQUITY?, in this volume on Neoplatonic commentary.

137

approach has been the methodology and outcome of Socratic *elenchus* (the systematic, inferential cross-examination of interlocutors by Socrates in the early Platonic dialogues, leading to the exposure of inconsistency in their belief-sets (Vlastos, 1994). Another has been the question of the cogency of the critique of the (Platonic) theory of Forms in the first part of the *Parmenides* and also whether Plato thought this critique could be answered (Owen, 1953, 1985; Vlastos, 1954).

The inverse of this way of reading the dialogues (that is, as explicit vehicles of Platonic philosophy) is the "esoteric" approach. The key mark of this approach is the belief that Plato's most profound and systematic doctrines were not found in the dialogues but were taught through oral instruction to advanced students in Plato's school, the Academy. The unwritten doctrines centered on two mathematico-ontic principles, the One and the Undivided Many; the system of ideas based on these principles is held to underpin Platonic philosophy as a whole, including (what we call) metaphysics, epistemology, and ethics, categorical distinctions not drawn by Plato. This view draws on evidence in Aristotle and the later ancient Platonic tradition for Plato's unwritten doctrines. For this interpretation, the written dialogues are intended only as preliminary (or "propaideutic") to systematic oral instruction. The dialogues offer provisional indications of the kind of doctrines and philosophical system taught comprehensively in the Academy. The provisional character of the dialogues is signalled by explicit indications of doctrinal incompleteness (e.g., *Rep.* VI, 504a–506a; *Plt.* 284d; *Ti.* 48b–c, 53d), as well as being illustrated by contrast with reports of the more systematic oral doctrines. The dominant role in the Platonic dialogues of Socrates and other main speakers (such as the Eleatic Stranger), by contrast with the interlocutor, is sometimes taken as exemplifying the fundamentally didactic and dogmatic character of Platonic philosophizing. This approach, broached in the early nineteenth century, was developed systematically by Konrad Gaiser and Hans-Joachim Krämer; current leading exponents are Thomas Szlezák (e.g., 1985, 1999) and Giovanni Reale (e.g., 1997).

The third interpretative response is one that attaches the highest importance to the fact that Plato wrote in dialogues and to the specific character and form of those dialogues. For this view, the dialogues are neither a full explication of philosophical doctrines or method nor a deliberately incomplete and preliminary version of a system of oral instruction. The key thought is, rather, that the dialogues are written in such a way as to stimulate the reader to think for himself or herself about the ideas discussed. The dialogues present genuine (and not simply "propaideutic") philosophizing but they are not supposed to be offering fully worked-out, authoritative conclusions. It is for the reader to take the argument further, either by responsive interpretation or by independent philosophical enquiry. This approach draws on several salient features of the dialogues themselves, taken as offering a model for philosophical activity or a guide to interpretation. These include the presentation by Socrates of his characteristic form of dialogue as a method of "shared search" (*suzētēsis*)[2] and one which is, in principle, incomplete and ongoing, as is indicated by the unresolved, "aporetic" conclusions of many dialogues. They also include Socrates' characterization of his

---

2. See e.g. *Chrm.* 166c–d; *Grg.* 505e–506a; *Prt.* 348c5–e1; *Sph.* 218b–d; *Phlb.* 19a–c; *Plt.* 258b–c, 285c–d; *Tht.* 150a–151e.

dialectical method in the *Theaetetus* as "maieutic" (midwifely), designed to bring to birth the ideas of the others rather than supplying them with fully developed ideas of his own (*Tht.* 149–151). Other texts often cited in support of this reading are the criticisms made of writing as a medium for philosophical communication in the *Phaedrus* (275–278) and the *Seventh Letter* (340–344; cf. Gill, 1992). Writing is there said to give readers a false impression of having knowledge which they have not acquired for themselves by active dialectical enquiry. The Platonic dialogue is thought to be designed to use writing as a catalyst to independent enquiry in a way that counteracts the normal drawbacks of the medium – an idea that goes back to Schleiermacher in the early nineteenth century (Szlezák, 1997).

This way of reading dialogues can also be found in antiquity. David Sedley (1996, pp. 98–103) has shown how a Platonist commentator of the late first century BCE saw the *Theaetetus* not just as the origin of the idea of philosophy as a maieutic process but also as a dialogue which was written in a maieutic (midwifely) way, stimulating readers to draw their own conclusions. In modern times, there have been many forms of this style of reading, some by scholars who hold versions of the scholarly approaches already outlined (for instance, analytic or esoteric). Of the three ways of reading the dialogues surveyed here, I think that the third is the one that is being pursued most vigorously in current Plato scholarship. It has also given rise to some of the most penetrating studies of specific Platonic dialogues and of philosophically suggestive features of their form.

Within this line of interpretation, a major point of distinction is between those who think that Plato as author has a clear and determinate view about the intended conclusion of the reader's reflection and those who stress, rather, the openness of the outcome. Those who take the first line include followers of Leo Strauss. "Straussians" believe that the meaning of Platonic dialogues does not lie on their surface, and that sustained interpretative attention is required to decode that meaning, based on the assumption that each detail of argument or dramatic presentation subserves an overall purpose (a view prefigured by Proclus, p. 136 above). In most Straussian accounts (e.g., Strauss, 1964; Bloom, 1968), this is combined with the assumption that this sustained independent interpretation, if correctly carried out, will lead to certain, very definite, conclusions. A reading of the *Republic*, for instance, should lead to the con-clusion that philosophers should *not* engage in politics in conventional societies and that programmes of social reform, of the kind undertaken in many Western countries in modern times, are fundamentally misguided (cf. Ferrari, 1997; also, more critically, Burnyeat, 1985).

For other scholars, writing from a variety of standpoints, the intended outcome of interpretation or reflection is taken to be less predetermined. This view is shared by some whose approach is, broadly, literary-philosophical. These scholars focus on, for instance, the implications of the studied anonymity of the Platonic dialogue form and of Plato's life-long presentation of philosophy as inseparable from shared dialectical enquiry.[3] Versions of this view are also sometimes adopted by esoteric or analytic scholars. Rafael Ferber (1991), for instance, adopts the esoteric approach in a relatively

---

3. See, e.g., Gonzalez, 1995; Griswold, 1988, 2002; Press, 1993, 2000; Stokes, 1986.

non-dogmatic form, and maintains that both Plato's written teachings and the ideas in the dialogues were presented by Plato only as a provisional attempt to formulate knowledge of truth and not as an authoritative system (cf. Gill, 1993). Analogously, Michael Frede (1996), writing from an analytic standpoint, argues that Plato's continuing use of the dialogue form throughout his writing career signifies a disavowal of philosophical authority. Even in a dialogue such as the *Sophist*, the central part of which reaches determinate, and conceptually powerful, conclusions (about the nature of false statement), Plato signals the limitations of what the dialogue achieves. Plato does so especially by alluding to a further dialogue, the *Philosopher*, which will offer a more positive and definitive account of philosophical knowledge than the *Sophist* – but which is never written. The implication is that it is up to us, as responsive readers, to work out for ourselves what the *Philosopher* should have contained (cf. Sayre, 1992). Although modern pioneers of the analytic approach, such as Owen and Vlastos, were not inclined to see the dialogue form as being of special philosophical importance, more recent analytic scholars have been more disposed to think that it is and that analytic readings can be advanced in this way. Gill and McCabe (1996), a collection mostly by analytic scholars, is centered on the aim of examining the relevance of the dialogue form for the key conceptual issues of the late dialogues – a group of dialogues which received specially close attention from analytic scholars. The idea that it is very important to reach an independent understanding of conceptual problems raised by the dialogues has, in fact, been fundamental for the analytic approach; and it is now more widely recognized that study of the distinctive features of the dialogues can form an integral part of that process.

The Dialogue Form and Periodization

As is indicated in the preceding survey of approaches, the view taken of the role of the dialogue form in Plato is closely bound up with the larger interpretation of Plato's philosophical aims and methods. I explore this connection further by showing how the question of the dialogue form is linked with one of the key issues of current Platonic scholarship: that of periodization, and the question whether and in what sense Platonic philosophy develops. Subsequently, I offer and defend my own view on that issue by exploring further the third approach just outlined, the interpretation of Platonic dialogues as maieutic.

A common way of subdividing the Platonic dialogues, at least in modern times, is into early, middle, and late; this subdivision is also linked with certain widely held views of the function of the dialogue form in the relevant period. The main aim of the early dialogues (like "Socratic dialogues" by other ancient authors such as Aeschines and Xenophon) is taken to be to perpetuate the character, themes, and mode of argument of the historical Socrates. The "Socratic dialogue" is, in some sense, a dramatic genre, though we do not know if these dialogues were written for performance, recitation, or private reading. The drama of the early Platonic dialogues centers especially on the recreation of Socrates' trial-speech and his response to imprisonment before execution (*Apology, Crito*). It also centers on Socrates' characteristic method of dialectic (*elenchus*) either with relatively naïve interlocutors (e.g.,

Euthyphro, Laches) or in gladiatorial contests with more intellectually sophisticated figures (*Protagoras, Gorgias*). The representation of the figure of Socrates and his interaction with others is elaborated in the middle dialogues, which dramatize his tough-minded response to the prospect of death (*Phaedo*), to sexual desire and alcohol (*Symposium*), or to the dialectical challenge of an immoralist (*Republic*, Book I). At the same time, these dialogues are often seen as vehicles by which Plato puts forward in a more constructive and explicit way ideas (for instance about Forms or the immortality of the soul) which go beyond the thinking of the historical Socrates, even if they have their roots in Socratic enquiries. In the late dialogues, Plato is sometimes seen as retaining the dialogue form only as a convention in works which have become virtual monologues (*Laws*) or, indeed, actual monologues (*Timaeus-Critias*). A more positive view of the function of the late dialogues, held particularly by analytic scholars, is that they are used to demonstrate Plato's intellectual independence, both from Socrates and from his own earlier ideas. In the *Theaetetus* and *Philebus*, Plato dramatizes again the Socratic method of dialectical cross-examination, but with certain methodological and conceptual modifications (Burnyeat, 1977; D. Frede, 1996b). In the *Parmenides, Sophist, Statesman*, we find explicit or implied criticism of the middle period theory of Forms and related theories,[4] combined with the exploration of new forms of dialectical enquiry (notably, definition of real kinds by "division"); the function of the dialogue form in the late works is taken to display these diverse forms of intellectual independence and creativity.

Views of this type are relatively common in modern Platonic scholarship. Ideas about periodization are also often associated with accounts of the development of Plato's philosophy during his writing-career. To some extent, this concern goes back to antiquity. Aristotle identifies certain ideas as Socratic (for instance, the denial of *akrasia* or weakness of will in the *Protagoras*), while treating the theory of Forms in the *Republic* as Platonic (Vlastos, 1991, pp. 91–8). However, this way of reading the dialogues is by no means universal in antiquity. Later Platonists and the Stoics, whose ethical ideas are strongly influenced by Platonic thought, do not seem to draw a clear distinction between Socratic and Platonic versions of the idea that virtue is fundamental to happiness (Annas, 1999, ch. 2). Unitarianism was an assumption of much ancient commentary in the later Platonic school; hence, when commenting on the *Theaetetus*, Platonists tried to find consistency between the epistemological ideas of the *Theaetetus, Meno*, and *Republic* (Sedley, 1996). They looked for consistency between dialogues seen in modern scholarship as belonging to different phases of Plato's thought.

The attempt to track the stages of the development of Plato's thought on key issues has been a central preoccupation of English-language scholarship, especially in the analytic approach. A related aim has been to correlate this with a chronological ordering of the dialogues, especially through the study of style-markers which are independent of changes in content (that is, stylometry; cf. Brandwood, 1992). Vlastos,

---

4. Explicit criticism, *Prm.* 129a–135c; implied criticism, e.g. *Sph.* 246b–249d; on the question whether there are changes in Plato's later political theory, see Gill, 1995, 301–4; Rowe, 2000; and in this volume Lane, PLATO'S POLITICAL PHILOSOPHY.

for instance, set out an influential four-stage framework for subdividing the dialogues (elenctic, transitional, middle, late). This framework was designed to identify a phase in which Plato's aim was to dramatize Socratic method and ideas (the elenctic dialogues) and then to chart his progressive emancipation from Socratic method and ideas (Vlastos, 1991, ch. 2). Owen focused, rather, on the idea that the late dialogues were dominated by Plato's critique and rejection of his earlier (middle-period) theory of Forms and dualistic epistemology. He argued at one point (Owen, 1953) that the apparently dualist *Timaeus* should be re-dated as middle to ensure that the late period (inaugurated by the critique of the theory of Forms in the first part of the *Parmenides*) was seen as consistently critical of idealist metaphysics and epistemology. That move has not been generally followed. A more common response among later analytic interpreters (such as Sayre, 1983; McCabe, 1994; and D. Frede, 1996b) has been to read the late dialogues as, by implication, rethinking Platonic philosophy in a way that replaces middle-period dualism with more unified conceptual frameworks for understanding epistemology, the cosmos, or metaphysical categories.

This project of trying to track Platonic development and its chronology has recently been subjected to strong criticism from within English-language scholarship. John Cooper, in the introduction to the Hackett collected translation of Plato (1997, pp. viii–xviii), has highlighted the weak evidential support for many of the assumptions used to construct a chronology of the dialogues; the Hackett collection is ordered on the basis of Thrasyllus' (first century BCE) arrangement. Charles Kahn (1996), writing from a broadly unitarian standpoint, has criticized both aspects of the analytic periodization of the Platonic works: the distinction between Socratic and Platonic works and that between middle-period and critical Platonic works. One of the most cogent features of his critique has been directed at the idea that stylometry can be used to construct a Platonic chronology by which to map philosophical development on a linear, dialogue-by-dialogue basis. He argues, persuasively, that the only solid outcome of Platonic stylometry, one achieved about a century ago, was to establish three broad stylistic groups – which *may* be chronologically distinct. These are: group 3 (late dialogues) – *Laws, Philebus, Sophist, Statesman, Timaeus-Critias*; group 2 (middle), *Phaedrus, Parmenides, Republic, Theaetetus*; group 1 (early) all other dialogues. He argues that stylometry provides no means for identifying a precise chronological sequence within each group (Kahn, 1996, pp. 42–8, cf. 2002), a claim reinforced on stylometric grounds by Paul Keyser (1991). Kahn's arguments, if accepted, have radical implications for the future study of Platonic development, bearing, in particular, on the limits of what we know about this development.

How do these recent debates on chronology and development relate to the question of the interpretation of the dialogue form? They do so, in part, because, as indicated earlier, the understanding of the function of the dialogue form has, typically, rested on a specific picture of Platonic development, with certain assumptions about which dialogues should go in each group. For instance, the *Symposium* and *Phaedo* are widely seen as middle-period, "Platonic," works, but, as Kahn underlines (1996, p. 46), they belong in stylometric group 1, although their specific chronological position in that group cannot be determined by stylometric means. Kahn himself offers a new concept to characterize the function of most of the group 1 dialogues, seeing their discussions as "proleptic" (anticipatory) of the metaphysical framework which is presented in full and explicit form in the *Republic*. In effect, Kahn seeks to revise the Socrates–Plato divide, presenting most of the dialogues seen by Vlastos as representations of Socratic *elenchus* as partial and indirect statements of Platonic theory. Kahn's move has been criticized from an analytic standpoint by M. M. McCabe (2002), who suggests that, when different Platonic dialogues seem to have comparable content, they are better understood as "metaleptic," coming after and criticizing previous ideas and thus encouraging readers to think out the issues for themselves. A more general point is that the more we see the dialogue form as used in an artful or indirect way, the less straightforward is the task of interpreting Plato's thought, or tracking his development, from the dialogues. This idea is also implicit in esoteric or Straussian interpretations, which lay little stress on development; but recent debate has also brought out the importance of this point for those who read the dialogues rather as explicit vehicles, that is, doctrinal or analytic readers.

A Maieutic Response to the Question of Periodization

I now offer a fuller response to the issue of periodization, drawing out the implications for the interpretation of the dialogue form (cf. Gill 1996 and 2002b). I do so from the third interpretative standpoint outlined earlier (p. 138), in which the dialogues are read as maieutic, designed to promote independent philosophical reflection in the reader. In doing so, I refer to four related principles which I have offered elsewhere (1996, p. 285) as a basis for analyzing Platonic thinking about dialectic and the search for knowledge and thus for illuminating the written dialogues which center on the representation of dialectic.

1. Objective knowledge of the most important kind (about the essential principles of reality) can only be achieved in and through participation in dialectic, that is, philosophical dialogue conducted through systematic, one-to-one question and answer.
2. Dialectic can only achieve this goal if the participants (a) bring to dialectic the appropriate qualities of character and intellect, and (b) engage effectively in the mode of dialectic that is appropriately related to the subject under discussion.
3. The proper understanding of any given philosophical problem depends on situating this problem correctly in relation to (a) the fundamental principles of reality, and (b) the fundamental principles of dialectical method.
4. Each dialectical encounter has its own integrity and significance and constitutes a context in which substantial progress can be made towards understanding the fundamental principles of reality and philosophical method.

I want to suggest that these principles can help us to explain certain recurrent features of the dialogue form and that they provide a basis for analyzing the philosophical outlook that underlies Platonic deployment of dialectic. They enable us, first, to define a different kind of "unitarianism" from that discussed earlier, namely a unitarianism of philosophical outlook rather than the content of the ideas throughout the dialogues. Second, they help us to see the philosophical significance of Plato's practice of presenting each dialogue as a distinct dialectical encounter. Third, they provide a basis for a periodization of Plato's works based on variations in type of dialogue – in particular in the extent to which the dialectic responds to different or opposing views. I conclude by characterizing the philosophical outlook that is, in my view, implied in these dialectical principles and in Plato's use of the dialogue form.

As suggested earlier (p. 140), it is often supposed that the dialogue form is used quite differently in different phases of Plato's writing career and that the role of the dialogue form may be more important at some periods than at others. However, we can also see certain important types of continuity in this respect. One is that, as indicated in principle 1 above, philosophy, whether represented or described in the dialogues, is always conceived as taking the form of dialectic, that is, one-to-one question-and-answer using a specific method to carry out an agreed enquiry. The form of dialectic varies: it may be *elenchus*, hypothesis, collection and division or some version of dialectic that is more technical (*Parmenides*) or more informal (*Republic, Laws*) (cf. Berti, 2002; Robinson, 1962; Sayre, 1969). Other styles of discourse, such as myth, may be incorporated into the overall dialectical project (Morgan, 2000); the (incomplete) *Timaeus-Critias-Hermocrates* trilogy seems to have been conceived as three correlated types of philosophical myth. Hence, the continuing presentation of the mode of discussion as "shared search" (*suzētēsis*) remains intelligible and justifiable. The idea that search must be "shared" is underlined in various ways, as suggested in principle 2 above. In some cases, the incapacity or unwillingness of the interlocutor to engage in the relevant type of dialectical enquiry leads to well-marked breakdown in discussion or to *aporia* (unresolved difficulty). The fact that this is, for both partners in discussion, a genuine "search" is marked throughout the dialogues, though in different ways. Even in cases where the discussion does not terminate in *aporia*, the limits of the knowledge achieved by the main speaker is sometimes underlined, by contrast with the kind of comprehensive understanding sought through dialectic (principle 3 above). For instance, in the *Republic*, Socrates emphasizes that he only has (fallible) "opinions" about what constitutes complete knowledge of the Good (VI, 506b–507a). In the *Philebus*, Socrates underlines the fact that the dialectical methods he employs fall short of a fully comprehensive and systematic, "god-given" type of dialectic (*Phlb.* 14b–20a, esp. 16c–17a).[5] Hence, the "shared search" presented throughout the dialogues is a continuing one which the reader is invited, explicitly or implicitly, to continue. Thus, what is often seen as the distinctively Socratic philosophical standpoint, of continuing quest through dialectic for knowledge not yet attained, is pervasive throughout the whole Platonic corpus.

These considerations help to explain Plato's retention of the dialogue form, namely as a mode of representing dialectical shared search. They can also serve to explain why each dialogue is marked as an independent dialectical encounter, with its own fresh cast of characters (apart from Socrates), context, subject-matter and (sometimes) mode of dialectic. This mode of presentation is not characteristic of the only other complete surviving examples of "Socratic dialogues", those of Xenophon (*Memorabilia*),

5.   Cf. D. Frede (1996a), pp. 226–39, esp. 232–3; see also p. 140 above (M. Frede on allusions to the *Philosopher* in the *Sophist*).

in which each episode is simply part of a continuing narrative; thus, this mode seems to reflect a distinctively Platonic conception of the form. Although there are internal references within the trilogy *Theaetetus-Sophist-Statesman* and the projected trilogy *Timaeus-Critias- [Hermocrates]*, there are no other explicit references across dialogues. Even apparent references, such as that in the *Phaedo* to the *Meno* or in the *Timaeus* to the *Republic*, are best taken as allusion to other (fictional) discussions rather than cross-references to Platonic texts.[6] This formal feature is too consistently maintained to be merely accidental. Part of the point seems to be to underline (as suggested in principle 4 above) that any given dialectical encounter provides a context in which the "shared search" for knowledge of reality can be carried forward. The studious absence of cross-referencing within the dialogues, despite Plato's own awareness of his developing corpus of works, seems to reflect the point signaled in the *Phaedrus* and *Seventh Letter* (p. 139 above). This is that philosophy must be an active, independent process of shared enquiry, conducted through strenuous engagement in a certain form of dialectic. It cannot rely on conclusions reached by others in another context, or indeed on conclusions reached by the main speaker in another dialectical encounter, though he may draw in a generalized way on ideas developed elsewhere. Thus, although the Platonic works hold up as an ideal a kind of complete and systematic knowledge (principle 3 above), the dialogues themselves do not purport to articulate that system, but present themselves as localized, separate, aspirations to such knowledge. In this way too, they negate any impression of being authoritative and thus of making it unnecessary for the reader to undertake such independent enquiries for herself. It also follows, I think, that interpretation of the dialogues should focus, in the first instance at least, on responding to the distinctive character and significance of the argument in any one dialogue, rather than trying to explain that argument by reference to other dialogues or by a system of thought supposedly embodied in (or behind) the whole set of dialogues. Correspondingly, certain recent studies, including those from an analytic standpoint, have focused on drawing out the internal logic and significance of a single dialogue (e.g., Burnyeat, 1990; Notomi, 1999). Indeed, a series of such studies is in preparation for publication by Cambridge University Press, with M. M. McCabe as General Editor.

So far, I have stressed aspects of the dialogue form, which seem to be linked with important features of Platonic thought about dialectic, which run throughout the whole corpus. But I think that the "maieutic" reading of the dialogues can also lead us to form a fresh view of the periodization of the dialogues, and one that is compatible with three-group division which (as Kahn has argued, p. 142 above) is the only secure outcome of stylometric research. The basis for this periodization is "dialogue" in a rather broader sense than that of dialectical method, namely the kind of dialogue that takes account of positions and approaches different from, or opposed to, one's own. The elenctic dialogues of stylometric group 1 (often regarded as the core "Socratic" dialogues) purport to show Socrates engaging very closely with the ideas of his interlocutors. However, the argument is so highly directed by Socrates and so uniformly negative or aporetic in its outcome that it is open to question how far such *elenchus*

---

6. See *Phd.* 72e–73a; *Meno* 81a–86b; *Ti.* 81e–86b; also *Tht.* 183e; *Sph.* 217c; cf. Gill, 2002b.

really engages with the positions of the respondents (as stressed by Beversluis (2000); on which see Gill (2001)).

There is a marked difference in this respect in the dialogues of stylometric group 2: *Parmenides, Phaedrus, Republic, Theaetetus*. In the *Parmenides*, the main questioner (Parmenides) both criticizes the theory of Forms which is presented positively in other Platonic dialogues and also deploys what seems to be a radically new version of dialectical argument. In the *Phaedrus*, in sharp contrast to the wholly negative treatment of rhetoric in the *Gorgias*, Socrates twice adopts the mode of rhetoric as a vehicle for ideas about love and also offers an account of what would constitute a rational, systematic form of rhetoric. The *Theaetetus*, while deploying *elenchus* again, does so in a very different, "maieutic" manner (cf. Burnyeat, 1977). This process involves an articulation of a version of Protagorean subjectivism (combined with Heraclitean flux-doctrine) that is so fully developed that readers have sometimes mistaken it for Platonic doctrine rather than seeing it as designed, ultimately, for dialectical refutation (Burnyeat, 1990, pp. 10–19; Fine, 1996). The *Republic* dramatizes this contrast in styles of dialogue. Book I shows Socrates refuting the immoralist through *elenchus* – though leaving him quite unconvinced; Books II–X show him constructing a complex argument, combining ethics, epistemology, psychology, and politics in a quite new way that seeks to meet and answer the immoralist's substantive claims. In the dialogues of stylometric group 3, the focus mainly falls on the evolution of new figures (the Eleatic and Athenian Strangers, Timaeus and Critias) whose modes of discourse and whose conceptual projects diverge in significant ways both from each other and from those of the dialogues of groups 1 and 2. These discussions sometimes include a more explicitly collaborative form of dialectic, seeking common ground between opposed positions, notably in the *Philebus*. This might include standing back from positions previously adopted in the dialogues, as in the critical comments on "the friends of the Forms" in the *Sophist*, 246a–249d. But even when there is not explicit engagement with opposed (or formerly opposed) positions, there is, as in the *Timaeus-Critias* or *Laws*, a readiness to embrace areas such as cosmology or detailed constitutional theory formerly eschewed by Socratic-Platonic dialectic. This progressive move towards ever fuller dialogue with different positions and methods also supports the maieutic reading of the dialogues because it embodies an exemplary willingness to explore new and divergent conceptual frameworks and to evolve procedures for determining what is valid in those frameworks as well as in one's own previous standpoint.

I conclude by considering what kind of philosophical outlook is implied in the version of the maieutic reading of Plato outlined here and in the four principles of Platonic thought about dialectic offered earlier. Typically, Plato is seen as author of one of the classic objectivist theories in the history of philosophy, that of the theory of Forms, with a correlated theory of knowledge and associated idealist implications for the study of psychology, politics, and the cosmos. However, some modern philosophers who have shown interest in the form of Platonic dialectic in the dialogues have seen there the expression of a rather different outlook. Donald Davidson, for instance, sees in the method of *elenchus*, both in the early dialogues and the *Philebus*, a method of seeking truth through agreement between participants that implies an intersubjective conception of knowledge, thus anticipating Davidson's own position. Hans-Georg Gadamer finds in the "shared search" of Socratic dialectic, including that in the *Republic*, a prefiguring of his ("hermeneutic") view that truth arises out of the dialectical sharing of "interpretations," each one framed from an inevitably localized perspective.[7] The formulations of the principles of dialectic offered earlier are designed to express what I have called an "objective-participant" or "inter-objective" standpoint (1996, pp. 284–6). In this standpoint, objective knowledge of truth is taken as the goal and ultimate outcome of dialectic. But this is coupled with the recognition that the only effective means of moving towards such knowledge is through engagement in ever more searching and profound forms of dialectical enquiry. The dialogues can be seen both as representing this process and as aiming to promote such engagement among its readers. Of the very diverse and contrasting ways in which the dialogue form is currently understood, this seems to me to be the most promising.

Bibliography

Works Cited

Annas, J. (1999). *Platonic Ethics: Old and New*. Ithaca: Cornell University Press.

——. and Rowe, C. (eds.). (2002). *Perspectives on Plato: Modern and Ancient*. Cambridge, Mass.: Harvard University Press.

Berti, E. (2002). "Si può parlare di un'evoluzione della dialettica platonica?" *Plato* 2 (Internet Journal of the International Plato Society: http://www.nd.edu/~plato).

Beversluis, J. (2000). *Cross-examining Socrates: A Defense of the Interlocutors in Plato's Early Dialogues*. Cambridge: Cambridge University Press.

Bloom, A. (trans.). (1968). *The Republic of Plato* (with notes and an interpretive essay). New York: Basic Books.

Brisson, L. (1998). *Le Même et l'autre dans la structure ontologique du Timée de Platon: un commentaire systématique du Timée de Platon* (3rd edn.). Sankt Augustin: Academia Verlag.

Brandwood, L. (1992). "Stylometry and Chronology." In R. Kraut (ed.), *The Cambridge Companion to Plato* (pp. 1–50). Cambridge: Cambridge University Press.

Burnyeat, M. (1977). "Socratic Midwifery, Platonic Inspiration." *Bulletin of the Institute of Classical Studies*, 24, 7–16.

——. (1985). "Sphinx Without a Secret." *New York Review of Books*, 32 (May 30), 30–6.

——. (1990). *The Theaetetus of Plato*, translated by M. J. Levett, revised and with an introduction by M. Burnyeat. Indianapolis: Hackett.

Cherniss, H. (1936). "The Philosophical Economy of the Theory of Ideas." *American Journal of Philology*, 57, 445–56.

Cooper, J. (ed.). (1997). *Plato: Complete Works*. Indianapolis: Hackett.

Cousin, V. (ed.). (1864). *Procli philosophi opera inedita* (2nd edn.). Paris.

Davidson, D. (1985). "Plato's Philosopher." *London Review of Books*, 1 Aug. 1985. Reprinted in T. Irwin and M. C. Nussbaum (eds.), (1993) *Virtue, Love and Form: Essays in Memory of Gregory Vlastos = Apeiron*, 26 (3–4) (pp. 179–94). Edmonton, Alberta: Academic Printing and Publishing.

Ferber, R. (1991). *Die Unwissenheit des Philosophen oder Warum hat Platon die "ungeschriebene Lehre" nicht geschrieben?* Sankt Augustin: Academia Verlag.

7. See Davidson, 1985, 1993; also Scaltsas, 1989; Gadamer, 1980, and 1986, ch. 3; cf. Renaud, 1999; and Gill, 2002a.

Ferrari, G. R. F. (1997). "Strauss's Plato." *Arion*, 5 (2), 36–65.

Fine, G. (1996). "Conflicting Appearances: *Theaetetus* 153d–154b." In C. Gill and M. M. McCabe (eds.), *Form and Argument in Late Plato* (pp. 105–33) Oxford: Clarendon Press.

Frede, D. (1996a). "The Hedonist's Conversion: The Role of Socrates in the *Philebus*." In C. Gill and M. M. McCabe (eds.), *Form and Argument in Late Plato* (pp. 213–48). Oxford: Clarendon Press.

——. (1996b). "The Philosophical Economy of Plato's Psychology: Rationality and Common Concepts in Plato's *Timaeus*." In M. Frede and G. Striker (eds.), *Rationality in Greek Thought* (pp. 29–58). Oxford: Clarendon Press.

Frede, M. (1996). "The Literary Form of the *Sophist*." In C. Gill and M. M. McCabe (eds.), *Form and Argument in Late Plato* (pp. 135–51). Oxford: Clarendon Press.

Gadamer, H.-G. (1980). *Dialogue and Dialectic: Eight Hermeneutical Studies on Plato*. (trans. P. C. Smith). New Haven: Yale University Press. (Original work published as separate essays between 1934 and 1974.)

——. (1986). *The Idea of Good in Platonic-Aristotelian Philosophy*. (trans. P. C. Smith). New Haven: Yale University Press. (Original work published 1978.)

Gill, C. (1992). "Dogmatic Dialogue in *Phaedrus* 276–7?" In L. Rossetti (ed.), *Understanding the "Phaedrus."* Proceedings of the Second Symposium Platonicum (pp. 156–72). Sankt Augustin: Academia Verlag.

——. (1993). "Platonic Dialectic and the Truth-Status of the Unwritten Doctrines." *Methexis*, 6, 55–72.

——. (1995). "Rethinking Constitutionalism in *Politicus* 291–303." In C. Rowe (ed.), *Reading the Statesman*. Proceedings of the Third Symposium Platonicum (pp. 292–305). Sankt Augustin: Academia Verlag.

——. (1996). "Afterword: Dialectic and the Dialogue Form in late Plato." In C. Gill and M. M. McCabe (eds.), *Form and Argument in Late Plato* (pp. 283–311). Oxford: Clarendon Press.

——. (2001). "Speaking up for Plato's Interlocutors. A Discussion of J. Beversluis, *Cross-examining Socrates*." *Oxford Studies in Ancient Philosophy*, 20, 297–321.

——. (2002a). "Critical Response to the Hermeneutic Approach from an Analytic Perspective". In G. Reale and S. Scolnicov (eds.), *New Images of Plato: The Idea of Good* (pp. 211–22). Sankt Augustin: Academia Verlag.

——. (2002b). "Dialectic and the Dialogue Form." In J. Annas and C. Rowe (eds.), *Perspectives on Plato: Modern and Ancient* (pp. 145–71). Cambridge, Mass.: Harvard University Press.

——. and McCabe, M. M. (eds.). (1996). *Form and Argument in Late Plato*. Oxford: Clarendon Press.

Gonzalez, F. (ed.). (1995). *The Third Way: New Directions in Platonic Scholarship*. Lanham, Md.: Rowman & Littlefield.

Griswold, C. (ed.). (1988). *Platonic Writings, Platonic Readings*. New York: Routledge. (2nd edition, University Park, Pennsylvania: University of Pennsylvania Press, 2002.)

Kahn, C. H. (1996). *Plato and the Socratic Dialogue: The Philosophical Use of a Literary Form*. Cambridge: Cambridge University Press.

——. (2002). "On Platonic Chronology." In J. Annas and C. Rowe (eds.). *Perspectives on Plato: Modern and Ancient* (pp. 93–127). Cambridge, Mass.: Harvard University Press.

Keyser, P. (1991). Review of G. Ledger, *Recounting Plato. Bryn Mawr Classical Review*, 2 (7), 404–27.

Morgan, K. (2000). *Myth and Philosophers: From the Presocratics to Plato*. Cambridge: Cambridge University Press.

McCabe, M. M. (1994). *Plato's Individuals*. Princeton: Princeton University Press.

——. (2002). "Developing the Good: Prolepsis or Critique in the *Euthydemus*?" *Plato* 2 (Internet Journal of the International Plato Society: http://www.nd.edu/~plato).

148

Notomi, N. (1999). *The Unity of Plato's Sophist: Between the Sophist and the Philosopher.* Cambridge: Cambridge University Press.

Owen, G. E. L. (1953). "The Place of the *Timaeus* in Plato's Dialogues." *Classical Quarterly*, NS 3, 79–95.

——. (1985). *Logic, Science and Dialectic: Collected Papers in Greek Philosophy.* (M. C. Nussbaum, ed.). London: Duckworth.

Pradeau, J.-F. (2002). *Plato and the City: A New Introduction to Plato's Political Thought* (trans. J. Lloyd). Exeter: University of Exeter Press. (Original work published 1997.)

Press, G. (ed.). (1993). *Plato's Dialogues: New Studies and Interpretations.* Lanham, Md.: Rowman & Littlefield.

——. (2000). *Who Speaks for Plato? Studies in Platonic Anonymity.* Lanham, Md.: Rowman & Littlefield.

Reale, G. (1997). *Towards a New Interpretation of Plato* (trans. J. Catan and R. Davies). Washington, DC: Catholic University of America Press. (Original work published 1984; translation based on 10th edn.)

Renaud, F. (1999). *Die Resokratierung Platons: Die Platonische Hermeneutik Hans-Georg Gadamers.* Sankt Augustin: Academia Verlag.

Robinson, R. (1962). *Plato's Earlier Dialectic.* Oxford: Clarendon Press.

Rowe, C. (2000). "The *Politicus* and other Dialogues." In C. Rowe and M. Schofield (eds.), *Cambridge History of Greek and Roman Political Thought* (pp. 233–57). Cambridge: Cambridge University Press.

Sayre, K. (1969). *Plato's Analytic Method.* Chicago: Chicago University Press.

——. (1983). *Plato's Late Ontology: A Riddle Resolved.* Princeton: Princeton University Press.

——. (1992). "A Maieutic View of Five Late Dialogues." In J. C. Klagge and N. D. Smith (eds.), *Methods of Interpreting Plato and his Dialogues.* (= *Oxford Studies in Ancient Philosophy* suppl. vol.) (pp. 221–43). Oxford: Clarendon Press.

Scaltsas, T. (1989). "Socratic Moral Realism: An Alternative Justification." *Oxford Studies in Ancient Philosophy*, 7, 129–50.

Sedley, D. (1996). "Three Platonist Interpretations of the *Theaetetus*'. In C. Gill and M. M. McCabe (eds.), *Form and Argument in Late Plato* (pp. 79–103). Oxford: Clarendon Press.

Shorey, P. (1904). *The Unity of Plato's Thought.* Chicago: University of Chicago Press.

Stokes, M. (1986). *Plato's Socratic Conversations: Drama and Dialectic in Three Dialogues.* Baltimore: John's Hopkins University Press.

Strauss, L. (1964). *The City and Man.* Chicago: University of Chicago Press.

Szlezák, T. A. (1985). *Platon und die Schriftlichkeit der Philosophie: Interpretationen zu den frühen und mittleren Dialogen.* Berlin: de Gruyter.

——. (1997). "Schleiermachers 'Einleitung' zur Platon-Übersetzung von 1804." *Antike und Abendland*, 3, 46–62.

——. (1999). *Reading Plato* (trans. G. Zanker). London: Routledge. (Original work published 1993.)

Tarrant, H. (1993). *Thrasyllan Platonism.* Ithaca: Cornell University Press.

Vlastos, G. (1954). "The Third Man in the *Parmenides*." *Philosophical Review*, 63, 319–49.

——. (1991). *Socrates: Ironist and Moral Philosopher.* Cambridge: Cambridge University Press.

——. (1994). *Socratic Studies.* (M. Burnyeat, ed.). Cambridge: Cambridge University Press.

Further Reading

Blondell, R. (2000). *The Play of Character in Plato's Dialogues.* Cambridge: Cambridge University Press.

Coventry, L. (1990). "The Role of the Interlocutor in Plato's Dialogues: Theory and Practice." In C. Pelling (ed.), *Characterization and Individuality in Greek Literature* (pp. 174–96). Oxford: Clarendon Press.

Derrida, J. "Plato's Pharmacy." In B. Johnson (trans.). *Dissemination, With Introduction and Additional Notes* (pp. 61–171). Chicago: University of Chicago Press.

Findlay, J. N. (1974). *The Written and Unwritten Doctrines*. New York: Humanities Press.

Gaiser, K. (1980). "Plato's Enigmatic Lecture on the Good." *Phronesis*, 25, 5–37.

Haslam, M. (1972). "Plato, Sophron, and the Dramatic Dialogue." *Bulletin of the Institute of Classical Studies*, 19, 17–38.

Kahn, C. H. (1983). "Drama and Dialectic in Plato's *Gorgias*." *Oxford Studies in Ancient Philosophy*, 1, 75–121.

Klagge, J. C. and Smith, N. D. (eds.). (1992). *Methods of Interpreting Plato and his Dialogues*. (= *Oxford Studies in Ancient Philosophy* suppl. vol.). Oxford: Clarendon Press.

Nightingale, A. (1995). *Genres in Dialogue: Plato and the Construct of Philosophy*. Cambridge: Cambridge University Press.

Rutherford, R. B. (1995). *The Art of Plato: Ten Essays in Platonic Interpretation*. London: Duckworth.

Schmid, T. (1998). *Plato's Charmides and the Socratic Ideal of Rationality*. Albany, NY: State University of New York Press.

Sedley, D. (1995). "The Dramatis Personae of Plato's *Phaedo*." In T. Smiley (ed.), *Philosophical Dialogues: Plato, Hume, Wittgenstein* (pp. 3–26) (= *Proceedings of the British Academy 85*). Oxford: Clarendon Press.

Tigerstedt, E. N. (1977). *Interpreting Plato*. Uppsala: Almquist and Wiksell International.

Weingartner, R. H. (1973). *The Unity of the Platonic Dialogue*. Indianapolis: Bobbs-Merrill.

9

Plato's Ethics: Early and Middle Dialogues

TERRY PENNER

Socrates and Plato: Conflicting Psychologies of Action

There is a considerable change of tone and method between what we find in most of Plato's early dialogues and what we find in that great ethical masterpiece of Plato's middle period, the *Republic*.[1] Thus in a typical early dialogue, we find Socrates examining and refuting answers of others to ethical questions of the sort: "What is courage?" ("What is temperance?" "What is piety?") and "Is virtue teachable – and if so how?"[2] and suggesting (surely with ironic exaggeration), that he himself is quite as ignorant about the correct answers to his questions as his initially confident interlocutors turn out to be by the end of the dialogue. This is not to deny that we find Socrates there clearly enough committed to beliefs of his *own* – such as "Virtue is knowledge," "No one errs willingly," and "All desire is for the good." The point is merely that by the end of most early dialogues, Socrates has apparently shown all the answers anyone has offered to his main questions to be failures. The results of these dialogues are all, in form, negative.

In the *Republic*, by contrast, at least from Book II onwards, we find the character Socrates offering (and sustaining) a *positive* answer to the question "What is justice?" – doing so, moreover, by means of an extraordinary and quite unprecedented device: examining what justice would be in a certain ideal city constructed in thought.[3] But

---

1. For the dating of Plato's dialogues, see C. Gill, THE PLATONIC DIALOGUE, in this volume.
2. Other questions: What is love (or friendship)? Is virtue a science or expertise? What is rhetoric – that is, what is the art of persuasion, and is *it* an expertise or science? Or is it what moderns would call a pseudo-science (n. 5 below)? What is literary criticism, and is *it* an expertise or science that can be had independently of the truth about the subject-matter the literature deals with? Or is it a pseudo-science too? Is Achilles the better person, or Odysseus? And is the person good in some area the one who errs willingly in that area, or the one who errs unwillingly? If young people should devote themselves to the pursuit of human goodness and therefore knowledge or expertise, what is the relevant knowledge or expertise? Is Socrates an atheist and corruptor of the young? And would Socrates be acting well and justly in trying to escape?
3. Extraordinary because of the particular way in which justice in the individual is modeled on justice in an ideal state: see the sections below on psychological well-adjustment in the *Republic*.

not only is the "What is it?" question given a positive answer. The *Republic* also offers – as its central argument indeed – an extended argument for a positive answer to the question "Does the just life make us happier than the completely unjust life?"

Associated with this change of tone and method in the *Republic* is (a) a certain widening of Plato's interests beyond the area of individual ethics, together with (b) certain developments – and even (c) reversals – in doctrine. Thus, (a) *Rep.* II–X shows an interest in details of political organization that is entirely absent from the early dialogues. Again, (b) in a development of the early period insistence on the objectivity of the sciences, the Plato of *Rep.* II–X engages in some elaborate theorizing about the metaphysics and epistemology of the unchanging objects of the sciences – the abstract objects he calls "Forms," which he contrasts sharply with the ever-changing phenomena of the perceptible world. This contrast between changing perceptibles and unchanging abstract objects (intelligibles) – which Plato also speaks of as a contrast between *becoming* and *being* – is quite absent from the early dialogues (except for the *Phaedo*, the *Cratylus*, and the *Symposium*). And (c) *Rep.* II–X unveils a whole new psychology of desire and voluntary action that actually *contradicts* the views espoused in the early dialogues (with the exception of the *Phaedo* and parts of the *Gorgias*). Where the early dialogues mostly insist that all desire is for the good, at *Rep.* IV, 437d–438a we are told that thirst is desire just for *drink* – not for hot drink or cold drink, or much drink or a little drink, and, above all, not for good drink. We are not to allow an objector to tell us that thirst is for good drink (drink that is good) on the grounds (the objector says) that *all desire is for the good.* Who the objector is will be all too obvious to anyone familiar with the early dialogues. It is the view of the character Socrates in most of the early dialogues that all desire is for the good.[4] Thus Plato in the *Republic* is precisely *rejecting* the view of most of the early dialogues.

These changes notwithstanding, there is also remarkable continuity between the ethical views of the early dialogues and those of the *Republic*. Questions of human goodness and the good for humans remain very much a matter of objective knowledge or science throughout Plato's dialogues, whether this shows up (as in the early dialogues) via the analogy of human goodness to various forms of expertise, or (as in the *Republic*) via the reference to Forms. In either version, the emphasis is on science – as opposed, say, to tradition, religious or not. Thus the ethics implicit in the theology of the traditional myths is roundly criticized (*Rep.* II–III) – or even ridiculed (*Euthyphro*). At the same time, the sophistic enlightenment (with which Aristophanes' *Clouds* had identified Socrates) is also criticized. Thus rhetoric, as practiced by the politicians and orators of the day, and often represented in the "new learning" of the late fifth century as a way to achieve success in personal and political life, is argued throughout to be

4.   That is, all desire that leads to action. One may feel a desire for *drink* that one does not act on; but when such a desire leads to action, it is arguably only because the drink in question is seen as (part of) the good in the particular situation confronting the agent (*Lys.* 220d8–e2, 221c5–d2, *Grg.* 467e–468e). In the view we find in most of the early dialogues, even when thirsty, one acts on the desire for good, not the desire for drink.

at best (what we would call) a pseudo-science.[5] Finally, the idea that there is some *understanding* to be gained from the works of the great epic and tragic poets of the day is treated with the same disdain throughout.

Even so, the changes noted above between most early dialogues and *Rep.* II–X deserve some explanation. Some commentators,[6] following Aristotle on the historical Socrates, suggest that these changes and developments are best explained by supposing that most early dialogues give us a Plato still under the very considerable influence of the methods and doctrines of the historical Socrates, while *Rep.* II–X gives us a Plato who carries forward in a new way many of the same ethical concerns that animated Socrates, but who also has preoccupations that are distinctively his own.

One thing Aristotle tells us is distinctive of the views of the historical Socrates is the view that virtue is knowledge. This is certainly the suggestion of the *Apology*, even though the *Apology* also has it that Socrates is the wisest person there is, and that his wisdom consists in his acknowledging that he himself has no knowledge. Thus the virtue which is knowledge is something at which we can at best *aim*. (A kind of ideal object, as the Forms will later be.) The knowledge in question (that no one has) appears to be the knowledge of the good and the bad – of virtue and vice. (As for other sorts of knowledge, Socrates has no problem with the idea that cobblers, carpenters, and doctors have knowledge of their own particular subject-matters.)[7] What the *Apology* tells us is that the best chance of making children, or others, good people lies in making sure they are examined – and refuted – every day in their opinions about virtue (human goodness). "The unexamined life," as he famously puts it, "is not worth living" (*Ap.* 38a5–6).

5.   The boast of the rhetorician Gorgias is that, without any grasp on the science of medicine, he can persuade patients to undergo surgery where his brother, the doctor, fails (*Grg.* 456a–c). More generally, by what Socrates calls a "knack of flattery" (463b), Gorgias professes to gain clients a supposed good they *think* they want; but Gorgias feels free to express complete indifference to the science relevant to the good in question. This over-extends rhetoric in the following way (derived from *Grg.* 466a–468e): Without that knowledge which a science has of the means–end structures within its area, rhetoric is in danger of securing for its clients what they *think* is a means to their end in that area – when it isn't. (This applies also to the science of the good and the bad, where presumably means-end structures are pretty complex.) To profess indifference to knowledge of means-end structures relevant to the clients' desires is precisely to court disaster. To secure an apparently wanted means that, through ignorance, leads to no end the client wants – that is no exemplification of a science of getting people what they want. Rhetoric – without science – gains one no real good. See Penner (1988, 1991). A true rhetoric, *with* the science of the real good, would be another matter: cf. *Grg.* 517a, *Phdr.* 261c–262c.

6.   Halliwell (1994), Irwin (1977, 1995), Penner (2002: contra Kahn (1996)), Santas (1979), Vlastos (1991).

7.   At any rate, he is content, for purposes of the analogy with virtue that he wishes to set up, to treat these sciences as well enough instantiated in actual carpenters, doctors, etc. The use of the idea that these sciences are autonomous, and require no knowledge of the (human) good, if intended in no more than an expository way – to introduce the idea of virtue as a science – would not therefore clash with the claim in the *Republic* that there is no knowledge of any science without knowledge of the Form of the Good.

Virtue, it appears, is entirely an intellectual matter. In this picture, there does not seem to be any room – or need – for the training of character, or the training of people's motivations and their desires. By contrast, the Plato who wrote *Rep.* II–X obviously held that virtue is, at any rate in its beginning, a matter *primarily* of character and of the training of one's emotions and desires. Thus the primary education of children considered in Books II–III of the *Republic* does not look much like dialectic. Indeed, it looks more like the formation of character by largely non-intellectual means – rigorously censored stories about gods and heroes, censored music, and carefully supervised physical activities. For the Plato of the *Republic*, then, character training is the absolute basis of virtue (however much it remains the case that the person of complete virtue must also, in the end, have expert knowledge of the good). Indeed the guardians of Plato's ideal state go on having their character tested even while they are engaged in their final studies to become guardians of that ideal state. Thus character disqualifies some human beings for human goodness, regardless of their beliefs. This is not the picture apparently embraced by Plato when, still under the formidable influence of his master, he was writing many of the early dialogues.

The Socratic picture must surely seem altogether strange to us, at least at first glance. How could mere *intellect* be sufficient to make us good persons? The answer has to do with the Socratic theory of desire – or as we might put it, the Socratic psychology of action. According to Socrates, all desires productive of action are desires for the good. They are desires for one's *own* good (*Meno* 77c8–d1, d7, *Grg.* 468b6 with d3) – one's own *real* good, not just one's own *apparent* good (what one *thinks* of as one's own good: *Grg.* 468c2–5, d1–6).[8] The early dialogues seem clearly enough to identify the agent's good with his or her own happiness (*Euthd.* 278e3ff., esp. 279a2–3, a5, 280a4–c4, d4–e2, 281b2–4, 282a1–b7; *Symp.* 204e1–205a8). But then if every voluntary action proceeds from desire for one's own *real* good, good people will not differ from bad people in the fundamental desire that generates their actions (*Meno* 78b5–6). On the

8. If one's action did not lead to one's real good, but just to what *seemed* to one to be the real good (that is an apparent good), then, Socrates holds, one did not want to do the action one did (*Grg.* 468c–d). One wanted to do instead the action that would have led to that real good for the sake of which one did the action. Plato's point here may be put as follows: Wanting to do something is not a two-place relation between a person and an action, but a three-place relation between a person, an action, and the real good to which the action (in favorable circumstances) is the means. See Penner (1991), Penner and Rowe (1994).

Prior to Penner (1991), most scholars took it as obvious that, for Socrates as for Aristotle, the claim that all desire is for the good was the claim that all desire was for the *apparent* good, i.e., for what the agent *thought* was best for the agent – even if, unbeknownst to the agent, it was *not* in fact best for the agent. (Helen wanted the running away with Paris *under the description* "good".) On such a view, she *did* want the running away with Paris that ended by making her miserable. (If she didn't *want* to do it, why *did* she do it?)

On the quite different view here derived from the *Gorgias*, Helen had no desire for that action. Instead her desire was the (incoherent) desire to do that action which is both the best action for her all things considered (whatever that might be – she couldn't be quite sure *what* it was) and the action she *took* to be the best, namely running away with Paris. But the action she *did* do, the one that made her miserable, is not that really best action she wanted to do.

154

Socratic psychology of action we are all the same in this respect: In everything we do, we are more or less reflectively looking to the happiness of our own life.

But if one person will not differ from another in the fundamental desire that produces all action, how is it that some act virtuously, some viciously? If we do not differ in the end we all seek, then presumably we differ only in the means to that end which we choose, believing them to be the best available to us at the time. But on that showing, the difference can only reside in our more or less reflective beliefs as to what particular action is the best means open to us, at the time of action, to our own real happiness. That is, differences between people which we think of as differences in their motives and intentions are, on the Socratic view, the consequence solely of their beliefs. Hence, on this view, if Smith wants to harm me, and Jones wants to help me, that is not because of any difference in fundamental desires, but solely because Smith holds the belief that harming me will lead to his real good (perhaps because of another more general belief about the uses of *harm to others* for being happy), while Jones holds the belief that *helping* me will lead to his real good (perhaps because Jones, like Socrates himself, believes that harming others always results in harm to you: *Ap.* 25d6–e5.) For Socrates, then, Jones's virtue is knowledge, Smith's vice ignorance. Notice the following corollary: there is really only one way to change Smith's behavior. This is to engage in dialectic with him as a way of changing his beliefs. Virtue thus becomes knowledge. To become more virtuous is to come to understand better what is and is not a means to one's own real good.

But, now, if Plato endorses this Socratic view of the nature of desire and human goodness in the early dialogues, why does he abandon it when he comes to *Rep.* II–X? Because at some point – perhaps (though this is a mere conjecture) under the influence of the Pythagorean philosophers he met on his first visit to Italy and Sicily some eleven years after Socrates' death – he has come to a new view about the human psyche (*Grg.* 493a1–494a5), a view according to which Plato concludes in *Rep.* IV that human action does not always flow from an agent's fundamental desire for his or her own good, but sometimes also flows from other more irrational – and (we might say) more physiological – desires, such as thirst, hunger, and the desire for sex (cf. point (c) on page 152). This is the parts-of-the-soul doctrine of *Rep.* IV.

According to this doctrine, Reason, the Rational Part of the soul, acts solely from its fundamental desire for the (real) good of the entire individual. (So far, the Platonic rational part of the soul is exactly like the Socratic individual as a whole.) To leave aside for now the desires of the spirited part,[9] the appetitive part desires food, drink,

9. The desires of the spirited part seem to be mainly desires to support Reason in its attempts to control the appetitive desires. But then why not simply have desires of Reason attempting to control appetite? (Plato's arguments are in any case not very good for there being this third part of the psyche. Why then does he persist in positing this third part?) Already in the *Gorgias* (e.g., 505b–c), Socrates is at least *suggesting* an analogy between punishing (*kolazein*) unruly members of society and disciplining (*kolazein* : "to discipline" cf. *akolasia*: "indiscipline", more usually "self-indulgence") unruly bodily appetites in the soul. If the *Republic* then develops an explicit and extensive analogy between city and soul, and it is natural to depict the punishing of unruly citizens as the action of the military that serve the rulers, rather than of the rulers themselves, it may have come to seem natural to Plato that he seek in the soul an agency for disciplining appetites distinct from the Rational part.

sex, and the like – generally speaking entirely independently of Reason's beliefs about what is good for the individual as a whole. Appetite – the desire for insulin-rush, let us say – moves me to take this cookie. Reason says "This will be bad for the individual as a whole." But the appetite for insulin-rush doesn't quit; and being too much for Reason, leads me to take the cookie – against my better judgment. So too with Leontius, at *Rep.* IV, 439e–440a, whose Reason says it is best not to act on certain base erotic desires – to view a pile of corpses – at the same time as his appetite leads him, cursing, to run over and view the corpses.[10]

The most important feature of this doctrine of the tripartite soul is not the claim that the soul has *parts* (a point on which Aristotle *criticizes* Plato) but the claim that action is sometimes produced by desires other than the fundamental desire for good: more physiological, non-rational desires, such as thirst, hunger, and sexual desire (a point on which Aristotle *follows* Plato). On this new view, these irrational desires will sometimes (non-intellectually) *overcome* one's desire for good (this is what Aristotle called *akrasia*, or "weakness of will"), and sometimes they will (non-intellectually) *corrupt* either one's desire for good (this is what Aristotle called *akolasia*, or "wickedness") or one's fundamental beliefs about the good (Plato's version of *akolasia* – very much on display in *Rep.* VIII–IX). As a consequence, Plato in the *Republic* comes to the view that moral education will require not just rational discussion, but the control and redirection (by at least some non-rational means) of one's irrational desires and emotions, so that they neither *overcome* the desires of Reason nor *corrupt* Reason's beliefs about the good. The good person becomes the person of good character. For Socrates, by contrast, there is no such thing as Aristotelian *akrasia* and no such thing as *akolasia*. There is only ignorance.[11]

Such then is the background, in contrasting psychologies of action, for the difference between the Socratic view that virtue is knowledge and the Platonic view that the training of character (in at least partly non-intellectual ways) is a necessary precondition to the acquiring of that wisdom which, in Plato as in Socrates, is necessary to virtue.

The Desire for Good in Platonic Ethics

But what about ethics? Does the Plato who wrote *Rep.* II–X also hold different ethical views from the Socratic Plato who wrote many of the early dialogues? The suggestion to be made here is that in the main lines of the *Republic*, we find no changes in ethical

---

10.   Plato represents this case as Appetite opposing not Reason, but the Spirited part. (See preceding note.) It is true that some scholars deny that Plato is presenting the case of Leontius as a case of acting contrary to one's desire for what is best. But this seems a desperate measure to avoid the clear implications of the text. It is true that at VI, 506e–507a, Plato is still saying that all desire from which action proceeds is desire for good. But it is probable (VI, 505d) that Plato is in this context simply speaking of actions one would *choose* to do (as opposed to those actions forced on us by our irrational desires) – something we know happens also in the opening sentence of Aristotle's *Nicomachean Ethics*.

11.   But see Devereux (1995).

theory that are not expected consequences of the change in psychology of action, wherein added to the agent's rational desires for his or her own good, there are also irrational desires that, in someone not properly educated, will corrupt Reason's beliefs and overcome Reason's desires.

It is true that there is a feature of the description just given which leaves many commentators dissatisfied, since they want to deny that the desire for good that we find in the *Republic* is in this way egoistic. (Three paragraphs back, we claimed that the good my Reason desires is *my* good.) According to many commentators, however, the Platonic Form of the Good that, in the *Republic*, stands over all the other Forms, comes to direct the philosopher's thought and aspiration onto a higher and more general level – to something closer to the idea of most modern philosophers, according to which the good desired by the good person is not the person's *own* good, but the good *generally*, including the good of one's fellow citizens and the good of others quite generally. In most interpretations, this flows from the idea – not adopted here – that the Forms are "self-predicational" in a certain absolute (non-relative) way, so that the Form of the Good is, first, *itself* a good thing, and, second, a good thing which is not good *for me* (or relative to me) or – for that matter – good *for you*, or good *for* anyone. It is good *period*. Hence the good desired by those whose characters and intellects have been appropriately trained becomes not the good *for* anyone, even for one's fellow-citizens or for humans quite generally, but a whole new kind of good: an *impersonal* (and ideal) good – not perhaps quite identical with *moral good*, but as close to it as Plato ever comes.

A second suggestion may be influencing interpreters here – a particularly strong way of understanding the idea of the "transcendence" of the Forms. The suggestion is that the Form of the Good or the Form of Beauty are more than simply the real natures of the good or of beauty. (That is, they are not analogous to what a Form of Happiness would be if we imagined such a thing in Plato – something giving us precisely the real nature of human happiness that is the object of the Socratic science of the good and the bad.)[12] If we take the Form of the Good or the Form of Beauty as more than just an object of Socratic sciences, what the Good Itself and the Beautiful Itself will turn out to be – if they are strongly "transcendent" in this way – is not just abstract objects (intelligibles as opposed to perceptual phenomena) which, whether one knows it or not, one who desires or loves wishes to partake in. Instead, the Form of the Good will be a whole new otherworldly good, going beyond any human good (and indeed beyond the good of anything in the phenomenal world), a good which few humans get to contemplate let alone consciously desire to be part of their lives. A Form of the Good, conceived along the lines of this suggestion, *could* be *some* sort of moral good beyond any creature.[13]

12. Cf. *Tht.* 175c for something like this idea in another middle dialogue.
13. Similarly, on the strong "transcendence" view of the Forms, which some find at *Symp.* 210a–211c, what we are to do is to turn away from all attachments to beautiful perceptibles to form a new attachment to an ideal object in another world, which object is itself the most beautiful of beautiful objects – as Vlastos (1965) puts it, winning hands down all beauty contests with beautiful phenomena. By contrast, on the reading favored here, love for beautiful perceptibles is really attachment to these perceptibles for love of that real nature of beauty that resides in them. (Just so, one reading of the *Lysis* has it that when Lysis "makes much of"

The issues here are highly controversial, with perhaps a majority of scholars taking the line that the Form of the Good is this kind of self-predicational and "strongly transcendent" being.[14] Nevertheless it may be pointed out against such a view of the effect that the Form of the Good has on Plato's ethics, that this valiant and ingenious effort to stop Plato's ethics from being egoistic in its goals[15] destroys the intended parallel between Reason and the rulers of the Ideal City. For, as will be made clear below, it is central to Plato's use of the Intellectual Ruling Class as a model for the Rational Part of the psyche that as the directing desire of the Rulers is for the good of the entire city, so the directing desire of Reason should be for the good of the entire individual. But then (as claimed two paragraphs back) the good that my Reason seeks must be my own good, as the happiness it seeks must be my own happiness.

If we set aside considerations of the self-predicational and the "strongly transcendent" notion of the Forms, the best evidence for a *non*-egoistic good in the *Republic* concerns a minor, if important, detail in the construction of the ideal city – Plato's insistence on making sure that those selected to rule are those that in fact have a better life available to them than ruling, namely, a life of study of the Forms (VII, 519b–521b). Not being eager to rule, such rulers won't look to benefit themselves by ruling, but merely to do what is necessary and just during such times as they are forced to abandon their studies. Do we not have in this feature of the construction of the ideal city a picture of people acting justly *and contrary to what is most in their self-interest?* Is this not a picture of human goodness that runs contrary to the idea that the just life is the happiest life? Or is it merely a detail in the construction of the ideal city that Plato hoped to get away with, allowing himself to be seduced by the epigram that the only people you want to have as rulers are people who see less advantage to ruling than to doing something else? Or – splitting the difference – do we see here a symptom of the emerging tension in Plato's thought as he turns more and more to an interest in the goals of politics?[16]

Menexenus, what he loves in Menexenus is the real good – the "first friend" – that, at best, the two seek together, especially in argument. Similarly, when Lysis desires to drink, what he desires in that action is the real good to which that action is the best means: Cf. n. 3 above.)

How can it be that we all desire the real (and even transcendent) nature of the good (the Form) if what we each desire is *our own* real good? The desire for the real nature of the good, more fully expressed is the desire that the real nature of the good (the Form) be realized in our own lives.

14.   Annas (1981), Cooper (1977), Irwin (1977, 1995), Santas (2001), White (1979).

15.   Most treatments of the *Republic* seem anxious to avoid making it egoistic in its goals – even Irwin (1977, 1995), who follows Penner (1973b) in making at least *Socratic* ethics egoistic.

16.   *Ep.* VII, 324b–325c, tells us of Plato's initial determination to enter politics when his mother's cousin Critias (leader of the oligarchic "Thirty Tyrants") and her brother Charmides undertook to reform the Athenian government. This ambition was aborted when Plato saw how his relatives treated his "older friend" Socrates.

For Socrates' holding himself back *altogether* from political life, see especially *Ap.* 31c–32a, 32e (on political activity as an actual obstruction to that care for the soul that consists in the examined life). For Plato's gradual return of interest, at least in the politics of *ideal* societies, see *Ep.* VII, 324b–326b. The *Gorgias* too, esp. 501b1ff. with 515a–521a, shows signs of a

At any rate, the present treatment will suppose that even if in this passage Plato should feel some temptation to abandon the universality of the claim that the aim of people's rational desires is always their own self-interest, the *Republic* as a whole cannot be doing so. For even aside from the egoistic implications of the city/soul model, the *Republic*'s main point surely remains that the just person is always happier than the unjust – so that there is in this respect no change between the conception of the good in Socrates and the conception of the good in the *Republic*. For one to desire real good is to want the real good we all aim at to be realized in one's own life.

If this seems to anyone to make Plato's just person a selfish person, it needs to be pointed out that selfishness is something quite different from pursuing one's self-interest. For selfishness is a policy *of not caring about the good of others*. Neither Socrates nor Plato would have thought this policy a sensible way to go about securing one's own best interests. Indeed, it was Socrates' belief that in the long run it is never in your interest to harm others (*Ap.* 25c–26a, *Grg.*, *Rep.* I, 335b6–e6, cf. *Tht.* 173a7–b3). Still, modern moral philosophers – many of them anxious to have something to say (or do) to those who wrong others and appear to get away with it[17] – tend to view with distaste this suggestion that there is nothing disreputable about looking to one's own self-interest.

We see here that in spite of the clear enough distinction between selfishness and self-interest, moral philosophers tend to remain uneasy about Plato as a role model for the moral philosopher. In his justly celebrated inaugural lecture, "Duty and Interest" of 1928, H. R. Prichard points out how important it is to the *Republic* that Plato has Socrates, both in Book I and in the remaining nine books of the *Republic*, accept as legitimate the question whether the unjust or the just are happier. Therein, Prichard avers, Plato grants, in effect, that we cannot claim justice to be a virtue unless we can show that it is *in our interest* to be just. But, like most modern moral philosophers, Prichard does not think such a self-interested approach towards justice or morality can possibly be justified. Indeed Prichard suggests that the *Republic* in accepting this question sets moral philosophy off on the wrong foot altogether. The question is not what is in our self-interest, but what is *right*. While it would be nice to be able to assure ourselves that "Honesty is the best policy," such a view, Prichard thinks, is hardly to be relied upon, and moral philosophers must accordingly redirect their audience's attention away from questions of self-interest to questions of right and wrong. In so doing, they must turn away from the moral philosophy of the *Republic*.

---

cautious return of political interest. See also *Rep.* VI, 495a–497a, for implicit Platonic regrets about Critias and Alcibiades, and even criticisms of Socrates' holding himself back from politics.

The *Republic*'s view that rulers need payment of some sort (I, 345b–347e) and that it would not be in the philosopher-king's interest to rule if a city is to be well-ruled (VII, 520d–521a and 519d–520a) does not cohere with the view in the *Gorgias* (515d–520e) that ruling is the one art where one does not need to be paid. Perhaps the two former views speak more to conventional ideas of good (as does *Rep* IV, 419a–421c, with V, 465e–466c), while the view in the *Gorgias* speaks to what is true by nature?

17. Might this anxiety itself not flow from a certain sort of self-interest?

It is true that Prichard sees some hope for Plato in a distinction Plato draws at the beginning of Book II, 357a–358d, between (a) things good in themselves and without further consequences (e.g., harmless pleasures), (b) things good in themselves and good for their consequences (e.g., thinking, seeing, and being healthy), and (c) things good only in their consequences (e.g., medical treatment and money). Prichard thinks that in placing justice along with health in group (b), Plato is showing *some* interest in justice as a good *in itself*, i.e., as close to a moral good. But it is not clear how health or harmless pleasures could be moral goods. So perhaps Prichard takes more solace from this passage than he should.

Let us pursue the evidence on the nature of Plato's ethics in some of the details of the treatment of justice in the *Republic*.

Peculiarities of the Treatment of Justice as Psychological Well-adjustment

Book I of the *Republic* has all the earmarks of a dialogue from the Socratic period which has been slightly edited to serve as a preface to the rest of the *Republic*. It begins by Socrates examining and refuting answers to the question "What is justice?" given by the young man Polemarchus and the sophist Thrasymachus.[18] But before long, Plato allows Thrasymachus to redirect the main question away from "What is justice?" to "Does justice or injustice make one happier?" Socrates gives his arguments on the side of justice. But those arguments do not satisfy the two young men Glaucon and Adeimantus (who are in fact Plato's older brothers). At the beginning of Book II, which constitutes a whole new beginning to the enterprise of the *Republic*, the two brothers throw down to Socrates the challenge to show (what they would themselves like to believe) that: "the completely just life will be happier than the completely unjust life, even when all the rewards of a *reputation* for justice are stripped from the just person and added to the unjust person." – a tall order.

In responding to this challenge, Socrates ranges over a wide range of topics, some of them noted above: the division of labor and the organization of an ideal society into an intellectual ruling class, a military class, and a class of workers (Books II–IV); the division of the psyche into Reason, the Spirited part, and Appetite; the place of doctors and judges in a good society (Book IV); equality of women; eugenics, communism of property, wives, and children among rulers; Knowledge vs. Opinion (Book V); Ideas

18. One of the most noteworthy features of Book I is Socrates' constantly inserting into his handling of the accounts of Polemarchus and Thrasymachus an idea that was surely initially very far from their minds – the idea that justice is some form of expertise, akin to medicine, navigation, and the like. Such an idea seems totally foreign to their own, respectively, traditional(?) and positivistic accounts of justice. Socrates simply reads this idea – the idea that virtue is knowledge – into their account. The idea is also rather out of keeping with *Rep.* II–X. (But we should note that there is an appearance in Book I of the later idea of justice as instead a form of psychological well-adjustment: 351a7–352a8.)

or Forms; testing of the character of future rulers; higher education of the rulers, including a curriculum of studies – with philosophical dialectic as the highest study (Books VI–VII); the sociology of the degeneration of political societies and of individual character (Books VIII–IX); the relative merits of narrative and dramatic poetry; the censoring of dramatists; the immortality of the soul; punishments and rewards in the afterlife; and the soul's freedom of choice in the afterlife concerning what will be it's next incarnation (Book X). But Plato threads his way through all these digressions and near-digressions with his eye always on the challenge to show the just life happier.

But though this question of the happiness of the just has become the main question of *Rep.* II–X, Plato insists again at the beginning of Book II on returning to what Book I has said is the prior question, "What is justice?" And what an extraordinary answer Plato gives, mainly in Books II–IV, to the question "What is justice?"! Justice in the individual, Plato seems to be telling us here, is *a certain sort of well-adjustment of different parts of the soul to each other.*

Someone might object, "But what has psychological well-adjustment to do with justice? Can one not be psychologically well-adjusted but act unjustly? And can one not act justly by sheer will-power, even though somewhat psychologically ill-adjusted? Has Plato not illegitimately changed the subject from the notion of justice as *we* understand it, to some other notion (well-adjustment) which doesn't seem to be a notion of justice at all? We want to know whether *justice* will make us happier, and all Plato tells us, in reply is 'Yes, psychological well-adjustment *will* make us happier!'"

So oddly irrelevant does the Platonic reply here seem, that some are inclined simply to throw up their hands and suppose that in *Rep.* II–X Plato is *not*, after all, so much interested in the question whether just individuals are happier than unjust individuals as he is in a question in political philosophy, namely, "How should one go about constructing in thought an ideal state?" At any rate, this is how the *Republic* is often taken – as not so much an ethical treatise (with digressions) as a treatise in utopian political philosophy (with digressions).

But to treat the *Republic* as primarily a work of utopian political philosophy, however imaginative and daring, is to misconstrue the main aim and direction of the *Republic*, not to mention Plato's literary art. True, Plato *does* have an interest in the ideal conditions for a just political society just as a matter of finding ways to optimize political arrangements within the city. We see this in Book V's digressions on the equality of women and on communal family life for the guardians, in the fragmentary account of the subject-matter of the *Republic* that shows up at the beginning of the *Timaeus*, and in the evident political longing expressed in his discussions of the philosopher king – and perhaps even in Plato's own motives for his three visits to the courts of Dionysius I and Dionysius II. (Cf. also n. 16 above.) Nevertheless, the *Republic*'s purpose in studying justice in an ideal state is tightly constrained by the need to say what justice is in the individual. That is, whatever Plato's interest in the ideal state from other points of view, or in other works, it must be insisted that the ideal state shows up in the *Republic* primarily in the service of determining what justice in the individual is, and whether the just individual is happier than the unjust individual. But to maintain this, we shall have to see how Plato could have thought that his examination of the ideal state could

161

provide insight into what justice is in the individual and whether it is always more beneficial to the individual than complete injustice.[19]

Broadly speaking, Plato thinks that justice in the ideal city has to do with the behavior of the citizens of that city towards each other. Members in each of its classes are to play their own role and not interfere with others playing their own role. By modern lights, this does not seem terribly off the mark as an account of social justice. For the idea of doing your fair share and not interfering with others is not so different from the idea of justice as fairness between different members of the society (though perhaps the *Republic*'s account emphasizes rather more the importance of a person's *role* in society, as opposed to the *rights* of the person within society). Thus Plato does not yet appear to have *changed the subject* on us, even if his views about the subject are *somewhat* different from ours. Real trouble will only arise later.

This account of justice in the ideal city is particularized in terms of its three classes: the intellectuals command, with knowledge, what is best for the city as a whole; the soldiers follow the orders of the intellectual class in defending the city against external and internal enemies; and the workers deal with more narrowly practical needs of the city while going along with the commands of the rulers and soldiers.

At this point, Plato could have suggested that we read off from this account of the justice *internal to* the city, an account of the justice of the individual citizen in terms of that citizen's *external* relations to other citizens. This does not seem so unusual an idea: to understand the justice of individuals within a just society in terms of their behavior towards other individuals within that society. If Plato had done this, the result would, again (as two paragraphs back) not be that different from our notion of justice.

But this is not what Plato does. Instead, he tells us that if justice in a city is a matter of the internal structural relations within the city, then justice in the individual is *also* a matter of internal structure – the internal structural relations within the *individual's* psyche. As the ideal city has three parts (the guardians who have knowledge and look to the good of the entire city; the military who defend the city from danger from outside as well as from within; and the worker class who do their own thing while going along with the commands of the guardians), so too, in parallel, does the individual psyche have three parts (Reason whose job is to have knowledge and look to the good of the entire person; the Spirited part which follows Reason's orders and protects the entire person against unthinking impulses of the Appetitive Part; and the Appetitive Part itself). And as justice in the ideal city is an internal structuring, in accordance with which each of its three parts (classes) fulfills its own function and

---

19. The issue here is not whether "the *Republic* is not at bottom a work of political philosophy at all" (see Lane, PLATO'S POLITICAL PHILOSOPHY, in this volume), if that would exclude the genuine interest in political arrangements which evidently spills out everywhere in the *Republic* (cf. para. 3 of this chapter, as well as paras. 2 and 6 of the present section). Rather it is whether the interest in political arrangements represents a primary interest of the *Republic*, or that interest – within the work itself – is strictly subordinated to pursuit of the two central questions, "What is justice in the individual?" and "Does Complete Justice make the individual happier than Complete Injustice?"

does not interfere with other parts as they try to fulfill theirs, so too justice in the individual is the same internal structuring of the parts of the psyche, in which each of its three parts fulfills its own function and does not interfere with the functions of the other parts. Hence, instead of justice being, as we expected, a relation *external* to – between – the citizens of the just city, it is a relation *internal* to *any* individual – whatever city he or she be a citizen of. It is, as we have said, a kind of psychological well-adjustment – a certain well-adjustment of the three parts of the psyche to each other.

Thus we are, after all, stuck with the problem of defending Plato against the charge of changing the subject from justice as we all know it to something like psychological well-adjustment.[20] The oddity of this turn away from justice as *we* conceive it – we tend to conceive it less in terms of our psychology and more in terms of the relations we stand in towards others – will be intensified if, following Cooper (1977, sec. 1), we note that, by Plato's account of justice, most citizens of the just city *are not just at all*. For, by the account of the three classes Plato gives, only the members of the intellectual class have the knowledge of the good of the whole city that we have seen must be present by the above account of justice. Plainly, Plato has little interest in what we may suppose is the justice of the ordinary citizen of the ideal city. What he is interested in is merely the internal structure of the ideal city as a whole, and the very same internal structure in the individual, no matter what state the individual is a citizen of. One can hardly fail to wonder at how Plato came to such an extraordinary account of justice in the individual.

But suppose for the moment that we grant Plato this account of justice. Then, he thinks, it is going to be fairly straightforward to show that the just person is happier, even if the unjust person is the one who gets all the rewards of *reputation* for being just. For he makes clear at the very end of Book IV that he thinks he has available an analogy between health and medicine that will do the trick. (This analogy is also to be found in the *Crito* and *Gorgias*.) It's simple: As health is a certain well-adjustment of

---

20.   See Sachs (1963) with Penner (2005). It must be granted that Plato has Socrates tell us at IV, 435c–d that this psychological well-adjustment account of justice is not accurate, and that a longer, fuller road must be taken to get that account; and that at VI, 504d–506a, he spells out what is lacking in this account. What is lacking is something greater than justice: the Form of the Good, from which justice and all other things become "useful and beneficial" to us. Proponents of the "strongly transcendent" reading of the Forms noted above may be tempted here to say that Plato is turning away from the psychological well-adjustment account of justice to some much more unworldly Forms of Justice and the Good. But on the reading followed here, it is only being said that for the psychological well-adjustment in which justice consists to be true justice, one needs to add, to any justice we derive from Book IV, knowledge of the real nature of the Good. This says that the just person's Reason must seek *with knowledge*, the real good of the whole individual. Just so, *Euthd.* 280b3–281b4, and *Meno* 87e5–88d3 say that for courage (on some characterization) to be a good, it must be used with wisdom – the knowledge of the good. The point in the *Republic* is thus simply that justice more fully characterized *remains* psychological well-adjustment – but a well-adjustment directed by the full knowledge of the real nature of the good that is to be gained from knowledge of the Form of the Good.

bodily elements to each other, and no one can be happy with those parts not properly adjusted to each other – since life is hardly worth living, no matter how much money or how many other advantages one has, if one's body is ravaged by ill-health – so too, one whose psyche does not have its parts well adjusted to each other stands no chance of happiness, no matter how much money or how many other advantages one has.[21]

If we can accept this analogy between health and well-adjustment of the soul, then these arguments will establish that the just life is happier than the completely unjust life. (The brilliant Books VIII and IX show Plato attempting to confirm his conclusion by examining various unjust forms of city, both less unjust and completely unjust, and the corresponding forms of psyche, evidently arguing that the just life is happier and more pleasant than the many forms of unjust life.)

But even if we succeed in convincing ourselves that Plato can answer H. W. B. Joseph's question whether the reasonably well-adjusted person who acts unjustly only on a certain few occasions – when he can get away with it – isn't happier than the completely just person, we are still stuck with the feeling that justice as *we* understand it *has very little to do with psychological well-adjustment*. So the question remains: Why is the *Republic*'s answer to the question, "What is justice?" so peculiar?

Psychological Well-adjustment as what the Socratic Science of Justice must become given the new Platonic Psychology of Action

The explanation to be offered here is continuous with the claim above that there is no change from Socratic to Platonic ethics that does not flow from the change in the psychology of action. It makes the Platonic account of justice a straightforward adaptation of the *Socratic* account of justice to the requisite changes in the psychology of action.

First, then, let us try to offer an account of what Socrates would have said justice is. There is not much discussion of justice in the early dialogues. But the *Hippias Minor*, like *Republic* I (see n. 18 above), treats justice straightforwardly as a science. And, in the *Protagoras*, we find material from which a fuller account can be extrapolated. Here Plato depicts Socrates taking on the views of Protagoras about virtue and its teachability – views not altogether dissimilar from those in the *Republic* about how the young are to become virtuous. (The main difference is that where the *Republic* wants the intellectual ruling class in charge of education, Protagoras seems to be appealing to the democratic ideal of the whole adult citizen body beneficially educating the young – an ideal Socrates ridicules at *Ap.* 24c–25c, as at 19d–20c he seems to ridicule the idea of education by the sophists.) The methods of education Protagoras employs, however, are largely similar to those we find in *Rep.* II–X: reproof; reformative punishment; education; beatings; the reading of good poets; and music and gymnastic exercise only of the sort to encourage harmony of soul.

---

21. Again, echoes of the *Euthydemus* and *Meno* passages cited in n. 20. Cf. also *Rep.* VI, 505a–b.

In his response, Socrates studiously avoids everything in the large educational canvas painted in Protagoras' Great Speech (320c–328d) except for "one little thing" Socrates needs to be clear on before he can grasp the whole picture (329d). This "one little thing" had come up when Protagoras argued that while the other arts that the city needs can each be practiced by only a few with specialist training, there is one thing that every citizen needs if there is to be a city: "justice, temperance, piety – which together I call the one thing human virtue" (324e–325a, 329c). Are you saying, Protagoras, that virtue is one thing, and justice, temperance, and piety are (distinct) parts of it? Or that what we have in the names "justice," "temperance," "piety," and so forth is just five different names for the same thing? The rest of the *Protagoras* is consumed by Socrates pursuing this question so seemingly irrelevant to the main direction of Protagoras' Great Speech. Why does Socrates do this?[22]

If we look at how Socrates shows that courage is identical with wisdom (358d–360e, correcting 349d–351b), we get some idea of how his thought works. The many think that the courageous and the cowardly go towards different things, since the courageous go towards the fearful – into battle – and the cowardly away from the fearful – away from battle. But Socrates points out (359c–d with 358c d) that the courageous don't go towards the fearful thinking it *fearful*. Rather, they go towards the fearful thinking it *good* to go towards the fearful, just as the cowardly run away from the fearful thinking *that* good to do. Everyone goes towards what they think good, pleasant, and fine, and no one errs willingly (in going towards such things). That is, all desire is for the good. So the difference can only be that the courageous are wise about the good, the cowardly ignorant. That is, courage is wisdom about the good, cowardice ignorance of the good (360c–d). Thus courage and wisdom are not two distinct parts of the one thing virtue. "Courage" and "wisdom" are two different names of the same thing.

Now this argument is itself derived from an earlier argument designed to show that what the many call "being overcome by pleasure" (351b–357e) or "being overcome by fear" or "being overcome by oneself" (359d) is really ignorance of what pleasures, or goods, are worth trading for what in life. The upshot is that what Plato elsewhere calls "temperance" is also identical with wisdom, so that "temperance," "courage," and "wisdom" are different names for the same thing, namely, the science of what goods or pleasures are worth trading for what in life (the "measuring art"). It is true that, for historical reasons, we call this science "courage" in situations involving fear, and "temperance" in situations involving temptation to indulge one's bodily appetites. But the same applies to calling the planet Venus "The Morning Star" at dawn, and "The Evening Star" at dusk. Our using different names on different occasions is no argument that they stand for different things.

---

22.   Plato is so good at portraying opposing points of view, such as those of Protagoras, that some scholars think Plato in the early dialogues does not intend us to embrace the positions put forward by Socrates, but rather a composite of the views of all interlocutors. At that rate, Plato in the *Protagoras* is actually endorsing the views of Protagoras pretty well as much as those of Socrates. See O'Brien (1967) and Kahn (1996). (Such an approach to Plato's intentions would hardly be defensible for the *Ion* or *Hippias Minor*, let alone for the *Apology* or *Crito*.)

The result is that we see Socrates here endorsing the claim (also at *Prt.* 329d, 349b) that "courage," "temperance," "wisdom," "piety," and "justice" are five different names of the same thing – the knowledge of what is worth trading for what in life.[23] What is more, what we have said above should have led us to expect this result. If the fundamental desire leading to action is exactly the same in everyone – desire for their own good – there is nothing left for the good person to be but one *good at* getting his or her own good. (Cf. *Hippias Minor*, not forgetting at 376b, that no one errs willingly at getting their own good.) Hence, virtue is knowledge. Indeed every virtue is the very same knowledge.

But then what would Socrates say about justice, given the above account of the unity of all virtue? It seems plain enough (especially from *Rep.* I) that Socrates would accept the usual view of injustice – that it consists in getting the better of others – more precisely in (trying to) get one's own good by depriving others of their good. ("Trying to" has been inserted here since, as we have seen above, it is also Socrates' view that harming others is *never* in one's interest, so that there is in fact no such thing as getting one's own good by harming others.) This being so, it may be suggested that if Socrates had given an account of justice parallel to the accounts he gives of courage and temperance in the *Protagoras*, he would have said justice is the same knowledge they are, and that the *word* "justice" is, for historical reasons, used for that knowledge in situations where there is a temptation to try to get one's own good by harming others. (The *Crito* in fact shows Socrates all but identifying harm with injustice.)

If this is right, we can now say what we would expect to happen to this account of justice if, as in *Rep.* II–X, the psyche begins to admit of irrational desires causing actions in opposition to what was in Socrates the fundamental desire causing *every* voluntary action. Truths reached by dialectic and the examined life would no longer be sufficient to ensure good action. One would need one's character to be trained and the irrational desires controlled by Reason. (Either that, or without such training and control one would not be able to apprehend the requisite truths.) But the aim would still be the same – the achieving of one's own good in the wisest way possible and without the effort to gain one's own good at the expense of harming others (since harming others will always result in harm to you). That, I believe, is what we have in the idea of justice as psychological well-adjustment. It is precisely what we would expect from a Socratic account of justice modified to take account of the change in psychology that comes with the doctrine of the tripartite soul.

So there is the same aim in the *Republic* as in the early dialogues – to get what is really best for oneself. The difference is only that in the early dialogues, this can be done solely by intellect, while in the *Republic* it needs also character.

It is worth mentioning that this difference in psychology of action between the early dialogues and *Rep.* II–X shows up also in the conception of the ideal city with which Plato works there. For the ideal city Plato discusses is not the ideal city Socrates first describes – rural, decent, and unwarlike, if rude – and which Glaucon describes as providing its citizens with a diet no more interesting than that provided to pigs

---

23. So Penner (1973a, 1992a), followed by Irwin (1977, 1995), Taylor (1976, 1991); contra Vlastos (1973).

(II, 372a–d). The ideal city Plato chooses to discuss is rather the "fevered" city, where people have the kinds of desires, and cravings for luxuries that can only be satisfied by wars of conquest – with the result that the "ideal" city turns out to require the ability to wage war in order to acquire extra goods by conquest, and hence also to require a military class. Once again one asks: Why should one who is interested in justice start from the premise that members of a just city will be warlike?[24] The reason, one may suspect, is that the ideal city has to be parallel to the just psyche. The just psyche has all these unruly appetites to contend with – appetites that, in the absence of justice, sometimes *overcome* Reason (chiefly in Book IV) and appetites that sometimes *corrupt* Reason, making it treat, as good, things that are in fact bad. The result is that, corresponding to these structural facts about the psyche, the ideal city must have *its* parts contending with base desires and the craving for luxuries. (As remarked in note 9, the need for the military in the model is simply that it is politically implausible to have the intellectual class being the ones who control unruly workers.)

Such, then, is the case for supposing that justice in the *Republic* is psychological well-adjustment – because that is the state of soul, replacing Socratic intellectual knowledge of the good, which enables one to achieve one's own maximum good in situations of temptation to try to get one's own good at the expense of others. If the psychology of action has changed, the ethics involves no further changes.

The Development of Greek Ethics Through Plato

In conclusion, it may be useful to see Socratic and Platonic ethics in the context of the development of moral theory of the fifth and early fourth centuries. (I adapt here a scenario from Prichard.) First we have traditional morality where laws and conventions are thought of as handed down by the gods. Then we have the sophistic enlightenment that, as Aristophanes notes, points out that laws are in fact made up by men, so that it becomes rational to ignore these laws and conventions, instead simply fixing on (and announcing: Cf. nn. 5, 8 above) what one thinks one wants and then using sophistic and rhetorical techniques to satisfy those supposed wants. In this contest between traditional morality and the Sophists, Socrates did not align himself with tradition – even if he did hold that some of the things held to be good by convention would also, surprisingly, turn out also to be good by nature. So this "corrupter of the young" was falsely assimilated to the Sophists in the public mind. But Socrates also does not align himself with the Sophists. He argues that what the Sophists took as the easy part is in fact the hard part – knowing what one wants, that is, knowing what the real good is. Hence his exclusively dialectical pursuit of knowledge of the real good – a pursuit to be engaged in every day. Socrates also takes it, for reasons connected

---

24. And, what is more, warlike in a way that disregards the need for the city to be just in its *external* relations to other states? Of that external justice, there is scarcely a word in the *Republic* – another odd feature of Plato's notion of justice, at least from a modern point of view. Would we not expect Plato's description of a just city to include that it be fair and even-handed in its treatment of other states? But that we do not find.

with his psychology of action, that such knowledge (could one but gain it) would also be sufficient for human goodness and for the human's maximization of his or her own happiness. As for Plato's account of human goodness (justice) – provided we resist certain interpretations of the Form of the Good noted above – that differs from the Socratic account solely in the different psychology of action that is operative. In the new Platonic psychology, what one needs if one is to achieve human goodness and one's own maximum good is *character* and *the training of one's irrational impulses* – in addition to that *knowledge of the good* that, in Socrates, was self-sufficient.

Bibliography

Works Cited

Annas, J. (1981). *An Introduction to Plato's Republic*. Oxford: Clarendon Press.

Cooper, J. (1977). "The Psychology of Justice in Plato's *Republic*." *American Philosophical Quarterly*, 14, 151–7.

Devereux, D. (1995). "Socrates' Kantian Conception of Virtue." *Journal of the History of Philosophy* 33, 381–408.

Halliwell, S. (1994). "The Cambridge Companion to Plato." *Dialogos*, 1, 128–34.

Irwin, T. (1977). *Plato's Moral Theory*. Oxford: Clarendon Press.

——. (1995). *Plato's Ethics*. Oxford: Oxford University Press.

Kahn, C. (1996). *Plato and the Socratic Dialogue*. Cambridge: Cambridge University Press.

Nettleship, H. (1925). *Lectures on the Republic of Plato* (2nd edn.). London: Macmillan. (First edition 1906.)

O'Brien, M. J. (1967). *The Socratic Paradoxes and the Greek Mind*. Chapel Hill: University of North Carolina Press.

Penner, T. (1973a). "The Unity of Virtue." *Philosophical Review*, 82, 35–68.

——. (1973b). "Socrates on Virtue and Motivation." In E. N. Lee, A. P. D. Mourelatos and R. Rorty (eds.), *Exegesis and Argument* (Festschrift for Gregory Vlastos). [*Phronesis*, suppl. vol. 1], (pp. 133–51) Assen: Royal van, Gorcum/New York: Humanities Press.

——. (1987). *The Ascent from Nominalism: Some Existence Arguments in Plato's Middle Dialogues*. Dordrecht: Reidel.

——. (1988). "Socrates on the Impossibility of Belief-Relative Sciences." *Proceedings of the Boston Area Colloquium in Ancient Philosophy*, 3, 263–325.

——. (1990). "Plato and Davidson: Parts of the Soul and Weakness of Will." In D. Copp (ed.), *Canadian Philosophers, Canadian Journal of Philosophy*, suppl. vol., 16, 37–45.

——. (1991). "Desire and Power in Socrates: The Argument of *Gorgias* 466a–468e that Orators and Tyrants have no Power in the City." *Apeiron*, 24, 147–202.

——. (1992a). "What Laches and Nicias Miss: and Whether Socrates thinks Courage is only a Part of Virtue." *Ancient Philosophy*, 12, 1–27.

——. (1992b). "Socrates and the Early Dialogues." In R. Kraut (ed.), *The Cambridge Companion to Plato* (pp. 121–69). Cambridge: Cambridge University Press.

——. (2002). "The Historical Socrates and Plato's Early Dialogues: Some Philosophical Questions." In J. Annas and C. J. Rowe (eds.), *New Perspectives on Plato, Modern and Ancient*. Cambridge, Mass.: Harvard University Press.

——. (2005). "Platonic Justice and the Meaning of 'Justice.'" *Journal of the International Plato Society*, 5, 1–76. online at: <http://www.nd.edu/~plato/plato5issue/contents5.htm>.

Penner, T. and Rowe, C. J. (1994). "The Desire for Good: Is the *Meno* consistent with the *Gorgias*?" *Phronesis*, 39, 1–25.

Penner, T. and Rowe, C. J. (2005). *Plato's Lysis*. Cambridge: Cambridge University Press.

Reshotko, N. (ed.). (2003). *Desire, Identity and Existence*. Kelowna, BC: Academic Printing Press.

Sachs, D. (1963). "A Fallacy in Plato's *Republic*." *Philosophical Review*, 72, 141–58.

Santas, G. (1979). *Socrates: Philosophy in Plato's Early Dialogues*. London: Routledge.

——. (2001). *Goodness and Justice: Plato, Aristotle, and the Moderns*. Malden, Mass.: Blackwell.

Taylor, C. C. W. (1976). *Plato: Protagoras*. Oxford: Clarendon Press.

——. (1991). *Plato: Protagoras* (revised edn.). Oxford: Clarendon Press.

Vlastos, G. (1965). "Degrees of Reality." In R. Bamrough (ed.), *New Essays on Plato and Aristotle* (pp. 1–18). New York: Routledge & Kegan Paul.

——. (1973). "The Unity of the Virtues in the *Protagoras*." *Review of Metaphysics* 25, 415–58. Reprinted with an appendix in Vlastos (1981).

——. (1981). *Platonic Studies*. 2nd edn. (pp. 221–69). Princeton: Princeton University Press.

——. (1991). *Socrates: Ironist and Moral Philosopher*. Cambridge: Cambridge University Press.

White, N. P. (1979). *A Companion to Plato's Republic*. Indianapolis: Hackett.

Further Reading

White (1979) is a fine commentary on the *Republic* from a point of view quite different from the present one. Also quite different, and quite excellent, is Santas (2001). A more traditional, and very readable take on the *Republic* is to be found in Nettleship (1925). For contrasting views on the early dialogues, see Santas (1979) and Penner (2002) with the references in those places.

169

10

Plato's Political Philosophy: The *Republic*, the *Statesman*, and the *Laws*

MELISSA LANE

If Socrates is said to have invented ethics, it is his pupil Plato who has been credited by posterity with the invention of political philosophy.[1] Socrates taught Plato that the fundamental question of how to live well[2] was both a question demanding philosophical inquiry (as opposed to being answered authoritatively by poetry, law, or tradition), and a question which trenched on the claims of existing political regimes to be good regimes. For if those regimes failed to promote the practice of philosophy which could uniquely identify (and perhaps even constitute) the human good, their principles of organization and value must be faulty.

Distinguishing Socrates from Plato is a hazardous business, since all our evidence of Socrates' views is indirect and most of it comes from Plato's dialogues themselves. Nevertheless, most readers of Plato today assume that the "Socrates" who figures as a character in Plato's *Republic* is not to be identified with the historical Socrates. And since Socrates does not appear in the *Laws* and appears only at the beginning of the *Statesman*, all three dialogues we are considering as the core of Plato's political philosophy are generally regarded as expressing the ideas of Plato rather than those of Socrates.[3] On these terms, we can say that Plato did not follow his teacher in restricting himself in

1. According to Cicero (*Tusc.* 5. 4): "Socrates, however, called philosophy down from heaven and placed it in the midst of our cities, even introduced it into our homes, and forced it to ask questions about our life, morals, and the good and bad in things." For an argument that political philosophy was invented by pro-democratic thinkers in Athens rather than by the critic of democracy Plato, see Farrar (1988); the contrary case – that political philosophy was a genre invented by Plato in order better to express his critique of Athenian democracy – is put strongly by Ober (1998); and see also Nightingale (1995).
2. "*Eu prattein*" ("do well") are the closing words of the *Republic*, linked etymologically to eudaemonia, the state of happiness or, literally, being well treated by the gods.
3. Many scholars take the fact that both the method and certain assumptions or positions in the *Republic* diverge so far from the relatively unified group of "early" dialogues, to indicate that the "Socrates" of the *Republic* has become a mouthpiece for Plato's views, although it has become fashionable to point out that one cannot necessarily identify the views of a dialogue's author with those expressed by any one character within the dialogue. It remains true that, whatever one thinks as to whether any of the dialogues can be taken to express the views either of (Plato's version of) the historical Socrates or of Plato himself, the texture and project of the *Republic* are in important ways very different from most other dialogues in which Socrates appears (see the section on the *Republic* below).

political matters to a critique of the ethics and (by implication) the politics of Athens. He went further, offering in two dialogues full-scale reconstructions of what a good city might look like. And he also went beyond Socrates in his explorations of what philosophy itself should be, drawing on Pythagorean and Eleatic sources as well (the Pythagoreans were themselves steeped in political concerns).

In sum, Plato searched for a political art (*politikē technē*), a form of knowledge which can use power to produce ethical good, as opposed to using power for the gratification of desire or honor (Wallach, 2001, p. 1). The fundamental axiom of his political thought is the claim that knowledge must govern or "rule" human action – indeed, that genuine knowledge is the most important and perhaps (as is argued in the *Statesman*) the sole proper criterion of good rule. This was the consistent orienting principle of Plato's political thought, one which he took to be antithetical not only to Athens, but also to all other regimes of his own day. It informs all three of the dialogues to be considered in this chapter.

Yet the three dialogues differ from each other along at least two crucial dimensions. First, their projects and purposes are quite different. The point of the *Republic* is to show that knowledge in the ruling group or element is the key to well-being and health in the city and soul alike. The burden of the *Statesman* is to explicate what such ruling knowledge could consist in, and what the nature of such rule could be. And the purpose of the *Laws* is to show how knowledge can be embedded in the structure of the city itself, so that the city like the dialogue becomes an instantiation of the very principle that it advocates – the principle that knowledge must rule (Nightingale, 1993). Second, the psychology, epistemology, and metaphysics which Plato uses to underpin his political arguments changes in crucial respects between the three dialogues. Yet his concern with distinct questions about politics in each means that it may be too swift to claim (as do Bobonich, 2002, pp. 1–8 and *passim*; and Rowe, 2003, p. 92) that it is changes in psychology and epistemology that drive the changes in Plato's politics, and not vice versa. Differing political projects may themselves imply and generate different views of motivation and possible knowledge.

The matrix resulting from changes on both axes yields a corpus of political philosophy which is at once one and many, both unified by common themes and internally differentiated. The achievement of unity in the city is, as Jean-François Pradeau (2002) has shown, a major concern for Plato, as is the more general philosophical status of being one or whole despite having many parts (Harte, 2002; McCabe, 1994). So it is only fitting that both his political philosophy itself and the principal works in which he expressed it are achievements of this kind.

Despite their different casts of characters, the *Republic* and the *Laws* are a common order of magnitude longer than all of Plato's other dialogues, and the fact that both depict aspects of an envisaged admirable city at great length has led readers so minded to identify them as the core texts of Plato's political philosophy. The case for treating the *Statesman* as a third such core political text is different, and more recent. Whereas the *Republic* and the *Laws* build legal and political edifices on the foundational claim that knowledge should rule, the *Statesman* excavates the meaning of that foundation itself. It is accordingly a shorter and more abstract dialogue, one that offers painstaking clarification (and in some respects revision, as will be shown below) of a limited but vital contention in Plato's political thought.

171

But while there is a case for calling the *Republic*, the *Statesman* and the *Laws* a distinct body of work constituting "Plato's political philosophy,"[4] two caveats must be entered to that case before it is further pursued. The first is that these are not alone among Plato's works in having a political dimension. All his dialogues do. In part, this is because politics and indeed everyday life were saturated with ethical terms in ancient Athens, albeit terms which Plato rejected, and because his philosophical investigations of virtue and nature themselves bear on political questions. But further, an Athenian jury condemned Socrates to death. The resulting dilemmas – is philosophical knowledge at war with the equality of democratic opinion? If so, how can democracy tolerate philosophy, and how can philosophy tolerate democracy? – pervade the Platonic corpus as a whole.

The second point is the converse of the first. For while all of Plato's works bear on politics, all of them also address questions other than politics. One might say that Plato treats politics, but also puts it in its place: that of a crucial but instrumental human concern, which like all purely human concerns is further subordinated to what is divine. If Plato invented political philosophy, he also insisted that it is at once connected to the rest of philosophy (psychology, epistemology, ethics, and metaphysics) and that it does not exhaust the purpose of philosophy. Our three dialogues illustrate the former point by each resting most heavily on a particular philosophical plank ethics in the *Republic*, epistemology in the *Statesman*, theology in the *Laws*. And they illustrate the latter point by showing (each in its own way) that the reasons to be concerned with politics are located in what lies beyond politics – the eschatological future life of the soul in the *Republic* and the *Laws*, general dialectical or philosophical ability in the *Statesman*.

Republic

Having contended that the *Republic* belongs in the corpus of Plato's political philosophy, we must immediately confront a challenge. For it has been argued that, given that the text is governed by an ethical question – why should anyone bother being just? – it is not at bottom a work of political philosophy at all (Annas, 1999; see the discussion of this question in Penner, PLATO'S ETHICS, in this volume). On this view, the sketch of Kallipolis (as the ideal city described in the *Republic* is sometimes called) is a mere cartoon, meant as an illustration of the possibilities of governing one's soul rather than as a blueprint for a political regime.[5]

---

4.   Whereas an author like Klosko (1986) spent most of his time on the *Republic* and treated the *Statesman* and the *Laws* cursorily as stages of decline, the more recent contribution of Samaras (2002) interprets the sequence as building up to the *Laws* as a climax. Samaras adds a brief consideration of the *Timaeus* and *Critias* between the *Statesman* and the *Laws*. Wallach (2001) treats a far greater number of dialogues as integral to his account of Plato's political thought.

5.   "Blueprint" here is a shorthand way of capturing what most participants in this debate take a "political" dialogue to be; for criticism of the idea that the politics of the dialogue involve a "blueprint" at all, see Waldron (1995, pp. 159 and *passim*), though he adheres to the view being

It is right to point out that ethics motivates the *Republic*, and that concern for the fate of the individual immortal soul concludes it. Socrates goes so far as to say that even if Glaucon is right that the city they have described does not exist "anywhere on earth" (and cannot do so without the help of "divine good luck"), "perhaps . . . there is a model of it in heaven, for anyone who wants to look at it and to make himself its citizen on the strength of what he sees" (IX, 592b). True political philosophy describes the city in which the philosopher would wish to be an active citizen, and so long as that city does not exist, the philosopher will restrict himself to sculpting its order in his own soul rather than seeking to take part in public life.

Nevertheless, to conclude that politics in the *Republic* is at best a sideshow is mistaken. By placing politics in its ethical and eschatological contexts, that text shows just why and how politics matters so profoundly – and so why existing regimes are so dangerously perverse. While it can be argued that ethics overshadows politics in the *Republic*, it is equally true to say that politics there infiltrates ethics, showing that there exist a politics of self-care and a politics of friendship as well as the conventional politics of the city. All of these political regimes, large and small, are instruments necessary to give people the chance to be as happy as they can be. Although only true philosophers can and will be truly happy – since happiness depends on the harmonious rule of reason which only they can secure for themselves – other people will be as happy as possible in this life only if they live in Kallipolis, and only there are they likely to have the opportunity to do better for themselves by choosing rationally for the life to come. So Plato is not merely using politics to illustrate tricky points in ethics. He is genuinely seeking to invent a political philosophy, one which can expose why virtually all of the political arguments of his day (both for and against democracy) are shallow and bankrupt, "sophistry" rather than "philosophy." It is in the *Republic* that Plato invents a new conceptual language – rooted in a psychology, an epistemology and a metaphysics – which underwrites his profound critique of democratic and indeed all existing politics as indifferent to value, to virtue, and to knowledge.

But if the *Republic* takes this giant step forward in the corpus of Plato's writings, it grows out of questions worried over repeatedly in other dialogues. In several dialogues Socrates raises the question of whether there is any master knowledge: a kind of knowledge that would govern the entire course of life and specifically the good of the soul, in the way that medical knowledge is acknowledged to govern the good of the body (e.g., *Prt.* 313a–b; see generally on the "master knowledge" aporetic dialogues, Sprague, 1976). He also suggests that if knowledge is the criterion that Athenians accept when they are choosing doctors or ship captains, should it not *a fortiori* be the criterion used when making political decisions? (Socrates in the *Gorgias*, 502d–e: good orators with philosophical knowledge would "set their sights on making the citizens as good as possible through their speeches," as opposed to the Athenian orators who are "bent upon the gratification of the citizens and . . . slight the common good for the sake of

---

criticized here, that the dialogue is ethical *as opposed to* political: he says that "the construction of an ideal society is imagined by Socrates and his friends not as the articulation of a political proposal but as a way of answering an ethical challenge" (p. 143). See also Lane (1999, pp. 120–1, 134–5).

their own private good.") But the difficulty lies in knowing whether there is any such overall knowledge relevant to the success and happiness of life, and what its content might be.

The *Republic* triumphantly answers this question by linking the conception of Forms which emerges in other dialogues (notably the *Phaedo*) with the conception of the knowledge of choiceworthiness – or goodness – which emerges in the "master knowledge" dialogues. The rulers should know the Form of the Good, but only the philosophers can know this – hence the philosophers should rule. These pathetic creatures who skulk in corners and appear to sophists like Callicles (*Grg.* 484c–485e) and even to decent young men like Adeimantus (*Rep.* VI, 487c–d) to be politically useless, utterly irrelevant to the real business of life, are in fact the principal hope for any city's salvation.

Yet even here lies danger, in two directions. The first is how to prevent exploitation of the ruled by the rulers: how can rulers be kept gentle guard-dogs rather than becoming rapacious wolves? Virtually anyone who wants power may want it, or come to want to use it, to exploit the ruled rather than serve them. Books II–IV outline an answer, which is then deepened in the second "philosophical" description of the ideal city in Books V–VII, and which is not always recognized as being as startling as it is. For Socrates does not rely on the fact that the rulers will be wise (Books II–IV) and even genuinely philosophical (Books V–VII) as a sufficient safeguard of their justice toward the ruled. Rather, the ruling guardians must be deprived of any possibility of exploiting those they rule, by the drastic expedient of being deprived themselves of family bonds and private property. Only if rulers have no children or relatives to favour, and no chance of accumulating property to favour them with, will those they govern be truly safe. To put it in the terms of Book I, only a shepherd without prospect of wealth or family will care for his sheep for their sake rather than his own.

The second danger takes the form of a paradox. It was argued in response to the first danger that only those who do not want to rule and have no private incentive to want to rule, can be trusted to rule. How then can the reluctant potential rulers be induced to rule? Book I already sketches one answer to this. Socrates states that "wages must be provided to a person if he's to be willing to rule, whether in the form of money or honor [money being rejected in Book V when communism for the guardians is introduced] or a penalty if he refuses" (347a). But, he continues, "good people won't be willing to rule for the sake of either money or honor. . . . So, if they're to be willing to rule, some compulsion or punishment must be brought to bear on them . . ." (347b). This is amplified in one direction in Book IV (419a–421c), when Socrates retorts to Adeimantus – who is troubled that the rulers, deprived of money and luxury, will not be happy – that justice will be most easily found when the whole city is happy. This in turn depends on the rulers playing their part along with the other groups of citizens, though Socrates later pointedly observes to Adeimantus' brother that the guardian-rulers will enjoy victory and public acclaim and so happiness more than that of Olympic victors (V, 465d–e). It is amplified in a different direction in Book VI (499b–d), in the thought that philosophers unwilling to rule may sometimes be "compelled" by chance or necessity (which Greek thought did not sharply distinguish) to rule, or existing kings may be inspired by "a god" to love philosophy. But the problem is nowhere fully resolved. A good political regime is vital if the majority of people – all but the philosophers – are to be able to be as non-miserable as they can be, yet the prospects of establishing such a regime are hazardous, chancy, and extremely dim.[6]

Let us return to the ethical frame of the argument, as set out especially in Books I–II and IX. The text opens with a discussion about the nature of justice at the home of a wealthy metic living in the Piraeus, the Athenian port which stands outside the walls of the city proper. This discussion, in which three interlocutors successively replace one another in the role of being questioned by Socrates, anticipates many of the points made in the remainder of the text. For present purposes the crucial part is the exchange between Socrates and Thrasymachus, a "sophist" who aggressively exposes what he sees as the argumentative ploys used by Socrates against the previous speaker. Thrasymachus takes the position that justice is the advantage of the strong as defined by them for their purposes in controlling and exploiting the weak: if shepherds care for their flock, it is only to fatten them for a more valuable kill. Socrates tries to argue that acting justly is in fact in the interests of the just person. But two of the listeners are not fully convinced. While Thrasymachus argues that the strong pull the wool over the eyes of the weak (justice is never in the interests of the ruled), these two youths pose a slightly different problem. For them, the weak may have reason to be just rather than unjust if they know they can't get away with flouting the laws publicly. But the best thing for the weak would be to be able to get away with acting unjustly. While it is better for them to pull the wool over their own eyes than not to do so if the only alternative is to be destroyed, it would be better still for them to deceive their fellows instead of themselves by getting unjust gains at no reputational cost.

These two interlocutors – brothers bearing the names of Plato's actual brothers, Glaucon and Adeimantus – therefore challenge Socrates more fully to answer the question, why be just? They explain that while they do not believe that it is better to be unjust, they equally don't believe that the case that justice is what really benefits the individual has been made well enough by any of the poets or philosophers who have addressed the question. No wonder that many of the young are cynical about doing what their elders tell them is right and living on the straight and narrow path; even these two, who have withstood the temptations of injustice, are not immune to the vaunting of its attractions. The rest of the *Republic* is Socrates' response to this request, in the form of an attempted proof that justice – not the apparent attractions of injustice – is what most truly benefits the individual.

In passing we should note that it is crucial to the dialogue's structure (and to what distinguishes it from the "Socratic" dialogues) that the youthful brothers at no point themselves defend the contention that it is better to be unjust – they merely say that they have not heard it be sufficiently well refuted and ask Socrates to do so. In the aporetic dialogues, Socrates characteristically insists that the person he is questioning

---

6.   One line of commentators, inspired by Leo Strauss, has indeed held that the real, hidden message of the *Republic* is that the realization of the ideal city is impossible – contrary to Socrates' repeated assertions in Book V of the ways in which the regime will be "possible" and "beneficial." See Strauss (1987) and the representative debate between Bloom (1977) and Hall (1977). The view taken here is that it is possible to realize the ideal city, though this may depend on divine aid (see below).

must say sincerely what he actually believes. Here, Glaucon and Adeimantus are at pains to deny that they themselves believe that it is better (for oneself) to act unjustly rather than justly. Instead of putting energy into refutation, therefore, Socrates is free to put his energy into constructive argument – and the brothers, who assert that they have been tempted by, but never succumbed to, the claim that injustice really pays, are presented as free to be persuaded.

Socrates' response is, in a nutshell, to argue that justice is what really benefits the individual because justice contributes along with the other three cardinal virtues to the harmony of the soul. The just person is at peace with himself because and insofar as his soul is well-ordered; the unjust person is miserable because his soul is divided and disordered. And the proper order of the soul is for it to be governed by knowledge. This is where the brothers' ethical question "why justice," intersects with the classic Socratic problematic about knowledge ruling. Each person's happiness depends on their soul being ruled by knowledge. But only in the case of true philosophers is their reason capable of doing the job alone. For most people, the possibility of happiness and justice depends on their reason being supplemented by surrogate reason from outside: either because their own reason has not attained the true objects of knowledge which the surrogate reason has done, or because their own reason is too weak to do the job on its own. "[I]t is better for everyone to be ruled by divine reason, preferably within himself and his own, otherwise imposed from without, so that as far as possible, all will be alike and friends, governed by the same thing" (IX, 590d). Being governed by such surrogate external reason may not be enough to make a non-philosopher really just or happy. But it will get them as close as they can get, and in particular will save them from the out-of-control appetites that would otherwise render their misery complete.

Such a portrait of complete misery is drawn in Book IX – the tyrant – and is identified as the epitome of the unjust person, in contrast with the philosopher who is the epitome of the just. In virtue of his ability to satisfy all his lusts – the very ability which Glaucon and Adeimantus had heard described as admirable for those who can attain it – he is miserable. The objects of lust do not confer happiness. Only a well-ordered soul ruled by reason can do that, so being ruled by lust and greed, the tyrant forfeits his chance for happiness. At this point the argument has come full circle – from the temptations of tyranny described by Glaucon and Adeimantus in Book II, to the abhorrence with which Glaucon meets the description of the tyrant in the terms just sketched in Book IX. But the *Republic* does not end there. The brothers had originally challenged Socrates to prove that justice pays in itself, not in virtue of the rewards which a reputation for justice might attract. Glaucon vividly posed the challenge by telling the story of the ring of Gyges (II, 359c–360d), a ring which makes its bearer invisible and so allows him to profit from injustice; he also imagines a just person who, conversely, is maligned and maltreated so as to suffer from all manner of worldly evils – reviled and poor, is his justice any real consolation? In Books IX and X Socrates completes the argument by pointing out the usual benefits which being just brings in its train, together with the more unusual ones – namely, the benefit justice confers on you not only in this life but in the next. The myth of Er is one of several eschatological myths in Plato. Here, in a neat and important twist, what justice gains you after death is not a divinely conferred reward, but rather the ability to choose wisely – unclouded by lust or ambition – among the various lives on offer for the next life. It is the link between justice and wisdom – that is, between virtue and knowledge – rather than justice alone which is the key to happiness in the *Republic*.

The skeleton of the argument should now be clear. At its core are two central ribs, one psychological, the other epistemological. We may say that the psychology of the *Republic* pluralizes, politicizes, and platonizes the soul. For what does it mean for souls to be potentially divided and so badly or well-ordered? The idea that injustice arises from a divided and disordered soul contradicts the thesis of many Socratic dialogues that evil (including injustice) is done only out of ignorance, a thesis which denies the possibility of acting against what you know to be right or best (the possibility of *akrasia* or "weakness of will"). In the *Republic*, evil may be done due to ignorance – one may have a well-enough-ordered soul but one's reason is not sufficiently well cultivated to have attained moral knowledge. But evil may also be done out of disorder of the soul, and this is explained for the first time by a pluralization of the soul: each soul has parts.

By analogy with social-functional classes in the city, it is argued that there are three parts of the soul. Appetite and reason are obvious candidates for two of these; indeed, the thought that appetite can sometimes oppose reason is at the heart of the folk understanding of *akrasia* which Socrates so counter-intuitively denies in other dialogues. The third part is harder to isolate; Danielle Allen (2000, pp. 245–6) has shown how the argument identifying this as the *thumos* or spirited part serves to transform the Athenian political and psychological landscape, by prompting readers to reject the results of angry Athenian punishments and seek instead to find their honor in the course of reason. Each of these "agent-like" parts of the soul has a characteristic goal and is capable of a primitive form of practical reasoning to attain that goal (Bobonich, 2002, pp. 217–22). This is one reason that "appetite" is a better translation of *epithumia* than "desire," because all three parts have their own characteristic "desires." Appetite seeks satisfaction for particular bodily wants and chooses objects which it believes will satisfy those wants, believing further that the satisfaction of wants constitutes the good life. *Thumos* seeks honor and evaluates what it takes to be occasions to display courage in order to achieve that goal, believing further that the attainment of honor constitutes the good life. Reason seeks knowledge including knowledge of the good, believing (when properly educated) that the attainment of such knowledge constitutes the good life.

Such a psychic structure is not only plural, but also political. By this is meant that the soul is figured as a mini-polis, a political unit in which order and rule must be established. What must most be avoided is *stasis*, or factional uprisings against good rule – in the case of the soul, this happens when *thumos* allies itself with appetite instead of with its natural ally, reason. And it is the thesis that reason is the best ruler of the soul which constitutes the soul's platonization. The soul is not ideally a democracy. The justification for the rule of reason is not that it has been chosen by the other two parts to rule, but because its rule is the best and only path to happiness for the individual. Freedom, as Socrates concludes in Book IX, can only be given to children or to cities once a constitution or "*politeia*" has been established in them (IX, 590e).

This account has been called inconsistent and contradictory (Williams, 1973). If each individual has a tripartite soul, how can the city consist of three distinct "parts" or social groups each corresponding to a single part of the individual soul? Jonathan Lear (1998 [1992]) has resolved this apparent inconsistency by offering a psychodynamics of the interaction between soul and city, showing how the apparently static model of Books II–IV comes to life in the psycho-civic-dramas of regime degeneration in Books VIII–IX.[7] Each timocrat, say, does have three parts to his soul, but the *thumos* or honor-loving part is predominant, setting the goals for the person as a whole, and so stamping its character on the city where he and those like him predominate.

Why, though, should reason be willing to rule in the soul, given the acute and unresolved problems in the text as to why and indeed whether philosophers would be willing to rule in the city? This is the second objection. The best explanation as to why reason should be ready to rule in the soul appeals to the fact that reason in Plato is an intrinsic orderer, inherently motivated to promote the existence of good order in the world. But if this were enough also to answer the question as to why the philosophers would be willing to rule in the city, the reiteration of the roles of chance, necessity, and compulsion in bringing them to do so would be pointless. The disjuncture between the willingness of psychic reason and living philosophers to rule can be explained as follows. By ruling in the soul, reason is performing a natural ordering function: its role in the soul is indeed that of innate and intrinsic orderer. But it is not natural, in the Platonic sense of what is teleologically best, that one person's reason should have to order the soul of another. The political relationship, that is, is not natural. It is necessary only because of the weakness, perversion, or failure of the reason of the person who needs (in Platonic terms) to be ruled.

So reason, which would be teleologically driven to contemplate the Forms and establish justice in its own bearer's soul, is forced to turn away from those perfections in order to compensate for the weaknesses of reason in others. This conduces to justice in that it enables reason everywhere to be bolstered in its rightful task of ruling, and so enables the city as a whole to be as happy as possible. And it may be required by justice if so doing repays a debt incurred in the education of the philosophers. But if it can be explained as a surrogate procedure required by "goodness," it forms no part of "bestness," and so reason's intrinsic ordering function does not solve the problem of why the philosophers should be willing to rule.

We have here begun to trench on the ultimate metaphysical teaching of the *Republic*, that is, the Form of the Good. For to say that reason's proper object is knowledge, as was said above, is not yet to have said enough. As was shown at the outset of this discussion of the *Republic*, the question raised by many other dialogues is – knowledge of what? What kind of knowledge is it that is capable of governing our lives for the best?

"What kind" can mean "what nature" or "what content," and the *Republic* addresses both of these meanings for the question above. First, the nature of the knowledge relevant to politics and appropriate as an object for reason. This knowledge must remain stable across many different contexts, if it is to be useful for political life. So,

---

7. Ferrari (2003) has challenged Lear's account, arguing that these processes are not evident in the text of the dialogue and offering a different interpretation of the city–soul relationship (and the problems it raises) from those given not only by Lear but also by the classic paper to which Lear himself had responded (Williams, 1973): this challenge cannot be assessed here, but the present author remains persuaded of the value of Lear's insight.

Socrates argues, it cannot owe anything to those contexts in themselves: it cannot be relative or situational. Plato therefore infers that there must be objects of knowledge which are by nature context-independent, unaltered by changes in time and space. It is the absolute nature of these objects that enables them to serve as a standard and touchstone by which the philosophers orient themselves in the world of action. These objects are the Forms. There is not exactly a "theory of Forms" in the *Republic* – the remarks made about them are called provisional and insufficient. Yet the aspiration to knowledge which is timeless and context-independent, and which is also value-relevant and so relevant to action, is embodied unforgettably in Socrates' contrast between those who love ordinary sensuous objects and those who love the Forms.

But there are many Forms – the beautiful, the just, alongside the more problematic example in Book X of the Form of the couch (on Book X, see Burnyeat, 1999). Which one – what content – is the most fundamentally relevant to political knowledge? The *Republic* sweeps to an answer by means of a grand metaphysical analogy in Book VI. Just as the light of the sun makes physical objects visible, so the light of the Good makes the Forms intelligible – that is, visible to the mind's eye. The Good, because intelligibility and purpose can only be understood in light of (in terms of) goodness. As the *Timaeus* suggests, the world can be explained only insofar as it is good; where goodness runs out, so does explanation, and we are left confronting sheer, mere matter.[8]

Grasping the Good is, therefore, the fundamental aim of reason and so the orienting purpose of any well-ordered soul. Putting the Good into practice is the special task of politicians in the city as it is the task of each person in his or her own life. Loving and seeking after the Good – even if one does not have full contemplative knowledge of it – is itself enough to quiet and tame all other possible desires in the soul. And this is why those who are converted to the cause of reason and philosophy – even if they lack a full philosophical education – will themselves be just.

Contrary to those who have followed Sachs (1963) in claiming that Plato has simply performed a bait and switch, substituting justice as psychic harmony for the conventional interpersonal justice which he is supposed to be defending, the *Republic* takes pains to point out that people who are psychically just will have no motive to behave unjustly towards others. Having defined justice in the soul as in the city as each part doing its own work, Socrates assures Glaucon that they can dispel any "doubts" as to whether justice in the soul is the same as in the city "by appealing to ordinary cases" (IV, 442d–e): "For example, if we had to come to an agreement about whether someone similar in training and nature to our [just] city had embezzled a deposit of gold or silver that he had accepted, who do you think would consider him to have done it?" (443a). Glaucon is quick to agree that no one would suspect the psychically just person of such embezzlement, nor, in response to further questions by Socrates, of "temple robberies, thefts, betrayals of friends in private life or of cities in public life . . . [being] untrustworthy in keeping an oath or other agreement . . . [or engaging in] adultery, disrespect for parents, and neglect of the gods" (443a).

8. For a different account of explanation in the *Timaeus*, grounded in mathematics rather than explicit appeal to the good, see in this volume Brisson, PLATO'S NATURAL PHILOSOPHY AND METAPHYSICS.

Put simply, the psychically just have no desire for the fruits of injustice, their desire being oriented solely toward the good. The just man "puts himself in order, is his own friend, and harmonizes the three parts of himself like three limiting notes in a musical scale . . ." (IV, 443d). Socrates' friendship for Glaucon and Adeimantus can aid them to befriend themselves in this way, even if they must cling only to an intimation of the Good rather than a full and complete contemplative knowledge of it. Such friendship, embedded not in elenchus but in constructive conversation, is in one sense political, since it involves Socrates using his reason to improve and bolster that of the youths. But it is more natural than ordinary politics since it is based on a potential affinity of reason and virtue, and the aspiration to a truly mutual friendship in virtue akin to that which Aristotle would later idealize.[9] The politics of friendship aims, we might say, to outgrow the need for politics at all. Where friendship succeeds, it can implement ethics at least in individual souls; where it fails or is impossible, the full politics of Kallipolis must await the chance or necessity of the rule of philosophers.

Statesman

The *Republic* is framed as an inquiry into the definition of justice and its bearing on happiness; the *Statesman*, as an inquiry into the definition of the eponymous person with genuine political knowledge. For the former, the purpose of an inquiry into ruling knowledge is to establish justice and happiness; for the latter, the purpose of the inquiry is simply to define the nature of that knowledge which could rule more precisely. In particular the *Statesman* makes two points which go unnoticed in the *Republic*: ruling knowledge is not simply knowledge of the good, but knowledge of the good in time (the *kairos*); and such inherently flexible knowledge of the *kairos* must be made authoritative over the unchanging and approximate requirements of fixed laws (Lane, 1998, pp. 132–3, 139–45, 193–202). So for the *Statesman*, the antithesis of the true statesman is the sophist conceived as a politician – the person who pretends to knowledge but exercises rule without it. Such a sophist may be found in any kind of regime lacking genuine knowledge, which is to say in all regimes existing in Plato's day. In the *Republic*, in contrast, the antithesis of the true statesman, that is to say, of the philosopher-ruler, is as we have seen the tyrant – not simply any person who rules without knowledge, but specifically that ignorant ruler whose appetites and power are most spectacularly unbridled.[10]

The same equation – those who know should rule – lies at the heart of both dialogues. In the *Republic*, the relevant knowledge is defined as knowledge of the good, and attention is focused on the perspective of the rulers – how they will be educated, the puritanical conditions in which they must live (eugenic breeding, no recognized

---

9.   In this volume, see Pakaluk, ARISTOTLE'S ETHICS.
10.   So in *Republic* VIII, democracy is the next-to-worst of the imperfect regimes, better only than tyranny. In the *Statesman* (303a–b), democracy without true knowledge is the best of bad regimes (defined as regimes not governed by a true statesman) since democrats have less power of action than tyrants and oligarchs and so can do in their ignorance the least harm.

families, no property) in order to exclude the greed which would shatter their unity as a group. In the *Statesman*, the relevant knowledge is defined as knowledge of the good in time, and attention is focused on defining that knowledge as opposed to other forms (and pretences) of knowledge – the true statesman becomes a cipher, his perspective being reduced to the nature of his knowledge alone. The effort of definition itself commands attention in the latter dialogue; the loose methods of analogy which Socrates had used in the *Republic*, contrast with the precise methodological instructions and corrections issued by the Eleatic Stranger in the *Statesman*. And whereas the myth of Er cemented the reasons for the individual to be just and virtuous, the "myth" of the *Statesman* – a fabrication from three legends with a particular version of the legendary rule of Kronos at its core – instead serves to define the conditions of political life for what has earlier been called the "human herd." The *Republic*'s myth teaches that justice pays; the *Statesman*'s, that politics is necessary, non-grandiose, and must be carefully distinguished from the other arts (Lane, 1998, pp. 117–25).

We saw earlier that it is not implausible (though ultimately unpersuasive) to argue that the *Republic* is essentially an ethical rather than political dialogue. One could make no such argument about the *Statesman*. This is a philosophical dialogue *about* politics (Migliori, 1996, p. 197), whereas the *Laws*, as we shall see below, is largely a work *of* politics. Another way to put the differences between the projects of the *Republic* and the *Statesman* is to say with Malcolm Schofield (1999, p. 37) that whereas the *Republic* begins with the question of the good or best political regime and discusses statecraft as a way to bring this regime about (and so becomes preoccupied with the question of how would-be rulers could gain the knowledge needed to do so), the *Statesman* in contrast begins with the more general question of the nature of political expertise in rule as such, saying nothing about how someone might acquire it and relatively little about what the city ruled by it would be like. The *Statesman*'s project is at once more general and more narrow.

In return for this narrowness of focus, which excludes some of the fundamental challenges of political life, the *Statesman* offers a more complex understanding of the nature of political knowledge and indeed of the nature of knowledge itself. The methods of division and of example which are employed (along with the myth) lay out the structure of knowledge of the relationship between different arts in terms of differentiation and interrelationship. The *Statesman*'s knowledge is located within this structure and consists in grasping the structure as a whole.

The price of this systematic investigation is the abandonment of virtually all meaningful dialectical interaction; at the outset the Stranger announces his preference for monologue, or if need be, for dialogue with a suitably tractable interlocutor, and his anonymity strips him of the political entanglements which the character of Socrates would have brought to mind for any Greek reader. The *Republic* seeks to redirect ambitious youth to the life of philosophy by offering them a compelling argument in the mouth of the charismatic Socrates; in the *Statesman*, a younger boy serves mainly as a foil for a Stranger whose city is renowned for metaphysics rather than ethics, and whose age is not specified – he appears ageless, anonymous, the voice of pure discriminating reason. (We shall see later that the *Laws*, in contrast to both, is a conversation among old men [Schofield, 2003, pp. 4–6 and *passim*]; lacking either political ambition to be tamed, or the impetus to set out on a comprehensive philosophical quest, they devote themselves to reflection on their experiences of political life.)

But perhaps the most startling apparent contrast between the *Statesman*, on the one hand, and the *Republic* and *Laws* on the other, is their characterization of the rule of law. While law is not flagged as a problematic topic in the *Republic*, it is relied upon as a form of surrogate reason, both in the envisaging of how the philosophers will proceed to rule, and in the law-making which Socrates and his interlocutors themselves engage in as "founders" of the ideal city. And in the *Laws*, as we shall see later, law is conceived as more than merely a surrogate for reason: it is called the embodiment of divine reason itself. Toward the end of the *Statesman*, however, the Stranger homes in on the distinction between sophists and statesmen by recalling that their whole discussion has been guided by the crucial criterion involved: the possession or lack of expertise. So whereas, he suggests, existing regimes classify themselves as democracies or oligarchies, tyrannies or monarchies, on the basis of criteria such as the wealth of the rulers, the voluntary willingness of the subjects to be ruled, or the use of written laws, none of these criteria is relevant to the definition of statecraft (293a–e). The true statesman might force things on his subjects, or dispense with the use of laws altogether, without forfeiting his claim to be practicing an art which benefited subjects by making them better.

Here Young Socrates is driven to object, in the name of fundamental Greek assumptions rather than specifically democratic ones: he does not question the use of force on unwilling subjects, but finds it hard to accept that one could rule without laws (293e) – this may simply strike him as an oxymoron.[11] In response the Stranger develops the thought that law is inherently imperfect, in that it is unable to address itself to individual peculiarities or changing circumstances. Statecraft, it will emerge, is defined by its ability to judge when something should be done or not done, whereas law can only repeat the same order over and over. Yet in the absence of the true statesman, or when people are (wrongly) fearful that a true statesman would harm rather than benefit them, the second-best plan is to stick to existing laws rigidly rather than suffer them to be changed for selfish or stupid reasons by someone ignorant. The "sophists" include both those who preside over the second-best constitutions in which law is observed, and those who make a bad situation worse by attempting to change the laws without knowledge: they comprise all politicians except the true statesman. As Christopher Rowe has persuasively if controversially argued, these second-best

11.   The idea that rule without law would seem to Young Socrates an oxymoron now seems to this writer the most attractive explanation of why he objects to this point in particular (and not, e.g., to the argued irrelevance of force vs. voluntariness). This is not incompatible with Lane (1998, pp. 148–52), which argues against Gill's (1995) reading of Young Socrates as a spokesman for Athenian constitutionalism, on the ground that the Athenians did not conceive their laws as a "restraining framework" which could not be changed. But it now seems to me clear that the *use* of law would seem to Young Socrates to be a feature of any possible and existing regime; it is left to the Eleatic Stranger to point out that the mere existence of laws is not what distinguishes regimes, but rather their stance in either observing or failing to observe their laws.

regimes have no means of access to the laws which a true statesman would prescribe: their virtue as "second-best" lies only in their sticking to whatever laws they happen to have (Rowe, 1995, ad. loc.; Rowe, 2001, pp. 68–74; but see criticism in Samaras, 2002, pp. 171–80).

Once this criterial point (Cooper, 1999, p. 101) has been established – that nothing is relevant to the definition of an expert except his expertise – it can be admitted that the statesman will indeed use laws to establish the necessary common opinion between divergent groups of citizens. In this passage the two summative accounts of statecraft – the one, its definition in relation to the rival arts, as the master art which governs when each of the other arts should act (305c–d); the other, as the political weaver of civic unity (305e) – come together. The statesman was defined against his closest rivals – rhetors, generals, and judges – in terms of his knowing the "*kairos*" – the right moment or opportunity – when it is fitting to use or pronounce persuasion or force, war or peace, guilt or innocence. Now it turns out that as political weaver, his task is to embed recognition of the *kairos* in the judgments of the citizens, modifying their natural tendencies to misjudge in characteristic ways (some too boldly, others too timidly) so that both groups can be made virtuous (courageous or moderate) and united by common opinion and by marriages (Lane, 1998, pp. 171–82).[12] Defined by his expert knowledge of the *kairos* (which Aristotle would call "the good in time"), the *Statesman* can unlike ordinary sophistic lawmakers shape the laws and modify them when necessary so that the good can be achieved despite the flux of circumstance.

Images used by the Stranger suggest that the statesman will not be a permanent resident of the city whose laws he frames. He is compared to an athletics coach or trainer, and to a doctor, both of whom may go away for a while leaving written prescriptions (laws) for their patients to follow, yet who should be obeyed if on return they order the written prescriptions to be discarded or changed. The practice of voluntarily or compulsorily leaving the city for which they had written laws was not unknown among Greek lawgivers. The idea of a lawgiver or statesman who stands outside the city that he shapes here becomes central to Plato's political thought.

Whereas readers tend to contrast this itinerant eponymous statesman with the resident and (eventually) native philosopher-rulers of the *Republic*, this is a mistake. For as Socrates' eagerness to convince even the guardians to believe the "noble lie" about the city's origins in the *Republic* (III, 414d) shows, the *Republic*'s rulers belong within the city rather than outside. It is Socrates and his interlocutors in the *Republic* who are the real counterparts to the statesman of the *Statesman*, as to the interlocutors of the *Laws*. Once the superiority of knowledge over law has been vindicated by the *Statesman*, the dialogue is content to consider the statesman as a legislator when he needs to be, but stresses throughout that his role is to be outside the city, an occasional sojourner there rather than a resident or native ruler. As this dialogue brings out more

---

12. Arends (2001, pp. 136–8) has rightly criticized the translation in Lane (1998), of 307d, contrasting it with the correct translation by Rowe (reprinted in Cooper, 1997), which runs as follows: "this disagreement, of these classes of people, is a sort of play; but in relation to the most important things, it turns out to be a disease which is the most hateful of all for cities."

clearly than most, Plato's political thought is framed and located most comfortably at the level of the statesman who shapes, founds, and then withdraws, not that of the ordinary or regular participant in political life.

The *Laws*

If the *Republic* is a work of soaring moral-political imagination, and the *Statesman* one of painstaking methodologico-political clarification, the *Laws* is a work of comprehensive "theologico-political" (Laks, 2000, p. 292) reflection and prescription. It is unique among Plato's dialogues in its setting, and in the fact that Socrates plays no role in it. Whereas many dialogues show Socrates talking primarily with Athenian citizens (as in the *Republic*) or depict visitors and "strangers" to Athens (as in the *Statesman*), this one presents an "Athenian Stranger" in conversation with two fellow old men, the Spartan Megillus and the Cretan Clinias, while walking to the top of Mt. Ida in Crete to sacrifice at Zeus's shrine. It has been observed that this presents a deliberate form of inter-cultural dialogue, between old men who escape the wise lawmaker's ban on legal questioning and dissent among the young, but who lack the philosophical bent of the Eleatic Stranger (Gill, 2003). While the conversation begins with the Athenian Stranger simply proposing that they occupy themselves with discussion of laws and constitutions (in fact, it famously begins with the word "*theos*," as the Stranger asks his companions whether their people ascribe the authorship of their laws to god or man), it takes a new turn at the end of Book III, when Clinias reveals that he has been chosen as one of ten men of Cnossos (a city in Crete) to frame the legislation for the new colony of Magnesia. The rest of the conversation, which consists of nine further books (and according to ancient testimony was left on wax tablets at Plato's death, which has been taken to imply that it was unfinished), constructs a model legislative framework for this new colony.

It is important to note that, like the ideal city of the *Republic* (II, 369a; IX, 592a–b), the city of the *Laws* is founded "in speech" (III, 702e) rather than in actuality; the purpose is to advise Clinias for his later practical deliberations rather than to enact those deliberations themselves. Yet it matters equally that the colony in view will be populated by "volunteers," whose fallibility and flawed education is not seen to pose a mortal threat to the new city, whereas the *Republic* is driven to suggest that everyone over the age of ten should be exiled to the countryside in order to start the new order off with a clean slate. Here, the people come first and the city's rule must be adjusted to suit them (within limits: in both dialogues, hopelessly bad people are to be exiled), whereas in the *Republic*, the rulers come first and it is their character and knowledge that determine the nature of the city. Indeed, in the *Laws* the people will themselves play an active role in ruling themselves, a balance between "monarchy" and "democracy" being a crucial aspect of the constitution (III, 693e). The philosophers who must be ever-present and ever-watchful in the *Republic* contrast with the statesman who withdraws in the *Statesman*, and both contrast with the *Laws* where the constitution for Magnesia involves no single ruler or group of rulers in whom knowledge uniquely resides.

It is important to note here that the Athenian Stranger's claim – repeated several times in the text – that the city of Magnesia is of the "second rank," is never made explicitly with reference to the *Republic*. In Book V of the *Laws*, the first-ranking "ideal society" is described as a "community of wives, children and all property," a phrase undeniably evocative of the *Republic*. But this community is specified as "put into practice as widely as possible throughout the entire state" (739c), as opposed to the *Republic* where it is explicitly restricted to the guardian-rulers. Book IX of the *Laws* by contrast does seem implicitly to suggest that the city of the *Laws* is second-best, as compared not to the city of the *Republic* but to that of the *Statesman*. The prelude to laws about violence explains the necessity of laws by saying that: "no man has sufficient natural gifts *both* to discern what benefits men in their social relationships *and* to be constantly ready and able to put his knowledge to the best practical use" (875a) (emphasis in the English translation used but not in the Greek).

So it will be difficult for anyone to grasp the theoretical truth that the aim of the true *politikē technē* is "not the interest of private individuals, but the common good"; and even if someone could grasp this and gain a position of absolute control over a city, "his human nature will always drive him to look to his own advantage and the lining of his own pocket" (875b). This sounds like a critique of the possibility of the *Statesman*'s ideal ruler ever coming to exist. But the Athenian continues to affirm both the superiority of such rule by knowledge (rather than law) and the possibility that the "grace of God" could bring it about:

> But if ever by the grace of God (*theia moira*) some natural genius were born, and had the chance to assume such power, he would have no need of laws to control him. Knowledge is unsurpassed by any law or regulation; reason, if it is genuine and really enjoys its natural freedom, should have universal power: it is not right that it should be under the control of anything else, as though it were some sort of slave. But as it is, such a character is nowhere to be found, except a hint of it here and there. That is why we need to choose the second alternative, law and regulation, which embody general principles, but cannot provide for every individual case. (875c–d)[13]

It is striking that the *Republic*, too, invokes the need for a "divine dispensation" (*theou moiran*, VI, 493a) in order to save the soul of a potential philosopher (and so potential ruler or founder of Kallipolis) from corruption. Paradoxically, then, it is the political projects of the *Republic* and the *Statesman* – where theology is far less emphasized – which are said to depend for their very possibility of realization on divine intervention. Magnesia, which requires no divine dispensation to be established (despite the Athenian's pious prayer for divine favor, IV, 712b, and as opposed to the regime ruled by the "natural genius" described above), is therefore not a theocracy (a regime *ruled*

---

13. See Schofield (2003, pp. 7–11), contrasting this passage with IV, 712b–715e and XII, 957c (where the rule of law is identified with reason and divinity) and comparing all three with the *Statesman*. Schofield suggests that the *Laws'* theological framework and its limited philosophical ambitions go together.

by the gods), nor is it a regime actually *needing* the gods to exist. It is rather a regime resting on *belief in* the gods. This belief is both paradigmatically rational and a belief in the divinity of reason, or the rationality of the divinity(ies), which is why André Laks (2000, p. 262) for his part calls Magnesia a "noocracy."

Why the central role here for belief in theology? In the absence of philosophers to rule and to respect, the people need to fear the gods. It is not simply that theology is a practical way to secure moral principles among a general population (as argued by Schofield, 2003, p. 13), though the *Laws* does rely on this as a method. Respectful fear (*aidos*) of the gods is to be fundamental to the motivational structure of the virtuous citizen. But it is only essential because the external surrogate reason of the philosophers of the *Republic* is here absent. Law in the *Laws* is the embodiment of reason, but to be efficacious in the city it must be internalized in the souls of the citizens. Belief in the gods internalizes ideal rulers in the soul who surpass even the philosopher-rulers of the *Republic*. Whereas the *Republic* has difficulty in establishing why the philosophers will be willing to rule, as we saw above, the *Laws* can assert that the gods care for humans because care is a virtue and treat them justly because justice is a virtue (900d). The gods' rule is perfectly virtuous; unlike mortal rulers, they have no need to control their appetites in order to be proof against bribery, injustice, or indifference.

The proof of this comes in the "prelude" addressed to an imagined youthful atheist, which occupies virtually the whole of Book X, and seeks to rebut the atheistic claims that either there is no god, or the gods do not care about humans, or the gods can be bribed by prayers and sacrifices. The Athenian invokes the primacy of soul in the cosmos, as immortal and the oldest of all generated entities, in order to show that rational intelligence is fundamental and pervasive, and that this rational intelligence will necessarily be virtuous and love virtue.

We saw that the *Republic* is built on fundamental contentions in two key areas: psychology and epistemology. The *Statesman* makes psychology virtually a function of epistemology, to the extent that it treats the subject at all. Now the *Laws* reverses the emphasis: it has little concern with epistemology (except for a notable emphasis on ignorance as one cause of evil, e.g., IX, 863c–e) but a deep and abiding concern with psychology. The roles of pleasure and shame as effective motivating experiences in the soul are stressed, against the one-sided Doric emphasis on fear; true virtue, which is the Stranger's proclaimed goal for the constitution – that it should foster virtue in the citizens – consists not in repressing the pleasures but in rationally shaping them to its own ends. Pleasure and pain, *thumos* (anger or spiritedness), and ignorance are all mentioned as human mental and emotional states (*pathē*) which can undermine reason and so the rational purposes of the law. But the *Laws* does not treat any of these as independent parts of the soul with their own evaluative purposes, nor does it invoke their dominance in the soul as demarcating different classes of citizens.

This new psychology underpins a new emphasis in the way that the law is said to operate. In the *Republic*, education and law are both treated as essential, but the links between them as such are not explored at any length. The *Laws* treats the principal and ideal function of all laws as educative: the "prelude" part of the law aims to persuade the citizens to act as it prescribes, so that the need for the coercive aspect of law can be reduced so far as possible, though never entirely abolished. The famous passages contrasting the operation of "free doctors" (that is, doctors treating free men) and "slave doctors" (that is, doctors treating slaves) are most naturally read to support the idea that the laws, like free doctors, seek to be efficacious through rational persuasion of those they govern (IV, 720a–e; IX, 857c–e). But some critics have challenged the rationality of the actual preludes contained (as examples) in the text of the *Laws*, and have gone on to argue that Plato is not here envisaging rationally autonomous citizens who operate primarily on the basis of rational argument: with their behavior so controlled and prescribed, restrictions on their ability to travel abroad, strict military discipline, is Plato really depicting a city of potentially rational and virtuous citizens, or a city of thought-policed robots?

Cases for and against the rationality of the preludes as described, and as exemplified, have been made powerfully on both sides.[14] The present writer contends that while the preludes are conceived as rational, and (with allowances for context) are mostly presented as exercises in rational persuasion, Plato also consistently in the *Laws* (as in the *Republic*) insists on, and dramatizes, the fact that compulsion and persuasion cannot always be so readily distinguished in theory or separated in practice. Socrates is compelled to explain the community of wives, children and property in the *Republic* (V, 449a–450b); it is less often noticed that the *Laws* also involves two notable dramatic references to compulsion should persuasion fail. In Book VI (753a) the Athenian proposes to Clinias that he should himself become a citizen of the new colony of Magnesia, "with your consent (failing which, you'll be gently compelled)." In Book XII, Clinias and Megillus agree in turn that they must get the Athenian himself to join the colony by refusing "to let him leave us," and using "entreaties and every ruse we can think of" (that is, persuasion and deception) to accomplish that aim (969c). In Book IV also, the young dictator whose rule is called the easiest and quickest way to change the laws of a state, is said to combine "persuasion with compulsion" (711c).[15]

In short, the role of persuasion is important, but not unaccompanied by compulsion whether by legal penalties or by other forces. And its role is rather to shape the character of the citizens than to acknowledge their independent right as the ultimate judges of political power, in the way that practices of persuasion in the Athenian assembly and lawcourts did. The rule of law in Plato's vision here takes over the authority of the democratic Athenian assembly, and accords authority to the citizens only insofar as they are themselves molded to recognize its own rationality and authority (Allen, 2000, pp. 179–90). "Voluntary" acceptance of rule by the citizens of a true *politeia* – as contrasted with the "unwilling" subjects of the factional regimes of tyranny, oligarchy and democracy – does not exclude a role for compulsion in molding that acceptance (VIII, 832c–d).

---

14. For the case against, see for example Stalley (1994), and the more moderate Laks (2000, pp. 289–90), both criticizing Bobonich (1999 [1991]). Samaras (2002, pp. 310–25) advances the debate by arguing that while the theory of preludes is indeed one of rational persuasion (even if not all preludes in the text exhibit this), Plato's commitment to rational persuasion here does not commit him to a liberal view of individual choice or freedom.

15. Nevertheless, one place where persuasion and compulsion are conjoined in the *Republic* – in order to get the rule of philosophers started in the first place – is avoided in the *Laws* by the assumption that the colonists will be (screened) volunteers (IV, 708aff.; V, 741a).

Given that the psychology of the *Laws* does lay emphasis (though not sole emphasis) on rational persuasion, it underpins a politics in which citizens can play diverse roles. The establishment of the magistracies in Book VI involves law-wardens, commanders, a Council and its subdivisions, stewards for the city, the land, and the markets, officials for education and competition in music and gymnastic, and judges. All these are to be elected by various forms of restricted nomination and suffrage, many involving property class: democratic equality must have its share in the city, though it is less correct and perfect than the kind of equality which is proportional to worth, but its share cannot be complete as in the Athenian practice of selection by lot. In Book XII the *euthunai*, or scrutineers of the law-wardens, are given a far more exalted role than the office of that name in Athens; they are the guardians who must guard the guardians. And Book XII also introduces the famous or infamous "Nocturnal Council" (a more accurate name would be the less sinister "Dawn Council," as they are to meet near dawn), a group of experienced and wise elderly men, each accompanied by an apprentice younger man. They have no magisterial power in the city but are charged with reviewing its laws, partly in light of embassies to the outside, in order to make sure that they remain as rational as possible.

Although the Stranger acknowledges that many details must be omitted and left to the law-wardens to determine, what strikes any reader of Books VII–VIII is the extraordinary level of detail which is in fact provided. The Athenian declares earlier that, "Nothing, so far as possible, shall be left unguarded" (VI, 760a), and in fact, nothing so far as possible is to be left unregulated: infants' clothing, children's games, pregnant women's diet, all are prescribed so as to begin shaping the experience of pleasures and pains from the very moment of conception, going on to agricultural and market laws to safeguard the food supply. Books IX, XI, and part of XII are the principal locus of the penal laws and the discussion of punishment, which is consistent with Platonic principles of punishment elsewhere in the corpus in holding that punishment should aim at improving the offender's soul. The Athenian also keeps faith with the Socratic paradox that no one does injustice willingly, coping with its radical implications for the penal code by reassigning the distinction between voluntary and involuntary criminal action to the notion of injury effected rather than that of (always involuntary) injustice intended.

Throughout the work is reiterated the theme of age, contrasting the political difference between old men who can be trusted on the basis of experience, and young men who may be rash in their judgments of city, self, and gods, and who need to be tempered to respect the law. Also reiterated is the theme of the divinity of reason which can be embodied in laws, and so guide mortal nature with a divine cord. These two themes together help to show that the supposed Actonian pessimism about absolute power corrupting absolutely is not in fact present in the *Laws*. The passage where it is most often discerned (IX, 875b–d) says that any man with knowledge and power will be driven by his "human nature" to use that power for his own advantage. But this does not exclude the possibility raised in the "golden cord" puppet image (I, 645a) that his "human nature" might be controlled by something divine in him. If the emphasis on divinity in political affairs distinguishes the *Laws* from other Platonic works, this very emphasis makes it possible for the dialogue to keep faith with the aspiration to rulers with knowledge and virtue which characterizes them all.

Conclusion

In writing these three dialogues Plato explored what political philosophy could and should be from different angles and according to different understandings of philosophy itself. Yet all Plato's political explorations pursue the basic thought that knowledge alone can make action virtuous and so make people happy and their lives worth living. It follows that whoever possesses such knowledge – which Plato assumes throughout his work to be potentially and at most only a few people – must ensure that somehow or other it governs the actions of all.

Plato's political philosophy, as enunciated in the three major works considered in this chapter, goes beyond the criticism of Athenian democracy with which it presumably began, to inquire into the ethical basis of power and the true significance of all existing constitutional forms. The dialogues speak through many voices to explore the possibility of constructing a politics aiming at virtue, for souls who are divided, in a world constrained by necessity and requiring the divine or semi-divine guidance of reason in the form of philosophy, statecraft, or law.[16]

Bibliography

Works Cited

N.B. The Latinization of the Greek title of the *Statesman*, by which it is sometimes called, is the *Politicus*.

Allen, D. S. (2000). *The World of Prometheus: The Politics of Punishing in Democratic Athens*. Princeton: Princeton University Press.

Annas, J. (1999). *Platonic Ethics: Old and New*. Ithaca, NY: Cornell University Press.

Arends, F. (2001). "Review Article – The Long March to Plato's *Statesman* Continued." *Polis*, 18, 125–52.

Bloom, A. (1977). "Response to Hall." *Political Theory*, 5, 293–313.

Bobonich, C. (1999 [1991]). "Persuasion, Compulsion, and Freedom in Plato's *Laws*." In G. Fine (ed.), *Plato vol. 2: Ethics, Politics, Religion and The Soul* (pp. 373–403). Oxford: Oxford University Press.

——. (2002). *Plato's Utopia Recast: His Later Ethics and Politics*. Oxford: Clarendon Press.

Burnyeat, M. F. (1999). "Culture and Society in Plato's *Republic*." In G. B. Peterson (ed.), *The Tanner Lectures on Human Values*, vol. 20 (pp. 215–324). Salt Lake City: University of Utah Press.

Cooper, J. M. (1999). "Plato's *Statesman* and Politics." *Proceedings of the Boston Area Colloquium in Ancient Philosophy*, 13, 71–104.

——. (ed.) with Hutchinson, D. S. (assoc. ed.). (1997). *Plato: Complete Works*. Indianapolis: Hackett.

Farrar, C. (1988). *The Origins of Democratic Thinking: The Invention of Politics in Classical Athens*. Cambridge: Cambridge University Press.

16.   Thanks to the editors, Adam Rachlis, and Malcolm Schofield for comments on previous versions.

Ferrari, G. R. F. (2003). *City and Soul in Plato's Republic*. Sankt Augustin: Academia Verlag.

Gill, C. (1995). "Rethinking Constitutionalism in *Statesman* 291–303." In C. J. Rowe (ed.), *Reading the Statesman*. Proceedings of the Third Symposium Platonicum (pp. 292–305). Sankt Augustin: Academia Verlag.

——. (2003). 'The *Laws* – Is it a Real Dialogue?'. In S. Scolnicov and L. Brisson (eds.), *Plato's Laws: From Theory into Practice*. Proceedings of the Sixth Symposium Platonicum (pp. 42–7). Sankt Augustin: Academia Verlag.

Hall, D. (1977). "The *Republic* and the 'Limits of Politics.'" *Political Theory*, 5, 293–313.

Halliwell, S. (ed., tans., and notes). (1993). *Plato: Republic V*. Warminster: Aris and Phillips.

Harte, V. (2002). *Plato on Parts and Wholes: The Metaphysics of Structure*. Oxford: Clarendon Press.

Klosko, G. (1986). *The Development of Plato's Political Theory*. London: Methuen.

Laks, A. (2000). "The *Laws*." In C. Rowe ad M. Schofield (eds.), *The Cambridge History of Greek and Roman Political Thought* (pp. 258–92). Cambridge: Cambridge University Press.

Lane, M. [S.] (1998). *Method and Politics in Plato's Statesman*. Cambridge: Cambridge University Press.

——. (1999). "Plato, Popper, Strauss, and Utopianism: Open Secrets?" *History of Philosophy Quarterly*, 16, 119–42.

Lear, J. (1998 [1992]). "Inside and Outside the *Republic*." In J. Lear. *Open-minded: Working Out the Logic of the Soul*. Cambridge, Mass.: Harvard University Press.

McCabe, M. M. (1994). *Plato's Individuals*. Princeton: Princeton University Press.

Migliori, M. (1996). *Arte politica e metretica assiologica: commentario storico-filosofico al "Politico" di Platone*. Milan: Vita e Pensiero.

Nightingale, A. (1993). "Writing/Reading a Sacred Text: A Literary Interpretation of Plato's *Laws*." *Classical Philology*, 88, 279–300.

——. (1995). *Genres in Dialogue: Plato and the Construct of Philosophy*. Cambridge: Cambridge University Press.

Ober, J. (1998). *Political Dissent in Democratic Athens: Athenian Critics of Popular Rule*. Princeton: Princeton University Press.

Pradeau, J.-F. (2002). *Plato and the City. A new Introduction to Plato's Political Thought*. Trans. by J. Lloyd with foreword by C. Gill. Exeter: University of Exeter Press. (Originally published as *Platon et la cité*, 1997).

Rowe, C. J. (ed., trans. and notes). (1995). *Plato: Statesman*. Warminster: Aris and Phillips.

——. (2001). "Killing Socrates: Plato's Later Thoughts on Democracy." *Journal of Hellenic Studies*, 121, 63–76.

——. (2003). "Socrates, the Laws, and the *Laws*." In S. Scolnicov and L. Brisson (eds.), *Plato's Laws: From Theory into Practice*. Proceedings of the Sixth Symposium Platonicum (pp. 87–97). Sankt Augustin: Academia Verlag.

Sachs, D. (1963). "A Fallacy in Plato's *Republic*." *Philosophical Review*, 72, 141–58.

Samaras, T. (2002). *Plato on Democracy*. New York: Peter Lang.

Schofield, M. (1999). "The Disappearing Philosopher-King." In M. Schofield, *Saving the City: Philosopher-Kings and Other Classical Paradigms* (pp. 31–50). London and New York: Routledge.

——. (2003). "Religion and Philosophy in the *Laws*." In S. Scolnicov and L. Brisson (eds.), *Plato's Laws: From Theory into Practice*. Proceedings of the Sixth Symposium Platonicum (pp. 1–13). Sankt Augustin: Academia Verlag.

Sprague, R. K. (1976). *Plato's Philosopher-King: A Study of the Theoretical Background*. Columbia, SC: University of South Carolina Press.

Stalley, R. F. (1994). "Persuasion in Plato's *Laws*." *History of Political Thought*, 15, 157–77.

Strauss, L. (1987). "Plato". In J. Cropsey and L. Strauss (eds.), *History of Political Philosophy*. 3rd edn. Chicago: Rand-McNally. (Original work published 1963.)

Waldron, J. (1995). "What Plato Would Allow". In I. Shapiro and J. Wagner DeCew (eds.), *Theory and Practice* (= *Nomos* 37). New York: New York University Press.

Wallach, J. R. (2001). *The Platonic Political Art: A Study of Critical Reason and Democracy*. University Park, Pa.: Pennsylvania State University Press.

Williams, B. (1973). "The Analogy of the City and Soul in Plato's *Republic*." In E. N. Lee, A. P. D. Mourelatos, and R. Rorty (eds.), *Exegesis and Argument* (pp. 196–206). New York: Humanities Press.

Further Reading

Benardete, S. (1984). *The Being of the Beautiful: Plato's Theaetetus, Sophist, and Statesman.* Chicago: University of Chicago Press.

——. (1989). *Socrates's Second Sailing: On Plato's Republic.* Chicago: University of Chicago Press.

Burnyeat, M. F. (1992). "Utopia and Fantasy: The Practicability of Plato's Ideally Just City." In J. Hopkins and A. Savile (eds.), *Psychoanalysis, Mind and Art: Perspectives on Richard Wollheim* (pp. 175–87). Oxford: Oxford University Press.

Morrow, G. R. (1960). *Plato's Cretan City: A Historical Interpretation of the Laws.* Princeton: Princeton University Press.

Rosen, S. (1995). *Plato's Statesman: The Web of Politics.* New Haven, Conn.: Yale University Press.

Saunders, T. (1991). *Plato's Penal Code: Tradition, Controversy, and Reform in Greek Penology.* Oxford: Clarendon Press.

Strauss, L. (1975). *The Argument and the Action of Plato's Laws.* Chicago: University of Chicago Press.

Tuana, N. (ed.). (1994). *Feminist Interpretations of Plato.* University Park, Pa.: Pennsylvania State University Press.

Vlastos, G. (1977). "The Theory of Social Justice in Plato's *Republic*." In H. F. North (ed.), *Interpretations of Plato* (= *Mnemosyne* suppl. vol. 50) (pp. 1–40). Repr. in G. Vlastos, *Studies in Greek philosophy.* vol. 2: *Socrates, Plato, and their Tradition* (pp. 69–103) (D. W. Graham ed.). Princeton: Princeton University Press.

Yunis, H. (1996). *Taming Democracy: Models of Political Rhetoric in Classical Athens.* Ithaca, NY: Cornell University Press.

11

Plato's Metaphysics and Dialectic

NOBURU NOTOMI

Did Plato do Metaphysics?

Plato is often admired or attacked as a champion of metaphysics. What is the power of his thinking that fascinates philosophers and makes them resist? Plato's philosophy has long been stimulating philosophical spirits, and has thereby framed the Western tradition of metaphysics. Metaphysics, in turn, became a central theme in Platonic studies. This theme is more difficult to deal with than one might suppose, however, since Plato himself never describes his own project as "metaphysics," as Leibniz, Kant, and Heidegger, for instance, do. Discussing Plato's metaphysics inevitably raises the question of what philosophy is. But this question is exactly what Plato invites us, readers of his dialogues, to consider, so as to engage in philosophy with him. Here we should not take metaphysics for granted, nor should we project our modern conception onto Plato. Instead, this chapter will investigate a basic question: did Plato do metaphysics, and if so, in what way? For this question is, I believe, crucial to the understanding of Plato's metaphysical impact. Let us begin by looking briefly at the meaning of metaphysics.

Plato was clearly innocent of the specific area of philosophy called "metaphysics." This concept was born later, at earliest when his pupil Aristotle wrote a set of treatises or lecture notes, which were three centuries later edited and entitled *Ta meta ta phusika* (which means what comes after the treatises on natural things, i.e. physics). The later tradition reinterpreted this title as dealing with what is beyond (*meta*) natural things. In those treatises Aristotle discusses "being as being" with its focus on "substance" (the primary being), and the god(s) as the first principle, which exists beyond natural things. He calls this "first philosophy," in contrast to physics, which deals with things changing in time and space (see M. L. Gill, FIRST PHILOSOPHY IN ARISTOTLE, in this volume). Metaphysics was established on the basis of what Aristotle inherited from Plato, although in some respects Aristotle clearly departed from Platonic thinking. For while the separation of the two domains – the unchanging principles and the changing or changeable things – originates in Plato, Aristotle drastically alters their ontological status.

The title "Plato's metaphysics" is, strictly speaking, not only anachronistic but also misleading in a sense, since we find no independent treatise in Plato that deals with metaphysics. The Aristotelian division of philosophy hardly applies to Plato's works, which are all given in dialogue form. Each dialogue treats multiple issues in a single line of conversation. The *Republic*, for example, starts with the mundane topic of senility, and then raises ethical problems concerning justice and looks for a definition of it. The dialogue also covers politics, education, literary criticism, sociology, psychology, ontology, epistemology, and sciences. All these topics are closely interconnected with each other, so that it is almost impossible to single one out. At the climax of the dialogue, however, comes what we might call metaphysics: Socrates introduces a theory that posits things in themselves, namely, beauty itself, justice itself, and goodness itself. These are called "forms," and the arguments for forms have traditionally been treated under the name of Plato's theory of forms (in this chapter, I use the word "form" as representative of the related vocabulary including "idea"; "Form" with the initial capital letter F is often used for Plato, in contrast with Aristotelian or Socratic "form," but this is a sheer convention of some modern scholarship).

Despite the risk of anachronism, there are also good reasons, both historical and philosophical, for discussing Plato's metaphysics; for based on Aristotle's report, the theory of forms has traditionally been recognized as that. The theory of forms and the living dialogue create a tension, which culminates in the philosophical method called "dialectic," and in this tension lies the essence of Plato's metaphysical thinking. In this chapter I will demonstrate how the tension between the two illuminates what Plato's metaphysics is, or rather what metaphysics *can be* for Plato.

Aristotle's Account of Plato's Theory of Forms

As a member of Plato's Academy from his youth, Aristotle was familiar with the basic thinking about forms. It is Aristotle, a severe critic, who framed our view on "Plato's metaphysics." Especially the first book of the *Metaphysics*, in dealing with the history of philosophy, summarizes Plato's position (A.6; similar accounts are given at M.4, 1078b12–17, and M.9, 1086a32–b13). So let us observe what Aristotle presents there as the kernel of his master's thought.

Aristotle introduces and critically examines the views of his predecessors, from Thales to Plato, on first principles. They discovered only one or a few of the four causes, namely, material, formal, efficient, and final causes, while Aristotle succeeds in finding all the four. Aristotle turns to Plato after examining the Pythagoreans, who believed that numbers are the principles of all things (A.5). Here I introduce the first three sections of A.6, which are most relevant to our argument.

The first section (987a29–b14) starts with a comment connecting Plato to the Pythagoreans: he basically followed them but with two important departures. In his youth he learned Heracliteanism from Cratylus and maintained its doctrine even at a later stage, that "all sensible things are ever in a state of flux and there is no knowledge about them." Moreover, Plato adopted Socrates' method of seeking universals through definition:

> Plato accepted his (sc. Socrates') teaching, but held that the problem applied not to any sensible thing but to entities of another kind – for this reason, that the common definition could not be a definition of any sensible thing, as they were always changing. Things of this other sort, then, he called forms, and sensible things, he said, were apart from these, and were all called after these; for the multitude of things which have the same name as

the form exist by participation in it. Only the name "participation" was new; for the Pythagoreans say that things exist by imitation of numbers, and Plato says they exist by participation, changing the name. (*Met.* A.6, 987b4–13)

Three factors – Heracliteanism, Socrates, and Pythagoreanism – are said to shape Plato's basic thoughts: first, sensible things are always changing and can never be grasped by knowledge; second, unchanging forms exist separately as the objects of universal definition and of knowledge; third, sensible things exist by participating in the forms. This account has become the standard understanding of Plato's theory of transcendent forms, but at the same time we must keep in mind that this quasi-historical account is made to fit Aristotle's own philosophical scheme.

Socrates' philosophy shows primary influence, especially in those dialogues where Socrates asks about moral properties, "What is it?" (*ti estin*) and seeks definitions, with most inquiries ending in *aporia*. Many modern scholars take this philosophical activity to become the starting point for Plato: he tries to answer this difficult question by proposing forms. Forms are never changing and can therefore be objects of universal definition. Actually, the *Euthyphro*, one of the earlier dialogues, which examines piety, uses the word "form" (*idea, eidos*) for the objects of definition (5d, 6d–e). Socrates asks his interlocutor to state the form itself: by looking upon that form itself and using it as a model, one is supposed to be able to explain why any pious action is pious. Similarly, the *Lysis* introduces "the first friend, that for the sake of which we say that all the rest are friends too" (219c–d). These expressions indicate that the notion of "form" develops from the single object for definition required by the Socratic question. However, they do not indicate ontological separation or transcendence, for which other factors are needed (cf. Allen, 1970).

As for the Heraclitean influence, Aristotle's account is often doubted because the flux theory shows scarcely a trace at the earlier stage. Also, it becomes the target of severe criticism later in the *Theaetetus*, although it is disputed (since antiquity; cf. Sedley, 1996) what message should be drawn from this criticism: the flux theory may either remain valid within the sensible world, or be rejected as invalid altogether (cf. Burnyeat, 1990). Aristotle's account seems to be committed to the first option.

Next, apart from the two cores of Pythagoreanism, namely, transmigration of the soul (apparent in the *Gorgias, Phaedo, Phaedrus*, and elsewhere) and general interest in mathematics and numbers (in the *Republic* and *Timaeus*, in particular), it is unclear how deep the Pythagorean influence on Plato is. Despite Aristotle's report, the relation between sensibles and forms does not necessarily correspond to that between things and numbers, since the Pythagoreans often *equate* things with numbers (rather than separating them). Aristotle gives priority to Pythagoreanism because such an exposition was fashionable in the Academy (certainly on Plato's initiative); the essence of Plato's philosophy was cast back to various and often vague Pythagorean origins. Thus, Aristotle's account, though it may sound authoritative, presents Plato's theory *as he understands it*.

For the origins of Plato's theory, we must take at least two more important factors into account, namely, Parmenides and Protagoras, whose omission betrays the defects of Aristotle's account as *historical*. Parmenides is no doubt a predecessor most important for Plato, as testified in the *Parmenides* (main speaker) and *Sophist* (target of examination). Parmenides argued that there is one absolute being, which allows neither plurality nor any change in time and space. Plato's characterization of the transcendent forms reflects the one being of Parmenides. Separation of forms from sensibles must come from, or at least be based on, the Parmenidean distinction between the unchanged being and many changing appearances. On the other hand, the famous sophist Protagoras remains a chief antagonist for Plato. Connected with the Heraclitean flux theory, Protagorean relativism is formally rejected in the *Theaetetus*: the equation of appearance with reality and of opinion with knowledge is to be repudiated (in my view, however, Protagoreanism continues to be a major target in the *Sophist*).

In the next section, Aristotle adds Plato's view on mathematics:

> Further, besides sensible things and forms he says there are the objects of mathematics, which occupy an intermediate position, differing from sensible things in being eternal and unchangeable, and from forms in that there are many alike, while the form itself is in each case unique. (*Met.* A.6, 987b14–18)

Clear as the statement is, it is controversial whether Plato admits an intermediate ontological status for mathematical objects, such as numbers and geometrical figures. The only direct treatment of them appears in the Simile of the Line in the *Republic* (VI, 510b–511e), but there Plato's words are ambivalent and bewilder interpreters. Many modern scholars are inclined to deny their independent status intermediate between forms and sensibles. Aristotle's account may be his own interpretation and response to what Plato puts as a difficulty to be considered (cf. Burnyeat, 1987).

Then, in the third section, Aristotle proceeds to an account of the composition of forms. Before examining this section, let us see the conclusion Aristotle draws from the account: concerning the first principles, Plato uses only two of the four, namely, formal and material causes. Thus, Aristotle formulates Plato's metaphysics in terms of his own scheme of "form and matter," which themselves are the major legacy of Plato's metaphysics. At the same time the metaphysical system given here leaves many issues open. In fact, Aristotle himself reports its openness: "But what the participation or the imitation of the forms could be they left *for our common inquiry*" (987b13–14). The theory of forms was a theme to be discussed in a shared research project in the Academy.

The Unwritten Doctrines

In the third section, Aristotle's formal account crucially differs from what we see in Plato's own dialogues:

> Since the forms are the causes of all other things, he thought their elements were the elements of all things. As matter, the great and the small were principles; as substance, the one; for from the great and the small, by participation in the one, come the numbers (or the forms). (987b18–22)

The one is not a natural number; the Greeks usually begin to count number from two, whereas one is the unit of numbers. It is the ultimate formal principle, from which numbers and forms come to be. On the other hand, "the great and the small," elsewhere called "the indefinite dyad," is regarded as the material principle that accepts formal characters.

This report, however, has no clear equivalent in Plato. In several places, Aristotle presents this fundamental theory, or what he sometimes calls "the Unwritten Doctrines" (*agrapha dogmata*) (*Phys.* IV.2, 209b14–15), whose contents were also hinted at by several ancient authors. A natural conjecture is that Plato discussed such ideas with his colleagues in the Academy, who heard, interpreted, and criticized them as his metaphysical doctrines. Although little is known about Plato's activities in the Academy, a famous episode is recorded by Aristoxenus, a pupil of Aristotle. Once Plato announced that he would give a lecture "On the Good," and people gathered in expectation to hear about ordinary good things, such as wealth, health, and happiness. Their expectation was soon dashed, however, since Plato discussed only mathematics, and concluded that good is one. Hearing this, people were greatly disappointed. Then some scorned the affair and others criticized it (*Harm.* II, 30–31).

When the Neoplatonists, beginning with Plotinus, deepened Plato's ontology, they used these materials as supplementary to the dialogues. Such fundamental principles as the one and the indefinite dyad fit their hierarchical systematization of beings: the supreme good (identical with the one) is the fundamental principle, from which all beings successively emanate. Here we should bear in mind that most Platonists (after Middle Platonism) made much use of Aristotle in their interpretation of Plato. The way Aristotle understands Plato's metaphysics, including the oral tradition, was deeply implanted in the Platonist tradition. (See Brisson and Pradeau, PLOTINUS, and Hoffmann, WHAT WAS COMMENTARY IN LATE ANTIQUITY?, in this volume.)

The fragmentary state of the evidence makes it difficult to reconstruct exactly what the doctrines are. In the search for clues in the dialogues, some scholars, relying on Aristotle's identification of the second kind, the "unlimited," with the dyad (*Phys.* III.6, 206b27–28), suggest that the doctrines correspond to the ontological division of all things into four kinds in the *Philebus* (23c–27c): limit, unlimited (*apeiron*), the mixture of the two, and the cause of the mixture. In addition, the Neoplatonists emphasized the transcendence of the form of the good, expressed as "beyond being" in the Simile of the Sun in the *Republic* (VI, 509b), and sought its proofs in the later dialogues, especially the *Sophist* and the *Parmenides*.

Modern scholarship, especially German philology since the nineteenth century, focused exclusively on the dialogues, and tended to ignore the oral tradition as unreliable or irrelevant. Against this, scholars of Tübingen University, starting in the 1960s, began to advocate a new esotericism. They seek the essence of Plato's metaphysics in the indirect tradition, while they downgrade the dialogues, taking the meaning of "unwritten" to indicate Plato's intentional decision not to put his fundamental doctrines in the written documents (they appeal, controversially, to his criticism of written speeches at *Phdr.* 274b–278b and *Ep.* VII, 341a–345c). Assuming that Plato held a rigid system of metaphysical doctrines, they try to uncover the hidden meanings in the writings. They push in an esoteric way the strong temptation since Aristotle to see a metaphysical system in Plato's thinking. Yet the Unwritten Doctrines might well be his seminal ideas or suggestions for further inquiry.

It seems necessary to take the indirect testimony into account, but that should not lead to the extreme. While Plato was well aware of the danger of blindly trusting in written words (which is opposed to philosophy as one's own thinking and shared research), this by no means implies that he never puts his fundamental thoughts in his writings. The dialogues remain the main source for our understanding of Plato's metaphysics.

Analytical and Dialogical Readings

In addition to the tension between systematic formulation and lively thinking, there is another kind of tension within scholarly approaches to the dialogues, between analytical argument and dialogical reading.

Since the second half of the twentieth century, analytic interpretation of Plato has flourished. The most famous analysis appeared in Gregory Vlastos' article in 1954, "The Third Man Argument in the *Parmenides*." Vlastos formulates in a clear, analytical fashion the hidden assumptions that yield an undesirable infinite regress in the first part of the *Parmenides*:

> "I suppose you think *there is one form in each case* on the following ground: whenever some number of things seem to you to be large, perhaps there seems to be some one character, the same as you look at them all, and from that you conclude that the large is one."
>
> "That's true," he said.
>
> "What about the large itself and the other large things? If you look at them all in the same way with the soul's eye, *some one large again appears*, by which all these appear large?"
>
> "It seems so."
>
> "So another form of largeness will make its appearance, which has emerged alongside largeness itself and the things that partake of it, and in turn another over all these, by which all of them will be large. Each of your forms will no longer be one, but unlimited in multitude." (132a–b)

Vlastos extracts from this brief text two premises that contradict each other when put side by side. The first premise is what he calls the self-predication assumption: "Any Form can be predicated of itself. Largeness is itself large. F-ness is itself F." The second is the non-identity assumption: "If anything has a certain character, it cannot be identical with the Form in virtue of which we apprehend that character. If x is F, x cannot be identical with F-ness." These premises are so basic and so indispensable for Plato's theory of forms that any contradiction between them causes a logical consequence fatal to the theory. Concluding that Plato cannot avoid this consequence, Vlastos praises his honesty as a philosopher in admitting perplexities in his own thought.

Scholars were stimulated to respond to this provocative thesis over decades. Some agreed with Vlastos that the contradiction is inevitable and that Plato must have abandoned his own theory of transcendent forms after the *Parmenides* (the

197

"developmentalist" view), while others tried to remove the alleged contradiction and saw basically the same theory in the later dialogues ("unitarian"). Many scholars were keen on finding fault with self-predication, which appears in several dialogues from early to late (e.g. *Prt.* 330c–e, *Sph.* 255a–b). A self-predicative sentence, such as "largeness itself is large," may look odd in light of the modern notion of predication, but Plato obviously holds that the expression "is large" can properly be said in a primary way of the form largeness and then of many sensible things in a derivative way (cf. *Phd.* 100c). It is highly questionable whether the verb "to be" in Plato, here or elsewhere, is thoroughly analyzable in terms of the modern distinction between identity, predication, and existence (or between complete and incomplete uses). If it cannot be, we must seek another way to understand Plato's argument.

Vlastos' analytical reading, which inspires and provokes philosophical responses, has much in common with Aristotle's reading. In fact, the catchword "the Third Man Argument" comes from Aristotle's report, which uses the form of *man* (*SE* 22, 178b36–179a10), but not from Plato's own argument. In fact, the Greek text – the conversation between Parmenides (questioner) and Socrates (respondent) – allows alternative readings, which may lead to different lines of interpretation. For example, the two phrases italicized in the above quotation allow different renderings: "each form is one / again won't some one thing appear large"; these may fit their context more (cf. Gill, 1996). Plato's text contains far richer possibilities than Vlastos' verdict.

Analytic philosophers share the assumption that they can extract arguments from the dialogue to reconstruct Plato's theory. For that purpose, they normally identify the main speaker – Socrates, the Eleatic visitor, or the Athenian visitor – with the author Plato. However, this way of reading the dialogues is now under fire. Some critical reactions and alternative approaches have been proposed over the past few decades. They reconsider the dialogue form, in which Plato puts his philosophical thinking, and emphasize the dramatic characters, contexts, and modes of discourse. Each dialogue should be read as a whole, not any part in isolation. They point out the cost the analytical approach pays by abstracting from Plato's argument. (See C. Gill, THE PLATONIC DIALOGUE, in this volume.)

Using various methods (occasionally contrary to each other), the new trend sometimes goes so far as to deny the possibility of seeing any "argument" in Plato's dialogues. The tendency to avoid "philosophical" parts, especially those concerning the forms, is noticeable in the literary reading. We should remember that the Analytic method is valid and stimulating wherever the logic of arguments is to be clarified. Accordingly, the Dialogical reading should be pursued in combination with analysis of philosophical arguments. Analytical interpreters recently take more account of context and mode. For example, while the Third Man Argument used to be treated in isolation, recent studies place the argument within the whole dialogue, especially in connection with the second part of the dialogue (Gill, 1996; Meinwald, 1991). Also, the second regress argument (*Prm.* 132c–133a), which is often deemed the same type as the first, is reconsidered in its context and shown to have a different argumentative structure (Schofield, 1996).

Now, following the dialogical suggestions, let us examine how particular contexts and modes of discourse convey Plato's metaphysical thinking.

Modes and Contexts for Presenting the Forms

We find several passages concerning transcendent forms in a group of dialogues, namely, the *Phaedo, Symposium, Republic, Phaedrus*, and possibly *Cratylus*. These are usually called the middle dialogues because they show some common features as distinct from those of the earlier and later ones.

Here we face a difficult question: how should we discuss the theory of forms, not from Aristotle's viewpoint or on his Procrustean bed, but as the origin of and stimulus for metaphysical thinking? Since each dialogue is an independent and self-contained whole like a universe (a favorite metaphor of the Neoplatonists), we should carefully examine various modes and contexts in which the forms are presented.

First, the *Phaedo* is often regarded as the first dialogue that presents the transcendent forms. In depicting the last day of Socrates' life in prison, his dialogue concerning how philosophers face death appeals to the existence of forms, such as justice, beauty, and goodness themselves (65dff., which we shall discuss below). On the other hand, the forms are reintroduced later in the dialogue as a fresh "hypothesis" for the final proof of the soul's immortality (100b–107b). When Socrates has to avoid the deadlock caused by the severe criticism against the permanent existence of the soul (86e–88b), hypothesis is adopted as a philosophical method: posit a proposition as a hypothesis, and examine whether other propositions agree with it; when the hypothesis itself needs explanation, hypothesize a higher proposition (100a, 101d–e). The transcendent forms are posited in the following hypothesis: "If there is anything beautiful besides the beautiful itself, it is beautiful for no other reason than that it participates in that beautiful, and I say so with everything" (100c).

This hypothesis provides an explanatory scheme concerning how things come to be, pass away, and *are* in this world. When Simmias, who is large in relation to Socrates, becomes small in relation to Phaedo, the largeness that Simmias has in him by participating in largeness itself (often called "immanent form, character") is replaced by smallness in him. A more sophisticated theory finally demonstrates the immortality of the soul by means of the form of life. In this way, the forms are discussed in different parts of the dialogue. The final argument leaves them as postulates rather than as proved.

Next, the *Symposium* describes a succession of encomia on Love by the participants in a party, which culminates in the speech of Socrates. He praises Love by relating the dialogue he once had with a mystic woman named Diotima (201d–212c). Diotima revealed to Socrates the transcendent character of beauty itself as the ultimate mystery; the ascent from many bodily beauties to eternal beauty (209e–212a). She emphasizes the extreme difficulty in following this course and reaching the ultimate form. Here the form is intentionally introduced in a mode utterly different from ordinary philosophical argument or sober proof.

Then, the *Republic* first introduces the forms when Socrates is obliged to defend his bold thesis that the philosopher should be a ruler or the ruler a philosopher in the ideal state. His interlocutor Glaucon asks what the philosopher is, and Socrates replies that he is a lover of seeing the truth. Truth consists in knowing the forms:

"Since the beautiful is the opposite of the ugly, there are two."

"Of course."

"And since they are two, each is one?"

"I grant that also."

"And the same account is true of the just and the unjust, the good and the bad, and all the forms. Each of them is itself one, but because they manifest themselves everywhere in association with actions, bodies, and one another, each of them appears to be many."

"That's right." (V, 475e–476a)

Here Socrates undertakes to distinguish between knowledge and opinion by appeal to their different objects (V, 476a–480a). Knowledge, being unfailingly true, deals with what is always the same, whereas opinion, lying between knowledge and ignorance, deals with many things that both are and are not something at different times, in different respects, or from different points of view. This argument appears to be straightforward to many scholars, who use it for the standard interpretation of the theory of forms. However, we should be more cautious about its context. Socrates here intends to persuade a supposed opponent called a lover of sights, who does not believe in the beautiful itself and other forms as distinct realities, but sees many beautiful things only. Glaucon replies on behalf of the lover of sights, and Socrates tries to persuade *him* to admit the existence of forms, starting from ordinary experiences without assuming the forms. The argument is clearly intended as persuasion, or at least constitutes only an early stage of the whole process culminating in the form of the good.

The later stage puts forward the form of the good as the greatest subject of learning for the philosopher-ruler. However, Socrates abruptly confesses his ignorance of the good itself, and asks permission to present similes (or images):

"By Zeus, Socrates," Glaucon said, "don't desert us with the end almost in sight. We'll be satisfied if you discuss the good as you discussed justice, moderation, and the rest."

"That, my friend," I said, "would satisfy me too, but I'm afraid that I won't be up to it and that I'll disgrace myself and look ridiculous by trying. So let's abandon the quest for what the good itself is for the time being, for even to arrive at my own view about it is too big a topic for the discussion we are now started on. But I am willing to tell you about what is apparently an offspring of the good and most like it." (VI, 506d–e)

Then he proposes three similes in succession, namely, the Sun, the Line, and the Cave, to illuminate what the form of the good is like. First, the form of the good is compared to its offspring, the sun (VI, 507a–509c); just as the sun makes our sight possible in the sensible world, so the good is the cause of knowledge, truth, and being in the intelligible world. Next, the line proportionally divided into four sections represents the different stages of our cognition (VI, 509c–511e): imaging and belief (in the sensible domain), and thought and knowledge (in the intelligible). Finally, our human condition is compared to a life deep inside a cave (VII, 514a–521b). We are seated facing the wall, on which various shadows are projected from the light behind. We are used to taking those shadows to be real, but once released and forced to turn our heads to the back, we get perplexed but finally behold the things that cast the shadows. Ascending out of the cave and seeing the outside world correspond to education to see the forms, above all, the form of the good (the sun outside), while descending back into the cave corresponds to the philosopher's duty to engage in politics. The subsequent educational program of mathematics and dialectic is designed to redirect our soul's eye from ordinary experiences and to lead us up to the understanding of forms themselves. The metaphor of image and model, representing the relation between sensible thing and intelligible form, prevails in the similes, which are themselves images. The interpretation of these similes is extremely difficult, especially how they relate to each other. For example, the fourfold division of the line at first sight appears to correspond to the four stages inside and outside the cave, but there are several details that refuse such easy matching. The three similes presumably illustrate different aspects of the form of the good, which resist translation into a standard argument or a theory. Thus, the presentation of forms in the *Republic* is again carefully situated in particular contexts, and Plato uses various modes of presentation. Any attempt to generalize Plato's theory of forms from these arguments requires extraordinary caution.

Finally, the *Phaedrus* shows characteristics both of the middle and the later dialogues; the great Myth of the destiny of our soul depicts the world of transcendent forms (246a–257a), and the dialectical method of division and collection, which Plato uses in his late dialogues, is formally introduced (to be considered in the final section of this chapter). In the Myth, the soul is likened to "the natural union of a team of winged horses and their charioteer." It marches with Zeus and other gods in heaven to observe all the forms, and feasts on them. Occasionally the soul's steersman loses control of the bad-tempered horse, so that the soul eventually falls down to the earth. Its wings are wounded in the fall. For their recovery, the soul needs love, to recollect the forms through looking at the traces of the celestial beauty in the beloved person. The forms are thus described in the cosmic, divine, mystic, and ethical myth as the original sphere where our soul aspires to return.

Our survey of the main appearances of forms in the middle dialogues has revealed their peculiar features. The theory of forms, though usually abstracted and interpreted from these passages, is presented in various contexts and modes, which may prevent us from straightforward treatment. Hypothesis, mystic report, persuasion, simile, and myth, all these modes seem to indicate some fundamental difficulties in talking about forms, and Plato's awareness of them. Plato makes full use of the dialogue form, as appropriate discourse for such warning.

The more cautiously we look at Plato's treatment of forms, the harder we find it to discuss the theory directly as philosophical argument. However, this by no means implies, as some literary scholars suggest, the inadequacy or impossibility of an attempt to discuss Plato's metaphysics or theory of forms. On the contrary, how to speak about forms is itself a main issue for Plato's metaphysics. We should consider these modes and contexts themselves as his serious attempts at metaphysics. By means of the dialogue form Plato keeps warning us not to take our philosophical attempt for granted, but encourages us to consider together what philosophy is.

Metaphysical Impact as Awakening Our Soul

A crucial question is why and how Plato posits forms as separate and transcendent reality. A few suggestions have already been given by Aristotle, who ascribes logical and epistemological motivations to Plato: to answer the Socratic question for universal definition and to meet the condition for the objects of knowledge. Also, the strict ontological requirement for the one being, broached by Parmenides, may have shaped Plato's frame of thought: one form stands over many sensible things. However, these are not sufficient to explain Plato's various attempts to present forms in the dialogues. Here let us set about our own consideration by focusing on Plato's expressions for forms and their ethical implications. Although entirely missing in Aristotle's account and most traditional interpretations, ethical questions, which are inherited from Socrates, clearly motivated Plato. (On this topic, see also Penner, PLATO'S ETHICS, in this volume.) For the main examples of forms concern moral properties, such as justice, moderation, beauty (or fineness), and goodness, while many others are introduced chiefly to illustrate them. Plato's main concern lies in how to live well as a philosopher.

Let us begin by examining Plato's expressions for forms. He uses several words, namely, "form" (*eidos*), "idea" (*idea*), "shape" (*morphē*), and "kind" (*genos*), along with such phrases as "thing itself" (*auto*), "itself by itself" (*auto kath' hauto*), and "what it is" (*ho estin*). Scholars often claim that this variety in vocabulary indicates Plato's intention to avoid fixing technical terminology: to keep his thinking vivid and living, Plato chooses expressions with different nuances in accordance with the contexts and stages of discourse. He employs the two representative terms, "form" and "idea," almost equivalently, whereas Aristotle tends to use the latter in his criticisms of Plato and the former as the positive concept denoting the internal structure and essence, paired with "matter," in his own philosophy. On the other hand, since the word "idea" has acquired a new connotation of being present in one's mind, particularly in early modern philosophy, many scholars tend to avoid unnecessary confusion by avoiding the word; for Plato himself clearly rejects the notion that forms reside in one's mind as thoughts (*Prm.* 132b–c). The common Greek words, "form" and "idea," have their etymological origin in "seeing" (*idein*). Why does Plato use the words that are originally linked with vision?

Visible forms of things are what we encounter in our ordinary life: something appears to us, for example, beautiful, large, and equal. Moreover, we experience courage, justice, goodness and other moral characters in particular actions or persons. For example, in Achilles, a model soldier, we see courage, and in Odysseus wisdom. We mold our own form of life by looking upon those moral characters as models. By performing courageous actions, we make ourselves courageous and seen as such. Yet visible characters suffer various changes. Something appears fine in a certain respect at a certain time, but the same thing appears not fine soon afterward or in another respect. Here the variety and instability of sensible things, to which Plato draws our attention, comprises several kinds of change: change in time and space, difference in respects, relation to different things, and perspective of observers. Although the philosophical meanings of these qualifications are, as scholars rightly point out, different in kind, sensible things are in any case bound to suffer some or all of these deficiencies, never to remain the same. The conflicting visual appearances first cause confusion in our cognition, but they may also generate a skeptical attitude in deciding what should be done in molding one's own character; for if a certain type of action appears to be both just and not just, anyone would wonder whether that should be performed. Seeing this sort of confusion and mistrust, Protagorean relativism may appeal to us – that there is no such absolute entity as justice or goodness, since everything is relative to observers and circumstances. This attitude never admits the absolute status of the beautiful, the just, and the good by themselves, but only sees many beautiful things, which are not beautiful as well. Staying in the realm of many visible things keeps us away from forming a *good* life.

We should transcend this dimension of what necessarily suffers "is and is not," and turn our soul's eye around to be activated to behold a new dimension of what always and absolutely "is." That means to admit real forms that never suffer any change, contradiction, restriction, or perspective (cf. *Symp.* 210e–211b). Once the two dimensions are separated, it turns out that visible things are grounded in, and caused by, the forms. The "forms" or "ideas" are seen with the soul's eye, that is, by intellect, instead of the physical eyes. To see the forms of beauty, justice, goodness, and others leads us "to live well" (*to eu zēn*), a famous motto which Socrates advocates (*Cri.* 48b). Plato for this purpose proposes the new dimension of absolute and eternal beings, as completely separated from the sensibles. Separation is the central feature of Plato's forms, but at the same time supports the two world view, for which he is often criticized by modern philosophers. In order to investigate his ethical motivations further, let us concentrate on the first part of the *Phaedo*. The context is Socrates' last dialogue concerning his own death, that is, his soul's departure to the other world.

Separation is indicated, perspicuously in the *Phaedo* but in other dialogues as well, by adding "itself" (*auto*) to each word: beauty itself, justice itself, and so forth. This is exactly what Aristotle ridicules: in his criticism of the theory of forms, he states that adding "itself" does not make any difference to each thing, but only unnecessarily duplicates entities, such as "man-itself" in contrast to "man" (cf. *EN* I.6, 1096a34–b3, *Met.* Z.16, 1040b32–34). This criticism is repeated in the history of philosophy under the name of Ockham's razor. However, the emphatic word "itself" bears a particular significance in the ethical argument of the *Phaedo*. When Socrates advocates his thesis that true philosophers practice and welcome death, he defines death in the following way:

> "By death do we not mean simply the departure of soul from body? Being dead consists, does it not, in the body having been parted from the soul and come to be itself by itself, and in the soul having been parted from the body, and *being* itself by itself (*autēn kath' hautēn*). Can death possibly be anything other than that?" (64c; translation based on Hackforth)

Death is the state of the soul's being itself by itself, that is, in complete separation. Separation means here purification (*katharsis*) of the soul from all bodily senses and desires, which always divert our attention from the soul and its inquiry into true beings. Here the soul and the body rather indicate two opposite directions of our life: whereas the care for the body concerns only how to increase wealth, fame, and what belongs to us, the care for the soul (*epimeleia tēs psuchēs*) makes us as good as possible (cf. *Ap.* 29d–e). The soul is our own self (cf. *Alc.* 1 127d–133c), and therefore, the soul's being itself by itself constitutes our truly being ourselves. Consequently, to practice and willingly accept death is to care for our own self through separation of the soul (cf. *Phd.* 107c, 115b–e).

Only the separated soul performs its proper function, contemplation, free from any bodily disturbances. The pure state of contemplation, called wisdom (*phronēsis*, as distinct from the Aristotelian practical wisdom), concerns justice, beauty, goodness, and things themselves by themselves. Here transcendent forms appear as the proper objects for the soul. To admit the existence of the forms is to admit that the soul, or the true self, really exists. Although our ordinary life is contaminated with bodily desires and inclinations, the contemplation of the forms will restore our true self (as depicted in the Myth of the *Phaedrus*). We should remember that in the Platonist tradition the aim of human life is to become like a god as much as possible. The digression on philosophers in *Theaetetus* 176a–b most clearly presents this view, but some other dialogues contain similar ideas (e.g., *Rep.* VI, 500b–d; X, 613a–b; cf. Sedley, 1999; and in this volume Betegh, GREEK PHILOSOPHY AND RELIGION). Through philosophical efforts to behold the forms, we human beings strive to live as good a life as we can.

In the subsequent section of the *Phaedo*, Socrates buttresses this ethical motivation by the theory of recollection (72e–77b). Since we see equal things also appearing unequal, we are aware that they are always deficient in being, compared with the equal itself. Recollection is the recovery of our prenatal knowledge of the forms through sense perceptions. Forms are the final objects, for which our life aspires in philosophical inquiry (cf. Scott, 1995, 1999). Then, the crucial conclusion is drawn that the possibility of the soul's being itself by itself (after death) and the existence of the forms are equal necessities: they stand or fall together (76d–77a). Following this parity assumption, the two realms of beings are sharply separated (78b–80b): the true beings that always remain the same, and the changing things that never remain the same. While the latter are visible by sensation, the former are invisible and can be grasped only through pure reasoning. The soul is cognate with the unchanging reality.

In this way, the existence and separation of transcendent forms is originally required to establish our own self as *being* really what it is. Facing death, or the ultimate separation of the soul, Socrates' discourse reveals the separate reality as correlative to his true self. This view is finally confirmed by the final proof of the soul's immortality on the hypothesis that uses the form of life (105c–107a). Since the soul is the principle of life, the goodness of the soul makes our life bliss.

Separating reality from our ordinary experience is a continuous process that will not be complete until death. The philosopher's life is lived in seeking for this separation. Similarly, recognizing forms is a continuous movement we must experience, from inside the cave out into the real world. In this movement, we are ourselves changed to see reality from different viewpoints, and eventually beyond any perspective. Shadowy vision in this world is to be transformed into correct discernment according to the forms (cf. *Rep.* VII, 520c).

In the *Republic*, philosophers who behold the forms are compared to people awake in contrast to the lovers of sights who are sleeping but take themselves to be awake (V, 476c–d). Plato's metaphysics awakens us and urges our soul to behold truth and reality. Plato is thus challenging us, his readers, and invites us to the philosophical journey upwards through dialogue. His discourse on the forms provides not a system of doctrines to be analyzed and explained, but manifold stimuli or catalysts for our own thinking towards reality.

Criticisms of the Theory of Forms in the *Parmenides*

Various contexts and modes of discourse prove to be Plato's devices for taking us – those who wish to join him in doing philosophy – beyond our ordinary perspective in order to live philosophers' lives. By contrast, the *Parmenides* for the first time presents the theory of forms in a direct way and puts it under critical examination. The tension becomes obvious in the dialogue itself, between the discourse dependent on particular contexts and the argument independent of any viewpoint. It turns out that this tension, represented in the *Parmenides* and later crystallized as "dialectic," is the essence of the impact that Plato's metaphysics produces.

In an indirect report of the remote dialogue, Socrates in youth proposes transcendent forms as an answer to the one-many problem: how can one thing be many? In reply to Zeno's paradoxical argument, Socrates denies that a thing's being both one and many is problematic, *if* it participates in forms. The great Parmenides then requests clarification of this theory from Socrates, and eventually refutes all his suggestions.

The proposed formulae concerning the forms remind us of the middle dialogues, especially the *Phaedo* and *Republic*, and this makes us wonder about Plato's intention. Does this theory properly represent his own philosophical theory in the middle dialogues? If so, how much validity do Parmenides' criticisms have? Does the theory of transcendent forms contain fatal problems that force the philosopher to abandon or modify it in the later dialogues? To what extent is Plato aware of those problems? If, on the other hand, the proposed theory is different from that in the middle dialogues, perhaps Plato is criticizing certain misunderstandings of his followers. Notwithstanding the difficulties that Socrates confronts, Parmenides emphasizes that forms must exist if dialectic and philosophy are to be preserved, and urges the inexperienced Socrates to engage more in dialectical practice (134e–135d). Scholars' interpretations differ substantially on how to see Plato's philosophical career: positions are normally taken between unitarian, developmentalist, and somewhere in between. The first part of the *Parmenides* provides a test for any interpreter of Plato's philosophy.

Here we can notice the dialogue's peculiar mode of presentation that clearly differs from the earlier ones. To subject the forms to systematic treatment is a conspicuous scheme of the *Parmenides*. This new mode reveals Plato's main concern in the dialogue, namely, to bring the previous modes into question. His critical investigation aims at two issues: the scope of forms and the metaphorical expressions for them.

The first issue is raised when Parmenides asks Socrates what forms there are (130b–e). There is a form itself by itself, in the case of likeness, justice, beauty, goodness and other things of that sort. But Socrates is uncertain whether substances like human beings, fire, and water have forms in the same way. Finally, he confidently denies the existence of forms for hair, mud, dirt, and other such trivial things. Parmenides comments that Socrates' assurance is due to his youth. Here the scope of forms is explicitly called into question for the first time in Plato's dialogues.

Before the *Parmenides*, different kinds of forms have been proposed: moral properties, physical characters, mathematical objects, and artifacts. Each context of discussion has naturally limited the range of forms, but once proposed as a theory, this thinking must be elucidated. In *Republic* X, when Socrates tries to define imitation, he appeals to the theory of forms as usual procedure:

> "For we are, as you know, in the habit of assuming that the form which corresponds to a group of particulars, each to each, is always one, and in that case we call them by the same name (as that of the form)." (596a; translation based on Smith, 1917)

As an illustration, Socrates uses the forms of bed and table, at which craftsmen look in making physical beds and tables; those physical beds and tables are, in turn, imitated by artists in pictures. A similar example, the form of shuttle for weaving, appears in the *Cratylus* (389b–c). Yet one may wonder, distancing oneself from the particular context of discourse, in what way forms of artifacts can exist. In fact, the key passage quoted above is often misunderstood as admitting a single form corresponding to *every* single word. The notion that everything has a form is obviously absurd, and cannot escape Ockham's razor. This is the context to which the question about the extent of forms is directed in the *Parmenides*.

In addition to the status of mathematical objects mentioned before, the later Platonists had to face another difficult question of whether negative properties like badness and not-being truly have forms (rather than being privations of positive forms) – Plato occasionally mentions such negative forms along with positive ones (for example, "ugly, unjust, bad" in *Rep.* V, 475e–476a quoted above, p. 200; for "not-being," see the delicate treatment in the *Sophist*). The *Parmenides* thus reveals the tension regarding forms between particular discourse and general theory. This tension pushes us for a shared philosophical inquiry, as pursued in the Academy.

Also, Parmenides' criticisms target the metaphorical expressions used in the previous consideration of forms. He first questions the key term "participation" (*methexis*) of sensible things in the form (130e–131e). If many things literally take *part* in a form, does each have a part of the form or the whole of it? If a part, the form will be divisible; but if the whole, the single form will be present in many places at once (but *how?*). This argument challenges the common metaphorical expression for the relationship between many sensibles and a single form. How to analyze the part–whole relation becomes a central philosophical issue in the later dialogues, beginning with the second part of the *Parmenides* (cf. Harte, 2002).

The regress of largeness (the so-called Third Man Argument) next arises when Parmenides explains how to posit the form, in terms of seeing (132a–b, quoted above, p. 197); by looking at many large things and largeness itself together with the soul's eye, we can observe another largeness. Here the metaphor of seeing, prevalent particularly in the *Republic*, contributes to the undesirable regress.

Also, the distinction between transcendent and immanent forms seems deliberately blurred in the final criticism (133a–134e; cf. Fujisawa, 1974). When the *Phaedo* originally puts forward the visible character that participates in the transcendent form,

206

expressed, for example, as "the smallness *in* Simmias" or "the smallness that Simmias *has*," its relationship to the form is left open. After hypothesizing the form with the word "participate" (*metechein*) (100c, quoted above, p. 199), Socrates says:

> "I simply, naively and perhaps foolishly cling to this, that nothing else makes it beautiful other than the presence (*parousia*) of, or the sharing (*koinōnia*) in, or however you may describe its relationship to that beautiful we mentioned, for I will not insist on the precise nature of the relationship, but that all beautiful things are beautiful by the beautiful." (*Phd.* 100d)

The status of immanent form as distinct from transcendent form raises controversy (cf. traditional view of Devereux, 1994, against Fine, 1984, 1986). Some scholars suggest that the more developed account of the ontological triad of model, receptacle, and image, in the *Timaeus*, overcomes this problem.

Furthermore, implications in the expressions, "model" (*paradeigma*) and "itself by itself," are put under examination. Parmenides elicits another infinite regress from the model–image relation (132c–133a: cf. Schofield, 1996); then he demonstrates that complete separation ends in incommunicability between the two realms (133a–134e): if there is knowledge itself, that divine knowledge is not concerned with things in our world.

Thus, Plato may be critically examining the ways he has presented forms. Although rich contexts and metaphorical expressions initiate us into intimate thinking about forms, once that thinking is subjected to the common ground of philosophical argument, we cannot but face literal difficulties.

The Academy and the Later Development of Dialectic

Plato's metaphysics develops in the later dialogues, driven by the tension between dynamic thinking and universal theory. Many questions are left open, by which Plato provokes, besides himself in his later works, subsequent philosophers, beginning with his pupil Aristotle. Plato invites us to respond, not just to learn his great system. The tension that has come to light in the *Parmenides* promotes inquiry in two directions which surely influenced each other: the philosophical activities in the Academy and Plato's later development of dialectic.

First, whether the target of criticism in the *Parmenides* is Plato's own theory or its inferior imitations, the argument obviously reflects open discussions and criticisms of forms among his fellow researchers in the Academy. Surprisingly, his successors in the school, Speusippus and Xenocrates, are reported to have abandoned the theory of forms and instead developed their own metaphysical theories. Aristotle criticizes, in his lost work *Peri Ideōn*, five arguments proposed to prove the existence of forms (including the Third Man Argument). They are briefly mentioned in *Metaphysics* A.9, 990b8–17 (also in M.4, 1079a4–13) and substantially documented in a commentary on it by Alexander of Aphrodisias (cf. Owen, 1957; Fine, 1993). Of those arguments some can be traced back to Plato's own works, but others may have been given by other Platonists. Aristotle's critical attitude indicates the open and lively atmosphere at the Academy, in which Plato's seminal ideas on forms were scrutinized and developed

207

into a universal understanding. The critique of forms advanced not only Plato's think-ing, but more importantly, that of the critics, especially Aristotle. Now we can clearly see that Aristotle's formulation of Plato's metaphysics is his own interpretation of and response to his master. This impact promotes further common and lively argument, aiming for universal truth and reality.

Second, the shift appearing in the *Parmenides* from particular modes and contexts to more general arguments points to the development of Plato's main philosophical method, namely, dialectic (which means the art or knowledge of holding dialogue). The word "dialectic" (*dialektikē*) was originally coined by Plato out of the ordinary Greek verb "*dialegesthai*" (to engage in dialogue), which is a preferred mode of philo-sophical inquiry for Socrates. By asking the question "What is a virtue?" and cross-examining an answerer's opinions, he involves people in philosophical inquiry. Socratic dialogue, by using definition, distinction, induction, and analogy, clarifies the issue and forces the interlocutors to admit their own ignorance. Plato's dialectic is, on the other hand, a philosophical art of argumentation (*logos*) to deal with a structured whole of reality. Dialecticians are those who have a synoptic view on all things (*Rep.* VII, 537c). This demand for system and totality encourages universal thinking, one pole of the metaphysical tension. The educational program of the philosopher-ruler in the *Republic* claims that dialectic is the highest knowledge, which deals with forms through forms themselves and ends in forms (VI, 510b, 511b–c). Nevertheless, this notion is not fully described, nor directly applied to that dialogue.

Later dialectic develops mainly in logical, epistemological, and ontological directions. For logic, the second part of the *Parmenides* demonstrates dialectical exercises through systematic use of hypothesis on a large scale. It examines consequences from both positive and negative hypotheses, and trains the reader in detecting ambiguities, logical problems, and proper ways of argument. The *Phaedrus* officially introduces the methods of collection and division – that is, the search for a certain unity over many things and the proper division of a genus into species, so as to grasp the essence of things (265c–266c, 273d–e). These methods are put to use in the *Sophist* and *Statesman* to define, through division, the arts of a sophist, a statesman, and a philosopher. (On division and definition in the late dialogues, see, in this volume, Modrak, PHILOSOPHY OF LANGUAGE, sec. on Plato.)

As the highest knowledge of the philosopher, dialectic plays a double role, as the *Sophist* demonstrates (253b–e; cf. Notomi, 1999). In addition to pursuing proper divi-sion of generic forms into specific forms for definition, it can discern the relationship between forms, especially the greatest kinds, such as being, sameness, and otherness. Forms participate in or differ from each other, to structure the whole sphere of reality. Proper discernment of their relationship provides the basis of truth and knowledge. Also, the *Statesman*, in using dialectical arguments for defining the statesman, elucidates the necessity and importance of dialectic: discernment of basic "elements" not only explicates each particular issue, but advances the dialectical practice itself, which contributes to the understanding of *all things* (285c–287a). Through such arguments as might seem unimportant (e.g., definition of the art of weaving), dialectic displays its general application in philosophy.

Finally, dialectic is ontologically and cosmologically significant. The *Philebus* proposes a more refined dialectical method to deal with the one-many problem. It certainly indicates a new stage of consideration about forms (which many scholars regard no longer as the transcendent forms of the middle dialogues, but as concepts or classes). The cosmology of the *Timaeus*, comprising the form (model), the receptacle, and the image, together with the world-making god called the Demiurge, reflects the fourfold ontological division in the *Philebus* (mentioned above). These highly expert arguments represent the later stage of dialectic.

We can observe that the tension between the lively dialogues and scientific dialectic corresponds to that between living discourse in particular contexts and modes on the one hand, and pure universal reasoning beyond any perspective on the other. Plato's dialogues awaken us, readers, and encourage us to practice universal argument. If philosophy is ascent from our perspectival world to the universal truth, the tension embodied in later dialectic is the essence of Plato's metaphysics.

If you wish to appreciate the offspring of Plato's metaphysics, you can visit the gallery of our contemporary interpretations (some are mentioned here and several others are listed in the Bibliography). But in that gallery, you must yourself become an artist and produce your own works. The final product should be your own form of life, or the being of yourself.

Bibliography

Works Cited and Related Works

Allen, R. E. (ed.). (1965). *Studies in Plato's Metaphysics*. London: Routledge & Kegan Paul.

——. (1970). *Plato's "Euthyphro" and the Earlier Theory of Forms*. London: Routledge & Kegan Paul.

——. (1997). *Plato's* Parmenides. Revised Edition. Translated with Commentary. New Heaven, Conn.: Yale University Press.

Annas, J. (1999). *Platonic Ethics: Old and New*. Ithaca, NY: Cornell University Press.

Burnyeat, M. F. (1987). "Platonism and Mathematics: A Prelude to Discussion." In A. Graeser (ed.), *Mathematics and Metaphysics in Aristotle* (pp. 213–40). Bern and Stuttgart: Haupt.

——. (1990). "Introduction." *The Theaetetus of Plato*, with a translation of Plato's *Theaetetus* by M. J. Levett, revised by M. F. Burnyeat. Indianapolis: Hackett.

Cherniss, H. F. (1944). *Aristotle's Criticism of Plato and the Academy*. (vol. 1). Baltimore: Johns Hopkins University Press.

——. (1957). "The Relation of the *Timaeus* to Plato's Later Dialogues." *American Journal of Philology*, 78, 225–66 = in R. E. Allen (ed.), (1965) *Studies in Plato's Metaphysics* (pp. 339–78). London: Routledge & Kegan Paul.

Cohen, S. M. (1971). "The Logic of the Third Man." *Philosophical Review*, 80, 448–75. Repr. in G. Fine (ed.), (1999) *Plato*. (vol. 1): *Metaphysics and Epistemology* (pp. 275–97). Oxford: Oxford University Press.

Devereux, D. (1994). "Separation and Immanence in Plato's Theory of Forms." *Oxford Studies in Ancient Philosophy*, 12, 63–90. Repr. in G. Fine (ed.), (1999) *Plato*. (vol. 1): *Metaphysics and Epistemology* (pp. 192–214). Oxford: Oxford University Press.

——. (2003). "Plato: Metaphysics." In C. Shields (ed.), *The Blackwell Guide to Ancient Philosophy* (pp. 75–99). Oxford: Blackwell.

Fine, G. (1984). "Separation." *Oxford Studies in Ancient Philosophy*, 2, 31–87.

——. (1986). "Immanence." *Oxford Studies in Ancient Philosophy*, 4, 71–97.

——. (1990). "Knowledge and Belief in *Republic* 5–7." In S. Everson (ed.), *Cambridge Companion to Ancient Thought.* (vol. 1): *Epistemology* (pp. 85–115). Cambridge: Cambridge University Press. Repr. in G. Fine (ed.), (1999) *Plato.* vol. 1: *Metaphysics and Epistemology* (pp. 215–46). Oxford: Oxford University Press.

——. (1993). *On Ideas: Aristotle's Criticism of Plato's Theory of Forms.* Oxford: Oxford University Press.

——. (ed.). (1999a). *Plato.* (vol. 1): *Metaphysics and Epistemology.* Oxford: Oxford University Press.

——. (ed.). (1999b). *Plato.* (vol. 2): *Ethics, Politics, Religion, and the Soul.* Oxford: Oxford University Press.

——. (2003). *Plato on Knowledge and Forms. Selected Essays.* Oxford: Oxford University Press.

Fujisawa, N. (1974). "*Echein, Metechein,* and Idioms of 'Paradeigmatism' in Plato's Theory of Forms." *Phronesis,* 19, 30–58.

Geach, P. T. (1956). "The Third Man Again." *Philosophical Review,* 65, 72–82. Repr. in R. E. Allen (ed.), (1965) *Studies in Plato's Metaphysics* (pp. 265–77). London: Routledge & Kegan Paul.

Gill, M. L. (1996). "Introduction." In *Plato, Parmenides.* Trans. by M. L. Gill and P. Ryan. Indianapolis, Ind.: Hackett.

Hackforth, R. (1955). *Plato's Phaedo.* Translated with an Introduction and Commentary. Cambridge: Cambridge University Press.

Harte, V. (2002). *Plato on Parts and Wholes: The Metaphysics of Structure.* Oxford: Oxford University Press.

Krämer, H. J. (1990). *Plato and the Foundations of Metaphysics.* (ed. and trans. J. R. Catan). Albany, NY: State University of New York Press.

Kraut, R. (ed.). (1992). *The Cambridge Companion to Plato.* Cambridge: Cambridge University Press.

Meinwald, C. C. (1991). *Plato's* Parmenides. Oxford: Oxford University Press.

——. (1992). "Good-bye to the Third Man." In R. Kraut (ed.), *The Cambridge Companion to Plato* (pp. 365–96). Cambridge: Cambridge University Press.

Nehamas, A. (1975). "Plato on the Imperfection of the Sensible World." *American Philosophical Quarterly* 12, 105–17. Repr. in G. Fine (ed.), (1999a) *Plato.* (vol. 1): *Metaphysics and Epistemology* (pp. 171–91). Oxford: Oxford University Press.

Notomi, N. (1999). *The Unity of Plato's* Sophist: *Between the Sophist and the Philosopher.* Cambridge: Cambridge University Press.

Owen, G. E. L. (1953). "The Place of the *Timaeus* in Plato's Dialogues." *Classical Quarterly,* NS 3, 79–95. Repr. in R. E. Allen (ed.) (1965) *Studies in Plato's Metaphysics* (pp. 313–38). London: Routledge & Kegan Paul. Also in G. E. L. Owen, (1986) *Logic, Science and Dialectic: Collected Papers in Greek Philosophy* (pp. 65–84). (M. C. Nussbaum, ed.). Ithaca, NY: Cornell University Press.

——. (1957). "A Proof in the *Peri Ideon.*" *Journal of Hellenic Studies,* 77, 103–11. Repr. in R. E. Allen (ed.) (1965) *Studies in Plato's Metaphysics* (pp. 293–312). London: Routledge & Kegan Paul. Also in G. E. L. Owen, (1986) *Logic, Science and Dialectic: Collected Papers in Greek Philosophy* (pp. 165–79). (M. C. Nussbaum, ed.). Ithaca, NY: Cornell University Press, 1986.

Patterson, R. (1985). *Image and Reality in Plato's Metaphysics.* Indianapolis, Ind.: Hackett.

Robinson, R. (1953). *Plato's Earlier Dialectic.* 2nd edn. Oxford: Oxford University Press.

Ross, W. D. (1924). *Aristotle's* Metaphysics. A Revised Text with Introduction and Commentary. (2 vols.). Oxford: Oxford University Press.

——. (1951). *Plato's Theory of Ideas.* Oxford: Oxford University Press.

Schofield, M. (1996). "Likeness and Likenesses in the *Parmenides.*" In C. Gill and M. M. McCabe (eds.), *Form and Argument in Late Plato* (pp. 49–77). Oxford: Oxford University Press.

Scott, D. (1995). *Recollection and Experience: Plato's Theory of Learning and its Successors.* Cambridge: Cambridge University Press.

——. (1999). "Platonic Recollection." In G. Fine (ed.), *Plato.* (vol. 1): *Metaphysics and Epistemology* (pp. 93–124). Oxford: Oxford University Press.

Sedley, D. (1996). "Three Platonist Interpretations of the *Theaetetus.*" In C. Gill and M. M. McCabe (eds.), *Form and Argument in Late Plato* (pp. 79–103). Oxford: Oxford University Press.

——. (1999). "The Ideal of Godlikeness." In G. Fine (ed.), *Plato.* (vol. 2): *Ethics, Politics, Religion, and the Soul.* (pp. 309–28). Oxford: Oxford University Press.

Smith, J. A. (1917). "General Relative Clauses in Greek". *Classical Review*, 31, 69–71.

Szlezák, T. A. (1999). *Reading Plato.* (trans. G. Zanker). London and New York: Routledge. (Original work published 1993.)

Vlastos, G. (1954). "The Third Man Argument in the *Parmenides.*" *Philosophical Review* 63, pp. 319–349. Repr. in R. E. Allen (ed.), (1965) *Studies in Plato's Metaphysics* (pp. 231–61). London: Routledge & Kegan Paul.

——. (ed.). (1971). *Plato: a Collection of Critical Essays* (vol. 1): *Metaphysics and Epistemology.* Garden City, NY: Anchor Books.

——. (1981). *Platonic Studies.* 2nd edn. Princeton: Princeton University Press.

Wedberg, A. (1955). *Plato's Philosophy of Mathematics.* Stockholm: Almquist & Wiksell.

——. (1971). "The Theory of Ideas." In G. Vlastos (ed.), *Plato: A Collection of Critical Essays* (vol. 1): *Metaphysics and Epistemology* (pp. 28–52). Garden City, NY: Anchor Books.

White, N. P. (1992). "Plato's Metaphysical Epistemology." In R. Kraut (ed.), *The Cambridge Companion to Plato* (pp. 277–310). Cambridge: Cambridge University Press.

Further Reading

For Aristotle's view on Plato's theory of Forms, see Ross (1924), Cherniss (1944), Owen (1957), and Fine (1993); the last two deal with his arguments in the lost *Peri Ideōn* or *On Ideas.* Analytical arguments are collected in Allen (ed.) (1965), Vlastos (ed.) (1971), and Fine (ed.) (1999a). For the controversy over the "Third Man Argument," see Vlastos (1954), Geach (1956), Cohen (1971), and Meinwald (1992) among many. More general treatments of the *Parmenides* are given in Allen (1997), Meinwald (1991), and Gill (1996). The two main contributions of the Tübingen-Milano school are translated into English: Krämer (1990) and Szlezák (1999).

12

Plato's Natural Philosophy and Metaphysics

LUC BRISSON

Plato's position on the knowledge of nature has been the subject of divergent evaluations.[1] Many scholars believe that Plato's influence in this area was disastrous, in that the central hypothesis he defends, that genuine reality is represented by intelligible forms, of which sensible things are mere images, leads more to metaphysics and even to mysticism than to the study of natural phenomena (e.g., Lloyd, 1968, 1991). It may be, however, that Plato's procedure of making mathematics the model of knowledge and describing the stability manifested in the sensible world in mathematical terms, makes him a precursor of modern science (Brisson, 2000).

These two contradictory positions can be explained by the very structure of Plato's thought. In this regard, I would like to develop the following three positions:

1. Plato wants to account for the sensible world, a task that had been attempted before him by those who were interested in nature.
2. Plato was disappointed by the conclusions of his predecessors: for example, Anaxagoras in the *Phaedo*, and Parmenides and Zeno in the *Parmenides*.
3. As a result of this disappointment, Plato inaugurated metaphysics; this led him to go beyond nature, and set forth the hypothesis of the Forms and of the soul, but the goal was still to explain nature.

1. This chapter was already written when I became aware of A. Gregory's (2000) and T. K. Johansen's (2004) books. In both cases, I disagree on the question of "teleology," which I believe constitutes an anachronism. The question of *telos* is explicit in Aristotle, but not in Plato. Plato does talk about the goodness of the demiurge and the beauty of his product at *Ti.* 28–30, and he says that the god made one choice rather than another, because it was better or best (e.g., 75e), or because it served some good purpose (e.g., eyelids 45d). But the demiurge is good because he is a god who is always doing what is best; and his product is beautiful because it is the image of an intelligible model. The demiurge chose to organize the cosmos mathematically – a cosmos whose stability we can grasp – because using mathematics would result in a good and beautiful product, the best that can be done with recalcitrant "necessity," and not because he was driven by an Aristotelian final cause. Those who interpret the *Timaeus* teleologically are right in a way, but since they rely only on teleology they miss what is truly distinctive and important about Plato's explanations: their mathematical component.

212

Such a procedure entails a two-stage explanation. In the first stage, Plato borrows the explanation of nature from his predecessors, although he thoroughly transforms it by associating the elements with geometrical figures. In the second stage, he goes beyond nature, by bringing in the soul and the Forms.

Going Beyond Nature in Order to Explain it

The term *phusis* (nature), a noun of action, brings together three notions, origin, process, and result – in other words, the growth of a thing in its totality, from its birth until its maturity and death. In their writings, to which the title *Peri phuseōs* was subsequently given, thinkers prior to Plato engaged in inquiry (*historia*) not into the nature of a thing in particular, but into the nature of the totality of things, that is, the universe. For them, the point (at least from an Aristotelian perspective) was to discover the "material principle," from which all things were engendered. In short, prior to Plato, we cannot really speak of "metaphysics," understood as going beyond nature,[2] since none of the attempts to account for nature goes beyond nature.[3]

Yet Plato shows himself to be unsatisfied by these attempts. In the *Phaedo*, he criticizes the position of Anaxagoras, which, in his view, does not go far enough. Socrates, who has just narrated how disappointed he was by reading Anaxagoras' book, and how discouraged he is by the explanations so far proposed of causality in nature – that is, in the domain of sensible things – explains why he is leaning towards the hypothesis of the existence of intelligible realities (*Phd.* 100c–d). In the first part of the *Parmenides*, Socrates responds to the paradoxes encountered by Parmenides and Zeno in their analysis of the sensible world (*Prm.* 127d–e), which are also described in the second part of the dialogue. If we suppose such a structure, the second part of the *Parmenides* is not a random rhapsody of arguments, but a coherent set of deductions following an overall plan. We understand, then, how the series of eight deductions form the conceptual structure of a cosmology that serves as their background. We are not dealing with a cosmological description, as we find in the *Timaeus*, but with an inventory of the suppositions and definitions on which such a description relies. In other words, while the *Timaeus* is presented in narrative form, the *Parmenides* provides the "tool box" required for the construction of a cosmological model.[4]

Convinced that Parmenides' thesis that the world is a unique whole (*Prm.* 127e–128a) is untenable, Socrates, according to Plato, introduces the hypothesis of the existence of the Forms. In fact, for Plato's Socrates, our universe contains an indeterminate number of things, which, although distinct and different from one another,

2. As I have tried to show in Brisson (1999).
3. On pre-Platonic natural philosophy, see in this volume Hussey, THE BEGINNINGS OF SCIENCE AND PHILOSOPHY IN ARCHAIC GREECE, and Curd, PARMENIDES AND AFTER: UNITY AND PLURALITY.
4. On this interpretation of the second part of the Plato's *Parmenides*, see Brisson (2002). For alternative readings of the second part of the *Parmenides* different from mine, but which also see the deductions as following some overall plan, see Sayer (1978) and Gill (1996).

share a considerable number of characteristics. It is the recognition of this community that leads Plato's Socrates to hypothesize the existence of intelligible realities separated from sensible things, in which the sensible things participate. Since the intelligible reality does not change, and is not subject either to generation or to corruption, it exists in itself, i.e., independently of other things; it should therefore be considered not as an effect, but as the cause of its own being. These realities are defined as Forms (*eidē*). The very term suggests a visual metaphor which Plato uses very widely, when he discusses our grasp of the intelligible.

This distinction between true being and sensible reality is formulated with the help of spatial metaphors: in the *Republic*, we read of the "intelligible place" (*Rep.* VI, 509d2; see also 508c2 and VII, 516b–c, 532d1), and in the *Phaedrus* of a place which is located beyond the heavens (*Phdr.* 247c). Yet this separation cannot be complete, simply because the Forms are supposed to exist in order to solve the paradoxes constantly raised by sensible things. Sensible realities receive their names from the intelligible realities. Above all, sensible realities can be known only through the intelligible. Of sensible realities, we can have only opinion; but opinion is situated midway between the absence of knowledge and true knowledge. True knowledge has intelligible reality as its object, and is obtained by recollection, understood as the rediscovery of a knowledge-content that was apprehended when the soul was separated from the body. This rediscovery, which in this world is triggered by the perception of a sensible object corresponding to intelligible reality, culminates in an intuition assimilated to intellectual vision.

Plato, therefore, was the first to suppose the existence of separate realities. Such a separation may correspond to a religious experience. However, the fact that the upper world consists of Forms rather than of gods explains why, whereas the religious phenomenon seems to be universal, the metaphysical approach is so infrequent. The same idea also enables us to understand how metaphysics, even when assimilated to theology, constitutes a radical critique of the traditional representation of the divine. One cannot either address prayers or offer sacrifices to an utterly separate god. Therefore, as the history of the expression seems to imply, it is separation from nature that enables us to define metaphysics. By the same token, metaphysics is quite naturally associated with theology, from which it is nevertheless distinct and whose dissolution it in the long run entails.

However, if we admit that true reality consists of the intelligible forms, it follows that the knowledge of sensible things cannot be considered as a science in the strict sense of the term. Yet to attribute an inferior status to this knowledge is not equivalent to denying its existence. After all, in the majority of his work Plato speaks of sensible things and tries to supply an explanation for them. We are therefore justified in raising the question of Plato's attitude towards the "branches of knowledge" of his time, such as mathematics, medicine, etc.: Was it that of an enlightened amateur, or of a "genuine scientist"?[5]

---

5. That is, "scientist" in the modern sense of the term. On the development of Greek mathematics and medicine in Plato's time, see Mueller, GREEK MATHEMATICS, and Pellegrin, ANCIENT MEDICINE, in this volume.

Technē, epistēmē and alēthēs doxa

Before we try to answer this question, we should consider an important evolution in Plato's approach to the knowledge of sensible things.

Technē

At first, Plato, like Socrates, found a model of access to the sensible in the *technai*. In ancient Greek, the term *technē* designates a very wide variety of skills and competences, which extend from the figurative arts to rhetoric, from medicine and navigation to architecture, and which include the work of blacksmiths, joiners, and cobblers. These skills and practices have always existed in one form or another, and they are characterized by their specialization, since no expert lays claim to knowledge in its totality.

In the first Platonic writings, the mention of *technai* has two primary functions (see Balansard, 2001). It makes possible the preparation of an effective opposition to all kinds of false knowledge, and it proposes models of know-how. Every *technē* implies an activity (*ergon*), which may consist in the production of an object (a flute, for instance, or a boat), or else deal with the use of these objects (music, navigation), or with the care (*therapeia*) of certain natural objects (land, livestock, or human bodies). *Technē* seeks to control the totality of its object – for instance, the human body – but it must be limited to a particular area; it is on this condition that its competence and autonomy are guaranteed. Within the limits of its own domain, *technē* possesses full knowledge of the rational procedures of its intervention, which it can account for publicly, and which it can transmit by teaching. From this point of view, the *technai* display a normative character. In addition, they lay claim to efficacy (*dunamis*) when they intervene in their object. Because they are always a "know-how," the *technai* are able to serve as a model for ethics and for politics.

At this point, two problems arise that call into question the use of *technē* as a model of knowledge. On the one hand, the objects of all *technai* pertain to the sensible world, which, for Plato, is subject to perpetual change, and for this reason cannot be the object of language and thought. Moreover, every *technē* contains in its principle the pursuit of the interests of the person practicing it, which is not the case for a certain number of fields of knowledge, in which interest does not come into consideration at all.

This is why, without completely abandoning the advantages he had derived from the *technai*, Plato, beginning with the *Meno*, turns towards another paradigm: that of mathematics (this is the thesis of Vlastos, 1988). If human beings are to know sensible things and speak about them, sensible things must display a stability that allows that. Yet it is only mathematics, whether pure or applied, that enables human beings to explain and describe this stability.

Pure mathematics, considered as an object of study in itself, enables the soul to tear itself away from the sensible, even if, within the framework of Greek practice, which gives precedence to construction (by ruler and compass) over calculation, the mathematician must construct figures, and even if mathematics is ultimately based on axioms (more or less explicit), which cannot be demonstrated. In other words, the ideal character proper to mathematics allows Plato to make us understand why it is

215

necessary to hypothesize the existence of intelligible forms, of which sensible things are mere images.

Epistēmē

Moreover, in a way that remains mysterious even today, mathematics appears as traces of the intelligible within the sensible, in so far as it manifests the symmetry that ensures genuine stability to the realities perceived by the senses. All human beings can do is to observe and describe this stability, in the framework of such different branches of knowledge as cosmology, astronomy, physics, chemistry, and biology. Such an inventory of the branches of knowledge is anachronistic, for we do not find any constituted branch of knowledge in Plato having as its name one of those we have enumerated (except perhaps astronomy), and therefore, necessarily, we find no system in which these branches of knowledge could take their place. What is more, in ancient Greek, there is no pair of contrasting terms designating on the one hand the exact description of sensible realities, and on the other the intuition of intelligible realities.

This division of reality among models, which constitute true reality, and copies, which contain only a derived reality, entails a strictly parallel distinction on the level of knowledge and of discourse. This is explained at *Timaeus* 29b–c and 51d–e, where the intellect, which has as its object the intelligible forms, is opposed to true opinion, which has for its object sensible things perceived by the senses. This epistemological opposition alternates, moreover, with the following sociological one: "[in true opinion] every human being has a share, we must say, whereas in intellectual intuition [*nous*] it is the gods [who have a share] and, among human beings, only a small class" (*Ti.* 51e). This tiny class of people is obviously the philosophers.

Alēthēs doxa

In short, science (*epistēmē*) deals with true reality, which is the model of every sensible reality of the same type. This true reality is perceived by the intellect (*nous*). The knowledge that results from this process, like the discourse that transmits this knowledge, is certain, and is reserved for philosophers. True opinion (*alēthēs doxa*), by contrast, is concerned with copies of true reality. These derived realities are perceived by sensation (*aisthēsis*), which, through the intermediary of recollection, leads towards the intelligible. The knowledge that results from sensation, however, cannot achieve certainty, for it has only changing images as its objects. The same holds true of the discourse that transmits this knowledge, and which Plato qualifies as a "likely story" (*eikos muthos*) or "likely discourse" (*eikos logos*), simply because this discourse cannot be true in the full sense of the word, since it deals with images, and not with the true reality which is its model.

Mathematics, pure and applied

Even if we cannot give a determinate status to mathematical or geometrical objects as such, they nevertheless each have a Form that corresponds to them – that of Two or of the Circle, for instance. Be that as it may, we must admit the essential role of mathematics since it mediated between the sensible and the intelligible. Mathematics enables the soul to rise up from the sensible to the intelligible, and its action enables the presence of the intelligible within the sensible to be ensured. In Plato – and this is a very important characteristic – mathematics plays a pivotal role in the process of education.

In the *Republic* (II, 372d–IV, 427c), after demonstrating the existence of a warrior class, from whom are selected those who will become the philosophers who will lead the city, Socrates describes to Glaucon the program of education that will be used to train these philosophers. The warriors, some of whom are destined to become philosophers, will first be initiated into pure mathematics,[6] the various branches of which are reviewed.

Arithmetic (VII, 522c–526c) enables us to begin to apprehend something superior to the sensible. Each sensible perception brings with it the sensible perception of its opposite; and the mind cannot become conscious of the unity and plurality latent in diversity until sensation gives it information on the contrary attributes of the same object. Although such consciousness of unity remains rudimentary, this is truly an act of pure intelligence.

Geometry (526c–527c) is just as indispensable for the achievement of higher education, for it enables us to reach results that are abstract, universal, and even, one might say, eternal. Experience shows, moreover, that whereas arithmetic makes the mind more agile, geometry educates it.

Geometry is immediately understood as plane geometry. But we must also consider geometry in three-dimensional space – the geometry of solids, that is to say stereometry (527d–528e) – for that is required for the application of mathematics to astronomy, which is the science of solids in motion.

We then move on to the geometry of bodies in motion, which interests astronomy (529a–530c). The sky can be seen as an immense moving picture. Like geometry, however, astronomy must go beyond phenomena, in order to determine the general principles that account for the motion of solids. It must therefore abandon the contemplation of the heavens, in order to take an interest in the real problems, which are mathematical in nature, by studying abstract theorems.[7]

The theory of music can be elevated not only above disputes between musicians, but also above the limits imposed upon it by the Pythagoreans, who were interested only in the harmonies perceptible to the ear. Those who wish to become philosophers must rise to the universal and abstract contemplation of harmonic ratios themselves, as we can see from the *Timaeus*, where such ratios account for the regularity of the movements of the heavenly bodies which emit no sound; hence the importance of harmonics (530c–531c).

As we have seen, mathematics presents two faces, as inseparable as those of a coin: one is oriented towards the intelligible, which it allows us to reach; and the other is

6.   On this subject, see Pritchard (1995).
7.   On this subject, see the polemical work edited by J. P. Anton (1981). See also Mueller (1992).

oriented towards the sensible, where it represents the "traces of the intelligible." At this level, mathematics intervenes in every area of knowledge.

Cosmology

In the *Timaeus*, Plato develops a cosmology. He sets forth a simple, yet coherent and rigorous representation of the universe, the properties of which appear as the logically-deduced consequences of a limited set of presuppositions, even if such presuppositions remain implicit and poorly explained in this dialogue. Moreover, the *Timaeus* appears as the first cosmology in which such a description is carried out with the help of mathematics, and not merely with the help of ordinary language. Aristotle, particularly in the *De Caelo* and the *Physics*, never stops criticizing Plato's mathematization of the universe. However – and it is in this respect that the *Timaeus* is anchored in tradition, including myth – Plato's description of the universe remains tied to a description of the origin of man, and even of the origin of society, as is illustrated by the myth of Atlantis, summarized at the beginning of the dialogue and narrated in the *Critias*.

For Plato, a cosmology that aims to set forth a simple representation of the universe must be able to answer these two questions: On what conditions is the sensible world knowable? How can we describe it? These questions are inspired by the following conviction: incessant change cannot be considered to be true reality. In order to become an object of knowledge and discourse, the sensible world must, even in its transformations, display something that does not change, something that is genuinely permanent, and which is therefore identical in every case. Plato responds to this demand by making the following hypothesis, which presents a double aspect: there exists a world of intelligible forms, immutable and universal realities that are the object of true knowledge and discourse, and there is a world of sensible realities, which participate in the forms, of which they are mere copies.[8]

Since resemblance may be defined as identity reduced to certain aspects, sensible things, if they are only images of the intelligible forms, must simultaneously display a certain resemblance to the intelligible forms and be dissimilar to them, lest they be confused with the corresponding intelligible forms. The demiurge guarantees resemblance, whereas *chōra* explains difference. We must hypothesize the existence of *chōra*, in order to explain why sensible things are different from the intelligible forms, in which they nevertheless participate (*Ti.* 52c–d).

Chōra is that which supplies a location for sensible things, which are thereby situated in exteriority, separate from one another. An analysis of the discourse which deals with sensible things enables Plato to show how *chōra* is the stable receptacle in which sensible things appear, and from which, after a certain lapse of time, they disappear (*Ti.* 52b). Moreover, some of Plato's images and metaphors, like the "mother" and the "nursemaid," suggest that *chōra* is in a sense constitutive of sensible things. Sensible things display thus a certain consistency, which explains why they are impenetrable, and so cannot occupy the same place at the same time. In this way *chōra* enables us to explain why sensible things, although they must resemble the intelligible, are different

---

8. On participation, see Notomi, PLATO'S METAPHYSICS AND DIALECTIC, in this volume.

from it: they are located somewhere, and they are subject to a certain consistency, if we take this term in a very wide and imprecise sense. So *chōra* includes a double aspect, both spatial and constitutive, as we shall see below; and this is why we must resist the temptation to identify *chōra* with a kind of defective matter (*hulē*), as Aristotle did. In itself, *chōra* is bereft of measure and proportion, but as a result of this it can accept all kinds of measures and proportion.

Nevertheless, *chōra* is never described in the *Timaeus* as such and in its pure state. When the demiurge undertakes to introduce measure and proportion into it, it already presents traces of the four elements (*Ti.* 52d–53c), which are agitated by a mechanical movement bereft of order and of measure. Plato calls this principle of resistance *anankē*, a term that is usually translated "necessity," but which should be understood as the set of unavoidable consequences which, in the sensible world, impose severe limits upon every rational intention. By admitting the persistent presence of "necessity" in the universe, with which first the demiurge, and then the world soul must deal, Plato acknowledges that the order presupposed by his cosmological model cannot but remain partial and provisional. We are thus far from Leibnizian optimism. Since order reigns over only a part of the universe, all cosmological explanations are condemned to remain partial and provisional.

In the sensible world, permanence is manifested with the following characteristics: causality, stability, and symmetry. There is causality if every event depends on a cause; stability if the same cause always produces the same effect; and symmetry if this relation of causality remains invariant despite incessant transformations. This invariance, which can be expressed in terms of mathematical ratios, in fact constitutes the essential part of the sensible world that human beings can come to know and describe. Nevertheless, the knowledge and discourse that have sensible things as their object maintain a relation of copy to model with the knowledge and discourse that have intelligible forms as their object. This relation is similar to that of sensible things with regard to intelligible forms. This knowledge and the discourse that expresses it are never true, but remain probable, for they deal only with images, and not with true reality. The demiurge fabricates the universe, which is a living being endowed with a soul and a body, by keeping his eyes fixed on the intelligible.

Astronomy

Why does Plato consider the universe to be a living being – that is, as a being endowed with a soul? In ancient Greece, the main problem in cosmology, as we have seen, is to account for what is orderly in the sensible world although it changes constantly, and above all for the most regular movements observed in it, those of the celestial bodies. In this case, however, how can we explain both the existence of movement and of the order this movement manifests?

It was Newton who, in 1687, formulated the law of gravitation: two bodies exert a force of attraction upon one another proportional to their masses and inversely proportional to the square of their distance. The law of inertia, according to which a body which is not subject to any force can only be at rest or display rectilinear and uniform motion, had to await Galileo to be formulated, and Newton to be extended to celestial bodies. If these laws are not available, one must hypothesize a motion that is not perceived by the senses, but which accounts for the origin and the persistence of the totality of movements in the universe, and especially of the most noble of them, those that animate the celestial bodies. According to Plato, this reality is the same in nature as the principle of spontaneous movement in living beings: it is a soul.

This hypothesis is just as plausible as that of the existence of "movement at a distance." In living beings, which are, by definition, endowed with the principle of spontaneous movement which Plato calls "soul," a certain regularity within change manifests itself: a member of a given species engenders another member of the species, lives a specific number of years, displays certain characteristics, etc. Moreover, the human soul is endowed with an intellect, which ensures it a behavior coherent and in conformity with intentions that are more or less well-defined. An analogous line of reasoning allows us to associate these two domains of facts, and suppose that the sensible world has a soul endowed with reason (*Ti.* 30a–c), as is the case for humans. Since this is so, we can better understand how the demiurge goes about fabricating the body and soul of this living being which includes all living beings – that is, the universe.

The world soul, which ensures the permanence of the mathematical order established by the demiurge within the universe, displays the following characteristics, whenever it comes to exert absolute power (*Ti.* 34c): it is an intermediate reality, which resembles a series of overlapping circles (the most "noble" of plane figures, for it presents the greatest symmetry), which are interrelated mathematically with one another, and which explain all motion in the universe, whether psychic or physical.

This reality intermediate between the sensible and the intelligible represents, within the sensible, the origin of all orderly motion, the circular movements of the heavenly bodies, and the rectilinear movements of sublunary realities. Thus, the *Timaeus* presents the constitution of the world soul as if it were the construction of an armillary sphere, i.e., a globe made up of rings or circles, representing the movement of the heavens and the stars (mentioned at *Ti.* 40d). We must bear this image in mind to comprehend what follows.

By bringing in mathematical relations (geometrical, arithmetical, and harmonic), which are also used in music, at the level of the world soul, Plato is merely trying to account for the two characteristics of permanence and regularity, characteristics that have been observed since earliest antiquity in the heavenly bodies, and that have led human beings to regard them as divine. In order to account for these two character-istics, Plato formulates two postulates: 1) The movements of the heavenly bodies fol-low a circular trajectory, so that their motion is permanent. 2) These motions obey laws defined by three types of mathematical relations known at the time, so that their movement is regular, despite appearances to the contrary (see Knorr, 1990).

In the *Timaeus* (38c–39e),[9] Plato proposes an astronomical system of astonishing simplicity. Indeed, this astronomical explanation brings only the following two elements into play: the circular movement of the celestial bodies, a hypothesis which was accepted until Kepler (the law of orbits, in 1609), and three types of mathematical relations: geometrical, mathematical, and harmonic. The extraordinary complexity

---

9. For a table of celestial motions in the *Timaeus*, see Cornford (1937, pp. 136–7).

of the movements which seem to affect the celestial bodies is thus reduced to two elements of mathematical nature: circles and means.

Physics and chemistry

The demiurge adapts this soul to the world's body (*Ti.* 34b, 36d–e), which appears as a gigantic sphere, since, as the copy of a perfect original, this body must have the perfect and symmetrical form. In the geometry of three-dimensional space, no form is more symmetrical than the sphere.

The elements

In conformity with a traditional opinion that probably goes back to Empedocles, and which was to continue down to the eighteenth century, Plato takes for granted that the body of the universe is fabricated exclusively from the four elements: fire, air, water, and earth (*Ti.* 56b–c). Yet he goes much further. On the one hand, he sets forth a mathematical argument, to justify the fact that there must be four elements. Above all, he is conscious of showing a high degree of originality (*Ti.* 53e) by establishing a correspondence between the four elements and the four regular polyhedra – that is, he transposes the whole of physical reality and the changes that affect it into mathematical terms.[10]

These four polyhedra are themselves constructed from two types of surfaces, which themselves result from two types of right-angled triangles.

The mathematical constitution of the elements

The two types of right-angle triangles which play a role in the beginning are the right-angled isosceles triangle, which is half of a square (Figure 12.1b), and the right-angled scalene triangle, which is half of an equilateral triangle of side x (Figure 12.1a).

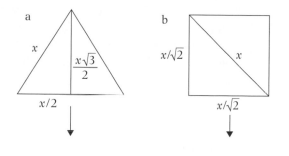

Figure 12.1

10. It should be noted that the construction of the first regular polyhedra is attributed to Theaetetus (415–369 BCE), a contemporary of Socrates, whom Plato depicts in the prologue of the dialogue which bears his name (*Theaetetus*); this indicates that Plato devoted considerable attention to the development of mathematics in his time.

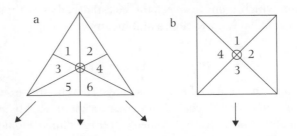

Figure 12.2

These two elementary right-angled triangles enter into the construction of two other types of surface: the square and the equilateral triangle. A square results from the union of four right-angled isosceles triangles (*Ti.* 55b) (Figure 12.2b); and an equilateral triangle is the result of the union of six right-angled scalene triangles *Ti.* 54d–e) (Figure 12.2a). In order to constitute a square, two right-angled isosceles triangles would have sufficed, just as would two right-angled scalene triangles have sufficed to constitute an equilateral triangle. We may suppose, however, that, in the case of the square and of the equilateral triangle, Plato wants to find a center of axial symmetry (cf. Euclid, *Elements*, XII,18, scholium), which would ensure that none of the triangles that make up the square or the equilateral triangle could have preeminence over the others. This may perhaps be an implicit criticism of Pythagoreanism, in which right and left had opposing values.

Equilateral triangles are used to construct three regular polyhedra: the tetrahedron (*Ti.* 54e–55a, 4 equilateral triangles, Figure 12.3a), the octahedron (*Ti.* 55a, eight equilateral triangles, Figure 12.3b), and the icosahedron (*Ti.* 55a–b, 20 equilateral triangles, Figure 12.3c), associated respectively with fire, air, and water. In addition, squares are used to make up the cube (*Ti.* 55b–c, 6 squares, Figure 12.3d), which is associated with earth. Finally, there is a fleeting mention of the dodecahedron, the regular polyhedron that is most similar to the sphere (*Ti.* 55c), the geometrical figure associated with the body of the world (cf. *Ep.* XIII [apocryphal], 363d).

All the properties of the polyhedra associated with the four elements may be gathered together in an easily readable table (see Table 12.1). Two observations result from an attentive reading of Table 12.1:

a   b  c 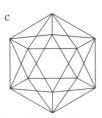 d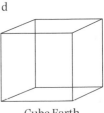

Tetrahedron Fire   Octahedron Air   Icosahedron Water   Cube Earth

Figure 12.3

Table 12.1

Element	Regular solid	Number of faces	Number of right-angled triangles
fire	tetrahedron	4 equilateral triangles	24 scalenes
air	octahedron	8 equilateral triangles	48 scalenes
water	icosahedron	20 equilateral triangles	120 scalenes
earth	cube	6 squares	24 isosceles

1. The regular polyhedra that correspond to the various elements are described exclusively as a function of the number of faces that make up their envelope; and
2. the edges of these faces are defined on the basis of an original value that corresponds to the length of the hypotenuse of the elementary right-angled triangles that compose them; but this value remains indeterminate (*Ti.* 57c–d). Such indeterminacy has considerable importance, for two reasons: on the one hand, it reduces the explanatory power of the geometrical model proposed by Plato, by going against its simplicity; on the other hand, however, it allows the varieties of one and the same element to be better explained.

Plato wants to show how the cosmological model he proposes, and which can be reduced to four elements, assimilated to regular polyhedra composed of equilateral triangles and squares, themselves made up of regular scalene and isosceles triangles, allows for the description of the objects of the entire sensible world, which are mere varieties of the four elements, or their combination, and even for the description of their properties. At *Ti.* 58c–61c, we find a few examples that will illustrate this point (Table 12.2). The most complex substances found in the universe are, indeed, only varieties of the four elements. The entire material structure of the universe is reducible to the four elements and ultimately to two kinds of equilateral triangles.

The mutual transformation of three of these elements

In order to account for the mutual transformations of these polyhedra – the tetrahedron (associated with fire), the octahedron (associated with air), and the icosahedron (associated with water) – Plato takes into consideration only the number of surfaces which constitute their envelope. The correspondences established between the number

Table 12.2

Element	Polyhedron	Sides	Weight	Mobility	Sharpness
Earth	Cube	6 Squares	Heavier	Stable	Malleable
Water	Icosahedron	20 Triangles	Heavy	Less mobile	Sharp
Air	Octahedron	8 Triangles	Light	Mobile	Sharper
Fire	Tetrahedron	4 Triangles	Lighter	Very mobile	Sharpest

Table 12.3

---

1 [fire] = 4 Δ
2 [fire] = 2 × 4 Δ = 8 Δ = 1 [air]
1 [fire] + 2 [air] = 4 Δ + 2 × 8 Δ = 20 Δ = 1 [water]
2½ [air] = 2½ × 8 Δ = 20 Δ = 1 [water]

---

of equilateral triangles making up the surface of these polyhedra enable the formulation of the mathematical equivalencies that explain how the elements are transformed into one another, and how generation and corruption in the sensible world occur.

Such an explanation is based upon the following presupposition: the two types of right-angled elementary triangles can neither be created nor destroyed. Consequently, in every transformation, the number of triangles of each species implicated in a transformation is conserved. In addition, only the elements which correspond to polyhedra whose faces are forms of equilateral triangles can be transformed into one another. It follows that water, air, and fire can be transformed into one another. Earth, which corresponds to the cube, whose faces are squares, is affected only by processes of decomposition and recomposition. In short, the transformation of the elements is considered as a function of the surfaces making up the regular polyhedra, and not, as would be natural, as a function of their volumes. The rules of the mutual transformation of fire, air, and water can be summarized in a relatively simple table (Table 12.3). Such a solution is surprising, for it takes into consideration only the surfaces surrounding the polyhedra, even though these polyhedra are volumes.

How can we explain this surprising solution? Three explanations can be advanced:

1. As we can still note in Euclid, what defines a polyhedron is its form, i.e., its limit, which corresponds to the set of its faces.
2. The indeterminacy of the length of the hypotenuse of the elementary right-angled triangles that compose the equilateral triangles makes it difficult to explain the mutual transformation of polyhedra whose faces are not equilateral triangles of the same surface. In other words, only elements of corresponding varieties (whose faces are equilateral triangles of the same dimension) can be transformed into one another.
3. The mathematics known in Plato's time encountered numerous difficulties when it came to extracting square roots, and it was unable to extract cube roots.

The problem of change

The explanations proposed so far do not suffice to account for the mechanical changes that affect the whole of the sensible world, because they lack the following axioms:

1. Everything that is corporeal must be somewhere (*Ti.* 52b).
2. The universe is not uniform, and the motion observed in it originates in the lack of uniformity found within it (*Ti.* 57e). This lack of uniformity can be explained in

two ways. A weak interpretation justifies it by the fact that there exist four regular polyhedra that cannot fit perfectly into one another. A stronger interpretation states that this non-uniformity results from the fact that the length of the hypotenuse of the elementary right-angled triangles remains indeterminate; it follows that the dimensions of the elementary polyhedra that make up all sensible things can be different. This lack of uniformity thus explains the incessant change to which the sensible world is subject, a change the world soul will try to set in order, but only where it can.

3.   There is no void in the sensible world (*Ti.* 58a, cf. 79c), or, what amounts to the same thing, everywhere is filled with something, that is something corporeal.

4.   The world sphere envelops all that is corporeal. Within this sphere, the four elements are distributed in four concentric layers (*Ti.* 33b, 53a, 48a–b), and between those layers exchanges are explained as follows. Since there is no void, the particles, which have a certain weight, cannot spread to infinity towards the outside, while, on the inside, they can only circulate within the always-filled interstices, originating from the absence of homogeneity among the elements. The result is a chain reaction (*Ti.* 58b; cf. 76c and *Laws* X, 849c), which entails a process (*Ti.* 58b) displaying the two movements that govern all transformations of one body into another, which we have mentioned above: division and condensation, decomposition and recomposition.

We must ultimately imagine the Platonic universe as a vast sphere filled with a homogeneous fluid, bereft of all characteristics – that is, *chōra*. Yet the greatest part of it is enclosed within envelopes that delimit the outer surface of each of the four regular polyhedra: tetrahedron, octahedron, icosahedron, and cube. These elementary components tend to be distributed in four concentric layers; but this tendency runs counter to the movement of rotation that carries along the whole of the sphere. The result of this movement is the displacement of the regular polyhedra, or a modification of nature, with fire becoming air, air becoming water, and *vice versa*. This representation introduces a contradiction: in the Platonic universe, we must consider both the continuity that characterizes *chōra*, and the discontinuity the regular polyhedra inevitably establish. Platonic physics is thus neither atomistic like that of Leucippus and Democritus, nor a physics of continuity, like that of Parmenides, Zeno, and Melissus; it is intermediate between the two.

We must acknowledge that since the mechanical movements of the sensible world are dominated by a soul that displays a particularly rigorous mathematical structure, and since the demiurge has fashioned *chōra* mathematically, introducing the regular polyhedra into it, every transformation of one body into another can be explained in terms of mathematical interactions and correlations. Mathematics allows us to apply to the sensible world certain predicates of the intelligible world in which it participates; the sensible world thus acquires permanence and regularity. Ultimately, it is mathematics that accounts for the participation of the sensible world in the intelligible world. And if the sensible world is indeed an image of the intelligible, it must therefore be constructed mathematically; from this point of view, mathematics fixes the limits of Platonic cosmology. Nevertheless, it remains true that Plato was able to use the most elaborate concepts offered by the mathematics of his time; we must consequently

225

recall that the limits of Plato's cosmology coincide with the limits of the mathematics of his time.

Ultimately, nothing guarantees that the mechanical motion just described will always display enough regularity and order to allow people to think about it, speak of it, and act within it. Therefore, Plato makes the world soul prolong the action of the demiurge; this hypothesis not only explains why and how the motion of the sublunary bodies is orderly, but also how and why it is also constantly subject to mathematical laws, giving it the possibility of displaying a certain regularity and permanence. The more the world soul is ruled by rigorous mathematical laws, the more the motions that affect the sublunary sensible world are likely to be orderly.

Biology

If we define biology as knowledge that deals with living beings, we face a whole series of problems when we take up the question in Plato. For him, a living being is one endowed with a soul, where the soul, as we have already seen, is defined as the self-moving principle of all spontaneous motion, physical as well as psychic. Since they are immortal, all souls present themselves as substitutes for the world soul, the constitution of which is described at *Ti.* 35a–b.

Beings endowed with a soul are nevertheless classed hierarchically. At the summit are the gods and daemons; then come human beings – men and women – and the animals that live in the air, on the earth and in the water; plants are ranked at the bottom. Thus, when we wish to speak of biology, we are forced to make a distinction. We must separate human beings and animals, since they are distinct both from plants, which possess only an appetitive soul, and from the gods (including the world and the celestial bodies) and the daemons, whose body is not subject to corruption. Nevertheless, if, as Plato believes, one and the same soul passes through various animal bodies, then the difference between human beings and beasts is radically attenuated. It is a human soul, displaying the same structure as that of gods and daemons, which animates the bodies of men, women, and even all animals (according to the definition given above) that live and move in the air, on the earth and in the water. As a result, men, women, and all the animals are human beings, originally male, but subject to a process of degeneration as a function of the use they have made of their reason in a previous life.

Human beings are constituted on the same model as the universe (*kosmos*): they possess a soul, whose rational part displays the same two circles that constitute the world soul; these circles have the same mathematical proportions as the world soul. The human body is fabricated out of the four elements that constitute the world's body, and only of these four elements. We could therefore say that the human being is a microcosm (a mini-universe). Two features enable us to establish a distinction between this microcosm and the world. Contrary to the body of the world, a human body is subject to destruction; and the human soul experiences a history that makes it pass into different bodies, as a function of its contemplation of the intelligible, both when it is separated from all bodies and when it occupies a body (*Ti.* 90e–92c). Very generally, then, a human being can therefore be considered as a composite, which provisionally associates a human soul with a body of masculine or feminine sex.

The constitution of the body

Two types of basic tissues make up the body of human beings: marrow and flesh. In order to fabricate marrow, the demiurge first chooses smooth regular triangles, which can produce fire, water, air, and earth of the most exact form. He mixes these perfect triangles together in order to constitute the marrow, with which he fabricates the brain, spinal marrow, and bone marrow; marrow is valued to this extent: it is here that the various parts of the soul will come to be anchored, as we shall see below. Then the demiurge continues his work: after irrigating and watering down pure earth, sifted with marrow, the demiurge fabricates the substance of bone, which he uses to fashion the skull, the spinal column, and all the other bones.

This time using elements composed of ordinary triangular surfaces, the demiurge then undertakes to constitute flesh, out of a mixture of water, fire, and earth, to which he adds a leaven made up of salt and of acid, which also consists of ordinary triangles. Flesh, when it dries, causes the appearance of a film, which is the skin. On the skull, the moisture, which comes out through the holes pierced in the skin by fire and is forced back under the skin by the air, takes root and gives birth to hair. Out of a mixture of bone and flesh without leaven, the demiurge fabricates the tendons, which he uses to attach the bones to each other. Finally, he fabricates the nails out of a mixture of tendons, flesh, and air.

The human body is thus reduced to the four elements corresponding to the four regular polyhedra, which are themselves constructed out of surfaces resulting from the arrangement of two types of right-angled triangles: isosceles and scalene. The mathematical qualities of these two basic triangles explain the difference between marrow, the anchor-point of the soul in man, and flesh, which is a completely mortal substance. Here even biology is mathematized, at least down to its most elementary level.

The destruction of the human body by illnesses is also described in mathematical terms at its most basic level, since it is ultimately explained by a dissociation or transmutation of its constituents, which can also be associated with the four elements, associated with the four regular polyhedra. Death occurs when the marrow in which the soul is anchored is gravely damaged; in this case, the bonds that hold the soul to the body relax and let go.

Three systems, the circulatory system (*Ti.* 77c–78a), the respiratory system (*Ti.* 78a–80d), and the nutritive system (*Ti.* 80d–81e), explain the orderly functioning of the human body, which is destroyed by several types of illness (*Ti.* 82b–86a).

The circulatory system is described by means of the metaphor of a garden. The description takes place in two stages. First to be mentioned are the networks of vessels (*Ti.* 77c–e) which transport the blood to all the parts of the body. Then Plato describes the circulation, within these vessels (*Ti.* 77e–78b), of the blood that results from the decomposition, through fire, of food. The circulation of blood has a double function: it ensures the nutrition of all the parts of the body, and it is the vehicle of sensation. The general term "vessels" is used here, for the distinction between veins and arteries was not established until Harvey in 1628.

The respiratory system (*Ti.* 78a–80d) is described on the model of a lobster pot. This pot contains two parts: a central cavity made of fire, which is inside the trunk, and two tunnels made of air, which pass through the nose and the mouth (*Ti.* 78a–d). This entire structure is subject to an alternative movement, which causes the thorax to rise and fall, and which continues as long as life does. Air, followed by fire, is in fact subject to a circular motion; it is breathed in through the nose and mouth, and breathed out through the body (*Ti.* 78d–79a) in a circular motion Plato assimilates to several other species of motion (79a–80c). The circularity of all the motions mentioned is explained by the will to account for their permanence.

Plato then moves on to the nutritive system (*Ti.* 80d–81e). Blood plays the main role in nutrition, and it results from the decomposition of food by fire, which gives blood its red color. This food may be in the form of drink or solid food (*Ti.* 80d–e) which is taken exclusively from plants. Fire, which, as we have just seen, follows air in the respiratory process, dissolves the food when it passes through the stomach, and forces the blood resulting from this decomposition to introduce itself into the vessels adapted to this purpose. Transported through all the parts of the body, the blood nourishes the marrow, flesh, and the whole of the body (*Ti.* 80e–81b). Mortal illnesses occur when the marrow, in which the various parts of the soul are anchored, because it is nourished inappropriately, degenerates and decomposes (*Ti.* 81b–e).

The illnesses that destroy the human body are divided into three groups. Some illnesses are due to an excess, a defect, or a poor distribution of the elementary components (i.e., the four elements) that constitute the human body (*Ti.* 81e–82b). Other illnesses come from the decomposition of tissues (flesh and tendons) which, as they liquefy, pollute the blood (*Ti.* 82b–84d). A third group of illnesses pertains to each of the elements that make up the human body: earth, water, air, and fire. These are fevers (*Ti.* 86a), certain illnesses that concern the breath (*Ti.* 84d–85a), and those relative to phlegm (*Ti.* 85a–b) and bile (*Ti.* 85b–86a).

Observation and Experimental Verification

The strength of Greek science resides essentially in its formal dialectical and demonstrative techniques. The ancient Greeks devoted considerable effort to developing an axiomatic system, and to using mathematics as the privileged instrument for understanding natural phenomena.

The empirical method also achieved considerable progress among the Greeks, in both research and practice. History and geography were the first domains to engage in the careful and exhaustive gathering of information; but this practice was soon extended first to medicine, and then to several domains: zoology, botany, and so on.

Nevertheless, empirical observation must be carefully distinguished from theoretical observation. Even if both types of observation overlap, all theoretical observation presents a deliberate character. In this regard, Aristotle rightly insists on the distinction between the observations carried out by fishermen in the context of their activity, and those undertaken in order to carry out a scientific investigation on fish. We must add another distinction, between observation properly so called, and awareness of its importance for research. To carry out detailed research on animals, plants, minerals, stars, musical notes, or illnesses, is one thing, but quite another to have an explicit methodology that attributes a precise role to empirical data within scientific research.

The two concerns just mentioned are present in Plato, albeit not at the level of self-awareness, and not to the same extent as in Aristotle. This general attitude can also be found in the *Timaeus*. Although several propositions made by Plato could be subjected to verification and eventually turned out to be false, the following nevertheless reveal that Plato was sensitive to a certain form of observation, and was not immediately opposed to all experimental verification. This is true of the movement of "planets" (*Ti.* 39a–d), of the greater density of gold than bronze (*Ti.* 59b–c), of the relation between the rapidity of a sound and its pitch (*Ti.* 67b), and above all the need for circular motion (*Ti.* 79e–80d) in a world that contains no void. These examples suggest that despite all the technical problems he had to face, Plato, in the *Timaeus*, formulates statements that truly pertain to cosmology, and that conflict neither with logic nor with sensory experience.

In ancient Greece, the search for certainty was often counterbalanced by an absence of empirical information. In addition, "evidence" and "experiments" were frequently used to corroborate a theory rather than to test it. In short, competitive debate, or *agōn*, seems ultimately to have furnished the framework in which the sciences of nature were developed in ancient Greece. The point was to establish a model of explanation, on the level of discourse, by presenting convincing arguments for it, rather than to impose it on the level of reality, by testing it against the facts to determine whether it could withstand the test or could better explain the facts than some other theory.

Two types of explanation, some technical and the others theoretical, can be advanced to explain Plato's reticence with regard to experimental verification.

Technical limits

The measuring operation may be considered the fundamental act of science. In order to progress, science must define particularly abstract concepts beforehand, among the first of which are units of measure. Let us note, for example, the tremendous importance assumed for the development of science by such units of measure as temperature expressed in degrees, acceleration, energy, electric charge, entropy, quantity of information as measured in bits, etc., and the elaboration of instruments allowing them to be measured. In Plato's time, known standards of measure, which concerned only length, weight, volume, and time, did not display any universality, since they varied as a function of individual cities, and remained highly unreliable, given the primitive nature of measuring instruments. In addition to the lack of appropriate abstract measures, another factor, no less decisive, also came into play: mathematics in Plato's time was in a particularly primitive state, and several of its developments now considered essential were still lacking. However, several examples dating from Hellenistic times reveal the ingenuity that was used to surmount or to get around these difficulties.

In view of what has just been said, it should be evident that, even if they attained a fairly advanced level in geometry, even if they succeeded in accomplishing technical exploits, as is shown by their architecture, their sculpture, and their ceramics, and although their methods of navigation implied the use of technical procedures, albeit primitive, the Greeks of Plato's time did not have available the tools which could have enabled them to conceive, define, and to put into practice experiments intended to verify their hypotheses in the domain of scientific knowledge.

Theoretical prejudices

Experimental verification, that absolutely decisive procedure of questioning Nature, escaped Plato, who, after setting forth his theory of colors, exclaims:

> To want to test [a physical phenomenon] under the control of experience (*skopoumenos basanon lambanoi*) would mean being unaware of the difference between men and the gods, for only a god . . . possesses the necessary knowledge and power, whereas among men none is capable . . . nor will they ever be in the future. (*Ti.* 68d–e)

For Plato, experimental verification thus implies the exact reproduction of Nature, a task that is as impossible for us as it was for him.

Let me mention just one particular aspect of a theory of verification, within the framework of a purely local, controlled, and repeatable experiment. Today, experimentation exhibits the following characteristic: in the course of an experiment, only a very limited number of parameters is allowed to vary, on the assumption that all the rest of the universe, with its enormous complexity, and its large number of variables, will exercise no influence on the experiment in progress: *ceteris paribus*, "everything else does not count." To reach this *ceteris paribus*, all the experimenter's ingenuity must be brought into play, which sometimes leads him to construct gigantic instruments such as particle accelerators. Now Plato, who clearly had neither the instruments, nor the units of measure, nor the mathematical language which would have enabled him to do so, did not try to carry out this type of experiment. This defect explains why the models of explanation he proposed in the *Timaeus* remain bereft of all operative value.

By neglecting observation, and especially by refusing experimental verification, Plato condemned his explanations to impotence. Why, indeed, should one prefer the explanations he proposed to others that were intuitively more plausible and used ordinary language, less abstruse than the mathematics whose use was reserved for a small number of specialists? On the level of the history of science, therefore, Plato remains an ambiguous figure – very modern when he appeals to mathematics and when he complies with the rigors of deductive argumentation, but very traditional when he holds observation to be worth little, and experimental verification to be impossible.

Bibliography

Works Cited

Anton, J. P. (ed.). (1981). *Science and the Sciences in Plato*. Buffalo, NY: Caravan Books. (Articles by Vlastos, Mourelatos, Turnbull and Mueller on *Republic* VII, 528e–530c.)

Balansard, A. (2001). Technē *dans les dialogues de Platon. L'empreinte de la Sophistique*. Introduction in English by Luc Brisson. Sankt Augustin: Academia Verlag.

Brisson, L. (1999). "Un si long anonymat." In J.-M. Narbonne and L. Langlois (eds.), *La métaphysique. son histoire, sa critique, ses enjeux* (pp. 37–60). Collection Zétésis. Paris: Vrin / Québec: Presse de l'Université Laval.

——. (2000). "Le rôle des mathématiques dans le *Timée* selon les interprétations contemporaines." In A. Neschke-Hentschke (ed.), *Le Timée de Platon. Contributions à l'Histoire de sa réception* (pp. 295–315). Louvain: Bibliothèque Philosophique de Louvain / Paris: Peeters.

——. (2002). "Is the World One? A New Interpretation of Plato's *Parmenides*." *Oxford Studies in Ancient Philosophy*, 22, 1–20.

Cornford, F. M. (1937). *Plato's Cosmology*. London: Routledge & Kegan Paul.

Gill, M. L. (1996). "Introduction." In M. L. Gill and P. Ryan (trans.), *Plato. Parmenides* (pp. 1–109). Indianapolis: Hackett.

Gregory, A. (2000). *Plato's Philosophy of Science*. London: Duckworth.

Johansen, T. K. (2004). *Plato's Natural Philosophy. A Study of the Timaeus-Critias*. Cambridge: Cambridge University Press.

Knorr, W. (1990). "Plato and Eudoxus on the Planetary Motions." *Journal for the History of Astronomy*, 21, 313–29.

Lloyd, G. E. R. (1968). "Plato as a Natural Scientist." *Journal of Hellenic Studies*, 88, 78–92.

——. (1991). "Plato on Mathematics and Nature, Myth and Science." In G. E. R. Lloyd, *Method and Problems in Greek Science* (pp. 335–51). Cambridge: Cambridge University Press. (Originally published 1983 in Japanese.)

Mueller, I. (1992). "Mathematical Method and Philosophical Truth." In R. Kraut (ed.), *The Cambridge Companion of Plato* (pp. 170–99). Cambridge: Cambridge University Press.

Pritchard, P. (1995). *Plato's Philosophy of Mathematics*. Sankt Augustin: Academia Verlag.

Sayer, K. M. (1978). "Plato's *Parmenides*: Why the Eight Hypotheses are not Contradictory." *Phronesis*, 23, 123–50.

Vlastos, G. (1988). "Elenchus and Mathematics: A Turning-point in Plato's Philosophical Development." *American Journal of Philology*, 109, 362–96. Repr. in H. H. Benson (ed.). (1992), *Essays on the Philosophy of Socrates* (pp. 137–61). Oxford: Oxford University Press.

Further Reading

Brisson, L. (1992). Platon, *Timée / Critias*. New translation (in French), introduction and notes, with the collaboration of Michel Patillon for the translation. GF 618. Paris: Flammarion.

Broadie, S. (2000). "Theodicy and Pseudo-history in the *Timaeus*." *Oxford Studies in Ancient Philosophy*, 21, 1–28.

Burnyeat, M. F. (2000). "Plato on Why Mathematics is Good for the Soul." In T. Smiley (ed.), *Mathematics and Necessity: Essays in the History of Philosophy* (pp. 1–82). Oxford: Oxford University Press/British Academy.

Calvo, T. and Brisson, L. (eds.). (1997). *Interpreting the* Timaeus-Critias. Proceedings of the Fourth Symposium Platonicum. Sankt Augustin: Academia Verlag.

Natali, C. and Maso, S. (eds.). (2003). *Plato Physicus. Cosmologia e antropologie nel* Timeo. Amsterdam: Hakkert.

O'Brien, D. (1984). *Theories of Weight in the Ancient World. Four essays on Democritus, Plato and Aristotle. A Study in the Development of Ideas*. (vol 2): *Plato, Weight and Sensation. The Two Theories of the* Timaeus. Paris: Les Belles Lettres / Leiden: Brill.

Sedley, D. N. (1997). "Becoming Like the God." In T. Calvo and L. Brisson (eds.), *Interpreting the* Timaeus-Critias (pp. 327–39). Proceedings of the Fourth Symposium Platonicum. Sankt Augustin: Academia Verlag.

Vlastos, G. (1975). *Plato's Universe*. Oxford: Clarendon Press.

Zeyl, D. J. (2000). *Plato. Timaeus*. Translation with Introduction. Indianapolis: Hackett.

Part III

Aristotle

13

The Aristotelian Way

PIERRE PELLEGRIN

The ancients themselves regarded Plato and Aristotle as the two greatest philosophers who had ever lived. This evaluation has endured into modern times, as witnessed by the judgment of Coleridge cited in the Introduction to this volume, among many others. Aristotle, in fact, initiated a "style of thought" that has deeply marked the history of philosophy to the present day; and, of the two "greats" in question, he has indisputably exercised the deeper and more lasting historical influence on western thought. Dante, who made him the "master of those who know," was not mistaken. We can gain access to this "Aristotelian thought" by considering some historical and biographical facts about Aristotle himself.

Aristotle was born in 384 BCE, in Stagira, a Chalcidean city. Though Greek by language and culture, he was therefore a subject of the king of Macedonia, with whom his father, a physician, maintained friendly relations (cf. Pellegrin, 1996). It is remarkable, for that matter, that with the exception of Socrates and Plato all the great Greek philosophers came from the periphery of, or from outside, the Greek politico-cultural sphere. This closeness of Aristotle's family to the Macedonian dynasty is doubtless at the root of one of the most notable episodes of Aristotle's life, namely the teaching he lavished on the Macedonian prince who would become Alexander the Great. For Philip, Alexander's father, Aristotle was no doubt only a "second choice": if he wanted to give his son a Greek education, but without his having to leave Macedonia, he probably could not call on people as well-known as Plato or Isocrates, who were hardly inclined to leave Athens. When he became the prince's tutor, Aristotle had not yet founded the Lyceum and was not yet recognized as a major philosopher. About the relations between teacher and pupil – who studied with Aristotle from the age of 13 to 20 – we know little for certain, and it is better to leave aside the many stories on the subject.

Yet there is one point on which to reflect. Alexander was the principal agent in a radical change in world history, which historians have marked by saying that his reign completes the "classical" period and begins the "Hellenistic" one. Among the many changes, we are above all interested in the political transformation of the Greek world. The city, which was the basic political unit of the classical Greek world, gives way to large kingdoms and persists only as a municipal entity. Alexander himself wanted to put an end to Greek ethnocentrism, which regarded all non-Hellenes, or at least all non-Greek speakers, as "barbarians." He thus conceived a great project of political and even "biological" fusion – since he encouraged his officers to marry Persian women – between the Greco-Macedonians and the peoples under Persian domination. Aristotle was not the theorist of this new world being born before his eyes. On the contrary, he buttressed the city by taking it to be the most developed form of human association. Further, following a theory of climates, other versions of which are found in Plato and in the Hippocratic treatise *Airs, Waters, Places*, Aristotle thought that due to their environment only the Greeks were able to combine liberty with intelligence and to live in a city, whereas the barbarians were, at least in tendency, of a slavish nature. This Aristotelian backwardness in politics is perhaps the main reason for the relative disinterest in Aristotle's political philosophy among later generations, since it rests upon a historically moribund reality. The *Politics* was not translated into Arabic. Aristotle was the last of the "classical philosophers," not the first of the Hellenistic ones. In his conception of the world, he, whose Greekness has been questioned, remained strictly Greek.

The second "great man" to whom Aristotle must be related is obviously Plato. The young Aristotle met Plato at about 17, when he came to Athens and became a member of the Academy. It seems certain that Aristotle was a critical student, but it is hard really to judge what his attitude was toward Plato, because the tradition offers two contrary pictures of it. On one picture, Aristotle was a quasi-orthodox Platonist whose criticism of the theory of Forms was in the end no more virulent than that found in Plato's dialogues themselves, especially beginning with the *Parmenides*. On the contrary one, interpreters have regarded Aristotle as the anti-Platonic philosopher *par excellence*. An interesting example of this interpretive dichotomy concerns the question of when exactly Aristotle founded his own school, the Lyceum. Some holding that he did so during the lifetime of Plato – who then, according to Diogenes Laertius, compared him to a colt kicking out against its mother – while according to others he did not decide to found his own school until the headship of the Academy, having first eluded him in favor of Speusippus, eluded him for the second time, in favor of Xenocrates. This second hypothesis seems more solid, and today it is generally agreed that the Lyceum was founded in 335. Behind the biographical anecdote lies a fundamental difference in interpretation of immense consequence. The Neoplatonic philosophers who dominated the philosophical scene at the end of antiquity, all of whom commented on Aristotle (cf. Hoffmann, WHAT WAS COMMENTARY IN LATE ANTIQUITY?, in this volume), inclined toward a conciliatory attitude, according to which, on the one hand, there is no divergence between Plato and Aristotle, and, on the other, the study of Aristotle is a preliminary to that of Plato for the student of philosophy. In late antiquity and in the Byzantine world, treatises on the "harmony of Plato and Aristotle" came almost to constitute a literary genre.

In this area two aspects must be distinguished. First, there is the extent to which Aristotle adhered to Platonist theses. For example, one of the most tenacious commonplaces of the history of philosophy – and one that is far from being wholly false – is that Aristotle replaced the supra-sensible Platonic forms with a form that is involved in matter. There is also the question of differences of *structure* between Platonic and Aristotelian thought.

On the first point, as we have seen, tradition in antiquity wavered, with a majority tending to regard Plato and Aristotle as in theoretical harmony. Modern and contemporary interpreters, on the contrary, have most often held that the positions of Aristotle and those of Plato were irreconcilable. Let us consider a few of the great divergences that the tradition has claimed to discover between the two philosophers. Theodor Gomperz sought to explain what seemed to him to be an internal tension in the Aristotelian corpus as a struggle between two tendencies in Aristotle, or rather between two coexisting personalities in him, whom Gomperz called "the Platonist" and the "the Asclepiad" (cf. Gomperz, 1920). The speculative boldness transmitted to him by the company of Plato was tempered by an empirical tendency inherited from Aristotle's physician father. In the same vein, many interpreters have opposed the eminent role that Plato gives to mathematics to a supposed experimental bent in Aristotle. When we look at things more closely, the contrast between Plato and Aristotle is not as definite as it seems. Aristotle is far from having neglected mathematics, and if it is not "invasive" in his works, that is mainly because it is not, or not mainly, a theoretical tool but a particular science alongside others, as we shall see again below. As for the idea that Aristotle wished to introduce into philosophy an empiricism acquired from the company of physicians, it is in one sense the reverse of the truth. Far from having wished to "medicalize" philosophy, Aristotle on the contrary attempted to put medicine back under the control of philosophy (cf. Pellegrin, ANCIENT MEDICINE AND ITS CONTRIBUTION TO THE PHILOSOPHICAL TRADITION, in this volume). One might add that Aristotle retains the main requirements of "scientific" knowledge according to Plato, in particular the universality and necessity of its propositions as well as the immutability of its object (cf. Bodnár and Pellegrin, ARISTOTLE, PHYSICS, AND COSMOLOGY, in this volume).

In a word, discussion of the degree of convergence between Plato's theses and those of Aristotle leads to undecidable questions rather than indisputable results. By contrast, what clearly distinguishes Aristotle from Plato in the domain of epistemology is Aristotle's fundamental and unshakeable confidence in perception. One of his basic ideas, in fact, is that nature has sufficiently furnished us with the instruments needed to give us adequate knowledge of reality. This is not to imply that Aristotle was not aware of the risks of error to which perception exposes us; but for him these errors are foreseeable and avoidable. In the cognitive domain, the "power of perception," to borrow the title of a book by Deborah Modrak (Modrak, 1987), is immense: first because perception gives us an accurate picture of things as they are, then because perception serves as a kind of model for every other cognitive process, and finally because perception is a necessary condition for all other kinds of knowledge. Here there is a real break with Platonism. From our modern point of view, we can render two contrary verdicts on this aspect of Aristotelianism. Many have extolled Aristotle's "return to the real" after the speculative excesses of Plato that led to the mystical doctrines of the Neoplatonists. Thus those, and they are many, who believe that modern science is fundamentally empirical – which is a manifest untruth – see in Aristotle a scientist or a "proto-scientist" in the modern sense. Those who are more informed both about the history of science and about the very nature of scientific knowledge know that science begins and develops in the face of perceptual evidence. Thus the anti-Aristotelian movement of the Renaissance did not have simply, or even mainly, anti-religious motives, as has too often been said and taught – because Aristotle had been annexed by the Thomists – but rather scientific ones. Furthermore, it is very striking that the makers of the new world, as against Aristotle's world – which was the world of our perception, with the earth motionless at the center, objects defined by their qualities, etc. – sought their inspiration and their models in the Platonist tradition (cf. Koyré, 1957).

When one comes to what were called above the "differences in structure" between Platonism and Aristotelianism, no further doubt is possible: Aristotle is indeed entirely opposed to his teacher on some fundamental points. It is at this level that one must seek what is most characteristic of "Aristotelian thought." We shall consider two of these points.

Aristotle did not doubt for one instant that he represented the ultimate perfection of human thought. Many philosophers have taken the same position about their own thought. It is true nonetheless that Aristotelianism, in contrast to Platonism, is a deeply historical way of thinking. In the introduction we applied the term "teleological" to this form of historicism, in so far as Aristotle sees his own system as the culminating point of the history of thought. According to Aristotle, all philosophers, or almost all, have expressed some part of the truth, a truth he said was hard to attain and also hard to miss entirely (*Met.* α.1, 993a30). Aristotle's position here accords with what he thought about the powers of perception: through our sense-organs, reality constrains even the most unwilling, such as the Eleatics, to see it as it is (cf. *Phys.* I.5, 188b30). This contrast between Plato, who thinks afresh at the end of a history made up of errors, and Aristotle, who takes his place in a historical development of the discovery of the truth, recurs throughout the history of philosophy: from this viewpoint Descartes is on Plato's side and Hegel on Aristotle's.

But the most pronounced structural contrast between the two philosophers concerns their conception of scientific knowledge itself, this term being understood in the ancient sense. For Plato, what in the *Republic* he called dialectic is the science of everything. The other sciences are, pedagogically, ways of access to it and, theoretically, derivative from it. Aristotle, on the contrary, conceived of knowledge as irremediably divided. The basic thesis of his epistemology is that there is one science (*epistēmē*) per genus (*genos*), and a discipline that concerns several genera is not itself a science, even if several sciences can make use of it. Thus we do not demonstrate geometrical properties within and by means of arithmetical science, and if Aristotle indeed alluded to a kind of general mathematics, it remained a theoretical phantom. In practice this system is more flexible than it seems to be, since it leaves some room for sciences subordinate to one another and for sciences whose objects are concerned with several genera because they can be considered from different points of view: thus optics depends on geometry when we consider light rays as straight lines and on physics when we consider their material composition. A still deeper division separates what Book E of the *Metaphysics* calls theoretical, practical, and productive sciences. Leaving aside the latter, which are in fact rational techniques like architecture, we see that the theoretical sciences, of which the three great types are mathematics, physics, and theology, have a different kind of rationality than practical sciences like politics and ethics (see Keyt, ARISTOTLE'S POLITICAL PHILOSOPHY, in this volume).

This division of knowledge into irreducibly different types has extraordinarily important consequences. It is no longer the philosopher who is the best mathematician, but neither is he the one who should busy himself with ruling the city. At most the philosopher can participate in molding the legislator. Plato already sent advisers to princes, but in the hope that someday philosophers would take power. Aristotle confines their role to that of teachers and advisers.

238

What Aristotle objects to in Plato is certainly what has been called his "idealism," which drove him to posit supra-sensible entities that in the end are useless. But it is also, and perhaps primarily, that his thinking rests on a confusion between notions and methods that must be distinguished. Thus at the beginning of the *Politics*, Aristotle criticizes the Platonists – without naming them, however – because they appeal to a notion of "power" that is a conceptual grab-bag into which anything may be put, whereas the power of slave-master, the husband, the father, the king, and the magistrate are properly distinguished, because these powers are "of different kinds." Historically, this Aristotelian organization of knowledge has had an extraordinary influence, especially on the institutional plane. Upon it was modeled the organization of studies at the Museum in Alexandria, for example. In its partition by disciplines – physics, metaphysics, psychology, politics, etc. – a book like this one is, from a certain viewpoint, more Aristotelian that Platonic; but the reasons are pedagogical rather than theoretical.

Here we also find a kind of oscillation in history between a unitary vision of the sciences and a return to a plural conception of knowledge. At the beginning of the twentieth century, for example, the physical sciences claimed to absorb all the sciences, not just biology (with the "chemistry of life") but also psychology and those sciences known as "social." The Platonic dialectician then donned the garb of the physicist. This unification on a physicalist basis was already present in Descartes. Today the practice, if not the theory, of the sciences seems oriented rather to a pluralist approach. We are, to that extent, in an Aristotelian age: this situation perhaps partly explains the infatuation with Aristotle that emerged in the second half of the twentieth century. Thus the sciences of our day are all discovering (or rediscovering) Aristotelian roots both individually and in their organization.

For the historian of philosophy, the Aristotelian corpus displays certain specific traits. The most important are the result of the way these texts were transmitted. The history of this transmission is of the most romantic sort, and it is impossible completely to disentangle the true from the legendary in the accounts that have come down to us. Theophrastus, Aristotle's successor as head of the Lyceum, left his library containing Aristotle's works in particular to Neleus of Skepsis, the son of his former co-disciple Coriscus. This is no doubt the same Coriscus whom Aristotle often takes as an example of an individual man. As the kings of Pergamum, the Attalids, wanted to build a library able to rival that of Alexandria, and to that end conducted a veritable hunt for books, the heirs of Neleus, fearing their possessions would be stolen from them, hid Aristotle's works in a cellar, from which they were not removed until a century and a half later by a certain Appellicon of Teos, who was in the employ of the king Mithridates. Appellicon had copies made of Aristotle's texts. When Mithridates was defeated by the Romans, the library in question ended up in Rome in the hands of Tyrranion, a remarkable man who was Cicero's librarian and the tutor of his son, who took up the project of editing Aristotle's works. But the enterprise was really brought to completion only by Andronicus of Rhodes, the eleventh successor to Aristotle as head of the Lyceum (from about 70 to 50 BCE). Andronicus corrected and edited the texts of Aristotle and, most important, set them in the order in which they have been transmitted to us. All later editions are thus merely reincarnations of that of Andronicus of Rhodes (see Mejer, ANCIENT PHILOSOPHY AND THE DOXOGRAPHICAL TRADITION, in this volume).

Why dwell at such length on what seems, at first sight, a mere series of anecdotes? We can, in fact, draw some significant elements from it. First, according to this history, the works of Aristotle that we know remained unknown to the educated public for two centuries after the death of the master. No doubt Andronicus exaggerated things a little for the sake of a kind of publicity for the edition he published. But on the whole it seems established that what the educated public knew before Andronicus was "another" Aristotle, one who wrote works for publication, including a certain number of dialogues in the Platonic manner. This Aristotle is more or less completely lost to us. A second very important point: the Aristotle we have has thus been subject to two kinds of intervention. For one thing, the texts were not originally intended for publication, but rather sprang from Aristotle's teaching, and were doubtless partly re-written, especially to take account of comments of the students. Then Andronicus put the texts in a systematic order that seemed adequate to him but does not reflect the place Aristotle intended to give to each of them. This editorial task also implies many adjustments, divisions, and additions on the part of an editor who, like those of his time, did not have a modern editor's respect for the letter of the text.

In brief, contrary to what holds in the case of Plato, we do not have a text that is, strictly speaking, from Aristotle's own hand (or, more precisely, dictated by him, since the ancients did not write but rather dictated the works published under their names). If there is, indeed, a *style* recognizable in all the Aristotelian treatises, we can by no means speak of it as *Aristotle's* style, whereas we know the style of Plato through the dialogues. The most important consequence of this is that a chronology of Aristotle's texts cannot be established on the basis of stylistic evidence, as has been done for Plato's dialogues (see C. Gill, THE PLATONIC DIALOGUE, in this volume). When, therefore, two passages present different views and consequently can be presumed to have been written at different times in Aristotle's life, we can tell which is earlier only by relying on doctrinal criteria.

It was only in the twentieth century that historians of philosophy really applied themselves to the problem of Aristotle's doctrinal development. The founding work on the question is that of Werner Jaeger, *Aristotle: Fundamentals of the History of his Development*, first published in German in 1923. Jaeger's central idea is that the various Aristotelian texts can be dated according to their greater or lesser distance from Platonism, with the more Platonic passages belonging to an earlier period of Aristotle's activity, when he was more influenced by the teaching of the Academy. This method encounters two difficulties. First, determining the "degree of Platonism" of a text is very difficult for multiple reasons (for example, the presence of Platonic echoes in the vocabulary used by Aristotle is not a sign of greater proximity to Platonism). Second, and above all, Jaeger's position rests on a psychological and theoretical supposition whose truth is not at all evident: why should Aristotle have moved away from the Platonism to which he more or less adhered in his youth? Why should he not rather have rejected Platonism when he was young, to draw nearer to it later, as some think (cf. Düring, 1966, Owen, 1965)? The fundamental flaw in the many studies devoted to Aristotle's chronology is thus that one looks for, and finds, in the Aristotelian corpus support for a preconceived idea of Aristotle's intellectual history. For example, many have found it entirely "natural" that, after the mystical tendencies of youth, as witnessed for instance by a dialogue like *Eudemus, or the Immortality of the Soul*, in which Aristotle is said to have held that the best thing humans can do is to die as swiftly as possible so that their souls can return to their true homeland, Aristotle became more "positive" and, for example, developed his studies as a naturalist. Such a position is clearly weak. The best thing is thus to leave aside all chronological hypotheses in reading the Aristotelian corpus, while recognizing that Aristotle very likely did evolve in the course of his philosophical career.

Our tendency to see Aristotelian doctrine as highly systematic could even be regarded as the effect of an illusion due to the intervention of Andronicus. This supposed systematicity may be one of the sources of the image of a rigid and dogmatic Aristotle, often contrasted with a flexible and seductive Plato. The truth is more nuanced. Aristotle is not a dogmatist, in the pejorative sense, but a searcher. This is seen, for example, in his practice of dialectic and in the role he gives to doxographies in his philosophical work. For Aristotle, dialectic is no longer the supreme science it was in the *Republic*; rather it becomes, like rhetoric – to which dialectic is, according to Aristotle, very close – a discipline that codifies discussion between two disputants on any given question. Dialectic thus still has the universal value it had for Plato, but it loses its scientific character because it is not confined to one genus. Now, one function of dialectic that has much interested commentators is its role in establishing the principles of the sciences. According to the letter of Aristotle's text (*Top.* I.2, 101a36), dialectic "examines" the notions involved in the principles in light of "reputable opinions" (*endoxa*), that is, opinions granted by everyone, or by most people, or by the wise, or by the majority of them. In short, far from being a man of the school or sect, Aristotle continues, in the Socratic tradition, to submit philosophical activity to the scrutiny of the man in the street. As for Aristotle's use of doxography, it conforms to what was said above: all opinions must be taken into account because all – except those of paradox-seekers such as the Sophists – express a side of the truth. This is the main reason for the presence of extensive doxographies at the beginning of almost all the Aristotelian treatises.

From this also stems one of the remarkable characteristics of Aristotle's school, the Lyceum, which was a storehouse of knowledge and objects: carrying on a practice already present in the Academy, it collected the political constitutions of numerous cities and barbarian peoples (the sources say 250 or 255) as well as lists of "customs." Each of Aristotle's assistants was in charge of a particular discipline and of its history (Eudemus was in charge of geometry, arithmetic, and astronomy; Theophrastus of biological sciences; some others of music, literary criticism, etc.). Aristotle seems, moreover, to have begun a new relation to writing by owning a library himself, which no one, with few exceptions (e.g., Euripides), had done before. He was known as "the reader."

In fact, the Lyceum operated as the first university in the quasi-modern sense of the word, much more than did the Academy or the Hellenistic philosophical schools. This was due, fundamentally, to Aristotle's conception of knowledge: anyone interested in a particular subject could come to the Lyceum without having to give up that interest. On the contrary, he found his place in the global research program of the school. Until the end of antiquity, the Lyceum remained one of the great philosophical schools (cf. Moraux, 1973, 1984). This can be seen in every period of ancient history. One example: Galen's father thought that a complete education for his son should include instruction by a Peripatetic teacher; and when Galen arrived in Rome, he found a very active Peripatetic intellectual circle, which had connections in the highest circles of Roman society.

But Aristotle's glory days would come much later. Nowadays we still think within the intellectual framework put in place by the Renaissance and modern science. This science was largely constructed in opposition to Aristotelianism. The attacks directed against it, because of their passion, their excessiveness and, often, their bad faith, are in fact a tribute to the conceptual strength of the Peripatetic philosophy. Starting with the first rediscovery of the Greek texts, which took place in the time of the Crusades, Western Christian thinkers, or at least the best of them such as Albertus Magnus and Thomas Aquinas, found in Aristotle not just a mass of knowledge to which they did not have access but also an effective way of thinking for their own time. Here we find again characteristics of Aristotelianism we mentioned earlier: its encyclopedic tendency, and its way of articulating different kinds of knowledge. Marie-Dominique Chenu has convincingly shown the true reasons for the Aristotelian revival of the thirteenth century (Chenu, 1954). Thomas Aquinas obviously continued to believe that God can intervene in the world wherever and whenever He pleases, even overturning the order of nature. But the new world born around the cities in fact lived in a nature that was coherent, autonomous, and no longer explicitly dependent on special divine decrees for each of its events. A Platonist vision, as revised by Augustine, that related all of reality and all events to a first principle as their single source was no longer adequate to this new world. But, as we have seen, it is characteristic of Aristotelianism to articulate, if not without difficulty or obscurity, a global vision of being and distinct domains of reality, to which different cognitive aims correspond. Here we find again the cardinal rule of Aristotelian epistemology, which confines every science to a single genus. The benefits of such a vision were such that Thomas Aquinas did not hesitate to pay an enormous price to annex Aristotle: the reconciliation of Aristotle's thought with a Judaeo-Christian theology completely alien to it. Thus Aristotelianism lived on and continued to speak. As Pico della Mirandola put it, "Sine Thoma mutus esset Aristoteles."

Bibliography

Texts, Translations, and Reference Works for Aristotle

Aristotle's works are cited by Bekker numbers: page and column of *Aristotelis opera* edited by Immanuel Bekker published by the Prussian Academy (1831–70). Berlin: G. Reimer. The first two volumes include the text of Aristotle edited by Bekker (2 columns); vol. 3 contains some Latin translations; vol. 4: contains excerpts from the commentators; vol. 5 is the *Index Aristotelicus* by H. Bonitz, which has been separately published (listed below). All subsequent editions of the Greek text use the Bekker numbers.

Concordance

Bonitz, H. (1870). *Index Aristotelicus*. 2 edn., 1955. Berlin. Repr. Graz: Akademische Druck-u. Verlagsanstalt.

Modern editions of Aristotle are in the series Oxford Classical Texts (various editors). Oxford: Clarendon Press. A number of the main texts have been edited with commentary by W. D. Ross. Those used are cited in the separate bibliographies in this section.

English translation of Aristotle

Barnes, J. (ed.). (1984). *The Complete Works of Aristotle*. The revised Oxford translation. (2 vols.). Princeton: Princeton University Press.

Ancient Commentaries

Commentaria in Aristotelem Graeca (cited as CAG). Various editors. (23 vols.) Berlin: G. Reimer, 1882–1909.

These works are currently being translated into English in the series Ancient Commentators on Aristotle. R. Sorabji (General Editor). Ithaca, NY: Cornell University Press / London: Duckworth.

Medieval Commentaries

Averroes. Junctas edition Venice 1562–74. Repr. by Minerva, Frankfurt am Main 1962.

Aquinas

Commentaries on Aristotle are published by Marietti. Some of these commentaries have been translated into English. The Dumb Ox Books intend to bring out all the Aristotelian commentaries in English.

Some of the English translations currently available are:

Blackwell, R. J., Spath, R. J., and Thirlkel, W. E. (trans.). (1963). St. Thomas Aquinas. *Commentary on Aristotle's* Physics. Introduction by V. J. Bourke. London: Routledge & Kegan Paul.

Foster, K., O.P. and Humphries, Fr. S., O.P. (trans.). (1951). *Atistotle's* De Anima *with the Commentary of St. Thomas Aquinas*. Introduction by Ivo Thomas, O.P. London: Routledge & Kegan Paul.

Litzinger, C. I., O.P. (trans.). (1993). St. Thomas Aquinas. *Commentary on Aristotle's* Nicomachean Ethics. Foreword by Ralph McInerny. Notre Dame, Ind.: Dumb Ox Books 1993. (Translation originally published 1964.)

Works Cited

Chenu, M.-D. (1954). *Introduction à l'étude de saint Thomas d'Aquin*. Paris: Vrin.

Düring, I. (1966). *Aristoteles. Darstellung und Interpretation seines Denkens*. Heidelberg: Universitätverlag.

Gomperz, T. (1920). *Greek Thinkers: A History of Ancient Philosophy* (trans. L. Magnus and G. G. Berry) (4 vols.). London: J. Murray. (Original work published in German 1896–1909.)

Jaeger, W. (1923). *Aristoteles, Grundlegung einer Geschichte seiner Entwicklung*. Berlin: Weidmannsche Buchhandlung. (English version *Aristotle: Fundamentals of the History of his Development*. (trans. R. Robinson). 2nd edn. Oxford: Oxford University Press. 1948.

Koyré, A. (1957). *From the Closed World to the Infinite Universe*. Baltimore: Johns Hopkins University Press.

Modrak, D. (1987). *Aristotle. The Power of Perception*. Chicago: University of Chicago Press.

Moraux, P. (1973, 1984). *Der Aristotelismus bei den Griechen*. (2 vols.) Berlin: de Gruyter.

Owen, G. E. L. (1965). "The Platonism of Aristotle." *Proceedings of the British Academy*, 50, 125–50. Repr. in G. E. L. Owen, (1986). *Logic, Science, and Dialectic: Collected Papers in Greek Philosophy* (M. C. Nussbaum, ed.) (pp. 200–20). London: Duckworth / Ithaca, NY Cornell University Press.

Pellegrin, P. (1996). "Aristote, Hippocrate, Œdipe." In R. Wittern and P. Pellegrin (eds.), *Hippokratische Medizin und antike Philosophie* (pp. 183–98). Hidelsheim, Zürich / New York: Olms.

Further Reading

Gottschalk, H. B. (1987). "Aristotelian Philosophy in the Roman World from the Time of Cicero to the End of the Second Century AD." *ANRW* II.36(2), 1079–174.

Grayeff, F. (1974). *Aristotle and his School*. London: Duckworth.

Lynch, J. P. (1972). *Aristotle's School*. Berkeley: University of California Press.

Natali, C. (1991). *Bios Theoretikos. La Vita di Aristotele e l'Organizzazione della sua Scuola*. Bologna: Il Mulino.

14

Aristotle's Logic and Theory of Science

WOLFGANG DETEL

Knowledge and Analysis

Aristotle's logic and theory of science have been handed down to us in two texts that are nowadays called *Prior Analytics* and *Posterior Analytics*, respectively. But Aristotle himself usually refers both to his logic and his theory of science as "analytics" (e.g., *Top.* VIII.11, 162a11–12; *Met.* Z.12, 1037b8–9; *EN* VI.3, 1139b27; *Rh.* I.2, 1356b10), and the very first sentence of the *Prior Analytics* announces an enquiry about demonstrative knowledge which is the specific topic of the *Posterior Analytics*: "First we must state the subject of the enquiry and what it is about: the subject is demonstration, and it is about demonstrative knowledge" (*APr.* I.1, 24a10–11). Hence, for Aristotle the procedure of analysis (*analusis*) is crucial for both logic and the theory of science, and his logic called *syllogistic* is simply a part of his theory of scientific knowledge and demonstration. We can only understand in which way Aristotle puts analysis to work in logic and science if we first look briefly at his basic notion of knowledge (*epistēmē*).[1]

Aristotle took over from Plato the idea that *knowledge in the proper sense* is about universal facts in the universe. However, while *knowledge of universal facts* is, for Aristotle, certainly a basic kind of knowledge, *scientific* knowledge consists in knowing the *causes* of given facts, the causes being, of course, themselves facts (*APo.* I.2, 71b9–16): First we have to establish the facts; and "when we know the fact we seek the reason why" (*APo.* II.1, esp. 89b29–31). In this way, science (*epistēmē*) is, on the one hand, a specific state of the knowing subject, and, on the other hand, the set of specific theories we have – according to adequate methods – established and grasped if we are in the specific epistemic state called science.

Aristotle cares a lot about reliable methods of establishing facts; but his main concern in the *Analytics* is the methodology of finding causes for given facts. Given that all animals have a stomach we want to know *why* that is so. A first idea might be that all animals take in food from outside and therefore need an organ for receiving and digesting food, and this is just the stomach (*PA* III.14, 674a12–19). Given that all statues made of metal are heavy we want to know why. An answer might be that all these statues are of bronze and bronze is a pretty heavy metal. Finding out about causes of given facts clearly comes down, *linguistically* speaking, to looking for adequate

---

1. For his discussion of names and assertions, another preliminary topic, see Modrak, PHILO-SOPHY OF LANGUAGE, in this volume.

premises for a given *conclusion.* More specifically, if we note, as Aristotle did, the standard form of a predication *C is an A* inversely as *A belongs (as a property) to C's* (let us abbreviate this by AC), scientific knowledge of AC provides, in the simplest case, premises AB and BC for AC such that the new term B points to the cause. For instance, why does being heavy (A) belong to statues of metal (C)? Because there is a property *consisting of bronze* (B) such that being heavy belongs to all things consisting of bronze (AB) and consisting of bronze belongs to statues of metal (BC).

It is at this point that we can see how the procedure of analysis enters the picture. The underlying idea is that, in general, knowledge of a domain entails knowing all the simplest parts of this domain (*Phys.*I.1, 184a9–14; *Met.* H.1, 1042a5–6), and the method of theoretically dividing a domain into its simplest parts is called *analysis* (*EN* III.3, 1112b20–24). Analysis can be applied, for instance, to means–end relations in ethics (*ibid.*) and to two-dimensional diagrams in geometry (*Met.* Θ.9, 1051a21–26),[2] but is used most prominently in logic (*APr.* I.44, 50b30, 51a1–3) and science (*APr.* I.32, 47a3–5; *APo.* I.12, 78a7; I.32, 88b15–20; II.5, 91b12–13). In particular, if we seek, in a scientific enterprise, the causes of given facts, this is an important case of analysis: we try to analyze given facts in terms of further facts that point to causes of the given facts. Linguistically speaking, we try to analyze, in the simplest case, a given proposition AC by providing a third term B such that AB and BC are premises of the conclusion AC and thus, AC is analyzed into AB and BC. The two premises have one term, the *middle term,* viz. B, in common; the other two terms, viz. A and C, are called *extremes.* If there are no more middle terms such that AB and BC can themselves be analyzed, AB and BC are *immediate,* i.e. are the *simplest* logical parts of AC. This can be illustrated by the formula:

D   A: AB – BC: C

If, however, there are more middle terms such that the premises AB and BC can themselves be further analyzed, the analysis has to be continued until we get to immediate premises. This amounts to, as Aristotle calls it, *thickening* AC by filling AC with all the middle terms we have found (*APo.* I.23, 84b19–85a1). For instance, let B, D, E be all the middle terms we can find for AC, such that AB and BC are premises of AC and AD and DB are in turn immediate premises of AB, while BE and EC are immediate premises of BC, then this can be illustrated by the formula:

D*   A: AD – DB – BE – EC: C

To be sure, this kind of analysis is analysis in empirical sciences, *not* in syllogistic. Even from the thin description of this sort of analysis that I have presented so far it becomes evident that scientific analysis is basically a *bottom-up procedure,* not a top-down procedure; it starts from given facts or conclusions, and looks for causes and premises,

---

2.   In geometry, circle and straight line are the simplest parts of the geometrical continuum; this is why proofs in geometry have to use compasses and ruler: constructing diagrams by using compasses and ruler comes down to analyzing the diagrams into their simplest parts.

and maybe for causes of these causes and premises of these premises. Analysis looks for *sufficient* premises of given conclusions and is, therefore, *not* a deductive method.

The Relation Between Prior and Posterior Analytics

So far, we have been talking in a quite informal way. Interestingly, Aristotle's definition of a deduction at the beginning of the *Analytics* looks quite informal too: "A deduction (*sullogismos*) is a discourse in which, certain things being posited, something other than the things laid down follows of necessity in virtue of the fact that they are these" (*APr.* I.1, 24b18–20; similarly *Top.* I.1, 100a25–27). Some scholars are worried about this definition, since it does not seem to be connected with a notion of logical validity. It has even been argued that Aristotle's definition of deduction reflects an early stage in the development of his theory of science and demonstration that did not presuppose formal syllogistic as presented in the *Prior Analytics* (Barnes, 1969, 1981; Solmsen, 1929). There is a good deal of evidence for this chronological guess. The *Prior Analytics* is in many technical respects far more developed than the *Posterior Analytics*, and it is obviously designed to solve a number of proof-theoretical problems posed by an informal sketch of a theory of demonstration. The most important of these problems is *which* premises are *good* premises for a given conclusion and *why* they are good ones. It is primarily these questions that the syllogistic seeks to answer. This implies also that the initial informal concept of deduction be restricted to a formal notion of deduction based on the idea of logical validity. In addition, given the idea that scientific knowledge is primarily concerned with the universal it is small wonder that a logic that is supposed to provide a sound logical foundation for the theory of science is mainly concerned with analyzing the logical relations between universal and particular quantified propositions. That is why, to use modern terms, Aristotle's syllogistic is, not a propositional logic, but a first-order predicate logic.

All this is, of course, fully consistent with the view that in the *Analytics* as we read it today, syllogistic is the official logic of the theory of science. That is, we must take the syllogistic (the *Prior Analytics*) to be what Aristotle says it is: *theoretically* preliminary to the theory of science (the *Posterior Analytics*) (see e.g., *APr.* I.4, 25b26–31; Smith, 1989, p. xiii; Detel, 1993, vol.1, pp. 110–14).

Syllogistic

In presenting a logic that is helpful for a theory of science, Aristotle first determines a canonical form of syllogistic propositions: A *syllogistic proposition* is either a universal affirmative or a universal negative or a particular affirmative or a particular negative proposition, i.e. has one of the following four forms:

1. A belongs to every B (in short AaB);
2. A belongs to no B (in short AeB);
3. A belongs to some B (in short AiB);
4. A does not belong to some B (in short AoB)

(where A and B are usually one-placed universal terms and a, e, i, o are the *syllogistic relations*) (*APr.* I.2, 25a4–5).

As we have seen, the basic form of an argument based on an analysis, for instance in science, consists of two premises and a conclusion. Therefore, Aristotle looks, in his syllogistic, at forms of ordered sequences of three syllogistic propositions. In particular, he examines deductions having as premises two syllogistic propositions sharing one term, and this is the case, if the common term is either subject of one premise and predicate of the other, or subject of both premises, or predicate of both premises. In this way, he gets exactly three different forms of such sequences – called *syllogistic figures* – concerning a given conclusion AC.[3] In general terms, these figures are as follows:

(1) $A \times B, B \times C \Rightarrow A \times C$; (2) $B \times A, B \times C \Rightarrow A \times C$; (3) $A \times B, C \times B \Rightarrow A \times C$ (where x is one of the four syllogistic relations and A, B, and C are variables for universal terms).

The logical tradition usually calls an ordered sequence of syllogistic propositions that has the form of one of the three syllogistic figures a *mood*. Clearly, there are 192 (= $3 \times 4 \times 4 \times 4$) moods.

It is the *most important task of Aristotle's syllogistic* to determine *which of the 192 moods are syllogistically valid*. And it is in formulating and solving this problem that we can see Aristotle as being the first thinker to fully grasp the idea of a formal logic. The crucial proposal is that there are four deductions in the first figure that are *perfect*, i.e. such that the conclusion follows *evidently* of necessity from its premises. These *perfect deductions* are:

A1   AaB, BaC $\Rightarrow$ AaC (*Barbara*)
A2   AeB, BaC $\Rightarrow$ AeC (*Celarent*)
A3   AaB, BiC $\Rightarrow$ AiC (*Darii*)
A4   AeB, BiC $\Rightarrow$ AoC (*Ferio*)

Aristotle justifies his claim that **A1** and **A2** are perfect deductions by saying: "we have already explained in which way we say: being predicated of all" (*APr.* I.4, 25b39–40, cf. I.1, 24a18), and: "it has been defined in which way we say: being predicated of none" (*APr.* I.4, 26a27; cf. I.1, 24a18–19).[4] Although Aristotle did not have a clear notion of meaning, it seems evident that *he in fact justified the logical validity at least of* **A1** *and* **A2** *by pointing to the meaning of the syllogistic relations a and e*: in general terms,

3.   This procedure might provide an explanation why Aristotle never mentions a fourth syllogistic figure that could be constructed by changing the order of the terms in the premises, i.e., $B \times A, C \times B \Rightarrow A \times C$ (he does discuss deductions of this form, though, but treats them as deductions of the first figure) (Patzig, 1968, Smith, 1989).
4.   Indeed it suffices to talk about A1 and A2 alone because, as Aristotle later correctly notes, A3 and A4, although belonging to the perfect deductions the validity of which can be justified by the way we talk about the syllogistic relations, can nevertheless be proved on the basis of A2 (the proofs are presented in *APr.* I.7, 29b1–14).

deductions are logically valid if they are valid only in virtue of the meaning of the logical constants they contain. That is why we can use, in doing formal logic, variables for the non-logical vocabulary, as Aristotle does for the first time in the history of thought: such is the conception of formal logic.

Furthermore, it is evident that given the way we use the syllogistic relations we can propose:

L1 $AeB \Rightarrow \neg (AiB)$
L2 $AaB \Rightarrow \neg (AoB)$

Finally, Aristotle takes it that the principle of indirect proof (which he calls the principle of *deductions leading to the impossible*) is valid, for instance in the following form:

RI   Let R, S, T be three syllogistic propositions, then,
if the deduction $\neg T, S \Rightarrow \neg R$ is valid, the deduction $R, S \Rightarrow T$ is valid too.

There is no justification of **RI** in the *Prior Analytics* (only a discussion in I.29), but since **RI** follows from the principle of the excluded middle which is in turn extensively defended in *Met.* Γ, we can recognize **RI** as at least indirectly justified.

Assumptions **A1 – A2, L1 – L2** and **RI** are a sufficient logical foundation for approaching the next challenge the syllogistic has to meet: to *prove syllogistically* which moods of the second and third syllogistic figure are syllogistically valid. It is in connection with grasping the notion of a logical proof and with constructing effectively such proofs that the conception of analysis again proves to be helpful. And it is here that we can see how Aristotle puts analysis to work *in his syllogistic*.

The basic idea is that if $R, S \Rightarrow T$ is a deduction that is not perfect, a *syllogistic proof* of this deduction consists in *analyzing it into perfect or already proved deductions*. This kind of *syllogistic analysis* comes down to filling the gap between premises and conclusion of the deduction with perfect or proved deductions. The general scheme for the syllogistic analysis of the deduction D $(R, S \Rightarrow T)$ is accordingly the proof formula:

P $R, S: D_1 (R,S \Rightarrow X_1) - D_2 (X_2,X_3 \Rightarrow X_4) - \ldots - D_n (X_{n-1},X_n \Rightarrow T): T,$

where the Ds are perfect or proved deductions such that the first of them starts with the premises of the deduction that is to be proved and all following ones use as premises two of the syllogistic propositions that show up before in the row (R, S, or the X_i) until T is reached. In this way, deduction D is indeed analyzed into deductions $D_1 - D_n$. Proofs in Aristotle's syllogistic are analyses, not of syllogistic propositions into other syllogistic propositions, but of deductions into other deductions.[5]

---

5.   Aristotle does not use the notion of analysis in this context, but says rather that the imperfect deductions are *completed by*, or *reduced to*, perfect deductions and conversion rules by *making them perfect by certain supplementary assumptions* (the supplementary assumptions simply being perfect deductions and conversion rules) (e.g. *APr.* I.5, 28a1–9; I.6, 29a14–17, I.7, 29b1–2). But this *is* the description of a kind of analysis; indeed, it would be odd to assume that Aristotle calls his syllogistic theory *Analytics* without being willing to see the most important part of this theory as a case of analysis.

The first deductions Aristotle proves are not moods, but simpler deductions with only one premise, namely the *conversion rules* (*APr*. I.2, 25a14–25):

K1 AeB $\Rightarrow$ BeA; **K2** AiB $\Rightarrow$ BiA; **K3** AaB $\Rightarrow$ BiA.

The conversion rules are frequently used in proofs of valid deductions in the second and third figure (these deductions are called *imperfect* because they need to be proved). Hence, it is possible that in the proof formula **P** stated above R = S or $X_i = X_{i+1}$. According to Aristotle, among the 188 moods that must be checked for logical validity, only 14 prove to be syllogistically valid. Two typical proofs or logical analyses run as follows:

(a) Proof of BaA, BeC $\Rightarrow$ AeC (Camestres, second figure):
  BaA, BeC: **K1** (BeC $\Rightarrow$ CeB) – **A2** (CeB, BaA $\Rightarrow$ CeA) – **K1** (CeA $\Rightarrow$ AeC): AeC
(b) Proof of AiB, CaB $\Rightarrow$ AiC (Disamis, third figure):
  AiB, CaB: **K2** (AiB $\Rightarrow$ BiA) – **A3** (CaB, BiA $\Rightarrow$ CiA) – **K2** (CiA $\Rightarrow$ AiC): AiC

These proofs obviously satisfy formula **P**, i.e., are genuine logical analyses.[6]

Interpretations of Aristotle's Syllogistic Logic

Aristotle's *Prior Analytics* contains much more than just the so-called *assertoric syllogistic* outlined above. Much of this additional material is designed to help solve problems emerging from the theory of science. Most prominently, since a scientific theory often uses *modal propositions* (primarily *necessary* ones) Aristotle develops a *modal syllogistic* (*APr*. I.8–22) that leaves unsolved, though, a number of serious problems. For instance, Aristotle seems to use the modal operators in an ambiguous way: sometimes he reads **NAaB** (where N abbreviates *necessary*) as *it is necessary that AaB* (the so-called *de-dicto*-reading), but sometimes as *Every necessary-A belongs to B* (the so-called *de-re*-reading). This is one of the reasons why scholars have sometimes extreme difficulties understanding why Aristotle calls some modal deductions valid or invalid, respectively (Patterson, 1995; Striker, 1994).

Assertoric and modal syllogistic are supposed to show *how every deduction comes about*, as Aristotle says. But in addition, there are two more projects in *Prior Analytics* I (cf. *APr*. I.32, 47a1–4): first, to define a way in which deductions may be found (chs. 27–31), and second, to show how a given informal deduction can eventually be transformed into a deduction *in the figures* (chs. 32–45) (this transformation is another kind of *analysis*). *Prior Analytics* II is best seen as discussing technical concepts of dialectic in terms of syllogistic theory and as trying to solve further proof-theoretic difficulties showing up in the *Posterior Analytics* (Smith, 1989).

For a long time scholars tried to read Aristotle's syllogistic as an axiomatic system in the modern sense (Lukasiewicz, 1957; Patzig, 1968), the perfect deductions being

---

6. Aristotle does not only show which moods are syllogistically valid, he also shows which are invalid. And he does this pretty much in the same way modern logicians do it – by providing countermodels.

the axioms and the imperfect deductions the theorems. But according to this reading we would need some more deduction rules to get from axioms to theorems, including theorems from *propositional* logic. There are no such rules to be found, though, in the text of the *Prior Analytics*. Therefore, according to the axiomatic reading Aristotle's syllogistic is formally incomplete. However, it is much more natural, and corresponds much more closely to formula **P** that is actually used in the text, to look at the perfect deductions as *inference rules* that are inferentially primitive (but are, of course, semantically justified as truth-transmitting). This interpretation looks at syllogistic as a system of natural deduction in the modern sense (Corcoran, 1974b; Smiley, 1973; Smith, 1989). It presupposes what Aristotle seems in practice to assume, namely that *no* universal term is empty. Under this reading Aristotle's syllogistic proves to be both sound and formally complete (Corcoran, 1974b).

Knowledge of Facts

Knowledge of facts is, for Aristotle, the foundation of scientific knowledge (*APr.* I.27, 43b1–38; *APo.* I.23, 84b19–85a1).[7] Accordingly, Aristotle is concerned, not only with the methods of establishing scientific knowledge, but also with scientific methods of establishing knowledge of facts. For instance, he recommends to state facts in such a way that they can be more easily incorporated into scientific inquiries; thus, we should use an adequate terminology and should avoid homonymy and ambiguities (*APo.* II.13, 97b30–36; II.17, 99a4–15) (Lennox, 1994). Sometimes facts can even be deductively established, and this is one of the reasons why we must carefully distinguish between deductions from symptoms and deductions from causes (*APo.* I.13, 78a22–b11). Sometimes scientific research starts from facts that most people recognize. For instance, asked *what thunder is* most people would say *that* thunder is a certain noise in the clouds. Propositions describing these facts are, therefore, a sort of *definitions* (so-called *nominal* definitions) that do not need justification and can serve as possible *conclusions* of scientific explanations (*APo.* II.10, 93b29–32, 94a14).[8]

One way of establishing universal facts is *induction*. Aristotle claims that "we learn either by induction or by demonstration and that it is impossible to consider universals except through induction" (*APo.* I.18, 81a39–b2). He even says that, in a sense, we become familiar with the immediate premises of science by induction (*APo.* II.19, 100b3–4). Scholars disagree about how Aristotle conceived of induction. Is it a form of *argument* leading from a finite set of singular premises to a universal conclusion (Ross, 1957), pretty much in the modern sense? A minority of scholars denies this and claims that an Aristotelian induction is simply a list of singular facts sharing a structure and is, therefore, not an argument at all (Engberg-Pedersen, 1979). According to this view, universal assumptions cannot be inferred from singular propositions, but

7. That facts are a domain of *knowledge* is explicitly suggested at the beginning of *APo.* I.13.
8. For a sophisticated and far-reaching analysis of the status of facts in zoology, especially concerning the classification of animals, see Pellegrin (1986). Pellegrin shows that these facts do not have scientific status and cannot be related to a taxonomic project (in sharp opposition to the traditional interpretation).

must rather be already presupposed for classifying singular facts and establishing an induction. Indeed, there is not a single passage in which Aristotle unambiguously calls the *transition* from singular to universal propositions an induction. We must be careful not to read formulas like *this is evident by induction* or *secured by induction* (*Phys.* I.2, 185a14; *Top.* IV.2, 122a19) as pointing to a procedure of deducing or concluding; rather, these formulas are fully consistent with the claim that it is by looking at certain singular facts or propositions as *heuristic devices* that we can make a good *guess* about a universal. Looking at some things *and* classifying them under *presupposed* universals as swan and white (the finite list of these things *thus described* forming the induction) we may *guess*, not conclude, that all swans are white. This guess holds good as long as we do not encounter a swan that is not white (*Top.* II.3, 110a32–36; VIII.2, 157a34–b33; *APr.* II.26, 69b1–8; *APo.* I.4, 73a32–34; II.7, 92a37–38).

Aristotelian Causes

As already mentioned, Aristotle thinks that science builds on the knowledge of facts to explain them by finding out about their causes (*aitiai*). It is important, though, not to confuse Aristotelian causes with causes in the modern sense. To be sure, there is no agreement among modern philosophers about how best to analyze the difficult notions of cause and causation, but the standard view is that causes are earlier than, and sufficient for, their effects and are based on natural laws. It follows that if we know some cause and the appropriate natural law, we can predict that the effect will come about. Aristotelian causes are in important respects different. Here are some examples: (i) the fact that statues are of bronze is an Aristotelian cause of the fact that these statues are heavy; (ii) the fact that the moon is in the middle between sun and earth is an Aristotelian cause of the fact that the moon is eclipsed, and (iii) to stay healthy is an Aristotelian cause of walking after dinner and other activities suggested by medicine and dietetics; finally, (iv) the fact that a string is divided according to the ratio 1:2 is an Aristotelian cause for the fact that the string produces an octave. In such cases, the cause is not later than, and sufficient as well as necessary for, its effect (*APo.* II.12, 95a10–24; II.13, 97a35–b24) and does not involve a notion of natural laws (it is only later in Stoic philosophy that the concept of a natural law begins to emerge, see Frede, 1989). Therefore, knowing an Aristotelian cause does not permit us to predict its effects; rather, from effects we can infer their Aristotelian causes (*APo.* II.12, 95b22–37). All this is a clear indication that Aristotelian causes are not causes in the modern sense. Aristotle's key idea is that a *cause* of an effect is a fact that can *answer the question why* the effect comes about. And he feels that there are *four kinds of answers to why-questions*: one points to the *material* of the thing in question (as in case (i)), another points to the *origin of its movement* (as in case (ii)), a third mentions it's *aim* (case (iii)), and a fourth looks at its *form* (case (iv)). This is the *Aristotelian doctrine of the four causes*: the material, efficient, teleological and formal cause (cf. *Phys.* II.3).[9] Hence, a fact BC is an *Aristotelian cause* of another fact AC iff the B-property of C can

9. On causes in Aristotle's *Physics*, see Bodnár and Pellegrin, ARISTOTLE'S PHYSICS AND COSMOLOGY.

be classified as material, origin of movement, aim or form in relation to the A-property of C.

A short additional note about the teleological cause seems in order. From early modern times on many philosophers and scientists have seriously criticized the notion of a teleological cause because this cause seems to exercise an influence of the future on the past. This objection is, however, clearly based on falsely reading the modern understanding of a cause into the notion of an Aristotelian cause. According to Aristotle, BC is a teleological cause of AC if, roughly, there is a regular development of states of C such that usually BC is the final and most developed state of C and AC is a regular former state in the development of C such that AC is necessary for reaching BC. This is one way of explaining why C gets into state AC. This idea is empirically contentful, consistent and by no means absurd; in particular, it in no way involves that the future can exercise any influence on the past or the present (Gotthelf, 1987b).

Aristotelian causes and their effects are connected, not by a natural law, but by a universal empirical regularity. That is to say: BC's being an Aristotelian cause of AC involves that AaB is a universal fact of the universe. A full explanation of AC has therefore to mention, not only the cause BC, but also the regularity AaB (cf. *Phys.* II.8).

Demonstration

The opening sentence of the *Analytics* shows that the idea of a demonstration, and of scientific knowledge based on demonstrations, lies at the heart of Aristotle's logic and theory of science. To adequately understand this idea it is important not to confuse valid deductions, proofs, and demonstrations – even more so, since the Latin formula *quod erat demonstrandum* is nowadays well known for resuming *proofs*. But for Aristotle a deduction is, as we have seen, *syllogistically valid* iff it is a perfect or imperfect deduction in the technical sense; a valid deduction is, in turn, a *proof* iff its premises can be taken to be true; and finally, a proof is a *demonstration* iff its premises reveal an Aristotelian cause. Aristotle himself uses the same term (*sullogismos*) for both valid deductions and proofs, but a different term (*apodeixis*) for demonstrations.

According to the *Analytics*, every demonstration is a sort of valid deduction (*APr.* I.4, 25b29–31) and so has the form of one of the syllogistic figures (*APr.* I.23, 41b1–5; I.25, 41b36f.); there is *no* demonstration without middle term (*APo.* I.23, 84b23–25), and in particular the first syllogistic figure proves to be most important for demonstrative sciences (*APo* I.14). That is why syllogistic plays a crucial role for Aristotle's theory of science. His notion of a demonstration shows clearly that he conceived of the crucial scientific activity as constructing *logically valid explanations of given facts revealing universal relations between (Aristotelian) causes and effects.*[10] We can

10. This idea has been rediscovered in the twentieth century philosophy of science in the famous article by Hempel and Oppenheim on the structure of a hypothetical-deductive explanation (note that the authors do not rely, in this article, on a modally qualified notion of cause, but only on the idea of a universal empirical regularity, pretty much like Aristotle some 24 centuries earlier), see Hempel and Oppenheim (1948).

use examples (i) to (iv) for Aristotelian causes mentioned in the preceding section to construct demonstrations that instantiate this idea:

(i)*   Statues of metal are heavy because, first, bronze is heavy and, second, statues of metal consist of bronze;[11] symbolic notation:
       (a)   being heavy **a** *being of bronze*;
       (b)   *being of bronze* **a** statues of metal;
  ⇒   (c)   being heavy **a** statues of metal

(ii)*   The moon is eclipsed because, first, whenever something in the sky is in the middle between sun and earth it is eclipsed, and, second, the moon is in the middle between sun and earth; symbolic notation:
       (a)   being eclipsed **a** *being in the middle between sun and earth*
       (b)   *being in the middle between sun and earth* **b** moon
  ⇒   (c)   being eclipsed **b** moon

(iii)*   To digest food requires walking after dinner etc. because, first, staying healthy requires walking after dinner etc, and, second, it is the aim of digesting food to stay healthy; symbolic notation:
       (a)   walking after dinner etc. **a** *staying healthy*
       (b)   *staying healthy* **a** digesting food
  ⇒   (c)   walking after dinner etc. **a** digesting food

(iv)*   A string produces sounds in an octave because, first, producing sounds in an octave requires being divided according to the ratio 1:2 and, second, this string is divided according to the ratio 1:2; symbolic notation:
       (a)   producing sounds in an octave **a** *being divided according to ratio 1:2*
       (b)   *being divided according to the ratio 1:2* **b** string
  ⇒   (c)   producing sounds in an octave **b** string
       (where **a** is the relation *belongs to all* and **b** the relation *belongs to*).

Obviously, all four arguments are demonstrations, i.e. valid explanatory deductions in the technical Aristotelian sense: they are proofs in one of the syllogistic figures, their minor premises (b) points to one of the Aristotelian causes for fact (c), and their major premises (a) states a universal relation between cause and effect. In many cases the conclusion of a demonstration, i.e. of a scientific explanation, is itself a universal fact (as in (i)* and (iii)*); in this case, both the major and the minor premises must also be universal. But Aristotle feels that there are sometimes also scientific explanations of singular facts (as in (ii)* and (iv)*) (for examples see *APr.* I.33, 47b21–34; II.27, 70a16–20; *APo.* I.24, 85b30–35; I.34, 89b13–15; II.11, 94a37–b8); in this case, while the major premise remains universal, the minor premise can be singular too. Some of the singular facts that can be demonstrated are even contingent, for instance the fact that the Persian war came upon the Athenians (*APo.* II.11, 94a37–b8). This is not inconsistent with Aristotle's claim that there is no demonstration and no

---

11.   For much more sophisticated examples of explaining phenomena by referring to matter, for instance, the formation of metals in the ground, see Gill (1997) in her illuminating discussion of *Meteor.* IV.12.

demonstrative knowledge of the contingent (*APo.* I.6, 75a18–21; I.30). The Athenians could have decided not to attack Sardis, and in this case the Persians would probably not have waged a terrible war with the Athenians; but given that the Athenians first sacked a big city like Sardis, and given the military strength of the Persians and their struggle for power, it was necessary, and we can explain demonstratively, that the Persians made war with Athens. To be sure, Aristotle thinks that demonstrations of universal facts are better and more scientific than demonstrations of particular facts (this is the claim of *APo.* I.24); but nevertheless, he does by no means exclude scientific explanations of particular facts.

Constructing demonstrations remains a *bottom-up procedure*; as Aristotle often emphasizes, first we state the facts we want to explain, and then we look for their causes by searching for premises that logically imply, and explain by pointing to an Aristotelian cause of, the given fact (e.g. *APo.* II.1–2). Sometimes there are *different demonstrations* for a given fact: there is *not* a unique demonstration for every given fact. And doing good science involves usually constructing *whole nets of connected demonstrations*, for in many cases the premises of a given demonstration can themselves be demonstrated; in these cases the question what the *decisive* cause is supposed to be becomes urgent (all this is extensively discussed in *APo.* II.16–18).

Principles

Constructing demonstrations is first to analyze, by way of a bottom-up procedure, a given fact or conclusion until all immediate deductive premises of the conclusion are discovered, and then to decide which of these premises can be classified as Aristotelian causes. The immediate premises every given demonstration depends on are called *primitives* (*prōta*) or *principles* (*archai*) (of this demonstration) (*APo.* I.2, 72a5–9). More generally, we can talk about principles of a whole scientific area, i.e., of the whole net of connected demonstrations that make up the scientific theory of this area. Aristotle calls principles of this sort *definitions* (*horismoi*) (*APo.* I.2, 72a19–22).

But if we define, say, the cold and the hot, or numbers of some kind, this does not in itself imply that they *exist*. Some sciences, such as geometry, can sometimes prove that certain entities exist (in the case of geometry, for example, by showing how they can actually be constructed); but every specific science must assume without proof that the fundamental entities in its domain exist. Sometimes it is evident that these entities exist; for example, it is evident that the cold and the hot exist. But sometimes this is less evident, as in the case of numbers (*APo.* I.10, 76b15–23). Nonetheless, these existence assumptions, although not being parts of demonstrations, are principles of a sort that have to be assumed. Aristotle calls them *suppositions* (*APo.* I.2, 72a19–21).

Finally, what about the inference rules provided by syllogistic or the more general logical principles like the principle of the excluded middle? Since demonstrations are valid deductions, these principles are also to be presupposed for any specific science that proposes demonstrative explanations. Like suppositions, they do not show up as parts (i.e., premises or conclusions) of demonstrations; but unlike suppositions, they hold in every demonstrative science. This is the third kind of principles Aristotle recognizes; he calls them *postulates* (*APo.* I.2, 72a15–18).

The way Aristotle determines the three kinds of principles is not without problems, and consequently scholars have different views about how exactly the principles have to be interpreted. Thus, it is doubtful whether definitions have existential impact, whether suppositions are nothing more than existence assumptions, and whether all postulates hold in all sciences or some of them hold in more than one, but not necessarily in all, sciences. It seems rather clear, though, that definitions in the full sense, i.e., as highest premises of actually constructed nets of demonstrations, do have existential impact, while this might not be evident for nominal definitions. Moreover, the examples of suppositions Aristotle hints at suggest that at least an important kind of scientific supposition is existence assumptions about fundamental entities of specific sciences (more precisely, if G is the specific domain or *genus* of a specific science, about Gs). And finally, at least the paradigm cases of postulates, i.e., logically valid inference rules, hold obviously in all sciences.

In any case, definitions are the only principles that are parts of demonstrations. Consequently, Aristotle devotes a considerable part of the second book of the *Posterior Analytics* to a discussion of the relation between demonstrations and definitions (*APo.* II.1–10). The way Aristotle describes this relation is crucial for our understanding of his theory of science; but first of all it should be emphasized that in the framework of this theory definitions are *not*, as older readings have it, analytic propositions in the modern sense (i.e., propositions that are true in virtue of the meanings of the words they contain); rather, definitions are, for Aristotle, universal propositions having *empirical* (or *mathematical*) content.

Definitions and Demonstrations

Aristotle claims that there is a close connection between definitions and demonstrations. "What is an eclipse? Privation of light from the moon by the earth's screening. Why is there an eclipse? Or: Why is the moon eclipsed? Because the light leaves it when the earth screens it" (*APo.* II.2, 90a15–17). "What is thunder? Extinction of fire in clouds. Why does it thunder? Because the fire in the clouds is extinguished" (*APo.* II.8, 93b8–9). "In all these cases it is evident that what it is and why it is are the same" (*APo.* II.2, 90a14–15). These examples show how we have to understand the close relation between *the what it is* (definitions) and *the why it is* (demonstrations): the definiens of a good definition that has explanatory power is just the middle term pointing to an Aristotelian cause in the corresponding demonstration.

Let us assume, as Aristotle does, that thunder or a certain noise in the clouds that we used to call thunder (A) is adequately defined by extinction of fire in the clouds (B) (so that A:=B is true, which implies, of course, AaB and BaA), then for any C such that A and B belong to C we get the demonstration A:=B, BC ⇒ AC. In particular, dependent on the way we determine the extremes we get a particular or a universal demonstration, respectively: If A is thunder and C some clouds up there, then we explain, why there is thunder in those clouds up there: because there is an extinction of fire in the clouds up there and thunder *is* an extinction of fire in the clouds, i.e., we get the particular demonstration A:=B, BbC ⇒ AbC. If, however, we take *certain noise in the clouds* (A) and *thunder* (C) as extremes and the explanatory middle term (B) again as *extinction of fire in the clouds*, then we can explain why thunder is a certain noise in the clouds: because thunder is an extinction of fire in the clouds and the certain noise in the clouds we used to call thunder *is* an extinction of fire in those clouds, i.e. we get the universal demonstration A:=B, BaC ⇒ AaC (in *APo.* II.8, Aristotle offers both alternatives as possible symbolization).

The decisive message we get from these and other examples is that "without a demonstration you cannot become aware of what a thing is" (*APo.* II.8, 93b17–18). That is to say, whether a given universal syllogistic proposition is a definition can only be determined if it shows up as an explanatory premise in a demonstration we have actually constructed. However, as Aristotle adds in discussing the demonstrative explanation of thunder sketched above, "if there is another middle term for this, it will be from among the remaining accounts" (*APo.* II.8, 93b12–14): we must remind ourselves that it may be possible to explain, in turn, the premises of our explanation of thunder; in this case, we will get higher definitions out of our demonstrations. So there might be mediate definitions: only if, in the context of the entire theory of thunder possibly consisting of a hierarchy of demonstrations, we get finally to the highest immediate definitions, have we discovered definitions as *principles*. The crucial point here is that Aristotle does *not* think that we first grasp the definitions as principles and then try to explain, and demonstrate, certain phenomena by using the definitions; on the contrary, *it is only from successful explanatory demonstrations and whole theories that we can get a grip of the principles of a science.*

In particular, to grasp definitions as highest principles, we have to carry out a thorough scientific analysis of the whole domain in question. While this is basically a bottom-up procedure, it obviously provides many more premises than conclusions. Therefore we can, *after* having completed the analysis and the construction of the corresponding demonstrations, take the premises we have established and *deduce* from them, in a *top-down* manner, more conclusions. Doing this for *every* proposition about the given domain, i.e., showing how a given domain can be analyzed into *all* its elements, is to *axiomatize* our theory in an *Aristotelian* way. As Aristotle remarks correctly, in the end the number of premises and conclusions will be, in this sort of axiomatization, more or less equal (*APo.* I.32, 88b4–7). Aristotle's idea of an axiomatization is not to compress the content of a whole theory into as few axioms as possible, but rather to analyze, and thereby to see more clearly through, the content of a scientific theory.

Having grasped the principles of a scientific domain is to be in the highest epistemic state, *insight* (*nous*) (*APo.* II.19, 100b7–12); therefore, insight can itself be called the principle of knowledge (*APo.* II.19, 100b12–16). More generally, as has been mentioned above, p. 246, having insight into a given domain is to have knowledge of the simplest parts of this domain. In particular, in science insight is the "assumption of immediate premises" (*APo.* I.33, 88b35–89a4). But since it is on the basis of experience that notions of universals are formed in the soul, the principles *as being universal propositions* can be grasped (in a weak sense) by experience (*APr.* I.30; *APo.* II.19). However, experience cannot give us insight into the *immediacy*, *deductive position*, or *causality* of universal syllogistic propositions. Therefore, to grasp principles in the full sense, i.e., to come to see which propositions are the highest immediate explanatory definitions of a departmental science, requires the actual construction of the net of demonstrations that make up this departmental science. *Therefore, doing science successfully does not begin, but rather ends up with, having insight in the fullest sense.*

Necessity

At the beginning of the *Posterior Analytics* Aristotle makes it clear that knowledge of a thing is not only awareness of what the cause of the thing is, but also an awareness that "it is not possible to be otherwise" (*APo.* I.2, 71b9–12), i.e., that it is *necessary* (*anankaion*). This is a truism, of course, since demonstrative conclusions are logically necessary in relation to their premises. But Aristotle proceeds to claim that *premises* of demonstrations are necessary too (*APo.* I.6, 74b15–18). Some scholars read a passage in the *Posterior Analytics* (I.4, 73a21–24) even as arguing that the necessity of demonstrative premises *follows* from the necessity of its conclusion, although Aristotle emphasizes elsewhere that this is not a valid inference in modal syllogistic (*APo.* I.6, 75a1–4). It is important to be clear about the precise sense in which Aristotle calls demonstrative premises necessary and even necessarily true, if only to avoid the impression that the necessary truth of definitions and other demonstrative premises implies their epistemological certainty.

It is telling that in the crucial passage that describes the key features of demonstrative premises necessity is missing: Demonstrative premises have to be "true and primitive and immediate and more familiar than and prior to and explanatory of the conclusion" (*APo.* I.2, 71b21–23). Scholars have argued, correctly, that two of these six features, viz. immediacy and explanatory power, entail the other four (see Barnes, 1975, pp. 98–9; Detel, 1993, vol. 2, pp. 62–3). Basically, therefore, highest demonstrative premises are immediate and point to Aristotelian causes. We must conclude, then, that the necessity of demonstrative premises is closely tied to these two characteristics. Indeed, Aristotle is making two different claims: First, if a necessary conclusion can be *deduced* from premises, it does *not* follow that the premises are necessary (*APo.* I.6, 75a1–4); but second, if a necessary conclusion can be *demonstrated* from premises, it *does* follow that the premises are necessary too (*APo.* I.4, 73a21–24; I.6, 74b15–17). And AB is supposed to be a *necessary demonstrative premise* iff A belongs in itself to B or B belongs in itself to A. As Aristotle's examples show, *belonging in itself* is, metaphysically speaking, an *essential* relation. But he explains this relation *epistemologically* by saying that A *belongs in itself* to B iff AaB and BaA are true and A belongs to the definition of B (*APo.* I.4, 73a34–b5). And he adds that if A belongs in itself to B, then A is not said about B as underlying subject (which comes down to saying that A is at least partially (in case of a definition A:=B even fully) identical with B), and A belongs to B because of itself (which comes down to postulate a causal relation between A and B) (*APo.* I.4, 73b6–17).

Obviously, this is one of the important points at which metaphysics enters the theory of science.[12] Understanding the necessity of demonstrative premises and definitions

---

12. Another such point is the metaphysical argument in *APo.* I.22 that is designed to show that every scientific analysis must come to an end, i.e., that the sequences of ordered deductions and demonstrations must be finite and that, therefore, scientific principles exist.

as being founded on essential relations in the metaphysical sense does *not* have dramatic epistemological implications, though. In particular, it does *not* imply that demonstrative premises are epistemologically certain; rather, they are, *if true at all*, metaphysically necessary and necessarily true, which is consistent with assuming that it might turn out that they are false. If syllogistic propositions are, according to the criteria provided by the theory of science, definitions or highest immediate explanatory premises in an actually constructed theory, then this is a good reason to assume that these premises are metaphysically necessary and represent essential relations. Therefore, the necessity of demonstrative premises does not follow from the necessity of the conclusion, but from the very notion of a successful demonstration (see *APo.* I.6, 74b5–17).

This has a rather interesting impact for Aristotle's concept of essences. The traditional simple view is that the essence of a thing (for instance, of a species) can be captured by one immediate defining formula pointing to a single unified cause of other properties of the thing. But it seems clear that in many cases just one definition does not have the explanatory power to demonstrate the properties of the thing in question. We need a lot more immediate *and* demonstrated premises within the demonstrative net in order to actually complete the explanations. In these cases, then, the essence of a thing is itself a complex matter (see Charles, 1997; Detel, 1997; Gotthelf, 1997).

Science and Dialectic

In the very first sentence of his *Rhetoric*, Aristotle proposes to distinguish both rhetoric and dialectic from science. Indeed, Aristotle conceives of dialectic as an art of reasoning that includes the capability of discussing *any* problem from *any* domain that we may come across (*Top.* I.1, 100a18–20). In many cases, the dialectician will examine both a given proposition and its negation, but typically he will not look for causes. All this does not go for science (*APo.* I.11, 77a31–35). Moreover, in examining, and trying to refute, a thesis put forward by an opponent, the dialectician may proceed from any assumption the opponent agrees with, without being obliged to care about the *truth* of the assumption (dialectic *ad hominem*) (*APr.* I.1, 24a22–b2). Hence, dialectical premises are not scientific premises. On this account, it seems that dialectic has nothing to do with science.

However, in the *Topics*, reasoning is defined as *dialectical* if it *reasons from noted beliefs* (*endoxa*) that are "things which are accepted by everyone or by most people; or by the wise – either by all of them, or by most, or by the most famous and distinguished" (*Top.* I.1, 100b21–23). This is, obviously, not dialectic ad hominem, but *dialectic proper*: a method of reasoning that relies exclusively on types of testimony which anyone has access to. Aristotle thinks that a proper dialectical examination can sometimes be helpful for finding out about the truth (*Top.* I.2, 101a35–37). Consequently, Aristotle himself argues often dialectically in a quite explicit way, not only in his ethical works, but also in the *Physics* (see his comment at *Cael.* III.4, 303a20–24) and, interestingly, also in the second book of the *Posterior Analytics*, where he devotes five chapters in a row to working through the problems concerning the relation of definitions and demonstrations (*APo.* II.3–7). Some scholars even argue that for Aristotle dialectic proper is, in ethics as well as in physics, *sufficient* for reaching the principles (Owen, 1961). This is certainly an exaggeration (Bolton, 1987). Aristotle does feel, though, that dialectical reasoning proper is sometimes *necessary* for scientific work. It can often provide a more precise and adequate interpretation of given proposals and in this way set the stage for developing *scientific* answers for the problems that have been dialectically worked through (*Top.* I.2, 101a37–b4; *Phys.* IV.4, 211a7–11). Thus, the dialectical reasoning in *APo.* II.3–7 clearly sets the stage for determining, in a satisfying way, the exact relation between definitions and demonstrations (*APo.* II.8–10). It is in this sense that dialectic may even discuss the principles of science (*Top.* I.2, 101a37–b4). On this view, there seems to be an important connection between dialectic and science.

We should not conclude from this evidence, though, that Aristotle's account of the relation between dialectic and science is inconsistent. Clearly, dialectical reasoning may be sometimes helpful for, but remains different in method from, science. The adequate way of establishing scientific principles and in particular scientific definitions cannot be provided by dialectic (Bolton, 1987). But since in many cases what all people believe is true and what nobody believes is false (*EN* X.2, 1173a1–2; *Met.* α.1, 993a30–b4), scientists should see to it that the beliefs of experts and of most of the other people remain consistent (*Top.* I.10, 104a5–13) and that as many widely accepted beliefs as possible be proved to be true (*EN* VII.1, 1145b3–7). It is in this way that *science* is, on Aristotle's view, *closely connected to common sense and dialectical premises.*

There is a striking specific application of this view in the *Posterior Analytics*. Nominal definitions, being propositions that a specific scientific theory may try to demonstrate, are sometimes called "general" (*logikoi*) propositions that most people believe to be true. This indicates that Aristotle takes them to be dialectical starting points of scientific reasoning. More importantly, in trying to find adequate premises that we can use to demonstrate dialectical nominal definitions Aristotle points to accepted background theories that render the major term of the given nominal definitions more precise, thereby providing, at the same time, the theoretical framework that all possible demonstrations have to fit with. For instance, the claim that thunder is a certain noise in the clouds is a nominal dialectical definition. But for this definition to become a scientific theorem that may be demonstrated, we have to fill in the background theory of noises (cf. *De An.* II.6, II.8; *Cael.* II.9) that provides the scientists with a precise interpretation of the major term *noise*. Any demonstration that explains why thunder is a certain noise in the clouds has to be consistent with this background theory. If such a demonstration can be established, it shows, how *and* under which interpretation the nominal definition can be demonstrated (*APo.* II.8). This is a model of the way science is supposed to show why, *and* under which interpretation, beliefs accepted by most people are true.

Fallibility

Aristotle was certainly convinced that it is not impossible for human beings to grasp the truth, even in complex scientific inquiries; in this sense, he was not a skeptic. But at the same time he emphasizes that "it is difficult to be aware whether one knows or not" (*APo.* I.9, 76a26), for "as the eyes of bats are to the blaze of day, so is the reason in our soul to the things which are by nature most evident of all" (*Met.* α.1, 993b9–11). Consequently, Aristotle feels that in our struggle to offer adequate scientific explanations, a lot of things can go wrong, and sometimes we cannot decide once and for all whether something went wrong. As already indicated, the simplest case in question is the attempt to establish a universal fact, say AaB. This is true only as long as we do not find a thing that is B, but not A. Furthermore, in trying to find, by way of a bottom-up analysis, immediate premises, how can we make sure that we have found premises that are truly immediate? In discussing how scientific theories may increase Aristotle talks about the discovery of new facts that may force us to extend the highest premises of our theory (*APo.* I.12, 78a14–22). Obviously, he takes into account that we may, at every stage of our scientific research, discover new facts; it follows that we can never make sure that we have found immediate premises because the discovery of new facts may point to new middle terms that enable us to demonstrate propositions we took before to be immediate. This is why Aristotle justifies his claim that "it is difficult to be aware whether one knows or not" by remarking: "For it is difficult to be aware whether we know from the principles of a thing or not – and that is what knowing is" (*APo.* I.9, 76a26–30).

Aristotle looks also at logical ways to refute given universal propositions. For instance, he examines in which way *ignorance*, i.e., *error through deduction*, comes about (*APo.* I.16–17). In this context, he envisages situations in which valid deductions entail false conclusions, in particular conclusions that are inconsistent with other universal propositions assumed to be true. In such cases we have, as Aristotle correctly remarks, to determine which of the premises are false. So there is sufficient evidence that Aristotle is talking about different ways of examining the truth-value of given scientific propositions by looking at their logical implications. Indeed, this is something Aristotle himself does several times in his own scientific works (see, e.g., *Cael.* II.13, 293a23–30; II.14, 297a2–6; III.7, 306a5–17; *Met.* Λ.8, 1073b32–1074a6).

There are a number of other ways our scientific research can fail. Thus, we may be inclined to demonstrate in a circular manner (*APo.* I.3); we may be, in determining scientific principles, satisfied with stating their truth or even their plausibility (*APo.* I.6); we may sometimes cross, within a sequence of demonstrations, the specific domain of a departmental science (*APo.* I.7); sometimes scientists raise unscientific questions (*APo.* I.12), and sometimes they don't use perception and induction at all, or take them to be sufficient for doing science (*APo.* I.18). Some scientists think they can get definitions without constructing demonstrations (*APo.* II.3–7), and some think that the Platonic method of dividing concepts is logically valid (*APo.* II.5); some take it that there is, for every explainable fact, a simple and unique demonstration, and some take it that there are, for every explainable fact, two or more demonstrations (*APo.* II.16–18). For Aristotle, all these assumptions or inclinations are methodological mistakes that are often not easy to detect. In sum, Aristotle does reflect in different respects on our weak epistemic condition, and he takes many scientific proposals and explanations, at every point of our scientific research, to be rather fragile and fallible (Detel, 1993).

261

Applicability

Ancient biology and geometry do not seem to argue in a syllogistic way, and it seems hard to see how they could do so. Neither does Aristotle himself, in his own biological works, seem to follow the methodological rules he recommends in the *Analytics*. This is the application problem. Recent work on Aristotle's biology indicates, though, that on a closer look he in fact does use a great number of rules proposed in the *Analytics*; in particular, he seems to assume that his arguments *can* at least rather easily be reconstructed in a formal syllogistic way, and it has been shown that such reconstructions can actually be offered (Bolton, 1987; Detel, 1997; Freeland, 1990; Gotthelf, 1987a, 1997; Lennox, 1987; McKirahan, 1995; and in this volume Lennox, ARISTOTLE'S BIOLOGY; see however Modrak, 1996). In general terms, in reading Aristotle's logic and theory of science we should proceed from the assumption that there is a *conceptual unity* of these disciplines with his metaphysics and his empirical studies like biology or meteorology (Pellegrin, 1986, p. 50).

The case of geometry proves to be a lot harder. One of the main problems is that Euclidean proofs use two-placed predicates that cannot easily be symbolized syllogistically. Nevertheless, there is evidence that Aristotle himself *thought* that syllogistic is applicable to geometry, too (*APo.* II.11, 94a20–35). Of course, the easiest way of dealing with this claim is simply to declare it trivially wrong, and that is indeed what most scholars are inclined to do. But if we look more closely at the examples Aristotle hints at we can see that there may be a way out of this problem: these examples suggest that a syllogistic symbolization of geometrical proof is supposed to be extremely general, such that the entire idea of the proof is contained in the middle term of the demonstration (Detel, 1993, vol. 1, pp. 172–81; Mendell, 1998).

In any case, Aristotle's crucial idea is that formal logic must be an essential part of a theory of science that is supposed to provide the foundation for rationally reconstructing scientific practice; and this idea proved to be extremely influential and fruitful throughout the history of science, although syllogistic turned out to be too restricted in scope to support this idea sufficiently.

Readings of Aristotle's Theory of Science

The first principles of science in the *Analytics* have been thought, by centuries of commentators, to be something like a priori truths grasped by special acts of intellectual insight that guarantee the epistemic certainty of the principles.[13] And, so the story goes on, once we have grasped the principles we can try to deduce, or to demonstrate, further theorems in a top-down procedure that guarantees, because of the logical validity of our deductions, the truth of all the theorems too. This traditional outline of Aristotle's idea of science and scientific activity can be called the *axiomatic reading*. Indeed, Aristotle tells us that knowledge and insight are epistemic states "by which we

---

13. For literature on this point see Detel, 1998, pp. 157–8, n. 2.

grasp the truth" and so are "always true" (*APo.* II.19, 100b6–8). He stresses that we must be more aware of, and more convinced by, the principles of science than by their conclusions (*APo.* I.2, 72a15–b4), and that these principles must somehow be assumed, although they cannot be proved or demonstrated (*APo.* I.2). And an appropriate scientific theory is supposed to rely, of course, on methods and proposals that avoid all the methodological mistakes that are marked so explicitly by Aristotle. These and similar remarks have been taken to confirm the axiomatic reading of the *Analytics*.

Recently scholars have suggested an alternative interpretation: "There are hints that the theory of the *Posterior Analytics* was meant to provide the proper formal account and presentation of the finished system" (Barnes, 1975, p. x; see also Barnes, 1969, 1981; and Bauman, 1998). According to this picture, it is extremely important not to confuse the aspect of discovery and scientific research, on the one hand, and the aspect of learning, teaching, and presenting an established scientific theory, on the other hand. Discovery and research use induction and empirical investigation, and they look primarily at *phenomena*, i.e., at what most people think to be true (see Owen, 1961; Wieland, 1962). Essences of things are nothing else than the set of properties that turn out, in our scientific research, to be causally basic properties of these things; and "insight" as a mode of discovery is absent from the *Posterior Analytics*. From the point of view of this *pedagogical reading* of the *Analytics*, Aristotle seems to be a "whole-hearted empiricist" (Barnes, 1975, p. 259). Influential scholars see the pedagogical reading as "the new orthodoxy and the now accepted interpretation of the *Posterior Analytics*" (Bolton, 1987, p. 121; Sorabji, 1980, pp. 188, 194).

Finally, some scholars have emphasized that Aristotle sees our scientific activity as aiming, not at the production of entirely new discoveries, but rather at *deepening given knowledge* by providing explanations of well-known phenomena. This is why questions of justification are almost absent from the *Posterior Analytics* (Burnyeat, 1981; Kosman, 1973; Lear, 1988; Lesher, 1973): Our given knowledge is not *justified* by explanations and demonstrations; rather, explanations and demonstrations *deepen* our given knowledge and help us to *better understand* phenomena that we already take to be the case.

There is a nice little remark Aristotle makes about hitting the truth: "no one is able to attain the truth adequately, while every one says something true about the nature of things" (*Met.* α.1, 993a31–b4). This applies also to the three interpretations of his theory of science just outlined. The beginning of wisdom in reading the *Analytics* consists in distinguishing descriptions of an *ideal of science and scientific activity* that shows what a *perfect scientific theory* should look like, and descriptions of the *epistemic condition human researchers are in* at every moment of their scientific activity and career. It is precisely by developing a perfect ideal of science that one can indicate in which way we may fail in doing science and in which respect we can never make sure once and for all that we have achieved perfect scientific knowledge. In his theory of science we can see Aristotle doing *both* things: sketching what perfect scientific knowledge comes down to, *and* indicating in which way our human epistemic condition is fragile and fallible. For only by doing both these things can we *improve* our fragile epistemic condition and come *closer* to perfect knowledge. This is the basic assumption of a *complex reading* of the *Analytics* (Detel, 1998, pp. 176–7).

From this point of view the axiomatic reading focuses exclusively on Aristotle's ideal of knowledge. Claiming that knowledge and insight are always true is a proposal about what perfect knowledge and insight perfected by analysis should be: if it is *really* perfect knowledge, it is, and remains, true. That is how we define perfect knowledge. But the crucial flaw of this reading is to take Aristotle's thoughts about perfect science to cover the epistemic condition of human scientific research too.

The pedagogical reading, on the other hand, correctly emphasizes that Aristotle talks, for instance, in the very first sentence of the *Posterior Analytics*, about the context of teaching and learning that every adequate scientific theory belongs to. It is also true that Aristotle seems to think that teaching and learning a scientific theory requires presenting the theory in a deductive and demonstrative frame so that the student can see how its proposals depend on each other. But it is clearly wrong to suggest, as the pedagogical reading has it, that there is a sharp methodological distinction between perception, induction, and dialectical reasoning as belonging to the context of discovery, and deduction and demonstration as belonging to the context of teaching, learning, and presenting the theory. This is obviously inconsistent with Aristotle's claim, so decisive for his view of science, that scientific activities aim primarily at the discovery of causes; the discovery of causes and highest premises, however, necessarily requires the construction of demonstrations. Therefore, deductions and demonstrations belong to the context of discovery too.

Finally, it is true that Aristotle is, in the *Analytics*, mainly interested, not in the knowledge of facts, but in the knowledge of causes of given facts that deepen our knowledge of facts simply by explaining them causally. But we should not overlook that Aristotle does reflect, even in the *Analytics*, also on methods of establishing facts, and that, in general, questions of justification are by no means completely absent from the *Analytics*. This holds even for scientific principles. Aristotle certainly thinks that scientific principles are *given* in the restricted sense that they cannot be *proved* or *demonstrated*. But *postulates* and *suppositions* can be *justified* in logic and first philosophy. Thus, Aristotle himself justifies, for instance, the law of the excluded middle in the *Metaphysics* (Book Γ) and the validity of syllogistic inferences in the *Prior Analytics* (Book I). Likewise, it is the job of first philosophy to justify existence claims about fundamental entities of scientific domains, as Aristotle demonstrates too, for instance, in the case of mathematical entities (*Metaphysics* M). Finally, *definitions* in the sense of highest explanatory principles and demonstrative premises cannot be *demonstrated* or *proved* either, but at the same time there is a clear double sense in which they can be *justified* even within the departmental science they belong to: as universal propositions, they can and must be justified by induction or deduction (*APo.* II.19), and as immediate explanatory premises they must be justified by showing that they sit at the top of actually constructed analyses and sets of demonstrations making up a whole scientific theory.

One way of characterizing the *complex reading* of Aristotle's theory of science is to say that Aristotle conceived of science, and of scientific activity, as an *epistemic culture*. In general, a *culture* is a *set of practices* that are based *on shared background assumptions* and are taught and learnt; in particular, an *epistemic* culture consists of practices that are designed to evaluate claims to knowledge and to produce justified knowledge; at the same time, an epistemic culture relies specifically on shared background assumptions about what perfect knowledge is, and its methods and results are transmitted by teaching and learning them. Outlining the complex reading this way makes clear that it preserves the advantages of the three other readings sketched above while at the same time avoiding their narrowness.

Epistemological Status of the *Analytics*

In Aristotle's classification of all sciences (*Met.* E.1) dialectic, logic, and theory of science are missing. Aristotle does not seem to count them among the sciences. This has provoked a debate among scholars (e.g., Ackrill, 1981, p. 79; Barnes, 1982, p. 25; Ross, 1923, p. 20). The suggestion offered by the Aristotelian *tradition* is that Aristotle considered these disciplines as mere *tools* of the sciences. But Aristotle himself gives us some clues that help to understand better how he looked at the status of logic, dialectic, and the theory of science.

Specific sciences proper are defined by the specific domain, or *genus* (*genos*), they deal with. Genera are, in Aristotle's view, radically different from each other: they "have no path to one another, but are too distant and without common measure" (*Met.* I.4, 1055a6–7). Different genera are therefore separated from each other in such a way that the gap between them is, at least in any direct way, impassable (though there may be analogies between them). At the same time, any genus is a space of specific differences and includes contrary kinds (*eidē*), the relation of contrariety being defined, by a theory of opposites, as the maximum difference between attributes such that contrary attributes cannot coexist in the same subject in the same relation (*Met.* I.4). Every specific science can, therefore, be defined *uniquely* by its specific genus, and it explores the contrary kinds of its specific domain. The notions of a genus (*genos*) and a kind (*eidos*) are not, however, taxonomic concepts in the modern sense of genus and species. In his biology, for instance, Aristotle applies the term *genos* often to things that count as species in the modern taxonomic sense. Animal classifications are, in Aristotle's view, outside science, the central project of Aristotle's biology being what we might call an etiological moriology (Balme, 1962; Pellegrin, 1986). It is on the basis of the radical separation of scientific genera from each other that Aristotle insists that scientists are not permitted to cross over, in their explanations and demonstrations, from one genus to another (*APo.* I.7).

Aristotle's theory of science is, therefore, a variety of an *anti-reductionist scientific pluralism* that puts emphasis on the *specificity* and *uniqueness* of domains and terminologies that are constitutive for every specific science (although there are cases of subordination of one science to another within the same genus; for example, optics is subordinate to geometry). There are indications that Aristotle conceived of scientific genera as being *abstracted* from natural things by scientific activity. Thus, for example, part of establishing the science of biology is that scientists look at natural things *qua* living things, and part of establishing the science of geometry is that scientists look at natural things *qua* dimensional entities (*Met.* M.3, 1077b17–1078a26; *Phys.* II.2, 193b31–194a12). This is not to say that Aristotle entertains an anti-realistic position about scientific genera; rather, he feels that natural things are bearers of a great variety of structures and can therefore be looked at in different ways. It is up to the scientist what kind of structure he wants to look at, thereby abstracting from other parameters that are also given in natural things.

In any case, logic and the theory of science do not explore a specific domain; for "neither of them deals with the nature of any definite subject, but they are mere faculties of furnishing arguments."[14] In addition, logic and the theory of science do not seem to be looking for *causes* either. In these crucial respects they differ, like dialectic, from sciences proper.

More importantly, recognizing and following general *methodological* rules is a matter, not of science, but of *education*. Thus, the wrong demand that everything should be demonstrated (discussed in some detail in *APo.* I.3) is due to "want of education, for not to know of what things one may demand demonstration, and of what one may not, argues simply want of education" (*Met.* Γ.4, 1006a5–8). Likewise, it is "the mark of an educated man to look for precision in each class of things just so far as the nature of the subjects admits" (*EN* I.3, 1094b24–25). In general, concerning every study and investigation, there are, according to Aristotle, two different kinds of proficiency: one is a kind of acquaintance with the subject, provided by sciences proper; the other is what "may be properly called educated knowledge of the subject. For an educated man should be able to form a fair judgment as to the goodness or badness of an exposition in nearly all branches of knowledge, and not merely in some special subject." Therefore in the sciences, in particular in the natural sciences, "there must be certain canons, by reference to which a hearer shall be able to criticize the method of a professed exposition, quite independently of the question whether the statements made be true or false." Indeed, in general "to be educated is to do this, and the man of general education we take to be such" (*PA* I.1, 639a1–15) (George, 1993). These illuminating remarks show how Aristotle conceives of the true status of logic and a theory of science: learning and mastering these disciplines is, not to be a scientist, *but to be educated in the most general sense*; logic and theory of science are the very core of *paideia*. One important aspect of this general education is a *rational critical attitude* towards the *structure* and *validity* of proposed arguments. To use modern terminology, to be educated in this general sense, i.e., to use logic and scientific methodology in a critical and rational way, is to *move in the space of reason, to participate in the game of giving and asking for reasons*. The process of learning logic and scientific methodology is *to tame nature and to move from the realm of nature into the space of reasons*, and this is one of the most important *conditions for living a good life*. It is in this way that Aristotle lucidly and admirably shows us the true status, and the true importance, of the formal disciplines that he himself has the eternal merit of having invented.

Bibliography

Works Cited

Ackrill, J. L. (1981). *Aristotle the Philosopher.* Oxford: Oxford University Press.
Balme, D. (1962). "Genos and Eidos in Aristotle's Biology." *Classical Quarterly,* 12, 81–98.

14. See *Rh.* I.2, 1356a32–33. This remark is restricted to rhetoric and dialectic, though; but since syllogistic inference rules belong also to dialectic (*APr.* I.1, 24a26–28), this goes also for syllogistic logic, and therefore a fortiori also for the rules of scientific arguments developed in the *Posterior Analytics*.

Barnes, J. (1969). "Aristotle's Theory of Demonstration." *Phronesis*, 14, 123–52.

——. (1975). *Aristotle's Posterior Analytics*. Oxford: Clarendon Press. (2nd edn. 1994.)

——. (1981). "Proof and the Syllogism." In E. Berti (ed.), *Aristotle on Science. The Posterior Analytics* (pp. 17–59). Proceedings of the Eighth Symposium Aristotelicum. Padua: Editrice Antenore.

——. (1982). *Aristotle*. Oxford: Oxford University Press.

Bauman, R. W. (1998). *Aristotle's Logic of Education*. New York: Peter Lang.

Berti, E. (ed.). *Aristotle on Science. The Posterior Analytics*. Proceedings of the Eighth Symposium Aristotelicum. Padua: Editrice Antenore.

Bolton, R. (1987). "Definition and Scientific Method in Aristotle's *Posterior Analytics* and *Generation of Animals*." In A. Gotthelf and J. G. Lennox (eds.), *Philosophical Issues in Aristotle's Biology* (pp. 120–66). Cambridge: Cambridge University Press.

Burnyeat, M. F. (1981). "Aristotle on Understanding Knowledge." In E. Berti (ed.), *Aristotle on Science. The Posterior Analytics* (pp. 97–139). Proceedings of the Eighth Symposium Aristotelicum. Padua: Editrice Antenore.

Charles, D. (1997). "Aristotle and the Unity and Essence of Biological Kinds." In W. Kullmann and S. Föllinger (eds.), *Aristotelische Biologie* (pp. 27–42). Stuttgart: Steiner.

Corcoran, J. (ed.). (1974a). *Ancient Logic and Its Modern Interpretations*. Dordecht: Reidel.

——. (1974b). "Aristotle's Natural Deduction System." In J. Corcoran (ed.), *Ancient Logic and Its Modern Interpretation*. (pp. 85–131). Dordecht: Reidel.

Detel, W. (trans. and notes). (1993). *Aristoteles Analytica Posteriora*. (2 vols.). Berlin: Akademie Verlag.

——. (1997). "Why All Animals Have a Stomach: Demonstration and Axiomatization in Aristotle's *Parts of Animals*." In W. Kullmann and S. Föllinger (eds.), *Aristotelische Biologie* (pp. 63–84). Stuttgart: Franz Steiner.

——. (1998). "Aristotle's Posterior Analytics and the Path to the Principles". In N. Avgelis and F. Peonidis (eds.), *Aristotle on Logic, Language and Science* (pp. 155–82). Thessaloniki: Sakkoulas Publications.

Engberg-Pedersen, T. (1979). "More on Aristotle's Epagoge." *Phronesis*, 24, 301–19.

Frede, M. (1989). "La notion de cause." *Revue de métaphysique et de morale*, 104, 483–511.

Freeland, C. A. (1990). "Scientific Explanation and Empirical Data in Aristotle's *Meteorology*." In D. Devereux and P. Pellegrin (eds.), *Biologie, Logique et Métaphysique chez Aristote* (pp. 287–320). Paris: Éditions du CNRS.

George, M. I. (1993). "The Notion of Paideia in Aristotle's *De Partibus Animalium*." *American Catholic Philosophical Quarterly*, 67, 299–320.

Gill, M. L. (1997). "Material Necessity and *Meteorology* IV.12." In W. Kullmann and S. Föllinger (eds.), *Aristotelische Biologie* (pp. 145–61). Stuttgart: Steiner.

Gotthelf, A. (1987a). "First Principles in Aristotle's *Parts of Animals*". In A. Gotthelf and J. G. Lennox (eds.), *Philosophical Issues in Aristotle's Biology* (pp. 167–98). Cambridge: Cambridge University Press.

——. (1987b). "Aristotle's Conception of Final Causality." In A. Gotthelf and J. G. Lennox (eds.). *Philosophical Issues in Aristotle's Biology* (pp. 204–42). Cambridge: Cambridge University Press.

——. (1997). "The Elephants Nose: Further Reflections on the Axiomatic Structure of Biological Explanation in Aristotle." In W. Kullmann and S. Föllinger (eds.), *Aristotelische Biologie* (pp. 85–96). Stuttgart: Steiner.

Gotthelf, A. and Lennox, J. G. (eds.). (1987). *Philosophical Issues in Aristotle's Biology*. Cambridge: Cambridge University Press.

Hempel, C. G. and Oppenheim, P. (1948). "Studies in the Logic of Explanation." *Philosophy of Science*, 15, 135–75.

267

Kosman, L. A. (1973). "Understanding, Explanation, and Insight in the *Posterior Analytics*." In H. D. Lee, A. P. D. Mourelatos and R. Rorty (eds.). *Exegesis and Argument*: (Festschrift for Gregory Vlastos), *Phronesis* suppl. vol. 1 (pp. 374–92).

Kullmann, W. and Föllinger, S. (eds.). (1997). *Aristotelische Biologie*. Stuttgart: Steiner.

Lear, J. (1988). *Aristotle. The Desire to Understand*. Cambridge: Cambridge University Press.

Lennox, J. G. (1987). "Divide and Explain: The *Posterior Analytics* in Practice." In A. Gotthelf and J. G. Lennox (eds.), *Philosophical Issues in Aristotle's Biology* (pp. 90–119). Cambridge: Cambridge University Press.

——. (1994). "Aristotelian Problems." *Ancient Philosophy*, 14, 53–77.

Lesher, J. (1973). "The Meaning of 'Nous' in the *Posterior Analytics*." *Phronesis*, 18, 44–68.

Lukasiewicz, J. (1957). *Aristotle's Syllogistic from the Standpoint of Modern Formal Logic*. Oxford: Clarendon Press.

McKirahan, R. (1995). *Principles and Proofs: Aristotle's Theory of Demonstrative Science*. Princeton: Princeton University Press.

Mendell, H. (1998). "Making Sense of Aristotelian Demonstration." *Oxford Studies in Ancient Philosophy*, 16, 161–225.

Modrak, D. K. (1996). "Aristotle's Epistemology: One or Many Theories?" In W. Wians (ed.), *Aristotle's Philosophical Development: Problems and Prospect*. (pp. 151–70). Lanham: Rowman & Littlefield.

Owen, G. E. L. (1961). "*Tithenai ta phainomena*." In S. Mansion (ed.), *Aristote et les problèmes de méthode* (pp. 83–103). Louvain: Publications Universitaires de Louvain.

Patterson, R. (1995). *Aristotle's Modal Logic: Essence and Entailment in the Organon*. Cambridge and New York: Cambridge University Press.

Patzig, G. (1968). *Aristotle's Theory of the Syllogism* (trans. J. Barnes). Dordrecht: Reidel. (Original work published 1962.)

Pellegrin, P. (1986). *Aristotle's Classification of Animals* (trans. A. Preus). Berkeley: University of California Press. (Original work published 1982.)

Ross, W. D. (1923). *Aristotle's Prior and Posterior Analytics*. Oxford: Clarendon Press.

——. (1957). *Aristotle*. London, New York: Methuen.

Smiley, T. (1973). "What is a Syllogism?" *Journal of Philosophical Logic*, 2, 136–54.

Smith, R. (trans. and notes). (1989). *Aristotle. Prior Analytics*. Indianapolis: Hackett.

Solmsen, F. (1929). *Die Entwicklung der aristotelischen Logik und Rhetorik*. Berlin: Weidmann.

Sorabji, R. (1980). *Necessity, Cause, and Blame. Perspectives on Aristotle's Theory*. London: Duckworth.

Striker, G. (1994). "Assertoric vs Modal Syllogistic." *Ancient Philosophy*, 14, 39–51.

Wieland, W. (1962). *Die aristotelische Physik*. Göttingen: Vandenhoeck and Ruprecht.

Further Reading

Ancient and Renaissance commentators

Alexander of Aphrodisias

Wallis, M. (ed.). (1883). *In Aristotelis Analyticorum Priorum Librum I Commentarium* (CAG, 2.1). Berlin: Reimer.

Philoponus

Wallis, M. (ed.). (1905). *In Aristotelis Analytica Priora Commentaria* (CAG, 13.2). Berlin: Reimer.

——. (ed.). (1909). *In Aristotelis Analytica Posteriora Commentaria* (CAG, 13.3). Berlin: Reimer.

Zabarella

Zabarella, J. (1597). *In duos Aristotelis libros Posteriorum Analyticorum Commentaria*. Cologne: Lazarus Zetzner. (Repr. Hildesheim: Olms.)

Modern authors

Avgelis, N. and Peonidis, F. (eds.). (1998). *Aristotle on Logic, Language and Science* (pp. 155–82). Thessaloniki: Sakkoulas Publications.

Barnes, J., Schofield, M., and Sorabji, R. (eds.). (1975). *Articles on Aristotle*. (vol. 1): *Science*. London: Duckworth.

Charles, D. (2000). *Aristotle on Meaning and Essence*. Oxford: Oxford University Press.

Corcoran, J. (1994). "The Founding of Logic." *Ancient Philosophy*, 14, 9–24.

Devereux, D. and Pellegrin, P. (eds.). (1990). *Biologie, Logique et Métaphysique chez Aristote*. Paris: Éditions du CNRS.

Ferejohn, M. (1991). *The Origins of Aristotelian Science*. New Haven: Yale University Press.

Frede, M. (1974). "Stoic vs. Aristotelian Syllogistic." *Archiv für Geschichte der Philosophie*, 56, 1–32.

Gill, M. L. (1989). *Aristotle on Substance. The Paradox of Unity*. Princeton: Princeton University Press.

Gotthelf, A. (ed.). (1985). *Aristotle on Nature and Living Things*. Pittsburgh/Bristol: Mathesis.

——, and Lennox, J. G. (eds.). (1987). *Philosophical Issues in Aristotle's Biology*. Cambridge: Cambridge University Press.

Hintikka, J. (1973). *Time and Necessity: Studies in Aristotle's Theory of Modality*. Oxford: Clarendon Press.

Irwin, T. (1989), *Aristotle's First Principles*. Oxford: Oxford University Press.

Kakkuri-Knuuttila, M. and Knuuttila, S. (1990). "Induction and Conceptual Analysis." *Acta Philosophica Fennica*, 49, 294–303.

Kullmann, W. (1974). *Wissenschaft und Methode. Interpretationen zur Aristotelischen Theorie der Naturwissenschaft*. Berlin: de Gruyter.

Lennox, J. G. (1994). "Putting Philosophy of Science to the Test: The Case of Aristotle's Biology." *Proceedings of the Biennial Meetings of the Philosophy of Science Association*, 2, 239–47.

Matthen, M. (ed.). (1988). *Aristotle Today. Essays on Aristotle's Ideal of Science*. Edmonton: Academic Printing and Publishing.

McKirahan Jr., R. D. (1995). "Aristotle's 'Metaphysics' from the Perspective of the *Posterior Analytics*." *Proceedings of the Boston Area Colloquium in Ancient Philosophy*, 11, 275–97.

Mignucci, M. (1975). *L'argomentazione dimostrativa in Aristotele. Commento agli Analitici Secondi*. (vol. 1). Padua: Publicazione Istituto di storia della filosofia e del Centro per ricerche di Filosofia medievale.

Owen, G. E. L. (1986). *Logic, Science, and Dialectic* (M. C. Nussbaum ed.). Ithaca: Cornell University Press / London: Duckworth.

Pellegrin, P. (1987). "Logical Difference and Biological Difference: The Unity of Aristotle's Thought." In A. Gotthelf and J. G. Lennox (eds.), *Philosophical Issues in Aristotle's Biology* (pp. 313–38). Cambridge: Cambridge University Press.

——. (1990). "De l'explication causale dans la biologie d'Aristote." *Revue de Métaphysique et de Morale*, 105, 197–219.

Smith, R. (1982). "The Axiomatic Method and Aristotle's Logical Methodology." *Southwest Philosophical Studies*, 8, 49–59.

Sosa, E. (1983). "Classical Analysis." *Journal of Philosophy*, 80, 695–710.

Wians, W. (ed.). (1996). *Aristotle's Philosophical Development: Problems and Prospects*. Lanham, Md.: Rowman & Littlefield.

269

15

Aristotle's Physics and Cosmology

ISTVÁN BODNÁR AND PIERRE PELLEGRIN

Aristotle, at *Met.* **E**.1, 1026a6–22, contrasts what he calls *phusikē epistēmē* (physical science) with the other theoretical sciences, the mathematical sciences, and theology. The upshot of the comparison is that physics is similar to theology, because both theology and physics treat substances – entities which are capable of separate exist-ence on their own – but this similarity does not allow for an identification of the two theoretical disciplines, because physics, unlike theology, treats changeable substance, whereas theological inquiry investigates the domain of the eternal and immutable divine entities. This, as Aristotle also stresses, means that if there were no unmovable, non-physical entities, physics would be first philosophy: it would give an account of everything there is in the world by inquiring into the principles of everything.

Such a position has its own theoretical coherence, but also shows the trace of crisis in the history of philosophy from its beginning to Aristotle. In a famous passage in the *Parts of Animals*, Aristotle, criticizing the Socratics for having restricted themselves to ethics and politics, claimed to revive the pre-Socratic tradition in the investigation of nature (*historia peri phuseōs*, cf. Hussey, THE BEGINNINGS OF SCIENCE AND PHILOSOPHY IN ARCHAIC GREECE, in this volume). This kind of philosophy, which considered all beings as coming from a small number of principles – principles which were mainly material, being either substances like water or fire, or qualitites like hot and cold, thick and thin – had been toppled by the attack of the Eleatics, according to whom no being can either come from not-being or return back to not-being. Aristotle re-established the possibility of physics on a new basis. On Aristotle's account, nature, or natural beings taken as a whole, is no longer considered the totality of being, and the domain of changeable entities is no longer considered self-sufficient. As it turns out, it needs for its continued existence and changes the causal influence of immutable entities – the prime movers. Nevertheless, for all this causal dependence, physics remains a separate theoretical inquiry: what changes there are in the domain of changeable entities will fundamentally depend on the constitution of these entities. Even if a thorough and exhaustive knowledge of the supra-sensible domain were possible, it would not provide an understanding of the various processes in the changeable realm. For that, a genuine study of the entities endowed with change is indispensable. Physics and theology are different from each other because they are concerned with different and irreducible objects, even if these objects are related to each other.

Now the changes any changeable entity will undergo depend on two main factors: external influences exerted on the object, and also some salient inherent characteristics of the changing object itself. An explanation of every physical process, then, has to

270

appeal to both kinds of factors. A discussion of the constitution and the internal characteristics of changeable objects – which also will include the causal influence these objects can exert on one another – is a prerequisite of physical inquiry.

So far we have considered what could be called an epistemological answer to Parmenides' critique. What is established, through the Aristotelian division of sciences, is the possibility of a theoretical science of changeable being, a science that inherited the constraints of Eleatic and Platonic knowledge (eternity and immutability of the object of science, necessity of the connections displayed by science).

But Aristotle's answer to the Parmenidean challenge is also a *cosmological* one. Because he abandoned the cosmogonic explanations of previous philosophers, including Plato, Aristotle is the first, and in a sense the last *cosmologist*,[1] at least in antiquity (cf. Solmsen, 1960). Setting aside the question of the origin of the universe, Aristotle takes the world to be perfect and eternal – predicates related to each other, because something that is not perfect could not be eternal – and also finite and spherical in its form. This global perfection is compatible with some local imperfections. The reproduction of living beings within the boundaries of eternal species, for instance, is but an imperfect imitation of the individual eternity of the celestial bodies. In this very reproduction many accidents may take place, which can produce offspring of various degrees of monstrosity. Those imperfections are restricted within the boundaries of what commentators, but not Aristotle himself, have called the "sublunary region." For Aristotle's world is composed of a set of concentric spheres the center of which is the center of the earth, which is the only immobile point in the universe. The outermost sphere is that of the fixed stars on which constellations are attached and which completes a full revolution in one day. Beyond the sphere of the fixed stars there is neither space nor place nor void nor time (*Cael.* I.9, 279a11). Below this sphere are the planets which are set within spheres which give them their movements. Aristotle adopts with some emendations the theory of concentric spheres posited by Eudoxus and revised by Callippus. This theory aims to explain how it is possible that the sphere of the fixed stars has a uniform circular motion, whereas that of the planets – "planet" means "wandering" in Greek – is not. Eudoxus proposed the hypothesis of several concentric spheres that have different axes, orientation of motion, and speeds. Each planet is therefore dependent on a system of several spheres, and its final trajectory is the result of the composition of the motions of these spheres. (Cf. Duhem, 1913; and Mendell, 2000).

The last of these spheres, viz. the one closest to us, is the sphere of the moon. Above this sphere – in the region called "supralunar" by commentators and merely designated by the expression "the things above" by Aristotle himself – the movements are complex but absolutely regular. Within the sublunary region, by contrast, one can find a certain degree of disorder. This disorder is one of the obstacles Aristotle had to overcome to build up a science that can be applied to the realities of the sublunary region. One example: in the sublunary region, due to the presence of perishable matter, all the phenomena are in some respects indeterminate, and the necessary connections are not valid "always" but only "for the most part."

1. For a brief overview of the later Stoic cosmology, see in this volume Brisson and Pradeau, PLOTINUS, p. 590.

It is within this closed and cyclical world that Aristotelian physics has its significance, and in particular that the theory of change is understandable. What is, then, the domain of physical science?

When he refers to the *Physics* as a treatise, Aristotle mainly speaks of *ta peri phuseōs* and *ta phusika*. W. D. Ross, in the introduction of his edition of the *Physics* (Ross, 1936), mentions that these expressions, when used as titles, may refer to three things: either a set of texts that includes at most the first four books of our *Physics*, or the eight (or seven) books of our *Physics*, or the complete set of all the physical treatises the most complete list of which is given in a passage of the *Meterology*, a text that deserves to be quoted almost in full:

> We have already discussed the first causes of nature, and all natural motion, also the stars ordered in the motion of the heavens, and the corporeal elements . . . and becoming and perishing in general. There remains for consideration a part of this inquiry which all our predecessors called meteorology. It is concerned with events that are natural, though their order is less perfect than that of the first element of bodies. . . . When the inquiry into these matters is concluded, let us consider what account we can give, in accordance with the method we have followed, of animals and plants, both generally and in detail. (*Meteor.* I.1, 338a20–339a8)

Let us have a look at each stage of this list: "the first causes of nature, and all natural motion" refers to the treatise we know as the *Physics*. "The stars ordered in the motion of the heavens" corresponds, in our corpus, to the first two books of *On the Heavens*. "The corporeal elements . . . and becoming and perishing in general" corresponds to the last two books of *On the Heavens* and to the treatise *On Generation and Corruption*. Then comes the "meteorology" which, according to Aristotle, deals with many phenomena – rain, snow, hail, winds, rivers, tides, earthquakes, rainbow, etc., but also shooting stars, comets, aurora borealis, milky way, etc. – all situated in the sublunary region, according to Aristotle. "Animals and plants" refers to Aristotle's zoological treatises and his lost book on plants. At *Meteor.* I.1, 339a8, Aristotle concludes that "when that has been done we may say that the whole of our original undertaking [i.e., physics] will so to speak have been carried out."

The Principles of Physics

Being a science in the true Aristotelian sense of the term, physics must both concern a genus and be based on principles (see Detel, ARISTOTLE'S LOGIC AND THEORY OF SCIENCE, in this volume). The genus is that of the natural beings, that is, beings insofar as they have an internal principle of change and rest. Concerning the principles, the first chapter of the *Physics* explicitly says that physics must establish its own principles just as the other sciences do, that is, by proceeding from particular to universal. These principles are of two kinds.

First, any physical investigation will have to rely on two important preliminary assumptions: the presupposition of plurality, and of motion. These presuppositions cannot be established by physics itself; it is the task of another kind of knowledge – of first philosophy, according to some interpreters, but more probably of dialectic – to discuss and defend them (*Phys.* I.2, 184b25–185a20). The defense of plurality, against Eleatic arguments to the contrary, invokes Aristotle's theory of categories. According to the theory of categories, items which can be said to be do not constitute a single genus. Entities come in a variety of ten different kinds, and among them the fundamental divide is that between substances (entities belonging to the first category), and non-substances or attributes (entities belonging to the other nine categories). Accordingly, if there were only a single item which is, we would have to discard the insights of the theory of categories, since the single existing thing could fall into only one of the categories, and it could not be characterized by attributes falling into any of the other categories. The other categories would have to remain uninstantiated in such a monistic setup. But such an inquiry is not part of physics either.

The other kind of principle is considered in Book I of the *Physics*, chs. 5–9. Given that the object of physics is defined by its mutability, Aristotle introduces a unified account of change: in any process of change or motion an underlying subject (a *hupokeimenon*) acquires a form (an *eidos*) it previously lacked. Before the change the subject is characterized by the privation of the form (the *sterēsis*). In such cases the two end-points of change stand to each other as opposites. This is true also in cases in which change does not start from one of the extremes, or does not reach an extreme at the end of the process: as Aristotle submits, intermediate points combine both opposites, and can do duty *in lieu* of these opposites (*Phys.* V.1, 224b28–35). Such opposition, however, does not hold in the case of celestial revolutions: these revolutions go on forever, without beginning or end, and are not characterized by the opposition of starting point and end point, or of any point along the circumference of their circular paths. (See *Cael.* I.4 and II.3.)

At first sight, this account differs from the one Aristotle can give about non-substantial change within the framework of the *Categories* only in its terminology. Once the same framework is applied also to cases of substantial change, and an underlying *matter* (*hulē*) is identified in processes of the generation and perishing of substances, substantial entities, which the *Categories* treats as simple unanalyzed entities, turn out to be constituted out of matter and form.[2]

For substantial change, a substance needs to have generatable and perishable matter. Indeed, in processes of generation and perishing the subject of the change will be neither the object itself, nor the independently existing substance(s) from which the object is generated or into which it perishes. Only those cases count as substantial

---

2.   As a consequence of this additional level of analysis, Aristotle no longer needs to maintain a fundamental distinction of the *Categories*. He does not distinguish between entities which *can be predicated of* a subject – wider kinds predicable of individuals or of less general kinds – and entities which *are in* subjects, i.e., inhere in them. Once substances are analyzed into matter and form, the form can be said to be in the matter, and to be predicated of the matter. Similarly, in the parlance of the works where the analysis of substances into their matter and form is present, the inherent attributes of a substance are said to be predicated of the substance (see, e.g.. *Met.* Z.3, 1029a20–24). On this relation between form and matter, which arguably creates difficulties for Aristotle, see Gill, FIRST PHILOSOPHY IN ARISTOTLE, in this volume.

generations in which "the whole changes without anything perceptible remaining as the same substratum" (GC I.4, 319b14–16, trans. Williams). This means that in these cases the underlying matter has to be something which is not perceptible in itself, even though it may possess perceptible attributes. Aristotle's examples for such attributes which remain unchanged through a process of substantial change are transparency and coldness (or, with Williams' emendation, transparency and wetness) of air and water. Aristotle stresses in 319b21–24 that in such cases, even though they are present in both the preexisting entity and the outcome, such overarching attributes cannot serve as the substrate of generation and perishing.

In some cases, the matter of the product is generated at the same time as the product itself – organs are generated as an integral part of the generation of living beings. But then the generation of this matter also needs to be accounted for. At the last remove the division into matter and form has to account for the generation of homogeneous masses from one another, where one homogeneous mass is completely replaced by another one through the process. Aristotle's examples at 319b16–17 for such rock bottom generations are the biological change of seed into blood, and the elemental changes from water into air, or from air into water.

Accordingly, these cases will invoke a matter which cannot exist on its own, and can feature only as the material component of an entity endowed with form.[3] But Aristotle introduces matter not only as the bearer of substantial change. In the case of non-substantial changes, even though the underlying subject of the change is a substance, Aristotle submits that the substance, in order to be able to undergo the change in question, needs to be constituted of the right kind of material – matter that can engage in locomotion, or undergo qualitative and quantitative changes.

It is important to stress here that Aristotle's claim can be taken in at least two different ways, depending on which matter the claim is about. The claim makes excellent sense about the *proximate matter* – that collection of entities that are organized directly by the form into the substance the entity is. Whatever capacities the substance has, must be accounted for by the capacities of the material component of the substance. With Aristotle's example, if a living being is able to perform an array of life functions, it has to be constituted of the right kind of matter – in this case, of the right kind of organs – which have the capacity of performing these functions. In this case there is a strict one-to-one correspondence between the capacities of the entity and those of its matter.

---

3. Cf. also GC I.5, 320b20, where Aristotle rejects the existence of a common corporeality – i.e., of a corporeal entity which could exist on its own, and would constitute the substrate of homogeneous elemental masses. It is a further point whether the material component of elemental masses is a factor common to these elements – which would be the traditional doctrine of prime matter – or whether what counts as the material component in a generation and perishing depends on the actual pair of elements generated from each other. This latter option would have the consequence that the material component of elements could not be identified for individual elements, but only for pairs of elements. But Aristotle's wording at GC I.5, 320b12–14, is apparently more committed, saying that the material component is "numerically one and the same for all of [the elements], although it is different in account for each of them."

But Aristotle's claim is presumably about *remote matter*, or even about the remotest matter: whatever serves as the fundamental material component of the constituents of the material counterpart of the substance in question. We are inclined to take Aristotle's claim this way, because it is not formulated with a strict one-to-one correspondence in mind. To remain with our example, the capacities of the life functions can be located at the level of the organs of the organism, whereas the tissues constituting these organs will have a host of different capacities, out of which, due to the forms organizing these tissues into different organs, organs with different capacities will emerge. If we take Aristotle's claim in this way, it will stress that the emerging capacities of a substance, corresponding to the capacities of its proximate material component, will be rooted in the different, fundamental capacities of some ultimate material, manifest in the potentialities of the elements – fire, air, water, and earth – and their combinations.[4]

The Science of Natural Beings

Physics, as we have seen, studies a genus – it is the science of natural beings, the main characteristic of which is to be *mobile*. Insofar as physics is a science, it offers explanations that are included within a universally valid framework of causal explanation.

Explanations about the features or the behavior of an entity refer to a factor responsible for this feature or behavior – they specify the cause (*aition* or *aitia*) of the feature or behavior. Different causes can be quoted for the same feature or behavior, because different causes explain in different ways. These different ways are grouped by Aristotle under four headings, the so-called four causes.

When the matter or the form of an entity is specified as the responsible factor for a state of affairs, it is introduced as material or formal cause. The separation of the material and formal causes as distinct types implies that if something is explicable in terms of matter or form, explanations in terms of form will be different in kind from those in terms of matter. As a rule there is a collaboration between these causes – matter provides the potentialities that are actualized by the form – but this is not such that the two types of explanation would overlap. Rather, these causally relevant entities give rise to a hierarchic structure of explanation. In order for a form to be realized, one needs to have suitable matter. This suitable matter brings with it the required features into the composite of matter and form. These features, then, are on the one hand the contribution of the matter, and as such the matter is the (material) cause of these features of the composite entity, whereas on the other hand they are indispensable presuppositions for the realization of the form, and to that extent their

4. Note that the claim is about composite entities, constituted of matter and form. Pure forms will be actualities which are not tied to the capacities of a material component. Indeed, even within composite entities Aristotle's claim does not exclude the existence of some fundamentally novel actualities, provided some forms which can exist independently of matter can enter the constitution of composite entities: cf. the vexed question of Aristotle's discussion of the active intellect in *De An.* III.5. On this topic, see Caston, ARISTOTLE'S PSYCHOLOGY, in this volume.

presence is prompted by the form. To this extent the form is at the same time a *final* cause for the potentialities that are present in order to make its emergence possible. Such dependence relations between matter and form are labeled by Aristotle as cases of *hypothetical necessity*. To use Aristotle's example, if there is to be a house, one needs bricks, slabs, mortar etc.: this means in each case material with suitable properties within a definite range.

Explanations often specify entities beyond the role played by the matter and the form of the entity itself. These cases are grouped by Aristotle as efficient (or moving) causes on the one hand and as final causes on the other. Efficient causes operate in a straightforward manner by initiating processes and bringing about their effects, whereas final causes account for processes and entities by being what these processes and entities are for, their objective end or goal.

Efficient causes possess the active capacity to bring about change or rest, while they exert this causal power on a subject or on some preexisting matter with the matching passive capacity to undergo the change or remain at rest. (Cf. *Met.* Θ.8, 1049b5–10, and Θ.1, 1046a11–13). But efficient causation need not issue from the outside. An efficient cause can also be internal. In such cases it will be, in a specific function, one of the parts of the entity in question, or it can even be identical with the formal aspect of the entity.

But, as we have noticed, mobility is the main characteristic of natural beings. Now not every sort of mobility makes a being a natural being. A nature (*phusis*), according to Aristotle, is an inner principle or source (*archē*) of change and being at rest (*Phys.* II.1, 1928b8–32). This means that when an entity moves or is at rest according to its nature (*phusei* or *kata phusin*) we need not specify any other cause of the event. We have to describe how – to what extent, through what other processes, and due to what agency – the preconditions for the process of change or being at rest are present, but once we have provided an account of these preconditions, we have given a complete account of the process. The nature of the entity is in and of itself sufficient to induce and to explain the process, if nothing external interferes.[5]

Such natural processes of change or rest are contrasted with cases in which the process is effected by constraint or force (*biai*), against the nature of an entity (*para phusin*). In such cases both the active potentiality of the external constraint and the passive potentiality on which this external constraint is operative need to be specified. Natures, then, in a way do double duty – once a nature is operative, neither an independent further active, nor an independent further passive capacity needs to be invoked – but this, as will be clear from Aristotle's discussion, needs a host of qualifications.

---

5. This should be contrasted to modern essentialism, in which the nature – the complex of essential features – of an entity can give rise to fundamentally different behavior under different circumstances, where these circumstances cannot be described as only providing preconditions or creating obstacles for the natural course of events. This fundamental difference between modern essentialism and Aristotle's explanations in terms of natures is discussed by Sarah Broadie in Waterlow (1982, ch. 1). On nature in its application to living things, see Lennox, ARISTOTLE'S BIOLOGY, and for a discussion of nature in his political philosophy, see Keyt, ARISTOTLE'S POLITICAL PHILOSOPHY, section on "Nature," in this volume.

As internal principles of change, natures need to fall into one of the four classes of causes – otherwise they would constitute an exceptional, fifth kind of causal efficacy. As it turns out, they can feature in any of the four causal functions. However, when nature is an explanatory factor as matter – when the natural motion or rest of an entity is explained by the matter the entity is made of – behind the nature as matter there is a further explanatory factor, a feature of this matter itself, which in turn at some level of analysis is determined by the form of the matter or some part of the matter.[6]

Hence one could make the more restricted claim that natures are operative ultimately as forms of the entity or of some embedded constituent of the entity, as final causes or as efficient causes. One can further add that form and final cause often coincide. A first efficient cause is not the same entity as the effect, but is nevertheless the same in form (or in species, *eidei*) (*Phys.* II.6, 198a24–27, cf. *Met.* H.4, 1044a32–b1). This is the principle of synonymy, which we will discuss below. Natures as internal principles of motion and rest, although not necessarily moving causes themselves, stand in an exclusive relationship to the efficient or moving causes of these motions and rests. In some cases when Aristotle is not specifying the first moving cause, he can assert the identity of nature and moving cause. Accordingly, the soul of living beings will be identified as the substance (i.e., form) and the moving cause of these organisms.[7] In other cases, as we shall see, even though the nature is not identical with the moving cause, it will be linked to it in an intimate manner.

Motion, Causal Interaction, and Causational Synonymy

At the beginning of Book III of the *Physics*, Aristotle writes: "since nature is a principle of motion and change, and that is the subject of our inquiry, we must not neglect what motion is. For if it is unknown, nature too would be unknown" (200b12–15). Because motion or change (*kinēsis*) is mentioned in the definition of nature, a discussion of nature will also include an account of what motion is. The *Categories* include alongside the other categories the categories of action and passion, which can house processes and motions, provided every motion occurs as the effect of a mover on an entity moved. Once the further analytical tools of matter, form, potentiality (or capacity, *dunamis*), and actuality (or activity, *energeia*) are available, each motion can be reassigned to the category in which the motion as such effects a change. This can occur in five of the categories: (1) substance; (2) quality; (3) quantity; (4) place; and (5) relation. Time, which in some manuscripts is also on the list of categories of *Phys.* V.1, is involved in

---

6. Cf. the claim of *Phys.* II.1, 192b34, that nature always is in a substrate, and further, see *Phys.* II.1, 193a36–b8, where Aristotle submits that form, rather than matter, is the internal source of motion and rest, because it is related to matter as actuality to potentiality. This latter claim is reformulated in *Met.* Δ.4, 1015a15–16, where Aristotle claims that matter is called nature on account of having the capacity to receive form, which is nature in the strict sense.

7. See e.g. *De An.* II.4, 415b8–27, where after identifying the soul as substance (i.e., as form), and as moving cause, the passage specifies a meaning in which the soul is also a special final cause, as the beneficiary (*hōi*) of the processes in the living being.

all forms of motion (see e.g., *Phys.* V.4, 227b24–26, and VIII.8, 262a2–5), but there is no motion in respect of time. Changes of relations are, on the other hand, accidental, as they occur also in entities in which no change occurs at all, if the entity to which they stand in relation undergoes some change (*Phys.* V.2, 225b11–13). Hence Aristotle can claim that there are as many types of motion and change as there are kinds of being (*Phys.* III.1, 201a8–9 = *Met.* K.9, 1065b13–14), meaning only the first four of these kinds. He calls these changes generation and corruption for change according to substance, alteration for change according to quality, augmentation and diminution for change according to quantity, and locomotion for change according to place.

There is an interesting variation in Aristotle's vocabulary, which has caused a lot of ink to flow. In some passages he uses the general term "motion" (*kinēsis*) as the generic term for all kinds of changes, whereas other passages restrict *kinēsis* to changes according to quality, quantity and place, and use the term *metabolē* as the general term to cover the *kinēseis* and the change according to substance. This has been, among commentators, the origin of some chronological hypotheses about the final form of Aristotle's doctrine. We will not decide on a matter that is actually undecidable. There is nevertheless a difference between generation and corruption on the one hand and all other changes on the other, which reflects the difference between substance and all the other categories.

Within the four domains in which genuine change can occur, change always requires the existence of a potentiality that can be actualized. But change is neither identical to this potentiality, nor to the lack of a property, nor, without further qualifications, to the actuality which is acquired when the potentiality is actualized (*Phys.* III.2, 201b33–35). It is a special kind of actuality, the actuality of the potential in so far as it is potential (*Phys.* III.1, 201a27–29). Aristotle's formulation strongly suggests that the potentiality actualized in the process of change is not a separate and independent potentiality for motion, alongside the entity's potentiality for the end-state of the process: the process of, say, house-building, and the end result, the house, are different actualizations of the same potentiality of a set of materials that is buildable into a house. Not only would Aristotle's definition be uninformative and circular otherwise – amounting to the tautologous claim that change is the actualization of the capacity for change – the further qualification in the definition, that change is the actuality of the potential *in so far as it is potential*, would be completely idle. This further restriction is meant to select those among the different types of realizations of the same potentialities which, as Aristotle stresses, are the incomplete actualities of these potentialities. Aristotle can further add that the potentiality actualized in the process is an incomplete potentiality only (*Phys.* III.2, 201b32–33). Accordingly, potentialities for change are readmitted into the ontology. Nevertheless, they do not feature as potentialities in their own right, but as the incomplete variants of the fundamental potentiality for an end result.

It is important to note that potentiality in this discussion throughout excludes actuality. In a formulation closely matching the formulation of the principle of non-contradiction, Aristotle asserts that "some things are the same [= have the same properties, are the same substances] both in potentiality and in actuality, but not at the same time or not in the same respect, as e.g. [a thing is] warm in actuality and cold in potentiality" (*Phys.* III.1, 201a19–22). Hence Aristotle's definition can pick out this intermediate entity, which is the actuality of a potentiality that can no longer be present as potentiality once it has been replaced by the corresponding property in actuality.

If a motion has a mover, it is the duty of the entity effecting change to confer the requisite form on the object changed, as *Phys.* III.2, 202a9–11, puts it. But there are further important requirements for such a change to occur. First of all, these motions or changes occur through the interaction of two potentialities. One, the passive potentiality, is in the object undergoing change, the other, the active potentiality, is in the entity initiating change. The two potentialities need to match each other: when there is a potentiality for being heated in the object undergoing change, the process needs to be initiated by another object possessing an active potentiality for effecting heat. This is true to the extent that Aristotle can claim that the definition of passive potentiality is dependent on that of the active potentiality (*Met.* Θ.1, 1046a11–13). These two potentialities need to work in tandem, and, consequently, Aristotle can claim that there is only a single process going on, which is located in the entity moved. When a process of instruction occurs, it is identical to a process of knowledge acquisition, which happens in the mind of the learner. Hence although action and passion retain their categorical difference, because their account is different, what they subsist in, the motion, will be the same (*Phys.* III.3, 202b19–22).

Aristotle, however, does not only require the presence of a matching pair of active and passive capacities, but subscribes to an even stronger principle, that the cause must have the property it brings about in the effect. In Aristotle's favorite example: the human in actuality produces a human from the human in potentiality. The principle – which we could term the principle of causational synonymy – comes from Plato (see, e.g., *Phd.* 100b–101d), but Aristotle has his own reasons for endorsing it, as his science attests to the presence and operation of causally active forms at each level of analysis of the physical world.[8]

Hence, Aristotle's forms are the causally significant components of the substance effecting a change. Accordingly, when it comes to specifying the moving cause of an artifact, Aristotle refers to the art of the craftsman as the fundamental component operative in the change (See *GC* I.7, 324a29–35; *Phys.* II.3, 195b21–25). In cases where a living being is generated, it is the parental form which is transmitted to the newly emerging living being.[9]

It is, nevertheless, important to note that Aristotle restricts the principle of causal synonymy in different and subtle ways. Most importantly, there is a domain of cases in which a property of an object is actualized but is exempted from the requirements of this principle. The actualization of a property can be the continuation of a previous causal process to the extent that Aristotle claims it is the *second actuality*, following

---

8. On the earlier history of the principle of causational synonymy, see Mourelatos, THE CONCEPT OF THE UNIVERSAL IN SOME LATER PRE-PLATONIC COSMOLOGISTS, pp. 61–4.

9. In the generation of the elements, Aristotle describes their generator as "that which produces weight," or "that which produces lightness," at *Cael.* IV.3, 310a31–32. But elements are also exhaustively characterized by the pair of elemental properties hot–cold and dry–moist, and these are also causally operative in the processes when one elemental mass transforms another element, see *GC* I.7, 324b5–14; and cf. *Phys.* VIII.5, 257b9–10.

upon a previously acquired *first actuality*. To elucidate this distinction Aristotle contrasts the possession of knowledge, and the actual use of knowledge one has acquired beforehand (*De An.* II.5, 417a21–b27). In such a case the emergence of the second actuality does not require an additional external efficient cause. The operation of this first actuality, through which the actuality is reinforced and raised to a higher, more complete realization, can be the mere extension of the operation of the original efficient cause. Alternatively, the entity which has acquired this first actuality can already itself be causally responsible for its own activities, including the ones that bring it to a level of higher actuality. It is important to note that these claims are far from trivial: they rest on further claims that the very definitions of these first actualities (what it is to be an element, an animal, or knowledge) inseparably include these activities.

Second, the principle is couched in terms that do not include locomotions: it is substantial, qualitative, or quantitative form that is claimed to be transmitted through the efficacy of the cause. It is easy to see why: the way its location belongs to an entity is different from the way its other qualifications belong to it. Hence it would be extremely awkward to speak of a transmission of this qualification in the same way that one speaks of the transmission of the other three. Locomotions, then, form a separate case, which is not subsumed without further elucidation under the general scheme for causation.

Third, the principle of causational synonymy is restricted to substances at the end of *Met.* Z.9,[10] and in the first half of the same chapter the non-standard presence of some causally relevant forms may also be envisaged. Aristotle's example is that there is heat in motion, which produces heat in the body (*Met.* Z.9, 1034a26–27) when the doctor rubs the patient in the appropriate manner. This heat in the motion can be the presence of an active potentiality in the motion which is able to elicit heat in the body, without heat being predicable of motion itself.

All these restrictions notwithstanding, Aristotle can claim that the principle of causational synonymy remains universally valid. This is so, because all three restrictions above specify cases where Aristotle can claim that a preceding, more prominent cause has already satisfied the requirement: in the case of second actualities the first actuality was called into existence by a synonymous cause in the first place; locomotions, qualitative, and quantitative changes, even if not caused by a synonymous entity, can be part of a larger pattern of causation, in which a substance is caused by a substance of the same kind; and causal chains producing substances can be claimed to start out invariably from synonymous substances. This means that the two major paradigms of such causation are natural generation and artificial production, and in both cases the forms – the nature of the natural entity, and the art of the craftsman

---

10. Cf. *Met.* Λ.3, 1070a4–5, which announces the principle of synonymy for substantial items only, and *GC* I.5, 320b17–20, where the principle of causal synonymy is relaxed to the almost non-committal requirement that in some cases an instance of the same entity in actuality is causally efficacious, whereas in other cases the cause is an actuality, but not of the same kind as the effect. Aristotle's example for the latter is the process effecting rigidity: this does not require a cause that is actually rigid.

exercising his art[11] respectively – are the causally operative entities initiating change. This has wide-ranging consequences for the status of forms in several respects. First, the causal relevance of these forms shows that not just any arrangement or configuration can qualify as a full-fledged form. True, privations are also forms in some sense (*Phys.* II.1, 193b19–20), but this is not the same sense in which the causally operative forms, describable in evaluative terms, can be called forms. Moreover, the causal relevance of forms allows Aristotle to switch (e.g., in *GC* I.7) without further notice between the craftsman and the craft itself as the appropriate specification of the efficient cause in these cases. We should note that with the latter Aristotle specified causes that are unmoved. They do not effect motion by being in motion themselves, and since they are in one-sided contact with the entity they effect motion in, they are not under any reactive influence during this process either.

Aristotelian Kinematics

Most of the treatise called *Physics* – whether constituted as we have it by Aristotle himself or by later editors – is, quite naturally, devoted to a study of change. Many other notions considered in the *Physics*, like place, time, infinity, void (the conclusion about the void is that there is no void at all in the universe) are considered in their relation to change. Now Aristotle proposes in the *Physics* a subtle and grandiose theory of change and particularly of locomotion. This Aristotelian kinematics will be definitely toppled only by modern physics originating with Galileo.

Among changes, Aristotle recognizes the priority of locomotion (*phora*), and the priority of circular locomotion to all the other forms of locomotion. According to him any locomotion is either circular, or rectilinear, or a form mixed of the two. He considers such an affirmation as evident, on the assumption that a straight line and a circle are the only simple lines, and that, therefore, the simple movements are the movements which take place along a simple path. Furthermore, he postulates that all locomotions are either simple or composed of simple locomotions. Such a position has been criticized since Antiquity, within the Aristotelian school itself. Thus Simplicius (*In Cael.* 13.25) says that Xenarchus of Seleukia, a Peripatetic of the first century BCE, claimed that the helix of the cylinder was also a simple line "because any of its parts corresponds to any other." But, according to Aristotle, circular locomotion is simpler than rectilinear because it can be infinite and eternal. More precisely, Aristotle says that a rectilinear movement going eternally from A to B and from B to A is not a single

---

11. Aristotle can refer to the causally operative form in the mind of the craftsman as identical to the form of the emerging artificial object, but this is clearly a partial description only (*Met.* Z.7, 1032b11–14; for a restricted, more circumspect identification of form and craft, see *Met.* Λ.4, 1070b33 and *Met.* Λ.10, 1075b10): the form of the object in the craftsman's mind needs to include all the relevant information of the rules of the trade about how to effect this particular form in the matter; it has to be embedded in (a workable portion of) the craft itself (see *Phys.* II.1, 193b12–17, for the difference of the forms of the cause and of the effect in artificial change).

movement since there is a stop at each extremity, as we shall see later. There is in any case no actual infinite line in Aristotle's world.

Moreover, among the circular locomotions, only one that is uniform, i.e. with a constant speed, can be eternal, since a locomotion that accelerates or decelerates during an infinite time would have an infinitely great or small speed.

It is quite important to understand that the foundation of this doctrine is cosmological. Aristotle argues at the opening of *Physics* Book VIII that motion and change in the universe can have no beginning, because the occurrence of change presupposes a previous process of change. With this argument Aristotle can establish an eternal chain of motions and refute the claim that there could have been a previous stationary state of the universe. But the eternal presence of motion in the universe, Aristotle argues, needs to rely on an eternal cause that guarantees its persistence. If motion were present in the universe only through an unending succession of processes of finite duration, the occurrence of every constitutive process within the series would be contingent, rendering the whole series a contingent one. Hence he postulates that the infinite succession of finite processes in the universe depends on an eternal motion (or on several eternal motions), namely the eternal revolution of the heavenly spheres, which in turn depends on one or several unmoved movers (*Phys.* VIII.6, 258b26–259a9).

The priority of the eternal celestial revolutions, furthermore, guarantees the causal finitude of the universe. This is so, even though there are infinite causal chains: since male parents are the efficient causes of their offspring, and Aristotelian species are eternal, behind every single individual of the species there is an infinite series of male ancestors, each causally responsible for the subsequent members in the series. Nevertheless the finite sublunary universe on its own would already have reached a deadlock, a state of complete separation of the elemental masses into their con-centrically arranged natural places, were it not for the constant excitation caused by the celestial motions, producing heat in the sublunary domain, especially in the immediate vicinity of the sun (see *Cael.* II.7, 289a19–35; and cf. the special case of the physician's rub causing heat in the body of the patient mentioned above, which will turn out to be analogous to the most fundamental interaction between the celestial and the sublunary domains).[12] Given the role of celestial motion in sublunary change, Aristotle will be entitled to assert that the cause of the human being is his or her father, and besides, the sun and its annual path along the ecliptic.[13]

The eternal celestial revolutions provide a causal support mechanism for each and every sublunary being, embedded in finite causal chains of sublunary processes. This eternal maintenance, in turn, allows for the presence of infinite sublunary causal chains,

12. According to Aristotle, the sun is not warm by itself, warmth being produced by the friction of its movement on the air due to its motion. This is true for all the celestial bodies (*Cael.* II.7, 289a19).

13. See *Met.* Λ.5, 1071a14–17, where Aristotle also mentions that the sun and its motion along the ecliptic are moving causes but are not instances of the same form as their effects – i.e., the principle of causational synonymy does not hold in their case. For an almost cryptically shorthand form of the same example, see *Phys.* II.2, 194b13.

like the infinite series of male ancestors any individual has. But the dependence of this infinite sublunary causal chain on the eternal celestial motions can always be spelled out in terms of the dependence relations that hold among eternal revolutions and finite sublunary causal chains.

Besides the distinctions between circular, rectilinear, and mixed movements on the one hand, and uniform and non-uniform movements on the other, there is a third crucial distinction: that between natural movements and movements against or contrary to nature. Each of the elements that compose the universe – earth, water, air, fire, and the fifth element which constitutes the celestial spheres – has a natural place. Fire naturally goes upward, earth downward, whereas air and water end up in the intermediate regions due to their natural tendency. The fifth element has a natural tendency to move in a circle around the center of the universe. Aristotle calls "natural place" the place toward which an element naturally goes, and "natural motion" the motion which leads this element to its natural place. An unnatural, or violent, movement, on the contrary, takes the mobile away from its natural place, as, for instance, the motion of a heavy body thrown upward does. When going away from its natural place the movement has a tendency to lose its "force" – as the stone which eventually stops its upward trajectory and falls down – whereas the movement which leads a thing toward its natural place increases its "force." In this respect the qualities "heavy" and "light" are not relative terms, but absolute ones (cf. O'Brien, 1981). Earth is heavy and fire is light, but one cannot say that fire is less heavy than earth, since fire is not heavy at all; or that earth is less light than fire, since earth is not light at all. We must notice that this is not true only of "pure" elements (which cannot be found in everyday life, since the element earth is not the earth we put in flowerpots, but a component that cannot be perceived except in combination with some others) but it is also true of the bodies we see around us. Those bodies act according to their main component: bodies which are mainly composed of earth go naturally downward, whereas fiery bodies go naturally upward. One of Aristotle's major presuppositions is that the division of motions into those that are natural and those that are contrary to nature is exhaustive. There are no changes to which the nature of the entity would be indifferent or neutral. We must note, however, that Aristotle's account of heavenly motions requires a class of locomotions of such an intermediate status, because he holds both that there is no forced motion in the celestial domain, and at the same time that planetary motions are the result of the composition of rotations of several different spheres, each of which performs a part of these motions as its own, whereas the other component is as it were superadded to it (*Cael.* II.12, 293a9–11; cf. *Met.* Λ.6, 1072a9–18).

By means of these three distinctions, Aristotle intends to build up a theory of change that includes kinds of changes that seem absolutely heterogeneous to each other, not only all the changes that occur in living beings – locomotion, and also growth, assimilation of food, decay, etc. – but also the movement of projectiles and all the transformations of inanimate objects. The fundamental insight of the Aristotelian theory of movement is that everything moved is moved by a mover which is in immediate contact with what is moved. This contact is of one of two great kinds: in the case of living beings the mover is internal; in the other cases the mover is external and the contact is by contiguity. This is consistent with the Aristotelian conception of a world deprived of void. The moved is moved as long as the mover moves it. To make this situation intelligible, Aristotle, once again, appeals to his distinction between actuality and potentiality. He does not say that movement is simply produced by the mover, for the mobile must to some extent have the movement in itself. As we pointed out earlier, Aristotle's analyses of actuality show that two things may have the same actuality; thus the instructor's teaching is the same actuality as the student's learning (*Phys.* III.3, 202b6−8). Movement will, therefore, be the common activity of the mover and the moved. Consequently, movement is not something that can continue to exist by itself, since its existence depends on the persistence of the action of the mover. Rest, and most particularly, natural rest, on the contrary, is, according to Aristotle, a *state*. This is one of the main differences between Aristotelian and modern kinematics.

In Book VII of the *Physics*, Aristotle makes this contiguity of the mover and the moved a little clearer, in the case of the three kinds of movement (in the narrow sense of this word): locomotion, alteration, and quantitative change. In the case of locomotion, for instance, he distinguishes four kinds of locomotion, of which all the others are varieties or compositions: pulling, pushing, carrying, and twirling. Packing and combing, for example, are two forms of pushing – pushing together and pushing apart. But one can go further and say that carrying and twirling are reducible to forms of pulling and pushing as well: these are the two fundamental forms of locomotion. In the case of alteration, Aristotle gives the example of sense perception in which the perceived object alters the sense. The result is that, in this case too, there is a common activity of the mover and the moved which are in contact either with or without an intermediary, since "color is continuous with the light, and the light with sight" (*Phys.* VII.2, 245a7). When considering the requirement of contiguity in the case of augmentation and diminution, Aristotle clearly has in mind vital processes.

This kinematics, which is at the same time a dynamics, bestowed to following generations a set of problems which were obstacles to the development of modern science. Let us consider two of those problems.

Projectile motion is not easy to deal with from an Aristotelian perspective, because once a javelin has left the hand, it seems to continue its trajectory "by itself," and, therefore, it seems that there is no further contiguity between the mover and the moved. In such a case, Aristotle says, it is the medium, namely the air, which transmits the impulsion given by the hand and continues to transmit it up to the end of the movement. To be sure, Aristotle is not very explicit about how and the reason why the air keeps and transmits movement. In the treatise *On the Heavens* III.2, he merely remarks that "the force uses air as an instrument": air is able to transmit the causal influence it receives from the mover to further pockets of air, exerting a force that would later be called the *vis impressa*. This theory has been criticized, and even ridiculed, since antiquity. Thus Philoponus recommends to soldiers to use bellows as a propeller for their javelins . . . (*In Phys.* 641.19). But the case of natural motion is no less obscure. We might even want to paraphrase this as the query: Whence does the force effecting these motions originate? Take the example of a falling stone. Aristotle describes its movement downward, i.e., toward the center of the earth, if there is no obstacle, as a natural movement – a movement toward its natural place. The stone indeed is mainly composed of earthy ingredients and is, therefore, heavy by nature. Aristotle also notices that this movement accelerates, contrary to what happens in the case of the unnatural movement of the javelin. Finally, Aristotle thinks that the speed increases proportionally to the weight of the falling body. We will return to this.

Aristotle's Theory of the Continuum

On the occasion of his analysis of motion in the *Physics*, Aristotle provides the history of science with one of his most remarkable contributions in proposing a theory of the continuum of unprecedented generality. According to him, indeed, every change is continuous, and when this continuity is interrupted this means that the change has also been interrupted to be replaced by rest or another change. Here too the historical context is crucial. In the last three books of the *Physics* Aristotle criticizes two adversaries who have not much in common, namely Zeno of Elea and the Atomists. We have, then, a play with three protagonists.

Aristotle himself mentions that Atomism claimed to answer the Parmenidean challenge (*GC* I.8). For the atoms, being ungenerated, imperishable, and immutable, in a way inherited the characteristics of Parmenidean being. Their aggregations make the different things that exist in the universe.[14] Zeno of Elea, the second great Eleatic figure after Parmenides, shares an important position with Aristotle on this question: both of them claim that the doctrine of indivisible magnitudes is incoherent. For if a continuous magnitude is taken to be composed of indivisibles – i.e., if it is not indefinitely divisible – there are but two possibilities. Either the indivisible is truly a magnitude and, in that case, why can it not also be divided? or the indivisible is not truly a magnitude and, in that case, how can an addition of non-magnitudes result in a magnitude? From this refutation of the theory of indivisible magnitudes Zeno draws the radical conclusion that a continuum is unintelligible. According to what we know of his positions – here we have to remember that our main source for Zeno's doctrine is precisely Aristotle's *Physics* and the commentators of the Aristotelian *Physics* – Zeno bases his criticism of a continuum on a criticism of an essentially continuous reality, viz. motion. If, on the one hand, a continuum – in this case length and time – is composed of indivisibles, how can an arrow that has been launched go from one place to another? If, on the other hand, a continuum is infinitely divisible, how can a motion begin, since there is always a moment before the moment at which the motion begins? All this is based on the impossibility of there being an actual infinity.

Aristotle objects both to the hypothesis of indivisible magnitudes and to Zeno. It is worth mentioning that mathematicians had already made an attempt, actually a successful one, to circumvent Zeno's critique. Eudoxus is the author of a general theory of proportions that encompasses commensurable as well as incommensurable magnitudes (Cf. Euclid's *Elements* Book V, def. 5, and, in this volume, see Mueller's GREEK MATHEMATICS, pp. 700–4). Accordingly, this definition sees no difficulty in speaking about magnitudes being in the same ratio no matter whether they are commensurable or incommensurable with each other. Aristotle not only knew of this general theory of mathematical ratios, but he also regarded it as a revolutionary

14. On fifth-century atomism, see Curd, PARMENIDES AND AFTER, in this volume.

novelty of the previous generation (*APo.* I.5, 74a18). In the last books of the *Physics*, and particularly in Book VI, he lays down a general theory of continuous physical magnitudes which, though definitely refuting the doctrines of indivisibles, reestablishes, against Zeno, the possibility of movement, and, by the same token, the possibility of physics.

Aristotle's theory is a general one too, because he does not merely apply the notion of a continuum to lengths, surfaces, and volumes, as mathematicians before him did, but also to time and change, in claiming of magnitudes, times, and changes that either all of them are composed of indivisibles, or none of them is (*Phys.* VI.1) (cf. Waschkies, 1991).

In Book VI of the *Physics*, Aristotle proposes a rich and surprising theory of the continuum, which, as Simplicius says, goes beyond the common conception of what a magnitude is (*In Phys.* 925.7ff.). This theory puts together two theses apparently incompatible with each other. On the one hand, in every continuous line there is nothing but points, and when a line is divided by an intersection with another line, such a division is made at a point. On the other hand, a line is not made of points, because points having no extension are not parts of the line. This is true for a continuous time and instants (called "nows" by Aristotle), and for a continuous movement and what would correspond to an instant in the domain of movement, which Aristotle calls "*kinēma*". Using the evident truth, that "a thing is divided into what it is made of" (VI.1, 231b10), he objects that if these magnitudes consisted of indivisible entities like points or "nows," they would have to be divisible into these very components. But relations between length and points, time and instants are neither a relation between a whole and its parts (points are not segments of the line), nor a relation between a container and something contained (points are not in a line as water is in a glass), nor a relation between components and a compound (points are not to a line as an atom of hydrogen is to water or, in Arisotelian terms, as earth is to flesh). To describe such a relation Aristotle uses a term which was to have a remarkable fate in mathematics in saying that point and instant are "limits" of the line and of the time.

Aristotle's answer to Zeno's paradoxes is, in fact, based on a new approach to the relationship between the finite and the infinite. According to Zeno, if there is an infinite number of points in a finite line, a mobile which traverses a finite magnitude AB has to go through an infinite number of places intermediary between A and B. By Aristotle's lights this argument confuses two kinds of infinity, which are carefully distinguished in the *Physics*. The finite line is not composed of an infinite number of finite magnitudes, that is, in Aristotelian terms, the infinite which is in the finite line is not an infinite "by addition" but "by division." Aristotle also says that any magnitude is infinite, not in actuality, but by division (*Phys.* III.6, 206a16). This doctrine becomes clearer if we refer to two different operations that Aristotle contrasts with each other in Book III of the *Physics*. On the one hand one finds what Aristotle calls "the bisections of a magnitude" (III.7, 207b11), that is the fact that any magnitude can be divided in two parts, these parts being in turn divisible, and so on. In a more general formulation, we have: "if we take a determinate part of a finite magnitude and add another part determined by the same ratio, we shall not traverse the given magnitude" (III.6, 206b7–9), which is, after all, a version of the first of Zeno's argument on the impossibility of motion (the moving object, before reaching the end of a finite length, must first reach the half of this length, and so on, cf. VI.9, 239b11). This infinite divisibility of a magnitude shows, better than any other example, what is the status of the infinite in Aristotle: "the infinite exists in no other way but potentially" (III.6, 206b12). On the other hand, Aristotle remarks that "every finite magnitude is exhausted by means of any determinate quantity however small" (206b11), which is taken as an *axiom* by Archimedes (*On the Sphere and Cylinder* I, axiom 5; cf. Euclid, *Elem.* V, def. 4). One can see here the rejection of any infinitesimal approach of mathematics as well as of physics, and the foundation of the science of the continuum on the idea that it is irreducible to the discontinuum.

Aristotle shared with almost all the Greek thinkers the conviction that infinity would be contrary to perfection and an obstacle to scientific knowledge. With his doctrine of the indefinitely divisible continuity he found a way to integrate infinity within his finite universe.

One of the major positions of Aristotelian kinematics is that every change happens in time and takes a certain amount of time. Since an instant is not a certain amount of time but the limit of a time, there can be no movement in an instant. It is, therefore, impossible to determine the very instant at which a movement begins, because once such an instant has been determined, one can always imagine an instant previous to it which would be the true beginning of the movement. The same is true of a state of rest following a movement: it is impossible to assign a first instant for it without falling into an infinite regress. Now it is always possible to interrupt a movement by cutting it at some instant in a time. Aristotle devoted attention to the problem of the unity of a movement. According to him, a movement has three components: the mobile, that "in which" the movement takes place (the trajectory of a locomotion, for example) and the time in which the movement is completed. A movement is "absolutely one" as long as none of these factors has been changed. A locomotion from A to B and from B to A, for instance, is not absolutely one since it is interrupted. Any movement which is one is, by the same token, continuous, and this does not mean that it has to be uniform. The beginning of a movement may therefore be defined negatively as the instant at which the preceding movement (or rest) ends.

One case has been taken to contradict this doctrine. Aristotle sometimes recognizes that a change occurs instantaneously, for instance, the freezing of water (*Phys.* VIII.3, 253b26). But freezing is an event, and not a change, that happens at the end of a continuous change (or of several continuous changes, if the process is interrupted), viz. the cooling of the water.

The Causes of Elemental Motions

Book VIII of the *Physics* argues for the thesis that for each motion, whether natural or contrary to nature, there must be a mover. We have seen that in cases of forced motion movers are present in a perspicuous way, and that this is not necessarily so with natural motions. Apart from the cases in which the nature of the entity is at the same time its moving (efficient) cause – i.e., apart from living beings, whose nature, the soul, is their form and an efficient cause as well – the mover is inconspicuous in the remaining large class of natural motions, the natural motions of the elements, namely, the falling of heavy bodies and the movement upward of light ones. For in the case of the falling stone this motion must also have an external mover, since the stone is not a living being, and, therefore, the cause cannot be its "soul." But if the center of the earth exerted an attraction on the stone, the stone would have to receive this attraction through a medium – air, for example. And what is the role of the stone in the motion? It must obviously have a salient role to be called an entity which moves according to its nature. Similarly, how will we explain the acceleration of natural motion, e.g., of a falling body? Aristotle says that "Earth moves more quickly the nearer it is to the center of the earth" (*Cael.* I.8, 277a28). Why is that so, given Aristotle's kinematics?

Simplicius (*In Phys.* 1212.30) takes Aristotle to assimilate this coming nearer to the natural place to an actualization: when earth goes downward and fire upward "they go towards their proper actuality" (*Phys.* VIII.4, 255a30), because the actuality of the heavy and the light is to be respectively up and down (see 255b11). The passage in which Aristotle deals with this question in the most explicit, if not the clearest, way is *Cael.* IV.3. In this chapter Aristotle describes the motion of each body towards its natural place as "a motion towards its own form" (310a33). Then comes a controversial passage:

> For something to move to its own place is for it to move to its like. For the successive members of the series are like one another: water, I mean, is like air and air like fire . . . [and in the other direction] air is like water, but water is like earth; for the relation of each outer body to that which is next within it is that of form to matter (310b10–15, trans. J. L. Stocks)

Stocks' interpretation should probably be adopted: "The 'place' (centre and extremity as explained) gives form to the body, and the body in reaching its place attains its form, i.e., completes the transition from potentiality to actuality. In a sense, then, if the potential is like the actual, it moves 'to its like'" (Stocks n. 3 ad loc.).

Nevertheless, the nature, the internal principle of motion and rest of the elements is not the moving cause of these motions, Aristotle claims, because if it were, then it would be up to the elementary masses to determine when they perform such a motion. Moreover the principle of causational synonymy rules out that a homogeneous mass, without an internal demarcation of the moved component and the mover, could possibly move itself (*Phys.* VIII.4, 255a5–18). This is so because in case one part of a homogeneous body could move another part, this would mean that change would occur even though no transmission of a causally relevant property from the active part to the exactly similar passive one could be specified. This implies that even though the question why the elements move to their natural places can be answered by an appeal to their respective natures as causes ("the cause is that they are naturally towards somewhere, and this is what it is to be light and to be heavy" *Phys.* VIII.4, 255b13–17), this does not yet specify their mover. Since their thrust is in a single direction, the elements cannot circumvent fairly simple obstacles they encounter on their way (a sealed container can retain air under water; the roof stays put pressing down on the walls of a building, etc.); hence whoever removes these obstacles is causally responsible for the ensuing elemental motions. But someone who removes an obstacle will not be the proper moving cause, without further qualification. For the

288

identification of the moving cause of these locomotions Aristotle invokes his distinction of two potentialities. Some heavy material is potentially light, since it can be transformed into a light material in a process of generation, but the emerging light material is still potential in a sense until it has acquired its full-fledged status, which involves that it has arrived at that region of the cosmos which is its natural place, or is as near to its natural place as the element can get within the cosmos (see Gill, forthcoming).

This will then suggest that the natural locomotion of the elements is a possibly postponed, completing stage within a single overarching process, and hence in these cases Aristotle can identify the cause of the second stage of the process with the efficient cause of the first stage, the entity which generated the element in the first place (*Phys.* VIII.4, 256a1, and *Cael.* IV.3, 310a31–32).

Unmoved Movers

Once it is established that there is a mover for each change, the finite causal chains can be followed up to the primary instance of motion, the celestial revolutions, the sun's motion along the ecliptic responsible for seasonal changes being foremost among them. Whether the cosmos has unmoved or moved movers, moreover, and whether the universe is causally closed or needs some continuous external causal influence for its preservation, depends then ultimately on the status of celestial motions.

Revolutions in the celestial realm are the natural motions of the special element that constitutes the celestial spheres. This, however, does not exclude that they are in need of an external unmoved mover: the motions of the sublunary elements also occur under the influence of a moving cause. Nevertheless, the celestial bodies cannot be moved by an external mover of the same sort as the sublunary elements. These celestial bodies are eternal and ungenerated; hence Aristotle cannot appeal to the entity which produced them as responsible for their locomotions. As they do not encounter any hindrance during their revolutions, there is no room for an admittedly accidental mover which would remove the obstacles. Nevertheless, as celestial revolutions are motions, albeit eternal ones, they include some component of potentiality, which is actualized in the motion, and hence this potential component is in need of an actuality as a mover. This requirement implies that whatever can be the mover of these eternal motions needs to be in actuality without any restrictions (*Met.* Λ.6). Moreover, such an entity has to possess an infinite power,[15] which it communicates to the moved celestial sphere; hence it cannot be divisible and cannot have extension (*Phys.* VIII.10).

All this testifies to the exceptional status of the first movement, and behind it, of the first mover in the universe. The mover of these spheres is a pure actuality, but this actuality is not what is transmitted in causation. As we have seen above, this would not be exceptional yet: locomotion need not be caused on the transmission model of causation. But all such locomotions could be embedded in larger patterns of causation which observed the principle of causational synonymy, and it is exactly such a larger

---

15. The word used here for power is *dunamis*, but as the unmoved mover is nothing but actuality it cannot refer to an intrinsic infinite *potentiality* of the mover.

pattern of causation which is missing in the case of celestial motions. Instead, what we hear in *Met.* Λ.6 is that the mover moves as an object of love and striving, which comes perilously close to abandoning the claims of *Physics* VIII about an unmoved mover which is an efficient cause of the motions of the cosmos.

Nevertheless, this role of the unmoved mover is paralleled by the ultimate unmoved factor of the self-motion of animals, the object of desire, which moves the faculty of desire, and then this faculty in turn causes the locomotion of the animal (see *De An.* III.10, 433a9–30; cf. *MA* 6). Although the details of this account do not carry over to the celestial case without difficulty,[16] Aristotle may feel entitled to use it as setting out, in the terminology of his physics, the mode of operation of a supra-physical entity without which the universe cannot function and persist.

Bibliography

Texts, Translations, and Commentaries

Allan, D. J. (1936). *Aristotelis De Caelo libri IV*. Oxford: Clarendon Press.

Charlton, W. (1970). *Aristotle's Physics Books I and II*. Clarendon Aristotle Series. Oxford: Clarendon Press. (2nd edn. 1992.)

Dalimier, C. and Pellegrin, P. (2004). *Aristote, Traité du ciel*. Text, Translation, and Notes. Paris: Flammarion.

Diels, H. (1882, 1885). *Simplicius. In Aristotelis Physicorum commentaria* (CAG 9, 10). Berlin: Reimer.

Fobes, F. H. (1919). *Aristotelis Meteorologicorum libri IV*. Cambridge, Mass.: Harvard University Press.

Guthrie, W. K. C. (1971). *Aristotle. On the Heavens*. Loeb Classical Library. Cambridge, Mass.: Harvard University Press / London: Heinemann.

Heiberg, I. L. (1894). *Simplicius. In Aristotelis De Caelo commentaria* (CAG 7). Berlin: Reimer.

Joachim, H. H. (1926). *Aristotle, On Coming-To-Be and Passing-Away (De Generatione et Corruptione)*. A Revised Text with Introduction and Commentary. Oxford: Clarendon Press.

Lee, H. D. P. (1952). *Aristotle. Meteorologica*. Loeb Classical Library. Cambridge, Mass.: Harvard University Press / London: Heinemann.

Moraux, P. (1965). *Aristote. Du Ciel*. Text, translation, notes. Paris: Les Belles Lettres.

Nussbaum, M. C. (1978). *Aristotle's De Motu Animalium*. Text with Translation, Commentary, and Interpretive Essays. Princeton: Princeton University Press.

Pellegrin, P. (2000, 2002). *Aristote, Physique*. Translation and Notes. Paris: Flammarion.

Ross, W. D. (1936). *Aristotle, Physics*. A Revised Text with Introduction and Commentary. Oxford: Clarendon Press.

Ross, W. D. and Fobes, F. H. (1929). *Theophrastus. Metaphysics*. Oxford: Clarendon Press. (Repr. in 1982 by Olms.)

Stocks, J. L. (1930). *Aristotle, De Caelo*. Oxford: Clarendon Press.

16. Indeed, Theophrastus *Met.* 8–9, 5a28–5b10, remarks that the fact that the mover of the celestial revolutions is an object of striving would imply that the first change the unmoved mover effects would be the very striving in the souls of the celestial bodies, and not the celestial revolutions.

Vitelli, H. (1887, 1888). *Philoponus. In Aristotelis Physicorum commentaria* (CAG 16, 17). Berlin: Reimer.

Williams, C. J. F. (1982). *Aristotle's De Generatione et Corruptione.* Clarendon Aristotle Series. Oxford: Clarendon Press.

Works Cited

Berti, E. (1985). "La suprématie du mouvement local selon Aristote: ses conséquences et ses apories." In J. Wiesner (ed.), *Aristoteles Werk und Wirkung* (Festschrift for Paul Moraux). (vol. 1, pp. 123–50). Berlin: de Gruyter.

De Gandt, F. and Souffrin, F. (1991). *La Physique d'Aristote et les conditions d'une science de la nature.* Paris: Vrin.

Duhem, P. (1913). *Le système du monde.* Paris: Hermann.

Gill, M. L. (forthcoming). "The Theory of the Elements in *De Caelo* III and IV." In A. C. Bowen and C. Wildberg (eds.), *A Companion to Aristotle's Cosmology: Collected Papers on the* De Caelo.

Mendell, H. (2000). "The Trouble with Eudoxus." In P. Suppes, J. M. E. Moravcsik, and H. Mendell (eds.), *Ancient and Medieval Traditions in the Exact Sciences* (pp. 59–138). Stanford: CSLI Publications.

O'Brien, D. (1981). *Theories of Weight in the Ancient World. Four Essays on Democritus, Plato and Aristotle. A Study in the Development of Ideas.* (vol. 1): *Democritus Weight and Size.* Paris: Les Belles Lettres and Leiden: Brill.

Solmsen, F. (1960). *Aristotle's System of the Physical World. A Comparison with his Predecessors.* Ithaca, NY: Cornell University Press.

Waschkies, H.-J. (1991). "Mathematical Continuum and Continuity of Movement." In F. De Gandt and F. Souffrin, F. (eds.), *La Physique d'Aristote et les conditions d'une science de la nature* (pp. 151–79). Paris: Vrin.

Waterlow, S. (1982). *Nature, Change, and Agency in Aristotle's* Physics. Oxford: Clarendon Press.

Further reading

Bodnár, I. (1997). "Movers and Elemental Motions in Aristotle." *Oxford Studies in Ancient Philosophy*, 15, 81–117.

Gill, M. L. and Lennox, J. G. (eds.). (1994). *Self-Motion: From Aristotle to Newton.* Princeton: Princeton University Press

Graham, D. W. (1999). *Aristotle's Physics VIII.* Clarendon Aristotle Series. Oxford: Clarendon Press.

Hussey, E. (1983). *Aristotle's Physics III–IV.* Clarendon Aristotle Series. Oxford: Clarendon Press.

Judson, L. (ed.). (1991). *Aristotle's Physics. A Collection of Essays.* Oxford: Clarendon Press.

Legatt, S. (1995). *Aristotle, On The Heavens I and II, with an Introduction, Translation and Commentary.* Warminster: Aris and Phillips.

16

Aristotle's Biology and Aristotle's Philosophy

JAMES G. LENNOX

Introduction

The first book of *On the Parts of Animals* (*PA*) begins by outlining its purpose, which is to establish a set of standards for judging natural investigations (639a15). The next four chapters pursue this purpose, discussing the appropriate level of generality for such studies, the modes of causality and necessity to be used, the method of division, the means of identifying natural kinds, and much more. Judging by the questions asked and the examples used, Aristotle is focused exclusively on the investigation of animals – yet he never describes his focus in such terms. Rather, he claims to be developing standards for *natural* inquiry, and in particular for inquiry into those natural things that come to be and pass away. It is not until the fifth chapter, which begins by dividing up the natural domain into those things that are eternal and those that come to be and pass away, that the discussion is said to be about animals in particular.

> Since we have completed stating the way things appear to us about the divine things, it remains to speak about *animal nature*, omitting nothing within our power, whether of lesser or greater esteem. For even in the study of animals disagreeable to perception, the nature that crafted them likewise provides extraordinary pleasures to those who are able to know their causes and are by nature philosophers. (*PA* I.5, 645a4–10)

The opening sentence of this chapter contrasts those naturally constituted substantial beings (*ousiai*) that are eternal with those that partake of generation and perishing (644b23–24), and describes the former as divine, setting the context for the contrast in the above quotation. But now, and finally, the discussion is said to be about *animal* nature (*peri tēs zōikēs phuseōs*), even about the natures of animals disagreeable to the senses.

The puzzle is, of course, why a discussion that appears to be exclusively zoological in focus is consistently characterized as developing standards not *merely* for the study of living things, but for the investigation of nature quite generally. One way of responding to this puzzle is to say that it derives from an anachronism. Biology, it is sometimes said, is a new science, an invention of the nineteenth century. To imagine that a set of treatises written in ancient Greece with titles such as *On the Parts of Animals*, *On the Generation of Animals* (*GA*), *On Animal Locomotion* (*IA*) or *History of Animals* (*HA*), constitutes an early stage in the history of biology projects our labels on to alien territory, and causes the reader to search in vain for the principles and methods of biological science where there could not possibly be any.[1]

This answer is easy, but wrong-headed. By any reasonable modern definition of biology, Aristotle's "animal studies" are biological.[2] They are, that is, general, theoretical investigations of the living world, aimed at systematically organizing data collected by careful and controlled observation and experiment (if systematic dissection done for the sake of answering anatomical and functional questions is a form of experiment) and at integrated causal explanation of these data. Though Aristotle clearly sees them as part of a *wider* investigation of nature, they appear to be (this is what *PA* I is all about) a *distinctive* part with *distinctive* standards of investigation. (On the place of biology in Aristotle's broader investigation of nature, see Bodnár and Pellegrin, ARISTOTLE'S PHYSICS AND COSMOLOGY, in this volume.)

For a less easy but more adequate response, we need to turn to Aristotle's metaphysics. Modern metaphysical prejudices are reductionist. We expect someone who is talking about general principles of natural investigation to be focused primarily on the ultimate material constituents of the world. After all, is that not the *obvious* way to achieve generality?

Obvious to us, perhaps – but not to Aristotle. Suppose only a subset, and a rather impoverished subset at that, of the principles that govern natural processes operate at the level of nature's material constituents. Suppose that a full and complete understanding of *all* the principles and causes of natural things emerges only in the domain of *living* nature. If *this* were your point of view, an essay devoted to defining the standards appropriate to animal investigation would at the same time be seen as providing standards proper to the investigation of nature in its most robust sense.

I shall argue later that these are Aristotle's suppositions, and that this explains the fact that *PA* I.1–5 is in fact about the proper way to investigate animals and to judge such investigations and yet does not get around to saying so until chapter 5. We find the converse pattern in Book II of Aristotle's *Physics*. It purports to be a full-blown development of the principles for natural investigation. But this very quickly turns into a defense of the study of both material and formal nature, and of giving priority to the formal nature, which turns out to be that for the sake of which natural changes occur, as well. This focus on teleologically organized composites of matter and form carries over to the discussion of causality and chance in chapters 3–7 and to the argument for the extension of teleological reasoning to the study of nature in chapters 8 and 9. Though this book purports to be developing an adequate account of the

---

1.   Coleman (1977, p. 1): "Biology was introduced in the nineteenth century. First came the word; a century of incessant activity was needed to create a thriving science." Cunningham (1999, p. 22): "And yet a little reflection will remind us that biology, as a term, as a discipline, as a domain of knowledge, is of very recent construction."
2.   According to Webster's *New World Dictionary, College Edition*, for example, "biology" refers to "the science of living organisms and life processes, including the study of growth, structure, and reproduction." When I use the phrase "Aristotle's biology," I mean to suggest there is a group of treatises within the Aristotelian corpus that makes a contribution to such a science. I don't mean to suggest that it looks at all like ours.

principles and causes of nature generally, the focus seems to be on *living* nature; in chapter 8, for example, he claims to be arguing for the extension of teleology to *nature*, not, or not merely, to *plants* and *animals*. And yet the examples he uses to illustrate the teleology of nature are all organic. Again, or so I shall argue, this makes good sense from an Aristotelian perspective. The focus *is* on living nature, where form and goal-directed actions are dominant. Of course the materials that go into the constitution of animals also often require teleological explanation, but always by reference to form and function. One will have to explain how material elements, operating according to their own natures, nevertheless change, meld, and are organized into living systems of tissues and organs.

So the answer to our puzzle seems to be this: when Aristotle thinks of the study of nature, he is thinking, first and foremost, of the study of *living* nature. One often sees this habit of thought in unexpected places. In *Metaphysics* E.1, for example, he is attempting to distinguish first philosophy, the study of being *qua* being, from the two other domains of theoretical knowledge, the studies of nature and of mathematics. In characterizing the study of nature (*phusikē epistēmē*), as the study of combinations of matter and form, he gives a list of examples:

> for example eye, face, flesh, bone, animal generally, leaf, root, bark, plant generally (for of none of these is there an account without change, but always the account includes matter). (1026a1–3)

These – animals, plants, and their parts – are the sorts of thing the natural scientist studies. Of course, a full understanding of them must include an understanding of the materials that constitute them as well; and we will see that Aristotle takes this obligation very seriously.

Biology and the Theory of Knowledge[3]

But if Aristotle believes that the study of nature is first and foremost the study of living nature, and if the investigation of nature is, as *Metaphysics* E.1 states, one form of theoretical understanding (*theoretikē epistēmē*), then an investigation of Aristotle's study of animals has an important role to play in any investigation of his epistemology, or theory of knowledge. This is true not only because the investigation of animals is aimed at theoretical knowledge, but because it is by far Aristotle's most sustained theoretical investigation, comprising (depending on which treatises you include) between 25 and 30 percent of Aristotle's extant writings. Moreover his single sustained contribution to epistemology, the *Posterior Analytics* (*APo.*), presents a theory of *scientific* knowledge, so that having a series of treatises that report the results of a sustained

---

3. Wolfgang Detel's discussion of Aristotle's *Analytics* in this volume, ARISTOTLE'S LOGIC AND THEORY OF SCIENCE, serves as valuable background to this section, especially in that we share the view that the biological works are conscious exercises in demonstrative science and thus valuable examples of Aristotle's theory of demonstration in practice.

scientific investigation carried out by its author may help us in understanding that work.[4]

At first pass, however, exploring Aristotle's biology for help in understanding his theory of knowledge seems unpromising. Notoriously, Aristotle's account of "demonstrative understanding" in the *APo.* applies paradigmatically to axiomatized, deductive systems based on self-evident first principles. If there were anything in fourth-century BCE Greece that would help us in understanding such a theory, surely it would be geometry, not biology.[5]

But here is where Aristotle's investigations of animals can help to shed light on the *Analytics* program. For they help us to see that the above description of the *Posterior Analytics* is a misleading caricature. In fact, a detailed comparison of its explorations of knowledge, inquiry, causality, division, definition and demonstration with Aristotle's biological inquiries, causal demonstrations, divisions and definitions provides us with a richer and more realistic picture of the *Analytics* program. The full case for this claim is to be found in research done over the past three decades.[6] Here there is only room for an outline of that case, and then one example.

The *Posterior Analytics* contains two books. The above caricature is a caricature of only one thread of the first six chapters of the first book. The second book announces itself as a sustained discussion of the different inquiries that are components of all scientific research.

4. I realize I am here sending up many red flags, which I will acknowledge without attempting to "run them down." There is an ongoing debate about how properly to characterize the *Posterior Analytics*. It is clear from the opening paragraph of the *Prior Analytics* that Aristotle saw the four books of our two "*Analytics*" as constituting a single project (see Detel, loc. cit.). The temptation to read the first two (*APr.*) as "formal logic" and the second two (*APo.*) as "philosophy of science" or "epistemology" should be resisted. But the previous sentence introduces *another* red flag. Twentieth-century philosophy has developed in such a way that the theory of knowledge and the philosophy of science appear to be very different enterprises. However, not only is this not the case for Aristotle, but it is arguably not generally true of the history of philosophy before Kant (see Burnyeat, 1981). Moreover, saying that *APo.* presents a theory of scientific knowledge will raise eyebrows. By adding the adjective "scientific" here, I mean to capture the idea that this work is concerned with such topics as the nature of proof, forms of inquiry and their relations, explanation, causality, and induction; and that it exemplifies these ideas by drawing on the practices of branches of mathematics and natural philosophy. Aristotle clearly intends it to be an abstract enough presentation to find application across the mathematical and natural sciences, occasionally using an example from each domain to illustrate a single abstract philosophical point. It is a matter of much dispute whether Aristotle imagines that the same is true of first philosophy or metaphysics.
5. Were this true it would be extremely unfortunate, since there is virtually nothing of Greek geometry extant before Euclid, who lived a generation after Aristotle. The burden of the next paragraph, however, is that it is not true. (For what we do know about geometry, see Mueller, GREEK MATHEMATICS TO THE TIME OF EUCLID, in this volume).
6. See Balme (1987a, 1987b); Bolton (1987, 1997); Charles (1990, 1997, 2000); Detel (1997, 1999, this volume); Gotthelf (1987, 1997a, 1997b); Kullmann (1974, 1985, 1997, 1999); Lennox (1987a, 1990, 1997a, 1997b, 2001a, 2001b, 2001c); Lloyd (1990, 1996); Pellegrin (1982, 1986).

> The things about which we inquire are equal in number to the things we understand. We inquire about four things: *the fact, the reason why, if something is, what something is.* (*APo.* II.1, 89b23–25)

Moreover, these four inquiries are *paired*, and there is a natural *sequence* in each pair.

> When we know *the fact* we inquire about *the reason why* (e.g., knowing *that* it is eclipsed or *that* the earth moves, we inquire into *the reason why* it is eclipsed or *why* the earth moves). (*APo.* II.1, 89b29–31)

> And having come to know *that* it is, we inquire *what* it is (e.g., Then what is a god? Or what is a man?). (*APo.* II.1, 89b34–35)

Though it cannot be captured in a readable translation, it is important to know that what I have rendered "the fact," above, is literally "the that" – so in Greek it is obvious that the example, "that the moon is eclipsed," illustrates the first inquiry. More importantly, the last quoted passage above indicates that Aristotle is aiming to understand how these pairs of inquiries are related. For having begun to illustrate the distinction between inquiry *if* or *whether* something is and *what* it is with the question "whether there is or is not a centaur or a god," he then characterizes the knowledge achieved as "knowing that it is." This is codified in the next chapter by noting that "factual" inquiries take two forms, unqualified and predicative, the former being "existential" inquiries – are there centaurs? – the latter being "attributive" inquiries – is the moon suffering eclipse? Moreover, it becomes clear that Aristotle sees these two sequenced pairs of research as intimately connected to one another. He first connects them by means of his syllogistic concept of "middle term," the term which is common to the two premises in a syllogistic proof, and which thus warrants the conclusion:

> Thus it results that in all our research we seek either if there is a middle term or what the middle term is. For the middle term is the cause, and this is in every case what is sought. (*APo.* II.2, 90a7–9)

That is, in any valid syllogistic inference the middle term shared by the premises is the warrant for the conclusion. In scientific explanation, however, the middle term must also identify the cause of the fact given in the conclusion. If what we seek to explain is the periodic sound of noise in the clouds, the middle term needs to identify the cause of the connection between that noise and clouds. Moreover, on Aristotle's account of the relationship between causal demonstration and scientific definition, knowing that cause will give us a grasp of the essence of thunder.

> There is a difference between saying why it thunders and what thunder is. In the one case you will say: Because the fire is extinguished in the clouds. But: What is thunder? – A noise of fire being extinguished in the clouds. Hence the same account is given in different ways: in one way it is a continuous demonstration, in the other a definition. (*APo.* II.10, 94a4–8)

Now one may explore the unfolding of these complicated ideas about inquiry within the *Posterior Analytics* itself. Aristotle recurs regularly to a number of standard examples

296

– especially research about thunder and eclipses, but also, and importantly, seasonal loss of leaves in broad-leafed plants. But these examples present many problems – it is safe to say they raise as many interpretive questions in understanding Aristotle's theory as they help resolve. So it is worth asking whether Aristotle's sustained theoretical investigation into animals can be used as a resource for understanding his theory of research itself.

The following three passages – one from the *History of Animals* (a better though less familiar translation would be *Inquiry into Animals*), one from *On Animal Locomotion* and one from *On the Parts of Animals* – suggest that the answer is "yes." For they suggest that the entire biological project is organized in accordance with the theory of inquiry developed in *APo*. II. If that is so, we will be able to use these investigations as a resource for seeing how, and how well, the *Analytics* theory of scientific knowledge works when embodied in Aristotle's most sustained investigation of nature. We will not be forced to depend solely on the schematic, problematic, and sometimes fictitious, examples Aristotle occasionally alludes to in the *Analytics* itself.

Let us begin with a passage in the first book of the *History of Animals*. After five chapters in which Aristotle lays out the kinds of differences among animals to be studied and sketches the ways in which they are to be investigated, he makes the following sweeping programmatic statement about the investigation to come, and where it fits in the entire scientific study of animals.

> These things, then, have now been said by way of outline to provide a taste of what things need to be studied, and what it is about them that needs to be studied, in order that we may first grasp the differences and the attributes belonging to all animals. After we do this, we must attempt to discover the causes. For it is natural to carry out the investigation in this way, beginning with the inquiry into each thing; for from these inquiries it becomes clear both about which things (*peri hōn*) the demonstration (*tēn apodeixin*) should be and from which things (*ex hōn*) it should proceed. (*HA* I.6, 491a7–14)

The natural way to proceed, then, is to begin with inquiry (*historia*), with the aim of grasping the differences between, and attributes of, all the animals; and then to attempt to discover their causes. This is natural because, given that our goal is demonstrative understanding, we want to end up with a clear distinction between the *explananda* (the *peri hōn*) and the *explanans* (the *ex hōn*). The *History of Animals* characterizes itself as a contribution to the first of these two inquiries, and looks forward to investigations that aim to discover the causes – the reasons why animals have the attributes they have and differ in the ways that they do. In the language of the *Posterior Analytics*: *HA* establishes the *fact*, e.g., *that* all animals with lungs have windpipes, or *that* all cetacea have lungs and are viviparous, typically seeking to identify groups by means of discovering co-extensive differentiae with the aid of the method of division.[7] Works such as *Parts of Animals* or *Generation of Animals* seek to establish the reason why – the cause – of the fact. If he is following the method described in the *Analytics*, these causal

---

7. On the use and significance of this methodology in *HA*, see Gotthelf (1988, 1997a); and Lennox (1987a, 1990, 1991).

explanations should at the same time gives us an essential definition of what it is to be a windpipe or to be viviparous.

His causal investigations stress that they presuppose that the preliminary work of inquiry, establishing the facts at the most general level possible, has been accomplished. Here are two explicit statements to that effect, one from the beginning of his study of the causes of the differences in animal locomotion, one from the beginning of his study of the causes of the differences among the parts of animals.

> Clearly there needs to be a study of all of these [questions about animal locomotion] and any others of the same kind; for *that* (*hoti men*) these things are thus is clear from our inquiry into nature (*tēs historias tēs phusikēs*); *the reason why* (*dioti de*) must now be investigated. (*IA* 1, 704b7–10)

> From which parts and from how many parts each of the animals is constituted has been exhibited more clearly in the inquiries about them (*en tais historiais tais peri autōn*); it is the *causes* owing to which each animal has this character that must now be examined, on their own and apart (*chorisantas kath' hauta*) from what was said in the inquiries. (*PA* II.1, 646a8–12)

Each of these passages explicitly describes the study of animals with which Aristotle is engaged in the language of Aristotle's theory of research in *APo*. II.1. Indeed, the passage from *HA* I.6 does so by insisting that the *natural method* to use is to first get clear on the differences and attributes to be demonstrated ("establish the fact *that* . . .") before going on to find the causes ("the reason why, i.e., the cause") to be appealed to in these demonstrations.

The *IA* and *PA*, on the other hand, refer to themselves as carrying out the project of discovering the causes that provide the reasons why the various kinds of animals are differentiated as they are, and acknowledge that they are going on to do this precisely because the factual investigation into the locomotion and parts of animals has been accomplished and recorded in "the inquiries into animals," i.e., our *HA*. (Note, by the way, another instance of the puzzle with which we began – what are usually called by Aristotle inquiries into *animals* are, in the *IA* 2 passage quoted above, referred to simply as inquiry into *nature*.) In every case, Aristotle emphasizes the distinction on which we are focused, making it all but certain that he is reminding us of his philosophy of scientific research.

These programmatic statements, so clearly reflecting the theory of inquiry presented and defended in *APo*. II, gives us good reason to expect that the investigation of animals may provide us with a sustained investigation carried out in ways that self-consciously reflect the theory of research outlined in *APo*. II. Looking at the biological works in this light has turned out to be an extremely fruitful tool both for investigating their structure and methods, but equally for the investigation of Aristotle's theory of scientific research and theory of knowledge.[8]

By pursuing this line of research into Aristotle's investigation of animals one gets a very precise sense of why Aristotle insists, in the *Analytics*, that the proper use of

---

8. See the work cited in note 6. The first comprehensive investigation of this relationship in modern times is that of Kullmann (1974).

division is both necessary for the pursuit of knowledge and why he is equally insistent that it is by no means sufficient (cf. *APr.* I.31; *APo.* II.13, 96b25–97a6). As many studies, following up on the pioneering work of David Balme (1961, 1987), have now established, the *History of Animals* is a work that from first to last works by means of division of animal differences. It is organized as a study of four kinds of animal differences first mentioned in *HA*'s first chapter as the principle objects of study (at 486b22–487a14) – differences in parts (Books I–IV), in modes of activity (Books V, VI, IX), in ways of life (Book VII) and in characters (Book VIII). These in turn are sub-divided; discussion of the non-uniform parts of animals with blood (I.7–III.1) is followed by that of their uniform parts (III.2–22); with a discussion of the parts of animals without blood concluding the discussion of differences in parts (IV.1–8). Book IV concludes with a discussion of differences in sensory faculties, voice, and differences related to sex.[9]

It is only once Aristotle begins to distinguish differences among, say, uniform parts that various groupings of animals play an important role in organizing the discussion. And in so far as there are relatively stable general groupings of animals, these are identified by noting their possession of stable correlations among differentiae – for example, there are a large number of different animals all of which have wings, feathers, beaks (bony snouts without lips or teeth), and two fleshless legs, a combination which has been given the name "bird."[10] In other cases such groups have not been generally recognized, and Aristotle simply refers to them by means of some of their most important correlated differences – the four-legged and live-bearing animals, for example.

What is clear from the practice of the *History of Animals* is both the value of division and its limitations. Division by itself does not provide you with the *axes* of division; rather they are presupposed. Division does not give you the kinds – something must be done with the products of divisions in order for a researcher to recognize *theoretically significant* kinds. Why group animals together based on their possession of four legs and the ability to produce living offspring rather than eggs? Certainly each of these traits is the product of a division, one of modes of locomotion and one of modes of reproduction. But those divisions do not tell you that animals with four legs that bear living young constitute a scientifically significant group.

A second limitation of division is its indifference to the distinction between causally fundamental characteristics and proper attributes, to use the language of the *Analytics*. Yet being able to distinguish these is absolutely fundamental to Aristotelian science. A careful comparative study of the *History of Animals*, on the one hand, and works such as *On the Parts* or *On the Generation of Animals* again provides insight into how Aristotle understands and deploys this distinction in his actual scientific practice.[11] And as we have seen above, Aristotle draws explicit attention to its importance for his biological

9. This is an overview. For a more detailed account, look at Gotthelf (1988) and Lennox (1991, 2001a).
10. Compare *HA* I.6, 490b7–491a6, II.15, 505b26–506a10, and IV.8, 534b12–15.
11. For work on this subject, each reaching somewhat different results, compare Bolton (1987); Charles (2000, ch. 12); Gotthelf (1997b); Kullmann (1974); Lennox (1987a), also in Lennox (2001a).

investigations in a number of key texts within those investigations themselves. To study in detail the interplay between definition, causal demonstration, and division in the biology is to see Aristotle working through just those problems which form the central question of *Posterior Analytics* II – how precisely are definition, causal demonstration, and division related to one another in the quest for scientific understanding?

Biology and Metaphysics

One reason our predecessors did not arrive at this way of proceeding is that there was no "what it is to be" (*to ti ēn einai*) and no "defined substantial being" (*to horizisthai tēn ousian*). Democritus touched on it first, not however as necessary for the study of nature, but because he was carried away by the subject itself; while in Socrates' time interest in this grew, but research into the natural world ceased, and philosophers turned instead to practical virtue and politics. (*PA* I.1, 642a24–31)

These words conclude a long and complex defense by Aristotle of a new way of investigating the natural world. The approach he is recommending appears to require, first, the development of certain metaphysical preliminaries and, second, the application of those metaphysical preliminaries to the investigation of nature.

In the introduction to this chapter, I indicated that in order to understand Aristotle's habit of using the term "nature" when what he seems to be primarily focused on is *living* nature, one needs to understand his metaphysical presuppositions. It is now time to give some substance to that claim.

From a modern standpoint, two treatises in the Aristotelian corpus treat topics we would now relegate to metaphysics: his *Metaphysics* and his *De Anima*. The first is an investigation into being – not into this or that sort of being, but into being as such (on this topic, see also Gill, FIRST PHILOSOPHY IN ARISTOTLE, in this volume). The second investigates the soul, that is, the source (*archē*) of life (on this topic, see also Caston, ARISTOTLE'S PSYCHOLOGY, in this volume). The two end up being closely related studies, because Aristotle's is a metaphysics that elevates living being to a place of ontological primacy, and the principle and cause of living being – *psuchē*, soul – to a place of metaphysical primacy. As a consequence of Aristotle's exploration of the question "What is being?," the study of living things becomes the most elevated of natural investigations.[12]

12. Aristotle's metaphysical inquiries result in biology's pride of place in natural philosophy; and perhaps natural philosophy's pride of place among forms of knowledge. Among Aristotle's three theoretical forms of knowledge, metaphysics is said to be first philosophy, while the study of nature is called second philosophy. Indeed, Aristotle says that if there were nothing apart from naturally constituted things, the study of nature would be first philosophy (*Met.* E.1, 1026a7–32). Therefore, the claim that his metaphysical views somehow derive from his biological investigations has the connection exactly the wrong way around. Studies exploring connections between Aristotle's *Metaphysics* and his zoological treatises include Balme (1987a, 1987c); Charles (1990, 1997, 2000); Cooper (1987, 1988); Freeland (1987), Furth (1988); Gill (1989); Gotthelf (1985a); Kosman (1987); Lennox (1985, 1987b, 1990, 1997a); Lloyd (1990, 1996); Pellegrin (1982, 1986); Witt (1985).

Any view on the argument of the central books of the *Metaphysics* will, of course, be controversial. On that subject I must be somewhat dogmatic here, and hope this will be forgiven in the interests of pursuing the primary interest in this chapter: How might an investigation of Aristotle's biological works help us to better understand that argument, and (conversely) how does that argument inform his investigation of living things?

First philosophy is distinguished from other theoretical inquiries because it aims to discover the principles and causes of being *qua* being (E.1, 1025b3–4; cf. Γ.1, 1003a20–32). *Met.* Z–Θ narrow the focus to the *primary* being, substantial being (*ousia*). As Aristotle puts it:

> Indeed the thing sought long ago, now and always, and that is always puzzling – what is being? – comes down to this: what is substantial being? (Z.1, 1028b3–4)

Z.2 famously begins this inquiry with a list of bodies to which substantial being seems most obviously to belong:[13]

> This is why we say the animals, plants, and their parts are substantial beings, and natural bodies such as fire, water, earth, and each thing of this sort; and again as many things as are parts of these or come from these, either from parts of them or all of them, e.g., the heaven and its parts, stars, moon, and sun. But whether these are the only substantial beings or whether there are others – or whether *none* of these are, but *rather* others – must be investigated. (1028b8–16)

It is open, then, for these prima facie candidates to be eliminated. And indeed it looks as if by Z.16 not only universals, but the parts of animals and the elements, have been eliminated, or at least demoted.

> It is clear that most of the things believed to be substantial beings are potentialities; this is true of the parts of animals (for none of these can exist when separated; when separated they all exist as matter) and also of earth, fire, and air. For none of them is one; rather they are like heaps, until concocted and some one thing comes to be from them. (1040b5–10)

I take the point to be that there are good reasons to think the items mentioned here fail certain tests for substantial being. Animal parts on their own fail the *independence* test; elemental bodies on their own fail the *unity* test.

---

13.   Or "to be present in". The Greek verb *huparchein*, can have either sense, and here it makes a major difference. Is Aristotle saying that these are the things that seem obviously to be labeled "substances"; or is he saying these are the things that most obviously seem to have substantial being within them? Taken in the latter way, even at the level of what is manifest and obvious, there is no obvious answer to the inquiry into what substantial being is, but only to the inquiry about where to look for such a thing. Taken in the former way, this is a list of things that appear to be substances. Of course, one can still go on to inquire into what about them makes them substances; but nevertheless there would already be an answer to the question "What is substantial being?"

Now at this point it would be a very good thing to know more about how Aristotle thinks of the relationship between animals and their parts, and between elements unconcocted and the unity that emerges when they are concocted.[14] It would also help to understand why concoction is able to provide a unity that elevates a merely potential substantial being to an actual one. Such understanding is available by examining the explanatory function of concoction in *Parts of Animals, Generation of Animals, Parva Naturalia* and *Meteorology* IV. In doing so, one discovers that the parts of animals fall into two broad categories, uniform (flesh, bone, semen, sinew) and non-uniform (eye, hand, wing). *PA* II.1 is a sustained account of this distinction, and *GA* II.6 is a discussion of the development of many of them out of nutritive blood. The non-uniform parts typically have complex functions that require them to be made of a number of uniform parts (the hand, as Aristotle notes, requires soft flesh, hard bone, flexible sinews and semi-hard nails (cf. *PA* II.1, 646b10–26).

The uniform parts such as flesh, bone, teeth, or hair, are constituted by concoction from the elemental bodies; they are not, however, mere combinations of amounts of the actual elements involved. Concoction, rather, produces an emergent entity, a uniform or homogenous material, the parts of which, no matter how often divided, will continue to display the emergent properties of that uniform entity, properties not found in any of the components, either singly or in combination. *Meteorology* IV.1–7 explains in detail what concoction is and how it produces uniform bodies with these emergent properties; chapters 8–11 provide a classification of these emergent uniform materials by reference to a list of 18 pairs of dispositional properties, and then relates these emergent properties back to the elemental constitutions out of which concoction produces them. This sustained discussion has added philosophical importance in that it accomplishes these tasks by deploying a thoroughly "bottom up" explanatory strategy, appealing to the efficient causes of heating and cooling and consequent condensing, evaporation, and drying, and never once mentioning the goals or functions of the uniform structures that emerge, even when those structures are in fact organic.

However, the last chapter of *Meteorology* IV, chapter 12, also makes it clear that what has preceded is not a *complete* account of any such materials as have a function within a structured system of non-uniform parts. It is a sustained philosophical discussion of the centrality of teleological explanations in any case where one must understand the function for the sake of which the uniform part was concocted. It concludes by directing the reader to texts such as *PA* II.1 for a fuller understanding. Indeed, *PA* II.1 stresses that even to think of the more complex nature as "emergent" gets the priority relations wrong.

> In generation things are opposed to the way they are in substantial being; for things posterior in generation are prior in nature, and the final stage of generation is prior in nature. (646a24–26)

And with respect to organisms in particular,

---

14. See the claim at *Met*. Z.17, 1041b11–33, regarding the relation of flesh and bone to the elements.

Thus animals have been constituted from both of these parts [uniform and non-uniform], but the uniform parts are for the sake of the non-uniform; for of the latter there are functions and actions, e.g., of eye, nostril, and the entire face, of finger, hand, and the entire arm. (*PA* II.1, 646b10–14)

These *functional* parts, such as eye and finger, moreover, are only truly such when they are capable of acting for the sake of the organism – "none of the parts of a corpse is any longer such – I mean, e.g., any longer an eye or a hand" (I.1, 641a3–4).[15] In the end, then, the *being* of these parts, all the way down to the elements, is parasitic on the being of a living thing – with the stress on *living*. For as the just-cited passage about corpses makes clear, it is not in virtue of being a part of a *body* that an eye is an eye, but in virtue of its capacity to make a functional contribution to the life of an *organism*. It may well be a primary task of *De Anima* to understand the centrality of life to the being of these paradigmatic natural substances, a subject I will take up in the next section.

There have been hints throughout *Metaphysics* Z that animals and plants have a special status that needs to be explored. For example:

Among the things that come to be, some do so by nature, some by art, and some spontaneously – but all come to be *by* something, *from* something, and *something*. . . . Those generations are natural of which the generation is from nature; but that *from* which it comes to be is what we call matter, while that *by* which is some one of those things that *are* by nature, and *that which comes to be* is a human being or a plant or some other thing of that sort, *which we declare to be substantial beings most of all*. Now generally there is both a *nature from which* and a *nature in virtue of which*; for that which has come to be, e.g., a plant or an animal, has a nature; and that *by which* it comes to be, *the nature spoken of in virtue of the form*, is alike in form [to what has come to be] though in another; for a human being generates a human being. (Excerpts from *Met.* Z.7, 1032a12–26)

Notice that plants and animals are here said to be paradigmatic examples of things generated by nature, though again the focus is on natural things that reproduce, as we would say – where the agent and the product are one and the same in form. As Aristotle stresses both in *De Anima* and *Generation of Animals*, this ability to replicate form allows organisms to "participate in the eternal and divine" – organisms come to be and pass away, but their form lives on in their offspring. (cf. *De An.* II.4, 415a22–b2; *GA* II.1, 731b24–732a1)

In passages like this in Z there is an apparent tension between the insistence that the composite outcomes of natural generation are most of all *ousiai* (substantial beings,

---

15. Distinguishing uniform from non-uniform parts by assigning functions only to the latter is an over-simplification. An organized yet uniform part (e.g., the liver) may be, functionally, an organ. Later in *PA* II Aristotle argues that bones are only truly bones when they are parts of a functioning skeleton (II.9, 654a32–b2), that flesh is the organ of touch perception (II.8, 653b20–26), and that brain is an organ for maintaining the proper temperature in the organism (II.7, 652b6–26). It is thus not surprising to find that at *GA* II.1, 734b24–31, he applies the homonymy principle, the principle that to be an organic part the structure must be able to function, indifferently to face and flesh.

e.g., Z.8, 1034a4) and that their formal nature is most of all *ousia* (this tension drives the dialectic of Z.10–11, for example). There are places, however, where Aristotle seems to declare that he is speaking in his own voice.

> That there is a certain state of *aporia* about definitions, and due to what cause, has been discussed. And for this reason to reduce everything in this way, i.e., to abstract away the matter, is unhelpful; for some things are equally "this in this" or "these disposed thus." And the comparison to the animal, which the younger Socrates used to make, is not a good one, for it leads away from the truth, and to the supposition that a human being can exist without its parts, just as the circle can exist without the bronze. But the cases are not alike; for an animal is something that is perceptible, and cannot be defined without change, nor therefore without its parts somehow being in a certain state. For it is not the hand in every possible condition that is a part of a human being, but the hand able to perform its function, and so ensouled – if it is not ensouled, it is not a part. (*Met.* Z.11, 1036b21–32)

The suggestion here seems to be that while the fact that circularity can be found in any number of materials allows matter to be ignored in the definition of a circle, it would be wrong to think that the connection between soul and body in a plant or animal is similar to that between circularity and (say) bronze. Once you say that to be an animal is to be capable of perception, you are at once saying that it is a being with instrumental parts capable of undergoing certain changes and performing certain functions. To be ensouled is to be a body capable of such functions. The relation of soul and body is utterly unlike the relation of mathematical figure and body. It will be noticed that this argument is the complement of that made in *Parts of Animals* I and II – just as the eye of a corpse is no true eye, so too there can be no vision in the absence of the material preconditions of vision. The definition of the eye, or of an entire animal, requires reference to the functional capacities of appropriate bodies.

Interestingly, when Aristotle announces "another sort of beginning" (1041a6) in Z.17, one in which we will focus on substantial being as a source and cause (1041a10), he begins by reminding us about the theory of inquiry in *Posterior Analytics* II.[16] "The reason why (*to dia ti*) is always sought in this manner, [by asking] the reason why one thing belongs to another" (1041a12–13). The central problem of the chapter, however, is that the objects of the inquiry we are currently engaged in appear to lack this predicative structure. After reviewing the familiar "thunder" example from *APo.* II, he begins to discuss these more difficult cases of inquiry:

> "And why are these things, e.g., these bricks and stones, a house?" It is now apparent that [when one asks such a question] one is inquiring into the cause (and this, speaking logically (*logikōs*) is what it is for it to be), which in some cases is what it is for, as perhaps in the case of a house or a bed, and in other cases what first moved it; for this too is a cause. This latter cause is sought in the case of coming-to-be and perishing, while the former is also sought in the case of being. (1041a26–33)

---

16.   "Readers of Z.17 should bone up on *Posterior Analytics* II.1–2 and 7–11" Burnyeat (2001, p. 75).

This sort of inquiry, which leads us to conclude that goals and agents are the causes we are seeking, not surprisingly also leads ultimately to form (1041b8).[17] But the relationship of form to the materials it "causes" to be some complex object is puzzling. If as a meteorologist you are investigating thunder, you begin by assuming that thunder picks out a certain range of noises that belong in some way or other to clouds, and you are seeking the cause of that connection. When you discover that fire is extinguished in the clouds at the very time that the noise we call thunder occurs, and you have prior knowledge that extinction of fire causes such a noise, you have your cause. But when you ask what it is that causes bricks and mortar to be a house, your inquiry is very different. First, in a sense it is inappropriate to say these materials "belong to" the house – properly speaking, they *are* the house, in a way that the clouds are not thunder. Second, if what it is that makes those materials a house is the function the house performs (hinted at above and stated explicitly in *Metaphysics* H.2, 1043a14–21), it is not the cause of the house in the way that extinguishing of fire is the cause of a noise in the clouds. It is with this very puzzle that *Met.* Z ends.

> It would seem that this [cause we are seeking] is something other than an element, and it is surely the cause of one thing being flesh while another is a syllable, and similarly in other cases. And this is the substantial being (*ousia*) of each thing; for this is the primary cause of being (*aition prōton tou einai*). Now since some things are not substances, but all those that are substances (*ousiai*) are constituted in accordance with nature and by nature, it would appear that this "nature" is substantial being (*ousia*), which is not an element but a source (*archē*), (1041b25–31)

There are many puzzles in this chapter, and I want to suggest features of Aristotle's biological works that might help in solving them. If Aristotle is serious that the key to understanding substantial being is understanding the causal relationship between formal natures and material natures, then there is no better place to look for help than to the biological works.[18] The *Parts of Animals* is devoted in large part to explaining the differences in the constitution, position, and operations of the organs and tissues of animals by appeal to their functional, that is, formal natures. The term "nature" is used over 200 times in that work, referring sometimes to the material constituents of the animal and sometimes to its form. Formal natures are both *agents* and *goals*. As an agent, for example, the nutritive soul is a capacity the function of which is to transform nutrients first into blood and then into the appropriate tissues and then to transport them, in appropriate amounts, to appropriate places. But these processes are all taking place for the sake of the maintenance of an organism with those very living capacities

---

17.   Though the reference to form is in all the manuscripts, it has for reasons both of syntax and sense been suspected of being a gloss. Cf. Burnyeat (2001, p. 60, n. 124), for the arguments and a couple of suggestions in favor of its retention.

18.   Cf. Burnyeat (2001, p. 61): "It follows that the substantial being *of* such things, as the primary cause of their being the natural things they are, just is that internal principle of change and stability – their nature. Aristotle means, but does not expressly say: nature as form."

– they are the goal. Assuming (and regularly reminding us) throughout that "nature does nothing in vain, but always what is best, from the possibilities, for the substantial being of each kind of animal" (*IA* 2, 704b14–16), Aristotle treats formal natures as the causes of animals being as they are:

> So then, what the nature of the horns is for has been stated, and the cause on account of which some animals have them while others do not; but since the necessary nature is of such a character, we must say how the nature according to the account (*hē kata ton logon phusis*) has made use of the things that belong of necessity for the sake of something. (*PA* III.2, 663b22–24)

The discussion then proceeds to explain how it is that nature provides materials, which could just as easily have been used for hoofs or teeth, to the top of the head for the construction of horns. The formal nature of horned viviparous quadrupeds is a cause in no merely "formal" manner![19] Moreover, when Aristotle says repeatedly that nature does what is best for each kind of animal's substantial being (*ousia*), he seems clearly to be referring to the formal nature of the animal. If that is so, then once again we see that nature is portrayed both as an agent and as a goal in these passages.

Discussions of a number of other fundamental questions in Aristotle's *Metaphysics* have been enriched by studying his zoological works carefully. Allan Gotthelf investigated all the texts in *Parts of Animals* in which Aristotle referred to some feature as in the substantial being (*ousia*), or in its account (*logos tēs ousias*), or in the being (*einai*) or the what-it-is-to-be (*to ti ēn einai*) of some kind of animal. Antecedently one might have thought the references would all be to features on the side of "soul" and "form," but his investigation showed decisively otherwise. Being able to perceive, fly, and swim were mentioned; but so too were being blooded, having a lung, and having long and slim bodies.

What does one make of that? An easy solution would be to suppose that these terms are being used in a different manner than in the *Metaphysics* – but these are philosophical expressions and this is a desperate solution. Another possibility is that these passages recommend that we take seriously Aristotle's suggestion that, at least in the case of natural things, the relationship between body and soul, form and matter, is an intimate one and that definitions will reflect this fact. Two points discussed earlier encourage us to think in this direction. First, Aristotle urges us to recognize that a wing that cannot take flight is a wing in name only – the account of a wing must include an account of its biological function. Second, and conversely, marble wings do not take flight – the account of a wing must include an account of the appropriate materials for instruments of flight, the feathers, hollow bones, connection to appropriate

---

19.   For a fuller discussion and defense, see Lennox (1997a, 1997b). For a defense of form as efficient cause in the context of Aristotle's theory of animal generation, see Code (1987, pp. 51–60). A topic that would require a chapter to itself simply to review the current status of discussion is Aristotle's understanding of teleology as goal causation. A review of the literature up to 1992 prepared by Allan Gotthelf can be found in the Balme (1990, pp. 172–3).

muscles of appropriate organisms, etc. To call an animal blooded is to say much more than that they are made up of a red, viscous fluid; it is to say things about their modes of perception, nutrition, and reproduction, and even about the number of limbs they can have. To say an organism is perceptive is to say it has to have certain sorts of organs constituted of certain sorts of materials organized in appropriate ways (cf. Charles, 2000, chs. 11–12; Ferejohn, 1994).

Likewise, on the issue of whether Aristotle's forms are general or particular – where the *Metaphysics* has seemed to endorse and disparage both answers – the biological works, and especially *Generation of Animals*, have once again been helpful in dealing with the difficulty (cf. Balme, 1987a, pp. 18–19, 1987c; Cooper, 1988; Furth, 1988; Witt, 1985). Book IV of that work includes a discussion of inheritance, and attempts to provide an explanation for the complex patterns of family resemblance maintained through the generative process. Arguably, that discussion describes resemblances between individual children and their parents as formal likenesses, a view that conflicts with some understandings of what Aristotle could mean by a "formal likeness."

I will close this section with one final example of the metaphysical rewards of exploring Aristotle's scientific account of living things. Explorations of *Meteorology* IV, a book devoted to explaining the generation and constitution of "uniform" or "homogenous" things – including uniform parts of animals and plants – have raised questions about how seriously Aristotle takes material level accounts of natural things (cf., Freudenthal, 1995; Furley, 1989, ch. 12; Gill, 1997). For *Meteorology* IV self-consciously approaches uniform parts from "the bottom up," not even referring to them as "parts" until it looks toward the biological works in the last chapter. Blood, semen, bone, sinew, hair, and many more stuffs are discussed in detail – but with not one word about their biological functions. In the final chapter of *Meteor.* IV, Aristotle describes what he has done, and prepares us for a different look at these "uniform things" when we move on to our next investigation, that of plants and animals, a preparation that includes one of the most rich and complex discussions of teleology in the entire corpus. Only as he looks forward to zoology and botany does he begin to refer to certain "uniforms" as uniform parts of organisms (cf. Furley, 1989, pp. 132–48; Gill, 1997, pp. 145–62).

If the same philosopher who tells us that natural things are to be investigated "like the snub," i.e., as composites of matter and form, can *also* carry out a purely material level investigation of this kind, it constrains our interpretation of his remarks about natural inquiry. Nor does *Meteorology* IV stand alone in this respect. *Generation of Animals* V begins with a philosophically rich discussion of when investigation should be primarily teleological, and when not. We quickly learn why he is discussing this issue. For he announces that the rest of Book V will provide accounts of features of animals that do *not* come to be for the sake of anything, but simply and only due to material necessity. Once more, a careful study of the zoological corpus constrains philosophical interpretation – in this case interpretation that puts excessive emphasis on Aristotle's teleological worldview. A teleologist he certainly is, but one who clearly believes that teleology has its limits, and that even when it is an inappropriate explanatory tool, there is plenty of scientific work to be done.

Soul, Life, and Reason

As we have seen, the *ontology* of substantial beings is not the core of the argument of the *Metaphysics*. Aristotle is much more concerned to determine what the *principles* and *causes* of substantial being are – which, it seems, will have prior claim to the label substantial being. And if living beings are primary candidates for substantial being, then a study of the principle and cause of living being is an investigation of overarching importance. That, of course, is how *De Anima* (*De An.*) advertises itself:

> Let us assume that knowledge is among the noble and honorable things, but that one sort is more so than another either in virtue of its precision or by being of better and more wonderful things; on that assumption we might reasonably hold that the inquiry about the soul is among primary branches of knowledge for both reasons. And knowledge of the soul seems to contribute greatly to all truth, but most of all to truth about nature; for [the soul] is a sort of first principle (*hoion archē*) of animals. And we are seeking to study and to know both its nature and its being, and then whatever things are attributed to it, among which some seem to be proper affections of the soul, others of animals as well on account of the soul. (*De An.* I.1, 402a1–12)

A number of features of this passage, and indeed of the chapter it introduces, are intimately related to the themes of this chapter. Notice, first, that the ground for the claim that knowledge of soul will make a major contribution to truth about nature (without qualification) is that it is "a sort of first principle of animals." The qualification here is, I believe, an indication that Aristotle will, by the end of Book I, be insisting on a thesis about the soul his readers will find somewhat unorthodox, namely that it is also a principle of *plant* life. That aside, we once more see that for Aristotle the investigation of nature is, first and foremost, an investigation of *living* nature.

Second, note the distinction between studying the nature and being of soul and studying its attributes, and within this latter category between attributes belonging to the soul itself and those belonging also to animals because they are ensouled. While it will take us too far afield to pursue the implications of these distinctions for Aristotle's investigation of nature, it is worth noting that the chapter continues by opening up the question of whether there is a single method (*mia tis methodos*) for the investigation of a thing's being and what it is (*tou peri tēn ousian kai tou ti esti*), in the way that demonstration is a method for knowing a thing's proper attributes; or whether there will need to be a distinct mode of inquiry in each case. That is, we are plunged into questions about whether the principles of inquiry and demonstration established in the *Posterior Analytics* are applicable everywhere, including here, or not. Reading this passage, in light of the complications about stating a universal definition of the soul which engages Aristotle in the first three chapters of *De An.* II, one can see that he is self-consciously concerned with the pressures that may be put on his theory of scientific knowledge by investigation of the soul.

It is hard *not* to hear echoes of *APo.* II.7–8 in this passage as well. Having, in the first six chapters of *APo.* II explored the question of how definition, demonstration, and division are related, Aristotle begins chapter 7 with the question: "Then how will a definer exhibit (*deixei*) the being (*tēn ousian*) of a thing or what it is (*to ti estin*)?"

308

(92a34–35). And when, in the following chapter, he begins working on a positive resolution to this question, he points out that a preliminary step is, in one way or another, getting a grip on the subject being investigated. Sometimes this is accomplished "by grasping something of the thing itself – of thunder, that it is a sort of noise in the clouds; of an eclipse, that it is a sort of privation of light; of man, that he is a sort of animal; *of soul, that it is a self-moving thing*" (93a21–24). If one considers *De Anima* as an inquiry aimed at a scientific definition of soul, one is forced to return to the very questions that we saw were central to *Metaphysics* Z. And that is precisely what Aristotle does.

> Perhaps it is first necessary to determine into which of the kinds [to place soul] and what it is; I mean whether it is a particular and a substantial being, or a quality, or a quantity, or one of the other divisible categories; and next whether it is among things which exist potentially or is rather a complete actuality of some sort – for this is no small difference. (*De An.* I.1, 402a23–27)

Having been told that this is the first thing to determine, it comes as no surprise that the beginning of his positive account in *De An.* II.1 opens as it does:

> Enough said, then, of the deliverances of our predecessors about soul; we return again to the beginning and attempt to determine what soul is and what would be the most common account of it. We say that substantial being (*ousian*) is one kind of being, and substantial being is in one way as matter and in itself is not a particular thing, in another way it is shape and form, and in a third way it is the composite of these. And the matter is potentiality, while the form is complete actuality (*entelecheia*), and that in two ways, as knowledge is and as studying is. Now bodies would seem most of all to be substantial beings (*ousias*), and of these most of all natural bodies, since these are first principles of the others. And among natural things some have life, some do not; and by life we mean the capacity of self-nourishment as well as growth and decay. Every natural body having life would, then, be a composite substantial being (*ousiai . . . hōs sunthetē*). And since it is a body of such a kind [we are considering], that is, one having life, the body would not be a soul; for the body is not among the things that are said of a subject, but rather it exists as subject and matter. Therefore soul must be substantial being in the sense of form of a natural body having life potentially. But substantial being is complete actuality. Therefore soul is complete actuality of such a body. But "complete actuality" is spoken of in two ways, as knowledge is and as studying is. Thus it is clear that soul is complete actuality as knowledge is. (*De An.* II.1, 412a3–24)

It is clear that certain results of the *Metaphysics* Z–Θ are being deployed here, in order to locate soul in just the ways requested in the first chapter of *De An.* I – it is in the category of substantial being, but things in that category can have the status of matter, form or composite. Though the argument for treating soul as form is open to various interpretations, it looks as if Aristotle's view is that natural bodies with life have life in virtue of soul, and thus (given the options) their body has the status of underlying subject and matter within the composite, which means soul must have the status of form. When he then goes on to assert that substantial being is complete actuality, it seems he is talking about substantial being as form; which allows him the quick inference to soul being complete actuality; and though I have not given it, he goes on to provide a plausible argument for deciding in which of the two senses of complete actuality soul is such.

De Anima, as I have characterized it so far, would seem to have an obvious relationship to Aristotle's investigations of animals. Animals are living things; knowledge of the soul is knowledge of the first principle of life; the soul must, then, be among the first principles of the scientific study of animals. And so much seems to be true. Indeed, the opening of *De Sensu* says as much:

> Since we have previously defined soul by itself and the powers of each of its parts, we must next investigate the animals and all things with life, which of their activities are distinctive and which common. So then let that which has been stated about the soul be assumed (*hupokeisthō*); we must now speak about the rest, and first of all about the primary things. (*Sens.* 1, 436a1–6)

But at the same time Aristotle insists that a significant portion of the investigation of the soul is outside the purview of the natural philosopher.

> However, it is not the case that all soul is a source of change, nor all its parts; rather, of growth the source is the part which is present even in plants, of alteration the perceptive part, and of locomotion some other part, and not the rational; for locomotion is present in other animals too, but thought in none of the others. So it is clear that the natural scientist should not speak of all soul; for not all of the soul is a nature, but some part of it, one part or even more. Further, none of the abstract objects can be objects of natural study, since nature does everything for the sake of something. (*PA* I.1, 641b5–11; cf. *Met.* E.1, 1026a17).

Natural philosophy takes as its subject things that change in virtue of a source within themselves. In so far as soul is such an inherent source of change – of growth, alteration, locomotion – it is a proper object for natural study. But reason (*nous*) is denied that status. Though it cannot be done here, a good case can be made that Aristotle honors this argument in the breach (cf. Lennox, 1999). So the connection of the study of the soul to Aristotle's animal studies, which include the study of human beings with rational souls, must be more complicated than it appears at first glance. For Aristotle's investigations of animals are from first to last *natural* investigations, while at least part of the investigation of soul falls beyond the expertise of the natural philosopher.

From a historical standpoint this is not, of course, an unusual position to take. Even today there are distinguished practitioners of the philosophy of mind who see what they do as essentially unconnected to what the natural sciences have to say about our brains and nervous systems. Aristotle seemed to have doubts about whether understanding the functions of the human heart, which on his account was the central organ of cognition, would involve understanding human reason, just as certain philosophers today have similar doubts about whether understanding the brain will involve understanding the mind.

Conclusion

In this chapter I have tried to indicate ways in which careful attention to Aristotle's investigations of animals has been, and can be, a valuable aid to understanding his investigations of knowledge and of being, i.e., the *Posterior Analytics* and the *Metaphysics*. Conversely, I have argued that his biological studies are illuminated when seen in the light of his views about the nature of inquiry and demonstration in the former work and the nature substance, matter, and form in the latter.

A pivotal text in trying to understand the relationship between Aristotle's epistemological and metaphysical views, on the one hand, and his science of living things on the other, is *De Anima*. In the penultimate section of this discussion I have raised a number of questions about its relationship to the *Metaphysics* and *Posterior Analytics* on the one hand, and to Aristotle's various studies of animals on the other. There are, of course, many other respects in which attending to Aristotle's investigations of animals can inform work on Aristotle's philosophy, and vice versa. The bibliography appended to this chapter provides the reader with a guide to some of the best work of this kind. There is much work still to be done.

Bibliography

Texts, Translations, Commentaries, Indexes

Balme, D. M. (2003). *Aristotle: Historia Animalium.* (vol. 1): *Books I–X Text* (Prepared for Publication by A. Gotthelf). Cambridge: Cambridge University Press.

——. (1991). Aristotle. *History of Animals, Books VII–X.* Cambridge, Mass.: Harvard University Press.

——. (1992). *Aristotle. De Partibus Animalium I and De Generatione Animalium I (with passages from II.1–3)* (With a Report on Recent Work and an Additional Bibliography by A. Gotthelf). Oxford: Oxford University Press.

Bodson, L. (1990). *Aristote: De Partibus Animalium, Index Verborum, Listes de Fréquence.* Liège: Centre Informatique de Philosophie et Lettres.

Drossaart Lulofs, H. J. (1965). *Aristotelis De Generatione Animalium.* Oxford: Oxford University Press.

Düring, I. (1943). *Aristotle's* De Partibus Animalium: *Critical and Literary Commentaries.* Göteborg: Elanders boktryckeri aktiebolag. Repr. New York: Garland Publishing, 1980.

Langkavel, B. (1868). *Aristotelis Opera.* (vol. 1): *De Partibus Animalium.* Leipzig: Teubner.

Le Blond, J. M. (1945). *Aristote, philosophe de la vie: Le livre premier du traité sur les Parties des Animaux.* Paris: Aubier.

Ogle, W. (1882/1987). *Aristotle on the Parts of Animals.* New York: Garland.

——. (1912). *Aristotle: De Partibus Animalium.* In W. D. Ross and J. A. Smith (eds.), *The Works of Aristotle Translated into English.* (vol. 5.). Oxford: Oxford University Press.

Peck, A. L. (1961). *Aristotle: Parts of Animals.* Introduction, text, translation. Loeb Classical Library. Cambridge, Mass.: Harvard University Press / London: Heinemann.

——. (1963). *Aristotle: Generation of Animals.* Introduction, text, translation. Loeb Classical Library. Cambridge, Mass.: Harvard University Press / London: Heinemann.

——. (1965). *Aristotle: Historia Animalium, Books I–III.* Introduction, text, translation. Loeb Classical Library. Cambridge, Mass.: Harvard University Press / London: Heinemann.

———. (1970). *Aristotle: Historia Animalium, Books IV–VI.* Introduction, text, translation. Loeb Classical Library. Cambridge, Mass.: Harvard University Press / London: Heinemann.

Thompson, D. W. (1910). *Aristotle: Historia Animalium.* In W. D. Ross and J. A. Smith (eds.), *The Works of Aristotle Translated into English.* (vol. 4). Oxford: Oxford University Press.

Works Cited

Balme, D. M. (1961). "Aristotle's Use of Differentiae in Zoology." In S. Mansion (ed.), *Aristote et les problèmes de méthode* (pp. 195–212). Louvain: Publications Universitaires de Louvain.

———. (1987a). "The Place of Biology in Aristotle's Philosophy." In A. Gotthelf and J. G. Lennox (eds.), *Philosophical Issues in Aristotle's Biology* (pp. 9–20). Cambridge: Cambridge University Press.

———. (1987b). "Aristotle's Use of Division and Differentiae." In A. Gotthelf and J. G. Lennox (eds.), *Philosophical Issues in Aristotle's Biology* (pp. 69–89). Cambridge: Cambridge University Press.

———. (1987c). "Aristotle's Biology was not Essentialist." In A. Gotthelf and J. G. Lennox (eds.), *Philosophical Issues in Aristotle's Biology* (pp. 291–312). Cambridge: Cambridge University Press.

———. (1990). "Matter in Definition: A Reply to G. E. R. Lloyd." In D. Devereux and P. Pellegrin (eds.), *Biologie, Logique et Métaphysique chez Aristote* (pp. 49–54). Paris: Éditions du CNRS.

Bolton, R. (1987). "Definition and Scientific Method in Aristotle's *Posterior Analytics* and *Generation of Animals.*" In A. Gotthelf and J. G. Lennox (eds.), *Philosophical Issues in Aristotle's Biology* (pp. 120–66). Cambridge: Cambridge University Press.

———. (1997), "The Material Cause: Matter and Explanation in Aristotle's Natural Science." In W. Kullmann and S. Föllinger (eds.), *Aristotelische Biologie* (pp. 97–124). Stuttgart: Steiner.

Bowen, A. (ed.). (1991). *Science and Philosophy in Classical Greece.* New York: Garland Press.

Burnyeat, M. F. (1981). "Aristotle on Understanding Knowledge." In E. Berti (ed.), *Aristotle on Science: the* Posterior Analytics. Proceedings of the Eighth Symposium Aristotelicum (pp. 97–139). Padova: Editrice Antenore.

———. (2001). *A Map of* Metaphysics Zeta. Pittsburgh: Mathesis.

Charles, D. (1990). "Meaning, Natural Kinds and Natural History." In D. Devereux and P. Pellegrin (eds.), *Biologie, Logique et Métaphysique chez Aristote* (pp. 145–67). Paris: Éditions du CNRS.

———. (1997). "Aristotle and the Unity and Essence of Biological Kinds." In W. Kullmann and S. Föllinger (eds.) (pp. 27–42). *Aristotelische Biologie.* Stuttgart: Steiner.

———. (2000). *Aristotle on Meaning and Essence.* Oxford: Oxford University Press.

Code, A. (1987). "Soul as Efficient Cause in Aristotle's Embryology." *Philosophical Topics,* 15, 51–60.

Coleman, W. (1977). *Biology in the Nineteenth Century: Problems of Form, Function, and Transformation.* Cambridge: Cambridge University Press.

Cooper, J. M. (1987). "Hypothetical Necessity and Natural Teleology." In A. Gotthelf and J. G. Lennox (eds.), *Philosophical Issues in Aristotle's Biology* (pp. 243–74). Cambridge: Cambridge University Press.

———. (1988). "Metaphysics in Aristotle's Embryology." *Proceedings of the Cambridge Philological Society,* 214, 14–41.

Cunningham, A. (1999). "Aristotle's Animal Books: Ethology, Biology, Anatomy, or Philosophy?" *Philosophical Topics,* 25, 17–42.

Detel, W. (1997). "Why All Animals Have a Stomach: Demonstration and Axiomatization in Aristotle's *Parts of Animals.*" In W. Kullmann and S. Föllinger (eds.), *Aristotelische Biologie* (pp. 63–84). Stuttgart: Steiner.

———. (1999). "Aristotle on Zoological Explanation." *Philosophical Topics,* 25, 43–68.

312

Devereux, D. and Pellegrin, P. (eds.). (1990). *Biologie, Logique et Métaphysique chez Aristote.* Paris: Éditions du CNRS.

Ferejohn, M. (1994). "The Definition of Generated Composites in Aristotle's *Metaphysics.*" In T. Scaltsas, D. Charles, and M. L. Gill (eds.), *Unity, Identity, and Explanation in Aristotle's* Metaphysics (pp. 291–318). Oxford: Clarendon Press.

Freeland, C. A. (1987). "Aristotle on Bodies, Matter and Potentiality." In A. Gotthelf and J. G. Lennox (eds.), *Philosophical Issues in Aristotle's Biology* (pp. 392–407). Cambridge: Cambridge University Press.

Freudenthal, G. (1995). *Aristotle's Theory of Material Substance: Heat and Pneuma, Form and Soul.* Oxford: Clarendon Press.

Furley, D. (1989). "The Mechanics of *Meteorologica* IV: A Prolegomenon to Biology." In D. Furley. *Cosmic Problems: Essays on Greek and Roman Philosophy of Nature* (pp. 132–48). Cambridge: Cambridge University Press.

Furth, M. (1988). *Substance, Form and Psyche: An Aristotelean Metaphysics,* Cambridge: Cambridge University Press.

Gill, M. L. (1989). "Aristotle on Matters of Life and Death." *Proceedings of the Boston Area Colloquium in Ancient Philosophy,* 4, 187–205.

———. (1997). "Material Necessity and *Meteorology* IV 12." In W. Kullmann and S. Föllinger (eds.), *Aristotelische Biologie* (pp. 145–62). Stuttgart: Steiner.

Gotthelf, A. (ed.). (1985a). *Aristotle on Nature and Living Things* (Festschrift for David M. Balme). Pittsburgh: Mathesis.

———. (1985b). "Notes Towards a study of Substance and Essence in Aristotle's *Parts of Animals* II–IV." In A. Gotthelf (ed.), (pp. 27–54).

———. (1987). "First Principles in Aristotle's *Parts of Animals.*" In A. Gotthelf and J. G. Lennox (eds.), *Philosophical Issues in Aristotle's Biology* (pp. 167–98). Cambridge: Cambridge University Press.

———. (1988). "*Historiae* I: *Plantarum et Animalium.*" In W. W. Fortenbaugh and R. W. Sharples (eds.), *Theophrastean Studies* (pp. 100–35). New Brunswick: Rutgers University Press.

———. (1997a). "The Elephant's Nose: Further Reflections on the Axiomatic Structure of Biological Explanation in Aristotle." In W. Kullmann and S. Föllinger (eds.), *Aristotelische Biologie* (pp. 85–96). Stuttgart: Steiner.

———. (1997b). "Division and Explanation in Aristotle's *Parts of Animals.*" In H.-C. Günther and A. Rengakos (eds.), *Beiträge zur antiken Philosophie* (Festschrift for Wolfgang Kullmann). (pp. 215–30). Stuttgart: Steiner.

Gotthelf, A. and Lennox, J. G. (eds.). (1987). *Philosophical Issues in Aristotle's Biology.* Cambridge: Cambridge University Press.

Günther, H.-C. and Rengakos, A. (eds.). (1997). *Beiträge zur antiken Philosophie* (Festschrift for Wolfgang Kullmann). Stuttgart: Steiner.

Kosman, L. A. (1987). "Animals and Other Beings in Aristotle." In A. Gotthelf and J. G. Lennox (eds.), *Philosophical Issues in Aristotle's Biology* (pp. 360–91). Cambridge: Cambridge University Press.

Kullmann, W. (1974). *Wissenschaft und Methode.* Berlin: de Gruyter.

———. (1985). "Different Concepts of the Final Cause in Aristotle." In A. Gotthelf (ed.), *Aristotle on Nature and Living Things* (Festschrift for David M. Balme) (pp. 169–76). Pittsburgh: Mathesis.

———. (1997). "Die Voraussetzungeben für Studium der Biologie nach Aristoteles." In W. Kullmann and S. Föllinger (eds.), *Aristotelische Biologie: Intentionen, Methoden, Ergebnisse* (pp. 43–62). Stuttgart: Steiner.

———. (1999). "Aristoteles' wissenschaftliche Methode in seinen zoologischen Schriften." In G. Wöhrle (ed.), *Geschichte der Mathematik und der Naturwissenschaften,* (vol. 1, pp. 103–23). Stuttgart: Steiner.

Kullmann, W. and Föllinger, S. (eds.). (1997). *Aristotelische Biologie.* Stuttgart: Steiner.

Lennox, J. G. (1985). "Are Aristotelian Species Eternal?" In A. Gotthelf (ed.), *Aristotle on Nature and Living Things* (Festschrift for David M. Balme) (pp. 67–94). Pittsburgh: Mathesis.

——. (1987a). "Divide and Explain: the *Posterior Analytics* in Practice." In A. Gotthelf and J. G. Lennox (eds.), *Philosophical Issues in Aristotle's Biology* (pp. 90–119). Cambridge: Cambridge University Press.

——. (1987b). "Kinds, Forms of Kinds, and the More and the Less in Aristotle's Biology." In A. Gotthelf and J. G. Lennox (eds.), *Philosophical Issues in Aristotle's Biology* (pp. 339–59). Cambridge: Cambridge University Press.

——. (1990). "Notes on David Charles on *HA*." In D. Devereux and P. Pellegrin (eds.), *Biologie, Logique et Métaphysique chez Aristote* (pp. 169–83). Paris: Éditions du CNRS.

——. (1991). "Between Data and Demonstration: The *Analytics* and the *Historia Animalium*." In A. Bowen (ed.), *Science and Philosophy in Classical Greece* (pp. 261–95). New York: Garland Press.

——. (1994). "Aristotelian Problems." *Ancient Philosophy*, 14, 53–77.

——. (1997a). "Material and Formal Natures in Aristotle's *De Partibus Animalium*." In W. Kullmann and S. Föllinger (eds.), *Aristotelische Biologie* (pp. 163–81). Stuttgart: Steiner.

——. (1997b). "Nature does nothing in vain. . . ." In H.-C. Günther and A. Rengakos (eds.), *Beiträge zur antiken Philosophie* (Festschrift for Wolfgang Kullmann) (pp. 199–214). Stuttgart: Steiner.

——. (1999). "The Place of Mankind in Aristotle's Zoology." *Philosophical Topics*, 27, 1–16.

——. (2001a). *Aristotle's Philosophy of Biology: Studies in the Origins of Life Science*. Cambridge: Cambridge University Press.

——. (2001b). *Aristotle: On the Parts of Animals I–IV*, translation and commentary. Oxford: Oxford University Press.

——. (2001c). "Aristotle on the Unity and Disunity of Science." *International Studies in the History and Philosophy of Science*, 15(2), 133–44.

Lloyd, G. E. R. (1987). "Empirical Research in Aristotle's Biology." In A. Gotthelf and J. G. Lennox (eds.), *Philosophical Issues in Aristotle's Biology* (pp. 53–64). Cambridge: Cambridge University Press.

——. (1990). "Aristotle's Zoology and his Metaphysics. The *status quaestionis*. A Critical Review of Some Recent Theories." In D. Devereux and P. Pellegrin (eds.), *Biologie, Logique et Métaphysique chez Aristote* (pp. 7–36). Paris: Éditions du CNRS.

——. (1996). *Aristotelian Explorations*. Cambridge: Cambridge University Press.

Marcos, A. (1996). *Aristóteles y Otros Animales*. Barcelona: Promociones y Publicaciones Universitarias.

Pellegrin, P. (1982). *La Classification des animaux chez Aristote: statut de la biologie et unité de l'aristotélisme*. Paris: Les Belles Lettres.

——. (1985). "Aristotle: A Zoology Without Species." In A. Gotthelf (ed.), *Aristotle on Nature and Living Things* (Festschrift for David M. Balme) (pp. 95–115). Pittsburgh: Mathesis.

——. (1986). *Aristotle's Classification of Animals: Biology and the Conceptual Unity of the Aristotelian Corpus* (trans. Anthony Preus). Berkeley: University of California Press.

——. (1987). "Logical Difference and Biological Difference: The Unity of Aristotle's Thought." In A. Gotthelf and J. G. Lennox (eds.), *Philosophical Issues in Aristotle's Biology* (pp. 313–38). Cambridge: Cambridge University Press.

Preus, A. (1975). *Science and Philosophy in Aristotle's Biological Works*. Hildesheim: Olms.

Ross, W. D. (1924). *Aristotle's Metaphysics*. A Revised Text with Introduction and Commentary. Oxford: Oxford University Press.

Simpson, G. G. (1964). *This View of Life*. New York: Harcourt, Brace, and World.

Witt, C. (1985). "Form, Reproduction, and Inherited Characteristics in Aristotle's *Generation of Animals*." *Phronesis*, 30, 46–57.

Further Reading

See Works Cited for bibliographical details.

Bowen (ed.). (1991): A fine collection of essays on the theme of the relationship between philosophy and the special sciences in classical Greece.

Charles (2000): An impressive reading of the *Posterior Analytics* with chapters on its relationship to Aristotle's biological writings.

Furth (1988): A lively exploration of Aristotle's metaphysics always with an eye on the insights to be gleaned from the biological works.

Gotthelf (ed.). (1985a): A festschrift honoring David M. Balme, the pre-eminent interpreter of Aristotle's biology in the twentieth century, it includes a number of fine essays on the relationship between Aristotle's biological writings and his logic, metaphysics, and natural philosophy.

Gotthelf and Lennox (eds.). (1987): A rich collection of essays that focus on the biological writings as a source of insight into Aristotle's metaphysical and epistemological thought.

Günther and Rengakos (eds.). (1997): A collection of essays honoring Wolfgang Kullmann, the author of *Wissenschaft und Methode* (Kullmann (1974)), the first thoroughgoing study of the biological works from the standpoint of their relationship to Aristotle's *Posterior Analytics*.

Kullmann and Föllinger (eds.). (1997): The published proceedings of a conference organized by the editors on the topic of Aristotle's biology.

Lennox, J. G. (2001a): This volume collects together a dozen previously published essays on the relationship between Aristotle's general views about the nature of science and his biological studies.

Lloyd (1996): This volume, by one of the field's pre-eminent scholars, includes a number of essays on the relationship between Aristotle's natural science and his more general philosophical views.

Marcos (1996): An excellent introduction to the general theme of the relevance of Aristotle's systematic study of animals to other aspects of his philosophy.

Pellegrin (1982, English trans. 1986): This volume argues vigorously for understanding Aristotle's animal investigations in Aristotle's own terms, and for the misunderstandings that arise from not doing so.

17

Aristotle's Psychology

VICTOR CASTON

Aristotle's psychology – what he calls the "study of the soul" (*hē tēs psuchēs historia*) – occupies a prominent place both in his own philosophy and in the Western philosophical tradition as a whole. In his own system, psychology is the culmination of metaphysics and natural science. For Aristotle, living things are the paradigm of natural objects and substances in general, and so offer the best case for the application of his theories. Psychology also serves as a foundation for the rest of his philosophy, in so far as it provides a framework for understanding thought, speech, and action, and to various extents his logic, rhetoric, politics, and ethics all draw on these views. Its influence on subsequent philosophers has also been great. During the Roman empire, later Platonists appropriated many of his doctrines, especially those concerned with cognition. In medieval scholasticism, they become part of a common legacy, shared widely by philosophers who differ in many other respects. They thus belong to the backdrop against which early modern philosophers attempted to distinguish themselves, a point of reference and a point of departure to which some twentieth century philosophers sought to return, in their efforts to shake free of Descartes' grip. Many still regard Aristotle's theory as offering an attractive middle course, which avoids the extremes of both extravagant dualism and crude materialism. With so much at stake, it is not surprising that there has been heated controversy about Aristotle's psychology in recent years, as regards both its precise nature and its viability.

Some misunderstandings can be avoided at the outset by being careful about the words "soul" and "mind." We tend to associate the first with religious traditions, in which the soul is regarded as a separate substance, divinely implanted in us and capable of immortal life. The second term, "mind," is often construed in a similarly dualistic way, although it owes more to Descartes than to religion. Here the assumption is that "the mental" and "the physical" are mutually exclusive, where the mental is characterized as ineradicably private and subjective. Neither of these preconceptions is at work in Aristotle. In inquiring after the nature of the soul or *psuchē*, Aristotle is looking for nothing other than the basis or *archē* of life – that in virtue of which living things are alive and behave in the ways distinctive of living things, *whatever that should turn out to be*. He does not prejudge the question of whether this is a separate immaterial substance (as Plato thought), or a material one (as Democritus thought), or something else altogether. For all we know at the outset, the soul might be inseparable from the body, or alternatively, it might be capable of separate existence. Such conclusions are to be established by argument, based on what it is to be alive and the characteristics that distinguish living from nonliving things. The fact that this is

Aristotle's starting point, and not questions about skepticism and certainty, explains why he is not preoccupied with many of the issues that preoccupy Descartes.

The soul, then, is that by which we perceive, feel, think and act,[1] since these are all activities peculiar to living things. To this extent, Aristotle's use of "soul" is quite similar to our use of "mind." We commonly say that we perform these activities "with our minds," without implying anything Cartesian about dualism or privacy. But the two are not precise equivalents. As the basis of *life*, the soul for Aristotle is also that in virtue of which we grow, digest, reproduce, and breathe.[2] In fact, he criticizes his predecessors for not having paid attention to this, and pointedly insists that *plants* also have a soul, even though he regards them as incapable of perception, thought, feeling, or action.[3] In so far as it studies vital capacities as well as mental ones, psychology has a broader scope for Aristotle than philosophy of mind does for us. But apart from this difference in extension, they will have much in common. Many of the issues that arise in connection with the mind – for example, mechanism, reduction, and emergence – have structural analogues for vital phenomena more generally. The differences between these phenomena will make a difference, of course, as to how we answer these questions in each case. But this is something Aristotle himself emphasizes. The unity of the phenomena that psychology studies is only a loose one. We cannot give a single, general account of the soul, he believes, that will apply across the board and still be substantive and illuminating. Instead, we must attend to the specific activities that are characteristic of different kinds of living thing. In certain ways, perception and thought differ from digestion. But in other ways, perception has more in common with digestion, and Aristotle will regard thought as the odd one out. By keeping all of these phenomena together within a single area of study, we are less likely to generalize falsely about the nature or peculiarity of the "soul" and the "mind."

The Soul–Body Relation

One of the chief concerns of Aristotle's treatise *De Anima* is the relation of the soul to the body.[4] Aristotle wants to account for the way in which they can be said to be "one," as well as the way in which they differ; and he repeatedly returns to the question of whether there is any sense in which the soul can be said to be "separable" (*chōristos*). His own solution appeals to the central concepts of his metaphysics. He regards the body as the *matter* and the soul as the *form* of a living thing (*De An.* II.1,

---

1.   *De An.* I.5, 411a26–30; II.2, 413b11–13; II.3, 414a29–b1.
2.   *De An.* I.5, 410b16–411a2, 411a30; II.2, 413a21–b8; II.3, 414a31; II.4, 415a22–b2, b23–26, 416a6–b29; III.12, 434a22–26. See also "On Length and Shortness of Life" and "On Youth, Old Age, Life and Death and Respiration" in his *Parva Naturalia*, as well as the treatment of reproduction in *Generation of Animals*.
3.   *De An.* I.4, 409a9–10; I.5, 411b27–28; II.2, 413a25–b1; II.3, 414b32–415a3; III.12, 434a26.
4.   For Aristotle's treatment of this topic in his biological works, see Lennox, ARISTOTLE'S BIOLOGY AND ARISTOTLE'S PHILOSOPHY, esp. the "Biology and Metaphysics" section, in this volume.

412a15–b6) – hence, the description of his view as "hylomorphism," literally, "matter-form-ism." The two are correlative to one another. The parts and materials that make up a concrete object are its matter, while the way they are organized into a whole that can function in the appropriate ways is its form. If we grant this, he claims, then there is no more point to asking whether soul and body are one than there is in the case of wax and its shape (412b6–8). The soul is not itself a certain kind of body (as the Atomists think), but neither can it exist without a body (as the Platonists think). It is something that *belongs to* a body of a given sort and so *inheres in* it (II.2, 414a17–22). Most, if not all, of what living things do or undergo will thus be the activity of body and soul together (I.1, 403a3–19, b17–19). The only exception Aristotle is willing to consider is the understanding (*nous*); and even this will not be separable, if it always requires the power of representation, which is necessarily embodied (403a8–16). In general, psychological states are also to be understood hylomorphically, just like the composite living thing that has them, as "enmattered structures" (*enhuloi logoi*) that must be defined in terms of both their formal organization and their material realizations. Being angry, for example, is at once a desire for reprisal *and* a boiling of the blood around the heart (403a24–b9).

Hylomorphism is widely regarded as the sort of middle course for which Aristotle is famous, a nuanced solution that does justice to the intuitions on each side, without going to either extreme. Others see it instead as a beguiling, but ultimately hopeless, attempt to have things both ways.[5] We cannot hope to resolve this question, though, without a more precise understanding of the position itself, and on this antecedent question there is a dismaying range of responses in the literature. Scholars differ over even quite basic questions, such as whether Aristotle is a materialist or a dualist,[6] not to mention more refined ones, like whether he is committed to functionalism,[7] psychophysical supervenience,[8] or emergentism.[9]

Before exploring these debates, it may help to see why one simple answer will not do. At the opening of *De Anima* II.1, Aristotle suggests that body and soul are each

5. This accusation is leveled in Williams (1986), although the worry is already present in Ackrill's seminal article (1972–3). A different charge of incoherence is pursued at length in Granger (1996).
6. For a nonreductive materialism: Caston (1997); Charles (1984); Irwin (1991); and Wedin (1992, 1996). For a dualist reading: Hamlyn (1978); Heinaman (1990); Robinson (1983); and Sisko (2000).
7. For a functionalist reading: Irwin (1991); Shields (1990). Against a functionalist reading: Burnyeat (1992); Code and Moravcsik (1992); Granger (1990); Heinaman (1990).
8. For the supervenience of psychological states on material states: Charles (1984, pp. 214, 246); Shields (1988, pp. 106, 131–4; and 1993, p. 165); Wedin (1992, 1996); and, with qualifications, Caston (1992 and 1997, pp. 332–7). Against supervenience: Burnyeat (1992, p. 23); Granger (1990, 1993); Heinaman (1990, p. 101 (though cf. p. 90)).
9. For the suggestion that Aristotle is an emergentist, see Ackrill ((1972–3) 1979, p. 74); Caston (1997, pp. 326–8, and 1999b); Heinaman (1990, p. 91); Robinson (1983). (Note that both Robinson and Heinaman take emergentism to be *incompatible* with materialism and supervenience, while I take it to imply both). Against an emergentist reading, see Miller (1999); Sisko (2000).

"substances" or *ousiai* and that the individual composed from these two is a third (412a6–b9). There could not be a clearer statement, one might think, of substance dualism. But the traditional translation of "substance" is misleading. The Greek, as Aristotle uses it, signifies something's *being*, what something *is*, and the point he is making is that there is a systematic ambiguity when we speak about what a thing is: in one way, it is the *kind* or *type* of thing it is and what it is to be that sort of thing; in another way, it is the matter that *constitutes* or *composes* such things; and in yet another, it is the compound of the two, that is, this sort of nature *as realized by* that sort of matter.[10] Body and soul are therefore not "substances" in the way that substance dualism requires. They are not two species of a single genus, each of which can exist independently on its own. Rather, each is a substance in a fundamentally different sense, as matter and as form, and both must be conjoined for there to be an individual at all. We can approach this point in another way. If hylomorphism committed Aristotle to substance dualism, he would be a substance dualist not only with regard to humans, animals, and even plants, but *all natural bodies*. The distinction between matter and form is not peculiar to living things, but applies to all natural substances across the board. In applying it to living things, Aristotle is therefore treating them *on a par* with the rest of the natural world. In none of these cases can a form exist independent of matter. Form is not an additional ingredient alongside the materials that constitute an individual, which can be separated from the rest. It is rather the *organization* of these materials into a certain kind of thing, that in virtue of which they are such a thing and possess the relevant capacities (*Met.* Z.17). It cannot exist apart on its own.

These same considerations suffice to show that Aristotle cannot be an eliminative or reductive materialist either. His analysis presupposes that there *is* such a thing as the soul, not to mention psychological phenomena; and that there is a fundamental, *irreducible* distinction between the soul and the body, and more generally between their formal and material contributions in the analysis of psychological phenomena. On the other hand, because the soul is necessarily the form *of the body* and psychological phenomena have *both* a formal *and* a material aspect, he must nevertheless be some kind of materialist, though of a nonreductive sort.[11] We might say that Aristotle rejects "type identity," while accepting a certain "token identity." Soul and body constitute *distinct types*: what it is to be animate is different from what it is to be embodied, since one consists in being organized in a certain way, the other in being composed of certain kinds of material and parts. Nevertheless, an individual living thing is *both* animate *and* embodied – each of these is rightly said to be something the living individual *is* (and thus its being or *ousia*) – and so the *same token* instantiates both types. Aristotle extends the same analysis to psychological phenomena. My anger on a particular occasion is both a desire for reprisal *and* a boiling of my blood, even though *what it is* to desire reprisal differs from *what it is* to have one's blood boil.

---

10.   For more on being and substance, see M. L. Gill, FIRST PHILOSOPHY IN ARISTOTLE, in this volume.
11.   I am bracketing for the moment (as Aristotle often does himself) the question of whether thought constitutes a genuine exception to this rule. See pp. 335–41 below.

Between these two extremes, there is still a wide range of options, depending on how the matter–form relation is to be understood. It is in this connection that technical concepts such as functionalism, supervenience, and emergentism have been invoked in recent years.

Functionalism

Functionalism, perhaps the predominant approach in philosophy of mind over the past 30 years, has also been the subject of intense debate among Aristotle scholars. The functionalist interpretation of Aristotle was initially embraced quite widely, encouraged by the endorsement of Hilary Putnam, one of functionalism's early pioneers.[12] But during the past decade, it has suffered something of a backlash, triggered by Myles Burnyeat's polemic, "Is an Aristotelian Philosophy of Mind Still Credible?" (1992). It ends with this defiant challenge: "Hence all we can do with the Aristotelian philosophy of mind and its theory of perception . . . is what the seventeenth century did: junk it . . . new functionalist minds do not fit into old Aristotelian bodies" (p. 26).

The subsequent debate has produced a large and wide-ranging literature.[13] But little of it in fact concerns functionalism as such. The focus has instead been on other theses, which are allegedly presupposed or implied by functionalism, such as supervenience or multiple realization. But if we consider functionalism in its own right, two things become immediately clear: (i) such an approach contains deep insights about Aristotle's psychology, which deserve recognition; yet (ii) in the technical sense, Aristotle cannot be a functionalist.

According to functionalism, each mental state is defined by its *functional role*, that is, by all the ways in which it can interact causally, in mediating between sensory inputs, behavioral outputs and other mental states. What *plays* or *realizes* this role will be – or, at least, is generally expected to be – some material state. But it is not specified as such in the definition. What is required is that it be a state whose causal powers *suit* it to play the functional role in question. Consequently, even if a role is always realized by a certain type of material state, it will not be *identified* as such. In fact, there might even be several types of material state that are suited to play the same role. Functional definitions thus leave open the possibility of *multiple realization*. The specification of a functional role constrains the kind of states that could play it, without guaranteeing that there is a unique realization or, for that matter, several. Nothing in the definition

---

12.   Putnam (1975c) describes his own view as "substantially the same" as Aristotle's, "although stated a bit more precisely with the aid of the vocabulary of contemporary scientific methodology and cybernetics" (1975b, p. xiv; cf. 1975c, p. 302 and 1975a, p. 279). He never intended the precise details involving Turing machines to be attributed to Aristotle, only the general strategy of functional analysis (Nussbaum and Putnam, 1992, p. 48). See also Block (1980, pp. 171, 177).
13.   See e.g., Bradshaw (1997); Broackes (1999); Broadie (1992); Burnyeat (1995, 2001, 2002); Caston (2005); Code and Moravcsik (1992); Cohen (1992); Everson (1997); Freeland (1992); Granger (1990, 1992); Johansen (1998); Lloyd (1992); Magee (2000); Miller (1999); Nussbaum and Putnam (1992); Price (1996); Sisko (1996, 1998); Sorabji (1992, 2001); Whiting (1992); Woolf (1999).

320

explicitly requires either outcome.[14] Functional explanations are, to this extent, autonomous from material ones. The essence of mentality consists not in what realizes or constitutes these states, but in what they *do*.

If we consider Aristotle's psychology from this perspective, three themes become salient. First, Aristotle's conception of form in general is a functional one, in a suitably broad sense of the term. In *Meteorology* IV.12, he characterizes forms, and hence what each thing *is*, in terms of what each thing can *do*. Nothing can properly be said to belong to a kind *K* unless it is able to perform the activities characteristic of *K*s – if it is not able to satisfy this condition, it can be called a *K* only "homonymously" or by courtesy, due to extrinsic similarities. Aristotle applies this view explicitly to living things (*De An.* II.1, esp. 412b10–413a3), and employs functional analysis to explore the specific organization of different kinds of souls. Each, in fact, is *defined* by its capacities, such as the capacity to digest, to perceive, to think and to move (*De An.* II.2, 413b11–13). Second, matter plays a subsidiary role for Aristotle too. Every living thing, as something that undergoes change, must be embodied. The *type* of matter is constrained only by its function, through what Aristotle calls "hypothetical necessity" (*Phys.* II.9; *PA* I.1). A substance of a certain kind *K must* have a suitable type of matter, *if* it is to perform the activities characteristic of *K*s. Just as a saw cannot be made of just anything, but must be made of a metal such as iron (*Phys.* II.9, 200a10–13), so too a given soul cannot exist in just any type of body; it must be in a body of the right sort (*De An.* I.3, 407b20–26; II.2, 414a22–27). Beyond meeting this suitability requirement, however, the type of matter is not important to what a thing is, and, in the abstract, more than one type of matter might conceivably do. An axe might be made from various kinds of metal (*PA* I.1, 642a9–11), and perhaps a human could be constituted from something other than flesh and bones (*Met.* Z.10–11). Third, for Aristotle psychological explanations are "from the top down" – they give primacy to form. One begins by looking at the type of activities a living thing can perform, in order to develop a functional analysis of the capacities required for such activities. Only then can one turn to the details of how these activities are implemented in specific materials, and how these might malfunction in various ways. Psychological explanation thus presupposes a material account. But it also possesses a kind of autonomy, which constrains the explanatory role of the material account, rather than vice versa.

Each of these themes is central to Aristotle's psychology. But they still do not amount to functionalism. Functionalism is primarily a thesis about mental *states*: they are to be defined holistically, by specifying the functional role of all the states simultaneously via the Ramsey-Lewis method of theoretical identifications, purely in terms of their causal relations to one another.[15] This removes all mental terms from the definiens,

---

14. It is worth emphasizing that multiple realizability only entails *epistemic* possibility: *for all we know*, there might be several types of material state that satisfy the definition, since it does not explicitly specify a certain type of material state, much less one that uniquely satisfies it. But it does not follow that multiple realization is a genuine *physical* possibility in any given case, as is sometimes alleged. Epistemic possibility is just a question of what is "left open" by the definition, due to its abstractness.

15. For the classic statement of the Ramsey-Lewis method, see D. Lewis (1970); and for its application to functionalism, D. Lewis (1972), and Loar (1981).

leaving a topic-neutral characterization of mental states that can be used to identify the underlying material states. Aristotle's main emphasis, in contrast, is not on mental or psychological states, but on the *soul* and the *capacities* that constitute it. And while he does discuss the proper definition of psychological states (*De An.* I.1, 403a25–b19), the schema he endorses does not approach a functional definition either in spirit or detail. It makes no attempt to capture the holistic nature of psychological states or their functional roles.[16] Nor does he define them by their causal roles, by specifying all of their causes and effects in different circumstances. He does require that the definition state the efficient cause of a psychological state, along with its matter, form, and aim – that is, each of his four *aitia* or explanatory factors (403a26–27).[17] But his own emphasis, moreover, is not on the efficient cause, but on matter and form, and this directly conflicts with functionalism. The example he provides, a definition of anger, shows this clearly (403a30–b1). It lacks the abstractness of functionalist definitions, because it specifies the matter as the *blood's* boiling.[18] It also violates topic-neutrality, because it specifies the form as a *desire* for reprisal. Aristotle therefore does not attempt to eliminate *either* psychological *or* material vocabulary from his definitions, one of the key motivations behind contemporary functionalism.

Supervenience and homonymy

Even if we put functionalism to one side, the debate has raised important questions about related issues, which are of independent interest. Burnyeat's two main objections to functionalist interpretations, for example, turn on the modal status of the relation between the body and the soul. One of them claims that on Aristotle's theory it lacks the necessity that functionalism requires. The other claims that it lacks the contingency that functionalism requires.

The first objection concerns whether the mental or the psychological *supervenes* on the physical, whether, that is, a subject's psychological states *necessarily covary* with its physical or material states. If there is supervenience, then given certain material states, certain psychological states must obtain of necessity: there cannot be a difference in the latter without some difference in the former.[19] Against this, Burnyeat and others

---

16. In *Rh.* II.1–11, Aristotle does offer some relational characterizations of various emotions. Even if these were intended as proper definitions for purposes of psychology (or parts of such definitions), they do not make the critical move towards picking out psychological states in terms of their *causal role*. They mainly concern the structure of the emotion's intentional content.

17. Someone might suggest that the aim or *telos* of a psychological state corresponds to its causal effects, of which it is the efficient cause. But this is still a far cry from specifying a state's causal role. What is at issue for functionalism is the full range of effects a state can have within one's psychological economy, not just the ultimate aim intended (such as reprisal in the case of anger).

18. Heinaman (1990, pp. 100–2).

19. It is worth emphasizing that "supervenience," as I am using it here, signifies nothing more than this pattern of covariation. To claim that the mental supervenes on the physical, then, is much weaker than to claim that it is a causal consequence of the physical, much less a logical consequence or somehow metaphysically dependent. For more on supervenience, see the classic articles by Kim (1984, 1990).

have argued that Aristotle rejects supervenience, citing *De An.* I.1, 403a21–22.[20] It is possible to be in same sort of material state that one is in when angry *without being angry*: here would be a difference in one's psychological condition without a corresponding difference in one's material conditions. On Burnyeat's interpretation, a change in perception likewise does not require any change in one's material state, but only a change in external objects. Others argue that understanding does not supervene on bodily states.[21]

Aristotle does not, of course, speak directly of supervenience. But various remarks commit him to it. To begin with, he thinks that souls supervene on bodies. He castigates his predecessors for speaking as if any type of soul could be present in any type of body. On the contrary, he urges, "each body seems to have its own form and structure" (*De An.* I.3, 407b20–24; cf. II.2, 414a22–28). Anything, that is, which has a certain kind of body must have a certain kind of soul: there cannot be difference in souls without a corresponding difference in bodies. The generation of substances quite generally, in fact, supervenes on material changes, and so *a fortiori* the generation of living things and their souls (*Phys.* VII.3, esp. 246a4–8); and similar remarks apply to the demise and destruction of living things. Aristotle does not make a blanket statement with regard to the supervenience of psychological states. But the passage cited above, as evidence against supervenience, actually favors it on closer inspection. Aristotle says that *whenever* we are in that same bodily state, we *are* angry, even if the sorts of external stimuli that normally provoke anger are absent. Indeed, we can have emotions such as fear even when there are *no* external stimuli of the relevant sort; but if we are not in the right state, even pronounced stimuli will not result in an emotional reaction (403a19–25).[22] We will consider perception and thought more closely in the sections below. But nothing there is incompatible with supervenience either.

If anything, Aristotle is faced with the opposite problem. The fact that a body of the relevant sort must have a soul seems to imply that it is *essentially* alive or ensouled. But then when a living thing dies, *that body* will cease to exist as well – it cannot exist as such, whatever else survives, without the soul that necessarily accompanies it. What was flesh will no longer be flesh except "homonymously," that is, in name alone.[23] If so, then living things seem to be quite unlike the artifacts that figure in Aristotle's examples, such as a bronze sphere, where the matter has that form *only contingently* and can be identified independently of the compound into which it enters. This poses a second problem for the functionalist interpretation, Burnyeat argues (1992, p. 26; cf. 17), because it presupposes "the artifact model": it requires that material states be identifiable independently of psychological states and contingently related to them.

If homonymy is a genuine problem, though, it would threaten a good deal more. Aristotle's account of substantial change, of how substances come to be and cease to

---

20. Burnyeat (1992, p. 23); Heinaman (1990, p. 101).
21. Robinson (1991, p. 211); Shields (1993, p. 165); Sisko (2000).
22. For a closer examination of the evidence for supervenience, see Caston (1997, pp. 332–7).
23. *Meteor.* IV.12; *GA* II.1, 734b24–31; *Met.* Z.10, 1035b23–25; cf. *GC* I.5, 321b28–32.

be, holds that the matter of a substance underlies these transformations. To do this, though, the matter must exist before the substance has come to be and must remain after the substance has ceased to be. In short, it must be capable of existing independently of the substance to which it belongs. And since living things are the paradigmatic substances for Aristotle – indeed, they may be the only genuine substances for him – the same should apply here. But it does not, if what was said about homonymy above is correct: the matter of a living thing cannot exist independently. If so, then what Aristotle says about homonymy is at odds with one of the main tenets of his metaphysics, concerning substantial change. Either (a) Aristotle is grossly inconsistent, or (b) he has abandoned his views about substantial change, or (c) he has a different understanding of homonymy, which allows that *some* of the matter of a living thing can exist independently of it. Of these, (c) is plainly the best option.[24]

Yet how can some matter exist independently of a living thing, while some does not? One attractive solution suggests that we distinguish two kinds of matter: (i) *functional matter*, such as hands or uniform parts, like flesh and bones, which are specified by reference to the function of the substance as a whole, and thus its form; and (ii) *compositional matter*, such as earth and fire, from which the functional matter, and thus ultimately the substance, is formed. Functional matter cannot exist apart from the functioning whole, except homonymously, in name alone, because it cannot play that function apart from the substance in question. But compositional matter *can* exist independently of that substance, because it can be specified without reference to the functioning whole – indeed, it must be able to, if it is to underlie substantial change. In fact, Aristotle draws just this sort of distinction between two senses of the word "flesh." We use the word in one sense to refer to the form, to what it is to be flesh and be able to do things characteristic of flesh. But in another sense, we use it to refer to the matter that constitutes flesh (GC I.5, 321b19–22). Aristotle can therefore appeal to homonymy when speaking of *functional* matter, while accounting for substantial change in terms of *compositional* matter.[25]

Compositional matter is not only important for problems concerning homonymy. It is important for supervenience as well. The soul and its capacities trivially supervene on the functional matter of living things, since functional matter by definition implies the presence of the functional whole. It is a substantive question, however, whether the soul and its capacities supervene on the *compositional* matter of living things, and so whether psychological states supervene on material states. It is significant, then, that the evidence for supervenience mentions the elements, and not merely flesh, bones, or vital heat (see Caston, 1997, p. 336).

24.   Compare Ackrill's discussion of the alternatives ([1972–3] 1979, pp. 70–5).
25.   For a full and clear statement of this solution, see Whiting (1992), based on her (1984), esp. pp. 223–34; the same solution appears in Irwin (1988, pp. 241–5), framed in terms of "proximate" and "non-proximate" matter. Chapter 4 of Gill (1989) appeals to the distinction (pp. 127–30, cf. 163), but Gill does not regard it, or the rest of *Met.* Z, as representing Aristotle's final view; rather, it poses a problem for him, which is only solved later in *Met.* H and Θ on a different basis. For a close examination of different conceptions of matter and the ways in which they relate to supervenience and homonymy, see Lewis (1994).

Mental causation and emergentism

Another objection to functionalism, which has broader ramifications, concerns causation. Aristotle cannot be a functionalist, it is argued, because he regards psychological states and the soul itself as efficient causes. Functionalists, in contrast, locate the real causal power in the underlying material states: for them, it is claimed, causal explanation works "from the bottom up," not "from the top down," as Aristotle prefers.[26] Some think that supervenience also precludes psychological states from being efficient causes in their own right. If so, then questions of mental causation will still pose a difficulty for these interpretations, even if functionalism has been abandoned.

Part of the problem here is due to the metaphorical use of "up" and "down," which is bound to cause confusion unless we distinguish carefully the different issues involved. If psychological states supervene on material states, there is a sense in which the "lower" material states of a living thing *determine* or even *necessitate* which "higher" psychological states it has: given certain material states, it must have certain psychological states. But these higher states are not *caused* by the lower ones. Consider the analogy Simmias offers in Plato's *Phaedo* (92e–93a; cf. 85e–86c). Whenever a musical instrument like a lyre is in a certain physical state, each string having a specific length and tension of its own – it *follows necessarily* that the instrument has a certain tuning or *harmonia*. But the tuning is not a causal consequence of the strings' tension, so much as something that covaries with it: for the strings to have a different tuning, they would have to have a different tension. Determination "from the bottom up" is an ontological issue about which properties or states a thing has, given others that it has. It says nothing about causal responsibility. It might be that causal responsibility always resides on the lowest level, and that these lower states are primarily what drives things. But it also might not. There is nothing inherent in supervenience that requires higher-level states to be epiphenomenal, incapable of bringing anything about in their own right. In some cases, it might be the higher-level states, and not the lower-level ones, which are causally responsible – there might, that is, be *downward causation*, even though there is determination from the bottom up. Which higher-level states a thing has will be determined by the lower-level states it has. But the causal powers of the lower-level states themselves are not sufficient to explain the result. In this sense, the higher-level states have genuinely new, *emergent* causal powers that are not reducible to the lower-level ones, even though they supervene upon them. In the nineteenth and twentieth centuries, emergentists such as John Stuart Mill and C. Lloyd Morgan argued that this was in fact the way that chemistry was related to physics: which chemical properties a substance had depended on which physical properties it had; but their causal powers could not be explained by their physical properties alone, at least not before the advent of quantum mechanics.[27]

---

26. Code (1987); Code and Moravcsik (1992); Granger (1990, 1996); cf. Cohen (1992, pp. 71–2). For a clear statement of the problem of mental causation for functionalism generally, see Block (1990).

27. For an excellent treatment of emergentism, historically and systematically, see McLaughlin (1992).

Aristotle believes that the soul, unlike the tuning of an instrument, has causal efficacy in its own right, which is not reducible to bodily properties (*De An.* I.4, 407b34–408a5).[28] The most dramatic case concerns organic rather than mental phenomena. Aristotle argues that the soul alone is responsible for the cohesion of a living thing: on their own, the material elements that constitute it would disperse to their natural places (*De An.* II.4, 416a6–9). But he likewise regards mental states, such as desire and *phantasia*, as the proper efficient causes of action and speech; the underlying material states have a merely instrumental role (*MA* 6, 700b17–20; *De An.* III.10, 433b13–27).[29] Aristotle is thus committed to "downward causation." Not all of the effects of a living thing are brought about by it in so far as it is material. Some are the result, at least in part, of a psychological state, precisely in so far as it is psychological.

Whether or not downward causation is compatible with functionalism, it is compatible with supervenience; to accept both supervenience and downward causation is just to accept emergentism. Downward causation, then, need not commit Aristotle to either vitalism or dualism; and indeed neither view fits his overall approach in psychology. The four material elements *jointly exhaust* the constitution of living things, as they do everything else in the sublunary world.[30] In this sense, all living things are fully material, without remainder. Form is not reducible to matter, but it is not a ghostly element injected into the material world either. Aristotle ridicules any theory that explains mental phenomena by introducing "mind dust" – a soul-element, in effect – whether material or immaterial.[31] Form is rather the organization of existing material at each level of complexity into new substances with new capabilities (*Met.* Z.17). The substantial natures that result are ultimately *based* on configurations of the four elements, even though they are *irreducible* to them. This is not peculiar to life and consciousness. It holds equally for inanimate matter as well. The 18 chemical properties Aristotle discusses in *Meteorology* IV.8–9 already go well beyond the four elemental qualities of the hot, cold, moist and dry, even though they are based on them. The theory of the elements is not enough, therefore, to account for the behavior of even relatively simple bodies. For Aristotle, chemistry, biology, and psychology have a crucial explanatory role as well. He thus tends towards a form of *emergentism*: a position committed to downward causation, while upholding the supervenience of higher states, including psychological states, on lower, material ones. If so, then for Aristotle psychological states would have genuinely new causal powers of their own, which are not reducible to those of the underlying material states, *without being basic*. Which psychological states a living thing has will still be a function of its material states.

28.   This has been recognized by a number of recent authors: Nussbaum (1986, pp. 277–81) (rejecting her earlier view in her 1978, pp. 88, 152–53, 188); Code (1987, *passim*, 1991, p. 111), Code and Moravcsik (1992, p. 139); Granger (1990, 1996); and Caston (1997, pp. 329–31). For an exploration of the *harmonia* theory in Plato and Aristotle and its later aftermath, see Caston (1997).
29.   For a closer examination of the evidence, see Caston (1997, pp. 326–32).
30.   *Meteor.* IV.12, 389b26–28. Cf. I.2, 339a19–20, a27–28; GC II.7, 334b16–20; PA II.1, 646b12–24.
31.   *De An.* I.3, 406b15–25; I.4, 409a10–15; I.5, 409a31–411a2.

Perception

In addition to the soul–body relation, the topic of perception constitutes one of Aristotle's central concerns. Nine chapters of *De Anima* are devoted exclusively to it (*De An.* II.5–III.2), as well as a separate essay, "On Perception and Perceptibles," in the short essays referred to as the *Parva Naturalia*. These views have ramifications as well, since he regards many of our other mental abilities – such as *phantasia*, desire, memory, and dreams – as grounded in the perceptual system,[32] and considers understanding to be analogous to perception in certain important ways (*De An.* III.4, 429a13–18).

In *De Anima* II.6, Aristotle distinguishes three kinds of perception, depending on whether what is perceived is "exclusively," "commonly," or "extrinsically" perceptible. Something is *exclusively perceptible* if it can be perceived by only one sense, such as sight or taste. Colors, flavors, tones, odors and so on fall into this class. Something is *commonly perceptible* if it can be perceived by more than one sense. Aristotle lists motion and rest, number, shape, and extension as belonging to this group.[33] Both of these kinds of object are intrinsically perceptible. Other kinds of object, such as the son of Diares, are also perceptible, but only *extrinsically*. They are something that we perceive only in virtue of other features, which are themselves intrinsically perceptible. Aristotle regards what is exclusively perceptible as fundamental, and it is with respect to these that the nature of each sense is to be defined (418a24–25). Such perception is always true, while the others are subject to error in varying degrees.[34] Given its exclusive concern with sensible qualities, its infallibility, and its foundational role, it is not unreasonable to think of this basic form of perception as "sensation," even though the terminology is not Aristotle's, in contrast with the complex activity that constitutes our ordinary perceptual experience (and typically involves all three forms of perception). In developing his causal model of cognition in *De Anima* II.5, II.12, and III.4, Aristotle is concerned almost exclusively with perception in this most basic sense.

The causal model

Aristotle takes sensation to be about what brings it about, namely, a particular sensible quality. The color of an object – jade green, say – intrinsically has the ability to affect a transparent medium like air or water, which in turn affects the eye of a perceiver, causing him to see that color. Aristotle is thus committed not only to the reality of sensible qualities, but to their causal efficacy. It is color, primarily, which is capable of being seen, because it is this quality that can affect the eye in the right way so as to produce sight (*De An.* II.7, 418a26–b2).[35] He explicitly rejects the view of subjectivists,

---

32. See e.g., *De An.* III.7, 431a12–14; *Mem.* 1, 449b24–25, 450a10–12; *Insomn.* 1, 459a16–19.
33. *De An.* II.6, 418a17–18; III.1, 425a14–20; *Sens.* 1, 437a8–9. Contrast Plato's list of "commons" at *Tht.* 185c–d.
34. *De An.* II.6, 418a11; III.3, 427b12 (but cf. 428b18–25); III.6, 430b29–30; *Sens.* 4, 442b8–10; *Met.* Γ.5, 1010b2–3.
35. This is well-emphasized by Sarah Broadie (1992). For alternative accounts of his realism and its ramifications, see Everson (1997, ch. 3), and Broackes (1999).

who hold that there would not be colors, flavors, and so on, if perceivers did not exist. But his rejection is qualified. On Aristotle's view, sensible qualities would still exist without perceivers. But since they would not actually be sensed, they would not fully realize their nature. They would instead exist only at the "first level" of actuality: they would *actually* be *capable* of producing sensation, but they would not actually be producing it.[36]

When a sense is acted on by a sensible quality, both are brought into activity, one sensing, the other being sensed. Aristotle explains this as he does any agent–patient interaction (*Phys.* III.3). The activity of the patient (the sense) and the activity of the agent (the sensible quality) are "one and the same" and take place in the patient. But their "being is different" – what it is to be the one and what it is to be the other are distinct (*De An.* III.2, 425b26–426a26). And just like other agent–patient interactions, it consists in the patient (the sense) taking on the form of the agent (the sensible). Initially, they are only potentially alike, but as a result of the interaction the sense comes to actually be the sort of thing the sensible is already.[37] This change does not alter the nature of the sense, causing it to lose its perceptual capacity. To the contrary, the sense realizes its nature through this change, by exercising its capacity, like a builder building (II.5, 417a21–b19). But sensation differs from other changes, such as a plant's being warmed or cooled, in so far as it receives the form "without the matter." Just as a bronze signet ring produces a sealing in wax, but does not make it another seal, so a sense is "informed" with the form of the sensible, without becoming an exact replica of its object (*De An.* II.12, 424a17–24, a32–b2). Aristotle ridicules views that require an internal replica. We do not have a stone in our soul, he replies, but only the form of the stone (*De An.* I.5, 409b23–410a13; III.8, 431b20–432a3).

The literalism–spiritualism debate

The precise implications of these views are, not surprisingly, the subject of considerable controversy. Some maintain that the sense organ literally takes on the form of the sensible quality it senses, so that, when I look at a rose and then an azure sky, some part of my eyes literally turns crimson first and then azure. Receiving form "without the matter" is, on this view, an entirely ordinary alteration. Aristotle's phrase indicates that the organ receives only the form of the sensible object and not *its* matter, so that there is no influx of matter from the object (as Empedocles imagined). But in addition to being an ordinary alteration, this change is also a perceiving, because it takes place in the appropriate part of a sentient being, namely, a functioning sense organ. Such a view has, for obvious reasons, come to be called "literalism."[38]

Against this, Myles Burnyeat and others have argued that there is *no* physiological change that occurs during perception. In coming to see azure, *all* that occurs is my

---

36. *De An.* III.2, 426a15–26; *Met.* Γ.5, 1010b30–1011a2; Θ.3, 1047a4–10; *Cat.* 7, 7b22–8a12. One might worry whether these views compromise Aristotle's realism: see Irwin (1988, pp. 313–14).

37. *De An.* II.5, 416b32–417a20, 418a5–6. Cf. III.4, 429a13–18.

38. Slakey (1961); Sorabji ([1974] 1979, pp. 49–50, esp. n. 22 (cf. pp. 54–6)); Everson (1997). Slakey already identifies this view as "the literal interpretation" (pp. 473–4).

coming to see it. Perception is still an embodied process on this view – it is a change *of* or *in* a bodily organ. And it is a "physical" change in so far as Aristotle views it as a completely natural change. But there is no *material process* underlying this change that can be described in topic-neutral terms. The only material conditions necessary for perception are standing conditions, such as having an undamaged eye, a clear and illuminated medium which is not obscured by intervening objects, and so on. The ability to perceive, on Burnyeat's view, is a *basic* power of matter that does not involve any further underlying changes. It is for this reason, he urges, that Aristotle's philosophy of mind is no longer credible. It presupposes a view about matter, and its basic powers, that we can no longer accept, much less find intelligible: for us, matter is not "pregnant with consciousness," something that is just, in itself, capable of perception. For Aristotle, Burnyeat claims, it is. Such a position has come to be called "spiritualism," because it regards perception, with Thomas Aquinas, as a "spiritual" change – one that is physical and embodied, but not a material change.[39]

Much of the debate here turns on close analyses of key texts and cannot be treated, even cursorily, in such a brief space.[40] Even so, there is good reason to think that literalism and spiritualism do not exhaust the possibilities, and that both in fact are mistaken.

The arguments for spiritualism are largely negative. The most ambitious arguments claim that certain of Aristotle's doctrines, such as the distinction of perception from ordinary alterations or the causal efficacy of sensible qualities, *preclude* literalism.[41] But both overstate the case. Perception is not an alteration in the customary sense, according to Aristotle, because it does not destroy our ability to perceive, but rather realizes it, "just as a builder does when building" (*De An.* II.5, 417b6–15). But we wouldn't infer from this that a builder can build without any material change going on, seated, as it were, with arms folded. On the contrary, the builder realizes his building ability *precisely through* material changes such as hammering and sawing. Such changes are not only essential. They in some sense *constitute* his activity as a builder. But then this doctrine cannot rule out such changes in perception either. The second argument, in contrast, which concerns the efficacy of sensible qualities, *does* preclude material alterations from playing an independent causal role. But it does not rule out the *presence* of underlying material alterations, as a supervenience base – that is, it overlooks the possibility that Aristotle is an emergentist. Material alterations might well underlie perception, then, without being in causal competition with sensible qualities and so undermining their causal role.

Aristotle is not in fact silent about material changes in perception, as is sometimes thought. Having classed perception as a state or "affection" of the soul (*De An.* I.1, 403a3–8), he says that the body *undergoes* something *along with* all the affections of the soul, a change that can therefore be distinguished from the affection itself (a16–19, cf. b17–19). In *Generation of Animals* he also clearly states that visible objects affect the eye *both* in so far as they are moist *and* in so far as they are transparent (V.1,

---

39. Broadie (1992); Burnyeat (1992, 1995, 2001, 2002); Johansen (1998); Magee (2000).
40. I offer a detailed analysis in "The Spirit and the Letter: Aristotle on Perception" (2005).
41. For the first argument, see esp. Burnyeat (2002), and for the second, Broadie (1992, pp. 143–5, 150–1).

779b26–780a7). Change in the latter respect constitutes seeing. But this does not preclude change in the former respect, a material – indeed, elemental – change, and these changes, he goes on to explain, have consequences for how we see.

Literalism is not without its difficulties. Literalism is not merely committed to underlying material changes in perception. It is committed to *a quite specific change*: it claims that when we perceive a sensible quality *F*, our organ comes to be *F* in just the same sense that the object is *F*. But Aristotle seems to reject this. If the exact same qualities were exemplified, the object would be *replicated* within the subject, and Aristotle ridicules such views mercilessly. We do not have a stone or a human in our soul when we come to know one, or good and not-good, or any other predication (*De An.* I.5, 409b23–410a13; III.8, 431b21–29). Whatever it means when Aristotle claims that the sense "becomes like" the sensible quality *F*, therefore, the sense cannot become *F* in the same sense that the object is, since that would result in an internal replica. But then Aristotle rejects literalism.

This leaves a crucial gap. Aristotle might be committed to underlying material changes in perception, without being committed to internal replicas. This is clear from his account of understanding. When we think of objects which are large and far away, we do so by means of changes within us that embody the *proportions* of the objects in question, without having the exact same magnitudes, or even necessarily magnitudes along the same dimensions (*Mem.* 2, 452b9–16). These internal changes *model* or *represent* the objects we think about, by having physical magnitudes that embody the same proportions and, perhaps more fundamentally, by sharing certain causal powers in common. Having the same proportions is one way of being similar to something in a precise sense without necessarily being a replica. It is worth noting, then, that Aristotle appeals to proportions extensively in his account of sensible qualities. Colors, sounds, odors, and temperatures are all treated as proportions of contrary qualities. Crimson, for example, is a mixture of white and black in one proportion, purple another.[42] A sense organ could thus become like a sensible quality by taking on the same proportions as the quality possesses, yet avoid replicating it by exhibiting those proportions in a different set of contraries: the eye might take on the proportion that crimson has, but exemplify it not in black and white, but in other contraries, such as hot and cold or viscous and runny. So there is textual as well as logical space for alternative material changes in perception.[43]

Consciousness

There has been debate within the scholarly literature as to whether Aristotle had a concept of consciousness.[44] In a sense, each side is right. Aristotle clearly distinguishes

---

42. *De An.* III.2, 426b3–7; *Sens.* 3, 440b1–26; 4, 442a13–31; *GA* V.7, 786b25–787b20; *APo.* II.2, 90a18–22; *GC* II.7, 334b14–16. On this point, see Sorabji (1972).

43. For this line of interpretation, see Bradshaw (1997); Bynum (1987); Caston (2005); Lear (1988, pp. 109–16); Modrak (1987, pp. 56–62, cf. 28); Price (1996); Silverman (1989); Tweedale (1992, pp. 226–30); Ward (1988).

44. *Against*: Hamlyn (1993, p. xiii, and 1978, p. 12); Rorty (1979, pp. 38–61); Wilkes (1988, pp. 20–1). *For*: Hardie (1976); Kahn ([1966] 1979); Modrak (1980–1, 1987, ch. 6).

being awake and alert from being asleep or knocked out, where the notion of consciousness comes close to that of perceiving. On the other hand, he does not use any single word to pick out the phenomena we have in mind, and he does not share the epistemological concerns distinctive of the Cartesian conception, such as privacy or indubitability. But in another sense, these observations are all beside the point. Aristotle has a good deal to say about the higher-order awareness we have of our own mental states, and this is a sense of "consciousness" which is clearly of interest today.

Aristotle asks how we are able to perceive that we see at the opening of *De Anima* III.2 (425b12–25), and he offers a set of arguments to show that it is by perception itself. The details are controversial, but virtually all commentators have taken them to rule out a distinct *capacity* of higher-order awareness, such as an inner sense.[45] This would put *De Anima* in conflict with his essay "On Sleep and Waking," though, where he argues that we do this not in virtue of vision, but rather a common sense (2, 455a15–22). But the arguments in *De Anima* III.2 are better read as ruling out a distinct *activity* of being aware that we are perceiving. Instead, we perceive that we see an azure sky *by the very same perceptual act* by which we see the sky. Higher-order awareness is thus *intrinsic* to each act of perception. It does not belong to any particular sense modality as such, but to the common perceptual ability that underlies the system as a whole.[46]

Phantasia

After Aristotle completes his discussion of perceptual abilities in *De Anima* III.2, he turns to the topics of thought (III.4–6) and desire and action (III.9–11). But not immediately. In *De Anima* III.3, he introduces a new ability, distinct from all the rest, which he calls "*phantasia*." This ability will play a central role not only in his accounts of thought and desire, but also in his accounts of memory, dreams, passions, and aspects of perceptual experience that go beyond mere sensation. But as the first chapter of *De Anima* already makes clear, it has especially significant consequences for the understanding. This, among all mental capacities, is the most likely to be "separable." But, Aristotle warns, if it requires *phantasia*, even the understanding cannot exist apart from the body (I.1, 403a8–10). And it does in fact require *phantasia*. In the last part of *De Anima* and in the *Parva Naturalia*, Aristotle repeatedly claims that we do not ever think without a *phantasma*,[47] the state we have when we are using *phantasia* (III.3, 428a1–2).

"*Phantasia*" and "*phantasma*" are most commonly rendered "imagination" and "image." But these translations are loaded and potentially misleading. Like the cognates "fantasy" and "fancy," they have a long history of theoretical usage in philosophy,

---

45. See e.g., Hamlyn (1993, pp. 121–2); Kosman (1975, pp. 500–2); Modrak (1980–1); Osborne (1983).

46. For a detailed defense of this reading, see Caston (2002).

47. *De An.* III.8, 432a9, and *Mem.*1, 449b31–450a14; cf. also *De An.* III.7, 431a15, b2; and III.8, 432a4–5, a12–14.

psychology, and poetics, especially in the past four centuries, which strongly colors our associations. But Aristotle stands at the beginning of this history, which evolves well beyond his original concerns. When we speak of imagination, for example, we often have in mind a source of creativity and invention. But these are not a part of Aristotle's concerns when he introduces *phantasia*. And while it has connections to mental imagery and visualization, it may be wrong to think of a *phantasma* as something which is viewed with the mind's eye. Many interpretations do make just this assumption, conditioned by the translation "image." But it is not part of the meaning of the Greek. Such questions can only be resolved by looking at Aristotle's actual usage and the details of his theory.

Although Aristotle is not the first to use the term, "*phantasia*" is a technical term. Derived from the passive verb "*phantazesthai*," it signifies the capacity through which things are made to *phainesthai*, to appear or seem to us to be the case. It thus has more to do with things appearing a certain way in experience than with inventing imaginary scenes. Plato actually defines *phantasia* as "a belief that comes about through perception" (*Sph.* 264a–b; cf. *Tht.* 152a–c). Aristotle rejects the claim that it is a kind of belief, but he too is thinking along similar lines. The sun *appears* to be a foot wide, he argues, even though we believe and in fact know that it is not, but larger than the earth (*De An.* III.3, 428a24–b9), just as the two lines in a Müller-Lyer diagram (to use a modern example) continue to *look* unequal even after we have convinced ourselves that they are in fact equal. The way things appear to us has a certain independence from what we believe. Because of this, Aristotle regards *phantasia* as more rudimentary than belief and even more closely connected with perceptual experience than Plato had claimed.

What enables us to have experiences of this sort? It is not simply perception, since things can appear to us other than they are. Yet it is something *like* perception and clearly plays a part in perceptual experience, more broadly conceived. This, according to the last third of *De Anima* III.3, is what *phantasia* is. Aristotle proposes that it is a trace or echo of perceptual activity. It thus bears a similar content to perception, even after the original perceptual encounter has ended, and so is able to falsely represent how things are in the world (428b10–429a9). In the *Parva Naturalia*, Aristotle explicitly compares *phantasmata* to representations, suggesting that they are reproduced from perceptual activity, like an impression from a signet ring (*Mem.* 1, 450a27–32). In these essays, he also discusses the physiology more extensively, beginning with how the traces persist in the peripheral organs, where they can bring about after-images and other perceptual illusions (*Insomn.* 2), and then how they proceed to the central perceptual organ (which, for Aristotle, is the heart). Along the way, they are subject to distortion, resulting in dreams that can deviate wildly from our waking experience (*Insomn.* 3). Because these *phantasmata* can be stored for long periods in the walls of the heart (*Mem.* 1, 450a32–b11), we are able to remember experiences long past, as well as search for and retrieve particular items (*Mem.* 2). There are even a few tantalizing details about the mechanisms of representation itself, at least as regards magnitudes and their ordering (*Mem.* 2, 452b7–453a4).

The richness of detail in the last third of *De Anima* III.3, corroborated by the *Parva Naturalia*, has rightly led many interpreters to emphasize this part of Aristotle's account. But it has also traditionally been construed in terms of mental images, especially before the rise of behaviorism, when introspection was still dominant in psychology. On this interpretation, *phantasmata* are not merely representations that bear the content of mental acts. The way they represent objects is by being *viewed internally*, by being themselves the *objects* of an internal mental act. Consequently, they are like the percepts from which they are copied by subjectively *resembling* them, though they are fainter and less vivid (cf. *Rh.* I.11, 1370a28–29). The echoes of British empiricism here are not accidental. Such interpretations often allude explicitly to Hobbes' characterization of the imagination as a kind of "decaying sense" or Hume's description of it as a "faint and languid perception."

Growing concerns about mental images in the twentieth century have led to a re-examination of this reading. The most influential critiques were advanced by Malcolm Schofield (1978) and Martha Nussbaum (1978). Both allow that Aristotle in places treats *phantasmata* as mental images, but deny that this is essential to their function. Schofield emphasizes Aristotle's sensitivity to ordinary language, especially skeptical or non-committal uses of the phrase "it appears that" in waking experience, which is more evident in the middle section of *De Anima* III.3 (427b6–428b9). He concludes that *phantasia* is a "loose-knit, family concept" (p. 106), best understood as a passive capacity for having "non-paradigmatic sensory experiences" (pp. 101–2). Nussbaum similarly regards Aristotle as lacking a "canonical theory" (p. 222). But she emphasizes the more positive role *phantasia* plays in Aristotle's account of action, both later in *De Anima* (III.9–11) and in *De Motu Animalium* (6–11). Here, she contends, Aristotle treats *phantasia* as a capacity to perceive objects *as* certain sorts of things, in particular *as* something worth pursuing or avoiding. Both stress the interpretive character of *phantasia* and its pervasive role in ordinary perceptual experience, as opposed to dreams and visualization.

With the resurgence of interest in representational theories of mind in the last quarter of the twentieth century, the pendulum has swung back, at least in part. Deborah Modrak (1987), Michael Wedin (1988) and Dorothea Frede (1992) defend the overall coherence of Aristotle's theory against Schofield's and Nussbaum's critiques. But while both Modrak and Frede accept the traditional view that *phantasmata* are images, Wedin's account marks more of a new departure by construing Aristotle's account along "cognitivist" lines. *Phantasia* is not a full-fledged faculty in the Aristotelian sense, but a system of internal representation that subserves the other faculties, where representations or *phantasmata* are not themselves objects of *phantasia*, or indeed Humean images at all. Instead, they are to be understood as physical states of the body, which possess their content in virtue of their similarity to an object, together with their role in the cognitive system as a whole.

There is much to be said for this general approach. Aristotle explicitly treats *phantasmata* as representations that underwrite the content of mental states generally. This naturally includes imagistic experience and visualization. But active visualization is not necessary for these representations to bear their content and so perform their cognitive role. To use a scholastic distinction, they are that "by which" (*a quo*) mental states are about objects. But they are not in general something "towards which" (*ad quem*) mental states are directed – in general they are not themselves the objects of mental states. Criticisms of representational theories, from the early modern period on, often assume that a representation must be the object of some internal mental state in order to represent another object. But Aristotle does not appear to think that this is necessary. It may simply be that *by which* our mental states are directed at objects, without itself being an object of a mental state at all. The question of subjective resemblance, therefore, need not arise: *phantasmata* do not represent by being looked at and compared to the objects they represent.[48] To the extent that Aristotle does appeal to similarity, it is objective, *physical* similarities that matter, such as possessing magnitudes with the same proportions as those of the object or having similar causal powers with respect to the cognitive system.[49] In fact, Aristotle also explains similarity in artistic representation by reference to causal powers, in distinguishing signs from likenesses (*Pol.* VIII.5, 1340a18–35).[50]

The suggestion that *phantasia* is a form of internal representation that underlies mental states quite generally also fits the contexts in which Aristotle invokes it. On several occasions, he raises puzzles concerning intentionality and mental content, which he uses as a basis for rejecting other theories – any adequate theory, he believes, must have a solution to them. He rejects both pre-Socratic and Platonic accounts, for example, because they cannot solve *the problem of presence in absence* in its full generality – the problem, that is, of explaining how we can remember or think of objects that are absent, whether they are simply absent from our immediate environment, or no longer existent, or have never existed at all. But a solution can be found, he believes, if we posit internal representations or *phantasmata*.[51] Similarly a theory must have a solution to *the problem of error*, of explaining how it is possible for the content of our mental states to deviate not only from immediate stimuli in our environment, but from the way things are in the world more generally. This is the task Aristotle sets explicitly in the opening section of *De Anima* III.3 (427a17–b6). This passage, though overlooked by most discussions, makes clear the structure of the entire chapter. Aristotle taunts his predecessors for not being able to explain how error is possible given their simple causal account of cognition, according to which "like is known by like." On such a view a mental state is invariably about what brings it about and so always corresponds to actual conditions in the world – it cannot err or deviate from the way things are. What makes this critique especially interesting is that Aristotle's *own* account of the most basic forms of perception and thought does not differ in this regard and Aristotle accordingly takes both sensation and understanding to be incapable of error.[52] The difference is that Aristotle does not think that all cognition can be *reduced* to these two basic activities – the simple causal model of cognition that underlies them does *not* account for content in general. A different kind of activity is required: *phantasia*. In the second section of the chapter (427b6–428b9), he argues that *phantasia* is distinct

---

48. There are of course cases where we do reflect on the content of our mental states – for example, when we wonder whether we are genuinely remembering or not (*Mem.* 1, 450b20–451a14), or whether we are dreaming (*Insomn.* 3, 462a5–7) – and in such cases, we do consider the similarity of their content to that of perceptual experiences. But it does not entail that *phantasmata* possess their content in the first place by subjective resemblance.

49. Similar proportions: *Mem.* 2, 452ab11–22. Similar causal powers: *Insomn.* 2, 460b23–25; *MA* 7, 701b17–22; 11, 703b18–20.

50. For more extensive discussion and defense of these claims, see Caston (1998a).

51. *Mem.* 1, 450a27–32; 2, 452b11–16; *Peri Ideōn* 81.25–82.6 Harlfinger.

52. For sensation, see n. 34 above; for understanding, n. 55 below.

from perception, thought, or any combination of the two. The way it is generated from perception, he argues in the third section (428b10–429a9), explains why its content is similar to perception, yet also capable of deviating from actual conditions in the world. *Phantasia* can represent the world falsely as well as truly (428b17) and thus is a key factor in explaining the complex behavior of animals (428b16–17, 429a4–8).[53]

Thought

Aristotle's "noetic" – his account of *nous* or thought (*De An.* III.4–8) – is one of the most influential parts of his entire psychology. It is also one of the most controversial, as it is decisive for several issues of larger importance, including dualism and personal immortality. Given the predominance of these metaphysical issues in the literature, it is worthwhile to start with his views on content and intentionality instead, which have received comparatively less attention.

The content of thought

Aristotle's treatment of thought resembles, in certain large-scale features, his treatment of perception. Just as he distinguished a basic form of perception, which we called "sensation," from other forms of perception, he also singles out a basic form of thinking from more complex ones that include propositional thought and reasoning. This basic form of thinking or *nous* is perhaps best thought of as "understanding." Its object is always a nature or essence,[54] about which one *cannot be in error*: either one grasps it or one doesn't.[55] Its infallibility, like the infallibility of sensation, can be traced to the simple causal model that underlies both accounts. Understanding is about the object that brings it about, which causes the understanding to become like it in form, without becoming the object itself (*De An.* III.4, 429a13–18; *Met.* Λ.7, 1072a30).

For humans, each act of understanding is grounded in *phantasia* and so ultimately perception. Without any sensory experience, humans could not learn or grasp anything (*De An.* III.8, 432a3–8). But we also retain the contents of such experiences in memory, which allows us to have the objects of understanding available within us and so think whenever we want (II.5, 417b19–26; III.4, 429b5–9). The objects of understanding are said to be "in" *phantasmata*. Hence, their contents in some sense depend on quasi-perceptual content (see p. 332 above) which therefore constrain what we are capable of understanding.[56] But even if concepts are not without *phantasmata*, they are not reducible to *phantasmata* either (III.8, 432a12–13), since understanding is "of the universal" (II.5, 417b22–23). This difference is plainly due to the interaction of *phantasmata* and the understanding, but on this crucial question Aristotle says very little. According to one common interpretation, it consists in the literal "abstraction"

53. A close reading of the chapter and its structure can be found in Caston (1996).
54. *De An.* III.4, 429b10–22; III.6, 430b27–29.
55. *De An.* III.6, 430a26–27, b27–28; *Met.* Θ.10, 1051b15–32, 1052a1–4; cf. *Int.* 1, 16a9–13. The metaphor of touch is used at *Met.* Θ.10, 1051b24–25; cf. Λ.7, 1072b21.
56. See e.g., *De An.* III.7, 431b18–19; *Mem.* 1, 450a7–14.

of intelligible forms from material *phantasmata*, by stripping away or removing the matter to yield disembodied forms, freed from their particularity. But the only process Aristotle explicitly describes is more like selectively attending, or better *ignoring*, parts of a *phantasma*'s content, as we do when we use diagrams in geometry and ignore those features which are irrelevant to our purposes (*Mem.* 1, 450a1–10).

This basic form of thought is contrasted with a more discursive form he refers to as *dianoia*. This type of thinking involves the "combination and division" of basic concepts, to produce a new compound unity,[57] which is capable of falsehood as well as truth.[58] The analogy Aristotle draws with words and sentences suggests that he takes both combination and division to be forms of predication, where one concept is either applied to another or withheld from it. Understanding, in contrast, is like uttering a single word.[59] Aristotle offers few further details. Apart from the cryptic remarks at *De An.* III.6, 430b20–23, for example, very little is said about how the mind "divides" concepts. Even combination is not entirely clear, as "combining" and "dividing" ordinarily signify symmetric operations, whereas predication is nonsymmetric.[60] One would also like to know more about the basic "simple" concepts, which are uncombined and undivided (or perhaps even indivisible).[61]

The metaphysics of understanding

Aristotle devotes considerably more attention to the metaphysics of understanding: the nature of the understanding as both a capacity and an activity, its relation to the body, and the existence of a second understanding, the so-called "agent intellect," which he says is alone immortal (*De An.* III.5, 430a23). It will be possible here only to outline the major issues.

Aristotle begins *De Anima* III.4 by confronting a question that has dogged him throughout the treatise, namely, whether the understanding is "separable" (*chōristos*). Until this point, he has offered only hedged and qualified remarks.[62] Plainly, it is separable in so far as it is *conceptually distinct* from other capacities. The question now is whether it is *spatially distinct* as well (429a10–13). He concludes that it does not have an organ of its own, but is "uncompounded" with the body (Anaxagoras' phrase), on the grounds that if it had any actual qualities of its own prior to its exercise – as it would, if it were compounded with the body – these would block it from understanding things that we can in fact grasp (429a18–27).[63] Prior to grasping something, there

---

57. *De An.* III.6, 430a27–28, b5–6; 8, 432a10–12. Cf. III.11, 434a9–10.
58. *De An.* III.6, 430a27–28, b1–4; III.8, 432a10–12; *Int.* 1, 16a9–18.
59. *Int.* 1, 16a9–18; *De An.* III.7, 431a8–10, a14–16. On Aristotle's psychosemantics more generally, see Charles (2000) and Modrak (2001).
60. For some speculations along these lines, see Caston (1998b).
61. On this question, see Aubenque (1979) and Berti (1978).
62. *De An.* I.1, 403a3–b19; I.4, 408b18–29; II.1, 413a4–7; II.2, 413b24–27; II.3, 414b18–19, 415a11–12.
63. Aristotle actually claims that the understanding grasps *everything*. But his argument only requires that being mixed with the body would prevent us from thinking *some* things we actually can think. See Caston (2000).

is nothing more to the understanding beyond the ability itself, like a slate on which nothing has yet been written (429a24–27, 429b31–430a2). This makes it even less vulnerable than our perceptual abilities. If anything, highly intelligible objects strengthen our ability rather than debilitate it (429a29–b5).[64]

On the face of it, this conclusion sounds like a strong affirmation of dualism. But its exact import is less clear in context. To begin with, it does not imply that the human understanding can exist on its own, independently of the body. In the very next chapter, he claims that this intellect is *perishable*, in contrast with another, which "alone is immortal and eternal" (*De An.* III.5, 430a22–25). Nor does it imply that the understanding can function independently of the body's involvement. As we have seen, all human understanding presupposes *phantasmata* – it actually grasps its objects "in" *phantasmata* – and so cannot take place without certain bodily activities.

Aristotle's stated conclusion is more modest and limited in any case. It need mean no more than this: that there is no *organ* of understanding, that is, no *discrete part* of the body that is dedicated to its functioning, as there is for each of the other capacities that make up the soul. It is in this sense that Aristotle can claim that there is nothing more to the understanding, prior to actually grasping something, than its "nature," namely, the mere ability itself to understand. Beyond the equipment we already possess for other functions, there is no special apparatus for understanding that exists even when it is not being exercised. To go back to the question Aristotle raises at the beginning of the chapter, the ability to understand would be separate *only* in the sense of being conceptually distinct from our other abilities. It cannot further be located in some particular part of our bodies. It is part of the form of the body, but it is not the form *of part* of the body, as he had intimated earlier (cf. II.1, 413a4–7). Such a claim is compatible with various forms of materialism (even if it runs counter to our own view that the brain is the seat of cognitive activity).

Some have felt that the understanding must be an "immaterial faculty" in a stronger sense, though, which no materialist could countenance.[65] But it is difficult to give these claims a precise meaning. There is a temptation to imagine an incorporeal *organ*, something analogous to a bodily sense organ, but dematerialized and, as it were, diaphanous. Such a view would conflict with Aristotle's stated argument, however. For an immaterial organ would have to be something *actual*, beyond the mere ability of understanding, which would exist even when it is not being exercised – otherwise, it would be an "organ" only in name, and there would be nothing to distinguish this view from the minimalist reading given above. Yet if this organ is something actual prior to acts of understanding, it will have characteristics of its own, which would obstruct the full range of understanding, against what Aristotle claims.

Any interpretation, in fact, other than the minimalist reading will confront the same objection. If the understanding, prior to its exercise, is nothing more than the mere ability to understand, there cannot be anything more to the understanding, whether material or immaterial, that exists between episodes of understanding. The capacity to understand is something that belongs to the human being as a whole, without any additional special apparatus.

64. For close examinations of this argument, see Caston (2000); Shields (1997); Sisko (1999).
65. See Hamlyn (1978); Robinson (1983); and now Sisko (2000).

Aristotle's argument has consequences for his views about cognition more generally. One of the most interesting features of the argument is the way it links the *constitution* of the understanding to the *contents* it is able to entertain. It rests on certain assumptions about how forms must be received for cognition to take place, and how the constitution of material organs affects performance in specific ways. Such assumptions are clearly important in trying to evaluate his views on mental content.[66]

The "agent intellect"

These difficulties pale, however, when we come to *De Anima* III.5, a chapter of a mere 16 lines. In it, Aristotle argues that there must be a *second* understanding, traditionally referred to as the "agent intellect" (*nous poiētikos* or, in Latin, *intellectus agens*), which alone is "immortal and eternal" (430a22–23). There is not a phrase in the chapter whose interpretation has not been disputed. But plainly it is decisive for many of the issues we have been raising. If each person has an agent intellect of their own, Aristotle is committed not only to personal immortality, but to a genuinely robust substance dualism, where the human soul, or part of it at any rate, can exist after our demise, independent of the body. It is not surprising that over the last 2,300 years it has occasioned more controversy than any other passage in the corpus.[67]

The chapter consists of two parts: an extended inference, arguing for the existence of the second understanding (430a10–17); and a compendious list of its attributes (a17–25). In every kind found in nature, Aristotle claims, there is (i) something that serves as matter and has the potential to become each of the things in that kind and (ii) something that is the productive cause that makes all the things in that kind, comparable to the way that art (*technē*) is related to matter and light makes potential colors into actual ones. This distinction, he argues, is also found in the soul: one understanding has the capacity to become all things, another to make all things. The latter understanding is not only separate, inviolable, and unmixed, it is also by its very essence in actuality – it is not the case that it sometimes thinks and sometimes does not. Thus, even though the capacity to understand precedes the activity of understanding in the individual, in the universe as a whole the activity of understanding is prior. This second understanding, taken separately just by itself, is alone "immortal and eternal." The other understanding is perishable.

The identity of the second understanding is very much in dispute. One tradition, championed by Thomas Aquinas and dominant throughout the twentieth century, holds that (a) each human being has an "agent intellect" of his own, which guarantees some form of continued existence after death.[68] But this isn't the only way to construe Aristotle's conclusion that the distinction between agent and patient can also be found

---

66. For an attempt to spell out some of these assumptions more precisely, see Caston (2000).

67. The most detailed account of ancient interpretations is still Kurfess (1911). In English, see Blumenthal (1996, ch. 11); Brentano (1977, pp. 4–24); Kal (1988, pp. 93–109).

68. Thomas Aquinas *ST* 1a q. 79 a. 4–5; *SCG* II.76–78; *In III De An.* lect. 10; *Quaest. De An.* a. 5; *De Spir. Creat.* a. 10. For representative examples from the twentieth century, see Rist (1966), and Ross (1949, pp. 148–53).

"in the soul." It need not imply that both understandings can be found within *each* human soul, but only among souls generally.[69] The fact that this second understanding is supposed to be eternal and in actuality by its very essence suggests that (b) it belongs to a different kind of soul, either (1) one of the higher intelligences, as many of the medieval Arabic and Italian Renaissance commentators held,[70] or (2) God himself, as Alexander of Aphrodisias maintained (second–third century CE).[71] There is extensive overlap, in fact, between the attributes of the second understanding and those of the divine understanding listed in *Metaphysics* Λ.7–9, which is held to be unique.[72] On either (b1) or (b2), personal immortality is out of the question, as is substance dualism.

On *any* of these readings, though, Aristotle's naturalism would be in doubt. For they all take the second understanding to play a direct and essential role in the production of ordinary human thoughts, and this would seem to preclude a naturalistic account, whether the second understanding is supposed to be a higher intelligence, like God, or a human intellect capable of existing independently from the body. This consequence has been combated recently by Michael Wedin, who argues that Aristotle's account is "stubbornly naturalistic" (1988, p. 194). In fact, it is thoroughly functionalist and cognitivist in spirit, he claims, especially the distinction between two kinds of understanding. Aristotle first explains the basic features of cognitive activity by positing a single, unified faculty of understanding in *De Anima* III.4. But he goes on to raise two puzzles at the end of the chapter (429b22–430a9), which prompt him to offer a deeper analysis, at a "lower, sub-personal level." *De Anima* III.5 offers us, in effect, a distinction between two "subsystems" within a single, unified mind that together allow us to think spontaneously, as self-movers. This move does not threaten naturalism, according to Wedin, because the "productive mind" is not *literally* divine, eternal, or independent of the body. It is active whenever it exists, but it does not exist forever or function continuously (pp. 178–9, 189–90). It is eternal only in the sense that a mathematical object is, in so far as both are defined abstractly without reference to the body; yet neither can exist or function without a body (pp. 190–3). Productive mind is separable only in so far as it is not the actuality or form of a discrete organ (pp. 182–3, 186).

Some may reject such an interpretation as overly deflationary: it is difficult not to take "eternal" as meaning existing at all times. But it would be wrong to blame Wedin's commitment to "stubborn naturalism." The real culprit is the nearly universal assumption that the second understanding is instrumental in the production of ordinary thoughts. Absent this, it is easy to offer a naturalistic reading without being deflationary. The second understanding can be literally eternal, and even God, if the causal mechanisms of human thought involve nothing more than the first intellect together with the lower faculties. One of the greatest difficulties for the tradition, in fact, has always been to specify what the second understanding is required to *do*. Suggestions run the gamut, including the abstraction of universals from images (which is itself

---

69. If anything, the logical structure of the argument requires that they belong to distinct kinds of soul: see Caston (1999a, pp. 205–11).
70. See Davidson (1992) and Kessler (1988).
71. See Moraux (1942).
72. See Caston (1999a, pp. 211–12).

explained in diverse ways), selective attention, the ability to think spontaneously, and even free choice. But these are entirely speculative. Aristotle says *nothing* determinate about how the second understanding would produce thoughts – in fact, this intellect is never expressly referred to outside *De Anima* III.5. And that chapter, beyond its initial distinction between an understanding that "becomes all things" and another that "makes all things," only offers analogies to art and to light, which have proven extremely malleable throughout the tradition. So commentators have searched for lacunae in Aristotle's account that need to be filled. But if the second understanding played such a critical role in the production of human thoughts, it would not have been to his credit to have introduced it in this way. It would be little more than a *deus ex machina*, a magical problem solver, mentioned only in an exceedingly telegraphic and cryptic manner. Worse, many proposals are difficult to reconcile with what Aristotle actually *does* say, in particular about the parallel between understanding and sensation. Whether one takes the "agent intellect" to act directly on our receptive understanding or indirectly by acting on an object of understanding (which in turn acts on the receptive understanding), nothing comparable is found in sensation. Aristotle makes no similar call for an "agent sense," whose causal intervention is required if sensible objects are to have any effect on our capacity to sense.[73] Instead, the sensible object acts directly to produce a sensation of itself. If the object of understanding cannot act similarly, as is traditionally assumed, then the parallel Aristotle draws between sensation and understanding and their respective objects cannot run deep at all: the simple causal model used to explain sensation will be inadequate for understanding. But what *exactly* is inadequate about this model in the case of understanding? What is it about the object of understanding that prevents it from acting in a parallel fashion? And which differences between the two activities demand the introduction of a new agent that is itself *a kind of understanding*, rather than an object? What, finally, will remain of Aristotle's prominent claim at the opening of *De Anima* III.4 that the understanding is "related to its objects in just the same way" that sensation is to its objects (429a15–18)?

These difficulties are avoided if we deny that the second understanding is part of what *we* would call the causal mechanisms of thought.[74] The capacities Aristotle discusses at length in the *De Anima* are sufficient on their own to produce thought. Human understanding does in fact work on the same model as sensation: the object of understanding is able, on its own, to act on the receptive understanding, causing us to grasp it, just as objects of sensation act on the senses. The second understanding is *not* a part of this account at all, but is introduced only against the backdrop of "the whole of nature" (430a10). At this point in his discussion, as at the climax of his other great works (*Met.* Λ.7–9, *EN* X.7, and *EE* VIII.2–3), Aristotle considers his subject in its larger, theological context. On this reading, the second understanding is simply God, who is said to be eternal and pure activity (*Met.* Λ.7, 1072a25–26, b27–28;

---

73. Although this did not stop some medieval commentators from worrying about this: see Dewender (1996) and Pattin (1988), and in English, Kennedy (1966); MacClintock (1956).
74. See Caston (1999a), as well as Frede (1996), which gives an allied reading, though different in both its motivations and details.

cf. Λ.9, 1075a10). His role as the Prime Mover, moreover, as something that is ultimately responsible for all movement in the universe, shows how Aristotle might have regarded him as "producing" all thoughts. According to Aristotle, God makes the heavenly spheres move "in the way a beloved does" (Λ.7, 1072b3), by being the object of their striving, an endpoint towards which all their efforts tend. Aristotle explicitly regards this kind of final cause as an efficient cause (*poiētikon kai kinētikon*, Λ.10, 1075b8–10, b30–35). But it is not a triggering cause, as moved movers are, which can only bring about change by direct contact (*GC* I.6–7). God is an unmoved mover, a standing condition that helps to explain certain general patterns of change, rather than the occurrence and peculiarities of particular episodes. The intermittent and imperfect exercise of our capacity for understanding is something that can be fully appreciated only by reference to the most complete and perfect example of understanding, God. It is only then that we understand what understanding really is. But episodes of understanding – why I succeed in understanding something on this occasion rather than fail, or why I have an understanding of this thing rather than something else – must be accounted for in entirely non-transcendent terms, by reference to the objects in my surrounding, my cognitive history, and my very human capacities. These are, one and all, the capacities of an embodied being, even if they are not all forms of a specific part of the body, and they all perish with the body at death. In this way, a naturalistic account of the causal mechanisms of human thought can be preserved. The idiosyncratic sense in which the second understanding is "productive" depends heavily on *Aristotle's* views about explanation, and in particular the central importance that teleology has for him. But it does not interfere with what we would call the causal account of thought.

Bibliography

Works Cited

Ackrill, J. L. ([1972–3] 1979). "Aristotle's Definitions of *psuchē*." *Proceedings of the Aristotelian Society*, 73, 119–33. Repr. in J. Barnes, M. Schofield, and R. Sorabji (eds.), (1979). *Articles on Aristotle*. (4 vols.). vol. 4: *Psychology and Aesthetics* (pp. 65–75). London: Duckworth.

Aubenque, P. (1979). "La pensée du simple dans la *Métaphysique* (Z.17 et Θ.10)." In P. Aubenque (ed.), *Études sur la Metaphysique d'Aristote* (pp. 69–88). Proceedings of the Sixth Symposium Aristotelicum. Paris: Vrin.

Berti, E. (1978). "The Intellection of 'Indivisibles' According to Aristotle, *De Anima* III.6." In G. E. R. Lloyd and G. E. L. Owen (eds.), *Aristotle on Mind and the Senses* (pp. 141–63). Proceedings of the Seventh Symposium Aristotelicum. Cambridge: Cambridge University Press.

Block, N. (1980). "What is Functionalism?" In N. Block (ed.), *Readings in Philosophy of Psychology*. (2 vols.). (vol. 1, pp. 171–84). Cambridge, Mass.: Harvard University Press.

——. (1990). "Can Mind Change the World?" In G. Boolos (ed.), *Meaning and Method* (Festschrift for Hilary Putnam) (pp. 137–70). Cambridge: Cambridge University Press.

Blumenthal, H. J. (1996). *Aristotle and Neoplatonism in Late Antiquity: Interpretations of the De Anima*. Ithaca, NY: Cornell University Press.

Bradshaw, D. (1997). "Aristotle on Perception: The Dual-Logos Theory." *Apeiron*, 30, 143–61.

Brentano, F. (1977). *The Psychology of Aristotle*. (R. George, ed. and trans.). Berkeley: University of California Press. (Original work published 1867.)

VICTOR CASTON

Broackes, J. (1999). "Aristotle, Objectivity and Perception." *Oxford Studies in Ancient Philosophy*, 17, 57–113.

Broadie, S. (1992). "Aristotle's Perceptual Realism." In J. Ellis (ed.), *Ancient Minds* (pp. 137–59) (= *The Southern Journal of Philosophy*, suppl. vol. 31.)

Burnyeat, M. F. (1992). "Is an Aristotelian Philosophy of Mind Still Credible? (A Draft)." In M. C. Nussbaum and A. O. Rorty (eds.), *Essays on Aristotle's De Anima* (pp. 15–26). Oxford: Clarendon Press.

——. (1995). "How Much Happens when Aristotle Sees Red and Hears Middle C? Remarks on *De Anima* 2.7–8." In M. C. Nussbaum and A. O. Rorty (eds.), *Essays on Aristotle's De Anima* (pp. 421–34). First paperback edition, including an additional essay by M. F. Burnyeat. Oxford: Clarendon Press. (Original work published 1992.)

——. (2001). "Aquinas on 'Spiritual Change' in Perception." In D. Perler (ed.), *Ancient and Medieval Theories of Intentionality* (pp. 129–53). Leiden: Brill.

——. (2002). "*De Anima* II.5." *Phronesis*, 47, 28–90.

Bynum, T. W. (1987). "A New Look at Aristotle's Theory of Perception." *History of Philosophy Quarterly*, 4, 163–78.

Caston, V. (1992). "Aristotle and Supervenience." In J. Ellis (ed.), *Ancient Minds* (pp. 107–35). (= *The Southern Journal of Philosophy* suppl. vol. 31).

——. (1996). "Why Aristotle Needs Imagination." *Phronesis*, 41, 20–55.

——. (1997). "Epiphenomenalisms, Ancient and Modern." *The Philosophical Review*, 106, 309–63.

——. (1998a). "Aristotle and the Problem of Intentionality." *Philosophy and Phenomenological Research*, 58, 249–98.

——. (1998b). "Aristotle on the Conditions of Thought." *Proceedings of the Boston Area Colloquium in Ancient Philosophy*, 14, 202–12.

——. (1999a). "Aristotle's Two Intellects: A Modest Proposal." *Phronesis*, 44, 199–227.

——. (1999b). "Comment on Fred D. Miller, Jr., 'Aristotle's Philosophy of Perception.'" *Proceedings of the Boston Area Colloquium in Ancient Philosophy*, 15, 214–30.

——. (2000). "Aristotle's Argument for Why the Understanding is not Compounded with the Body." *Proceedings of the Boston Area Colloquium in Ancient Philosophy*, 16, 135–75.

——. (2002). "Aristotle on Consciousness." *Mind*, 111, 751–815.

——. (2005). "The Spirit and the Letter: Aristotle on Perception." In R. Salles (ed.), *Metaphysics, Soul, and Ethics* (Festschrift for Richard Sorabji) (pp. 245–320). Oxford: Oxford University Press.

Charles, D. (1984). *Aristotle's Philosophy of Action*. Ithaca, NY: Cornell University Press.

——. (2000). *Aristotle on Meaning and Essence*. Oxford: Clarendon Press.

Code, A. (1987). "Soul as Efficient Cause in Aristotle's Embryology." *Philosophical Topics*, 15, 51–59.

——. (1991). "Aristotle, Searle, and the Mind–Body Problem." In E. Lepore and R. van Gulick (eds.), *John Searle and his Critics* (pp. 105–13). Oxford: Blackwell.

Code, A. and Moravcsik, J. (1992). "Explaining Various Forms of Living." In M. C. Nussbaum and A. O. Rorty (eds.), *Essays on Aristotle's De Anima* (pp. 129–45). Oxford: Clarendon Press.

Cohen, S. M. (1992). "Hylomorphism and Functionalism." In M. C. Nussbaum and A. Rorty (eds.), *Essays on Aristotle's De Anima* (pp. 57–73). Oxford: Clarendon Press.

Davidson, H. A. (1992). *Alfarabi, Avicenna, and Averroes on Intellect: Their Cosmologies, Theories of the Active Intellect, and Theories of Human Intellect*. New York: Oxford University Press.

Dewender, T. (1996). "Sensus agens." In J. Ritter and K. Gründer (eds.), *Historisches Wörterbuch der Philosophie*. (11 vols.). (vol. 9: pp. 618–22). Basel: Schwabe.

Everson, S. (1997). *Aristotle on Perception*. Oxford: Clarendon Press.

342

Frede, D. (1992). "The Cognitive Role of *phantasia* in Aristotle." In M. C. Nussbaum and A. O. Rorty (eds.), *Essays on Aristotle's De Anima* (pp. 279–95). Oxford: Clarendon Press.

Frede, M. (1996). "La théorie aristotélicienne de l'intellect agent." In G. Romeyer-Dherbey (ed.), *Corps et âme: Sur le De Anima d'Aristote* (pp. 377–90). Paris: Vrin.

Freeland, C. (1992). "Aristotle on the Sense of Touch." In M. C. Nussbaum and A. O. Rorty (eds.), *Essays on Aristotle's De Anima* (pp. 227–48). Oxford: Clarendon Press.

Gill, M. L. (1989). *Aristotle on Substance: The Paradox of Unity.* Princeton: Princeton University Press.

Granger, H. (1990). "Aristotle and the Functionalist Debate." *Apeiron*, 23, 27–49.

——. (1992). "Aristotle's Perceptual Realism." In J. Ellis (ed.), *Ancient Minds* (pp. 161–71). (= *The Southern Journal of Philosophy*, suppl. vol. 31).

——. (1993). "Aristotle and the Concept of Supervenience." *The Southern Journal of Philosophy*, 31, 161–77.

——. (1996). *Aristotle's Idea of the Soul.* Boston: Kluwer.

Hamlyn, D. W. (1978). "Aristotle's Cartesianism." *Paideia*, second special issue, 8–15.

——. (1993). *Aristotle De Anima, Books II and III (with passages from Book I).* Trans. with Introduction and Notes. 2nd edn. Clarendon Aristotle Series. Oxford: Clarendon Press. (1st edn. 1968.)

Hardie, W. F. R. (1976). "Concepts of Consciousness in Aristotle." *Mind*, 85, 388–411.

Heinaman, R. (1990). "Aristotle and the Mind–Body Problem." *Phronesis*, 35, 83–102.

Irwin, T. (1988). *Aristotle's First Principles.* Oxford: Clarendon Press.

——. (1991). "Aristotle's Philosophy of Mind." In S. Everson (ed.), *Psychology* (pp. 56–83). Cambridge: Cambridge University Press.

Johansen, T. K. (1998). *Aristotle on the Sense-Organs.* Cambridge: Cambridge University Press.

Kahn, C. H. ([1966] 1979). "Sensation and Consciousness in Aristotle's Psychology." *Archiv für Geschichte der Philosophie*, 48, 43–81. Repr. in J. Barnes, M. Schofield, and R. Sorabji (eds.), *Articles on Aristotle.* (vol. 4): *Psychology and Aesthetics* (pp. 1–31). London: Duckworth.

Kal, V. (1988). *On Intuition and Discursive Reasoning in Aristotle.* Leiden: Brill.

Kennedy, L. A. (1966). "Sylvester of Ferrara and the Agent Sense." *The New Scholasticism*, 40, 464–77.

Kessler, E. (1988). "The Intellective Soul." In C. B. Schmitt, Q. Skinner, and E. Kessler (eds.), *The Cambridge History of Renaissance Philosophy* (pp. 485–534). Cambridge: Cambridge University Press.

Kim, J. (1984). "Concepts of Supervenience." *Philosophy and Phenomenological Research*, 45, 153–76. Repr. in J. Kim (1993). *Supervenience and Mind: Selected Philosophical Essays* (pp. 53–78). Cambridge: Cambridge University Press.

——. (1990). "Supervenience as a Philosophical Concept." *Metaphilosophy*, 21, 1–27. Repr. in J. Kim (1993). *Supervenience and Mind: Selected Philosophical Essays* (pp. 131–60). Cambridge: Cambridge University Press.

Kosman, L. A. (1975). "Perceiving that we Perceive: *On the Soul* III, 2." *The Philosophical Review*, 84, 499–519.

Kurfess, H. (1911). *Zur Geschichte der Erklärung der aristotelischen Lehre vom sog.* ΝΟΥΣ ΠΟΙΗΤΙΚΟΣ *und* ΠΑΘΗΤΙΚΟΣ. PhD. diss., Tübingen.

Lear, J. (1988). *Aristotle: The Desire to Understand.* Cambridge: Cambridge University Press.

Leszl, W. (1975). *Il "De ideis" di Aristotele e la teoria platonica delle idee.* Edizione critica del testo a cura di Dieter Harlfinger. (= Accademia Toscana di Scienze e Lettere "La Colombaria," Studi 40.) Florence: Leo S. Olschki Editiore. [Cited as Harlfinger.]

Lewis, D. (1970). "How to Define Theoretical Terms." *Journal of Philosophy*, 67, 427–46. Repr. in D. Lewis (1983). *Philosophical Papers.* (2 vols.). (vol. 1, pp. 78–95). New York: Oxford University Press.

343

———. (1972). "Psychophysical and Theoretical Identifications." *The Australasian Journal of Philosophy*, 50, 249–58. Repr. in D. Lewis (1999). *Papers in Metaphysics and Epistemology* (pp. 248–61). Cambridge: Cambridge University Press.

Lewis, F. A. (1994). "Aristotle on the Relation between a Thing and its Matter." In T. Scaltsas, D. Charles, and M. L. Gill (eds.), *Unity, Identity, and Explanation in Aristotle's Metaphysics* (pp. 247–77). Oxford: Clarendon Press.

Lloyd, G. E. R. (1992). "Aspects of the Relationship between Aristotle's Psychology and his Zoology." In M. C. Nussbaum and A. O. Rorty (eds.), *Essays on Aristotle's De Anima* (pp. 147–67). Oxford: Clarendon Press.

Loar, B. (1981). *Mind and Meaning*. Cambridge: Cambridge University Press.

MacClintock, S. (1956). "Sensation and the *Sensus Agens*." In S. MacCintock, *Perversity and Error: Studies on the "Averroist" John of Jandun* (pp. 10–50). Bloomington, Ind.: Indiana University Press.

Magee, J. M. (2000). "Sense Organs and the Activity of Sensation in Aristotle." *Phronesis*, 45, 306–30.

McLaughlin, B. P. (1992). "The Rise and Fall of British Emergentism." In A. Beckermann, H. Flohr, and J. Kim (eds.), *Emergence or Reduction? Essays on the Prospects of Nonreductive Physicalism* (pp. 49–93). Berlin: de Gruyter.

Miller, F. D., Jr. (1999). "Aristotle's Philosophy of Perception." *Proceedings of the Boston Area Colloquium in Ancient Philosophy*, 15, 177–213.

Modrak, D. K. W. (1980–1). "An Aristotelian Theory of Consciousness?" *Ancient Philosophy*, 1, 160–70.

———. (1987). *Aristotle: The Power of Perception*. Chicago: University of Chicago Press.

———. (2001). *Aristotle's Theory of Language and Meaning*. Cambridge: Cambridge University Press.

Moraux, P. (1942). *Alexandre d'Aphrodise: Exégète de la Noétique d'Aristote*. Liège: Faculté de Philosophie et Lettres.

Nussbaum, M. C. (1978). *Aristotle's De Motu Animalium*. Text with translation, commentary and interpretive essays. Princeton: Princeton University Press.

———. (1986). "Rational Animals and the Explanation of Action." In M. C. Nussbaum, *The Fragility of Goodness: Luck and Ethics in Greek Tragedy and Philosophy* (pp. 264–89). Cambridge: Cambridge University Press.

Nussbaum, M. C. and Putnam, H. (1992). "Changing Aristotle's Mind." In M. C. Nussbaum and A. O. Rorty (eds.), *Essays on Aristotle's De Anima* (pp. 27–56). Oxford: Clarendon Press.

Nussbaum, M. C. and Rorty, A. O. (eds.). ([1992] 1995). *Essays on Aristotle's De Anima*. First paperback edition, including an additional essay by M. F. Burnyeat. Oxford: Clarendon Press, 1995. (Original work published 1992.)

Osborne, C. (1983). "Aristotle, *De Anima* 3.2: How do We Perceive that We See and Hear?" *Classical Quarterly*, NS, 33, 401–11.

Pattin, A. (1988). *Pour l'histoire du sens agent: La controverse entre Barthélemy de Bruges et Jean de Jandun, ses antécédents et son évolution*. Étude et textes inédits. Leuven: University Press.

Price, A. W. (1996). "Aristotelian Perceptions." *Proceedings of the Boston Area Colloquium in Ancient Philosophy*, 12, 285–309.

Putnam, H. (1975a). "Language and Reality." In H. Putnam *Philosophical Papers*. (3 vols.). (vol. 2): *Mind, Language and Reality* (pp. 272–90). Cambridge: Cambridge University Press.

———. (1975b). *Philosophical Papers*. (3 vols.). (vol. 2): *Mind, Language and Reality*. Cambridge: Cambridge University Press.

———. (1975c). "Philosophy and our Mental Life." In H. Putnam *Philosophical Papers*. (3 vols.). (vol. 2): *Mind, Language and Reality* (pp. 291–303). Cambridge: Cambridge University Press.

Rist, J. M. (1966). "Notes on Aristotle *De Anima* 3.5." *Classical Philology*, 61, 8–20.

Robinson, H. (1983). "Aristotelian Dualism." *Oxford Studies in Ancient Philosophy*, 1, 123–44.

——. (1991). "Form and the Immateriality of the Intellect from Aristotle to Aquinas." In H. Blumenthal and H. Robinson (eds.), *Aristotle and the Later Tradition* (pp. 207–26). (= *Oxford Studies in Ancient Philosophy*, suppl. vol.) Oxford: Clarendon Press.

Rorty, R. (1979). *Philosophy and the Mirror of Nature*. Princeton: Princeton University Press.

Ross, W. D. (1949). *Aristotle*. 5th edn. London: Methuen & Co. (Original work published 1923.)

Schofield, M. (1978). "Aristotle on the Imagination." In G. E. R. Lloyd and G. E. L. Owen (eds.), *Aristotle on Mind and the Senses* (pp. 99–141). Proceedings of the Seventh Symposiuim Aristotelicum. Cambridge: Cambridge University Press.

Shields, C. (1988). "Soul and Body in Aristotle." *Oxford Studies in Ancient Philosophy*, 6, 103–37.

——. (1990). "The First Functionalist." In J.-C. Smith (ed.). *Historical Foundations of Cognitive Science* (pp. 19–33). Amsterdam: Kluwer.

——. (1993). "Some Recent Approaches to Aristotle's *De Anima*." In D. W. Hamlyn *Aristotle De Anima, Books II and III (with passages from Book I)*. Trans. with Introduction and Notes. 2nd edn. Clarendon Aristotle Series. Oxford: Clarendon Press. (1st edn. 1968.)

——. (1997). "Intentionality and Isomorphism in Aristotle." *Proceedings of the Boston Area Colloquium in Ancient Philosophy*, 11, 307–30.

Silverman, A. (1989). "Color and Color-Perception in Aristotle's *De Anima*." *Ancient Philosophy*, 9, 271–92.

Sisko, J. (1996). "Material Alteration and Cognitive Activity in Aristotle's *De Anima*." *Phronesis*, 41, 138–57.

——. (1998). "Alteration and Quasi-Alteration: A Critical Notice of Stephen Everson, *Aristotle on Perception*." *Oxford Studies in Ancient Philosophy*, 16, 331–52.

——. (1999). "On Separating the Intellect from the Body: Aristotle's *De Anima* III.4, 429a10–b5." *Archiv für Geschichte der Philosophie*, 81, 249–67.

——. (2000). "Aristotle's ΝΟΥΣ and the Modern Mind." *Proceedings of the Boston Area Colloquium in Ancient Philosophy*, 16, 177–98.

Slakey, T. J. (1961). "Aristotle on Sense Perception." *The Philosophical Review*, 70, 470–84.

Sorabji, R. (1972). "Aristotle, Mathematics, and Colour." *Classical Quarterly*, ns, 22, 293–308.

——. ([1974] 1979). "Body and Soul in Aristotle." *Philosophy*, 49, 63–89. Repr. in J. Barnes, M. Schofield, and R. Sorabji (eds.) (1979). *Articles on Aristotle*. (vol. 4): *Psychology and Aesthetics* (pp. 42–64). London: Duckworth.

——. (1992). "Intentionality and Physiological Processes: Aristotle's Theory of Sense-Perception." In M. C. Nussbaum and A. O. Rorty (eds.), *Essays on Aristotle's De Anima* (pp. 195–225). Oxford: Clarendon Press.

——. (2001). "Aristotle on Sensory Processes and Intentionality: A Reply to Myles Burnyeat." In D. Perler (ed.), *Ancient and Medieval Theories of Intentionality* (pp. 49–61). Leiden: Brill.

Tweedale, M. (1992). "Origins of the Medieval Theory that Sensation is an Immaterial Reception of a Form." *Philosophical Topics*, 20, 215–31.

Ward, J. K. (1988). "Perception and Λόγος in *De Anima* ii 12." *Ancient Philosophy*, 8, 217–33.

Wedin, M. V. (1988). *Mind and Imagination in Aristotle*. New Haven: Yale University Press.

——. (1992). "Content and Cause in the Aristotelian Mind." In J. Ellis (ed.), *Ancient Minds* (pp. 49–105). (= *The Southern Journal of Philosophy*, suppl. vol. 31).

——. (1996). "Keeping the Matter in Mind: Aristotle on the Passions of the Soul." In F. A. Lewis and R. Bolton (eds.), *Form, Matter, and Mixture in Aristotle* (pp. 1–38). Oxford: Blackwell.

Whiting, J. (1984). *Individual Forms in Aristotle*. PhD. diss., Cornell University.

——. (1992). "Living Bodies." In M. C. Nussbaum and A. O. Rorty (eds.), *Essays on Aristotle's De Anima* (pp. 75–91). Oxford: Clarendon Press.

Wilkes, K. (1988). "—— ——, yìshì, duh, um and consciousness." In A. J. Marcel and E. Bisiach (eds.), *Consciousness in Contemporary Science* (pp. 16–41). Oxford: Oxford University Press.

Williams, B. (1986). "Hylomorphism." *Oxford Studies in Ancient Philosophy*, 4, 189–99.

Woolf, R. (1999). "The Coloration of Aristotelian Eye-Jelly: A Note on *On Dreams* 459b–460a." *Journal of the History of Philosophy*, 37, 385–91.

Further Reading

Nussbaum, M. C. and Rorty, A. O. ([1992] 1995) (details above) is a valuable collection of essays.

In addition:

Barnes, J., Schofield, M., and Sorabji, R. (eds.). (1979). *Articles on Aristotle*. (vol. 4): *Psychology and Aesthetics*. London: Duckworth.

Lear, J. (1988). *Aristotle: The Desire to Understand*. Cambridge: Cambridge University Press.

Lloyd, G. E. R. and Owen, G. E. L. (eds.). (1978). *Aristotle on Mind and the Senses*. Proceedings of the Seventh Symposiuim Aristotelicum. Cambridge. Cambridge: Cambridge University Press.

18

First Philosophy in Aristotle

MARY LOUISE GILL

What is First Philosophy?

The title of Aristotle's *Metaphysics* (*ta meta ta phusika*) literally means "the things after the physical things." This was not Aristotle's own title.[1] In *Metaphysics* A.1 he calls the project *wisdom* (*sophia*) and says it is knowledge of the first causes and principles (982a1–3). Though not his own title, "metaphysics" is in one respect a suitable description of Aristotle's project. His arguments in the *Metaphysics* frequently rely on his physical theory — especially the theory of change, nature, and the four causes, and his treatment of terrestrial and celestial motion.[2] Aristotelian physics (and natural philosophy more generally) is a theoretical science, whose domain is things subject to change, both perishable (sublunary) and imperishable (heavenly). These same objects (together with some others) are also the domain of wisdom, though they are studied from a different perspective, as we shall see. The *Metaphysics* assumes that its audience is versed in Aristotle's natural philosophy. The *Metaphysics* comes *after* the works on natural philosophy in the sense that it uses their findings in developing its own argument. This science comes after physics in the order of learning (Burnyeat, 2001, pp. 111–24).

But in another respect the title "metaphysics" is misleading. Aristotle's *Metaphysics* relies not only on his investigations into natural philosophy but also on his *Organon* (the so-called "logical" works like the *Categories*, *Topics*, and *Analytics*), works primarily devoted to methodology, but which also lay out, at an abstract level, the logical and causal relations between entities. The audience of the *Metaphysics* is expected to be acquainted with these works as well. As we shall see, Aristotle often opens his treatment of topics in the *Metaphysics* with a framework adapted from the logical works. So the

---

1. Perhaps the title is due to Andronicus of Rhodes (first century BCE) or an earlier Hellenistic editor. On the tradition about the transmission of Aristotle's texts, see Pellegrin, THE ARISTOTELIAN WAY, in this volume. The arrangement of the corpus relies on the Hellenistic division of philosophy into logic, physics, and ethics. Sometimes physics was divided into physics proper and theology. The fact that Aristotle occasionally calls his project "theology" might explain why the *Metaphysics* was grouped with his works on natural philosophy. The title has often been taken to designate the place of the *Metaphysics* in Aristotle's collected works, after the physics. See Ross (1953, p. xxxii, n.2).

2. See Bodnár and Pellegrin, ARISTOTLE'S PHYSICS AND COSMOLOGY, in this volume.

title "metaphysics" is too narrow: the work presupposes knowledge of the *Organon*, as well as physics.

That metaphysics comes after physics in the order of learning should not obscure the fact that Aristotle regards metaphysics as explanatorily *prior* to natural philosophy. On several occasions he distinguishes what is more knowable *to us* from what is more knowable *by nature* or *simply*.[3] Things more knowable to us are, he says, more accessible to perception, whereas things more knowable by nature are further from perception, but *explain* the more familiar things. The correct procedure, he says, is to start an inquiry with things more knowable to us, things to which we have direct perceptual access, and through the study of them to arrive at their causes and principles, which are more knowable by nature. This methodology is advocated in the *Posterior Analytics* and practiced in the natural sciences (start with the observable or agreed facts, proceed to their explanation),[4] but it also appears to hold between physics and metaphysics, for the following reason.

The domain of physics is restricted to things subject to change. But Aristotle gives arguments to show that the continuity of celestial motion and of generation and destruction in the sublunary realm is ultimately caused by movers that are separate from physical things and not themselves subject to change (*Met.* Λ.6–10). Investigation of these unmoved movers – the principles and first causes of motion – falls outside the domain of physics. It is the task of another theoretical discipline, distinct from physics, to study the separate and unchangeable principles on which all changeable things depend – principles Aristotle regards as divine. He calls the discipline *theology* (*Met.* E.1, 1026a18–19). He also calls it First Philosophy (*philosophia prōtē*).[5]

First Philosophy is not restricted to the investigation of divine substance. At the end of *Metaphysics* E.1, Aristotle says that this science will also investigate what is *as* (or *qua*) *being*, both what it is (*ti esti*) and the things that belong to it as being (1026a31–32). *Metaphysics* Γ.1 and the beginning of E.1 say more about this general project (cf. *Met.* K.3, 1061a28–b17). Aristotle carefully distinguishes it from the special sciences. The special sciences mark off some genus of being – for instance, physics studies things subject to change, geometry studies magnitudes, and arithmetic numbers. These disciplines investigate the same objects or overlapping domains of objects but they treat them from different perspectives, ignoring those features not relevant to the discipline. Thus geometry considers objects simply as extended. Physics considers those same objects but insofar as they change. Zoology considers a subset of those objects that are self-movers. First Philosophy investigates the objects of physics and their causes and principles, but it considers them from a highly abstract perspective – simply *as being*.

Some scholars think that Aristotle has two sorts of metaphysical projects, which are distinct, one described in *Metaphysics* Γ, which they call *general* metaphysics or

---

3. E.g., *APo*. I.2, 71b33–72a5; *Phys.* I.1; *Met.* Z.3, 1029b3–12.

4. See Detel, ARISTOTLE'S LOGIC AND THEORY OF SCIENCE, and for the application in biology, see Lennox, ARISTOTLE'S BIOLOGY, pp. 294–300 in this volume.

5. In addition to references to his project as First Philosophy within the *Metaphysics*, references to it occur in Aristotle's works on natural philosophy: *Phys.* I.9, 192a34–b1; II.2, 194b14–15; *Cael.* I.8, 277b9–12, refer forward to the project. *MA* 6, 700b6–9 refers back to it. *Met.* Z.11, 1037a10–17, refers to physics as second philosophy.

ontology, since it investigates everything that is insofar as it is; the other called *special* metaphysics or *theology*, since it treats the most valuable genus of being, divine substance.[6] On this view Aristotle lays out the general science in *Metaphysics* Γ and pursues it in the central books of the *Metaphysics* (Z, H and possibly Θ). General metaphysics is thought to anticipate special metaphysics, since Z mentions an investigation of separate, immaterial, non-sensible substances, to be undertaken later.[7] Z seems to prepare the way for that more specialized study.

Metaphysics Λ is the obvious place to look for Aristotle's treatment of special metaphysics. Yet scholars have found this text disappointing. First, he spends half the book traveling the same ground explored in ZHΘ. Why include these chapters, if the topic of First Philosophy is divine immaterial substance? Why not rely on the argument in ZHΘ, and move directly to theology in Λ? *Metaphysics* Λ, contrary to expectation, builds up to divine substance from observations about ordinary sensible substances, perishable and imperishable. Indeed, Λ appears to argue for a first unmoved mover, relying on considerations from physics. A second source of disappointment is that Aristotle's theology is expected to investigate what it is to *be* in the primary sense – what it is to be a divine substance. This paradigmatic being is supposed to explain the derivative sorts of being of substantial forms and material substances.[8] Instead, the being of divine substance, though of a rarefied sort (pure actuality or activity), seems not to differ in kind from that of mundane substances.

My view, which I sketch in this chapter, is that Aristotle is committed to a single science of First Philosophy, which is the investigation of being *qua* being.[9] That is the study of all being, and therefore includes divine substance, which is the first cause and principle of being. That first cause is adequately treated in *Metaphysics* Λ, but the bulk of Aristotle's project, which he reworks in Λ.1–5, is carried out in Z, H, and Θ.

The Science of Being *qua* Being

First Philosophy differs structurally from the special sciences. Whereas they mark off a part of being – a genus – and undertake to explain facts about objects that fall within that genus, Aristotle insists (against Plato) that being is *not a genus* (*APo.* II.7, 92b14; *Met.* B.3, 998b22). Being divides immediately into the categories (substance, quantity, quality, and the rest), which are themselves the highest genera (cf. Matthews, 1995). *Metaphysics* Γ.2 articulates the structural relations among beings with a device known as *focal meaning* (*pros hen legomenon*).[10] The idea is that there is a primary sort of being, and that other sorts of beings are determined as what they are in relation to it.

6. Frede (1987), Owens (1978), Patzig (1979). On this issue, see Menn (Forthcoming).
7. Z.2, 1028b30–31; Z.11, 1037a10–13; Z.16, 1040b34–1041a3; Z.17, 1041a7–9.
8. See Frede's Introduction in Frede and Charles (2000, pp. 2, 50). For a critique of the prevailing views on Λ, see Menn (Forthcoming).
9. My perspective on First Philosophy is indebted to the penetrating study by Sefrin-Weis (2002), who reconstructs Aristotle's project of First Philosophy as articulated in *Metaphysics* A, B, Γ, E, and the relevant chapters of K.
10. The label comes from Owen (1960).

Focal meaning must be distinguished from two other notions, which Aristotle defines in the *Categories*: *homonymy* and *synonymy* (*Cat.* 1). Two or more items are *homonymous*, if they share the same name, but the account of why the name applies to them is different. For instance, the rising ground bordering a river and a financial institution are both called a "bank," but for different reasons. Two or more items are *synonymous*, if they share the same name, and the name applies to them for the same reason. For instance, a human being and a horse are called "animal" synonymously, because the name applies to both for the same reason: both are called "animal," because they are living things that can move themselves. If things belong to the same genus, they are synonymous with respect to that genus.

Focal meaning is a special kind of homonymy.[11] One or more items are focally related to a single item, if they share the same name, but neither for the same reason nor merely for a different reason. In giving the reason why the name applies to a secondary item, we must mention the primary item. Aristotle illustrates with the name "medical." A doctor, a patient, an instrument, an instruction, and a practice are all called "medical" with reference to a primary case, medical knowledge. We mention medical knowledge in the account of the others. A doctor is called "medical" because she *possesses* medical knowledge, a patient because he is a *recipient* of medical knowledge, and an instrument because it is *used in the application of* medical knowledge (Γ.2, 1003a34–b4). We must therefore first understand what medical knowledge is, if we are to understand the things that are focally related to it. Still – and this is the important and controversial point – we cannot simply derive the others from an analysis of the focal term. The focus determines *part* of what the secondary item is. Full understanding requires that we uncover what else that entity is and how it is related to the primary term.

Aristotle claims that "being," like "medical," is said in many ways, but not merely homonymously. Instead, entities are said to "be" with reference to a primary case, the being of *substance*.[12] Some things are beings because they are *affections* of substance,

---

11. This claim is controversial, since many scholars think that focal meaning is, ultimately, a kind of synonymy. I am persuaded by the arguments of Sefrin-Weis (2002), who challenges the widely accepted view of Owen (1960, 1965) and more recent views, including Bolton (1994, 1996) and Code (1996, 1997). For an earlier critique of Owen along similar lines, see Berti (1971), who focused on the evidence from the *Eudemian Ethics*.

12. "Substance" is the traditional translation of *ousia* in Aristotle. The Greek word is an abstract noun derived from the feminine participle (*ousa*) of the verb "to be" (*einai*). The translation of *ousia* as "substance" is misleading, because the noun "substance" derives from the Latin verb "to stand under," which captures only one function of an Aristotelian *ousia*, being an underlying *subject* (Greek: *hupokeimenon*). More serious is the loss of the etymological connection with *being* and the clouding of the connection with Plato, who used the word *ousia* for the entities he regarded as most real: Forms. Some scholars prefer the translation "substantial being," but this is cumbersome. I will therefore retain the traditional "substance," but readers should keep in mind the association with being. On the word's etymology, see Collinge (1971). István Bodnár, to whom I owe the reference, has suggested to me that Collinge's derivation of *gerousia* ("council of elders") could in principle be transferred to *ousia*. The fundamental issue is how old or new the etymological development is, and we unfortunately lack data on this.

350

some because they *lead to* substance or because they are *destructions, privations, qualities* or *productions* of substance (1003a33–b10). Although being resembles medical in that secondary items are understood via the primary item, being differs from medical in that things investigated simply as *beings* are considered apart from any specific content. We study the secondary beings by investigating the nature of their dependence on the primary entity. First Philosophy inquires into the *causal structure* of reality (cf. Sefrin-Weis, 2002, chs. 9 and 10).

Categories and Change

A schematic and partial framework of Aristotle's ontology is laid out in the *Categories*. There Aristotle argues that things like a particular man and a particular horse are primary substances. They are the ultimate *subjects* on which everything else depends for its existence. Non-substantial properties (such as quantities and qualities), which characterize substances, and substantial species and genera, which identify them specifically and more generally, all depend on the primary objects for their existence. Remove the primary substances – the basic subjects – and everything else is removed as well (*Cat.* 5, 2a34–b6). The *Categories* treats its primary objects as atomic entities and does not analyze them further.[13]

In the *Physics* Aristotle tackles the problem of change and analyzes substances into matter and form. Parmenides had denied the possibility of change, arguing that change would involve the emergence of something out of nothing. Aristotle agreed with his predecessor that there is no absolute becoming. His task was to account for change without admitting the emergence of something from nothing. In *Physics* I.7 Aristotle argues that every change involves three principles: a pair of opposites – a form ϕ and privation $\sim\phi$[14] – and an underlying subject x. A change brings something new into the world: ϕ replaces $\sim\phi$. But the change is not a mere replacement, with the pre-existing entity perishing into nothing and the product emerging out of nothing, because part of the product was there all along – the subject x, which was characterized first as $\sim\phi$ and then as ϕ. In non-substantial changes (changes of quality, quantity, or place) the continuant is a *Categories*-type primary substance, such as a particular man or a particular horse, and the form and privation are pairs of terms, which are properly opposed, in one of the categories of quality, quantity, or place. The relation between a non-substantial property or privation and the underlying subject is *accidental*, because the subject remains what it is in its own right when one of the pair of opposites replaces the other. Socrates remains a man when he becomes dark from pale or musical from unmusical. I will speak of the relation between a predicate and a subject in such cases as *categorial predication*. Below we shall examine the more subtle varieties of predication Aristotle sets out in the *Posterior Analytics*.

Aristotle claims that substantial generation can also be analyzed in terms of three principles. In this case a substance is the *product* of the change and so cannot be what persists through it. *Matter* is introduced as the persisting subject, and *form* is the positive

---

13. For a different view about the *Categories*, see Devereux (1992).
14. The designation "$\sim\phi$" applies to any state on a range that leads to ϕ.

member of a pair of opposites. A new substance (e.g., a statue) comes to be when matter (e.g., bronze) acquires a form (a shape) it originally lacked. Items in the first category are analyzed in the *Physics* into matter and form to account for their substantial generation, and the relation between them appears to be analogous to that between a non-substantial property and a *Categories*-type primary substance. Thus Aristotle appears to extend categorial predication to the relation between form and matter. The *Metaphysics* agrees with the *Physics* in treating items in the first category as *composites* of a subject (matter) and a predicate (form), often called *hylomorphic complexes*.

What Being is Primary?

Once *Categories*-type primary substances are analyzed into matter and form, their primacy becomes questionable: Is the composite primary? A hylomorphic complex can be analyzed into matter and form, and so is presumably posterior to them. Is one of its components primary? Given the emphasis on subjecthood in the *Categories*, matter claims priority, since form is predicated of it. In *Metaphysics* Z.3 Aristotle lays out an argument that matter alone is substance on the subject-criterion, but he rejects the conclusion, pointing out that there are further criteria for substance, which matter fails to satisfy. So the form and the composite seem to have a better claim than matter to be substance (1029a26–30). Many scholars think that *Metaphysics* Z awards primacy to form, the component that determines what a composite is.

I disagree with this widespread assessment of Z. I will argue that Z presents objections to each of its candidates for substance: matter (Z.3), the composite (Z.4–11), and form (Z.13–16). The strategy of Z is to show that we can save none of them, if we think of matter and form on the categorial scheme of predication. Form cannot be predicated of matter in the way that a non-substantial property is predicated of a *Categories*-type primary substance (e.g., as whiteness is predicated of Socrates). I will argue that no solution to the problem of primacy is forthcoming as long as the categorial scheme of predication is applied to substance. To salvage substantial being, *Metaphysics* H and Θ re-conceive of matter and form on a different model: *potentiality* and *actuality*.

Aristotle prepares the way for this reassessment in E.2 (cf. *Met.* Δ.7). He says that *being* has a variety of meanings: (1) accidental; (2) truth; (3) the scheme of the categories; and (4) potentiality and actuality (1026a33–b2). *Metaphysics* E itself treats accidental being and being as truth, and concludes that neither serves the present purpose (E.4, 1027b33–1028a6). That leaves (3), categorial being, and (4), potential and actual being. Aristotle's task is to investigate the causes and principles of being itself *qua* being (E.4, 1028a3–4), and he does so first in terms of categorial being. I argue that this approach fails for substantial being. He then appeals to potential and actual being, a scheme that proves more successful.[15] I will outline the strategy in ZHΘ and then turn finally and very briefly to the theology in *Metaphysics* Λ.

15. Other scholars argue that the investigation of categorial being and the investigation of potentiality and actuality are two distinct investigations with different goals. See Witt (2003) and Yu (1997).

Overview of *Metaphysics* Z

Z opens with two introductory chapters. Z.1 argues that the study of being must in the first place be a study of substance, since other sorts of beings (qualities, quantities, and so on) depend for their existence and for what they are on substances. To understand those other entities, then, we must understand substance first. ZHΘ focus mainly on that first task.

Z.2 lists examples of substance, including things people widely agree on: animals and plants and their parts, the four elements – earth, water, air, and fire – and the heavenly bodies. Other examples are proposed by particular individuals or schools, such as Platonic Forms, numbers, and the limits of bodies. Part of the task, says Aristotle, is to determine which items belong on the list and which not, and whether there is (or are) some other substance(s) apart from the perceptible ones. But first, in order to evaluate the claims, he needs to address a different sort of question: What is substance? What is it about those entities that makes them seem to be substances?

Z.3 states that "substance" (*ousia*) is understood in a variety of ways, but especially four: (1) essence, (2) universal, (3) genus, and (4) underlying subject. These are criteria one might reasonably think a primary substance should satisfy.[16] Some of them (universal, genus) will be rejected; others (essence, subject) will be kept and clarified. *Metaphysics* Z is structured loosely around this list. Z.3 examines the claim that being an underlying *subject* makes something a substance. Z.4–12 spell out what an *essence* is and argue that a primary thing and its essence are identical. Z.13–16 examine and reject the claim that a *universal* is substance. The *genus* receives no separate treatment but appears to be rejected together with the universal.[17] Z.17 starts anew and considers substance as a principle and cause that explains why matter constitutes a composite.

Subject

Aristotle defines a *subject* in Z.3 as that of which other things are predicated but not itself predicated of anything else (1028b36–37). Take a statue. Three items have a claim to be a subject: the matter (bronze), the form (the shape of the statue), and the composite of both (the bronze statue) (1029a2–5). Aristotle then complains that his definition is unclear, and that in consequence matter alone turns out to be substance (1029a9–10). The bulk of the chapter demonstrates why this is so, and introduces further constraints on substance to avoid that outcome.

---

16. A number of scholars contend that this fourfold list specifies what might count as the *substance of* a substance – what component of, say, Socrates counts as his substance? I disagree. When Aristotle says that the essence, etc., seem to be the substance of each thing (*ousia . . . hekastou*), he is asking for the *reason why* the examples in Z.2 are regarded as substances. For a helpful discussion of this issue, see Devereux (2003, pp. 161–6).

17. In his summary of Z in H.1, Aristotle mentions the genus together with the universal (1042a13–16) and says that neither is a substance (1042a21–22).

The main argument in Z.3 is puzzling, if one brings to Z the insights of Aristotle's physics and reflects on his example: the bronze statue. One expects Aristotle to ask about the bronze statue: what counts as the underlying subject? The statue? No, the statue is a shape predicated of bronze. The bronze should trump the others as the underlying subject. But is the bronze the *primary* underlying subject? The bronze is a compound of more basic material ingredients, copper and tin, combined in a certain ratio. And those metals are themselves compounds of the Aristotelian elements water and earth. Are water and earth primary? Scholars since antiquity have reasoned that, since Aristotle thinks that earth, water, air, and fire can be transformed into one another, there must be a yet more ultimate subject that survives their transformations, an entity traditionally known as *prime matter* – something that is nothing in its own right but underlies all material bodies in the sublunary realm.[18]

In Z.3 Aristotle strips off properties to arrive at matter, but not through repeated hylomorphic analysis. Instead he first removes the qualities, then the quantities (length, breadth, and depth), and says we see nothing left, unless there is something determined by these. And so, he says, matter must appear to be the only substance (1029a11–19). He then defines matter as something that has no categorial being in its own right (*kath' hauto*): It is neither something, nor so much, nor anything else by which *being* is determined (1029a20–21). "For," he says, "there is something of which each of these is predicated, whose *being* (*to einai*) is *different* from that of each of the predicates" (1029a21–23). This subject is nothing in its own right: all categorial properties (including their negations) belong to it *accidentally* (1029a24–26).

Contrary to expectation, matter is reached as it were directly, as soon as all categorial predicates (including substantial predicates) have been removed. This is not prime matter – something reached by stripping off layers and layers of form. Some scholars have thought that Z.3 presents Aristotle's *concept* of matter, of which bronze is an example.[19] But bronze is not a good example of the matter advertised in Z.3. To be sure, the shape of a statue is accidental to the bronze (since the bronze can survive its removal), but the bronze is something in its own right: bronze. Bronze cannot cease to be bronze and still be what it is.

The passage is less peculiar, if we recognize, first, that Aristotle is relying on categorial predication, and second, that he is reflecting on the subject-predicate model from a highly abstract perspective – simply in terms of *being*, the perspective of First Philosophy. His claim is that his initial definition of a subject leads to a curious result. When all categorial being is removed, there *is something* whose *being is different* from all categorial being: a bare subject. A bare subject cannot be substance, he objects, because substance must be *separate* and a *this* (*tode ti*). So the form and the composite have a better claim than matter to be substance (1029a27–30).

18. Aristotle's commitment to prime matter has been disputed since the mid-twentieth century. See, e.g., Charlton (1970), Furth (1988), Gill (1989), and King (1956). Versions of the traditional interpretation have been defended by, e.g., Happ (1971) and Robinson (1974). See S. Cohen (1984, and 1996, ch. 3), for the attractive suggestion (which I also reject) that prime matter has some essential properties, such as extension. Cf. Sorabji (1988, ch. 1).
19. E.g., Dancy (1978), Frede and Patzig (1988).

Z.3 does not elaborate on separation and *thisness*.[20] In Z.1 Aristotle said that non-substantial properties are *not separate* from substance but depend on a definite subject of which they are predicated (1028a22–29). Substance alone is separate (1028a34–35). These claims suggest that things fail to be separate if they depend for their existence on some definite subject to which they belong. Something is separate if it is a definite subject of which properties are predicated, but does not depend for its existence on any of them. If this is what Aristotle means by separation, why is matter in Z.3 not separate? Matter is a subject to which properties belong, and it does not depend for its existence on any of them. More likely matter fails because it is not a *definite* subject. The being of matter, though *distinct* from all categorial being, is nothing definite, since it has no categorial being in its own right. Apparently, for a subject to be substance, it must be something definite.

Z.1 also mentions *thisness*. Aristotle said that being is said in many ways. In the first place it signifies what something is (*ti esti*) and a *this* (*tode ti*), and then the other categories (1028a10–13). *Thisness* is a distinguishing feature of substance. Scholars often take *thisness* to indicate particularity. Although Aristotle's use of the phrase in the *Categories* supports this claim (*Cat.* 5, 3b10–18), its application is probably not so restricted. Reflection on the phrase itself suggests another relevant factor. The phrase can be literally translated in two ways: "some this" or "this something." In either case one term presumably indicates a kind, and the other something that falls under that kind. The item marked off could be either a particular that falls under a kind (some horse, this horse) or a determination of a wider kind (a sort of horse, this sort of horse). That *thisness* does not simply mean "particular" seems assured, since matter in Z.3 fails the test.[21] A bare subject is surely a *particular*. Matter's lack of *thisness* is rooted in a different fault. As literal translations of *tode ti* suggest, something counts as a *this* only if it is something determinate or particular that falls under a kind. Matter in Z.3 may be a particular, but it does not fall under a kind, since it has no categorial being, and *a fortiori* no substantial being, in its own right.

In fact Aristotelian matter is not a bare subject. Bronze, and any other instance of matter, has some categorial being in its own right. That is why Aristotle regularly refers to matter as one way to be substance.[22] Z.3 demonstrates that if matter is conceived as a *bare* subject it cannot be substance, even though its being is independent of all categorial being. Later we shall see that, according to Z, any sort of matter that constitutes a composite is distinct in being from it. This fact will cause serious

20. On separation, see the debate between Fine and Morrison, esp. Fine (1984) and Morrison (1985). See also the recent assessment in Reeve (2000, §1.1). On *thisness*, see Frede and Patzig (1988, vol. 2, p. 15), and Gill (1989, pp. 31–4).

21. Note, too, that form passes the test. If *tode ti* means particular, Aristotle's designation of form as *tode ti* decides the question whether form is a particular or a universal. I doubt that the status of form can be decided simply on that ground, because, as we have noted, *tode ti* can be construed as something determinate (e.g., Arabian) that falls under a kind (horse). On that construal a *tode ti* is a lowest kind, something that cannot be further differentiated. Nothing prevents an entity of that sort occurring in more than one subject.

22. Even after rejecting the bare subject as substance in Z.3, Aristotle speaks of matter as one of three ways to be substance (1029a30–33); cf. Z.10, 1035a1–2; H.1, 1042a32–b3.

mischief – indeed it will prevent both the composite and the form from being primary substance.

Essence

Z.4 turns to the next topic on the agenda: *essence*. Aristotle says he will first speak "logically" (*logikōs*) about it. He then gives a curious argument. What is the essence of *you*? The essence of each thing, he says, is what it is said to be *kath' hauto* ("in virtue of itself"). To be you is not to be musical, since you are not musical in virtue of yourself. What you are in virtue of yourself is your essence. But your essence is not everything you are in virtue of yourself. It is not what something is *kath' hauto* in the way that white is to surface. Nor is the essence from both: being a white surface. The account of the essence of each thing must specify the thing without mentioning it. So, for example, if being a white surface is being a smooth surface, then the being for white is the same as the being for smooth (1029b13–22).

Why, having started out using *you* as his example, does Aristotle switch halfway through the argument to talk about a white surface? We know from later in Z that he thinks your essence is your *form* – your soul (Z.7, 1032b1–2 with Z.11, 1035b14–16). Why does he not appeal to matter and form here? He could have argued: Your accidental properties (like musicality) are not your essence. Your matter is not your essence. The combination of your form and your matter is not your essence. Your essence is your form. The argument from exclusion would have been clear. But that is not Aristotle's procedure. Instead of mentioning matter and form, he tries to make his point with some obscure remarks about a white surface. Why does he do this?

Some scholars argue that Z operates at two distinct levels of discourse.[23] Call this *the two-levels hypothesis*. Aristotle said at the outset that he would first speak "logically" about essence. One level has been dubbed "logical." A striking feature of the envisaged logical sections is that Aristotle restricts his terminology to vocabulary from the *Organon* – "substance" (*ousia*), "essence," "definition," "subject" and "predicate," "genus" and "species" (*eidos* in its *Organon* sense), "universal" and "particular," and the categories (Burnyeat, 2001, p. 8). These sections do not mention matter and form, which notoriously also go unmentioned in the *Organon*. Matter and form are conspicuously absent from the whole of Z.4–6. Those sections of Z that do appeal to matter and form have been labeled "metaphysical."

What difference in aim is supposed to distinguish the logical and metaphysical levels? The most plausible suggestion is that the logical level develops the *structure* for a metaphysical theory, whereas the metaphysical level fills in that structure by defending a particular metaphysical theory. The distinction is thus between *form* and *content*. On this view our passage at the beginning of Z.4 ignores matter and form, because Aristotle is working out, at a formal level, what an essence is, without privileging

---

23.   Burnyeat (2001), Code (1997, esp. pp. 6–8), Loux (1991, esp. ch. 3 and the summary, pp. 109–11).

his own metaphysical theory in advance. The account is supposed to be rich enough to capture alternatives (e.g., Plato's theory as well as his own) and neutral among competitors.

Our passage evidently does rely on the *Organon* and is in that sense "logical." In particular, Aristotle uses a distinction between two sorts of *kath' hauto* predicates and accidental predicates from *Posterior Analytics* I.4. There he says that Y belongs to X *kath' hauto* in one way, if Y is predicated of X, and Y must be mentioned in the account of what X is (call Y an *essential* predicate of X, since Y must belong to X if X is to be what it is). For instance, *animal* is an essential predicate of Callias, because animal is predicated of Callias and must be mentioned in the account of what Callias is (73a34–37; cf. *Met.* Δ.18, 1022a25–29). Y belongs to X *kath' hauto* in a second way, if Y is predicated of X, and X must be mentioned in the account of what Y is (call Y a *special* predicate of X: the account of Y – the predicate – must mention the kind of thing of which it is predicated) (73a37–b3). For instance, *odd* is a special predicate of *number*, because odd is predicated of number, and number must be mentioned in the account of what odd is. *Snubness* is a special predicate of *nose*, because snubness is predicated of the nose, and the nose must be mentioned in the account of what snubness is. Snubness, Aristotle tells us in Z.5, is *concavity in a nose* (concavity in the legs is something else: bowleggedness). Y is an *accidental* predicate of X, if Y is predicated of X, but neither term is mentioned in the account of the other. Aristotle's favorite example of an accidental predicate is *white* predicated of *man*. What I have so far been calling "categorial predication," applicable in Aristotle's theory of change, corresponds to what the *Posterior Analytics* calls accidental predication.

Our passage in Z.4 can be clarified by means of the *Posterior Analytics* distinctions. First Aristotle excludes your accidents (like being musical) from your essence. Then he says that your essence is what you are *kath' hauto*, but not everything you are *kath' hauto*. Your essence is not what you are *kath' hauto* in the way that *white* is to *surface*. White is predicated of surface, and surface must be mentioned in the account of what white is. Aristotle thinks that whiteness (and other colors) can occur only in surfaces and that the definition of whiteness must specify that primary recipient (*Met.* Δ.18, 1022a29–32, with Z.5, 1030b23–28). There is something to which *you* belong as a special predicate, in the way that white belongs to surface, which must similarly be mentioned in the account of what you are. What you are *specially* contributes to your *being*, but is not part of your *essence*.

The distinction between *being* and *essence* is important. The *being* of an entity is everything the entity is *kath' hauto* – both essentially and specially. The *essence* of an entity is simply what it is essentially, *kath' hauto* in the first way. Our passage in Z.4 mentions neither matter nor form, but your *essence* turns out to be your form and not your matter.

The two-levels hypothesis explains why Aristotle ignores matter and form in parts of *Metaphysics* Z, but I think it misconstrues his project. Aristotle has a reason to ignore matter and form in certain parts of his argument, because the subject-matter of First Philosophy is *being*. You and a bronze statue are substances – beings in the first category. Matter and form are relevant to the analysis of these. But other sorts of entities besides substances are included in the domain of First Philosophy. First Philosophy studies entities in the non-substance categories (qualities, quantities, etc.)

and it studies categorial compounds, like *white man*. Aristotle avoids mentioning matter and form when he speaks generally about the whole domain of his science.

That Aristotle is interested in all beings, and not merely those in the first category, becomes evident from his remarks that directly follow our passage in Z.4:

> Since there are also compounds (*suntheta*) corresponding to the other categories (for *there is some subject for each of them*, e.g., for quality and quantity and when and where and motion), we must consider whether there is an account of the essence for each of them. (1029b22–26)

You served as an example to introduce the question about the essence of compounds in all the categories, including accidental compounds like *white man*, whose components are a non-substantial property and a substance, not form and matter. Aristotle's discourse is abstract, but he is not presenting the formal framework for a metaphysical theory to be filled in later with his own theory of substance. He is working out a theory of *being* and is asking what counts as being in the primary sense and why. The whole discussion in Z (indeed in the *Metaphysics* as a whole) takes place at a single level, the level of *being*, and Aristotle aims at impartiality between *sorts of beings*. Matter and form are introduced when he focuses particularly on items in the first category (to which he will turn in Z.7). But items in the first category are part of a larger field, which includes items in non-substance categories (like *white*) and categorial compounds, like *white man* as well.[24]

Aristotle's task in Z.4–6 is to show what an entity must be like to count as a primary being. He argues in Z.4 that if an entity E is something primary, it is not analyzed as Y predicated of X, where X differs in being from Y (1030a2–11). Anything that can be so analyzed fails to be primary, because it must be explained in terms of its more basic components. Accidental compounds like *white man* are not primary, since the account of *white man* mentions two things, *white* and *man*, which are defined independently of each other. *Snubness* is not primary. Snubness is not itself a compound (it is a quality), but it is analyzed as Y in X, concavity in a nose (Z.5).

In Z.6 Aristotle argues that something succeeds as primary, if it and its essence are one and the same (1032a4–6). As I understand the Z.6 criterion, the essence of a primary thing is *predicated* of that thing and *exhausts* what the subject is: the essence and the being of the subject are identical.[25] There is nothing else that the subject is *specially*, which contributes to its being and must therefore be mentioned in its defining account. In the case of primary things, *being* and *essence* coincide. Only those entities whose being is exhausted by their essence are primary, because they are explained

---

24.   See esp. Aristotle's summary at the end of Z.4, 1030b11–13.
25.   In Z.6 Aristotle uses Platonic Forms as candidates for primary things. In the Platonic context the Z.6 criterion is called Self-Predication: The Form F is F (Justice is just, Largeness is large). In my view, the Z.6 criterion and Platonic Self-Predication both involve genuine predication. Many scholars read the Z.6 Thesis as an identity claim, without insisting that predication is also involved. See Code (1985, 1986) and Lewis (2003). Some scholars argue that the Z.6 criterion is something weaker than identity: M. Cohen (1978), Dahl (2003), Spellman (1995). My view shares much in common with Matthews (2003).

through themselves, not through anything more basic. Most entities fail to be primary, because their *being* and *essence* are distinct. Those entities must be defined with reference to their more basic components – both what they are *essentially* and what they are *specially*.

The Problem of Matter

Many scholars think that Z.7–9 are latecomers to *Metaphysics* Z, which intrude on the main argument. I do not share this view. Z.7–9 strike readers as intrusive, because they treat *becoming*, a topic that seems more appropriate to physics than to First Philosophy.[26] But in fact Aristotle has a good reason to include Z.7–9. Substantial generation, though proper to physics, is also vital to Aristotle's developing argument in Z. It reveals that matter precludes the primacy of material composites.

How does matter jeopardize composites? Aristotle claimed in Z.3 that even a bare subject differs in *being* from its predicates. Ordinary Aristotelian matter, like bronze, is something in its own right (bronze is bronze). He will argue that, whatever the matter is, it differs in being from the composite it constitutes. Recall that in the *Physics* Aristotle claimed that all changes are analyzed by means of three principles – a pair of opposites and an underlying subject. The subject survives the change and is characterized first by one opposite and then by the other. In substantial generations the continuant is matter. Matter pre-exists the change, constitutes the product, and persists when the product is destroyed. Reflection on matter in substantial generation reveals that composites in the first category resemble the accidental compound *white man*. This is because the matter that persists through generation and the composite it constitutes have *different persistence conditions*. The bronze that constitutes a statue exists before the statue was made and can survive when the form of the statue has been removed. Even if we focus on matter and form *qua being*, and disregard their specific content, the fact that matter outlasts the composite shows that it makes a *distinct* contribution to what the composite is: Matter contributes to the composite's *being*.

For this reason matter must be mentioned in the account of what a composite is. Aristotle asks in Z.7:

> Is matter among the things [mentioned] in the account? We say what brazen spheres are in both ways, mentioning the matter, that it is bronze, and the form, that it is such and such shape, and this is the genus into which [a brazen sphere] is first placed. So a brazen sphere has matter in its account. (1033a1–5)

In Z.8 he extends this conclusion to living organisms and their species and genera (1033b24–26). He repeats the point about species in Z.10. A species like *man* or *horse* is a universal composite composed of form and matter taken universally (1035b27–30).[27]

---

26. But see Buchheim (2001, pp. 220–7), who argues that becoming is crucial for Aristotle's metaphysical project. See also Ferejohn (2003).

27. Aristotle uses the word *eidos* for both species (e.g., *man*) and substantial form (e.g., human soul). Driscoll (1981) brought clarity to the whole issue and showed why it is important to keep the two notions distinct.

The analysis of substantial generation demonstrates that *Categories*-type primary substances, such as a particular man and a particular horse, plus their species and genera – man, horse, animal – fail to be primary in Z's sense. The aim of Z.7–9 is to show this, and also to argue that form is not generated (Z.8, 1033a28–b19). The argument that form is not generated (and so does not contain matter) is one step in Aristotle's larger argument to prove that form need not be defined with reference to matter, an argument he completes in Z.11 (1036a26–b7). Form is not like *snubness*: it need not be defined with reference to its primary recipient. Composites, however, are analyzed as Y predicated of X (*this in that*), and X is distinct in being from Y (1036b21–32). Whereas soul is the same as the essence of soul, and so satisfies the Z.6 criterion, man is not the same as the essence of man (Z.11, 1037a33–b7; cf. H.3, 1043b2–4). So composites in the first category are not primary but must be explained in terms of their more basic components. Aristotle concludes his treatment of essence in Z.11 by denying primacy to composites. The award goes to form, whose being is exhausted by its essence.

The Status of Form

Many scholars take the conclusion of Z.11 to be Aristotle's final conclusion in Z: primary substance is form. Although that is Aristotle's verdict in the section on essence, the status of form comes into question in the third section, whose official target is the (Platonist) claim that substance is a *universal*. In Z.13 Aristotle argues that no universal is a substance, a conclusion he repeats at the end of Z.16 (1041a3–5).

The main problem for form is *subjecthood*. Aristotle claimed in Z.3 and repeats in Z.13 (1038b15–16) that substance is a basic *subject*, something of which other things are predicated but not itself predicated of anything else. Form is predicated of matter, which is one sort of subject (1038b5–6). Aristotle claimed in Z.3 and demonstrated in his treatment of generation in Z.7–9 that matter is distinct in being from the composite it constitutes, and so distinct in being from the form of that composite. We have seen that matter deprives the composite of substantiality on the essence criterion, because the composite is analyzed as *this in that*. Like the accidental compound *white man*, the being of a composite is determined in two ways – by its constituent form and matter. Form satisfies the essence criterion: its being is exhausted by its essence. But matter deprives form of substantiality in a different way, because form is predicated of it. Form fails to satisfy the subject criterion. Substantial form can be defined through itself, but it depends for its existence on matter of which it is predicated.

This is not the occasion for a detailed analysis of Z.13 (for my analysis, see Gill, 2001). Z.13 is a pivotal chapter for scholars who share the view that Aristotle concludes in Z that primary substance is form. For some this chapter proves that Aristotelian forms are not universals but particulars.[28] Others reconstruct the chapter to show that form, though it is a universal, escapes the objections brought against universals

---

28. E.g., Frede and Patzig (1988, vol. 1, pp. 36–57; vol. 2, pp. 241–63), Irwin (1988, sec. 140), Spellman (1995), and Witt (1989, pp. 155–62).

in this chapter.[29] I think Aristotle's objections to the universal are devastating for form, whether form is a universal or a particular. Form is excluded as primary by the categorial scheme of predication, according to which it is predicated accidentally of matter. The problem is the same whether form is predicated of one bit of matter or many. On my interpretation, Z.13–16 show that even form cannot be substance.

If I am right, Z reaches a dead end in Z.16: None of the candidates for substance is primary. Not the matter. Not the composite. Not the form. The impasse is created by the categorial scheme of predication, which Aristotle extends to substantial being. He needs a different approach. Z.17 makes a fresh start, and Aristotle pursues the thread in H.1–5, using the concepts of potentiality and actuality.

Potentiality and Actuality

First Aristotle maps his concepts of potentiality and actuality onto his categorial scheme of predication. This strategy is useless in salvaging anything as primary substance, but let us follow his lead. Recall the model of change in the *Physics*. Aristotle analyzed change by means of three principles – a pair of terms properly opposed (ϕ and $\sim\phi$), and an underlying subject x, which is first in the privative state, then in the positive state. All terms and their combinations can be tagged as actualities – the goal (ϕ), the product (ϕx), the privation ($\sim\phi$), the pre-existing subject ($\sim\phi x$), and the persisting subject (x).[30] In addition, the change x undergoes from $\sim\phi$ to ϕ is labeled an actuality – an incomplete one. Change is an incomplete actuality, because it is directed toward a goal (ϕ) beyond itself. The goal terminates and completes the change.[31]

A potentiality is defined with reference to the actuality for which it is the potentiality. The potentiality for health differs from the potentiality for music. A potentiality for ϕ applies to a subject x, only if x is suited to be in the positive state: x must be the right kind of subject to be ϕ. Not all subjects are potentially healthy (living organisms are; inorganic materials are not). Any subject that is potentially ϕ is also potentially $\sim\phi$, and it retains that dual potentiality whether or not it is actually ϕ. Thus bricks, which are potentially a house, are still potentially a house whether or not they compose an actual house.

In *De Anima* II.5 Aristotle distinguishes levels of potentiality and actuality. A subject x has a first-level potentiality for ϕ, if it is suited to be ϕ but is actually $\sim\phi$. When x is actually ϕ its actuality is first-level. Typically ϕ is itself a capacity for some activity (ϕ-ing). So ϕx is not only at the first level of actuality; it also has a second-level potentiality, which may or may not be exercised. The activity (ϕ-ing) is a second-level

29. There are many versions of this approach, including Woods (1967) (cf. his 1991); Lewis (1991, ch. 11), Loux (1991, ch. 6). Cf. Wedin (2000, ch. 9).
30. The privation is defined with reference to the positive term – e.g., sickness is defined with reference to health (Z.7, 1032b2–6).
31. On this topic, see Gill (1989, ch. 6), Kosman (1969, 1984), Waterlow (1982, ch. 3), and, in this volume, see Bodnár and Pellegrin, ARISTOTLE'S PHYSICS AND COSMOLOGY, esp. pp. 277–81.

actuality. Unlike a change, which leads to a state beyond itself, and so is incomplete, an activity is complete as soon as it starts and for as long as it lasts.

The re-description of matter and form in terms of potentiality and actuality does not overcome the puzzles in Z. Consider a house, which has some claim to be a substance. A builder builds a house out of bricks, stones, and wood. Before he starts, the materials lying in a heap have a first-level potentiality to be a house: they are the right sorts of materials to be a house, but they lack the form of a house. Once the house has been built, the same materials constitute an actual house. The actuality is first-level. Aristotle specifies the form of a house as "a vessel capable of protecting goods and bodies" (H.2, 1043a16–18). This form enables the house to perform its function of actually protecting goods and bodies. This activity is a second-level actuality.

A house is not a genuine unity. The bricks, stones, and wood organized into a house are actually a house, and they have a second-level potentiality to be actively a house. But those materials – the suitable x – are not only potentially and actually a house. They are also *actually* bricks, stones, and wood, and they can retain that identity when the house is torn down. Let's call these compositional materials the *remnant matter*.[32] If the materials can remain what they were when the organization is removed, that organization is *accidental* to what they actually are in themselves, namely, bricks, stones, and wood. The being of the house is determined in two ways, by its form and by its matter, as *this in that*.[33] This example reveals that the subject x remains a troublemaker, even when Aristotle re-describes the situation in terms of potentiality and actuality.

The relation between matter and form in living organisms differs from that in artifacts, but the difference on which Aristotle focuses in *Metaphysics* Z and H.1–5 merely relocates the problem. On numerous occasions Aristotle insists that the material parts of living organisms, if separated from the whole, are what they were in name only – *homonymously*. For instance, a severed arm is an arm in name only and no better than a sculpted or painted arm. What is true for each bodily part is true for the whole body (*De An.* II.1, 412b17–25). A human corpse is not a human body with the soul removed. It is a human body in name only (*Meteor.* IV.12, 389b31). When an organism dies, what is left is not the organic matter. The matter, as well as the composite, is destroyed when the organism dies. Aristotle's homonymy principle indicates his conviction that the relation between form and matter in living organisms is *not* an accidental relation. On the contrary, the form determines the properties and capacities the matter must have to carry out the various organic functions. Since the form determines the matter, the relation between form and matter in living organisms is *essential*.[34] Let us call the matter, whose identity is determined by the form of the organism, the *functional matter*. Functional matter has certain second-level potentialities in virtue of the form of the object whose matter it is.

---

32. This vivid label is Wedin's (2000).
33. See Aristotle's three ways of defining a house at H.2, 1043a14–21.
34. The classic discussion of this topic is Ackrill (1972–3). In this volume, see Lennox, ARISTOTLE'S BIOLOGY AND ARISTOTLE'S PHILOSOPHY, pp. 300–10 and Caston, ARISTOTLE'S PSYCHOLOGY, pp. 320–4.

The problem of duality persists, however. Even if the functional matter is determined as what it is by the form of the whole object whose matter it is, the functions belong to some lower level subject, the remnant matter, which survives when the whole is destroyed.[35] In *Metaphysics* Z.10, Aristotle says that Callias is destroyed into flesh and bones (1035a18–19, a33). If flesh and bones survive the destruction of a living organism, they wreck the unity of the whole, even if they are functionally organized into an organic body within the animal. The being of the composite is determined in two ways, by the form (soul) and by the remnant matter (flesh and bones).

In *Generation of Animals* II.1, Aristotle confronts this issue. Flesh, he says, is like a face. After the organism dies, flesh is called flesh only homonymously (734b24–31). Thus he includes the uniform parts, like flesh and bone, with the nonuniform parts, like a face and an arm, as constituents of the functional matter. Still the problem does not go away. What about the matter of flesh – compositional flesh (*GC* I.5, 321b19–32) or the earth and water of which flesh is composed? If hylomorphic analysis uncovers remnant matter, however remote, that is the *x*-factor. The remnant matter undermines the composite on the essence criterion and it undermines substantial form on the subject criterion.

Form–Matter Predication

In the second half of *Metaphysics* H.6 Aristotle sketches what appears to be a new conception of matter and form in terms of potentiality and actuality. His discussion concerns a bronze sphere. Is it a unity? At the end of the chapter he says:

> But, as we have said, the ultimate (*eschatē*) matter and the form are the same and one, the one in potentiality, the other in actuality, so that it is like seeking what is the cause of oneness and of being one; for each thing is some one thing, and the thing in potentiality and the thing in actuality are somehow one, so that the cause is nothing else unless there is something that caused the movement from potentiality to actuality. And all those things that have no matter are simply just some one thing. (1045b17–23)

Why do I think the conception is new? Aristotle is talking about a bronze sphere, not a compound of form and functional matter (on this point, see Loux, 1995). His interest is the unity of the form and what I have so far been calling the remnant matter, the matter that persists when a composite is destroyed. His claim is that somehow the bronze and the spherical shape are one and the same, the one in potentiality, the other in actuality. Whereas on the categorial scheme of predication X and Y were two things, Y predicated of a distinct X, his present claim is that X and Y are somehow one. How can they be? Aristotle elaborates his answer in Θ.7.

In *Metaphysics* Θ.7 Aristotle considers the relation between the compositional matter (e.g., bronze) and the form of the product (the shape of the statue). He argues that the relation differs from that between an ordinary substance and its non-substantial

---

35.   On this topic, see the discussions by S. Cohen (1984, and his more detailed 1996), and Lewis (1994). Rhenius (2006) gives a rigorous critique of Lewis's position.

properties. He speaks of two sorts of predication: categorial predication and form-matter predication.

Aristotle signals his distinction by appeal to ordinary Greek usage. He says that people correctly prefer adjectives to nouns in specifying both an object's non-substantial properties and its matter. We call a man "healthy," not "health," and "musical," not "musicality." Similarly, we call a box "wooden," not "wood," and a statue "brazen," not "bronze."[36] Categorial predication holds as before between a substance and its non-substantial properties. The substance is a definite subject, a *this* (*tode ti*), and a non-substantial property is predicated of it. In such cases, Aristotle says, the ultimate thing is a substance (*ousia*) (1049a29–34). The situation is different for form and matter. He says:

> In the case of things that are not so [i.e., not related as non-substantial properties to a substance], but the thing predicated is some definite form (*eidos ti*) and *this* (*tode ti*), the ultimate thing is matter (*hulē*) and material substance (*ousia hulikē*). And calling [a thing] "that-en" with reference to its matter and its affections turns out to be quite correct. For both are indefinite (*aorista*). (1049a34–b2)

Form–matter predication is not ordinary predication. The item predicated is said to be some definite form and *this* (*tode ti*), and the matter of which it is predicated is variously characterized as *indefinite* (1049b2), *potential* (1049a21, a23), a *universal* (1049a28),[37] and not a *this* (1049a27–29). The indefiniteness of matter differs from the indefiniteness of the bare subject in Z.3. Here Aristotle compares the indefiniteness of matter to that of a thing's non-substantial properties. Non-substantial properties have definite content. Their indefiniteness is rooted in their dependence on a definite object to which they belong. Matter on the new predication model is indefinite in a similar way. We can specify the matter (spell out its content), but like non-substantial properties it depends for its existence on the definite object whose matter it is. This shared indefiniteness explains why people are correct to prefer adjectives to nouns in specifying both an object's properties and matter.

To understand the new form–matter relation, it is helpful to consider Aristotle's account of mixture in *On Generation and Corruption* I.10. He argues that the ingredients of a mixture exist actually before they are combined but are only potentially present in the compound (*GC* I.10, 327b22–31). Think of cake. The ingredients of cake are eggs, flour, sugar, butter, milk, and so on. These exist separately and actually before they are mixed, but once they are combined and the batter is baked, the product is a spongy stuff in which the ingredients are no longer actually present. Aristotle was not an

---

36. Once before, in Z.7, Aristotle considered this linguistic point (1033a5–23). On that occasion his aim was to give a rationale for the fact that linguistic usage conflicts with the metaphysical facts dictated by the categorial scheme of predication: If bronze is a definite subject of which the shape of a statue is predicated, it should be perfectly correct to call the statue "bronze," just as we call a musical man "man." The fact that Greek usage favors "brazen statue" and "wooden box" was something Aristotle tried to explain away in Z.7.

37. Contrary to modern editors, I read *katholou* ("universal") at 1049a28 with all the manuscripts.

atomist: an analysis of compounds does not yield elemental particles. He says that the ingredients are only *potentially* present in the compound. They are potentially present, because components of that sort are left behind when the compound is destroyed.[38] The original ingredients make a contribution to the compound: some of its properties are due to the ingredients. For example, the original ingredients of cake account for its flavor, moisture, weight, consistency, color, and so forth. The important point is that those properties *characterize* the higher level compound: there is no remnant matter to which the form of that higher compound belongs.

On the new model in Θ.7 the matter is not an independent subject to which the formal properties belong. Instead, the matter is something *potential* and *determinable*, which the form differentiates into a particular object.[39] In place of remnant matter, Aristotle introduces what I call *generic matter* (Gill, 1989, ch. 5). This generic matter can be thought of either as something determinable, which the form differentiates into the object, or as a collection of material properties that characterize the higher level object. An advantage of the new matter–form relation is that a statue is not *two* things with different persistence conditions, but just *one* thing – the statue. The proximate generic matter of the statue is a collection of properties that belong to it.[40] The material properties that connect an object with its simpler origins account for certain aspects of the thing's behavior, but they do not contribute to the nature of the higher level object.

Form and Functional Matter

Aristotle's re-conception of remnant matter as generic matter in H.6 and Θ.7 allows composites of matter and form to be unified objects.[41] That account, though vital to his defense of the substantiality of living organisms, also applies to material stuffs like the metals and artifacts like bronze spheres, which are not genuine Aristotelian substances. To see why living organisms are genuine substances, whereas stuffs and artifacts are not, we must consider Aristotle's further analysis of potentiality and actuality in *Metaphysics* Θ.

Θ.1 opens by reminding us of the main project of ZHΘ. Aristotle is investigating being in the primary sense, the being of substance (1045b27–32). It is in relation to

---

38.   In fact, the components extracted are typically not of the sort used in its production, but elements – earth, water, air, and fire – that composed the original ingredients. Cf. Aristotle's cyclical model of generation and destruction at *Met.* H.5, 1044b29–1045a6.

39.   Cf. Brunschwig (1979) and Jaulin (1999). Both scholars treat matter as determinable, like a genus. We differ on the status of the material genus. See Gill (Forthcoming).

40.   In Θ.7 Aristotle insists that an object is called "that-en" only with reference to the next item down, not to anything lower. A box is called neither "earthen" nor "earth," but "wooden" (1049a22). This is because the lower level matter is *transformed* into matter at the next level up, contributing some of its properties to it, and so on up the chain. For this reason the product is characterized by the properties of its proximate generic matter alone. See further Gill (Forthcoming).

41.   For a different account of the unity of composites, see Scaltsas (1994).

this being that other sorts of beings (qualities, quantities, etc.) are understood. Θ, like the preceding books, investigates substantial being, but it adopts a new approach to that investigation. In Θ.1 Aristotle distinguishes two potentiality–actuality models (1045b32–1046a4).[42] The first model treats potentiality in the strictest sense, which applies to change, but he says it is not the most useful for the present project. Even so, he devotes the first five chapters of Θ to it. In Θ.6 (1048a28–30) he indicates that the first model helps to clarify the second, which he will apply to substance.

The first potentiality–actuality model concerns the transition from a first-level potentiality to a first-level actuality (a change) and the product that results from that change. In Θ Aristotle is primarily interested in the *causal principles* of such changes. He identifies two, one active and one passive.

Change involves a mover and a moved, and each is characterized by a special sort of potency (*dunamis*).[43] Aristotle defines an active potency as "the principle of change in another thing or [in the thing itself] as other" (Θ.1, 1046a10–11). A passive potency is a principle of passive change by another thing or by the thing itself as other (1046a11–26). Active and passive potencies correspond in their goal: a state φ to be realized in the patient. But active and passive potency pairs are initially opposed – the agent is φ (or has φ in mind), and the patient is ~φ. By means of the change the agent brings the patient into a state that corresponds to the agent's own active potency (φ).[44] The active potency typically belongs to an entity other than the object changed but, in the special case of self-change, as when a doctor cures himself, the active potency belongs to the mover itself considered *as other*. The doctor acts in virtue of his knowledge of health (φ); he undergoes a change in virtue of his privation of health (~φ). By means of a change the doctor, as the patient, acquires health (φ). Aristotle regards an active potency as a first moving cause: it does not itself bring about the outcome, but

42. On this topic, see the classic paper by Kosman (1984). See also Gill (1989, chs. 6 and 7, and 2003).

43. I translate the same Greek word *dunamis* sometimes as "potentiality" and sometimes as "potency." I use "potentiality" in discussing Aristotle's distinctions between *dunamis* and *energeia / entelecheia* ("actuality"). I prefer "potency" in discussing an object's principle of active or passive change, because it lends itself more naturally than "potentiality" to active and passive construal. Although I use two translations, I do not intend thereby to distinguish two independent meanings of *dunamis*. Some scholars do think Aristotle has two distinct notions, either causal power and possibility (Charlton (1991), Freeland (1986)), or causal power and potentiality (inactive power) (Witt (2003)). I think there is a single core / focal notion of *dunamis* in Θ, that of active power to change something else (1046a10–11; cf. Δ.12, 1019b35–1020a2). The other sorts of *dunamis* are defined with reference to that. Frede (1994) argues that there is only one notion of potentiality – causal power – in Θ, which Aristotle uses in various ways. Although I agree that there is a generic sameness among the notions (see 1049b5–10, quoted below, p. 367, where Aristotle claims that *nature* is in the same genus as *dunamis*: the genus is presumably simply causal potency), I think there are specific differences among the notions that fall under that kind, and that one of those is the core notion.

44. Bodnár and Pellegrin (this volume) call this the principle of causational synonymy. For the background of this notion, see Mourelatos, THE CONCEPT OF THE UNIVERSAL IN SOME LATER PRE-PLATONIC COSMOLOGISTS, pp. 61–4.

its presence in the agent enables the agent to do so. An active potency is what Aristotle calls an *unmoved* mover.

The second potentiality–actuality model resembles the first in all its basic components. Like the first model, the second employs an active potency and a passive potency; and like the first, the second concerns two main actualities – a motion and a product. But unlike the first, the second model involves an agent and a patient that act and suffer in respect of the *same form* (ϕ), and unlike the first, the second concerns a motion that is not a change, but an activity.

Metaphysics Θ.8 specifies a potency, which Aristotle calls a *nature* and contrasts with the active potency familiar from Θ.1. He says:

> I mean by potency not only the one that has been defined, which is called an active principle of change in another thing or as other, but generally every principle of motion and rest. For *nature* is also in the same genus as potency; for it is a principle of active motion, yet not in another thing but in the thing itself *as itself*. (1049b5–10)

The single modification, that the principle of active motion is in the thing itself *as itself*, yields a scheme quite different from the previous one. In contexts of change the agent acts on a subject deprived of a certain positive character. By means of a change the patient comes to be other than it previously was and is assimilated to the positive state of the agent. On the second potentiality–actuality model the agent and the patient act and suffer in virtue of the same positive character, and in natural cases active and passive potencies are located in the same individual. For instance, a living organism has a perceptive soul, which is an active potency, and its body possesses sense organs, which have a corresponding passive potency. When the organism perceives, perception is a joint operation of its active and passive potencies. Perception does not change the perceiver – the perceiver does not become *other* than it previously was. Perception and the organism's other natural functions are *activities* that express the organism's nature.

The major difference between living organisms and all other material objects is that their active potency, the cause of their characteristic behavior, is internal, not external to them. Whereas an ax depends for its activity on someone who wields the ax, a living organism is both the active source and subject of its activities. Living organisms have an autonomy that other material objects lack.

Primary Substances

The analysis of substantial being in terms of potentiality and actuality reinstates many composites as primary substances. Living organisms like Socrates and the horse Bucephalus are unified objects, despite their composition from matter. Matter does not prevent their unity after all. By treating the lower level (generic) matter as something determinable and not as a definite subject to which properties belong, Aristotle can argue that the matter that connects an object with its simpler origins simply characterizes the object and does not contribute to what it is. He can then argue that the nature of the functional matter is *exhausted* by the form of the organism. There is nothing else of which the functions are predicated which contributes *specially* to what they are.

Predicating the form of the functional matter is therefore not a case of predicating one thing of another (Y in X, where X is distinct in being from Y). The being of a living organism and its essence are, after all, identical. The form of an organism just is the organism's active potency and its matter is its functional body, which is essentially (and exhaustively) determined by the corresponding passive potency. An organism acts on itself as itself and the motion is its characteristic activity, its mode of living.

The residual material properties (with reference to which parts of the organic body are called "*x*-en") remain independent of the form. These properties still have an important role to play. Recall what Aristotle said in H.6: "For each thing is some one thing, and the thing in potentiality and the thing in actuality are *somehow* one" (1045b20–21). Why only "somehow" one? I have argued that the form and the matter of living organisms are characterized by active and passive versions of the same functional properties. But because organisms are generated out of simpler matter and will be destroyed into simpler matter, they also possess dispositional properties of the proximate generic matter. For this reason complex organisms easily degenerate into simpler stuff. The residual material properties tend to subvert the unity of the whole, with the result that the unity is unstable and must be constantly maintained (see Gill, 1989, ch. 7). Those material properties account for the fact that material substances grow tired, weaken, and finally collapse.[45] Because an organism tends to degenerate, staying the same is considerable work. So an organism's characteristic activity is more than an expression of what it is. Such activity is also its means of self-preservation and renewal. This dynamic preservation is the joint manifestation of its active and passive potencies, and that activity maintains the organism as the unified thing that it is.

Theology

I have argued that living organisms are primary substances, whose characteristic behavior is caused by an inner principle, an active potency, which Aristotle calls their nature (*phusis*). These substances are perishable, and the source of their perishability is their proximate generic matter. This matter is not a distinct subject within the object, but a potentiality *of* the higher level object. That potentiality can cease to be actualized. When the potentiality to be the higher object ceases to be actualized, the organism dies – it is reduced to simpler stuff.

Living organisms do not depend on a cause beyond themselves to explain their natural behavior. Their active principle is internal. What does still need explanation, however, are the complex patterns of generation and perishing in the terrestrial realm. This question prompts Aristotle to discuss the heavens and to appeal to an ultimate divine principle, a first unmoved mover.

In *Metaphysics* Λ.5 Aristotle mentions two external moving causes of human beings, the father and the sun in its oblique course (1071a14–17). The sun plays a vital role

---

45. See Aristotle's discussion of the heavenly bodies in *Met.* Θ.8. Because they do not have the same sort of matter as sublunary objects, they never tire of their proper activity, as do perishable things. Matter of perishable things, which is their potentiality to be and not to be, is the cause of tiring and perishability (1050b20–28).

in substantial generation and destruction. Its twofold motion – its daily westward motion with the sphere of the fixed stars and annual eastward motion along the ecliptic, resulting in longer and shorter days – translates itself down to the sublunary realm in the elemental change witnessed in seasonal variation. The sun's complex motion accounts for the orderly cyclical pattern of generation and destruction in the sublunary realm.[46]

Metaphysics Λ.1 distinguishes three sorts of substances: perceptible perishable substances, like plants and animals; perceptible imperishable substances, like the sun and stars; and unmoved substance, which he argues is separate from physical things (1069a30–b2). Aristotle argues in the following way: What ensures the continuity of generation and destruction in all its splendid variety? His answer: the complex eternal circular motions of the heavenly bodies. What ensures the continuity of those motions? His answer: an unmoved mover, one for each heavenly sphere (Λ.6, 1071b3–11; Λ.8). The Prime Mover is first introduced as the cause of the eternal rotation of the outermost sphere, the sphere of the fixed stars (Λ.7, 1072a23–26; 1072b3–10). But this first mover accounts for more than the continuous rotation of the outermost sphere. In Λ.10 Aristotle asks in what way the good is contained in the universe: Is it contained in something separate by itself or in the order of the parts? Or is it contained in both ways, like an army, whose good is both in the order and the general? Aristotle says that the good is contained in both ways, but it is more the general, since the general does not depend on the order, whereas the order depends on him (1075a11–25). Aristotle's Prime Mover is the principle of cosmic order (see Kahn, 1985). The Prime Mover's constant activity guarantees that things continue to behave according to their natures for the good of one another and for the good of the whole.

Aristotle argues that the Prime Mover is a pure actuality – a second-actuality or activity. He excludes from it all vestiges of potentiality. If the first mover contained any potency (*dunamis*), its activity might fail, and it would depend on something else to ensure the continuity of its activity (Λ.9). The Prime Mover's divine being does not differ in kind from the active being of ordinary terrestrial substances. The difference is that Aristotle's God always enjoys the activity that we earthly substances achieve only sometimes and for a short time (Λ.7).[47]

Bibliography

Texts and Commentaries

Jaeger, W. (1957). *Aristotelis Metaphysica*. Oxford Classical Text. Oxford: Clarendon Press.
Further texts and commentaries on the Greek text of the *Metaphysics* are listed in Works Cited: Ross (1953); and Frede and Patzig (1988) (on Book Z).

46. On the role of the sun in the continuity of generation and destruction and its patterned variety, see GC II.10, esp. 336a31–b24. Cf. *Met.* Λ.6, 1072a9–18.
47. I thank István Bodnár and Paul Coppock for valuable comments on this paper. To Heike Sefrin-Weis I owe special thanks (see n. 9 above) for re-orienting my thinking about Aristotle's conception of being in the *Metaphysics*.

Works Cited

Ackrill, J. L. ([1972–3] 1997). "Aristotle's Definitions of *Psuchē*." *Proceedings of the Aristotelian Society*, 73, 119–33. Repr. in J. L. Ackrill, *Essays on Plato and Aristotle* (pp. 163–78). Oxford: Oxford University Press.

Berti, E. (1971). "Multiplicité et unité du bien selon *EE* I.8." In P. Moreau and D. Harlfinger (eds.), *Untersuchungen zur Eudemischen Ethik* (pp. 157–84). Proceedings of the Fifth Symposium Aristotelicum. Berlin: de Gruyter.

Bolton, R. (1994). "Aristotle's Conception of Metaphysics as a Science." In T. Scaltsas, D. Charles, and M. L. Gill (eds.), *Unity, Identity, and Explanation in Aristotle's Metaphysics* (pp. 321–54). Oxford: Clarendon Press.

——. (1996). "Science and the Science of Substance in Aristotle's *Metaphysics* Z." In F. A. Lewis and R. Bolton (eds.), *Form, Matter, and Mixture in Aristotle* (pp. 231–80). Oxford/Malden, Mass.: Blackwell. Corrected version of special issue of *Pacific Philosophical Quarterly*, 76 (1995).

Brunschwig, J. (1979). "La forme, prédicat de la matière?" In P. Aubenque (ed.). *Études sur la Métaphysique d'Aristote* (pp. 131–66.). Proceedings of the Sixth Symposium Aristotelicum. Paris: Vrin.

Buchheim, T. (2001). "The Functions of the Concept of *Physis* in Aristotle's *Metaphysics*." *Oxford Studies in Ancient Philosophy*, 20, 201–34.

Burnyeat, M. F. (2001). *A Map of Metaphysics Zeta*. Pittsburgh, Pa.: Mathesis.

Charlton, W. (1970). *Aristotle's Physics I, II*. Oxford: Clarendon Press.

——. (1991). "Aristotle and the Uses of Actuality." *Proceedings of the Boston Area Colloquium in Ancient Philosophy*, 5, 1–22.

Code, A, (1985). "On the Origins of some Aristotelian Theses about Predication." In J. Bogen and J. E. McGuire (eds.). *How Things Are* (pp. 101–31). Dordrecht: Reidel.

——. 1986. "Aristotle: Essence and Accident." In R. E. Grandy and R. Warner (eds.), *Philosophical Grounds of Rationality: Intentions, Categories, Ends* (pp. 411–39). Oxford: Clarendon Press.

——. (1996). "Owen and the Development of Aristotle's Metaphysics." In W. Wians (ed.). *Aristotle's Philosophical Development* (pp. 303–25). Lanham, Md.: Rowman and Littlefield.

——. (1997). "Aristotle's Metaphysics as a Science of Principles." *Revue Internationale de Philosophie*, 201, 357–78.

Cohen, M. (1978). "Individual and Essence in Aristotle's *Metaphysics*." In G. C. Simmons (ed.). *Paideia*: Special Aristotle Issue (pp. 75–85). Brockport, NY.

Cohen, S. (1984). "Aristotle's Doctrine of Material Substrate." *Philosophical Review*, 93, 171–94.

——. (1996). *Aristotle on Nature and Incomplete Substance*. Cambridge: Cambridge University Press.

Collinge, N. E. (1971). "The Senate and the Essence: γερουσία and οὐσία." *Glotta*, 49, 218–29.

Dahl, N. (2003). "On Substance Being the Same as its Essence in *Metaphysics* vii 6: The Argument about Platonic Forms." *Ancient Philosophy*, 23, 153–79.

Dancy, R. (1978). "On Some of Aristotle's Second Thoughts about Substances: Matter." *Philosophical Review*, 87, 372–413.

Devereux, D. (1992). "Inherence and Primary Substance in Aristotle's *Categories*." *Ancient Philosophy* 12, 113–31.

——. (2003). "The Relationship between Books Zeta and Eta of Aristotle's *Metaphysics*." *Oxford Studies in Ancient Philosophy*, 25, 159–211.

Driscoll, J. (1981). "ΕΙΔΗ in Aristotle's Earlier and Later Theories of Substance." In D. J. O'Meara (ed.). *Studies in Aristotle* (pp. 129–59). Washington, DC: Catholic University of America Press.

Ferejohn, M. (2003). "Logical and Physical Inquiries in Aristotle's *Metaphysics*." *The Modern Schoolman*, 80, 325–50.

Fine, G. (1984). "Separation." *Oxford Studies in Ancient Philosophy*, 2, 31–87.

Frede, M. (1987). "The Unity of General and Special Metaphysics: Aristotle's Conception of Metaphysics." In M. Frede, *Essays in Ancient Philosophy* (pp. 81–95). Minneapolis: University of Minnesota Press.

——. (1994). "Aristotle's Notion of Potentiality in *Metaphysics* Θ." In T. Scaltsas, D. Charles, and M. L. Gill (eds.), *Unity, Identity, and Explanation in Aristotle's Metaphysics* (pp. 173–93). Oxford: Clarendon Press.

Frede, M. and Charles, D. (eds.). (2000). *Aristotle's Metaphysics Lambda.* Oxford: Clarendon Press.

Frede, M. and Patzig, G. (1988). *Aristoteles Metaphysik* Z. *Text. Übersetzung und Kommentar.* (2 vols.). Munich: C. H. Beck.

Freeland, C. (1986). "Aristotle on Possibilities and Capacities." *Ancient Philosophy*, 6, 69–89.

Furth, M. (1988). *Substance, Form and Psyche: An Aristotelean Metaphysics.* Cambridge: Cambridge University Press.

Gill, M. L. (1989). *Aristotle on Substance: The Paradox of Unity.* Princeton: Princeton University Press.

——. (2001). "Aristotle's Attack on Universals." *Oxford Studies in Ancient Philosophy*, 20, 235–60.

——. (2003). "Aristotle's Distinction between Change and Activity." *Axiomathes* 14 (2004). 17–36. Repr. in J. Seibt (ed.), *Process Theories: Crossdisciplinary Studies in Dynamic Categories* (pp. 3–22). Dordrecht: Kluwer.

——. (Forthcoming). "Form–Matter Predication in *Metaphysics* Θ.7." In M. Crubelier, A. Jaulin, D. Lefebvre, and P.-M. Morel (eds.), *Aspects de la puissance: Platon/Aristote.* Grenoble: Millon.

Happ, H. (1971). *Hyle: Studien zum aristotelischen Materie-Begriff.* Berlin: de Gruyter.

Irwin, T. H. (1988). *Aristotle's First Principles.* Oxford: Clarendon Press.

Jaulin, A. (1999). *Eidos et Ousia: De l'unité théorique de la Métaphysique d'Aristote.* Paris: Klincksieck.

Kahn, C. (1985). "The Place of the Prime Mover in Aristotle's Teleology." In A. Gotthelf (ed.). *Aristotle on Nature and Living Things.* Pittsburgh, Pa.: Mathesis.

King, H. R. (1956). "Aristotle without *Prima Materia*." *Journal of the History of Ideas*, 17, 370–89.

Kosman, L. A. (1969). "Aristotle's Definition of Motion." *Phronesis*, 14, 40–62.

——. (1984). "Substance, Being, and *Energeia*." *Oxford Studies in Ancient Philosophy*, 2, 121–49.

Lewis, F. A. (1991). *Substance and Predication in Aristotle.* Cambridge: Cambridge University Press.

——. (1994). "Aristotle on the Relation between a Thing and its Matter." In T. Scaltsas, D. Charles, and M. L. Gill (eds.), *Unity, Identity, and Explanation in Aristotle's Metaphysics* (pp. 247–77). Oxford: Clarendon Press.

——. (2003). "Friend or Foe? – Some Encounters with Plato in *Metaphysics Zeta*." *The Modern Schoolman*, 80, 365–89.

Loux, M. J. (1991). *Primary Ousia: An Essay on Aristotle's Metaphysics* Z *and* H. Ithaca, NY: Cornell University Press.

——. (1995). "Composition and Unity: An Examination of *Metaphysics* H.6." In M. Sim (ed.), *The Crossroads of Norm and Nature: Essays on Aristotle's Ethics and Metaphysics* (pp. 247–79). Lanham, Md.: Rowman and Littlefield.

Matthews, G. (1995). "Aristotle on Existence." *Bulletin of the Institute of Classical Studies*, 233–8.

——. (2003). "Being Frank about Zeta." *The Modern Schoolman*, 80, 391–7.

Menn, S. (Forthcoming). *The Aim and Argument of Aristotle's Metaphysics.*

Morrison, D. (1985). "Separation in Aristotle's Metaphysics." *Oxford Studies in Ancient Philosophy*, 3, 125–57.

Owen, G. E. L. (1960). "Logic and Metaphysics in some Earlier Works of Aristotle." In G. E. L. Owen and I. Düring (eds.), *Aristotle and Plato in the Mid-Fourth Century* (pp. 163–90). Göteborg: Elanders Boktryckeri Aktiebolag. Repr. in G. E. L. Owen (1986). *Logic, Science, and*

371

Dialectic: Collected Papers in Greek Philosophy (M. C. Nussbaum, ed.) (pp. 180–99). London: Duckworth / Ithaca, NY: Cornell University Press.

——. (1965). "The Platonism of Aristotle." *Proceedings of the British Academy*, 50, 125–50. Repr. in G. E. L. Owen (1986). *Logic, Science, and Dialectic: Collected Papers in Greek Philosophy* (pp. 200–20). (M. C. Nussbaum, ed.). London: Duckworth / Ithaca, NY: Cornell University Press.

Owens, J. (1978). *The Doctrine of Being in the Aristotelian Metaphysics.* (3rd edn.). Toronto: The Pontifical Institute of Medieval Studies. (Original work published 1951).

Patzig, G. (1979). "Theology and Ontology in Aristotle's *Metaphysics.*" In J. Barnes, M. Schofield, and R. Sorabji (eds.), *Articles on Aristotle.* (vol. 3): *Metaphysics* (pp. 33–49). London: Duckworth. (Originally published as "Theologie und Ontologie in der 'Metaphysik' des Aristoteles." *Kant-Studien* 52 [1960–1].)

Reeve, C. D. C. (2000). *Substantial Knowledge: Aristotle's Metaphysics.* Indianapolis, Ind.: Hackett.

Rhenius, R. (2006). *Aristotles' essentieller Hylomorphismus: Materie, Form, und die Einheit der Komposita.* Berlin: Akademie Verlag.

Robinson, H. (1974). "Prime Matter in Aristotle." *Phronesis,* 19, 168–88.

Ross, W. D. (1953). *Aristotle's Metaphysics.* A Revised Text with Introduction and Commentary. (2 vols.). With corrections. Oxford: Clarendon Press. (Original work published 1924.)

Scaltsas, T. (1994). *Substances and Universals in Aristotle's Metaphysics.* Ithaca, NY: Cornell University Press.

Scaltsas, T., Charles, D., and Gill, M. L. (eds.). (1994). *Unity, Identity, and Explanation in Aristotle's Metaphysics.* Oxford: Clarendon Press.

Sefrin-Weis, H. (2002). *Homogeneity in Aristotle's Metaphysics.* Dissertation, University of Pittsburgh.

Sorabji, R. (1988). *Matter, Space, and Motion: Theories in Antiquity and their Sequel.* London: Duckworth.

Spellman, L. (1995). *Substance and Separation in Aristotle.* Cambridge: Cambridge University Press.

Waterlow, S. (1982). *Nature, Change, and Agency in Aristotle's Physics.* Oxford: Clarendon Press.

Wedin, M. (2000). *Aristotle's Theory of Substance: The Categories and Metaphysics* Z. Oxford: Oxford University Press.

Witt, C. (1989). *Substance and Essence in Aristotle.* Ithaca, NY: Cornell University Press.

——. (2003). *Ways of Being: Potentiality and Actuality in Aristotle's Metaphysics.* Ithaca, NY: Cornell University Press.

Woods, M. J. (1967). "Problems in *Metaphysics* Z, Chapter 13." In J. M. E. Moravscik (ed.), *Aristotle: A Collection of Critical Essays* (pp. 215–38). Notre Dame, Ind.: Notre Dame University Press.

——. (1991). "Universals and Particulars in Aristotle's *Metaphysics.*" In H. Blumenthal and H. Robinson (eds.), *Aristotle and the Later Tradition* (pp. 41–56) (= *Oxford Studies in Ancient Philosophy* suppl. vol.).

Yu, J. (1997). "Two Conceptions of Hylomorphism in *Metaphysics* ZHΘ." *Oxford Studies in Ancient Philosophy,* 15, 119–45.

——. (2003). *The Structure of Being in Aristotle's Metaphysics.* Dordrecht: Kluwer.

Further Reading

An excellent general book, which locates the *Metaphysics* in Aristotle's wider philosophy:
Lear, J. (1988). *Aristotle: The Desire to Understand.* Cambridge: Cambridge University Press.

A guide to some of the main issues debated in the *Metaphysics* and survey of recent literature:
Gill, M. L. (2005). "Aristotle's *Metaphysics* Reconsidered." *Journal of the History of Philosophy,* 43, 223–51.

Useful collections of papers cited above are:
Frede, M. and Charles, D. (eds.). (2000); Scaltsas, T., Charles, D., and Gill, M. L. (eds.). (1994).

See also:
Barnes, J., Schofield, M., and Sorabji (eds.). (1979). *Articles on Aristotle.* (vol. 3): *Metaphysics.* London: Duckworth.

Translations and Philosophical Commentaries

Bostock, D. (1994). *Aristotle's Metaphysics.* Books Z and H. Clarendon Aristotle Series. Oxford: Clarendon Press.
Kirwan, C. (1993). *Aristotle's Metaphysics.* Books Γ, Δ, and E (2nd edn.). Clarendon Aristotle Series. Oxford: Clarendon Press.

19

Aristotle's Ethics

MICHAEL PAKALUK

With the exception, apparently, of a few passages in Book V, on justice, and the double treatment of pleasure, in VII.11–14 and X.1–5, Aristotle's *Nicomachean Ethics* (*EN*) is a remarkably coherent book.[1] At the beginning Aristotle tells us what he aims to do; he then carries this out, in a systematic fashion, with deviations from the general plan readily explainable; and then, at the end, he declares that he has succeeded (by his lights) in carrying out what he had originally proposed. The treatise's general coherence is, moreover, underwritten by frequent editorial references backwards and forwards.

EN ostensibly has the character of a search backwards (*zētēsis*, cf. I.13, 1102a13); its apparent aim is, simply, to identify the ultimate good of human life, which Aristotle variously calls "the highest achievable good" (I.4, 1095a16); "the good" (I.2, 1094a23); "the best thing" (1094a23); "the human good" (1094b7, 1098a16); "doing well" (I.4, 1095a19); or "happiness" (1095a20). The treatise might therefore more appropriately be called, not "Ethics", but rather something like "What the ultimate good of human life is." Anything more that we would wish to regard as *ethics* is, at best, introduced by Aristotle as it were incidentally, in the course of his attempt to identify this ultimate good.

Aristotle's search for this good has the four elements that must compose any systematic search. First, one must give a rough description of *what* one is looking for; second, one must specify a *field* in which to conduct the search; third, one must *proceed systematically* through the specified field; and, fourth, one must *verify* whether a suspected candidate is in fact the object sought.

---

1. Four treatises on ethics have come down to us as attributed to Aristotle: the *Nicomachean Ethics* (*EN*); *Eudemian Ethics* (*EE*); *Magna Moralia* (*MM*); and *On Virtues and Vices* (*VV*). One might also add the reconstructed *Protrepticus* (*Protr.*), which is ethical insofar as it argues for a certain view of what makes life worth living. But *VV* is certainly spurious; *MM* probably so; and *EE*, often suspected of being inauthentic, is nonetheless so frequently corrupt in its text, or obscure in its meaning, that rarely may *it* be used with confidence to clarify *EN*, rather than the reverse. Yet *Protr.* and *EN* seem to agree in outlook and spirit. Hence I shall focus here on *EN* and take that treatise to express Aristotle's considered ethical views. (Kenny (1978), is the starting point for discussions of the dating and authenticity of the treatises. Perhaps the best discussion of the two treatments of pleasure, which attempts to reconcile them, is Owen (1971–2).)

Similarly, at the beginning of *EN* Aristotle, first, sets down two basic criteria which, he thinks, would need to be satisfied by an ultimate good: it must be truly ultimate (*teleiotaton*), in the sense that it cannot be worth having for the sake of anything else, whereas anything else worth having must be worth having for the sake of it; and it furthermore must be self-sufficient (*autarkēs*), in the sense that, if we were to have this good, then we would need nothing else (I.7, 1097a30–b21).

Second, he delimits the field of the search, chiefly by means of his famous "Function Argument": we should look for the ultimate good, Aristotle argues, among those activities that are expressions of the various human virtues; the ultimate good will be one such activity, the most ultimate of these (1098a17–18); and, using a simple account of human psychology, he derives a list of the virtues (I.13).

Third, Aristotle systematically examines these virtues and their corresponding activities; this investigation constitutes the bulk of the treatise, Books III–IX. Fourth, and finally, when he has completed this systematic examination, he looks back on what was established and, relying mainly on the criteria (of ultimacy and self-sufficiency) that he had articulated at the beginning, he picks out one such activity as the ultimate good: the ultimate human good, Aristotle concludes, is the activity that we can engage in through the virtue of speculative wisdom (X.7). This conclusion is broadly consonant with the viewpoint of the *Protrepticus* (hinted at too elsewhere in the corpus, such as at *Met.* A.1–2), where an impassioned Aristotle insists that "Humankind possesses nothing divine or blessed that is of any account except what there is in us of mind and understanding: this alone of our possessions seems to be immortal, this alone divine. By virtue of being able to share in this faculty, life, however wretched and difficult by nature, is yet so cleverly arranged that human beings seem to be gods in comparison with all other creatures" (*Protr.* B109 Barnes = p. 45 Ross).

Goodness is Goal-like

In order to understand this claim correctly, however, it is important to attend to some of Aristotle's remarks in the opening chapters of *EN* (I.1–2), on the nature of goals, which constitutes Aristotle's development of the Platonic notion of a "craft" (*technē*).

It is clear from the examples he gives that Aristotle regards a goal (*telos*) as *a repeatable result of a certain kind, which serves as a principle of organization for the actions of someone who (or something which) has a corresponding role or ability.* Bridle makers make bridles, repeatedly; generals win battles, repeatedly. To say that "victory in battle is the goal of a general," is to say that any action of a general, insofar as he is acting as a general, can be understood as directed at some particular victory (whether planned, merely, or in fact achieved; whether his own or won by an allied general – there is no need to take a goal to be egoistic in the first place). Human action as directed toward a goal is periodic in character, and the great bulk of it consists of preparation for attaining a goal. The goal is that around which the other activity is organized. Thus, a general wins battles only periodically, during campaigns, and most of his activity directed at winning battles will involve something besides fighting a battle, e.g. troop training; troop movement; logistics; preparation of weapons; etc. Similarly, to claim that "activity of speculative wisdom is the goal of a (good) human being" is, so far, to claim no more than that any action of a (good) human being, insofar as he is acting well as a human being, can be understood as directed at some particular exercise of speculative wisdom (whether planned, merely, or in fact achieved; whether his own, or that of a comrade).

It follows from this that if, with Aristotle, we refer to the ultimate human goal as "happiness" (*eudaimonia*, a term which means, literally, "being blessed by (or with) a god"), then happiness is a repeatable result of a certain kind, achieved by someone who has a corresponding role or ability; it is not something that (as we might imagine) comes about once for all, or randomly. Happiness occurs at intervals within a life well lived, and its occurrence organizes the other activities of such a life. To say that "happiness is activity of speculative wisdom" is to say that activity of that sort, periodically attained, should serve as the organizing principle of human life.[2]

It becomes necessary to distinguish, then, between *happiness* and a *happy life*: a happy life would presumably be one in which happiness is attained with a sufficient frequency (although, again, perhaps by a friend rather than by oneself) and with sufficient reliability, so that the life as a whole can count as happy.[3] (Note, however, that Aristotle does not say with any precision what degree or manner of attainment of happiness suffices to make a life happy. Nor should we expect him to do so: How many victories need a general win, or how frequently need he win them, to be successful as a general? The question is just about meaningless.)

Additionally, we should distinguish betweens goals that are attainable by an individual, acting on his own, and those that are attainable only through joint action with others, who consequently form along with oneself an "association" (*koinōnia*, see VIII.9–12) for the attaining of that goal. We seek a goal in association with others when it is either not possible at all, or practically speaking unworkable, to achieve that goal through one's own efforts. We seek a goal through a *larger* association, when it is either not possible at all, or practically speaking unworkable, to achieve that goal through the efforts of a smaller association. Thus: each farmer in Athens needed to defend his farm against attacks from other city-states; this is not something that he could practically speaking do by his own efforts; hence farmers and other citizens would be part of a militia, which jointly provided for individual defense. Again, each city-state in Greece needed to defend itself against Persian attacks; this is not something that the separate militias might effectively do on their own; hence, the city-states formed a league for common defense.

Aristotle regards happiness – the activity of speculative wisdom – to be a goal that is either not attainable at all by an individual's efforts, or not practically speaking so attainable. He regards it, rather, as something that is attainable through what he regards as the common efforts of the natural, complete unit of human association, that is, the city-state. This makes sense: the natural, universal goal for human beings,

2. In contrast it is perhaps most common in English to take "happiness" either subjectively, to indicate a feeling, or objectively, to signify a condition of a life taken as a whole. An influential article, which argues that Aristotle intends *eudaimonia* in the latter sense, is Kraut (1979a).
3. The distinction is correctly stressed in an important article by Heinaman (1988).

is something that is to be attained, Aristotle thinks, by the natural, complete unit of association. Hence, at the very beginning of *EN*, he is clear that the goal he is seeking after is the object of "political craft" (*politikē*, I.2, 1094b11) and properly the ultimate goal of political administration; and throughout *EN* he appeals to the intentions and efforts of legislators – indeed, *EN* seems to be addressed principally to legislators (cf. X.9; I.13, 1102a7–10, II.1, 1103b3–4; II.3, 1105a12).[4]

A reader of today might object to this idea: Isn't it obviously possible for an individual, on his own, to engage in activity of speculative wisdom? What could be easier than to take up a book of philosophy (say) and start thinking about it? The contrast with military defense is evident, and this hardly requires the joint action of citizens in political society. But, as is clear from the opening book of the *Metaphysics* (A.1, 981b14–24), in saying that the activity of speculative wisdom is a goal, and achievement, of political craft, Aristotle is thinking about the much larger picture, of how it is that an individual might be free, in the first place, to pick up that book of philosophy and think about it. Aristotle's view is that the achievement of the ultimate goal of human life requires leisure (*scholē*, *EN* X.7, 1177b4–22), that is, a temporary freedom from concern for the necessities of life; but that there is leisure at all is an achievement of political society; and that leisure is put to its proper use by citizens (education, thinking, and culture – rather than, say, military training, or hedonistic enjoyment) is also an artifact of a good system of laws and education.

Thus, throughout *EN* Aristotle takes it for granted that the ultimate goal of human action is something that is properly sought and attained in a stable and soundly constituted political society. But this forestalls, at least, a worry that is commonly felt by readers of *EN*. It is thought that *EN* is a treatise on "ethics," in our sense, and then it is noted, with consternation, that one fails to find in *EN* any direction, except of a rather vague sort, as to what sorts of actions are to be done and what sorts to be avoided. Ethics would seem to involve the articulation and justification of rules for action, but nothing like this is found in *EN*. (Is suicide ever permissible? What constitutes stealing, and why is it wrong to steal? What is the reason why murder is forbidden? Under what conditions is sexual intercourse licit? And so on.) Indeed, apart from some very rough remarks in Book V, where injustice is analyzed as a kind of inequality, Aristotle seems simply to take various moral principles for granted, for instance, that adultery is always wrong (II.6, 1107a11–15).

The worry arises largely because we presume that there is such a thing, in some form or other, as a "moral law," and we expect a treatise on Ethics to discuss moral laws. But for Aristotle the relevant law governing action is simply the law of political society (hence it becomes a serious question, for him, whether a good human being and a good citizen are the same thing, cf. *Pol.* III.3); and he regards it as fairly obvious (correctly so) that such things as theft and murder need to be outlawed in a stable and soundly constituted political society. In general, what *we* take to be a matter of morality, *he* takes to be primarily a matter of legislation, and he presumes that

---

4. On the relationship between Aristotle's ethics and political philosophy, see Keyt, ARISTOTLE'S POLITICAL PHILOSOPHY, in this volume.

constraints on action that might appear difficult to understand or justify, if considered as applying simply to an individual, will seem relatively easy to accept, if regarded as binding on political society as a whole. (Recall that, on Plato's lights, the position taken by an amoralist such as Thrasymachus is simply that *he* should be able to behave as if a tyrant, and therefore as if he lived apart from political society, with all of political society ministering to *his* wants.)[5] In a sense, then, in *EN* Aristotle defers, to a later consideration of legislation, many of the issues that we would want to investigate as matters of personal conduct (just as it is in Plato's *Laws*, not the *Republic*, that we find anything like a code of conduct). And, in fact, Ethics seems to have been regarded by Aristotle as seamlessly linked to Politics (cf. *EN* X.9).[6]

In general, it is difficult to overestimate the importance, for Aristotle's ethics, of the notion that *goodness has the character of a goal*.[7] That he will insist on this is clear from the opening lines of *EN*: "Every craft and every discipline, and similarly action and plan, seems to aim at a particular good, which is the reason why (*dio*) the good has been pronounced, correctly so, to be 'what everything desires.' But there appears to be a certain difference among goals. . . ." (I.1, 1094a1–4) What is of interest here is not whether the passage, as is often alleged, commits a "quantifier shift" fallacy, in arguing from "all/some" to "some/all"[8] – clearly, Aristotle might be justly charged with such a fallacy only if he thought that "There is a single good that everything aims at" follows directly, and with no further premises, from "Everything aims at some good or other." But his phrasing does not suggest this (the inferential particle *dio* generally indicates only that a later claim *receives support* from an earlier one, not that it is *deductively implied* by that earlier claim); and elsewhere in *EN* Aristotle indicates that a fairly subtle argument, with diverse and controversial premises, would be required to move from the one claim to the other (cf. VII.13, 1153b25–32; X.2, 1172b35–1173a5). Rather, what is interesting about the passage is how Aristotle immediately moves from talk of *goods*, to talk of *goals*: Aristotle makes use of the claim that "the good is what everything desires" as a justification for ceasing to talk about goods. In fact, it is the notion of "ultimacy" or "finality," not that of goodness, which dominates the first book of *EN*; goodness is introduced and examined principally in Aristotle's intricate refutation in I.6 of the Platonic claim that goodness is something common (*koinon*, 1096a28, b25) and separately existing (*chōriston*, 1096b22).

To hold that goodness is "in common" is to hold that, for any two things that are good, there is some attribute or property which they both share; and, in consequence of this, these things differ in goodness "as regards more and less" (*mallon kai hētton*, cf. VIII.1, 1155b15), that is, the one may be properly said to have more, less, or the same degree of goodness as the other. Aristotle holds, rather, that the term "good" takes on

---

5.   See the related remarks by Lane, PLATO'S POLITICAL PHILOSOPHY, in this volume.
6.   See Bodéüs (1993), for an influential statement of a view of this sort. Note that it is not claimed that Aristotle is a legal positivist: he clearly asserts in *EN* V.7 that only in some cases is something wrong only because it is proscribed; in other cases the explanation for its being wrong will need to refer also to the characteristics (that is, the "nature") of the act proscribed, or of the agents involved.
7.   On this point see the very helpful discussion in White (1988).
8.   The charge is perhaps stated most pointedly in Geach (1972, pp. 1–2).

a different meaning, amounting to a difference in kind, when it is applied across things that differ in kind. The term "good" in the phrase "a good knife" signifies something different, and incommensurable, with what that term signifies in the phrase "a good piano." The doctrine looks obscure and puzzling until we translate it into talk of goals or "ends," in which case it becomes mundane: of course, what a knife is meant to do (its "goal") is different in kind from what a piano is meant to do, and thus, similarly, what makes a knife such that it can do the one is different in kind from what makes a piano such that it can do the other. These notions, too, are introduced right at the beginning of *EN*: "Since there are many [kinds of] actions and crafts and disciplines, there are also many [kinds of] goals" (I.1, 1094a6–8; cf. I.7, 1097a16–18).

If goodness is not "in common," in the way explained, then, quite generally, classifications having to do with goods – that is to say, goals – will not behave in the same way as those involving attributes that are in common. In particular, in a discussion within ethics we should not expect to find genus-species trees that behave in the same way, or orderings of attributes that could be displayed using devices such as Venn diagrams. Rather, what will be the case is that the relevant good, or goal, will serve as a kind of standard for predication, and other usages will be obliquely related to this (what is sometimes called "central case" or "ideal type" analysis). Hence the distinction between an "unqualified" use of a term (the use of that term *simpliciter*, or *haplōs*), and a "qualified" use of a term (*secundum quid*), becomes the most important device of classification for ethics; and, indeed, Aristotle employs it frequently. The central case is prior because it is most explanatory: each of the various oblique cases may be understood in relation to the central case (because each in some sense "wishes to be" what is found in the central case), whereas no oblique case quite illuminates any other oblique case in the same way, and each is too impoverished to illuminate the central case. Because the central case is thus prior, it is "universal," as binding together the various oblique cases into a single class (for example, no one would take such opposite phenomena as *cowardice* and *reckless boldness* to go together, if courage did not serve to unite them).

One reason Plato wished to insist that goodness is "in common," is that this view coheres best with the view that there is a separate Form or Idea of Goodness, in which particular goods participate, and from which they derive their goodness. All particular goods, then, would have the same thing in common (namely what each derives from its participation in the Form), and they would vary in degree, as goods, depending upon their closeness to, or distance from, the Form. Aristotle of course will elsewhere give logical and metaphysical arguments against separate Forms: in the Ethics perhaps his principal argument against a Form of goodness is simply that such a Form seems irrelevant for action (I.6, 1096b35–1097a14). This criticism is decisive if, again, goodness has the character of a goal.

Criteria of an Ultimate Good

We distinguished four stages in the ostensible project of *EN*, the search for the ultimate goal of human life, and we may get a fair sense of the scope and plan of the treatise by briefly examining each of these in turn.

The first stage was to set down criteria to identify what one is looking for, and a criterion of this sort is adumbrated already at the beginning of I.2:

> If, then, there is a goal of practical matters which is such that (i) we wish for it on account of itself, and (ii) we wish for other things on account of it, (iii) and it is not the case that we wish for everything on account of something else (since thus there will be an infinite progression, the consequence being that striving is empty and vain), it is clear that this would be the good and the best thing. (1094a18–21)[9]

Aristotle holds that something that satisfies (i) and (ii) "has the nature of a goal" or is "goal-like" (*teleion*, I.7, 1097a25–30); and we should take (iii) to be setting down a third requirement, that is, that the thing under consideration is not, in turn, wished for on account of something else. Aristotle adds some slight refinements in I.7:

> We say that that which is to be sought in its own right is "more goal-like" than that which is to be sought on account of something else; and also that that which is never reasonably chosen (*haireton*) on account of something else is "more goal-like" than those things that are reasonably chosen both in their own right and on account of something; and also, then, we say that a thing is "without qualification goal-like" if it is always reasonably chosen in its own right and never on account of something else. (1097a30–34)

Both of these passages imply initially a threefold division of goods not unlike that which Plato draws in *Rep.* II (357b–d): goods that are purely instrumental, in the sense that we would not want them, except for their consequences; goods we want both in themselves and because of their consequences; and the sort of good that, as Plato says, "we would welcome, not from desiring its consequences, but greeting it for the sake of itself." But note that Plato uses the indicative mood to specify the first two classes (goods that we *do* want only for their consequences, or additionally for their own sake) and the optative in specifying the third class (a good that we *would* want, even apart from its consequences). This suggests that a further distinction could be made in this last class, which the refinements in the I.7 passage, involving temporal qualifications ("always," "never"), are meant to achieve. These temporal qualifications are consistent with Aristotle's conception of an end as being, as was said, a repeatable instance of a general kind. An end which, in none of its instances, is further subordinated to something else, is more goal-like than one which, in some of its instances, is reasonably so subordinated – even if there in fact are, or we could conceive of, instances in which the latter might be sought, without its being further subordinated.

Note that even if it is necessary, if striving is not to be "empty and vain," that there be goals that are not in every instance additionally sought for the sake of something else, nothing would guarantee that there be a goal that is, as Aristotle puts it, "goal-like without qualification," that is, which is *never* sought for the sake of anything else.

---

9. A provocative examination of this passage may be found in Wedin (1981).

That is why Aristotle provisionally provides a space for such an end, by using the term *eudaimonia* ("happiness"): *eudaimonia*, he points out, is taken to be the sort of end that is never additionally sought for the sake of something else, whereas other goal-like things, in some of their instances, are reasonably sought for its sake (I.7, 1097a34). (The claim would not be convincing if put forward using any of the other expressions that Aristotle tends to use as equivalent to *eudaimonia*, such as "the human good" or "the highest good".) But he need not have taken this additional step; he might simply have said that the ultimate goal of human life would simply be the *most* goal-like thing, even if nothing is goal-like without qualification. And, indeed, sometimes he prefers to speak in this way (e.g., 1097a36; 1098a18, cf. I.8, 1099a30).

A second mark of the ultimate human good is, Aristotle thinks, that it is "self-sufficient." Now we can distinguish between self-sufficiency as pertaining to a good possessed or enjoyed, and self-sufficiency as pertaining to the subject who has or enjoys some good, and Aristotle is quick to say that, by the mark of "self-sufficiency," he does not mean the latter: it will not be an isolated individual, but rather someone with family and friends at least, who has and enjoys the ultimate human good (I.7, 1097b8–14). But a *good* is self-sufficient, if it is such that taken on its own (i) it makes a life one that is worth choosing and (ii) it makes someone lacking in nothing (1097b14–16). Clearly this is a distinct criterion from the first: true enough, a purely instrumental good becomes entirely dispensable, once we have that for the sake of which we employ that instrument; but there is no reason to think that possession of the most goal-like of a class of non-instrumental goods would make those others dispensable. So, again, to make the point go through, Aristotle has to rely on the force of the term *eudaimonia*, because it does seem as though, if we possessed *eudaimonia* (happiness), then everything else would be unnecessary.

Note that we need not, however, take self-sufficiency to be an all-or-nothing attribute: it would presumably make sense to regard some goods as more or less self-sufficient than others, if, to a greater or lesser extent, their possession rendered other goods dispensable. Furthermore, a good might presumably be self-sufficient, to a certain extent, because it implied a reeducation of our desires, or a change in what we wanted, and not simply because it somehow captured, or combined into one, everything that we wanted, taking those wants to remain fixed. From various passages in the *Protrepticus*, it is clear that Aristotle views the self-sufficiency of the ultimate human good in the first way: "Then what is it among existing things for the sake of which nature and god have brought us into being? Pythagoras, when asked about this, answered, 'To observe the heavens,' and he used to say that he was an observer of nature and had come into life for the sake of this. And when somebody asked Anaxagoras for what end one would choose to come into being and live, he is said to have answered the question by saying, 'To observe the heavens and the stars, moon and sun in them,' everything else being worth nothing" (DK 59B18 and *Protr.* B19 Barnes = p. 42 Ross). The suggestion is that things that we once valued come to seem to be worthless once we contemplate the heavens. And this would be consistent with the general tenor, too, of Plato's thought: for Plato, the contemplation of the Forms is self-sufficient, not because that activity contains what one wanted (such as sex and pleasures from eating) *before* undergoing the training and self-discipline which led, eventually, to that contemplation; rather, a glimpse of the Forms makes us lose our desires for other things.

Note that, on this conception, the more self-sufficient a good one possesses, the greater the simplicity and detachment which is displayed in one's life (cf. X.8, 1178b33–1179a22).[10]

A Particular Activity in Accordance with Virtue

The second stage in the ostensible project of the treatise was to delimit the field in which to conduct the search for the ultimate good: What sort of thing are we looking for? Aristotle's view is that the ultimate human good will be found within the field: *activities in accordance with a virtue* (that is, which we can do only through having virtue). That is to say, the ultimate human end will be something that one achieves only through the putting into practice of a virtue, and which counts as the actualization of that virtue.

Negatively, Aristotle supports this conclusion by eliminating, through what he calls "published" considerations (I.5, 1096a3), popular contenders for the ultimate end: it cannot be bodily pleasure, which would be slavish and animalistic; or honor, which is conferred for the sake of virtue and therefore is not ultimate; or wealth, which clearly is instrumental (I.5, 1095b14–1096a9).

Positively, Aristotle reaches this conclusion through what is known as the "Function Argument" (I.7, 1097b22–1098a20). That argument presupposes that, generally, the good of a thing will be located in some kind of result, achievement, or product (*ergon*) for which the thing is designed. For instance, the "good of a shoemaker" will be located in the shoes that he produces: shoemakers exist to make shoes; a shoemaker does well if he makes good shoes; and a person who is a shoemaker, then, insofar as he is a shoemaker, achieves what he "desires", as a shoemaker, if he makes good shoes. Note that, on this conception, something is a "good of X" or a "good for X", not in the first instance because it contributes to a state of *satisfaction* of X, or remedies some kind of deficiency in X, but rather because it serves as a kind of offshoot or realization of X, which is *brought about* in the right sort of way by X. The "Function Argument" might therefore just as well be called the "Product Argument". It is indebted, yes, to Plato's similar argument at the end of *Republic* I, but also to Plato's conception in the *Symposium* of procreative activity as following naturally upon virtue.[11]

Immediately before the Function Argument, Aristotle had concluded that the ultimate human goal would be something that is "goal-like without qualification" and

10.   Note that scholars debate whether I.7, 1097b16–20 gives yet a third criterion of the ultimate good, a criterion of "greatest preferability" – that it is the sort of thing that is to be reasonably preferred when or if it is compared singly with other goods. Possibly the passage is simply intended to clarify the first criterion. A full discussion, with an excellent survey of the vast secondary literature, may be found in Lawrence (1997).

11.   Aristotle sometimes wishes to distinguish between an *ergon* in the sense of a "product" and an action (*praxis*): a product is where there is an end of action apart from that action itself (I.1, 1094a3–5, cf. VI.4). So in that sense happiness, something sought not for the sake of something else, could not be a product: "achievement" might be a better term. Yet the word "product" is useful here as highlighting the distinctness between the achievement of a virtue and the virtue through which we achieve it.

"self-sufficient." After the Function Argument, he asserts that a goal of this sort will be found among activities we can only achieve through virtue. The point of the Function Argument, then, is simply to advance Aristotle's overall project by just this one step. It tells us to look at those activities that correspond to the virtues of a thing, if we are to find the ultimate good of a thing.[12]

The argument does this through pointing out the logical interrelationships, as Aristotle conceives them, between "good for," "function" (or "product"), "good," and "virtue." That which is *good for* a thing of a certain kind, as was said, is its *function* (or *product*), that is, what a thing of that kind is designed to produce. A *good* thing of that kind will produce a good product, whereas a bad thing will produce a bad product. A good thing of a certain kind is one that has those attributes that enable it to produce its product well. Those attributes simply are the *virtues* of a thing of that kind. Thus, it is on account of the virtues of a thing that it will succeed in producing a good product, and thus achieving what is good for it. Hence, if we wished to discover what was *good for* a thing, it would suffice to look at its virtues – those traits that contributed to its being a good thing of that kind – and then to look at what it was made able to produce, through the agency of those virtues. Its good would have to be something it was rendered able to produce, by a trait that served to make it a good thing of that kind.

Aristotle takes these relationships and claims to hold generally, and thus also in the case of human beings. Suppose a human being has a function. Then he is designed to produce something, and what he is designed to produce will be what is "good for" him, as a human being. A good human being will produce this well, a bad human being will produce it poorly or not at all. But a good human being is rendered good precisely by having the virtues. Thus, what is "good for" a human being will be something that he produces through employing the virtues. Thus, if we look at the various virtues, and see what is brought about through employing them, then – applying the criteria already set down for an ultimate good – we shall be able to discover the ultimate good of a human being.[13]

The argument takes it for granted that human beings have a function (or "product"), but Aristotle in passing provides a couple of compressed arguments for this presupposition: "Could it be that there are certain products and actions belonging to a builder, or a shoemaker, but that there are none that belong to a human being, and that he is naturally bereft of anything to do? And just as, for an eye or hand or foot (and, generally, for each of his parts) there is evidently some particular task, so shouldn't one posit as well some particular task for the human being, apart from all of these?" (I.7, 1097b28–33). That is, apparently: human beings could not acquire occupations or roles, if these were not grafted onto some antecedent natural function; and the ascription of a function to a part makes sense only if we presuppose some function for the whole. (The arguments are of course controversial and open to objection. That Aristotle argues with such compression shows that he is relying, at this point, on his

---

12. For an alternative but complementary view, see Lawrence (2001).
13. This construal of the Function Argument, I believe, defuses the objection raised by Glassen (1957), that Aristotle tries to answer the question, "What is the good of a human being?" by changing the subject and telling us "What is it that makes a human being good?"

audience's agreement with the teleological understanding of nature that he defends in *Physics* II.)[14]

In the *Republic* Plato had stipulated that the function of a thing is that which "it alone can do, or it alone can do well" (I. 352e–353b). Taking up this idea, plausible and intuitive if one accepts a teleological view of nature, Aristotle argues that the human function has to be something that human beings alone can do; but they alone (assume: of things in the sublunary realm, which is our sphere of action) have a rational aspect to their soul; and (as he presumes, along with Plato, cf. *Rep.* I. 353d) the task of the soul is to live; and thus the human function must be, or involve, the activity of life of the rational aspect of the soul; and virtues would be traits through the employment of which a human being might carry out that sort of activity well.[15]

This conclusion allows Aristotle to generate a list of virtues (I.13). There are: (i) traits that help the soul carry out its rational activity well, in the sense that these traits pertain directly to that aspect of the soul: practical wisdom (intelligence as regards the ordering of temporal matters) and philosophical wisdom (intelligence as regards atemporal matters) (cf. VI.1, 1138b35–1139a17). Then (ii) there are traits that help the soul carry out its rational activity, by insuring that the non-rational parts of the soul are duly responsive to the rational parts. These are the "virtues of character," principally, courage (*andreia*); chaste moderation of appetite (*sōphrosunē*); generosity (*eleutheriotēs*); and justice (*dikaiosunē*).

The Systematic Examination of the Virtues

As was said, the bulk of *EN* consists, then, of an examination of the characteristic activities and effects of these virtues, because Aristotle wishes to work systematically through his delimited field of investigation, before reaching a conclusion about which "activity in accordance with virtue" is the ultimate end of a human being. Of course, given his characteristic, encyclopedic aspirations, in carrying out this search Aristotle also intends to touch upon all of the more salient elements of the moral life: the nature of pleasure and pain (VII.11–14, and X.1–5); moral psychology (III.1–5); weakness of will (VII.1–10); and friendship (VIII and IX).

Aristotle thinks of the emotions and virtues as ideally composing a natural moral constitution (cf. *sustēma*, IX.8, 1168b32) of a human being, and the order in which he considers the virtues reflects this. Roughly, the virtues that he considers earlier in his discussion are meant to be under the *control* of the virtues he considers later, and the earlier ones work so as to *enable* the activity of the later ones. He begins by considering first the virtues that pertain most directly to the non-rational aspect of the soul, courage and moderation (cf. III.10, 1117b23–24), and he concludes by comparing

14. On Aristotle's teleological conception of nature in the *Physics*, see in this volume Bodnár and Pellegrin, ARISTOTLE'S PHYSICS AND COSMOLOGY, pp. 275–7; and for a discussion of nature in his biology, see Lennox, ARISTOTLE'S BIOLOGY, pp. 300–10.

15. Useful discussions of the Function Argument may be found in Gomez-Lobo (1989), Kraut (1979b), and Whiting (1988).

the two architectonic intellectual virtues. This very ordering of the virtues is meant to be an argument that the ultimate human end will be the activity of one of these intellectual virtues.

Although Aristotle seems to regard his list of the virtues as exhaustive, he nowhere gives an argument for this view. Moreover, there are difficulties as regards his manner of individuating the virtues. For instance, he takes courage to be, most centrally, the correct handling of feelings of fear and boldness, by someone who is put in the position of potentially losing his life, in a glorious fashion, on the field of battle (III.6, 1115a32–35). Courage shown by sailors at sea, for instance, or the "courage" we might think is shown by, say, desperately ill persons who nonetheless persevere cheerfully, is something Aristotle regards as incidental. The reason is presumably that, again, he thinks of human beings as intended by nature to live in political society; hence, it is necessary to make implicit reference to the requirements of a stable political society, in order to explain the virtues – and a good military defense, requiring courage, is necessary for a stable political society. Similarly, generosity is required for reciprocity and the correct use of commercial goods among friends; justice for reciprocity and market relations among strangers; and so on.

Aristotle famously defines a virtue of character as a stable characteristic (*hexis*) of the soul, which consistently achieves in action a standard that is intermediate (*meson*) as between extremes, where that standard is established by practical reason, or is the standard that would be accepted by a person who has good practical reason (II.6, 1106b36–1107a6). This "Doctrine of the Mean" seems not to be a counsel of moderation ("nothing in excess") – since otherwise there would be no need to appeal to a standard set down from without, by practical reason – but rather an observation about the nature of the contrariety that one finds in the domain of the virtues: although virtue and vice are opposed, unlike typical cases of opposition each virtue will have *two* opposites (one at each extreme) rather than one. Thus opposed to courage are both cowardice and foolhardiness; opposed to generosity are both profligacy and stinginess; and so on. Of course the Doctrine of the Mean has practical implications, to which Aristotle draws attention with much shrewdness, such as that a person should determine to which extreme he is, by temperament or upbringing, more disposed to go, and then attempt to overcompensate for this, by acting as if he would go to the *other* extreme (II.9, 1109a30–35).[16]

It is fruitful to interpret Aristotle's discussion of the various virtues as a sustained polemic against Plato, intended to eliminate competitors for the ultimate human goal. Plato typically holds to a strong version of the unity of the virtues – he tends to think of the various virtues as merely different manifestations of one and the same kind of knowledge – and at different points courage; chaste moderation; greatness of outlook (magnanimity, *megalopsucheia*); and justice get identified with this single essential trait. Aristotle, in contrast, aims to deflate these various virtues, by assigning them rather humdrum civic responsibilities, falling within discrete domains: courage manages feelings of fear and boldness relevant to military defense; chaste moderation handles

---

16. The precise significance of the Doctrine of the Mean is much debated. See Broadie (1991, pp. 95–103) and Urmson (1973).

our desire for pleasures of touch associated with natural activities for sustaining and reproducing the species; justice deals with economic exchanges and civic penalties; magnanimity is an attitude toward honor and standing in society. It would be absurd to take any one of *these* operations, on its own, so evidently contributing to some total effect of political society, to be the ultimate human good. (And note that, for Aristotle, these various virtues typically go together and are united, not logically or essentially, but because they form part of a coherent natural system, IV.13, 1144b21–1145a2.) So, again, the field is cleared for the two architectonic intellectual virtues: the ultimate human goal would have to be the activity of one of these.

The Activity of Speculative Wisdom

It is relatively easy to conclude, of the two intellectual virtues, that the activity of philosophical wisdom is more goal-like, and thus that it constitutes the ultimate goal:

> If happiness is an activity in accordance with a virtue, one might reasonably expect that it be in accordance with the best virtue; but this would be the virtue of the best part. Whether, then, this be mind (*nous*) or some other thing, which in fact by nature seems to rule and exercise authority and take thought of noble and divine things, and whether this is in fact itself divine or rather the most divine of the things in us, the activity of this part, as governed by its appropriate virtue, would be ultimate happiness. That this is speculative activity we have already said. (X.7, 1177a12–18)

Aristotle confirms this conclusion by applying the criteria he had set down earlier. Speculative activity which is expressive of philosophical wisdom is most goal-like, because (i) it is never chosen for the sake of anything else, since, Aristotle claims, "nothing results from it, apart from the activity of speculation" (1177b2), and (ii) we seek everything else for its sake, because we do everything else that we do in order to procure leisure, and speculative activity, Aristotle thinks, is what we should use leisure for, rather than amusements and pleasurable diversions, cf. X.6, 1176b9–1177a11. (Presumably, in saying that "nothing results from it", he means *by its own tendency or nature*: I might do math problems, for instance, to help myself fall asleep, but that I fall asleep is something "incidental" to that activity. On the other hand, that a city be protected is not incidental to the activity of courage.)

Furthermore, it is more self-sufficient than any other activity. Why? "Both a philosophically wise person, and a just person, and anyone with any of the other virtues, needs those things that are necessary for living; however, after being sufficiently equipped with such things, a just person needs those towards whom and with whom he can act justly, and likewise also a moderate person, and a courageous person, and each of the other virtuous sorts, but a philosophically wise person is capable of engaging in speculative activity on his own" (X.7, 1177a28–33). Sometimes Aristotle is criticized here for adverting to a notion of self-sufficiency that he had rejected earlier, viz. self-sufficiency as involving the activity of a person on his own, apart from friends, relatives, or fellow citizens. But in fact the point is directed at the activity (the good), not the agent (the subject of the good): the activity of speculation depends upon fewer things that are outside itself, and thus as an activity it is more self-sufficient. It does not follow from this that the activity will typically be possessed or enjoyed by individuals on their own, and, in fact, Aristotle's doctrine that happiness needs to be shared with friends to be enjoyed, implies the contrary (IX.9, IX.12). His claim that "a happy person needs friends" is not the absurd claim that, supposing that someone is happy, he will still stand in need of friends, but rather that any human activity that counts as happiness must be social, from the nature of human life itself.

The activity which proceeds from the virtue of philosophical wisdom is happiness, but a *life* of such activity, that is, consisting of that activity alone, is something super-human: having bodies, Aristotle concedes, we must tend to bodily needs, to keep ourselves alive (X.7, 1177b26–30). Nevertheless, it does not follow that we should hold back from pursuing happiness, insofar as we are able; rather, our goal should be to be active in that way to the greatest extent possible (1177b31–33). For the worth of that activity, Aristotle contends, exceeds whatever all the other parts in us can achieve, and, in any case, to aim to engage in the activity of speculative wisdom is not, properly speaking, to choose the well-being of only one part of us, since each human being appropriately identifies himself with that part or aspect of him which thinks (1177b34–1178a4). Furthermore, every sort of thing has a proper function or activity, which will involve principally just one part or aspect of it, to which the rest of it is directed and subordinated (and towards which that thing is urged by its proper pleasure); and for a human being, that activity is thinking, and a life organized to bring this about is best (1178a5–8).

Although Aristotle does not waver from his view that happiness is speculative activity governed by the virtue of philosophical wisdom, he acknowledges in passing that the activity of practical wisdom can serve as an organizing principle, too, for a human life, and that that sort of life would be a happy life in a qualified and secondary sense (X.8, 1178a9–10). But objectively considered such a life should be ranked after, and not preferred over, a life subordinated to philosophical wisdom (and presumably, too, in a properly ordered political society, life of that sort is directed towards speculative activity). Aristotle's reasons for this ranking occupy the bulk of X.7–8: a life organized around speculative activity is divine in character (1177b26–1178a8); it is the most self-sufficient (1178a9–b7); it is the sort of life which the gods live, yet everything in the universe strives to be like the gods, so that this sort of life has more of the character of an end (1178b7–32); and a life of that sort, precisely because it is similar to the life of the gods, is more dear to the gods (1179a22–32). This appeal to the gods is an expression of Aristotle's general view, which he shares with Plato, that every kind of thing strives to imitate the divine in the manner in which it is suited (cf. *De An.* II.4, 415a26–b7; *GC* II.10, 336b27–34; *GA* II.1, 731b24–35).[17] That Aristotle in this way grounds his last arguments about happiness on his theology, and the ordering of nature that is entailed by that theology, confirms that the purpose all along of the *Ethics* has been to identify objectively the ultimate end of the human species.

---

17.   On this topic, see Betegh, GREEK PHILOSOPHY AND RELIGION, in this volume.

Conclusion

So then, the ostensible project of *EN* is to examine systematically the activities that correspond to the various virtues, in order to see which one qualifies as the ultimate end. The activity corresponding to any virtue, Aristotle thinks, is goal-like (*teleion*): it is worth doing for its own sake, apart from anything that follows from it. But the activity corresponding to the virtue of philosophical wisdom is the most goal-like (*teleiotaton*) in this class. Such activity, therefore, is the ultimate goal of human life and what counts as happiness for us – which is the ostensible conclusion of the treatise.

But this conclusion seems to leave us with various difficulties. There is a difficulty about *balancing*: How should someone reasonably trade off the pursuit of the *most* goal-like activity with the pursuit of other activities that are goal-like but subordinated to it? There is a difficulty too about *motivation*: to say that speculative activity is the most goal-like is to say, at least, that other activities are done for the sake of that; but then how can one coherently do those other activities for their *own* sake as well (it might seem problematic to say that X is done for its own sake *and also* for the sake of Y)? Moreover, there is an *ethical* difficulty: if all other goal-like activity is subordinated to speculative activity, then why wouldn't it be advisable to do something contrary to one of the other virtues, if doing so would increase one's opportunity for speculative activity (a stock example is: supposing one could get away with it, why shouldn't someone kill a wealthy relative to gain a large inheritance, so that one has more leisure for speculative activity)?

In view of these difficulties some commentators have proposed what is called an "inclusive" interpretation of *EN*.[18] On the ostensible project of the treatise, Aristotle is looking for a single kind of activity, which in its various repetitions counts as the human goal, and he examines the various virtues as a stage in *selecting out* that activity. According to the inclusive interpretation, in contrast, Aristotle regards the ultimate goal as a complex, attained once for all over a lifetime, which includes all activities worth doing in their own right, and he examines the various virtues in order to *collect together* all activities of that sort. The inclusive interpretation gets textual support principally through interpreting the terms *teleion, teleiotation* (which we have been rendering "goal-like", "most goal-like") as, rather, "complete" and "most complete" (which the Greek allows), in which case Aristotle, in looking for our ultimate goal, is looking for the most *complete good*.[19] Furthermore, this interpretation takes the self-sufficiency criterion of the ultimate good as actually to imply its completeness, since, if it lacked any of the goods worth having in their own right, it would not be self-sufficient.

The inclusive interpretation would resolve the difficulty about balancing by making it unimportant: what matters most in a happy life is that one engage in all inherently

---

18. The *locus classicus* for this interpretation is Ackrill (1974).
19. And therefore when Aristotle entertains the suggestion that there are multiple ends (e.g., at I.7, 1097a30), he does so with a view toward collecting these together, to create the most complete good, rather than selecting out from these a single, most ultimate end.

valuable activities, and presumably there would be many suitable ways of balancing them. Furthermore, since on the inclusive interpretation inherently good activities are related to the ultimate end as parts to whole, then the motivational difficulty seems to be solved as well: it is coherent to hold that one is choosing a *part* both for its own sake and also for the sake of the whole which it composes. Finally, the ethical difficulty also seems to be solved: if the ultimate good contains *all* the activities of the various virtues, then none can be slighted: to kill the wealthy relative would simply be to fail to achieve the complete human good.

Against the inclusive interpretation one might urge that to take *teleion* as "complete," in those passages where the ultimate good is discussed, is at odds with the fundamental theme of *EN* that a good simply is something that is goal-like (not "complete"); and nothing compels that we understand the self-sufficiency requirement to imply completeness, since, as we have seen, a good can be self-sufficient by effecting a change in desires, as much as by satisfying all antecedent desires.[20] Furthermore, the inclusive interpretation would resolve the difficulties mentioned only by creating a new one, involving the overall coherence of *EN*: even if Books I–IX admit of an inclusive interpretation, undeniably Book X is not putting forward such a view. And if, in reply, a proponent of the inclusive view were to concede that, although Aristotle takes the ultimate good to be a complex good, he nonetheless wishes in Book X to regard this complex as *ordered*, with speculative activity occupying the *highest position*, then all the difficulties crop up again: we need to know how to balance the lower goods in the complex against the highest; and there seems to be a new, not evidently intelligible sense in which a lower good in the complex is to be sought "for the sake of" the highest; and there seems to be no reason why, if both are not attainable together, we might not trade off one of the lower goods in the complex to attain more of the highest good.

One might additionally maintain that the inclusive view is unnecessary: Aristotle, it would seem, is not insensitive to the difficulties in his ostensible conclusion, and in Book X he offers a solution, which at least requires serious consideration.

Aristotle seems to understand his conclusion, that the ultimate good is speculative activity, as implying a "transvaluation of values." One might have supposed that speculative activity was simply one among many good pursuits, perhaps even less valuable than others because of its apparent uselessness. Therefore, before encountering Aristotle's arguments, one might have looked upon speculative activity as something praiseworthy but optional: good to do, if one has spare time and sufficient means. But the force of the argument of *EN* is to give an entirely different place to speculative activity. In claiming that it is our ultimate goal, Aristotle is claiming that it is what we are "meant" to do; ideally, we would simply engage in that constantly. But given that we are composite beings, with a body and its needs, we unfortunately need to allot some time – no more than is necessary, and this will be little – to taking care of the body. So the rule of action implied by this transvaluation of values, which posits

---

20. Heinaman (1988) argues persuasively that in fact the self-sufficiency criterion implies just the opposite, that is, that the ultimate good *cannot* be an inclusive good.

speculation as the ultimate end, is this: *engage in speculation, unless clear necessity (construed austerely) requires us to do otherwise.*[21]

Note that all of the virtues besides speculative wisdom come into play only as a consequence of this necessity. It is in buying and selling that we need justice; in defending the city that we need courage; and in ordering the whole machinery of the economy that we need practical wisdom. These virtues, then, come into play, as it were, "on a hypothesis": *given* that we are (regrettably) constrained to take time out from our chief activity (speculation), *then* we should act in those domains in accordance with the various other virtues.

Yet this then implies straightforward solutions to the stated difficulties. Balancing: use the rule of action stated above. Motivation: the sense in which we do an action in accordance with one of the other virtues (act courageously, justly, and so on) *for the sake of* speculative activity is that the virtuous action is piggybacked onto a necessary activity (fighting a war, conducting business), which we must attend to before devoting ourselves to speculative activity; it is the activity regarded as necessary which, strictly, is for the sake of speculative activity. The difficulty about ethics: for an action to be coherently done (one might maintain) it has to be sought as an action of a certain kind; but since (in the stock example) the person kills his relative to gain the opportunity to speculate, his action is correctly construed as an instance of "doing business"; but *on the hypothesis* that he is "doing business," he should do so rightly, which excludes surreptitiously killing a relative and collecting the inheritance. Actions of that sort are not rightly done to advance speculative activity, then, for the same reason that they are not rightly done at all.

On this last point, one is tempted to suspect that Aristotle simply presumes, as basic, that one should never do anything "shameful" or "base" (*aischron*), and actions contrary to the virtues are "base."[22] One might even try to give a sophisticated, "internalist" defense of that presupposition's being basic: good behavior has its own reasonability, one might insist, apparent to those who are already good, and inaccessible to those who are not; to engage in ethics is simply to get clearer, then, about certain sorts of commitments, built into one's character, that one already has; hence, no one who was raised poorly and lacked the requisite commitments would be suitably positioned even to deliberate about ethics.[23] However this strategy begs the question of why being raised well implies becoming the sort of person who *without qualification* rejects doing actions contrary to the virtues.

Alternatively one might suspect that the reason that Aristotle in no *single* passage argues for absolute proscriptions against vicious behavior, is that he takes it as nearly *everywhere* supported, as something *overdetermined* by the subject matter of Ethics.[24]

---

21. See Lawrence (1993) for a discussion along similar lines.
22. Perhaps this is an inheritance from Plato: see *Grg.* 474c–475e.
23. The classic statement of this view is M. Burnyeat, "Aristotle on Learning to be Good," in Rorty (1981).
24. Aristotle's remarks in I.3–4 about the rough character of generalizations in ethics do not imply that he is not committed to the principle that "one should never act unjustly." For a vigorous discussion of this point see Kaczor (1997).

Indeed, it seems open to Aristotle to reach that conclusion in various ways. For instance, speculative activity is the ultimate end *for a human being*; thus it must be sought and possessed in a human way, which implies, as was said, that it be sought and possessed in the context of political society: and surreptitious murder is not compatible with stable political society. Or, again, speculative activity should serve as the organizing principle of a life well-lived; but other activities are correctly organized as tending towards it, only if they are *intelligently* subordinated to it, yet (Aristotle might say) practical intelligence requires that we treat things in the way they deserve, by those with the requisite authority, and in the example either the relative does not *deserve* to be killed, or he does but the agent could not with *propriety* decide upon and execute the sentence.[25]

Then, too, there are responses which could draw upon the rich doctrine of friendship that Aristotle builds into his *Ethics*. Thus, as was said, Aristotle holds, no doubt rightly, that, whatever a person understands by happiness, he must take that activity to be one that he shares in with friends: since no one can be happy without friends (IX.9, 1169b17–18); and each person wishes especially to do, with his friends, what he takes happiness to be (12, 1172a1–6). But no one who surreptitiously murdered a relative could maintain a friendship of the best sort, as having to hide this from his friends (violating *frankness, parrhēsia*, 2, 1165a29), or, if he told them, they would no longer love him as good or be able to trust him (VIII.3, 1156b25–29; 1157a20–24); and, the murderer would hate himself, and thus destroy his self-love, from which his affection for his friends is derived (IX.4, 1166b11–13, b25–29). Or, again, it is not clear that someone who committed a murder could succeed in loving *himself*, on the grounds that he would not, in a sense, even be *the same moral agent* as the person who later wanted to put bloodshed aside and devote himself innocently to contemplation.

Admittedly, explanations of this sort – and more are easily imagined – can seem unsatisfactory, because of their contingency, but Aristotle might plead that presumably it is enough, for the purposes of practical reasoning, if they rest upon obvious and inescapable attributes of human nature and human social life.[26]

Bibliography

Works Cited

Ackrill, J. L. (1974). "Aristotle on *Eudaimonia*." *Proceedings of the British Academy*, 60, 339–59.
Bodéüs, R. (1993). *The Political Dimensions of Aristotle's Ethics*. (J. E. Garrett, trans.). Albany, NY: State University of New York Press.
Broadie, S. (1991). *Ethics with Aristotle*. Oxford: Oxford University Press.
Foot, P. (2001). *Natural Goodness*. Oxford: Oxford University Press.
Geach, P. (1972). *Logic Matters*. Oxford: Blackwell.

25.   Clearly this explanation puts heavy weight on the difficult notions of "desert" (*to axion*) and "fittingness" or "propriety" (*to prepon*); Aristotle relies crucially on these notions throughout *EN* (see especially X.8, 1178a13), yet he never analyzes them. For an attempt of an explanation, if not an analysis, see Lear (2004).

26.   For a recent philosophical development of an outlook of this sort, see Foot (2001).

Glassen, P. (1957). "A Fallacy in Aristotle's Argument about the Good." *Philosophical Quarterly*, 7, 319–22.

Gomez-Lobo, A. (1989). "The Ergon Inference." *Phronesis*, 34, 170–84.

Heinaman, R. (1988). "*Eudaimonia* and Self-Sufficiency in the *Nicomachean Ethics*." *Phronesis*, 33, 31–53.

Kaczor, C. (1997). "Exceptionless Norms in Aristotle? Thomas Aquinas and Twentieth-Century Interpretations of the *Nicomachean Ethics*." *Thomist*, 61, 33–62.

Kenny, A. (1978). *The Aristotelian Ethics*. Oxford: Clarendon Press.

Kraut, R. (1979a). "Two Conceptions of Happiness." *Philosophical Review*, 88, 167–97.

——. (1979b). "The Peculiar Function of Human Beings." *Canadian Journal of Philosophy*, 9, 467–78.

Lawrence, G. (1993). "Aristotle and the Ideal Life." *Philosophical Review*, 102, 1–34.

——. (1997). "Nonaggregatability, Inclusiveness, and the Theory of Focal Value: *NE* 1.7.1097b16–20." *Phronesis*, 42, 32–76.

——. (2001). "The Function of the Function Argument." *Ancient Philosophy*, 21, 445–75.

Lear, G. R. (2004). *Happy Lives and the Highest Good*. Princeton: Princeton University Press.

Owen, G. E. L. (1971–2). "Aristotelian Pleasures." *Proceedings of the Aristotelian Society*, 72, 135–52.

Rorty, A. O. (ed.). (1981). *Essays on Aristotle's Ethics*. Berkeley, Cal.: University of California Press.

Urmson, J. O. (1973). "Aristotle's Doctrine of the Mean." *American Philosophical Quarterly*, 10, 223–30.

Wedin, M. (1981). "Aristotle on the Good for Man." *Mind*, 90, 243–62.

White, N. P. (1988). "Good as Goal." *Southern Journal of Philosophy*, 27, suppl., 169–93.

Whiting, J. (1988). "Aristotle's Function Argument: A Defense." *Ancient Philosophy*, 8, 33–48.

Further Reading

Barnes, J., Schofield, M., and Sorabji, R. (eds.). (1977). *Articles on Aristotle*. (vol. 2): *Ethics and Politics*. New York: St. Martin's Press.

Bostock, D. (2000). *Aristotle's Ethics*. Oxford: Oxford University Press.

Broadie, S. and Rowe, C. (eds. and trans.). (2002). *Aristotle: Nicomachean Ethics*. Oxford: Oxford University Press.

Cooper, J. (1975). *Reason and Human Good in Aristotle*. Cambridge, Mass.: Harvard University Press.

Gauthier, R.A. and Jolif, Y. (eds. and trans.). (1958–9). *Aristote: L'Éthique à Nicomaque*. 2nd edn. 1970. Louvain: Publications Universitaires.

Hardie, W. F. R. (1980). *Aristotle's Ethical Theory*. 2nd edn. Oxford: Clarendon Press.

Kraut, R. (1989). *Aristotle on the Human Good*. Princeton: Princeton University Press.

Litzinger, C. I. (trans.). (1993). *Thomas Aquinas: Commentary on Aristotle's Nicomachean Ethics*. South Bend, Ind.: Dumb Ox Books.

Pakaluk, M. (ed. and trans.). (1998). *Aristotle: Nicomachean Ethics VIII and IX*. Oxford: Clarendon Press.

——. (2005). *Aristotle's* Nicomachean Ethics: *An Introduction*. Cambridge: Cambridge University Press.

Rorty, A. O. (ed.). (1981). *Essays on Aristotle's Ethics*. Berkeley, Cal.: University of California Press.

Urmson, J. O. (1988). *Aristotle's Ethics*. Oxford: Blackwell.

20

Aristotle's Political Philosophy

DAVID KEYT

Introduction

Aristotle's *Ethics* and *Politics* are two volumes of a single work on what Aristotle calls "the philosophy of things human" (*EN* X.9, 1181b15). The intimate connection of the two treatises is signaled by the fact that the opening and closing chapters of the *Nicomachean Ethics* (I.1–3, X.9) discuss political science and its final paragraph outlines a program of a work on politics. Aristotle even calls the *Ethics* a political treatise (*EN* I.2, 1094b10–11; *Rh.* I.2, 1356a25–27; [*MM*] I.1, 1181a24–28, b24–28). It is easy to see why. Many of the virtues it catalogs such as bravery, munificence (*megaloprepeia*), and justice relate one way or another to a political community (see *EN* III.8, 1116a17–29; IV.2, 1122b19–23; V.1, 1129b17–19); the life of moral virtue is for Aristotle a political life (see *EN* X.8, 1178a9–28 especially a27); and the theory of the *Ethics* cannot be put into practice without the aid of statesmen (*politikoi*) and lawgivers (*EN* X.9). The *Politics*, on the other hand, presupposes a treatise on ethics. Justice is one of its main concepts, and the ideal political community sketched in *Politics* VII and VIII presupposes an account of virtue and happiness. The *Politics* refers six times to a work on *Ethics* (II.2, 1261a31;[1] III.9, 1280a18; 12, 1282b20; IV.11, 1295a36; VII.13, 1332a8, 1332a22).[2]

The expression *philosophia politikē* (political philosophy) occurs but once in Aristotle's extant writings (*Pol.* III.12, 1282b23); his more usual term for political philosophy is *hē politikē* [*sc. epistēmē*] (political science). Aristotle gives an account of the general nature of political science in the *Nicomachean Ethics* (I.1–3; 13, 1102a5–13; VI.8; X.9, 1180b28–1181b23), and enumerates in the *Politics* (IV.1–2) the various problems with which it has to deal. Political science, we are told in the former treatise, is the most sovereign (*kuriōtatē*) and architectonic science; its end, or goal, which is nothing less than the supreme human good, includes (*periechei*) the ends of all the other sciences (*EN* I.2; *kuriōtatēs*: 1094a26; *periechoi*: 1094b6). The other arts and sciences are under it as manual craftsmen (*cheirotechnai*) are under architects (*Met.* A.1, 981a30–b1; *EN* VI.8, 1141b29). It assigns to each of the other arts and sciences its role within the political community: it decides whether an art or science is to be taught, to what extent, and to whom; and it uses the other arts as means to its own end (*EN* I.2,

---

1. Unless otherwise indicated all references are to the *Politics*.
2. For more on the relation of the two treatises see Newman (1887–1902, vol. 2, pp. 385–401).

1094a28–b5). For example, it uses military strategy to further its own end of peace (*EN* X.7, 1177b5–6). Political science, so characterized, is the art of legislation (*EN* I.2, 1094b5, VI.8; 1141b24–25);[3] and its works are laws (*EN* X.9, 1181a23).

As treatises in practical philosophy, the *Ethics* and the *Politics* aim at usefulness as well as knowledge (I.3, 1253b14–18, 11, 1258b9–10; *EN* I.3, 1095a5–6; II.2, 1103b26–29; X.9, 1179a35–b4; *Met.* α.1, 993b20–21). Those for whom they are useful are statesmen and lawgivers (IV.1, 1288b27, 1289a7; V.9, 1309b35–36; VI.5, 1319b33; *EN* I.13, 1102a8, a18, a23; III.1, 1109b34). The true statesman (*politikos*) in Aristotle's view pursues, through legislation, the goal of political science (*politikē*) – the supreme human good. He wishes to make his citizens good people who do noble things (*EN* I.9, 1099b29–32, 13; 1102a7–25). To fashion good law the true statesman will thus need to understand human goodness and how it is attained – the subject of the *Ethics*. But good law is impossible outside a good political community. So he will also need to understand how political communities are organized – the subject of the *Politics*. The link between the supreme human good and the legislation of statesman and lawgivers is habituation. According to the *Ethics* the supreme human good is happiness; happiness is activity in accordance with the moral and intellectual virtues;[4] the moral virtues are acquired by habituation; such habituation is guided by law; and law is fashioned by statesmen and lawgivers (*EN* I.7; II.1; X.9).

Aristotle's characterization of political science in the opening pages of the *Nicomachean Ethics* matches in its very words his characterization of the political community in the opening paragraph of the *Politics*, to which we now turn.

The polis

The *Politics* begins with an argument. Using the same terms as in *Nicomachean Ethics* I.2, Aristotle claims that the polis is the community that is most sovereign (*kuriōtatē*) of all and that includes (*periechei*) all the others; and then, on the basis of the principle that every community aims at some good, he infers that the polis aims at the most sovereign good (I.1, 1252a1–7; *periechousa*: 1252a6).[5] The inclusion of one community

---

3. In *EN* VI.8 Aristotle divides *politikē* in the broad sense into two species. One is the art of legislation; the other has as its two subspecies deliberation and adjudication and is said to be *politikē* in the narrow sense. This is the reverse of what one would have expected on the basis of Aristotle's use of the word in *EN* I.2 where *politikē* is used for the legislative art.

4. Among the intellectual virtues the most important are practical and theoretical wisdom (*phronēsis* and *sophia*). Aristotle thinks that to act in accordance with moral virtue and practical wisdom is entirely and exclusively human (*EN* X.8) but that we are like gods when we engage in theoretical activity (*theōria*) (*Met.* Λ.7, 1072b13–26; *EN* X.7, especially 1177b26–1178a2). This idea raises at least two questions. The first is the relation of the lower to the higher form of activity in the best (and happiest) life for an individual. The second is the place of theoretical or philosophical activity in an ideal polis. This second question is addressed on pp. 402–6 below; the first is discussed in Keyt (1983 and 1989), and in this volume in Pakaluk, ARISTOTLE'S ETHICS.

5. For a more concrete picture of the ancient Greek polis see Ehrenberg (1969).

in another of which Aristotle speaks is not the inclusion of the members of the one community among the members of the other, but the inclusion of the end, or goal, of the one community in the end, or goal, of the other. An army, for example, is included in a polis in so far as its end – victory or plunder or conquest – is included in the end of the polis (*EN* VIII.9, 1160a14–29), not as the Lacedaemonians are included among the Peloponnesians (*Top.* VII.1, 152a16–18). The sovereignty referred to is that of authority and power (IV.9, 1294b33–34). Furthermore, we know from the *Ethics* that the most sovereign good is good life and happiness (*EN* I.4, 1095a14–20). In the very first paragraph of the *Politics*, then, Aristotle subscribes to a maximalist conception of a political community, according to which the achievement of good life and happiness is the proper goal of its power and authority, including its power to coerce. This is a controversial conclusion demanding further defense, for the all-inclusiveness of the polis that Aristotle postulates expresses the very point political philosophers dispute. We return to this issue below. The portrait of the polis that Aristotle sketches in this opening paragraph, one should note, is highly idealized. He is hard pressed to cite a single example that fits his description, and acknowledges that few, if any, real poleis have good life and happiness as their end (VII.2, 1324b3–9; 14, 1333b5 14).

It is sometimes claimed that Aristotle's argument plays upon an ambiguity in the word "polis" (Mulgan, 1977, pp. 16–17). Aristotle, so it is claimed, uses the word "polis" in an inclusive and an exclusive sense corresponding to the two aspects of his dual characterization of the polis. In the inclusive sense the word "polis" refers to the most inclusive community; in the exclusive sense it refers to the most sovereign community. Aristotle's conclusion, according to this analysis, is invalid because the word "polis" shifts its meaning from one premise of his argument to another. In terms of modern political philosophy Aristotle shifts from speaking of the whole of society in one premise to speaking of the state, the monopolizer of legitimate coercion, in the other (for details see Keyt, 1991b, pp. 253–6). But this account of two senses of "polis" may not be right. When Aristotle says that man is (1) the only animal that laughs (*PA* III.10, 673a8) and (2) the only animal that possesses reason (VII.13, 1332b4–5), he is not giving the word "man" (*anthrōpos*) two senses. Similarly, if Aristotle believes that the most sovereign community and the community that includes all others are the same community, he can refer to this community as the polis without equivocation. But this identity seems to follow from Aristotle's view, to which we now turn, that the polis is a natural entity.

Nature

Aristotle remarks that in constructing a polis a statesman or a lawgiver, just like a weaver or a shipbuilder, must have suitable matter (*hulē*), and indicates that the matter in question is a population, especially a citizen population, and a territory (VII.4, 1325b37–1326a8). His idea seems to be that a lawgiver brings a polis into being by imposing form upon matter, a constitution (*politeia*) upon citizens (*politai*). (For the notion that the form of a polis is its constitution see III.3, 1276a17–b13.) By this analysis a polis is an artifact of (practical) reason. Since art and reason are usually opposed to nature in Aristotle (VII.14, 1333a23; *Phys.* II.6, 198a10; *Met.* Z.7,

1032a12–13; *EN* III.3, 1112a31–33), one would expect him to deny that the polis is a natural entity.

But, contrary to expectations, Aristotle famously claims that the polis *is* a natural entity (I.2, 1252b30, 1253a2, a25; VII.8, 1328a22). This is one of the three basic theorems of his political philosophy, the other two being that man is by nature a political animal and that the polis is prior by nature to the individual (I.2, 1253a2–3, a19; III.6, 1278b19; see also Keyt, 1991a and Depew, 1995). His principal argument for his first theorem is the following: the household, being grounded on the natural instincts for self-preservation and procreation, exists by nature; the village comes to be from and is the completion of the household; so the village exists by nature; the polis comes to be from and is the completion of the village; so the polis too exists by nature (I.2, 1252a24–b34). The idea seems to be that one community is the completion of another if it serves a wider range of purposes than the other. Thus, the household, the village, and the polis serve respectively daily purposes, non-daily purposes, and the purposes of a whole life (I.2, 1252b12–16; *EN* VIII.9, 1160a21–23).

We can now understand why Aristotle identifies the most inclusive community with the most sovereign. When a natural entity has an end, it always has a part whose function it is to realize that end. To realize its end of generating progeny, for example, every plant and animal has a reproductive soul (*De An.* II.4, 416b23–25; *GA* II.1, 735a17–19). Thus, if the most inclusive community is a natural entity and has good life and happiness as an end, it must have a part whose function it is to realize this end. Aristotle thinks that this part is its governing class (see IV.4, 1291a24–28), or sovereign element (III.6, 1278b8–14; 7, 1279a25–28), and stops just short of identifying the part with the whole: "A polis and every other composite," he says, "seems to *be* most of all its most sovereign element (*to kuriōtaton*)" (*EN* IX.8, 1168b31–32).

Aristotle's argument for the naturalness of the polis obviously depends upon some principle of the transitivity of naturalness, but it has proved difficult to formulate a principle that is not open to obvious objections (see Keyt, 1991a, pp. 130–1). One recent proposal is this: a community that comes to be from another and that serves natural ends that are more inclusive or of a higher order than those served by the other exists by nature if the other exists by nature (Miller, 1995, p. 42; see also Saunders, 1995, pp. 67–8). There are two major problems in applying this principle. The first is to establish that some initial community exists by nature; the second is to determine whether something is or is not a natural end. Consider the following application of the principle. Walking seems to be as natural as procreation. Given that people have an impetus (*hormē*) to associate with one another (I.2, 1253a29), a walking club would thus seem to exist by nature. Are dancing and singing natural ends? If so, then by the proposed principle a group of strolling minstrels that comes into being when a walking club begins to sing while it walks exists by nature. But if even groups of strolling minstrels exist by nature, the proposed principle loses its plausibility. The concept of natural existence becomes so attenuated as to be virtually meaningless (Robinson, 1962, p. xxii). On the other hand, not to count singing and dancing as natural ends seems *ad hoc*, designed simply to restrict the application of the proposed principle.

The concept of natural existence is important because it paves the way for the notion of an *unnatural* condition. Only a natural entity can be in an unnatural condition: a horse can be blind and deaf, but not a statue of a horse. Whether a man is in a natural or an unnatural condition, Aristotle explains, depends upon the relation of rule and subordination between his soul and his body and between his reason and his emotions (I.5, 1254a34–b9). Similarly, whether a polis is in a natural or an unnatural condition depends on the relation of rule and subordination among the sections of its population, which is determined by its political organization (*taxis*), or constitution (III.1, 1274b38; 6, 1278b8–10; IV.1, 1289a15–18). Some constitutions, Aristotle maintains, are according to nature (*kata phusin*), whereas others are contrary to nature (*para phusin*) (III.17, 1287b37–41).

To understand this distinction we need to recall Aristotle's identification of the forced and the unnatural.[6] "What is by force (*bia(i)*) and what is contrary to nature," he says, "are the same" (*Cael.* III.2, 300a23; see also *Phys.* IV.8, 215a1–3; V.6, 230a29–30; *GA* V.8, 788b27). Fire in an Aristotelian cosmos moves upward toward its natural place by nature but downward only by force and contrary to nature (*GC* II.6, 333b26–30 and elsewhere). The identification of the forced and the unnatural is a feature both of animate and inanimate nature (*GA* II.4, 739a4; III.8, 777a18–19; V.8, 788b27) and extends even to human beings (*EE* II.8, 1224a15–30; *Rh.* I.11, 1370a9).[7] The constitutions that Aristotle thinks contrary to nature are precisely those that are based on force (III.3, 1276a12–13; 10, 1281a23–24).

Nature supplies the normative element of Aristotle's political philosophy and keeps it from being entirely descriptive and pragmatic. Aristotle believes that nature and justice are connected, and subscribes to two principles relating them: a positive principle linking the just and the natural (I.5, 1255a1–3; III.17, 1287b37–39; VII.9, 1329a13–17) and a negative principle linking the unjust and the unnatural (I.10, 1258a40–b2; VII.3, 1325b7–10; and see I.3, 1253b20–23). (For both principles together see I.5, 1254a17–20 and III.16, 1287a8–18.) Though these justice-of-nature principles go unexplained and unsupported in the *Politics*, they are not ultimate principles for Aristotle. They follow syllogistically from his natural teleology supplemented by one further premise. According to Aristotelian teleology "nature makes everything for the sake of something" (I.2, 1252b32; *PA* I.1, 641b12, 5, 645a23–26; *Phys.* II.8), where this something, the end, or goal, of the making, is something good (I.1, 1252b34–1253a1; *Phys.* II.2, 194a32–33; 3, 195a23–25; *Met.* A.3, 983a31–32 and especially *Somno* 2, 455b16–25). To reach the positive principle we need a premise relating goodness and justice (for which see III.12, 1282b16–17; 13, 1283a38–40 together with Keyt, 1996, pp. 131–2). We then have the following syllogism:

Everything natural is good.
Everything (within the sphere of social conduct)[8] that is good is just.
Therefore, everything (within the sphere of social conduct) that is natural is just.

---

6. On Aristotle's distinction between what is natural and what is contrary to nature, see Bodnár and Pellegrin, ARISTOTLE'S PHYSICS AND COSMOLOGY, in this volume, esp. pp. 275–7.
7. On the role of nature in animate things, see in this volume Lennox, ARISTOTLE'S BIOLOGY, esp. pp. 300–10.
8. This restriction is necessary because the sphere of justice is narrower than the realm of nature.

The negative principle, that everything (within the sphere of social conduct) that is unnatural is unjust, can be derived similarly *mutatis mutandis* (for details see Keyt, 1996, p. 132).

One might question the validity of this syllogism. For it is not clear that its middle term has the same meaning in both premises. According to Aristotelian teleology the good that nature pursues is the good of the individual tree, mollusk, or human being (*Phys.* II.7, 198b8–9), whereas the just is not the individual's good, but another's good (*EN* V.1, 1130a3–4; 6, 1134b5–6). This problem underscores the importance for Aristotle of establishing that man is by nature a social or political animal whose good is tied to the good of others. Without this basic theorem the syllogism grounding his positive justice-of-nature principle would commit the fallacy of four terms.

Aristotle's political naturalism should be read as a response to the opposite challenges of Protagorean relativism and Platonism. Protagorean relativism is the view that "whatever things *appear* just and fine to each polis *are* so for it as long as it holds by them" (Plato, *Tht.* 167c4–5). For Protagoras there is no external or absolute standard of judgment; any constitution that appears just and fine to those living under it is just and fine for them.[9] Such a view is anathema to both Plato and Aristotle. Like Aristotle, Plato tries to avoid it by an appeal to nature (*Laws* X, 888d7–890d8), though his concept of nature is radically different from Aristotle's. For Plato the realm of nature is the world of Forms (*Phd.* 103b5; *Rep.* X, 597b5–7, c2, 598a1–3; *Prm.* 132d2); and "the just by nature" (*Rep.* VI, 501b2) is the Form of justice, an incorporeal entity (*Phd.* 65d4–66a10; *Sph.* 246b8) existing beyond time and space (*Ti.* 37c6–38c3, 51e6–52b2).[10] Aristotle wishes to avoid relativism without invoking such a suprasensible standard. This he endeavors to do by bringing nature down to earth. He identifies nature with the sensible world (*Met.* Λ.1, 1069a30–b2) and seeks his standard in this world.[11] This is a noble project with which many contemporary philosophers will be in sympathy. Its full-scale pursuit in the *Politics* gives the treatise its greatness as a work of philosophy.

Distributive Justice

The two main concepts in Aristotle's political philosophy aside from the strictly political, referred to in Greek by terms on the stem *polit-*, are nature and justice. Having discussed nature, we turn now to justice. Aristotle devotes an entire book of the *Ethics* to this topic: *Nicomachean Ethics* V = *Eudemian Ethics* IV. In this book he first distinguishes universal from particular justice – the lawful (*to nomimon*) from the equal (*to ison*) (*EN* V.1, 1129a34; 2, 1130b9) – and then divides particular justice into distributive and corrective (*EN* V.2, 1130b30–1131a1), the former being concerned with establishing equality, the latter with restoring it.

9.   On this topic, see in this volume Barney, THE SOPHISTIC MOVEMENT, pp. 87–90.
10.   On the role of Forms in Plato's political thought, see Lane, PLATO'S POLITICAL PHILOSOPHY, esp. pp. 172–80.
11.   The difference between Plato and Aristotle is beautifully illustrated in Raphael's famous painting *The School of Athens*.

The focus of Aristotle's political philosophy is on distributive justice. The *Politics* can be read as an application of the abstract theory of distributive justice laid out in *Nicomachean Ethics* V.3, which is in its turn a development of a Platonic idea (*Grg.* 507e6–508a8; *Laws* VI, 756e9–758a2). (Aristotle refers explicitly to *Nicomachean Ethics* V.3 at *Politics* III.9, 1280a18, and 12, 1282b20.) Distributive justice, according to this theory, is a kind of geometric proportion involving at least two persons, *A* and *B*, and two things, *C* and *D*. A distribution in which *C* and *D* are allotted to *A* and *B* respectively is just if the ratio of *C* to *D* is the same as that of *A* to *B*:

$$\frac{C}{D} = \frac{A}{B}$$

The ratios imply a basis of comparison both of the persons and of the things. Persons do not stand in ratios to each other *per se* but only in certain respects such as height, age, wealth, and so forth; nor do things. The basis of comparison of the things is their positive or negative value, and that of the persons is their worth (*axia*). When this factor is taken into account, the formula becomes:

$$\frac{\text{The value of } C}{\text{The value of } D} = \frac{\text{The worth of person } A}{\text{The worth of person } B}$$

Finally, the dummy names "*C*" and "*D*" can be eliminated in favor of definite descriptions of *C* and *D*:

$$\frac{\text{The value of the thing allotted to } A}{\text{The value of the thing allotted to } B} = \frac{\text{The worth of person } A}{\text{The worth of person } B}$$

A distribution is just according to Aristotle's theory if it follows this formula – if the value of the thing it allots to one person stands to the value of the thing it allots to another as the worth of the one person stands to the worth of the other. (For a detailed analysis see Galston, 1980, pp. 145–50.)

The things distributed by the formula are the apportionable goods: honor, money, and safety (*EN* V.2, 1130b2, b30–33). The greatest of these in Aristotle's eyes is honor (*EN* IV.3, 1123b20–21), which includes not only respect and tokens of esteem (*Rh.* I.5, 1361a27–b2) but also political office (III.10, 1281a31). Political office is the greatest of the apportionable goods because the political community is the primary arena of distribution. Those who win office in such a community make and administer the laws regarding property, military service, and even political office itself, and thus control all further distributions of the apportionable goods.

The basic offices in an ancient Greek polis were those of assemblyman (*ekklēsiastēs*) and juror (*dikastēs*). To be a full citizen (*politēs haplōs*) was to have the right to sit in the assembly and to serve on juries (III.1, 1275a22–33, b13–21). Full citizenship was thus the basic apportionable good and the focus of disputes over distributive justice. The parties to such disputes were those with a prima-facie claim to full citizenship. In ancient Greece these were the freeborn adult male natives residing in a polis. The voices of women, children, aliens, and slaves – the majority of the population – were not heard.

Disputes over distributive justice, Aristotle says, are not over the principle of distributive justice itself (III.12, 1282b18–21; V.1, 1301a26–27; EN V.3, 1131a10–14), nor over the value of the things being distributed (III.9, 1280a18–19), but over the worth of the claimants to a share of the distribution. "All agree," Aristotle says, "that the just in distribution must be according to worth of some sort, though all do not recognize the same sort of worth; but democrats say it is freedom, oligarchs wealth or good birth, and aristocrats virtue" (EN V.3, 1131a25–28). Disputes break out, in other words, because people evaluate worth by different standards. It is useful here to borrow the distinction from John Rawls (1971, pp. 5–6, 9–10) between the formal and abstract *concept* of distributive justice expressed by the formula above and the various concrete *conceptions* of distributive justice that result when the worth mentioned in the formula is evaluated according to various standards. Thus, the democratic conception of justice evaluates worth according to the standard of freedom; the oligarchic, according to the standard of wealth. Oligarchs and democrats share the same concept of distributive justice, but not the same conception.

Not being a Protagorean relativist, Aristotle thinks there is a correct standard of worth. What is it? This is a central question of Aristotle's political philosophy. He begins to address it in *Politics* III.12 by seeking criteria for evaluating the various standards. In a complex argument he rejects the idea that, other things being equal, "superiority in any good" (height, physical beauty, good complexion, good birth) is a rational ground for distributing political offices unequally. His first thought is that a rational basis for distributing political office is provided only by those personal qualities such as justice and political virtue that fit a man for political office. So the first criterion he considers is fitness. But later in the same chapter Aristotle acknowledges the importance of freedom and wealth in a political community – "there could not be a polis," he says, "wholly of needy people, any more than of slaves" (III.12, 1283a18–19) – and endorses freedom and wealth as reasonable standards of worth. Since Aristotle never argues that free status or wealth fits a man for political office, his idea seems to be that they are reasonable standards because they contribute somehow to a political community. He seems, then, to have introduced a second criterion: contribution (III.9, 1281a4; 12, 1283a1–2). The two criteria are not the same since a person who is unfitted to participate in a certain activity might still make a contribution to it. A person with no athletic skills might provide the equipment for the team. (On these two criteria see Newman, 1887–1902, vol. 1, pp. 249–50, and Irwin, 1988, pp. 427–8.)

Neither criterion can be applied until the nature of a political community is clarified. Some people, Aristotle notes, think of a political community as a joint-stock company whose end is to enrich the shareholders (III.9, 1280a25–31; IV.8, 1294a11; *Rh.* I.8, 1366a5); others regard it as a free society where one is able "to live as one wishes" (VI.2, 1317b11–12; IV.9, 1294a11; *Rh.* I.8, 1366a4); still others look upon it as an ethical community directed to education and virtue (IV.8, 1294a9–11; *Rh.* I.8, 1366a5–6). A contribution to one of these enterprises might be the destruction of another. A focus upon return on capital might contribute to the success of a joint-stock company but destroy an ethical community. Similarly, a quality that fits a man for a leadership position in a joint-stock company, such as competitiveness, might disqualify him for such a position in an ethical community. Thus, in searching for the correct standard of worth Aristotle is led to the prime question, What is a political community? Or, as Aristotle phrases it, What is a polis (III.1, 1274b33–34)? The search for the correct standard of worth becomes in the end a search for a definition of what it is to be a polis (see *Top.* VII.3, 153a15–16 and *Met.* Z.5, 1031a12).

The search is conducted in *Politics* III.9. What Aristotle seeks in this chapter is a real definition of "polis" *per genus et differentiam*. He takes it for granted that a polis is a kind of community (I.1, 1252a1; III.3, 1276b1), so his task is to find the feature that differentiates a polis from other species of the same genus. This feature is its end, or goal. He tries to find it by an elimination argument. In such an argument one rules out each distinct possibility in turn until only one remains, which must, then, be the correct one. Aristotle considers six possibilities: property, self-preservation, mutual defense, trade, prevention of injustice, and good life. He eliminates five on the ground that, taken severally or jointly, they differentiate at most an alliance, not a political community (1280b8–33; see also II.2, 1261a24–25), and infers that the sixth possibility, good life, is the true end. A polis, he concludes, is "a community of households and clans in living well, for the sake of a perfect and self-sufficient life" (1280b33–35; see also VII.8, 1328a35–37).

Aristotle is now in a position to determine the correct standard of worth. Combining his definition of "polis" with the contribution criterion, he claims that "those who contribute most to such a community have a larger share in the polis than those who are equal or superior in freedom and birth but unequal in political virtue, or those who exceed in wealth but are exceeded in virtue" (III.9, 1281a4–8). In saying that those possessing political virtue "have a larger share in the polis" than the free or the wealthy, he acknowledges again that the free and the wealthy also have a share, albeit a smaller one, and that the correct standard of worth, though heavily weighted in favor of virtue, must include freedom and wealth as well as virtue. The standard that Aristotle endorses as the correct one is "virtue fully furnished with external means" (IV.2, 1289a31–33; VII.1, 1323b41–1324a1).

Since this conclusion stands or falls along with Aristotle's definition of "polis," we need to examine the elimination argument that leads to his definition. Aristotle's argument seems to be vulnerable on at least two scores. First, his list of the possible ends of a polis is incomplete. An end he mentions elsewhere, for example, but fails to mention in *Politics* III.9 is that pursued by Sparta: conquest and war (II.9, 1271b2–3; VII.2, 1324b5–9, 1325a3–4; 14, 1333b12–14). Second, in eliminating the first five candidates he relies on the controversial assumption that a polis is more than an alliance and hence must have a higher end than an alliance. Philosophers who adopt a minimalist view of a political community will think such an assumption begs the question. They argue that a polis *is* simply a kind of alliance along with commercial and military alliances. Just as a military alliance is an alliance of poleis, a polis is an alliance of households. Aristotle himself mentions two such minimalists, Lycophron (III.9, 1280b10–12) and Hippodamus (II.8; see especially 1267b37–39).

Not only does Aristotle's argument seem to fail, but its conclusion seems patently false. (A bad argument can have a true conclusion.) For good life is not an end that very many political communities pursue. Aristotle does not offer any examples. But one way to defeat a definition, as Aristotle points out in the *Topics*, is to show that it is not true of every member of the species being defined: "for the definition of 'man' must be true of every man" (*Top.* VI.1, 139a25–27).

But perhaps this requirement on definitions is too stringent. Having two feet might be part of the definition of "man" (see *Top.* I.7, 103a27; V.4, 133a3, b8) even though some humans are born without them. The definition of a natural entity defines it in a natural, rather than an unnatural, condition. Since the polis is a natural entity, a definition of it cannot be refuted by citing poleis of which the definition is not true, if these poleis are in an unnatural condition, as all those are that have constitutions based on force. This is no doubt the reason that Aristotle claims, not that his definition of "polis" is true of every polis, but only that it will be acceptable to those who "give thought to good government" and "inquire accurately" (III.9, 1280b6, b28).

Aristotle's theory of distributive justice thus comes to rest upon an account of what it is to be, not just any polis, but a polis in a natural, rather than an unnatural, condition. Aristotle sketches a picture of such a polis in *Politics* VII and VIII.

"The polis of our prayers"

The ostensible subject of *Politics* VII and VIII is the best constitution (VII.1, 1323a14; 2, 1325a15; 9, 1328b34; 13, 1332a4), but Aristotle's discussion in these two books ranges far beyond the strictly constitutional.[12] What he actually describes is a polis ideally situated on ideal territory, with an ideal population, an ideal educational system, *and* an ideal constitution. He describes, not merely an ideal constitution, but each of the four causes of "the polis of our prayers" (VII.4, 1325b36): final (VII.1–3, 13–15), efficient (VII.4, 1325b40–1326a5), material (VII.4–7, 11–12), and formal (VII.8–10). The constitution is the fourth (III.3, 1276a17–b13).

The final cause of the best polis, its end or goal, is to live well (I.2, 1252b30; III.9, 1280a31–32) or happily (VII.1, 1323b1; 13, 1331b38–39), where happiness is "an actualization and a sort of perfect use of virtue" (VII.8, 1328a37–38; see also VII.13, 1332a7–10; *EN* I.7, 1098a7–20; *EE* II.1, 1219a38–39). We say more about this below. The efficient cause of a polis is the lawgiver who designed its constitution.

The material cause of a polis is its population, especially its citizen population, and its territory (VII.4, 1325b37–1326a8). The number of full citizens of an ideal polis should be determined by the function (*ergon*) of such a polis (VII.4, 1326a13–25), that is, by its end, or final cause; and the size of its total population including women, children, resident aliens, and slaves should be determined in turn by the number of its full citizens. Thus, the body of its full citizens should be small enough to be self-sufficient for living well in the context of a political community while its total population

12. The relation of books VII–VIII to the rest of the *Politics* is a matter of controversy. Some scholars reject the traditional order in which the two books, rather illogically, immediately follow three closely connected books dealing with imperfect constitutions and constitutional preservation and destruction, and place them, where they seem to belong, immediately after Book III on the general theory of constitutions. For opposing views see Kraut (2002, pp. 181–9) and Simpson (1998, pp. xvii–xx).

should be large enough for the polis to be self-sufficient in the necessities of life (VII.4, 1326b2–9). Aristotle does not offer any numbers, though he does think that the 5,040 full citizens of Plato's second-best polis of the *Laws* would require an unrealistically large territory the size of Babylon to carry a population large enough to support so many people living in idleness along with their wives and servants (II.6, 1265a10–17). (For the enormous size of Babylon see III.3, 1276a27–30.) So much for the quantity of full citizens in an ideal polis. As for their quality, they must have the psychic capability of acquiring the moral and intellectual virtues: they must be spirited (*thumoeideis*) and intelligent (*dianoētikoi*) Greeks rather than spirited but intellectually deficient Europeans or intelligent but spiritless Asians (VII.7, 1327b20–36). The lawgiver develops their psychic capability, makes them into men of virtue, by habituation and instruction (VII.7, 1327b36–38; 13, 1332a38–b11; see also *EN* II.1, 1103a14–18; X.9).

An ideal territory is superlatively self-sufficient (VII.5, 1326b26–30, but see VII.6, 1327a25–27), has a healthy climate (VII.11, 1330a38–b17), is easy to defend (VII.5, 1326b39–1327a3), and is large enough to allow the citizens of a polis founded on it to live at leisure freely and temperately (VII.5, 1326b30–32). Such a polis should ideally have walls (VII.11, 1330b32–1331a18) and access to the sea (VII.6). One historical polis that came close to satisfying Aristotle's physical requirements, to judge from its ruins, was his own native city of Stagira.

The social, economic, and political structure of Aristotle's ideal polis – its constitution and its formal cause – is outlined in *Politics* VII.8–10. Aristotle begins by distinguishing the proper parts of a polis from those things that are not parts but are indispensable for its existence. Its proper parts are the men (women are ignored throughout VII.8–10) who can share in its end, or goal. Thus, the proper parts of the ideal polis are the men who are capable of living a life of virtuous activity. Many who are indispensable for the existence of the ideal polis are incapable of living such a life. The lives of artisans, merchants, and shopkeepers are "sordid and opposed to virtue," while farmers lack the leisure necessary "for the growth of virtue and for political activities" (VII.9, 1328b39–1329a2). The proper parts of the ideal polis are its citizens. Those who are indispensable but not proper parts are mere accessories. Since no free native in the ideal polis is to be excluded from full citizenship (VII.13, 1332a34–35), the accessories must be either slaves or aliens. The farmers will ideally be slaves (VII.9, 1329a25–26; 10, 1330a25–28), while craftsmen, merchants, and shopkeepers will presumably be resident aliens (*metoikoi*) or foreign visitors, as they are in Plato's second-best polis of the *Laws* (VIII, 846d1–847b6, XI, 920a3–4). Each of the full citizens will own land (VII.9, 1329a17–19; 10, 1329b36–37, 1330a9–25) (which will not, however, shield them from the vicissitudes of fortune (VII.10, 1330a5–8)). Citizenship is thus distributed according to the Aristotelian standard: virtue fully furnished with external means (VII.1, 1323b40–1324a2). So in Aristotle's view the ideal polis must be ideally just. It should also be remarkably stable. Since the free, the wealthy, and the virtuous are exactly the same men, the divisions among free natives that regularly lead to faction will be nonexistent.

Aristotle assigns trade, industry, and agriculture to slaves and aliens so that his citizens may have leisure from material concerns for happy lives, lives of virtuous activity (II.9, 1269a34–36; 11, 1273a32–35; VII.9, 1329a1–2). But which virtues do they have to exercise? Certainly all the moral virtues. They are brave, temperate, just (VII.1, 1323a27–34, b32–36; 9, 1328b38), even great-souled (*megalopsuchoi*) (VII.7, 1328a9–10; VIII.3, 1338b2–4). They must also have practical wisdom since no one can possess the moral virtues without it (*EN* VI.13, 1144b30–1145a6). So much is clear. But do they possess theoretical wisdom? Are they able to engage in theoretical activity (*theōria*)? This has been doubted, primarily because the *Politics*, in spite of containing an entire book on educational theory, contains but a single allusion to higher education (VIII.2, 1337a42: *ta peritta*, the extraordinary things, for which see Susemihl and Hicks, 1894, pp. 571 and 619; and Kraut, 1997, p. 176). When this fact is coupled with Aristotle's admission that some people are able to develop their practical but not their theoretical reason (VII.14, 1333a23–29), it is easy to conclude that the majority of his citizens are not men of theoretical wisdom and that the theoretical life is not the goal of the ideal polis (Kraut, 1997, pp. 138–40; 2002, pp. 197–202; Lord, 1982, pp. 196–202; Solmsen, 1964, pp. 217–18). As sensible as this interpretation sounds, it is probably mistaken. Aristotle does not say or necessarily imply at *Politics* VII.14, 1333a23–29, that some of his *citizens* will be incapable of developing their theoretical reason; he implies only that some *people* are incapable. Moreover, theoretical wisdom appears to be among the virtues that Aristotle expects in his citizens. In discussing the virtues needed for work and leisure, war and peace, he says that "bravery and endurance are needed for work, philosophy for leisure, temperance and justice at both times" (VII.15, 1334a22–25; see also a28–40). The philosophy needed exclusively for leisure cannot be the virtue of the entire intellect, of practical and theoretical reason together, as some have maintained (Newman, 1887–1902, vol. 1, pp. 346–7, vol. 2, p. 255, vol. 3, p. 450) or the virtue of practical reason alone; for these are needed for both work and leisure. It must then be the virtue of theoretical reason, whose exercise is theoretical activity (*theōria*). This interpretation is supported by the fact that the properties attributed to philosophy in the *Politics* are those attributed to theoretical activity in the *Nicomachean Ethics*: painless pleasure, self-sufficiency, leisuredness (compare II.7, 1267a7–12 with *EN* X.7, 1177a17–b26, and note the use of "philosophy" as a stylistic variant for "theoretical activity" at 1177a25). It seems, then, that the theoretical life is the highest end of the ideal polis (Newman, 1887–1902, vol. 1, p. 200; Stewart, 1892, vol. 1, pp. 59–62; Susemihl and Hicks, 1894, pp. 48–9, 619) just as it is of each individual human being (*EN* X.7). There is thus no need to evade the clear meaning of Aristotle's oft repeated principle that the goal of the best man and of the best polis are the same (VII.2, 1324a5–8; 3, 1325b30–32; 14, 1333b37; 15, 1334a11–13).

Aristotle's ideal city sets the standard for naturalness and, consequently, for Aristotelian justice. We can now explain why the ideal polis is in a completely natural condition. First of all, the end of the ideal city is the highest end of human life, theoretical activity. Second, its constitution distributes military, political, and religious offices to its adult male citizens in a manner that corresponds to the natural stages of life (VII.14, 1332b35–38). In his physical prime a citizen serves as a hoplite in the armed forces; in his mental prime he heads a household and participates in the political life of his polis as a full citizen; when he grows old, he becomes a priest (VII.9, 1329a2–17). Third, the constitution distributes political office only to the naturally superior sex (I.5, 1254b13–14; 12, 1259b1–3). And, finally, it assigns natural slaves to natural masters. The social and political structure of the ideal polis is to Aristotle's eye completely natural because it reflects what he takes to be the natural hierarchy of human beings and the natural stages of life.

In an Aristotelian universe, temporally infinite in both directions, one might expect superb instances of every type of natural object to crop up from time to time – completely healthy horses, for example, with no weaknesses or abnormalities, and completely natural poleis. This leads one to wonder just how distant Aristotle thinks his ideal polis is from historical reality. Plato, after all, conjectures that *his* ideal polis may exist in some corner of the world or some point in time (*Rep.* VI, 499c7–d6); and Aristotle is able on occasion to look beyond parochial time (II.5, 1264a1–5; VII.10, 1329b25–35). Aristotle never addresses the question of historical reality, though he does insist that political ideals should presuppose nothing impossible (II.6, 1265a17–18; VII.4, 1325b38–39), which means that in his eyes the ideal polis lies within the realm of possibility. But there are many degrees of possibility ranging from mere logical consistency to political feasibility. So the question arises of the closeness of the possibility demanded by Aristotle to historical reality. Scholarly opinion on this matter spans a wide spectrum: the ideal polis is an unapproachable ideal (Yack, 1993, p. 3); it is an approachable but unattainable standard, possible in principle but unattainable in practice (Miller, 1995, p. 252); it is a present possibility (Kraut, 1997, p. 140); it is not only possible but practical (Stalley, 1991, pp. 198–9); it is a practical model for the foundation of a new Greek polis (Ober, 1998, p. 328n). One might wonder whether Aristotelian ideas do not imply the existence of the ideal polis at some point in time. For in addition to the idea mentioned above that it would be odd if a type of natural entity never, throughout the whole of infinite time, appeared in a completely natural condition, there is the Aristotelian principle that every possibility is realized at some point in time (*Cael.* I.12; *Top.* II.11, 115b17–18; *Met.* Θ.3, 1047a10–14; 4, 1047b3–6). Though the scope of this principle is restricted – the possibility that a given cloak will be cut up will never be realized if the cloak wears out first (*Int.* 9, 19a12–14) – Aristotle's ideal polis seems to fall within its scope; for the principle applies at least to natural entities (Waterlow, 1982, pp. 141–58), of which the ideal polis is one kind (VII.8, 1328a21–25).

We cannot leave Aristotle's ideal polis without considering its unattractive features: slavery, the subordination of women, ethnic prejudice, contempt for industry and trade, and denigration of labor. These are all reflective of popular Greek values of the fourth century BCE (Keyt, 1991b, pp. 267–8): the polis of our prayers is the polis prayed for by ancient Greek males. But it was not left to modern times to question these values. The report of diverse voices is a part of Aristotelian methodology. We need look no further than the *Politics* itself for an indictment of Aristotle's ideal. Aristotle reports the view of those who consider slavery unjust (I.3, 1253b20–23), examines one of Plato's arguments for placing women on an equal footing with men (II.5, 1264b4–6; see *Rep.* V, 451d–457c), discusses the democratic view that artisans are fit for full citizenship (III.5), refers to the barbarian Egyptians with respect (VII.10, 1329a40–b5, b23–25), and ranks the constitution of barbarian Carthage just below the best constitution (IV.7, 1293b14–19). (For the division of the human race into Greek and barbarian see *Cael.* I.3, 270b7–8, and Plato, *Plt.* 262c10–d6.) Not only does Aristotle report a contrary voice on the subject of slavery, but as we shall see in the next section his defense of natural slavery is at odds with his own principles. The other repugnant features of Aristotle's ideal we shall not pursue.

Slavery

Aristotle's defense of natural slavery serves at least two purposes. The first relates to the naturalness of the polis. Aristotle needs to prove that the household is natural as a step toward proving that the polis is natural; this involves showing that the various relations in the household – husband and wife, master and slave, father and child (I.2, 1252a24–b15; I.12) – are natural; and the most problematic of these is that of master to slave. The second purpose relates to the justice of Aristotle's ideal polis. The leisure of its citizens is secured by the labor of slaves; so unless slavery can be justified the ideal polis, instead of being perfectly just, will be grossly unjust.

Aristotle's defense of natural slavery turns on a notion that he defines but does not label, which we shall call "weak-mindedness." A person is weak-minded if he completely lacks the deliberative part of the soul (I.13, 1260a12) and "shares in reason to the extent of apprehending it but without possessing it" (I.5, 1254b22–23). Aristotle thinks there are many such people. Their only function being bodily labor (I.5, 1254b18–19), they are no more than ensouled tools (*EN* VIII.11, 1161b4). Aristotle claims that they stand, in respect of ruling and being ruled, to the fully rational as the body stands to the soul and as beast to man (I.5, 1254b16–20). He thinks it is natural for the body to be ruled despotically by the soul and for lower animals to be ruled despotically by humans (I.5, 1254b2–13). So he infers that it is natural for the weak-minded to be ruled despotically by the fully rational (I.5, 1254b16–23). But despotic rule is the rule of a master over slaves (I.7, 1255b16–18; IV.11, 1295b19–22). The conclusion now follows that it is natural and (by the positive justice-of-nature principle) just for the weak-minded to be slaves and to be ruled by a master (I.5, 1255a1–3). But the rule of a master (*hē despoteia*) is rule with a view to the advantage of the master and only incidentally with a view to the advantage of the slave (III.6, 1278b32–37).

The basis of Aristotle's argument is a threefold association that is repeated often enough in the *Ethics* and *Politics* to appear a commonplace: master is to slave as soul is to body and as a craftsman is to his tools (see, in addition to the above, *EN* VIII.11, 1161b4; *EE* VII.9, 1241b17–19, b22–24; 10, 1242a28–29). In *Politics* I.13 Aristotle raises a problem about this threefold association that effectively undermines it. The problem is this. An intemperate and cowardly slave will fail to fulfill the function of a slave (I.13, 1260a33–36). A good slave must, then, be temperate and have the bravery of a subordinate (for which see I.13, 1260a23). But the moral virtues are higher than the virtues of a tool or the virtues of the body (I.13, 1259b22–25); temperance, for example, is more valuable than the sharpness of a knife or the health and strength of a body. But if a slave were simply a tool or simply a body, his virtues could not exceed those of a tool or those of the body; the goodness of a slave would consist simply of his health and strength and ability to do his work. Since this is not the case, a slave cannot by nature be simply a tool or a body.

Aristotle expresses the problem as a dilemma: if there is a virtue of a slave higher (*timiōtera*) than that of a tool or of bodily service, such as temperance, bravery, or justice, a slave will not differ (in nature) from a free man; but if not, a (natural) slave has no share in reason and, consequently, is not human[13] (I.13, 1259b21–28). The implicit conclusion of this dilemma is that either slaves do not differ in nature from free men or else they are not human. So if slaves *are* human, they do not differ in nature from free men. In other words, nature does not divide mankind into free and slave, the very position Aristotle set out to refute.

It should be noted, furthermore, that Aristotelian principles, correctly applied, entail the correct moral stance with respect to the weak-minded. Aristotle's characterization of the weak-minded as those who share in reason to the extent of apprehending it but without possessing it (I.5, 1254b22–23) resembles his characterization of the orectic soul: "the appetitive and in general the desiderative (*orektikon*) part [of the soul] shares [in reason] in a way, in so far as it listens and is obedient to it" (*EN*. I.13, 1102b30–31; see also *Pol.* VII.14, 1333a16–19; 15, 1334b17–28.) The weak-minded, then, are analogues, not of the body, but of the orectic soul. But Aristotle maintains that "the soul rules the body with a despotic rule whereas mind rules desire (*orexis*) with a political and regal rule" (I.5, 1254b4–6). It would seem to follow that the weak-minded, being analogous to the orectic soul, should be ruled with a political and regal rule (Newman, 1887–1902, vol. 2, p. 146). But regal and political rule, unlike despotic rule, is exercised with a view to the advantage of the ruled rather the ruler (III.6, 1279a17–21; 7, 1279a25–39). Thus, Aristotelian principles yield the correct moral stance: the weak-minded should be ruled with a view to their own advantage.

Constitutions

One important element of Aristotle's political naturalism, as we said before, is his idea that the condition of any given polis is either natural (and hence good) or unnatural (and hence bad). To be in a natural condition it is necessary in Aristotle's view for a polis to have a constitution that is according to nature. (But not sufficient: other requirements are that its constitution be stable and its citizens law-abiding.) So we come finally to the main subject of the *Politics*: constitutions.

Aristotle defines a constitution in two ways: as an arrangement (*taxis*) of the inhabitants, primarily the citizens, of a polis (III.1, 1274b38–41) and as an arrangement of political offices (III.6, 1278b8–11). The latter is the more fundamental definition: a constitution arranges the citizens of a polis by arranging the political offices that they fill. Such an arrangement sets the distributive principle for full citizenship, the eligibility conditions for each office, and the end, or goal of the polis (IV.1, 1289a15–18), which it is the function (*ergon*) of the polis (VII.4, 1326a13) to attain.

Some constitutions in Aristotle's view are correct (*orthai*), others deviant (*parekbaseis*). Those that are correct aim at the common advantage (*to koinē(i) sumpheron*); those

---

13.   Implied by Aristotle's words: "if not, this is absurd since they are humans and share in reason."

that are deviant seek only the rulers' own advantage (III.6, 1279a17–20). Since under any constitution there are either one, few, or many rulers, there are six types of constitution in all: kingship and its deviation, tyranny, have one ruler; aristocracy and its deviation, oligarchy, have only a few; and so-called constitution (or polity) and its deviation, democracy, have many (III.7, 1279a25–39, b4–6).

Aristotle thinks this initial classification of constitutions is based on accidental rather than essential properties (III.8, 1279b34–39) and superimposes upon it one following ethical and socio-economic rather than numerical principles (III.7, 1279a39–b4, b7–10; III.8). Virtue is the ethical principle; wealth and poverty (or wealth and freedom) the socio-economic. Aristotle thinks that virtue comes in various degrees (*EN* VII.1, 1144a15–27), the higher the degree the rarer. Military virtue, the virtue of a hoplite, is more common than complete virtue (III.7, 1279a39–b2); and complete virtue more common than the transcendent virtue (*hē huper hēmas aretē*) of heroes (*EN* VII.1, 1145a18–27). Kingship is now defined, in terms echoing Aristotle's description of the virtue of heroes,[14] as rule by a man of transcendent virtue (I.12, 1259b10–17; III.13, 1284a3–12; IV.2, 1289a41–b1; VII.14, 1332b16–23); aristocracy as rule by (a few) men of complete virtue (IV.7, 1293b3–5); and so-called constitution as rule by (many) men of military virtue (III.7, 1279a37–b4). These are of course idealized definitions. As for the deviant constitutions, democracy is defined as the rule of the (many) poor (or free) and oligarchy as the rule of the (few) wealthy (III.8, 1279b34–1280a6; IV.4, 1290b17–20). In defining democracy Aristotle oscillates between poverty (see III.7, 1279b8–9; 8, 1279b18–19) and freedom (see IV.4, 1290b1; 8, 1294a11; VI.2, 1317a40–41), the differentiae of proletarian and egalitarian democracy respectively. Aristotle does not revise his initial definition of tyranny as the rule of one man for his own advantage (III.7, 1279b6–7), though he obviously regards tyranny as the rule of one *vile* man (V.11, 1315b4–10; Keyt, 1999, pp. 170–1). The six constitutions form a moral hierarchy, the better the correct constitution the worse its deviation: kingship, aristocracy, polity, democracy, oligarchy, and tyranny (IV.2, 1289a38–b5).

The most interesting and controversial part of Aristotle's classification is his division of constitutions into correct and deviant. Thomas Hobbes, for example, thinks the division is entirely subjective. "[*Tyranny* and *Oligarchy*]," he says, "are not the names of other Formes of Government, but of the same Formes misliked. For they that are discontented under *Monarchy*, call it *Tyranny*; and they that are displeased with *Aristocracy*, call it *Oligarchy*" (1651, ch. 19, p. 95). To evaluate Aristotle's idea we need to understand his notion of the common advantage. To begin with, whose advantage is it? The common advantage is not the advantage of every inhabitant of a given polis. The common advantage does not include the advantage of slaves (III.6, 1278b32–37), nor apparently the advantage of resident aliens or foreign visitors. Aristotle equates the common advantage with the common advantage of the citizens (III.13, 1283b40–42). But the common advantage can hardly be the advantage exclusively of full citizens. The full citizens of a polis are its rulers, and the common advantage is distinguished from the rulers' own advantage. Nor can it be the advantage of full citizens

14. Both the king and the hero are said to have an "excess of virtue" *(aretēs huperbolē)* (III.13, 1284a4; *EN* VII.1, 1145a23–24).

together with their wives and children, for it is difficult to drive a wedge between a man's own advantage and that of his household. The concept of the common advantage implies a body of second-class citizens – free unenfranchised native-born adult males. Aristotle, indeed, asks whether such men are to be called "citizens" (III.5, 1277b33–39), mentions the citizen who is ruled (*ho archomenos politēs*) rather than ruler (III.5, 1278a16–17), and speaks of citizens under kingship and tyranny (III.14, 1285a25–29; V.11, 1314b12–13), who can only be second-class citizens, the king and the tyrant being the only full citizens in a kingship and a tyranny. The common advantage seems, then, to be the advantage of all the first- and second-class citizens in a polis.

But now a second question arises. For, as Aristotle points out, the word "all" is ambiguous; it can be taken either collectively or distributively (II.3, 1261b16–32, V.8, 1307b35–39). ("They all lifted the stone" can mean either "They lifted the stone together" or "Each in turn lifted the stone by himself.") The question, then, is whether the common advantage is the advantage of all the citizens collectively or distributively. The latter is Aristotle's answer. The common advantage is associated with living finely (*to zēn kalōs*) (III.6, 1278b21–24); that is, with living a life of virtue and happiness. But happiness, Aristotle claims, is not like evenness, which can be present in a whole without being present in either of its parts (i.e., $2 = 1 + 1$); a whole cannot be happy, unless all or most or some of its parts are happy (II.5, 1264b17–22). Thus, the common advantage is not the advantage of the citizens collectively. That it is also (ideally at least) not the advantage distributively of most rather than all citizens is suggested by the following passage: "Even if it is possible for all to be good without each citizen individually being good, the latter is more choiceworthy; for all being good follows from each being good" (VII.13, 1332a36–38). (For more on the common advantage see Miller, 1995, pp. 194–224).

A third question concerns a broad-based democracy in which every free native-born adult male is a full citizen and where the common advantage and the rulers' own advantage are the same. Such a democracy, contrary to Aristotle's classification, would seem to be correct rather than deviant. Aristotle, indeed, allows for such a "good" democracy (VI.2, 1318a3–10; Keyt, 1999, pp. 202–3), but he thinks that egalitarian democracy usually degenerates into proletarian democracy in which the poor use their superior numbers to virtually disenfranchise the rich (VI.2, 1317b3–10).

By Aristotle's justice-of-nature principles constitutions that are according to nature (*kata phusin*) are just (III.6, 1279a17–19) and those that are contrary to nature (*para phusin*) are unjust (III.11, 1282b8–13). We can now explain why Aristotle thinks that correct constitutions are according to nature and deviant constitutions contrary to nature (III.17, 1287b37–41). The correct constitutions are according to nature because they distribute political office according to a standard of worth validated by the ideal polis, which, for the reasons given earlier, is pre-eminently natural. This standard is of course the Aristotelian standard: virtue fully furnished with external means (VII.1, 1323b40–1324a2). (Only men of virtue, we might add, will rule with a view to the common, rather than their own, advantage.) That the deviant constitutions are contrary to nature is a consequence of their despotism and the Aristotelian equation of the forced and the unnatural. Seeking only their own advantage, the rulers under a deviant constitution treat those outside the constitution, the second-class citizens, as slaves (III.6, 1279a19–21; IV.11, 1295b19–23). Since no free man will endure such treatment willingly (see IV.10, 1295a17–23), these outsiders obey their rulers only because they are forced to (III.3, 1276a12–13; 10, 1281a23–24).

Like a modern political theorist, Aristotle distinguishes between a constitution and the laws made under it (IV.1, 1289a11–25; see also II.12, 1273b32–34, 1274b15–19; III.11, 1282b8–13; 15, 1286a2–4). The laws in his view reflect the constitution (IV.1, 1289a13–15) and its justice or injustice: democracies have democratic laws, oligarchies oligarchic laws, (un)just constitutions (un)just laws (III.10, 1281a37; 11, 1282b10–11; IV.9, 1294b6–7; V.9, 1310a14–18). He notes, however, that when a constitution changes, the tendency of people, acting out of habit, to continue observing the pre-existing laws often gives the new constitution the cast of the old (IV.5, 1292b11–21).

The importance of education now emerges. For laws that are not obeyed and constitutions that are not honored are worthless (IV.8, 1294a3–7; V.9, 1310a12–18). For a polis to survive its citizens must be habituated to obey its laws and educated in the spirit of its constitution (II.8, 1269a20–21; *MA* 10, 703a29–34). This is part of what Aristotle means when he says that the constitution is a certain way of life of a polis (IV.11, 1295a40–b1). Thus, education is a prime topic of Aristotle's political philosophy; an entire book of the *Politics* is devoted to it.

The Good Man and the Good Citizen

We shall conclude with a brief word about Aristotle's famous distinction between the good man and the good citizen. The function of a citizen, Aristotle maintains, is to preserve the constitution of his polis. A good citizen, then, is one who performs this function well (for the inference see *EN* I.7.1098a11–12). Among other things a good citizen is disposed to obey the laws of his polis, to be just in the broad sense of the term (*EN* V.1, 1129b11). But the disposition to obey democratic laws is different from the disposition to obey oligarchic laws. The virtue of the good citizen is thus relative to the constitution under which he lives. On the other hand, the virtue of a good man in Aristotle's view is always one and the same. The virtue of the good citizen must, then, be distinct from that of the good man (III.4, 1276b26–34; V.9, 1309a36–39). The two coincide, Aristotle claims, only in the full citizens of the ideal polis (III.5, 1278a40–b5; IV.7, 1293b1–7). For it is only in the ideal polis that citizens will be disposed to obey laws that are without qualification just, and it is only the full citizens – the rulers – of such a polis who must possess practical wisdom, or *phronēsis*, the intellectual virtue characteristic of a good man (*EN* VI.8; 13, 1144b30–32). The younger citizens, those serving as hoplites, who are in their physical but not their mental prime, being intellectually immature have true opinions in lieu of practical wisdom, and consequently are not yet good men and are not yet qualified to be full citizens, or rulers (III.4, 1277a14–16, 1277b25–30; VII.9, 1329a2–17; 14, 1333a11–13).

Aristotle does not draw out the consequences of his analysis. One obvious consequence of his definition of a good citizen is that such a person can be at most a reformer, never a revolutionary. He can work to improve the constitution under which he lives – to moderate an extreme democracy like Athens, for example – but, devoted as he is to the preservation of the constitution of his polis, he cannot strive to replace it with a better constitution. It also follows that a good man living under a deviant constitution – under a democratic constitution, for example – cannot be a good citizen. A good man is just without qualification, whereas a good citizen of a democracy will be disposed to obey democratic laws, which, though just from the standpoint of democracy, are without qualification unjust (III.11, 1282b8–13).[15]

Bibliography

Works Cited

Depew, D. J. (1995). "Humans and Other Political Animals in Aristotle's *History of Animals*." *Phronesis*, 40, 156–81.

Ehrenberg, V. (1969). *The Greek State*. 2nd edn. London: Methuen.

Galston, W. A. (1980). *Justice and the Human Good*. Chicago: University of Chicago Press.

Hobbes, T. (1651). *Leviathan*. London: Crooke.

Irwin, T. H. (1988). *Aristotle's First Principles*. Oxford: Clarendon Press.

Keyt, D. (1983). "Intellectualism in Aristotle." In J. P. Anton and A. Preus (eds.), *Essays in Ancient Greek Philosophy* (vol. 2, pp. 364–87). Albany: State University of New York Press.

——. (1989). "The Meaning of ΒΙΟΣ in Aristotle's *Ethics* and *Politics*." *Ancient Philosophy*, 9, 15–21.

——. (1991a). "Three Basic Theorems in Aristotle's *Politics*." In D. Keyt and F. D. Miller (eds.), *A Companion to Aristotle's Politics* (pp. 118–41). Oxford: Blackwell.

——. (1991b). "Aristotle's Theory of Distributive Justice." In D. Keyt and F. D. Miller (eds.), *A Companion to Aristotle's Politics* (pp. 238–78). Oxford: Blackwell.

——. (1996). "Aristotle and the Ancient Roots of Anarchism." *Topoi*, 15, 129–42.

——. (1999). *Aristotle Politics: Books V and VI*. Oxford: Clarendon Press.

Keyt, D. and Miller, F. D. (eds.). (1991). *A Companion to Aristotle's Politics*. Oxford: Blackwell.

Kraut, R. (1997). *Aristotle Politics: Books VII and VIII*. Oxford: Clarendon Press.

——. (2002). *Aristotle: Political Philosophy*. Oxford: Oxford University Press.

Lord, C. (1982). *Education and Culture in the Political Thought of Aristotle*. Ithaca: Cornell University Press.

Miller, F. D. (1995). *Nature, Justice, and Rights in Aristotle's Politics*. Oxford: Clarendon Press.

Mulgan, R. G. (1977). *Aristotle's Political Theory*. Oxford: Clarendon Press.

Newman, W. L. (1887–1902). *The Politics of Aristotle*. (4 vols.). Oxford: Clarendon Press.

Ober, J. (1998). *Political Dissent in Democratic Athens*. Princeton: Princeton University Press.

Rawls, J. (1971). *A Theory of Justice*. Cambridge, Mass.: Belknap Press.

Robinson, R. (1962). *Aristotle Politics: Books III and IV*. Oxford: Clarendon Press. Repr. with a supplementary essay by D. Keyt, 1995.

Saunders, T. J. (1995). *Aristotle Politics: Books I and II*. Oxford: Clarendon Press.

Simpson, P. L. P. (1998). *A Philosophical Commentary on the Politics of Aristotle*. Chapel Hill: University of North Carolina Press.

Solmsen, F. (1964). "Leisure and Play in Aristotle's ideal State." *Rheinisches Museum für Philologie*, 107, 193–220.

Stalley, R. F. (1991). "Aristotle's Criticism of Plato's *Republic*." In D. Keyt and F. D. Miller (eds.), *A Companion to Aristotle's Politics* (pp. 182–99). Oxford: Blackwell.

15. I am grateful to Fred D. Miller, Christine Keyt, and the editors of this volume for helpful comments on earlier drafts of this chapter.

411

Stewart, J. A. (1892). *Notes on the Nicomachean Ethics of Aristotle.* (2 vols.). Oxford: Clarendon Press.

Susemihl, F. and Hicks, R. D. (1894). *The Politics of Aristotle.* London: Macmillan.

Waterlow, S. (1982). *Passage and Possibility.* Oxford: Clarendon Press.

Yack, B. (1993). *The Problems of a Political Anima: Community, Justice, and Conflict in Aristotelian Political Thought.* Berkeley: University of California Press.

Further Reading

Aubenque, P. (ed.). (1993). *Aristote Politique: Études sur la Politique d'Aristote.* Paris: Presses Universitaires de France.

Lord, C., O'Connor, D. K., and Bodéüs, R. (eds.). (1991). *Essays on the Foundations of Aristotelian Political Science.* Berkeley: University of California Press.

Nichols, M. P. (1992). *Citizens and Statesmen: A Study of Aristotle's Politics.* Lanham, Md.: Rowman & Littlefield.

Patzig, G. (ed.). (1990). *Aristoteles Politik.* Proceedings of the Ninth Symposium Aristotelicum. Göttingen: Vanderhoeck and Ruprecht.

Swanson, J. A. (1992). *The Public and the Private in Aristotle's Political Philosophy.* Ithaca: Cornell University Press.

Taylor, C. C. W. (1995). "Politics." In J. Barnes (ed.), *The Cambridge Companion to Aristotle* (pp. 233–58). Cambridge: Cambridge University Press.

Part IV

Philosophy in the Hellenistic Age

21

Philosophic Schools in Hellenistic and Roman Times

THOMAS BÉNATOUÏL

What was a philosophical "school" in antiquity? The terms used in the Greek texts allow us to distinguish several dimensions in the concept, even if in the end they became interchangeable. *Scholē* originally designated the leisure one enjoys to educate oneself and to participate in the political and cultural life of one's city: "school" is thus at first a phase of life and an occupation for a man who is free and able to provide for his own needs. The term *scholē* subsequently came to designate more narrowly an institution for apprenticeship, like the English word. Still, a philosophical "school" was not merely that: it was in the first instance a set of received teachings (*diatribē*), and above all a "school of thought" (*hairesis*) as well as a "succession" (*diadochē*) of teachers – a continuous tradition of thinkers who had cultivated and transmitted to students a doctrine and a method specific to a first teacher, the founder of the school. The philosophical school thus constituted a social model for the legitimation and spread of truth, which in Greece succeeded other more religious and political models, from which the school nonetheless borrowed certain features (Détienne, 1996). The famous words attributed to Aristotle, "I am a friend of Plato but even more of truth," express both a universal attitude and the historically specific articulation of social relations and intellectual activities that constitute the ancient "philosophical school."

Although there were also schools of rhetoric and, above all, of medicine (see Pellegrin, ANCIENT MEDICINE, in this volume), it was in philosophy that the scholastic model played the most important and enduring role, so much so that ancient historians of philosophy attempted to assign all philosophers to a small number of mostly artificial scholastic lineages: our most important source for the history of ancient philosophical schools, Diogenes Laertius' *Lives and Opinions of the Famous Philosophers*, provides the best example of such a construction.[1] In fact, only in the Hellenistic period did the great majority of practicing philosophers belong to organized and flourishing schools, the nature of which we shall try to penetrate gradually, by considering first their institutional history, then their internal organization and activities, and finally the practice of philosophy that developed in them.

---

1. See Mejer, ANCIENT PHILOSOPHY AND THE DOXOGRAPHICAL TRADITION, in this volume, and Mansfeld (1999).

A Brief History of Philosophical Schools in Antiquity

The origins

The four great philosophical schools of the Hellenistic period were founded in Athens between the beginning and the end of the fourth century BCE. Yet embryonic schools existed earlier and elsewhere. Most of the pre-Socratic philosophers had had disciples who had learned and then developed or modified the doctrine of their teacher. For example, this was the case with Thales, in Miletus (Ionia) in the sixth century BCE, who had his kinsman Anaximander for a student, who himself taught his doctrines to Anaximenes. Similarly, in the fifth century in southern Italy, Parmenides had Zeno and Melissus as students. But it was Pythagoras, a little earlier and in the same region, who was the first to gather around himself a real group of disciples. On the model of certain religious sects (Burkert, 1982) or military brotherhoods (Détienne, 1963), the "Pythagoreans" were defined by the passing of tests of initiation, respect for ritual rules fixed by Pythagoras, adherence to his secret doctrines, and by a communal life that could extend to the sharing of all their belongings. By contrast, fifth-century sophists such as Protagoras, Hippias, and Gorgias, were itinerant professors imparting mainly rhetorical and political knowledge in the form of short lessons for all who were willing to pay them.[2] As Jean-Pierre Vernant (1982, ch. 4; cf. Détienne, 1996, ch. 6) has remarked, Greek philosophy would hesitate throughout its entire history between these two original pedagogical models: religious initiation and public debate.

Socrates in particular mixed these two models. More than any other figure, he drew numerous apprentice philosophers to Athens, even after his death. Among all of his followers who gathered circles of students around themselves, only Plato gave birth to a real institution for teaching and research that survived him for many generations: founded near the Academy in 387, it is the first of the four great Athenian philosophical schools. Aristotle studied in it for 20 years and subsequently founded his own school in the Lyceum, in 335. Epicurus's school, the Garden, dates from 306, and it is around 301 that Zeno of Citium begins to teach in the Painted Colonnade (*Stoa*). The habit thus took hold of calling the four great schools and their members after the locales where their instruction took place in Athens.[3]

The Hellenistic golden age

How were these schools able to perpetuate themselves after the death of their founders? Following Wilamowitz-Moellendorff (1965, pp. 263–91) it was long thought that the philosophical schools – except for the Stoa – were religious societies dedicated to the

---

2. See Barney, THE SOPHISTIC MOVEMENT, in this volume.

3. *Peripatos*, the name commonly given to Aristotle's school (also called "Lyceum"), means a space provided for strolling, in a public or private location (Lynch, 1972, p. 74). Students of a school are usually called after its name (Academics, Peripatetics, Stoics) except for the Pythagoreans, the Epicureans (and the first Stoics, who are sometimes called "Zenonians"). The epithet "Platonists" appears only from the second century CE onward (Glucker, 1978, pp. 206–20).

cult of the Muses, which allowed them to be officially recognized by the City of Athens and to develop, within a stable institutional framework, instruction comparable to that of a modern university, and even certain religious activities (Boyancé, 1936). Today, however, this analysis is thought to lack for evidence.[4] Philosophical schools seem rather to have been a kind of private foundation or brotherhood, dedicated to teaching and philosophical reflection: the head of the school, or "scholarch," was the sole owner of the property it used (land, furniture, books, statues). He usually lived in the school and had to arrange for his heirs to continue to put it to the service of philosophy: this comes out clearly in the wills of the Peripatetics Theophrastus and Lyco, and in that of Epicurus, which have been preserved for us by Diogenes Laertius (5.52–53, 70 and 10. 16–17). The first two give the "promenade" of the Lyceum to a group of eminent school members to pursue and develop its philosophical activities; the third must leave the Garden to a member of his family, but gives its usufruct to Hermarchus, his successor as head of the school. Like many founders and heads of schools, the latter was not an Athenian citizen and therefore had no right to own real estate in Athens. Unlike the Academy and the Garden, which were founded by Athenians, the Lyceum, beginning with Theophrastus, controlled a private parcel of land only by special dispensation; and no source mentions real estate in connection with the Stoa (Ludlam, 2003), the heads of which mostly came from Asia Minor, where Epicurus, an Athenian born on Samos, had himself long taught before coming to Athens. The intellectual reputation of the city in fact drew disciples from the whole of the Hellenistic Greek world.

Thus, it was mainly, if not only, the existence of the scholarchate and the transmission of this office from one member of the school to a "successor" that guaranteed the unity and longevity of a philosophical school. Each scholarch normally held this office for life and designated his successor from among the leading members of the school or allowed the latter to elect the new scholarch. Sometimes disciples who had been passed over for the succession left their teacher's school to open their own. In addition to these dissidents, also teaching at Athens were the heirs of the Socratic schools, such as Diodorus Cronus, Stilpo of Megara, and Diogenes of Sinope (the Cynic) and his successors (see Decleva Caizzi, MINOR SOCRATICS, in this volume).

The Hellenistic philosophical scene nevertheless was largely dominated by the great philosophical schools, although the Lyceum seems to have essentially dedicated itself first to historical and scientific investigations,[5] and later to rhetorical and biographical ones, playing only a minor role in philosophical debate after Theophrastus and Strato, of whose successors little is known. By contrast, we know more or less

---

4.   See the criticisms of Lynch (1972), Glucker (1978), and the more nuanced assessments of Isnardi Parente (1986), Natali (1991) and Dorandi (1999b).

5.   In this domain (mathematics, astronomy, medicine, geography, grammar, philology) it was not the Athenian schools but the Alexandrian Museum and its famous library that constituted the most active center in the Hellenistic world: this was not a philosophical school but a research institution created (and financed) by the king, Ptolemy I, who was inspired by Peripatetic thinkers like Demetrius of Phaleron and Strato of Lampsachus. Thus Alexandrian authors (biographers, historians) often came to be called "Peripatetics" even though they had not studied at the Lyceum.

precisely who were the scholarchs of the three other schools down to the first century BCE (Dorandi, 1999a). It was at this time that the succession seems to have been interrupted in the Stoa and the Academy, with Panaetius of Rhodes, Stoic scholarch until about 110 BCE, and Philo of Larissa, who died in 84 BCE, having fled Athens when it was besieged by Sulla on behalf of Rome in 88 (Glucker, 1978). Philo's great rival, Antiochus of Ascalon, for his part left for Alexandria before returning to Athens to found there a school claiming to be the true heir of the "Old Academy." As far as the Garden is concerned, the last scholarchs whose names are known to us date from the same period (Zeno of Sidon, who died around 75, Phaedrus, then Patro); but the succession seems to have continued until a much later period (D.L. 10.9), as attested, for example, by a letter from the empress Plotina that asks Hadrian to authorize the nomination of a scholarch for the Garden who was not a Roman citizen (Glucker, 1978, pp. 365–6).

From the beginning of the empire to the end of antiquity

The interrupted succession in the Stoa and the Academy, and its obscurity in the Garden, does not mean that these schools were entirely unrepresented in Athens, but it testifies to the displacement of the Hellenistic world's center of gravity toward Rome, where Panaetius, for example, spent a great part of his life, due to his connections with the Scipionic Circle, and where Philo seems to have ended his days. Greek philosophers established themselves, taught and worked in Rome under the protection of cultivated aristocrats. The best example is the Syrian Philodemus of Gadara, a student of Zeno of Sidon and the animating spirit of a very active Epicurean circle based at Piso's villa in Herculaneum. It was also Rome where Pythagoreanism revived in the first century BCE, and where Andronicus of Rhodes compiled an edition, based on manuscripts brought back from Greece by Sulla, of the Aristotelian treatises used within the Lyceum: this work is a sign, maybe even a cause, of the rebirth of Aristotelianism in the first century BCE.

For all that, Rome did not simply replace Athens. What we see is rather a decentralization of the schools: the most influential philosophers rarely taught in Athens, recalling the situation before the time of Socrates. At Rhodes in particular (where Aristotle's disciple Eudemus had opened a Peripatetic school as early as 322 BCE), there was, in the first century BCE, a Stoic school directed by Posidonius, the most influential student of Panaetius, and an Epicurean school that displayed a certain intellectual independence from the Garden (Sedley, 1989). In the same period, many philosophers were teaching in Alexandria, which remained until the end of Antiquity one of the world capitals for philosophy and particularly for Platonism, although this latter philosophy, more than the others, continued to be associated with Athens, where Ammonius (the teacher of Plutarch of Chaeronea (50–125 CE)), Calvenus Taurus, and Longinus taught. During this period, nevertheless, it is Stoicism that dominates, due not so much to the prestige of its teachers as to its influence on many Roman statesmen and writers (Gill, 2003). The ancient slave Epictetus, educated in Rome by Musonius Rufus, a Roman politician and Stoic teacher, gained fame for his austere life and opened a school in Nicopolis in Greece.

Alongside these "private" schools, gathered around a philosopher whose influence has preserved his name for us, there were in many cities, such as Alexandria, Tarsus, and Pergamum, municipal chairs of philosophy (usually one for each of the four great schools), the holders of which were appointed and paid by the city to provide for the higher education of young citizens (Hadot, 1984, ch. 5). In the same spirit, in 176 CE Marcus Aurelius created *imperial* chairs of rhetoric and philosophy in Athens (one or perhaps two for each school). The holder of each chair was appointed for life by the leading citizens in recognition of his learning and paid from the imperial treasury (Lucian, *Eunuchus* 3–4), but he taught in his own house, as did other philosophers whose income depended on the generosity of their students. Though they attracted many candidate philosophers and many students to Athens, we know very few of the names of holders of the imperial chairs. Among them, only one was an influential philosopher: the Peripatetic Alexander of Aphrodisias, at the beginning of the third century CE.

The best-known and most original philosophers of the third and fourth centuries CE were in fact Platonists who gathered groups of disciples. Plotinus (205–70) studied philosophy in Alexandria, then opened a school in Rome, where he resided in the household of a rich aristocrat (see Brisson and Pradeau, PLOTINUS, in this volume). Iamblichus (240–326) studied in Rome and taught his synthesis of Platonism and Pythagoreanism at Apamea in Syria, where he had many students. It is only in the fifth century that Athens regained its preeminence, relative to Rome and Alexandria, through the impulse of Plutarch of Athens (died 432). Set up in his residence south of the Acropolis, his school was wealthy, attracted many students, and became the most active and influential Platonic school of late Antiquity. A succession even developed in it that was comparable to those of the Hellenistic schools, including Syrianus, Proclus (412–85), Marinus, Isidorus, Zenodotus and Damascius (died 529)[6] (see Hoffmann, WHAT WAS COMMENTARY IN LATE ANTIQUITY?, in this volume). This school presented itself as the heir to Plato's Academy, although it had no connection with it, either legal or material, nor with the imperial chairs of philosophy.[7] In this period, the principal adversaries of the Platonists had for a long time been not the other philosophical schools but rather the Christians, who were hostile to the defense of paganism undertaken by the Platonists (Hadot, 1998c). In 529, the emperor Justinian decreed a prohibition of teaching by pagans. Yet the Platonist schools did not immediately disappear (Lynch, 1972, pp. 163–8). Some of their leading members, like Simplicius, left to teach in Persia before being allowed to return to Athens, where they had no successors. In Alexandria, the last pagan Platonist teacher, Olympiodorus, was succeeded by Christians, like Elias, David and Stephanos, who was then (after 610) called to teach in the imperial "University" in Byzantium.

6.   No succession of such length is attested for any of the very many schools opened between the first century BCE and the fifth century CE. Organized around a famous teacher, most did not survive the death of the founder or his first successor.

7.   See the corrective accounts of Lynch (1972, pp. 177–89) and Glucker (1978), particularly the refutation of the thesis of the "golden chain," i.e., that a continuous institutional succession holds for heads of the Academy from Plato to Damascius.

Life in the Schools

What did life consist of in the philosophical schools? How was instruction conducted, who were the students, and what were they taught? We have very little information on this subject, "such matters being universally known at the time and seemingly unworthy of mention" (De Witt, 1936). In addition, practices must have been fairly diverse depending on the school and the period. We can nevertheless attempt to give a general idea of what the teaching of philosophy was like in the Hellenistic schools.

Teachers and students

A substantial proportion of the students in the schools consisted of ephebes, young Greeks of good families, whose education for citizenship, organized by the city, comprised physical, military, rhetorical, and philosophical training. Joining the ephebes were curious older people with professions, and foreign students and visitors, particularly young Roman aristocrats, many of whom completed their education in Athens in the first century BCE or in Marseilles a century later (Strabo 14.5.81). Not all of these students were attached to a school, but all attended the public lectures that the various scholarchs gave (alongside rhetors) in the gymnasiums, under the colonnades, or in a hall reserved for courses, the *exhedra* (Vitruvius, *On Architecture* 5.11.2). The most charismatic philosophers, such as Theophrastus, Arcesilaus, or Aristo of Chios, attracted larger audiences than the rest. It was for the sake of these young men in training that many cities later created municipal chairs of rhetoric and philosophy. For example, before learning medicine, Galen (born in 129 CE) studied the four great philosophical doctrines with four professors in Pergamum. In this period, students were not always numerous or assiduous: Taurus complains that philosophers had to wait at the doors of their rich students until noon (Gell. *NA* 7.10.5).

Among the external "auditors" (*akroatai*) of the public lectures, some developed a taste for philosophy and for a particular teacher, becoming his disciples (*zēlōtai*) for several years. The existence of one or two women disciples is attested for many schools, but not for the Lyceum or the Stoa (D.L. 2.86; 3.46; 6.96; 10.5). Disciples entered a community of "companions" (*hetairoi*) or "friends" (*philoi*) devoted to the practice of philosophy. Among them the "youngest" (*neaniskoi*), still in training, were distinguished from some more or less substantial number of philosophers who were "older" (*presbuteroi*), who frequently lived together, gave courses, and administered the school, sometimes rotating offices (D.L. 5.4), the scholarch often being only the *primum inter pares* and the official representative of the school, particularly in the public courses. The leading members of the school were often linked by familial relations (Natali, 1991, pp. 71–3), on which the school relied in order to persist. In the same spirit, the scholarchs of the Academy were buried within the school and the birthdays of Socrates and Plato were celebrated each year. In his will (D.L. 10.18), Epicurus provided for festivals celebrating his memory, those of his first companions and of his family: it was a matter of binding the school community together in the manner of a family or a religious brotherhood, and of recalling the model for imitation provided by the life and thought of the founders (Clay, 1998, pp. 67–102).

Teaching and research

It must be emphasized that the disciples learned not just arguments and doctrines but also attitudes and behavior in accordance with them, in conformity with the ancient conception of philosophy as a way of life (Hadot, 2002). As Seneca says (*Ad Luc.* 6.6, trans. R. M. Gummere), "Cleanthes could not have been the express image of Zeno if he had merely heard his lectures; he shared his life, saw into his hidden purposes, and watched him to see whether he lived according to his own rules." Philosophers like Zeno and Xenocrates were famed as much for their temperance as for their doctrines. Likening the work of the philosopher to that of the physician, they undertook to improve the conduct of their circle, as is witnessed by many anecdotes preserved by Diogenes Laertius, and by Philodemus's work *On Frank Criticism*, which shows how emulation and the correction of faults should be managed among Epicurean disciples (Konstan et al., 1998), who were guided by the maxim, "Act in all things as if Epicurus were watching" (Sen., *Ad Luc.* 25.5).

Of course, alongside this constant practical training, the scholarchs and their assistants gave more theoretical courses. Certain scientific disciplines, or rhetoric, were considered prerequisites or indispensable complements to philosophical instruction in the Academy and the Lyceum, while they were held to be useless or even harmful in the Garden and in the Stoa at its start (Hadot, 1984, ch. 2). The students also had to prepare themselves for argument, on the occasion of dialectical contests,[8] and for handling various logical methods, such as division (*diairesis*) at the Academy (Epicrates, in Athenaeus, *Deipnosophistai* 2.59D) or formal procedures of demonstration (*sullogismos*) in the Lyceum and the Stoa. As for courses in philosophy in the proper sense, they most often took a dialectical form in the Hellenistic period: the teacher discussed a question or "thesis" – sometimes by interrogating a student in the Socratic manner – and proposed a demonstration or refutation of the thesis (or both in the skeptical Academy of Carneades), then answered the students' questions (Hadot, 1998b). In the imperial period, by contrast, in the schools of Epictetus, Taurus, Plotinus, or Proclus, philosophical lectures focused on the explication of texts of past philosophers like Chrysippus, Aristotle, or Plato (Hadot, 1998a and 2002; Sedley, 1997). With Epictetus, a student began by reading and commenting upon the text, then was corrected by the teacher, who might then discuss for its own sake the question addressed in the text; this was also what Plotinus did (Porphyry, *Life of Plotinus* 13; Goulet-Cazé, 1982). In the Neoplatonic schools, the students followed a genuine course of study of the works of Aristotle, Plato, and of religious texts, each of them commentated upon according to a systematic hermeneutical method.[9]

Having become companions of the scholarch after a sufficiently long stay in the school, disciples left it to teach their knowledge elsewhere or remained to assist the scholarch in training younger disciples and in polemics with other schools. Another important activity for the disciples was editing the works of the scholarch. For teachers like Pyrrho, Carneades, and Epictetus, who held to the Socratic model and wrote nothing, disciples often took it upon themselves to record their teachings in writing. Also,

---

8. Their rules were codified by Aristotle in *Topics* VIII (Moraux, 1968).
9. For more details, see Mejer and Hoffmann, in this volume.

some schools dedicated themselves not just to teaching, discussion, and the philo-sophical life, but also to scientific research, principally mathematical in the Academy, more empirical and historical in the Lyceum (zoology, law, biography). These invest-igations required the collection of many materials (specimens, maps) and particularly books (Natali, 1991), so much so that the activities of these schools depended greatly on their libraries, and the loss of these may have been one of the causes of their decline, especially of the Lyceum (Sedley, 2003, p. 25).

Philosophers and political life

Far from being shut in upon themselves, philosophical schools maintained constant relations with the established political powers, if only because they participated in the training of young citizens, receiving payment and honors in return. For his good influ-ence on the youth, Athens honored Zeno both before and after his death (D.L. 7.6–12). But cities might also ask philosophers, as they also did orators, to serve as ambas-sadors to foreign powers: the most famous example is the journey to Rome in 155 BCE by Carneades, Diogenes of Babylon and Critolaus (scholarchs of the Academy, the Stoa, and the Lyceum) to ask for the abrogation of a fine against Athens.

If this episode remains exceptional because it involved the scholarchs of the schools, the latter nonetheless did not disdain political activity.[10] One of the avowed aims of the Academy, and to a lesser extent the Stoa, was the training of politicians, and many passed through them. The Lyceum and the Garden claimed rather to stand apart from politics and to dedicate themselves respectively to the "theoretical" (or "scholastic") life (Bodéus, 1993) and to the enjoyment, among friends, of a peaceful philosophical life. Still, Athens was twice led by men from these schools. Demetrius of Phaleron, a student of Theophrastus, governed Athens from 317 to 307 BCE in the name of the king of Macedonia, and seemed so much to favor the philosophical schools that, after his fall, the philosophers had to flee Athens because of a new law forbidding them to lead schools without the permission of the Assembly. (The law was repealed after a year.) Later, between 88 and 87 BCE, the Peripatetic Athenion and the Epicurean Aristion played an important part in rallying Athens to the cause of Mithridates against Rome, which provoked the siege of the city by Sulla and the ruin of most of the schools (Ferrary, 1988).

In the Hellenistic period, however, political power was concentrated in the hands of kings who were heirs to the generals of Alexander the Great rather than in city assemblies. These kings actively sought out the company of philosophers. Zeno several times received visits and generous gifts from the king of Macedonia, Antigonus Gonatas (D.L. 7.6–8). Scholarchs such as Zeno, Cleanthes, and the Academic Lacydes gener-ally declined the invitations of kings, to whom they preferred to send one of their disciples. Thus the Stoic Sphaerus left for the court of Ptolemy in Alexandria, which was frequented also by the Epicurean Colotes, Stilpo of Megara and some Cyrenaics. These philosophers might become advisers to the prince, as Sphaerus was to the kings of Sparta (Erskine, 1990). This role became characteristic of Stoic philosophers in

10. See Brown, HELLENISTIC COSMOPOLITANISM, in this volume, for a discussion of Stoic and Epicurean attitudes about politics.

republican, then in imperial Rome (Rawson, 1989): for instance, Augustus had for advisers Athenodorus of Tarsus, who was his tutor, and Arius, two Stoics who also wrote philosophical works and ended their careers as the governors of cities. Philosophers enjoyed thereafter varying degrees of favor from the succeeding Roman emperors: from Nero to Domitian, several Stoic philosophers and politicians were exiled or ordered to commit suicide because of their criticisms of the powerful, while under Hadrian and Marcus Aurelius, philosophy was in favor and its professors received privileges.

Specific Characteristics of Philosophy in the Hellenistic Schools

We must now examine the effects of the scholastic organization we have just described on the intellectual activity taking place in its midst. What did "philosophizing" mean for a leading member of a philosophical school? Was this practice recognized as legitimate or genuine philosophy by all thinkers?

Teaching and dogmatism

Even though the greater part of ancient philosophical teaching was oral, the composition of written works was an important philosophical activity. Some works, such as Plato's dialogues, were intended to present the thought of the school to the public at large and to attract students. Others, like those works of Aristotle that have survived, were the texts for courses restricted to disciples, whence their more technical and sometimes tentative character. In the Hellenistic period, this distinction between "exoteric" and "acroamatic" works (Gell. NA 20.5.5) gave way to a variety of works that were for the most part dogmatic and authoritative – that is, they transmitted an organized body of truths to an actual or potential disciple. This is particularly the case with the writings of Epicurus, which presented different versions of his doctrine depending on the level of advancement of their audience, from mnemonic maxims to *On Nature* (which examined, in 37 books, every detail and problem of the doctrine), including summaries for novices, students in a hurry, and those in need of an aide-mémoire (Hadot, 1969; Wolff, 2000). Hellenistic philosophers thus wrote not only treatises on questions bearing on the three parts of philosophy (methods of knowing and of discourse [logic], the study of Nature [physics], theoretical and practical ethics) but also numerous "summaries" and "introductions" to promote the spread of their doctrines (Mansfeld, 1999).

To convince students to abandon current opinions and to adopt their doctrine rather than some other one, philosophers had, above all, to resort to various techniques of persuasion (Lloyd, 1979, chs. 2 and 4). Most allowed the use of rhetoric in discourses addressed to large audiences, even if the Stoics refused to make long, ornate speeches. But it was dialectic, in the first instance, by means of question-and-answer or syllogisms, that was used in the oral or written lessons. The Stoics developed dialectic a great deal, in order to prove their theses on the basis of their students' opinions and to refute all objections (LS 31P), but also to elaborate their system, which claimed absolute coherence (Cic., *Fin.* 3.74). The Epicureans, on the other hand, adopted an analogical method of induction from sensations to ground their theses. But all held that the ideal disciple should have no doubts at all about the doctrine and should know how to respond to all the skeptics' refutations, relying especially on "common notions" or "preconceptions": elementary ideas shared by all men and made explicit by philosophers (Epict. *Diss.* 1.22).

Yet some were not convinced that these theoretical efforts were indispensable to attaining the goal of philosophy, the good life. All the Hellenistic schools, except perhaps the Lyceum, recognized the primacy of ethics and of practice. The therapeutic function of doctrines was explicit and primary; works recalled the exemplary lives and the moral precepts of the founders of the schools. Even in Plato's time, however, Diogenes of Sinope questioned the ethical efficacy of the philosophical schools (D.L. 6.24). Following him, the Cynics rejected, throughout all of antiquity, the schools' approach to philosophy (see, for example, Lucian, *Demonax*) in favor of a "short cut to virtue" (D.L. 6.104): an austere and solitary life aiming for self-sufficiency. Their teaching came down to aggressively censuring the habits of those they encountered (Goulet-Cazé, 1990). Some ancient historians of philosophy thus denied to Cynicism the status of a "school of thought" (*hairesis*) (D.L. 6.103). In the schools, however, there were some who were sympathetic to Cynic criticism: the Peripatetic Dicaearchus emphasized that Socrates did not teach in a school setting (Plut. *An seni* 796D) and Epictetus ceaselessly reminded his students of the dangers of school education: syllogisms and the texts of authors were not to be studied to shine intellectually in the school, but rather to know how to live outside of it (Colardeau, 2004).

Succession and orthodoxy

As David Sedley has emphasized, the primary effect of the principle of "succession" is the authority it confers on the thought of the school's founder. The main task of succeeding scholarchs was not to propose new doctrines but to spread, clarify and sometimes to develop the doctrines of the founder (who himself generally claimed to be extending a tradition of thought and not to be "original"). The Stoic Chrysippus gave evidence of his independent spirit when he said to his master "that all he wanted was to be told what the doctrines (*dogmata*) were; he would set out the proofs for himself" (D.L. 7.179, trans. Hicks). Yet this remark also shows that the defense of the school's "dogmas" was not incompatible with important philosophical work: the need to show the truth of all the founder's doctrines, to defend them against the attacks of the school's adversaries, led to many innovations and internal debates in every school. Even among the Pythagoreans, the "acousmatic" disciples, who claimed to adhere, without examining them, solely to those precepts heard from the founder's own lips, were challenged by the "mathematicians," who sought to systematize his scientific and philosophical doctrines. Later, the many debates among the Stoics about the definition of representation or the relations between reason and the passions were simultaneously debates about the theses and texts of Zeno (Sedley, 2003), just as the Epicureans discussed the status of rhetoric, for example, by way of interpreting what Epicurus had said about it (Sedley, 1989).

The doctrine of the school was thus enriched by the contributions of each debate and each scholarch. If that of the Garden claimed always to remain as close as possible to the texts of Epicurus (Erler, 1993), the philosophy of the Stoa was much more open to evolution, while holding inviolable a great many of the principles posited by Zeno. Among Zeno's first disciples, several disputed some of his theses and did not recognize the authority of Cleanthes, his official successor. Chrysippus, the third scholarch, developed from Zeno's teaching a systematic and deepened doctrine, which became almost in its entirety that of the school, without Chrysippus becoming an authority beyond all criticism. In the Academy and the Lyceum the founders had left their disciples greater liberty in research and discussion. It is difficult to extract a systematic doctrine from Plato's dialogues, so much so that his successors felt themselves entitled to drop the theory of Forms and, beginning with Arcesilaus, to argue against the Stoics that man cannot attain to any certain knowledge and that philosophy should not recognize any authority (Cic. *Tusc.* 5.83) (see Lévy, THE NEW ACADEMY AND ITS RIVALS, in this volume). The successors of Aristotle, for their part, extended the spirit of his investigations to areas he did not treat in a complete or satisfactory way, such as botany, and Theophrastus and Strato did not hesitate to question the coherence of the principles of his physics.

From the first century BCE on, we observe attempts to make the authorities of several schools converge. The Stoics Panaetius and Posidonius accord great authority to Plato and to Aristotle, who in this period return to center stage (Frede, 1999). Antiochus of Ascalon broke with the skeptical Academy and claimed to rediscover the original doctrine of the "Old Academy," said to be common to Plato, his immediate successors, Aristotle, and even Zeno, despite the distortion imposed on it by the latter.[11] The case of Antiochus also shows how new philosophers more and more present their own thought as the rediscovery of ancient doctrine (see Zambon, MIDDLE PLATONISM, in this volume). The skeptic Aenesidemus thus claims to revive the philosophy of Pyrrho. Posidonius, for his part, traces certain aspects of Stoic doctrine to Pythagoras, by way of Plato as intermediary. These tendencies toward "archaism" (Boys-Stones, 2001) and "eclecticism" (Dillon and Long, 1988) developed gradually during the Christian era and went hand in hand with the spread of commentary as a method of philosophical reflection: the Neoplatonists in particular appropriated Aristotle as much as Plato and sought, in their rivalry with the Christians, to trace back their own doctrines to very ancient (and sometimes mythical) authors.

Polemics and doxography

We have already indicated the fundamental role of controversies between schools in the formation of their doctrines and methods. The presence in Athens of numerous rival philosophers during almost all of the Hellenistic epoch certainly explains the great philosophical vitality of the period (Cic. *Tusc.* 2.4). The main debate was the one between the naturalism of the Stoa and the skepticism of the New Academy (see Lévy, in this volume). Its intensity resulted partly from the fact that both schools claimed to inherit and develop the thought of Socrates, which nourished many Hellenistic debates: not having delivered any genuine teaching, Socrates could be claimed as an

---

11.   See Sharples, THE PROBLEM OF SOURCES, section titled "The Debate about Happiness," in this volume.

authority by many divergent philosophies (see Decleva Caizzi, in this volume). Only the Epicureans rejected the authority of Socrates and they polemicized as much against the Stoa as against the New Academy.

Apart from their share of logical objections, empirical counterexamples, and historical and mythological arguments, Hellenistic polemics were fought with two original weapons. First, there were personal attacks on the rival philosopher's way of life, justified by the importance of ethics in philosophy; thus, for example, the debates over the life – debauched or simple and generous – of Epicurus, which were supposed to undermine or legitimate his hedonism (D.L. 10.3–11). Then there were accusations of doctrinal plagiarism, which allowed the denunciation of the rival philosophy for a lack of specificity and consistency. Epicurean atomism was thus often attacked as an unrigorous copy of that of Democritus, and Carneades followed by Antiochus tried to show that Stoic ethics, stripped of its artificial terminology, amounted either to the ethics of Aristotle or an ethics of indifference, since according to them no intermediate solution was coherent (Cic. *Fin.* 4–5).

Polemics, which in writing gave rise to numerous works of refutation ("*Against X*"), therefore bore not only on the truth of theses but on their place in the whole of actual and possible doctrines. From this flows the importance granted to doxography, that is, the more or less systematic collection of the different philosophical opinions that had been advanced on each question (Mansfeld, 1999, and in this volume Mejer). Already, Aristotle began his courses with a summary of the opinions of his predecessors, to show how his own resolved their contradictions (Mansion, 1980). In the Hellenistic period, the philosophical use of doxography was often polemical. Chrysippus, for example, proposed a "division" of possible ethical positions showing that the Stoic was the only viable and serious one, while the contemporary "division" by Carneades had opposite aims (Algra, 1997; Lévy, 1999).

The intensity and reflexivity of these Hellenistic polemics stirred up many critiques outside the schools. Philosophers were reproached with being as sure that they possessed the truth as they were unable to reach agreement (Lucian, *Icaromenippus* 5–10), or with founding new schools only to make money by attracting students (Diodorus of Sicily 2.29.6). This confusion of the bewildered student who does not know who to believe is sometimes also found among the philosophers of the Roman period, in the form of a suspicion of polemics, tinged with syncretism or skepticism. Just as Galen will show that epistemological disputes between medical schools went hand in hand with agreement about therapies (*On Sects* 4.7–8), Cicero and Seneca emphasize that disagreements over ethical doctrines often mask a basic agreement about the practical attitudes of the wise man. More radically, the Pyrrhonian skeptics claimed to show that the dissension (*diaphōnia*) among philosophers was irreducible. Using doxography to free himself from dogmatism, Sextus Empiricus thus proposed a systematic refutation of all known doctrines (*Against the Professors*), supposed to show that none is more (or less) plausible than another, so that peace of mind can only be found outside of them and the schools (see Brunschwig, PYRRHONISM, in this volume). But did not this skepticism and its sectaries themselves constitute a new *hairesis* in the dissonant concert of the philosophical schools (D.L. 1.20 and 9.70)? Of course, the Pyrrhonists and their adversaries were not in agreement on this point . . .

426

Bibliography

Works Cited

Algra, K. (1997). "Chrysippus, Carneades, Cicero. The Ethical *divisiones* in Cicero's *Lucullus*." In B. Inwood and J. Mansfeld (eds.), *Assent and Argument. Studies in Cicero's Academic Books* (pp. 107–39). Leiden: Brill.

——, Barnes, J., Mansfeld, J., and Schofield, M. (eds.). (1999). *The Cambridge History of Hellenistic Philosophy*. Cambridge: Cambridge University Press.

Bodéus, R. (1993). *The Political Dimensions of Aristotle's Ethics*. Albany: State University of New York Press. (Original work published 1982.)

Boyancé, P. (1936). *Le culte des muses chez les philosophes grecs*. Paris: de Boccard.

Boys-Stones, G. (2001). *Post-Hellenistic Philosophy*. Oxford: Oxford University Press.

Burkert, W. (1982). "Craft versus Sect: The Problem of Orphics and Pythagoreans." In B. F. Meyer and E. P. Saunders (eds.), *Jewish and Christian Self-definition in the Graeco-Roman World* (pp. 1–22). Philadelphia: Fortress.

Clay, D. (1998). *Paradosis and Survival. Three Chapters in the History of Epicurean Philosophy*. Ann Arbor: University of Michigan Press.

Colardeau, T. (2004). *Étude sur Épictète*. La Versanne: Encre marine. (Original work published 1903.)

De Witt, N. W. (1936). "Organization and Procedure in Epicurean Groups." *Classical Philology*, 31, 205–11.

Détienne, M. (1963). "Des confréries de guerriers à la société pythagoricienne." *Revue de l'histoire des religions*, 163, 127–31.

——. (1996). *The Masters of Truth in Archaic Greece* (trans. J. Lloyd). New York: Zone Books. (Original work published 1967.)

Dillon, J. and Long, A. A. (eds.). (1988). *The Question of "Eclecticism"*. Berkeley: University of California Press.

Dorandi, T. (1999a). "Chronology." In K. Algra et al. (eds.), *The Cambridge History of Hellenistic Philosophy* (pp. 31–54). Cambridge: Cambridge University Press.

——. (1999b). "Organization and Structure of the Philosophical Schools." In K. Algra et al. (eds.), *The Cambridge History of Hellenistic Philosophy* (pp. 55–62). Cambridge: Cambridge University Press.

Erler, M. (1993). "*Philologia medicans*. Wie die Epikureer die Texte ihres Meisters lasen." In W. Kullmann and J. Althoff (eds.), *Vermittlung und Tradierung von Wissen in der griechischen Kultur* (pp. 281–303). Tübingen: Narr.

Erskine, A. (1990). *The Hellenistic Stoa: Political Thought and Action*. London: Duckworth.

Ferrary, J.-L. (1988). *Philhellénisme et impérialisme. Aspects idéologiques de la conquête romaine du monde hellénistique, de la seconde guerre de Macédoine à la guerre contre Mithridate*. Rome: École Française de Rome.

Frede, M. (1999). "Epilogue." In K. Algra et al. (eds.), *The Cambridge History of Hellenistic Philosophy* (pp. 771–97). Cambridge: Cambridge University Press.

Gill, C. (2003). "The School in the Roman Imperial Period." In B. Inwood (ed.), *The Cambridge Companion to the Stoics* (pp. 33–58). Cambridge: Cambridge University Press.

Glucker, J. (1978). *Antiochus and the Late Academy*. Göttingen: Vandenhoeck and Ruprecht.

Goulet-Cazé, M.-O. (1982). "L'arrière-plan scolaire de la *Vie de Plotin*." In L. Brisson, M.-O. Goulet-Cazé, R. Goulet, and D. O'Brien, *Porphyre: Vie de Plotin*, vol. 1 (pp. 229–327). Paris: Vrin.

THOMAS BÉNATOUÏL

——. (1990). "Le cynisme à l'époque impériale." *ANRW* II 36.4, 2720–833.

Hadot, I. (1969). "Épicure et l'enseignement philosophique hellénistique et romain." In Association Guillaume Budé (ed.), *Actes du VIIIe Congrès* (pp. 347–54). Paris: Les Belles Lettres.

——. (1984). *Arts libéraux et philosophie dans la pensée antique.* Paris: Études augustiniennes.

Hadot, P. (1998a). "Théologie, exégèse, révélation, Écriture dans la philosophie grecque." In P. Hadot, *Études de philosophie ancienne* (pp. 27–58). Paris: Les Belles Lettres.

——. (1998b). "Philosophie, dialectique, rhétorique dans l'Antiquité." In P. Hadot, *Études de philosophie ancienne* (pp. 159–93). Paris: Les Belles Lettres.

——. (1998c). "La fin du paganisme." In P. Hadot, *Études de philosophie ancienne* (pp. 341–74). Paris: Les Belles Lettres.

——. (2002). *What is Ancient Philosophy?* (trans. M. Chase). Cambridge, Mass.: Harvard University Press. (Original work published 1995.)

Isnardi Parente, M. (1986). "L'Accademia antica: interpretazioni recenti e problemi di metodo." *Rivista di Filologia e di Istruzione Classica,* 114, 350–78.

Konstan, D., Clay, D., Glad, C., Thom, J., and Ware, J. (eds.). (1998). *Philodemus: On Frank Criticism.* Atlanta: Society of Biblical Literature.

Lévy, C. (1999). "Permanence et mutations d'un projet aristotélicien: la doxographie morale d'Aristote à Varron." *Méthexis,* 12, 35–51.

Lloyd, G. E. R. (1979). *Magic, Reason and Experience.* Cambridge: Cambridge University Press.

Ludlam, I. (2003). "Two Long-running Stoic Myths: A Centralized Orthodox Stoic School and Stoic Scholarchs." *Elenchos,* 24, 33–55.

Lynch, J. P. (1972). *Aristotle's School. A Study of a Greek Educational Institution.* Berkeley: University of California Press.

Mansfeld, J. (1999). "Sources." In K. Algra et al. (eds.), *The Cambridge History of Hellenistic Philosophy* (pp. 3–30). Cambridge: Cambridge University Press.

Mansion, S. (1980). "Le rôle de l'exposé et de la critique des philosophies antérieures chez Aristote." In S. Mansion (ed.), *Aristote et les problèmes de méthode* (pp. 35–56). Louvain: Publications Universitaires de Louvain.

Moraux, P. (1968). "La joute dialectique d'après le huitième livre des *Topiques.*" In G. E. L. Owen (ed.), *Aristotle on Dialectic: The* Topics (pp. 277–311). Oxford: Oxford University Press.

Natali, C. (1991). *Bios theoretikos. La vita di Aristotele e l'organizzazione della sua scuola.* Bologna: Il Mulino.

Rawson E. (1989). "Roman Rulers and the Philosophic Adviser." In J. Barnes and M. Griffin (eds.), *Philosophia Togata I. Essays on Philosophy and Roman Society* (pp. 233–57). Oxford: Clarendon Press.

Sedley, D. (1989). "Philosophical Allegiance in the Greco-Roman World." In J. Barnes and M. Griffin (eds.), *Philosophia Togata I. Essays on Philosophy and Roman Society* (pp. 97–119). Oxford: Clarendon Press.

——. (1997). "Plato's *Auctoritas* and the Rebirth of the Commentary Tradition." In J. Barnes and M. Griffin (eds.), *Philosophia Togata II. Plato and Aristotle at Rome* (pp. 110–29). Oxford: Clarendon Press.

——. (2003). "The School from Zeno to Arius Didymus." In B. Inwood (ed.), *The Cambridge Companion to the Stoics* (pp. 7–32). Cambridge: Cambridge University Press.

Vernant, J.-P. (1982). *The Origins of Greek Thought.* Ithaca: Cornell University Press. (Original work published 1969.)

Wilamowitz-Moellendorf, U. von (1965). *Antigonos von Karystos.* Berlin: Olms. (Original work published in 1881.)

Wolff, F. (2000). "Être disciple d'Épicure." In *L'être, l'homme, le disciple* (pp. 253–88). Paris: Presses Universitaires de France.

Further Reading

See Mejer, ANCIENT PHILOSOPHY AND THE DOXOGRAPHICAL TRADITION, in this volume, "Works Cited" and "Further Reading," for additional references.

André, J.-M. (1987). "Les écoles philosophiques aux deux premiers siècles de l'Empire." *ANRW* II. 36–1, 5–77.

Brunt, P. A. (1975). "Stoicism and the Principate." *Papers of the British School at Rome*, 43, 7–35.

Burkert, W. (1972). *Lore and Science in Ancient Pythagoreanism* (trans. E. L. Minar). Cambridge, Mass.: Harvard University. (Original work published 1962.)

Centrone, B. (2000). "Cosa significa essere pitagorico in età inperiale." In A. Brancacci (ed.), *La filosofia in età imperiale. Le scuole e le tradizione filosofiche* (pp. 137–69). Naples: Bibliopolis.

Cherniss, H. (1945). *The Riddle of the Early Academy.* Berkeley: University of California Press.

Clarke, M. L. (1971). *Higher Education in the Ancient World.* London: Routledge.

Collins, R. (1998). *The Sociology of Philosophies. A Global Theory of Intellectual Change*, Cambridge, Mass.: Harvard University Press.

Daly, L. W. (1950). "Roman Study Abroad." *American Journal of Philology*, 71, 40–58.

Dclorme, J. (1960). *Gymnasion. Études sur les monuments consacrés à l'éducation en Grèce.* Paris: De Boccard.

Donini, P. (1994). "Testi e commenti, manuali e insegnamento: la forma sistematica e i metodi della filosofia in età postellenistica." *ANRW* II. 36–7, 5027–100.

Dorandi, T. (1991a). *Ricerche sulla Cronologia dei Filosofi Ellenistici.* Stuttgart: Teubner.

Gottschalk, H. B. (1987). "Aristotelian Philosophy in the Roman World." *ANRW* II. 36–2, 1079–174.

Habicht C. (1997). *Athens from Alexander to Antony* (trans. D. L. Schneider). Cambridge, Mass.: Harvard University Press. (Original work published 1995.)

Hadot, I. (1970). "Tradition stoïcienne et idées politiques au temps des Gracques." *Revue des études latines*, 48, 133–79.

Manning, C. E. (1994). "School Philosophy and Popular Philosophy in the Roman Empire." *ANRW* II. 36–7, 4995–5026.

Marrou, H.-I. (1982). *A History of Education in Antiquity* (trans. G. Lamb). Madison: University of Wisconsin Press. (Original work published 1948.)

Meyer, B. F. and Saunders, E. P. (1982). *Jewish and Christian Self-Definition.* (vol. 3): *Self-Definition in the Graeco-Roman World.* Philadelphia: Fortress.

Mitsis, P. (2003). "The Institutions of Hellenistic Philosophy." In A. Erskine (ed.), *A Companion to the Hellenistic World* (pp. 464–76). Oxford: Blackwell.

Natali, C. (2000). "Schools and Sites of Learning." In J. Brunschwig and G. E. R. Lloyd (eds.), *Greek Thought: A Guide to Classical Knowledge* (trans. C. Porter). Cambridge, Mass.: Harvard University Press. (Original work published 1996.)

Nock, A. D. (1933). *Conversion. The Old and the New in Religion from Alexander the Great to Augustine of Hippo.* Oxford: Clarendon Press.

Pélékidis, C. (1962). *Histoire de l'éphébie attique des origines à 31 avant Jésus-Christ.* Paris: de Boccard.

Sedley, D. (1976). "Epicurus and his Professional Rivals." *Cahiers de Philologie*, 1, 119–59.

——. (1981). "The End of the Academy. A Review of J. Glucker, *Antiochus and the Late Academy.*" *Phronesis*, 36, 67–75.

——. (2003). "Philodemus and the Decentralisation of Philosophy." *Cronache Ercolanesi*, 33, 31–41.

Snyder, G. (2000). *Teachers and Texts in the Ancient World.* London: Routledge.

22

The Problem of Sources

ROBERT W. SHARPLES

The Extent of the Problem

To a varying extent we are dependent on ancient secondary sources for our know-ledge of all the Hellenistic philosophical schools.[1] The surviving writings of Epicurus are either summaries requiring expansion and elucidation (the *Letters* and still more the *Principal Doctrines*) or fragmentary and in need of reconstruction (the papyrus fragments of his major work *On Nature* preserved among the charred remains of the Epicurean library at Herculaneum buried, and hence preserved, by the eruption of Vesuvius). We have nothing at all of the original writings of the early Stoics, apart from quotations in later ancient sources and a few fragments on papyrus; and there is good reason to suppose that what, with the benefit of hindsight, appears as a distinc-tion between "orthodox" early Stoicism and heretical variants is in fact evidence for competing interpretations of the views of Zeno, the founder of the school, one of which eventually prevailed (with the result that later sources disparage the philosophical merits and interest of the defeated views: cf. Boys-Stones, 1996, esp. pp. 88 and 94). Diogenes Laertius gives us an extensive summary of Stoic doctrines, but one which is of limited usefulness just because it *is* a summary of doctrines; like many other ancient reports of the views of philosophers, it gives us the conclusions of arguments, but not the reasons that led to their adoption (cf. Furley, 1999, p. 433).[2] As for the Academic Sceptics, not only did Carneades himself not commit his doctrines to writing, but our knowledge even of the writings of his followers is at second-hand, and the same phe-nomenon of competing interpretations occurs as in the case of the Stoics, in the rivalry between Clitomachus and Metrodorus (cf. LS, vol. 1, p. 448). And for both Pyrrho himself and neo-Pyrrhonian skepticism before Sextus Empiricus we are dependent in part on secondary sources and in part on the writings of Sextus himself, which by their very extensiveness may dominate our thinking and make us less alert to variations in the earlier thinking of the school – or indeed to variations in Sextus' own thought at different periods of his career (cf. Bett, 1997, pp. xii–xxxii).

In this respect the Hellenistic period is not untypical of all Greek philosophy before the Roman period. From the fourth century BCE the writings of two major figures

---

1. On the schools themselves, see Bénatouïl, PHILOSOPHIC SCHOOLS IN HELLENISITIC AND ROMAN TIMES, in this volume.
2. On Diogenes Laertius as a source and as a biographer, see Mejer, ANCIENT PHILOSOPHY AND THE DOXOGRAPHICAL TRADITION, in this volume.

survive, complete (Plato) or to a substantial though oddly selective extent (Aristotle, whose published works are lost but whose school-treatises survive). But the works of many others from that period and earlier are lost; and that more texts survive from the Roman period (though many do not) is due to the general tendency of new books to drive out old ones – except in the case of old books which are deemed to be classics and preserved by a continuing tradition: and the Stoic and Epicurean traditions were eclipsed in late antiquity by Neoplatonism.

It has been calculated (Runia, 1989, pp. 23, 35–6) that of 316 known philosophers writing in Greek in the period 600 BCE to 600 CE, the works of only Plato, Plotinus, and possibly Marcus Aurelius survive in their entirety, and of the remainder no less than 256 are known to us only through quotations and/or second-hand reports conveyed by other authors. But dependence on secondary evidence lays traps for the unwary; it is the purpose of this chapter to indicate some of these, and to do so with the aid of specific examples. If the reports of one particular writer, Cicero, seem to have particular prominence in what follows, it is because he is both a major source for our knowledge of the philosophy of the Hellenistic period and a skilled writer and advocate; the latter role, as we shall see, complicates our use of him in the former.

Collections of Fragments

Since so much of our evidence is second-hand, those studying Hellenistic philosophy are necessarily dependent on collections of fragments and testimonia (the strict distinction being that fragments are verbatim quotations; but in practice, and given the difficulties of distinguishing between quotation and paraphrase, "fragments" is often loosely used to refer to both). Such collections have their own pitfalls (well pointed out by Mansfeld (1999, p. 27); and see in this volume the chapter by Mejer).

The standard reference collection of evidence for the Stoics is still von Arnim (*SVF*) (1903–24), though this is being replaced by the work of the Utrecht Stoics project (directed by J. Mansfeld), and the general reader will use LS (Long and Sedley, 1987). Von Arnim presents in his first volume the evidence that is linked to specific Stoics before Chrysippus, and then in a second volume and most of a third all that which relates either to Chrysippus himself or, in von Arnim's view, to the early Stoics in general. (The latter part of the third volume contains evidence explicitly connected with Chrysippus' successors). Chrysippus was regarded as having codified the doctrines of the school (D.L. 7.183), and this to some extent justifies von Arnim's arrangement; he does moreover specify in his preface (vol. I, p. v) how he uses different sizes and styles of type to distinguish between (i) verbatim quotations of Chrysippus in later sources, (ii) reports of Chrysippus' views, and (iii) "texts which seemed in some way useful for understanding Chrysippus' teaching." But scholars have not always heeded von Arnim's warning, and have sometimes tended to treat his collection as if all the material in it was Chrysippus' actual words. The problem of determining the status of any given text as evidence for Stoicism is exacerbated by the fact that Stoic terminology became something of a standard philosophical language for later antiquity – carrying with it, to some extent but not altogether, a tendency to see issues in Stoic terms. Nor is the danger confined to that of treating as authentically Stoic texts in class

(iii) which von Arnim did not intend to present as such; the arrangement of his collection invites readers to see Stoic doctrine as less susceptible to change over time than it actually was, and to read later formulations back into the earlier period of the school (see Bobzien 1998a and 1998b, and the following section "The Reporter's Own Agenda").

Other collections of evidence can also have dangers for the unwary. For example, the recent collection of the evidence relating to Aristotle's colleague Theophrastus, the use of whom by Epicurus in particular has been emphasized by Sedley (1998, pp. 166–85), includes all references to him by name in ancient and medieval sources up to 1450 CE (Fortenbaugh et al., 1992; for the methodology see vol. 1, pp. 4–14.). The mere fact of the inclusion of a piece of evidence thus implies no judgment as to its reliability, and readers are expressly directed to the commentary for discussion of these issues. This collection also includes the context of each report in the ancient source from which it comes, in so far as this is relevant to assessing the report; the reports themselves vary between quotation, paraphrase of Theophrastus' own words, and reporting of his views in the reporter's own terms. Clearly, the mere occurrence of particular terms and expressions in reports of the third type says nothing in itself about Theophrastus' own terminology; individual instances need to be examined in detail. It is intrinsically more difficult in the case of references to an author writing in prose to distinguish between an actual report and its context, and to decide whether a report is verbatim quotation (except where this is explicitly indicated in the ancient source) than it is in the case of prose writers quoting from poetical authors.

There are moreover dangers in ignoring the original context of a report. Epiphanius, bishop of Salamis in Cyprus in the fourth century CE, gives a report (*Haer.* III 2.9.35–39 = *On Faith* 9.35–39) of the physical theories of various Peripatetics, concluding with Critolaus, who went with Carneades and the Stoic Diogenes of Babylon on the notorious philosophical embassy to Rome in 156 BCE. There seems good reason to suppose that the report was originally formulated by Critolaus himself, and that the views it attributes to Aristotle are in fact Critolaus' own interpretation of Aristotle's views (cf. Sharples, 2002, pp. 22–3). Wehrli, the editor of the fragments of Critolaus, however argued (1969b, p. 66) that the report is Pythagorean, rather than an accurate report of Critolaus' views, and supports this by Cicero's claim at *Fin.* 5.14 (= fr.11 in Wehrli, 1969b) that Critolaus' views differed from Aristotle's. But the context of *that* passage is ethics rather than physics. Wehrli indeed notes this (1969b, p. 64); but it calls into question the validity of his using it in the way he does to discredit Epiphanius' report. True, it mentions no specific ethical doctrine in connection with Critolaus, unlike the philosophers who precede and follow him in the list. Perhaps then Cicero intended a general comment on Critolaus' doctrines, because he had no specific ethical information to give (though such there was: see pp. 440–1); but the point at least needs arguing.

Sometimes, indeed, the limitations of a collection of fragments may result from the progress of knowledge. The continual process of decipherment of the papyri from Herculaneum, and in particular the re-reading of already edited texts with new technological aids, means that the papyrus texts in the most recent standard collection (Arrighetti, 1973) can no longer always be relied upon. As work on the decipherment and reconstruction of the Herculaneum papyri continues, the writings of the Epicurean

432

Philodemus will become an increasingly important source, and not just for Epicurean-ism. His practice – to a varying extent, indeed, in different works – of summarizing the views of predecessors before criticizing them may make him a particularly valuable source as more information becomes available (cf. Janko, 1995, pp. 87–92; Obbink, 1996, p. 18 and n.3, pp. 81–2, 88, 98–9, 523). Even so, the state of the texts may lead to difficulties in practice in distinguishing between Philodemus' views and those he is reporting from others (Obbink, 1996, p. 282). Epicurus, on the other hand, never quoted from anyone, at least if we may believe D.L. 10.26.

Even when we can be sure that we have correctly identified what in a secondary source reflects the original author whose views are being reported, and what does not, fragmentary evidence can still mislead. As Mansfeld (1999, p. 27) notes, some ancient sources, by identifying a standard set of views associated with a school and then con-centrating on cases where individuals diverged from these, may give an impression that there was more disagreement than was in fact the case. (Cf. also Sharples, 1998, esp. pp. 271–2; and on fragments in general Kidd, 1986, 1998.)

The Reporter's Own Agenda

Even those who set out to write the history of philosophy as such, rather than to develop their own philosophical arguments, can only escape from their own philo-sophical preconceptions with difficulty, if at all. This is not to say that the attempt is not worth making; still less that all interpretations are equally valid. The moral is rather that it is better to be aware of our own presuppositions than to be uncon-sciously at their mercy. For this reason alone all history of philosophy needs to be philosophically informed. But the study of earlier philosophical theories from a purely historical perspective is a relatively recent development (cf. Mansfeld, 1999, p. 16). Even today philosophers who refer to their contemporaries and their recent predeces-sors do so, generally speaking, not with the aim of establishing exactly what those other philosophers think, but as a means to an end, that of developing their own positions and arguments. Their own preoccupations influence what they emphasize in the contributions of other philosophers, and how they interpret those contributions. And in classical antiquity (and in the Middle Ages, both Islamic and Christian) it was the use of predecessors for philosophical purposes, rather than the establishing of an accurate historical record, that was paramount. The tendentiousness of Aristotle's treatment of his predecessors, and above all of Plato, is well known; but the practice certainly did not stop, or start, with Aristotle. Plato's Socrates is infuriatingly ready to regard people as committed to what he sees as the implications of their views, in spite of their protests (e.g., Plato, *Grg.* 466e). The extreme case is when writers themselves invent arguments for a position they oppose, in order to demolish them; this happens now, and it happened in antiquity too. Sometimes indeed it is hard to tell whether an author is reporting or fabricating. (A case in point is the objection to Alexander of Aphrodisias' own account of responsible action attributed by him to his opponents, and then refuted, in his *On Fate* chs. 26ff.; cf. Sharples, 2001a, p. 563 and n.347).

The philosophical writings of Cicero are a primary source for the Hellenistic period. Cicero's philosophical works are for the most part dialogues, in which the supporters

433

of rival views are presented arguing against one another; and there is a direct connection between this form of writing, Cicero's own Academic skepticism, and his practice as an orator and advocate. He explicitly states (*De Or.* 3.80 = LS 68L; cf. *Tusc.* 2.9) that the Peripatetic and Academic practices of arguing respectively for both sides of a question or against all views proposed are helpful as rhetorical training; and an advocate needs to be aware of the arguments on both sides of the case in order to present the most convincing possible case for the side he is representing. As we shall see, Cicero did not leave his courtroom skills behind him when he came to write philosophy; and that is a fact we neglect at our peril. Not that we should go to the other extreme and dismiss Cicero as lacking integrity as a reporter: not only would this be to deprive ourselves of a major source of information, but we should also realize that, in presenting the views of others in the light of his own understanding of the issues, Cicero is simply doing what is natural for those engaged in philosophical debate. Stokes' comment (1995, p. 170) on Cicero's presentation of the Epicurean theory of pleasure in *De Finibus* 1 is pertinent: "Not all, and indeed few critics in antiquity were so careful as Cicero here to distinguish for the attentive reader where they are reporting and where they are conducting dialectical criticism."

Cicero was not indeed the first to use rhetorical devices in philosophical debate (cf. Mansfeld, 2001, pp. 241–2). But in his expert hands they may mislead us all the more effectively. While Cicero certainly used earlier written sources, he did not simply translate them into Latin mechanically, or compile his philosophical works by the mere unreflective concatenation of material from different sources. (For one place where we can see Cicero at work, selecting and rearranging material from his source, see Obbink, 1996, p. 97.)

Even Lucretius, who follows his Epicurean source-texts closely, can alter the force of an original argument, as when he treats the analogy with visible minima as an actual argument for indivisible minimal parts of the atom rather than as, in itself, a clarification of their nature (cf. LS 9A and 9B with LS's comment at vol.1, p. 42). He can also beg a question or anticipate an argument in the interests of effective exposition, for example when at 1.150 he adds to Epicurus' argument that nothing comes from nothing the comment that it does not do so by divine agency, which is not strictly relevant where the claim that nothing comes from nothing is being advanced as part of the proof of the basic atomic theory (cf., Asmis, 1983, p. 57; Classen, 1968, pp. 80–1; Gottschalk, 1996, p. 234). Sedley (1998, pp. 198–9) defends Lucretius on the grounds that to say that nothing comes from nothing is to remove one argument for the need to invoke divine agency for what would otherwise be inexplicable; but it may also be appropriate to say, with Asmis, that Lucretius is influenced by the requirements of exposition rather than by those of logic. Lucretius goes on to argue that the fact that things do not come to be in an arbitrary way shows that they come from definite "seeds" (1.169 = LS 4B). So too does Epicurus at the corresponding point in his own exposition in *Letter to Herodotus* 38. But Lucretius has already indicated at 1.59 that he will use "seeds" as one of his terms for atoms, which Epicurus does not do (Sedley, 1999, pp. 363–4); and if the reader takes the term thus, Lucretius will have introduced a reference to the atomic theory into an early stage of the very argument that is meant to establish it. This is more likely to be deliberate rhetorical design than the result of carelessness (cf., Asmis, 1983, p. 59; Classen, 1968, p. 83); from the outset

Lucretius anticipates features of his theory which he has yet to demonstrate, which is a good technique for instruction and persuasion, but not for logical demonstration. (Indeed Classen (1968, pp. 81–2) argues that Lucretius must be judged by *more* stringent standards than Epicurus because he is seeking to convince a general public rather than writing for those who are already members of the school familiar with Epicurus' doctrines.) But for our present purpose the question whether or not Lucretius' approach is legitimate, and indeed the question whether or not it is deliberate, are beside the point: comparison with surviving texts of Epicurus shows that Lucretius changes the expression of Epicurus' arguments in subtle ways – and if he does so where we can check, he may also do so where we cannot. (Cf. Classen (1968, pp. 80–3) and Sedley (1998, pp. 193–9), and in general for the relation between Lucretius and Epicurus, cf. Sedley, 1998.)

However, the philosophical preoccupations of the reporter may not always be the correct, or complete, explanation for the distinctive character of a report. A major source for the Stoic theory of fate and responsibility has been the treatise *On Fate* by Alexander of Aphrodisias, which does not actually name the Stoics anywhere, and argues against a determinist position which is, in comparison with what we can reconstruct from other sources for the early Stoa, at the least selective both by disregarding some aspects and by giving particular emphasis to others. This has been explained by saying that Alexander is interested in arguing against determinism as a philosophical thesis, rather than against a historical position, and that this is why he does not name its proponents (cf. Sharples, 1983, pp. 19–20); but the view has gained support, particularly in the writings of Susanne Bobzien (1998a, pp. 372–5; 1998b), that the Stoic theory changed and developed over time, and that Alexander is engaged in polemic with a particular form of the theory advanced nearer his own time (c. 200 CE) and in some respects closer to more modern formulations (such as Laplacean determinism) than Chrysippus' own statements had been. It has long been recognized that we risk misinterpretation – at the very least, the introduction of a false emphasis – if we encumber Sophocles in the *Oedipus Tyrannus* with our own philosophical baggage deriving from two millennia of debate about responsibility and divine predestination (Dodds, 1966, p. 42), and that Aristotle's approach to material necessitation is not that of nineteenth-century science (Balme, 1939; 1992, pp. 82–3). It may be that we need to take the same lesson to heart when dealing with the early Stoa as well. But the corollary where Alexander is concerned is that the way in which an author presents the views of his opponents is not always to be explained by his own preoccupations; sometimes it may be due to formulations of those views, by the opponents themselves, which are not otherwise well known to us.

Cicero and Epicurus: The Atomic Swerve

Against the Stoic dilemma that either everything including human action must be predetermined or else some uncaused motion must occur, Carneades argued that human action can be free and yet not uncaused because the cause of the action is in the voluntary motion itself. And by the same token he argued that Epicurus did not need the random swerve of atoms to maintain freedom from determinism (Cic. *Fat.*

21–25 = LS 20E). David Sedley has argued not only that Carneades was right, but also that Epicurus was himself ready to dispense with the swerve. Both claims seem questionable. I have discussed the issue elsewhere (Sharples, 1991, pp. 7–8, 175–7; 1991–3, pp. 178–82), but I mention it again here because to do so will highlight issues in the use of secondary evidence, and of Cicero's evidence in particular. (Cf. also Everson 1999, pp. 554–7; Purinton, 1999, esp. pp. 285–99.)

Sedley finds Carneades' view convincing, and the Epicurean atomic swerve unsatisfactory. However, while there are certainly problems – of which Epicurus himself may or may not have been aware – in reconciling the randomness of the swerve with responsible human action, it is at the very least arguable that in postulating the swerve Epicurus was right, and that in saying it was unnecessary Carneades was wrong. Either all that happens is predetermined, or else events must occur that are to some extent at least independent of their chronological antecedents, and to that extent they must occur with no prior cause. In terms of the atomist picture of continually colliding and rebounding atoms, whose trajectories will be determined by the prior movements of themselves and of the other atoms with which they collide, this must amount to a deviation or swerve of an atom from its previous path. Whether this deviation is caused by some higher agency, for example by a power of the human soul independent of its underlying atomic make-up, is a separate issue, though there are problems in incorporating such a view into Epicurus' atomic theory. What does seem clear is that on the atomic level each swerve must be uncaused, because if it were caused it could on that level be caused only by prior atomic movements, and if it were caused by these it would at least in principle be predictable and the very point of its introduction would be lost.

Cicero, however (*Fat.* 22 = LS 20E2), presents the causelessness of the atomic swerve as something Epicurus is *compelled* unwillingly to accept. This might give the impression that Epicurus himself found the causelessness of the swerve an embarrassment. In fact, however, Cicero's statement is not in itself evidence of anything of the sort. Cicero himself ridicules the claim that the swerve has no cause (*Fat.* 46–48); and when he presents Epicurus as embarrassed by this, he is engaging in court-room rhetoric. What better way to call an opponent's view into question before an audience than to suggest that even he would be happier not to hold it?

Some caution is indeed needed here. Sedley (LS vol. 2, p. 110) has pointed out that there is little evidence that Epicurus did himself assert that the swerve has no cause; the only place where absence of cause is attributed to Epicurus himself is Cic. *Fin.* 1.19. But, first, our sources are limited and tendentious, and, second, we need not indeed suppose that Epicurus made the claim that the swerve has no cause explicitly. The context in which it would be appropriate to do so is in reply to the Stoic claim that to deny determinism is to introduce uncaused motion; and that claim is, it would seem, later than Epicurus' introduction of the atomic swerve, perhaps even a response to it (however, on one ancient text that has been thought to imply this, cf. Boys-Stones, 1996). Epicurus was worried not by Stoic determinism but by the deterministic implications, as he saw them, of Democritus' atomism. My claim is only that the claim that the swerve has no cause reflects what Epicurus hoped it would achieve more accurately, even though in the terms of a subsequent debate, than does the claim that an uncaused swerve is redundant.

436

In arguing thus I am influenced by my own view that human free will requires a radical denial of physical determinism, just as those who find Carneades' position on this particular issue plausible are in effect accepting a position in that debate akin to Richard Taylor's "agent causation" (cf. Taylor, 1967, p. 369). There is nothing surprising in this; it is a consequence of the "principle of charity" that modern interpreters will tend to understand ancient philosophers in ways that they themselves find philosophically plausible. The question is always how far charity should extend. The views of modern interpreters also affect their assessment of ancient criticisms of particular philosophical positions: for example, scholars whose own view of the free-will problem is that responsibility and determinism are compatible have sometimes regarded ancient criticisms of the similar Stoic position as simply misunderstanding or misrepresenting the Stoics' views (Frede, 1982, pp. 276–98; Rist, 1969, pp. 112ff.) – which is true, *from a Stoic viewpoint*. The need for the historian is to be aware that different positions are taken on many issues by philosophers even now, and to use that awareness to arrive at an understanding of the views of both sides in ancient debates.

Sedley further argues that Carneades (as reported by Cicero) suggests that Epicurus would be better off without the atomic swerve, and that since Carneades as a skeptic has no positive views of his own, he must argue entirely on the basis of the beliefs of those he is criticizing (LS vol. 2, p. 110). But while the Academic skeptics certainly argue on the basis of their opponents' principles, this does not mean that *every* principle they appeal to is one that their opponents would accept. For example, Cicero reports the following:

> "[P] If the sage will ever assent to anything, he will sometimes have opinions; but [Q] he will never have opinions; therefore [R] he will not assent to anything." Arcesilaus approved this conclusion, for he endorsed both the first and the second (premise). (Cic. *Acad.* II. (*Lucullus*) 66–77 = LS 69G2)

The Stoics would certainly accept that [Q] the sage will not hold opinions (defined as assent to a proposition of which one does not actually have knowledge); but they would not accept [P]. And the reason for that can be seen by spelling out the implicit reasoning on which [P] is based:

[A] The wise man will sometimes assent.
[B] Certainty is impossible.
[C] To assent to what is uncertain is to have opinion rather than knowledge.
[D] The wise man will sometimes assent to what is uncertain. [from A and B]
[E] The wise man will sometimes have opinions. [from C and D]

The Stoics would accept [A] and [C], but not the implicit premise [B].

It is true that [B] is the basic claim – or, if we are to avoid dogmatism, the basic finding – of skepticism, and so it might be argued that it is a special case and not evidence for a general readiness on the part of Academic Skeptics to introduce into their arguments other premises that their opponents would not accept. But we also know from Cicero (*Fat.* 17–20, 26–28 (= LS 70G), 37–38) that Carneades was prepared to argue against both Epicurus and the Stoics that they were jointly wrong in their shared view that the truth of the prediction of an event is incompatible with that event not being predetermined.

Cicero's tendentious presentation of the view of others is not confined to Epicureanism. He preserves for us a valuable piece of information; the Stoic Chrysippus argued that the predictions of diviners should be formulated not as conditionals ("If someone was born at the rising of the Dogstar, that man will not die at sea") but as negated conjunctions ("not both: someone was born at the rising of the Dogstar, and that man will die at sea": Cic. *Fat.* 15 = LS 38E). Sedley has shown (1982, pp. 253–55) that Chrysippus intended thereby to indicate that the signs that foretold the future were not themselves the direct causes of the future events, but rather were found regularly to be connected with events of that type (cf. Cic. *Div.* 1.118 = LS 42E) – divination being regarded by the Stoics as an empirically based science, however odd this may seem to us. In this respect divination is to be contrasted with sciences such as medicine and geometry which do concern themselves with causes or explanations (though the question whether medicine should involve itself with causal explanations or just with observations was itself debated: cf. Cambiano, 1999, pp. 604–13). But Cicero, even while preserving the basic information, misses the point entirely, mocking Chrysippus for his presumption in telling astrologers how to formulate their propositions, and saying that the doctors and geometricians might as well follow the same advice.

Importing Distinctions: Dicaearchus on the Soul, Plutarch on the Octopus

Cicero's discussion of the atomic swerve shows that we often have to deal with the possible influence of the philosophical views of interpreters at more than one level: for example, those of the ancient reporter and those of the modern scholars interpreting the report. (And the latter will also enter in to any attempt to assess the former.) It also highlights the fact that while we cannot expect an ancient writer to take an explicit position on a question (in this case, that of uncaused events) in terms in which it was not yet formulated when he wrote, neither can we disregard the question in our own assessment of his thought as if it was equally unfamiliar to us. (That is why philosophers are prepared, where historians might not be, to compare synchronically views advanced in widely differing periods. There is an excellent discussion of this issue, though in relation to periods of ancient philosophy before and after that with which we are here concerned, in O'Brien, 1993.)

We are told by some sources that Aristotle's pupil Dicaearchus defined the soul as a harmony of the bodily elements (texts collected in Dicaearchus fr. 12 in Wehrli, 1967; cf. fr. 11); by others that he denied its very existence (texts collected in frr. 7 and 8 Wehrli). Leaving aside the question whether the reference to the bodily elements is a later intrusion into the reports, as suggested by Gottschalk (1971, pp. 186–8), the most plausible explanation of the contradiction seems to be that Dicaearchus' view of the soul was epiphenomenalist, regarding it as something that is produced by and supervenes on the structure of the body, and that the reports claiming that he denied its existence altogether reflect the views of those (notably Platonists) for whom the issue was whether the soul existed in its own right and whether it could do so in

438

separation from the body. The reports, in other words, cannot be assessed independently of the reporters' own starting-points and philosophical agendas. But the case of Dicaearchus may also serve to show the difficulty of establishing the position of an ancient philosopher where a modern distinction is concerned, especially when our knowledge of that philosopher's views is itself at second hand. Caston (1997, pp. 345–6) argues that Dicaearchus' doctrine of the soul is epiphenomenalist, in a sense of that term that distinguishes it from an emergentist view: both imply that the soul supervenes on the bodily structure, but the latter claims, while the former denies, that the soul has causal powers of its own. This however seems in principle difficult to establish. For to do so involves reading into ancient secondary sources (specifically, pseudo-Plutarch, *On Desire and Grief* 5) distinctions of which those sources were probably themselves unaware while formulating their reports; in which case, even if Dicaearchus himself took a clear position on the issue, can we rely on the sources to have transmitted it? (Cf. Sharples, 2001b, pp. 156–9.)

The case of Dicaearchus highlights another problem in using the evidence of Cicero. For while Cicero is one of those who report that Dicaearchus denied the existence of the soul altogether (Dicaearchus fr. 7 and fr. 8c–f in Wehrli, 1967), elsewhere he attributes to him the view that the soul engages in prophecy most effectively when functioning separately from the body in sleep (frr. 15 and 16 Wehrli). It may be possible to find ways to reconcile these two claims (for an exploration of how this might be done see Sharples, 2001b, pp. 165–8); it may also be, as Wehrli (1967, p. 46) suggested, that Cicero has misattributed to Dicaearchus a view actually put forward by Cicero's own contemporary Cratippus. But the important point for present purposes is that Cicero himself shows no interest in reconciling the apparently conflicting claims. He refers to the views of earlier philosophers as and when it suits his argument; he is concerned with the immediate context rather than with the consistency of the historical record. And this is exactly what one would expect both from a writer whose interest is philosophical rather than historical and from a rhetorician whose interest is in the immediate debate. (Cf. Sharples, 2001b, pp. 171–3; and, for another instance where Cicero's concentration on the immediate context may mislead interpreters who regard his philosophical writings as more systematic than they actually are, cf. Sharples, 1995a, p. 271.)

Apparent contradictions in reports by a single ancient source may sometimes be explained by the reporter's imposing distinctions which the thinker being reported would not accept or would not draw in the same way. For example, referring to the octopus' changing color for reasons of camouflage, Plutarch at one point seems to attribute to Theophrastus (fr. 365C in Fortenbaugh et al., 1992) the view that this is a purposeful action on the octopus' part, at another (fr. 365D) the view that it is a mechanical reaction brought about physiologically through fear. But for a Peripatetic like Theophrastus, nature brings about purposeful results through mechanical causes; the two are not opposed, and the further one descends in the hierarchy of living creatures the less of a distinction there will be between them (cf. Sharples 1995b, p. 41).

Sometimes the effect of the philosophical standpoint of an ancient source can be reinforced by that of modern critics. For example, Cicero and Plutarch report that Strato, the third head of Aristotle's school, denied conscious purpose in nature (Strato, frr. 32, 33 and 35, in Wehrli, 1969b). They do indeed go further and say, respectively, that nature for Strato "lacked form" (*figura*) and that Strato made chance prior and nature posterior. But it is still important for us in interpreting these reports to remember that *for Aristotle too* there is no conscious purpose in nature (cf. Furley, 1999, p. 416 n.7; Repici, 1988, pp. 117–56). For some modern interpreters have argued, on the basis of this ancient evidence, that Strato irretrievably damaged the Aristotelian tradition, and brought about its decline, by introducing materialism. But both their reading of Aristotle himself and their judgment of Strato may reflect their own anti-materialistic tendencies – be they Platonizing, Thomistic, or Hegelian.

The Debate About Happiness

Cicero was a pupil of the Academic Philo of Larissa and a fellow-student of Antiochus of Ascalon, who broke with the skeptical Academy and claimed to restore an "old philosophy," dogmatic in character, which was shared by Plato, Aristotle, and the Stoics, though Plato was its purest exponent.[3] Antiochus has been seen by some modern scholars as constructing an artificial synthesis from the ideas of different schools. But in his own historical setting his position does not seem so unreasonable; the two main groups of philosophers active in his time who are excluded from the "old philosophy" are the Academic Skeptics on the one hand and the Epicureans, who identified the good with pleasure, on the other, and it is certainly true that Plato, Aristotle, and the Stoics have it in common that they are not skeptics and that they are not hedonists. Moreover, recent work by David Sedley (1998, pp. 76–7; 2001) has shown that what has previously seemed to be Antiochus' misattribution to the Old Academy of the Stoic theory of two physical principles, God and Matter, may in fact have a sound historical basis, not so much where Plato himself is concerned as for the fourth head of the Academy, Polemo, who was the teacher of the Stoic Zeno. Antiochus may have been a more accurate historian than has been thought.

He was not however setting out to be a historian, except incidentally, but to develop a philosophical position. And his reports need to be read in that light. One issue that preoccupied him was that of the sufficiency of virtue for happiness, a thesis maintained in different ways both by the Stoics and by Antiochus himself.[4] The issue is discussed by Aristotle at length in *Nicomachean Ethics* I.8–10, arriving at a position which is finely nuanced; virtue is not sufficient for happiness but it is sufficient to avoid wretchedness (cf. Annas, 1993, pp. 36–7, 413–18). Antiochus constructed a picture in which Aristotle's successors, rather than Aristotle himself, were responsible for "weakening" virtue. Part of the basis for this was Theophrastus' treatise *On the Happy Life* (Cic. *Acad.* I.33; cf. *Fin.* 5.12). We do not ourselves possess the treatise, and so cannot judge. But it is then rather surprising to find Vitruvius citing Theophrastus on the educated person's contempt for fortune (*On Architecture* 6, prologue §2). We cannot resolve the discrepancy; but it seems at least possible that Antiochus, or Cicero himself, wanted to emphasize a range of competing positions, and that his approach to Theophrastus was at least in part influenced by the desire to find representatives for

3. See Zambon, MIDDLE PLATONISM, in this volume.
4. On this topic, see also Bett, STOIC ETHICS, in this volume.

440

these, with the consequent oversimplification. Such a process is not after all unknown in teaching and writing even today. To take but one example, it has become customary to emphasize the contrast between ancient Greek eudaemonist ethics and Kantian ethics; but this may involve oversimplification on both sides, corrected by several of the contributions in Engstrom and Whiting (1996). Another example may be Galen's contrast between the doctrine of a tripartite soul, attributed by him to both Plato and Posidonius, and the doctrine of a unified soul, which he attributes to Chrysippus (cf. Gill, 1998). Nor is the effect of later philosophical debates on the tradition confined to the creation of over-simplified contrasts; Stephen White (2002, 2004) has shown how the preoccupations of later (and hostile) reporters have led, not only to a failure to appreciate the contributions in ethics of the Peripatetics Hieronymus and Lyco in their own proper historical perspective, but to a failure to realize that they made much of a contribution at all.

The desire to produce clearly contrasted positions may affect not only the reporting of predecessors but the development of doctrine itself. Critolaus claimed that the goal of life was made up of all three of the standard kinds of goods, those of the soul, those of the body, and external goods (Critolaus frr. 19–20 in Wehrli 1969b). This at least does seem to go beyond anything Aristotle indicates, at least in the *Ethics* (*Rh.* I.5, 1360b14ff. is another matter; cf. Rist, 1989, pp. 137–8, a reference I owe to Roger Crisp); Diogenes Laertius 5.30 does attribute such a view to Aristotle, but this simply shows that, on this as on other issues, the report of Aristotle's views in Diogenes is part of the same tradition as Critolaus. (Thus both Diogenes and the report in Epiphanius which may be due to Critolaus – above, p. 432 – attribute to Aristotle the view that divine providence is concerned only with the heavens and not with the terrestrial region.) Cicero's complaint in *Fin.* 5.14 that Critolaus adopted an un-Aristotelian position can, therefore, be seen as having some justification; and we know that Critolaus was attacked in turn by others (Arius Didymus(?) ap. Stob. *Ecl.* 2.7.14 = 2.126,22– 127,2 Wachsmuth. Cf. Annas, 1993, p. 415). It seems likely that here, as elsewhere in his teaching, Critolaus interpreted Aristotle in a way that was intended to distance his views from those of the Stoics and to emphasize their distinctive features (cf. Sharples, forthcoming).

Mistakes and Misrepresentations, Simple and Less Simple

Sometimes, however, straightforward error and misunderstanding are the only plausible explanation. Diogenes Laertius (7.127 = Posidonius F173 EK) reports that while the Stoics in general held that virtue is sufficient for happiness, Panaetius and Posidonius claimed that "health and resources and strength" were also needed. It may be that all they were claiming was that these were needed in order to practice virtue; but even this would be a divergence from the traditional Stoic position, according to which – and in conflict with traditional Greek ideas – even a slave could be virtuous. It may also be, as John Rist has suggested (1969, p. 9), that there is some confusion at work here in the sources between two meanings of the Greek word *chreia*, which may mean either that the virtuous person has *need* of material resources, or just that he will be able to make *use* of them.

However, two other reports go further. Diogenes Laertius 7.103 (= Posidonius F171 EK) claims that Posidonius regarded health and wealth as goods. This seems unlikely in itself, and is made even more doubtful by the fact that Seneca (*Ep.* 87.35 = F170 EK; cf. 87.31) attributes to Posidonius the very same argument for wealth and health not being good (that they can sometimes do harm) that Diogenes attributes to the ortho-dox Stoics with whom he contrasts Posidonius. Some sort of misunderstanding seems to have occurred (cf. on this Edelstein and Kidd, 1988–99, vol. 2, pp. 639–41; Kidd, 1986, pp. 8–9, 24–6). Even more extreme is the report by Epiphanius (*Haer.* III 2.9.46 = *On Faith* 9.46 = F172 EK) that "Posidonius of Apamea said that the greatest good among men was wealth and health." Either this is a further exaggeration of a mis-understanding like that already found in Diogenes; or, conceivably, a comment by Posidonius on the mistaken views of mankind has been presented as a statement of his own view (cf. Edelstein and Kidd, 1988–99, vol. 2, pp. 641–2).

The possibility of textual corruption is always present. To take but one example, Aëtius 2.9.3 reports Posidonius as saying that what is outside the world (i.e., void, empty space) is not infinite but sufficient (*all' hoson*) for it to dissolve into (when it is periodically turned entirely to fire and hence expands). The text of Aëtius has to be reconstructed from later sources (cf. Mansfeld and Runia, 1997), but here those sources agree. However, almost all other sources say that for the Stoics the void was infinite; and for *all' hoson* Kidd (Edelstein and Kidd, 1988–99, vol. 2, pp. 391–4 commentary on Posidonius F97ab EK) therefore suggests reading *kath' hoson*, which would indicate that the space outside the world is not infinite *for that reason*; a finite world does not need infinite space to expand into even when turned to fire, but that does not in itself preclude the void's being infinite.

Sometimes distortions are more subtle. Chrysippus' use of the analogy of a cylinder to explain how predetermined actions can still be our responsibility is recorded both by Cicero, *Fat.* 39–43 (LS 62C) and by Gellius, *NA* 7.2.6–13 (LS 62D). The cylinder and cone roll only if they are pushed; but the fact that they roll, and the way in which they roll, are due to their shape. Similarly our actions are the result of external stimuli, but the way in which we react depends upon our nature. However, while Gellius makes it clear that for Chrysippus our nature is as much predetermined as the external stimulus is, both alike being part of the determinist nexus of causes and effects, in Cicero's account what is emphasized is that external factors contribute to our action but do not determine it, the fact that our nature and the external factors *together* do so being left unclear. Cicero writes as if the fact that external factors do not on their own determine our action, a fact on which both Chrysippus and those who deny determin-ism can agree, were the important one. It has sometimes been thought that this shows the influence of an attempt by Antiochus to minimize the difference between Chrysippus and those who denied determinism; but this is questionable, and the one-sidedness of the account may rather, as Donini (1989, pp. 139–43) has argued, reflect the frag-mentary state of our text of this work of Cicero, the complete version having presented Chrysippus' view in a way that emphasized different aspects at different points in order to emphasize its supposed inconsistency (cf. Sharples, 1991, pp. 20–2, 187–8, 192–4, and references there).

At *On Fate* 39 Cicero writes that "Chrysippus, like a respected arbitrator, seems to have wanted to strike a balance, but in fact inclines rather to those who want the movements of the mind to be free from necessity. However, by the expressions he uses he slips into difficulties such that he unwillingly supports the necessity of fate." Arguably Chrysippus' own words might be a better indication of his real position than what Cicero, from a different and hostile philosophical perspective, suggests he wanted to claim but admits he did not actually say. Chrysippus did indeed hold that, while everything is fated, not everything that is fated is necessary (cf. LS §38). But that is not the distinction Cicero is making in this passage; for just before it he has contrasted two groups, those who claim that fate necessitates everything and those who claim that voluntary mental movements do not involve fate *at all*. It is the position of this latter group that he goes on, in the passage quoted, to suggest – tendentiously, as I suppose – that Chrysippus wanted to adopt but failed to do so. (But the passage is highly controversial; cf. Hankinson, 1999, pp. 530–31.)

The claim that fate is only an initiating cause is also mentioned as a possible interpretation of Chrysippus by Plutarch (*St. rep.* 47, 1056B = LS 55R), who refers to it in order to point out that it conflicts with Chrysippus' general belief in the universality of fate. This treatise of Plutarch is devoted to finding as many ostensible inconsistencies as possible in the writings of the Stoics in general and of Chrysippus in particular; it has the incidental advantage – which was certainly not the one Plutarch envisaged – of preserving for us a considerable number of verbatim quotations of works of Chrysippus whose text is otherwise now lost. Not surprisingly given this aim, Plutarch's interpretations are sometimes tendentious; for example, he claims that Chrysippus' criticism of Aristo of Chios, who claimed that the different virtues are a single virtue in relation to different contexts, is inconsistent with Chrysippus' own endorsement of Zeno's definitions of the virtues as practical wisdom in different contexts. But what Plutarch has failed to note is that for Zeno the content of the practical wisdom will be different in different contexts, so that Zeno's definitions allow for distinctions that Aristo's position does not. (Cf. LS vol. 1, p. 384; Donini, 1999, p. 718; and on Plutarch's treatise in general Boys-Stones, 1997; Kidd, 1998.)

In §37 of the same treatise (= LS 54S) Plutarch reports Chrysippus as considering why misfortunes may occur, even though the universe as a whole is ordered by divine providence, and as asking whether this is because some details are neglected, as happens in a large household, or because they are in the charge of inferior spirits (*daimonia phaula*). Both suggestions, and in particular the second, seem (as Plutarch naturally points out) inconsistent with Chrysippus' general view, and one must ask, with Babut (1969, pp. 261–2) whether Plutarch has reported as a genuine question what was in fact a rhetorical question inviting the answer "no." It may not be irrelevant that earlier in the treatise (§10 = LS 31P) Plutarch criticizes Chrysippus for setting out positions opposed to his own so effectively that he undermined his own case (and also for inconsistency, in doing this while saying that one should express a rival position in a way that emphasizes its inadequacy, *and* for behaving unphilosophically – in proposing to treat rival views unfairly). Plutarch indeed *himself* goes on to liken the "inferior spirits" to evil and maddened governors and generals, thus implying that Chrysippus too intended them to be not just negligent but positively evil; but that is not necessarily the implication of the actual words that he quotes.

However, even in this treatise Plutarch's treatment, or mistreatment, of Chrysippus is not simply arbitrary or purely destructive. George Boys-Stones has argued that

Plutarch's approach reflects his belief that the Stoic position is untenable, and more specifically that in attempting to live their philosophy the Stoics are attempting to put into practice what is contradictory and therefore impossible; they can only live their philosophy by re-interpreting it in a way which would involve discarding their mistaken divergences from the true Platonic tradition (Boys-Stones, 1997, especially p. 47 n.12). One may compare Alexander of Aphrodisias' treatment of his opponents in *On Fate*, both in arguing that their doctrines are and must be in conflict with their actual practice (18 188.17ff., 19 190.15ff.) and in dismissing their interpretations of such concepts as chance and responsibility ("what depends on us") as simply failing to take account of agreed and evident facts (7 172.9ff., 13 181.10ff., 14 182.20ff.). Indeed at one point Alexander accuses his opponents of simultaneously deceiving both themselves and their audience (8 173.22–3).

The nature of the gods according to Epicurus is a topic of current scholarly debate (cf. LS vol. 1, pp. 145–9, and Mansfeld, 1999, pp. 456–7, 472–4). It is uncertain whether Epicurus himself located the gods in our minds, as the product of streams of atomic images flowing there, or whether he left their location unclear. But Obbink (1996, p. 7 n.5) has pointed out that the specific claim that Epicurus' gods are located in the spaces between world-systems (the *intermundia*) occurs nowhere earlier than Cicero, and does not seem to have been present in Cicero's sources; and later references for the most part seem to derive from Cicero. Whether or not Obbink is right in suggesting that Cicero engaged in "willful misinterpretation" of Lucretius' description of the abode of the gods (3.18–25), this provides another example of the way in which an influential author's formulation of someone else's doctrine can itself become canonical. And we may note that it is none other than Cicero himself who provides the evidence that suggests that the gods are in our minds after all (LS 23E7).

Conclusion

The uncertainties inherent in the nature of our sources for Hellenistic philosophy should not lead us to despair of the possibility of interpreting and understanding the views that were put forward in the period and the reasoning behind them. They should rather lead us not to take statements in the ancient secondary sources too readily at face value, and cause us to realize that a closer approximation to certainty is possible on some points than on others. The assessment of the sources, and the study of misrepresentation and misunderstanding and the reasons for them, is also a study that has a peculiar fascination of its own.

Bibliography

Works Cited

Algra, K., Barnes, J., Mansfeld, J., and Schofield, M. (eds.). (1999). *The Cambridge History of Hellenistic Philosophy*. Cambridge: Cambridge University Press.

Annas, J. (1993). *The Morality of Happiness*. New York: Oxford University Press.

von Arnim, H. (ed.). (1903–24). (Cited as *SVF*). *Stoicorum Veterum Fragmenta* [Fragments of the Early Stoics]. (4 vols.). Leipzig: Teubner.

Arrighetti, G. (ed.). (1973). *Epicuro: Opere.* 2nd edn. Turin: Einaudi.

Asmis, E. (1983). "Reason and Rhetoric in Lucretius." *American Journal of Philology,* 104, 36–66.

Babut, D. (1969). *Plutarque et le stoïcisme.* Paris: Presses Universitaires de France.

Balme, D. M. (1939). "Greek Science and Mechanism. I, Aristotle on Nature and Chance." *Classical Quarterly,* 33, 129–38.

———. (1992). *Aristotle: De partibus animalium I and De generatione animalium I.* 2nd edn. Oxford: Clarendon Press.

Bett, R. (1997). *Sextus Empiricus: Against the Ethicists.* Oxford: Clarendon Press.

Bobzien, S. (1998a). *Determinism and Freedom in Stoic Philosophy.* Oxford: Clarendon Press.

———. (1998b). "The Inadvertent Conception and Late Birth of the Free-will Problem." *Phronesis,* 43, 133–75.

———. (2000). "Did Epicurus Discover the Free Will Problem?" *Oxford Studies in Ancient Philosophy,* 19, 287–337.

Boys-Stones, G. R. (1996). "The *epeleustikē dunamis* in Aristo's Psychology of Action." *Phronesis,* 41, 75–94.

———. (1997). "Thyrsus-bearer of the Academy or Enthusiast for Plato? Plutarch's *De Stoicorum repugnantiis.*" In J. Mossman (ed.), *Plutarch and his Intellectual World* (pp. 41–58). London: Duckworth.

Cambiano, G. (1999). "Philosophy, Science and Medicine." In K. Algra et al. (eds.), *The Cambridge History of Hellenistic Philosophy* (pp. 585–613). Cambridge: Cambridge University Press.

Caston, V. (1997). "Epiphenomenalisms: Ancient and Modern." *Philosophical Review,* 106, 309–63.

Classen, C. J. (1968). "Poetry and Rhetoric in Lucretius." *Transactions of the American Philological Association,* 99, 77–118. Repr. in C. J. Classen (ed.), *Probleme der Lukrezforschung* (pp. 331–74). Hildesheim: Olms, 1986.

Dodds, E. R. (1966). "On Misunderstanding the *Oedipus Rex.*" *Greece and Rome,* 13, 37–49.

Donini, P. L. (1989). *Ethos: Aristotele e il determinismo.* Alessandria (Torino): Dell'Orso.

———. (1999). "Stoic Ethics (VIII–XI)." In K. Algra et al. (eds.), *The Cambridge History of Hellenistic Philosophy* (pp. 705–38). Cambridge: Cambridge University Press.

Edelstein, L. and Kidd, I. G. (eds.). (1988–99). (Cited as EK). *Posidonius: The Fragments.* (3 vols.). 2nd edition. Cambridge: Cambridge University Press.

Engstrom, S. and Whiting, J. (eds.). (1996). *Aristotle, Kant and the Stoics: Rethinking Happiness and Duty.* Cambridge: Cambridge University Press.

Everson, S. (1999). "Epicurean Psychology". In K. Algra et al. (eds.), *The Cambridge History of Hellenistic Philosophy* (pp. 542–59). Cambridge: Cambridge University Press.

Fortenbaugh, W. W., Huby, P. M., Sharples, R. W. (Greek and Latin), and Gutas, D. (Arabic) (eds.). (1992). *Theophrastus of Eresus. Sources for his Life, Writings, Thought and Influence.* (2 vols.) Leiden: Brill.

Frede, D. (1982). "The Dramatisation of Determinism: Alexander of Aphrodisias' *De Fato.*" *Phronesis,* 27, 276–98.

Furley, D. J. (1999). "Cosmology." In K. Algra et al. (eds.), *The Cambridge History of Hellenistic Philosophy* (pp. 412–51). Cambridge: Cambridge University Press.

Gill, C. (1998). "Did Galen understand Stoic Thinking on Emotions?" In J. Sihvola and T. Engberg-Pedersen (eds.), *The Emotions in Hellenistic Philosophy* (pp. 113–48). Dordrecht: Kluwer.

Gottschalk, H. B. (1971). "Soul as Harmonia." *Phronesis,* 16, 179–98.

———. (1996). "Philosophical Innovation in Lucretius?" In K. A. Algra, P. W. van der Horst and D. T. Runia (eds.), *Polyhistor* (Festschrift for Jaap Mansfeld) (pp. 231–40). Leiden: Brill.

Hankinson, R. J. (1999). "Determinism and Indeterminism." In K. Algra et al. (eds.), *The Cambridge History of Hellenistic Philosophy* (pp. 513–41). Cambridge: Cambridge University Press.

Janko, R. (1995). "Reconstructing Philodemus' *On Poems*." In D. Obbink (ed.), *Philodemus and Poetry* (pp. 69–96). New York: Oxford University Press.

Kidd, I. G. (1986). "Posidonian Methodology and the Self-sufficiency of Virtue." In H. Flashar and O. Gigon (eds.), *Aspects de la philosophie hellénistique* (pp. 1–28). Vandoeuvres, Geneva: Fondation Hardt.

——. (1996). "What is a Posidonian Fragment?" In G. W. Most (ed.), *Collecting Fragments/ Fragmente sammeln* (pp. 225–36). Göttingen: Vandenhoeck and Ruprecht.

——. (1998). "Plutarch and his Stoic Contradictions." In W. Burkert et al. (eds.), *Fragment-sammlungen philosophische Texte der Antike* (pp. 288–302). Göttingen: Vandenhoeck and Ruprecht.

Long, A. A. and Sedley, D. N. (1987). (Cited as LS). *The Hellenistic Philosophers*. (2 vols.). Cambridge: Cambridge University Press.

Mansfeld, J. (1999). "Sources" and "Theology". In K. Algra et al. (eds.), *The Cambridge History of Hellenistic Philosophy* (pp. 3–30, 452–78). Cambridge: Cambridge University Press.

——. (2001). Review of J. Leonhardt, *Ciceros Kritik der Philosophenschulen*. *Mnemosyne*, 54, 241–2.

Mansfeld, J. and Runia, D. T. (1997). *Aëtiana: The Method and Intellectual Context of a Doxographer* (vol. 1): *The Sources*. Leiden: Brill.

Obbink, D. (ed.). (1996). *Philodemus On Piety, Part 1*. Oxford: Clarendon Press.

O'Brien, D. (1993). "Non-being in Parmenides, Plato and Plotinus: A Prospectus for the Study of Ancient Greek Philosophy." In R. W. Sharples (ed.), *Modern Thinkers and Ancient Thinkers* (pp. 1–26). London: University College London Press.

Purinton, J. S. (1999). "Epicurus on 'Free Volition' and the Atomic Swerve." *Phronesis*, 44, 253–99.

Repici, L. (1988). *La natura e l'anima: saggi su Stratone di Lampsaco*. Turin: Tirrenia.

Rist, J. M. (1969). *Stoic Philosophy*. Cambridge: Cambridge University Press.

——. (1989). *The Mind of Aristotle*. Toronto: University of Toronto Press.

Runia, D. T. (1989). "Aristotle and Theophrastus Conjoined in the Writings of Cicero." In W. W. Fortenbaugh and P. Steinmetz (eds.), *Rutgers University Studies in Classical Humanities* (vol. 4): *Cicero's Knowledge of the Peripatos* (pp. 23–8). New Brunswick: Transaction.

Sedley, D. N. (1982). "On Signs." In J. Barnes, J. Brunschwig, M. Burnyeat, and M. Schofield (eds.), *Science and Speculation* (pp. 239–72). Cambridge: Cambridge University Press / Paris: Editions de la maison des sciences de l'homme.

——. (1998). *Lucretius and the Transformation of Greek Wisdom*. Cambridge: Cambridge University Press.

——. (1999). "Hellenistic Physics and Metaphysics." In K. Algra et al. (eds.), *The Cambridge History of Hellenistic Philosophy* (pp. 355–411). Cambridge: Cambridge University Press.

——. (2001). "The Origins of Stoic God." In D. Frede and A. Laks (eds.), *Traditions of Theology* (pp.41–83). Leiden: Brill.

Sharples, R. W. (ed.). (1983). *Alexander of Aphrodisias On Fate*. London: Duckworth.

——. (ed.). (1991). *Cicero On Fate and Boethius Consolation of Philosophy IV.5–7 and V*. Warminster: Aris and Phillips.

——. (1991–3). "Epicurus, Carneades and the Atomic Swerve." *Bulletin of the Institute of Classical Studies*, 38, 174–90.

——. (1995a). "Causes and Necessary Conditions in the *Topica* and *De Fato*." In J. G. F. Powell (ed.), *Cicero the Philosopher* (pp. 247–71). Oxford: Clarendon Press.

——. (1995b). *Theophrastus of Eresus: Sources for his Life, Writings, Thought and Influence*. (Commentary volume 5): *Sources on Biology*. Leiden: Brill.

——. (1998). "Theophrastus as Philosopher and Aristotelian." In J. M. van Ophuijsen and M. van Raalte (eds.), *Theophrastus: Reappraising the Sources* (pp. 267–80). New Brunswick: Transaction.

——. (2001a). "Schriften und Problemkomplexe Zur Ethik" [Writings and connected Problems on Ethics: in English]. In P. Moraux (ed. J. Wiesner). *Der Aristotelismus bei den Griechen* (vol. 3): *Alexander von Aphrodisias* (pp. 511–616). Berlin: de Gruyter.

——. (2001b). "Dicaearchus on the Soul and on Divination." In W. W. Fortenbaugh and D. C. Mirhady (eds.), *Dicaearchus* (pp. 143–73). New Brunswick: Transaction.

——. (2002). "Aristotelian Theology after Aristotle." In D. Frede and A. Laks (eds.), *Traditions of Theology* (pp.1–40). Leiden: Brill.

——. (forthcoming). "Natural Philosophy in the Peripatos after Strato." In W. W. Fortenbaugh and S. A. White (eds.), *Aristo of Ceos*. New Brunswick: Transaction.

Stokes, M. C. (1995). "Cicero on Epicurean Pleasures." In J. G. F. Powell (ed.), *Cicero the Philosopher* (pp.145–70). Oxford: Clarendon Press.

Taylor, R. (1967). "Determinism." In P. Edwards (ed.), *Encyclopedia of Philosophy* (vol. 2, pp. 359–73). New York: Macmillan.

Wachsmuth, C. and Hense, O. (eds.). (1884–1912). *Stobaeus, Johannes, Anthologium.* (5 vols.). Berlin: Weidmann.

Wehrli, F. (1967). *Die Schule des Aristoteles* (vol. 1): *Dikaiarchos.* 2nd edn. Basel: Schwabe.

——. (1969a). *Die Schule des Aristoteles* (vol. 5): *Straton von Lampsakos.* 2nd edn. Basel: Schwabe.

——. (1969b). *Die Schule des Aristoteles* (vol. 10): *Hieronymos von Rhodos: Kritolaos und seine Schüler.* 2nd edn. Basel: Schwabe.

White, S. A. (2002). "Happiness in the Hellenistic Lyceum". In *Apeiron* suppl. vol. 35, 69–93.

——. (2004). "Lyco and Hieronymus on the Good Life." In W. W. Fortenbaugh and S. A. White (eds.), *Lyco of Troas and Hieronymus of Rhodes: Text, Translation and Discussion* (pp.389–409). New Brunswick: Transaction.

Further Reading

Mansfeld, J. (1998). "Doxographical Studies, Quellenforschung, Tabular Presentation and other forms of Comparativism." In W. Burkert et al. (eds.), *Fragmentsammlungen philosophische Texte der Antike* (pp. 16–40). Göttingen: Vandenhoeck and Ruprecht.

Most, G. W. (ed.). (1997). *Collecting Fragments/Fragmente sammeln.* Göttingen: Vandenhoeck and Ruprecht.

447

23

The New Academy and its Rivals

CARLOS LÉVY

The notion of "skepticism" is a convenient instrument for historians of philosophy, but its use poses real problems. Everyone who has worked a little on ancient philosophy knows that thinking before the Hellenistic period contained elements of skepticism – for example, the Democritean Metrodorus of Chios declared, "none of us knows anything and we do not even know if we know or if we do not know" (DK 68B1) – but that skepticism as a systematic construction awaited the turmoil following Alexander's conquests to manifest itself in two different forms: the Middle and New Academy, on the one hand, and Pyrrhonism on the other.[1] A supplementary paradox: Arcesilaus, who took the initiative in orienting the Platonic school toward skepticism, and Pyrrho himself would have been very surprised if someone had regarded them as "skeptics." No term in this family is to be found in the fragments that have come down to us about the New Academy, and as for Pyrrhonism in its original form, the word *skeptosunē* occurs in only one line (fr. 59 Di Marco) of Timon, Pyrrho's disciple, but most specialists agree that there it bears no technical meaning. Let us add, lastly, that the astonishment of Arcesilaus and the first Pyrrhonists would have turned to genuine anger if someone had told them they represented two different forms of a single current of thought. The notion of skepticism, in the sense we give it, in fact appears only with neo-Pyrrhonism, for which the work of Sextus Empiricus constitutes our most important testimony. It is therefore best not to make too central the concept of skepticism when speaking of the New Academy. The majority of recent studies of the latter have interpreted its struggle against Stoicism, the chief target of its attacks, as a confrontation between skepticism and dogmatism, and it is true that this aspect predominates in the testimonies that have come down to us. But, in attacking Stoic epistemology, they aimed not just to refute that theory of knowledge, but to bring down the whole system. Now, this system was defined above all by the idea that the *logos* is manifest in the

---

1. Sextus Empiricus, *PH* 1.220, says that for the most part three Academies were distinguished – the Old (that of Plato and his immediate successors), the Middle (that of Arcesilaus), and the New (that of Carneades) – and that some added a fourth (that of Philo of Larissa) and even a fifth (that of Antiochus of Ascalon). In practice the expression "New Academy" is often currently used to designate the period from Arcesilaus to Philo of Larissa. Glucker (1978) has shown that Sextus's distinctions have no institutional validity and that the Academy as an institution disappeared after Philo of Larissa. For developments in Platonism after the Hellenistic Period, from the first century BCE to the third century CE, see Zambon, MIDDLE PLATONISM, in this volume.

world and that no rationality exists anywhere but in the eternally repeated cycles of cosmic history, which was ontologically unacceptable to philosophers of the Platonic tradition. We shall therefore ask, throughout this chapter, to what extent logic was merely the battlefield on which the dialecticians of the Academy sought victory in a conflict of an ontological nature.

As scholarch of the Academy, Arcesilaus was heir to a philosophical tradition of great richness. Not even to mention the various sects that appealed to the authority of Socrates, to the variety of the Platonic works themselves were added the (very dogmatic) interpretations that were given to them by the Old Academy, which seems to have tried to shield Platonism from Aristotelian critiques by developing new concepts, such as that of the Ideal Numbers. We have no testimony that explicitly tells us that Arcesilaus tried to revolt against any elements in this tradition. Diogenes Laertius says that Arcesilaus admired Plato and owned his books. When he abandoned the school of Theophrastus for the Academy of Crates and Polemo, he compared his new teachers "to gods or to survivors from the Race of Gold" (D.L. 4.22). The reason he gave for this is interesting: he approved of the fact that the philosophers of the Academy held the mob in contempt and worried very little about the vulgarization of their teaching.

> They were not eager for public favor, but were like the flute player Dionysodorus, who was said to have boasted one day that no one had heard his tunes, as those of Ismenias were heard, on shipboard or at a fountain. (D.L. 4.22)

Arcesilaus thus drew from his Platonist teachers the idea that philosophy should have an aristocratic character, and from this perspective he could only see the new systems that appeared in the Hellenistic period as concessions to the mob: didn't they promise those who followed their precepts that they would attain truth and absolute happiness and thus to transform them into the equals of gods? One possible interpretation of the new orientation he gave to the Platonic school is that he saw in universal doubt at once the means to combat the philosophical tendencies he condemned and to perpetuate the intellectual strictness he had admired in his teachers. In spite of a few ancient testimonies to which we shall return, almost no one believes that his skepticism was a front concealing a dogmatic Platonism that he communicated to a few disciples. His skeptical interpretation of Plato certainly rested on the aporetic character of some dialogues, but also on all the formulations through which Plato, even in dialogues that have nothing aporetic about them, expressed how difficult it is for a mere mortal to approach the truth. Like Socrates, Arcesilaus wrote no philosophical works, and like him practiced refutation, the *elenchos*; but unlike Socrates he asserted that he had absolutely no certainties, not even the famous "I know that I know nothing." He thus proposed to surpass Plato in skepticism, which he justified through the idea that there was nothing dogmatic in Plato, or at any rate nothing similar to the dogmatism of the Stoics or Epicureans.

It would be too simple to imagine that for Arcesilaus and his successors there was on the one hand the relation to Plato and on the other the refutation of the philosophical systems arising in the Hellenistic period. Even if the evidence is scarce, it seems much likelier that his interpretation of Plato had its proximate cause in a philosophical environment of which certain elements (the rejection of all transcendence, and absolute dogmatism conceived of as a correlate of immanence) were by nature shocking to a thinker in the Platonic tradition and that, on the contrary, his criticism of the new doctrines was rooted in Platonic notions such as the imperative to investigate and the dialectical relation to the beliefs of others. But it is necessary to take into account another aspect, a historical and cultural one. Despite their very elementary structures, which has been well shown by J. Glucker (1978), the philosophical schools were institutions and, as such, the phenomena of rivalry, of struggle for a power that was no less important for being intellectual, were no strangers to them. The Academy, the oldest, the most prestigious of the schools, also the most specifically Athenian, could only be hostile to the Stoa, founded by a retired Phoenician importer of purple-dyed material, and to the Garden, which it saw as a late recrudescence of Democritus, just as it could only despise Pyrrho, the obscure painter from Elis turned philosopher of appearances. It is these relations, highly conflictual for reasons both philosophical and non-philosophical, that we propose to examine here.

The Academy and Pyrrhonism

Our use of the term "skeptic" to describe both the New Academy and Pyrrhonism obviously encourages a search for ties between the two streams of thought, and there are still today seekers who will not resign themselves to admitting that they are two entirely heterogeneous currents. The problem is not new, since in the catalog of Plutarch's treatises is the title of a work he devoted to the differences between the Academics and the Pyrrhonists, which has not come down to us. Similarly, Aulus Gellius (*NA* 11.5.6–8) wrote that "it is an old question and one treated by many Greek authors whether, and in what measure, the Pyrrhonists and the Academics differ from one another." The testimonies on which we can rely in order to assemble the elements of an answer to this question are scarce and hard to interpret. From the Academic side, Pyrrho is present only in the philosophical works of Cicero, where he is never cited as a skeptic. We find him many times over in the principal ethical doxographies alongside the dissident Stoics Herillus and Ariston, the three being regarded as the representatives of an ethic of absolute indifference. It is also made clear that their doctrines quickly fell into desuetude. These Ciceronian passages seem to us to include two elements that should be carefully distinguished: the idea of associating Pyrrho with these two dissidents may have been the work of people who used this regrouping as a polemical tool; the perception of Pyrrho as a moralist perfectly indifferent to everything that was not the absolute good – or at any rate was not what he regarded as such – was in itself not at all absurd. Like other Hellenistic philosophers, Pyrrho sought perfect internal serenity; he was simply the one who went the furthest in this direction, since he aimed "to slough off the man" (fr. 15a Decleva Caizzi), that is, to destroy not only opinions but even sensations, thinking thus to arrive at a state of insensibility, of apathy. What is surprising in the Ciceronian testimony is not so much his mention of Pyrrho as a moralist as his complete silence on the epistemological aspects of Pyrrhonist thought. To this, a certain interpretive current replies that Cicero's silence is not unjustified since Pyrrhonism did not originally include epistemology.

450

We cannot fully enter into this debate, but all the same it may be remarked that when the New Academy wished to justify its orientation, it spun out long genealogies including thinkers very distant from skepticism in the narrow sense of the term. Even if the ethical component of Pyrrhonism seemed more important to the Academics than the later epistemological aspects, the fact that they never mention Pyrrho except as an indifferentist does not necessarily reflect purely philosophical motives. That is all the more true since Arcesilaus and his successors could not ignore that they were explicitly accused of plagiarizing Pyrrho. The most famous testimony we have regarding this accusation is the line by the dissident Stoic Aristo, the same who found himself alongside Pyrrho in the Academic doxographies, and who wrote, parodying the Homeric description of the Chimera: "Plato before, Pyrrho behind, in the middle Diodorus" (frr. 32–35 Decleva Caizzi), which amounted to describing the thought of Arcesilaus as a monstrous assemblage of Platonism, Pyrrhonism, and Megarian dialectic. Sextus (*PH* 1.234) cites this line to prove that some accused Arcesilaus of practicing an esoteric dogmatism, transmitting the Platonic "dogmas" only to his most gifted disciples, but this interpretation is completely illogical. In fact, if the line is understood as expressing an opposition between the apparent teaching of Arcesilaus and the reality of his thought, it would have to be admitted that the esoteric doctrine was Pyrrhonism, not Platonism. What Ariston really meant to say was that Arcesilaus's doctrine had no originality, but was rather a jumble of elements borrowed from philosophers as different as they could possibly be. The idea that Arcesilaus "borrowed" at least a part of his doctrine was clearly current among the Pyrrhonists themselves. Like many other philosophers, Arcesilaus was accused by Timon both of vanity and of seeking the approval of the mob, a particularly serious accusation for an Academic, but, more specifically, he was reproached with having pilfered from Pyrrho. Such is the meaning of two lines (frr. 31–32 Di Marco) whose details give rise to divergent interpretations, but whose general sense is clear: like Ariston, Timon underlined the heteroclite character of Arcesilaus's thought and, in these two lines, highlighted by means of an epic parody the Pyrrhonist and Megarian components he claimed to coexist in the Academic's teaching.

The absence, after Timon, of strong personalities able to take control of the Pyrrhonist tradition allowed the Academy to reinforce its strategy of keeping quiet about the conflict that had brought it into opposition with Pyrrho's disciple, and of confining Pyrrhonism to the category of indifferentist doctrines, vanished ones to boot. Cicero is the most striking witness of this neo-Academic conviction that the Pyrrhonist problem no longer existed. What is paradoxical about the texts in which he expresses this is that, at just about the same moment, and apparently without Cicero's knowledge, Pyrrhonism was being reborn at the initiative of Aenesidemus, very probably a former disciple of the Academy. The latter, disappointed in the skepticism, too lax in his view, of the neo-Academics, undertook to revive skeptical thought by laying claim to Pyrrho. In fact, as far as we can tell on the basis of the scarce evidence we have, the neo-Pyrrhonism of Aenesidemus owed much more to neo-Academic skepticism than to original Pyrrhonism, but referring to Pyrrho above all allowed him, in a fashion that may be thought somewhat fantastical, to make room for skeptical radicalism. By choosing Pyrrho, but also Heraclitus, as emblems for his renovation of skepticism – the first ignored by the New Academy for the reasons we have given, the second regarded by the Stoics as their forebear – Aenesidemus constructed a pedigree for skepticism that owed nothing to that of the neo-Academics.[2] A trace of these ambiguities is to be found in the way Sextus Empiricus locates neo-Pyrrhonism in relation to the New Academy in *Outlines of Pyrrhonism* (1.220–235). He first firmly distinguishes the neo-Academics from the true skeptics, who for him can only be the Pyrrhonists, before affirming that Arcesilaus seems to him to have "entirely shared the doctrines of the Pyrrhonists." This attitude, from Sextus's point of view, was doubly advantageous: on the one hand, it reasserted the idea that Arcesilaus drew his inspiration from Pyrrho, all the while insinuating that the Academic had perhaps practiced a dogmatic Platonism behind a façade of skepticism; on the other, it introduced a rupture into the history of the New Academy between Arcesilaus, who was perhaps an authentic skeptic, and his successors, accused of being not skeptics but probabilists.

The New Academy and Epicureanism

A great fancier of luxury and pleasure, Arcesilaus, as an individual, was compared to a second Aristippus by Diogenes Laertius (4.40). Nonetheless, from a philosophical viewpoint Arcesilaus could not feel, either as a Platonist or as a skeptic, the slightest sympathy for the Epicurean system, which must have looked to him like a mixture of Democritean physics and Cyrenaic hedonism. This contempt for Epicurus on the part of the founder of the skeptical Academy shows through in an anecdote recounted by Diogenes Laertius. Arcesilaus, asked why people left other schools for that of Epicurus but never that of Epicurus for another, replied (D.L. 4.43): "If one is a man, one can become a eunuch, but if one is a eunuch, one cannot become a man." The philosophical distance between the Academy and the Garden was too great for their relations to have the complicated character of those between the Academics and the Stoics. The Academics could reckon that the Stoic system contained corrupted elements of Platonism; in the Epicurean they rediscovered everything that the Platonic tradition had always combated. Neo-Academic criticism of Epicureanism was organized around two sometimes contradictory axes. On the one hand, it was emphasized that Epicurus had contributed nothing new, while on the other he was vigorously condemned for having introduced particularly absurd and immoral ideas. As for the Epicureans, despite the contempt they affected for the other schools, they took a close interest, at least in the first century CE, in the history of the Academy, as is proved by the existence of a work by Philodemus devoted to the different scholarchs of the Academy (Dorandi, 1997).

In the realm of physics, our principal source for reconstructing the Academic–Epicurean confrontation is the first book of Cicero's *De Natura Deorum*. It contains the classic accusation of plagiarism: "What is there in the physics of Epicurus," asks the Academic Cotta, "that does not come from Democritus?" (*ND* 1.73). Further on it is said (1.120), more figuratively, that Epicurus diverted the Democritean source to water his own garden. At the most, Cicero grants that the doctrine of the *clinamen*

---

2. For further discussion, see Brunschwig, PYRRHONISM, in this volume.

(swerve) is not a borrowing from Democritus.[3] As far as concerns the Epicurean position on the gods, the Academic refutation centered on two complaints: absurdity and hypocrisy. The Epicureans assert an absurdity when they say that the gods are made of a "quasi-matter" and that they have human form, and they are accused of developing such a theology not from conviction but from cowardice, to avoid the accusation of atheism. To this was added a more specifically philosophical complaint: how can one assert both that the gods do not care about men and that it is necessary to feel piety toward them?

The methods we find applied in Book 2 of *De Finibus* are not fundamentally different. There too all originality is denied to Epicureanism, though in a more sophisticated way. In effect, the Academic Cicero traps the Epicureans in a dilemma. If they give the word "pleasure" its usual meaning, their thought is in no way different from that of the Cyrenaics, that is, it is a defense of all pleasures. By contrast, if by "pleasure" they mean the absence of suffering, their thought differs in no way from that of Hieronymus, who thus defined the supreme good. What the Academic pretends not to know is that Epicurean ethics is precisely all about the transition from kinetic pleasure, that immediate satisfaction of the senses that, according to Epicurus, is sought since birth, to catastematic pleasure, that perfect serenity attained through the wise calculation of pleasures. While the conception of pleasure in Epicureanism is fundamentally dynamic, the Academic demands from the Epicureans a definition in the Platonic tradition, based on the principle of division. Since they are neither willing nor able to accede to this demand, they are accused of practicing a philosophy that seeks to please the greatest number and which to do so renounces all intellectual strictness. For example, Plutarch (*Non posse suaviter vivi secundum Epicurum*, 1093D) reproaches the Epicureans with artificially banishing all intellectual pleasures, those provided by the reading of works of history, by mathematics, or again by music. In the same way, Epicureanism's effort to preserve the four traditional virtues by giving them a new conceptual foundation, since it bases them not on transcendent realities but on pleasure and utility, is made ridiculous by the Academic refusal to see Epicurean pleasure as anything but the immediate satisfaction of the senses. Just as Epicurus was accused of having developed a theology only to avoid the deserved reproach of atheism, so he is accused of having preserved only the name of virtue for fear of being charged with immorality. Finally, in the Roman, as in the Greek, context, the enemies of Epicureanism condemned its claim to found communities isolated from the world, and in particular from politics.

The Epicurean theory of knowledge, the canonic, gave occasion for fewer criticisms, probably because the Academics were too absorbed in refuting Stoic ideas in this area. In a general way, it may be said that this canon was assimilated to an absurd confidence in sensation. The example constantly given is that of the sun. Epicurus, convinced of the truthfulness of sensations, asserted in effect that the size of the sun is the size our eyes perceive it to be. This was constantly used by their adversaries in the Academy as the proof that Epicureanism was unable to understand anything at all about science. In addition, the Academics used the Epicurean canon as a dialectical

---

3. On Cicero as a source for Epicurean views on this topic, see Sharples, THE PROBLEM OF SOURCES, the section entitled "Cicero and Epicurus: The Atomic Swerve," in this volume.

weapon in their criticism of the Stoic theory of knowledge. Why, they asked the Stoics, don't you do the same as the Epicureans, who by asserting that all sensations are true show themselves to be more consistent than you, since your theory of representation states that most representations are true, without being able to define precisely what distinguishes false ones? On the question of knowledge, our evidence about the Academic criticism of Epicureanism is scarce, while in the opposite direction Lucretius, in Book 4 of *De Rerum Natura*, lets us see the care with which the Epicureans refuted skeptical arguments. Thus, regarding the argument, so frequently used by the Skeptics, about the square tower that from afar looks round, Lucretius explains (Lucr. 4.353–360) that the great mass of air occupying such an interval makes the angles become obtuse, then disappear. The atoms thus arrive at our eyes in a different position from the one they originally had.[4] But the work that best allows us to imagine the arguments and methods used by the Epicureans against the Academics is Plutarch's *Against Colotes*. Colotes of Lampsachus was one of the first disciples of Epicurus. He wrote a work in which he claimed to show that the doctrines of other philosophers had the effect of making life impossible. Arcesilaus was Colotes' favorite target, both as a skeptic and as representing a Platonic tradition Colotes could only condemn. Against Arcesilaus Colotes used the argument most often employed against Skeptics, that of *apraxia*, that is, the accusation of making action impossible by refusing to admit that we have certain knowledge that can guide us in our lives. But he also attacked the attempt at historical legitimation through which Arcesilaus wanted to show that, long before him, very illustrious philosophers, many pre-Socratics among them, had questioned the possibility of attaining to certain knowledge. There had thus been, since the beginnings of Epicureanism, a real will to mount a very fierce battle against the New Academy. If this aggressiveness did not elicit from the Academics as great a reaction as might have been expected, it is because the New Academy principally concentrated its efforts against Stoicism, regarding Epicureanism as an intellectually less developed and less interesting doctrine than Stoicism.

The New Academy and Stoicism

Carneades, who was after Arcesilaus the most brilliant representative of the skeptical Academy, was in the habit of saying, "If Chrysippus had not existed, I would not exist" (D.L. 4.62), thus parodying the line expressing the importance of Chrysippus in the history of the Stoa, "If Chrysippus had not existed, the Stoa would not exist" (D.L. 7.183). Carneades therefore did not hesitate to recognize the extreme importance of the anti-Stoic dialectic in his own thought. This dialectic has been at the center of the study of the New Academy since the two founding articles by P. Couissin, which were published in 1929 and whose importance to research is now much greater than at the time of their publication. The very existence of this dialectical relationship, so strong and so long-lasting, raises a certain number of questions.

Why was Stoicism the favored target of the New Academy? To understand this, we must take into account a set of both historical and philosophical reasons. Unlike the

4. See further, Morel, EPICUREANISM, the section entitled "The Criteria of Truth," in this volume.

Epicureans, who could seem to philosophers of the Platonic tradition like a resurgence of an old enemy, Democritus, Stoicism was rooted twice over in the Socratic-Platonic tradition. As a student of the Cynic Crates, Zeno of Citium belonged to one of the most powerful and original Socratic currents. As a student of Xenocrates and Polemo, he was a product of the Academy by the same right as Arcesilaus – whence the disputation, so prominent in neo-Academic dialectic, of the very identity of the Stoa. From the perspective of the neo-Academics, Zeno's decision to create a new school could only be a mark of vanity, if the Stoic teaching was of Socratic-Platonic inspiration, or a betrayal, if it constituted a break with that tradition. The Academy had already experienced a somewhat similar situation with the creation of Aristotle's Lyceum, but the growth of Stoicism took place precisely against the background of the Lyceum's decadence after Theophrastus. Athens, which had erred so often in the past, immediately recognized Zeno as a great philosopher, bestowing important honors on him. The king of Macedonia, Antigonus Gonatas, came to hear him in Athens and asked him to teach at home, promising to make him the preceptor of the whole Macedonian people. Such a situation could only exacerbate Academic concern about Stoic dogmas.

The dialectic practiced by the New Academy has been interpreted, roughly speaking, in two different ways. For Couissin and his successors it consisted in taking a Stoic thesis P and drawing from it a conclusion Q_2 entirely different from Q_1, the conclusion that the Stoics had drawn from it. From such a perspective, the Academic contributes no new proposition, no original concept; he only corrects the statements of his adversary and amends the sense of the notions the latter uses, and he defends Q_2 as a probable proposition. The Stoic, for his part, finds himself in a theoretical dilemma whose alternatives are equally unacceptable to him: either to abandon P or to adopt Q_2. The second interpretation, defended especially by A. M. Ioppolo (1986), lays much greater stress on the contribution of the Academic, who combats Stoicism not just by correcting the logical movement but by opposing Stoic concepts with specifically Academic ones derived from the Platonic tradition. Despite their obvious differences, these two interpretations have at least one point in common: they raise the question of the existence of certain convictions in neo-Academic thought. Couissin primarily insisted on the destructive work carried out by the New Academy in the interior of the Stoic system, but it is clear from reading the testimony of Cicero and Sextus Empiricus that the fundamental concepts of the neo-Academics, such as that of suspension of judgment and that of probability, were not simply results of Stoic subversion. They expressed the Academy's own convictions. In the other direction, those who have justly pointed out that many of the notions used by the New Academy existed well before the emergence of Stoicism, particularly in Plato and Aristotle, have neglected the fact that the emergence of Stoicism did have important semantic consequences. This school in fact succeeded more than any other in widely imposing not just its neologisms but also its new uses of old terms.

Trying to define the general thrust of the dialectic, one can conclude that what the New Academy most criticized in Stoic thought was the claim to be able to pass, within the world and without a genuine break, from the immediate deliverances of the senses to the highest intellectual realities, those that in Plato cannot be understood without reference to the Forms. The New Academy never explicitly used Platonic themes in its criticism of Stoicism, and yet it draws on a Platonic inspiration to the extent that it

455

always expressed a distrust not just of the senses but also of a reason that claimed to be able to attain to truth by working exclusively on the deliverances of the senses. The Stoic sage does not contemplate transcendent realities, but rather is simply the man in whom the transition from sensation to perfect reason has taken place. This itinerary, exceptional but in no way utopian, makes him the equal of the gods.

As far as the theory of knowledge is concerned, Academic criticism principally bore on the concept of "cataleptic" representation. By this term the Stoics indicated that most of the time nature does not deceive us, that it gives us in sensation faithful images of reality. Lucullus, who defends the Stoic theory of knowledge in Cicero's *Academica*, expresses this (*Acad.* II.19) very precisely: "There is, he said, very great truth in the senses, as long as they are sound and healthy and everything that impedes them and prevents them from acting is kept away from them." "Cataleptic" representations constitute the vast majority of those perceived by an individual in good health. They are, say the Stoics, intrinsic signs of manifest truth, in virtue of which they cannot be confused with those that characterize dreams, intoxication, or madness. Every "cataleptic" representation presents three characteristics: (a) it comes from a real object; (b) it is a faithful image of this object; and (c) it is such that it could not come from an object that did not exist or was not the one from which it came. Because they have this character of manifestness, "cataleptic" representations almost irresistibly elicit assent, which yet remains under our control and constitutes the instrument of our freedom. For the neo-Academics, the idea that most of our representations are images of the real, and that our senses thus deceive us only very exceptionally, is unacceptable. They also brought the full force of their dialectic to bear on clause (c), the one asserting infallibility. They worked strenuously to show, using every example of sensory error, that there is not a single representation of which one can assert with absolute certainty that it corresponds to a real object from which it seems to come. According to them, one must, with respect to any representation, however manifest and certain it may seem, practice *epochē*, that is, suspend one's judgment. The Stoics retorted that such an attitude condemns us to inaction, since all our actions, from the simplest to the most complex, are implicitly based on the idea that we live in a very real world and that the senses do not deceive us. They emphasized that the sensory errors invoked by the neo-Academics take place in exceptional states in which the subject's reason is disturbed by sleep, intoxication, or madness. To this argument from inaction, already used by the Epicureans, Arcesilaus and his successors replied that their dialectic took aim at the character of certainty that the Stoics attributed to representation and not at representation itself. In other words, they accepted as "probable," "plausible," (*eulogon* for Arcesilaus, *pithanon* for Carneades) the representations that the Stoics called "cataleptic," and they thought to make action possible on the basis of this notion of probability. Yet the confrontation between the Stoa and the New Academy was not confined to the interpretation of sensory representations. The Stoics held that "cataleptic" representations are the foundation on which an individual's entire intellect is built, and that their truth is the necessary condition for the elaboration from them of concepts and techniques as well as for the functioning of memory. Still more, "cataleptic" representation is the immediate model for what ought to be the relation to nature: the sage is he who adheres to reason with the same facility, the same confidence, with which the common run of mortals adheres to sensation.

Contrariwise, in the thinking of the New Academy the sage is one who, faced with any ethical or intellectual problem, is able to suspend judgment, as he does with regard to any sensory representation at all. One may say that the Academic sage is characterized by the critical distance he establishes between himself and the world, and the Stoic sage by the will to adhere to the order of a world that, for him, is perfectly rational. For the Stoics as for the neo-Academics, wisdom is the polar opposite of opinion, but for the former the best weapon against *doxa* is to understand and accept the world; for the latter it is to distrust it.

Things are not fundamentally different with regard to ethics. For the Stoics, nature in a way confers a birthright on every living creature, whether an animal or a human being, in furnishing it with *oikeiōsis*, that is, the *élan vital* that makes it strive, from birth, to persist in its own existence, to seek what is good for its nature and to flee from what is harmful to it. At the beginning, the human being, who does not become a rational being until the age of seven, is not fundamentally different from the animals, but as he grows up he perceives – or at any rate he should perceive – that the things he spontaneously sought out as good, those that in Latin are called *prima naturae*, have no absolute value but are indifferent in comparison with the only true good, knowledge of moral beauty. As a very simple example, for the Stoics life as a biological phenomenon has at best a relative value; it is a positive indifferent, a "preferable." It is better, as a general rule, to be alive than to be dead, but the short life of a virtuous being is preferable, from the ethical viewpoint, to the long life of a tyrant, which shows that life in itself cannot be regarded as a genuine good. In all this, said the neo-Academics, there was nothing but incoherence and hypocrisy. What shocked the philosophers of the Platonic tradition was, above all, the Stoic claim to base human ethics on a vital impulse common to man and animal. Just as they deconstructed the Epicurean system by calling upon the Epicureans to choose between the absence of suffering and sensual pleasure, they claimed that the Stoics could not at the same time affirm that man seeks certain objects that he regards as natural goods and claim that the latter have no value with respect to ethics. For the New Academy, in their hearts the Stoics recognized other goods besides virtue, but unlike the Peripatetics they did not have the courage to admit it. Other aspects of Stoic doctrine attracted the derision of the neo-Academics. They regarded the moral radicalism that led the Stoics to assert that all moral faults are equally grave as an absurdity. Cicero, in *Pro Murena* (61), exploits it for a slightly cheap rhetorical effect by saying that for a Stoic "the crime of killing a rooster without need is as great as strangling one's grandfather." Similarly, they mocked the Cynical aspects of Zeno's *Republic*, a work written in a spirit of anti-Platonic polemic, in which the founder of Stoicism rejected commonly accepted social rules. Finally, they disputed that it was possible to eradicate completely the passions of the human soul, as the Stoics aspired to do, who held that the human soul contains no irrational element and that passion is a disease of reason whose cure is not impossible. The various aspects of this critique can all be related to the same idea: the rejection of Stoic immanentism, that is, in particular, the Stoic idea that man can attain moral perfection without recourse to any reality other than those he finds in the world.

But what exactly is this world? For the Stoics, there is no need to imagine a demiurge building the world in imitation of the forms. The world results from the action of *logos* on inert matter, there is no difference between God, providence, *phusis* and *logos*,

457

everything is material and everything is rational. There is no place for chance in this world, everything is governed by fate, everything has a cause, and so everything can be foreseen. This explains why the Stoics defended divination, even if they recognized that it gave rise to many abuses. What is more, nature created the world to make it "the city of men and gods," and conceived of everything in the interests of these beings, who are the only rational ones. The Stoics did not reject the gods of mythology; they regarded them not as an aberration but as a naïve and partial vision of divinity on the part of men who lacked the capacity to understand what it really is. All this obviously furnished subjects for criticism by the neo-Academics, who asserted that it was contradictory to claim that everything is determined by fate and at the same time to want to safeguard human freedom.[5] Carneades refused to grant the rather complicated distinction of causes through which Chrysippus sought to reconcile fate and freedom; he asserted rather that the human will cannot be inserted into fate, and that it is its own cause – a distant echo, perhaps, of the self-motion of the soul in Plato. Similarly, he held up to ridicule the belief in divination and held that by wishing to confuse God and the world the Stoics destroyed the very idea of divinity and that they might as well regard nature as a system of purely mechanical forces. In all this criticism of Stoic immanentism, the New Academy made abundant use of the sorites, the dialectical proceeding that allows an insensible transition from one proposition to its contrary. The sorites highlighted the contradictions of a Heraclitean conception of the world, Stoicism being perceived as neo-Heraclitean. Given their conclusion that the Stoic conception of the world was fundamentally mistaken, the neo-Academics could only urge them to pursue an investigation into the nature of things. All the same, it will be noticed that at no time did their dialectic, however universal its aspiration, attack the *Timaeus*, and that it thus left Plato as at least a possible solution to this shortcoming of Stoicism.

The New Academy and Middle Platonism

The thought of the New Academy amalgamated two different elements, Socratic-Platonic inspiration and radical skepticism, whose coexistence was possible only through the tension created by the confrontation with Stoicism. In time, the latter lost its central position and fissures began to open in neo-Academic skepticism. The successors of Carneades were divided over the interpretation of its teaching. Clitomachus, an "orthodox" interpreter of Carneadian thought, argued for the maintenance of *epochē* in all its rigor; while Philo of Larissa, the last scholarch of the Academy, in works written in Rome after his flight from Athens in 88 BCE, formulated innovations of which the most important was the assertion that things are knowable by nature, but they cannot be known on the basis of the Stoic criterion, the "cataleptic" representation. In other words, Philo affirms that the skepticism of the New Academy had essentially been an anti-Stoicism. Philo continued to criticize the "cataleptic" representation, and he asserted the unity of the Academy more strongly than

5. On the Soics and neo-Academics on fate and freedom, see Sharples, THE PROBLEM OF SOURCES, in this volume.

his predecessors, but he seems, to judge by the meager surviving evidence, not to have proposed any path of access to this knowledge whose possibility he theoretically admitted. Nevertheless, this development in the New Academy was to have important and paradoxical consequences. We have already mentioned Aenesidemus's decision to recreate an authentic skepticism by appeal to Pyrrho. Further, Antiochus of Ascalon, who had been a student of Philo of Larissa, broke with his teacher, holding that the doubt of the New Academy contradicted the teaching of Plato and his immediate successors. He claimed to revive the Old Academy, referring by this name to a tolerably heteroclite view amalgamating Platonic, Peripatetic, and Stoic elements. The innovations of Philo of Larissa and the eclectic dogmatism of Antiochus of Ascalon open the period that has been called Middle Platonism, featuring personalities as rich and diverse as Philo of Alexandria, Apuleius and Plutarch. After the death of Philo of Larissa around 84 BCE, neo-Academic inspiration seems to have disappeared, and Cicero presents himself as the representative of an abandoned doctrine. Yet, even within Middle Platonism, skeptical elements are present, alongside very dogmatic interpretations of Plato. With Philo of Alexandria, not only does the *De Ebrietate* contain a version of the skeptical Modes of Aenesidemus, but neo-Academic concepts like those of *epochē*, *pithanon* and *eulogon* are integrated into a fideist perspective, skepticism then being the expression of the nothingness of human reason before the divine omnipotence. As far as Plutarch is concerned, Jan Opsomer (1998) has shown the extent to which Platonic and neo-Academic themes are tightly entwined in this author who, more than any other, defended the idea of the unity of the Academy throughout all the vicissitudes of its history. Far from completely disappearing with Philo of Larissa, the skepticism of the New Academy thus exercised a definite influence on important philosophical currents, neo-Pyrrhonist skepticism and Middle Platonism, which in their own way perpetuated in the history of philosophy the two contradictory elements that New Academy strove to make coexist for two centuries.

Bibliography

Sources

General

Long, A. A. and Sedley, D. (eds.). (1987). (Cited as LS). *The Hellenistic Philosophers.* (2 vols.). Cambridge: Cambridge University Press.

Aulus Gellius

Rolfe, J. C. (ed., trans., notes). (1927–8). *Aulus Gellius. The Attic Nights.* (3 vols.). Loeb Classical Library. Cambridge, Mass.: Harvard University Press / London: Heinemann.

Cicero

Pease, A. S. (ed., comm.). (1955–8). *Cicero. De natura deorum* (2 vols.). Cambridge, Mass.: Harvard University Press.

Rackham, H. (ed., trans., notes). (1914). *Cicero. De finibus bonorum et malorum.* Loeb Classical Library. Cambridge, Mass.: Harvard University Press and London: Heinemann.

459

———. (ed., trans., notes). (1933). *Cicero. De natura deorum. Academica.* Loeb Classical Library. Cambridge, Mass.: Harvard University Press and London: Heinemann.

Reid, J. S. (ed., comm.). (1885). *Cicero. M. T. Ciceronis Academica.* London: Macmillan.

Diogenes Laertius

Goulet-Cazé, M.-O. et al. (ed., trans. comm.). (1999). *Diogène Laërce. Vies et doctrines des philosophes illustres.* Paris: Librairie générale française.

Hicks, R. D. (ed., trans., notes). (1972). *Diogenes Laertius. Lives of eminent philosophers.* Loeb Classical Library. Cambridge, Mass.: Harvard University Press and London: Heinemann.

Lucretius

Rouse, H. D. and Smith, M. F. (ed., trans., notes). (1975). *Lucretius. De rerum natura.* Loeb Classical Library. Cambridge, Mass.: Harvard University Press / London: Heinemann.

Philo of Alexandria

Gorez, J. (ed., trans.). (1962). *Philo of Alexandria. De ebrietate. De sobrietate.* Paris: Editions du Cerf.

Philodemus

Dorandi, T. (ed., trans., notes). (1991). *Filodemo. Storia dei filosofi: Platone e l'Academia (PHerc. 1021 e 164).* Naples: Bibliopolis.

Plutarch

Cherniss, H. (ed., trans., notes). (1976). *Plutarch. Plutarch's moralia,* XIII, 2. (Anti-Stoic treatise.). Cambridge, Mass.: Harvard University Press and London: Heinemann.

Einarson, B. and De Lacy, P. H. (ed., trans., notes). (1967). *Plutarch's moralia,* XIV (Anti-Epicurian Treatise). Loeb Classical Library. Cambridge, Mass.: Harvard University Press and London: Heinemann.

Pyrrho

Decleva Caizzi, F. (ed., trans., comm.). (1981). *Pirrone. Testimonianze.* Naples: Bibliopolis.

Sextus Empiricus

Annas, J. and Barnes, J. (trans.). (1994). *Sextus Empiricus. Outlines of Scepticism.* Cambridge: Cambridge University Press.

Bury, R. G. (ed., trans., notes). (1976). *Sextus Empiricus. Outlines of Pyrrhonism.* Cambridge, Mass.: Harvard University Press / London: Heinemann.

Pellegrin, P. (ed., trans., notes). (1997). *Sextus Empiricus. Esquisses pyrrhoniennes (Purrōneiai hupotupōseis).* Paris: Seuil.

Timon

Di Marco, M. (ed.). (1989). *Timone di Fliunto. Silli.* Introduzione, edizione critica, traduzione e commento. Di Rome: Edizioni dell' Ateneo.

Various neo-Academics

Mette, H. J. (1984). "Zwei Akademiker heute: Krantor und Arkesilaos." *Lustrum,* 26, 7–94.

———. (1985). "Weitere Akademiker heute: von Lakydes bis zu Kleitomachos." *Lustrum,* 27, 39–148.

Works Cited

Couissin, P. (1929a). "Le stoïcisme de la Nouvelle Académie." *Revue d'Histoire de la Philosophie*, 3, 241–76. English trans. in M. Burnyeat (ed.). (1983), *The Skeptical Tradition* (pp. 31–63). Berkeley: University of California Press.

——. (1929b). "L'origine et l'évolution de *l'epochè*." *Revue des Études Grecques*, 42, 373–97.

Glucker, J. (1978). *Antiochus and the late Academy*. Göttingen: Vandenhoeck and Ruprecht.

Ioppolo, A. M. (1986). *Opinione e scienza: il debattito tra Stoici e Accademici nel III e nel II secolo a. C.* Naples: Bibliopolis.

Opsomer, J. (1998). *In the Search of Truth*. Bruxelles: Verhandelingen van de Koninklijke Academic voor Wetenschappen, Letteren en Schone Kunsten van België.

Further Readings

Algra, K. A. (1997). "*Chrysippus, Carneades, Cicero: The Ethical Divisions in Cicero's* Lucullus." In B. Inwood and J. Mansfeld (eds.), *Assent and Argument. Studies in Cicero's Academic Books* (pp. 107–40). Leiden: Brill.

——., Barnes, J., Mansfeld, J., and Schofield, M. (1999). *The Cambridge History of Hellenistic Philosophy*. Cambridge: Cambridge University Press.

Allen, J. V. (1994). "Academic Probabilism and Stoic Epistemology." *Classical Quarterly*, 44, 85–113.

Annas, J. (1990). "Platon le sceptique." *Revue de Métaphysique et de Morale*, 95, 267–91.

——. (1992). "Plato the Sceptic." *Oxford Studies in Ancient Philosophy*. Suppl. vol., 43–72.

Assayas-Auvray, C. and Delattre, D. (eds.). (2001). *Cicéron et Philodème. La polémique en philosophie*. Paris: Editions Rue D'Ulm.

Barnes, J. (1982). "The Beliefs of a Pyrrhonist." *Elenchos*, 4, 5–43.

——. (1989). "Antiochus of Ascalon." In M. Griffin and J. Barnes (eds.), *Philosophia togata. Essays on Philosophy and Roman Society* (pp. 51–96). Oxford: Oxford University Press.

Barnes, J., Brunschwig, J., Burnyeat, M., and Schofield, M. (eds.). (1982). *Science and Speculation: Studies in Hellenistic Theory and Practice*. Cambridge: Cambridge University Press / Paris: Éditions de la Maison des Sciences de l'homme.

Besnier, B. (1993). "La Nouvelle Académie selon le point de vue de Philon de Larisse." In B. Besnier (ed.), *Scepticisme et exégèse* (Festschrift for Camille Pernot) (pp. 85–163). Fontenay-aux-Roses: Presses de l'École Normale Supérieure.

Bett, R. (1989). "Carneades' *pithanon*: A Reappraisal of its Role and Status." *Oxford Studies in Ancient Philosophy*, 7, 59–94.

Bonazzi, M. (2003). *Academici e Platonici. Il dibattito antico sullo scetticismo di Platone*. Milan: Edizioni Universitarie di Lettere Economia Diritto.

Brittain, C. (2001). *Philo of Larissa. The last of the Academic Sceptics*. Oxford: Oxford University Press.

Brochard, V. (1887). *Les sceptiques grecs*. Paris: Vrin.

Brunschwig, J. (1986). "The Cradle Argument in Epicureanism and Stocism." In M. Schofield and G. Striker (eds.), *The Norms of Nature: Studies in Hellenistic Ethics* (pp. 113–44). Cambridge: Cambridge University Press / Paris: Éditions de la Maison des Sciences de l'homme.

——. (1994). *Papers in Hellenistic Philosophy*. Cambridge: Cambridge University Press.

——. (1995). *Études sur les philosophies hellénistiques: épicurisme, stoïcisme, scepticisme*. Paris: Presses Universitaires de France.

Brunschwig, J. and Nussbaum, M. C. (eds.). (1993). *Passions and Perceptions*. Proceedings of the Fifth Symposium Hellenisticum: *Studies in Hellenistic Philosophy of Mind*. Cambridge: Cambridge University Press.

Burnyeat, M. F. (1980). "Can the Skeptic Live his Skepticism?" In M. Schofield, M. F. Burnyeat, and J. Barnes (eds.), *Doubt and Dogmatism: Studies in Hellenistic Epistemology* (pp. 20–53). Oxford: Oxford University Press. Repr. in M. F. Burnyeat (ed.). (1983) (pp. 117–48).

——. (ed.). (1983). *The Skeptical Tradition.* Berkeley: University of California Press.

——. (1984). "The Sceptic in his Place and Time." In R. Rorty, J. B. Schneewind, and Q. Skinner (eds.), *Philosophy in History. Essays on the Historiography of Philosophy* (pp. 225–54). Cambridge: Cambridge University Press.

Conche, M. (1973). *Pyrrhon ou l'apparence.* Villers-sur-Mer: Editions de Mégare.

Couissin, P. (1941). "Les sorites de Carnéade contre le polythéisme." *Revue des Études Grecques,* 54, 43–57.

Dal Pra, M. (1975). *Lo scetticismo greco.* 2nd edn. Rome-Bari: Laterza.

Decleva Caizzi, F. (1986). "Pirroniani ed accademici nel III secolo a.C." In H. Flashar and O. Gigon (eds.), *Aspects de la philosophie hellénistique* (pp. 147–78). Vandoeuvres-Geneva: Fondation Hardt.

——. (1992). "Aenesidemus and the Academy." *Classical Quarterly,* 42, 176–89.

——. (1992). "Sesto e gli Scettici." *Elenchos,* 13, 277–327.

Dorandi, T. (1997). "Gli Academica quale fonte per la storia dell'Academia." In B. Inwood and J. Mansfeld (eds.), *Assent and Argument. Studies in Cicero's Academic Books* (pp. 89–106). Leiden: Brill.

Flashar, H. (ed.). (1994). *Grundriss der geschichte der Philosophie. Die Philosophie der Antike* (vol. 4): *Die hellenistische Philosophie.* Bâle-Stuttgart: Schwabe.

Fowler, D. P. (1986). "Sceptics and Epicureans." *Oxford Studies in Ancient Philosophy,* 2, 237–67.

Frede, M. (1983). "Stoics and Skeptics on Clear and Distinct Impressions." In M. F. Burnyeat (ed.), *The Skeptical Tradition* (pp. 65–93). Berkeley: University of California Press.

——. (1984). "The Skeptic's Two Kinds of Assent and the Question of the Possibility of Knowledge." In R. Rorty, J. Schneewind, and Q. Skinner (eds.), *Philosophy of History* (pp. 255–78). Cambridge: Cambridge University Press. Repr. in M. Frede (1987), (pp. 201–22).

——. (1987). *Essays in Ancient Philosophy.* Oxford: Oxford University Press / Minneapolis: University of Minnesota Press.

Giannantoni, G. (ed.). (1981). *Lo scetticismo antico.* (2 vols.) Naples: Bibliopolis.

——. (1986). *Diogene Laerzio storico del pensiero antico.* Naples: Bibliopolis.

Gigante, M. (1981). *Scetticismo e epicureismo. Per l'avviamento di un discorso storiografico.* Naples: Bibliopolis.

Görler, W. (1994). "Älterer pyrrhonismus, Jüngere Akademie, Antiochos aus Askalon." In H. Flashar (ed.), *Grundriss der Geschichte der Philosophie. Die Philosophie der Antike* (vol. 4): *Die hellenistische Philosophie* (pp. 717–89). Bâle-Stuttgart: Schwabe.

Griffin, M. T. and Barnes, J. (eds.). (1989). *Philosophia togata. Essays on Philosophy and Roman Society.* Oxford: Oxford University Press.

Hankinson, R. J. (1995). *The Sceptics.* London and New York: Routledge.

Inwood, B. and Mansfeld, J. (eds.). (1997). *Assent and Argument. Studies in Cicero's Academic Books.* Leiden: Brill.

Ioppolo, A. M. (1981). "Il concetto di 'eulogon' nella filosofia di Arcesilao." In G. Giannantoni (ed.) *Lo scetticismo antico* (vol. 1, pp. 143–61). Naples: Bibliopolis.

——. (1986). *Opinione e scienza: il debattito tra Stoici e Accademici nel III e nel II secolo a.C.* Naples: Bibliopolis.

——. (1993). "The Academic Position of Favorinus of Arelate." *Phronesis,* 38, 183–213.

Krämer, H. J. (1971). *Platonismus und Hellenistische Philosophie.* Berlin: de Gruyter.

Lévy, C. (1978). "Scepticisme et dogmatisme dans l'Académie: l'ésotérisme d'Arcésilas." *Revue des Études Latines,* 56, 335–48.

——. (1992). *Cicero Academicus*. Rome: École française de Rome.

——. (1993). "La Nouvelle Académie a-t-elle été antiplatonicienne?" In M. Dixsaut (ed.), *Contre Platon* (vol. 1): *Le platonisme dévoilé* (pp. 139–56). Paris: Vrin.

——. (1993). "Le concept de doxa des Stoïciens à Philon d'Alexandrie. Essai d'étude diachronique." In J. Brunschwig and M. C. Nussbaum (eds.), *Passions and Perceptions*. Proceedings of the Fifth Symposium Hellenisticum: *Studies in Hellenistic Philosophy of Mind* (pp. 250–84). Cambridge: Cambridge University Press.

——. (1997). "Lucrèce avait-il lu Enésidème ?" In K. A. Algra, M. H. Koenen, and P. H. Schrijvers (eds.), *Lucretius and his Intellectual Background* (pp. 115–24). Amsterdam: Royal Netherlands Academy of Arts and Sciences.

——. (2001). "Cicéron et l'épicurisme. La problématique de l'éloge paradoxal." In C. Assayas-Auvray and D. Delattre (eds.), *Cicéron et Philodème. La polémique en philosophie* (pp. 61–75). Paris: Editions Rue D'Ulm.

——. (2001). "Enésidème et Sextus Empiricus: la question de la légitimation historique dans le scepticisme." In A. Brancacci (ed.), *Antichi e Moderni nella filosofia di età imperiale* (pp. 299–329). Naples: Bibliopolis.

Long, A. A. (1967). "Carneades and the Stoic telos." *Phronesis*, 12, 59–90.

——. (1986). "Diogenes Laertius, Life of Arcesilaus." In G. Giannantoni (ed.), *Diogene Laerzio storico del pensiero antico.* (pp. 429–49). Naples: Bibliopolis.

——. (1988). "Socrates in Hellenistic Philosophy." *Classical Quarterly*, 82, 150–71.

——. (1996). *Stoic Studies*. Cambridge: Cambridge University Press.

Mansfeld, J. (1990). "Doxography and Dialectic: The Sitz im Leben of the *Placita.*" In *ANRW* II 36.4, pp. 3056–229.

——. (1995). "Aenesidemus and the Academics." In L. Ayres (ed.), *The Passionate Intellect* (Festschrift for I. G. Kidd) (pp. 235–47). New Brunswick, NJ: Transaction.

Nonvel Pieri, S. (1978). *Carneade*. Padova: Liviana editrice.

Powell, J. G. F. (ed.). (1995). *Cicero the Philosopher*. Oxford: Oxford University Press.

Reydams-Schils, G. (1999). *Demiurge and Providence. Stoic and Platonic Readings of Plato's* Timaeus. Turnhout: Brepols.

Robin, L. (1944). *Pyrrhon et le scepticisme grec*. Paris: Presses Universitaires de France.

Schofield, M. (1986). "Cicero For and Against Divination." *Journal of Roman Studies*, 76, 47–65.

——. (1991). *The Stoic Idea of the City*. Cambridge: Cambridge University Press.

——. (1999). "Academic Epistemology." In K. Algra et al. (eds.), *The Cambridge History of Hellenistic Philosophy* (pp. 323–50). Cambridge: Cambridge University Press.

——. and Striker, G. (eds.). (1986). *The Norms of Nature: Studies in Hellenistic Ethics*. Cambridge: Cambridge University Press. Paris: Maison des Sciences de l'Homme.

——., Burnyeat, M. F., and Barnes, J. (eds.). (1980). *Doubt and Dogmatism: Studies in Hellenistic Epistemology*. Oxford: Oxford University Press.

Sedley, D. N. (1981). "The End of the Academy." *Phronesis*, 26, 67–75.

——. (1983). "The Motivation of Greek Skepticism." In M. F. Burnyeat (ed.), *The Skeptical Tradition* (pp. 9–29). Berkeley: University of California Press.

——. (1989). "Philosophical Allegiance in the Greco-Roman World." In M. Griffin and J. Barnes (eds.), *Philosophia Togata. Essays on Philosophy and Roman Society* (pp. 97–119). Oxford: Oxford University Press.

——. (1998). *Lucretius and the Transmission of Greek Wisdom*. Cambridge: Cambridge University Press.

Striker, G. (1980). "Sceptical Strategies." In M. Schofield, M. F. Burnyeat, and J. Barnes (eds.), *Doubt and Dogmatism: Studies in Hellenistic Epistemology* (pp. 54–83). Oxford: Oxford University Press.

——. (1981). "Über den Unterschied zwischen den Pyrrhoneern und den Akademikern." *Phronesis*, 26, 153–71. Repr. in English in Striker (1996), (pp. 135–50).

——. (1996). *Essays on Hellenistic Epistemology and Ethics*. Cambridge: Cambridge University Press.

Vander Waerdt, P. A. (1989). "Colotes and the Epicurean Refutation of Skepticism." *Greek Roman and Byzantine Studies*, 30, 225–67.

24

Pyrrhonism

JACQUES BRUNSCHWIG

Introduction

The word "Pyrrhonism," taken strictly, simply denotes the philosophy of Pyrrho of Elis (circa 365–270 BCE); in practice, it refers to a complex reality. Pyrrho (like Socrates) wrote no philosophical works. Did he, as is often said, found a skeptical "sect"? In one sense, he did not; in another, he did.[1] A good many ancient philosophers invoked his authority; but, except for the latest of them, Sextus Empiricus (second century CE),[2] most of them are little known and their works are generally lost. The most famous clearly left the Pyrrhonist tradition in a state different from that in which they found it. Their principal philosophical endeavor was to overturn the many forms, naïve or learned, of "dogmatism"; but they were also concerned to distinguish their views from philosophical tendencies, analogous to their own in some respects, that characterized the Platonic Academy under the direction of Arcesilaus (circa 315–240 BCE) and Carneades (circa 214–128 BCE) (see Lévy, THE NEW ACADEMY AND ITS RIVALS, in this volume). Further, after a certain time, the Pyrrhonist tradition was fruitfully allied with the empirical and methodical schools of medical thought (see Pellegrin, ANCIENT MEDICINE, in this volume).

This is why there is no good way to give a historical and philosophical account of Pyrrhonism within the bounds of a brief chapter. It would require a book, on the model of Brochard (1887), Hankinson (1995), or Bett (2000). Perhaps the least bad way would be to set out from the idea that Pyrrhonist thought is *reactive*, depending for its existence on what it criticizes; but this method would again lead to ill-proportioned exposition, due to the complexity of the debates at issue. Here we shall follow, in sequence, two guiding threads that appear to have some historical validity. First we shall trace what seems to be the *offensive* phase of Pyrrhonism's development; that is, the long work of assembling, reinforcing, and refining the Pyrrhonist arsenal; then we shall strive to see how Pyrrhonism, having reached the highest degree of offensive perfection of which it was capable, undertook to *defend itself* against the main objections brought against it.

---

1. See Sextus Empiricus, *Outlines of Pyrrhonism* [hereafter: *PH*] 1.16–17; Diogenes Laertius [hereafter: D.L.] 1,20. I shall refer to the ancient works when these are easily accessible; to modern collections (Long and Sedley = LS) when they are not.
2. Whence the place of the present chapter in this volume.

465

For a quick estimate of the divergence between the starting point and the end of the long Pyrrhonist tradition, it is enough to recall, to begin with, that the term "Pyrrhonism," by which seventeenth- and eighteenth-century philosophers frequently meant skepticism, did not have the same dominance among the ancients. The successors of Pyrrho used a diverse nomenclature (see *PH* 1.7, D.L. 9.69–70): "skeptics" (observers or examiners), "zetetics" (searchers), "ephectics" (practitioners of the *epochē* or suspension of judgment), "aporetics" (exploiters of *aporiai*, i.e., impasses). The label "Pyrrhonist," put in leading position by Diogenes Laertius, while Sextus puts it last, seems to have aroused some scruples, at least in later times (see Theodosius in D.L. 9.70): how could one really call oneself a Pyrrhonist if one could not know Pyrrho's "movements of thought"? And did Pyrrho not have precursors? Sextus replies to these arguments, but very cautiously (*PH* 1.7: "It *appears to us* that Pyrrho devoted himself to *skepsis more completely and more brilliantly than his predecessors*").

If, on the other hand, the term "skeptic" clearly predominates in Sextus, that is doubtless in order to distinguish the *skepsis* of the Skeptics from their rivals in the "skepticizing" Academy: rightly or wrongly, Sextus regards the Academics as dogmatists in reverse: they declare that it is impossible to find the truth (*PH* 1.2–3). (See Lévy's chapter in this volume.) The Pyrrhonists, who "continue to seek it," are the true "examiners."

Pyrrho and Timon

Diogenes Laertius's biography of Pyrrho (see 9.61–69) is vivid, if not always credible. We can fairly easily make out in it two rival pictures of the man: an eccentric guru and a modest, gentle sage. The guru accompanied his teacher and friend Anaxarchus, a favorite of Alexander the Great, to the East; he had bizarre ideas and behaved bizarrely. The modest, gentle sage lived peacefully in the country with his sister. The guru's ambition was to "strip off the man," but the modest, gentle sage humbly acknowledged that it was not easy, and that he did not always attain to it himself.

Perhaps this is why the ancients had some difficulty placing his character in the philosophic landscape of antiquity. The extravagant Pyrrho was the one who discovered a radically novel way to fulfill the program of "happiness" (*eudaimonia*) set for themselves by all the philosophical schools of Greece. The conventional Pyrrho was the one who took note, like many others before him, of the weakness of human knowledge. That is why he is readily inserted into a succession going back to Homer (D.L. 9.71–73) or, less fancifully, into a skepticizing lineage stemming from Xenophanes, Zeno of Elea, and Democritus (D.L. 9.72–73). Even his partisans do not go so far as to isolate him entirely: Timon, the most famous of his circle, energetically mocks all other philosophers, but is relatively indulgent toward some of them, above all Xenophanes. Later, Sextus takes care to compare Pyrrhonism with "neighboring" philosophies (*PH* 1.210–241), noting the differences, to be sure, but also highlighting the common traits that explain how they could sometimes have been conflated. Nor do modern historians hesitate to speak of Pyrrho's "precursors" or the "antecedents" of Pyrrhonism.

This assimilationist reading of the relations between Pyrrho and his predecessors pushes his thought toward epistemological questions. It is of a piece with an equally

466

assimilationist reading of his relations to his posterity, a posterity that is itself a critique of belief and knowledge. The problem is thus to understand the connection, for Pyrrho himself, between the ethical revolution and the "pre-neo-Pyrrhonist" skepticism we instinctively credit to Pyrrhonism's eponymous founder.

Nevertheless, perhaps one should lay it down as a principle, when dealing with a Pyrrho as with a Socrates, that the essential thing is to assess the effect they had on those who knew them, or even on those who heard tell of them. Consider a man like Timon, whose character was as different as could be from his (see his portrait in D.L. 9.109–115): what about his teacher could have struck him so powerfully? Would it have been a boundless curiosity and appetite for reflection about the problems of knowledge? That theme was already fairly well-worn at the time. Unprecedented, on the other hand, or almost so, was the nature he ascribed to happiness: not the possession of an absolute, supreme good, but rather the inner attainment of certain "privative" attitudes, such as *apatheia* (absence of affects), *adiaphora* (indifference), *ataraxia* (imperturbability), *astorgia* (freedom from attachments), *apragmosunē* (uninvolvement with the affairs of others), *aphasia* (silence or laconism). Epicurus, who was passionately interested in Pyrrho's "life style" (D.L. 9.64), may even have complimented him for being *amathēs* (ignorant) and *apaideutos* (uncultivated) (see Sedley, 1976). When Timon described his overwhelming encounter with his teacher, what he asked of him was the secret of his superhuman tranquillity (D.L. 9.65); and, in the answer he seems to put in Pyrrho's mouth (S.E. *M* 11.19–20), the latter expresses himself in terms so assured that modern interpretation (Burnyeat, 1980a) has had to lavish treasures of ingenuity on reconciling them with Pyrrho's "skepticism."

But Timon has left us not just traces of his enthusiasm. A famous and ceaselessly discussed text, a quotation or paraphrase transmitted by the Peripatetic Aristocles, summarizes the thought of Pyrrho (and/or the Pyrrhonists). We can hardly avoid quoting it here, in our own articulation of questions and replies, with the warning that every detail of our translation is subject to controversy.

> Pyrrho of Elis . . . did not himself leave anything written. It is his disciple Timon who says that it is necessary for those who want to be happy to consider the following three points: [Q1] first, what are the characteristics of things according to their nature; [Q2] second, what attitude should we take toward them [them = the things]; [Q3] lastly, what benefit those who take this attitude will find in it. [R1] As far as concerns things, Timon says [R1a] that Pyrrho declares them all to be equally indifferent, unstable and indeterminate; [R1b] that for this reason neither our sensations nor our opinions are true or false. [R2a] For this reason, therefore, we cannot have the least confidence in them [= the sensations and opinions], [R2b] but must rather be without opinions, without inclinations, without waverings, [R2c] saying of each thing that it in no way is more than is not, or that it at once is and is not, or that it neither is nor is not. [R3] For those who take this attitude, according to Timon, the benefit will be [R3a] first *aphasia*, [R3b] followed by *ataraxia*; [R3c] but Aenesidemus says that it is pleasure. Such are the main points of what they have said. (Eus. *Praep. Evang.* 14.18.2–5 = LS 1F2–6 = Caizzi 53)

From among the many comments called for by this testimony from Timon/Aristocles (hereafter: TA), here is a brief selection.

1. It is a pity that no later Pyrrhonist seems to have known of TA: one would be curious to know his reaction to so "un-Pyrrhonian" an initial question as Q1; for if there is any sphere in which a Pyrrhonist should practice the *epochē*, it is surely that which concerns the properties belonging to "things" "according to their nature," "truly," "in themselves."

2. Still, it may be suggested, even if Q1 was not a skeptical question, R1a might have been a skeptical answer to it. The adjectives it employs could imply that it is *we* who lack the cognitive means to distinguish things, to determine them, to decide whether or not they have this or that property. R1a would then express an epistemological skepticism. However, in order to answer Q1 in the terms in which the question was posed, I think R1a must rather have meant that the "things" do not exhibit "objective" differences,[3] and that it is we who all too hastily introduce distinctions between them that do not belong to them "according to their nature."

   Let us note in passing, albeit quickly, that one could retain the threatened link between R1a and the later "Pyrrhonist" tradition if one were to accept a proposed emendation to the text of R1b.[4] Instead of "for this reason (*dia touto*) neither our sensations nor our opinions are true or false," the emended text would mean "for the reason (*dia to*) that neither our sensations nor our opinions are true or false." The metaphysical thesis of the indeterminacy of things (R1a) would then have a cognitive basis (R1b), namely, the lack of determinate truth value of our sensations and our opinions. But it seems unclear that the fallibility of our cognitive faculties can ground a genuinely metaphysical thesis. Besides, the proposed emendation has not won universal acceptance, and more than one way has been found to render the inference, as presented in the received text, more or less acceptable.

3. To his own non-skeptical question Q1, then, Pyrrho would offer an equally non-skeptical answer, R1a. This claim will be found astonishing; but recent research tends to emphasize the divergence between Pyrrho and the (neo)Pyrrhonists. At most we could say that the indeterminacy thesis is dogmatic in one sense, while in another it is anti-dogmatic. It is anti-dogmatic in that it forbids us to decide in a determinate way on the "natural" properties of things; for example, to say that *such and such a thing is* F by nature rather than not F, or that *such and such another thing is* by nature not F rather than F. But it is dogmatic in that it itself takes a determinate position on the issue of whether or not things *in general* are distinct in nature from one another (as a matter of fact, Pyrrho does *not* say that things are in no way more distinct than non-distinct). In the terminology of recent discussions, one would call it a negative meta-dogmatic thesis.[5]

Among the remaining controversial questions, the following requires a few words: what *scope* did Pyrrho attribute to Q1 and R1? At first sight, TA is definitely universal: the Pyrrhonist thesis covers *all* determinations, distinctions, and characterizations of

3. It would therefore be a genuine "metaphysical thesis," a "thesis of the indeterminacy of things," as Bett (2000) maintains.
4. See Zeller (1909) and Stopper (1983).
5. On this terminology, see especially the precise explications supplied by Barnes (1992, pp. 4252 n. 54 and 4254 n. 72).

"things." For example, R2c infers from R1 that we must say (granting the translation proposed here) "of *each* <thing>, that it in no way is <F> more than is not <F>, or that it at once is <F> and is not <F>, or that it neither is <F> nor is not <F>." Why then are we *not* to say what the learned and the ignorant alike say all the time: this is F and that is not F? Very likely, due to a principle which (despite the philosophical disasters it has wrought) was explicitly or implicitly accepted almost everywhere in Greek thought (see Burnyeat, 1979). According to Bett (2000), who calls this principle "the invariability condition," we may formulate it as follows: something that is F only in certain circumstances (but not F in others), or F only in certain relations (but not in others) is, by that very fact, not "F by nature," not "really F."

TA denies that there are predicates that satisfy the invariability condition, that is, predicates true in all the circumstances and relations of the subjects of which they are true. If, however, we read the testimony as it is transmitted to us, keeping R1b and R2a in mind,[6] it seems that what Pyrrho explicitly condemns is the ordinary usage of predicates applied on the basis of a sensation or an opinion: here TA speaks neither of knowledge nor of science. By disqualifying sensations and opinions, Pyrrho attacks the information sources (or supposed such) that ground our perceptual judgments and value judgments, and that ordinarily guide our daily life.[7]

Does the Pyrrhonist critique take aim at perceptual judgments as well as at value judgments? The debate is spirited, even today. In favor of an interpretation restricted to ethical predicates, which is far from being universally accepted,[8] we may recall here that TA is framed by an original project that is overtly eudaimonistic. We may also recall the formulation of R3, which mentions *ataraxia* as among the benefits that adepts of the Pyrrhonist way can expect. In this circle that closes so visibly on itself, it is not very clear what role the critique of perceptual judgments could play. What would be particularly disturbing about believing and saying that snow is white? And what would be particularly reassuring about believing and saying that it is no more white than black? To understand this, we would have to sketch at least a few of the links, complex ones moreover, that later Pyrrhonists were to establish between a (general) *epochē* and *ataraxia* (for example, *PH* 1.29); but nothing like this appears in TA, an absence that seems insufficiently explained by its character as a summary.

Finally, on this point, we might profitably compare TA with the general description of Pyrrho's thought in D.L. 9.61: "He said that nothing is fine or vile, just or unjust, and similarly for everything, that nothing is <this or that> in truth, but only by custom and habit is it that men do all that they do; in fact, according to him, each

---

6. In Brunschwig (1994), on the basis of some grammatical observations, I suggested attributing the insertion of R1b and R2a to Timon, along with the "epistemological turn" stamped on Pyrrho's thought by this insertion. That debatable (and debated) hypothesis would naturally be out of place in a work such as the present one.

7. In the terminology of current discussions, one would say that his "skepticism" is of the "rustic" type, as opposed to the "urban" skepticism that leaves ordinary beliefs intact and only attacks the doctrines of philosophers and the learned. For these discussions, see Barnes (1982); Burnyeat (1983, 1984); Frede (1984, 1987); Brennan (1994).

8. Despite weighty supporters, such as Brochard (1887), Robin (1944), von Fritz (1963), Decleva Caizzi (1981), and Ausland (1989).

thing is no more this than that." Here we see that the universal vocabulary ("similarly for all," "nothing," "each thing") does not keep the examples adduced ("fine," "vile," "just," "unjust," "what men do") from being limited to the sphere of values and practical life. If we were to admit that Pyrrho himself had in mind only an *epochē* confined to ethical-political predicates, perhaps we would appreciate better the scope and power of the intellectual advances achieved in the Pyrrhonist tradition. If everything had been in place from the start, the Pyrrhonists would not have worked as hard, and we would have fewer occasions to wonder if one of our sources gives us a misleading account of a version of skepticism attested by another, or an exact account of a different version (see Barnes, 1992, p. 4253).

From Timon to Aenesidemus

The history of Pyrrhonism after Pyrrho and Timon was already a subject of discussion in antiquity (D.L. 9.115–116). According to some, Timon had disciples, whose successors formed an uninterrupted series of skeptical philosophers and empiricist physicians down to Sextus and his pupil Saturninus. Many of the figures mentioned are no more than names to us, and the listing raises some problems of chronology. According to others (as confirmed by the testimony of Cicero, *Off.* 1.6; *Fin.* 5.8), Pyrrho himself had waived his right to speak about such vital philosophical topics as duties and ends, and his influence suffered a long eclipse. But Pyrrhonism eventually resurged. The agent of this resurrection, according to the empiricist physician Menodotus, had been another physician, Ptolemy of Cyrene; but according to Aristocles, followed on this point by all modern commentators, the impetus was due to Aenesidemus, in the first century BCE. As nothing indicates that Aenesidemus, of whose life we know very little, was a physician, it may be suggested that Menodotus was concerned to give the leading role to one of his colleagues.

Above all, Aenesidemus is famous for the Ten Modes (or "tropes") for inducing *epochē* that are attributed to him (S.E. *M* 7.345) and of which several accounts remain (*PH* 1.31–163, D.L. 9.79–88, Philo of Alexandria, *On Drunkenness* 169–205), though unfortunately not his own.[9] Further, a fairly detailed summary of his *Pyrrhonian Discourses* in eight books, has survived, drawn up by the erudite Photius, the ninth-century patriarch of Constantinople (LS 71C, 72L).

The "modes of Aenesidemus" are so many means of inducing *epochē*, starting from the conflicts of appearances (in the great majority of cases, sensory appearances). To give a quick survey (though the texts are clear and abundant), we may say that they rest upon differences (1) between animals, (2) between men, (3) in the constitution of sense-organs, (4) in circumstances, (5) in positions and distances, (6) in mixtures, (7) in quantities, or again on differences depending (8) on relations, (9) on frequency or rarity, or (10) on traditions, customs, and cultural contexts.

Quite understandably, the Ten Modes focused the attention of ancient as they have of modern commentators. They presented a kind of *summa*, relatively well ordered

---

9. These texts are admirably collected, translated, and commented on in Annas and Barnes (1985).

and articulated, of argument-types employed by the Pyrrhonists against their dogmatic adversaries, at a particular moment in their historical course. But in a sense, this focus is regrettable: the list of the Ten Modes is visibly indebted to earlier material accumulated by generations of philosophers (whether Pyrrhonists or not) preoccupied with the recurrent problem of the conflict of appearances. Further, this list was certainly reworked later in various ways by Aenesidemus and/or his successors so as to systematize it further (see especially *PH* 1.38–39, on the reduction of the Ten Modes to three "superordinate" modes – that based on who judges, that based on what is judged, and that based on both – and of these to a single supreme mode, that of relation).

The texts dealing with the Ten Modes are, therefore, probably not the best source for an assessment of Aenesidemus's own contribution to the development of Pyrrhonism. For example, on the philosophical level the subtlest interpreters have discerned in Sextus's account, but also in that of Diogenes, an uneasy coexistence between two strategies that are in principle distinct.[10] On the one, which is properly speaking *relativist*, a conflict of appearances does not really induce *epochē*: x appears F to A and not F to B, and that is all there is to say about it. The question, "But is it or is it not F by nature?" does not arise. On the other, conforming more to Sextus's version of Pyrrhonism, this question is neither illegitimate nor absurd; it is merely *undecided*, at least so far, thus allowing the skeptic to claim that he "continues to search."

Photius's summary, thanks to its very marginality, has some chance of providing us with less hopelessly encumbered evidence. Based on a direct reading of Aenesidemus's major work, it supplies precious information about the scope of his reflections and the intentions motivating his labors.

Beginning with Book I, Aenesidemus laid out the most important events in the interval that separated him from Pyrrho: namely, the appearance of Academic skepticism and the long series of essentially epistemological debates that matched its successive representatives, Arcesilaus and Carneades, against the teachers of ancient Stoicism, Zeno of Citium and Chrysippus. This development perhaps had a personal dimension for him, if it is true, as has been generally believed on the strength of a passage from Photius, that he himself had been a member of the Academy before breaking with it, disgusted by its increasing concessions to Stoic dogmatism.[11]

What is certain is that Aenesidemus formulated his position with explicit reference both to Pyrrho (positively) and to the Academics (negatively). But these two reference points, far from being merely juxtaposed, were in interaction. For example, Aenesidemus gave prominent place to his exposition of Pyrrho's eudaimonist project; yet, in declining to assert even the most slightly metaphysical principle similar to Pyrrho's thesis of indeterminacy, he was no doubt tacitly taking the anti-dogmatism of the Academics into account. Again, he equally took into account the importance of epistemological questions in the concerns of the Academics and in their debates with the Stoics, going so far as explicitly to introduce a component of Pyrrhonist blessedness that echoed these debates in a way. Witness this rather remarkable phrasing from Photius: "He who philosophizes in the manner of Pyrrho is blessed *in all ways, but in particular* he

10.   See Annas and Barnes (1985, pp. 97–8); and also Striker ([1983] 1996); Bett (2000).
11.   This reconstruction, however, has been contested by Decleva Caizzi (1992).

has the wisdom (*sophos esti*) to know (*eidenai*) to the highest degree that he grasps nothing firmly (*kateilēptai*); and even with respect to things he knows, he is so scrupulous (*gennaios*) that he gives his assent no more to the affirmation than to the denial" (LS 71C3).

Aenesidemus's complaints against the Academics may, it appears, be summarized as follows:

1. They are dogmatic, in the sense that they unhesitatingly assert certain things and unambiguously deny others. Which things? According to the context of this passage (LS 71C5–6), at least general meta-dogmatic claims like "all things are ungraspable" (or even like "all things are graspable"), and no doubt also dogmatic claims about this or that particular thing.
2. The most recent Academics, especially, had adopted many Stoic dogmas, to the point where their discussions gave the impression of "Stoics fighting with Stoics" (LS 71C9). The only remaining bone of contention was the famous "cognitive impression" (*phantasia kataleptikē*), the Stoic criterion of truth.[12]
3. The Academics are unaware that their negative meta-dogmatic assertions and their positive dogmatic ones are in mutual conflict (LS 71C11–12).[13]

On all these points, Aenesidemus regards the Pyrrhonists, "aporetic and free from all dogma," as unassailable.

1. They eschew all general metadogmatic claims like "all things are ungraspable," "inaccessible," "graspable," or "accessible," or even "some are accessible." Aenesidemus recommends saying instead: "they are no more accessible than inaccessible, or they are sometimes accessible and sometimes not, or they are accessible to this man and not to that one."
2. They also eschew all particular dogmatic claims, especially, of course, all those of the Stoics about ethical, epistemological, or other matters. The formula recommended by Aenesidemus is therefore that things "are no more this than that, or that they are sometimes this and sometimes not, or that they are this for this man but not for that one, and even entirely nonexistent for this third one." Notice the differences between the formulas recommended by Aenesidemus and those favored by Pyrrho: while some of the latter ("each thing at once is F and is not F," "it neither is F nor is not F") seem to violate the principles of non-contradiction and excluded middle, Aenesidemus seems to want to acknowledge Aristotle's refinements to his formulation of the first one (*Met.* Γ.3, 1005b19: "it is impossible for the same predicate to belong to the same subject *at the same time and in the same relation*.")

12. A detail certainly worth setting next to the thesis (puzzling in any case) attributed to the Academic Philo of Larissa, who asserted that "in so far as one considers the Stoic criterion, that is, the cognitive impression, things are ungraspable, but that, in so far as one considers the nature of things themselves, they are graspable" (*PH* 1.235).
13. The text is uncertain. On a difficult point, Long and Sedley adopt an emendation suggested in conversation by F. Sandbach.

3. Finally, Aenesidemus claims that the Pyrrhonist position is completely consistent. Not only does it avoid the contradictions he detected in the Academic position, it is also forearmed against a type of contradiction with which some "skepticizing" formulations are constantly charged: how can one say "I know that I know nothing," "I affirm that I affirm nothing"? A few rare ancient philosophers, sensitive to distinctions in levels of knowledge and language, had found such claims perfectly acceptable;[14] others, much more numerous, had found them totally inadmissible.[15]

Aenesidemus is clearly aligned with the latter group; but to avoid the difficulty, he seems to have explored two distinct paths. The one that was to find the greatest favor in the later history of skepticism consisted in including skeptical pronouncements within their own scope: according to Aenesidemus, "the Pyrrhonist determines absolutely nothing, not even this very claim that nothing is determined." But he adds a somewhat embarrassed comment, seemingly aware that he is pressing an innovation to the limits of the sayable: "We put it this way, for lack of a way to express the thought" (LS 71C8). Another solution, which did not have the same success, is sketched in the passage cited above (LS 71C3): it takes advantage of the shades of meaning distinguishing different cognitive terms, in proportion to their force in ordinary usage or in their technical employment by this or that philosophical school. Ordinary verbs of knowing, e.g., *eidenai* and *gignōskein*, thus take on a weaker sense by their very contrast with those to which Stoic usage had typically given a stronger one, such as *katalambanein* ("to grasp") and *sunkatatithesthai* ("to give one's assent"). Hence it is no longer contradictory to say that one "knows," in a weak sense, that one can "know nothing," in a strong one.

Did Aenesidemus succeed in his project of constructing a "Pyrrhonism" genuinely "free from all dogma?" It must be admitted, if we examine the summaries (very brief ones, to be sure) that Photius gave of his *Pyrrhonist Discourses* II–VIII, that Aenesidemus did not refrain from "unambiguously" denying, not just the possibility of knowing a great many things, but the very existence of, among other things, several essential tools in the apparatus of positive dogmatism, such as truths, causes,[16] and signs.[17]

The lacunae or indefiniteness in Aenesidemus's Pyrrhonism may also explain one of the most enigmatic features of his reputation: his relation to Heraclitus. At *PH* 1. 210, Sextus reports that according to Aenesidemus, skepticism is a "path" toward the philosophy of Heraclitus: if contrary properties *appear* to belong to the same thing, then, it seems, one is but a step from thinking that they *actually belong* to the same thing, in accordance with the doctrine traditionally credited to Heraclitus. Sextus calls this slide "absurd," but he does not say that Aenesidemus thought it so.[18] It is doubtless

14. Socrates, according to Arcesilaus (Cic. *Acad.* I.45); the Stoic Antipater (*Acad.* II.28).
15. Metrodorus of Chios (*M* 7.88), Arcesilaus (Cic. *Acad.* I.45), Carneades (*Acad.* II.28).
16. Aenesidemus's Eight Modes against causes have been preserved in *PH* 1.180–185.
17. For a brief discussion of the Pyrrhonists on signs, see Modrak, PHILOSOPHY OF LANGUAGE, in this volume.
18. Moreover, Sextus several times mentions opinions, definitely dogmatic, which he attributes to "Aenesidemus in accordance with Heraclitus." Here we can do no more than mention this formulation, over which much ink has been spilled.

understandable that the author of the Ten Modes was tempted either to slide in this way himself or at least to understand that others could have: for if, for example, the same thing X appears F to A and not F to B, it is easy to suppose that this is not just because A is disposed in one way and B in another, but also because X has some *intrinsic* property that explains why it appears F to people who are disposed as A is, and some other property that explains why it appears not F to people disposed as B is.

Agrippa

After the very modest enlightenment afforded us by the Aenesidemean evidence, we are fortunate, so to speak, to know almost nothing of Agrippa, no doubt the greatest of the Pyrrhonists. Historically, he stands somewhere between Aenesidemus and Sextus; and his contribution to Pyrrhonism consists, for us, in a few lines expounding the Five Modes he introduced, not to supplant the Ten of Aenesidemus but to complete and enrich them. These Modes are attributed to him by D.L. 9.88–89. Sextus gives a barely less compressed account, attributing them merely to the "most recent" skeptics. This passage from Sextus is undoubtedly, along with TA, the only text that can and must be cited in full, unparaphrased, in an exposition of Pyrrhonism. Here it is (in a version that nothing assures us is from the hand of Agrippa himself):

> [1] The mode based on dissonance (*diaphōnia*) leads us to find that with regard to the matter under discussion there has arisen both among ordinary people and among the philosophers an undecided[19] conflict because of which we are unable either to choose a thing or reject it, and so fall back on *epochē*. [2] The Mode based upon infinite regress is that whereby we assert that the thing adduced as a proof of the matter proposed needs a further proof, and this again another, and so on to infinity, so that the consequence is *epochē*, as we possess no starting point for our argument. [3] The mode based on relativity, as we have already said,[20] is that whereby the object has such or such an appearance in relation to the subject judging and to objects considered at the same time, but as to its real nature we adopt *epochē*. [4] We have the mode based on hypothesis when the Dogmatists, being forced into an infinite regress, take as their starting-point something which they do not establish by argument but claim to assume as granted simply and without demonstration. [5] The Mode of circular reasoning[21] is the form used when the proof itself which ought to establish the matter of inquiry requires confirmation derived from that matter; in this case, being unable to assume either in order to establish the other, we adopt *epochē* with respect to both. (*PH* 1.164–169, Trans. by J. B. Bury, slightly modified)

Like the Aenesidemean modes, Agrippa's are "modes of *epochē*": the effect of each individually is to push us toward *epochē*, as indicated by most of the formulas terminating the particular accounts. But their scope is distinctly more universal: they allow us not just to exploit all sorts of conflicts among sensible appearances, but also to undermine any series of arguments whatever that purports to reach a determinate

---

19. *anepikritos*: on this translation, see below.
20. See *PH* 1.135–140, in the context of a discussion of the Ten Modes of Aenesidemus.
21. *ho de diallēlos*: literally, "the one through the other and the other through the one."

conclusion on any disputed question at all, whatever its nature.[22] Furthermore, a detail given in passing in the account of Mode 4 shows that the Modes of Agrippa could also function in combination with each other: when the dogmatist, forced by Mode 2 into an infinite regress, resorts to assuming a hypothesis that he takes for granted, the skeptic can then meet him with the specific criticism of this move recommended by Mode 4.

Based on this isolated remark and several arguments pressed here and there by Sextus, Agrippa has been celebrated for constructing, in his Modes, a philosophical net that leaves the dogmatist no escape, whatever proposition he may undertake to defend. Right after the *exposition* of these Modes (hereafter, E), Sextus sets himself to show, in effect, that "all matters under inquiry may be reduced (*anagein*) to these [Five] Modes" (*PH* 1.170–177, hereafter, A). But the relation between the passages A and E is strange in multiple respects, to the point where the best present-day commentator on the Five Modes has renounced the use of A, preferring to reconstruct a modified version of the Agrippan "net" on philosophically firmer foundations (Barnes, 1990, pp. 114ff.) While referring the reader to this magisterial study, to which I owe much, I shall here propose a different reading exercise, one whose more modest and certainly sketchier purpose will be to show, by comparing certain details of A and E, that Agrippa did not himself deliver, along with the Five Modes described in E, the systematic method of applying them that A purports to give. Perhaps he was unable to do so, or did not wish to, or again perhaps his words and personal commentaries were not transmitted to his successors. It will emerge from this exercise that in the later history of Pyrrhonism the Modes of Agrippa, despite their crystalline clarity, were the topic of reflective and coordinating *work* – rather laborious work, whose traces are all the more interesting for their very uncertainty. Here follow a few remarks along this line:

1. Unlike E, which neither does nor needs to concern itself with this, A aims to show that Mode 1, that of *diaphōnia* ("dissonance"), applies to all matters of inquiry. A, therefore, prefaces the exposition of this mode with a universal demonstration. But this demonstration proceeds, oddly enough, by a partition of the domain in question: all matters of inquiry are "sensible" or "intelligible" (perhaps rather, in Sextus's vocabulary, perceptible or imperceptible);[23] now, there is dissonance about everything that exists (only the sensible? Or only the intelligible? Or both?); therefore dissonance universally affects all matters of inquiry.

2. In E, Mode 1 comes into play when we "find (*heuriskomen*) that with regard to the matter under discussion there has arisen (*gegenēmenēn*) both among ordinary

---

22. Their connection with the difficulties raised by Aristotle regarding the possibility of demonstrative science in general (*APo.* I.3) has been noted several times. In particular, see Barnes (1990, pp. 120–2). On demonstrative science in Aristotle, see Detel, ARISTOTLE'S LOGIC AND THEORY OF SCIENCE, in this volume.

23. Perhaps we have here a kind of injection of Aenesidemus into Agrippa (see the beginning of Photius's summary: "there is no firm basis for cognitive grasping, neither by sensation nor by thought" LS71C1). No doubt one could say the same about the mode of relativity, which already fits rather uneasily into the Ten Modes of Aenesidemus (see Annas and Barnes, 1985, pp. 130–45) and fits still more uneasily into E as well as into A. But we cannot pursue this point here.

people and among the philosophers an *anepikritos* conflict." The word *anepikritos* is ambiguous: it can mean either "undecided" or "undecidable" (see Barnes, 1990, pp. 17–20). Here, the context invites the translation "undecided": the existence of the conflict and its *anepikritos* character are in the realm of facts, about which one *finds* that they *have held*. Are there "decided" conflicts? The text says nothing of them, and with good reason; for Mode 1 is supposed to lead directly to *epochē*, and "decided" conflicts, if such things existed, could hardly have that effect. On the other hand, A explicitly distinguishes dissonances according to whether they are *epikritos* or *anepikritos*, and that is no less easily understood: an *anepikritos* dissonance immediately induces suspension, as in E; but an *epikritos* dissonance (that is, *one that a dogmatist would call epikritos*) must be taken under consideration, for it is in this dialectical situation that the skeptic will ask his adversary to tell him "what would be the origin of the decision"; on the basis of the answer, depending on its content, he will bring to bear the other Modes besides Mode 1. The many future-tense verbs found in A ("What will the dogmatists say, from where will they obtain their decision – will it be from a sensible, or from an intelligible?") reveal that the question is now whether the matter under discussion is *decidable* (as, in principle, the dogmatist maintains) or *undecidable* (as the skeptic, thanks to his set of Modes, takes himself to be able to establish). Two distinct versions of skepticism are encapsulated, it seems to me, in this shift of meaning: in E, the situation of *undecided* conflict psychologically induces a de facto *epochē*; in A, the situation of *undecidable* conflict rationally induces a de jure *epochē*.

3. The partition, introduced at the beginning of A, between sensible and intelligible makes its effect felt in the rest of the passage. Among others, Mode 2, that of infinite regress, is explained separately depending on whether the regress affects terms that are all sensible (§171) or all intelligible (§176), which is a gratuitous restriction on the concept of an infinite regress. Similarly, the relativity of sensibles to sensing subjects and that of intelligibles to thinking subjects are, without any particular need, noted separately (§§175 and 177). Finally and above all, A shows that Mode 4 prohibits the dogmatist from positing a hypothesis taken for granted, and from thus escaping the pincers in which he was caught by the joint operation of Mode 2 and Mode 5;[24] but A shows this twice in a row, in much the same terms, once for the sensible (§172), then for the intelligible (§176). The importance this confers on Mode 4, in contrast to its less prominent role in E, would certainly explain why the reasons for its particular force might be expounded in A with a fairly unwonted wealth of detail (§§173–174).

4. We also find a non-negligible difference between E and A in their accounts of Mode 5, the *diallēlos*. In E, this mode is defined in clear and simple terms: there is *diallēlos*, that is, reciprocal reasoning, when two propositions are set forth as being so related that one is justified by the other and the other by the first. The more complex case of circular reasoning, in which a series of propositions loops back to its first member, is not mentioned. Nevertheless, whether reciprocal or circular reasoning is in question, the propositions that effect the closure of the *diallēlos* are themselves *individually* the same in each of their occurrences. In A, on the other

---

24. Which A mentions in proximity to each other (§172), surely for this reason.

hand, the notion of the *diallēlos* is transformed by the initial distinction between sensible and intelligible: first, its joint operation with infinite regress is presented twice over (§172 for sensibles, §176 for intelligibles); next, and above all, A presupposes that *diallēlos* is already present when a proposition belonging to one of these two types (e.g., the sensible proposition SP_1) is justified by a proposition belonging to the other (say, IP_1), then conversely (IP_1 being justified in turn by a proposition distinct from SP_1 but of the same type, say, SP_2), and so on, so that a series of alternating borrowings from the two types SP and IP here counts as a kind of *diallēlos*. This is, at the very least, a degenerate use of the concept of *diallēlos*.

These few remarks, and others one might add, show at a minimum that the author of A (no matter whether it is Sextus of one of his sources) is not that of E. The great Agrippa left something to be worked on by his successors, and they made of it what they could.

Sextus Empiricus

For us, as he was throughout history, Sextus Empiricus is the last and most important source for ancient skepticism. He is eulogized at the end of the skeptical "succession" in D.L. 9.116; and he is the only ancient skeptic whose work has been in large part transmitted to us.

Since it has been preserved, we may as well say a few words about it. The manuscript tradition divides his writings into two works:

1. *Outlines of Pyrrhonism* (*Pyrrhōneioi hupotupōseis* = PH), in three books (Book I: "general" presentation of skeptical philosophy; Books II and III: "special" presentation, articulated according to the division traditional in the Hellenistic schools, logic in II, physics and ethics in III);
2. *Against the Professors* (or *the Scientists*) (*Pros mathēmatikous* = *Adversus mathematicos* = M), in eleven books.

It is acknowledged that M brings together two distinct works. M Books 1–6 (to which nothing corresponds in PH) successively criticizes the arts characteristic of traditional education, namely, to begin with, two future elements of the medieval *trivium*, grammar and rhetoric,[25] then four disciplines that more vaguely herald the future *quadrivium*, geometry, arithmetic, astrology (not astronomy), and music.[26] M 7–11 reproduces the tripartite Hellenistic division of PH 2–3: logic (7–8), physics (9–10), ethics (11). M 7–11 had been preceded by a general presentation of skepticism, which was not PH 1 but corresponded to it in the same way that M 7–11 corresponds to PH 2–3.[27]

25. The third discipline of the *trivium*, logic, finds its place in the differing organization of M 7–11.
26. Cf. Plato, *Prt.* 318e.
27. See Janáček's numerous studies, esp. 1963. A bibliography, complete to the date of its publication, is to be found in Barnes (1992, pp. 4298–9).

This general presentation has not been preserved, which is obviously a great pity but may be a sign that, at some point or in some eyes, *PH* 1 had come to be regarded as making it otiose to preserve the books that corresponded to it.

One of the historically important features of Sextus' work is thus that it includes, on a large number of topics, several different treatments of the same theme. These doublets have turned the attention of scholars to problems of sources – Did Sextus draw on different sources? Did he work out different treatments on the basis of the same sources? What are the relations between his sources and those of Diogenes Laertius 9.61–116?[28] – and to problems of chronology – as between *M* 7–11 and *PH* 2–3, which was composed first? Which did the author write with the other one at hand?

In the wake of Janáček's meticulous investigations, a more or less general consensus had arisen in favor of dating the composition of *PH* before that of *M*. The criteria used by Janáček, essentially based on comparisons of style, vocabulary, and connecting particles in parallel passages, were a token of objectivity; to aspire to criticize so carefully constructed a monument in a few lines would obviously be ridiculous. Let us simply remark that a particular difference of style or vocabulary in two parallel passages may be as compatible with the anteriority of the one as of the other: if text A, for example, uses a more varied vocabulary than text B, that may be because Sextus, taking account of the literary genres and pedagogical purposes of his different works, wanted to simplify his vocabulary in writing B, or because he wanted to embellish it in writing A. Furthermore, recent commentators who have approached the chronological problems using philosophical criteria (of clarity, coherence, conceptual precision) have often reached conclusions contrary to Janáček's.[29] It seems the wind is beginning to shift on the question of Sextian chronology.

The problem is not purely scholarly. In the traditional view, *PH* really was an "outline," a youthful essay, introductory and not very personal in character; *M* 7–11, by contrast, was the *magnum opus* of a lifetime of work, a "summa" of ancient skepticism. Doxography and the collection of arguments and counter-arguments naturally having a great part in it, Sextus essentially appeared as a doxographer and compiler.

The reversal of the chronological relation between *M* 7–11 and *PH* may be at once the effect and the cause of a new estimation of *PH*. The "progress" and "improvements" detectable in it relative to *M*, whether in the general organization of its contents, in the choice and formulation of arguments, in the definition of concepts, or in any other area, do not entail, to be sure, that *PH* is later than *M*: Sextus could have used better sources when he composed *PH*; and, after all, later works are not necessarily better than youthful ones. At any rate, the detection of this "progress" has encouraged a re-reading of *PH*, freed from the obsession with chronology, but not without philosophical impact.[30]

28. On this matter, which we must here leave aside, the best account is that of Barnes (1992).
29. For a few detailed studies, see Glidden (1983); Brunschwig (1994, 1995); Bett (1997). For fuller treatments, see Bett (2000); Dye (2001).
30. A re-reading attested by several recent translations: Annas and Barnes (1994); Mates (1995); Pellegrin (1997). By a coincidence that is doubtless really not one, it happened that during the preparation of this chapter I had occasion to read two completely independent unpublished studies: Johnsen (2001), and Dye (2001). Both begin by throwing into relief, through a citation and a commentary, the "crucial" passage *PH* 1.4, which has no equivalent in *M*.

478

The exegetical benefit is paradoxically twofold. When Sextus treats the same subject twice, one reads the *PH* version with renewed care, without presupposing that the *M* version must be our touchstone. And where Sextus has not left us doublets, as in the case of *PH* 1, one pays the more attention to the only surviving version.

Sextus' work is abundant, generally well written, with a manifest and constant pedagogical care; nothing can replace reading and studying it for oneself. If we wished nevertheless to characterize schematically the version of Pyrrhonism it presents, we would draw attention, as suggested at the outset, to the importance of the *defensive* effort it embodies, by contrast with the construction of the *offensive* arsenal of Pyrrhonism, so far as we have been able to trace it by calling up the great figures of Pyrrho, Timon, Aenesidemus, and Agrippa.

The objections against which Pyrrhonism has always had to defend itself are essentially of two kinds: on the theoretical level, it has been charged with being incoherent, or even self-refuting; on the practical level, it has been accused of "making life impossible," in the sense that if one wished to refrain (and if one really could refrain) from holding any opinions, as the skeptic recommends and claims to do, one could neither live nor act: how can one live or act without *believing* that the door is to the right and the window to the left? How can one "live one's skepticism"? One can no doubt *think* in skeptical fashion at certain times, and *live* like everyone else at others; but one cannot do both at once.[31]

As concerns the accusation of incoherence, the gravest objection against which the Pyrrhonists had to defend themselves in antiquity was not that they upheld one proposition here, while they were upholding another that contradicted it.[32] More formidable, it seems, was the accusation that their assertions "refute themselves." Strangely enough, their reaction to this charge still remains today the subject of an "undecided dissonance" among the commentators. It is most often maintained that, far from rejecting the accusation, the skeptics accepted it, even with pleasure, while specifying that their formulas[33] and arguments,[34] even if they do refute themselves, do so only *after* having refuted what they were supposed to refute. Sextus frequently employs, in this context, the famous metaphors of purgative drugs that eliminate themselves after having eliminated noxious humors, of the fire that consumes itself after having consumed its fuel, or (this one taken up again by Wittgenstein) of the ladder that one kicks away after using it to climb onto the wall. These metaphors enabled the

---

31. See Burnyeat ([1980b], 1983) reconsidering Hume's "challenge."
32. Modern analyses, based as much on historical as on philosophical considerations, are more demanding on this point. Cf. Barnes (1992, pp. 4252ff). On a particular point, Bett (1997, incorporated also in 2000, p. 212) has shown that in *M* 11, the book dedicated to the criticism of the moralists, Sextus distanced himself from his "official" position by maintaining, not that we should suspend judgment about what is really good or bad (if there be such), but that nothing is really, or by nature, good or bad. This would seem to be a vestige of Aenesidemus's position.
33. For example, the famous *slogans* whose authentically skeptical meaning is specified by Sextus at *PH* 1.187–208.
34. For example, the formidable puzzle constituted by the demonstration that there are no demonstrations (cf. *PH* 2.188 and *M* 8.480).

skeptic both to benefit, in a first application, from the anti-dogmatic efficacy of skeptical formulations, and to remove, in a second, the dogmatic status their very assertion threatened to give them. Nonetheless, this interpretation has recently been criticized, with noteworthy arguments, by Castagnoli (2000), who undertakes to show that Sextus, far from admitting to the charge of self-refutation, perfected a very subtle means of *rejecting* it.[35]

I mention this discussion, which cannot be summarized here, only because it provides an occasion to mention a detail which its protagonists have perhaps not taken sufficiently into account, and which I should like to exploit in closing. Sextus dedicates a particularly important chapter (*PH* 1.3–15) to the question: "Does the skeptic dogmatize?" In the strong sense of the term "dogmatize," of course, his answer is negative. In support of this answer, he first advances, in two slightly different forms, the "self-cancellation" argument: "a formula such as 'No more (this than that)' (*ouden mallon*) asserts that it itself is, like all the rest, 'no more (this than that),' and thus cancels itself (*sumperigraphei*) along with the rest" (1.14). Nevertheless, Sextus at once adds: "And, most important of all (*to de megiston*), in his enunciation of these formulas the skeptic states what appears to himself (*to heautōi phainomenon*) and announces[36] his own impression (*pathos*) without expressing an opinion (*adoxastōs*), without making any positive assertion regarding the external realities." (1.15, trans. Bury, slightly modified.)

It is no doubt legitimate to lay particular emphasis on the transition ("And most important of all") that separates the self-cancellation argument from what I shall call the "*apangelia*" argument.[37] This transition intimates that, beyond the refined maneuvers of self-cancellation, the *apangelia* remains the high trump in Sextus' defensive game, the argument which, at the limit, makes the others needless. Furthermore, he hastened right from the start in the *PH* (1.4) to throw the *apangelia* over the *whole* of his work like a protective shield: "Our[38] task at present," he writes, "is to describe in outline (*hupotupōtikōs*) the skeptic doctrine, first premising that of none of our future statements do we positively affirm that the fact is exactly as we state it, but we simply report (*apangellomen*) each fact, like a chronicler (*historikōs*), as it appears to us at the moment (*kata to nun phainomenon hēmin*)." (Trans. Bury, slightly modified.)

Thus playing the *apangelia* card, the skeptic renders himself invulnerable: if he does not claim the dignity of "objective" truth for an assertion that merely makes public what appears so (*phainomenon*) to him and "reports" the *pathos* that he undergoes,

---

35. His distinction between *peritropē* ("self-refutation") and *perigraphē* ("self-cancellation") particularly merits reflection. He mentions (p. 264, n. 3) the principal defenders of the position he criticizes, among others Burnyeat (1980b), Hankinson (1995), and especially McPherran (1987), his main target.

36. *Apangellei*: one could also translate "reports" or "tells."

37. The word (which evokes the idea of "message", or "news" – not to mention "angel" and "evangel") appears only in *PH*, neglecting two irrelevant occurrences in *M* 2. Outside Sextus's work, it has an interesting equivalent in the *exomologēseis* ("avowals") invoked in the same context in D.L. 9.104.

38. This plural form, like those that follow, poses a problem that seems to have been barely studied. Whether it denotes the author of *PH* in particular (as is surely the case here) or all the skeptics collectively (as is surely the case elsewhere), can Sextus know that what appears so to *him* is also what appears so to *them*?

how can he be persuaded that he is wrong to have the impression that he has, or to undergo the experience that he does? The dogmatist "will show himself rash, by trying to upset another man's *pathos* by discourse;[39] for just as nobody can by discourse convince the joyful man that he is not joyful, or the man in pain that he is not in pain, so nobody can convince the man who is convinced that he is not convinced." (*M* 8.475, trans. Bury, slightly modified.) This discreet but decisive assimilation of the case of intellectual *pathos* to that of affective *pathos* enables the skeptic to disarm all of his adversaries' arguments in advance.

The other side of the coin is that his own arguments are in no better case. But this is a consequence he is ready to accept. In a passage at the end of *PH* 3 (280–281) that has not always been taken seriously enough, he presents himself, like the physician he is, as a "philanthropist," wishing to "cure by *logos, as best he can*, self-conceit and rashness," i.e., typical dogmatic ailments (trans. Bury, slightly modified). Just as the doctor applies remedies of various strengths to the sick, according to the severity of their illness, so does the skeptic use stronger or "milder" arguments depending on the degree of the dogmatists' afflictions. It is not out of the question that some dogmatists, like some patients, are incurable: the duty of the healer of souls, as of the body, is to take good care, not to produce results (Arist. *Top.* I.3, 101b5–10).

It is therefore possible, on the theoretical level, for the debate between skeptics and dogmatists to result, after a vehement exchange of arguments and counter-arguments, in a kind of draw. But if the superiority of skepticism to dogmatism does not (and cannot) consist in its greater *truth* about matters about which dogmatism pretends to be true, then in what does it consist?

We can suggest the following answer: it consists in skepticism's greater ethical efficacy. Pyrrhonism was, from the start, a program for happiness, and seems never to have forgotten it (except perhaps with Agrippa, but how can we know?). The question, from that moment forward, was the following: in what way is one happy when one is a skeptic, and in what way is one happier when one is a skeptic than when one is not?

To answer this question, the skeptic must first free himself from the charge of *apraxia*, the "impossibility of acting" to which his skepticism would supposedly condemn him: for how can he claim to be happy if his principles preclude those minimal conditions of happiness that the very possibility of living and of acting seem to be? Sextus appears not to be very troubled by this objection; if the skeptic suspends judgment regarding the existence of a criterion of truth, still he avails himself of a criterion of action – appearance – that offers no occasion for the slightest investigation, since it consists in an involuntary *pathos* (*PH* 1.23–24):

> Adhering then to appearances, we live in accordance with the normal rules of life, undogmatically (*adoxastos*), seeing that we cannot remain entirely inactive (*anenergetoi*). And it would seem that this regulation of life is fourfold, and that one part of it lies in the guidance of Nature, another in the constraint of the affects, another in the tradition of laws and customs, another in the instruction of the arts. (Trans. Bury, slightly modified)

The skeptic does not claim that this conformism will make him happy; it will merely allow him not to be inactive, and hence to live, even if not to live well (his criterion of

---

39. Or "argument" (*logos*); similarly in the following lines.

action is *not* a moral criterion, *PH* 1.17). It is just a matter of removing a preliminary obstacle, not of achieving the end.

How then are we to understand what enables Pyrrhonism to present itself (rightly or wrongly) as better placed than its rivals to assure the happiness of its adepts?[40] For that result, there seem to be two necessary conditions whose joint satisfaction is not a matter of course: in one sense, the attainment of Pyrrhonist happiness must depend on us, and only on us, on our work, on our efforts; and, in a different sense, this happiness must be unhoped for, surpassing what one can normally expect of the human condition. Although we have had to give the largest role in this chapter to theoretical skepticism, it is right to note, at least briefly, that the Pyrrhonists also worked a great deal in the field of ethics, as the rather tempestuous history of their reflections on the *telos* (the sovereign "end" of human existence) may show.

Through at least one of his aspects (his "guru" side), Pyrrho had set the bar very high: it is no doubt with respect to him that it was wondered whether his "end" was or not *apatheia*, the absence of all affect and feeling.[41] The term *ataraxia* ("imperturbability"), which figures among the "benefits" of the Pyrrhonist attitude according to TA, may already represent an attenuation of *apatheia*: for one can "feel" *pathē* without thereby being "troubled" or "perturbed" by them; their further history will show that the Pyrrhonists did full justice to this observation.

In this further history, at least two distinct positions may be discerned. According to D.L. 9.107, which attributes this position (already) to Timon as well as to Aenesidemus, the end was no longer defined in terms of a moral disposition, but rather in terms of an intellectual one: *epochē* itself is the "end" of the skeptics (see also *PH* 1.30), probably because it can be achieved by means of a dialectical competence that it is up to us to acquire. Still *ataraxia*, the moral disposition that previously constituted the end but which is not achieved by merely intellectual work, remains in close relation with the new "end": the text says that it "follows" *epochē* "like its shadow." On the other hand, the sequel of this passage (D.L. 9.108), while still purporting to be an exegesis of the position attributed to Timon and Aenesidemus, specifies that beyond the realm of things that depend only on us, there is a realm in which we necessarily undergo unavoidable *pathē* (such as hunger, thirst, and pain), which implies an unavoidable limitation of the "maximalist" ideal of *apatheia*.

The distinction between these two realms, and its consequences for the definition of the end, reappear in a slightly different form in the chapter Sextus devotes to the *telos* of skepticism (*PH* 1.25–30). Here, the end overtly divides into two components, an intellectual and an affective one, namely, "*ataraxia* in matters of opinion" and "*metriopatheia* [moderation of affects[42]] in those of unavoidable necessities." But let us

---

40. *M* 11 frequently stresses these two complementary themes: a dogmatist (who believes that some things are good by nature and others bad by nature) cannot attain *eudaimonia*; a skeptic, believing no such thing, can by that very means attain it. He will live "happily and unperturbed," *eudaimonōs kai atarachōs* (11.118).

41. D.L. 9.108 (where *apatheia* is contrasted with *praiotēs*, "mildness"). See also Cic. *Acad.* II. 42.130: Pyrrho said that the wise man "does not even feel" (*ne sentire quidem* = *apatheia*) the differences toward which the Stoic Aristo of Chios recommended *adiaphoria*, "indifference."

42. Here the shying from the standard term *apatheia* becomes patent.

consider a few more details. In the remainder of the chapter, we can in fact distinguish two explanatory developments (§§ 26–28 and 29–30), not precisely congruent and each dedicated to explaining this division.

In the first passage, Sextus first expounds what one might call the philosophical path to *ataraxia*. The founders of skepticism ("noble natures," as *PH* 1.12 describes them) sought to attain this end through the discovery of truth, a discovery supposed to put an end to "contradictions in things" and to impasses in investigation; but, falling into "contradictions of equal weight," they adopted *epochē* and the latter led them "by chance" (*tuchikōs*) to *ataraxia* in matters of opinion (quite generally). Yet Sextus also expounds what one might call an ethical path to *ataraxia*. Among the opinions affected quite generally by *epochē*, one class in particular immediately causes "disquiet" (*tarachē*): those in virtue of which we think that such and such things are good (or bad) "by nature." If, for example, one considers something one possesses to be good "by nature," one will be disquieted by the idea of losing it; and if it is something one does not possess, one will be just as much disquieted by the desire to have it. By ridding oneself of such "superadded" opinions, one will cease to "strain" in the slightest to pursue or to flee whatever it may be: suppress the cause of your *tarachē* and you will suppress its effect. By its specific effect on this kind of opinion, *ataraxia* contributes, and contributes unfailingly, to *metriopatheia*; thus the two components of the skeptical *telos*, *ataraxia* in matters of opinion and *metriopatheia* in the realm of the unavoidable, remain linked.

In the second explanatory passage, the separation between these same two components is much more definite. When Sextus now describes *metriopatheia*, he seems deliberately to avoid saying that those who stand in need of it are victims of *tarachē* and those who attain it enjoy *ataraxia*. The term *ataraxia* now occurs only in the description of the philosophical path; and this time the skeptics are said to have had the same experience as the painter Apelles, who, despairing of representing a horse's froth in his painting, finally hurled at the canvas the sponge he used to clean his brushes. The froth, hoped for and despaired of, was wonderfully captured by the mark of the sponge. Similarly, for those who practiced *epochē*, "*ataraxia* followed as if by chance (*hoion tuchikōs*), as a shadow follows the body" (*PH* 1.29, trans. Bury, slightly modified).

Reflecting on this striking "collage" of the invocation of chance (mentioned by itself in D.L. 9.107) and the image of the shadow (used by itself in *PH* 1.26), we might wonder whether it was not obligatory to choose between them; for in fact the shadow does not follow the body by chance, but by necessity, at least if the sun is shining. But perhaps Pyrrhonism owes its unique glamour precisely to the relation, so subtly woven of chance and necessity, by which it came to link its intellectual commitment to its moral benefit. After all, the incident of the sponge befell not just any painter, but the great Apelles. And all the same, it was he who had painted the horse.

Bibliography

Editions, Translations, Commentaries of Ancient Texts

Annas, J. and Barnes, J. (1985). *The Modes of Scepticism – Ancient Texts and Modern Interpretations*. Cambridge: Cambridge University Press.

——. (1994). *Sextus Empiricus: Outlines of Scepticism*. Cambridge: Cambridge University Press.

Bett, R. (1997). *Sextus Empiricus Against the Ethicists*. Oxford: Clarendon Press.

Decleva Caizzi, F. (1981). *Pirrone: Testimonianze*. Naples: Bibliopolis.

Long, A. A. and Sedley, D. N. (1987). *The Hellenistic Philosophers*. (2 vols.). Cambridge: Cambridge University Press. Traduction française par J. Brunschwig and P. Pellegrin (2001). Paris: Flammarion.

Mates, B. (1995). *The Skeptic Way: Sextus Empiricus's Outlines of Pyrrhonism*. New York and Oxford: Oxford University Press.

Pellegrin, P. (1997). *Sextus Empiricus: Esquisses pyrrhoniennes*. Paris: Seuil.

Modern Works Cited

Ausland, H. W. (1989). "On the Moral Origin of the Pyrrhonian Philosophy." *Elenchos* 10, 359–434.

Barnes, J. (1982). "The Beliefs of a Pyrrhonist". *Proceedings of the Cambridge Philological Society*, NS 28, 1–29 = *Elenchos* 4, 1983, 5–43.

——. (1990). *The Toils of Scepticism*. Cambridge: Cambridge University Press.

——. (1992). "Diogenes Laertius IX 61–116: The Philosophy of Pyrrhonism". In W. Haase and H. Temporini (eds.), *ANRW* II 36.6 (pp. 4241–301). Berlin/New York: de Gruyter.

Bett, R. (2000). *Pyrrho, His Antecedents, and His Legacy*. Oxford: Oxford University Press.

Brennan, T. (1994). "Criterion and Appearance in Sextus Empiricus: The Scope of Sceptical Doubt, the Status of Sceptical Belief." *Bulletin of the Institute of Classical Studies*, 39, 151–69.

Brochard, V. (1887). *Les sceptiques grecs*. Paris: Vrin.

Brunschwig, J. (1994). *Papers in Hellenistic Philosophy*. Cambridge: Cambridge University Press.

——. (1995). *Études sur les philosophies hellénistiques*. Paris: Presses Universitaires de France.

Burnyeat, M. F. (1979). "Conflicting Appearances." *Proceedings of the British Academy*, 65, 69–111.

——. (1980a). "Tranquillity Without a Stop: Timon, Frag. 68." *Classical Quarterly*, NS 30, 86–93.

——. (1980b). "Can the Sceptic Live his Scepticism?" In M. Schofield, M. Burnyeat, and J. Barnes (eds.), *Doubt and Dogmatism: Studies in Hellenistic Epistemology* (pp. 20–53). Oxford: Clarendon Press. Repr. in M. F. Burnyeat (ed.). (1983) (pp. 117–48).

——. (ed.). (1983). *The Skeptical Tradition*. Berkeley: University of California Press.

——. (1984). "The Sceptic in His Place and Time." In R. Rorty, J. B. Schneewind, and Q. Skinner (eds.), *Philosophy in History* (pp. 225–54). Cambridge: Cambridge University Press.

Castagnoli, L. (2000). "Self-bracketing Pyrrhonism." *Oxford Studies in Ancient Philosophy*, 18, 263–328.

Decleva Caizzi, F. (1992). "Aenesidemus and the Academy." *Classical Quarterly*, NS 42, 176–89.

Dye, G. (2001). *L'esprit du scepticisme*. Paris (unpublished thesis).

Frede, M. (1984). "The Skeptic's Two Kinds of Assent and the Question of the Possibility of Knowledge." In R. Rorty, J. B. Schneewind, and Q. Skinner (eds.), *Philosophy in History* (pp. 255–78). Cambridge: Cambridge University Press. Repr. in M. Frede (1987). *Essays in Ancient Philosophy* (pp. 201–22). Minneapolis: University of Minnesota Press.

——. (1987). "The Skeptic's Beliefs." In M. Frede, *Essays in Ancient Philosophy* (pp. 179–200). Minneapolis: University of Minnesota Press.

von Fritz, K. (1963). "Pyrrho." In Pauly-Wissowa, *Realencyclopädie der klassischen Altertumswissenschaft* XXIV, col. 89–106.

Glidden, D. (1983). "Skeptic Semiotics." *Phronesis*, 28, 213–55.

Hankinson, R. J. (1995). *The Sceptics*. London/New York: Routledge.

Janáček, J. (1963). "Die Hauptschrift des Sextus Empiricus als Torso erhalten?" *Philologus*, 107, 271–7.

Johnsen, B. C. (2001). "On the Coherence of Pyrrhonian Skepticism." *Philosophical Review*, 110, 521–62.

McPherran, M. L. (1987). "Skeptical Homeopathy and Self-refutation." *Phronesis*, 32, 290–328.

Robin, L. (1944). *Pyrrhon et le scepticisme grec*. Paris: Presses Universitaires de France. (Garland repr. 1980).

Sedley, D. N. (1976). "Epicurus and His Professional Rivals." *Cahiers de Philologie*, 1, 119–59.

Stopper, M. R. (1983). "Schizzi Pirroniani," *Phronesis*, 28, 265–97.

Striker, G. (1983). "The Ten Tropes of Aenesidemus". In M. F. Burnyeat (ed.), *The Skeptical Tradition* (pp. 95–115). Berkeley: University of California Press. Repr. in G. Striker (1996). *Essays on Hellenistic Epistemology and Ethics* (pp. 116–34). Cambridge: Cambridge University Press.

Zeller, E. (1909). *Die Philosophie der Griechen in ihrer geschichtlichen Entwicklung*. 4th edn. Leipzig: Reisland.

25

Epicureanism

PIERRE-MARIE MOREL

Introduction

Epicureanism gives the first impression of being a philosophy of nature, not just because the science of nature (*phusiologia*) holds a central place in it, but also because Epicurean ethics invite us to lead a life in conformity with nature. For instance, Epicurus' *Principal Doctrine* 25 exhorts us to relate each of our acts, in all circumstances, to the "goal of nature," if we want our actions to be coherent with our reasonings. Yet this relation to nature is not a matter of course. First of all, physical nature is, at bottom, nothing but atoms and void. The organization and beauty of our world are only effects of an initially disorderly movement of corpuscles. The world itself is destined for destruction and is only a distinctive specimen among an infinity of worlds to be found in an unlimited universe. There is no providence or teleology that could explain the local and precarious order in which we live. Physical nature is, therefore, not in itself a bearer of meaning: it is neutral, and in principle ought not to determine any norm capable of grounding a relation of conformity. Further, Epicureanism is characterized by a tension between the immediacy of the relation to nature afforded us by our affects of pleasure and pain, and the mediation represented by scientific knowledge of nature: the study of *phusiologia* is to reveal what does not appear to us and so to turn us away from common illusions, baseless fears, and superstition. It is thanks to an "affective" criterion, pleasure, that we are able to choose a happy life, but this life is accessible to us only through the intermediary of a kind of science of happiness. Because these difficulties affect the very principles of ancient Epicureanism, it is essential to understand how its exponents tried to resolve them.

The philosophical tradition founded by Epicurus (341–270 BCE) is one of the most homogeneous of antiquity. It did undergo a certain evolution, owing to successive polemics, to historical conditions, and to the literary and philosophical temperament of authors, particularly Lucretius. Nonetheless, the Epicureans, without renouncing their freedom of speech, appeal constantly and with great respect to their first teacher. He was the author of a considerable body of work, now largely lost. Still, Book 10 of Diogenes Laertius' *Lives and Opinions* contains a precious "life of Epicurus" and reproduces the three philosophical texts that constitute the basis of our documentary evidence: the *Letters* to Herodotus, Pythocles, and Menoeceus. These are followed by 40 *Principal Doctrines* on ethics. But Diogenes Laertius cites 41 titles of works by Epicurus and specifies that he is mentioning only his best works (10.27–28). Among these, *On Nature* (*Peri phuseos*), in 37 books, must have been the most important in all respects.

We have a few fragments of it, thanks to the excavations at Herculaneum and the papyrological studies based on them.[1]

Epicurus was not a solitary thinker, and around 306–305 he founded his own school, the Garden, in the immediate environs of Athens. His first-generation disciples, especially Hermarchus, who succeeded to the headship of the Garden, Colotes, Polystratus, and Metrodorus, contributed to deepening the doctrine. The influence of the Garden gradually extended beyond the circle of first-generation disciples and, in the first century before our era, Rome becomes the site of an important Epicurean revival, thanks to the debates between the great philosophical schools. Our main Epicurean witnesses to this phenomenon are Philodemus of Gadara and above all Lucretius. The former, a Greek philosopher from Syria, is the author of a very important body of work dealing with ethics, aesthetics, politics, logic, theology, and the positions of the various philosophical schools. The fragments of his treatises, preserved in the papyri of Herculaneum, constitute a source that is damaged but very precious for developments in Epicureanism and for its new areas of interest, such as poetry and the history of philosophical movements.[2] We know practically nothing about the life of Lucretius, and only the text of his poem, *On the Nature of Things* (*De rerum natura*), allows us to form an idea of his philosophical project. Lucretius himself claims to be a mere translator or imitator of Epicurus (Lucr. 3.6). We shall see that his undeniable fidelity should not conceal a great formal originality and a genuine intention to elaborate the doctrine on several fundamental points.[3] Further, we would not understand Epicureanism as well if we did not have available external, sometimes hostile, sources. These include the various polemical treatises on which Plutarch partly draws, but also the testimonies left us by Cicero in *De Natura deorum* (Book 1) and *De finibus bonorum et malorum* (Books 1 and 2). Finally, the fragments of Diogenes of Oenanda's mural inscription, in Lycia, attest to the persistence of the Epicurean tradition until the second century of our own era, even if they are contemporary with the retreat of its influence in the ancient world.[4]

Physics

The Democritean heritage

Epicurean physics is based on extremely simple principles: reality is constituted by bodies and void; bodies are either indivisible, i.e., atoms (*atoma*), or else composites of atoms. The atoms are unlimited in number, and the void in which they move is unlimited. Also, the All itself is unlimited. Worlds are likewise unlimited in number. The exposition of these principles takes up the first paragraphs (*Hdt.* 39–44) that follow the

1. The editions resulting from these studies are published, for the most part, in the journal *Cronache Ercolanesi* and in the collection, "La Scuola di Epicuro," Naples: Bibliopolis.
2. On Philodemus' position in the Epicurean tradition, see Auvray Assayas and Delattre (2001).
3. On this question, see Sedley (1998).
4. For more ample information on the Hellenistic schools and questions about sources, see Erler (1994); and in this volume the chapters by Bénatouïl, PHILOSOPHIC SCHOOLS IN HELLENISTIC AND ROMAN TIMES, and Sharples, THE PROBLEM OF SOURCES.

prologue to Epicurus' *Letter to Herodotus*. Now, the latter is the authoritative epitome for everyone who wants to acquire the knowledge needed for happiness. The science of nature, once reduced to its essentials, in fact promises a life free from disturbance to those who study its details, as it does to those who master only its basic principles (*Hdt.* 35–37). In Epicurus' eyes, then, this exposition represents what is most essential within the essential, what is most elementary within the elementary. The science of happiness that Epicureanism aims to build is thus in the first instance a physics.

Although Epicurus claims to demonstrate his own intellectual autonomy and to be exclusively his own student and no one else's (D.L. 10.13), this physical doctrine is, in its main lines, the one that Democritus of Abdera had elaborated before him.[5] This indirect connection is attested by several ancient sources, especially Cicero, Sextus Empiricus, and Clement of Alexandria. Diogenes Laertius (10.2) even relates that Epicurus threw himself into philosophy after discovering the books of Democritus. Epicurus nonetheless formulates many implicit criticisms against the real founder of atomism, whom he nicknames "Lerocritus," which would mean: he who exercises his judgment – or who disputes – about absurdities. He thus seems at once to appropriate Abderite physics and to revise it. This double attitude is probably in large part required by the need to answer the criticisms Aristotle had advanced against Democritus (see esp. Furley, 1967). Besides, Epicureanism will not content itself with revising Abderite physics: it will also dispute the hegemony of its primary explanatory principle, i.e., necessity.

The revision of physics

The Epicurean revision bears principally on three points: the infinity of atomic shapes, the structure of the atom, and the variations in the motions of atoms. Democritus had posited not only the infinity of atoms, but also that of their shapes, thus basing the whole explanation of events and physical structures on a limitless combination of shapes (see esp. Simpl. *In Phys.* 28.15 = DK 68A38). It is not certain, however, that Democritus pushed the doctrine of infinity to its ultimate conclusions. He may thus not have gone so far as to assert both that the atom is imperceptible by nature and that there could be an atom the size of a world. In any case, the Epicureans judged that his conception of atomic infinity was defective on this point. Epicurus holds for his part that the shapes are not absolutely infinite in number, but only inconceivably many, though there is an infinite number of atoms of each of these shapes (*Hdt.* 42–43; 55–56; Lucr. 2.479–588).

This disagreement is no mere detail: it reveals important methodological and epistemological differences. Epicurus makes clear in paragraph 56 of the *Letter to Herodotus* that it is not necessary, in order to explain the differences between sensible qualities, that sizes be strictly infinite. Thus he privileges a particularly economical method on the speculative level, and so defines a sort of principle of sufficient explanation, of which we find no trace in the testimonia and fragments of the Abderite corpus. Together with this, he invokes the testimony of sense-experience, which prevents us from admitting atoms large enough to be perceptible. Now, Democritus had developed

5.   On Democritus' physics, see Curd, PARMENIDES AND AFTER, in this volume.

a theory of knowledge that was very critical of sense-experience, and so he could not evaluate the atomic theory by reference to the testimony of the senses.[6] Furthermore, Lucretius makes clear that a strict infinity of shapes would have as consequence an infinity of variations between sensible qualities. Lacking the ability to discern boundaries between the latter, we would therefore perceive nothing distinct. Sensible impressions would vary infinitely. But no such thing takes place: simply by perceiving, we distinguish differences of temperature, of color, of odor, and of taste (Lucr. 2.500–521).

The revision of atomism also bears on the very structure of the atom. According to Democritus, the smallness and solidity of the atom attest to its physical indivisibility. We, therefore, have no really strong reason to reconsider the thesis that the Abderite atom, an indivisible polyhedron, lacks parts. Aristotle, however, objects that, in virtue of the continuity of space, the atom must be mathematically divisible (*Phys.* VI.10, 240b8ff.). Even if one postulates its physical indivisibility, as the atomists do, no body can cross a spatial boundary all at once. We must, therefore, be able to distinguish in it the parts that have not yet crossed the boundary from those that have done so. Thus, according to Aristotle, something indivisible "can neither move nor change in any way" (240b31). This objection is particularly cruel: the Abderites meant precisely to respond to the Eleatic negation of motion by raising the movement of atoms in the void to the rank of an unquestionable principle. Aristotle thus destroyed the very foundation of their physics. It is not surprising that Epicurus would have wished to answer this objection. He did so by conceding that the atom does, in one sense, have parts: "concurring with the doctrine of Leucippus and Democritus about the first bodies, he preserved their impassibility, but removed from them the property of being without parts, meaning thus to answer Aristotle" (Simpl. *In Phys.* 925.19–22). The atom thus has ultimate parts – the *minimae partes* of Lucretius – which are the units of measure, but which are inseparable from the whole they constitute and, because of this, incapable of producing by themselves any motions or aggregations. They are conceived by analogy with the ultimate threshold of sense-perception (*Hdt.* 59; Lucr. 1.599–634).

As far as the motions of atoms are concerned, the Epicurean texts also contain important refinements not found in the testimonia available to us on the Abderites: atoms move at equal speed in the void, no matter what their weight, their trajectories being modified by impacts (*Hdt.* 61–62; Lucr. 2.238–239); and an atom's own weight is the cause of its downward movement (*Hdt.* 61; Lucr. 2.190). According to Cicero (*Fat.* 20.46), the Epicureans differ on this point from Democritus, for whom only impacts are responsible for the motions of atoms. Nevertheless, it remains true that, for Democritus as for the Epicureans, there is no beginning to the presence of motion in the universe.

Finally, the doctrine of the swerve – *clinamen* in Latin, *parenklisis* in Greek – of atoms constitutes a decisive innovation relative to the first version of atomism.[7] Lucretius imagines the following situation (2.221–224): if weight was the only original

6. In truth, this point seems to pose a problem for Democritus himself, as he suggests by imagining a contradictory dialogue between the senses and reason (Gal. *Med. exp.* 15 Walzer-Frede = DK 68B125).
7. For the neo-Academic critique of the atomic swerve, see Sharples in this volume, section titled "Cicero and Epicurus: the Atomic Swerve."

principle of the motion of atoms, would not the latter fall downward through the infinite void, like drops of rain? How then could they collide with each other, and how could nature produce anything at all under such conditions? We must suppose that a minute swerve affects the first movement of these atoms in order to understand the spontaneous generation of corporeal combinations and, indirectly, the formation of worlds. The swerve is thus just as primitive as the relation between the weight and the downward motion of the atom. This doctrine also has an ethical side and, in Lucretius, grounds the possibility of free action. It thus has a central role in the theoretical structure of the Lucretian poem, but it also poses redoubtable problems of interpretation. In the first place, we do not know if Epicurus already held it, as Lucretius, Aëtius, and Diogenes of Oenanda assure us. The only extended and reasoned exposition we have of it is in Book 2 of *De Rerum Natura* (Lucr. 2.184–293) and we find no mention at all of the swerve in the surviving texts of Epicurus. On the whole, modern interpreters have taken the following positions: some think Epicurus may have come late to the doctrine of the swerve, which would explain its absence from the *Letter to Herodotus*; others judge that its absence from the surviving texts of Epicurus is due merely to lacunae; finally, others doubt that Epicurus is its author. In fact, it must be asked whether he really needed the doctrine of the swerve, or whether he thought himself to have solved by other means the difficulties it claims to solve. We shall come back to this question in connection with cosmogony and also the explanation of free action.

Further, it is fairly difficult to give a positive description of the process of the swerve solely by the light of the Lucretian passage, and even more so to explain the relation between the swerve and voluntary decision: the *clinamen*, due to its somewhat indeterminate character, makes room for the idea of a break in the mechanical chain of strictly physical causes (Lucr. 2.251–293), but gives no positive explanation of the process of decision itself. For instance, Lucretius' text does not make it completely clear whether the *clinamen* is a motion that is necessary for voluntary decision, or whether it happens after the decision, as a response to a stimulus. In this sense, it constitutes merely a condition of the possibility, not a true cause, of free action. Still, the essential thing is to understand the motivations to which this doctrine responds. As we have seen, in Lucretius it completes the description of the atomic mechanism. The Roman poet must also have been concerned to oppose the Stoic doctrine of fate. To these motives may be added one of the constant preoccupations of the Epicurean tradition: to contest Democritus' thesis that necessity is the principle of all things (D.L. 9.45 = DK 68A1; Arist. *GA* V.8, 789b2 = DK 68A66). Now, this rejection of necessitarianism forces a new representation of nature, of its organization, and of its power. It therefore contributes directly to the definition of Epicurean naturalism.

A new "nature"

The *clinamen*, as we have seen, is a condition of free action because it gives a physical ground for the possibility of a break in the chain of mechanical causes. Just as atoms possess a motive cause beyond weight and impacts, so we have a capacity to shield ourselves, at least partially, from the external necessity of external forces and the internal necessity of our passive tendencies (Lucr. 2.272–293). Lucretius thus indicates that there is natural necessity, but that it is neither all-powerful nor hegemonic.

Prior to the moral problematic, however, and as the Lucretian account dedicated to the *clinamen* shows, the rejection of necessitarianism relates first of all to a reconsideration of the Democritean conception of natural principles. True, the Abderite conception of necessity is more complex and more nuanced than the Epicureans seem to have recognized: retaining only the most compulsive dimension of Democritean necessity, they set it over against contingency, chance, and indeterminacy. In Democritus, the notion of necessity applies just as much to order – the organization of worlds, the causal chain of events – as to disorder, such as the motion of atoms outside of worlds. Chance is therefore an aspect of necessity. Nevertheless, and by the same token, chance as such has no specific causal function. For Lucretius, on the contrary, the indeterminacy characterizing the *clinamen* is the condition *sine qua non* of the genesis of all organization: without the *clinamen*, "nature would have created nothing" (2.224). The first principles of things are thus characterized by their inconstancy, and order, always precarious, is the outcome of a primal disorder.

From this it may seem paradoxical that Lucretius represents nature allegorically, making it in some fashion the organizing subject of the world. Nature is in fact a "creator" (*natura creatrix*: 1.629 and 2.1117) or "sovereign" (*natura gubernans*: 5.77), and she "demands" (*natura cogit*). She institutes the covenants or contracts that guarantee the relative constancy of phenomena, e.g., the stability of species. Must we see in these expressions, beyond their metaphorical aspect, a concession to a kind of intentional teleology or providentialism? In fact, nature has no other creative power than that which the atoms exercise in their own way, i.e., blindly. The atoms do not deliberate and do not decide anything, not only because they are inanimate and have no mental attributes, but also because they do not need to: organization emerges spontaneously from an infinity of trials eventually resulting in the realization of viable and stable structures (1.1023–1090). That is why nature "accomplishes everything herself, spontaneously, without any divine assistance" (2.1092).

In these circumstances, it is perfectly legitimate to speak of "nature" as a totality:[8] man is to understand the covenants of nature and to see them for what they are, i.e., decrees that are inviolable and in that sense necessary, whose cosmological manifestations are nonetheless contingent and precarious. Necessity, far from being hegemonic, is henceforth in the service of nature.

Cosmology and Anthropology

A cosmology of selection

The point of departure for the Epicurean explanation of the generation and internal organization of worlds is likewise an ambivalent relation to the thought of Democritus.

---

8. And not just in order to denote the essence or the physical foundations of things. While we find no trace in Democritus of a "nature" understood as a totality, Epicurus uses *phusis* to mean the essential properties of things, or the things themselves, as well as the totality of what exists. Sometimes Lucretius uses *natura* in the first sense, but the second is very definitely predominant for him.

Epicurus' *Letter to Pythocles* lets us form a good idea of the Garden's theses on this question (see also Lucr. 5.416–508). As in Democritus, the worlds are limitless and of multiple shapes. However, the Epicureans contribute an important correction: it is not enough to invoke, as the Abderite does, a primeval "vortex" (*dinē*) of atoms of whatever sort to explain the formation of a cosmic structure; we must assume the presence of appropriate seeds (*spermata*) (*Pyth.* 89–90). Although this point has been debated, these seeds are probably atoms, which means that Epicurus introduces a new limitation within the physics of the infinite that Democritus had elaborated: it is not just the infinity of the atoms and their combinations that explains, in principle as well as in fact, the existence of worlds, but also a kind of spontaneous selection within this infinity. It follows that the worlds can hardly be of all possible shapes. Democritus, for his part, thought that some lacked animals, plants, and wetness, that some lacked both sun and moon, though in others there were several (Hippol. *Haer.* 1.13 = DK 68A40).

Details of the formation of worlds are of little importance for Epicurus, since knowing about them is unnecessary for our happiness. Besides, the conditions necessary for such a process are variable. The essential thing is to account in the simplest possible way for a reality which then will give no more occasion for astonishment, any more than we should be astonished or made fearful by other celestial phenomena, such as eclipses or thunder. The Epicureans thus insist in various ways on the spontaneity of the transition from the initial disorder of atomic motions to the formation of a cosmic structure. This spontaneity is linked to the continuity that Epicurus discerns in the relation of the isolated atom to the atom in a composite. In fact, the fundamental category of Epicurean physics is "body," rather than the atom. This may be verified by observing the argumentative procedure of the *Letter to Herodotus*, which mentions bodies before it mentions atoms, and which lumps the latter in with the former: "among the bodies, some are composite and others are those of which the composites are made" (*Hdt.* 40–41). There is therefore no ontological gap between atoms and composites, but rather a functional distinction within the entirety of "body." By nature, atoms are both independent and apt to aggregate with each other to form bodies. The Lucretian terms for the atom confirm this: atoms are not simply "matter" (*materies* or *materia*); they are also the "first principles of things" (*primordia rerum*), the "first bodies" (*corpora prima*), the "seeds of things" (*semina rerum*) and their "generative principles" (*genitalia rerum*), all expressions that make reference to composites.

Thus, when he speaks of the formation of worlds and of their infinity, starting with paragraph 45 of the *Letter to Herodotus*, Epicurus suggests that the atoms have two causal roles: "It is not possible for the atoms which we have just described, out of which (*ex hōn*) a world can come to be or by which (*huph' hōn*) a world can be produced, to be exhausted in a single or a limited number of worlds..." The play with the prepositions *ex* and *hupo*, suggests that atoms, considered as ceaselessly in motion, are not just components ("out of which"), but also the real spontaneous agents or immediate moving principles ("by which") of the formation of worlds. It is not impossible, though it cannot be stated definitively, that the cosmogonical purpose of the Lucretian *clinamen* was retrospectively to make explicit this function of atoms.

492

Human life and the limits of conformity with nature

As Democritus had before them, the Epicureans extend their cosmogonical hypotheses to include a view of the genesis and development of humankind. Epicurean anthropology is an anthropology of spontaneous progress: the human species came out of the earth and the rise of social existence, language, technical skills, laws, and political institutions is part of the history of our world. It is thus not a process alien to nature. The latter, Epicurus says at the beginning of the anthropological passage in the *Letter to Herodotus* (75–76), "has been taught and compelled, abundantly and in many ways, by things themselves." Lucretius explains the institution of language, for example, by saying that nature (*natura*) caused the utterance of the various sounds of language and that utility (*utilitas*) led men to settle on the names of things (Lucr. 5.1028–1029).

This example, however, because it distinguishes two factors – nature and utility – shows the limits of the relation to nature: nature itself is in the process of becoming and it is diversified; so it cannot suggest to man immutable norms he could merely apply. Technical skills, to be sure, derive from an imitation of nature: the sun teaches men to cook their food and to soften it (Lucr. 5.1102–1104); nature, through the spontaneous sprouting of berries and acorns, provides the model (*specimen*) for sowing, and it is at the origin of our practice of grafting (1361–1367). Nevertheless, human progress is not an ever more faithful imitation of nature, but rather a continuous adaptation to natural conditions. Languages, for instance, though they have a natural origin, differentiate themselves because of the diversity of the feelings and experiences specific to each people (Epic. *Hdt.* 75–76). Human action in general is thus inspired and guided by nature, but it cannot rest content with merely *imitating* nature.

The definition of what is just, in the *Principal Doctrines* (KD 31–37), is a particularly revealing example of this phenomenon. On the one hand, Epicurus gives an apparently naturalist definition of justice: "the justice arising from nature is a pledge of mutual utility neither to harm one another nor to suffer harm" (*KD* 31). On the other, he seems to subscribe to a conventionalist, or even relativist, conception of the just or of justice: justice is not something that exists in itself, but is merely a certain contract (*sunthēkē*). It is an agreement that men, assembled together, draw up in a particular place at a particular time, concerning what it is proper to do and not to do, for the purpose of not harming each other (*KD* 33). The definition of justice also legitimately varies from one time to another and from one people to another, in such a way that what is regarded as just at a given time may not be so regarded in other times (*KD* 37–38). Actually, Epicurus' point of view cannot be assimilated to sheer relativism, for his conception rests on two constants: the correspondence between the just and the useful (*sumpheron*) and the fact that common interest is the sole criterion of usefulness in politics. The shared experience of what is useful in collective life allows us to give a real content to the preconception or pre-notion (*prolēpsis*) that we have of the just.[9] Thus, through a relation that is both natural and variable – what is useful to

9. On the role of preconceptions in Epicureanism, see also Modrak, PHILOSOPHY OF LANGUAGE, in this volume.

the community – the (natural) reality of common life is linked to the (conventional) reality of legal rules. Nature cannot determine norms in this matter, for the just varies with the changes of historical becoming.[10] Nature is content to mark limits – those within which the definition of common usefulness varies – and leaves to man the responsibility for legal decisions. The attribution to Epicurus of a form of legal naturalism (see especially Alberti, 1995), therefore, cannot completely avoid the conventionalist reading (defended, with qualifications, by Goldschmidt, 1977): without breaking away from nature, Epicurus rejects every conception of justice that claims to abstract from differences between peoples and from the movement of history (see Morel, 2000).

Epistemology

The origin of representations

We have seen that the fundamental objects of Epicurean physics are entities that are hidden or non-evident (*adēla*): atoms and void. Still, every proposition about these entities must be compared with the evidence of things that do appear (*ta phainomena*). We shall see below what the rules are for this comparison, but we can state now that the intellectual grasp of the principles is always dependent on the evidence of the senses. For instance, in the *Letter to Herodotus*, the unfolding of which seems to exclude all previously acquired theoretical knowledge, the appeal to sensory experience is mandated at the outset.

One might object to such a method that it uses means of knowing whose validity it has not previously established, and that it should seek, independently of physics, an epistemological justification for the transition from the visible to the invisible. Epicurean texts propose, as a reply to this objection, the physiological explanation of sensations: vision results from the reception of replicas (*tupoi*) or images (*eidōla*) originating spontaneously from the seen object. Because they are transmitted emanations that preserve the structure and properties of the object, these replicas allow us to form a representation or appearance (*phantasia*) which remains in "sympathy" (*sumpatheia*) with it. This same principle of sympathy also holds for the other senses (*Hdt.* 48–53; Lucr. 4.46–268). The appearance is, therefore, not purely subjective, and even less is it strictly mental: we perceive something that the object itself produces, and the process through which we perceive this thing can be described in the same way as any other natural process. Physics thus explains the way in which we represent to ourselves the phenomena that in turn undergird propositions about hidden entities. As we shall see, this justification for the appeal to the evidence of the senses is decisive on the epistemological level, for it applies derivatively to representations that are not immediately sensory. It thus allows for the definition of the criteria of truth.

10.   The view taken by Epicurus clearly does not amount to evoking the first human societies (on this point see Lucr. 5.1019–1027 and 1108–1160, and Hermarchus' genealogy, cited at length by Porphyry, *Abst.* 1.7–12): the variations of the just are also those of history in their course.

The criteria of truth

Because our sensations are physically similar to their objects, they can be called "true" prior to any judgment about their truth or falsity. The explanation of the origin of sensations thus leads to an assimilation of truth to reality. The truth of sensation, therefore, does not need to be guaranteed to a judgment that would be its criterion. Still, two objections may be raised. First of all, since sensation is defined as a passive reception, how can it by itself play the role of a criterion, that is, an active role, capable of grounding a critical attitude toward our own representations? Second, if sensation is true right from the start, how are we to account for perceptual errors? An apposite answer to the first objection specifies that the sensory impression does not actually become an appearance (*phantasia*) unless we "grasp [it] by applying ourselves to it through thought or else through the sense organs" (*Hdt.* 50). Sensation, like the mind's perception, is an *epibolē*, that is, a "projection" toward the object. The latter is thus not merely received but also "aimed at." Its image is at the same time a grasping-of-an-image (*phantastikē epibolē*: *Hdt.* 50–51). Consequently, sensation involves both the physical receptivity that makes it true, and the act of attention without which it could not indicate what is true. It is therefore not purely passive.

Still, how are we to exonerate this activity from all responsibility for producing perceptual errors, such as hallucinations and optical illusions? The Epicureans take a two-fold attitude, at once defensive and positive, in response to this standard objection. Lucretius defends the infallibility of sensations by showing that no sense, such as sight or smell, can be corrected by a different sense: sight cannot be corrected by hearing, or hearing by touch, or touch by taste, since each sense has a particular and distinct power (4.486–490). As for reason, it comes from sensation and so cannot refute it, since it would refute itself in claiming to refute its own origin (4.483–485; see also D.L. 10.32). We must therefore admit that error comes from some other mental movement distinct from sensation. If I see a square tower in the distance as round, it is not sensation itself that deceives me, but rather the belief I form when I have the sensation (Lucr. 4.353–363; S.E. *M* 7.208–209). Here once again we must go back to the physics: the flow of images (*eidōla*) from the square tower that I see in the distance conveys to me an image of a round tower because of the erosion they suffer in passing through the air over a long distance. Nevertheless, the image finally received is a real image, the actual presence of what is emanating from the object. The sensation is therefore not intrinsically false, for it is true, when I perceive the tower as round, I do perceive it as round, even if in itself it is square. The distortion of the images (*eidōla*) is an epistemologically neutral physical process. The error really comes from that which is "added by opinion" (*prodoxazomenon*) and is not subsequently subjected to a verification capable of confirming it (*Hdt.* 50). This judgment depends on sensations, but it is distinct from the latter. This is how it is with the erroneous judgment according to which the tower that we see from afar is really round, when we have no confirmation of it, not having varied our experience of the object. The sensation is not just non-false: it the first positive manifestation of what is true.

Sensation is therefore the first criterion of truth, but it is not the only one. Diogenes Laertius (10.31) reports that, according to Epicurus' *Canon*, the criteria of truth are sensations, preconceptions (*prolēpseis*) and feelings (cf. S.E. *M* 7.203–216). We do not have, in the Epicurean texts, an account expressly dedicated to preconceptions, but Diogenes Laertius' summary indicates that they have two correlative functions: the retention in memory of repeated sensations – the notion of man derives from the sensory experience we have had of individual human beings – and the anticipatory apprehension of objects that may correspond to later sensations – what appears to me in the distance may be a horse, an ox, or a man (10.33). As for affections (*pathē*), they disclose pleasure and pain in an evident manner (10.34) and for this reason play a central role in Epicurean ethics.

The method of judgment

This theory of the criteria of knowledge may seem at first sight to be a naïve empiricism. Its application, however, shows that it is no such thing, for the Epicureans in no way claim to reduce the knowledge of hidden entities to a direct extension of the perception of phenomena. Our eyes see shade and light, but they do not teach about the difference between them: "reason (*ratio animi*) alone must discern them, and the eyes are unable to know the nature of things (*natura rerum*)" (Lucr. 4.384–385). The *natura rerum*, which constitutes the very subject matter of Lucretius' poem, truly unveils itself only to the eyes of reason. All the subtlety of Epicurean methodology lies in the different modes of transition from conceptions (*epinoia*) to sensations and inversely: by acquaintance, analogy, resemblance, and composition (D.L. 10.32). These modes, and analogy in particular, relate propositions about hidden things to sensory evidence through a complex method for verifying beliefs. The testimony of Diogenes Laertius and Sextus Empiricus on the "canonic," Philodemus' treatise *On Signs*, as well as argumentative procedures used by Epicurus and Lucretius, allow us to understand its rules. When beliefs relate to what can be the object of a direct sensory experience, their truth is established by confirmation (*epimarturēsis*) and their falsity by non-confirmation (*ouk epimarturēsis*). Thus, when I believe that Plato is coming toward me, I still need confirmation or its opposite, non-confirmation, which sensory experience will provide me when the man I see has come near. When beliefs relate to hidden things, they can be the subject of a non-infirmation (*ouk antimarturēsis*) or an infirmation (*antimarturēsis*). In this case I must establish a relation of consequence between the invisible and sensory evidence. The latter cannot be directly confirmed, but it can be established by non-infirmation. Take for example the existence of the void. We assume the existence of motion. But this implies the existence of the void (*Hdt.* 40). Therefore, we posit the existence of the void. Thus the contrary hypothesis is infirmed and the conclusion is warranted. If the inference does not infirm the contrary hypothesis, it justifies a resort to multiple explanations, as in the case of celestial phenomena. Eclipses of the sun and moon, for example, can be explained by their being extinguished, or by their being hidden by other bodies. Furthermore, the different explanations of a single phenomenon may not only be compatible but may even be conjoined (*Pyth.* 96). It is a peculiarity of Epicurean epistemology that it allows that a single phenomenon may be explained in different ways (*Pyth.* 86–87, 93–96; *Hdt.* 79). On the one hand, the same phenomenon, such as thunder or earthquake, may be explained differently depending on which world it occurs in; on the other, within a single world, it may be open to a plurality of explanatory hypotheses. Given that a hypothesis is not infirmed and that it is compatible with the main principles of physics, then, even if other hypotheses also meet the same conditions, it fulfills its only true function: to preserve our *ataraxia* (absence of disturbance) by showing that it is pointless to invoke gods in order to explain natural events. It should therefore be regarded as sufficient.

Epicurean science is thus aware of its own limits. We can possess some certainties, since sensation and the representations directly derived from it are evident, and what is evident requires no proof. Nevertheless, the infinity of the All and the complexity and remoteness of some particular physical processes mandate the method just described. For instance, after comparing atomic combinations to those of the letters that make up the verses he is writing, Lucretius says further that atoms have more numerous powers to create the diversity of things (1.827–829). This indicates that human discourse is unable to encompass the totality of that for which it nonetheless gives an explanation. Knowledge of nature is thus in this sense imperfect. It is sufficient, however, to free us from anxiety in the face of the unknown and to ground the conditions for happiness.

Ethics

Natural philosophy and the happy life

We have seen that knowledge of nature is wholly oriented toward ethics. If knowledge did not make us happier, it would be useless. The task of philosophy, which is to lead us to happiness, is thus the only one that is absolutely necessary. It is the only indispensable activity, and thus the only activity that is entirely suited to our nature. Epicurus in fact shares with the philosophers of the intellectual generation preceding him – especially Plato and Aristotle – this idea that men tend by nature toward the attainment of their happiness, even if, more often than not, they employ inadequate means to it. The point of knowing nature is precisely to allow us to discern what goods and activities are well matched to our own nature.

Now, the image of nature the Epicureans found in Abderite atomism rules out, as they see it, the possibility of both living in conformity with nature and acting freely. Therefore, they defend a new conception of nature which, as we have seen, limits the power of necessity. The atomic swerve is one means contributing to this limitation, but not the only one. Epicurean texts invoke at least two other kinds of argument: from the consequences of necessitarianism and from its absurdity. The argument from the consequences consists in denying that happiness and moral conduct would be possible, under the hypothesis that physical necessity is all-powerful, because the latter would entirely eliminate the responsibility of the agent. Diogenes of Oenoanda, moreover, joins this argument to the appeal to the *clinamen*, by implicitly associating all the theoreticians of fate with Democritus: if everything is moved by necessity and the atoms have no free movement – i.e., no swerve – and one believes in fate, then we can no longer admonish or blame (fr. 54 Smith = LS 20G). In his *On Nature*, Epicurus takes aim at the Abderites themselves and asserts that they cannot say that "necessity and chance are the causes of all things" and at the same time continue to act, without bringing their doctrine into conflict with their actions. Now, this contradictory situation puts them, not in a state of happiness, but on the contrary in a state of internal disturbance (PHerc. 1056; Epic. *Nat.* 34.30 Arrighetti = LS 20C). Necessitarianism is thus as disastrous for happiness as for moral responsibility. Further, it leads to despair, as the *Letter to Menoeceus* makes clear: "For it would be better to follow the mythology about gods than be a slave to the fate of the natural philosophers: the former at least hints at the hope of begging the gods off by means of worship, whereas the latter involves an inexorable necessity" (*Men.* 134). The Epicurean sage, having learned physics, knows for his part that necessity is not hegemonic and that "what depends on us, with which culpability and its opposite are naturally associated, is free from any master" (*Men.* 133). The argument from the absurdity of necessitarianism consists in saying that one cannot coherently claim that necessity is the only cause: "the man who says that all events are necessitated has no ground for criticizing the man who says that not all events are necessitated; for according to him this [i.e., this last assertion] is itself a necessitated event" (Epic. *SV* 40). In fact, from the necessitarian's own viewpoint, the position contrary to his is justified to the extent that its own existence is necessary. It therefore expresses just as well as his own does the law of necessary determination.

This does not mean that we must deny all forms of necessity or, in particular, the mechanical character of strictly physical causality. Did the Epicureans want to develop an anti-reductionist theory of emergent properties and to shield mental motions and judgments from the chain of atomic motions (for this interpretation, see Sedley, 1983 and 1988)? They may, more modestly, have been extolling adaptation to the constraints of nature and to have thought that the possibility of free action was indirectly warranted by the arguments we have just sketched. Epicurus states that the Epicurean sage has faced the necessities of existence (*ta anankaia*), knowing how to give rather than to take his portion, for he is rich in the internal treasure of his self-sufficiency (*SV* 44). To be happy, then, one must acknowledge necessity, which assumes that not everything is subject to it: "Necessity is an evil, but there is no necessity to live with necessity" (*SV* 9). Epicurus' ethics thus adumbrates the distinction, made famous mainly by imperial Stoicism, between what depends on us and what does not.

Now, natural philosophy delineates the precise boundaries around what belongs to me, teaching that what lies beyond them is not to be feared. This is especially so in the case of death: physics teaches me that the soul is corporeal, composed of atoms, and that its cognitive functions depend on the proportion of its atoms found in the aggregate it makes together with the body. It therefore does not survive death, and I experience no sensations whatever once this boundary is passed. Knowing that death is the end of all sensation, and that no "I" persists if it cannot feel, I know that I am not contemporary with my own death. The latter is thus "nothing to me" and I experience no suffering because of it, so that it is no longer to be feared (*Men.* 124–127). Lucretius invokes, in support of this doctrine, the force of natural compacts and so gives a cosmological justification for the occurrence of death: the old man must yield his place because every thing must participate in the formation of something else, in conformity with the process of atomic compensation (Lucr. 3.962–972). Here again, the constraint of natural laws should not dishearten us: to know that every individual life has an end is also to turn away from the fruitless desire for immortality. In a general way, natural philosophy contributes to the preparation of what Philodemus (*Against the*

Sophists 4.9–14 = LS 25J) will call the "quadruple remedy" (*tetrapharmakos*) against the disturbances that keep us from happiness. The contents of this program, which underlies the structure of the *Letter to Menoeceus* and is repeated by *Principal Doctrines* 1–4, are the following: there is nothing to fear from the gods; death is nothing in relation to ourselves; the highest of all pleasures is attainable and is equivalent to the elimination of all suffering; we are able to endure suffering because it is not unlimited.

Men and gods

Theology offers a good example of the synthetic character of Epicurean philosophy and of its ability to include physics, the theory of knowledge, and ethics in the same movement. The first injunction in the *Letter to Menoeceus* is to see the gods for what they are, i.e., happy, indestructible living beings, and to attribute to them nothing inconsistent with these two fundamental properties (*Men.* 123–124). This ethical prescription makes a twofold appeal to physics. In the first place, it dissociates the gods from natural phenomena, especially celestial ones, which men generally attribute to their will or to their anger: a corollary of the beatitude of the gods is their indifference to the order of the universe and to human affairs (*Hdt.* 76–78).[11] In the second place, it assumes that the gods have a physical nature or status which explains their indestructibility and grounds their beatitude.

Unfortunately, the Epicurean texts are rather imprecise on this point. Consequently some commentators (see, for example: Long and Sedley, 1987, vol. 1, pp. 144–49) think the gods do not really differ from the representations we form of them, and that they are in fact mental constructs. God would therefore be nothing more than a flow of images corresponding to the concept we have of him. In the text that pays closest attention to the question of the physical status of the gods (Cic. *ND* 1.43–49 = LS 23E), the Epicurean Velleius states further that the form of the gods is not a solid body but a "quasi-body," the blood of which is "quasi-blood." This interpretation, which opts for a minimal relation to physics, is especially urged out of a concern to take account of anthropomorphic tendencies in the Epicurean conception of the gods: these tendencies suggest a spontaneous "transfer" on the part of our thinking, which tends to attribute to the gods the traits we perceive in vigorous and happy men. Velleius credits the gods with the human form, since it is the most beautiful (Cic. *ND* 1.46; see also the scholium to *KD* 1) and Philodemus assumes that they converse in Greek, because Greek is the language of sages (*On the Gods* 3, col. 14 Diels). We could thus reduce the tension between, on the one hand, the rational and critical theology, or the minimal religiosity, that is predominant in the *Letter to Menoeceus*, and, on the other hand, the acceptance of a kind of literally descriptive theology, compatible with certain traditional and popular representations of the gods.

However, the "conceptualist" interpretation, leaving aside the fact that it is not explicitly attested by any authentically Epicurean text, raises other problems. It precludes any positive account of the statement that the gods live in the "interworlds" (Lucr. 5.146–155; Cic. *ND* 1.18); or of the idea that their nature reconstitutes itself

---

11. See also *KD* 1; Lucr. 2.167–183, 1009–1104; 5.156–194, 1186–1240; 6.68–79; Cic. *ND* 1.45 = LS 23E4–5; Diogenes of Oenoanda, fr. 19-iii Smith.

at every instant through a continuous flow of atoms (as Velleius suggests in Cic. *ND* 1.49), which implies that they are corporeal. In addition, it is very hard to think of them as "living beings" if they are mere objects of thought. If they are images (*eidōla*), then in theory they should be lifeless, since images by themselves have neither sensation nor reason (Diogenes of Oenoanda, fr. 10 Smith; Plut. *On the Disappearance of Oracles*, 420B–C). Finally, the anthropomorphic aspects of theology may be understood by reference to the status of our natural preconception about the gods: Epicurus gives a rather indefinite content to this *prolēpsis* about the gods, mentioning only beatitude and indestructibility, but he does not forbid us to credit them with other attributes. The essential thing is not to attribute anything to them that is incompatible with these fundamental properties. Moreover, we must attribute to them anything that can contribute to the preservation of these properties (*Men.* 123). Our preconception about the gods, in this respect like our preconception about the just, constitutes a kind of framework for variation or a regulative notion, not a real *definition* of the divine. According to Lucretius, we can thus speak of Bacchus to refer to wine, or say that the Earth is the Mother of the gods, as long as we do not let ourselves be contaminated by the established religion (Lucr. 2.655–660). Epicurean anthropomorphism, therefore, does not express an ontological deficiency in the divine, but rather a logical consequence of the method of non-infirmation as applied to our preconception about the gods: the fact that gods have human form is not infirmed by their beatitude and indestructibility. Some members of the school – such the character of Velleius in Cicero (*ND* 1.48), and Demetrius of Laconia (*[The Shape of God]* col. 15 Santoro) – seem merely to have extended the viewpoint opened up by the Teacher of the Garden when they assert that the gods must *necessarily* be human in their form, since no other is found to have the faculty of reason. Velleius' further suggestion – the human form is also the most beautiful – is the final outcome of this logic. In any case, we can ascribe to the Epicureans a realist theology that is compatible with its anthropomorphic aspects.

Pleasure as an end

The assimilation of happiness to pleasure is the most well-known feature of Epicureanism and the one that has earned it the most criticism. Those that Cicero formulates in the second book of *De Finibus*, and the treatise by Plutarch entitled *That it is Impossible to Live Pleasantly if One Follows Epicurus*, provide good examples. This assimilation, however, is not an arbitrary theoretical dictum, for Epicurus takes great pains to justify it. Paragraphs 128–129 of the *Letter to Menoeceus* give a fairly precise idea of his argument. Let us start with the statement that knowledge of nature leads to knowledge of what is naturally suitable for us. Now, as we have seen, men by nature seek the life of happiness, which has for its end "the health of the body and the absence of disturbance (*ataraxia*) in the soul" (*Men.* 128). The absence of disturbance, since it is a state in which nothing is lacking, is absence of pain. The latter is therefore fundamentally the natural end that we pursue. But Epicurus seems to think that there is no intermediate state between pain and pleasure, doubtless because of his assimilation of pain to a state of lacking and because there is no intermediate state between lacking and the absence of a lack. The absence of pain therefore coincides with pleasure itself, so that the latter is the goal of the happy life, our first and congenital (*sungenikon* or *sumphuton*) good.

Not all pleasures, however, correspond to the same degree of pacification of the soul. Some texts, in fact, distinguish between "kinetic" pleasures, such as the pleasure of drinking when thirsty, and "static" or "catastematic" ones. The latter, absence of physical pain and *ataraxia*, express a state of stability in our constitution (*katastēma*) (LS 21Q–T). The fact that we can attain a threshold of equilibrium in pleasure clearly shows that the latter, far from condemning us to unlimited desires, determines a limit that makes it sufficient for happiness.

Pleasure, on the other hand, is not only the end-point of a process of mental pacification: it is also its precondition. This is what Epicurus suggests when he explains that "pleasure is the principle (*archē*) and the end (*telos*) of the happy life" (*Men.* 128). The "canonic" in fact confers a criterial role on feeling (*pathos*), and the principal feelings are precisely pain and pleasure. Now, feeling is a criterion that is at once cognitive and practical: it teaches us what is suitable to us and what is not, and it motivates our choice and avoidance (D.L. 10.34; *Men.* 129). As such, it establishes a direct connection between knowledge and action. Pleasure is therefore at both the beginning and the end of the activities that characterize the happy life.

The opponents of Epicureanism did not fail to denounce this hedonism, which seems at first sight to neglect concern for others, and to license an egoistic ethic at the expense of properly moral conduct. The Epicurean choice of a life surrounded by friends, withdrawn from public life (*KD* 27; *SV* 58; Lucr. 5.1120–1135), does not wholly remove this ambiguity. Friendship provides security above all and seems in that sense to have personal tranquility as its ultimate end (*KD* 27, 28, 40). The Epicurean reply may perhaps rest on a conception of human relations we might describe as an ideal of restricted sociability.[12] If, indeed, one regards friendship not as something merely auxiliary to happiness but as a precondition of the happy life, it no longer looks like just one means among others to assure one's own security. The portrait of the sage that concludes the *Letter to Menoeceus* fits this view: he lives among his fellows "like a god among men" (*Men.* 135). The Epicurean sage by definition, therefore, lives in a community – at least ideally – which implies that he does not have to *choose* friendship. The latter imposes itself of its own accord as a component of the good life. Furthermore, Epicurus makes it plain that it is friendship that provides the greatest pleasure (*KD* 40). Nevertheless, it remains true that friendship is only one particular sphere of sociability, and a fairly small one. It thus is not enough to prove that the life of pleasure is consistent with virtue in all its forms.

The solution is undoubtedly to be found in the Epicurean conception of prudence (*phronēsis*): if every pleasure is, in principle, good, it does not follow that every pleasure ought to be chosen. The choice of a pleasure assumes in the first place that one gives a privileged place, among pleasures, to those that are both natural and necessary to happiness; that is, those that can be attained through philosophy and friendship. These are distinct from pleasures that are necessary for the absence of bodily disturbance or for the satisfaction of vital needs, as well as merely natural desires – such as sexual desire. Natural desires in general are contrasted with vain desires (*Men.* 127). Choosing to pursue a pleasure requires, on the other hand, a prudent calculation of the consequences, an anticipatory comparison of the resulting pleasures and pains.

12.   On this topic, see also Brown, HELLENISTIC COSMOPOLITANISM, the section on Epicureanism.

This calculation is precisely where virtue comes in: prudence teaches that pleasure is inseparable from prudence itself, from probity and from justice (*Men.* 132). We must thus assume that pleasures that are harmful to others have consequences that are contrary to pleasure: reproach, punishment, and inner turmoil. Hence "the virtues naturally accompany the pleasant life and the pleasant life is inseparable from them" (*Men.* 132). It will be objected that the virtues are here merely the means or instruments of pleasure. Perhaps the Epicureans opted for a pragmatic attitude and thought it was futile, in order to establish the principles of moral conduct, to assign them any higher status. In any case, it seemed absurd to them to think of repressing pleasure, the only state perfectly natural to us, in the name of virtue.

Conclusion

Epicurean philosophy is a paradoxical naturalism: nature in itself is deprived of all final purpose, but human beings are to live according to the natural end of pleasure. Yet, Epicureanism overcomes this difficulty. In the first place, conformity to nature is not submission to a duty considered as an objective being, but rather refers to a factual state: disorder is just as natural as order, and the latter is only a temporary arrangement of the former. Now, it is through consciousness of this very state of things that we can bring order to our soul and preserve it from disturbance. Consequently, the Epicureans sought, in nature, not prescriptions but limits: those fixed by natural compacts, but also the limits of desires and of evils. We must also correct two fairly frequent misunderstandings: the picture of Epicurean ethics as purely intuitive or affective and the idea that physics is merely a theoretical preparation for the happy life. To live according to nature in fact assumes that one engages in rational discourse about it: natural philosophy grounds in reason what pleasure and suffering reveal in their own fashion as feelings. Further, *phusiologia* is no mere propaedeutic, because it is a synthetic attitude that never isolates ethics from physics and the theory of knowledge: physics, in the manner of the *Letter to Herodotus*'s argumentation, is to be boiled down to elementary theses that are memorized, internalized, and put into practice. It is thus actualized in the very activity of seeking happiness. For instance, one can and should not just think but even drill oneself and get used to thinking – continually and at every moment – that death is nothing to us (*Men.* 124). Because it is, in this sense, a philosophy for actual application, Epicureanism in its way overcomes the opposition of theory and practice: it is at the same time a science of nature and an attitude in conformity with nature. Its naturalism is inseparably both learned and lived.

Bibliography

Ancient Texts and Commentaries

Epicurus

Arrighetti, G. (ed.). (1973). *Epicuro, Opere*. Torino: Einaudi.
Bailey, C. (ed.). (1926). *Epicurus, The Extant Remains*. Oxford: Clarendon Press.
Usener, H. (ed.). (1887). *Epicurea*. Leipzig: Teubner.

Lucretius

Smith, M. F. (ed.). (1975). *Lucretius, De rerum natura,* with an English trans. by W. H. D. Rouse. Revised with new text, introd., notes and index by M. F. Smith. Loeb Classical Library. Cambridge, Mass.: Harvard University Press / London: Heinemann.

Epicurean tradition (selection)

De Lacy, Ph. And De Lacy, E. A. (eds.). (1978). *Philodemus, On Methods of Inference.* Naples: Bibliopolis.

Diels, H. (ed.). (1916). *Philodemos über die Götter.* Book 1. Abhandlungen der königlich Preussischen Akademie der Wissenschaften, philosophisch-historische Klasse 7. Berlin.

Long, A. A. and Sedley, D. N. (eds.). (1987). (Cited as LS). *The Hellenistic Philosophers.* Cambridge: Cambridge University Press.

Obbink, D. (ed.). (1996). *Philodemus on Piety, Part I.* Oxford: Oxford University Press.

Santoro, M. (ed.). (2000). *[Demetrio Lacone]. [La forma del dio]* (*PHerc.* 1055). Naples: Bibliopolis.

Smith, M. F. (ed.). (1993). *Diogenes of Oinoanda. The Epicurean Inscription.* Naples: Bibliopolis.

Works Cited

Alberti, A. (1995). "The Epicurean Theory of Law and Justice." In A. Laks and M. Schofield (eds.), *Justice and Generosity, Studies in Hellenistic Social and Political Philosophy* (pp. 161–90), Cambridge: Cambridge University Press.

Auvray Assayas, C. and Delattre, D. (eds.). (2001). *Cicéron et Philodème. La polémique en philosophie.* Paris: Editions Rue d'Ulm.

Erler, M. (1994). Chap. "Epikur"; "Die Schule Epikurs"; "Lukrez." In H. Flashar (ed.), *Die hellenistische Philosophie, Grundriss der Geschichte der Philosophie – Die Philosophie der Antike,* (vol. 4–1: pp. 29–490). Basel: Schwabe.

Frede, M. (ed.). (1985). *Galen, Three Treatises on the Nature of Science.* Trans. R. Walzer and M. Frede, with an Introduction by M. Frede. Indianapolis, Ind.: Hackett. [Cited as Walzer-Frede.]

Furley, D. J. (1967). *Two Studies in the Greek Atomists.* Princeton: Princeton University Press.

Goldschmidt, V. (1977). *La Doctrine d'Épicure et le droit.* Paris: Vrin.

Morel, P.-M. (2000). "Épicure, l'histoire et le droit." *Revue des Études Anciennes,* 102, 393–411.

Sedley, D. (1983). "Epicurus' Refutation of Determinism." In ΣΥΖΗΤΗΣΙΣ. *Studi sull'epicureismo greco e romano* (Festschrift for M. Gigante) (pp. 11–51). Bibl. della Parola del Passato, 16-I. Naples: Macchiaroli.

——. (1988). "Epicurean Anti-Reductionism." In J. Barnes and M. Mignucci (eds.), *Matter and Metaphysics* (pp. 295–327). Naples: Bibliopolis.

——. (1998). *Lucretius and the Transformation of Greek Wisdom.* Cambridge: Cambridge University Press.

Further Reading

Algra, K. A., Koenen, M. H., and Schrijvers, P. H. (eds.). (1997). *Lucretius and his Intellectual Background.* Amsterdam: Verhandelingen der Koniklijke Akademie van Wetenschappen.

Asmis, E. (1984). *Epicurus' Scientific Method.* Ithaca, NY: Cornell University Press.

Bailey, C. (1928). *The Greek Atomists and Epicurus.* Oxford: Clarendon Press.

Clay, D. (1998). *Paradosis and Survival. Three Chapters in the History of Epicurean Philosophy.* Ann Arbor, Mich.: University of Michigan Press.

Erler, M. (ed.). (2000). *Epikureismus in der Späten Republik und der Kaiserzeit.* Philosophie der Antike 11. Stuttgart: Steiner.

Giannantoni, G. and Gigante, M. (eds.). (1996). *Epicureismo greco e romano.* (3 vols). Naples: Bibliopolis.

Goulet, R. (2000). "Épicure." In R. Goulet (ed.), *Dictionnaire des philosophes antiques.* (vol. 3): *d'Eccélos à Juvénal.* Paris: Editions CNRS.

Konstan, D. (1973). *Some Aspects of Epicurean Psychology.* Leiden: Brill.

Mitsis, P. (1988). *Epicurus' Ethical Theory. The Pleasures of Invulnerability.* Ithaca, NY: Cornell University Press.

Morel, P.-M. (2000). *Atome et nécessité. Démocrite, Épicure, Lucrèce.* Paris: Presses Universitaires de France.

Salem, J. (1989). *Tel un dieu parmi les hommes. L'éthique d'Épicure.* Paris: Vrin.

——. (1990). *La Mort n'est rien pour nous. Lucrèce et l'éthique.* Paris: Vrin.

Warren, J. (2004). *Facing Death. Epicurus and his Critics.* Oxford: Clarendon Press.

504

26

Stoic Logic

KATERINA IERODIAKONOU

Introduction

Logic as a part of philosophy

According to most Stoic philosophers, logic is a part of philosophy, the other parts being physics and ethics (Aët. 1, prooem. 2 = LS 26A; D.L. 7.39 = LS 26B1). The Stoics distinguish these three parts of philosophy, because each part has its own particular subject-matter and aim, yet they are at the same time inseparably intertwined. But what is the subject-matter of Stoic logic? The Stoics do not use the term "logic" (*logikē*) as we do nowadays. Logic for them is the study of *logos*, that is, the study of reason as revealed in articulate speech. Thus, logic as a part of philosophy is meant to examine everything to do with rational discourse.

The Stoics divide logic into rhetoric (*rhetorikē*) and dialectic (*dialektikē*): rhetoric is the art of speaking well in the form of whole, continuous speeches; dialectic, on the other hand, is the art of conducting discussions by means of short questions and answers, but in a much broader sense, it is also defined as the science of what is true, what is false, and what is neither true nor false (D.L. 7.41–42 = LS 31A1–5). Dialectic itself is subdivided into the topics of significations and utterances, that is, it separately studies what is signified by our utterances and the utterances themselves. The study of what is signified covers what gets said by using all sorts of utterances, but mainly by using declarative sentences, and hence propositions, the relations between them, the arguments composed of such propositions, and especially their validity. Often, though, it also covers how we distinguish true from false impressions (*phantasiai*), because on the Stoics' view it is on the basis of criteria for true impressions that we are able to determine which propositions are true. The study of utterances includes purely linguistic and grammatical phenomena, that is, a physical account of sound appropriately formed by the speech organs, a discussion of the phonemes or letters of the alphabet, an analysis of the parts of speech, an examination of the criteria for good style (D.L. 7.43–44 = LS 31A7–9). Therefore, although "dialectic" is the Stoic term most closely corresponding to our sense of "logic," the Stoics include under dialectic a good deal that we would call epistemology, philosophy of language, grammar, and linguistics. In what follows we will mainly be concerned with the narrow sense of dialectic that fits, more or less, our modern understanding of logical studies.

Thus defined, Stoic logic aims at a systematic understanding of the rules of rationality, which can assist us to think clearly and correctly, and protect us from being misled by fallacious arguments in all kinds of rational discourse. In other words, logic is meant to help people discuss and argue correctly, ask and answer questions methodically, explore all the arguments for and against a given thesis, distinguish the true from the false, clarify ambiguous statements, solve paradoxes. In general, the aim of logic is the establishment of a true and stable understanding of the world, an understanding that is supposed to be essential to human beings if they are to live a well-reasoned and ordered life (D.L. 7.46–48 = LS 31B).

Hence, logic turns out to be both a prerequisite for the proper understanding of the physical world and a necessary component of a moral life. Given the Stoics' belief in the rationality of nature, logic becomes inseparable from the other parts of philosophy, and this for the following reason: whereas the end of physics is knowing the world and its order, and that of ethics is living in accordance with the natural order, logic aims at distinguishing the true from the false, and thus makes it possible to find out the truths in the domains of reality which belong to the other parts of philosophy. That is why the Stoics come to understand logic as a particularly important part of philosophy, and that is exactly why they insist that the philosopher must be, more than anything else, a dialectician:

> The reason why the Stoics adopt these views in logic is to give the strongest possible confirmation to their claim that the wise man is always a dialectician. For all things are observed through the study conducted in discourses, whether they belong to the domain of physics or equally that of ethics. As to logic, that goes without saying. (D.L. 7.83 = LS 31C)

To show the special role of logic in the interrelation between the three parts of philosophy, the Stoics moreover compare logic to the shell of an egg, to the surrounding wall of a fertile field, to the fortification of a city, or to the bones and sinews of a living being (D.L. 7.40 = LS 26B3; S.E. *M* 7.19 = LS 26D).

Although the Stoics regard logic as a genuine part of philosophy, they certainly do not consider it as a mere auxiliary instrument to ethics and physics. In fact, there seems to have been a considerable dispute over the issue whether logic is a part (*meros*) or merely an instrument (*organon*) of philosophy, a dispute which, although it took place most probably only in late antiquity, helps us to reconstruct the reasoning behind the Stoics' insistence on regarding logic as an integral constituent of philosophy (Alexander, *In APr.* 1.4–4.29; Ammonius, *In APr.* 8.15–11.21; Philoponus, *In APr.* 6.19–9.20). For it becomes clear that, given the subject-matter and aim of Stoic logic, the Stoics have every reason to believe that their logic does not simply provide the other sciences with demonstrative methods. Rather, Stoic logic deals with a particular domain of reality of its own, which is distinct both from the subject-matter of physics and that of ethics, namely it deals with propositions and their interrelations; for, as we will shortly see, the Stoics view propositions as states of affairs which, although they do not exist as bodies do, definitely are part of reality in that they obtain and, if true, are facts. Furthermore, in its concern with truth, Stoic logic goes beyond the bounds of a science aiming only at producing proofs for scientific theorems; among other things, it is meant to enable us to distinguish between the true and the false quite generally.

The Stoic logicians and their sources

To better understand the emergence of Stoic logic, it is useful to get an idea of the logical background out of which it historically developed. There are two philosophical schools that could have influenced Stoic philosophers in their logical interests: first, of course, Aristotle and his followers, mainly Theophrastus and Eudemus, and second, the Megarians, like Diodorus Cronus and Philo of Megara.[1]

Indeed, the prevailing view in the nineteenth century was that Stoic logic should be considered as a mere supplement to Aristotle's logical theory; for Stoic logic, so it was alleged, does nothing more than either copy Aristotelian logic or develop it in a vacuous and formal way. It is only since about the middle of the twentieth century, after the important advances in symbolic logic, that it has become obvious how Stoic logic essentially differs from Aristotelian logic. It has even been suggested that the Stoics could not possibly have been influenced by Aristotle, because after the death of Theophrastus Aristotle's esoterical writings, and therefore his logical works, were no longer available and were only recovered in the first century BCE.

I think it is extremely implausible to assume that Aristotle's logical writings were not available to the early Stoic logicians. But, even if the Stoics were familiar with these treatises, there can be no doubt about the originality of the Stoic logical system; just studying Stoic logic and comparing it with what we know about Aristotelian logic provides us with adequate proof that they are two radically different systems. It is true, on the other hand, that Theophrastus and Eudemus published treatises about what they called syllogisms "based on a hypothesis" (*ex hupotheseōs*), which Aristotle (*APr.* I.29, 45b15–20) had promised to write about, but never did, and these syllogisms have a great deal in common with the types of syllogisms the Stoics discuss. However, there is no evidence that the Peripatetic logicians anticipated the outstanding feature of Stoic logic, namely constructing a logical system to prove the validity of a whole class of arguments, though of a different kind than those Aristotle focused on in his syllogistic.

As far as the Megarians are concerned, the historical connections between them and the Stoics are well-documented. Zeno knew both Diodorus and Philo well, and Chrysippus wrote treatises in which he criticized their logical views. However, although Diodorus and Philo were not exclusively concerned with the study of logical puzzles or paradoxes, in connection with which they are usually mentioned, but also put forward original views, for instance about logical modalities and the truth conditions of conditional propositions, they never came close to constructing a logical system as elaborate and sophisticated as that of the Stoics.

But what do we actually know about the Stoic philosophers who were particularly instrumental in the development of Stoic logic? The philosopher who immediately comes to mind, of course, is Chrysippus: "He [Chrysippus] became so renowned in dialectic that it was the general opinion that if the gods had dialectic, it would be no different from that of Chrysippus" (D.L. 7.180 = LS 31Q). Indeed, to confirm Chrysippus' reputation as the principal Stoic logician, one needs only to go through the long list of logical books attributed to him by Diogenes Laertius (D.L. 7.189–198). But Chrysippus

---

1. On the Megarians, see Decleva Caizzi, MINOR SOCRATICS, in this volume.

was not alone among the Stoics in his interest in logic. For though it may have been the case that Zeno and Cleanthes, before Chrysippus, were not logicians in the sense that they constructed a formal logical system, they both used valid arguments of a considerable level of logical complexity in order to establish their philosophical theses; and, given the rather standardized patterns of their arguments, one might think that they must have been aware of the logical forms in virtue of which these logical arguments are valid. Also, logical studies in the Stoic school certainly did not die with Chrysippus; there were later Stoic logicians, and they did not simply parrot Chrysippus' doctrines. There is some evidence that Stoic philosophers, like Posidonius, Athenodorus and Epictetus, made further additions to the Chrysippean system, and even that they diverged from Chrysippus' logical theses on lesser issues.

Having said that, however, it is not at all easy to distinguish between Chrysippus' own views and those of his successors, given the state of the surviving evidence; for instance, our ancient sources usually attribute the logical doctrines to the Stoics in general, and not to individual Stoics. Moreover, the fact that most of our sources for Stoic logic are quite hostile and late makes our project of reconstructing the Stoic logical system seem extremely problematic. But it is not impossible. Needless to say, though, there is always plenty of space for different interpretations of the surviving texts, and thus plenty of disagreement among modern scholars on many points of detail.

The Stoic Logical System

Lekta *and* axiōmata

The main characteristic of Stoic logic is that the inferences it studies are about relations between items that have the structure of propositions. Whereas Aristotle focused his attention on inferences that involve relations between terms, and thus introduced a logical system similar to what we nowadays call "predicate logic,"[2] Stoic logic marks the beginning of what is now called "propositional logic." To say, though, that Stoic logic is propositional may be somewhat misleading; for, to start with, the Stoics have quite a different understanding of what a proposition is, or to use their own term, of what an *axiōma* (assertible) is: "They say that an *axiōma* is a complete *lekton* which, as far as it itself is concerned, can be asserted" (S.E. *PH* 2.104 = LS 35C2).

So in order to fully grasp the Stoic definition of an *axiōma*, we first need to get some idea about the Stoic notion of a *lekton* (sayable).[3]

Lekta (Sayables)

The term *lekton* is derived from the Greek verb "*legein*," i.e., "to say," and it is, therefore, what has been or gets said or something which can be said. In fact, the Stoics distinguish between what gets said by uttering or using an expression and the

---

2. On Aristotle's logic, see Detel, ARISTOTLE'S LOGIC AND THEORY OF SCIENCE, in this volume.
3. On the sayables in the Stoic theory of meaning, see also Modrak, PHILOSOPHY OF LANGUAGE.

expression itself which we utter or use in saying something. For instance, they distinguish between the expression "Cato is walking," which is used to say that Cato is walking, and what gets said by using this expression, namely that Cato is walking (Sen. *Ep.* 117.13 = LS 33E). So the kind of item which gets said by using the appropriate expression in the appropriate way, the Stoics call a *lekton*.

The Stoics also talk about a *lekton* as the state of affairs signified, i.e., the signification (*sēmainomenon*), distinguishing it from the utterance which is the signifier (*sēmainon*), and from the corporeal entity which the *lekton* is about (*tunchanon*) (S.E. *M* 7.11–12 = LS 33B). Thus *lekta* are items that are placed between mere vocal sounds or written sentences on the one hand and the objects in the world on the other; very roughly speaking, *lekta* are the underlying meanings in everything we say, as well as in everything we think. For *lekta* are defined by the Stoics also as the content of our thoughts: "They say that a *lekton* is what subsists in accordance with a rational impression" (D.L. 7.63 = LS 33F2; S.E. *M* 7.70 = LS 33C).

But not everything that gets thought gets said, and not everything that can be said gets thought. There are indeed many things that never get thought or said, although they are there to be thought or said. In other words, Stoic *lekta* are not mind-dependent items; at the same time, though, they certainly do not exist in the way bodies exist in the world. The Stoics stress that *lekta* are incorporeal, like void, place, and time (S.E. *M* 10.218 – LS 27D), and in order to characterize their mode of being, they introduce the notion of subsistence (*huphistanai*), as opposed to existence (*einai*). Reality, they claim, is not just constituted by corporeal entities, but also by predicates true of bodies and propositions true about bodies. Hence, *lekta* are given in Stoic ontology some status, namely the status, not of bodies, but of incorporeal somethings.

The Stoics divide *lekta* into complete and incomplete (D.L. 7.63 = LS 33F). Incomplete *lekta* include predicates, like for instance what is meant by "writes," for it is simply a thing to say about something. On the other hand, questions, oaths, invocations, addresses, commands, curses, are all complete *lekta*. But for the Stoic logical system the most important kind of a complete *lekton* is what we call a proposition, for example, that Socrates writes, and this the Stoics call an *axiōma*.

Axiōmata (Assertibles)

So let us return to Sextus' definition of a Stoic *axiōma*: "They say that an *axiōma* is a complete *lekton* which, as far as it itself is concerned, can be asserted" (S.E. *PH* 2.104 – LS 35C2). And let us also quote the definition that Diogenes attributes to Chrysippus himself: "An *axiōma* is that which is true or false, or a complete state of affairs which, so far as itself is concerned, can be asserted, as Chrysippus says in his *Dialectical definitions*" (D.L. 7.65 = LS 34A). It thus seems that the property of being true or false is what differentiates an *axiōma* from other types of complete *lekta*, but an *axiōma* is mainly defined by the fact that it is the kind of item such that in saying this sort of thing one is asserting something.

Why do we then prefer the translation "assertible" rather than the more common term "proposition?" It is true, of course, that Stoic *axiōmata* and propositions as we conceive them share common characteristics. For instance, they are expressed by complete indicative or declarative sentences, they are either true or false, and they are incorporeal. But we should also underline the differences between *axiōmata* and propositions. For instance, while a proposition is timelessly true or false, an *axiōma* is asserted at a particular time and has a particular tense; that is to say, an *axiōma* can in principle change its truth-value without ceasing to be the same *axiōma*. For example, the *axiōma* "It is day" is true when it is day and false when it is not (D.L. 7.65 = LS 34E). The *axiōmata* that change their truth-value are called by the Stoics "changing" (*metapiptonta*). For example, the conditional "If Dion is alive, Dion will be alive" is a changing *axiōma*; it is not true at all times, for there will be a time when the antecedent will be true and the consequent false, and thus the conditional will be false (Simpl. *In Phys.* 1299.36–1300.10 = LS 37K). Also, since Stoic *axiōmata* include token reflexive elements, like for instance "this" or "I," they may cease to exist and presumably also, though this is not clearly stated, begin to exist at definite times. For a Stoic *axiōma* requires the referent of a referring expression as its subject, otherwise it is said to be destroyed; the destruction of an *axiōma* is its ceasing to be expressible. For example, the *axiōma* "This man is dead" is destroyed at Dion's death, if "this man" refers to Dion (Alexander, *In APr.* 177.25–178.1 = LS 38F).

Being a particular class of *lekta*, *axiōmata* do not exist as bodies do, but they can be said to subsist. In addition, the Stoics make a further distinction: if an *axiōma* is false, it only subsists (*huphistanai*), but if it is true, it is a fact and thus also can be said to be present or there (*huparchein*). In this sense true *axiōmata* correspond to the world's having certain features, and they are available to be thought and expressed whether anyone is thinking about them or not. On the other hand, since false *axiōmata* are said to subsist, the philosophical question of how false statements and thoughts are possible gets a reasonable answer; false *axiōmata* are the contradictories of facts, and hence have some status.

Finally, *axiōmata* are divided into simple and non-simple *axiōmata*.

Simple axiōmata

According to Sextus, simple *axiōmata* are those which are not composed either of a repeated *axiōma* or of several *axiōmata*; e.g., "It is day" or "Socrates is talking" (S.E. *M* 8.93–98 = LS 34H).

Simple *axiōmata* are again divided into definite (*hōrismena* / *katagoreutika*), indefinite (*aorista*), and intermediate (*mesa* / *katēgorika*). Definite *axiōmata* are those that are expressed through demonstrative reference (*deixis*), i.e., through a non-verbal, physical act of indicating something simultaneously with the utterance of a sentence with a demonstrative, e.g., "This one is walking." Indefinite *axiōmata* are those that are governed by some indefinite constituent, i.e., they are composed by one or more indefinite pronouns and a predicate, e.g., "Someone is walking." Intermediate *axiōmata* are those that are neither indefinite as to the subject, for they mark off its specific kind, nor definite, for they are not pointing at the subject itself, i.e., they consist of a nominative case and a predicate, e.g., "A man is walking" or "Socrates is walking."

As for their truth conditions, definite *axiōmata*, such as "This one is walking," are true whenever the predicate, such as "walking," belongs to the thing identified by "this one" (S.E. *M* 8.100 = LS 34I). That is to say, of course, that definite *axiōmata* are our means of stating with precision the particular facts in the world. The truth of the indefinite *axiōmata* is contingent upon those of the corresponding definite ones; for instance, "Someone is walking" comes out true when a definite one of the form "This one is walking" is true (S.E. *M* 8.98 = LS 34H10). It is interesting that the Stoics rejected proper names as subjects of definite *axiōmata*, for on their view proper names signify qualities and could fail to refer; for instance, the "Socraticity" of Socrates marks off a specific individual, but not something necessarily present now, as does "this one."

The above classification by Sextus does not seem to be an exhaustive division of simple *axiōmata*; it is rather a division of affirmative simple *axiōmata*. Diogenes Laertius proposes instead six classes of simple *axiōmata*, of which the last three classes are similar to the ones discussed by Sextus, while the first three classes are all different kinds of negative *axiōmata* (D.L. 7.69–70 = LS 34K): First, a negative *axiōma* (*apophatikon*) consists of a negative particle and an *axiōma*, e.g., "Not: it is day." A special case of this is the double negation or super-negation (*huperapophatikon*), which is the negation of a negative *axiōma*, e.g., "Not: not: it is day." Second, the denial (*arnētikon*), is composed of a denying particle, like "no one," and a predicate, e.g., "No one is walking." Third, the privative (*sterētikon*), is composed of a privative particle and a potential *axiōma*, e.g., "This man is unkind," i.e., "un" and "This man is kind."

It seems, therefore, that the Stoics think of negative *axiōmata*, as well as of the double negation, as simple *axiōmata*. That is to say, introducing a negative particle does not, by itself, make an *axiōma* non-simple, though negation can also apply to non-simple *axiōmata*. The negation of a simple *axiōma* is itself simple, that of a non-simple *axiōma* non-simple. It is also important to note that the scope of the negative particle is, according to the Stoics, the entire *axiōma*; that means, for instance, that an *axiōma* of the form "It is not day" was regarded as affirmative and not as negative. Hence, the negative particle "not" was not regarded by the Stoic logicians as a connective (*sundesmos*); for such connectives bind together parts of speech, and the negative particle does not do that (D.L. 7.58).

Finally, Stoic negation is truth-functional; that is to say, the negative particle "not," if added to true *axiōmata*, makes them false, whereas if added to false *axiōmata* makes them true. Moreover, an *axiōma* and its negation form a pair of contradictories (*antikeimena*). Thus, contradictories are *axiōmata* one of which exceeds the other by a negative, provided that the negative is prefixed and controls or governs the whole *axiōma* (S.E. *M* 8.88–90 = LS 34G); e.g., "It is day" and "Not: it is day" are contradictories.

Non-simple axiōmata

Non-simple *axiōmata* are those that are composed either of a repeated *axiōma* or of several *axiōmata* that are combined by one or more connectives (S.E. *M* 8.95). The main types of non-simple *axiōmata* studied by the Stoic logicians are the following (D.L. 7.71–74 = LS 35A; S.E. *M* 8.125–127):

1. A conjunctive *axiōma* (*sumpeplegmenon*) is one which is conjoined by the conjunctive connective "and" or "both ... and ... ," e.g., "Both it is day and it is light." The Stoics gave the obvious truth-conditions for conjunctions, i.e., the truth of the conjunction depends solely on the truth or falsity of the conjuncts, and not on their content. A conjunctive *axiōma* is true if and only if all its conjuncts are

true. However, it seems that this Stoic view was not generally accepted, but was in need of defense. For opponents failed to understand that a conjunctive *axiōma* should be treated as one assertion, and claimed that if some of the conjuncts were true and others false, it naturally should be described as "no more true than false," though they allowed that it might perhaps be called true if most of the conjuncts were true.

2. A disjunctive *axiōma* (*diezeugmenon*) is one that is disjoined by the disjunctive connective "or" or "either . . . or . . . ," e.g., "Either it is day or it is night." The Stoics understand the disjunctive relation as exhaustive and exclusive. That is to say, the minimal requirement for the truth of a disjunction was that one and only one disjunct is true.

3. A conditional *axiōma* (*sunēmmenon*) is one linked by the conditional connective "if" (*ei*), e.g., "If it is day, it is light." A conditional, according to the Stoics, is true when there is "connection" (*sunartēsis*) between the antecedent and the consequent, i.e., when the contradictory of its consequent conflicts with the antecedent. For instance, the conditional "If it is day, it is day" is true, since the contradictory of its consequent "Not: it is day" conflicts with its antecedent "It is day." A conditional is false when the contradictory of its consequent does not conflict with its antecedent. For instance, the conditional "If it is day, I am talking" is false, since the contradictory of its consequent "Not: I am talking" does not conflict with its antecedent "It is day."

Hence, Chrysippus assigned to the conditional connective "if" a strong sense, compared to what our sources attribute to Philo of Megara and Diodorus Cronus. For Philo claimed that a conditional is true simply when it does not have a true antecedent and a false consequent, e.g., "If it is day, I am talking." In fact, this use of the conditional connective "if" is equivalent to what we nowadays call "material implication" and is clearly truth-functional. Diodorus, on the other hand, said that a conditional is true when it neither was nor is able to have a true antecedent and a false consequent. On this view the conditional "If it is day, I am talking" is false, since when it is day but I have fallen silent it will have a true antecedent and a false consequent; but the conditional "If there are no partless elements of things, there are partless elements of things" is true, for it will always have the false antecedent "There are partless elements of things." On the Stoic view, however, both the conditional "If it is day, I am talking," and the conditional "If there are no partless elements of things, there are partless elements of things" are false, since in them there is no connection between the antecedent and the consequent (S.E. *PH* 2.110–113 = LS 35B).

The Stoic interpretation of the conditional connective "if" has the disadvantage of rendering at least part of their logic non truth-functional. On the other hand, it is able to adequately express intelligible connections in nature and avoid cases that are counter-intuitive, such as the conditionals "If it is day, I am talking" or "If there are no partless elements of things, there are partless elements of things." Similarly, the Stoics' interest in adequately expressing intelligible connections in nature shows in Chrysippus' decision not to use the conditional when discussing astrological predictions merely based on empirical observation of the correlations between astral and terrestrial events. For example, it may be that it is not the case both that Fabius was born at the rising of the dog-star and that Fabius will die at sea. Chrysippus would not express this as "If Fabius is born at the rising of the dog-star, he will not die at sea," precisely because he was not convinced that there was a necessary causal connection between being born at that time of the year and dying on dry land. This is the reason why Chrysippus preferred in such cases the negated conjunction, i.e., "Not: Both Fabius was born at the rising of the dog-star and Fabius will die at sea" (Cic. *Fat.* 12–15 = LS 38E).

Needless to say, non-simple *axiōmata* can be composed of more than two simple *axiōmata*, either because the constituent *axiōmata* are themselves non-simple, or because certain connectives, namely the conjunctive and the disjunctive connective, are two-or-more-place functions. For instance, the Stoics use the conditional "If both it is day and the sun is above the earth, it is light," or the three-place disjunction "Either wealth is good or it is evil or it is indifferent."

But we find in our sources more kinds of non-simple *axiōmata*, apart from conjunctions, disjunctions, and conditionals; most of these additional non-simple *axiōmata* may have been introduced after Chrysippus. For instance, a subconditional *axiōma* (*parasunēmmenon*) is one which is joined by the connective "since" (*epei*). A subconditional is true when the consequent follows from the antecedent, and the antecedent holds, e.g., "Since it is day, the sun is above the earth," when said in daytime; it is false when it either has a false antecedent, or has a consequent which does not follow from the antecedent, e.g., "Since it is night, Dion is walking." A subdisjunctive *axiōma* (*paradiezeugmenon*) is a non-simple *axiōma* which is indistinguishable in its linguistic form from a disjunctive *axiōma*, but which is true either when its subdisjuncts do not conflict with each other or when the contradictories of its subdisjuncts are not mutually incompatible. For example, the subdisjunctive *axiōma* "Either you are running or you are walking or you are standing" is true, because the contradictories of the disjuncts are not mutually incompatible (Gell. *NA* 16.8.12–14 = LS 35E). A causal *axiōma* (*aitiōdes*) is one which is joined by the connective "because" (*dioti*), e.g., "Because it is day, it is light" (D.L. 7.72). The truth conditions of this kind of non-simple *axiōma* unfortunately have not survived.

Modalities

Although Stoic logic does not deal with *axiōmata* of the form "It is possible that it is day," simple and non-simple *axiōmata* are standardly classified as possible, impossible, necessary, and non-necessary. For the Stoic logicians regarded, like truth and falsehood, modalities too as properties of *axiōmata*; so, according to their view, an *axiōma* may in principle change its modal value, since it has it at a time.

Stoic modal logic developed out of the debate over Diodorus Cronus' famous Master Argument (*kurieuōn logos*), which Epictetus discusses in the following text:

> These seem to be the sort of starting-points from which the Master Argument is posed. The following three propositions mutually conflict: "Every past truth is necessary"; "Something impossible does not follow from something possible"; and "There is something possible which neither is nor will be true." Diodorus saw this conflict and exploited the convincingness of the first two to establish the conclusion that "Nothing which neither is nor will be true is possible." Now some will retain the pair "There is something possible which neither is nor will be true" and "Something impossible does not follow

from something possible," but deny that "Every past truth is necessary." This seems to have been the line taken by Cleanthes and his circle, and was in general endorsed by Antipater. Whereas others will retain the other pair, that "There is something which neither is nor will be true," and that "Every past truth is necessary," but hold that something impossible does follow from something possible. To retain all three is impossible because of their mutual conflict. So if someone asks me, "Which of them do you retain?" I shall answer "I don't know; but my information is that Diodorus retained the first pair I mentioned, the circles of Pathoides (I think) and Cleanthes the second pair, and Chrysippus and his circle the third pair." (Epict. *Diss.* 2.19.1–5 = LS 38A)

Thus, it seems that the Stoics made various attempts to rebut Diodorus' view that nothing is possible which neither is nor will be, reacting to the threat of a weakened form of logical determinism entailed by such a claim. In addition, Alexander of Aphrodisias (*In APr.* 177.25–178.1 = LS 38F) gives us some further information about Chrysippus' attack on the second premise of the Master Argument. For in order to show that nothing precludes that something impossible follows from something possible, Chrysippus is reported to have used as an example the conditional "If Dion is dead, this one is dead," and this for the following reasons: First, the antecedent "Dion is dead" is possible, since it will be true at some time. Second, the consequent "This one is dead" is impossible, for any *axiōma* that neither is nor ever can be true is impossible, and "This one is dead" is necessarily either false, namely as long as Dion is alive, or destroyed, namely when Dion is dead. Third, the conditional is true according to all the different truth-conditions for conditionals.

Reacting both towards Diodorus' definition of the possible as "that which is or will be" and Philo's definition as "that which is predicated in accordance with the bare fitness of the subject, even if it is prevented from coming about by some necessary external factor" (Alexander, *In APr.* 183.34–184.10 = LS 38B; Boethius, *Int.* 234.22–26 = LS 38C), Chrysippus proposed his own account of the possible: A possible *axiōma* (*dunaton*) is that which admits of being true, and is not prevented by external factors from being true, e.g., "Dion is alive" (D.L. 7.75 = LS 38D; Boethius, *Int.* 234.27–235.4). Given this definition of the possible, Chrysippus defined the other three standard modal properties of *axiōmata* so as to yield the expected logical relations; for instance, that the necessary is something of which it is not possible that it is not the case, or that the possible and the impossible as well as the necessary and the non-necessary are contradictory to each other.

Hence, an impossible *axiōma* (*adunaton*) is defined as that which does not admit of being true, or admits of being true but is prevented by external factors from being true, e.g., "The earth flies." A necessary *axiōma* (*anankaion*) is that which is true and does not admit of being false, or admits of being false but is prevented by external factors from being false, e.g., "Virtue is beneficial." A non-necessary *axiōma* (*ouk anankaion*) is that which is capable of being false, and is not prevented by external factors from being false, e.g., "Dion is walking."

Two further modalities were also studied by the Stoic logicians; namely, plausibility and probability (D.L. 7.75–76): A plausible *axiōma* (*pithanon*) is that which invites assent to it, e.g., "If someone gave birth to anything, she is its mother." A probable or reasonable *axiōma* (*eulogon*) is that which has higher chances of being true than false, e.g., "I shall be alive tomorrow."

514

Arguments

The Stoics define an argument (*logos*) as a complex or a compound of premises (*lēmmata*) and a conclusion (*epiphora* / *sumperasma*). The following is a typical Stoic argument (S.E. *PH* 2.135–136 = LS 36B2; D.L. 7.76–77 = LS 36A1–3):

If it is day, it is light.
But it is day.
Therefore it is light.

They call the first premise "leading premise" (*hēgemonikon lēmma*: Galen, *Inst. Log.* 7.1), while they call the second premise "co-assumption" (*proslēpsis*). It was the orthodox Stoic view that an argument must have more than one premise, though it seems that Antipater admitted in his logic single-premise arguments (*monolēmmatoi*) (S.E. M 8.443 = LS 36C7), as for instance (Apul. *Int.* 184.16–23 = LS 36D):

You are seeing.
Therefore you are alive.

In addition, the Stoics discussed arguments in terms of their modes (*tropoi*), which are the abbreviations of particular arguments; for instance, the mode of the previous argument is the following:

If the first, the second.
But the first.
Therefore the second.

The ordinal numbers here stand for *axiōmata*, and have exactly the same role as the letters of the alphabet in Aristotelian logic. Finally, the Stoics also used the so-called "mode-arguments" (*logotropoi*), in which the *axiōmata* are given in full when first occurring, but are then replaced by ordinal numbers, obviously for purposes of simplicity and clarity:

If Plato is alive, Plato is breathing.
But the first.
Therefore the second.

Of arguments some are valid or deductive (*perantikoi* / *sunaktikoi*), others invalid or non-deductive (*aperantoi* / *asunaktoi*). Invalid arguments occur when the contradictory of the conclusion does not conflict with the conjunction of the premises (D.L. 7.77 = LS 36A4). For instance, the argument:

If it is day, it is light.
But it is day.
Therefore Dion is walking.

515

is invalid, because the contradictory of its conclusion, i.e., "Not: Dion is walking," does not conflict with the conjunction of its premises, i.e., "Both if it is day it is light and it is day." In other words, the validity of an argument depends on the truth of the corresponding conditional formed from the conjunction of the premises as antecedent and the conclusion as consequent (S.E. *PH* 2.137 = LS 36B3; S.E. *M* 8.416, 421). To take again the previous argument, it is invalid because the corresponding conditional "If both if it is day it is light and it is day, Dion is walking" is false, at least according to Chrysippus' truth-conditions for conditional *axiōmata*.

Further, some arguments are true, others false (D.L. 7.79 = LS 36A8–9; S.E. *PH* 2.138–139 = LS 36B4–6). True are those arguments which deduce correctly from true premises, e.g.,

If virtue benefits, vice harms.
But virtue benefits.
Therefore vice harms.

False arguments are those which either have some false premise, or are invalid, e.g.,

If it is day, it is night.
But it is day.
Therefore Dion is alive.

Syllogistic arguments

Of valid arguments, some are just called "valid," others "syllogistic" (*sullogistikoi*). The Stoics define syllogistic arguments as those which either are what they call "indemonstrable" (*anapodeiktoi*), or can be reduced to the indemonstrables (D.L. 7.78 = LS 36A5).

Indemonstrables or simple syllogisms

Indemonstrable arguments are those whose validity is not in need of demonstration, given that it is obvious in itself (D.L. 7.79–81 = LS 36A11–16; S.E. *M* 8.223–227; *PH* 2.157–158). The lists of indemonstrable arguments which are to be found in our ancient sources vary, but there is no doubt that Chrysippus himself distinguished five different types of such arguments, each type being characterized by a particular basic form in virtue of which the arguments are understood to be indemonstrable. As to other surviving lists of types of indemonstrables, they reflect the criticisms and alterations that the standard list seems to have undergone at the hand of later Stoics in the centuries following its introduction; they differ from Chrysippus' list in adding extra types of argument, as well as in objecting to the usefulness or application of others (Cic. *Top.* 57; Martianus Capella 4.419–420; Boethius, *Cic. Top.* 358; Cassiodorus, *Inst.* 119.3–4).

The basic logical forms of the five standard indemonstrables are described and illustrated by examples in our texts as follows:

516

1. A first indemonstrable argument is constructed out of a conditional and its antecedent as premises, and the consequent as conclusion, e.g.,

   If it is day, it is light.
   But it is day.
   Therefore it is light.

2. A second indemonstrable argument is constructed out of a conditional and the contradictory of its consequent as premises, and the contradictory of its antecedent as conclusion, e.g.,

   If it is day, it is light.
   But not: it is light.
   Therefore not: it is day.

3. A third indemonstrable argument is constructed out of a negated conjunction and one of its conjuncts as premises, and the contradictory of the other conjunct as conclusion, e.g.,

   Not: both Plato is dead and Plato is alive.
   But Plato is dead.
   Therefore not: Plato is alive.

4. A fourth indemonstrable argument is constructed out of a disjunction and one of its disjuncts as premises, and the contradictory of the other disjunct as conclusion, e.g.,

   Either it is day or it is night.
   It is day.
   Therefore not: it is night.

5. A fifth indemonstrable argument is constructed out of a disjunction and the contradictory of one of its disjuncts as premises, and the other disjunct as conclusion, e.g.,

   Either it is day or it is night.
   Not: it is day.
   Therefore it is night.

Of course, the types of indemonstrable arguments include many more arguments than the simple examples above suggest. For instance, if in each type of indemonstrable the simple *axiōmata* that we use to construct the premises are not affirmative, as they are in the above simple examples, but either both negative or negative and affirmative respectively, we get different combinations of premises, and hence different indemonstrable arguments of the same type. That is to say, in the case of the first indemonstrable, if, instead of having as first premise the conditional "If it is day, it is light," we use the conditionals "If not: it is day, not: it is light" or "If not: it is day, it is light" or "If it is day, not: it is light," together with the appropriate affirmative or negative *axiōmata* as second premises, we still get different arguments of the same first type of indemonstrables. In addition, it becomes clear that many more arguments are included in each type of the five indemonstrables, if we consider the cases in which the *axiōmata* of the premises are themselves non-simple, as, for instance, in the case of the Chrysippean argument discussed in the following text:

> According to Chrysippus (that arch-enemy of irrational animals!) the dog even shares in their legendary "dialectic." At any rate, this man says that the dog applies himself to a multiple fifth indemonstrable when he comes to a triple fork in the path, and, after sniffing the two paths which his quarry did not take, sets off at once down the third without even sniffing it. For, the ancient philosopher says, the dog is in effect reasoning: "Either my quarry went this way, or this way, or this way. But neither this way, nor this way. Therefore this way." (S.E. *PH* 1.69 = LS 36E)

But why did Chrysippus decide to suggest this particular list of the five types of indemonstrable arguments? It is certainly not the case that Chrysippus was trying to introduce the smallest possible number of different types of indemonstrable arguments. For one could easily dispense with the second indemonstrable on the basis of the first indemonstrable and the logical principle which the Stoics call "the first *thema*," a principle of contraposition of the conclusion with a premise which we will shortly discuss; similarly, the fifth indemonstrable seems to be redundant, since we already have the fourth indemonstrable, if we avail ourselves again of the first *thema*. Rather, it has reasonably been suggested that Chrysippus included in his list of the five indemonstrables all types of argument which just rely on the argumentative force of the different basic types of connectives known to him. In the case of the third indemonstrable, for instance, to use a negated conjunction just is to say that if one of the conjuncts holds the other does not; or again, the fourth and fifth indemonstrables just rely on what it means to use the disjunctive connective, namely to say that if one of the disjuncts holds the contradictory of the other holds too, and if the contradictory of one disjunct holds the other disjunct holds too.

Non-simple syllogisms

But not only are the indemonstrable arguments, according to the Stoics, syllogistic; our sources discuss Stoic examples of syllogistic arguments which are not themselves indemonstrable. For instance, we find the following example of a syllogistic argument which, though it also has two premises and a conditional as its first premise, is more complex than the first or the second indemonstrables (S.E. *M* 8.230 = LS 36G3):

If it is day, if it is day it is light.
But it is day.
Therefore it is light.

We also find a Stoic example of a non-simple syllogism with three premises (S.E. *M* 8.234 = LS 36G6):

518

If things evident appear alike to all those in like condition and signs are things evident,
  signs appear alike to all those in like condition.
But signs do not appear alike to all those in like condition.
And things evident do appear alike to all those in like condition.
Therefore signs are not things evident.

In fact, given the complexity of this syllogistic argument, Sextus also gives us its mode
(S.E. *M* 8.235 = LS 36G7):

If both the first and the second, the third.
But not the third.
But also the first.
Therefore not the second.

Another Stoic example of a non-simple syllogism with three premises is the following
(S.E. *M* 8.466; *PH* 2.186; cf. *M* 8.281):

If proof exists, proof exists.
But if proof does not exist, proof exists.
But also either proof exists or does not exist.
Therefore proof exists.

And we are again given its mode (S.E. *M* 8.292):

If the first, then the first.
But if not the first, then the first.
But also either the first or not the first.
Therefore the first.

Syllogistic are also, according to the Stoics, the so-called "indifferently concluding
arguments" (*adiaphorōs perainontes logoi*), of which our ancient sources provide us the
following example (Alexander, *In Top.* 10.10–12):

Either it is day, or it is light.
But it is day.
Therefore it is day.

Besides these non-simple syllogisms, there are also the so-called "duplicated arguments"
(*diaphoroumenoi logoi*); their first premise is a non-simple *axiōma*, which is constructed
out of the same simple *axiōma* used twice or more times (Alexander, *In Top.* 10.7–10;
D.L. 7.68–69; S.E. *PH* 2.112), e.g.,

If it is day, it is day.
But it is day.
Therefore it is day.

519

Finally, arguments of the following kind are also regarded by the Stoics as syllogistic (Origen, *Cels.* 7.15 = LS 36F):

If you know that you are dead, you are dead.
But if you know that you are dead, not: you are dead.
Therefore not: you know that you are dead.

All these non-simple syllogisms, the Stoics seem to have held, are formed by combination of simple syllogisms or indemonstrables, and thus they can be reduced to them by purely logical means. Indeed, to demonstrate the syllogistic validity of any argument whatsoever, the Stoic logicians considered it necessary to reduce it to one or more of the indemonstrable arguments. This procedure of reducing non-simple syllogisms to indemonstrable arguments was called by the Stoics "*analusis.*"

Analysis

To go by its very name, analysis is a method of reducing something to something more basic or prior, i.e., in this case a method of reducing the non-simple syllogisms to the indemonstrables, which are regarded as the first principles of the Stoic logical system. To carry out this procedure, the Stoic logicians had, according to our ancient sources, at least four logical rules which were called "*themata*" (D.L. 7.78 = LS 36A5; Galen, *Plac.* 2.3.18–19 = LS 36H), and in Latin "*constitutiones*" or "*exposita*" (Apul. *Int.* 191.5– 10 = LS 36I). We only know the first and the third Stoic *thema*, and it is on the basis of extremely meager evidence that modern scholars have suggested their different reconstructions of the other two.
　The first *thema* is the following:

> If from two propositions a third is deduced, then from either one of them together with the contradictory of the conclusion the contradictory of the other is deduced. (Apul. *Int.* 191.6– 10 = LS 36I)

It can be formalized in the following way:

$$\frac{P_1, P_2 \vdash C}{P_1, \text{ctrd } C \vdash \text{ctrd } P_2}$$

The third *thema* is the following:

> When from two propositions a third is deduced, and extra propositions are found from which one of those two follows syllogistically, the same conclusion will be deduced from the other of the two plus the extra propositions from which that one follows syllogistically. (Alexander, *In APr.* 278.12–14 = LS 36J; cf. Simpl. *In Cael.* 237.2–4)

It can be formalized in the following way:

$$\frac{P_1, P_2 \vdash C; E_1, \dots, E_n \vdash P_2}{P_1, E_1, \dots, E_n, \vdash C}$$

As to the second and fourth *themata*, we try to reconstruct them mainly on the basis of a logical principle, the so-called "dialectical theorem" (*dialektikon theōrēma*) or "synthetic theorem" (*sunthetikon theōrēma*), which is most probably Peripatetic and which is supposed to do, according to our ancient sources (Alexander, *In APr.* 284.10–17), the same job as the second, third, and fourth *themata* together:

> When we have the premises from which some conclusion is deducible, we potentially have that conclusion too in these premises, even if it is not expressly stated. (S.E. *M* 8.231 = LS 36G4; cf. Alexander, *In APr.* 274.21–24; 278.8–11; 283.15–17)

Indeed, the only two examples of Stoic analysis that have survived, and are both reported by Sextus Empiricus, make use of this dialectical theorem in order to reduce certain non-simple syllogisms to indemonstrable arguments, and thus prove their syllogistic validity. In particular, the first example of analysis (S.E. *M* 8.232–233 = LS 36G5) deals with the first non-simple syllogism which we mentioned earlier, namely:

If it is day, if it is day it is light.
But it is day.
Therefore it is light.

The second example of analysis (S.E. *M* 8.235–236 = LS 36G7) deals with the second non-simple syllogism that we have previously mentioned, namely:

If things evident appear alike to all those in like condition and signs are things evident,
    signs appear alike to all those in like condition.
But signs do not appear alike to all those in like condition.
And things evident do appear alike to all those in like condition.
Therefore signs are not things evident.

Let us then discuss in detail the second of these examples, so that we get a clearer idea of how Stoic analysis actually functions, and how we are supposed to apply the Stoic *themata*. To this purpose, it would be easier to use, as Sextus himself does, the mode of the non-simple syllogism, namely:

If both the first and the second, the third.
But not the third.
But also the first.
Therefore not the second.

Sextus suggests that this argument can be reduced to two indemonstrables of different types, namely to a second and a third indemonstrable argument, by going through the following two steps:

1. By combining the first premise, which is a conditional, with the second premise, which is the contradictory of the conditional's consequent, we get a second indemonstrable which has as its conclusion the contradictory of the conditional's antecedent:

521

If both the first and the second, the third.
But not the third.
Therefore not: both the first and the second.

2. By combining the conclusion of this indemonstrable, which is a negated conjunc-
    tion, with the third remaining premise, which affirms one of the two conjuncts,
    we get a third indemonstrable which has as its conclusion the affirmation of the
    other conjunct:

Not: both the first and the second.
But the first.
Therefore not: the second.

Hence, the dialectical theorem in this case validates the use of the conclusion of the
second indemonstrable, that is to say the use of the negated conjunction, in the construction of the third indemonstrable; for, according to this logical rule, the negated
conjunction which is deduced from some of the premises of the argument is implicitly
contained in the argument, though it is not expressly stated. And it is obvious that we
may similarly use the third *thema*; for a single application of the third *thema* on the
second and third indemonstrables, which we have constructed, could help us deduce
the non-simple syllogism whose validity we try to prove.

To summarize, Stoic analysis starts with a non-simple syllogism and continues
with a series of arguments which are either indemonstrables or arguments directly
derived from the indemonstrables by appropriate application of one of the Stoic *themata*.
Indeed, there are several ancient texts that suggest that the Stoic logicians, and in
particular Chrysippus, believed that their standard list of five indemonstrables is complete in the sense of containing all that is required for reasoning. It is said, for instance,
that every argument is constructed out of these indemontrables (D.L. 7.79 = LS 36A11),
and that all other arguments are thought to be validated by reference to them (S.E.
PH 2.156–157; 166–167, 194). Therefore, we may certainly infer that some claim
of completeness was made by the Stoic school, but it is not at all clear what precisely
the Stoics' definition of completeness was, if they ever offered one.

Valid arguments, in the narrow sense

After all, the Stoics themselves admit that we cannot apply the method of analysis
to all valid arguments, that is to say we cannot reduce all valid arguments to the
five indemonstrables by using the four Stoic *themata*. For, as we have already said,
there are arguments in Stoic logic which are just valid, but not syllogistic (D.L. 7.78 =
LS 36A6). It seems that, according to the Stoics, the validity of such arguments is
guaranteed not by their own analysis, but by their being equivalent to syllogistic arguments. To explain what I mean, let us briefly discuss the two groups of arguments of
this kind for which we have some evidence: the so-called "subsyllogistic arguments"
(*huposullogistikoi logoi*), and the "unmethodically conclusive arguments" (*amethodōs
perainontes logoi*).

Subsyllogistic arguments differ from syllogisms only in that one or more of their constituent *axiōmata*, although being equivalent to those in a syllogism, diverge from them in their linguistic form (Gal. *Inst. Log.* 19.6). The example given by Diogenes Laertius to illustrate the class of valid arguments in the narrow sense most probably is a subsyllogistic argument; for if it were not for the first premise which slightly diverges from the linguistic form of a negated conjunction, the argument would have been a third indemonstrable (D.L. 7.78 = LS 36A6):

"It is day and it is night" is false.
But it is day.
Therefore not: it is night.

Alexander of Aphrodisias also seems to discuss an example of a subsyllogistic argument in the following text:

> For while "If A then B" means the same as "B follows from A," they [i.e. the Stoics] say that there is a syllogistic argument if we take the expression "If A then B. But Λ. Therefore B," but that the argument "B follows from A. But A. Therefore B" is not syllogistic but concluding. (Alexander, *In APr.* 373.31–35)

In general, what emerges from the Stoics' treatment of subsyllogistic arguments is that the Stoic logicians tried to eliminate unnecessary ambiguities by standardizing language, so that the form of a sentence would unambiguously determine the type of *axiōma* expressed by it. For one and the same sentence may express *axiōmata* that belong to different classes, and equally two different sentences may express the same *axiōma*. But if there is some agreement to fix language use in a certain way, it becomes possible to easily discern the logically relevant properties of *axiōmata* and their compounds by simply examining the linguistic expressions used.

The case, however, of the unmethodically concluding arguments is more perplexing; for it is difficult to be certain about the actual kinds of argument which belong to this group as well as about the reasons on the basis of which the Stoics consider them as valid. For instance, it seems that the following argument is a Stoic example of an unmethodically concluding argument (Alexander, *In APr.* 22.17–23; 345.28–29; *In Top.* 14.27–15.3; Gal. *Inst. Log.* 17.2):

Dio says that it is day.
But Dio speaks truly.
Therefore it is day.

On the other hand, our evidence is unclear as to whether the following unmethodically concluding argument is of Stoic origin (Alexander, *In APr.* 21.31–22.7; 344.14–15; *In Top.* 14.21–27):

A is equal to B.
C is equal to B.
Therefore A is equal to C.

523

And similarly, in the following case (Alexander, *In APr.* 344.31–34):

A has the same parents as B.
B has the same parents as C.
Therefore, A has the same parents as C.

Moreover, it is uncertain which the corresponding syllogisms are on the basis of which these arguments are, according to the Stoics, valid. For the first example Alexander of Aphrodisias (*In APr.* 345.30–346.4) suggests that we add an appropriate universal premise, while at the same time combining the existing two premises into one, so that one may construct the following syllogism:

Everything that someone says when speaking truly is the case.
Dio, speaking truly, says that it is day.
Therefore it is day, as Dio says.

But it is difficult to see why this would be a satisfactory solution for the Stoic logicians.

Invalid arguments

According to the Stoics, invalid arguments arise in four ways: by disconnection, by redundancy, by being propounded in an invalid schema, and by deficiency (S.E. *M* 8.429–434 = LS 36C1–5):

1. Arguments are invalid by disconnection (*kata diartēsin*) when premises have no connection with one another or with the conclusion, e.g.,

    If it is day, it is light.
    But wheat is being sold in the market.
    Therefore it is light.

2. Arguments are invalid by redundancy (*kata parolkēn*) when they contain premises which are superfluous for drawing the conclusion, e.g.,

    If it is day, it is light.
    But it is day.
    But also virtue benefits.
    Therefore it is light.

3. Arguments are invalid by being propounded in an invalid schema (*en mochthērōi schēmati*), e.g.,

    If it is day, it is light.
    But not: it is day.
    Therefore not: it is light.

524

4. Arguments are invalid by deficiency (*kata elleipsin*) when they contain premises that are incomplete, e.g.,

> Either wealth is bad, or wealth is good.
> But not: wealth is bad.
> Therefore wealth is good.

For the first premise should be "Either wealth is bad, or wealth is good, or wealth is indifferent"; and moreover, a premise is missing.

Paradoxes

Finally, the Stoics discussed some arguments which they called "sophisms," and among which we also find what we nowadays consider as logical paradoxes:

> A sophism (*sophisma*), they say, is a plausible argument deceitfully framed to make us accept the false or false-seeming or non-evident or otherwise unacceptable conclusion. (S.E. *PH* 2.229 = LS 37A2)

There is abundant evidence of the Stoics' interest in solving logical paradoxes; just going through the list of Chrysippus' logical works shows that he in particular took them very seriously (D.L. 7.192–198 = LS37B). After all, the surprising conclusions of these seemingly rather simple arguments were a challenge to the Stoics' conception of basic logical notions, such as truth and falsehood, so that it soon became clear that solving the paradoxes would require careful reappraisal of some parts of their logical system. More specifically, the Stoics were intrigued by the paradoxes which had already puzzled the Megarians, for instance the Liar and the *Sorites*.

The Liar

Various versions of the Liar paradox were known in antiquity, but there is no single text that gives us with certainty the precise formulation of the argument. For instance, the following passage from Cicero's *Academica*, which most probably is our oldest testimony on the Liar, has a devastating lacuna at a crucial point: "If you say that you are lying, and you say so truly, are you lying *** telling the truth?" (Cic. *Acad.* II.95 = LS 37H5; cf. Gell. *NA* 18.2.9–10).

Different suggestions have been made in order to emend the text in a satisfactory way; one such plausible suggestion which fills up the lacuna and presents us with a real paradox reads as follows: "If you say that you are lying, and you say so truly, you are lying, and if you are lying, you are telling the truth." Presumably it was Eubulides who invented this paradox in the fourth century, and a version of it seems to have been known to Aristotle (D.L. 2.108). But there is no doubt that it was Chrysippus who more than anyone else in ancient times tried to solve it. For it is clear from our ancient sources that Academic Skeptics in his day used this paradox to challenge the Stoic view that all *axiōmata* are either true or false, and thus to question the Stoic logicians' faith in the Principle of Bivalence (Cic. *Acad.* II.95 = LS 37H5; Plut. *Comm. not.* 1059D–E = LS 37I).

525

But did Chrysippus find a solution to the Liar paradox? Some modern scholars have claimed that Chrysippus is a forerunner of the medieval *cassantes*, i.e., those who believed that the Liar's statement "I am lying" is not an *axiōma*, because it is meaningless. Against this, it has been convincingly argued that Chrysippus must have thought that such a statement is an *axiōma*, since there are cases in which it has a clear-cut meaning and a definite truth-value, given the conditions under which it is uttered. The peculiarity of the case of the Liar, at least as it is presented by Cicero, seems to be, not only that we are not able to find out what the truth of the statement is, but that in this case there is no truth of the matter. So perhaps Chrysippus' view was that in cases like this the statement is neither true nor false. However, if this is correct, the solution would put the very notion of an *axiōma* under great pressure and would force a reconsideration of its definition.

The *Sorites*

The name of the *Sorites* comes from the Greek noun "*sōros*," which means "heap" or "pile." As it becomes clear from the following text, this paradox exploits the vagueness of certain predicates, like for instance "heap":

> Wherefore I say: tell me, do you think that a single grain of wheat is a heap? Thereupon you say No. Then I say: what do you say about 2 grains? For it is my purpose to ask you questions in succession, and if you do not admit that 2 grains are a heap then I shall ask you about 3 grains. Then I shall proceed to interrogate you further with respect to 4 grains, then 5 and 6 and 7 and 8; and I think you will say that none of these makes a heap. Also 9 and 10 and 11 are not a heap . . . If you do not say with respect to any numbers, as in the case of the 100 grains of wheat for example, that it now constitutes a heap, but afterwards when a grain is added to it, you say that a heap has now been formed, consequently this quantity of corn becomes a heap by the addition of the single grain of wheat, and if the grain is taken away the heap is eliminated, And I know of nothing worse and more absurd than that the being and not-being of a heap is determined by a grain of corn. (Gal. *Med. exp.* 17.1 = LS 37E3)

According to Cicero, Chrysippus claimed that this paradox does not pose any real difficulty, because the wise man knows at which moment he should stop replying to questions of the form "Are so-and-so many grains a heap?":

> "That doesn't harm me," he says, "for like a skilled driver I shall restrain my horses before I reach the edge, all the more so if what they're heading towards is a precipice. In like manner I restrain myself in advance and stop replying to sophistical questions." (Cic., *Acad.* II.94 = LS 37H3)

In addition, the Stoic logicians concerned themselves with sophisms of the following kinds, which at least are far less problematic:

The Veiled Man

> Chrysippus: Next you're going to hear the quite fascinating Veiled Argument. Tell me, do you know your own father? Customer: Yes. Chrysippus: Well, if I place someone veiled in front of you and ask "Do you know this person?" what will you say? Customer: Obviously

that I don't know him. Chrysippus: But in fact this person is your very own father. So if you don't know this person, you clearly don't know your own father. (Lucian, *Vit. auct.* 22 = LS 37L)

The Horned Man

If you have not lost something, you have it still. But you have not lost horns. Therefore you still have horns. (D.L. 7.187)

Unfortunately, there is no evidence as to the way in which the Stoics tried to solve these sophisms.

Conclusion

As I indicated at the beginning of the chapter, it was only towards the middle of the twentieth century that Stoic logic began to be studied on its own merits and not as an appendix to Aristotle's syllogistic. To a great extent it was the revival of interest in the logical contributions of the Stoics that convinced scholars to investigate more carefully the other parts of Stoic philosophy, namely ethics and physics. The literature on Stoic logic that has since been published has managed to reconstruct a logical calculus, which still surprises us with its sophistication and its similarities to modern systems of logic. At the same time, though, it also has become clear that we should not fail to take seriously into account what differentiates Stoic logic from its modern counterparts. For only in this way can we get a better understanding of how the history of logic has evolved in close connection to the other parts of philosophy, and more importantly, only in this way do we have a chance to appreciate the peculiar features and insights of ancient logic.[4]

Bibliography

Collections of Fragments and Translations

von Arnim, J. (ed.). (1903–1924). (Cited as *SVF*). *Stoicorum Veterum Fragmenta*. (3 vols.). vol. 4: indexes by M. Adler. Leipzig: Teubner.

Hülser, K.-H. (ed.). (1987–8). *Die Fragmente zur Dialektik der Stoiker*. (4 vols.). Stuttgart / Bad Cannstatt: Frommann-Holzboog.

Long, A. A. and Sedley, D. N. (eds. and trans.). (1987). (Cited as LS). *The Hellenistic Philosophers*. (2 vols.). Cambridge: Cambridge University Press.

Editions of Works of Individual Authors

Alexander of Aphrodisias

Hayduck, M. (ed.). (1891). *Alexandri Aphrodisiensis in Aristotelis Analyticorum priorum librum I commentarium*. CAG, 2.1. Berlin: Reimer.

4. I would like to thank Fabio Acerbi, Susanne Bobzien, Walter Cavini, and Michael Frede for their helpful comments on an earlier version of this chapter.

527

Wallies, M. (ed.). (1891). *Alexandri Aphrodisiensis in Aristotelis Topicorum libros octo commentaria.* CAG, 2.3. Berlin: Reimer.

Ammonius

Wallies, M. (ed.). (1890). *Ammonii in Aristotelis Analyticorum priorum librum I commentarium.* CAG, 4.6. Berlin: Reimer.

Aristotle

Ross, W. D. (ed.). (1964). *Aristotelis Analytica priora et posteriora.* Oxford: Oxford University Press.

Boethius

Minio-Paluello, L. (ed.). (1965). *De Interpretatione vel Periermenias: Translatio Boethii.* In *Aristoteles Latinus.* 2.1–2 (pp. 1–38). Bruges/Paris: Desclèe de Brouwer.

Orelli, J. C. and Baiter, J. G. (eds.). (1837). *In Ciceronis Topica Commentaria.* In *M. Tulli Ciceronis opera quae supersunt,* 5.1. Zürich: Füssli.

Cassiodorus

Mynors, R. A. B. (ed.). (1937). *Cassiodori senatoris institutiones.* Oxford: Oxford University Press.

Cicero

Wilkins, A. S. (ed.). (1903). *M. Tulli Ciceronis: Topica.* Oxford: Oxford University Press.

Diogenes Laertius

Long, H. S. (ed.). (1964). *Diogenis Laertii Vitae philosophorum.* (2 vols.). Oxford: Oxford University Press.

Galen

Kalbfleisch, K. (ed.). (1896). *Galenus: Institutio logica.* Leipzig: Teubner.

Gellius

Marshall, P. K. (ed.) (1968). *Aulus Gellius: Noctes Atticae.* Oxford: Oxford University Press.

Martianus Capella

Willis, J. (ed.). (1985). *Martianus Capella.* Leibzig: Teubner.

Philoponus

Wallies, M. (ed.). (1905). *Ioannis Philoponi in Aristotelis Analytica priora commentaria.* CAG, 13.2. Berlin: Reimer.

Sextus Empiricus

Mutschmann, H. and Mau, J. (eds.). (1954–62). *Pyrrhonei Hypotyposes.* In *Sexti Empirici Opera* 1. Leipzig: Teubner.

Mutschmann, H. and Mau, J. (eds.). (1955–61). *Adversus Mathematicos.* In *Sexti Empirici Opera* 2 and 3. Leipzig: Teubner.

Simplicius

Heiberg, J. L. (ed.). (1894). *Simplicii in Aristotelis De caelo commentaria.* CAG, 7. Berlin: Reimer.

Further Reading

Barnes, J. (1985). "*Pithana Sunēmmena.*" *Elenchos*, 2, 454–67.

——. (1990). "Logical Form and Logical Matter." In A. Alberti (ed.). *Logica, mente e persona* (pp. 7–119). Florence: Leo S. Olschki.

——. (1997). *Logic and the Imperial Stoa.* Leiden: Brill.

——. (1999). "Aristotle and Stoic Logic." In K. Ierodiakonou (ed.). *Topics in Stoic Philosophy* (pp. 23–53). Oxford: Clarendon Press.

Bobzien, S. (1996). "Stoic Syllogistic." *Oxford Studies in Ancient Philosophy*, 14, 133–92.

——. (1997). "The Stoics on Hypotheses and Hypothetical Arguments." *Phronesis*, 42, 299–312.

——. (1999). "Logic. The Stoics." In K. Algra, J. Barnes, J. Mansfeld, and M. Schofield (eds.), *The Cambridge History of Hellenistic Philosophy* (pp. 92–157). Cambridge: Cambridge University Press.

Brunschwig, J. (1994). "Remarks on the Classification of Simple Propositions in Hellenistic Logics." In *Papers in Hellenistic Philosophy* (pp. 57–71). Cambridge: Cambridge University Press.

Cavini, W. (1996). "Essere ed essere vero: sull' uso assoluto di *huparxō* nella logica stoica." In M. Funghi and D. Manetti (eds.), *Hodoi dizēseōs – Le vie della ricerca* (Festschrift for Francesco Adorno) (pp. 141–5), Florence: Olschki.

Crivelli, P. (1994). "Indefinite Propositions and Anaphora in Stoic Logic." *Phronesis*, 39, 187–206.

Döring, K. and Ebert, T. (eds.). (1993). *Dialektiker und Stoiker. Zur Logik der Stoa und ihrer Vorläufer.* Stuttgart: Steiner.

Ebert, T. (1991). *Dialektiker und frühe Stoiker bei Sextus Empiricus – Untersuchungen zur Entstehung der Aussagenlogik.* Hypomnemata 95. Göttingen: Vandenhoeck and Ruprecht.

Frede, M. (1974). *Die stoische Logik.* Göttingen: Vandenhoeck and Ruprecht.

——. (1974). "Stoic vs. Aristotelian Syllogistic." *Archiv für Geschichte der Philosophie*, 56, 1–32.

——. (1994). "The Stoic Notion of a *Lekton.*" In S. Everson (ed.), *Companions to Ancient Thought* (vol. 3): *Language* (pp. 109–28). Cambridge: Cambridge University Press.

Ierodiakonou, K. (1990). *Analysis in Stoic Logic.* (dissertation London).

——. (1990). "Rediscovering some Stoic Arguments." In P. Nicolacopoulos (ed.). *Greek Studies in the Philosophy and History of Science* (pp. 137–48). Dordrecht: Kluwer.

——. (2002). "Zeno's Arguments." In T. Scaltsas and A. S. Mason (eds.), *The Philosophy of Zeno* (pp. 81–112). Larnaca: The Municipality of Larnaca.

Kneale, W. and Kneale, M. (1962). *The Development of Logic.* Oxford: Oxford University Press.

Łukasiewicz, J. (1935). "Zur Geschichte der Aussagenlogik." *Erkenntnis*, 5, 111–31.

Mates, B. (1953). *Stoic Logic.* Berkeley: University of California Press.

Mignucci, M. (1999). "The Liar Paradox and the Stoics." In K. Ierodiakonou (ed.), *Topics in Stoic Philosophy* (pp. 54–70). Oxford: Clarendon Press.

Milne, P. (1995). "On the Completeness of non-Philonian Stoic Logic." *History and Philosophy of Science*, 16, 39–64.

Mueller, I. (1979). "The Completeness of Stoic Propositional Logic." *Notre Dame Journal of Formal Logic*, 20, 201–15.

Schofield, M. (1983). "The Syllogisms of Zeno of Citium." *Phronesis*, 28, 31–58.

Sedley, D. N. (1984). "The Negated Conjunction in Stoicism." *Elenchos*, 5, 311–16.

27

Stoic Ethics

RICHARD BETT

Introduction

The proper interpretation of the role of *nature* is among the most central, difficult, and debated topics in the study of Stoic ethics. Our sources make clear that, at several points in the exposition of their ethical system, the Stoics make an appeal to nature. We are told of numerous different Stoic formulations of the end or goal of life (the *telos*); most of them refer to some form of attunement to, or connectedness with, nature as the ideal to be strived for. Again, the Stoics have a complicated story to tell about human development – a development that might optimally result in the attainment of this ideal – in which the types of impulses given to us by nature figure prominently. And even for those who fall short of the ideal (which the Stoics were inclined to think included almost everyone who has ever lived), it is, they believe, possible to achieve a measure of what they call "value" (*axia*) by means of the judicious selection of a variety of items labeled "things according to nature" (*ta kata phusin*). The concept of nature, then, will play a central role in the present survey. I focus first on the Stoics' conception of the ethical ideal, and of the character of the person who attains it. This is followed by an account of their picture of the optimal course of human development. The final main section is devoted to the condition, as the Stoics see it, of those of us who fail to achieve the ideal, and the ways in which we differ from those who do achieve it.[1]

Stoic philosophy, including Stoic ethics, underwent various developments over the several centuries in which it flourished. Most obviously, in the transition from the Hellenistic to the Roman periods ethics gradually came to occupy center stage, eventually to the almost complete exclusion of other areas of philosophy; in the earlier phase of Stoicism, by contrast, the other areas were treated as on a par with ethics (and, as will shortly become clear, strongly interconnected with it). There was also a gradual

---

1.   Diogenes Laertius (D.L.) (7.84 = LS 56A) opens his survey of Stoic ethics with a division of topics that, he claims, was adopted by a number of authoritative Stoics beginning with Chrysippus. This reflects the Stoics' pervasive concern with taxonomy. However, given the extremely interconnected character of all these topics, any such division is bound to be to some extent arbitrary; besides, it is not entirely clear how the topics in Diogenes' list are to be divided up (see Inwood, 1999, p. 113, n.56). For both reasons, I have felt no need to adhere to Diogenes' ordering. On Diogenes Laertius as a source, see Mejer, ANCIENT PHILOSOPHY AND THE DOXOGRAPHICAL TRADITION, in this volume.

decrease in the rigidity of the Stoics' ethical outlook, along with a gradual increase in interest in discussing conditions below the ideal, and in offering advice to ordinary non-ideal practitioners. The detailed plotting of these and other developments is too large a task for the present survey. The evidence suggests that Stoic ethics, like Stoic philosophy in general, first reached its fully elaborated state with Chrysippus. I will concentrate mainly on this "canonical" version of Stoic ethics, with occasional glances forward to the later Greek and Roman Stoics and, less frequently, backward to the ideas of the original Stoic Zeno. As we shall see, these excursions will sometimes be necessary in order to fill out the picture. There are also interesting and difficult questions about the relations between Stoicism (including the developments within it just mentioned) and the political and economic conditions of later antiquity. It has often been said that the ethical ideals prevalent in Hellenistic philosophy, including Stoicism, are a reaction to the demise of the city-state, and the resulting political impotence of almost everyone in the Greek world, that occurred in the wake of Alexander's conquests; at a general level the claim is attractive, but it deserves detailed scrutiny. Again, though, limitations of space forbid me from undertaking that project.[2]

The Sage versus the Rest of Humanity

The Stoics spend considerable time describing the cognitive and ethical condition of a character referred to as "the sage" (*ho sophos*).[3] We are repeatedly told that "the sage does everything well." This follows, according to one report, from the sage's "accomplishing everything in accordance with correct reason and in accordance with virtue, which is a skill relating to the whole of life"; by contrast, the common person – that is, everyone except the sage – "does everything badly and in accordance with all the vices" (Stob. 2.66,14–67,4 = LS 61G).[4] As a result of this unerring conduct, and the

---

2. For a reassessment of this issue, see Brown, HELLENISTIC COSMOPOLITANISM, in this volume. Other topics of considerable interest have had to be omitted. Most notably, there is the question of how, or in what sense, the Stoics can reconcile moral responsibility with their determinist – and indeed, providentialist – picture of the universe. There are also a number of intriguing issues in Stoic political theory. However, it is fair to say that these topics are not as central to the subject as those on which I do focus. On freedom and determinism, see Bobzien (2001), and in this volume, Sharples, THE PROBLEM OF SOURCES; on political theory see Schofield (1991).

3. Despite the Greek masculine pronoun, I prefer the gender-neutral translation "sage" to the traditional "wise man." Stoic theory does not accept the kind of gulf between men's and women's natures alleged by, for example, Aristotle; and at least some Stoics appear to have recognized the consequence that the highest levels of human attainment were as open to women as to men. Cleanthes wrote a book called *On the Fact that Virtue is the Same for a Man and for a Woman* (D.L. 7.175); and the Roman Stoic Musonius Rufus took up related topics in works entitled *Whether Daughters Should be Educated in the Same Way as Sons* (the answer is yes) and *That Women too Should Philosophize* (preserved in summary by Stobaeus: 2.235,23–239,29 and 2.244,6–247,2).

4. All translations are my own, including passages that appear in Long and Sedley (1987); the English versions in this chapter and in Long and Sedley are therefore not identical.

state of character that gives rise to it, the sage is said to achieve happiness; the rest of us are doomed to unhappiness. This rigid and stark division between just two types of people, sages and non-sages – the former, not surprisingly, being extremely rare – is a consequence of a number of Stoic theses about virtue, the good, and the *telos*.

Virtue and vice

The Stoics hold that the only things truly good are the virtues (and, according to some accounts, certain other items necessarily connected to the virtues, such as virtuous actions and virtuous persons). Conversely, the only things truly bad are the vices. This leaves a huge number of things that we might have considered either good or bad in a third, intermediate category, namely the indifferent: for example, health, wealth, or reputation, along with their opposites, all qualify as indifferents (D.L. 7.101–103 = LS 58A). As we shall see in more detail later, this does not mean, at least for orthodox Stoics, that such things make, or should make, no difference to our motivations and behavior. But it does mean that they are irrelevant to our attainment of happiness (*eudaimonia*); one can be happy without health or wealth, or unhappy with them – indeed, one's loss or gain of health or wealth makes no difference to whether or not one is happy. The attainment of the good, on the other hand, guarantees happiness; indeed, some Stoics are said to have *defined* the good in terms of its capacity to produce happiness (S.E. *M* 11.30).

Perhaps surprisingly, this relegation of everything except virtue and vice to the category of the indifferent is said to have been supported by the conclusion that virtue is the only thing truly beneficial, and vice the only thing truly harmful (LS 58A). Health, wealth, and the like are described as no more beneficial than harmful, on the ground that benefiting is not "peculiar to" (*idion*) health or wealth, nor harming "peculiar to" sickness or poverty. That is, health and wealth are not, just as such, guaranteed to benefit, nor sickness and poverty guaranteed to harm (there are cir-cumstances in which sickness or poverty is preferable to health or wealth); only virtue is guaranteed, just as such, to benefit, and vice to harm. One might have expected the moral to be that health and wealth benefit only some of the time, or from some points of view, whereas virtue benefits invariably. This is the position taken in two passages of Plato to which the Stoics are clearly indebted (*Meno* 87e–89a, *Euthd.* 280e–281e); here it is argued that health and wealth are not *inherently* beneficial, but can *become* beneficial when used with wisdom. But the Stoics, though clearly relying on the same kinds of considerations, draw the stronger conclusion that only virtue benefits (and only vice harms), period; for them, there is apparently no such thing as a merely temporary or contingent benefit or harm.

The Platonic precedent goes further than the point just mentioned. Like Socrates in a number of Platonic dialogues, the Stoics also conceive of virtue in strongly intel-lectualist terms. This is clearly connected with their conception of the human soul – or at least, of the "ruling part" (*hēgemonikon*) of the soul – as rational through and through, by contrast with the conception suggested elsewhere in Plato (the *Republic*, for example) and in Aristotle, according to which the soul has both rational and non-rational elements; if the soul is nothing but reason, then it is hard to see what virtue could consist in other than in the perfection of one's reason. In any case, we are repeatedly told that the Stoics took the virtues to be species of knowledge (*epistēmai*) and skills (*technai*) (e.g., Stob. 2.63,6–7 = LS 61D1). This point, in turn, is connected with yet another thesis of Socratic or Platonic origin, the inseparability of the virtues. (There was some internal dispute among the Stoics about how strongly to understand their interconnection; but Chrysippus, at any rate, seems to have opted for inseparability rather than outright unity.) That the Stoics adhered to some version of this thesis might have been inferred from the inherently systematic character of knowledge in general, on the Stoic view (Stob. 2.73,21–74,1 = LS 41H2–3, which actually cites the virtues as an example of this systematicity). However, we are also told explicitly (Plut. *St. rep.* 1046E = LS 61F1; Stob. 2.63,8–10 = LS 61D1) that, on the Stoic view, anyone who has any one virtue has all of them, and moreover, that to act in accordance with any one virtue is to act in accordance with all of them. The general idea is clear enough: in order to settle what action or actions any one virtue dictates in a given situation, the perspectives associated with the other virtues are also necessary. For example, the question of what risks or hardships it is appropriate to undertake in a given situation – in other words, the question of what the virtue of courage dictates – cannot be settled without attending to the worth of the various objectives that the act of undertaking them would promote; but for that purpose the other three canonical Stoic virtues – practical wisdom, moderation, and justice – are just as relevant as courage itself. The evidence suggests that Chrysippus went even further, arguing that each of these four virtues *includes* the perspectives that one would normally associate with the other three. This matter and the whole topic of the unity of virtue are well discussed in Cooper (1998).

The Telos *(Zeno, Cleanthes, Chrysippus)*

Why should virtue, so understood, be thought both necessary and sufficient for happiness? And why should the *lack* of virtue, so understood, be taken as entailing the active presence of vice (and unhappiness), with nothing between the two? To answer these questions, we need to begin to look at Stoic accounts of the *telos*, the end or goal of life;[5] it is here that the theme of nature begins to be important. The sources ascribe numerous different formulations of the *telos* to different Stoics, and two different formulations to Zeno, the school's founder; it is the earlier formulations that are relevant in the present context. Stobaeus tells us that Zeno gave as the *telos* "living in agreement" (*homologoumenōs zēn*, Stob. 2.75,11–12 = LS 63B1). He goes on to say that Zeno's successors, beginning with Cleanthes, took this to be an abbreviated way of saying "living in agreement *with nature*," and themselves preferred the longer, more explicit formulation; Chrysippus, he adds, devised the further version "living according to experience of things that happen by nature," thinking this to be clearer still. But

---

5. The Stoics distinguish between the *telos* and the "aim" or "target" (*skopos*); the latter is a certain optimal condition, specifiable without reference to any particular person, whereas the former is the actual exemplification of that condition in one's own life. See Stob. 2.77,1–5; 2.77,25–27 = LS 63A3. But this distinction and its ontological complexities need not detain us here.

Diogenes Laertius, while agreeing about Cleanthes' and Chrysippus' formulations, says that Zeno already defined the *telos* as "living in agreement with nature," citing Zeno's book *On Human Nature* (7.87 = LS 63C1).[6]

There is reason to believe that Zeno's shorter formulation was not in fact simply an abbreviation of "living in agreement with nature" (here I am in agreement with Striker (1996a, pp. 223–4) against Inwood (1995, p. 654)). For Stobaeus glosses the phrase "living in agreement" with the words "that is, living in accordance with a single consistent reason – on the assumption that those who live in conflict are unhappy" (2.75,12–76,1 = LS 63B1). It appears, then, that with this formulation Zeno had in mind the *internal* consistency or harmony of one's reason, rather than (as Stobaeus claims his successors understood him) agreement *with nature*. On the other hand, since Zeno apparently did also offer the longer formulation, we must assume that he took this internal consistency somehow to amount to the same thing as "living in agreement with nature"; for the *telos* is the *one* thing towards which one's life is or ought to be directed – by definition there cannot be more than one of them. If so, his successors' conflation of the two formulations (if it happened) would have been a simplification rather than a distortion.

We are also told that there was some question as to how to understand the word "nature" in the phrase "living in agreement with nature": does it refer to the nature of the universe, or to human nature specifically (D.L. 7.89 = LS 63C5)? Zeno's answer to this question is not reported. But his use of the two distinct, yet supposedly equivalent, formulations of the *telos* would be easily understood if the "nature" he had in mind was human nature; to render one's reason fully consistent might well be thought of as the perfection of one's nature as a human being. Chrysippus, however, is reported to have taken "nature" to refer both to human and to cosmic nature; his explanation of this, as summarized by Diogenes Laertius (7.88 = LS 63C3–4), is worth quoting in full.

> Therefore the *telos* becomes living consistently with nature – that is, in accordance both with one's own nature and with that of the whole – doing nothing that is habitually forbidden by the common law, which is correct reason permeating all things, being the same as Zeus, who is the leader of the administration of the things that are. Now this itself is the virtue of the happy person and a smooth flow of life, whenever everything is done according to the harmony of the spirit in each person with the will of the administrator of the whole.

Among other things, this passage links the *telos* with virtue and with happiness, and this is no surprise (compare, e.g., Stob. 2.77,16–21 = LS 63A1–2); it also makes clear an important connection between the Stoics' ethics and their cosmology or theology.

6. One further distinction may be worth mentioning here, to forestall a possible misunderstanding. The Introduction included a reference to "things in accordance with nature," which are the kinds of things (such as health or wealth) that we generally have reason to select. The phrases "in agreement with nature" and "in accordance with nature" are by no means equivalent in Stoic ethics. I am currently focusing exclusively on the former; I address the latter, and the differences between the two, in the section titled "The Indifferent and Progress towards the Good."

534

We shall return to the subject of the *telos*, and some additional formulations of it offered by later Stoics (see pp. 540–7). But we are now in a position to make better sense of the issues left aside a few paragraphs back – why virtue should be thought necessary and sufficient for happiness, and why there is nothing between virtue and vice.

The sufficiency of virtue for happiness

The picture suggested is as follows. For the reasons noted earlier, virtue is to be understood as the perfection of one's reason. Now, to perfect one's reason is just to bring it into a state of supreme order and consistency. This order and consistency, as we have seen, is captured in Zeno's shorter formulation of the *telos*; it is also echoed by other passages that stress the consistency and orderliness of the sage's disposition and behavior (e.g., D.L. 7.89 = LS 61A; Plut. *Virt. mor.* 441C = LS 61B8; Sen. *Ep.* 120.11 = LS 60E8). Along with consistency, as some of these passages indicate, is firmness or unchangeability; another passage, quoting Chrysippus, also alludes to the "fixity" (*pēxis*) that comes with the attainment of happiness (Stob. 5.906,18–907,5 = LS 59I). Once one has achieved virtue, then, one's soul is as ordered and as stable as could possibly be hoped for. As we saw, it is plausible to think that Zeno saw this condition as the fulfillment of one's nature as a human being; and, given the Stoics' conception of nature as providentially ordered according to a rational plan, it is not surprising that they would think of humans as naturally designed to achieve a state of perfect psychic order and stability (analogous to that of Zeus himself – Plut. *Comm. not.* 1076A–B, partially reproduced as LS 61J) – where this state, in turn, is understood as perfected rationality.

But this state is also a state in which one is "in agreement with nature" as a whole, not simply with one's own human nature. One's own nature, of course, is a part of nature in its entirety; and the whole of nature is itself a unified system, rationally ordered down to the last detail. Now it might be suggested, for this reason, that in living in agreement with one's own nature, one is thereby automatically fulfilling one's role in, and so living in agreement with, nature as a whole. However, while true, this is less significant than it may seem, because those who *fail* to live in agreement with their own natures are also nonetheless fulfilling their roles in nature as a whole; their failure is as much a part of the rationally ordered plan as one's own success. One's own success might perhaps be thought of as a sort of *collusion* with the divine will; but all of us, successes or failures, have a place in the plan of the universe, since that plan covers everything that happens. The real reason why the perfection of one's reason is also a state of agreement with (universal) nature is slightly different. This is that included in the perfection of one's reason is a process in which one comes to *understand* the nature of the whole universe; one's actions are shaped by one's understanding of this nature, and one is motivated to act in such a way as to be in conformity with it and to advance its goals to the best of one's ability. Those who lack this understanding do in fact have a place in the plan of the universe; but those who have this understanding are *aware* of their place in this plan, and willingly follow the path ordained for them. This is not to say that they know every event that is going to occur; the Stoics stress that even the sage will often have to make choices under conditions of uncertainty. But they do know the general outline of the plan, and they do know, of

535

every event that does in fact occur, that it is part of that plan. And, given their willing attachment to the plan, this means that they can never be disappointed; no matter what happens, they are content with the outcome.

Why there is nothing between virtue and vice

Sages are happy, then, in that their own natures are fulfilled, and in that they are, in a very strong sense, in tune with the world in which they live. One may now wonder why this should have anything to do with virtue, as commonly understood; the explanation of this will have to wait until a later stage. But we have at least some explanation of why happiness – that is, "a smooth flow of life" (D.L. 7.88 = LS 63C4; S.E. *M* 11.30) – should be thought to accompany the perfection of one's rationality. And we can now also get some idea of why there should be thought to be a fundamental and exclusive division between those who have, and those who have not, achieved this state of perfection. Those who have not achieved it are out of touch with themselves and with the world in general. They lack the psychic order and stability of the virtuous, and they lack the sage's willing identification with the course of events that unfolds in the world; it is therefore not at all the case that they can never be disappointed, and they cannot be said to enjoy "a smooth flow of life." Now, since vice is defined, in simple opposition to virtue, as inconsistency or disharmony of the soul (Cic. *Tusc.* 4.29 = LS 61O1), it follows that anyone who lacks virtue is in a state of vice. Moreover, corresponding to the inseparability of the virtues is the inseparability of the vices; if one lacks any one virtue, one lacks all of them, and the lack of any given virtue entails the presence of the corresponding vice. Hence, as we saw earlier, anyone who is not a sage is both unhappy and guilty of all the vices. This is not to deny that some people are *closer* to achieving virtue than others; the Stoics recognized the possibility of progress (*prokopē*) in this direction, and we shall return to this topic. But still, for those not in a state of virtue – however close to or far from attaining that condition they may be – it is just as true of any one of them as of any other that they are in a state of vice, and that they lack happiness. It is in this sense that, as the original Stoics maintained, "all failures are equal" (D.L. 7.120 – though a pair of minor later Stoics, Heracleides of Tarsus and Athenodorus, are said to have disagreed (7.121)).

The position may now seem less paradoxical and extreme than it looked at first. But the picture now needs to be filled out by an account of the development towards the state of virtue that the Stoics think will ideally take place, and of the differences that they take to exist between the kinds of decision-making open to the sage and to the rest of us.

The Ideal Course of Human Development

The Stoics have much to say about a state labeled *oikeiōsis*. There have been many attempts to translate this term: "appropriation" (Long and Sedley, 1987), "congeniality" (Inwood and Gerson, 1997) and "affiliation" (Inwood and Donini, 1999) are some recent examples. It is characterized in one source (though this does not appear to be a formal definition) as "a perception and apprehension of what is one's own (*tou oikeiou*)"

(Plut. *St. rep.* 1038C). It is an orientation, or set of orientations, given to us by nature (either from birth or in the course of our natural development), and has recently been well described as "a foundation in nature for an objective ordering of preferences" (Baltzly, 2000).

Initial oikeiōsis – *Self-preservation*

Our initial *oikeiōsis* takes the form of a natural orientation towards our own constitutions, from which it follows that we have, from the moment we are born, a natural impulse towards self-preservation (D.L. 7.85 = LS 57A1–2; Cic. *Fin.* 3.16; Plut. *St. rep.* 1038B = LS 57E). This is supported by an a priori teleological argument: of the various imaginable options as to how humans (and other animals) might be designed, it is by far the most likely that a providential nature would design us so as to have this kind of fondness for ourselves (D.L. 7.85–86 = LS 57A2–4). But it is also supported by observations of a broadly empirical kind. Animal and infant behavior is said to support the hypothesis of a natural impulse towards self-preservation (rather than, as the Epicureans claimed, towards pleasure) (Cic. *Fin.* 3.16–17; Sen. *Ep.* 121.5–9). In addition, we are said to be endowed with a *perception* of ourselves and all our parts; this theme is prominent in the meager remains of the later Stoic Hierocles' *Elements of Ethics* (see, e.g., LS 57C). On these various grounds, then, the Stoics conclude that our natures initially incline us to do whatever is needed for our survival at minimum, but also, more ambitiously, for our health and flourishing.

Developed oikeiōsis – *Reason and virtue*

But the story does not end there. The natural development of human beings (and here the parallel with other animals ends) also includes the emergence of reason, and this profoundly affects the character of our *oikeiōsis*. Seneca speaks of a number of different stages in the development of our constitutions, and of a different *oikeiōsis* corresponding to each stage (*Ep.* 121.14–16). The specifics of this account may be Seneca's own creative supplement to the original Stoic position. But it is clear that that position included the notion that our *oikeiōsis* does not remain constant, and that there is a shift away from the initial narrow attachment to our own self-preservation. Instead, as reason comes on the scene, acting rationally itself comes to be what we are naturally oriented towards (D.L. 7.86 = LS 57A5; Cic. *Fin.* 3.21–22 = LS 59D4–6). Now reason, as we saw earlier, is both the source of and the awareness of the good; the only good is virtue, and virtue just is a state of perfected reason. Thus the gradual emergence of reason is identical with progress towards the good, and also towards our understanding of the good. This does not happen automatically, but requires concerted effort on our part; however, our natures do incline us in that direction (Sen. *Ep.* 120.4). And, again to recall, once we achieve the state of perfected reason and virtue, our natures have achieved *their* perfection; however, this state is also one of harmony with, and understanding of, nature as a whole.

What happens to the initial orientation towards self-preservation when (or if) we achieve this state of perfected reason? Though the sources are not as explicit on this point as they might be, it clearly does not by any means disappear. As we shall see in the next section, there is a whole host of activities, described as "according to nature" and directed towards our continued existence as healthy, prosperous members of the human species, in which it is in the sage's interest, just as much as in the interest of the rest of us, to engage; it is fair to think of these as the developed expression of the natural impulse towards self-preservation that has been with us since birth. But what happens as one achieves the state of perfected reason is that these activities come to be seen in a wider context. One's orientation is now no longer towards one's self-preservation alone; rather, as noted in the previous paragraph, it is towards doing whatever reason or virtue dictates – which is also towards doing (in so far as this is within one's capabilities) whatever nature as a whole, or Zeus, dictates. Most of the time there will be no conflict between these two; that is, we will generally have reason to assume that the continuation and enhancement of our normal flourishing *is* what nature as a whole (or Zeus) dictates. But there will be exceptions to this, and in these cases the orientation of the sage's fully developed nature will go *against* the activities that a pure impulse towards self-preservation would dictate. Epictetus quotes Chrysippus as saying "If I really knew that it was fated for me now to be ill, I would even have an impulse towards that" (*Diss.* 2.6.9 = LS 58J). Chrysippus does not take himself to be a sage, and treats this imagined state of knowledge as purely counterfactual; for him, acting so as to preserve his health is always, or almost always, going to be the course that reason recommends. And even the sage, as was noted earlier, will regularly have to act in ignorance of the specific events that Zeus or nature has in store. But sometimes it will be clear to the sage (and on rare occasions it may even be clear to the non-sage) that reason, virtue, or nature dictates an action contrary to one's self-preservation – for example, the sacrifice of one's life for the good of humanity as a whole.

Oikeiōsis *and other-regarding motivations*

This last example points towards one further feature of the Stoics' account of *oikeiōsis*. Several texts refer to an *oikeiōsis* towards other human beings. The most obvious instances of this are the natural attachments that we have towards our children and, in general, towards those related to us (Hierocles 9.3–10 = LS 57D1; Cic. *Fin.* 3.62 = LS 57F1). But it is also suggested that we have a natural attachment towards *all* other human beings, which explains our coming together into societies (Hierocles 11.14–18 = LS 57D2; Cic. *Fin.* 3.63 = LS 57F2). At least the latter aspect of this "social *oikeiōsis*," as it has been called, is probably to be understood as developing along with – indeed, as part of – the development of reason; that is, it is simply a component in the picture already outlined. This is certainly what is suggested by a passage of Cicero's *On Duties*, a work heavily indebted to the Stoic Panaetius. The passage refers to this natural fellowship of human beings, and especially of parents towards their children; but this is cited in the course of an account of the development of the four cardinal virtues, and is explicitly said to be something that our reason (itself identified with the higher development of our nature) is responsible for (*Off.* 1.11–14). And once this "social *oikeiōsis*" is in place, we will rank the common advantage above our own advantage (*utilitatem* – Cic. *Fin.* 3.64 = LS 57F3; cf. Epict. *Diss.* 2.10.3–4 = LS 59Q3). We can now see why virtue, understood in the abstract as the perfection of one's reason, should be thought to include the kinds of qualities, such as justice, that essentially involve the fair, considerate or humane treatment of others – qualities that popular thought would have regarded as among the virtues, and that the Stoics themselves agreed were virtues. We can also see how, in a deeper sense, concern for others is compatible with – or even inseparable from – self-interest. As Epictetus puts it, Zeus "has designed the nature of the rational animal in such a way that it cannot achieve any of its own goods unless it contributes something to the common advantage" (*Diss.* 1.19.13). Our own good is virtue, and virtue includes acting in the interests of others; that is just the way that human beings, together with the universe, function.

There may, however, be limits to the coherence of this account. Justice, and perhaps other virtues as well, seem to require the *impartial* treatment of all who are affected, regardless of the level of one's personal connections with them. It is not easy to see how this is to be built on a foundation of natural attachments; even if we accept that there is a natural attachment to all other human beings, we must surely also admit that the degree of such attachments will vary greatly, depending on the closeness to oneself (in various senses) of any given person. We have a passage of anti-Stoic polemic that effectively exploits this tension between what is empirically plausible and what is ethically desirable (Anon. *In Tht.* 5.18–6.31 = LS 57H). On the Stoic side, Hierocles speaks of a person's being surrounded by a series of concentric circles, each containing different groups of people. The largest circle includes the entire human race. The smaller circles include sub-groups of humanity, and the smaller the circle, the closer one's attachment to the people it contains; the smallest circle (except for the one that simply contains oneself) includes only one's immediate kin (quoted in Stob. 4,671,7–673,11 = LS 57G). Hierocles urges us constantly to draw the circles together as much as possible – in other words, to treat the people in the larger circles as if they were members of the smaller circles, and so to move as far as one can towards equality in one's attachments. But this metaphor seems to concede that complete equality is not a practical possibility.

The rarity of the sage

We have been speaking at some length of the achievement of perfect rationality. It is worth repeating that this state of perfection is generally regarded as an extremely rare accomplishment. This may not have been true in the very earliest period; in his *Republic* Zeno described a city of sages, and it is by no means certain that he regarded this as an unattainable utopia.[7] But Chrysippus is quoted as acknowledging at one point that his ethical pronouncements will strike us as on the level of fiction, not on the level of ordinary humanity (Plut. *St. rep.* 1041F = LS 66A); it may have been Chrysippus' much more detailed delineation of the sage's condition that made fully apparent the extraordinary difficulty of attaining this condition. Diogenes Laertius reports (7.91) that Chrysippus, Cleanthes, Posidonius, and Hecaton all stated that virtue is teachable, and then adds "that it is teachable is clear from the fact that people become good from being bad." This makes it sound as if the attainment of goodness

---

7. However, see now Brouwer (2002), which argues that neither Zeno nor any other Stoic took *himself* to be a sage.

is something observable and common. However, it is not clear that this additional comment closely reflects anything that the Stoics in question said. Certainly the more standardly reported view is that the sage is rarer than the Phoenix (a mythical bird of which there is just one specimen alive at any given time). Starting at least as early as Panaetius, the Stoics had an interest in offering advice that might be of some practical use to those who are not sages. The standards for sagehood were not relaxed; but, as noted in the Introduction, the need to talk about (and to) others besides the sage was increasingly recognized (see, e.g., Cic. *Off.* 1.46 = LS 66D; Sen. *Ep.* 116.5 = LS 66C). This was not, however, more than a shift of emphasis; the resources for discussing the condition of the non-sage, and how one might progress towards the condition of the sage, were present in Stoic ethics from the start. The next section takes up these matters.

The Indifferent and Progress towards the Good

Distinctions within the indifferent

We have seen that the Stoics recognize nothing as either good or bad besides virtue and vice respectively; all the other things that we might be inclined to regard as having positive or negative value they consign to the category of the indifferent, on the grounds that these things make no difference to whether or not one achieves happiness. This does not, however, mean that they are or ought to be without effect on our motivations – or, for that matter, that they lack value. Within the category of the indifferent the Stoics make a threefold distinction among indifferents that are "in accordance with nature" (*kata phusin*), "contrary to nature" (*para phusin*) and neither. Examples of the first group are health, strength, and the proper functioning of one's sense organs; examples of the second group are disease, weakness, and disability (Stob. 2.79,18–80,3 = LS 58C1–2 – complete version only in vol. 2). Indifferents that are in accordance with nature are said to have "value" (*axia*), and those contrary to nature to have "disvalue" (*apaxia*); to have value, in the relevant sense, is to be the kind of thing that one has reason, in normal circumstances, to select (*eklegein*, Stob. 2.83,10–84,2 = LS 58D).[8] Indifferents that have a considerable amount of value are called "preferred," and those that have a considerable amount of disvalue are called "dispreferred" (Stob. 2.84,18–24 = LS 58E1–2); this leaves those with neither value nor disvalue, as well as those with a small amount of either, in the category of neither preferred nor dispreferred.[9] A preferred indifferent is therefore something that there is typically strong reason to select.

The extremist Stoic Aristo of Chios is reported by Sextus Empiricus to have objected to the very notion of preferred indifferents – and, by implication, to the whole idea of assigning value or disvalue to indifferents (*M* 11.64–67 = LS 58F). The main reason,

---

8.　Not to be confused with "choosing" (*haireisthai*), which is the appropriate stance to take towards the good.

9.　D.L. 7.106 equates being preferred with having value; but this is probably a simplification of the more complex account preserved in Stobaeus.

according to Sextus, is that the things labeled "preferred indifferents" are not invariably worth selecting; for example, sickness will be preferable to health if the healthy are being forced by a tyrant to participate in atrocities. It is not entirely clear that this was Aristo's own reasoning, rather than Sextus' elaboration on Aristo's basic contention; Diogenes Laertius 7.160 also makes clear that Aristo was opposed to distinctions of value within the indifferent, but does not offer this or any other reasoning in favor of this opposition. However, if Aristo did justify his view in the way Sextus suggests, he was missing the point. The orthodox Stoics are quite happy to accept that preferred indifferents are not invariably to be selected over dispreferred ones; indeed, to recall, that was precisely the basis on which they refused to call such things beneficial and therefore good. The labels "preferred" and "dispreferred" apply to types rather than to individual instances; to call health a preferred indifferent is to say that it is *by nature such as to be* (generally) worth selecting, and the existence of occasional instances in which sickness is preferable to health does not undermine this in any way.

The Kathēkon – *Meaning and definition*

The taxonomy of the indifferents, then, gives us a naturally based framework for decision and action.[10] However, it does not take us very far by itself. Another Stoic concept of great importance in this area is that of the *kathēkon*. This term is not easy to translate. Zeno is said to have offered an explanatory etymology, *kata tinas hēkein* (D.L. 7.108 = LS 59C2), but this too has been understood in multiple ways. The interpretation that I find most satisfactory is to translate the etymology as "coming down on certain persons" – that is, a *kathēkon* is an action that it *falls to* a certain person to do, or that it is that person's *place* to do – and to translate *kathēkon* itself, in line with this, as "incumbent" (see Cooper, 1996, p. 269 with n.22). Cicero translates *kathēkon* by *officium*, which in turn has generally been translated "duty." As the etymological gloss (interpreted in the way just mentioned) suggests, this is by no means wholly misleading. However, the term "duty" has connotations in modern moral philosophy, and in standard contemporary usage, that cannot be assumed to be part of the Stoic concept; I shall therefore avoid referring to *kathēkonta* as duties.

More helpful than an inspection of the word *kathēkon* itself is the definition given of it. We are told that a *kathēkon* is an action "which, when it has been done, has a reasonable defense" (D.L. 7.107, Stob. 2.85,14–15 = LS 59B1). Now, as Brennan (1996, p. 330) points out, it is token or individual actions, not types of actions, that are the things that are actually done; hence the term "when it has been done" (*prachthen*) makes clear that a *kathēkon* is a token action, not a type – my giving my mother a special gift on her seventieth birthday, for example, rather than the action-type "honoring one's parents." *Kathēkonta*, then, are actions that admit of a certain type of justification, labeled "reasonable" (*eulogos*); the crucial question is what is meant here by "reasonable."

---

10. It should not be supposed, incidentally, that this taxonomy is limited to items that are, in an intuitive sense, "natural" rather than products of society; our sources make clear that preferred indifferents include such things as wealth, reputation and lofty social class, and dispreferred indifferents their opposites (e.g., D.L. 7.106).

On one view, the "reasonable" justification in question is a justification that it would be open to any sensible person to provide, a justification that proceeds by giving reasons of a common-sense variety for the action. And on this view, one might expect that the actions that qualified as *kathēkonta* would be actions that promoted the preferred indifferents and avoided the dispreferred indifferents. However, there are several reasons for thinking that the Stoics must have intended the term "reasonable" in a much more stringent sense. First, the word *eulogos* and cognates appear in several other contexts in Stoic ethics where it is clear that it is "reasoning" of the *sage's* variety that is at issue (see Brennan, 1996, pp. 326–7); in the absence of any indication of an ambiguity in usage, one would expect it to have the same connotation here. Second, Diogenes says, in what sounds like an alternative way of putting the same point, that *kathēkonta* are those actions that "reason enjoins us to do" (*logos hairei poiein*, 7.108 = LS 59E2). Presumably "reason" in this context means "reason functioning as it should"; but for the Stoics this, in turn, can only mean "reason functioning in the perfect way exemplified by the sage." Finally, if "reasonable" were understood in the more relaxed way suggested above, then it would follow that there would be some cases in which a *kathēkon* was in fact a *wrong* action, despite admitting of a reasonable justification. However, it seems clear (*pace* Inwood, 1999, pp. 109–10) that there are no actions that are *kathēkonta* and wrong; rather, the sources repeatedly indicate that the *kathēkon* is just whatever action is in fact the correct action to perform in the circumstances (see, e.g., Cic. *Fin.* 3.59 = LS 59F4; Stob. 5.906,18–907,5 = LS 59I, with Brennan, 1996, p. 329).[11] It appears, then, that the "reasonable" justification that the Stoics speak of in this context is the justification that the infallible reason of the sage would generate. If so, there is no reason to assume that one's *kathēkonta* will always be those actions that secure the preferred indifferents; if, in a given circumstance, sickness is preferable to health, then it is the action that makes one sick, not the one that keeps one healthy, that will be the *kathēkon*.

The kathēkon *and rules*

Unfortunately, there seems to be some confusion on this point in our sources. We occasionally find lists of types of action cited as examples of *kathēkonta*; Diogenes Laertius, for example, lists honoring one's parents, brothers and country, and spending time with friends (7.108 = LS 59E2). However, if the *kathēkon* is the correct action in any given circumstance, this cannot be right; for there will be some circumstances in which honoring one's parents, etc., will be the *wrong* thing to do. Indeed, the Stoics were emphatic on the non-existence of any exceptionless rules, at least at this level of generality; hence their reported view that the sage will even engage in incest and cannibalism if circumstances warrant (which was gleefully exploited by the Stoics' opponents – e.g. S.E. *M* 11.191–195).

On the other hand, a great many Stoics wrote books called *On the* Kathēkon, and these books do appear to have been devoted to practical guidance, including

11.   Long and Sedley (1987) include a passage of Philo of Alexandria which appears to imply that *kathēkonta* can be wrong (59H); but there is no reason to think that Philo is following strict Stoic doctrine.

prominently the provision of rules of conduct. As suggested earlier, Panaetius appears to have given a greatly increased emphasis to this aspect of Stoic ethics; but books with this title are attested for Stoics all the way back to Zeno (see Sedley, 1999, esp. p. 137). Our main surviving evidence of this side of Stoic ethics consists of two long letters of Seneca (*Ep.* 94, 95); but it is clear that this was always considered an important topic. Now, it is difficult to see, in light of the point just mentioned, how these rules could have been anything more than provisional and defeasible guidelines; the only thing that is a *kathēkon* in all circumstances whatever is living virtuously (D.L. 7.109 = LS 59E4) – anything more specific will always admit of exceptions. (For this interpretation, and for reference to several others, see Inwood (1999); on this specific point see also Brennan (1996, p. 331).) However, as a matter of general policy, it clearly makes sense, for example, to take care of one's health; this, then, will normally be a *kathēkon*, and it might well be helpful to have an account of such types of action, including an account of why they are normally *kathēkonta* and how one can learn to spot the exceptions. It is this kind of agenda that appears to be reflected in a distinction, also reported in Diogenes Laertius, between *kathēkonta* that are not dependent on circumstances and *kathēkonta* that *are* dependent on circumstances – where taking care of one's health is the leading example of the former, and mutilating oneself and getting rid of one's property are examples of the latter (7.109 = LS 59E3). Again, this cannot be a distinction between actions that are invariably *kathēkonta* and actions that are not; as we have seen, taking care of one's health is not invariably the right thing to do. Rather, it must be a distinction between actions that are *kathēkonta* when special circumstances do not obtain (i.e., normally), and those that are *kathkonta* only when special circumstances do obtain (see Sedley, 1999, p. 132).

The sage's "Right actions"

The performance of *kathēkonta* – much of the time – is well within the capabilities of the non-sage. For to say that an action *has* a reasonable justification is not to say that the agent must be capable of *giving* that justification. By definition, the non-sage does not have a full understanding of what makes certain actions *kathēkonta*. But such a person can nonetheless do the kinds of things that will, for example, preserve his or her health, and these very often will in fact be *kathēkonta*. The difference between the sage and the non-sage, then, is not in the performance of *kathēkonta* – indeed, someone on the verge of becoming a sage might even succeed in performing *nothing but kathēkonta* (Stob. 5.906,18–907,5 = LS 59I) – but in the frame of mind in which they are performed. Quite simply, the sage's actions are all expressions of virtue or perfected reason; they may often be externally indistinguishable from the actions of a non-sage, but they derive from the stable and harmonious disposition described earlier, and that makes all the difference. The Stoics use the term "right action" (*katorthōma*), and also the term "perfect (*teleion*) *kathēkon*," to designate that special sub-class of *kathēkonta* that are expressions of the sage's virtue (Stob. 2.85,18–86,4 = LS 59B4). Stobaeus gives acting with practical wisdom and with justice as instances of "right actions." Unfortunately, he again creates the potential for confusion by listing "marrying, being an ambassador, engaging in dialogue and things like this" as instances of *kathēkonta* that are *not* "right actions." In fact, any one of these actions would be a "right action" if performed by a sage; for, to recall, *everything* that the sage does is an expression of virtue. However, it is true that they are not "right actions" in and of themselves.

The telos *(Diogenes and Antipater) and the duality of "nature"*

It should be clear by now that the sage's attitude towards the indifferents is not one of complete lack of interest. On the contrary, as we have seen, the *kathēkon* will in most cases involve the securing or retaining of preferred indifferents, or the avoidance of dispreferred indifferents; hence the "right action," the action that the sage will perform, will in most cases consist in the securing or retaining of preferred indifferents, or the avoidance of dispreferred indifferents, in a virtuous way – that is, as an expression of perfected reason. Again, the crucial difference between the sage and others is the frame of mind, or the state of character, that gives rise to these actions. Now, some Stoics after Chrysippus actually incorporated this point into their formulations of the end. According to Diogenes of Babylon, the end is "reasoning well (*eulogistein*) in the selection and rejection of the things in accordance with nature"; and Antipater is reported to have devised two different formulations (to which we will shortly return), both specifying a similar kind of orientation to the things in accordance with nature (Stob. 2.76,9–15 = LS 58K). The differences among these various formulations probably reflect a complicated debate on the topic with the Academic Carneades (see Long and Sedley, 1987, commentary on section 64; Striker, 1996b). But it is clear that all of them reflect a conception of virtue as involving the correct attitude towards the indifferents – a conception that was present in Stoicism from the start.

Carneades was not the only one to find something problematic in this conception. If selecting and rejecting the things in accordance with nature (normally selecting them, but in special cases rejecting them) is what the sage is supposed to do, how can it be claimed that the *achievement* (or, in special cases, the successful avoidance) of the things in accordance with nature is something that the sage considers irrelevant to happiness? Why aim for things that, by one's own account, make no difference whatever to one's level of well-being? This objection is pressed in a number of ways by several different authors (see Long and Sedley, 1987, section 64). The Stoics reply that it is not, in fact, the achievement or avoidance of the things in accordance with nature that one is aiming for; rather, what one is aiming for is the condition in which one performs the selection or rejection of these things in an infallible way – in other words, the life of the virtuous person. But to many there seemed to be something deeply paradoxical about attaching supreme importance to a condition in which one selects various things, but no importance to the things themselves. The Stoics, for their part, never climbed down on this point; we find it restated, essentially unchanged, in Seneca (*Ep.* 92.11–13 = LS 64J).

It should also be clear by now that the concept of nature plays a role in this account at two different points (see Striker, 1996a, p. 224). On the one hand, there are the things "in accordance with nature," which are a certain subset of the indifferents – the more significant of them constituting the *preferred* indifferents; these are the kinds of things that, other things being equal, will tend to promote the flourishing of human beings. On the other hand, there is the life "in agreement with nature," the achievement of which is the end; this is the life of the sage, whose perfected rationality constitutes the highest development of human nature, and who is also in harmony with the cosmic nature that governs everything. Now, as we have seen, the virtuous and perfectly rational person who is living "in agreement with nature" will generally pursue the things "in accordance with nature." However, there is by no means a complete correspondence between the achievement of the former and the pursuit of the latter. First, to repeat, there are some cases where pursuing the things "in accordance with nature" is the wrong thing to do, and hence *not* something that a person living "in agreement with nature" would do. Second, what really matters to the sage (and what distinguishes the sage from others), is the virtue or perfect rationality with which these things are pursued, not their actual attainment; the things "in accordance with nature" are, after all, only indifferents, whereas virtue or perfect rationality, the achievement of which is both necessary and sufficient for living "in agreement with nature," is a good.

Despite the fact that the two terms "in accordance with nature" and "in agreement with nature" have clearly distinct meanings and functions – but perhaps understandably – there is a tendency for their usage to be run together. Cicero, in a passage on *oikeiōsis* and natural human development referred to earlier (*Fin.* 3.20–22 = LS 59D2–6) uses both the terms "in agreement with nature" (*consentanea naturae*) and "in accordance with nature" (*secundum naturam*) to apply to the eventual attainment and understanding of the good; yet "in accordance with nature" also occurs in the same passage to refer to the preferred indifferents, pursuit of which is an early outgrowth of the initial impulse to self-preservation.[12] Stobaeus also at one point represents the end as "living in accordance with nature" instead of "living in agreement with nature" (2.77,19 = LS 63A1). And, if Stobaeus' quotations are to be trusted, even the Stoics' own formulations of the end illustrate the beginnings of a blurring of the distinction. Diogenes of Babylon, as we saw, gives as the end "reasoning well in the selection and rejection of the things in accordance with nature." Here "things in accordance with nature" clearly refers, as we would expect, to indifferents that have value; the sage, as an expression of perfected reason, will sometimes select these and sometimes reject them. But Diogenes' successor Antipater says that the end is "to live unceasingly selecting the things in accordance with nature and rejecting those contrary to nature," or alternatively, "unceasingly and unalterably doing everything in one's power towards obtaining the principal things according to nature" (Stob. 2.76,9–15 = LS 58K). And here it seems equally clear that "things according to nature" and "things contrary to nature" *cannot* refer to the indifferents that have value and disvalue respectively; for then it would not be the case that one should *invariably* select the former and reject the latter. Rather (if Antipater himself is not confused) these terms must refer to the things that, on any given occasion, the sage's *correct* understanding of nature would dictate that one select and reject. These will still, of course, be indifferents, not goods; but in this usage, unlike the standard usage of Diogenes, preferred indifferents will always warrant selection and dispreferred indifferents rejection.

---

12. In the same passage *kathēkonta* are said to originate *ab initiis naturae*, "from nature's starting-points." But this, too, is potentially misleading. The relation of the *kathēkon* to nature is complex; as we have seen, the performance of *kathēkonta* is not simply equivalent to the pursuit of the preferred indifferents – as Cicero's language might be taken to suggest.

Progress

How is one to progress towards the condition of the sage? The Stoics were happy to admit this possibility, despite their insistence on the equality of all vice and the absence of any middle ground between virtue and vice. As they say, someone who drowns two feet below the surface of the ocean is just as drowned as someone who drowns many fathoms down (e.g., Plut. *Comm. not.* 1063A = LS 61T); the analogy illustrates the equality of vice, but also the possibility of different degrees of closeness to virtue. We have little from the Hellenistic period on the details of how one might be expected to make progress in this area. But it is clear that this was taken to involve a progressively greater ability to discern what the *kathēkon* is on any given occasion – a grasp of general rules as well as a grasp of when to deviate from them – alongside a progressively greater consistency and order in one's own character. (The passage of Cicero cited in the previous paragraph is as good an illustration of this as any; for an analysis of this passage, and on the whole topic of moral progress, see Inwood and Donini (1999, sec. X).) The later period of Stoicism, in keeping with its more practical orientation, sees more extended attention devoted to the topic. Seneca offers a relatively detailed account of three stages of progress along the road to virtue (*Ep.* 75); there is some deviation here from the rigors of earlier Stoicism – for example, Seneca speaks (14) of a person being free from some of the vices but not yet from all of them – but the same basic points still apply. Epictetus also devotes a chapter specifically to the topic of progress (*Diss.* 1.4); but a great deal of his writing has to do, in one way or another, with the moral improvement of those of us who are not sages.

The passions

Another thing that is involved in the transition from vice to virtue – and this also receives considerable attention in Seneca's account – is the elimination of the passions (as the Greek term *pathē* is usually translated, though "emotions" is sometimes preferred). The Stoics offer a highly distinctive account of the passions as a species of defective belief; most, if not perhaps all, of these involve the mistaken view that something is good or bad which is in fact indifferent, together with an excessive and uncontrolled impulse to seek or avoid it. Naturally, the sage is altogether free of passions in this sense. This does not, however, prevent the sage from experiencing certain counterparts of the passions called "good feelings" (*eupatheiai*), which lack the objectionable elements of error and excess; to say, then, as popular conceptions of Stoicism might encourage one to say, that the sage is without emotions is at best an oversimplification. Whether this entirely exonerates the Stoic sage from the charge of being objectionably cold and aloof in interpersonal relations is another question; the answer suggested by a section of Epictetus' *Handbook* (3) – a passage that can plausibly be seen as inspired by the standard Stoic position – is not encouraging.[13]

13. See, however, Reydams-Schils (2002) for a recent attempt to defend at least the Roman Stoics against this charge.

In the case of everything that attracts you or that fulfils a need or that you are fond of, remember to say what sort of thing it is, beginning with the smallest things. If you are fond of a jug, say "I am fond of a jug"; for when it is broken you will not be disturbed. If you kiss your child or your wife, say that you are kissing a human being; for when it dies you will not be upset.

The Stoic account of the passions and "good feelings" has been the subject of much recent discussion; see in particular the numerous essays on Stoicism in Sihvola and Engberg-Pedersen, 1998.

Conclusion

Since antiquity, Stoic ethics has often been seen as impossibly high-minded, and the conception of nature with which it is intertwined questionable at best. Yet it has also been a source of inspiration in many periods, up to and including our own[14] – perhaps more so than any other ethical system developed by Greek philosophers. It is reasonable to suppose that the rigorous and uncompromising character of the Stoic ethical outlook has something to do with this. But its ability to speak to those who do not measure up to its ideals – however lofty those ideals may be – is surely another important factor.[15]

Bibliography

Works Cited

Baltzly, D. (2000). "Stoicism." In *The Stanford Encyclopedia of Philosophy* (online at: <http://plato.stanford.edu>).

Bobzien, S. (2001). *Determinism and Freedom in Stoic Philosophy*. Oxford: Oxford University Press.

Brennan, T. (1996). "Reasonable Impressions in Stoicism." *Phronesis*, 41, 318–34.

Brouwer, R. (2002). "Sagehood and the Stoics." *Oxford Studies in Ancient Philosophy*, 23, 181–224.

Cooper, J. M. (1996). "Eudaimonism, the Appeal to Nature, and 'Moral Duty' in Stoicism." In S. Engstrom and J. Whiting (eds.), *Aristotle, Kant, and the Stoics: Rethinking Happiness and Duty* (pp. 261–84). Cambridge: Cambridge University Press.

——. (1998). "The Unity of Virtue." *Social Philosophy and Policy*, 15, 233–74.

Inwood, B. (1995). Review of Julia Annas, *The Morality of Happiness*. *Ancient Philosophy*, 15, 647–65.

14. A striking twentieth-century example is Stockdale (1993).

15. The initial writing of this chapter coincided with a graduate seminar on Stoic ethics that I taught in the Fall Term of 2001. I would like to thank the participants in that seminar for pushing me to clarify and refine my ideas. I also thank Greg Burrill, Sean Greenberg, Geraldine Henchy and J. B. Schneewind for reading and commenting on a draft; and editors Pierre Pellegrin and Mary Louise Gill, as well as Adam Rachlis, for helpful advice on how to improve the penultimate version.

——. (1999). "Rules and Reasoning in Stoic Ethics." In K. Ierodiakonou (ed.), *Topics in Stoic Philosophy* (pp. 95–127). Oxford: Oxford University Press.

Inwood, B. and Donini, P. (1999). "Stoic Ethics." In K. Algra, J. Barnes, J. Mansfeld, and M. Schofield (eds.), *The Cambridge History of Hellenistic Philosophy* (pp. 675–738). Cambridge: Cambridge University Press.

Inwood, B. and Gerson, L. P. (ed. and trans.). (1997). *Hellenistic Philosophy: Introductory Readings*. 2nd edn. Indianapolis: Hackett.

Long, A. A. and Sedley, D. N. (1987). (Cited as LS). *The Hellenistic Philosophers*. (2 vols.). Cambridge: Cambridge University Press.

Reydams-Schils, G. (2002). "Human Bonding and *Oikeiōsis* in Roman Stoicism." *Oxford Studies in Ancient Philosophy*, 22, 221–51.

Schofield, M. (1991). *The Stoic Idea of the City*. Cambridge: Cambridge University Press.

Sedley, D. (1999). "The Stoic-Platonist Debate on *kathēkonta*." In K. Ierodiakonou (ed.), *Topics in Stoic Philosophy* (pp. 128–52). Oxford: Oxford University Press.

Sihvola, J. and Engberg-Pedersen, T. (eds.). (1998). *The Emotions in Hellenistic Philosophy*. Dordrecht: Kluwer.

Stockdale, J. (1993). *Courage Under Fire: Testing Epictetus's Doctrines in a Laboratory of Human Behavior*. Stanford: Hoover Institute.

Striker, G. (1996a). "Following Nature: A Study in Stoic Ethics." In G. Striker, *Essays on Hellenistic Epistemology and Ethics* (pp. 221–80). Cambridge: Cambridge University Press. (Originally published 1991.)

——. (1996b). "Antipater, or the Art of Living." In G. Striker, *Essays on Hellenistic Epistemology and Ethics* (pp. 298–315). Cambridge: Cambridge University Press. (Originally published 1986.)

Further Reading

Annas, J. (1993). *The Morality of Happiness*. New York: Oxford University Press.

Brunschwig, J. and Nussbaum, M. C. (eds.). (1993). *Passions and Perceptions: Studies in Hellenistic Philosophy of Mind*. Cambridge: Cambridge University Press.

Inwood, B. (1985). *Ethics and Human Action in Early Stoicism*. Oxford: Oxford University Press.

Long, A. A. (1986). *Hellenistic Philosophy: Stoics, Epicureans, Sceptics*. 2nd edn. Berkeley: University of California Press.

——. (2001). *Stoic Studies*. Berkeley: University of California Press. (Originally Published 1996 by Cambridge University Press.)

——. (2002). *Epictetus: A Stoic and Socratic Guide to Life*. Oxford: Oxford University Press.

Nussbaum, M. C. (1994). *The Therapy of Desire: Theory and Practice in Hellenistic Ethics*. Princeton: Princeton University Press.

Schofield, M. and Striker, G. (eds.). (1986). *The Norms of Nature*. Cambridge: Cambridge University Press.

Sharples, R. W. (1996). *Stoics, Epicureans and Sceptics: An Introduction to Hellenistic Philosophy*. London / New York: Routledge.

28

Hellenistic Cosmopolitanism

ERIC BROWN

Introduction

"When he was asked where he came from, he would say, 'I am a citizen of the world [*kosmopolitēs*]'" (D.L. 6.63). This story, told in antiquity about both Socrates (Cic. *Tusc.* 5.108) and Diogenes the Cynic (D.L. 6.63), records a neat disappointment of traditional Greek expectations. Ordinarily, a Greek would identify himself by the polis or city of his birth, and thereby affirm which institutions and which body of citizens held his allegiance. The polis depended on its citizens to defend the city from attacks, sustain its institutions of justice, and contribute to its common good. But the cosmopolitan denies allegiance to his polis and affirms instead his connection to the entire world.

Cosmopolitanism has long been associated with the Stoic and Epicurean philosophy of the so-called Hellenistic Age, the conventionally recognized period between the Macedonian Empire, which was divided after the death of Alexander the Great in 323 BCE, and the Roman Empire, whose birth can be dated to the victory at Actium of Octavian (later Augustus) in 31 BCE. But the traditional account of Hellenistic cosmopolitanism focuses on its negative aspect, the rejection of allegiance to the local polis, without inquiring much into its positive commitments, the connection to the entire world. This has been so for two reasons. First, a literal interpretation of world-citizenship is intelligible in negative terms, as a rejection of local citizenship, but seems to make no sense in positive terms in the absence of a world-state. Second, the origins of Hellenistic cosmopolitanism have traditionally been explained in a way that places its negative aspect front-and-center: it has been said that in the wake of Alexander the Great's conquests the traditional polis collapsed and could not command the allegiance that it had once received.

But the traditional account should be rejected. First, its explanation of the origins of Hellenistic cosmopolitanism is twice wrong. The widespread assumption that the polis collapsed under the imperial governments of Alexander's successors is at best controversial and at worst flatly mistaken. Focused attention on the Hellenistic period tends to show that there remained a significant sphere of political action in the local polis and significant opportunities for engagement on behalf of the local polis, and indeed, many philosophers in the Hellenistic period continued to recommend engagement in local politics. Moreover, and more decisively, the rise of philosophical cosmopolitanism *predates* the conquests of Alexander and the alleged collapse of the polis. As already noted, the earliest expressions of self-identified cosmopolitanism are attributed to Socrates and to Diogenes the Cynic.

The second inadequacy of the traditional account is its emphasis on the negative aspect of Hellenistic cosmopolitanism. Some closer attention to the Stoic assertions that the cosmos is like a polis and that a good human being lives as a citizen of the cosmos reveals positive commitments to benefit human beings as such in the absence of the world-state. And once we see the positive import of cosmopolitanism in a general concern to benefit human beings as such in place of a special concern to cultivate a common good with compatriots, we can recognize a similar positive cosmopolitanism in Epicurean thought.

Accordingly, this chapter aims to replace the traditional account with a new explanation of the origins of Hellenistic cosmopolitanism and a new appreciation of Hellenistic cosmopolitanism's positive import.

Socratic Roots of Cosmopolitanism

The story that Socrates identified himself as a citizen of the world is probably not true. In contrast to the same story told about Diogenes the Cynic, which is supported by a variety of sources, the portrayal of Socrates as a cosmopolitan is limited to Stoic contexts, and the Stoics not only saw themselves as cosmopolitans but also wanted to claim Socrates as an important source of their ideas. Still, the Stoics have a good point. The cosmopolitanism that is explicitly embraced by Diogenes the Cynic is Socratic.[1]

Socrates clearly believed that every human being is capable of the same virtue and that no human being should be done an injustice. Less obviously, the Socrates of Plato's early dialogues seems to hold the further belief that every human being is equally worthy of being benefited, regardless of conventional social and political status. First, Socrates rejects the life of traditional politics that gives Athenians special benefits that it does not give to foreigners. Second, although Socrates recognizes obligations to obey Athens and its laws, he does not argue for these obligations by reference to any duty to benefit Athenians. Third, he explicitly extends his life's work of examining people – which he recognizes as genuinely beneficial and thus as the proper work of politics (*Grg.* 521d6–8) – to *anyone*, Athenian or foreigner (*Ap.* 23b4–6). Of course, Socrates spends all of his time in Athens, and so he unavoidably benefits Athenians to a special degree, but we need not think that he stays in Athens out of an obligation to benefit Athenians. Rather, he sees himself as free to leave and decides to stay on the grounds that only Athens has the requisite respect for free speech that makes his career possible (*Grg.* 461e1–3; cf. *Ap.* 37c5–e2 and *Meno* 80b4–7). So understood, Socrates seeks to benefit human beings as best he can, and because he cannot benefit all human beings equally and cannot even benefit people very well at all if he leaves Athens, he realizes that the best he can do is to remain in Athens, seeking to examine *anyone* he comes across there. In other words, Socrates replaces ordinary politics and

---

1.   On the origin of the Cynics and Diogenes of Sinope (the Cynic), see Decleva Caizzi, MINOR SOCRATICS, and Bénatouïl, PHILOSOPHIC SCHOOLS IN HELLENISTIC AND ROMAN TIMES, in this volume.

its concentrated service of compatriots with extraordinary politics, which is a project to be shared as optimally as possible with all human beings.[2]

In these ways, the Stoics could have justified their portrayal of Socrates as a cosmopolitan. But this justification involves some heavy interpretation of Socrates' message. Socrates himself is silent about the negative thesis of cosmopolitanism, and he does not much advertise his positive commitment to all human beings in place of a special attachment to Athenians. (In fact, at one rhetorically touchy point he concedes special concern for Athenians (*Ap.* 30a3–5, and cf. 29d7–8 for a related, purely rhetorical concession).) If we are looking for an unequivocal embrace of cosmopolitanism that paves the way for the Hellenistic philosophers, we should look past Socrates to the man Plato allegedly called "Socrates gone mad" (D.L. 6.54), Diogenes the Cynic.

We do not know much of Diogenes aside from the colorful anecdotes that are told about him, but these anecdotes consistently reveal a man intent on challenging conventional values. We are told that he adopted unconventional dress, got by on handouts, and at one time or another indulged all his bodily functions in the marketplace. These stories suffice for us to understand his cosmopolitanism. Diogenes' affirmation of world-citizenship and his claim that "the only true political order (*politeia*) is in the cosmos" (D.L. 6.72) – if indeed this is his claim, and not the Stoicizing interpretation of later antiquity – fit neatly as part of a thorough campaign to overthrow standard obligations and customary prohibitions. Diogenes disdains the conventions of politics just as he disdains all conventions, and Cynic cosmopolitanism is readily intelligible as a negative thesis.

It is much harder to find in the historical record evidence that Diogenes the Cynic had positive commitments to the cosmopolis or to citizens of the world generally. Diogenes seems to recognize no community between him and the rest of the world, except insofar as he clearly desires to provoke others and to be heeded as a model. If we take this desire seriously, we might see Diogenes as a provocative teacher in the Socratic tradition, and if we see Diogenes as an educator, we can believe that he built into his understanding of a good human life a commitment to helping other human beings, without any special attention to compatriots. In this way, we could attribute to Diogenes a positive cosmopolitanism.

But it must be said that the positive side of Cynic cosmopolitanism is delivered entirely by our reflection on Diogenes' way of life. Diogenes rejects theory. He does not leave us reasons why we should reject conventional ties to the polis and embrace a life of trying to help others to live more natural lives. The few reported remarks that seem to give reasons (in D.L. 6.70–73; cf. 102–105) are probably unreliable, devised to emphasize the historical connections between Cynicism and Stoicism. And those remarks aside, Diogenes does not even leave a developed account of what is natural; there are only appeals to cultural variation as evidence of conventionality and mentions of animal behavior as evidence of naturalness. It was disputed in antiquity whether the Cynics had a philosophical school or simply a way of life (D.L. 6.103), and even today, anyone wishing to find in Cynicism interesting positive commitments must extract them from the lives Cynics lived and must provide the reasons for living such a life.

2.   On this topic, see also Morrison, SOCRATES, in this volume.

So it should not be said that Socratic philosophy brought the world cosmopolitanism as a finished philosophical position. It would also be over-simple to give the Socratics all the credit for putting cosmopolitanism on the philosophical agenda. Some Sophists, too, drew cosmopolitan conclusions from the distinction between nature and convention that the Cynics ruthlessly exploited (Antiphon DK 87B44; Hippias ap. Plato, *Prt.* 337c7–d3), and other intellectuals like Democritus (DK 68B247) made cosmopolitan claims. Still, there are clear Socratic tendencies toward rejecting ties to the local polis and taking on the project of improving the lives of human beings generally, without regard to their social or political status. The positive commitment is clearer in Socrates himself, the negative one in Diogenes the Cynic. These Socratic tendencies are the central influence on Hellenistic cosmopolitanism, just as Socratism looms largest for Stoic and Epicurean ethics more generally.

Stoic Cosmopolitanism

"The Stoics say that the cosmos is, as it were, a polis." So goes the report of many ancient authorities (including, e.g., Cicero, *ND* 2.154). A polis, according to the Stoic definition, is a place where human beings live or an organization of human beings (Stob. 2.103,17–20 Wachsmuth), put into order by law (Clement *SVF* 3.327; cf. Dio Chrysostom, *Or.* 36.20, 36.29). But law is right reason (Chrysippus, *On Law* ap. Marcianus *SVF* 3.314, with, e.g., Cic., *Leg.* 1.18), and because no extant city is actually put into order by right reason, no extant city actually deserves the name "polis" (e.g., Clement *SVF* 3.327). The only place where human beings live that *is* put in order by right reason is the cosmos as a whole, and so the cosmos – despite the fact that it is not a product of human work, as a "regular" city would be – is the only true claimant to the title "polis." This much seems clear, and it explains why the Stoics would say that "the cosmos is, as it were, a polis." But what is the significance of this doctrine?

First, the doctrine leaves its mark on the Stoics' conception of ideal politics. Zeno wrote a *Republic* (*Politeia*), which apparently imagined how a plurality of cities would be if every adult were a sage. In such a world, there would be no need for institutions of justice since every human would be in harmony with every other, living by the same right reason. Nor would there be any significant differences between the various cities, for all of them would in fact be ordered by the same right reason, parts of the same cosmopolis. What is more, in this ideal world of sages, every human action would harmonize with the right reason that pervades the whole and would thereby benefit every human being. This is unmistakably cosmopolitanism, though it is over-shadowed in our sources by the controversy over other especially Cynic tendencies (concerning sex and such) in Zeno's *Republic*. Because of this controversy, some later Stoics apparently denied Zeno's authorship of the *Republic* or insisted on its being written early in Zeno's career, but Chrysippus, the early standard-bearer for Stoic orthodoxy, endorsed the work's authenticity and defended some of the work's most notorious elements.

The cosmopolitanism of the ideal sketched by Zeno and endorsed by Chrysippus suggests that the doctrine of the cosmopolis is no mere metaphor for the Stoic goal of living in agreement with the cosmic nature and right reason, but it leaves unclear exactly how cosmopolitanism features in a Stoic ethic for here and now.[3] It might seem natural to interpret Stoic cosmopolitanism still further along Cynic lines. Since the Stoics deny that any extant polis is deserving of the name, we might suppose that they reject the traditional view that one should serve compatriots rather than human beings generally. Then we can get on with examining Stoicism for what Cynicism lacks, an account of why people should be positively committed to cultivating common goods with human beings as such, without regard to their conventional political or social status.

But there is a problem for this view: the Stoics do not follow the Cynics in rejecting engagement in local politics. "[The Stoics] say that the sage will participate in politics, if nothing prevents him – so says Chrysippus in the first book of *On Lives* – for they say that he will restrain vice and promote virtue" (D.L. 7.121). The rest of our evidence for Chrysippus' *On Lives* makes this perfectly clear. Consider three passages. First, Plutarch criticizes Chrysippus for emphasizing ways of making money (*St. rep.* 1043E):

> That he [*sc.*, the sage] does these things for the sake of trade and money, he [*sc.*, Chrysippus] has also made clear earlier [*sc.*, in Book One of *On Lives* (cf. *St. rep.* 1043B–D)] by positing three ways of making money which agree especially well with the sage: from kingship, from friends, and third, after these, from lecturing.

Second, much the same information is provided by Stobaeus' summary of Stoic ethics, although Chrysippus' *On Lives* is not named and the account of ways of making money is interrupted by a remark about family life (Stob. 2.109,10–24 Wachsmuth):

> [They say] that there are three principal lives, the kingly, the political, and third, the life concerned with knowledge. Similarly, there are also three principal ways of making money: from kingship, by which [the sage] will either be king or will thrive on kingly funds; second, from government, for he will engage in politics in accordance with guiding reason, for he will also marry and produce children, for these things accord with the nature of a rational animal, fit for community and loving others. Thus, he will make money both from government and from friends who are in authority. And concerning giving lectures and making money from giving lectures . . . they are agreed on making money from people for education and on occasionally taking fees from those who love learning.

Last, Plutarch elaborates on the first way of making money discussed in Chrysippus' *On Lives* (*St. rep.* 1043B–D):

> But Chrysippus himself in the first book of *On Lives* says that the sage will voluntarily assume kingship and make money from it, and if he is not able to be king, he will live with a king and will serve a king, a king like Idanthyrsus the Scythian or Leucon the Pontian . . . "For," he says, "while holding to these things [*viz.*, common conceptions? cf. S.E. *M* 11.22] let us again examine the fact that he will serve and live with princes, since we have maintained this too for reasons much like the very considerations which have caused

3. For a discussion of the Stoic ethical ideal of living in agreement with nature, see Bett, STOIC ETHICS, in this volume.

some not even to suspect it." And after a little: "And not only with those who have made some progress by being engaged in disciplinary activities and certain habits, for example at the courts of Leucon and Idanthyrsos."

With these three passages in front of us, we cannot say that the Stoic sage is a cosmopolitan by turning his back on local political engagement.

But two curious features of this evidence call for comment. First, notice the second way of making money. Does Chrysippus recommend sponging off friends? It certainly suits Plutarch's polemical purposes to make it sound that way (and cf. D.L. 7.189), but Stobaeus offers a more respectable version. If we keep in mind that the word "friends (*philoi*)" was frequently used in Hellenistic times of advisors at a kingly court (Konstan, 1997, pp. 93–108), then we can make sense of the reports. Chrysippus is saying that if the sage cannot be a king or an advisor to a king (the first way of making money), the sage will happily work in other political capacities, seeking support from royally connected advisors (the second way of making money). What is striking about both of these general ways of making money is the extent to which they count advising as a way of engaging in politics. Advising does not require holding a formal office, nor does it even require local citizenship. It is something one can do as a resident alien.

Which brings us to the second interesting feature of Chrysippus' ways of making money. He endorses advising *foreign* rulers. According to our third piece of evidence, Chrysippus says that one should carefully consider which court to serve as an advisor, favoring (but not limiting oneself to!) those kings who are making progress already, and he uses as examples of good kings rulers in Scythia and the Crimea, which are in the far reaches of the world as it was then known. So while Chrysippus does not reject local political engagement, he maintains a recognizably cosmopolitan position by urging consideration of engagement in politics abroad.

There is an important pattern of reasoning being suggested here, a pattern of reasoning that we can put in our own terms. The good human life includes helping other people to live better lives, and this is the principal reason given by the Stoics for engaging in politics at all. But because of what is required to help other people become better, one cannot help everyone become better in just the same way. So one must decide whom one is going to help. In deliberating on this question, the cosmopolitan seeks to help human beings as such. The best way to help human beings as such might involve staying here and helping these people most. But it might require emigrating, or otherwise sending benefits to others abroad. Either way, the cosmopolitan's purpose is the same, and it can be bumperstickered as "Think Globally, Act Locally."

The question facing such a cosmopolitan, and the question facing our interpretation of Stoic cosmopolitanism, is this: do one's compatriots count for anything special when one is considering where to help human beings? The answer to this question is perfectly clear in some Stoic writings. In the Stoic theory of "duties" in Cicero's *On Duties* (*De Officiis*), for example, anyone considering whom to benefit should reflect on the series of concentric circles of relations around one and should favor the closer relations by favoring, among others, fellow-citizens over foreigners (Cic. *Off.* 1.50–58). The evidence is equally clear in the other direction for the renegade Stoic Aristo, who is on record for the Cynic claim that that "the fatherland [*patris*] does not exist by nature" (Plut. *De exil.* 600E).

But the evidence on this question is much less clear for Chrysippus, the standard-bearer of early Stoic orthodoxy. Some passages that might represent Chrysippean doctrine suggest the possibility of special obligations to serve compatriots. Thus, for example, another passage in Stobaeus' summary of ethics, parallel to the one quoted above, suggests not only that the sage engages in the three ways of making money but also that he "consents to marry and to produce children, both for his own sake and for the sake of his fatherland [*patris*], and he abides both labors and death for it, if it be a moderate fatherland" (Stob. 2.94,7–20 Wachsmuth, quoting 14–17). These addenda may not be Chrysippean: they appear here not because of their link to the question of how one can make money but because of the doxographer's concern for other ways in which (at least some) Stoics talk of contributions to the polis. Furthermore, it is not obvious that the passage commits the Stoics to any special responsibilities to serve compatriots. Rather, it seems to say that if one cannot engage in the preferred careers and benefit human beings as such through an overtly political career or through lecturing and writing books, then one will have no special need to emigrate. In that case, one can contribute to the fatherland by starting a family and will not, if the fatherland is a reasonable place, shy from dangers in order to defend it (cf. D.L. 7.130). In other words, this passage and others like it might suggest that Chrysippus was less a Cynic on this question than Aristo, and closer to the more conventional attitudes of Cicero's *De Officiis*. But on the other hand, they might be saying only that cosmopolitan activities require favorable circumstances, and that in emergencies, the best one can do for human beings in general is to stand with one's neighbors. On the latter interpretation, the Cynicism embraced by Chrysippus' defense of Zeno's *Republic* extends also to his conception of whom one should help if one is lucky enough to choose.

In sum, the doctrine of the cosmopolis is more than a metaphor. The Stoics show a definite commitment to benefiting human beings as such by recognizing the need to deliberate about where one can do that best. Moreover, it seems quite possible that some orthodox Stoics like Chrysippus do not think that we have any special reason to benefit compatriots instead of human beings elsewhere, even though it is clear that some other Stoicisms like that of Cicero's *De Officiis* hold that one should deem one's compatriots more deserving of one's service than foreigners. The first position, which joins the Socratic impulse to benefit human beings with the Cynic rejection of the conventional status conferred by local citizenship, we may call strict cosmopolitanism. The second, which moderates the strict position by adding special consideration for compatriots, we may call moderate cosmopolitanism. Both are, it seems, Stoic possibilities.

Epicurean Cosmopolitanism

The Epicureans oppose the engaged versions of cosmopolitanism favored by Stoics. Epicurus sets up the end of pleasure, understood as the absence of physical pain and mental disturbance, and he concludes that politics and its many disturbances should be avoided (e.g., D.L. 10.119).[4] Live unnoticed, he counsels (Epic. fr. 551 Usener). In this way, Epicurus rejects the traditional service of compatriots, and thus demonstrates some sympathy for the negative thesis of cosmopolitanism. Yet there are three wrinkles that distinguish the Epicurean's withdrawal from the polis from the Cynic's.

The first is minor. Unlike the Cynics, Epicurus and his followers reject engaging in politics only conditionally. They realize that they need the security provided by local laws and institutions as much as anyone does, and they accept that if these laws and institutions are threatened with collapse, then their pursuit of freedom of disturbance requires them to enter the fray. The evidence does not explicitly tell us about exactly what kinds of imminent danger would call for engagement. Nor does it tell us whether certain disturbances might call for a move to another locale instead of engagement on behalf of the local laws and institutions. But the conditional commitment to the local polis is not inconsistent with a general insistence that Epicureans should choose where they live, not bound to hanging out by their fatherland in order to save their compatriots should the need arise, and so there is no reason to believe that the Epicurean's un-Cynic recognition that political institutions are valuable entails a rejection of cosmopolitanism.

Second, there is some reason to attribute to at least some Epicureans positive cosmopolitan commitments, for the Stoa's commitments to building communities as best one can with any group of human beings, regardless of social or political affiliation, are also to be found in the Garden. The key here is friendship. Epicurus declares friendship to be "by far the greatest of the things wisdom equips us with for the blessedness of life as a whole" (*KD* 27), and the Epicureans establish a community of friends who are for each other a bulwark against pain. If this community of friends, as far outside the sphere of conventional politics as it can safely be, is open to all human beings as such, it could be understood as the best one can do to share community with human beings as such, and in this case, the Epicureans are positive cosmopolitans.

There are hints supporting such an interpretation. One of the Epicurean *Sententiae Vaticanae* (*SV* 52, with emphasis added) has it that "friendship dances around the world, announcing to *all* of us that we should wake up to the blessing." Still more clear is the following evidence that at least some Epicureans could characterize their search for friends in cosmopolitan terms, in one of the inscriptions Diogenes of Oenoanda made much later in antiquity for all who could read them: "so-called foreigners really are not, for in relation to each section of the earth, each has its own fatherland, but in relation to the whole circumference of this world, the entire earth is the single fatherland of all and the world is one home" (fr. 30, col. 2.1–11 Smith).

But third, if this interpretation of Epicurean cosmopolitanism is sustainable, then we must ignore or impugn two pieces of evidence concerning Epicurus' beliefs. Clement reports that Epicurus supposed that only Greeks could philosophize (Epic. fr. 226 Usener), and Diogenes Laertius (10.117) reports Epicurus' belief that a sage could not arise in every people (*ethnos*). The Epicureans hold that all human beings have the same goal, and that the same pursuits (friendship, virtue) are the best means toward that goal. Moreover, Epicurus' successor Hermarchus suggests that the laws of justice, conventionally established to promote what is useful and thus different for different

---

4. On the Epicureans, see also Morel, EPICUREANISM, esp. the section titled "Pleasure as an End."

peoples, would be unnecessary if everyone were wisely conscious of what is useful. But if Clement and Diogenes Laertius are to be trusted, then Epicurus did not think that all people were capable of being wisely conscious of what is useful or that all people were capable of being friends. While this is consistent with negative cosmopolitanism's rejection of special obligations to serve compatriots, it sharply limits the cosmopolitan reach of Epicurus' positive commitments. The positive cosmopolitan is committed to human beings as such, and while this allows a commitment to all human beings insofar as they are potential members of a global community, it clashes with a belief that some human beings are naturally incapable of being members of that global community. With this belief – if he held it – Epicurus betrayed the Socratic roots of his project.

The Importance of Hellenistic Cosmopolitanism

On the traditional account, Hellenistic cosmopolitanism can seem a quaint doctrine, adopted by strange people to deal with strange times, and this might make us believe that if the Hellenistic philosophers' cosmopolitan ideas are relevant to us at all, they are relevant because of the Alexandrian power of contemporary economic globalization. But this account sells Hellenistic cosmopolitanism short.

The broad idea of positive commitments to all other human beings, transcending political boundaries, has been and should still be one of the most influential developments of the Hellenistic philosophers. We can see this first in political philosophy, which for hundreds of years has been shaped by Hellenistic cosmopolitanism and especially by a version of the late Stoics' tale of two cities, "the one great and truly common, by which gods and human beings are embraced . . . the other, to which the condition of our birth has assigned us" (Seneca *Otio* 4.1). Christians adopted this talk in contrasting Caesar's city with God's (*Matthew* 22:21), the one a local political authority with temporal aims and the other a potentially universal community of believers with other-worldly objectives (*Ephesians* 2:20), and in this form, political philosophers inherited the problem of weighing the authority of church and state. Political philosophers have also drawn deeply from Hellenistic cosmopolitanism in another idiom by extending the Stoic idea of a natural law of right reason that covers all human beings and orders all proper politics.

But the longest reach of Hellenistic cosmopolitanism is not in the particular field of political philosophy, but in the more general inquiry that was its original home. Most of us now believe that in order to live a good human life we should help other human beings as such, at least under certain circumstances. We face the questions of which other human beings to help and which circumstances call for help. As we face these questions, we should remember the way in which the Epicureans and the Stoics develop the Socratic challenge to conventional attitudes. These Hellenistic philosophers show us that we can aim to benefit human beings as such without attempting to live outside of a particular place and without trying to benefit all human beings in just the same way. In this way, these Hellenistic philosophers challenge us to show that we have special obligations to compatriots instead of lazily deciding that life as usual is a good life after all.

557

Bibliography

Sources

Smith, M. F. (ed.). (1992). *The Epicurean Inscription*. Naples: Bibliopolis.

Stobaeus. *Anthologii Libri duo priores* (ed. C. Wachsmuth). *Libri duo posteriores* (ed. Otto Hense). Berlin: Weidmann, 1884–94.

Usener, H. (ed.). (1887). *Epicurea*. Leipzig: Teubner.

Works Cited

Konstan, D. (1997). *Friendship in the Classical World*. Cambridge: Cambridge University Press.

Further Reading

Asmis, E. (forthcoming). "Choosing a Community: Epicurean Friendship and Stoic Cosmopolitanism."

Baldry, H. C. (1959). "Zeno's Ideal State." *Journal of Hellenic Studies*, 79, 3–15.

——. (1965). *The Unity of Mankind in Greek Thought*. Cambridge: Cambridge University Press.

Brown, E. (2000). "Socrates the Cosmopolitan." *Stanford Agora: An Online Journal of Legal Studies* 1, 74–87.

——. (2006). *Stoic Cosmopolitanism*. Cambridge: Cambridge University Press.

Moles, J. L. (1995). "The Cynics and Politics." In A. Laks and M. Schofield (eds.), *Justice and Generosity: Studies in Hellenistic Social and Political Philosophy* (pp. 129–58). Cambridge: Cambridge University Press.

——. (1996). "Cynic Cosmopolitanism." In R. B. Branham and M.-O. Goulet-Cazé (eds.), *The Cynics: The Cynic Movement in Antiquity and its Legacy* (pp. 105–20). Berkeley: University of California Press.

Nussbaum, M. C. (forthcoming). *The Cosmopolitan Tradition*. New Haven: Yale University Press.

Nussbaum, M. C., et al. (1996). *For Love of Country: Debating the Limits of Patriotism*. (J. Cohen, ed.). Boston: Beacon Press.

Schofield, M. (1991). *The Stoic Idea of the City*. Cambridge: Cambridge University Press.

Stanton, G. R. (1968). "The Cosmopolitan Ideas of Epictetus and Marcus Aurelius." *Phronesis*, 13, 183–95.

Part V

Middle and Late Platonism

29

Middle Platonism

MARCO ZAMBON

Middle Platonism: A Problematic Label

In order to outline the developments in Platonic philosophy between the first century BCE and the third century CE we use today the label "Middle Platonism." The label has only come into use recently and is controversial, because it involves the idea of an intermediate stage in the development of Platonic thought between the Academy and the so-called "Neoplatonism" inaugurated by Plotinus. Also the label implies that this intermediate step has at least some common features which allow us to grasp this version of Platonism as a unitary phenomenon. Both assumptions are debatable today.

The ancients had already attributed a change in doctrine to the last head of the Platonic Academy, Antiochus of Ascalon (Barnes, 1989): the abandonment of skepticism and return to a dogmatic understanding of Plato's teachings, in other words the conviction that Plato held *dogmata*, positive doctrines about the Divine, the cosmos and the soul. Middle Platonism is taken to begin with this turning to dogma and to end with Plotinus.

Historic reality seems somewhat more complex than the scheme we have just outlined. It is difficult to identify the context in which Middle Platonism began and an author who can be described as the "first Middle Platonist." Others besides Antiochus have been credited with founding Middle Platonism: Philo of Larissa, Posidonius of Apamea, Eudorus of Alexandria (Boys-Stones, 2001, pp. 99–101). Moreover, even though the Platonists of that era shared some common views, the positions they held are so varied and irreconcilable as to make it difficult to identify what doctrinal elements can properly be called "Middle Platonic."

In the light of this, it is perhaps safer to speak of "Platonisms" instead of "Middle Platonism." As examples of the diverse Platonisms of that age one may cite the Stoicizing version, taught by Antiochus and, to a lesser extent, by Atticus (Baltes, 1983); or the faithful heritage of the Academy propounded by Plutarch (Ferrari, 1995); or even the Pythagoricizing version of those thinkers who, like Eudorus (Dörrie, 1944), Moderatus and Numenius (Frede, 1987), are labeled in the ancient sources both as Platonists and as Pythagoreans. Finally, there was also a pro-Aristotelian version of Platonism, propounded for instance by Alcinous (Göransson, 1995), and an openly anti-Aristotelian version, like that of Atticus, Lucius and Nicostratus, which we can define as "orthodox," because it was hostile to all attempts to reconcile the thought of Plato and Aristotle.[1]

The assumption that Plotinus acts as a historic dividing line between two distinct phases in the history of Platonism is debatable. Actually, in the history of ancient Platonism, Plotinus is quite an isolated figure. The most innovative and original aspects of his thought were not taken on by his successors; besides that, Middle Platonic thinkers held doctrines that appear also in Plotinus and his successors (for example, negative theology and the doctrine of the One superior to being).

A turning point, however, in the Platonism of the Imperial Age did come about: we can make out the first signs around halfway through the first century BCE when, because of the damage following the Roman occupation, the Academy ceased to exist as an institution in Athens.[2] From that time onwards, being a Platonist no longer meant being a member of the Academy founded by Plato: instead, it meant trusting in the truth of the doctrine held in Plato's dialogues, which were seen as the main source for the knowledge of Platonic thought (P. Hadot, 1987). Starting from the second century CE we find evidence of the typical feature of Imperial Platonism, both before and after Plotinus, namely, the idea that Plato's doctrine – whatever it might be – counts as the exhaustive and authentic truth.

Plato's followers give him an authority superior to all other philosophers, regarding him as the bearer of ancient and complete knowledge – an attitude which has almost the character of a religious revelation. The job of the philosopher is thought of, not in terms of the development of the ideas of the master, but as the preservation and interpretation of a doctrine that is held to be contained, albeit sometimes implicitly and in enigmatic form, in the writings of Plato. This did not prevent Platonists of the Imperial Age from constructing different and original versions of Platonism; still, all of them share in the ideal of keeping completely faithful to what they believed was the authentic doctrine of their teacher.[3]

One may be tempted to follow in the steps of those scholars who think we should get rid of the modern distinction between "Middle" and "Neo" Platonism and go back to the ancient label of "Platonists" to differentiate the followers of Plato of the Imperial Age from the "Academics," the members of the school founded by Plato.[4] For the sake of clarity, however, it seems better to keep the label "Middle Platonism," conventional as it is, to indicate the historical development of Platonism from the end of the Academy up to Plotinus. The label will be used with this mere chronological meaning in what follows.

1. The opposition between an eclectic sort of Platonism and an orthodox one was proposed by Praechter (1916 and 1922), but is based on presuppositions which are now out-of-date: See I. Hadot (1990) and Donini (1988).
2. *Platonismus* (1987, §§32–4); Dillon (1979); Glucker (1978).
3. The language of the Platonists is interwoven with frequent quotations and allusions to the Platonic texts, but very different interpretations are possible with only slight variations in the form and context of a quotation: Whittaker (1987a).
4. On the history of the term *Platonici* as distinct from the term *Academici*, see Glucker (1978, pp. 206–25). On the Academy in the Hellenistic Age, see in this volume Lévy, THE NEW ACADEMY AND ITS RIVALS.

Literary sources

When the Roman siege put an end to the existence of the Academy, Athens had already ceased to be the only city where philosophy was taught. Alexandria, Apamea, Pergamum, Smyrna, Tyre and many other places, above all in the East of the Mediterranean area, were centers of activity of philosophy teachers, rhetoricians, doctors, state officials, and other cultivated people who, on very different levels of competence, were interested in philosophy.

The literary sources show a highly diverse panorama of pre-Plotinian Platonism. There are technical writings, related to school activity and providing the exegesis of Plato or other philosophers: commentaries, collections of questions, handbooks, lexica.[5] Some fragments of an anonymous *Commentary on the Theaetetus*, the exegetic writings of Plutarch (e.g., the *Platonic Questions* and the treatise *On the Generation of the Soul in the Timaeus*), the *Introduction to the Dialogues of Plato* by Albinus, the *Didaskalikos* of Alcinous, the handbooks of Nicomachus of Gerasa and Theon of Smyrna bear witness of this exegetical activity.

There are also polemical writings against rival schools of philosophy or other adversaries (e.g., the Christians), as well as works of a historical nature. The fragments of Atticus' treatise *Against Those Who Claim to Interpret Plato through Aristotle*, and of Numenius' *On the Defection of Academics from Plato*, as well as of Celsus' anti-Christian treatise, the *True Story*, give an idea of this kind of literature. We can also learn something about a widespread Platonic culture, even though often of modest level, from rhetoric works, from works on religion such as the *Discourses* of the rhetorician Maximus of Tyre, from the writings in the *Hermetic Corpus*, from the fragments of the *Chaldaean Oracles*, and finally from Gnostic and early Christian literature.

In particular the *Chaldaean Oracles* earned an extraordinary prestige among Platonists. The collection was put together around the time of Marcus Aurelius and claims to contain revelations either of divine origin or transmitted through the soul of Plato himself, and uttered in poetical form by mediums during evocation rituals. They convey a cosmogony and a psychogony resembling Numenius' interpretation of Plato's *Timaeus* (Liefferinge, 1999; Lewy, 1978).[6]

Most of the writings by Platonists before Plotinus, with the exception of some of the texts mentioned above and a few others, have been lost or are known to us only through quotations or testimony in later authors. We have a large *corpus* of writings only of Plutarch and Galen. The great variety of literary genres, the highly variable quality of the materials that we possess, the concentration of the evidence in the second century CE, together with the variety of philosophical options, all urge a certain caution in our attempt to reconstruct an overall picture of Platonism from the first century BCE to Plotinus.

5.   Donini (1994); Fuhrmann (1960); Sedley (1997).
6.   On the significance of the *Chaldaean Oracles*, see in this volume Hoffmann, WHAT WAS COMMENTARY IN LATE ANTIQUITY?

Philosophy as Exegesis: Dogmatic and Systematic Interpretation of Plato's Thought

All Platonists of the Imperial Age agree that Plato brought philosophy to perfection: Albinus, for example, states in his *Introduction* that "the doctrine [of Plato] is perfect and is similar to the perfect figure of the circle" (Alb. *Intr.* 4.149.13–14 Reis; see Reis, 1997). In the *Evangelical Preparation* by Eusebius of Caesarea we find two interesting testimonies of the way in which Plato's role was understood, one from the Platonist Atticus, the other from the Peripatetic Aristocles.[7] Atticus holds that Plato was sent by the gods to reveal philosophy in its entirety: Plato, in fact, "first and better than all others brought together in a unified form the limbs of philosophy . . . and he showed it as a body and a living being complete in every part." While his predecessors were only interested in partial aspects of philosophy, Plato dealt completely with every aspect.

A similar judgment is also expressed by Aristocles in his book *On Philosophy*: "If there has ever been someone who has philosophized in a complete and genuine way, this person was Plato." According to Aristocles Plato's predecessors only dealt with parts of philosophy. True, Socrates raised questions in various fields of philosophy; but he did not have time to answer them because of his untimely death. Plato, by contrast, understood that "the science of divine and human things is one and the same thing" and he dealt with both sides of this knowledge: cosmology and theology on one hand, human behavior and logic on the other.

The image of the circle and that of the living body articulated into all its parts capture the conviction that in Plato's teaching we get the complete truth, a teaching that enfolds in a coherent and ordered way all of reality. Without any hesitation these authors credit Plato with a division of philosophy into three parts: ethics, physics, and logic. This division is absent from his dialogues, but had become current in Hellenistic philosophy.[8] Philosophy became increasingly an interpretation and analysis of Plato's text: the problems which attracted most attention were raised starting from Plato and the presupposition that what Plato says is true if one understands it correctly. A problem for this effort was that Plato's dialogues do not lend themselves to the foundation of an encyclopedic and systematic conception of philosophy; nor do they supply clear and complete answers to every possible philosophical question. Throughout the Imperial Age an intense effort was made by Platonists to interpret the dialogues to show the ordered and systematic nature of the doctrine therein. Testimony of this intense work can be found in the many exegetic writings of which we have word, only a few fragments of which have come down to us.

In the fragments of an anonymous *Commentary on the Theaetetus* the author refers to some comments of his on the *Timaeus*, the *Phaedo*, and the *Symposium*;[9] the *Alcibiades* and the *Parmenides* were certainly commented upon; Atticus possibly composed a

---

7. Att. fr. 1 des Places = Eus. *Praep. Evang.* 11.1.2–2.5; Aristocl. fr. 1 Heiland = Eus. *Praep. Evang.* 11.2.6–3.9; *Platonismus* (1993, §§99–100).
8. On the tripartition of philosophy see P. Hadot (1979); *Platonismus* (1996, §101).
9. Anon. *In Tht.* 35.10–12; 48.7–11; 70.10–12 Bastianini and Sedley.

commentary on the *Phaedrus*;[10] Numenius commented on the myth of Er which ends the *Republic*.[11] However, all the Platonists before Plotinus share the conviction that the *Timaeus* is Plato's preeminent work, where he expounded his doctrine of principles, his theology, cosmology, and the doctrine of the soul.[12] We have testimony of exegetical works dedicated to this dialogue, from Eudorus,[13] Plutarch,[14] Calvenus Taurus,[15] Atticus and Longinus,[16] among others.

The commentators set themselves the task of solving the apparent contradictions between the dialogues: Plutarch argued for his interpretation of the Platonic doctrine of the soul by stating that it could resolve the apparent conflict between the *Timaeus*, where the soul is said to be produced by the demiurge, and the *Phaedrus*, where, on the contrary, the soul appears as having always existed.[17] Plato's dramatic and narrative style in the dialogues also presented a problem. Does this serve merely as rhetorical ornamentation or does it have a philosophical meaning? Not everyone agreed that the first part of the *Timeaus* (17a–27b) merited comment; some considered it a simple narrative.[18]

Another problem arose from the well-known claim of the *Timaeus* that the world is "generated" (28b–c): does this mean that the world had a starting point in time, as Plutarch probably held and Atticus certainly did? Or does the description of the temporal production of the cosmos serve only a didactic purpose, while in reality Plato thought that the world was eternal?[19]

The main strategy for the interpretation of Platonic texts, especially when Plato's words seemed obscure or philosophically irrelevant, was allegory, a strategy based on the principle that Plato often presented in an obscure or veiled way those doctrines that he did not want to be accessible. Only those who were worthy of understanding could do so. The Platonists of the Imperial Age held that Plato had stated his intention of presenting his doctrine "enigmatically," so that a casual, unprepared reader would not come to know it.[20]

---

10. Att. fr. 14 des Places = Procl. *In Ti.* 3.247.12–15 Diehl.

11. Num. fr. 35 des Places = Procl. *In Rep.* 2.128.26–131.14 Kroll.

12. On the *Timaeus* itself, see Brisson, PLATO'S NATURAL PHILOSOPHY AND METAPHYSICS, in this volume.

13. Plut. *De an. procr.* 3 (1013B); 16 (1019E; 1020C).

14. *Generation of the Soul in the Timaeus* (*De an. procr.*) is extant; also, five of the ten *Platonic Questions* are devoted to the *Timaeus* (II, IV, VII and VIII), while the others are devoted to the *Theaetetus* (I), *Republic* (III, IX), *Phaedrus* (VI), *Sophist* (IX).

15. Lakmann (1995).

16. On the Middle and Neoplatonic exegesis of the dialogues, see *Platonismus* (1993, §§78–81); on the *Timaeus*: Reydams-Schils (1999); Deuse (1983); Baltes (1976).

17. Plut. *De an. procr.* 8 (1015F–1016A); Plat. *Phdr.* 245c–246a; *Ti.* 34b–35a.

18. Procl. *In Ti.* 1.75.30ff.; 129.10ff. Diehl; *In Alc.* 18.13ff. Westerink; *In Rep.* 1.5.12ff. Kroll; *In Prm.* col. 658.34ff. Cousin.

19. Procl. *In Ti.* 1.276.30–277.7 Diehl; *Platonismus* (1998, §137); Zambon (2002, pp. 86–9); Baltes (1999a and 1976).

20. [Plat.] *Ep.* II, 312d. Numenius gives the oldest witness of the use of this pseudo-Platonic text, which the ancients held to be authentic: fr. 24.51–57 des Places. On the allegorical exegesis, see Buffière (1956); Pépin (1976); Lamberton (1989).

Before starting to interpret a text a reliable edition was needed and the exegete had to answer a series of preliminary questions: Was the work authentic? What was its literary genre? Who was its intended audience? What problem did it attempt to answer? What was the author's aim in writing it?[21] The Middle Platonists were indebted to the philological work of the Alexandrian scholars, but even so they had to work for a long time to establish a proper order for reading Plato's dialogues and to remove the spurious works. Among the various orderings, Thrasyllus' tetralogic ordering gained primacy and is still adopted by modern editors; but even that was not unreservedly accepted by everyone.[22]

If Plato's doctrine equals the truth itself and the best way to reach it is to study Plato's dialogues and learn to interpret them correctly, this requires long practice and a good literary and scientific background. The best place for this activity was a school. Even though the term "school" should not be taken in a narrow sense, we can characterize Platonic philosophy of the Imperial Age as a "school philosophy" or a "professor's Platonism" (Dörrie, 1960, 1966; Goulet-Cazé, 1989), meaning by this not the existence of widespread institutions of learning, but rather that most of the philosophers of the period used teaching methods in their writings. Inspired by the educational model that Plato himself had outlined for the philosopher-king in the *Republic*, the Middle Platonists also gradually developed a "training plan" for philosophers, which included knowledge of what would later be called the "liberal arts" (I. Hadot, 1984) and the study of a selection of the most important Platonic dialogues according to a systematic and propaedeutic order.

Albinus gives testimony to the fact that philosophy teachers disagreed about which Platonic dialogue should be read first; he proposed his own reading plan which he regarded as suitable for a student of the right age, with the right skills and both the desire to exercise virtue and the cultural preparation necessary to take on the serious study of philosophy. The first dialogue to be read is the *First Alcibiades*, because it reminds the student of the importance of self-knowledge; then the *Phaedo*, which provides the model of the philosophic style of life and outlines the essential themes of Platonic philosophy. Then he should read the *Republic*, which investigates and teaches virtue, and finally the *Timaeus*, which presents Plato's teaching on the divine order of the cosmos and the nature of divine reality (Alb. *Intr.* 4–5, 149.1–150.12 Reis).

Another reading plan, similar to this, can be found in the so-called "canon of Iamblichus," a list of ten dialogues crowned by the two held to be the most important (*Timaeus* and *Parmenides*). The "canon" is attributed to the Neoplatonic philosopher Iamblichus but counts in all likelihood as the consecration in written form of a

---

21. Starting from this set of questions, the practice was developed, already in Middle Platonism, of preceding the proper commentary with a series of preliminary points; an example of introductions of this type is Albinus' *Introduction* to Plato's dialogues. On this subject see Mansfeld (1994), and in this volume, Hoffmann.

22. Tarrant (1993); Festugière (1969); D.L. 3.56–62; a different plan is proposed by Alb. *Intr.* ch. 3, explicitly criticizing the order given by Thrasyllus. See *Platonismus* (1990, §§47–8).

practice that had already been in use for some time.[23] It is not possible to establish whether there was a precise and rigid succession in the readings of the dialogues in the schools, nor is it essential to our purposes: rather, what is well established and important here is that such a progression was considered necessary and fully consistent with the intentions of Plato himself.

Continuity or Rupture in the Platonic Tradition?

One of the most typical features of Platonism during the Imperial Age is the widespread production of historiographical and polemical works that aimed at defining the "school" of Plato, to mark it off from other schools. The problem of definition was first raised within Platonism itself. Had the disciples of Plato preserved the teachings of the master and were their own teachings legitimate instruments for the interpretation of the dialogues? None of the successors of Plato in the Academy had doubted being a legitimate heir of Plato, even though the doctrinal differences of the disciples concerning this or that Platonic doctrine were important right from the beginning.

Antiochus of Ascalon brought up the problem, stating that from Arcesilaus to Philo of Larissa the skeptical orientation of the Academy had caused the abandonment of the genuine teaching of Plato and a fracture in the tradition. Antiochus held, therefore, that skepticism should be abandoned and that Platonists should return to the true Platonic doctrine, that is, to the corpus of his *dogmata* (explicit doctrines). According to him, what Aristotle and the Stoics had taught coincided with Platonic teaching, albeit in a more confused manner. Along with the problem of the unity and continuity of the school of Plato there was also the debate, at times heated, about Aristotle. Could he be considered an authentic disciple of Plato or not? (*Platonismus*, 1987, §10; 1993, §84.)

These were not just historiographic issues. The solutions given to these problems involved different interpretations of Platonism. Plutarch, for example, who believed in the unity and continuity of the Academy, held a position consistent with skepticism, emphasizing the limits of human knowledge with regard to the reality of the divine and the order of the cosmos.[24] The anonymous author of the *Commentary on the Theaetetus* also stated that there had been no break in the transmission of the teachings of Plato by the Academy, because this teaching had always been, contrary to appearances, dogmatic (Anon. *In Tht.* 54.38–55.13 Bastianini and Sedley). Numenius took an opposing view and this position became the prevailing one, even influencing modern historiography on the skeptical tradition of the Academy: the immediate followers of Plato (Speusippus, Xenocrates, Polemon, and Aristotle) had already

---

23. The canon of Iamblichus included the *Alcibiades, Gorgias, Phaedo, Cratylus, Theaetetus, Sophist, Politicus, Phaedrus, Symposium, Philebus*. It is interesting to note that for many of the dialogues included in the canon, we have testimony of the existence of commentaries or other exegetic works already in Middle Platonic authors. On the subject, see *Platonismus* (1990, §50).
24. On the permanence of skeptical themes in Platonism during the Imperial Age see Opsomer (1998); Bonazzi (2003).

abandoned and betrayed Platonic teaching, damaging its unity (Num. fr. 24 des Places = Eus. *Praep. Evang.* 14.4–5). This position had a clear theoretical motivation: Plato, according to Numenius, unified in his teaching the wisdom of Pythagoras and Socrates and built up a doctrine that was fully consistent with that of all peoples and the ancient wise men. After Plato there could be no other option than absolute faithfulness to his teaching or the abandonment of the truth. Any positive development was held by Numenius to be, to all intents and purposes, impossible.

The dissent about Aristotle was particularly acute. His works presented much more systematic and complete teachings than the Platonic dialogues (above all his writings on logic, our *Organon*), as well as positions which were openly polemical against crucial themes of Platonism. Some (Plutarch, Alcinous, the anonymous commentator on the *Theaetetus*) thought they could integrate, at least in part, the teaching of Aristotle with that of Plato; others (Atticus, Lucius, Nicostratus, Numenius) vehemently opposed this attempt. The first group held that Aristotle did not really modify Plato, but merely explained and developed what in the dialogues was simply sketched or implied.[25] His anti-Platonism was explained in terms of misunderstanding, pride, or the student's desire to distinguish himself from his teacher.

Among the authors who opposed interpretations of Plato that relied on Aristotelian doctrine, Atticus is noteworthy because of the violence of his attack. In his treatise *Against Those Who Claim to Interpret Plato through Aristotle*, he claims that Aristotle had abandoned the teaching of Plato regarding the aim of philosophy, the providence of God, the generation of the world and the number of elements in the sensible world, the immortality of the soul and ideas (or Forms). Quite apart from the different solutions, it is worth noting that both the pro-Aristotelian Platonists and the anti-Aristotelian Platonists accepted a doctrine as true only if they thought it was coherent with the teaching of Plato and at least implicitly contained in it.

Another widespread idea was that the truth of the Platonic doctrine is confirmed by its roots in the distant past. Numenius and Celsus, for example, stated that it was in accordance with religious doctrines and ancient wisdom not only in the Greek tradition but also in all the ancient and prominent civilizations (Frede, 1987, 1994). The continuity established between the doctrines of Pythagoras and Plato,[26] as well as the reference to travels in the Orient and Egypt attributed to Plato by several sources, gave support to the conviction that the knowledge that humanity had received from the gods in ancient times was summed up in him. Being a Platonist meant, therefore, being faithful to a tradition of wisdom of a sacred nature, almost a

---

25. The topic of the presence in Plato of the doctrine of categories is discussed in Plut. *De an. procr.* 23 (1023E); Alc. *Didask.* 6.159.43ff. Whittaker and Louis; Anon. *In Tht.* 68.7–15 Bastianini and Sedley.

26. Some pre-Plotinian authors (Eudorus, Moderatus, Nicomachus, Numenius) are also known as "neo-Pythagoreans," because of their explicit claim of the dependence of Plato on Pythagoras's teaching. Their doctrines were developed within the Platonism of their era, even though often, by means of apocryphal texts, they were attributed to Pythagoras and his disciples. This is the case with the treatises of pseudo-Timaeus of Locri (ed. by Baltes) and pseudo-Archytas (ed. by Szlezák), which aimed at attributing the doctrines of the Platonic *Timaeus* and the Aristotelian *Categories* to disciples of Pythagoras.

revelation, which traced back, through Socrates, Pythagoras, Homer, Orpheus, the sages and the lawgivers of other peoples (e.g., Zoroaster and Moses), to the very origins of humanity.[27]

Common Doctrinal Topics in Middle Platonism

While bearing in mind the great variety of positions among the Middle Platonic authors even on fundamental issues, we can indicate at least some large thematic areas that characterize their doctrines. Compared with the Academic tradition, the Platonists of the Imperial Age show a much greater interest in theology. For instance, all of them accept the formula of the *Theaetetus*, according to which philosophy aims at "becoming similar to God, as far as possible."[28] Becoming similar to God was considered possible because it was assumed that the rational soul was of a nature homogeneous with the divine and able, therefore, to raise itself to the divine level through a process of moral purification and knowledge. This was what philosophy was for and this, in the Platonist's view, amounted also to the supreme good available to man.[29]

As we saw in the description of the reading order of the Platonic dialogues proposed by Albinus, the ideal path of Platonic philosophy started with self-knowledge as an immortal soul and culminated in the knowledge of the first principles of reality, presented in the *Timaeus*. Reading the *Timaeus* also provided a tripartite scheme of the principles that had great currency among Platonists, even though it was not the only one adopted. Following this scheme, the principles of reality are the demiurge, ideas and matter, often reinterpreted in Aristotelian terms as the efficient, formal and material cause of reality.[30]

The nature and the mutual relations of the three principles were dealt with in very different ways by the authors partly because of the constant effort towards the harmonization of topics coming from the various Platonic dialogues. For instance, in the *Timaeus* there was a recognizable doctrine of three principles of reality, but this had to fit together with a dualistic theory, based on the opposition between intellect and necessity stated in *Ti.* 47e–48a and confirmed by *Laws* X, 896d–e, which mentions

27. *Platonismus* (1990, §§64 and 69); Num. frr. 1a–c des Places = Eus. *Praep. Evang.* 9.7.1; Orig. *Cels.* 1.15; 4.51; fr. 8.13 des Places = Eus. *Praep. Evang.* 11.10.14; Orig. *Cels.* 1.14.16; 6.80; Lamberton (1989); Edwards (1990).

28. Plat. *Tht.* 176a–b; *Ti.* 90d; Alb. *Intr.* 5.150.10; 6.151.4 Reis; Alc. *Didask.* 2.153.8–9; 28.181.19–20 Whittaker and Louis; Stob. 2.7,3 = 2.49, 8–10 Wachsmuth. Eudorus was the first to adopt the formula "to become similar to God" as the expression of the goal of philosophy; cf. *Platonismus* (1996, §102); Merki (1952). The formula was probably contrasted with the Stoic conception of the end of philosophy: Anon. *In Tht.* 7.14–20 Bastianini and Sedley.

29. On assimilation to god, see Betegh, GREEK PHILOSOPHY AND RELIGION; and cf. Brisson and Pradeau, PLOTINUS, in this volume.

30. *Ti.* 27c–29d and the treatment in Alc. *Didask.* 8–10; Apul. *De Plat.* 1.5.190–6.193; *Platonismus* (1996, § 113.3). On the Aristotelian causes, see in this volume Bodnár and Pellegrin, ARISTOTLE'S PHYSICS AND COSMOLOGY, the section "The Science of Natural Beings."

two souls, one good and one bad, as the principles of reality. Thus some authors, Plutarch, Atticus, and Numenius, for example, superimposed a dualistic scheme on the tripartite scheme. The demiurge and the paradigm were identified with the good soul of the *Laws*, while matter was identified with the bad, disordered soul: from their mutual combination came into being the cosmos and the individuals provided with rational souls but also inclined towards evil.[31]

On the other hand, the *Republic* described the ascent towards a single intelligible principle, the idea of Good, which was declared to be the cause of all things and placed "beyond being with regard to dignity and power" (*Rep.* VI, 509b).[32] On the basis of this statement, Numenius, Alcinous, the authors of the *Oracles* and others investigated the transcendence of the first principle and denied that it was possible to reach the knowledge of it through the same cognitive means used to know other things (Num. fr. 2.7–16, 22–23 des Places = Eus. *Praep. Evang.* 11.21.7–22.2).

This paved the way to the careful distinction between the One-Good and Being developed later on by Plotinus and his successors, and a negative theology appeared side by side with the positive theology as an argument for the comprehension of the nature of the first principle.[33]

Is the idea of Good therefore identical to the demiurge of the *Timaeus* or does it belong to a different level of reality? Must we assume that there is only one principle for the whole of reality or should we admit that there are at least two, or even more? And what relation should we admit between Good, the demiurge and the Divine Soul that Plato talked about in the *Laws*? If, according to the definition in the *Sophist*, the soul is the principle of movement, could it be generated after the first principle – as a literal reading of the *Timaeus* would seem to imply – or, following the *Laws*, must it be conceived as an original principle on a par with the demiurge, the paradigm and matter? The Middle Platonic exegetes were faced with these and many other problems once they had affirmed, as they did, that in all the dialogues Plato had expounded a single coherent doctrine.

Two important doctrinal developments go back to pre-Plotinian Platonism: one is the interpretation of the Platonic demiurge, in the light of the *Sophist* and of Aristotle's theology, as a living intellect which contains in itself the object of its own thought, namely, the Ideas (Armstrong, 1960; P. Hadot, 1960). The other is the conception of the divine as a hierarchy of realities, a conception which distinguishes a primary god – the absolute principle – which is immobile, superior to being, and unknowable; a second god, a demiurgic intellect which contains ideas; and sometimes a third god, the World Soul, which is the principle that gives order and life to the sensible world. The theological scheme articulated into two or three gods was laid out in different forms by the authors who adopted it. Its development was probably linked to the diffusion of a theological interpretation both of the hypotheses contained in the *Parmenides* and of a

---

31. This is the doctrine which Plutarch expounds in his *De Iside et Osiride* (e.g., 45.369B–D); also Num. fr. 52 des Places = Calc. *In Ti.* 295–299; *Platonismus* (1996, §121).
32. On this passage see Baltes (1997); Whittaker (1969).
33. The idea of the transcendence and unknowability of the first principle was often discussed starting from *Ti.* 28c, *Ep.* VII, 341c and *Prm.* 142a; Nock (1962); Whittaker (1973, 1978); Tarrant (1983); *Arrhetos* (2002). See also Brisson and Pradeau, in this volume.

passage of the (pseudo)-Platonic *Epistle* II, which mentions "three kings" around which all things move (312e).[34]

Theology, cosmology, and anthropology made up an interconnected system of problems whose solutions were looked for in the Platonic dialogues. This was by no means a speculative exercise. Knowledge of the order of being was considered at the same time the condition and the effect of a well-ordered and happy life from the ethical point of view as well. It is in this close link between knowledge of the truth and a good life that we find, even in the Platonism of the Imperial Age, a persistent awareness of the political responsibility of the philosopher. Platonic philosophers thought it was their duty to offer guidance to their contemporaries on individual and collective virtuous behavior. First this was done by practicing and teaching philosophy, but some philosophers were also members of the magistrature or had the functions of priests at the local level, as Plutarch did; or they were in one way or another in touch with kings and emperors, as were Longinus and Plotinus.

There was also a political concern inherent in the struggle against the diffusion of more recent doctrines, which questioned the supremacy of Platonic teaching, in particular in the anti-Christian polemic *True Story* by Celsus (Andresen, 1955). Celsus' opposition to Christianity was the refusal of a novelty which was not rooted in the religious traditions and wisdom of ancient people and which altered the subordination of the sensible world to the intelligible (the incarnation of God's Word, the bodily resurrection), something which was perceived as a threat to the ethical and social order on which the peace in the Roman Empire was grounded.

Platonism as a Synthesis of Ancient Culture

The first centuries of the Empire were characterized by a laborious process of transformation that led Platonic philosophy to present itself as the collector and synthesis of the whole of the scientific, philosophical, sapiential, and religious heritage of the Greek culture. A hierarchical and highly structured conception of reality became dominant in the representation of divine reality, the natural world, society, and knowledge. The primacy and the sacredness of the figure and writings of Plato led either to a harsh struggle with rival authors and schools or to a conciliatory attitude prone to absorb into Platonism doctrinal contributions of the Peripatetic and Stoic traditions and the alleged Pythagorean tradition.

This complex work of assimilation and demarcation of the respective identities was carried out above all through the discussion and interpretation of the texts. The school, the books, the library, the debate, and public speech became the vehicles for philosophical training and the exchange of ideas. This does not mean, however, that Platonism became an "academic" discipline in the modern sense. The Platonists continued to advocate philosophy not just as a form of thought but also as a way of life, whose aim was to transform man and bring him to the style of life for which he alone was suited – life oriented towards the intelligible.

34. Also [Plat.] *Ep.* VI, 323d; Dodds (1928); Dörrie (1970).

The religious experience was by no means isolated from this movement towards synthesis. The rejection of traditions seen as foreign or subversive (Christianity, sometimes Judaism) was accompanied by an increase in the value given to mythical and ritual heritage, not just Greek but also barbarian, interpreted as a symbolic and partial expression of the same truth to which Plato's philosophy gave its all-embracing and final form. In the last resort, Platonism itself became with the *Chaldaean Oracles* in a certain sense a religion, and Plato was raised to the role of a divine being who reveals his philosophy to a few initiates.

Bibliography

Sources

Albinus

Reis, B. (ed.). (1999). *Der Platoniker Albinos und sein sogenannter Prologos. Prolegomena, Überlieferungsgeschichte, kritische Edition und Übersetzung.* Wiesbaden: Reichert.

Alcinous

Dillon, J. (1993). *Alcinous, The Handbook of Platonism.* Oxford: Clarendon Press.
Whittaker, J. and Louis, P. (eds.). (1990). *Alcinoos, Enseignement des doctrines de Platon.* Paris: Les Belles Lettres.

Anon. *In Tht.*

Bastianini, G. and Sedley, D. (eds.). (1995). *Commentarium in Platonis Theaetetum.* In *Corpus dei papiri filosofici greci e latini. Testi e lessico nei papiri di cultura greca e latina.* Part III: *Commentari* (pp. 227–562). Florence: Olschki.

Antiochus and Philo

Mette, H. J. (1986–7). "Philon von Larisa und Antiochos von Askalon." *Lustrum,* 28–29, 9–63.

Atticus

des Places, É. (ed.). (1977). *Atticus, Fragments.* Paris: Les Belles Lettres.

Eudorus

Mazzarelli, C. (1985). "Raccolta e intrepretazione delle testimonianze e dei frammenti del medioplatonico Eudoro di Alessandria. Parte prima. Testo e traduzione delle testimonianze e dei frammenti sicuri." *Rivista di Filosofia neo-scolastica,* 77, 197–209.
Mazzarelli, C. (1985). "Raccolta e interpretazione delle testimonianze e dei frammenti del medioplatonico Eudoro di Alessandria. Parte seconda. Testo e traduzione delle testimonianze non sicure." *Rivista di Filosofia neo-scolastica,* 77, 535–55.

Longinus

Brisson, L. and Patillon, M. (1994). "Longinus Platonicus Philosophus et Philologus. I. Longinus Philosophus." In *ANRW* II 36.7 (pp. 5214–99). Berlin: de Gruyter. "Longinus Philologus." In *ANRW* II 34.4, pp. 3023–108.

Männlein-Robert, I. (2001). *Longin Philologe und Philosoph. Eine Interpretation der erhaltenen Zeugnisse*. München-Leipzig: K. G. Saur.

Numenius

des Places, É. (ed.). (1973). *Numénius, Fragments*. Paris: Les Belles Lettres.
Petty, R. D. (1993). *The Fragments of Numenius*. Text, Translation and Commentary. Berkeley: University of California Press.

Chaldaean Oracles

des Places, É. (ed.). (1971). *Oracles chaldaïques. Avec un choix de commentaires anciens*. Paris: Les Belles Lettres.
Majercik, R. (1989). *The Chaldaean Oracles*. Text, Translation and Commentary. Leiden: Brill.

Plutarch

Plutarch. (1962–76). *Moralia*. Various editors. 15 vols. Loeb Classical Library. Cambridge, Mass.: Harvard University Press / London: Heinemann.

Pseudo-Archytas

Szlezák, T. A. (ed.). (1972). *Pseudo-Archytas. Über die Kategorien. Texte zur griechischen Aristoteles-Exegese*. Berlin: de Gruyter.

Pseudo-Timaeus

Baltes, M. (ed.). (1972). *Timaios Lokros: über die Natur des Kosmos und der Seele*. Leiden: Brill.

General Works and Bibliographies

Deitz, L. (1987). *Bibliographie du platonisme impérial antérieur à Plotin: 1926–1986*. In *ANRW* II 36.1 (pp. 124–82). Berlin: de Gruyter.
Dillon, J. (1996). *The Middle Platonists. A Study of Platonism 80 B.C. to A.D. 220*. 2nd edn. London: Duckworth.
Donini, P. (1982). *Le scuole, l'anima, l'impero: la filosofia antica da Antioco a Plotino*. Torino: Rosenberg and Sellier.
Festugière, A.-J. (1983). *La révèlation d'Hermès Trismégiste*. (3 vols.). Paris: Les Belles Lettres. (Original work published 1942–54).
Gersh, S. (1986). *Middle Platonism and Neoplatonism. The Latin Tradition*. (2 vols.). Notre Dame, Ind.: University of Notre Dame Press.
Krämer, H. J. (1964). *Der Ursprung der Geistmetaphysik. Untersuchungen zur Geschichte des Platonismus zwischen Platon und Plotin*. Amsterdam: Schippers.
Lilla, S. (1992). *Introduzione al medioplatonismo*. Rome: Institutum Patristicum Augustinianum.
Merlan, P. (1967). "Greek Philosophy from Plato to Plotinus." In A. H. Armstrong (ed.), *The Cambridge History of Later Greek and Early Medieval Philosophy* (pp. 11–132). Cambridge: Cambridge University Press.
Moraux, P. (1984). *Der Aristotelismus bei den Griechen. Von Andronikos bis Alexander von Aphrodisias*. (vol. 2): *Der Aristotelismus im I. und II. Jh. n. Chr.* Berlin: de Gruyter.

Special Studies

Andresen, C. (1955). *Logos und Nomos. Die Polemik des Kelsos wider das Christentum*. Berlin: de Gruyter.

Armstrong, A. H. (1960). "The Background of the Doctrine 'That Intelligibles are not Outside the Intellect.'" In *Les sources de Plotin. Dix exposés et discussions* (pp. 391–413). Geneva: Fondation Hardt.

Arrhetos (2002). *Arrhetos Theos. L'ineffabilità del primo principio nel medio platonismo* (F. Calabi, ed.). Pisa: Edizioni ETS.

Baltes, M. (1976). *Die Weltentstehung des platonischen Timaios nach den antiken Interpreten.* Part 1. Leiden: Brill.

——. (1983). "Zur Philosophie des Platonikers Attikos." In H.-D. Blume and F. Mann (eds.), *Platonismus und Christentum* (Festschrift for Heinrich Dörrie). Münster/Westfalen: Aschendorffsche Verlagsbuchhandlun. Repr. In M. Baltes (1999a) (pp. 81–111).

——. (1997). "Is the Idea of Good in Plato's *Republic* Beyond Being?" In M. Joyal (ed.). *Studies in Plato and the Platonic tradition* (Festschrift for John Whittaker) (pp. 3–23). Aldershot: Ashgate. Repr. in M. Baltes (1999a), (pp. 351–71).

——. (1999a). ΔΙΑΝΟΗΜΑΤΑ. *Kleine Schriften zu Platon und zum Platonismus* (A. Hüffmeier, M.-L. Lakmann and M. Vorwerk, eds.). Stuttgart-Leipzig: Teubner.

——. (1999b). "Γέγονεν (Platon. *Tim.* 28 B 7). Ist die Welt real entstanden oder nicht?" In M. Baltes (1999a) (pp. 303–25).

Barnes, J. (1989). "Antiochus of Ascalon." In M. Griffin and J. Barnes (eds.), *Philosophia Togata* I. *Essays on Philosophy and Roman Society* (pp. 51–96). Oxford: Clarendon Press.

Bonazzi, M. (2003). *Academici e platonici. Il dibattito antico sullo scetticismo di Platone.* Milan: LED.

Boys-Stones, G. R. (2001). *Post-Hellenistic Philosophy. A Study of its Development from the Stoics to Origen.* Oxford: Oxford University Press.

Buffière, F. (1956). *Les mythes d'Homère et la pensée grecque.* Paris: Les Belles Lettres.

Deuse, W. (1983). *Untersuchungen zur mittelplatonische und neuplatonischen Seelenlehre.* Mainz: Akademie der Wissenschaften und der Literatur.

Dillon, J. (1979). "The Academy in the Middle Platonic Period." *Dionysius,* 3, 63–77.

Dodds, E. R. (1928). "The *Parmenides* of Plato and the Origin of the Neoplatonic 'One.'" *Classical Quarterly,* 22, 129–42.

Donini, P. (1988). "The History of the Concept of Eclecticism." In J. Dillon and A. A. Long (eds.), *The Question of "Eclecticism." Studies in Later Greek Philosophy* (pp. 15–33). Berkeley: University of California Press.

——. (1994). "Testi e commenti, manuali e insegnamento: la forma sistematica e i metodi della filosofia in età postellenistica." In *ANRW* II 36.7 (pp. 5027–100). Berlin: de Gruyter.

Dörrie, H. (1944). "Der platoniker Eudoros von Alexandreia." *Hermes,* 79, 25–38. Repr. in H. Dörrie (1976), (pp. 297–309).

——. (1960). "Die Frage nach dem Transzendenten im Mittelplatonismus." In *Les sources de Plotin* (pp. 191–223). Genève: Fondation Hardt. Repr. in H. Dörrie (1976), (pp. 211–28).

——. (1966). "Die Schultradition im Mittelplatonismus und Porphyrios." In *Porphyre* (pp. 1–25). Genève: Fondation Hardt. Repr. in H. Dörrie (1976), (pp. 406–19).

——. (1970). "Der König. Ein platonisches Schlüsselwort, von Plotin mit neuem Sinn erfüllt." *Revue internationale de philosophie,* 24, 217–35. Repr. in H. Dörrie (1976), (pp. 390–405).

——. (1976). *Platonica minora.* München: Fink.

Edwards, M. J. (1990). "Atticizing Moses? Numenius, the Fathers and the Jews." *Vigiliae Christianae,* 44, 64–75.

Ferrari, F. (1995). *Dio, idee, materia. La struttura del cosmo in Plutarco di Cheronea.* Naples: D'Auria.

Festugière, A.-J. (1969). "L'ordre de lecture des dialogues de Platon au Ve/VIe siècles." *Museum Helveticum,* 26, 281–96. Repr. in A.-J. Festugière (1971). *Études de philosophie grecque* (pp. 535–50). Paris: Vrin.

Frede, M. (1987). "Numenius." In *ANRW* II 36.2 (pp. 1034–75). Berlin: de Gruyter.

——. (1994). "Celsus philosophus Platonicus." In *ANRW* II 36.7 (pp. 5183–213). Berlin: de Gruyter.

Fuhrmann, M. (1960). *Das systematische Lehrbuch. Ein Beitrag zur Geschichte der Wissenschaften in der Antike*. Göttingen: Vandenhoeck and Ruprecht.

Glucker, J. (1978). *Antiochus and the Late Academy*. Göttingen: Vandenhoeck and Ruprecht.

Göransson, T. (1995). *Albinus, Alcinous, Arius Didymus*. Göteborg: Acta Universitatis Gothoburgensis.

Goulet-Cazé, M.-O. (1989). "L'arrière-plan scolaire de la *Vie de Plotin*." In L. Brisson et al. (eds.), *Porphyre. La Vie de Plotin*. (vol. 1): *Travaux préliminaires et index grec complet* (pp. 229–27). Paris: Vrin.

Hadot, I. (1984). *Arts libéraux et philosophie dans la pensée antique*. Paris: Études Augustiniennes.

——. (1990). "Du bon et du mauvais usage du terme 'eclectisme' dans l'histoire de la philosophie antique." In R. Brague and J.-F. Courtine (eds.), *Herméneutique et Ontologie* (Festschrift for Pierre Aubenque) (pp. 147–62). Paris: Presses Universitaires de France.

Hadot, P. (1960). "Etre, Vie, Pensée chez Plotin et avant Plotin." In *Les sources de Plotin* (pp. 105–41). Genève: Fondation Hardt. Repr. in P. Hadot (1999). *Plotin, Porphyre. Études néoplatoniciennes* (pp. 127–81). Paris: Les Belles Lettres.

——. (1979). "Les divisions des parties de la philosophie dans l'antiquité." *Museum Helveticum*, 36, 201–23. Repr. in P. Hadot (1998). *Études de philosophie ancienne* (pp. 125–58). Paris: Les Belles Lettres.

——. (1987). "Théologie, exégèse, révélation, écriture, dans la philosophie grecque." In M. Tardieu (ed.), *Les règles de l'interprétation* (pp. 13–34). Paris, Les éditions du Cerf. Repr. in P. Hadot (1998). *Études de philosophie ancienne* (pp. 27–58). Paris: Les Belles Lettres.

Lakmann, M. L. (1995). *Der platoniker Tauros in der Darstellung des Aulus Gellius*. Leiden: Brill.

Lamberton, R. (1989). *Homer the Theologian. Neoplatonist Allegorical Reading and the Growth of the Epic Tradition*. Berkeley: University of California Press.

Lewy, H. (1978). *Chaldaean Oracles and Theurgy. Mysticism Magic and Platonism in the Later Roman Empire*. (New edition, M. Tardieu, ed.). Paris: Études Augustiniennes.

Liefferinge, C. van (1999). *La Théurgie des Oracles Chaldaïques à Proclus*. Liège: Centre International d'Étude de la Religion Grecque Antique.

Mansfeld, J. (1994). *Prolegomena. Questions to be Settled before the Study of an Author or a Text*. Leiden: Brill.

Merki, H. (1952). Ὁμοίωσις θεῶι: *Von der platonischen Angleichung an Gott zur Gottähnlichkeit bei Gregor von Nissa*. Freiburg, Switzerland: Paulusverlag.

Nock, A. D. (1962). "The Exegesis of *Timaeus* 28 C." *Vigiliae Christianae*, 16, 79–86.

Opsomer, J. (1998). *In Search of the Truth. Academic Tendencies in Middle Platonism*. Brussels: WLSK.

Pépin, J. (1976). *Mythe et allegorie. Les origines grecques et les contestations judéo-chrétiennes*. Paris: Études augustiniennes.

Platonismus. (1987). H. Dörrie (ed.), *Die geschichtlichen Wurzeln des Platonismus. Bausteine 1–35: Text, Uebersetzung, Kommentar*. Stuttgart-Bad Cannstatt: Frommann – Holzboog.

——. (1990). H. Dörrie and M. Baltes (eds.), *Der hellenistische Rahmen des kaiserzeitlichen Platonismus. Bausteine 36–72: Text, Uebersetzung, Kommentar*. Stuttgart-Bad Cannstatt: Frommann – Holzboog.

——. (1993). H. Dörrie and M. Baltes (eds.), *Der Platonismus im 2. und 3. Jahrhundert nach Christus. Bausteine 73–100: Text, Uebersetzung, Kommentar*. Stuttgart-Bad Cannstatt: Frommann – Holzboog.

——. (1996). H. Dörrie and M. Baltes (eds.), *Die philosophiche Lehre des Platonismus. Einige grundlegende Axiome / Platonische Physik (im antiken Verständnis) I. Bausteine 101–124: Text, Uebersetzung, Kommentar*. Stuttgart-Bad Cannstatt: Frommann – Holzboog.

——. (1998). H. Dörrie and M. Baltes (eds.), *Platinische Physic (im antiken Verständnis) II. Bausteine 125–150: Text, Uebersetzung, Kommentar.* Stuttgart–Bad Cannstatt: Frommann–Holzboog.

Praechter, K. (1910). "Richtungen und Schulen im Neuplatonismus." Repr. in K. Praechter (1973), (pp. 165–216).

——. (1916). "Zum Platoniker Gaios." *Hermes*, 51, 510–29. Repr. in K. Praechter (1973), pp. 81–100.

——. (1922). "Nikostratos der Platoniker." *Hermes*, 57, 481–527. Repr. in K. Praechter (1973), (pp. 101–37).

Praechter, K. (1973). *Kleine Schriften* (H. Dörrie, ed.). Hildesheim: Georg Olms.

Reis, B. (1997). "The Circle Simile in the Platonic Curriculum of Albinus." In J. J. Cleary (ed.). *The Perennial Tradition of Neoplatonism* (pp. 237–68). Leuven: University Press.

Reydams-Schils, G. (1999). *Demiurge and Providence. Stoic and Platonic Readings of Plato's Timaeus.* Turnhout: Brepols.

Sedley, D. (1997). "Plato's Auctoritas and the Rebirth of the Commentary Tradition." In J. Barnes and M. Griffin (eds.), *Philosophia Togata II. Plato and Aristotle at Rome* (pp. 110–29). Oxford: Clarendon Press.

Tarrant, H. (1983). "Middle Platonism and the *Seventh Epistle*." *Phronesis*, 28, 75–103.

——. (1993). *Thrasyllan Platonism.* Ithaca, NY: Cornell University Press.

Whittaker, J. (1969). "Ἐπέκεινα νοῦ καὶ οὐσίας." *Vigiliae Christianae*, 23, 91–104.

——. (1973). "Neopythagoreanism and the Transcendent Absolute." *Symbolae Osloenses*, 48, 77–86.

——. (1978). "Numenius and Alcinous on the First Principle." *Phoenix*, 32, 144–54.

——. (1987a). "Platonic Philosophy in the Early Centuries of the Empire." In ANRW II 36.1 (pp. 81–123). Berlin: de Gruyter.

——. (1987b). "The Value of Indirect Tradition in the Establishment of Greek Philosophical Texts or the Art of Misquotation." In J. N. Grant (ed.), *Editing Greek and Latin Texts* (pp. 63–95). New York: AMS Press.

Zambon, M. (2002). *Porphyre et le moyen-platonisme.* Paris: Vrin.

30

Plotinus

LUC BRISSON AND JEAN-FRANÇOIS PRADEAU

We are informed about the life and writings of Plotinus, who lived in the third century CE, through the work that Porphyry wrote nearly 30 years after his death: *On the Life of Plotinus and the Order of His Treatises*.[1] Porphyry's project was twofold: he wanted to teach the public about the life of his master to provide an introduction to his work and teachings. The biographical part of his work is a panegyric to the way of life practiced by Plotinus, whereas its bibliographical part explains how Porphyry himself collected his Master's treatises, in order to edit them. These explanations were all the more necessary because Porphyry was the posthumous editor of treatises which Plotinus had neither edited nor collected; nor had he even written them in the form Porphyry chose to give them.

The Life of Plotinus

Plotinus is supposed to have been born in 205 CE. The establishment of this date relies on the single testimony of the physician Eustochius, who was the only disciple near Plotinus when he died. According to some of the few testimonies we have in addition to Porphyry's biography, Plotinus came from "Lyco," in Egypt; this may have been Lycopolis, in Upper Egypt (modern-day Assiout). Yet Plotinus was not Egyptian. His name is Latin, and his culture seems to have been essentially Greek. We know nothing about his family origins or social status. His family was evidently wealthy and cultivated. Plotinus received a complete education and at the age of 27 set off in search of a philosophy teacher at Alexandria. He soon met Ammonius Saccas, whose classes he attended for ten years. Here again, we lack information: we are poorly informed about the status of philosophical schools at Alexandria, and even more so about Ammonius. He was a Platonist, probably influenced by Numenius, who had deliberately refused to produce written work; instead, he cultivated the silence and secrecy that were characteristic of neo-Pythagoreanism at the time. Plotinus and his two co-disciples, Herennius and Origen, vowed in their turn to reveal nothing of the teachings dispensed by Ammonius.[2]

---

1.   For Porphyry's *Life of Plotinus*, see Brisson et al. (1982, 1992).
2.   For some of what we do know about Ammonius and the philosophical school in Alexandria, see Hoffmann, WHAT WAS COMMENTARY IN LATE ANTIQUITY?, in this volume.

In 243, Plotinus left Alexandria and Ammonius' school to follow the court of the young emperor Gordian III, who was then preparing a campaign against the Persians. Porphyry reports that Plotinus had chosen to join this expedition to "try out both the philosophy practiced among the Persians and that which flourished among the Indians" (*Plot.* 3.15–17). At the age of 38, Plotinus could not bear arms; he joined the Emperor's court, probably at Antioch, and stayed there for perhaps a year. Opposed by Philip, Gordian died at Zaitha the following year. Plotinus hurriedly left the court and returned to Rome, where he settled permanently. He opened a school there, probably in 246. If we can believe Porphyry, Plotinus then taught, publishing no writings at all, for ten years.

Plotinus began to write his treatises in the course of the first year of the reign of Gallienus, at the age of 49. Nine years later, he had written almost half his works. Such is the testimony of Porphyry, who having arrived at Rome in 263, notes: "Now, beginning with the first year of the reign of Gallienus, Plotinus was led to deal in writing with the subjects that came up, and in the tenth year of the reign of Gallienus, when for the first time I, Porphyry, was allowed to make his acquaintance, he wound up writing twenty-one books" (4.9–13). Porphyry then lists these 21 treatises, specifying the place he assigned to them in the six "ninths" (*enneadas* in Greek), or themes into which his edition divides the totality of the Plotinian treatises.

Porphyry came to Rome probably from Athens, where he had studied with Longinus.[3] During the five years in which Porphyry followed Plotinus' instruction, from 263 to 268, Plotinus wrote 24 treatises (22 to 45). Before listing them, Porphyry claims to have influenced his teacher's production: "[A]nd I brought the Master himself to make a point of marking the articulations of his doctrine, and to write them more extensively" (*Plot.* 18.21–22). Porphyry does not hesitate to add that the best of the Plotinian treatises are those "the Master" wrote between 263 and 268, when his faithful disciple was by his side. However unencumbered by humility it may be, Porphyry's testimony attests a genuine diffusion of Plotinus' writings, which seem to have circulated in educated circles. The treatises were read and discussed, and polemics were engaged with adversaries from outside the school. In 265, Longinus published a treatise entitled *On the End; by Longinus in Answer to Plotinus and Gentilianus Amelius,* and at the time he seems to have possessed almost all Plotinus' writings. Also around 265, Porphyry reports that Plotinus was accused by "people who came from Greece" of plagiarizing Numenius. Copies of his treatises were therefore in circulation at Athens.

In 268, the emperor Gallienus was assassinated, and Claudius succeeded him. This turn of events no doubt had immediate repercussions on Plotinus' school, which was under the protection of Gallienus' wife Salonina and some of her associates. In 269, Amelius, Plotinus' other close disciple, left Rome for Apamea in Syria. In the same year, Plotinus, who was gravely ill, withdrew to Campania. He died there the following year, probably from tuberculosis. In 269 and 270, he wrote his last nine treatises, which he sent to Porphyry (treatises 46 to 54).

---

3. On Longinus, see Patillon and Brisson (2001).

Plotinus as Head of a School

The philosophy to which Plotinus devoted himself was a way of life that could certainly not be reduced to teaching or writing treatises. As head of his school, Plotinus was a guide, who instructed and governed a community that consisted of young people there to receive an education, well-off adults who came to be instructed, philosophers and scholars who were attracted by the Master's renown or by their interest in the debates that occupied his school. Within this community, instruction was coordinated with spiritual exercises, but it was also associated with religious practice, and civic instruction, so that the student's life was completely involved. Plotinus was regarded as a model, whose existence, as much as his doctrine, served to instruct and edify those who followed him. It was from this perspective that Porphyry wrote his *Life of Plotinus*, many of whose anecdotes and sayings thus served to emphasize the degree of perfection Plotinus had achieved. Porphyry's biography very often comes close to hagiography, because it seeks to maintain the memory of the virtues demonstrated by Plotinus' work and persona.

According to Porphyry, Plotinus thus incarnated to perfection the highest spiritual demands of his own doctrine; he had achieved what, according to his own treatises, the soul should achieve: union with the Intellect. The story of the "ecstasies," through which his soul was delivered from everything to unite with the intellect, thus bears witness to the aptitude of every soul, if it is willing to undergo a kind of spiritual training (*askēsis*), to find within itself the intelligible that is its true nature, and the Intellect that is its principle, and, ultimately the psychic power to turn towards the One, first principle of all things.

Plotinus' Treatises in the *Enneads*

Plotinus did not write the *Enneads*. The division of his work into 54 treatises is, as we have said, the work of Porphyry. When Porphyry published his *Life of Plotinus*, he certainly intended to edify his reader on the life and teaching of his Master, but also to present and justify his ordered edition of his writings: "Thus, our account of the life of Plotinus is finished. Now, since he himself confided to us the care of ensuring the ordering and the correctness of his books, and when he was alive, I promised him to discharge this task, and I also undertook this commitment before the other companions, first of all I have thought it well not to leave these books which had been produced pell-mell in chronological order" (*Plot.* 24.1–6). This was a genuine editorial task: Porphyry had revised the texts which had been circulated within the school, in order "to add punctuation to them and correct the mistakes that may have slipped into the expression" (26.37–39); he gave each text a title, and he appears to have taken the initiative to combine certain texts or to divide others, so as to achieve the exact distribution of fifty-four treatises in six *Enneads*.[4] Porphyry thus composed six *Enneads*,

4. The total of 54 is not fortuitous. Porphyry manifests a precise arithmological concern, which is characteristic of neo-Pythagorean speculations: 54 is the product of six (the perfect

and grouped them into three volumes: in the first volume, containing the first three *Enneads*, Porphyry collected the ethical, physical, and cosmological treatises; in a second volume, containing the fourth and fifth *Enneads*, the treatises concerning the soul and the intellect; finally, the last volume corresponds to the sixth *Ennead*, which is devoted to the One.

This composition, which obeys a rigorous numerical combination, serves a pedagogical project: reading the treatises, in this order, is supposed to educate Plotinus' reader, by leading him from the most common ethical questions to the most arduous doctrinal difficulties. Yet this order is not simply doctrinal or scholarly. The order is above all "psychagogic" – that is, it aims to lead the soul of the attentive reader to excellence. Ethical and physical questions are thus conceived as a kind of preliminary purification, which teaches the reader the necessity of recognizing what he is in himself: a soul, more closely related to the divine and intelligible realities to which it belongs than to the bodies or external possessions to which it is only partially and provisionally attached. To read Plotinus is not merely to learn a doctrine; it is to discover ourselves and to become better, to learn to separate ourselves from the sensible world, until finally, assimilated to the intelligible, we are able to contemplate the One, principle of all things (see esp. P. Hadot, [1966], 1999, p. 318).

A Platonic Commentator in a Stoic World

The whole of Plotinus' work presents itself as one vast commentary. The treatises from which Porphyry composed the *Enneads* tirelessly repeat that philosophy has already taken place. The truth is known; it was conceived and set forth by Plato, more than six centuries previously. This is why the spiritual experience to which Plotinus and then his editor Porphyry invited their readers assumed the form of a meditation on the Platonic dialogues. For us, the way Plotinus constantly appeals to the authority of Plato looks like a disconcerting devotion to the letter of the text. Yet if we were to stop here, we would perhaps miss what undertaking a commentary implied for a Neoplatonic author. He was fully aware of the difficulties, ambiguities, and even the lacunae of Plato's text; nevertheless, despite or perhaps because of the difficulties, he held this work to be the surest guide there is. If Plato's text is "true," it is above all because it can give meaning to human existence and guide it towards the perfection it can achieve. To read the Platonic dialogues, and above all to read them in a certain order, meant to define, in order to adopt, the path of self-transformation. Thus, much more than a *summa* of school dogmas to which one had to pledge allegiance, reading the dialogues proved to be the best means and surest path for the soul's ascent towards the principle

---

number, product of the first even number, two, and the first odd number, three) and of nine (the square of the first odd number). Porphyry divided the treatises so as to obtain this number. He maintains that Plotinus himself classified his treatises, but the disposition of the final edition seems to be entirely Porphyry's initiative. The question is still debated of whether the previous "chronological" edition of the treatises was or was not the work of Eustochius or Amelius. In this presentation, we shall refer to the chronological order rather than the systematic Porphyrian order of the *Enneads*.

from which it originated. Only associating with this principle could ensure the soul genuine happiness.

Plotinus' questions have a twofold context: the immediate context of his teaching, and the more extended context of elaborating a philosophical doctrine within a Greek and Roman culture under Stoic influence. In the context of his school, Plotinus had to guide and inspire his disciples, by examining with them questions of importance and urgency: what exactly *is* the reality in which we live? How, and to what end, is the whole universe ordered? What is our rightful place within it, and how can we best conduct our lives? Each of these general questions calls for its share of analyses, and only if these are all carried out can a doctrine demonstrate its philosophical pertinence. It must, for instance, be able to say exactly what the soul and the body are, of which we seem to be composed; or, again, how our soul is a part of the world it seeks to know; or how it came forth from the divine to which it can assimilate itself. From this viewpoint, the philosophical questions to which the treatises are devoted had already been agreed upon for centuries; as Plotinus repeats, they are as old as the masterworks of Plato.

What is more, they had been faced, even earlier by his most illustrious predecessors: the Pythagoreans, Empedocles, Heraclitus, Parmenides, Anaxagoras, and others. Thus, philosophy's vocation was no more to reflect on its reason for being than to find motives or to search for objects; all this had been given to it long ago. However, the responses were worthy of discussion; all the more so because third-century learned culture was so diverse. The philosophical landscape of late antiquity had lost the clear contours it possessed at the beginning of the third century BCE, when the Platonic, Aristotelian, Stoic, and Epicurean schools, which had all been recently instituted, differentiated themselves and confronted each other without doctrinal affiliations being retrospectively confused or suspected. Two or three centuries later, however, for reasons to do both with the geographical extension of philosophical culture, the multiplication of institutions, and the localities of teaching in the Greek and Roman world, and also with the progressive constitution of a common philosophical culture in the new Mediterranean empire, doctrines became inextricably mixed.

From the Hellenistic period to the century of Plotinus, scholarly and doctrinal encounters and combinations had been possible only thanks to the favor and cultural diffusion of Stoicism, which, for many centuries, imposed its conceptual language and its representation of the world upon the philosophical speculations of the Greeks and Romans. Thus, the questions inherited from the philosophers of the fifth and fourth centuries BCE, could, in Plotinus' time, be examined only if one took a stand about Stoic teachings, whether one wished to carry them further, occasionally modifying and correcting them, or to refute them, in order to link up once again with Plato. As each of Plotinus' treatises recalls in its own way, to deal with any given subject was to say what "they" think about it, and how "they" name and define it, before, eventually, showing how one must object to them. Long before Plotinus, Platonists had been reading and commenting on the Platonic works with Stoic tools and categories of analysis, so that their objections and doctrinal initiatives were, more often than not, formulated within the limits and in the very language of this common Stoic culture they were trying to escape.

Some Doctrinal Elements

At the beginning of the second century CE, Platonism experienced a veritable "Renais-sance," the conditions and implications of which were philosophical as much as reli-gious. Characteristic of this renaissance was that it seemed to arise in the very midst of Stoicism, like a dissatisfaction denouncing that doctrine's inability to achieve its own goals, whether in the field of understanding reality, the nature of things, or the acquisition of wisdom and virtue. Within a few generations, this "Middle Platonic" tradition had emancipated itself and developed sufficiently to present a philosophical and cultural alternative to the Stoic Roman empire, yet also sufficiently for Middle Platonism itself to experience profound perturbations (see Zambon, MIDDLE PLATONISM, in this volume). At the turn of the second–third centuries, by dint of a considerable revision in the practice of reading Plato, a new Platonic hermeneutic tradition was born, which was called "Neoplatonism"; for us, the first and principal representative of this movement was Plotinus.

Plotinus is distinguished from his Platonic predecessors not only by the context of his questions and the particular form of his treatises. His work is differentiated above all by specific doctrinal modifications. First of all, it breaks with several of the religious attitudes related to the Middle Platonic tradition of the second century. Plotinus rejects theurgy and is little inclined, and indeed frankly hostile, to Gnostic religious influ-ences. He also discredits most astrological teachings, as he does all irrational ritual practices, which he denounces as philosophical or scientific errors. Next, relying on the Stoic philosophical culture that was still current in his time, Plotinus renounces the highly ambiguous Middle Platonist hypothesis of a divine duality of principles, in order to defend the world's unity and coherence, and the unique order of all things. With this goal in mind, he had to completely revise the currently dominant interpreta-tion of the *Timaeus*, which, for more than two centuries, had been the dialogue of reference for the Platonists.[5] As the principle of all things, the Middle Platonists postu-lated a god mingled together with his own intellect, a divine Intellect thinking within itself the intelligible Forms that are the realities and paradigms of all things, a divinity that abandoned the task of producing all sensible things to the celestial intellect (the intellect of the world soul). Plotinus renounces this conception of the principles when he refuses to accord the rank of first principle to the Intellect; and by renouncing it he inaugurates the Neoplatonic tradition.[6]

In very brief summary, Plotinus' argument is as follows: the Intellect (*nous*), like the intelligible Forms that are inseparable from it, cannot be the first principle, nor the first activity. *Nous* suffers from duality, since it is thought which thinks itself and also thinks a multiplicity of intelligible forms within itself. So it must have a simple and primary cause: "there is something beyond the Intellect," Plotinus repeatedly claims. The then-dominant reading of the *Timaeus* accounts for this "something" only

5. On the *Timaeus* itself, see Brisson, PLATO'S NATURAL PHILOSOPHY AND METAPHYSICS, in this volume.
6. On the main figures after Plotinus, see in this volume Hoffmann, WHAT WAS COMMENTARY IN LATE ANTIQUITY?

imperfectly, and the explanation for it had to be sought in a dialogue other than the *Timaeus*: the *Parmenides*, which deals with "the One," as absolutely simple and beyond all things. The first hypothesis of the second part of the *Parmenides*, at 137c–142a, supposes the existence of a One without parts, and without beginning, bereft of all quality that might *multiply* it, bereft of all figure, situated in no place, and without motion. Plotinus intends to use this Platonic hypothesis to designate the first principle more appropriately, as that which is simple, consequently lacking all quality (and therefore "ineffable"), and the cause of all things; it is the cause of all the realities that come forth from it in succession.[7] Plato's *Parmenides* thus became, and was to remain for all the representatives of Neoplatonism, the dialogue of reference of Platonic exegesis. It was unanimously presented as an explanation of the way in which all things go forth from "the First." The structure of Plotinian doctrine is thus situated at the crossroads of the Middle Platonic reading, or rather revision, of the *Timaeus*, and of an unprecedented use of the *Parmenides*.

In Treatise 10, *On the Three Hypostases That Have the Rank of Principles*, Plotinus explains in a few lines (V.1 [10], 8.1–27) the way he himself conceived of his philosophical situation and project. Presenting himself as an exegete of Plato, he claims to be concerned to set forth a Platonic doctrine that the dialogues contain *implicitly*. In contrast to his predecessors, therefore, Plotinus no longer relies only on the *Timaeus*, but finds the principles of his exegesis in the *Parmenides*, as well as the ultimately adequate description of what is, in his view, the cause of all things: the One. With regard to the One, Plotinus follows the *Parmenides* (137c ff.), which develops all the consequences of the hypothesis that the One exists. If we wish to preserve the unity of the One, we cannot attribute anything to it: it is by definition without predicates. As soon as we affirm that the One is such-and-such a thing, or that it possesses such-and-such a quality, we add an attribute to it, and "multiply" it. We must therefore reach the disconcerting conclusion that we cannot even say that the One exists, since that would be equivalent to attributing being to it, or the predicate "existence." To speak about it (that is, to say anything other than "One" – but even this is too much, since we are giving it a name) is always to add something to it. Thus, we must conclude "that of it there is no name or definition. Of it there is neither science nor sensation nor opinion" (142a). The One, then, as Plotinus often repeats, is ineffable simplicity; that of which we can say nothing and to which we can attribute nothing without adulterating it.

Out of what remained, in the Platonic *Parmenides*, a provisional and aporetic hypothesis (soon replaced by another hypothesis concerning the One that exists), Plotinus chose to make the very definition of the principle from which the whole of reality proceeds: despite its ineffable simplicity, the One is the cause of all things. In addition, if one takes an interest in the following Platonic hypotheses, this use of the *Parmenides* allows the naming of two modes of being, or rather, since "being" is one of these two realities, two other realities that possess existence.[8] Three things exist: those

---

7. The simple is prior to all that is multiple or composite. O'Meara (1992) has devoted a lucid chapter to what he calls the Plotinian "PPS" (Principle of the Priority of the Simple).

8. Here, the term "existence" renders the Greek *hupostasis*, of which Plotinus makes a technical use. Nevertheless, as has been shown by Dörrie ([1955] 1976), in Plotinus this term does

three "first" realities corresponding to what Plotinus considers the object of the first three hypotheses of the *Parmenides*,[9] and which exhaust the totality of the real. It is then up to the treatises to say what is covered by each of these three realities which have an existence or "hypostasis," and to understand how they are related to each other.

This is precisely Plotinus' goal in Treatise 10, and he certainly does not confine himself, by way of Platonic sources, to the *Parmenides* alone, but instead makes of this dialogue the new matrix from which it becomes possible to reread the *Timaeus*, and also the *Republic* – that, too, is a re-casting of Middle Platonism. The conceptual tools, language, and arguments he uses to achieve this end are not simply those of Plato, any more than they are exclusively Stoic. Plotinus forges his doctrine by drawing upon various scholarly sources, and in his treatise he combines Stoic questions or arguments with an extremely deft mastery of the categories and terminology of Aristotle.[10]

"There are three things," says Plotinus, that are called "principles" and "genuine realities" because they alone have a real existence, or "hypostasis." The first principle is, simply, the One, then follows the Intellect (which is also being and life), and finally the Soul.[11] It is from these three primordial realities that an explanation of all things is possible.

As far as their nature is concerned, Plotinus gives sufficiently coherent definitions of the three realities for us to be able to present them briefly as follows, beginning with the cause of all things: the One, which is the First.

The One

Although his discourse on the One marks the break with Middle Platonism, inaugurating Neoplatonism, Plotinus does not content himself merely with adding a cause

---

not have the meaning it was to have in Porphyry (where the hypostases would henceforth be distinct and hierarchized levels of reality). Rather than *being* a hypostasis, Plotinus speaks of the three principal realities as *possessing* an hypostasis, or real existence (see, among others, *Enn.* V.9 [5], 5.46 or IV.7 [2], 8⁴.26, which explains how the soul "receives" an hypostasis). In this sense, *hupostasis* is a synonym for *ousia* (the reality, or "essence" of a thing), but with a subjective and substrative connotation, which partly explains its translation by Latin writers (*substantia*).

9. These are respectively *Prm.* 137c–142a, 142b–155e, and 155e–157b.

10. Plotinus often uses Aristotelian technical vocabulary, whether he borrows it from the Aristotelian works or from the discussion of commentators on Aristotle (for instance, Plotinus seems to know the commentaries of Alexander of Aphrodisias well). It is from Aristotle that he forges the essential part of his description of the Intellect that thinks itself, and it is also on the basis of Aristotelian concepts that he describes the principal modalities of relation that link the various realities among themselves; thus, the relation of actuality and potentiality enables him to show that the reality that precedes its product is always more active than it; elsewhere, the relation of form and matter enables him to establish that each reality informs what it produces.

11. In the strict sense, the One that precedes and causes all existence has no existence itself; to suppose that it has, or to speak of a "reality" in its case, is thus contrary to the hypothesis of its absolute simplicity. Plotinus runs into this difficulty several times, particularly in *Enn.* VI.8 [39], 7.47, where he uneasily accepts a "quasi-existence of the One" (*hē hoion hupostasis autou*).

of the divine Intellect that was his predecessors' ultimate principle. He attributes to this reality characteristics that are unprecedented, both in the Platonic tradition and in Greek thought as a whole: the One is that which engenders all things without being engendered by anything else – or rather, in a very particular sense, it engenders itself in all things. This singular hypothesis of a principle which proceeds from itself, something which thought can never grasp, receives varied explanations in the treatises, which are sometimes difficult to harmonize. Yet Plotinus is aware of this difficulty, all the more so because it seems to him inevitable that the One, or what is imperfectly named "the One," is precisely a principle of which there is no possible knowledge: neither the Intellect which the One engenders, nor *a fortiori* the Soul which the Intellect engenders, can grasp by reflexive or intellective activity a power that escapes all objective grasp.[12] The One is absolute power, both unlimited and simple. The only possible perception of it is comprehensive, in the particular sense that it is by unifying themselves, and re-discovering within themselves the unity from which they proceed, that the Intellect and the Soul will be able to unite with the One as with their good. In other words, the One is never known by and in something other than itself, as the first power or the first cause of existence and goodness, and of the beauty of all it has engendered. The most general of the difficulties concerning the status of the One is, then, the following: how can this "one" or this "First," from which absolutely everything proceeds, and which is the goal of all things, nevertheless remain distinct and immobile within itself, in autarchic perfection?

Intellect, Being, Life

Plotinus faithfully maintains the Middle Platonic axiom according to which the "intelligibles," or Forms, are not outside the Intellect that thinks them.[13] Yet it is the identification of the Intellect with being and life and in turn the hypothesis that there exists a principle beyond being that complicate the status of this second reality, and give it its properly Plotinian aspect. A discussion of being as such, henceforth hypostatized, must be engaged; for the fact that being is not the whole of reality (since there is the One), and that being, therefore, cannot be distinguished from the subject that thinks it, modifies the classical scheme of ancient theories of knowledge.

The question is no longer so much to know how a subject of knowledge (soul or intellect) knows an object (of the genus of being, a "being"), but how the first principle – the One – engenders one single thing which is being its intellection. For Plotinus is no longer content, like his Platonic or Aristotelian predecessors, to affirm that the

12. This is insisted upon particularly at *Enn.* VI.9 [9], 6.10–15: "It must also be admitted that it is infinite, not because its magnitude or its number cannot be measured, but because of the boundlessness of its power. For if you think of it as an Intellect or a god, it is more than that; again, if you unify it by reason, there again it is more than what you can imagine of it, because it has more unity than your thought of it; for it is by itself, and without any attribute."
13. Thus, among other passages: "Truly existent things, as such, each one of them, the things that truly are (*ta alēthōs onta*), are located in the 'intelligible place'" (*Enn.* V.6 [24], 6.14–15).

intellect has the totality of being as its object of thought,[14] nor even that everything that exists thinks in a certain way; but he maintains that Intellect and being are one and the same thing, and that the Intellect not only thinks being, but that it *is* being. He further affirms that the intelligible Forms, which constitute the Intellect as an "intelligible world," are, properly speaking, the only realities there are. Thus, the Plotinian treatises conceive the distinction of "two worlds," intelligible and sensible, explaining that what comes after the One is not so much a simple reality, or the product of a unique agent, as a multiplicity, that of the intelligible totality that Plato's *Timaeus* named the "intelligible living being" (30a–c).

Not only are the intelligible Forms the true realities, or beings, but they are in addition the only genuine living things: the Intellect is life. "If we are correct, it follows necessarily that being is alive, and that it lives with a life that is perfect" (*Enn.* III.6 [26], 6.15–16). In other words, intelligible being is not devoid of life, which might be thought to be a mere property of sensible and corporeal things, or one that only appears with matter. On the contrary, the intelligible is life itself, since sensible life is only an imperfect, provisional, and indeterminate image of it. The intelligible, not matter, is the principle of all development, all movement, and all determination.

Following the Middle Platonists and contrary to the Stoics, Plotinus maintains that Reality (*ousia*) is incorporeal. Yet there is more: by choosing to identify thought with a way of being and a way of life, or with reality and life themselves, Plotinus can also affirm that intellective activity is nothing other than the unfolding of life in the realm of being. Intellection is the vital deployment of being; it is the generation or the production of life. Stoic vitalism has not been sent packing, but has been assimilated by the Plotinian intelligible in such a way that one may, like the Stoics, say that all that exists lives by virtue of the same life; and that this life is the immanent dynamic principle by which the world itself determines itself or sets itself in order – with the addition, however, that this vital determination owes nothing to bodies or to matter, for it is intelligible.

The Soul

Because it is engendered by the Intellect, and is never completely separated from it, the Soul is still part of the intelligible. Yet in so far as it is a genuine reality, possessing an existence, it is also a productive power, and it engenders something. Soul is the cause of the sensible, and the cause of the existence and continuity of the sensible world, which is an image of the intelligible world. Again, Soul, in so far as it is itself intelligible, guarantees its sensible product a certain participation in goodness and in beauty, and in the rationality of the intelligible. Ultimately, however, in so far as Soul informs and animates the sensible, thereby exercising a demiurgic function, it is, to its own detriment, in contact with the pure indeterminacy of matter. Except for a "part" of itself which remains attached to the Intellect, and is in the intelligible, Soul is linked to the body it animates. As attested by the very first Plotinian treatises, Soul's

14.   What is meant here is that divine intellect is the highest being and identical with the object of its thought.

role and mode of being are ambiguous: Plotinus says that Soul has two lives, that it is "amphibious" and winds up "falling" or plunging into the sensible world it has engendered.

These are among the main doctrinal difficulties of the system. In the first instance, this is true since all souls are not incarnated equally: in particular, we must distinguish the soul of the world, which animates a perfect and incorruptible body, from the souls of living, changing individuals, ceaselessly affected and mortal. The former is so different from the latter that we are justified in wondering whether they have the same nature.[15] Another difficulty is that soul, as an intelligible reality, takes care of bodies which exist locally and temporally apart from one another, since souls seem to become "separate" from one another when they come down into the sensible. Plotinus must then prove that souls stay related, that they are "sisters" which all remain one single reality, and that they all exercise, by right if not in fact, the same functions.

He applies himself to the solution of these difficulties in the great treatise *On the Soul* (IV.3–5 [27–29]). The brief Treatise 21, *How it is Said that the Soul is Intermediary Between Indivisible Reality and Divisible Reality*, had already pointed out that the only way such difficulties could be solved was by admitting that: "It is in the intelligible that genuine reality (*hē alēthinē ousia*) is found; the Intellect is what is best in it, but souls are also within it, for they come here from above. The intelligible world contains souls without bodies, since this world contains souls that have come to be in bodies, and have been distributed among them" (IV.1 [21], 1.1–4). Although the soul represents the end of the intelligible procession, since no genuine reality exists after it, this does not mean that with it we reach the void, or not-being. There is something other than the intelligible: bodies that consist of matter, and living beings (humans, for instance) that are combinations of the intelligible and the sensible, yet which still participate in being, via the soul. It is therefore at the level of the soul, or rather at the limit it traces between the two "worlds," that the classic Platonic problem of participation is raised once again.[16]

These succinct reminders of what the three realities might be can now be completed by a summary of what is required by their mutual relations.

In the chapter we have already cited from Treatise 10, Plotinus mentions a kind of succession: first there is the One, then the Intellect which "comes from the One," and finally the Soul which, in its turn, comes from the Intellect. Here, as throughout Plotinus' works, the relations between the three realities are characterized by both exteriority and temporal succession. They are distinct, and they derive from one another. Modern commentators speak of "procession" to designate this process of successive generations. If Soul proceeds from the Intellect, which proceeds from the One (which, for its part, proceeds only from itself), then we must classify the three realities or principles hierarchically, according to their causal primacy: the One comes

---

15.   This is one of the numerous questions and difficulties encountered by the Plotinian doctrine of the soul; the most suggestive study on this subject remains Blumenthal (1971).

16.   This problem of participation is partially dealt with by means of the doctrine of the *logos*: Plotinus hypothesizes that it is not the Soul itself that is in direct contact with matter, but rather that something *of* itself, "reasons" or "rational formulas" – that is, Forms at the level of the Soul – inform matter. On this question, see most recently the explanations by Brisson (1999).

first, the Intellect second, and the Soul third. This is perhaps the only aspect of their mutual relations that can be appreciated appropriately; the two characteristics pointed out above (exteriority of the principles, and their chronological succession) are only approximations. As Plotinus often repeats, we cannot conceive that the three principles began to exist on a given day, or that their engendering involves a chronological successive generation, like a biological lineage. Similarly, we must not believe that these three realities exist separately from one another, as if they each had a place (which would hardly make sense, since they are incorporeal), or as if they were not inside one another, as they are.

However, despite the falseness of such representations, Plotinus constantly has recourse to them; otherwise, he says, we cannot speak. Yet such a local and chronological representation is not without value, since it enables the designation of most of the diverse mutual relations of the principles, which are thus hierarchically and locally distinguished by successive degrees of descent or ascent, equivalent to degrees of perfection. The One is above the Intellect, which is above the Soul, which is above the sensible, into which it descends. The Soul aspires only to rise back up in its entirety to the intelligible, when the Intellect directs its gaze towards the One. This hierarchical and vertical representation of realities, although it is the most common in the treatises, is nevertheless not the only one Plotinus uses.

Although he speaks most often of the Intellect as being "above" the Soul and "below" the One, or of procession as a "descent," and of contemplation as an ascent, Plotinus also uses a circular metaphor of encompassment or of centripetal gravitation, in which the One is the center encompassed by the Intellect; in its turn, the Intellect is surrounded by the Soul, which rotates around it. This is indicated, among other passages, by the following important passage from Treatise 28 (IV.4 [28], 16.23–31), *On Difficulties Concerning the Soul II*. Here, in an image which could clearly not be represented by a vertical stacking, Plotinus maintains that each principle or reality encompasses that from which it proceeds; and this reality then becomes the center around which it hovers. Plotinus affirms that reality does not leave behind that from which it proceeds, but is eternally turned towards its cause or its progenitor, which it also somehow contains.

Circular inclusion is therefore a much better image than vertical genealogy of a major hypothesis of Plotinian doctrine: all is in all, and each reality "possesses all things." In particular, this means that the Intellect, and even the One, are in the Soul.[17] In the tenth chapter of Treatise 10, Plotinus shows that the relation between realities is not one of exteriority or local separation, but that "just as these three realities are in the nature of things, we must consider that they are also in us" (*Enn.* V.1 [10], 10.5–7). Hence, of course, the human soul has the possibility of contemplating,

17. This also means that the intelligible is, to a certain extent, in the sensible, and Plotinus specifies that the sensible world rotates around the real world, which is the intelligible: *Enn.* VI.4 [22], 2. Treatises 22 and 23 demonstrate the universal immanence of the intelligible in the sensible, despite their separation: what is above (*ekei*) nevertheless remains, in a sense, present down here (*entautha*). In the same way, we must admit that the Intellect, although it does not "belong" to it, is still "in" the Soul, as is maintained at *Enn.* V.3 [49], 3.

rediscovering, and uniting with the principle that engendered it, without seeking it outside itself. Again, the metaphor of circular inclusion expresses rather well that the second and third realities – Intellect and Soul – have a double nature. Around a perfectly stable center, the Intellect already includes a share of multiplicity: that of a circle made up of parts. In turn, the Soul contains a multiplicity, *and* it is linked to that "outside," or "other" intelligence constituted by the sensible (as is indicated in the quoted text by the mention of "bodies").

Yet however multiple the Intellect may be, or however mobile and linked to the sensible the Soul may be, both of them nevertheless possess the One, which is both their object of contemplation and something *of* themselves, or their possession.[18] This mutual belonging of realities is accentuated by their common exercise of certain functions. As we shall see, each of the three realities engenders something related to it, without being identical to it. Each one produces or illuminates, dominates, and takes care of what it has produced; on the other hand, each reality desires what is above it, contemplates it, and strives to imitate it. Yet these activities, which constitute the first steps in the direction of the "descent" of the One towards the Soul, and the second steps of its "reascent," are nevertheless not dissociable. Another characteristic hypothesis of the Plotinian treatises is that they do not simply maintain, as the Middle Platonists did, that one principle produces another beneath it, by taking the preceding principle as a model, but that this contemplation is itself production in an immediate sense. In fact, they are one and the same activity: to contemplate is to seek to imitate the reality from which a given reality proceeds, and such imitation is production.

Thus, on the basis of these metaphysical principles, Plotinus sets an entire world in order, and the relations linking the three principles together provide a common foundation for the physics and the ethics the treatises seek to elaborate. The architecture of intelligible reality erected by the Plotinian treatises certainly proposes to resolve the questions and difficulties which the classical philosophical doctrines, essentially those of Plato, Aristotle, and the Stoics, had confronted. These difficulties were of both a physical and ethical nature, and we must understand that the Plotinian system of the three principles was forged in order to solve them.

The Organization of the Universe

Plotinus' doctrines in the field of physics must be re-situated within the context of polemics that have their origin in the Old Academy. Against Plato's *Timaeus*, Aristotle developed a criticism which would subsequently be widely accepted in philosophy. The world was no longer an artificial object, produced by a demiurge, but a natural being that lives and possesses the principle of its behavior within itself. This internal principle, whose name is "nature" (*phusis*) (see *Phys.* II.1, 192b1–24), may be considered from the point of view of form, and from that of matter. Nature, escaping all

---

18. This is recalled in the context of an ethical argument, in chapter 44 of *Enn.* IV.4 [28], where Plotinus says that the sage does not seek an illusory good thing outside himself, but, on the contrary, he knows that the only truly good thing is "that which he possesses" the One (via the Intellect, with which the Soul is united).

contingency and all intermittence, proceeds economically like a good steward, which, among all possibilities, always produces what is best (*Cael.* II.5, 288a2).[19]

The Stoics went even further along this path and extended the notion of nature, which for Aristotle applies to individual things within the universe, to a cosmic nature of the universe, by proposing a grandiose vision of the universe as a divine, living unity, organized according to rational laws and governed in its least details by Providence. As the basis of their physics, they postulate two principles: one has only the capacity to be affected: matter (*hulē*), lacking all determination, all movement, and all initiative. The other has the ability to act, and contributes form, quality, and movement to matter. This second principle is "reason" (*logos*). Nothing in the universe is "this" or "that"; nothing can even be called "this" or "that," without the presence of this principle independent of matter. In such a context, the *logos* can also receive the name "god," for its action makes it, as it were, the artisan of the universe, but an artisan whose art resides in all the productions of nature. By taking the demand for the determination of matter to its limit, Stoicism found itself forced to recognize the cause of the most elementary physical characteristics in the *logos* alone, corresponding to the four elements (fire, air, earth, and water), and to their combination in sensible things. This is why we may speak of Stoic "corporealism": the action of *logos* on matter and bodies remains a material, corporeal activity. This active principle of the *logos* also has a physical name for the Stoics: "fire." It is not concrete fire, but one which unites all its powers. It is an energy, and the other three elements (air, water, and earth), correspond to the three states in which it can be found: gaseous, liquid, and solid. Again, this fire is known as the *logos*, identified with god, can also be identified as an igneous breath, or the omnipresent *pneuma*. In all the parts of the world penetrated and informed by *pneuma*, fire, which is hot, is associated with expansion, and air, which is cold, with contraction. This oscillation, which animates all bodies and ensures their cohesion, is called "tension" (*tonos*), and this tension is diversified according to the regions of the universe. It assumes the name of "constitution," of "holding," or of "maintenance" (*hexis*) within inanimate solids; of "growth" (*phusis*) in plants, and of "soul" (*psuchē*) in animals (*SVF* 2.1013 = S.E. *M* 9.78). In all these cases, however, its function is to unify the totality of bodies, especially including the universe.[20]

Faced by this highly coherent doctrine, Plotinus expresses his faithfulness to Platonism by articulating his thought around three "hypostases" (the One, Intellect/ Intelligible, and Soul as hypostasis), which, although there is nothing corporeal about them, nevertheless represent the highest levels of reality. For this reason, reality cannot be reduced to the corporeal, as the Stoics would have it. The Soul contains the *logoi* which, within the Soul, are equivalent to the Forms; more precisely, the *logoi* are the Forms on the level of the Soul. The Soul depends causally on the Intellect, for it is through the intermediary of the Intellect that the One produces the Soul. Similarly, the Intellect, which in a way is responsible for the production of the sensible world, through the intermediary of the Soul, cannot be held responsible for the manner in which the soul governs the world.

---

19. Cf. Bodnár and Pellegrin, ARISTOTLE'S PHYSICS AND COSMOLOGY, in this volume, which discuss the natures of individual things within the cosmos, not of the cosmos as a whole.
20. This paragraph summarizes material in Brunschwig, 1997, pp. 534–48.

At this level, we are no longer dealing with the Soul considered as a hypostasis, but with souls in the sensible world: that is, the world Soul and the souls of individuals.[21] For although Plotinus insists on the unity of the Soul, the world Soul and the souls of individuals are not part of that Soul situated above them; they are images of it. The world Soul differs from the individual's soul because the body it produces and animates is better than the human body, and above all, it does not have the problems that trouble human souls, and even those of animals – although Plotinus, who believed in metempsychosis (see Deuse, 1983) was also interested in animal souls.

Beneath bodies, whose constitutive foundation, as it were, it represents, is matter, which according to all indications, emanates from the inferior part of the soul.[22] This hypothesis has considerable ethical consequences. By identifying the One with the primary Good, and matter with evil, Plotinus is obliged to explain how the Good seems necessarily to engender Evil. This is a question to which the treatises constantly return, to elaborate and deepen an ethical doctrine whose major argument is that of a liberation and a return, or a "conversion" (*epistrophē*).

Here Plotinus accepts without argument Aristotle's criticism, which, according to him, is directed not at the *Timaeus*, but at a false interpretation of the dialogue. He takes his distance from the "craftsman" metaphor[23] Plato uses when he depicts a demiurge who fabricates sensible things while keeping his gaze fixed on the intelligible forms. Since Plotinus rejects the action of a demiurge working like an artisan or an artist, he is led to confer the role of an agent, organizing matter and enabling the appearance of bodies, upon the Soul that animates the world. He thereby seems to incline towards Stoic materialism. Yet, to avoid falling into absolute immanence that denies the separation of the One, the Intellect, and the Soul – that is, the three hypostases – he undertakes to emphasize the role of the Intellect and the Intelligible, by showing that even the hypostasis Soul, to which the world Soul and the individual souls are attached, is not the absolute principle, but derives from a superior principle, the Intellect. The Intellect may be thought to resemble a demiurge who contemplates the Intelligible, yet without either deliberating or working.

Plotinus (*Enn.* III.2 [47], 2.8–24) explains how our universe is a living being, made up of matter and form. Its existence comes about because matter in its totality has received form, which prevails over its organization. However, in order to organize matter with the help of Forms, an agent is needed. In the case of the universe, which is not a technical work resulting from art, but a production of nature, this agent is not an artisan or artist who deliberates, calculates, and works, but the soul that informs matter, imposing the form of their organization upon the four elements (fire, air, water, and earth). In this text, we find the sketch of a critique of artisanal and artistic production. Such production depends on a power that is not present in the craftsman, but outside of him, because he must learn the art or the technique he practices. From this it follows that production in these areas is contingent and intermittent. Moreover,

---

21. Within this group, we must range the souls of gods, daemons, human beings, animals, and even those of plants.
22. Controversy on this subject persists. Against Corrigan (1986), O' Brien (1991, 1993, 1999) believes matter emanates. Narbonne (1993) upholds a much more nuanced position.
23. As Plotinus regards it.

such production implies reasoning and deliberation. As a result, the fabricated object must have an origin within time, and consequently it must be subject to destruction. Now, as far as the fabrication of the universe is concerned, contingency, generation, and corruption cannot be accepted; this explains recourse to the *logoi*.

To be able to organize matter, in order to produce the sensible universe, the Soul[24] incorporates intelligible organization as it contemplates it. Yet doesn't this conclusion presuppose that the natural production carried out by the Soul is subject to the same conditions as artificial production, as in the *Timaeus*? Doesn't it bring us back to the "craftsman" viewpoint, that Plotinus wished to set aside? Doesn't obliging the Soul to contemplate a transcendent model mean assimilating its action to that of an artisan or artist?

To be sure, an artisan or artist could not impose form upon matter without conceiving this form beforehand, or, more precisely, without receiving it in thought. The plan conceived by an architect is not a creation of his fantasy. It responds to specific demands, and it imposes itself upon his reflection like a necessity independent of him. To insist on the separate character of intelligible organization, and on the reality of this model, means recognizing the authority of such demands. Yet, if intelligible organization and the Forms are situated outside the thought of the craftsman, and if he himself is not their author, but must have received them, are they also outside the world Soul? Why could this Soul not be the place of the intelligibles, and discover them within itself? To oblige the soul to contemplate the intelligible organization in the Intellect, and to integrate it within itself – Is this not equivalent, if not to dissolving the Soul, at least to assimilating it to the Intellect,[25] and turning it into its instrument?[26]

These questions should be answered as follows: first, it is not necessary for the Soul to perceive the Forms of things within it to distinguish natural production from artificial. The Soul's organizing activity, although it presupposes the contemplation of the Forms, retains the privilege of extending to universality, thereby excluding the deliberation and calculations required for particular productions. Consequently, it is easy to understand why the intelligible organization, upon which the Soul's activity is modeled, was not to be found within itself, at least not in the same way. Indeed, the notion of the *logos* appears precisely in order to safeguard this separation; for the soul exercises its second function, that of organization, through the intermediary of the *logoi*.

At *Enn*. IV.3 [27], 10.10–42, Plotinus explains how, according to him, the universe is produced. The universe may be compared to a work of art, but one which is not produced from outside, by an artisan or an artist, as it was by the demiurge of the *Timaeus*. Instead, it is produced from within, by that organizing power of Nature. It is rather as if a piece of marble were to give itself the form of the Venus de Milo.[27]

---

24. First the hypostasis Soul, then the Soul of the world, and finally all the other particular souls.
25. At *Enn*. II.9 [33], 1.56, it is said that the Soul intelligizes (*noei*), and at *Enn*. VI.9 [9], 5.11–12 that the Intellect is found within the Soul.
26. Soul is sometimes considered as the *energeia* of the Intellect, which represents *ousia*; but *ousia* is not to be separated from its *energeia*.
27. See *SVF* 2.1044 = Alexander of Aphrodisias, *De mixt.* 225.18ff. Bruns.

Yet what is Nature? It is a power that corresponds to the lowest part of the world Soul, the part which comes into contact with matter. The organization to which it submits matter results from the action of rational formulas which, within the hypostasis Soul, correspond to the intelligible Forms. These formulas are in a state of dispersion, and not simultaneously, like the intelligible forms in the Intellect. Because the world Soul uses these rational formulas that exist within it in an inferior mode, it is able to organize matter so as to bring all bodies into being: both animate, for instance, a horse or a plane-tree, and inanimate, for instance, a stone. From this perspective, we can say that the sensible universe is an image of all the rational formulas the world Soul possesses. At this lower level, Plotinus established a very interesting distinction between the action of the soul in general, and that of the body. Both seek to render other realities similar to themselves, as a function of the rational formulas each contains; but whereas the soul is always awake, the body is awake only intermittently. Wood transmits heat only when it burns, whereas the soul perpetually maintains life within living beings. Plotinus' entire project is to explain how the sensible is impregnated by the intelligible, which thereby makes it beautiful.

From the outset, the opposition between nature (*phusis*) and art or technology (*technē*) prevents Plotinus from awarding technical products and works of art first place in the area of beauty, for the following four reasons:

1. For Plotinus, the process that explains the constitution of the universe is, so to speak, spontaneous, without any deliberation, reasoning, or calculation.[28] In contrast, artists and artisans are subject to uncertainty. They need to reflect, which is equivalent to an inability to be self-sufficient: "For to need calculation would be to diminish the Intellect's capacity to be sufficient unto itself; as in the arts, where calculation is appropriate for artists in difficult situations, whereas in the absence of difficulties, art is the master, and it does its job" (*Enn.* IV.3 [27], 18.3–4).
2. In order to produce, artists and artisans depend on knowledge, the acquisition of which comes from outside, and is characterized by contingency.
3. Artists use their hands and instruments, which at least implies that nature has come before them.[29]
4. Since the objects they produce imitate nature, they are not only bereft of life, but also of that internal power (*dunamis*) which even inanimate objects possess. This is why Plotinus speaks of indistinct and strengthless imitations (*amudra kai asthenē mimēmata*), and assimilates them to toys (*paignia*), despite all the skills artists use for their fabrication.

The Goals of the Human Soul

In the tradition of the philosophical problem discussed by Plato – particularly in the *Republic*, where the cardinal virtues moderation, courage, wisdom, and justice are

28. *Enn.* IV.3 [27], 10.14–17 and 26–27; V.8 [31], 7.2–44 and 12.21–22; II.9 [33], 4.12–16 and 12.17–18; VI.7 [38], 1.28–43; III.2 [47], 1.1–19.
29. *Enn.* IV.3 [27], 10.16–17; V.8 [31], 7.10–12; II.9 [33], 12.17–18.

enumerated and defined – by Aristotle, and by the Stoics, Plotinus, in his treatise *On Virtues* (*Enn.* I.2 [19]), shows how the ethical positions defended by Aristotelianism, Stoicism, and Platonism are contained within one another, so as to form a kind of system.

Plotinus begins by mentioning the civic virtues – that is, those of the citizen, corresponding to those emphasized by Aristotelianism, which consist in imposing measure on desires and passions. The civic virtues are virtues of a practical nature, and concern action and activity, or what is in accord or conformity with nature, in the Stoic sense of the rational law.[30] They imply a rational appreciation of the duties (*kathēkonta*, a Stoic term) people face in their everyday life. In other words, these virtues concern the soul which must live in a body, and in society.[31]

In this world, the soul suffers from two evils: union with inferior things, and the excessive nature of this union. Whereas the civic virtues cure people of excesses, the purificatory virtues allow them to reduce the soul's union with inferior realities to a minimum. We are then ourselves in a Stoic context, where the purificatory virtues consist in detaching oneself from things in the sensible world, in abstaining from actions accomplished together with the body, and in refusing to share its passions; thus, these virtues are identified with purification. They belong to the soul that distances itself from the body, in order to direct itself towards true being; that is, towards the intelligible. Thus, the idea here is of progress towards contemplation, understood in the Platonic sense of the contemplation of the intelligible. The purificatory virtues belong to the human soul – that is, to the soul united to the body. We acquire them in this life, and their goal is completely to free the soul from the passions which so far had only been given a measure. Their goal is assimilation to god – a Platonic formula.[32] The disposition corresponding to these virtues is impassibility (*apatheia*). At this second level, the soul, not content with imposing a limit and measure on the passions, undertakes to free itself from them completely. The purificatory virtues consist in detaching the soul, as far as possible, from the body. Of course, this liberation is on the level of judgment, and does not lead to real impassibility. Only death could lead to that complete impassibility equivalent to total liberation. Yet there is a paradox here: for in order to contemplate, one must live. This is why he who practices the virtues can only make progress towards this state of perfection; and this progress earns him the name of *daimōn*, a being situated between the human being, who is *spoudaios* when he practices the civic virtues, and the divinity, which the practitioner of the contemplative virtues assimilates.

For a Platonist, purification must not be sought for itself, but in order to enable contemplation. Whereas the civic virtues deliver the soul from the first form of evil – that is, excessive passions – the purificatory virtues deliver it from the second form of evil, which consists for it in uniting with inferior things. The civic virtues rule our relations with the things in this world, whereas the purificatory virtues put an end to these relations. The contemplative virtues belong to the person who is already contemplative, and whose soul henceforth contemplates the intelligible. Unlike the

---

30. On this topic, see Bett, STOIC ETHICS, in this volume.

31. On the political implications, see Brown, HELLENISTIC COSMOPOLITANISM, in this volume, esp. the section on the Stoics.

32. On this important topic, cf. Betegh, GREEK PHILOSOPHY AND RELIGION, in this volume.

preceding virtues, which indicated an effort or progress, the contemplative virtues are at rest. They are the virtues of the soul acting intellectually; for the soul only knows what is within it by turning towards the intellect. The soul possesses knowledge within itself, which it must somehow remember in the context of the process of recollection. Before even considering this third kind of virtue, Plotinus says that the disposition that follows from the contemplative virtues manifests itself in the absence of passions, since its goal is assimilation to god. The goal of these virtues is, therefore, that one act without the thought of detaching oneself from the passions even entering one's mind. The person who is able to act according to these virtues alone is a god (*theos*). With these virtues, the process of purification reaches its fullest achievement. The soul that is completely turned towards the intellect no longer experiences any affections, but gives itself over entirely to contemplation. For a Platonist, it is indispensable that virtue can be pursued to this level, since it consecrates the re-discovered unity between soul and intellect that corresponds to the intelligible world. The ideal of assimilation to god is thereby realized.

By means of the purificatory virtues, the purified soul unites with what engendered it, the Intellect, which is indissociable from the intelligible. This union follows upon the soul's conversion towards its principle; yet in it the soul is no longer a soul, but coincides with the intellect. Hence the particularly ambivalent status of these virtues, which are no longer virtues in the proper sense of the term, but are, so to speak, models (*paradeigmata*) of virtue.

In the long run, for truly divine and philosophical souls, contemplation must be accomplished in union, and the virtues will henceforth be only the memory of a path that has led the soul to assimilate itself to its principle, to dispossess itself of itself, and unite with the Intellect, and to become, like it, "*agathoeidēs*," or similar to the Good. The path towards human excellence thus takes on the appearance of a return, as if our souls somehow had to travel a path opposite to the one that gave birth to all things. They must free themselves from the body, rise back up to the intelligible, and finally unite with it, in order to turn towards that from which they came forth: the One.[33]

Bibliography

Works Cited

Blumenthal, H. (1971). *Plotinus' Psychology. His Doctrines of the Embodied Soul.* La Haye: Nijhoff.

Brisson, L. (1999). "*Logos* et *logoi* chez Plotin. Leur nature et leur rôle." *Les Cahiers Philosophiques de Strasbourg*, 8, 87–108.

——. Goulet-Cazé, M. O., Goulet, R., and O'Brien, D. (1982, 1992). *Porphyre, La Vie de Plotin* (2 vols.). Paris: Vrin.

Brunschwig, J. (1997). "La philosophie à l'époque hellénistique." In M. Canto-Sperber (ed.), *Philosophie grecque* (pp. 457–591). Paris: Presses Universitaires de France.

Corrigan, K. (1986). "Is There More Than One Generation of Matter in the *Enneads*?" *Phronesis*, 31, 195–203.

33.   The authors would like to thank Michael Chase for his translation of this chapter.

Deuse, W. (1983). *Untersuchungen zur mittelplatonischen und neuplatonischen Seelenlehre.* Wiesbaden: Steiner.

Dörrie, H. ([1955] 1976). "*Hupostasis*. Wort und Bedeutungsgeschichte." *Nachrichten der Akademie der Wissenschaften in Göttingen. Philol.-Hist. Klasse*, 1955, 35–93. Repr. in H. Dörrie, *Platonica minora* (pp. 12–96). Munich: Fink.

Hadot, P. ([1966] 1999). "La métaphysique de Porphyre." In *Porphyre*, Entretiens sur l'Antiquité classique XII, (pp. 125–63). Vandoeuvres-Genève. Repr. in P. Hadot. *Plotin, Porphyre. Études Néoplatoniciennes* (pp. 317–53). Paris. Les Belles Lettres.

Narbonne, J.-M. (1993). *Plotin, Les deux matières* (*Ennéade* II 4 [12]), Introduction, texte grec, traduction et commentaire. Paris: Vrin.

O' Brien, D. (1991). *Plotinus on the Origin of Matter. An Exercise in the Interpretation of the* Enneads. *Elenchos* supp. 22. Naples: Bibliopolis.

——. (1993). *Théodicée plotinienne et théodicée gnostique.* Leiden: Brill.

——. (1999). "La matière chez Plotin: son origine, sa nature." *Phronesis*, 44, 45–71.

O'Meara, D. J. (1992). *An Introduction to the Enneads.* Oxford: Clarendon Press.

Patillon, M. and Brisson, L. (eds.). (2001). *Longin, Fragments. Art rhétorique.* M. Patillon, (ed.), Rufus, *Art rhétorique.* Paris: Les Belles Lettres.

Further Reading

Greek text and translation

Armstrong, A. H. (1966–88). *Plotinus.* Loeb classical library. (7 vols.). Cambridge, Mass. Harvard University Press / London: Heinemann.

Henry, P. and Schwyzer, H.-R. (eds.). (1964–82). *Plotini Opera* [editio minor]. (3 vols). Oxford: Oxford University Press.

Bibliography

Dufour, R. (2001). "Plotinus: A Bibliography 1950–2000." *Phronesis*, 46, 237–411.

Studies

Atkinson, M. (1983). *Plotinus: Ennead V,1. On the Three Principal Hypostases. A Commentary with Translation.* Oxford: Oxford University Press.

Baltes, M. (ed.). (1987–2002). *Der Platonismus in der Antike.* (6 vols.). Stuttgart, Bad Cannstatt: Frommann–Holzboog.

Bussanich, J. (1988). *The One and its Relation to Intellect in Plotinus.* Leiden: Brill.

Dillon, J. (1996). *The Middle Platonists.* 2nd edn. London: Duckworth.

Dodds. E. R. (1928). "The *Parmenides* of Plato and the Origin of the Neoplatonic 'One'." *Classical Quarterly*, 22, 129–42.

Gerson, L. P. (1994). *Plotinus.* London: Routledge.

——. (ed.). (1999). *The Cambridge Companion to Plotinus.* Cambridge: Cambridge Univerity Press.

Hadot, P. (1993). *Plotinus or The Simplicity of Vision.* (M. Chase, trans., introduction by A. I. Davidson). Chicago: University of Chicago Press.

O'Meara, D. J. (1980). "Gnosticism and the Making of the World in Plotinus." In B. Layton (ed.), *The Rediscovery of Gnosticism.* (vol. 1, pp. 265–378). Leiden: Brill.

31

What was Commentary in Late Antiquity? The Example of the Neoplatonic Commentators

PHILIPPE HOFFMANN

Neoplatonic thought at the end of antiquity – like that of most of the schools of the Hellenistic and Roman period – has an essentially exegetical and scholastic dimension. Beginning with the classical and Hellenistic period, philosophy in Greece is inseparable from the existence of schools (private or public), often organized as places of communal life (*sunousia*), in which the explication of the texts of the school's founders came to be one of the main activities.[1] The practice of exegesis of written texts supplanted the ancient practice of dialogue. It was sustained through its application to canonical texts, and was put to everyday use in the framework of courses in the explication of texts. The social reality of the school as an institution, with its hierarchy, its *diadochos* (i.e., the successor to the school's founder), its structure as a conventicle in which communal life was practiced, its library, its regulation of time, and its programs organized around the reading of canonical texts, constitutes a concrete context into which we should reinsert the practice of exegesis, which is the heart of philosophical pedagogy and the matrix of doctrinal and dogmatic works.

A Network of Schools

From the third to the sixth century CE, from Plotinus, who taught in Rome, to the professors of the school of Alexandria (Ammonius, Olympiodorus, David, Elias) and to those of the school of Athens (Plutarch of Athens, Syrianus, Proclus, Damascius), we observe, from the West (Rome, Sicily) to the East (Apamea, Alexandria, Athens), a network of schools between which teachers and students often traveled, and a tight connection between Neoplatonic philosophy and the school organization, with the decisive works of Porphyry – a student of Plotinus who was active in Rome and in Sicily – and of Iamblichus, a native of Syria – to which we owe exegetical findings as fundamental as the rule of the *skopos* and the idea of a canonical double cycle of Plato's dialogues.

---

1.   See Bénatouïl, PHILOSOPHIC SCHOOLS IN HELLENISTIC AND ROMAN TIMES, in this volume.

Certain cities are prestigious: Apamea, where Numenius and Iamblichus taught; Alexandria, where the Neoplatonic school pursued its activities after 529, thanks to the policy of the Christian John Philoponus; and above all Athens, truly the "holy city." After sojourns in Apamea and Rome, the Platonic tradition in fact reestablished itself, after Iamblichus, in Athens with Plutarch of Athens, whose abode could have been the official residence of the succession until Proclus: thus the Platonic "Golden Chain," as Damascius called it, was preserved at the foot of the Acropolis, the foot of the temple of Athena. The biographical evidence we have allows us also to make out multiple links with social elites, and the formation of "university" families and matrimonial links sometimes weaving a Neoplatonic web around the Mediterranean periphery.

From a doctrinal viewpoint, the research of Ilsetraut Hadot (1978) has convincingly shown that there were no appreciable doctrinal differences between the schools of Athens and Alexandria, even if there perhaps remained a difference of emphasis between Athens, where the explication of Plato was a major activity, and Alexandria, from which came very numerous commentaries on Aristotle.

The Religious Climate

Some brief general considerations are needed to understand the particular character of Neoplatonic exegesis, that is, the intellectual, spiritual, and *pagan* religious "climate" in which texts were read (see, e.g., Festugière, 1966, and Saffrey, 1984b). First of all, a Neoplatonic academic community, in Athens or Alexandria in the fifth or sixth century, probably had some of the traits of a religious community. For example, in the case of the school of Athens, it was a "private" school, receiving bequests, living off the returns from real estate in Attica. And we know that Proclus did not disdain participation in municipal life in Athens.

As the life and work of the emperor Julian (fourth century) particularly shows, as also does a reading of Damascius's *Life of Isidorus*, Neoplatonism was for several centuries the philosophical backbone of the multiform movement – intellectual, cultural, religious, but also political – that was the "pagan reaction" to the establishment of a Christian empire. When the emperor Justinian, in 529, issued the edict forbidding the teaching of philosophy and law at Athens, it was not a *coup de grâce* delivered to a dying man, but rather a brutal measure taken against a Neoplatonic school doubtless in its full vigor after the policy of restoration carried out by the last successor of Plato, Damascius (Hoffmann, 1994), as attested by the immense commentaries on Epictetus and Aristotle (*Categories, Physics, De Caelo*) later composed – after the Persian exile, but where it is hard to say precisely – by Damascius's student, Simplicius. Philosophy and pagan religion were then tightly linked, and Neoplatonism became the refuge of the gods of the classical pantheon – reinterpreted in the framework of a system that, after the One-Good and at the summit of multiple levels of the intelligible, preserves a place for the "henads." At the moment when the cults were gradually prohibited, the temples closed, when visible official ceremonies disappeared, Athena appeared to Proclus in a dream, informing him of her intention to take refuge with him after the closing of the Parthenon, and of the probable removal to Constantinople of the statue of the goddess (Marinus, *Life of Proclus*, ch. 30). These philosophers of diverse origins (especially Easterners, from Egypt to Asia Minor by way of that Neoplatonic land, Syria) were "Hellenes," seemingly more by virtue of *paideia* than by their ethnic origin. For them, Greek was the *natural* language of philosophy – and the "terms" of propositions, the ten categories, were the most universal forms of human understanding, beyond the diversity of languages (of which Ammonius also took account, but in a secondary way).

Philosophy, Revelation, and Faith

A complex connection unites philosophy, theology, exegesis, and "revelation" – which is recorded in genuine "holy scriptures" (P. Hadot, 1987). At the same time as theology sets itself up as a "science" (Saffrey, 1996), a *style of life* develops, characterized by Pythagoreanism and wholly bent upon turning, beyond the divine classes and beyond being, in the direction of the One-Good. The reading and interpretation of canonical texts must be understood as part of a climate of *religio mentis*, which makes a growing place for supra-rational elements (Saffrey, 1981, 1984a): the *Chaldaean Oracles* are at once the ultimate revelations that the gods have made about themselves and the World, the touchstone of certain interpretations of texts of Plato and Aristotle, but also the "sacred book" on which are founded the practices of theurgy (Brisson, 2000; Lewy, 1956; van Liefferinge, 1999). Defense of traditional gods and curiosity about all kinds of divine manifestation, among both the Greeks and the barbarians; pilgrimages to holy sites or, as Michel Tardieu says, to "paysages reliques" (Tardieu, 1990); piety upheld toward the divinity of the Cosmos, sempiternal and uncreated; the conception of philosophy as "revelation": in such a context, interpreting such "authorities" as Plato and Aristotle amounts to unveiling – with no innovation – a meaning and a truth of which the gods and "divine men" are the source. And the authority of the philosophers who were at the base of the doctrinal synthesis of Neoplatonism – Plato and Aristotle – is itself completed by that of a Pythagoras, or of the poet Orpheus. The interpreter explicates what is *already there*: he is merely the vector of Truth. As the grandiose prologue of Proclus's *Platonic Theology* expresses it, there is furthermore no history of Truth, but only a history of its manifestation and of its unveiling – and Syrianus definitively established in Neoplatonism the presupposition of the "concord," *sumphōnia*, of philosophies (Saffrey, 1992). Against the Christianity adopted by the uncultivated masses, a minority of *pepaideumenoi* are in possession of theological science: it is in the (Platonic) order of things that the adherents of *doxa*, walled up by their appetites and passions, momentarily prevail over the philosophers (Saffrey, 1975). Against the Christians, the pagan philosophers have their "bible," their "sacred book" – the *Chaldaean Oracles*, bearers of revelation – and they gradually forge a properly Neoplatonic concept of Faith. The example of Simplicius's *Commentary on Aristotle's Physics* is emblematic of the connection between learned exegesis and religion: the "usefulness" of physics, Simplicius explains, is to provoke the awakening in souls of the anagogical triad of Love, Truth, and Faith (to which is added a fourth term, Hope); and the successive reading of the *Physics* and *De Caelo* leads the soul of the philosopher-exegete and those of his audience (or of his readers) to a "union" (*henōsis*), through

599

Faith and the "vital sympathy" correlative with it, with the divine Heaven and with the demiurgic intellect that produces the World (Hoffmann, 2000a).

The Course in Philosophy: A Day in Proclus's Life

Texts like the *Discourses* of Epictetus (e.g., 1.26.1 and 13; cf. 1.10.8), Porphyry's *Life of Plotinus*, or Marinus's *Life of Proclus* allow us to enter very vividly into the atmosphere of a philosophical school in antiquity, and, in the last example, of a Neoplatonic school. A lesson in philosophy, in principle, and in a schematic fashion, consisted of two distinct parts: first a disciple read, in the teacher's presence, a "magistral" text – by Plato, Aristotle, Chrysippus, or Zeno – as well as the earlier commentaries relating to the studied text, and this reading (*anagnōsis*) was accompanied by the teacher's own commentary: thus, Plotinus's course began with the reading of the exegetes of Plato and Aristotle (for example, Severus, Cronius, Numenius, Gaius, Atticus, Aspasius, Alexander of Aphrodisias, Adrastus), after which Plotinus set forth his own exegesis of the studied text (see Porphyry, *Life of Plotinus* 14.10–18). Then a kind of free discussion took place, the *diatribē*, in the course of which various questions were raised and discussed under the guidance of the professor.

It is even possible to sketch fairly concretely the course of a Neoplatonic philosopher's day, thanks to chapter 22 of the eulogy wrongly called the "Life of Proclus," by Marinus, Proclus's disciple (see Saffrey, 1987, pp. xx–xxi = 1990, pp. 149–51). Thus we may understand the existential framework in which, all through his life, Proclus's exegetical activity took place, consisting in continuous commentaries on canonical works (commentaries on the *Republic*, the *Timaeus*, the *Parmenides*) that we must carefully distinguish from his other writings, which constituted personal research and sometimes issued in magisterial syntheses (including works as different in their literary form as the *Elements of Theology* and the *Platonic Theology*). At dawn, Proclus paid homage, by prostrating himself, to the Sun, which is the "offspring" of the Good (Plato, *Republic* VI, 507a3), or its visible analogue (509b2–10, d2–3). A genuine vicar of the First Principle among men, at the head of the Platonic school, he began, with this act of philosophical piety toward the Sun (the subject of one of the Hymns: Saffrey, 1984c), a studious day that made him a professor "*in the highest degree similar to the Good.*" The first hours of the morning were dedicated to explicating authors making up the syllabus of the Neoplatonic philosophical *cursus*, organized around the "small mysteries" of philosophy (Aristotle) and the "great mysteries" (Plato). According to Marinus, he would give five – sometimes more than five – lessons explicating texts in a single day. The practice of textual exegesis, in the framework of instruction, preceded the personal work of writing and composition, and we know that Proclus wrote some seven hundred "lines" per day. A second prayer to the Sun marked midday, while the afternoon was given over to philosophical conversation with colleagues and the evening to "unwritten" lessons and to what we would call seminars. The day ended as it began, by a prayer to the Sun: thus, all philosophical activity took place in the light of the "offspring" of the Good, and one could say that an axis linked the First Principle, the Sun, and the Master, the exegetical and dogmatic authority at the heart of the Neoplatonic community. Table 31.1 (based on Saffrey, 1987, p. xx) allows us to see clearly how,

Table 31.1 A Neoplatonic professor's day

Hours of the day	Activities
Sunrise	Prayer to the Sun
First hours of the morning	Classes explicating authors on the school program
Late morning	Personal composition
Noon	Prayer to the Sun
Afternoon	Philosophical conversation with colleagues
Evening	Unwritten lessons and seminars
Sunset	Prayer to the Sun

concretely, exegetical activities fit into the daily life of a Neoplatonic professor, and how activities of *writing* were distinguished from purely *oral* communication – each being marked off by *silent* prayers to the Sun, beyond which the *ascensio mentis* initiated in the practice of exegesis was to be pursued.

But Proclus also wrote at night. He devoted his nights to meditation, prayer, and the composition of hymns in honor of the gods (Marinus, *Procl.* 24). Seven of these hymns have been preserved: they are dedicated to the Sun; to Aphrodite, mother of Love; to the Muses; to the gods of the *Chaldaean Oracles*; to Lycian Aphrodite; to Hecate and Janus; and to Athena of Good Counsel (Saffrey, 1994; van den Berg, 2001). Proclus himself may have gathered the collection of Orphic Hymns transmitted with his philosophical hymns.

Neoplatonic Pedagogical Thought

Neoplatonic instruction gives a central place to the notion of "authority": the authority of revealed texts, the authority of great philosophers (mainly Plato and Aristotle) who have "seen" the Truth, the personal and social authority of the Master and the Professor, who holds the correct doctrine and knows the meaning of the texts. Proclus, we have just seen, is described as the "vicar" of the One-Good and there is no doubt that the authority of the *diadochos* or *successor* – in every sense of the word – was immense. To be a professor was also to practice "assimilation to god," and this was, in the tradition of the *Theaetetus*, one of the six definitions of philosophy taught in the introduction to the philosophical *cursus*: the "assimilation" was practiced with regard to the "cognitive" faculties (imitation of divine omniscience) and with regard to the "vital" or "practical" faculties (providential solicitude for the imperfect souls of the students).[2] Deification by instruction, like deification by politics, corresponds to the exercise of "political" virtues – the virtues of a soul that uses its body in the manner of an instrument, and that lives in society – according to the Neoplatonic doctrine of the virtues; and it must therefore be realized that the very act of *teaching* – which consisted

2.   On the earlier history of this notion, see Betegh, GREEK PHILOSOPHY AND RELIGION, in this volume.

mainly of *commentary* on texts – was conceived as a *deification* of the professor, who guides his audience or his students on the path of their own deification (on all this, see Hoffmann, 1998, pp. 228–40).

The Doctrinal Fecundity of Exegetical Misinterpretations

In a mental universe very different from our own, a universe that condemns *originality* and enjoins a faithful respect for the Ancients, philosophical thought willingly saw itself as a mere unfolding of doctrines more or less explicitly (or implicitly) contained in texts that had *authority* (treatises of Aristotle, Plato's dialogues, etc.): Plotinus (*Enn.* V.1 [10], 8.10–14) presented himself as merely the "exegete" of very old doctrines of Parmenides and Plato, and even if the novelty of his thought in relation to classical philosophy is for us a manifest reality, it nonetheless remains that Plotinus – like his successors, for that matter – must have considered himself an authentic Platonist.[3] The appearance and development of new doctrines are not, in antiquity, the fruit of a departure claiming to be "original," but rather the result of exegeses that, if we may put it so, abandon themselves in good faith to the fecundity of errors and misinterpretations of the text on which they comment. In order for such distortions of meaning to attain their full fecundity, a constant and minute attention to the text itself is necessary: the role in it of the explication of the *letter* of the text (the *lexis*, as distinct from the *theōria*, i.e., the *meaning*, or rather the *doctrine*: Festugière, 1963) is known; and it has been possible to show the taste of certain exegetes, such as Damascius, for an interpretation that attends to the literary content of the dialogues, which perhaps led him to a better reading than others of the text of Plato (Westerink, 1971; and Hoffmann, 1994, p. 572).

A foundational study by P. Hadot (1968) has revealed the philosophical fecundity of misunderstandings or incomprehensions of the meaning of texts: they are the ancient and medieval way of producing "doctrines." Since philosophizing consisted essentially in conducting the exegesis of "Authorities," the search for truth was most frequently confounded with the search for the meaning of texts held to be authoritative on essential philosophical and theological questions, the truth *already* contained in these texts needing only to be made *explicit*. Hence, as the majority of philosophical and theological problems were posed in exegetical terms, theoretical developments proceeded according to a method we may describe as: (1) arbitrarily systematizing disparate formulations extracted from completely unrelated contexts; (2) amalgamating likewise disparate philosophical notions or concepts originating in different or even contradictory doctrines; and (3) explicating notions not to be found at all in the original. In such a context, it is frequently quite vain to try to interpret the philosophers of antiquity in terms of our modern, post-Hegelian concept of a "system" – even if, for example, a major work, Proclus's *Elements of Theology*, is a (successful) attempt to present *more geometrico* the whole system of reality, as it issues from the One-Good, according to Neoplatonic theology and ontology; and even if the *Platonic Theology* is the perfect and systematic fruit of generations of exegetical research conducted

---

3.   See Brisson and Pradeau, PLOTINUS, in this volume.

by Neoplatonic philosophers on the dialogues of Plato, and particularly on the *Parmenides* (Saffrey, 1984d).

The "Symphonic" Presupposition: Syrianus, and the Harmony of Plato and Aristotle according to Simplicius

Syrianus had written two works on Orpheus: *On the Theology of Orpheus* and *Harmony (sumphōnia) of Orpheus, Pythagoras and Plato with the Oracles* (i.e., with the *Chaldaean Oracles*). This latter treatise seems to have expounded the exegetical program that held sway in the Neoplatonic school in Athens, and doubtless also in the school of Alexandria: the rule of harmony among authorities, and of the harmony of "divine men" (Orpheus, Pythagoras, Plato) with the *Chaldaean Oracles* revealed by the gods themselves (Saffrey, 1992). Unfortunately, we have lost the contents of this treatise, but a reading of the Neoplatonic commentaries of late antiquity confirms that the search for *sumphōnia* between philosophers must have been the exegete's golden rule. The perfect doctrinal agreement between Plato and Aristotle was a postulate granted by all the Neoplatonic interpreters from Porphyry onward. A long evolution of inter- pretative methods, which had begun with Antiochus of Ascalon, here culminated and found its perfection (I. Hadot, 1978, pp. 68–9, 72–6, 148 n. 3, 195).[4] When, in particular, and at an earlier stage of the *cursus*, it came to commenting on Aristotle, the task of the good exegete (point 8 of the first introductory schema described below) was defined thus: "he must, when Aristotle contradicts Plato, not consider only the letter of the text (*lexis*) and condemn the discord (*diaphōnia*) of the philosophers, but take into consideration the spirit (*nous*), and seek to track down their harmony (*sumphōnia*) on the majority of questions" (Simpl. *In Cat.* 7.29–32). In fact, if the discords are verbal, and *purely verbal*, that is due to the difference of attitude of the two philosophers with regard to language, and thus to a difference of philosophical attitude, but not to a difference of *doctrine*: "It is necessary, in my opinion," Simplicius explains elsewhere,

> to consider at the same time the aim (*skopos*) and the words, and to understand that in these matters the divergence (*diaphora*) between the two philosophers bears not on the reality of things (*pragmata*) but on words (*onomata*): Plato, on account of his taste for precision, rejects the ordinary usage (*sunētheia*) of words, whereas Aristotle employs it – a method that, according to him, is in no way injurious to truth . . . (Simpl. *In Cael.* 69.11–15; cf. 15–29)

Plato scorns the language of the multitude, while Aristotle does not wish to abandon it (*In Cael.* 679.28–29). A difference in philosophical *method* underlies this difference in attitude toward language:

> thus, it is not reality itself (*pragma*), but the word (*onoma*), on which bears the present divergence (*diaphora*) between the philosophers; and it is likewise in most other cases. The

4. On Antiochus, see Lévy, THE NEW ACADEMY AND ITS RIVALS, and Zambon, MIDDLE PLATONISM, in this volume.

reason for it is, I believe, that often Aristotle wants to retain the ordinary meaning of words and sets out, in building his arguments, from what is manifest to the senses, whereas Plato displays several times over his contempt for ordinary significations, and rises gladly to intellectual contemplation. (*In Phys.* 1249.12–17)

As we shall see below (point 6 of the first introductory schema: Simpl. *In Cat.* 6.22– 30), Plato's attitude is "Pythagorean" because he "examines natural realities in so far as they participate in what is above nature," and he bases his demonstrations on intellection (*nous*), whereas Aristotle begins from sensation (*aisthēsis*), conscious of addressing himself to beings "who live with sensation," and he does not set himself apart from nature, studying the realities that are above nature only in their relation to nature. From an epistemological viewpoint, demonstrative perfection results from the conjunction of the two types of demonstration (that which begins from intellection and that which begins from sensation), which is strictly coherent with the principle of the *sumphōnia* of Plato and Aristotle (I. Hadot, 1978, p. 148; Hoffmann, 1987b, pp. 212–13).

An example of fecund misinterpretation: The composition of the substance of the heavens

The determination of the nature of celestial substance offers a perfect example of this conjunction of Aristotelian and Platonic methods of demonstration (Simpl. *In Cael.* 84.30–85, 31; cf. Hoffmann, 1987b, pp. 213ff.). Simplicius, commenting on Book I of *De Caelo*, wants to show the harmony on a fundamental point between the doctrines of the two authorities in a polemical anti-Christian context and in a spirit of traditional piety toward the Heavens and the Cosmos: the latter is not "born" at a moment of time – it has no temporal origin – and it is not consigned to destruction: it is unbegotten and incorruptible (as the *De Caelo* affirms). If Plato says it is "begotten," it is in so far as it proceeds ultimately from the One-Good. The Aristotelian assertion of the existence of a primary body, unbegotten and incorruptible, without change, growth or diminution, moved only in its circular motion, and distinct from the four sublunary elements, conflicts in no way with the teachings of the *Timaeus*, though it asserts no distinction between a sublunary and a supralunary sphere, and though it posits only the supremacy of fire in the Heavens – the latter also being composed of the other three elements (*Ti.* 40a). Where the modern historian reasonably sees a difference in doctrine, Simplicius – who reverts to a Proclian celestial physics whose origin lies in Treatise 40 of Plotinus – sees only a perfect *sumphōnia*: what Aristotle calls "primary body" is a mixture of the four elements under the pure form of principles (the "summits," *akrotētes*), which transcends the "sublunary" elements. This mixture is determined in its essence, characterized and denominated, according to the principle of "predominance," by the elementary "summit" predominating in it, and, as Plato says (*Ti.* 40a), what predominates on high is fire, in its purest form – light (*phōs*) that shines and does not burn, and which is as different from flame (*phlox*) as from glowing embers (*anthrax*) (*Ti.* 58c). The Aristotelian "primary body," or "aether," is such a mixture, the description of which coincides with the meaning attributed to Plato's text, and it is the reading of the *Timaeus* that guides that of *De Caelo*. This example illustrates the subtle exegetical mechanism by means of which texts are unduly reconciled in a *sumphōnia* that is a fecund misinterpretation. It is the Neoplatonists' joint reading of Plato and Aristotle that allows them to find a single, identical doctrine of celestial physics in the works of the two authorities: notice that the privilege accorded to Plato over Aristotle is decisive in this proceeding. And the religious horizon of this physics constructed through a reconciling exegesis is the reaffirmation of the piety handed down by the Ancients, and the "sympathetic" union (*henōsis*) with the Heavens and the Demiurge.

The Explication of Texts: The Neoplatonic *cursus* of Study

Aristotle, Propaedeutic to Plato

The heart of life in the Neoplatonic schools of Alexandria and Athens was constituted by daily lessons in the explication of texts (called *praxeis*), conforming to a strict program codified beginning with Iamblichus – to whom was owed the choice of twelve principal dialogues of Plato (Festugière, 1969). The program of the Neoplatonic *cursus* of studies may also be read as an ideal list of books – the core of fundamental books, to which was added the corpus of traditional commentaries – constituting a Neoplatonic library.

Without going into the details of all the questions raised by the contents of this *cursus*, let us recall its main stages (Goulet-Cazé, 1982, pp. 277–80; I. Hadot, 1978, pp. 148–9, 160–4; P. Hadot, 1979, pp. 218–21; Westerink, Trouillard, and Segonds, 1990, pp. xlviii–lvi ff.). Study began with the authors of the *trivium* and the *quadrivium* that made up a cycle propaedeutic to philosophical studies (I. Hadot, 1984). Then a set of preparatory ethical studies and prologues involved recourse to three hortatory discourses by Isocrates (discourses *To Demonicus*, *To Nicocles*, and *Nicocles*), to the Pythagorean *Carmen aureum* (commentary by the Alexandrian Hierocles), to the *Enchiridion* of Epictetus and to Porphyry's *Isagoge* – with which began the properly philosophical instruction, and on which we have several sixth century commentaries (Ammonius, David, Elias; edited by A. Busse, in the series Commentaria in Aristotelem Graeca (= CAG) vols. 4 and 18).

The chief part of the *cursus*, after Porphyry's *Isagoge* and various Introductions, was dedicated to the reading of Aristotle (the "small mysteries" of philosophy) and Plato (the "great mysteries"). Because the *Life* of Aristotle was placed at the beginning of the edition of the works of the Stagirite and could be read in that sort of volume, the Introduction to the Philosophy of Aristotle, given preceding the commentaries on the *Categories*, did not include a biography, but rather an elucidation of the names of the philosophical schools. The peripatetic philosophy, regarded as a propaedeutic to that of Plato (I. Hadot, 1991, 1992), and interpreted from this "symphonic" perspective, were studied in a sequence of readings as follows: the logical writings of the *Organon* (in an order to which we shall return later); then the "practical" writings, with the *Ethics* and the *Politics*; and finally the "theoretical" writings, which corresponded to Physics (*Physics*, *De Caelo*, *On Generation and Corruption*, etc.), to Mathematics (probably *De Lineis Insecabilibus* was read), and to Theology, that is, essentially the

Metaphysics, with which the "small mysteries" culminated. This sequence of readings derived from a very strict classification of the works of Aristotle, which left aside the treatises considered to be less philosophical, since they dealt with particular beings. Marinus tells us that Proclus put only two years into running through this Aristotelian propaedeutic cycle.

Reading Platonic dialogues

After the reading of Aristotle came that of Plato, based on a "choice" privileging – according to the canon attributed to Iamblichus – certain dialogues (Westerink et al., 1990, pp. lxviii–lxxiii): they constituted a processional and initiatory pathway leading from the "propylaea" (the *Alcibiades* I) to the "adytum" of the temple (the *Parmenides*). A first cycle was structured, fundamentally, by the Neoplatonic hierarchy of the virtues, and by the distinction between "political," "cathartic," and "theoretical" virtues. The "theoretical" part was itself divided in three, corresponding to the triad of names, notions, and realities, which plays a leading role in Neoplatonic ontology and in the doctrine of language. The theoretical study of realities was itself also divided into the study of *physical* realities and the study of *theological* realities. The first cycle thus included, in succession, the *Alcibiades* I (which served as an introduction, through the knowledge of oneself and the turning toward oneself), then the *Gorgias* (which corresponds to the practice of the "political" virtues, those of the soul that uses the body in the manner of an instrument, in the context of social life) and the *Phaedo* ("cathartic" virtues, corresponding to the separation of soul and body), the *Cratylus* and the *Theaetetus* ("theoretical" virtues trained through the study of *names* and of *notions*), the *Sophist* and the *Statesman* ("theoretical" virtues trained by the study of physical realities), then the *Phaedrus* and the *Symposium* ("theoretical" virtues trained by the study of theological realities), and it culminated with the *Philebus*, which provides a first instruction about the Good, preparatory to the reading of the *Parmenides*. Notice that this kind of selection, and classification, implies that in the *Statesman* only the cosmological myth is retained (corresponding to a physics) and in the *Symposium* and the *Phaedrus* only the development of the doctrine of Ideas or intelligible divine Forms. A long work like the *Republic* had no place in this scheme, but it was not on that account neglected or forgotten in Neoplatonic instruction, as demonstrated by the very existence of the great Commentary by Proclus on this dialogue, and the same may be said of the *Laws*. This first Platonic cycle was crowned by a second one, organized according to the division between physics and theology: it consisted in the study of the *Timaeus* and the *Parmenides*, to which Proclus devoted huge commentaries thanks to which we have partial access to the exegeses of his predecessors as well. Indeed, in many ways all of Neoplatonism is a perpetual commentary on the *Parmenides*, read word by word and ceaselessly meditated on: the Platonic dialogue is a sacred book, the reading of which "becomes the religious act *par excellence*" (Saffrey, 1984b, p. 171).

Beyond philosophy: Orphic Hymns *and* Chaldaean Oracles

Thanks to the *Parmenides*, the soul raised itself up to the One. But the *Parmenides* is not the final word of the course in philosophy: after the philosophical cycles the Orphic

Hymns (the only books possessed by the pagan monk Sarapion in Alexandria in the fifth century) and the *Chaldaean Oracles* were read and commented on (Festugière, 1966 [1971, pp. 583–4]; Goulet-Cazé, 1982, pp. 277–80). This collection of "theological" oracles, forged by theurgists (Julian, father and son) in the second century, during the reign of Marcus Aurelius, was a true "sacred book," destined to provide pagan theology at the end of antiquity with the equivalent of the Jewish and Christian sacred books: this pagan bible constituted the touchstone of all Neoplatonic exegetical enterprise, and the meanings attributed to the doctrines of Aristotle and Plato were founded on this revealed authority (P. Hadot, 1987 [1998]). Even if Plotinus paid no attention to these *Oracles*, their importance was the topic of a lively debate between Porphyry and Iamblichus, and they were commented upon by Proclus and Damascius. It is known that, in Byzantium, they attracted the interest of Psellos, and later in the fifteenth century, Georgius Gemisthus Pletho.

The Beginning of the Cursus: The Introductions Taught in the Framework of the Exegesis of Porphyry's *Isagoge* and Aristotle's *Categories*, and The General Principles of Exegesis

When he had received preparatory ethical instruction, the student in the Neoplatonic school began the study of philosophy with a set of six discourses which followed one another, each having, in various ways, the status of an "introduction," which led him to the heart of an Aristotelian propaedeutic integrated from the outset with the purest Neoplatonism. A brief overview of this complex structure (I. Hadot, 1987a [1990, p. 21ff.]; Hoffmann, 1998; Westerink et al., 1990, pp. xliii–lvi) shows the degree to which dogmatic instruction, exegesis of canonical texts, and psychagogical concerns are inseparable in the Neoplatonic school. The student thus studied, in succession: (1) a general Introduction to Philosophy, as a part of an introduction to the explication of Porphyry's *Isagoge*. The content of the different Introductions that have been preserved is well known, and it is enough to recall that they mainly taught, after a study of what a "definition" is, the six ancient definitions of Philosophy: knowledge of beings in so far as they are beings; knowledge of divine and human realities; assimilation to god as far as is possible for man; the practice of death; the art of arts and science of sciences; love of wisdom. They also expound a bipartite division of philosophy into a "theoretical" and a "practical" part. (2) An Introduction specifically to the *Isagoge*, developed in eight points, that is, the seven points addressed in principle in connection with Aristotle's *Categories* and other treatises of the Stagirite, plus an eighth point: "What is the form of instruction?" (3) Porphyry's *Isagoge*, which is an introduction at once to Aristotle's *Categories*, to logic, and to the whole of philosophy. It was important to elucidate correctly the "aim" (*skopos*) and the "utility" of the *Isagoge*, and it was the occasion to prepare for the explication of the *Categories*. In fact, in Neoplatonic instruction, the determination of the usefulness of the *Categories* was strictly connected to the determination of the usefulness, or rather several utilities, of the *Isagoge*, just as the aims of the two treatises are affiliate, since both alike bear on universal "signifying words." Ammonius taught several of the "utilities" of the *Isagoge*: the work is useful for the whole of philosophy, for the *Categories* (that is, for the reading of philosophical treatises containing the doctrine of universal predicates, that of Aristotle but also that of his Pythagorean source Archytas of Tarentum), "for all the treatises of philosophy," and "for the whole method of discovery that philosophy employs" (26.3–5). This last expression should be understood to refer to the four methods of dialectic (division, definition, demonstration, and analysis). And, adds Ammonius, even if there were no *written* philosophical treatises, the *Isagoge* would be useful "to the very methods used by philosophers, thanks to which the philosophers can discover every reality" (35.27–29). After Ammonius, the Alexandrians David and Elias rearranged these utilities under three or four heads, and Elias gave primary place to an anthropological consideration: the *Isagoge* is useful "for our very essence" (*ousia*) as living beings endowed with the capacity to communicate with one another by means of language. In a more immediate fashion, it was the pedagogical need for explanations preliminary to reading the *Categories* that led Porphyry to draw up – at the request of his audience, the Roman senator Chrysaorius – an "Introduction" to the *Categories*: the *Isagoge* is an explication of the most fundamental "five words" of Aristotle's logic (genus, species, differentia, property, and accident), and their *elucidation* is a necessary preliminary to that of the *Categories*. Then came (4) a general Introduction to the philosophy of Aristotle, which was to fix the general frameworks for the exegesis of the whole of Aristotle's philosophical corpus; this Introduction is imparted as the first part of the Introduction specific to the *Categories*, and it includes the ten points described below. The fifth stage consisted of the Introduction to the *Categories* proper, according to six or seven points that were also to be examined (some being optional) in connection with each of the Aristotelian treatises of the *cursus*. These schemas seem to have been expounded by Proclus in a lost treatise entitled *Sunanagnōsis*, "Explication of a Text under the Supervision of a Master" (Hadot et al., 1990, pp. 26, 34). Finally, (6), the reading of the *Categories* itself constituted the *beginning* of logic and the *prologue* to Philosophy as a whole: the general principles of exegesis were inculcated throughout all the previous Introductions.

The first introductory schema, in ten points, formed a general introduction to the philosophy of Aristotle, and to the exegesis of the whole set of treatises (see Hadot et al., 1990).

1. What is the origin of the names of the philosophical sects? The answer supplies a historical framework for the hermeneutic principle of the harmony (*sumphōnia*) of the philosophies of Plato and Aristotle, which is to guide all the reading of Aristotle. Aristotle is presented as the successor of Plato through the intermediary of Speusippus (Plato's successor as head of the Academy), and Olympiodorus went so far as to imply that the true successor of Plato, when it came to doctrine, would have been Aristotle rather than Xenocrates (who succeeded Speusippus).

2. How are the writings of Aristotle classified? The organization of the Aristotelian corpus proceeded from several distinctions: between "general," "intermediate," and "particular" works; between "syntagmatic" and "hypomnematic" works; between the dialogues and the works in which Aristotle speaks in his own name (*autoprosōpa*). The *division* allows us to discover the *sequence of readings* that constituted the program of exegesis for the whole Aristotelian corpus. The syntagmatic works were the only ones to which full dogmatic authority was

credited, because their doctrinal content is complete and they have a perfect literary form, as well as a title. They are divided into three classes: "theoretical" works, classified according to the threefold division into physics, mathematics, and theology; "practical" works, classified according to the threefold division into politics, economics, and ethics; "instrumental" works, also divided into three: those that appear to be "method" (*Poetics, Rhetoric, Topics, Sophistical Refutations*), those that bear on "method" (*Posterior Analytics*), and those that precede "method" (*Categories, De Interpretatione, Prior Analytics*). Based on this division, the logical writings were thus arranged according to an exegetical and pedagogical progression in the following order: the *Categories* (the doctrines of predicates and of the simple terms of the proposition), *De Interpretatione* (the doctrine of the "declarative statement" and of the premises constituting the syllogism), the *Prior Analytics* (the doctrine of the syllogism or deductive reasoning), the *Posterior Analytics* (which culminates in the teaching of the demonstrative syllogism, the "instrument" for discerning truth and falsity in *theory*, the good and the bad in *practice*), then the *Topics* and the *Sophistical Refutations* (notice that the "long" *Organon*, which included the *Poetics* and the *Rhetoric*, had no success in the worlds of late antiquity and Byzantium).

3. Where ought one to begin in grappling with Aristotle's treatises? With ethics (since without purifying one's ways one cannot think rationally), or with logic? The Neoplatonists answered that one ought to begin with logic (to which Porphyry's *Isagoge*, then the *Categories*, were an introduction), but that preparatory ethical instruction was to be given, as a preliminary, in an "unscientific" manner – the explicated reading of the Aristotelian *Ethics* being possible only later in the *cursus*.

4. What is the "end" (*telos*) of the philosophy of Aristotle? To this question, Simplicius replies that the "end" is happiness obtained by turning toward the One (the ascent back toward the First Principle) and by the *ethical* turn that consists in attaining perfection by the training in and practice of virtues. It is thus Book X of the *Nicomachean Ethics* that teaches the *telos*, and "demonstration," the keystone of the *Organon*, is the necessary instrument of an ascending movement that, through the interpretation of authoritative texts, is ethical and theoretical, but also spiritual and religious.

5. What are the means for attaining this end? They are the contents of the *cursus* itself (logic, ethics, physics, mathematics, theology).

6. What manner of expression is employed in Aristotle's writings? All the commentators describe Aristotle's style as compendious, concise, aporetic, and obscure. Plato and Aristotle practice inverse methods: Plato studies all things, and especially physical realities, based on the consideration of the divine intelligible Forms, and in this regard he conforms to the "Pythagorean" method (also known as "doing physics as a theologian"), whereas Aristotle sets out from current linguistic usage and the usual meanings of words, as well as from the consideration of particular sensible realities – the first that claim the attention of the novice, to whom it seems natural that the individual is "primary" substance. When he does theology, Aristotle remains a "physicist."

7. What is the source of Aristotle's obscurity? This obscurity, which Aristotle preferred to (Platonic) myth-making and (Pythagorean) symbolism, functions

609

to protect knowledge from being divulged (truth must be revealed only to those who are worthy of it), and furthermore it gives to those worthy of accession to Truth the opportunity to exercise and shape their sagacity (*agchinoia*). Obscurity has an initiatory and gymnastic value.

8. What qualities does an exegete of Aristotle need to have? According to Simplicius, the exegete should be at the same level of "greatness of thought" (*megalonoia*) as Aristotle. He should have a perfect and complete knowledge of the whole of Aristotle's work, as well as of his linguistic habits. He should not display sectarianism in his exegetical work, proceeding "as though he were a member of the philosopher's sect": his maxim should be, "*Amicus Plato sed magis amica veritas*" (Tarán, 1984). Above all, he is to seek, on most points, the deep harmony, the *sumphōnia*, between Aristotle and Plato, between whom disagreement can only be verbal, and can hardly concern doctrine itself. This principle of *sumphōnia* is the golden rule of Neoplatonic exegesis, and respect for it is the mark of the exegete "in love with knowledge," *philomathēs*, an epithet equivalent in the Platonic tradition to *philosophos*. This point is of the highest importance, because it describes the task of the exegete – minute and exhaustive explication of Aristotle's text, considered in all its detail and in the vast context of the corpus – and creates the conditions for a kind of autonomy for exegetical activity, accounting for the range of Simplicius's own commentaries.

9. What are the qualities needed by a good "hearer," that is, a good student of Aristotelian philosophy? He should be virtuous (*spoudaios* in the sense of Aristotelian metriopathy) or again with his behavior refined (*kosmios*) at the end of the preparatory ethical instruction, but not yet "scientific" (this "scientific" ethical instruction not being possible until later, when mastery of the syllogism allows for the rigorous study of the Aristotelian *Ethics*). The good student should meditate frequently on the fundamental notions of Aristotle's philosophy – which corresponds to a kind of spiritual exercise, already practiced with regard to the "five words" when the *Isagoge* was explicated – and he should engage in such meditation alone or in the company of friends equally "in love with knowledge." Finally, he should deny himself all "eristic" chatter, on pain of deserving punishment.

10. The tenth point was devoted to the list of six or seven points constituting the second introductory schema, which had to be expounded before the reading of *any* work by Aristotle – some points being optional, when the point was clear – and this schema is amply developed in the Neoplatonic introductions to the *Categories*, the inaugural treatise.

The six or seven points to be treated before reading any treatise by Aristotle

In the introduction to his Commentary on the *Categories*, Simplicius treats, in a manner both extremely probing and wholly exemplary, the *seven* points of the second introductory schema, in the following order:

610

1. What is the "aim" of the treatise, its intention (*skopos*)? This governing question, to which Iamblichus gave the force of law, orients all exegesis, and it is encountered in other types of commentary (patristic, medical, or rhetorical exegesis): all the doctrines and assertions of a philosopher whose works receive commentary should be coherent with this unique *skopos*. (A treatise, or a Platonic dialogue, cannot have several *skopoi*: the meaning of texts, like the World or Reality, is oriented toward a principle of unity.) Thus it will be explained that the categories are, in the human language proceeding from incarnated souls, the simplest "words" (*phōnai*) – established at the time of a "first institution" – and that these words signify, through mediation of simple and universal "notions" that are in the soul and that coincide with the *signifieds* of these words, the simplest and most universal "realities", that is, the "most generic genera," beyond which there are no more inclusive genera, since – as Aristotle himself teaches – being is not a genus (see Hoffmann, 1987a).[5]

    Another very interesting example is that of the *De Caelo* (Hoffmann, 1997, pp. 86–8). Simplicius confronts, and discusses, the interpretations of his predecessors, i.e., the commentators who preceded him in the study of the *De Caelo*: on one side, Alexander of Aphrodisias and in a more ancient time Theophrastus; on another side, Iamblichus and Syrianus. Alexander thinks that the *skopos* concerns the World and the simple bodies in it (earth, water, air, fire, and celestial substance), and he appeals to the authority of Theophrastus. By contrast, the Neoplatonic exegetes – Iamblichus and Syrianus – accord a distinct prominence to the "divine" body, and thus to the theological aspect of the treatise, thus privileging the first two books. According to Iamblichus, the treatise is mainly "about the celestial and divine body," even if it includes in a secondary way the theory of the Universe and that of the elements. Simplicius discusses Alexander's opinion as well as that of his Neoplatonic predecessors, and is led by the (Neoplatonic) twofold requirement of the unity of the *skopos* and the unity of the treatise itself to affirm the coherence of the four books and to integrate the study of the four sublunary elements within the horizon of the unique *skopos*, all the while recognizing the primacy of the divine Heavens – which generously communicates its perfections to the totality of the World: "it should not be held that the aim of the treatise (*skopos*) concerns the World: on the contrary, it concerns the simple bodies, of which the very first is the Heaven, in whose own goods it has made the World as a whole participate" (Simpl. *In De Cael.* 5.32–4).

2. What is the utility (*chrēsimon*) of the studied treatise? In the case here taken as an example, it will be said that the doctrine of the categories is useful for the construction of the apodictic syllogism or "demonstration," which is the instrument (*organon*) for distinguishing truth from falsity in the domain of "theory", good from bad in the domain of "practice" – theory and practice being the two "parts" of Philosophy, of which logic, based on the doctrine of the categories, is the "instrumental part." The categories are the "terms" of the proposition, the elements of the declarative statement (*logos apophantikos*) which, as a "premiss"

---

5. Cf. M. L. Gill, FIRST PHILOSOPHY IN ARISTOTLE, in this volume.

(*protasis*), is in turn an element of deductive reasoning or syllogism, of which a major type is precisely the apodictic syllogism. (On terms, see Aristotle in Modrak PHILOSOPHY OF LANGUAGE, in this volume; and on the syllogism, see Detel, ARISTOTLE'S LOGIC AND THEORY OF SCIENCE, in this volume.)

3. What place does the treatise occupy in the sequence of readings? Each treatise is situated, in virtue of its *skopos*, in a precise place in the *cursus* already described, according to a strict progression corresponding at once to the sequential unfolding of doctrinal instruction, to a pedagogical (or psychagogical) progression, and, fundamentally, to a spiritual and religious progression – since even the doctrine of the categories constitutes a "viaticum" toward the contemplation of the Forms and divine principles. In the sequence of the initial reading of the *Organon*, the *Categories* therefore comes first, immediately before *De Intrepretatione*, the *Prior* and the *Posterior Analytics*.

4. What justifies the title of the studied treatise? (See Hoffmann, 1997). In some cases the title is clear and needs no justification: thus *De Anima*, "On the Soul." Occasionally (*De Caelo*, "On the Heavens") its elucidation derives directly from the elucidation of the *skopos*, and Simplicius explains that Aristotle's treatise draws its title from the first and divine body that communicates its perfections to the whole World. In the case of the *Categories*, the question is much more complicated. A multiplicity of titles is actually discussed in the philosophical tradition. The Neoplatonic exegetes reject titles like "Pre-Topics" and "On the kinds of being." In the first case they do so because it implies a sequence and contiguity between the *Categories* and the *Topics*, and thus a "dialectical" reading of the *Categories* incompatible with the architecture of the *Organon* – inherited from the edition of Aristotle's writings by Andronicus of Rhodes – and with the Neoplatonic interpretation that is inseparable from it. In the second case, the title is rejected because "Plotinian" titles – those of the Porphyrian edition of the *Enneads* – imply a strictly ontological interpretation of the categories, which are thus seen as *realities* rather than as *signifying words*: so such a study belongs to the "theoretical" part of philosophy rather than to logic. The "good" title can thus only be "Categories." The word is not to be taken in its rhetorical sense ("accusation" as opposed to "defense," *apologia*), but in a "homonymous" sense given by Aristotle himself – who thus acts as *onomatothētēs*, or "name-giver". The categories are the predicates *par excellence*, the predicates that are predicates and nothing else and which signify the supreme genera in which participate all things at lower levels of reality – the interpretation of Aristotle's logic being aligned with a Platonic ontology from the outset, applying the principle of *sumphōnia*. It was also pointed out that the title, like the titles of Platonic dialogues and some titles of discourses by the sophist Aelius Aristides, is in the nominative case (rather than the usual construction, *peri* + genitive): such a formulation manifests the capacity of language to present *the things themselves*.

5. Are we dealing with an authentic work of the Philosopher? The dogmatic authority of the treatise depends on its authenticity, and this point is – when the question can arise – of prime importance. Various arguments are discussed (stylistic and doctrinal ones, but also the existence of cross-references in the corpus) in order

to establish the authenticity of the *Categories*. A structural argument plays an essential role: it is because it is *necessary* for the completeness of the *Organon* that the *Categories* is authentic. Without this inaugural treatise giving the terms of the proposition, the *Organon* would be "without a beginning" and "without a head."

6. What is the "division into chapters," that is, what is the structure of the treatise? A "syntagmatic" treatise is perfect from the twofold doctrinal and formal viewpoint, and it must have an organic unity. The literary perfection of the *Categories*, which is "tripartite," would therefore be affirmed; and the coherence of the four books of *De Caelo*, unified by the *skopos*, would be insisted upon.

7. To what part of Aristotle's philosophy does the treatise belong? The point is not in doubt in most cases (no hesitation, for example, in the case of the *Physics*, the *De Caelo*, or the *Metaphysics*), but it must be clarified in the case of the *Categories*, in conformity with what has been established in the study of several other points (the aim, the utility, the place in the sequence of readings): the *Categories* belong to the "instrumental part" of philosophy that is logic, and the categories should be carefully distinguished, as generic "beings" studied by ontology, from the "words" (*phōnai, lexeis*) that grammar studies.

Questions Preliminary to the Study of Plato

Although we have abundant commentaries on Plato, the only theoretical text that expounds the exegetical principles that should guide the reading of Plato is an anonymous work attributable to the second half of the sixth century, the *Prolegomena to the Philosophy of Plato*, which has been edited and studied by L. G. Westerink, J. Trouillard, and A.-Ph. Segonds (1990). We shall refer to the introduction to this edition (1990, pp. lix–lxxvi), as well as to the parallel presentation given by I. Hadot (1987a, [1990, pp. 30–4, 46]).

Here is a very brief summary of this Introduction to Plato, which occasionally derives from (lost) prolegomena composed by Proclus:

A. Biography of Plato
B. General introduction to Plato's philosophy, in ten points:

1. The character (*eidos*) of Plato's philosophy: this point consists of a summary history of Greek philosophy, intended to show the superiority of Platonism.
2. Why did Plato write, unlike Pythagoras and Socrates?
3. What reasons justify Plato's use of dialogue?
4. Of what elements are Plato's dialogues composed? A correspondence is set up between the elements of the dialogue and those of the cosmos: to the level of Matter (*hulē*) correspond the speakers of the dialogue, its time and its place; to the level of Form (*eidos*) corresponds its style; to Nature corresponds the form of the teaching, which may be either a mere exposition of Plato's opinions without investigation or demonstration, or an investigation, or a mixture of these two modes; to the Soul corresponds scientific demonstrations; "to the Intellect

corresponds the problem from which demonstrations project in the manner of a circumference;" to divinity corresponds the good at which the dialogue aims. Another correspondence is set up with a list of six causes: "to the material cause correspond the speakers, the time and the place; to the formal cause, the style; to the efficient cause, the soul; to the instrumental cause, the demonstrations; to the exemplary cause, the problems; to the final cause, the good aimed at by the dialogue."

5. From where are the titles of the dialogues drawn? From the speaker (*prosōpa*) or from realities (*pragmata*)?

6. What is the principle of division for the dialogues? (Not the dramatic situation or the argumentation, but the doctrine expounded.)

7. In what form (*tropos*) are the conversations in the dialogues (*sunousia*) presented? It is a question of studying the form of the action or the narration, the conversations being sometimes represented directly, sometimes reported by one or more intermediaries. An analogy is proposed between these successive reports and the degrees of knowledge in *Republic* VI.

8. What are the rules for determining the aim (*skopos*) of each of Plato's dialogues? Ten rules are laid down for determining the *skopos*.

9. What is the order of Plato's dialogues? Here is found a radical critique of the tetralogical order,[6] and a discussion of the canon of Iamblichus.

10. What are the methods of instruction? Fifteen methods are distinguished: divine inspiration, demonstration, definition, division, analysis, indication, image, example, induction, analogy, arithmetic, abstraction, addition, history, and etymology.

Prior to the reading of each Platonic dialogue a certain number of "preliminary points" were treated. We possess no summary list – unlike what is available for Aristotle – but examination of the introductions to the Neoplatonic commentaries on the various dialogues of Plato has allowed I. Hadot (1987a [1990, pp. 32–4, 46–7]) to reconstruct the following list, which includes eight points, of which some are identical to points examined before reading Aristotle's treatises:

1. How is the dramatic setting of the dialogue presented?

2. Who are the speakers of the dialogue, and what is their symbolic interpretation?

3. What is the general theme (*prothesis*) or the aim (*skopos*) of the dialogue?

4. What is the dialogue's place in the order of readings of Plato's dialogues?

5. What is the utility of the dialogue?

6. What is the division into parts or chapters of the dialogue?

7. What is the dialogue's manner of expression and philosophical character?

8. What is the form of the conversation in the dialogue, and what is its symbolic meaning? (Thus, the four conversations of the *Parmenides*, the first direct, the others indirect, are related to four ontological levels.)

---

6. On Thrasyllus and the tetralogical order of Plato's writings, see Mejer, ANCIENT PHILOSOPHY AND THE DOXOGRAPHICAL TRADITION, in this volume.

Commentaries composed from notes taken in the teacher's course (apo phōnēs) and commentaries composed by the exegete himself: The commentary as a spiritual exercise

The exegete might choose to compose his own commentary, when important issues are at stake: if the major part of the commentaries of Ammonius were published by his disciples (such as Asclepius and Philoponus), according to the *apo phōnēs* method (Richard, 1950), the importance of his investigations of the *De Interpretatione*, the "syntagmatic" character of which he demonstrated, pushed him to compose his own commentary personally, based on that of Proclus, and accompanied by what amounts to an edition of Aristotle's text. By contrast with the mass of commentaries *apo phōnēs*, often products of the school of Alexandria, which are editions of notes taken by auditors in the courses of professors, the commentaries of Simplicius, too, are, like the great commentaries of Proclus, the fruit of a personal labor of composition and writing: they are a genuine "*œuvre*," sometimes polemical, animated by a concern to summarize the philosophical tradition and to defend the ancestral religion of the Hellenes. And in such *written* commentaries it is not unusual to come across pages attesting to the literary, rhetorical cultivation of their author.

We must add another dimension of the act of writing: the practice of "spiritual exercises" in writing. We owe to it the *Meditations* of Marcus Aurelius – written variations, stylistically very polished, on the fundamental dogmas of Stoicism – but also many commentaries of late antiquity: for example, the Commentary by Simplicius on the *Handbook* of Epictetus, which Ilsetraut Hadot has shown to be a genuine spiritual exercise in writing (I. Hadot 1978, pp. 147–65; 1996, pp. 51–60). This observation may be applied to many other commentaries, and we must quote a striking passage in which Simplicius expresses the meaning for him of the act of reproducing (and of copying) long passages, word for word, from Iamblichus's commentary on Aristotle's *Categories*:

> As for me, I have even read the commentaries of some of the philosophers I have mentioned; and I have taken as a model the commentary of Iamblichus, with as much care as I was capable of, *in following him step for step and in frequently using the very text of this philosopher*. My aim, in making this copy (*apographē*), was on the one hand to acquire as far as possible, *by the very act of writing*, a more exact understanding of what Iamblichus was saying, and on the other to bring to greater clarity and measure this man's sublimity of thought, which is inaccessible to most people. Third, it was also in a certain manner to concentrate in a shorter form the abundant mass of commentaries of all kinds . . . (*In Cat.* 3.2–9)

This text clearly distinguishes two acts: the literal copying is a meditation that leads the philosopher's intellect to a "more exact," i.e., true, understanding of the difficult doctrines expounded by his predecessor, and this copying alternates with a labor of literary recomposition (simplification of expression and summary of earlier exegeses). Further, the use of the phrase "more exact intelligence" suggests that the act of copying (*apographē*) plays an essential role in awakening *Truth*, which is one of the three "anagogical powers" (Love, Truth, Faith) that determine the dynamism of prayer according to Proclus and Simplicius (Hoffmann, 2000a). This observation gains in interest when we observe, elsewhere in the work of the same exegete, that the literary whole comprising his commentaries on the *Physics* and on the *De Caelo* culminates in a final prayer in the first person, addressed to the Demiurge, which describes the Commentary itself as a "hymn" in honor of the Demiurge and the World. The hymn is meant for a god, which shows how much the exegesis of Aristotle was oriented toward Neoplatonic spirituality.

How Commentaries Were Composed

The exegesis proceeds according to a division into "lemmas" – shorter or longer sections of the text receiving commentary – and the commentator sometimes distinguishes between the explication of words (*lexis*) and the explication of points of doctrine (*theōria*) (Festugière, 1963 [1971]). Commentaries often deployed a huge documentation, and we know that Simplicius's commentaries abound with quotations and paraphrases of philosophers (beginning with the pre-Socratics) and earlier exegetes belong to the peripatetic and Neoplatonic traditions. Again, the notion of an "authority" – who might be cited through intermediaries – must be carefully distinguished from that of a direct "source": in his Commentary on the *Categories*, a large part of Simplicius's vast documentation comes from his principal if not exclusive sources, which are Porphyry's Commentary *Ad Gedalium* and Iamblichus's Commentary, itself dependent on Porphyry.

The quantitative extent of the commentaries of late antiquity also raises the question of the material media employed – the use during this period of large-format *codices* is known – but we are reduced to making prudent suppositions about the use of micrography to make whole folios or their margins (see below) hold large quantities of text: an important Byzantine manuscript of Aristotle's *Organon*, the *Vaticanus Urbinas graecus* 35 (copied for Arethas of Caesaria around 900) offers an example of micrography used for the transcription of marginal Neoplatonic commentaries, and it may be the heir of a much more ancient book-making tradition.

It may also be asked, still more concretely, what kind of books were used by the Neoplatonic commentators, and how the pages of commentaries were laid out (Hoffmann, 2000b). A major phenomenon of the history of commentaries in antiquity was the transition from the practice of putting the text commented upon and the commentary in separate books (rolls) to the practice of reuniting the commentary with text receiving commentary in the same book and on the same page – parceling the commentary out in the margins or encircling the text commented upon.

Three sets of items of evidence for the existence of commentaries written in the margins of manuscripts should be mentioned: the question is inseparably both codicological (since it is a matter of layout, the use of the space on the page) and literary (in the sense that the very composition of a commentary could take place directly in the margins of a copy, or could depend on sources distributed on the margins of another volume).

Thus the commentary on Hesiod's *Works and Days*, attributed to Proclus by the tradition and by the *Suda*, is in fact a commentary by Plutarch of Chaeronea, substantially annotated, in the margins of a copy, by Proclus, to whom the whole was then attributed: the study of this case allows us to understand the phenomenon of direct composition of a marginal commentary (Farragiana di Sarzana, 1978, 1981, 1987).

The *Life of Proclus*, by his disciple Marinus, furnishes an analogous case. The biographer informs us that Proclus, at his request, would record long commentaries of his own making in the margins of a commentary by Syrianus on Orpheus (see Brisson, 1987). This is what is described in a passage from chapter 27 of this *Life* (Saffrey and Segonds, 2001, p. 32):

> As one day I was reading in his presence the poems of Orpheus and heard him not only relating, in his explications, what Iamblichus and Syrianus said about them, but also adding many other developments more suited to Orphic theology, I asked the philosopher not to leave any longer without commentary a poetry so divinely inspired, but to comment on it too in a perfectly complete manner. And he replied to me that he had often wished to write a commentary, but that he had been obviously prevented by certain dreams: he had seen, he said, his teacher himself, who forbade him, with threats. Whereupon I thought of another way of proceeding: I begged him to consent to record his opinions in the margins of Syrianus's books. As our master, a perfect image of the Good, agreed to this, and made notes in the commentaries of Syrianus, we thus obtained, in the same book, a collection of all their opinions; and so there are also scholia and commentaries by Proclus on Orpheus which are of many lines, even though he was not able to annotate up to the end of the mythology, nor all of the *Rhapsodies*.

Proclus, therefore, had at hand a copy of Syrianus's commentary with margins large enough for him to be able to write in them scholia and commentaries corresponding to the exegesis he developed orally, in one of the last stages of the Neoplatonic cursus of study. As in the case of the commentary on Hesiod, we grasp a very interesting link between the process of literary composition and its codicological frame. Supplementary confirmation of these conclusions comes from the strange fact that the *Suda* attributes to both Syrianus and Proclus the same two works bearing on Orphism: *On the Theology of Orpheus* and *Harmony (Sumphōnia) of Orpheus, Pythagoras, and Plato with the Chaldaean Oracles*. It has been shown that these works are substantially due to Syrianus – and this fact is historically important, since the *Sumphōnia*, as we have seen, is like a manifesto of the exegetical presuppositions of the Neoplatonic school in the fifth and sixth centuries. Systematic examination of the quotations from the *Rhapsodies* by Damascius – who comments upon Orphic theology and integrates it into the Neoplatonic system by associating it with the testimony and authority of the *Chaldaean Oracles* – has been able to show that Damascius certainly had before him the famous copy of the commentaries of Syrianus (the *Sumphōnia* in particular) whose large margins contained the scholia and commentaries by Proclus (Brisson, 1991). Thus we glimpse the existence of a sacred book of the library in which the successors of Plato worked in the fifth and sixth century.

The sacred significance of such a book – preserved in all probability in the library of the school of Athens – in the eyes of these last pagan devotees, the Neoplatonic philosophers, is attested by an anecdote, reported by Damascius himself in his *Life of Isidorus* (= *Historia Philosopha*), which mentions – we may suppose – other copies of the same Orphic texts. In Alexandria, a "pagan monk" by the name of Sarapion lived in solitude, who cultivated poverty and whose spiritual life went far beyond the technical

617

subtleties of philosophy. On this account he possessed only two or three books, among them the poems of Orpheus, and these were the books that he sent to Isidorus, the teacher of Damascius, as an act of spiritual recognition (*Vita Isidori*, fr. 287 *Suda*; 231.5–6 and 233.2–4 Zintzen; see Festugière, 1966 [1971, p. 584]).

The third bit of evidence, which is more problematic, is no less interesting. In order to explain the composition and the thematic choices of Boethius, whose commentaries on Aristotle used Athenian sources, James Shiel (1958, 1987) has hypothesized that Boethius had before him a manuscript of Aristotle whose vast margins were filled with an anthology, arranged in "chains," of extracts from Neoplatonic commentaries, especially Porphyry's. This opinion has been disputed by another specialist, Sten Ebbesen (1987), who judges that the same literary and doctrinal phenomena can be explained by the use of *codices* including only commentaries – for example, a complete Porphyry. The question must therefore remain open, but taken together these several kinds of evidence open up stimulating perspectives on the concrete circumstances of the composition of ancient commentaries.

Bibliography

Works Cited

Brisson, L. (1987). "Proclus et l'Orphisme." In J. Pépin and H. D. Saffrey (eds.), *Proclus lecteur et interprète des Anciens* (pp. 43–104). Paris: Éditions du CNRS.

——. (1991). "Damascius et l'Orphisme." *Recherches et Rencontres*, 3, *Orphisme et Orphée* (Festschrift for Jean Rudhardt), 157–209.

——. (2000). "La place des *Oracles Chaldaïques* dans la *Théologie Platonicienne*." In A. P. Segonds and C. Steel (eds.), *Proclus et la Théologie Platonicienne* (pp. 109–62). Leuven-Paris: Actes du Colloque International de Louvain.

Ebbesen, S. (1987). "Boethius as an Aristotelian scholar." In J. Wiesner (ed.), *Aristoteles: Werk und Wirkung.* (Festschrift for Paul Moraux) (vol. 2, pp. 286–311). Berlin: de Gruyter. Repr. under the title, "Boethius as an Aristotelian Commentator." In R. Sorabji (ed.), *Aristotle Transformed. The Ancient Commentators and their Influence* (pp. 373–91). Ithaca, NY: Cornell University Press.

Farragiana di Sarzana, C. (1978). "Il commentario Procliano alle *Opere e i Giorni*. I. Plutarco Fonte di Proclo." *Aevum*, 52, 17–40.

——. (1981). "Il commentario Procliano alle *Opere e i Giorni*. II. Destinazione e fortuna dell'opera nella Scuola d'Atene e dopo la sua chiusura." *Aevum*, 55, 22–9.

——. (1987). "Le commentaire à Hésiode et la Paideia encyclopédique de Proclus." In J. Pépin and H. D. Saffrey (eds.), *Proclus lecteur et interprète des Anciens* (pp. 21–41). Paris: Éditions du CNRS.

Festugière, A.-J. (1963). "Modes de composition des Commentaires de Proclus." *Museum Helveticum*, 20. Repr. in A.-J. Festugière (1971) *Études de philosophie grecque* (pp. 551–74). Paris: Vrin.

——. (1966). "Proclus et la religion traditionnelle." In *Mélanges André Piganiol* (pp. 1581–90). Paris. Repr in A.-J. Festugière (1971) *Études de philosophie grecque* (pp. 575–84). Paris: Vrin.

——. (1969). "L'ordre de lecture des dialogues de Platon aux Ve/VIe siècles." *Museum Helveticum*, 26, 281–96. Repr in A.-J. Festugière (1971) *Études de philosophie grecque* (pp. 535–50). Paris: Vrin.

——. (1971). *Études de philosophie grecque*. Paris: Vrin.

Goulet-Cazé, M.-O. (1982). "L'arrière-plan scolaire de la *'Vie de Plotin.'*" In L. Brisson, M.-O. Goulet-Cazé, R. Goulet, and D. O'Brien (eds.), *Porphyre. La Vie de Plotin.* (vol. 1): *Travaux préliminaires et index grec complet* (pp. 229–80). Paris: Vrin.

Hadot, I. (1978). *Le problème du néoplatonisme alexandrin: Hiéroclès et Simplicius.* Paris: Études augustiniennes.

——. (1984). *Arts libéraux et philosophie dans la pensée antique.* Paris: Études augustiniennes.

——. (1987a). "Les introductions aux commentaires exégétiques chez les auteurs néoplatoniciens et les auteurs chrétiens." In M. Tardieu (ed.), *Les règles de l'interprétation* (pp. 99–122). Paris: Cerf. Repr. in I. Hadot, Ph. Hoffmann, P. Hadot, and J.-P. Mahé (1990). *Simplicius. Commentaire sur les "Catégories"* (pp. 21–47). Trans. (into French) directed by I. Hadot. (vol. 1): *Introduction. Première partie* [pp. 1–9, 3 Kalbfleisch]. Leiden: Brill.

——. (ed.). (1987b). *Simplicius: sa vie, son oeuvre, sa survie* (pp. 183–221). Berlin: de Gruyter.

——. (1991). "The Role of the Commentaries on Aristotle in the Teaching of Philosophy According to the Prefaces of the Neoplatonic Commentaries on the *Categories*." In H. Blumenthal and H. Robinson (eds.), *Aristotle and the Later Tradition* (= *Oxford Studies in Ancient Philosophy.* Suppl. vol. 1991) (pp. 175–89). Oxford: Oxford University Press.

——. (1992). "Aristote dans l'enseignement philosophique néoplatonicien. Les préfaces des commentaires sur les 'Catégories.'" *Revue de Théologie et de Philosophie,* 124, 407–25.

——. (1996). *Commentaire de Simplicius sur le "Manuel" d'Épictète.* Introduction and Critical Edition of the Greek Text. Leiden: Brill.

Hadot, I., Hoffmann, Ph., Hadot, P., and Mahé, J.-P. (1990). *Simplicius. Commentaire sur les "Categories."* Trans. (into French) directed by I. Hadot. (vol. 1): *Introduction. Première partie.* Leiden: Brill.

Hadot, P. (1968). "Philosophie, exégèse et contre-sens." *Akten des XIV. internationalen Kongresses für Philosophie* (vol. 1, pp. 333–9). Repr. in P. Hadot (1998) *Études de Philosophie Ancienne* (pp. 3–11). Paris: Les Belles Lettres.

——. (1979). "Les divisions des parties de la philosophie dans l'Antiquité." *Museum Helveticum,* 36, 201–23. Repr. in P. Hadot (1998) *Études de Philosophie Ancienne* (pp. 125–58). Paris: Les Belles Lettres.

——. (1987). "Théologie, exégèse, révélation, Ecriture, dans la philosophie grecque." In M. Tardieu (ed.), *Les règles de l'interprétation* (pp. 13–34). Paris: Cerf. Repr. in P. Hadot (1998) *Études de Philosophie Ancienne* (pp. 27–58). Paris: Les Belles Lettres.

——. (1998). *Études de Philosophie Ancienne.* Paris: Les Belles Lettres.

Hoffmann, Ph. (1987a). "Catégories et langage selon Simplicius – La question du *skopos* du traité aristotélicien des *Catégories*." In I. Hadot (ed.), *Simplicius: sa vie, son oeuvre, sa survie* (pp. 61–90). Berlin: de Gruyter.

——. (1987b). "Sur quelques aspects de la polémique de Simplicius contre Jean Philopon: de l'invective à la réaffirmation de la transcendance du Ciel." In I. Hadot (ed.), *Simplicius: sa vie, son oeuvre, sa survie* (pp. 183–221). Berlin: de Gruyter.

——. (1994). "Notice D3: DAMASCIUS." In R. Goulet (ed.), *Dictionnaire des Philosophes Antiques* (vol. 2, pp. 541–93). Paris: Éditions du CNRS.

——. (1997). "La problématique du titre des traités d'Aristote selon les commentateurs grecs. Quelques exemples." In J.-C. Fredouille, M.O., Goulet-Cazé, Ph. Hoffmann, P. Petitmengin, and S. Deléani (eds.), *Titres et articulations du texte dans les œuvres antiques* (pp. 75–103). Paris: Études augustiniennes.

——. (1998). "La fonction des prologues exégétiques dans la pensée pédagogique néoplatonicienne." In B. Roussel and J.-D. Dubois (eds.), *Entrer en matière* (pp. 209–45). Paris: Cerf.

——. (2000a). "La triade chaldaïque *Erōs, Alētheia, Pistis* de Proclus à Simplicius." In A. P. Segonds and C. Steel (eds.), *Proclus et la Théologie Platonicienne* (pp. 459–89). Paris: Les Belles Lettres.

———. (2000b). "Bibliothèques et formes du livre à la fin de l'Antiquité. Le témoignage de la littérature néoplatonicienne des Ve et VIe siècles." In G. Prato (ed.), *I Manoscritti greci tra riflessione e dibattito* (pp. 601–32). Florence: Edizioni Gonnelli.

Lewy, H. (1956). *Chaldaean Oracles and Theurgy. Mysticism, Magic and Platonism in the Later Roman Empire.* Le Caire: Institut français d'archéologie orientale. (2nd edn., 1978), M. Tardieu (ed.). Paris: Études augustiniennes.

Pépin, J. and Saffrey, H. D. (eds.). (1987). *Proclus lecteur et interprète des Anciens* (pp. 137–51). Paris: Éditions du CNRS.

Richard, M. (1950). "*Apo phōnēs.*" *Byzantion*, 20, 191–222. Repr. in M. Richard (1976–7). *Opera Minora* (3 vols.). Turnhout-Louvain: Brepols.

Saffrey, H. D. (1975). "Allusions anti-chrétiennes chez Proclus, le diadoque platonicien." *Revue des Sciences philosophiques et théologiques*, 59, 553–63. Repr. in H. D. Saffrey (1990) *Recherches sur le néoplatonisme après Plotin* (pp. 201–11). Paris: Vrin.

———. (1981). "Les Néoplatoniciens et les Oracles Chaldaïques." *Revue des Études augustiniennes*, 27, 209–25. Repr. in H. D. Saffrey (1990) *Recherches sur le néoplatonisme après Plotin* (pp. 63–79). Paris: Vrin.

———. (1984a). "La théurgie comme phénomène culturel chez les néoplatoniciens (IVe–Ve siècles)." *Koinōnia*, 8, 161–71. Repr. in H. D. Saffrey (1990) *Recherches sur le néoplatonisme après Plotin* (pp. 51–61). Paris: Vrin.

———. (1984b). "Quelques aspects de la spiritualité des philosophes néoplatoniciens de Jamblique à Proclus et Damascius." *Revue des sciences philosophiques et théologiques*, 68, 169–82. Repr. in H. D. Saffrey (1990) *Recherches sur le néoplatonisme après Plotin* (pp. 213–26). Paris: Vrin.

———. (1984c). "La dévotion de Proclus au Soleil." In *Philosophies non chrétiennes et christianisme* (pp. 73–86). Brussells: Éditions de l'Université de Bruxelles. Repr. in H. D. Saffrey (2000) *Le néoplatonisme après Plotin* (pp. 179–91). Paris: Vrin.

———. (1984d). "La 'Théologie Platonicienne' de Proclus, fruit de l'exégèse du 'Parménide.'" *Revue de Théologie et de Philosophie*, 116, 1–12. Repr. in H. D. Saffrey (1990) *Recherches sur le néoplatonisme après Plotin* (pp. 173–84). Paris: Vrin.

———. (1987). "Proclus, diadoque de Platon." In J. Pépin and H. D. Saffrey (eds.), *Proclus lecteur et interprète des Anciens* (pp. 43–104). Paris: Éditions du CNRS. Repr. in H. D. Saffrey (1990) *Recherches sur le néoplatonisme après Plotin* (pp. 141–58). Paris: Vrin.

———. (1990). *Recherches sur le néoplatonisme après Plotin.* Paris: Vrin.

———. (1992). "Accorder entre elles les traditions théologiques: une caractéristique du néoplatonisme athénien." In E. P. Bos and P. A. Meijer (eds.), *On Proclus and his Influence in Medieval Philosophy* (pp. 35–50). Leiden: Brill. Repr. in H. D. Saffrey (2000) *Le néoplatonisme après Plotin* (pp. 43–158). Paris: Vrin.

———. (1994). *Proclus. Hymnes et prières.* Paris: Arfuyen.

———. (1996). "Les débuts de la théologie comme science (IIIe–VIe siècle)." *Revue des Sciences philosophiques et théologiques*, 80, 201–20. Repr. in H. D. Saffrey (2000) *Le néoplatonisme après Plotin* (pp. 219–38). Paris: Vrin.

———. (2000). *Le néoplatonisme après Plotin.* Paris: Vrin.

Saffrey, H. D. and Segonds, A.-P. (2001). (with collaboration of Concetta Luna). *Marinus: Proclus, ou sur le Bonheur.* Texte établi, traduit et annoté. Paris: Collection des Universités de France.

Shiel, J. (1958). "Boethius' Commentaries on Aristotle." *Medieval and Renaissance Studies*, 4, 217–44. A reworked version (with a bibliographical update) in R. Sorabji (ed.) (1990) *Aristotle Transformed. The Ancient Commentators and their Influence* (pp. 349–72). Ithaca, NY: Cornell University Press.

———. (1987). "The Greek Copy of Porphyrios' *Isagoge* used by Boethius." In J. Wiesner (ed.), *Aristoteles: Werk und Wirkung.* (Festschrift for Paul Moraux) (vol. 2, pp. 312–40). Berlin: de Gruyter.

Tarán, L. (1984). "Amicus Plato sed magis amica veritas. From Plato and Aristotle to Cervantes." *Antike und Abendland*, 30, 93–124.

Tardieu, M. (1990). *Les paysages reliques. Routes et haltes syriennes d'Isidore à Simplicius*. Leuven/Paris: Peeters.

van den Berg, R. M. (2001). *Proclus' Hymns*. Leiden: Brill.

van Liefferinge, C. (1999). *La Théurgie, des* Oracles Chaldaïques *à Proclus*. Liège: Centre international d'étude de la religion grecque antique.

Westerink, L. G. (1971). "Damascius, commentateur de Platon." In *Le néoplatonisme* (pp. 253–60). Paris: Editions du CNRS. Repr. in L. G. Westerink (1980). *Texts and Studies in Neoplatonism and Byzantine Literature* (pp. 271–8). Amsterdam: Hakkert.

Westerink, L. G., Trouillard, J., and Segonds, A.-P. (1990). *Prolégomènes à la Philosophie de Platon*. Paris: Collection des Universités de France.

Further Reading

The Greek texts of the Neoplatonic commentators on Aristotle have been edited in the series, Commentaria in Aristotelem Graeca (cited as CAG), and a large number of them are currently available in English translation in the series, Ancient Commentators on Aristotle, directed by Richard K. Sorabji (published by Duckworth and Cornell). Collections of studies have been mentioned in the above bibliography of references.

The following will also be read with profit:

Busse, A. (1891). *Ammonius in Porphyrii isagogen sive quinque voces*. CAG 4.3. Berlin: Reimer.

Goulet-Cazé, M.-O. et al. (eds.). (2000). *Le Commentaire entre tradition et innovation*. Paris: Vrin.

Hadot, I. (1997). "Le commentaire philosophique continu dans l'Antiquité." *Antiquité tardive*, 5, 169–76.

Hadot, I. and Hadot, P. (2004). *Apprendre à philosopher dans l'Antiquité. L'enseignement du "Manuel d'Epictète" et son commentaire néoplatonicien*. Paris: Le Livre de Poche.

Hadot, P. (1974). "L'harmonie des philosophies de Plotin et d'Aristote selon Porphyre dans le Commentaire de Dexippe sur les *Catégories*." In *Plotino e il Neoplatonismo in Oriente e in Occidente* (pp. 31–47). Rome: Accademia nazionale dei Lincei. English version in R. Sorabji (ed.), (1990) *Aristotle Transformed: The Ancient Commentators and their Influence* (pp. 125–40). London: Duckworth / Ithaca, NY: Cornell University Press. Article repr. (in French) in P. Hadot (1999) *Plotin, Porphyre. Études néoplatoniciennes* (pp. 355–82). Paris: Les Belles Lettres.

——. (1976). "Le mythe de Narcisse et son interprétation par Plotin." *Nouvelle revue de psychanalyse*, 13, 81–108. Repr. in P. Hadot (1999) *Plotin, Porphyre. Études néoplatoniciennes* (pp. 225–66). Paris: Les Belles Lettres.

——. (1981). "Images mythiques et thèmes mystiques dans un passage de Plotin (V.8.10–13)." In *Néoplatonisme*. (Festschrift for Jean Trouillard) (pp. 205–14). *Les Cahiers de Fontenay* (École normale supérieure de Fontenay aux Roses), no. 19–22.

——. (1981). "Ouranos, Kronos and Zeus in Plotinus' Treatise against the Gnostics." In H. J. Blumenthal and R. A. Markus (eds.), *Neoplatonism and early Christian Thought*. (Festschrift for A. H. Armstrong) (pp. 124–37). London: Variorum Publications. [On the philosophical interpretation of the myth of Ouranos, Cronos and Zeus = the One, the Intellect of Spirit, the soul: a good example of the harmonization of traditional mythological data and of philosophical concepts].

——. (1993). *Exercices spirituels et philosophie antique*. Paris: Études augustiniennes. Revised and expanded edition. Paris: Michel, 2002.

——. (1995). *Qu'est-ce que la philosophie antique?* Paris: Gallimard/Folio.

Hoffmann, Ph. (trans.) & Luna, C. (2001). *Simplicius. Commentaire sur les* Catégories *d'Aristote. Chapitres 2–4* (Trans. [into French] by Ph. Hoffmann and Commentary by C. Luna). Paris: Les Belles Lettres.

Pépin, J. (1966). "Porphyre, exégète d'Homère." In *Porphyre. Entretiens sur l'Antiquité Classique* (pp. 231–66). Vandœuvres-Genève: Fondation Hardt.

Saffrey, H. D. (1981). "L'Hymne IV de Proclus, prière aux dieux des Oracles Chaldaïques." In *Néoplatonisme* (Festschrift for Jean Trouillard) (pp. 297–312). Fontenay-aux-Roses. Repr. in H. D. Saffrey (2000) *Le néoplatonisme après Plotin* (pp. 193–206). Paris: Vrin.

———. (1981). "Les néoplatoniciens et les mythes grecs." In Y. Bonnefoy (ed.), *Dictionnaire des mythologies et des religions des sociétés traditionnelles et du monde antique.* (vol. 2 [K–Z], pp. 157–63). Paris: Flammarion.

———. (1987). "Comment Syrianus, le maître de l'école néoplatonicienne d'Athènes, considérait-il Aristote?" In J. Wiesner (ed.), *Aristoteles: Werk und Wirkung* (Festschrift for Paul Moraux) (vol. 2, pp. 205–14). Berlin: de Gruyter. Repr. in H. D. Saffrey (1990) *Recherches sur le néoplatonisme après Plotin* (pp. 131–40). Paris: Vrin. Version in English, entitled "How did Syrianus regard Aristotle?" in R. Sorabji (ed.) (1990) *Aristotle Transformed: The Ancient Commentators and their Influence* (pp. 173–79). London: Duckworth/ Ithaca, NY: Cornell University Press.

———. (1992). "Proclus, les Muses et l'amour des livres à Athènes au Ve siècle." In H. J. Westra (ed.). *From Athens to Chartres. Neoplatonism and Medieval Thought.* (Festschrift for Edouard Jeauneau) (pp. 163–71). Leiden: Brill. Repr. in H. D. Saffrey (2000) *Le néoplatonisme après Plotin* (pp. 169–77). Paris: Vrin.

Sheppard, A. (1987). "Proclus' Philosophical Method of Exegesis: The Use of Aristotle and the Stoics in the Commentary on the *Cratylus.*" In Pépin, J. and Saffrey, H. D. (eds.), *Proclus lecteur et interprète des Anciens* (pp. 137–51). Paris: Éditions du CNRS.

Sorabji, R. (ed.). (1990). *Aristotle Transformed: The Ancient Commentators and their Influence.* London: Duckworth/ Ithaca, NY: Cornell University Press.

———. (2005). *The Philosophy of the Commentators, 200–600 AD: A Sourcebook.* (3 vols.). Ithaca, NY: Cornell University Press/ London: Duckworth.

Steel, C. (1992). "Le *Sophiste* comme texte théologique dans l'interprétation de Proclus." In E. P. Bos and P. A. Meijer (eds.), *On Proclus and his Influence in Medieval Philosophy* (pp. 51–64). Leiden: Brill.

Strange, S. K. (1987). "Plotinus, Porphyry, and the Neoplatonic Interpretation of the 'Categories'." *ANRW* II 36.2 (pp. 955–74).

Part VI

Culture, Philosophy, and the Sciences

Part XII

Critical Philosophy and the Sciences

32

Greek Philosophy and Religion

GÁBOR BETEGH

When one considers the relationship between philosophy and religion in antiquity, what springs into one's mind most readily is probably the trial and execution of Socrates. Socrates, who in many ways represents the paradigmatic figure of the philosopher, was tried on charges of impiety, found guilty, and executed by the Athenians. We could then continue by enumerating similar cases – the trials of Anaxagoras, Protagoras, and Diagoras, all three on charges of impiety. These infamous stories might very well suggest that the relationship between philosophy and religion was that of vehement and violent clashes: the philosopher, the free-thinking intellectual, did not respect the religious dogmas and institutions imposed by tradition, whereas the religious powers of the city brutally penalized all such transgressions.

On closer inspection it turns out however that, apart from the trial of Socrates, it is outstandingly difficult to establish even the most basic historical facts about these cases. It remains open to debate whether Anaxagoras and Protagoras were actually brought to trial, or whether the lyric poet Diagoras had anything to do with philosophy. But even if we take at face value everything that we can gather from later, mainly Hellenistic, sources, we have to realize that all these cases are concentrated in the very specific political and intellectual climate of Athens around the end of the fifth century BCE. When one broadens the perspective and examines the whole period from the sixth century BCE to the sixth century CE, from Ionia to Italy, one starts to realize, on the contrary, how exceptional these Athenian trials were, and in general how relaxed the relationship between religion and philosophy was. It turns out that all through antiquity, from Xenophanes to the late Neoplatonists, philosophers kept formulating their views about the nature of the divine, and these views always meant a vast departure from the traditional representations of the gods, and often incorporated a criticism of traditional religious attitudes. These views and criticisms were no less radical than the ones pronounced by Socrates, yet they did not result in open hostility. It starts to appear, then, that the trial of Socrates is not at all characteristic; what needs explanation is rather why in this particular case and in those specific historical circumstances the community reacted in such an extreme form.[1]

It is no less remarkable that, by and large, the philosophers' attitude towards traditional religiosity was a mixture of innovation, criticism, and conservativism. They were openly critical of many forms of traditional beliefs and certain forms of religious

---

1. On the case of Socrates, see the papers in Smith and Woodruff (2000), and especially Parker (2000); in this volume see Morrison, SOCRATES.

practice, but they were convinced (with some very rare exceptions) that the religious institutions sanctioned by tradition should be preserved. In a way, philosophers did exactly what the indictment against Socrates states – "they did not believe in the gods of the city and introduced new gods" – in so far as they propounded radically novel views about the nature and role of the divine. The philosophers themselves, however, most often presented their radical views as mere amendments, conceptual clarifications, or even as a return to a more ancient tradition. They conceived of their novel ideas as corrections that can render existing forms of religious worship genuinely meaningful.

Ancient lists of those who denied the existence of gods include Prodicus of Ceos, Theodorus of Cyrene, Critias of Athens and Euhemerus. As far as we can reconstruct it on the basis of the rather scanty evidence, the common strategy of these people was to explain the origin of the worship of the gods without reference to higher, divine powers. Prodicus, for example, said that early man deified "the fruits of earth and virtually everything that contributed to his subsistence." Some human beings were also deified because of their outstanding contribution to human culture: Demeter because she introduced corn, Dionysus because he introduced wine (Philod. *De Piet.* PHerc. 1428 fr. 19 trans. Henrichs and PHerc. 1428 col. 3.12–13 Henrichs (= DK 84B5)). So it is not the case that there is nothing corresponding to the recipients of traditional cults, but rather that they do not belong to a different, divine sphere of reality. Critias, on the other hand, was included in the lists of atheists on account of a theory expounded by a character in one of his plays. According to this theory a clever man introduced the idea of god in order to make people fear divine retribution for wrong-doing and thereby make them more law-abiding (S.E. *M* 9.54).[2]

Even if these views were not sustained by philosophical arguments, they could make the question "Whether the gods exist?" a legitimate philosophical topic (cf. e.g., Arist. *APo.* II.1, 89b33; Cic. *ND* 2.4; S.E. *M* 9.49; Aët. *Placit.* 1.7). As a reaction, all major philosophers from the time of Plato developed proofs *for* the existence of god(s), but no one *against* it. It seems that philosophical atheism in antiquity was a straw-man. It remains true, of course, that philosophers could still call one another "godless" on account of their contrasting characterizations of gods. Moreover, besides producing arguments for the existence of gods, philosophers were also keen to explain that their tenets were perfectly compatible with traditional forms of religiosity and could sustain institutional forms of religious practice – and these arguments, it seems, were not simple cover-ups to avoid charges of impiety. Thus, philosophers conceived their innovations and criticisms not as a rupture with traditional religiosity or a devastating attack from the outside, but as internal reforms grounded on a genuine understanding of the nature of the divine. The norm, as it turns out, was that the community and the religious authorities tolerated the philosophers' speculations, whereas the philosophers formulated their respective tenets within the traditional framework.

2.   Protagoras of Abdera is also a standard item on the ancient lists of atheists, although he apparently never said that "the gods do not exist." The famous opening sentence of his *On Gods* is agnostic also in this respect: "As to the gods, I cannot know either that they exist or that they do not exist, or what their form is; for there are many obstacles to knowing it: both the obscurity of the question and the shortness of life" (D.L. 9.51). On Protagoras, see Barney, THE SOPHISTIC MOVEMENT, in this volume.

The Framework of Greek Religion

Although the Greeks did not have a word corresponding to the English word "religion," religious phenomena were ubiquitous, organizing every moment of a Greek's life. There was a god supervising or protecting every human action, public or private, from morning to evening, from birth to death, and beyond death. Rivers, forests, seas, mountains, and the heavenly bodies were also identified as divinities or seen as inhabited by gods. It was Zeus who rained, and the sea stormed because Poseidon was angry. Although we are not sure how exactly Thales meant it, his dictum that "everything is full of gods" (DK 11A22) seems a fair representation of the Greek experience.[3]

The relationship between humans and gods was established and maintained through ritual. As all major and minor activities were put under the auspices of the gods, it was imperative to obtain the sanction of the relevant god for the successful performance of any action. It meant in practice that everyday private and public life was organized around sacrifices, ritual actions with the aim of gaining divine approval and cooperation. Large-scale public festivals also created and sustained social and political bonds between individuals as well as cities, and they offered spiritual comfort and distraction from everyday life with processions, sport, dramatic, and other competitions.

This emphasis on ritual can be contrasted with the absence of dogma. Each Greek city had "sacred laws," carved in stone or bronze and displayed at public places, to regulate ritual behavior and to fix the calendar of public festivals. The performative side of the cult was fixed and regulated, but not its interpretation. There was no attempt to constitute and codify a creed, a corpus of indisputable beliefs about the divine and its relation to humans. In the absence of a regulatory dogma, contrasting conceptions and representations of the gods co-existed without any feeling of antagonism. The poems of Homer and Hesiod certainly created a general frame of reference and a standard way of thinking about the gods, but later authors, epic poets, and tragic writers, had no qualms formulating alternative accounts and were not reproached for doing so. The idea of heresy is entirely alien to Greek religion. *Eusebeia*, commendable religious attitude, consisted not in fidelity to a code of belief but in the correct performance of ritual obligations and regularly honoring the gods with generous, though not excessive, offerings.

Another, related, feature of Greek religion is that it had no separate priestly caste. There were of course role distinctions in the performance of public rituals and in the maintenance of places of cult. Yet the leading roles were in principle open to everyone, and were in practice attributed on the basis of social, political and economic power, family membership, or in certain cases by lot. Cultic offices were not connected to special claims of authoritative knowledge about the gods and did not confer special powers on the priests to control and repress alternative views. In most cases, the political community retained the ultimate control over religious matters. Not a priest but a group of ordinary citizens raised the charges against Socrates, and not a clerical body but the assembly of the Athenians decided his case.

---

3.   Cf. Hussey, THE BEGINNINGS OF SCIENCE AND PHILOSOPHY IN ARCHAIC GREECE, in this volume.

Greek religion is also characterized by the co-existence of local variants. The "sacred laws" varied a great deal from one polis to another. Most of the festivals and cult places were also local. The mythical narratives about the gods were often connected to local cults and showed a considerable degree of variation. On the other hand, from the eighth century BCE onwards, some sanctuaries had attained a wider importance and were developed into Pan-Hellenic cult centers. Such cult centers, together with the poems of Homer and Hesiod, constituted shared points of reference and created a sense of identity. The recognition of the underlying unity did not however demand standardization; differences and variety were acknowledged as a fact.

The above characterization is formulated with constant reference to the polis as the framework of political and social life. It shows the resilience of the institutions of Greek religion that they could survive practically intact through the political and social changes of the Hellenistic age. It remains true, on the other hand, that the disruption of the polis brought with it the growing importance of mystery cults, which focused more on the individual and his or her spiritual needs.

This general framework opened up the possibilities and set the limits for the philosopher in matters of religion. The lack of a fixed corpus of beliefs made it possible for the philosopher to formulate radical views about the gods and still feel himself part of the tradition. The same can explain that the community could accept the philosopher's speculations provided that these did not undermine the belief in the social and spiritual importance of the established institutions of worship. The absence of a priestly caste meant that the philosopher did not need to compete in claims of knowledge with members of a fixed social group endowed with special authority and power. The rivals were the traditional poets, Homer above all, but there was no clergy to challenge and no high priest to control the philosopher's teachings. Remarkably, Socrates does not cross-question a priest but the religious fanatic Euthyphro in order to destroy unfounded claims of knowledge about "piety." Finally, the recognition of co-existing variants made the community more tolerant towards the alternative ideas offered by the philosopher, as long as these views were not felt to threaten the social cohesion and moral order created by shared institutions of cult.

In the absence of a separate clerical class philosophers were confident that it was *their* special competence to inquire into the nature of the divine and to define the correct human attitude towards the gods. Before philosophy emerged as a professionalized intellectual activity roughly in the generation of Socrates, the pre-Socratic "sage" could both be a religious teacher and engage in speculations that are philosophically interesting. Pythagoras and Empedocles are examples of this type. But theology remained a primarily phylosophical discipline even later. So Aristotle could claim that theology is first philosophy (*Met.* E.1), and Chrysippus could say that theology is the "fulfillment" (*teletai*) of philosophy (*SVF* 2.42).

Paradoxically, the very features that made the philosopher's enterprise possible became also his main targets. As we shall see in the last section of this chapter, the main thrust of the philosophical critique of religion concerns its ritualistic behavioral character. Furthermore, philosophical conceptions of the divine had universalistic claims, leaving very little room for local or individual variation. Because the philosopher had strong views about the nature of the divine, he thought he knew what others should consider true. The religious *beliefs* of the citizen in Plato's *Laws* are under much stricter control than in any existing Greek polis.[4] In a way, philosophers tried to fix what was left fluid by traditional forms of representation and seize the role left open by traditional religious institutions.

The Conceptualization of the Divine

As we have seen, the presence of gods was felt in every sphere of the world, and ritualized forms of honoring the gods created the fiber of public and private life. But who are, after all, these gods who permeate the world and are worshiped in cult? Of course, stories are told and poems are composed about their births, marriages, dealings, and fights with each other, as well as their involvement in human affairs. Their images are displayed in cult statues and on paintings. But what is the ground for these pictorial representations and how much can we accept of these often contradictory stories? After all, who or what is a god? What does its characteristic activity consist in, and what is its role in our world? And, on the whole, can we find answers to these questions, and if so, where shall we start? This approach to the gods and their traditional representations is characterized by critical reason, demands of coherence, and some form of reductionism; a way of thinking that we may call philosophical.[5]

The first author whose work prominently displays this attitude is Xenophanes of Colophon (ca. 570–475 BCE). His reflections on the nature of the divine already contain in germ many of the major tenets that later philosophers will work out in more detail and argue for with a more sophisticated conceptual apparatus. Xenophanes' theology comprises a critical and a constructive aspect. The critical aspect consists in an attempt to isolate and discard traits which popular belief commonly but mistakenly attributes to the gods. He shows that the origin of such attributions is that people tend to picture the gods in their own image: "Ethiopians say that their gods are snub-nosed and black; / Thracians that theirs are blue-eyed and red-haired" (DK 21B16, trans. Lesher, 1992). Clearly, such bodily traits are accidental and their differences do not affect a shared core notion of the gods. Xenophanes in a remarkable thought experiment carries the argument to the extreme and shows that practically all anthropomorphic features belong in this class:

> But if horses or oxen, or lions had hands
> or could draw with their hands and accomplish such works as men,
> horses would draw the figures of the gods as similar to horses, and the oxen as similar
> to oxen,
> and they would make the bodies
> of the sort which each of them had. (DK 21B15)

4. On the theology in Plato's *Laws*, see Lane, PLATO'S POLITICAL PHILOSOPHY, section on the *Laws*, in this volume.
5. I shall treat the notion of philosophical theology restrictively and shall not discuss cases in which an entity (the *archē* of the pre-Socratics or Plato's Forms) is called "divine" on account of some of its characteristics. For a defense of such a restriction, see Broadie (1999).

But how far can we go in stripping off non-essential features? What will remain as a shared, fundamental notion of the divine? Then again, this argument from "local variations" cannot prove that none of these contrasting accounts is correct, but only that we cannot rely on any of them in separating true from false. The outcome is two-fold. On the one hand, we come to understand that the basis of traditional representations is very shaky. On the other hand, the argument also shows that we are bound to the human perspective, and the human perspective has serious limitations, especially when it comes to understanding the gods (see e.g. DK 21B34).

The non-anthropomorphism of gods becomes a commonplace for later philosophers. But, remarkably, Plato still feels the need to emphasize that the cosmic god "needed no eyes, since there was nothing visible left outside it; nor did it need ears, since there was nothing audible there, either" and, for similar reasons, it did not need organs for breathing and eating, nor hands or feet (*Ti.* 33c–34a, trans. Zeyl 2000). Only the atomists continued to maintain, somewhat provocatively, that the gods have human shapes (Democritus: S.E. *M* 9.42; Epicurus: scholium to *KD* 1).[6]

Another crucial element in Xenophanes' criticism of popular representations of gods is ethical. He reproaches Homer and Hesiod for having attributed to the gods all kinds of immoral acts: "theft, adultery, and mutual deceit" (DK 21B11, B12). It is impossible to decide on the basis of the existing fragments whether Xenophanes considered the attribution of illicit actions as yet another aspect of ascribing anthropomorphic features to the gods, or whether instead he thought that immoral acts are incompatible with divine perfection. Probably both. This type of criticism has become especially emphatic in the dialogues of Plato. For Plato, and probably already for Socrates, the unquestionable major premise of all speculation about the gods is that: "A god really is good, and should be spoken of accordingly" (*Rep.* II, 379b1). Goodness conceived as the essential feature of the godhead entails that a god cannot do anything harmful either to other gods or to human beings.[7] Two conclusions follow necessarily. First, the view expressed by Homer and shared by most people that in human affairs the gods are the causes of good and bad alike, must be false. The gods can only be made responsible for what is good and beneficial for us; we ourselves are to be praised or blamed for the rest. The argument has crucial ramifications for ethical thinking as a whole, because it shifts the center of responsibility from divine to human agents. Second, the traditional stories in which gods are shown to hate and fight with each other, do injustices, and inflict punishments, must also be false. What is at issue here is not only the truth-value of the poetic representations of gods, but also their pragmatic role in forming the character of human beings. As Plato emphasizes, children grow up listening to these stories, and the divine beings presented there become powerful role models for them. So even when people commit such horrendous acts as inflicting harsh punishments on their fathers, they can simply point to Zeus and say that he did

---

6. On the Epicurean treatment of the gods, see Morel, EPICUREANISM, in this volume.

7. Empedocles is quite exceptional in this respect. He creates a dualistic scheme by positing two divine principles, Love and Strife, who, in addition to their respective physical functions, also represent opposite moral values. An enigmatic reference in Plato's *Laws* X (896e) has sometimes been interpreted as suggesting a comparable dualistic scheme. On the atomists' gods being harmful, see below.

the same to his father Kronos. Thus we have to condemn Homer and the other poets for speaking untruly about the gods and thereby corrupting the youth. Or – and this was the main line of defense both before and after the time of Plato – we have to say that, truly understood, Homer was speaking about something completely different and should be interpreted allegorically. So, for example, when Homer pictures the gods in fierce combat against each other in *Iliad* 20, in reality he is speaking about the interplay of physical elements in the cosmos.[8]

We can criticize the poetic accounts of the gods as being false, or we can declare that they speak about something else – either way we end up claiming that such stories are not directly informative about the gods. Along what lines could the philosopher then establish a substantive notion of divinity? The most common strategy was to isolate some traits of the gods from popular belief and set them as criteria for attributing further properties and functions. This method was there from the start but became explicit in the methodology of the Hellenistic schools when they took the "preconception" (*prolēpsis*) of god as the starting-point for theological inquiries. But we have already seen, for example, how Plato posits goodness as the core attribute of divinity, and then discards what is incompatible with it.

Another aspect of this strategy consists in amplifying the core feature (or features) and then identifying the divinity as that which shows the relevant feature at the highest degree. We find an early version of this reasoning in Xenophanes, who argues that the very notion of god entails that there is nothing greater (DK 21A28, A31 and C1). The same argument type appeared in many forms. Simplicius, for example, attributes the following argument to Aristotle:

> In general, where there is a better there is also a best. Since, then, among existing things one is better than another, there is also something that is best, which will be the divine. (Simpl. *In Cael.* 289.2–4 = Arist. *On Philosophy*, fr. 16 Rose)

Later authors, most prominently the Stoics, used this type of argument also with the aim of proving the existence of god:

> But that which is perfect and best will be better than man and fulfilled with all the virtues and not receptive of any evil; and this animal will not differ from god. God, therefore, exists. (S.E. *M* 9.88; cf. Cic. *ND* 2.33–39)

If we identify god as that which is the ultimate being in the relevant respect (goodness, greatness, power, etc.), will it not follow that there is only one god? Xenophanes' conclusion is inherently ambiguous: "There is one god greatest among gods and men" (DK 21B23.1). This wavering remains characteristic of later philosophers, too. Conceptual analysis, a theory of causes, reductionism, and requirements of theoretical parsimony in most cases drive the philosopher to the concept of a unique ultimate divinity. This one divine being, which is the first causal principle of the world and which stands in a fundamental relationship with the totality of things, is the god that

---

8.   For the different apologetic readings of this episode, see the scholium *Venetus B* to *Il.* 20.67, which probably goes back to Porphyry.

ultimately interests the philosopher. This tendency is manifest already in the pre-Socratic practice of calling the underlying principle of the world "divine." Aristotle explicitly claims that theology is the theoretical study of the first causes and first principles (see esp. *Met.* A.2, 982b28–983a10 and E.1, 1026a17–32). Then, in *Metaphysics* Λ, which contains his most elaborate discussion of the divine, he argues that there should be *one* ultimate divine substance on which the order of the whole world ultimately depends (Λ.7–8; see also *On Philosophy* fr. 17 Rose; *Phys.* VIII.6; *GC* II.10, 337a15–24).[9] Then he ends *Metaphysics* Λ with a quotation from Homer: "The rule of the many is not good; let there be one ruler" (10, 1076a4 quoting *Il.* 2.204).

Yet philosophers very often leave open the possibility that there are further, causally less relevant entities corresponding to traditional polytheistic conceptions. So Aristotle maintains that there are other, lesser celestial divinities of a fixed number. Indeed, he claims that, with due distinctions made, his conception of the eternal celestial substances corresponds to the intuition of primeval thinkers who spoke about a multitude of gods. The original insight subsequently got corrupted and this is how the mythical narratives about anthropomorphic gods were formulated "with a view to the persuasion of the multitude and to [their] legal and utilitarian expediency" (Λ.8, 1074b1–14). Similarly, Plato in the *Timaeus* draws the image of a first god, the divine craftsman, who is causally responsible for the entire visible universe. Yet he insists that there are also other, "younger" gods – the cosmos itself, celestial divinities, and even the gods of the traditional theogonies – who are situated at lower levels of the ontological hierarchy and who have more limited causal roles. According to Xenophon's testimony, Socrates made a comparable distinction between lesser gods and a unique first god who is causally responsible for the providential organization, structure, and maintenance of the whole world (*Mem.* 4.3.13).

The Stoics go even further. The Stoic god is the active principle that permeates and gives form to the other metaphysical principle, the completely passive and formless matter. This wholly immanent god is directly causally responsible for everything that exists and happens in the world, and can hence also be called "the common nature of things" or "the world itself."[10] Clearly, if god is defined as *the* active causal principle (or the world itself), it must be unique. The Stoics readily identified their god with Zeus, the one most powerful god of the tradition. On the other hand, they had no problem in speaking about gods in the plural. They considered the celestial bodies to be gods, and they also accommodated the traditional gods in their system via elaborate allegorical identifications.[11] What we find here is an attempt to mediate between a causal theory, positing one ultimate causal principle, on the one hand, and the traditional polytheistic pantheon, on the other.

A comparable effort is characteristic of the Neoplatonists. Following the Aristotelian conception, they considered theology as the study of the first causes, while in their highly speculative metaphysics they developed a complex hierarchy of causes. Yet, they,

---

9. See Bodnár and Pellegrin, ARISTOTLE'S PHYSICS AND COSMOLOGY, in this volume.

10. On the historical and philosophical connections between the Stoic god and Plato's *Timaeus*, see Sedley (2002).

11. See, e.g., D.L. 8.147; Cic. *ND* 2.63–69; Philod. *De Piet.* 1428 coll. 4.12–8.13 = coll. 356–360 (Obbink).

632

and especially the late Neoplatonists, also claimed that after the very first principle, the different levels of this hierarchy are identical with the different gods mentioned by Greek and non-Greek "theologians." The outcome, just to mention one example, is that the Neoplatonic "all-one," the second level in the triad of the so-called henadic principles, gets identified with the Chaos of Hesiod and the *Orphic Rhapsodies*, the Gaia of another Orphic theogony, the Night of Acusilaus and Epimenides, the Chthonia of Pherecydes of Syrus, the Thaute of the Babylonian myth, the Areimanios of the Persian magi and the Sand of the Egyptian mythology, not to mention the Mist of the Sidonians and the Air of the Phoenicians (Damascius, *De Principiis* 3.159.17ff.).[12] In part, this was clearly an attempt to show the unity of the pagan tradition in the face of the growing influence of Christianity. But, as we have just seen, this reconciliatory attitude had been characteristic of philosophical theologies from the start.

The contrast between the severely limited and always fallible human knowledge and the vast and secure divine knowledge was a commonplace of epic and lyric poets. Zeus, and sometimes lesser gods, was even described as having a comprehensive knowledge of everything (see e.g., *Od.* 20.75 "knows well all things"). On this traditional basis, but with significant reshaping, cognition, and rationality became the most essential functions of the philosophers' god. As Heraclitus puts it "The wise is one alone, unwilling and willing to be called by the name of Zeus" (DK 22B32). Then in the wake of Anaxagoras, it became customary for philosophers to call the divine causal principle of the world Mind or Intellect (*nous*). This is what we find, among others, in Plato, Aristotle, the Stoics, and with some restrictions, the Neoplatonists.

The doctrine of the intelligent divinity is a more refined form of anthropomorphism: we describe the god(s) by enlarging and extending our most noble capacities. The most valuable human capacity is thinking, to which philosophers add that it is also the most pleasant human activity. If so, the blessed divine being must show this capacity in the highest and purest form (e.g., S.E. *M* 9.23). Already Xenophanes claims about the greatest god that "whole he sees, whole he thinks, and whole he hears" (DK 21B24). What is more, this god can govern the world by mere thinking: "but completely without toil he shakes all things by the thought of his mind" (DK 21B25). The life of the divine is nothing but cognition. In their search for the best human life, Plato and Aristotle claimed later that a life of pure intellectual activity, and nothing but intellectual activity, is not a possibility for a human being – but it is the only life worthy of a god (*Phlb.* 22c; *EN* X.7, *Met.* Λ.9).

The divine, then, is both the ultimate causal principle and is essentially rational; this can explain that there is order, goodness, and beauty in the cosmos. Embryonic forms of this reasoning were present already in Heraclitus, but the subject became prominent in the generation of Socrates.[13] According to the Socrates of Plato's *Phaedo*, the

---

12. The issue is of course more complicated. Plotinus put all the gods in the second hypostasis (*Enn.* V.1 [10], 4) and used the tool of allegorical identifications very loosely. The introduction of the henads in the first hypostasis together with their identification with the gods, is probably due to Syrianus (Dodds, 1963, p. 257f.), and opened the gate for large-scale systematic allegory.
13. Diogenes of Apollonia seems to mark an important step in this development (DK 64B3, B5). The eye, Paley's favourite example for teleological design in biology, was described as the artifact of a creative and intelligent divinity already by Empedocles (DK 31B84 and B86). This

central task of the philosopher is to explain the cosmos as the work of a divine Mind. Roughly at the same time, the author of the Derveni papyrus, probably an Orphic initiation priest, tried to do the same in a religious context: he interpreted the traditional divine characters of the Orphic theogony as different cosmogonic functions of a divine Mind.

On the assumption that lasting regularity means order and the presence of a mathematically expressible pattern means rationality, Plato, Aristotle, and the Stoics concluded that the presence of the divine is particularly conspicuous in the motion of the heavenly bodies. In a way, this reasoning provided a philosophical underpinning for the traditional view that the heavenly bodies are divine beings. The Platonist author of the *Epinomis* went even further and proposed institutionalized forms of worship of the celestial divinities (988a).

The argument based on purposiveness and regularity in nature was also used as a proof for the existence of god. From the observable rational functioning of the cosmos, the purposefulness of its parts, and most importantly, the teleological structure of animals, one has to conclude that there must be an ultimate rational divine principle responsible for all this beauty and rationality. This argument, known as the argument from design, was used by Socrates (Xen. *Mem.* 1.4.2–19), developed further by Plato (*Laws* X and *Timaeus*), and gave occasion to the Stoics to list endless examples of providentiality in nature (S.E. *M* 9.75–123).

It nevertheless remained a formidable task for Plato, his followers, and interpreters, to explain how exactly the divine Mind and the order in the cosmos are related. The *Timaeus*, which can be read as a response to the task set by Socrates in the *Phaedo*, contains a narrative about the divine Mind-craftsman fashioning the cosmos from a previous chaotic state according to rational principles. Yet even Plato's immediate disciples disagreed whether or not we should take this story at face value. Aristotle read the *Timaeus* as a cosmogony (*Cael.* I.11, 280a30), and criticized it on the ground that the cosmos is eternal. Moreover, if the life of Aristotle's god is pure thinking, this also means that it cannot actively intervene in the functioning of the cosmos. But then how can it still function as a cause of the order in the world? Aristotle's solution is truly original. The divinity is the cause of order and goodness in the cosmos by being the object of desire. The subordinate components of the world desire the divinity and try to emulate its eternal perfection, and thereby their behavioral patterns become regulated.[14] The Stoics, as we have seen, espoused the opposite solution by affirming that the god actively and purposefully informs matter and thus creates temporally distinct cosmic orders. In this function, the Stoic god can genuinely be called a "divine craftsman" (Cic. *ND* 2.58).

The atomists took a distinct position also on this issue by holding that all that is regular and seemingly purposeful in the world is ultimately explicable by sheer mechanical causation. They did not deny that there are gods, or that the gods are intelligent, or even (as we shall see in the next section) that the gods have a crucial

---

is all the more significant as Empedocles is sometimes also quoted as an early Darwinist. The watch, the other stock example of later arguments from design, appears already in Cicero *ND* 2.87–88.

14. See *Met.* Λ.7; *GC* II.10, 336b25–337a8. The details are problematic and are hotly debated.

function in the life of individuals and societies. On the other hand, they firmly believed that the gods, whom they explained in physical terms as large living atomic images, have no role in the formation and functioning of the physical world.[15] Epicurus rejected the cosmological role of gods on the grounds that the toils of creating a cosmos and attending to its maintenance are simply incompatible with our preconception of gods as supremely happy beings.[16] As a later source formulates it "for otherwise [the god] would be wretched in the manner of a workman and a builder, burdened with care and fretting about the construction of the cosmos" (Aët. *Placit.* 1.7.7 trans. Runia).

The differences in attributing causal roles to the god(s) are reflected also in the divergent positions on the question whether the gods care for living beings, and above all, for humans. Socrates in Xenophon's *Memorabilia* 4.3 enlists numerous examples to demonstrate the godhead's providential love of mankind (*philanthropia*). For Plato, denying divine providence was a serious form of godlessness. The main character of the *Laws* presents a long argument to the effect that the god supervises not only the cosmos at large, but is mindful of the smallest of human matters (*Laws* X, 900d–903a). Similarly, the Stoics claimed that one either denies the existence of the gods, or must accept that the god (or gods) governs the world in a providential way. They argued that providentiality necessarily follows from superior power and perfect rationality; denying either of these attributes is a breach of our "preconception" of god. The Stoic can henceforth claim that Democritus and Epicurus – and one might add, Aristotle – in fact deny the existence of gods (Cic. *ND* 2.76–77; for lumping Aristotle with the atomists, see e.g., the Platonist Atticus fr. 3.52–57 des Places, quoted by Sharples, 2002).

Philosophical Piety

What is a pious act? Who is a pious individual? According to Euthyphro, the religious fundamentalist pictured in the Platonic dialogue of the same name, pious is the one who is dear to the gods (*theophilēs*, *Euth.* 7a). And when someone asked the Delphic oracle "How am I to make myself agreeable to the gods?" he was told that "By following the laws of the polis" (Xen. *Mem.* 4.3.16). The outcome is that the one who follows the laws of the city is pious. Clearly, such ready answers will not satisfy the philosopher. So Socrates immediately asks Euthyphro whether the pious is dear to the gods because he is pious, or is he pious because he is being loved by the gods? (*Euth.* 10a). Also, even if one accepts the Delphic answer and follows the laws of the polis, one can still wonder why it is dear to the gods if one carries out all the required sacrifices and religious actions required by the law. Do they need it or are they simply pleased by it, and if so, why? The seemingly unproblematic notion of piety becomes complicated in the hands of the philosophers.

We have just seen that the philosophers had something radically novel to say about the nature of the divine. But just as importantly, they had something novel to say

---

15. For an overview of the ancient evidence concerning the theology of the early atomists, see Taylor (1999, pp. 211–16).

16. Cic. *ND* 1.52; Epic. *Hdt* 76–77.

about the nature of man. Philosophical theology and philosophical anthropology developed hand in hand and the philosopher's conception of the commendable human attitude towards the divine is the outcome of this double process. We have already touched upon some of the crucial elements of this development. First, we have seen that philosophical theology helped to cultivate the notion of human beings as ethically autonomous agents who are responsible for their own fates. Another crucial element consists in emphasizing what is common between gods and humans. Traditional poets often described the human condition by *contrasting* it with the divine: our inevitable death, severely limited cognitive capacities, and incurable wretchedness were set against the immortality, wisdom, and happiness of the gods. Aspiring to more and trying to transgress the strict boundaries of human existence was a serious offense that deserved strict punishment from the gods. By contrast, it was central to the anthropology of many philosophers that even though the human condition is severely limited, there is an element of the divine in man. What is more, many of them taught, with significant individual variations, that the ultimate aim of a human being is to enhance the inner divine element and thereby become like god.[17] What counts as the utmost *hubris* in the traditional conceptions became the normative program of human life in the philosophical doctrines.

The ascent to divine status, based on a non-standard anthropology, was a crucial element in some mystery religions. The Orphic myth about the birth of mankind stressed that there is a portion of the god Dionysus in us. The reward of the proper way of life is that (possibly after a certain number of reincarnations) the divine aspect prevails and the mortal part is left behind. The Orphic initiate can thus tell the gods in the underworld that "I boast myself to be of your blessed race" and be told in response that "Happy and blessed one, you will be a god instead of a mortal" (fr. 488 Bernabé = A1 Zunz). Although the details are dauntingly difficult to interpret, it seems that Empedocles took over the eschatology of mystery religions, but integrated it into the explanatory scheme of his natural philosophy. Also, Aristotle is hesitant about who said first that "Mind (*nous*) is the god in us and mortal life contains a portion of some god," the philosopher Anaxagoras or his townsman Hermotimus, a mystic seer capable of shamanistic soul-journeys and an incarnation of Pythagoras' soul (Arist. *Protr.* fr 61 Rose; cf. *Met.* A.3, 984b15–22; D.L. 8.5). The view that the separation between divine and human is not absolute was apparently an interface between philosophers on the one hand and figures and movements functioning at the fringes of conventional religiosity on the other.

There are, however, a number of fundamental differences between the doctrine of salvation of the Orphics and the philosophical program of "becoming like god." First, philosophers, with the possible exception of Empedocles, preserved the idea that the

17. Some of the central texts are as follows: Plato, *Tht.* 176a–b; *Ti.* 90b–d; with Alcinous, *Handbook* 28; Plotinus, I.2 [19], 5–6; Aristotle, *EN* X.7–8; Seneca, *Ep.* 92.3; Epicurus, *Men.* 135. Arguably, the central assumptions are present already in Heraclitus' doctrine of divine fire coupled with the claim that the fiery (dry) soul is the wisest (DK 22B118). A good case can be made for Empedocles, too (see most recently Broadie, 1999, pp. 219–20). Socrates, on the other hand, apparently followed the more traditional view and emphasized the gap between gods and humans.

difference between god and man cannot ultimately be overcome. Becoming like god is not the same as becoming a god. Second, as in the polis religion, so too in mystery religions, the criterion of felicity was primarily performative: ritual purity and the proper execution of the required sacrifices and initiation rituals. As opposed to this, philosophers put the emphasis on the *nature* of the common trait in god and man. If intellect or mind is the divine element in us, it is by enhancing our rationality that we can become like god. As Plato says in the *Timaeus*:

> [I]f a man has seriously devoted himself to the love of learning and to true wisdom, if he has exercised these aspects of him above all, then there is absolutely no way that his thoughts can fail to be immortal and divine, should truth come within his grasp. (*Tim.* 90c, trans. Zeyl)

Intellectual perfection and the corresponding assimilation to god is also the way to become pious. This is for example the Aristotelian answer to the question set in the *Euthyphro*, "Who is dear to the gods?"

> Now he who exercises his intellect (*nous*) and cultivates it seems both in the best state and most dear to the gods (*theophilestatos*). For if the gods have any care for human affairs, as they are thought to have, it would be reasonable both that they should delight in that which was best and most akin to them (i.e. intellect) and that they should reward those who love and honor this most, as caring for the things that are dear to them and acting both rightly and nobly. And that all these attributes belong most of all to the wise man is manifest. He, therefore, is the dearest to the gods. (*EN* X.8, 1179a24–30)

Moreover, because the knower becomes like the known, the best way to think like a god is to think about the divine. Plato, Aristotle, the Stoics, and even the Epicureans, agree that the emulation of the divine must be based on a proper theology. When one considers that the primary meaning of the Greek word *teletai* is "the mystic rites at initiation," Chrysippus' saying that "theology is the *teletai* of philosophy" receives a new signification. Theology, the correct understanding of the nature of the divine, is the condition of becoming like god, being dear to the gods, and thereby of having a good life, and not the faultless performance of the ritual. Theology is the initiation ritual for a philosopher.

But if the commendable attitude towards the god(s) is the correct use of one's intellect, what function can the rituals prescribed by the laws of the polis still have? Most philosophers agreed that "the best first sacrifice to the gods is a pure mind and a soul without passions, but it is appropriate to begin the sacrifice with a moderate amount of the others [i.e. traditional material sacrifices] as well" (Porphyry, *Abst.* 2.61.1–3, the saying is sometime attributed to Theophrastus). Most philosophers accepted ritualized forms of worship upheld by tradition as a fact of human societies. This was sufficient basis even for the Skeptics to take part in cults (S. E. *M* 9.49; Cic. *ND* 3.5). The problem for the philosophers was not so much the practices but rather their interpretation. This was the real target already of Heraclitus' harsh criticism of popular religion (see Adomenas, 1999). As a matter of fact, the cults in Plato's ideal city in the *Laws* come very close to the actual Athenian practice. For Plato, the important point is that institutionalized forms of worship should enhance communal identity, so private shrines and cults are prohibited. More importantly, it is the most dangerous form of godlessness to believe that sacrifices and prayers are means to influence or bribe the gods (*Laws* X; cf. *Rep.* II, 365d–366a). Thus, the performance of sacrifice can be either a sign of piety or the worst form of godlessness depending on the interpretation the practitioner assigns to the act. The Stoic Zeno took a more radical stance towards traditional forms of worship when he declared that temples and cult statues should not be erected, because products of human craftsmen are not worth much, and therefore are not sacred either. This, however, could not stop the Stoics from worshipping the gods in the traditional way just as all other Greeks did (Plut. *St. rep.* 1034B). Plotinus apparently cared little for traditional cult activities. But ritual practice, in the form of theurgy, received a new significance for the later Neoplatonists in connection with a more pessimistic anthropology introduced by Iamblichus. According to this conception, the human soul completely descended into matter, and therefore the ritual manipulation of matter was needed for accessing the divine (e.g. Iamblichus, *De myst.* 2.2, with Steel, 1978).

The most interesting position in this respect is probably that of the Epicureans. Epicurus retained the normative concept of the assimilation to the gods. He, however, put the emphasis not so much on divine rationality, but rather on the blessed, tranquil existence of the gods – this undisturbed, joyful state is what the Epicurean sage should emulate. As we have seen above, the Epicurean gods do not intervene in human affairs. Yet they can be beneficial to human beings in so far as people with a correct understanding of the divine nature try to emulate a positive paradigm. A good life, once again, is ultimately dependent on a correct theology. But gods can be harmful as well. When one thinks of the gods as "terrifying tyrants," mainly because of one's own bad conscience, the fear of the gods will make one's life miserable (Philod. *De Piet.* coll. 71–87 Obbink). This view can function also as a philosophical account of divine justice: the gods help the betterment of the good, but harm the bad. What is the function of the rituals, then? Epicurus maintains that it is imperative to participate in public and private rituals, "not because the gods would be hostile if we did not pray," but because:

> [I]t is particularly at festivals that he [i.e. the wise man] progressing to an understanding of it [i.e. the nature of the divine], through having its name the whole time on his lips, embraces it with conviction more seriously. (Philod. *De Piet.* coll. 26–27 Obbink).

In other words, cultic activity puts the sage in the most appropriate psychological state to feel awe and thereby try to emulate the gods. Epicurus had startling views about the constitution and nature of the gods, and he had an original account of how they influence the life of individuals. Nonetheless, these unusual ideas provided the Epicurean with profound reasons to participate in the traditional religious festivals of the city – where he could also meet all the Platonists, Peripatetics, Stoics, and Skeptics, coming for somewhat different reasons based on somewhat different ideas.

Bibliography

Works Cited

Adomenas, M. (1999). "Heraclitus on Religion." *Phronesis*, 44, 87–113.

Bernabé, A. (2005). *Poetae Epici Graeci Testimonia et fragmenta*, Pars II, *Orphicorum et Orphicis similium testimonia et fragmenta*, fasc. 2. Leigzig: K. G. Saur Verlag.

Broadie, S. (1999). "Rational Theology." In A. A. Long (ed.), *The Cambridge Companion to Early Greek Philosophy* (pp. 205–24). Cambridge: Cambridge University Press.

Des Places, E. (ed. and trans.). (1977). *Atticus. Fragments.* Paris: Les Belles Lettres.

Dodds, E. R. (1963). *Proclus: The Elements of Theology.* 2nd edn. Oxford: Clarendon Press.

Henrichs, A. (1972). "Towards a New Edition of Philodemus *On Piety*." *Greek, Roman, and Byzantine Studies*, 13, 67–98.

——. (1974). "Die Kritik der Stoischen Theologie im P. Herc. 1428." *Cronache Ercolanesi*, 4, 5–32. (For Philod. *De pietate* PHerc. 1428 coll. 1–15.)

——. (1975). "The Doxographical Notes: Democritus and Prodicus on Religion." *Harvard Studies in Classical Philology*, 79, 93–123. (For Philod *De pietate* fr. 19.)

Lesher, J. H. (ed., trans. and commentary). (1992). *Xenophanes of Colophon: Fragments.* Toronto: University of Toronto Press.

Obbink, D. (ed. with commentary). (1996). *Philodemus: On Piety. Part 1.* Oxford: Clarendon Press.

Parker, R. (2000). "The Trial of Socrates: And a Religious Crisis?" In N. D. Smith and P. Woodruff (eds.), *Reason and Religion in Socratic Philosophy* (pp. 40–54). Oxford: Oxford University Press.

Rose, V. (1886). *Aristotelis qui ferebantur liborum fragmenta.* Leipzig.

Runia, D. T. (1996). "Atheists in Aëtius. Text, Translation and Comments on *De Placitis* 1.7.1–10." *Mnemosyne*, 59, 542–76.

Sedley, D. (2002). "The Origins of Stoic God." In D. Frede and A. Laks (eds.), *Traditions of Theology* (pp. 41–83). Leiden: Brill.

Sharples, R. (2002). "Aristotelian Theology after Aristotle." In D. Frede and A. Laks (eds.), *Traditions of Theology* (pp. 1–40). Leiden: Brill.

Smith, N. D. and Woodruff, P. (eds.). (2000). *Reason and Religion in Socratic Philosophy.* Oxford: Oxford University Press.

Steel, C. (1978). *The Changing Self.* Brussels: The Royal Academy.

Taylor, C. C. W. (ed., trans. and notes). (1999). *The Atomists. Leucippus and Democritus: Fragments.* Toronto: University of Toronto Press.

Zeyl, D. J. (trans.). (2000). *Plato's Timaeus.* Indianapolis/Cambridge: Hackett Publishing Company.

Zuntz, G. (1973). *Persephone. Three Essays on Religion and Thought in Magna Grecia.* Oxford: Clarendon Press.

Further Reading

Babut, D. (1974). *La religion des philosophes grecs.* Paris: Presses Universitaires de France.

Burkert, W. (1985). *Greek Religion. Archaic and Classical.* (trans. J. Raffarn). Oxford: Blackwell.

Cornford, F. M. (1912). *From Religion to Philosophy: A Study in the Origins of Western Speculation.* London: Arnold.

Drachmann, A. B. (1922). *Atheism in Pagan Antiquity.* London: Gyldendal.

Gerson, L. P. (1990). *God and Greek Philosophy.* London and New York: Routledge.

Kingsley, P. (1997). *Ancient Philosophy, Mystery and Magic.* Oxford: Oxford University Press.

Mansfeld, J. (1999). "Theology." In K. Algra, J. Barnes, J. Mansfeld, and M. Schofield (eds.), *The Cambridge History of Hellenistic Philosophy* (pp. 452–78). Cambridge: Cambridge University Press.

Most, G. W. (2003). "Philosophy and Religion." In D. Sedley (ed.), *The Cambridge Companion to Greek and Roman Philosophy* (pp. 300–22). Cambridge: Cambridge University Press.

Parker, R. (1996). *Athenian Religion: A History.* Oxford: Clarendon Press.

33

Philosophy of Language

DEBORAH K. W. MODRAK

Interest in and debates about Ancient Greek philosophy of language have intensified in the past 50 years as philosophy of language came to its own as a distinct and important area of philosophy. In contemporary philosophy of language, theories of meaning and theories of reference have been the primary focus of inquiry. Not surprisingly philosophers turning to the interpretation of Ancient Greek treatments of language have brought these concerns to the table and have raised questions, such as, does a particular author have a theory of meaning? Does a particular author have an adequate conception of reference? Some interpreters have found ancient discussions of these topics to be highly unsatisfactory from a modern perspective; others have defended the contributions to the philosophy of language made by Plato or Aristotle or the Stoics or the Epicureans. Representation as a topic is at the forefront of many ancient accounts of language. Whether this feature is a liability or an asset also remains a subject of ongoing debate among modern interpreters. Ancient Greek philosophy of language – and to what extent a "philosophy of language" should be attributed to ancient authors – is and is likely to remain for years to come a topic of inquiry and an occasion for lively disagreements.

Pre-Socratics and Sophists

Philosophy of language, in our sense, does not begin in the pre-Socratic period. Certain assumptions about the nature of language, however, shape several of the earliest works, most notably those of Heraclitus and Parmenides, and thus the foundation for Ancient Greek philosophy of language is laid. Heraclitus famously chides others for neither hearing nor comprehending the *logos* even though all things happen in accordance with the *logos* (DK 22B1). Here the multiple meanings of *logos* seem in play – *logos* as word, as account, as rule, and as reason. On the one hand, the *logos* in question is constituted by Heraclitus' words and he is expressing frustration that others do not attend to what he has to say; on the other hand, the *logos* for Heraclitus is regulative in an objective sense; it is also expressed in natural processes. Heraclitus' use of *logos* exploits the inherent ambiguity between word and object represented. A word is a sign, and what is signified typically is an object or state of affairs and yet the only way to indicate what is signified is by the use of the word. Thus Heraclitus uses "*logos*" both for his account and the reality that he claims to describe.[1]

In Parmenides, the appeal to the semantic features of language is even more explicit: "what is there for speaking and thinking must be" (DK 28B6). Human confusion and wrong-headed thinking is attributed to a mistaken application of terms: "for they established two forms in their minds for naming; of which it is not right to name one" (DK 28B8). Words conceived in accordance with what is and applied correctly are vehicles for truth but not all words meet these criteria. When they do not, words mislead and confuse. In Parmenides' poem, the goddess marks the transition from truth to opinion by drawing a distinction between her own trustworthy speech (*piston logon*) and the deceitful ordering of her words (*kosmon emon epeon apatelon*) (DK 28B8.50–53). Here we find two assumptions that will be made by many later Greek philosophers: the proper referents of terms are existents and, when words fail to pick out actual existents, they are vacuous and misleading.[2]

The sophists, by contrast, saw words as powerful tools for achieving one's ends by persuasion.[3] To play this role, words need not pick out actual existents; they need only have commonly accepted meanings. According to Protagoras "man is the measure of all things – of things that are, that they are, and of things that are not, that they are not" (S.E. *M* 7.60). The measure doctrine, while not explicitly about language, expresses an ontological thesis that fits very nicely with the notion that meaning is not determined by reference to extra-linguistic objects but by the speakers of the language. In a similar vein, Gorgias does not hesitate to express skeptical views about our ability to communicate truths and yet he also claims that as causal agents words are more powerful than physical forces. Even if there is an independently existing reality and the speaker has knowledge of it, there is no assurance that her words will refer to that reality or that their meanings correspond to it (S.E. *M* 7.65–86).

> For if things that are are visible and audible and generally perceptible, and in fact are external objects, and of these the visible are comprehended by vision and the audible by hearing, and not vice versa, how can these be communicated to another? For that by which we communicate is *logos*, but *logos* is not the objects . . . So just as the visible could not become audible and vice versa, thus since what is is an external object, it could not become our *logos*. But if it were not *logos*, it would not have been revealed to another. (S.E. *M* 7.83–85, trans. McKirahan)

This is an ingenious argument. Gorgias grants for the sake of argument the reality of the external world and then points out that language is not a feature of that world but of our experience. Moreover, *logos* is a secondary effect of the world's acting directly upon our senses. He goes on to argue that, because language is a response to

---

1. On Heraclitus' logos, see also Hussey, THE BEGINNINGS OF SCIENCE AND PHILOSOPHY IN ARCHAIC GREECE, in this volume.
2. See Mourelatos, THE CONCEPT OF THE UNIVERSAL IN SOME LATER PRE-PLATONIC COSMOLOGISTS, in this volume, who argues that several late pre-Socratics, and especially Democritus, developed a type–token distinction.
3. On this topic, see also Barney, THE SOPHISTIC MOVEMENT, in this volume.

perceptions, the causal chain goes in the wrong direction for language to be revelatory of the external reality that affects us and causes our utterances.

This fact about language does not limit the usefulness of speech as a tool for persuasion. The persuasive power of words, Gorgias contends, is such that there is nothing more powerful, nothing more able to move the mind or body of a person. In his effort to exonerate Helen, Gorgias argues that even if she was persuaded by Paris to flee to Troy, she is blameless, because words (*logoi*) can compel the soul and body to act. In support of the thesis that words can compel an agent to act, he cites a number of examples of words generating beliefs – the ability of astronomers to persuade us of things that would otherwise seem incredible, the acceptance of false claims by audiences at public speaking competitions and the shifting allegiances of the philosophers (*Encomium of Helen*).

In short, in the writings of Socrates' predecessors and contemporaries, we find several persistent ideas about meaning: words somehow get their meanings in relation to the world as perceived; words purport to represent things as they are; words may fail in this capacity; this failure is either due to human error or to the subjective character of language. These views provide the context for Socratic dialectic.

Socrates

Socrates made the search for the definitions of moral terms central to the philosophic enterprise. As portrayed by Plato, Socrates assumed that moral terms referred to realities that were such that proper definitions of them would provide analyses of the nature of justice, temperance, piety, and so forth. In the *Protagoras*, he says, "Here's a good first question: Is justice a thing or is it not a thing? I think it is. What about you?" (330c). Here we find the same realism about referents and the same normative assumptions about the correct use of words that we did in Parmenides' poem. The word is used correctly just in case the speaker succeeds in referring. The new wrinkle is the notion that definitions can correctly specify and analyze the actual referents of terms.

> Socrates: The same is true in the case of the virtues. Even if they are many and various, all of them have one and the same form which makes them virtues, and it is right to look to this when one is asked to make clear what virtue is. (*Meno* 72c, trans. Grube)

The proper Socratic use of a moral term will be regulated by a definition that ensures that its intended referent is its actual referent. On this picture, there is a fact of the matter about whether a speaker is using a word correctly that is not solely determined by linguistic practice. That a word is being used in a conventional way is simply irrelevant to the question of whether it is being correctly used in Socrates' sense, and thus he rejects lists of synonyms as definitions. Socrates presses individuals who claim to know what a particular moral term means to articulate the core concept that will be satisfied in every case where the term is correctly used. He then interrogates the proffered definition, and under scrutiny, the various efforts of interlocutors to spell out the meanings of moral terms are found wanting. Despite his failure to uncover definitions that would meet his criteria, Socrates appears to persist in the belief that such definitions are not only possible but required for morality.

Socrates and Plato

Elenchus, the cross-examination of an interlocutor's beliefs, as practiced by Socrates, however, tacitly embraces the distinction that Gorgias draws between words (*logoi*) and things. *Logoi* are fundamentally in the head and derivatively expressed in audible sounds and visible writing; things by contrast are simply in the world. Socrates examines the beliefs of his interlocutors in order to find the correct definitions of "just," "pious," etc. Treating beliefs as the well-spring for correct definitions is to treat *logoi* as objects that are internal to human thought.

Plato's Cratylus

The first philosopher to frame the question of the relation between words and things as a topic worthy of investigation in its own right was Plato. In the *Cratylus*, the Socrates character investigates and rejects two theories of meaning. The two are naturalism and conventionalism about names; both apparently had proponents at the time.[4] The naturalist view, which is attributed in the dialogue to a follower of Heraclitus, Cratylus, held that names either are correct because they capture the nature of their referents or they are meaningless sounds that fail to refer at all. The other view makes the correctness of names purely a function of convention. Both positions are ultimately rejected by the participants in the dialogue.

The first view to be investigated is conventionalism. The version of conventionalism that Socrates' interlocutor, Hermogenes, espouses is problematic, because he conflates several different positions. On the one hand, convention is taken by Hermogenes to be synonymous with agreement among speakers and to be supported by actual linguistic practice. Quite different sounds are used for the same things in different natural languages, and yet speakers of these languages have no difficulty understanding their own language. On this picture, meanings would be public, and correct use would be determined by social practice. On the other hand, conventionalism as interpreted by Hermogenes holds that an original dubbing fixes the referent of the sound, and should a speaker choose to use the sound "dog" to refer to the animal that the other members of her linguistic community call "horse" her idiosyncratic use of "dog" would be as correct as any other speaker's use of "horse." The failure to recognize that conventionalism need not sanction idiolects proves to be Hermogenes' undoing, as Socrates makes short work of showing him that he cannot maintain his account of the correctness of names unless he is willing to give up the realist beliefs he has about the truth conditions for sentences. Hermogenes is unwilling to do this. Had he been cleverer, he would have realized that he could consistently espouse the thesis that meaning is determined by social practice and a coherence account of truth. Or, alternatively he

---

4. On the fifth-century debate between naturalism and conventionalism, see Barney in this volume.

could have defended an account that embraced idiolects, a direct theory of reference where a causal chain links the referent of a term to an original act of naming, and a correspondence theory of truth. In the *Cratylus*, however, Hermogenes meekly follows Socrates' lead in examining a reformulated theory of meaning.

The radically subjective element of Hermogenes' theory is replaced by the view that words may be crafted correctly or incorrectly; a word may succeed in referring to a real object or it may fail to do so. Socrates then explores with him the cogency of a modified conventionalism where the original meanings of words are given by human beings but where correctness depends upon whether a term successfully describes the object it names (391a–427d). Socrates' initial examples, viz. proper names drawn from Homer and ordinary practice, seem to provide support for this theory, all the more, because many of these names contain descriptive elements and thus seem to be disguised descriptions (392d–395e). For instance, Astyanax, the name of Hector's son, is composed of the word for city (*astu*) and the word for ruler (*anax*). As the discussion progresses, however, the examples become more and more fanciful as Socrates shows that the words naming moral virtues and the arts and even "man" and "woman" are derived from other words indicating motion. Socrates applies the same technique to the syllables making up words and ultimately to the letters. This reduction leads to such nonsense that Socrates and Hermogenes abandon the attempt to save conventionalism. Although Hermogenes' views about the correctness of names, reference, and truth are shown to be a hopeless muddle, Plato presents this muddle to display a range of possible theories of meaning and to highlight the epistemic importance of questions about meaning and reference.

The discussion with Cratylus is much shorter. Cratylus' account of meaning is coherent. He is in a position to be a realist about truth, because he views names as disguised descriptions that pick out their referents by correctly describing them. The reason these descriptions succeed is that they stand in a natural relation to their referents. At the most basic level, this relation is resemblance – the resemblance between a spoken word and its object. If the original speakers of a language correctly assigned sounds to things, then the names they gave things are correct. The challenge facing Cratylus is to reconcile this picture of meaning and reference with the phenomenon of cultural change, and he fails to meet this challenge. Even if the original name-givers in a society assigned names correctly over time, Socrates points out, changes in the word for the sake of euphony or systematization would lead to many sounds no longer standing in an immediate relation to their meanings and hence their referents. The fiction of an original name-giver is a device for guaranteeing that the correct relation obtains between the meaning of a word and the object it represents. By showing the limitations of this device, Plato underscores the need to ground the relation between word and object in something other than phonetic imitation.

By the end of the *Cratylus*, Plato has called into question both naturalism and conventionalism about names, while at the same time maintaining that unless reference to objects by words succeeds, sentences cannot perform their function as truth-bearers. Conventionalism has been rejected on the grounds that, if language is a tool for marking real distinctions in the nature of things, it is not merely a matter of convention, for there is a fact of the matter as to whether a particular language divides reality up at its proper joints. Radical subjectivism has been rejected on the grounds that what a particular sequence of sounds uttered by a member of a linguistic community means is determined by public, interpersonal criteria, not by the whims of the speaker. Naturalism has been rejected because, in light of the historically conditioned nature of language, it has proven too difficult to tell a satisfactory story about the connection between a word and the object that it represents. In spite of the rejection of all the theories canvassed, an important and influential thesis about meaning and reference goes unchallenged: a correct name indicates the nature of the thing named (425d) and it is a verbal representation (*dēlōma*) of its referent.

Method of division

Throughout his career, Plato structured dialogues around the attempt to define a key term. However, in many of the later dialogues, Plato also advocates a method, the method of division, by which to arrive at a definition of the term in question. The object of the method of division is to produce a precisely worded definition that articulates an analysis of the concept. As described by Plato in the *Sophist* 218e−232a and elsewhere, division involves two processes − first, similar particulars are collected and grouped together under the most comprehensive term that seems to apply to them, for example, sophists fall under sophistry and types of sophistry under art (cf. *Plt.* 258b− 267c; *Phlb.* 16c−17a). In the *Sophist* the first example of division concerns the art of angling and concludes in a definition of angling:

> One half of all art was acquisitive − half of the acquisitive art was taking possession, half of possession-taking was hunting, and half of hunting was animal-hunting; half of animal-hunting was aquatic hunting; all of the lower portion of aquatic hunting was fishing; half of fishing was hunting by striking; and half of striking was hooking. And the part of hooking that involves a blow drawing a thing upward from underneath is called by a name that's derived by the similarity to the action itself, that it is called draw-fishing or angling − which is what we're searching for. (221a−c, trans. White)

At this point, division has produced a precisely defined concept that fits the particulars. The initial, pre-definitional understanding of angling was of a sort of fishing, a kind of whole; after the application of the method of division, angling is understood in terms of the genus and particular differentiae that define it.

The attempt to define the sophist's art proves much harder and initially results in six different definitions and finally, after the resolution of certain metaphysical puzzles, a seventh and truly adequate definition. The initial divisions appear to take the shape they do, because the particulars collected under "sophist" exhibit different characteristics. The Stranger initiates a search for the sophist and then as the result of employing six different strategies for dividing "art" and the subordinate universals produces six different definitions of the term "sophist" − each one of which seems to fit certain actual sophists. The second and third definitions differ only in that according to the second, the sophist travels from city to city as a merchant of ideas, and according to the third, the sophist stays in one city as a retailer of ideas. The third and fourth definitions differ only in that according to the third, the sophist retails the goods of another, and according to the fourth, the sophist retails his own work. The sixth definition is one that Plato would accept as a specification of Socrates' art: "a purifier of the soul from conceits that block the way to understanding" (232e). The inclusion of the sixth definition is evidence that the initial divisions represent an attempt to classify usages of the term as applied to individuals; since many of Plato's contemporaries considered Socrates a sophist, he would have been included in the initial collection of sophists under the term as used in common parlance (cf. Dover, 1971, p. 71).

The Stranger sets the first six definitions aside, however, on the grounds that they fail to capture the single nature shared by all sophists. At a deeper level, the defect revealed by the plethora of definitions is not that these definitions fail to delineate a concept that fits some persons called sophists, nor that taken jointly they fail to have exactly the same extension as *sophistēs* (sophist) in ordinary language, but rather that these definitions are too closely tied to the extension of the term as popularly used to articulate the common core concept that is at issue here.

> Well then, suppose people apply the name of a single sort of expertise to someone, but he appears to have expert knowledge of lots of things. In a case like that don't you notice that something's wrong with the way he appears? Isn't it obvious that if somebody takes him to be an expert at many things, then that observer can't be seeing clearly what it is in his expertise that all of those many pieces of learning focus on – which is why he calls him by many names instead of one? (232a, trans. White)

The seventh and final definition articulates the core notion shared by all the particular concepts that (correctly) fall under sophistry: "the art of contradiction making, descended from an insincere kind of conceited mimicry of the semblance-making breed, derived from image making, distinguished as a portion, not divine but human, of production" (268c–d). The final definition is such that it would apply to all the cases covered under the first five definitions but exclude the purifier of souls. The final definition would apply to all and only the types of activity that Plato believes to be genuine instances of sophistry. The proper definition is one that gets it right about the nature of the object. It is normative and need not hold of all the individuals falling under the extension of the term as ordinarily used. The term "sophist" is applied to a large number of individuals without distinguishing between them. The initial definitions produced by division make their differences explicit while the final definition, the one that captures "the genuine sophist," reveals the distinctive features of all forms of sophistry properly delimited.

Definition, for Plato, is a form of conceptual analysis, and the method of division is an analytic technique for arriving at truth, if properly and carefully applied. The object of division then is to discover the relations among linguistic concepts that reveal the structure of the extralinguistic world. This is why division begins with the collection of the particulars to which the concept is applied and extensional definitions that correspond to common usage. It also explains why division, if successful, terminates in a regulative definition that articulates the nature of the object in question. In the *Cratylus*, a well-formed language will provide a conceptual grid that articulates actual distinctions (cf. 389d). The method of division assumes that a non-vacuous term refers to a reality and that a philosophically perspicuous definition will articulate the nature of that reality. From the *Cratylus* to the *Sophist*, Plato maintains a distinction between the concepts and definitions of ordinary language and those that can be arrived at through reflection and dialectic. The latter divide the extralinguistic world up at its proper joints and thus provide a conceptual framework for knowledge and understanding. This conception of definition and the distinction between the meanings and definitions of ordinary language and epistemically rigorous definitions and meanings will profoundly influence the shape of later Greek philosophies of language.

Aristotle

The next philosopher to make important contributions to the study of meaning was Aristotle. Even more than Plato, Aristotle has a developed philosophy of language (Modrak, 2001). He shares several of the positions of his predecessors. Spoken sounds become words in virtue of having meaning for the speaker and the hearer. Words have meaning in virtue of a relation between the spoken sound and the world. This relation may be such that the word refers to an actual existent or it may be such that it only appears to pick out an actual object. Agreeing with Plato, Aristotle also differentiates between types of definitions. There are definitions that are wholly determined by the linguistic practices of a community of speakers. There are other definitions that are regulative in that they provide an objectively correct analysis of the object in question; Aristotle calls these "definitions of essence."

Aristotle's earliest attempt to address these issues is found in the *De Interpretatione*.

> Spoken words are the symbols of mental experience and written words are the symbols of spoken words. Just as all humans have not the same writing, so all humans have not the same spoken sounds, but the mental experiences, which these directly symbolize, are the same for all, as also are those things of which our experiences are likenesses. (*Int.* 1, 16a3–8)

Here Aristotle identifies all of the relevant items: the written word, the spoken word, the mental state that mediates the relation between word and object and thus accounts for meaning, the external object referred to, and a natural relation of likeness that explains reference. Unfortunately, the text is very compressed and its account of meaning has been widely criticized in the secondary literature. In recent years, happily, a few voices have been raised in Aristotle's defense (Charles, 2000; Irwin, 1982; Modrak, 2001). Arguably, this passage and other related passages in the *De Interpretatione* provide in rough outline a promising and potentially adequate theory of meaning.

The issues of the *Cratylus* seem very close to Aristotle's treatment of meaning. Not only does he (unlike the participants in the dialogue) distinguish between the language-specific nature of the phonetic sign associated with a particular content at 16a5, but he goes on to stress that sounds become words by convention: "no name is a name naturally but only when it has become a symbol" (16a26–27). Unlike Hermogenes, Aristotle distinguishes between the basic unit for meaning (the word) and the basic unit for truth (statement-making sentences). This puts him in a better position to answer Plato's challenge to develop a theory of meaning and reference that is consistent with realism about meaning and truth. In *De Interpretatione* 1, Aristotle treats the mental state that mediates meaning as a "black box"; he says next to nothing about it except that it is a likeness of the external object that is the source of meaning. Apart from a brief allusion to the psychological writings, Aristotle makes no further attempt in the *De Interpretatione* to explain how the inner state works. This has certain advantages: it allows him to focus on the object of reference and the word as a signific-ant phonetic sign without getting bogged down trying to explain how a mental state can have the psychological character and semantic function assigned it in his explanation of meaning.

Both written and spoken words are signs and meaning-bearers through linguistic practice. They are signs by convention (*kata sunthēkēn*). Aristotle's approach differs from that of either Hermogenes or Cratylus. Hermogenes fails to be clear about the relevance of social practice in determining a conventional name. Cratylus posits a direct relation between specific sounds and the things represented by those sounds; this means that he is unable to explain phonetic changes or phonetic differences among languages. According to Aristotle, the sound bears no intrinsic relation to the mental content associated with the sound or the external referent of the word. These relations are determined by the linguistic practices of a particular community. By distinguish-ing between the phonetic and semantic features of words, Aristotle is able to give a robustly realist account of the truth conditions of assertions without making implaus-ible claims about the sentence tokens used by different linguistic groups to make the same assertions about the world. Aristotle also deftly avoids the reduction of signi-ficant sounds (words) to meaning-bearing vowels and consonants. The word, Aristotle insists, is the bearer of meaning not its constituent elements.

Aristotle is also very clear that sentences not individual words make assertions, some of which are true or false.

> Just as there are in the mind thoughts which do not involve truth or falsity, and also those which must be one or the other, so it is in speech. For truth and falsity imply combination and separation. (*De Int.* 1, 16a9–11; cf. *Cat.* 4, 2a7–10, *Met.* E.4, 1027b18–28; Θ.10, 1051b1–17)

A statement is made true or falsified by extra-linguistic states of affairs.

> And while the true statement is in no way the cause of the object's existence, the object does seem in a way the cause of the statement's being true; it is because the object exists or does not that the statement is said to be true or false. (*Cat.* 12, 14b18–23)

While the words individually are not vehicles of truth, words make up sentences and the meaning of a sentence is a function of the meaning of its constituent words. The use of terms with meanings that fail to correspond to extra-linguistic realities defeat the claim to truth of the statements employing them. An epistemically adequate language will contain many words with meanings that correctly represent extra-linguistic realities. Meanings, on Aristotle's account, ideally meet two conditions: (a) the meaning of a simple term is a single coherent notion and (b) it is like the external object. Condition (b) is couched in the language of resemblance by Aristotle because resemblance is a real relation that insures that the concept corresponds to an extra-linguistic reality. When both conditions are met by a language (whether a natural language or one designed for a specific purpose), the language is epistemically adequate. These conditions may be and often are violated in one way or another by terms as employed in the well-formed sentences of a natural language. Despite this possibility, Aristotle remains optimistic about the prospects for epistemically adequate languages. He does not doubt that humans are able to use words to express truths about the world.

Having given a thumbnail sketch of a theory of meaning in *De Interpretatione* 1, Aristotle turns his attention not to straightforward cases of meaning and reference but rather to anomalous cases. The problematic cases he considers in the *De Interpretatione* include indefinite terms such as "not-man," compounded terms such as "man-and-horse," and terms having only nominal definitions such as "goatstag." According to Aristotle, the meaning of "not-man" is indefinite; by contrast, positive predicates such as "man" signify something definite (*Int.* 2, 16a29 31; 3, 16b11–15; 10, 19b9). Indefinite names have signification in a way (*pōs sēmainei*) Aristotle says (19b9), and he is tentative for good reason, because on his account of meaning, the coherence of the mental content (its expressing one notion) is only one necessary condition for meaning. In the case of negative names such as not-man, this condition is satisfied but in a way that makes it impossible to evaluate whether its meaning stands in a relation of likeness to a real object. Indefinitely many, arbitrarily selected individuals will satisfy the concept "not-man"; these individuals need not have any positive character-istics in common. There is no definition (*horismos*) or definable class under which they all fall; the group consisting of them is without determinate conceptual boundaries; it is *aoriston* (indefinite).

According to Aristotle, the simple sentence, "a man-and-horse is white," is either meaningless or equivalent to the compound sentence, "a man is white and a horse is white" (8, 18a18–25). Treated as a single term "man-and-horse" is non-referring and signifies nothing. (Aristotle arbitrarily assigns the name "cloak" (*himation*) to the putative concept of "man-and-horse" at 18a19, thus making it clear that this example is not about a centaur (*kentauros*) a mythical creature that is half horse and half man.) "Man-and-horse" fails to correspond to a concept expressing a single real essence; interpreted as a compound subject consisting of two terms, it encompasses two distinct essences. There are simply no actual individuals that satisfy the concept, man-and-horse, unless it is treated as a complex notion picking out at least one individual from each of two distinct kinds (humans and horses).

The superficially similar term "goatstag," however, expresses a single, coherent no-tion, because it has a nominal definition, albeit one that is not satisfied by any actual existent (cf. 1, 16a16–18). The significant difference between "man-and-horse" and "goatstag" or "centaur," for Aristotle, is whether there is a context that would allow a hearer to form a precise mental concept corresponding to a non-referring term or a sentence in which a non-referring term occurred (cf. *Int.* 3, 16b19–21). In the case of "a man-and-horse is white," the listener lacks such a context in contrast to a listener who is familiar with the mythical creature that is half goat and half stag. However, in order to satisfy the second condition on meaning, actual referents are required. When Aristotle turns his attention to terms that seemingly have meaning within a specified context such as myth but fail to pick out anything in the actual world, he solves this apparent puzzle by distinguishing between terms having genuine definitions (signification in the strict sense) and terms having only nominal definitions. Nominal definitions are adequate for the purposes of common linguistic practice, but they are not adequate for epistemically rigorous discourse, which requires that terms be such that they can be used in true sentences expressing real natures.

Having made meaning in the strict sense require a relation between the associated mental content (not the phonetic sign) and the world, Aristotle views all significant terms as referring terms: "Of expressions said without any combination, each signifies either substance or quantity or qualification or a relative or where or when or being-in-a-position or having or doing or being affected" (*Cat.* 4, 1b25–27). Aristotle's examples are instructive: man, horse for substance; four-foot, five-foot for quantity; white, grammatical for quality; double, half, larger for relation; in the Lyceum, in the agora for where; yesterday, last-year for when; is lying, is sitting for being in a position; has shoes on, has armor on for having; cutting, burning for doing; being cut, being burned for being affected. The variety of grammatical items listed is striking. The generic list contains nouns, adjectives, adverbs, and infinitives; the examples include prepositional phrases and active verbs and infinitives. Aristotle's intent is clear: any significant, simple term will find a place in one or another category of predicate. Moreover, Aristotle's subsequent treatment of each category makes it clear that what is being grouped is, on the one hand, a type of predicate or term, and on the other, features of the extra-linguistic world. Each (non-vacuous) predicate picks out a corresponding feature. The descriptive content of the meaning of the term determines which feature will be picked out. The simplest sentence consists in two terms (a subject and a predicate). If both pick out actual features of the world and if these features are combined in the world as in the statement, the statement is true. If, for instance, the bird is white, then the statement, "the bird is white," is true. If, however, the rock the bird is sitting on is white but the bird is brown, then even though both features mentioned in the sentence (bird, white) are actual, the statement is false.

Definition of essence

In order to differentiate between terms that are epistemically adequate and those that are not, in the *Posterior Analytics* and *Metaphysics* Aristotle recognizes several types of definition.[5] Of these, nominal definitions come closest to our everyday notion of definition. Any significant expression, irrespective of whether its referent actually exists, will have a nominal definition. Such definitions enable speakers of the same language to communicate with each other, even when the concepts they employ are confused, as in the case of "sophist" or when the concept only appears to refer to something as in the case of "goatstag" or "centaur." Surprisingly from a modern perspective, Aristotle is unwilling to call these formulae definitions in the strict sense (*horismoi*); he describes them as formulae (*logoi*) that signify the same as a name (*APo.* II.7, 92b26–28; cf. 92b5–8, b31–32). At the other end of the spectrum of types of

---

5. On definition, see also Detel, ARISTOTLE'S LOGIC AND THEORY OF SCIENCE, and Lennox, ARISTOTLE'S BIOLOGY, esp. the section "Biology and Theory of Knowledge," in this volume.

definition are definitions of essence. Unlike the nominal definition, a proper definition is an account of the cause of the thing's existence, and it is a statement of the
essential nature of the thing (II.8, 93a3–4; II.10, 93b29–94a10). These definitions
unpack a non-vacuous concept that captures a real nature. *Ex hypothesi* a definition of
essence must be satisfied by actually existing entities, which possess the essence in
question. Aristotle looks for some intrinsic characteristic of the definition of essence
that would differentiate it from a nominal definition. One indication, he finds, of the
difference between the two is that the nominal definition possesses only an artificial
unity, while the real definition is one essentially (93b35–37).

> Therefore there is an essence only of those things whose formula is a definition (*horismos*).
> And there is a definition not where a formula is identical in meaning to a word . . . but
> where there is a formula of something primary; and primary things are those which do
> not imply the predication of one element of another. (*Met.* Z.4, 1030a6–11)

Aristotle's account of definition is well suited to an account of a language to be used to
describe the world as it really is, but his account would seem to have considerably less
application in ordinary linguistic contexts.

This impression is somewhat misleading, because for Aristotle natural languages
are based on perceptions and beliefs about the extra-linguistic world. Thus, strict
definitions should be viewed as refinements of earlier, less perspicuous nominal definitions. In *De Interpretatione* 1, the mental state through which a meaning is associated
with a sound is itself a likeness of the extra-linguistic object. The words of a natural
language have significance in a social context but at base their meanings are determined by the action of the external world on the human mind. This is evident in
Aristotle's claim that the mental states will be the same for speakers of different languages. Since there is an extra-linguistic origin for linguistic concepts, there is typically
some truth in even the most conflated or confused concept. This explains why Aristotle,
like Socrates, believes that by examining our ordinary concepts we can arrive at truth.
In treatise after treatise, Aristotle begins with what appear prima facie to be linguistic
queries only to draw far-reaching conclusions about the topic at hand, be it natural
science or ontology or morality.

The terms of a natural language have, at a minimum, nominal definitions; they
may also have strict definitions that careful scientific/philosophical work will uncover.
Terms having strict definitions are required for the expression of truths. The sentences
of an Aristotelian science are true, because they correctly represent natures and states
of the extra-linguistic world. Aristotle's account of meaning taken together with his
theory of definition provides the right sort of foundation for his epistemological realism
and commitment to a theory of truth as correspondence between representations of
the world and the world.

Cognitive basis of meaning

Aristotle provides an account of human cognition in the psychological treatises that is
consistent with the role he assigns the mental state (*pathēma*) in *De Interpretatione* 1.
The *pathēma* is an apprehension of a meaning and a likeness of the external object. As

651

employed in the theory of meaning, the *pathēma* is an internal state, a psychic state of an individual. It is also the vehicle of a meaning shared by speakers of a common language. In the latter capacity, the *pathēma* is an intentional state. The psychological state that Aristotle identifies with the linguistic *pathēma* should be such that it satisfies both descriptions; it should also be such that it could be described as a likeness of an external object. In the psychological treatises Aristotle describes a cognitive capacity that allows the mind to store and utilize perceptual information; he calls this capacity *phantasia*.[6] In one of the few references to speech in the *De Anima*, Aristotle mentions *phantasia*:

> Consequently speech is the impact of the inbreathed air against that which is called the windpipe by the soul in these parts . . . what produces the impact must have soul in it and must be accompanied by an act of imagination for speech is a sound with a meaning (*sēmantikos*), and not merely the inbreathed air as a cough is. (II.8, 420b27–33)

Phantasia is a mode of sensory representation. As such, it is well situated to provide mental contents that are likenesses of objects that have been perceived. Yet such contents seem too specific to be sources of meaning. To remember a specific cat by the use of imagery seems straightforward; to use "cat" under appropriate circumstances seems to require a general concept that lacks the specificity of a particular cat.

Aristotle briefly addresses this challenge in the final chapter of the *Posterior Analytics*; his answer is that the human mind just is such that it can think through a perception of a particular to grasp the general concept (II.19, 100a13–14). This has some plausibility in the case of words naming natural kinds, but it seems somewhat less plausible when generalized to all non-vacuous concepts. Aristotle does not share these reservations. His account of thinking in the *De Anima*, moreover, provides him with a way to understand the relation between the perception of the particular and the grasp of the universal.

> Since there is no subject (*pragma*) that exists separately, so it seems, apart from magnitudes which are objects of perception, objects of thought (*noēta*) exist in perceptible forms, both the objects that are called abstract and those that are states and dispositions of perceptible objects. (*De An.* III.8, 432a3–6)

As this passage makes clear, all objects of thought are presented by means of perceptible forms. The universal exists as an object of thought, because it exists in some sense in the objects of perception. Thinking is a way of comprehending or representing the object presented sensorially through perception or *phantasia*. To apprehend the essence of water is to conceptualize a blue, fluid patch in a particular way; it is to represent water in terms of its essential properties. Similarly, if Socrates is perceived as short, snub-nosed and balding, the sensory representation of Socrates employed in thinking about the essence of human beings would include (some of) these idiosyncratic characteristics, but the thought would ignore them. To grasp a universal is to reinterpret the content of an appropriate sensory representation. Nevertheless, the sensory representation is a necessary component of the thought.

6.   See also Caston, ARISTOTLE'S PSYCHOLOGY, the section "Phantasia," in this volume.

According to Aristotle, likeness is the vehicle for meaning. The apprehension of a meaning is also the apprehension of a general concept. Aristotle is able to bring these two seemingly conflicting characteristics together by appealing to *phantasia*. The concept is a likeness of the external referent of the word, because at its core the comprehension of the meaning of the word is the apprehension of a sensory representation. The appeal to resemblance (Aristotle believes) is an appeal to a non-arbitrary relation having its source in the nature of things; in this case, it is to appeal to features that are shared by the internal state and the external object, and this naturalizes the relation between internal signs and the external objects to which they refer. This strategy is adopted not only by Aristotle but also by later Greek philosophers of language.

The dual character of the mental state mediating the relation between word and object in Aristotle's theory of meaning is less problematic on his cognitive theory than it would be otherwise. The internal state is a *phantasma* employed by the language user to represent an intelligible concept. The concept is a meaning as grasped by an individual. The concept is common to a number of speakers, because that particular meaning, although associated with a particular sound of a particular language, is the *logos* (account) of a type of external object (substance, quality, relation, etc.). Instances of the type are accessible by other persons speaking the same language or speaking another language. The *pathēma* is a likeness of the external object on two levels. As an object of *phantasia* and a sensory representation, the mental content resembles the object in a straightforward, sense-based way; as a *logos* or meaning, it is the apprehension of the sensory representation in a way that yields a universal concept. Under optimal conditions the meaning captures essential features of the external object, the *logos* as meaning corresponds to the *logos* as structural principle of the external object.

In Aristotle's theory of meaning, one finds the culmination of earlier views: *logos* as spoken word and as the assertion made in speech; a regulative notion of meaning where non-vacuous concepts require actual referents and correspondence to extra-linguistic realities; and finally the recognition of the importance of being clear about both the cultural dimensions of language and its role as the vehicle for truth. In these and other respects, Aristotle offers a theory that is both far more developed and more compelling than those of his predecessors and an account that, because it is all of a piece with earlier Greek concerns may strike a modern philosopher of language as either too realist or too psychologically based to be particularly helpful. Nevertheless, Aristotle's account of meaning and reference marks a significant advance in the philosophy of language.

Hellenistic Philosophy

Aristotle's Hellenistic successors follow in his footsteps in viewing meaning as a philosophically important topic and in addressing many of the same issues he does. Their accounts of meaning embrace some of the features of the *De Interpretatione* theory of meaning and diverge at other points. Both Epicureans and Stoics assign fundamental importance to two of the three relata in Aristotle's summary explanation of meaning. The word (in the form of its spoken or written token) and the external referent are real and their relation is required for signification. Both schools apparently use a quasi-technical term for referent (*to tunchanon*) (*SVF* 2.166; Plut. *Col.* 1119F). Both schools express reservations about the ontological status of the mental content associated with the sound. The Epicureans seek to deny any but the most tenuous status to concepts. The Stoics recognize the importance of mental objects to the theory of meaning and more generally to logic. They posit a special category of objects that are grasped by thought, expressible in language and called sayables (*lekta*); these objects do not exist but are said to subsist in relation to thought. Thus meanings, while not real in the sense of existing, are quasi-real as subsistents. Both Epicureans and Stoics, however, adopt a more naturalistic stance than Aristotle with respect to how a meaning comes to be associated with a particular bit of speech. Both, however, also allow social practice a role in shaping natural languages. They differ over whether common linguistic definitions can and should be modified by philosophers in the effort to arrive at concepts that more nearly capture real natures. The Epicureans prefer to accept the meaning commonly associated with the word, whereas the Stoics strive to produce definitions that are fully adequate analyses of their referents.

Epicureans

The Epicureans adopt a radically naturalistic stance with respect to language. Both Plato and Aristotle had viewed natural languages as cultural artifacts. In the *Cratylus*, Plato dramatizes this element by introducing a hypothetical name-giver who assigns sounds meanings for his society and in the *Philebus* he assigns the discovery of vowels and consonants to a god or a god-like person (18b). The Epicureans are at pains to reject this picture arguing that it is not only ridiculous but obviously false. As Lucretius says:

> Why should he [the original name-giver] have been able to indicate all things with sounds, and to utter the various noises of the tongue, yet others be supposed not to have had that ability at the same time? Besides, if others had not already used sounds to each other, how did he get the preconception of their usefulness . . . ? (Lucr. 5.1043–1049, trans. Long and Sedley)

Against this model of language as craft, the Epicureans defend the view that language is a natural consequence of the world's impact on human beings. This impact was such that originally humans uttered certain sounds that came to be associated with objects. In time, living in groups, humans agreed to the use of specific sounds in order to communicate better with one another. Additionally, philosophers and others with specialized knowledge gave names to entities that were not perceptible. Human languages develop as a result of the interaction between a creature having perceptual and vocal capacities of a certain sort and its environment. Epicurus accommodates both cultural and stipulative assignments of meanings to sounds within a naturalistic model. Unlike Plato's *Cratylus*, he need not insist upon core sounds that link the meaning of a word to a pre-linguistic vocal response to the environment. The naturalism about meaning defended by Epicurus and Lucretius is much more plausible than the Platonic parody of naturalism. A plausible historical account of the origin of language, however, is not by itself a compelling theory of meaning. The strong nominalistic strand in Epicurean thought, moreover, seems to constrain what they are entitled to say about meaning.[7]

In order to meet these challenges the Epicureans must: (a) identify the cognitive object through which a particular meaning is associated with a particular sound in a public language; (b) provide an account of universals (if meanings are universals); and (c) spell out their theory of meaning in a way that accommodates the epistemic role of language. The worry that they might not be able to specify an appropriate cognitive object was voiced by one of their ancient critics. Plutarch charges that the Epicureans have abolished meaning because they acknowledge only the roles played by the spoken word and the external object (*Col.* 1119F). The second problem – at least insofar as it is generalized to all universals – is also raised by ancient critics. The third problem arises because the Epicureans' flexibility about the various ways in which meanings come to be associated with sounds seems to weaken the connection between the world of objects and the world as represented in utterances. The Epicureans make perceptions and feelings the criteria of truth and so any evolution of meanings away from primal vocal responses to the environment would seem to be problematic.

Epicurus explains meaning by appealing to preconceptions:

> Preconception, [the Epicureans say], is as it were a perception, or correct opinion, or conception or universal stored notion, i.e., a memory of that which has frequently become evident externally; e.g., "Such and Such a kind of thing is a man." For as soon as the word "man" is uttered, immediately its pattern also comes to mind by means of preconception, since the senses give the lead. Thus what primarily underlies each name is something self-evident. Nor should we have named something if we had not previously learned its pattern by means of preconception. (D.L. 10.33, trans. follows Long and Sedley)

What precisely preconceptions are for Epicurus, however, is far from clear (Furley, 1967; Glidden, 1985; Laks, 1977; Long, 1971a, 1971b; Striker, 1977). On the most likely hypothesis, a preconception is a stabilized perceptual concept that is the direct consequence of bringing past perceptions to bear in a present perception. Since some images (*eidōla*) enter the body through pores much finer than those of the sense organs and these images act directly on the mind, Epicurus can explain the presence of preconceptions that are not easily traced back to ordinary perceptual experiences. Such preconceptions could function as basic concepts that are not constructed by the mind but are available to it. Despite being a spontaneous product of past perceptions and present stimulation, the preconception exists in the mind prior to the particular experience in which it is brought to bear.

Because the preconception is an enduring mental object, it is not subject to the vicissitudes of the sensorially presented object. Because a percipient has a concept of lion, for instance, she is able to categorize her visual perceptions of an approaching lion as the experience of seeing a lion while her perceptions may range from a blurry lion-like shape of indistinct color to a sharply defined lion shape in vivid colors. She is also able to talk about this experience because she has a concept of lion (D.L. 10.33; cf.

---

7. Cf. Morel's discussion of how the Epicureans meet these challenges in EPICUREANISM, in this volume.

Lucr. 4.749–756). The preconception gives Epicurus the tool he needs to explain the cognitive shift from the various and apparently conflicting perceptions of a particular lion to an apprehension that can be used to reason about lions and that can serve as empirical evidence for or against any claims made about the nature of lions. The origin of preconceptions in perceptions enables the Epicureans to explain the link between word and object. On the one hand, the encounter between humans and the world prompts certain spontaneous vocalizations and on the other, it prompts the formation of preconceptions that are conjoined with the vocalizations. Thus cries and other vocal responses are proto-words (sounds with associated meanings). It is on this base of spontaneous cognitive and vocal reactions to the external world that the linguistic refinements described by Epicurus take place. Preconceptions do the work of linguistic universals; however, the Epicureans remain firm about particulars being ontologically prior. In short, by appealing to preconceptions, the Epicureans can answer the first two challenges facing their account of meaning.

Epicurus may also have an answer to the puzzle about the epistemic role of language. In at least one place, he lists preconceptions with feelings and perceptions as criteria of truth (D.L. 10.31). Criteria of truth for Epicurus are spontaneous cognitive responses that occasion thought but are not structured by the mind. This suggests that there are certain basic meanings that just are preconceptions and such meanings would provide a linguistic foundation for true expressions. The picture he sketches seems to be a kind of semantic foundationalism where certain terms would be components of basic sentences expressing truths. Other true statements would be derived from the basic ones.

> For the primary signification (*ennoēma*) of each utterance must be seen and need no additional demonstration if we are to have something to which the inquiry or the problem or the opinion before us can be referred. (D.L. 10.38, trans. follows Hicks)

This approach to meaning would be consistent with Epicurus' conception of the role of basic cognitions in more complex ones: "Also, all notions (*epinoiai*) arise from the senses by means of confrontation, analogy, similarity and combination, with some contribution from reasoning" (D.L. 10.32; trans. Long and Sedley).

Just as, for the Epicureans, error enters, not at the level of basic perceptions, all of which are true, but at later cognitive stages when other cognitive operations are performed on them, error in linguistic representations would occur not at the most basic level but at subsequent stages of language development where cultural factors play a role and stipulative meanings are introduced. These changes are the source of "the multifarious conventions of language" which Epicurus cautions against in *Nat.* 28.31.10. In addition, as a way to protect the truth-bearing role of language, Epicurus may have made the spoken word the bearer of truth (S.E. *M* 8.13).

According to Plutarch, the Epicureans are left with only words and name-bearers, having abolished sayables (*Col.* 1119F). Since the Epicureans clearly accept that there are preconceptions associated with words, the point of the criticism may have been that, contrary to the view of the Epicureans, meanings are internal objects having the same structure as spoken language. The Epicureans apparently reject the linguistic model of the cognitive state associated with the spoken word and may have put in its place a sensory model. On their epistemology, this would strengthen the truth-preserving character of basic sentences, because mental linguistic representations would be more vulnerable to error than sensory-based preconceptions.

Epicurus differs sharply with Plato and Aristotle over the role of definition in fixing meanings and furthering understanding. Epicurus views definitions with the same level of suspicion that he views universals and other cognitive objects that are not firmly rooted in perceptual experience. Since words can only be defined by using other words, it is better (Epicurus believes) to stick with the notion that attaches to the word and not try to unpack it using other more general terms. Moreover, Plato and Aristotle had seen definition as a way to bring the meaning of the word in line with the object it represented. The proper definition might (and often did) shift the meaning of a term away from its common linguistic meaning. The Epicureans believe that the common linguistic meaning is more likely to correspond to the reality represented than any later refinement of the meaning through technical definition. Here as in other areas of his epistemology, Epicurus privileges the more immediate cognition over less immediate cognitions that involve additional mental processes.

Epicurus and his followers offer a clear alternative to the Platonic-Aristotelian approach to meaning. While it meets the challenges raised above, the Epicurean theory of meaning combines two positions that are uneasy bedfellows – the epistemic superiority of immediate experience and the endorsement of ordinary language. The advice to stay close to commonly accepted meanings is problematic, because the commonly accepted meaning may or may not (depending upon the history of the word) capture the experience(s) that initially prompted the formation of the concept. Also, preconceptions seem best suited to being perceptual concepts and much less adequate as general concepts of the sort associated with the names of abstract objects. Epicurus would no doubt grant this criticism but consider it a strength of his approach; however, viewed from a more neutral stance, it would seem to be a weakness.

Stoics

The Stoics made the study of signification one part of the study of logic; logic was divided into dialectic and rhetoric:

> Dialectic, they say, is divided into the topics of significations and utterance; and that of significations into the topics of impressions and derivatively subsistent sayables – propositions, complete sayables, predicates and similar actives and passives, genera and species, along with also arguments, argument modes and syllogisms, and sophisms which depend on utterance and on states of affairs. (D.L. 7.43, trans. Long and Sedley)

Just as Aristotle had included a discussion of meaning as part of his logical writings, so too the Stoics. The list above tracks the topics of Aristotle's *Organon*. There are differences, however; the Stoics introduce the notion of a sayable (*lekton*) and also have a distinct account of the impression (*phantasia*). In addition, apparently in response to the same query as the one raised in the *Cratylus*, the Stoics refused to include the study of "the correctness of names" under dialectic, preferring instead to focus on "what each existing thing is" and "what it is called" (D.L. 7.83); the topic of correctness was, however, discussed under grammar (Frede, 1978).

The Stoics offer a developed theory of signification. There are three items of note for them: the spoken word, what it signifies, and the referent of the word (S.E. *M* 8.11–12). The word and its referent are bodies and thus exist. What is signified, however, is said to subsist. What is signified "exists" as an intentional object of a rational impression or thought; the latter is a qualification of a material mind and hence exists but what the thought is about merely subsists. A meaning is expressible in language and is called a sayable. In contrast to Aristotle, the Stoics insist that names are by nature (*phusei*). Like Aristotle, they also appeal to resemblance to explain signification. The question is whether, for the Stoics, it is the sound that imitates the object for which it stands, or whether it is the associated sayable that imitates the object. If the latter is their position, then their theory of meaning might well be seen as an improvement on Aristotle's. Aristotle's internal state does double duty as image and meaning, whereas the Stoic sayable seems to be exactly the right sort of entity to be a meaning. The sayable is distinct from the thought of which it is the intentional content and from the external object to which the word refers.

However, there is also some evidence that the early Stoics gave a historical account of meaning according to which vocal sounds were natural imitations of things that were codified into language.

> [Are names] as the Stoics believe, of nature, the primary sounds (*phōnōn*) being imitations of the things of which the names are said? (*SVF* 2.146, trans. Long and Sedley)

This picture led to work on etymologies that may have been similar to, but more sophisticated than, the etymologies of the *Cratylus*. It is somewhat puzzling that after Plato had so clearly demonstrated the limitations of vocal resemblance as a vehicle of meaning that the Stoics embrace vocal resemblance. The explanation presumably lies in the emphasis they put on particulars. Only particulars are real. This ontological assumption apparently spawned the desire to link particular words audibly to their particular referents. The spoken word is a real particular; its auditory character is real; the word stands in a real relation of auditory resemblance to a real object to which the word refers. The sayable, by contrast, is not a concrete particular; it is an intentional object of an act of thought.

Significant sounds express sayables. Some sayables are incomplete and are the significata of individual words. Nouns signify either common qualities or peculiar qualities; verbs signify predicates (D.L. 7.58). Predicates must be asserted of something in order to express a complete thought (D.L. 7.64). Other sayables are complete. The Stoics say that complete sayables include judgments (*axiōmata*), syllogisms, and questions. All of these express assertions either directly or indirectly as queries in that they express complete thoughts; however being true or false is the defining feature of judgments – and thus "proposition" is a common translation of *axiōma* in this context. Beginning with these basic distinctions, the Stoics construct an elaborate and sophisticated theory of propositions and inference (D.L. 7.65–83).[8] This leaves them in an excellent position to frame their theory of meaning in a way that is consistent with their conception of truth.

---

8. On this topic, see Ierodiakonou, STOIC LOGIC, in this volume.

A detailed account of syntax is central to the Stoic approach. Their syntactic distinctions apply in the first place to surface grammar but they seem also to delineate types of sayables. There are five parts of speech, viz. the name, the appellative, the verb, the connective particles and articles (D.L. 7.57). At least some of these were explicated by appealing to the basic categories of existents, viz. substratum (common and individual) qualification, disposition and relative disposition. Names indicate individually qualified things and appellatives (common nouns) indicate commonly qualified things (D.L. 7.58). The other three syntactic categories are defined without explicit reference to the ontological categories. Arguably, however, each corresponds to an ontological category with verbs indicating dispositions, connective particles indicating relative dispositions, and articles indicating substrata (Graeser, 1978).

The Stoics also recognize a legitimate role for definition. A proper definition furnishes an analysis of the concept in question that is neither narrower nor broader than the concept. It provides an outline by which to link the concept to its external object (D.L. 7.60). The role of definition may have been primarily heuristic for the Stoics – a way to disambiguate commonly used expressions. Or, like Plato and Aristotle, they may have hoped to get clearer on the nature of the underlying reality by means of definition. Definitions seemed to have played an important role in their ethical theorizing (D.L. 7.199–200; Cic. *Tusc.* 4.53).

The Stoics face the challenge of reconciling their account of meaning and definition with their ontological commitments, because they (like the Epicureans) are unwilling to include universals among existents. Only particulars exist and each particular is a unique individual. These individuals, however, are also commonly qualified, and this provides the Stoics with the basis for an explanation of the use of universal terms. Universals are not real; they are concepts (*ennoēmata*) or figments (*phantasmata*) of the mind (*SVF* 1.65; D.L. 7.61). They arise in the mind, because the mind recognizes that particular bodies are qualified generically as well as individually. In a statement such as "Socrates is a man," the predicate "man" indicates that Socrates is commonly qualified in a particular way. The predicate is an incorporeal sayable that subsists in accordance with a rational impression (D.L. 7.63). The sayable, however, is an intentional object of thought and not, strictly speaking, a figment of the mind. Treated as a predicate, the universal term has a subsistent meaning, an abstract expression of a common qualification of the individuals that are qualified in a specific way, e.g., as humans.

Even so, the strong nominalistic thesis that the universal is a figment of the mind threatens to reduce the universal to an idea of a fictitious entity. One way out of this puzzle is to differentiate between the use of a universal term as a predicate and the use of a universal term as a subject. The Stoics seem particularly concerned about the latter. The use of a universal term as a nominative, especially in a definition, it might be argued, is evidence for the existence of an object (the universal) to which the name refers. In response, the Stoics propose to paraphrase the definition, "Man is a rational animal" as "If x is a man, x is a rational animal" (S.E. *M* 11.8–11). This paraphrase provides referents for the general terms that are individuals. The Stoics seem to grant, however, that the object of the definition is the species not the individual. The species is a figment of the mind caused by commonly qualified individuals. There is no need (according to the Stoics) to posit mind-independent universals to serve as the referents of thoughts about kinds or common characteristics. Either these thoughts are about commonly qualified individuals or they are about mental images caused by commonly qualified individuals.

To extend this conception of universals to the theory of meaning: the sayable that subsists in the case of a common noun such as "man" would be the predicate "man" that subsists in accordance with rational impressions of commonly qualified individual men. This cognition might prompt the formation of the universal concept (*ennoēma*) that functions as if (*hosanei*) it were a proper subject, a something (*ti*), in statements such as: "Man is two-footed." Although the vehicle for the concept exists as a corporeal state of a corporeal mind, the concept does not exist and it is unclear whether it even subsists. According to Alexander, the concept is neither a body nor an incorporeal (*SVF* 2.329). This is why the Stoics propose to avoid definitions that would reify the universal. By paraphrasing definitions by genus and differentia and predicating those of individuals, they are able to give an account of definition that uses only terms that refer either to existing individuals or correspond to subsisting sayables.

The Stoic treatment of meaning and related topics represents a sustained effort to clarify these notions. With the Stoics, philosophy of language comes of age as a core discipline within philosophy. Stoic logic, epistemology and psychology all have a decidedly linguistic character. By making the sayable a subsistent that is required for all forms of intellection, the Stoics assign a distinct ontological status to the intentional object of thought and make it proto-linguistic. The structure of the sayable is mirrored in the structure of the spoken language. The complete sayable, the proposition, is the basic building block of logic. The realism about objects of reference that characterized the earliest Greek views survives in the Stoic account but is integrated into an account of meaning that recognizes that the cognitive object is a proto-linguistic object; it is a sayable.

Skeptics

The Skeptics do not put forward substantive philosophical positions of their own on language or any other topic; for them, the task of the philosopher should be to undermine dogmatic claims made by others. They criticize various elements of the story told about meaning and truth by the Stoics. Sextus, a Pyrrhonian skeptic, challenges the evidence for sayables; any proof given for the existence of sayables would either beg the question or be equivalent to merely asserting that sayables exist in the face of the denial of this claim by Epicurus and others (S.E. *PH* 2.107). Moreover, the understanding of language will depend upon a prior grasp of the extralinguistic object because the association of a given sound with a particular object or a particular mental content cannot be through convention alone nor can it be by nature (S.E. *M* 1.37–38, 11.241–242). Were it by nature, Greeks would understand barbarians and conversely. Meanings can also be changed at the whim of speakers. Consequently, contrary to Stoic doctrine, there can be no science of dialectic understood as the knowledge of the things that signify and the things that are signified (S.E. *PH* 2.214). Since the Skeptics make arguments and attempt to persuade others, arguably they make certain assumptions about meaning and reference.

For if we abolished every sign it would necessarily result either that the words uttered by us against the sign signify nothing, or, if they are significant that the existence of a sign is conceded. But as it is, we make use of the distinction [between indicative and commemorative sign] and abolish one kind of sign but affirm the other [the commemorative] . . . (S.E. *M* 8.290; trans. follows Bury)

As a commemorative sign, the word triggers a response through association and memory. Whether the appeal to commemorative signs is consistent with Pyrrhonism is debatable (Allen, 2001; Glidden, 1983).[9] Notwithstanding, the Skeptics contend that their philosophizing carries no ontological baggage but merely accords with common linguistic practice (S.E. *M* 8.281–290). In this respect, they seem to be Gorgias' heirs.

Conclusion

There are several strands in Ancient Greek philosophy of language – realism about referents, truth and meaning, an emphasis on the revelatory aspect of language, a search for the cognitive basis for meaning and a recognition of the persuasive power of language. There is also a conflicting line of thought with fewer proponents, according to whom, words only appear to have meanings and refer to objects. On this view, the chief function of words is to be (or appear to be) useful for persuasion. Just as the pre-Socratic emphasis on *logos* and truth initiated the discussion of these topics by philosophers, Aristotle's account of meaning provided a framework in which the key elements were word, mental content, external object and the sign relation that would dominate Hellenistic discussions. The later treatments of language, especially the Stoic theory of meaning, are remarkably sophisticated. The explanatory power and comprehensiveness of the accounts put forward by Aristotle, the Epicureans and the Stoics are such that the attribution of a philosophy of language to them is clearly appropriate. The impact of Ancient Greek accounts of language on their philosophical successors was profound.

Bibliography

Editions and Translations of Ancient Texts and Commentaries

Aristotle

Ackrill, J. L. (trans. and comm.). (1963). *Aristotle's Categories and De Interpretatione.* Oxford: Clarendon Press.

Barnes, J. (ed.). (1984). *The Complete Works of Aristotle. The Revised Oxford Translation.* (2 vols.). Princeton: Princeton University Press.

Jaeger, W. (ed.). (1957). *Aristotelis Metaphysica.* Oxford: Clarendon Press.

Minio-Paluello, L. (ed.). (1949). *Aristotelis Categoriae et Liber De Interpretatione.* Oxford: Clarendon Press.

9.   On the distinction between indicative and commemorative signs, see also Pellegrin, ANCIENT MEDICINE AND ITS CONTRIBUTION TO THE PHILOSOPHICAL TRADITION, in this volume.

Ross, W. D. (ed.). (1964). *Aristotelis Analytica Priora et Posteriora.* Oxford: Clarendon Press.
——. (ed.). (1956). *Aristotelis De Anima.* Oxford: Clarendon Press.

Diogenes Laertius

Hicks, R. (ed. and trans.). (1925). *Diogenes Laertius Lives of Eminent Philosophers.* (2 vols.). Loeb Classical Library. Cambridge, Mass.: Harvard University Press / London: Heinemann.

Epicurus

Usener, H. (ed.). (1887). *Epicurea.* Leipzig: Teubner.

Hellenistic philosophers

Long, A. and Sedley D. (eds. and trans.). (1987). (cited as LS). *The Hellenistic Philosophers.* (2 vols.). Cambridge: Cambridge University Press.

Lucretius

Bailey, C. (ed.). (1947). *Titi Lucreti Cari De rerum natura libri sex.* (3 vols.). Oxford: Clarendon Press.

Plato

Burnet, J. (ed.). (1900–7). *Platonis Opera.* (5 vols.). Oxford: Clarendon Press.
Cooper, J. M. (ed. of English trans.). (1997). *Plato. Complete Works.* Indianapolis: Hackett.

Pre-Socratics

Diels, H. (1951–2). (Cited as DK). *Die Fragmente der Vorsokratiker.* (3 vols.). 6th edn revised by W. Kranz and often reprinted. Berlin: Weidmann. (Original work published 1903.)

Sextus Empiricus

Bury, R. (ed. and trans.). (1935–49). *Sextus Empiricus.* (4 vols.). Loeb Classical Library. Cambridge: Harvard University Press / London: Heninemann.

Stoics

von Arnim, J. (ed.). (1903–24). *Stoicorum veterum fragmenta.* (= *SVF*). (3 vols. vol. 4: indexes by M. Adler) Leipzig: Teubner.

Modern Authors

Allen, J. (2001). *Inference From Signs. Ancient Debates About the Nature of Evidence.* Oxford: Clarendon Press.
Atherton, M. (1993). *The Stoics on Ambiguity.* Cambridge: Cambridge University Press.
Charles, D. (2000). *Aristotle on Meaning and Essence.* Oxford: Clarendon Press.
Bolton, R. (1976). "Essentialism and Semantic Theory in Aristotle: *Posterior Analytics* II. 7–10." *Philosophical Review,* 85, 514– 44.
——. (1985). "Aristotle on the Significance of Names." In *Language and Reality in Greek Philosophy: Proceedings of the Greek Philosophical Society* (pp. 153–62). Athens.
DeMoss, D. and Devereaux, D. (1988). "Essence, Existence and Nominal Definition in Aristotle's *Posterior Analytics* II. 8–10." *Phronesis,* 33, 133–54.

Dover, K. (1971). "Socrates in the *Clouds.*" In G. Vlastos (ed.), *Socrates* (pp. 50–70). Garden City: Doubleday.

Frede, M. (1978). "Principles of Stoic Grammar." In J. Rist (ed.), *The Stoics* (pp. 27–75). Berkeley: University of California Press.

Furley, D. (1967). *Two Studies in the Greek Atomists.* Princeton: Princeton University Press.

Glidden, D. (1983). "Skeptic Semiotics." *Phronesis,* 28, 213–255.

——. (1985). "Epicurean *Prolēpsis.*" *Oxford Studies in Ancient Philosophy,* 3, 175–218.

Graeser, A. (1978). "The Stoic Theory of Meaning." In J. Rist (ed.), *The Stoics* (pp. 77–100). Berkeley: University of California Press.

Irwin, T. (1982). "Aristotle's Concept of Signification." In M. Schofield and M. Nussbaum (eds.), *Language and Logos* (pp. 241–66). Cambridge: Cambridge University Press.

Kahn, C. (1973). "Language and Ontology in the *Cratylus.*" In E. Lee, A. Mourelatos, and R. Rorty (eds.), *Exegesis and Argument* (Festschrift for Gregory Vlastos). *Phronesis,* supp. vol. 1. Assen: Van Gorcum.

Ketcham, R. (1979). "Names, Forms and Conventionalism: *Cratylus* 383–395." *Phronesis,* 24, 133–47.

Kretzmann, N. (1971). "Plato on the Correctness of Names." *American Philosophical Quarterly,* 8, 126–38.

——. (1974). "Aristotle on Spoken Sound Significant by Convention." In J. Corcoran (ed.), *Ancient Logic and Its Modern Interpretations.* Dordrecht: Reidel.

Laks, A. (1977). "Édition critique et commentée de la 'vie d'Épicure' dans Diogène Laërce (x, 1–34)." In J. Bollack and A. Laks (eds.), *Études sur l'Épicurisme antique.* Lille: Publications de l'Université de Lille III.

Long, A. A. (1971a). "*Aisthēsis, Prolēpsis,* and Linguistic Theory in Epicurus." *Bulletin of the Institute of Classical Studies,* 18, 114–33.

——. (1971b). "Language and Thought in Stoicism." In A. A. Long (ed.), *Problems in Stoicism* (pp. 75–113). London: University of London Athlone Press.

Manetti, G. (1993). *Theories of the Sign in Classical Antiquity.* (trans. C. Richardson). Bloomington: Indiana University Press.

Modrak, D. (2001). *Aristotle's Theory of Language and Meaning.* Cambridge: Cambridge University Press.

Moravcsik, J. (1973). "The Anatomy of Plato's Divisions." In E. Lee, A. Mourelatos, and R. Rorty (eds.), *Exegesis and Argument* (Festschrift for Gregory Vlastos). *Phronesis,* supp. vol. 1 (pp. 324–38). Assen: Van Gorcum.

Striker, G. (1977). "Epicurus on the Truth of Sense Impressions." *Archiv für Geschichte der Philosophie,* 59, 125–42.

Whitaker, C. (1996). *Aristotle's De Interpretatione: Contradiction and Dialectic.* Oxford: Oxford University Press.

663

34

Ancient Medicine and its Contribution to the Philosophical Tradition

PIERRE PELLEGRIN

In Greek and Latin antiquity, philosophy had a privileged relation to medicine. The rational medicine stemming from Hippocrates had what may be called a "theoretical reputation" equalled only by mathematics. In Plato's dialogues as much as in Aristotelian treatises, medicine figures as a science both established and incontestable. In virtue of this, it frequently serves as an example of a scientific discipline. This "strong" status of medicine will also make it a rival of philosophy, a rivalry that will take diverse forms in the different phases of the histories of medicine and of philosophy. To be sure, antiquity experienced a development, beginning especially with the Hellenistic period, in which the sciences were emancipated from theoretical tutelage to philosophy; but no science claimed to replace philosophy, conceived as all-embracing knowledge. Certainly one might regard Pythagoreanism, in its assertion that things are numbers (however one interprets this thesis), as attempting a kind of absorption of philosophy by mathematics. But, beyond the fact that the enterprise was abortive, it cannot be said that Pythagoreanism definitely set two disciplines in opposition to each other, one called "philosophy" and the other "mathematics." Things are otherwise with medicine. In fact, we shall see that in a certain way medicine and philosophy come to compete in the same arena, in that both claim to regulate the whole of human life. This becomes ever more true the more that philosophy, from Hellenistic and especially Roman times forward, sets itself the main goal of being an art of living. Further, philosophical discourse in this period notably incorporates medical terms, images, and maxims: it is a matter of healing passions, of moderating inclinations, of finding the life-regimen suitable to the subject's condition.

Before going into further details of the relations between medicine and philosophy, however, a few remarks are in place regarding ancient medicine in general. Historians have insisted on the existence, in Greece, of a rational medicine. Some, naïvely assuming their continuity, have included it in the same history with modern scientific medicine, finding anticipatory hints of Bernardian experimentalism in certain Hippocratic writings (Bourgey, 1953, esp. part 3). All that is certainly an exaggeration. We must remember, on the one hand, that the Greeks, like all other peoples, had great recourse to empirical therapists, indeed even to charlatans, as well as to a religious "medicine" dispensed in the great holy places; and, on the other, that Egyptian doctors, for example, were not wanting in theoretic boldness and constructed systems, both physiological and nosological, that bear comparison with certain Hippocratic treatises.

What seems most characteristic of Greek (and then Roman) medicine is its diversity, both synchronic and diachronic. If we consider the literary output of the ancient physicians, which remains very important even though only a part of it has been preserved, we find that at no time did any school or movement in medicine impose its hegemony. This was so even in Hippocrates' day, even though he dominated the medicine of his time and served as a model for all of ancient medicine, holding in it a place that no philosopher ever held in philosophy. Furthermore, the history of ancient medicine is punctuated by theoretical revolutions (not accompanied by corresponding revolutions in therapy) that preclude us from speaking – or continuing to speak – of "ancient medicine" as an undifferentiated but still significant unity. There are at least three "ancient medicines": Hippocratic medicine, Alexandrian medicine of the third century BCE, and the medicine of the sects and nosographies. Nor did philosophy remain self-identical from its appearance in the sixth century BCE to the end of antiquity; consequently relations between the two disciplines were radically transformed.

Hippocrates With and Against Philosophy

Hippocrates was born some ten years after Socrates. He is named as author of about 50 extant writings very different in their topics, doctrines, and dates. Ever since antiquity doubts have been voiced about the authenticity of some of them, but the general tendency was to attribute them, or most of them, to Hippocrates himself. Nowadays scholars are much more wary, and, in any case, the "Hippocratic question" – the problem of knowing which items in the Hippocratic corpus are from Hippocrates' own hand – is of reduced importance. It remains, nevertheless, that a majority of historians of ancient medicine maintain that there is a kind of "Hippocratic spirit" that distinguishes the works of Hippocrates and those in his circle from other treatises. It is often to these "Hippocratic" treatises that scientific features in the modern sense have been anachronistically attributed; for example, a combination of observation, even of experimentation, and reasoning.

Commentators have thus acquired the (bad) habit of giving a "positivist" reading of one of the discrepancies to be found among the works of the Hippocratic corpus. Through the controversy reported by the author of one of our treatises, the *Regimen in Acute Diseases*, we know that two schools, both located on the coast of Asia Minor, stood in opposition to each other: one, that of Hippocrates, was based in Cos, the other in Cnidos. In the wake of analyses too lengthy to expound here, historians accordingly came to identify a certain number of works in the Hippocratic corpus as "Cnidian": the *Diseases* II and III, the *Internal Affections* and the gynecological treatises. These treatises are incontestably of a more "archaic" character than the great treatises attributed to the school of Hippocrates. They are catalogues of diseases sorted by species and variants, with more or less the same expository structure: name, symptoms, prognosis, therapy. The treatises attributed to the school of Cos, by contrast, are marked by a notable expository diversity. Even when, as in the *Epidemics*, what we have are mere notes, recording individual cases observed by a no doubt itinerant doctor, giving even the locality of the case and the name of the patient, i.e., texts in no sense part of a theoretical or etiological account, we find neither the rigid exposition of the Cnidian treatises nor the stereotyped character of their therapeutic prescriptions.

It is nonetheless futile to attempt to find a difference of theoretical level between the Cnidian and the Coan treatises. In a revealingly titled book, Robert Joly (1966) has convincingly shown that the treatises of the Hippocratic corpus express, one and all, a prescientific way of thinking – customarily described, not so long ago, as "primitive" or "archaic" – immersed in what Auguste Comte called the "metaphysical age." The theory of humors, for example, one of the principal legacies of Hippocratic medicine to the Western medical tradition, projects an imaginary picture of the human body as the locus of the flux and concentration of fluids that eludes all experimental confirmation. The real basis of the difference between Cnidian and Coan treatises lies elsewhere. We may grasp it by considering treatises such as *The Art* and *Breaths*. Commentators have hardly been sympathetic to these treatises, finding their rhetorical virtuosity suspect. The last mentioned, for example, endeavors to prove that all diseases result from a maldistribution of gaseous fluxes in the body. To this end it deploys all the resources of the art of speechmaking, so advanced in those times, including the assonances that make discourse more elegant. It was thus held that it was a sophistic kind of discourse in which the author sought above all to display his skill as an orator, without much concern for the content of his remarks. This was reminiscent of the boasts of a Gorgias, undertaking to defend contrary theses with equal persuasiveness. The term, and concept, "iatrosophist" was therefore coined to denote the authors of such discourses.

Jacques Jouanna, in his edition of *The Art* and *Breaths* in the Budé Series, has irreversibly overthrown this notion. A treatise such as *Breaths* is indeed an epideictic discourse – that is, one delivered to an audience in order to persuade – but nothing proves that its content is a matter of indifference to its author. It is a case of a physician expounding the doctrine to which he adheres, one corresponding closely to the "level of Hippocratic science" (or of pre-Socratic philosophy), but expounding it in particular circumstances. Perhaps such exercises were linked to the institution of "public physicians" appointed by cities to deal with public health problems. Their recruitment, particularly in democratic cities where a popular assembly had the last word on everything, took place after a "competition" during which the physician was to convince the citizens that he was their man. Plato mocked the pretensions of the people to judge the technical abilities of experts. But we can give the institution of public physicians a different reading. It was, in fact, a matter of medicine's making its mark on the political space opened up by the founding of cities. As the groundbreaking works of Jean-Pierre Vernant (esp. 1965) have shown, when the city replaced earlier socio-political systems, rational argumentative discourse replaced authoritarian discourse based on tradition (usually with the backing of the gods) as the source of power. In other domains, the propagation of this form of rationality brought about the replacement of mythical accounts of the origins of the universe by pre-Socratic cosmogonies.

It is, therefore, not so much a theoretical progress that Hippocrates and, with him, the school of Cos made in medicine as a progress we might call rational. Whereas the school of Cnidos, so far as we can tell, seems to have remained within the traditional logic of an authoritative doctrine apparently transmitted through a family structure, it is notable that Hippocrates, even though he himself came from this type of structure – his grandfather, father, and sons were physicians – accepted *paying* students from outside his family. He may even have been the first to do so, though this cannot be stated with certainty. Thus his son-in-law Polybius – linked to the family by marriage, to be sure – was a physician: he would become the author of the famous treatise *On The Nature of Man*. It is therefore no exaggeration to say that Hippocrates was the one who aligned medicine with philosophy by making it share in the same sort of rationality as the latter. Medicine then lost, more or less rapidly but in the end definitively, all of its esoteric or initiational character and established itself in the public arena. The resemblances between medicine and philosophy then are striking. Both propose explanatory systems resting on demonstrations, and both develop through the competition of rival tendencies, which become, in the fourth century BCE for philosophy and less than a century later for medicine, duly constituted schools. No other discipline shared these traits with them for such a long period.

Yet one of Hippocrates' claims to glory in antiquity was that he established the theoretical autonomy of medicine by freeing it from the yoke of philosophy (cf. Celsus, preface to *De Medicina* 8). Before him, in fact, rational medicine was a province of philosophy, in the sense that pre-Socratic philosophy consisted in what was called "the investigation of nature" or "physics." Many of the pre-Socratic philosophers also represented themselves or were recognized as physicians. This was the case with Empedocles, Alcmeon of Croton, Archelaus, and perhaps even Parmenides. Vital phenomena were among those that physics undertook to explain on the same principles as other natural realities, usually by the mutual transformation of elementary principles. The conflict between medicine and philosophy in Hippocrates' time, and that up to the end of the "classic" period in philosophy, i.e., until the death of Aristotle, takes on the appearance of an attempt by medicine to escape from its theoretic tutelage to philosophy, and a parallel attempt by philosophy to reconquer its empire.

The question of the epistemological status of medicine in Aristotle, for example, is very complex – too complex, at any rate, to be treated here. We hardly know, in fact, where to place it in the apparently exhaustive classification of theoretical, practical, and productive sciences proposed in *Metaphysics* E. What is clear, on the other hand, is that for Aristotle "health and sickness are not the business of the physician alone, but also of the physicist, who must go far enough to give their causes . . . Those physicians who are educated and learned make some mention of physics and claim to derive their principles from it" (*Resp.* 21, 480b22). Though Aristotle does not reduce medicine to physics, as the pre-Socratics did, by making knowledge of the causes of health and sickness depend on a physical investigation – in the Aristotelian sense of the term – he thoroughly re-established philosophy's hold on medicine (cf. Bodnár and Pellegrin, ARISTOTLE'S PHYSICS AND COSMOLOGY, in this volume). Within the Hippocratic corpus itself we find both treatises that affirm the dependence of medicine on natural philosophy and others militating in favor of its theoretical autonomy. Thus the treatise *On Fleshes* – the title of which, *Peri Sarchōn*, is probably the result of an error in copying *Peri Archōn*, *On Principles* – and the treatise *Regimen* make a study of what we would call the general laws of nature a preliminary to all medical diagnosis and prognosis. The treatises *On the Nature of Man* and *On Ancient Medicine*, by contrast, denounce the reductionism of the philosophers. But the scope of this anti-philosophical critique must

667

be well understood. The author of *On the Nature of Man* rejects the postulate of some who hold that everything is constituted of a single element – the "Milesian" position – while *On Ancient Medicine* accuses the "new physicians" of falling under the influence of the simplifying assumptions of philosophers who explain everything by means of principles like the hot, the cold, the dry, the moist, etc. This is an anti-speculative critique rather than a properly theoretical one. What the physicians objected to in the philosophers was their reductionism, avoided by the physicians due to the diversity and complexity of the situations they confronted. Thus it is in the name of experience based on lengthy practice that *On Ancient Medicine* seeks to establish the dominion of medicine over everything that concerns human nature.

Hippocratic medicine thus did not threaten the explanatory monopoly of pre-Socratic and classical philosophy. As soon as it ventured into etiology, we see clearly that it adopted the presuppositions of this philosophy, whose "level" it shared, to use again R. Joly's term. It was later that medicine acquired the means to play a genuinely critical role, as we shall see. Nevertheless, medicine's challenge to a hegemonic philosophy was far from being insignificant. The very fact that a rational discipline, unanimously regarded as a "science," sets out to give itself its own theoretical foundations shows that with respect to philosophy, which had arrogated to itself a "right to concern itself with all things," as Hegel said, there are two kinds of dispute. First, there is internal disagreement, which is constitutive of philosophy itself, due to the fact of its agonistic origin and development. Even in the heyday of triumphant Neoplatonism, at the end of antiquity, no philosophical school ever imposed its hegemony in the Greco-Roman world, as Christianity would. The challenge of medicine, on the other hand, represents an external attack, to which we know, at least through one very important piece of evidence, that philosophy gave interested consideration. This is the passage in Plato's *Phaedrus* (269e–270e) in which he speaks of the Hippocratic method, according to which the nature of the whole must be known in order to know that of the part, the species of things to be known must be enumerated, and the relations of the thing to be known to things related to it must be examined. We must surely understand the Hippocratic method to be applicable to the human body, and particularly to the diseased body, even as, when taken up by philosophy, it is applicable to everything, or at least to many other things.

This Platonic passage is hard to interpret and has given rise to an important literature. The commentators have, in fact, asked what such theoretical injunctions meant and what they referred to – for example, to what "whole" is Plato alluding, the whole universe, the whole human body, or something else? It is not this kind of question that is of interest us, but rather that concerning the theoretical relation Plato describes between himself and Hippocrates, this Hippocrates who claimed to free medicine from the control of philosophy. It is hard to know how to read the passage, the interpretation of which lies between two extremes: (i) Plato is promoting the importation into philosophy, and more particularly into the investigation of the relations between rhetoric and the soul, of a method developed in medicine; (ii) Plato is mocking the physicians' claim to have originally developed a method that the philosophers acquired long ago, and that he himself had sketched a few pages above in discussing the procedures of division and collection (265c–266c). However that may be, whether he is admiring or mocking, Plato recognizes the existence of a Hippocratic method that leads to rational knowledge of the human body, a method that the physician of Cos had not borrowed from philosophy.

Alexandrian Medicine and the Hellenistic Philosophical Schools

We have seen that medicine is not easily classified in the Aristotelian system of the sciences, which collectively constitute philosophy. This will be equally true of the Hellenistic philosophical systems, like that of the Stoics, which divided philosophy into three parts – logic, physics, ethics – a division that persisted until the twentieth century. Medicine does not belong entirely to any of these parts, but mobilizes all of them. It was doubtless Galen who showed this best. The physician should obviously be a physicist, but he should also be a logician to be able to infer true judgments from his empirical observations. And Galen wrote several treatises on logic, of which the *Institutio Logica* has come down to us. In ethics, medicine will play an ever-larger role beginning with the Hellenistic period, competing directly with philosophy, as we shall see below. There is then a real rivalry between medicine and philosophy. But if, as the title (and clearly the content as well) of a Galenic treatise implies, "the good physician must also be a philosopher," we should not understand this injunction as turning medicine into a kind of reflection of philosophy. Medicine truly presents itself as a culmination of philosophy.

This is particularly clear in what has been called "Alexandrian medicine." After the dismemberment of Alexander's empire, the dynasty of the Ptolemies, which reigned in Egypt, successfully strove to make Alexandria the main intellectual center of the ancient world – whence the creation of the famous library and Museum, a kind of university, dedicated above all to philosophy and philology but not neglecting the other disciplines. Two great names dominate the medicine of this period, the beginning of the third century BCE: Herophilus of Chalcedon and Erasistratus of Ceos. We will take the first as our example. Herophilus is known primarily as a very great anatomist, due largely to his practice, innovative at the time, of human dissection, and even of human vivisection, practiced on condemned prisoners "pulled from the king's dungeons" (Celsus, preface to *Med.* 23). He is credited with the "discovery" (among others) of the difference between sensitive and motor nerves, the ventricles of the brain, the ovaries, etc. But we should be clear about the scope of these "discoveries": what should we make, for example, of an exact description of the ovary in the absence of any idea of what ovulation might be?

Herophilus is the very image of what in the following century will be called the "dogmatic physician," this epithet, then free from today's pejorative connotation, merely denoting someone who professes opinions (*dogmata*): a physician who thought that it is not the manifest causes – such as indigestion, sunstroke, etc. – that are the fundamental causes of diseases, but rather intervening changes at the level of the constituents of the body – tissues, humors, etc. These fundamental hidden causes can be known by a logical inference from symptoms. It is this procedure of inference, which the Skeptical philosophers as well as Galen called "indication" (*endeixis*) – defined as the inference to the hidden from the manifest, or to the invisible from the visible – that thus furnished the causes of diseases on which therapy strove to act. Having verified

669

such phenomena as fever, shivering, the change in appearance or consistency of certain parts of the body, etc., the dogmatic physician assigns to them, as their ultimate causes, an excess or deficiency of humors, the unseasonable attachment of some humor to an organ, or, if he cleaves to a corpuscular conception of the body's functioning, the clogging of the patient's pores or internal vessels by excessively large or numerous corpuscles. Dogmatism is thus not a doctrine but rather an attitude – we might even say a faith in human reason's capacity to make discoveries. All of the great physicians of the classical period, including Hippocrates, may thus be included among the dogmatists (Celsus, preface to *Med.* 15).

But the position of Herophilus is very different from that of Hippocrates, and this is in large part due to the progress of philosophical reflection. In Alexandria, the organization of studies was strongly influenced by the one that held sway in Aristotle's Lyceum. Strato of Lampsacus, the third head of Lyceum was also the teacher of Ptolemy II Philadelphus. The development, on the one hand, of Aristotelian physics – and especially of biology, which is the main part of it – and of anatomical and physiological investigations by physicians, on the other, meant that the investigation of causes – which is what was above all retained from Aristotelianism – could no longer restrict itself to the vague descriptions of humoral fluxes offered by the Hippocratic physicians. Stoicism too, which would become a prominent feature of the philosophical landscape beginning in the second half of the third century BCE, emphasized etiology. Commentators are not in agreement about the nature of the explanations offered by Herophilus, mainly because our sources are contradictory. Most of the evidence, especially that found in Galen, depicts Herophilus as a dogmatic physician, in the sense defined above.[1] Other fragments, including ones from Galen, describe him, by contrast, as a physician who was very cautious with respect to "hidden causes," and even make him a precursor of the Empiricist school to be discussed below. Heinrich von Staden, in his magisterial book on Herophilus (1989), proposes that he attributed a hypothetical status to explanations in physiology and pathology, which is perhaps to credit Alexandrian medicine with views that are too modern. A formulation that Galen credits to Herophilus says, doubtless with regard to observed phenomena, and especially those made accessible by the development of anatomy, "that these things are the first, even if they are not the first" (*Meth. Med.* X, 107 K), which, characteristically of the dogmatic position, is to acknowledge that the causes that explain phenomena are first "by nature," as Aristotle puts it. But it seems that Herophilus did not feel competent to determine the nature of the primary entities constituting all things (elements, qualities, or atoms). It is not, strictly speaking, a Skeptical position that is at issue, but Herophilus nonetheless contributed to preserving the theoretical autonomy of medicine as against philosophy.

The figure, already proclaimed by Aristotle (cf. *Pol.* III.11, 1282a3), of the biologist-physician, not to be found in the treatises of the Hippocratic corpus, was then established. The relations between medicine and philosophy were radically changed thereby. The situation may be described by paraphrasing Kant. Until the time of Aristotle, philosophers had succeeded in convincing many people, among them numerous

---

1.   The most explicit testimony, which lists the dogmatic ("rationalist") physicians, comes from a perhaps apocryphal Galenic treatise, *Introductio sive medicus* 4.

physicians, that medicine without philosophy was blind. The improvement, due to the results of medical investigation, in the identification of the causes of diseases, shows that, at least in physics, henceforth philosophy without medicine is empty. The most celebrated dogmatic physicians, says Celsus, "laid claim to the study of nature as well, judging that without it medicine was mutilated and powerless" (preface to *Med.* 9). Already surpassing the philosophers in physics, physicians, as we have remarked, were soon to become their redoubtable competitors in the realm of ethics.

Some have given a philosopho-centric reading of medicine's intervention in intellectual debate. For instance, G. E. R. Lloyd, in the account in the new edition (1991) of his article, "Who Is Attacked in *On Ancient Medicine?*" published in 1963, sets out to show that the polemic of *On Ancient Medicine*, discussed above, sets in opposition the two main tendencies of Greek philosophy and science: a deductive, axiomatic model and an empirical one. The whole Aristotelian tradition insisted on the importance of empirical examination. As early as the fourth century BCE, for example, the Aristotelizing anatomist Diocles of Carystos criticized the etiologizing excesses of physicians and their distrust of experience. Herophilus, it seems, did the same. Lloyd's analysis is perfectly acceptable as concerns philosophy and has the support of many texts, but it risks reducing medicine to a force supplementary to one of the two conflicting philosophical tendencies. It is in any case uncertain that such a view, even in its "hardest" version, really reduces the importance of medicine. On the one hand, one might, taking the inverse of Lloyd's view, show that medicine, from the Hippocratic period on, is itself shot through with the opposition between a theoretical and an empirical tendency; and that in treatises such as *Regimen* and *Fleshes* the theoretical approach calls philosophy, and in particular the "inquiry into nature," to its aid. On the other hand, if medicine is in a position to reinforce the so-called empirical tendency in Greek philosophy, and the latter must appeal to medicine in order to win out, or at least for reinforcement, that gives medicine the role of an arbiter in the intellectual debate.

The Theoretical Audacity of the Medical Schools

This decisive intervention by medicine in the philosophical debate takes a remarkable turn during the period of the development of medical "schools" or "sects," a period in which medicine demonstrated a theoretical boldness both unprecedented then and perhaps unequalled in later times. First we must say a few words about these "sects," long neglected by historians, no doubt because they saw in them excessive and ridiculous doctrines.

The terms "school" and "sect" translate the Greek words *hairesis*, a substantive corresponding to the verb *haireo*, "to choose" – a heretic being one who chooses a path other than the orthodox line. In a certain way the division of the medical landscape into sects assimilates medicine to philosophy, since the latter existed through the activity of rival schools. The first philosophical school to present most of the features that would characterize subsequent ones is Plato's Academy: its members led a largely communal life, at one in their admiration of the teacher, which wove between them very strong fraternal bonds. It seems, on the other hand, that Plato imposed no philosophical orthodoxy on his students, whereas one of the main traits of later schools, including Aristotle's Lyceum, was to turn their members into propagandists for the teacher's doctrine (Cf. Bénatouïl, PHILOSOPHIC SCHOOLS IN HELLENISTIC AND ROMAN TIMES, in this volume). In some fashion, medical schools already existed, even from the time of Hippocrates: these medical centers were in operation at least since the sixth century BCE, sometimes associated with religious sanctuaries dedicated to healing divinities; for instance, at Cyrene in present-day Libya, at Croton in Sicily and, as we have seen, at Cos and Cnidos. An exceptional personality such as Hippocrates might lend a theoretical and/or therapeutic "style" to the medical practice of a place, and thus found what we may call a "proto-school." With Herophilus, swiftly followed in this respect by Erasistratus, the period of the medicine of the sects truly begins. At Alexandria, Herophilus founded a school whose students would be charged with propagating the teacher's doctrine as well as his therapeutic practices, especially with regard to defending it against its eventual detractors. Thus have been preserved for us sources bearing on the divergences between Herophilians and Erasistrateans over the usefulness of bloodletting.[2] The schools of Herophilus and Erasistratus survived their founders: the school of Herophilus remained in Alexandria for about two centuries before emigrating to Laodicea in Asia Minor, and Galen, in the second century CE, still mentions the existence of Erasistratean physicians.

But it was just after the time of Herophilus that occurred an event of capital importance, not only for the history of ancient medicine but for the history of Greek thought and, ultimately, for the intellectual history of humanity in general. According to the most plausible version of the matter, a student of Herophilus, Philinus of Cos, founded the Empiricist sect or school.[3] Philinus had found in Herophilus himself certain views that steered him toward the doctrine he would develop, but we are faced with a genuine dissidence – dissidence being, in philosophy and henceforward in medicine, one of the processes by which new schools were formed. Empiricism sets out initially from a critique of earlier medicine, all representatives of which are collected under the epithet "dogmatists," a term we have already encountered. The dogmatic school, sometimes called "logical" or "rationalist," was not a true school, and no physician ever called himself "dogmatic." It was constituted by its critics, led by the Empiricists, who defined it by means of certain theoretical characteristics enumerated above.

The basic position of the Empiricists is that only what can be grasped through the senses is knowable, whereas everything inferred through "indication" offers only a baseless and illusory knowledge. By maintaining that reason is of no help in discovering hidden causes – that is, ultimately, in gaining knowledge of nature – the Empiricists scandalized the Greek rationalist consensus: a scandal from which we are not entirely set free, since only very recently have the Empiricists come to be regarded as anything but provocateurs or fools. In one sense, they are indeed the products of their

---

2.   Cf. the translation of Galen's treatise *Against the Erasistrateans* in P. Brain (1986).

3.   Celsus (preface to *Med.* 10) regards the sect as having been founded by Serapion of Alexandria (around 250 BCE), but there are at least two other candidates: a certain Zeuxis of whom Galen speaks in his commentary on Book I of Hippocrates' *Prorrhetic* (2.58 = XVI, 636 K): Zeuxis, "the most ancient of the Empiricists" (this reference seems to have escaped Deichgräber, 1930), and Acron of Alexandria, a disciple of Empedocles (cf. Galen *Subfig. emp.* 1.42 Deichgräber).

time, when Stoic and Epicurean dogmatisms were but the obverse of a feeling of doubt about the cognitive capacities of human beings:

> Before that period, there had certainly been no absence of critics to point out the shortcomings of human knowledge, but it is safe to say that various triumphs in the sciences, particularly in mathematics, had enabled philosophers, when they focused their inquiry on knowledge as such, to concentrate on questions about its nature, its origin, its instruments, and its structure of research and exposition, rather than on the question of its existence or possibility. The Hellenistic period, by contrast, was a period in which philosophers, particularly the Epicureans and the Stoics, became suddenly and vitally preoccupied with establishing that knowledge is possible, that our cognitive access to the world rests on an infallible base. (Brunschwig, 2000, p. 739)

Confining ourselves to the medical domain, it is at once the most ancient certainties and novel practices such as dissection that come to be doubted. Etiology, i.e., diagnosis, loses its entire basis: attempts to discover what is hidden being doomed to fail, not only does reasoning serve no purpose, but it is equally useless to practice anatomy or vivisection. If a cause (*aitia, aition*) can be assigned to diseases, it is in the immediate sense of the term *aition* – what is *responsible* for the illness in question. It is what the Empiricists called the "immediate cause": heat, cold, various excesses, fatigue, a trauma, etc. At once medicine, which, in the Greek intellectual landscape, had raised itself to the level of mathematics as a paradigmatic science, can no longer be regarded either as a science (*epistēmē*) or as an art (*technē*). For the Empiricist physician there are three ways to acquire sound knowledge: personal observation (*autopsia*); what has been observed and recounted by others and/or recorded in writing (*historia*); and what may be analogically derived from what has been observed – what the Empiricists called "transition to the similar": a treatment effective for one part of the body is "transferred" to another part similarly afflicted, etc. Moreover, the empiricists insist that only repeated observations can establish what they call a "theorem" – "a theorem is knowledge of a thing that one has seen a certain number of times, while together with the ability to distinguish the event contrary to it" (Gal. *Subfig. emp.* 2.46) – a term which must here be stripped of all theoretical connotation, leaving only its original etymological meaning, "what one sees," "spectacle."

The Empiricists were not empiricists in the modern sense of the term, and still less were they anti-rationalists who, for example, promoted a return to magico-religious medicine. It is very important to understand the attitude of the Empiricists toward rational procedure. Before trying to clarify this question, we must note that recourse to reasoning seems to have been the subject of a debate within the Empiricist school. Refuting the idea, propounded entirely without justification by Deichgräber (1930), the author of what remains the standard reference on the Empiricist school, according to which the Empiricist school was by nature incapable of any significant evolution, M. Frede (1988, p. 89) has shown that, while the first Empiricists took an extreme line in rejecting all recourse to reasoning, later physicians like Heraclides of Tarentum, whom Frede sees as "the most important Empiricist medical author,"[4] had a much

---

4. Heraclides is thought to have lived during the second and first centuries BCE.

more nuanced position. Not only must one resort to reason in order to reason against one's adversaries, as Galen says (*Subfig. emp.* 12.87), but we also may well wonder what kind of medicine it would be that dispensed entirely with inference.

The Empiricists like Heraclides of Tarentum must have been aware of the dangers of pure empiricism with which their predecessors were reproached. We find a trace of such criticisms in Galen. For instance, in his treatise on *Medical Experience*,[5] Galen points out (6.1ff.; 30.5ff. Walzer and Frede) that if the causal or non-causal character of the elements of a situation are not to be taken into account, then everything perceived must be put on the same level: what the patient did before the onset of the disease, but equally whether he was wearing a white cloak or a red one. Inference, however, need not take the form of "indication." That is, it need not be from something visible and graspable to something invisible and ungraspable – the Empiricists called this process, used by the dogmatic physicians, "analogism," a process so funda-mental to the practice of the dogmatists that they are also termed "Analogists" (Gal. *On Sects* 1) – but rather from what is graspable to what is graspable, whence the "epilogism" the Empiricists introduced in order to discover what is provisionally hidden, but the nature of which is not inaccessible to experience. Epilogism is in a way the most extreme form of reasoning acceptable to the Empiricists, or at least to the less extremist among them. Who could maintain, in any case, that repeated observation, which presupposes the judgment that cases observed with a view to establishing a "theorem" belong in fact to a single class, or the use of *historia*, which calls for a "criticism of sources," to say nothing of the transition to the similar, involve no reasoning at all? Further, when in the *Subfiguratio Empirica* Galen has the Empiricists say, "experience based on practice, i.e., expertise, comes only to men of the art, pursu-ant to some resemblances among the things they have found by experimentation" (*Subfig. emp.* 2.45), we see how far the experience on which Empiricism takes its stand is from the ordinary and unregulated experience to which the dogmatists would like to reduce it. It is a matter of a *reasoned* and systematic enterprise, of an experience in which external conditions are scrupulously taken into account.

In an article originally conceived as a commentary on the article by M. Frede cited above, M. Matthen makes an interesting remark (1988, p. 111): what the "clear-minded Empiricist" rejects is demonstration (*apodeixis*) in so far as it allows an infer-ence with a conclusion bearing on what is unobservable, "but some Empiricists [i.e., extreme Empiricists from the beginning of the Empiricist school] might also have banned reasoning as such, because they failed to distinguish between argument and proof." In the eyes of dogmatic ancient philosophers and physicians, to criticize the excesses of reason is also to criticize reason itself. This, by contrast, is true neither for the "clear-minded" Empiricists nor for us. In fact, to make one more step, the theoretical scope of the Empiricist doctrine is apparent. We can see in the position taken by the Empiricists, in effect, a very modern-style critique of a metaphysical (in the Comtian sense of the term) application of reason. To be sure, as Galen repeats often enough, the dogmatic physicians preach an alliance between reasoning and observation, even experimenta-tion, and he himself adopted such a position. But observation and experience as conceived and practiced by all these people are notoriously incapable of deciding

5. This text is preserved mainly in Arabic.

674

between rival theories, because, by their nature, these theories are unverifiable and unfalsifiable. Similarly, we may point out that the theoretical developments in medicine brought about by people like Herophilus and Erasistratus can have had only the feeblest consequences for therapy, obliging these bold theorists to fall back on traditional cures.[6] And Galen remarks several times over, with a bit of amusement, that in the end dogmatists and Empiricists meet again over matters of therapy. For instance, all agree that after the bite of a venomous animal one must cause the venom to bleed away, and thus not hurry to cicatrize the wound (*On Sects* 4.8).

We must say a little about the second great medical school that stood opposed to dogmatism, the Methodist school. Few are the historians who, before our recent times, have not regarded the Methodists as jokers at best and at worst as fools.[7] One example of this ill regard: some historians have purported to explain that the Methodist physicians enjoyed great credit among the dominant Roman classes – Cicero's physician was a Methodist – and even in the imperial palace because their simplistic theory had every appeal to Romans who were unrefined and little given to theoretical speculation. In fact, Methodism is an admirably subtle theory. The Methodists dismiss dogmatists and Empiricists equally: they reject, just like the Empiricists, explanations that resort to hidden entities, but they believe, as against the Empiricists, that experience – i.e., observation, in fact – is of no help in medicine. According to them, every illness itself indicates its own proper treatment, just as thirst indicates its own remedy, which is drink. All the same, this indication is to be read through a universally valid conceptual grid – that of "apparent communities."

This doctrine doubtless existed in several versions, which, for lack of texts, it would certainly be very difficult for historians to reconstruct exactly, but the most widespread would seem to be the following: Every pathological state of the body results from a state of compaction, of relaxation, or a mixture of compaction and relaxation. This presupposes that the body itself can be described in terms of condensation and rarefaction: "when the body is in a balanced state of condensation and rarefaction, the living person is in good health," says, for example, the pseudo-Galenic treatise *On the Best Sect* (26 = I, 180 K). It may be asked what purpose was served by such a construction. Now, we have seen that one of the dogmatists' main criticisms of the Empiricists was precisely that pure phenomena do not exist, and that perception can be put to use only by means of a theoretical construction that brings order to it. The doctrine of apparent communities escapes the pitfalls of phenomenalism without falling back into those of the search for inaccessible causes. This is surely what explains ch. 21 of *On the Best Sect*: it can happen that the symptoms are similar but that one should not use the same treatment, or that the same treatment should be used for apparently different conditions. The examples are interesting: the same treatment must not be used "as in the case of phrenitis, for that which results from compaction and that which results

6. Cf. my article, Pellegrin (2000). This idea had already been developed, a little earlier and unknown to me, in Mario Vegetti's excellent 1995 paper.
7. There have been, over the course of history, a few notable exceptions: In 1611 Prosper Alpinus published a *De Medicina Methodica* and Daniel Leclerc, in his *History of Medicine*, published in 1723, favors Methodist theses. At the present time, Jackie Pigeaud is one of the staunchest defenders of Methodism; cf., for example, Pigeaud (1991).

from relaxation," while one is to use the same treatment for pleurisy as for phrenitis "if they are both the result of compaction" (*Opt. Sect.* I.163 K). We are thus left with the impression that the Methodist school, the latest arrival of the three, took into account the criticisms addressed to the Empiricist school, whose suspicion of arbitrary theoretical speculation it nonetheless shared. For the Methodists, however, it is not only "apparent communities" that are indicative of the requisite treatment (a compacted state calls for intervention to make it cease, etc.). They also took account of the stage reached in the development of the illness, but in accordance with a predetermined schema, valid in all cases: every illness has a beginning (*archê, initium*), an increase (*auxēsis, epidosis, augmentum*), a paroxysm (*acmē, status*), and a decline (*parakmē, anexis, declinatio*).

The term "apparent" in the phrase "apparent communities" thus has an unexpected meaning. The author of the treatise *On the Best Sect* writes: "they do not mean by 'apparent' [in the phrase 'apparent communities'] what is grasped by the senses. In fact no disposition [what is at issue is no doubt the compacted and so forth] is grasped by the senses, but they call apparent what is graspable by oneself, even if it does not fall under the senses." And the author adds that for the Methodists "apparent" is "approximately" a synonym for "evident" (*enargēs*) ([Gal.] *Opt. Sect* 26 = I, 175–176 K). In other words, the manifest generalities avoid two objections: that of being grasped by the senses, with all the uncertainties attending sensible knowledge; and that of being rationally established on the basis of indicative signs. We shall return to the latter point below.

A historical problem, which takes up an ancient controversy, will let us complete this quick portrait of Methodism. The identity of the founder of the Methodist school has been, since antiquity, the subject of a dispute with an important theoretical stake. The two most serious candidates are Themison of Laodicea in the first century BCE, who was a disciple of the very famous Asclepiades of Bythinia, and Thessalus of Tralles in the first century CE (for Asclepiades, see Vallance, 1990 and 1994). Some even make Asclepiades himself the founder of Methodism. Asclepiades was at once celebrated and controversial, beginning even in his own time – he lived in the second century BCE – since he was considered now an outstanding physician, now a swindler. Of his doctrine we shall here recall only his "corpuscularianism": vital functions come down to fluxes of corpuscles in the body, inside appropriate cavities through "pores." Illnesses are thus due to perturbations of these fluxes, whatever their causes. How then, despite the highly dogmatic character of his doctrine – corpuscles and pores are invisible entities, disclosed by rational inference ("indication") – can Asclepiades have been suggested as the ancestor, or even the founder, of Methodism? The reason is that, for Asclepiades, the two main conditions that lead to illness are the drawing together of the particles constituting the body, which has the effect of clogging the pores, and the excessive separation of the same particles, which puts the body in a state of relaxation. The kinship with the Methodist "apparent communities" is clear. This allows Vallance (1990, p. 139) to highlight a parallel between Asclepiadian and Methodist descriptions of diseases, and to show that the Methodists conceptualized nosological realities "in Asclepiadean intellectual categories." To this convergence in theory may be added a historical and personal link, since Asclepiades was the teacher of Themison, one of the possible founders of Methodism. But the fundamental difference between

Asclepiades and the Methodists is no less remarkable for all that, especially for our approach to Methodism. Whereas normal and pathological states are described by Asclepiades in terms of the actions of corpuscles, the three Methodist generalities "suggest the resultant situation without referring to its aetiology at all" (Vallance, 1990, p. 134): where Asclepiades speaks, for example, of "obstruction" – where, that is, he gives the cause along with the effect – the Methodists are content to point out a compaction; and they do not describe this compaction as the effect of any cause whatsoever.

This yields an unexpected picture of Methodism as a kind of "dogmatism without dogmas," whose implicit position would be something like this: Let adventurous spirits like Asclepiades search for the causes of states of compaction, states of relaxation, and of mixed states; the Methodist physician, for his part, recognizes that etiology cannot be the subject of a true discourse. Did the Methodists go so far as to think that Asclepiadism could be seen as a *hypothetical* etiology, one that "worked" in taking account of pathological realities but that could eventually be replaced by another one? That is perhaps to "modernize" them a little too much; and, anyway, we have no texts stating this explicitly. This uncoupling of a possible but uncertain theory from its medical application is apparent, in any event, in the remarkable attitude of the Methodists toward a general theory of the living body. We have seen above that all consistent dogmatism had to rest, in the end, on a "physics." It is worth noting that the Methodists, without denying the possibility of such a physics, left its place empty, as it were: their description of the healthy body is, in a way, a minimal characterization – a state of equilibrium between condensation and rarefaction. The Methodists thus reject two attitudes. They do not want to rest therapy on a speculative and, in the end, metaphysical biology; but neither do they mean to declare theory impossible and to reduce the medical art to a pragmatic empiricism.

Obviously, this reconstruction is largely hypothetical, due to the scarcity of texts. But we can be reasonably sure of at least one thing, namely that the compatibility of the doctrine of Asclepiades with Methodist medicine was a subject of debate among the Methodists themselves. Thus, reading Caelius Aurelianus shows us that the later Methodists faulted Themison for not having sufficiently freed himself from Asclepiades.[8] Caelius shows how, by contrast, Soranus, a Methodist physician of the first century CE from whom we have a great treatise on gynecology, in some ways brought Methodism to completion, which led him to be more critical of Asclepiades than were his predecessors.

8. Caelius Aurelianus, a physician (writing in Latin), was formerly dated in the second century CE, but has been moved up to the fifth century CE by the majority of specialists. We have two treatises by him, *On Acute Diseases* and *On Chronic Diseases*, which are irreplaceable sources for the history of ancient medicine. The only modern edition is Drabkin (1950). On the strength of Caelius' own testimony, commentators have maintained that his works were Latin translations of works with the same titles, now lost, by Soranus of Ephesus: "Soranus, whom I have here undertaken to translate into Latin" (*Ac.* 2.8), "Soranus, whom I, in my mediocrity, wanted to render into Latin . . ." writes Caelius (*Ac.* 2.65). Perhaps this estimate will soon be revised, and these declarations seen as containing an element of literary fiction. But it is undeniable that Caelius is a Methodist, and that he does not refrain from showing that Methodism has a conflict-filled history.

Even the most provocative Methodist assertions have to be re-evaluated. Take their claim that medicine could be learned in six months (for example, cf. *On Sects* 9.24), which caused great scandal: is it not the sign of an acute awareness of the limits of medicine in their time? By accusing, even if not explicitly in these terms, the Empiricists of dogmatism, the Methodists largely side with Sextus Empiricus, who considers them to be the only medical school in accord with Pyrrhonian Skepticism (S.E. *PH* 1.238–240): they do not commit themselves on the nature of things, but they say how morbid states appear to them through the medium of their conceptual tools – the apparent communities and the phases of diseases. These conceptual tools are evident, but not through observation or experience.[9]

Medicine and Skepticism

With the Empiricist and Methodist schools, medicine begins a new relationship to philosophy, and in the first instance with a quite particular kind of philosophy: Skepticism. The problem of the relations between Skeptical philosophy and medicine is very complex, and much remains to be done to make possible its satisfactory treatment. Chronologically, Skepticism, whether Pyrrhonist or neo-Academic, predates the birth of the Empiricist sect, since Pyrrho was born around 365 BCE and Arcesilaus some 50 years later, while Philinus was active in the middle of the third century BCE. But this does rule out the hypothesis that Skepticism was of medical origin. Besides, it is hard to estimate the degree to which Skepticism influenced the birth of the Empiricist sect. As we remarked above, if Galen and a whole side of the doxography dedicated to Herophilus are to be believed, the main reason for the birth of Empiricist doctrine is to be sought in the history of medicine itself: it was from the doubts expressed by Herophilus about the possibility of penetrating to the causes of morbid states, or at least to some of them, that Philinus drew the impetus for his own thought. But the great Skeptical challenge to triumphant Greek rationalism was already on the intellectual scene, and could not have been entirely without effect. And in fact we find, especially in Galen, who remains our main source on the Empiricist and Methodist sects, passages showing that Empiricist physicians had assimilated several fundamental doctrines of Skepticism and sometimes expressed them in Skeptical terminology. Thus, to give one example, in the treatise *On Sects*, Galen reports that the Empiricists described "analogism" as reasoning which begins with *phainomena* and proceeds toward things that are "completely obscure," adding, "it was then that they had in their hands the discord that cannot be resolved (*anepikritos*), which is, they say, the sign of the ungrasped (*akatalēpsia*) – such is their language" (*On Sects* 5.11). Now what we have here is strictly Skeptical language. But Galen's testimony is to be taken with caution, not because it might be explicitly false, but because it does not necessarily distinguish between different periods of Skepticim and of Empiricism. It is, in fact, a matter of much more than mere borrowing; and it is a true fusion of Skepticism with medicine that we see, at a date that is the subject of debate among specialists.

9.   We can reaffirm most of the conclusions of Frede (1982), which is devoted to these problems, and especially to the rationalism of the Methodists.

The periodization of the Skeptical movement is, in fact, a difficult problem. Diogenes Laertius (9.115), for example, echoes a dispute among the ancients themselves over whether Timon, the disciple of Pyrrho, did or did not have any successors. But whether we hypothesize an uninterrupted succession of Skeptical philosophers, or a sort of resurrection of Pyrrhonism after a period of slumber, the presence of physicians among the protagonists is very important; and, according to a tradition reported by the Empiricist physician Menodotus, it was even a physician, doubtless himself also an Empiricist, Ptolemy of Cyrene, who revived the school (cf. Brunschwig, PYRRHONISM, in this volume). But certainly from the first century CE on, and perhaps earlier, there is genuinely a fusion, since the "heads" of the Skeptical school are also physicians and, according to the sources, usually Empiricist physicians. Victor Brochard (1923, p. 350) interprets this convergence in connection with a distinction between several phases of Pyrrhonist Skepticism:

> Aenesidemus and his immediate successors were, we believe, nothing but dialecticians: they pursued a purely negative aim and intended only to overturn dogmatism. . . . The Skeptics of the latest period are physicians: if they too wished to destroy dogmatism and philosophy, and in the same way, it was in order to replace it with art, based on observation, with medicine, i.e., with a kind of science. . . . They combat dogmatism as in our day the positivists combat metaphysics.

The first part of this verdict is no doubt too hasty, if it suggests that people like Aenesidemus confined themselves to a dialectical game, but the second is very interesting and connects with what was said above about Empiricism and Methodism. Skepticism militates for another use of reason, and when it implements its program, it does so through medicine.

On this point, it is quite remarkable that Sextus Empiricus seems simply no longer to make the distinction between philosophical and medical schools. At the end of Book I of *Outlines of Pyrrhonism*, for example, when he examines Skepticism's "neighbor philosophies" that aspired, or might have aspired, to take its place in the history of thought, he successively cites Heracliteanism, the philosophy of Democritus, Cyrenaic philosophy, Protagoreanism, the New Academy, and Empiricist medicine, which he compares to Methodism. Moreover, it has been maintained that when Sextus speaks of "dogmatists" in his study of signs, he is thinking sometimes of philosophers such as the Stoics and sometimes of physicians (cf. Allen, 2001).

This close link between philosophy and medicine is visible with particular clarity as regards a sphere mentioned above, which showed itself, beginning in the Hellenistic period, to be of the highest importance: that of signs. While in Aristotle the theory of signs was a sort of appendix to the account of the syllogism, in the Hellenistic period, especially in the two great "dogmatic" schools, the Epicureans and the Stoics, the appeal to signs becomes the basic method of scientific knowledge. The Stoics, for example, had a rich and complex semiology, found both in their theory of language and in the part of their logic concerning the inference in a connective proposition.[10] (On these topics, see Ierodiakonou, STOIC LOGIC, and Modrak, PHILOSOPHY OF LANGUAGE,

---

10. Thus I translate *sunēmmenon*, ordinarily rendered as "conditional."

in this volume.) It is remarkable that the most complete treatment of the notion of a sign that has come down to us is found in Sextus Empiricus. One can make out several "accidental" reasons for this, such as the loss of texts or Sextus' special interest, as a physician, in semiology; but there is also a more fundamental reason, which is that Pyrrhonian Skepticism is not an original philosophy with regard to what it needs to follow closely – the philosophies it attacks. Everything important, at least quantitatively, in Sextus' account is so because the corresponding subject is important to the "dogmatists." We have seen that signs occupy a central place in Hellenistic epistemology. Sextus therefore needed to linger fairly long over semiology. But there are certainly other reasons for this massive presence of signs in Sextus, born of the relations of Skepticism itself to the medicine of its time. Ancient authors, at least those of late antiquity, seem to have had the impression that the Pyrrhonian Skeptics emphasized even more the importance of signs. Thus we may cite this extraordinary definition of the sign in the *Suda*: "that through which the Skeptics apprehend that which is non-evident, and which they suppress by their arguments" (4.351). The sign, then, became a Skeptical affair.

The most elaborate version of Sextus' critique of the sign is in Book 2 (97–133) of *Outlines of Pyrrhonism*. Sextus there distinguishes two sorts of signs, indicative and commemorative. This distinction rests on another one, both being attributed to the "dogmatists." The first distinction is between what is clear (*prodēlon*) and what is obscure (*adēlon*), the obscure itself being divided into three categories: what is obscure once and for all (*kathapax*), for instance, whether the stars are even in number; what is on occasion (*pros kairon*) obscure – something is obscure in this way if it is evident by nature (these are the dogmatists speaking) but can on occasion be hidden, as Athens is from me at this moment – and what is obscure by nature but can be grasped by means of something else, for instance the invisible pores through which sweat passes. These are Sextus' own examples. Again according to the dogmatists, things that are clear need no sign; for example, "It is day." Things that are obscure once and for all are not grasped at all, and so do not have to be signified. There remain things obscure on occasion and things obscure by nature. The former are grasped by means of commemorative signs, the latter by indicative signs (*PH* 2.99). The dogmatists in fact define the commemorative sign as what has been observed "evidently" along with (*hama*) what it signifies, as smoke is a sign for fire, whereas the indicative sign is one that has not been observed with its signified, but rather "signifies from its nature and its own constitution" (*PH* 2.101), as the movements of the body signify the soul.

In *Outlines of Pyrrhonism* 2.102, Sextus states that the Skeptics accepted commemorative signs, which are "rendered credible by daily life"; and he gives two examples: smoke is a sign of fire, and "he who beholds a scar says there has been a wound." Now, a wound is not observed *along with* (*hama*) the wound, in the temporal sense of "along with." Moreover, in some cases, an expert eye is needed to distinguish a scar from, for example, an epidermal rash (think of an appendectomy scar years after the operation). Therefore there are probably scars that we know to be consequent upon wounds only after instruction, i.e., by appeal to the observations of others. This is what the Empiricist physicians called *historia*, as we have seen. "Along with" thus has here a sense that is both diachronic and collective. There is a technical employment of commemorative signs, mainly by physicians. We, therefore, understand, from these medical examples, what it means that the connection between a commemorative sign and its signified must be observed "in an adequate way." The example of smoke and fire is in fact misleading. Most of the commemorative signs used by Empiricist physicians, and doubtless Methodists as well, are not simply and immediately verified, but rather are based on observations that are repeated, careful, and free from all theoretical and, especially, causal apparatus. We may compare this with a remark by Sextus in *Adversus Mathematicos* 8.204: reddening, the curvature of vessels,[11] and thirst are not signs for the uninitiated, but are so "for Empiricist physicians." What are in question, then, are commemorative signs. The distinction between indicative and commemorative signs is thus not hard and fast: what for the vulgar or for bad physicians is an indicative sign, or no sign at all, can become a commemorative sign for the Empiricists, thanks to their repeated and careful observations.

On the problem of the sign, which is crucial as concerns the relations between philosophy and medicine, we may roughly summarize matters as follows. Both, in about the same period, made a transition from an epistemology that was mainly etiological to a logic that was essentially semiological. The best illustration of this, in philosophy, is the transition from Aristotelian syllogistic, in which the scientific syllogism, or demonstration, exhibits in its middle term the cause of the conclusion, to Stoic logic (Cf. Detel, ARISTOTLE'S LOGIC AND THEORY OF SCIENCE, and Ierodiakonou, STOIC LOGIC, in this volume). In medicine, it could be said that Hippocratic medicine is not a symptom-centered medicine, which sounds paradoxical, in so far as we suppose all medicine should cleave to symptoms. The weaknesses of the theoretical treatises in the Hippocratic corpus, from the modern scientific viewpoint, stem especially from their aspiration to account for the causes of morbid states, causes they discern, for example, in humoral movements. To reject etiology, for the Empiricists and the Methodists, is to refuse to "descend" from causes to effects, and is to put the symptom at the center of medical practice and theory. This is clear in the case of the Empiricists, since for them it is a matter of noting the usual links between symptom and treatment. The Methodists, who indeed have a kind of etiological schema – since all illness comes from a compaction, a relaxation, or a mixture of the two – nevertheless insist on the point that the illness is itself indicative of the treatment. Even dogmatic physicians inferred the non-visible from the visible, and were thus semiologists rather than etiologists.

This estrangement of physicians from the causal approach also reveals itself in the new face that medicine shows at the end of the Hellenistic period. We spoke above about "the medicine of the sects and nosographies," and we have seen what there were in the way of sects. Nosographies are treatises that name illnesses and classify them, allowing the physician to determine what condition his patient suffers from, based on the set of symptoms he presents. This practice endured until the nineteenth century and into our own day in psychiatry. These, then, are treatises on medical

---

11. The text is uncertain. I read *angeiōn* with Kalbfleisch; Hervet suggests reading *arthrōn* "of articulations," Bekker *aitiōn*, "of causes."

semiology, which must not be confused with the symptomatic descriptions of concrete cases that can be found in the Hippocratic *Epidemics*. The symptom defines the illness and determines the treatment. We can make out, in the background of such treatises, a long practice of observation and of recording correlations between symptoms and treatments, as advocated by the Empiricists.

Now, commentators have often concluded, from Sextus' statement that it was the "dogmatists" who introduced the distinction between indicative and commemorative signs, that this distinction was of philosophical, probably Stoic, origin (Brunschwig, 1980; Burnyeat, 1982). But no text states this, while our sources attibute the appeal to these two sorts of signs to the medical schools. Here are two particularly definite texts: "The Empiricists say that, among the things that are grasped, some are grasped by the senses, such as redness, others by memory (*hupomnēstikos*, which is the adverbial form of the adjective *hupomnētikos* translated above as "commemorative") in such a way that they are grasped through certain signs; by contrast [according to them] nothing is grasped in an indicative way (*endeiktikos*)" as among the rationalist physicians (Ps.-Galen, *Opt. secta ad Thrasybulum* ([Gal.] 14 = *Opt. Sect*. I, 149 K); "the commemorative sign, according to what the Empiricists say, is something apparent and known from a previous observation, useful for the remembering of something known" ([Gal.] *Def. med.* 176 = XIX, 396 K). That the distinction between indicative and commemorative signs is of medical origin, and enters philosophy through Sextus, is thus not an absurd hypothesis. It may be concluded from all this that, if philosophy and medicine together took a "semiological turn," medicine was not the little sister imitating her elder, but rather made a major contribution to the theory of signs. Presumably, it was medical practice, and their familiarity with symptoms, that enabled physicians to do this.

Ethics and Medicine

Finally, there is one last domain in which the relations between philosophy and medicine should be delineated, and to which we have already alluded several times: that of ethics. In the domain of ethics, indeed, it may be from medicine that came one of the common views best established among the ancients, namely that the passions are the effect of corporeal dispositions, and especially of a characteristic mixture of bodily humors. From among a great many texts, we may cite a very clearly titled little work by Galen: *The habits of the soul are the consequence of the dispositions of the body*, which attributes this thesis to the greatest philosophers. Galen claims, moreover, to have established experimentally that this doctrine is true "in every instance." A remarkable illustration of this psychological materialism is found in the conception the ancients had of what we call mental illnesses. "Mania," for example, which becomes, in the period of nosographical medicine, a particular nosological entity, but which previously denoted all types of "madness," is a fundamentally somatic affliction (cf. Pigeaud, 1987). Since, on the general view of the ancients, mastery of the passions is the main condition for the virtuous and happy life, it could seem, and actually did seem to many, that consulting a physician was a more effective means to ethical progress than recourse to the moralist.

It is hard for people who, like us, have been shaped by a Judaeo-Christian morality, particularly in its Kantian version, to understand the foundations of ancient morality. Let us recall two points that the ancients regarded as a kind of common ground, and that will be of great consequence for the relations between ethics and medicine. First, moral virtue is a natural state, while vice is a state counter to nature. This principle is enough to establish a strong parallel between virtue and health on the one hand and vice and illness on the other, of which the most famous expressions are undoubtedly Socrates's claims that the wicked should be healed, that he who acts badly has his soul in a bad state, and so on. It might be replied that these theses seemed paradoxical to the contemporaries of Socrates, which shows that they did not represent the majority view of the ancients. But what shocked people in Socrates' time was his claim that criminals are not responsible ("no one is wicked of his own free will"). The idea of the naturalness of virtue would have seemed more acceptable, and at any rate was defended by all the philosophers, perhaps with the exception of the Skeptics. The second point is that once this state of virtue is established, the subject attains a state of happiness he has no reason to leave. Once in a state of virtuous felicity, the ancient sage is not *tempted* to leave it, as the Christian saint is tempted by the attractions of evil. Here too the medical comparison suggests itself almost spontaneously: once we are in good health, only some *external* event can force us out of it.

If we connect these two ancient "common positions," we reach a point of contact between medicine and philosophy that Ludwig Edelstein has very rightly emphasized. Noting that, at least since Homeric times, popular morality regarded health as the sovereign good,[12] Edelstein (1967) takes aim at the pretensions of certain physicians to an annexation, pure and simple, of ethics. He cites in this regard Herophilus' statement in his work *On Regimen*, reported by Sextus Empiricus: "wisdom cannot display itself and art is non-evident and strength is unexerted and wealth useless and speech powerless in the absence of health" (S.E. *M* 9.50, trans. Bury). The retort of the philosophers is usually to affirm that health is not an end but a means. Two examples: for Aristotle, "no art asks questions about the end" and the physician's task is not whether one ought to be in good health, but whether one ought to walk in order to be in good health (*EE* II.11, 1227b28); and the Stoics took good care to distinguish goods from things to be preferred when insisting that health is among the latter. As against medicine, then, philosophy is neither conquering nor re-conquering: it is on the defensive. This problem of the reduction of ethical problems, and especially that of moral responsibility, to medical parameters will reappear throughout the whole history of thought.

We can certainly not agree with Galen that Plato took from Hippocrates the greater part of his "dogmas" (Gal. *De Usu Partium* 1.8 = III, 16 K). But it is no longer possible to accept unwarily Ludwig Edelstein's statement that "the assumption of an influence of Greek medicine on Greek philosophy must be regarded . . . as historically incorrect" (1967, p. 354). Philosophy was questioned by medicine. In the strategies it adopted to face this challenge, it profoundly transformed itself.

---

12.   Edelstein (1967) cites Sextus Empiricus in this connection: "that health is a good, and the prime good, has been affirmed by not a few of the poets and writers and generally by all ordinary folk" (S.E. *M* 9.49).

Bibliography

Sources

Caelius Aurelianus

Drabkin, I. E. (ed. and trans.). (1950). *Caelius Aurelianus, On Acute Diseases and On Chronic Diseases*: Chicago: University of Chicago Press.

Galen

Kühn, K. G. (ed.). (1821–33). (cited as K). Galen. *Opera omnia.* Medicorum Graecorum opera quae exstant. (20 vols.). Leipzig: Cnobloch. Repr. Hildesheim: Olms, 1964–5.
Singer, P. N. (trans.). (1997). Galen. *Selected Works.* Oxford: Oxford University Press.
Walzer, R. and Frede, M. (eds.). (1985). Galen. *Three Treatises on the Nature of Science.* (Introduction by M. Frede.) Indianapolis: Hackett.

Herophilus

von Staden, H. (1989). *Herophilus. The Art of Medicine in Early Alexandria.* Cambridge: Cambridge University Press.

Hippocratics

Festugière, A.-J. (1948). *Hippocrate. L'ancienne médicine.* Paris: Klincksieck.
Jones, W. H. S et al. (ed. and trans.). (1923–88). *Hippocrates.* Loeb Classical Library. (6 vols.). (vols. 1, 2, 4 by W. H. S. Jones; vol. 3 by E. T. Withington; vols. 5 and 6 by P. Potter). Cambridge. Mass.: Harvard University Press / London: Heinemann.
Jouanna, J. (ed. and trans.). (1988). Hippocrate *Des vents. De l'art.* Paris: Les Belles Lettres.
——. (ed. and trans.). (2003). Hippocrate *Airs-Eaux-Lieux.* Paris: Les Belles Lettres.
Littré, É. (ed.). (1839–61). *Oeuvres complètes d'Hippocrates.* (Greek text and facing French translation.). (10 vols.). Paris: Baillière.
Lloyd, G. E. R. (ed.). (1978). *Hippocratic Writings.* London: Penguin.

Works Cited

Allen, J. (2001). *Inference From Signs. Ancient Debates about the Nature of Evidence.* Oxford: Oxford University Press.
Barnes, J., Brunschwig, J., Burnyeat, M., and Schofield, M. (eds.). (1982). *Science and Speculation. Studies in Hellenistic Theory and Practice.* Cambridge: Cambridge University Press / Paris: Maison des Sciences de l'Homme.
Bourgey. L. (1953). *Observation et expérience chez les médecins de la Collection hippocratique.* Paris: Vrin.
Brain. P. (1986). *Galen on Blooletting. A Study of the Origins, Development and Validity of His Opinions, With a Translation of the Three Works.* Cambridge: Cambridge University Press.
Brochard, V. (1923). *Les Sceptiques grecs.* Paris: Alcan. 2nd edn. Paris: Vrin. (First published in 1887.)
Brunschwig, J. (1980). "Proof Defined." In M. Schofield, M. Burnyeat, and J. Barnes (eds.), *Doubt and Dogmatism: Studies in Hellenistic Epistemology* (pp. 125–60). Oxford: Oxford University Press.
——. (2000). "Pyrrhon." In J. Brunschwig and G. E. R. Lloyd (eds.), *Greek Thought. A Guide to Classical Knowledge* (pp. 739–44). Cambridge, Mass.: Harvard University Press.

Burnyeat, M. (1982). "The Origin of Non-deductive Inference." In J. Barnes, J. Brunschwig, M. Burnyeat, and M. Schofield (eds.), *Science and Speculation. Studies in Hellenistic Theory and Practice* (pp. 193–238). Cambridge: Cambridge University Press / Paris: Maison des Sciences de l'Homme.

Deichgräber, K. (1930). *Die griechische Empirikershule: Sammlung und Darstellung des Lehre.* Berlin: Weidmann.

Edelstein, L. (1967). *Ancient Medicine. Selected papers of Ludwig Edelstein.* Baltimore: Johns Hopkins University Press.

Frede, M. (1982). "The Method of the So-called Methodical School of Medicine." In J. Barnes, J. Brunschwig, M. Burnyeat, and M. Schofield (eds.), *Science and Speculation. Studies in Hellenistic Theory and Practice* (pp. 1–23). Cambridge: Cambridge University Press / Paris: Maison des Sciences de l'Homme.

——. (1988). "The Empiricist Attitude Towards Reason and Theory." in R. J. Hankinson (ed.), *Method, Medicine and Metaphysics* (pp. 79–97). Alberta 1988 (= *Apeiron*, Special Issue, 21). Edmonton: Academic Printing and Publishing.

Grmek, M. (ed.). (1995). *Histoire de la pensée médicale en Occident.* Paris: Seuil.

Joly, R. (1966). *Le niveau de la science hippocratique.* Paris: Les Belles Lettres.

Lloyd, G. E. R. (1991). *Methods and Problems in Greek Science.* Cambridge: Cambridge University Press.

Matthen, M. (1988). "Empiricism and Ontology in Ancient Medicine." In R. J. Hankinson (ed.), *Method, Medicine and Metaphysics* (pp. 99–121). Alberta 1988 (= *Apeiron*, Special Issue, 21). Edmonton: Academic Printing and Publishing.

Pellegrin, P. (2000, French version 1996). "Medicine." In J. Brunschwig and G. E. R. Lloyd (eds.), *Greek Thought. A Guide to Classical Knowledge* (pp. 414–32). Cambridge, Mass.: Harvard University Press.

Pigeaud, J. (1987). *Folie et cures de la folie chez les médecins de l'Antiquité gréco-romaine.* Paris: Les Belles Lettres.

——. (1991). "Les fondements du méthodisme." In P. Mudey and J. Pigeaud (eds.), *Les Écoles médicales à Rome* (pp. 7–50). Geneva: Librairie Droz.

Vallance, J. (1990). *The Lost Theory of Asclepiades of Bithynia.* Oxford: Oxford University Press.

——. (1994). "The Medical System of Asclepiades of Bithynia." *ANRW* II, 37.1 (pp. 693–727).

Vegetti, M. (1995). "Entre le savoir et la pratique: la médecine hellénistique." In M. Grmek (ed.), *Histoire de la pensée médicale en Occident* (pp. 67–94). Paris: Seuil.

Vernant, J.-P. (1965). *Mythe et pensée chez les Grecs.* Paris: Maspero.

Further Reading

Cooper, J. M. (2002). "Method and Science in *On Ancient Medicine*." In H. Linneweber-Lammerskitten and G. Mohr (eds.), *Interpretation und Argument* (Festschrift for Gerhard Seel) (pp. 25–57). Würzburg: Königshausen and Neumann. Reprinted in J. M. Cooper (2004) *Knowledge, Nature, and the Good* (pp. 3–42). Princeton: Princeton University Press.

Gill, M. L. (2003). "Plato's *Phaedrus* and the Method of Hippocrates." *The Modern Schoolman*, 80, 295–314.

Hankinson, R. J. (1998). *Cause and Explanation in Ancient Greek Thought.* Oxford: Clarendon Press.

Jouanna, J. (1999). *Hippocrates.* (trans. M. B. DeBevoise). Baltimore: Johns Hopkins University Press. (Originally published as *Hippocrate* 1992.)

Lloyd, G. E. R. (1973). *Greek Science after Aristotle.* London: Chatto and Windus.

——. (1979). *Magic, Reason and Experience.* Cambridge: Cambridge University Press.

35

Greek Mathematics (Arithmetic, Geometry, Proportion Theory) to the Time of Euclid

IAN MUELLER

Euclid's *Elements*

The earliest Greek texts which we classify as mathematical date from the late fourth century BCE shortly after the death of Aristotle, and, therefore, after the death of the two ancient Greek philosophers, Plato and Aristotle, whose writings relating to mathematics have – and deservedly have – attracted the greatest attention from scholars. The major mathematical text which is brought to bear in discussions of those two figures is Euclid's *Elements*, conventionally dated at 300 BCE. Since it is also the basis for much of the discussion of the history of earlier Greek mathematics, I am going to frame my discussion of the subject in terms of it. The *Elements* is often thought of as a geometrical work, but it is clearly more than that since Books VII–IX are a self-contained discussion of arithmetic, and Book V is a self-contained presentation of a general theory of proportion, that is of expressions of the form "a is to b as c is to d."

It is now generally agreed that nothing of great mathematical significance in the *Elements* is the invention of Euclid. Some scholars treat the *Elements* as essentially a compilation of previously existing works, which they try to identify at least by specifying an author; for such scholars Euclid's contribution took the form of relatively slight and sometimes careless revisions aimed at incorporating the treatises into a unified whole. Other scholars are more generous, but generally less precise in what they attribute to Euclid. Particularly important in this connection for students of philosophy is the question of whether the relatively high degree of rigor and stylistic formalization in the *Elements* is something which only came into mathematics in the late fourth century or whether it is something that can be supposed to have existed in the earlier fifth or even later sixth century.

First Principles

Euclid's first principles

At the beginning of Book I Euclid lists a series of definitions (*horoi*), postulates (*aitēmata*), and common notions (*koinai ennoiai*). Lists of definitions also occur at the beginning of Books II, III, IV, V, VI, VII (where they are obviously intended to cover VIII and IX as well), X, and XI (where they are obviously intended to cover Books XII and XIII), and they are the most common kind of "first principle" to be found in Greek mathematical texts. No other mathematical text in antiquity makes distinctions among the kinds of assumptions it employs.

Euclid's specifically geometric operations are given by the first three postulates, which license the connecting of two points with a straight line, the extension of a finite straight line, and the drawing of a circle with a given center and radius. One can think of these postulates as restricting the means of construction to an unmarked ruler and a compass which collapses when it is raised above the plane of reference. To these construction postulates are added the assertion that all right angles are equal and the following version of the parallel postulate (see Figure 35.1):

If angles CAB, DBA together are less than two right angles, then if AC and BD are extended past C and D, they will eventually intersect.

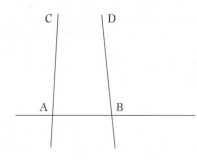

Figure 35.1

Since the postulates and their Book I consequences are applied in later Books, it is reasonable to say that the postulates underlie the whole of Euclid's geometry. In contrast after Book I new terms are introduced in definitions only when they relate to a new topic being introduced. But even when the domain of discussion is expanded to solid geometry or extended to numbers, Euclid never introduces any new assumptions other than definitions. This fact suggests that the idea of postulates was relatively new in Greek mathematics when the *Elements* were composed.

The manuscripts are quite discrepant in their common notions, and this textual uncertainty makes trying to give an account of the common notions especially problematic. Five common notions are printed in the standard edition of the *Elements*. The usual explanation of their presence, which has its roots in Aristotle's *Posterior Analytics*, is that they are supposed to embody principles of reasoning applicable to more than one subject – in the *Elements*, then, to at least numbers and geometric magnitudes. This explanation applies best to the first three, which also have the strongest claim to authenticity:

1. Things which are equal to the same thing are also equal to one another;
2. and if equals be added to equals, the wholes are equal;
3. and if equals be subtracted from equals, the remainders are equal.

It perhaps fits the fifth common notion, which says that the whole is greater than the part, but the fourth seems to be purely geometric, since it asserts the equality of things which coincide with one another and seems to envisage the fitting of one geometric figure on another.

Aristotle and Plato on first principles

The earliest author we know to have distinguished among kinds of first principles is Aristotle. Plato's most explicit description of mathematical first principles, which he calls hypotheses, comes in the famous Divided Line passage in Book VI of the *Republic*, where Socrates is describing a cognitive condition which he calls *dianoia* (thinking) and associates with those who deal with "geometries and calculations, and the like":

> [These people] hypothesize the odd and the even, and the figures and three kinds of angles, and other things akin to them in each inquiry, as [if] they know them, and they make them hypotheses and don't think it is necessary to give any account of them to either themselves or anyone else, as [if] they are evident to everyone. Beginning from these they move on through other things and end up in agreement at the thing which they set out to investigate. (*Rep.* VI, 510c–d)

If one were to interpret Socrates' remark about mathematical method as a description of Euclid's *Elements*, one would presumably have to say that the examples of hypotheses are definitions, the definitions of odd and even numbers at the beginning of Book VII, of figures such as the circle, semicircle, equilateral triangle in Book I and of the right, obtuse, and acute angles, also in Book I. And we can certainly say of these definitions as presented in our texts of the *Elements* that they are not explained or justified and even that they are not evident since they are explanations of words that are not known (at least with specific precision) to an audience. However, this seems an artificial construal of the method of mathematics. The definitions are more plausibly construed as ways of making precise for purposes of argument the meaning of terms which are already understood by the members of the audience either because they are already familiar with them or because they can be made familiar with them in an informal way, say with a picture. It does not seem that one can talk of such hypotheses as not understood, since no deductions from them would be possible if they weren't understood. Nor does it make sense to speak of them as being known or not known since they are just indications of what certain words mean.

It seems to me more likely that we should take Socrates to be thinking of a mathematics in which certain *things* are set out as subjects of discourse, odd and even numbers, various figures, right, acute, and obtuse angles, it perhaps being taken for granted that the kinds of numbers and angles are exhausted by the possibilities mentioned. These things would be explained in the sense that their nature would be indicated in an informal way, but those explanations would not approach the detail of arguments for propositions, such as that the sum of two odd numbers is even or constructions, such as producing on a straight line an angle equal to a given one. or a step-by-step calculation.

There are several passages in which Aristotle espouses a trichotomy of first principles. The passages do not obviously all espouse the same trichotomy, but I am inclined to think that the following passage expresses the core Aristotelian doctrine:

> Every demonstrative science[1] concerns three things: (a) the things it hypothesizes to be (these constitute the genus of which it studies the *per se* properties (*pathēmatōn*)); (b) the so-called common axioms from which first things it proves; (c) and third the properties (*pathē*) of which it assumes what each signifies. (*APo.* I.10, 76b11–16)

The fact that Aristotle espouses a trichotomy of principles and Euclid presents one in the first Book of the *Elements* has led scholars to inquire about the relation between the two trichotomies. The most striking coincidence between them is Aristotle's common axioms, one of Aristotle's examples of a common axiom being Euclid's third common notion. Moreover, Aristotle speaks of these axioms in a way that suggests they are a known feature of mathematics ("so-called common axioms" in this passage and "what are called axioms in mathematics" at *Met.* Γ.3, 1005a20). So it seems likely that by Aristotle's time some mathematicians were being explicit about general quantitative assumptions they were making, a feature of mathematics of which we find no clear trace in Plato. However, Aristotle also mentions as examples of common axioms the laws of non-contradiction and excluded middle, that is, fundamental logical laws. It seems *prima facie* unlikely that these axioms were ever made explicit in mathematics; if they were, it is unclear why we have no trace of their presence in mathematical texts. Hence I am inclined to think that Aristotle expanded a mathematical practice of making explicit principles common to all quantitative argumentation to include the most general principles of all, logical principles. If this is right, then it seems fair to say that Aristotle's trichotomy is not just a description of mathematical practice, but also a philosophically based normative account of what demonstrative science ought to be like. Of course, the extent to which his account departs from pre-Euclidean mathematical practice is not possible to determine with any precision.

It is striking that Aristotle speaks of the axioms as if they were the only *premises* of mathematical proof: a demonstrative science proves that the relevant properties hold of objects in its genus from the common axioms. It would seem that in the mathematics Aristotle knew there were no other starting points that Aristotle was willing to identify as assumed propositions. Now it seems to me entirely unlikely that mathematics ever had any kind of articulated deductive structure which did not involve definitions of some kind, some kind of explication of the nature of the things being talked about. The words "what each signifies" in the description of (c) just quoted makes clear that Aristotle associates some form of assumption about meaning with what he calls properties. And the material immediately preceding the quotation shows that the same is true of (a). For there Aristotle says that a science assumes about items in (a) both that they are (exist) and what they are or signify, whereas about those in (c) it assumes

---

1. Aristotle is officially concerned with more than mathematics when he talks about "every demonstrative science," but it is clear that in the passages where he is discussing the trichotomy of principles he is basing his discussion on a picture of mathematics, mainly geometry and arithmetic.

what they signify and proves that they exist (i.e., that they apply to objects in the genus). It seems to me very unlikely that Aristotle would only treat the common axioms as assumptions if he were reflecting on a text like Euclid's *Elements*, where definitions and postulates are laid out in parallel with common notions. The likelihood seems rather to be that Aristotle and presumably Plato as well are reflecting primarily on oral presentations which had somehow evolved to the point of articulating general quantitative assumptions, but still relied on informal explications of terminology. If this is right (and our date for Euclid is approximately right), then the extent of reduction to first principles that we find in Euclid's *Elements* is the culmination of a relatively rapid development of the last half of the fourth century. In the sequel I shall assume that the common notions we find in the *Elements* are a fourth-century development and that prior to the fourth century it was simply taken for granted that, e.g., things equal to the same things are equal to each other.

The situation with (a) is still more perplexing. Aristotle gives as examples of things that are hypothesized to exist monads or units (once plural, once singular) in arithmetic, and points and lines (or, in another passage, magnitude) in geometry. There is obviously a general sense in which Euclid assumes the existence of these things in the *Elements*, but the assumptions are completely tacit, so that no attempt to correlate (a) with Euclid's postulates can come to grips with Aristotle's examples in a satisfactory way. Aristotle's failure to mention anything like Euclid's postulates as first principles confirms the suggestion of the previous section that postulates are a quite late development in Greek mathematics and another expression of the increased interest in explicit formalization. The first three postulates are included in the *Elements* because analysis of a large number of geometric constructions led to the conclusion that they could be built up out of these three, and that these could not be further reduced to others. The presence of the parallel postulate appears to have the same kind of explanation: at some point in the fourth century it was recognized that one could not prove such theorems as the equality of the interior angles of a triangle to two right angles (I,32) unless one made some such assumption.[2] I shall discuss the reason for the inclusion of the fourth postulate on pages 691–4.[3]

Even if the postulates are post-Aristotelian, there might still have been some other kind of mathematical assumption that led Aristotle to introduce (a). However, the notion that every demonstrative science deals with a subject genus seems more likely to be a (very possibly correct) Aristotelian analysis of mathematical practice than a report on some explicit starting point adopted by mathematicians. It is Aristotle who sees a demonstrative science as dealing with a genus the elements of which it assumes to exist, and as proving properties of those elements. This characterization is more closely tied to Aristotelian theories of predication and the syllogism than it is to Euclid's geometry, in which objects are constructed out of more elementary objects on the basis of three fundamental constructions and properties are proved of those objects on the basis of the definitions and the common notions (and in some important cases the fifth postulate).

2. See Heath (1949, pp. 27–30) and Vitrac (1990–2001, vol. 1, pp. 306–10). For the proof of I,32 see pages 691–4.
3. The postulate is, in fact, provable; see, e.g., Hilbert (1971, pp. 20–1).

In the previous quotation from Plato I put the word "if" in square brackets to indicate that it is not clear whether Socrates is asserting or questioning that the hypotheses are known or evident. It seems more likely that he is questioning their status, since he calls them hypotheses and is in the process of contrasting *dianoia* with a higher cognitive condition which he calls *noēsis*. In *Posterior Analytics* II.19 Aristotle gives a very brief and cryptic description of our knowledge of first principles and associates it with a condition which he calls *nous*, a term which, like *noēsis*, is generally attached by philosophers to cognition of the highest order. On the whole, the authors of mathematical treatises give no indication of the cognitive status they assign to either their first principles or the conclusions drawn from them, and it would be easy to infer from their silence that they took both to be unquestionable. However, in a preface to the *Sectio Canonis* the author (the treatise comes down to us as a work of Euclid) says that the fundamental assumption that concordant pairs of notes stand in ratios of the form $n + 1$ to n or of n to 1 has been made reasonable (*eikos*); and in a prefatory letter to the *Quadrature of the Parabola* Archimedes says of a "lemma" (the so-called axiom of Archimedes: given a finite area F and two unequal areas A and B with A greater than B, then some finite multiple of A − B is greater than F) which he has used in his quadrature that it was used by earlier geometers to prove theorems (the examples which Archimedes gives are all found in *Elements* XII and do depend on something essentially equivalent to his lemma)[4] which have been believed no less than those proved without the lemma and that it is sufficient if his result is accorded the same sort of belief (*tan homoian pistin*). These two examples suggest, although they hardly prove, that mathematicians were not so dogmatic about their fundamental assumptions as Plato and Aristotle suggest.

Aspects of Euclid's Plane Geometry

The equality of the three angles of a triangle to two right angles (Elements I, 32)[5]

Major results of the first book of the *Elements* include the construction of a parallelogram equal to any given rectilineal area (I,45) and the Pythagorean theorem (I,47), according to which the square on the hypotenuse of a right-angled triangle is equal to the squares on the other two sides. Euclid also proves that the interior angles of a triangle are equal to two right angles (I,32) or more exactly (see Figure 35.2):

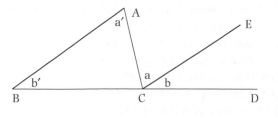

Figure 35.2

4. See pages 712–15.
5. With this section see also Mueller (2003).

If ACB is a triangle and BC is extended to D and CE is drawn parallel to BA, ∠ACD = ∠ABC + ∠BAC, so that (since angles ACB, ACD together are equal to two right angles) angles ACB, ABC, BAC together are equal to two right angles.

The proof invokes the equality of ∠ACE to ∠BAC and of ∠ECD to ∠ABC, equalities which depend on I,29, which itself requires the first application of the parallel postulate. I,29 says (see Figure 35.3):

If BAF and GCE are parallel, then:

(a)   ∠BAC = ∠ACE,
(b)   ∠HAF = ∠ACE, and
(c)   angles FAC, ECA together are equal to two right angles.

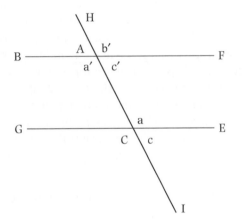

Figure 35.3

Any of I,29 (a), (b), and (c) implies the other two on the assumptions that:

I,13 Angles such as b′ and c′ ("adjacent angles") together are equal to two right angles.
I,15 Angles such as a′ and b′ ("vertical angles") are equal.

Euclid derives I,15, which follows from 1,13 plus common notions, using postulate 4. For, by I,13 angles b′, c′ together and angles a′, c′ together are each equal to two right angles; so if all right angles are equal, the two pairs are equal to each other, and ∠a′ = ∠b′. Hence I,29 and I,32 ultimately depend only on the fourth and fifth postulates, I,13, and common notions, and it seems likely that the two postulates were introduced together as part of the proof of something like I,29. To prove equality (a) of this proposition Euclid assumes that ∠a′ is not equal to ∠a and takes ∠a as the smaller. Then, by I,13, ∠a + ∠c′ is less than two right angles, and by the parallel postulate BAF and GCE extended will meet.

I,13 is "proved" with a picture (see Figure 35.4). If ∠FAH is equal to ∠FAC, then by the definition of a right angle, each is a right angle. If they are unequal, then let JA be

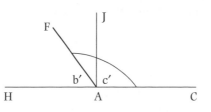

Figure 35.4

drawn at right angles to HAC. Then ∠FAH + ∠FAC = ∠JAH + ∠JAC, and the latter are two right angles.

With I,13 all of the following are equivalent: I,29(a), I,29(b), I,29(c), I,32, and the parallel postulate.

In his commentary on Book I of the *Elements* Proclus, citing Aristotle's pupil Eudemus as authority, credits the Pythagoreans, standardly taken to be Pythagoreans of the later sixth or earlier fifth century, with the discovery of the theorem that the interior angles of a triangle are equal to two right angles. Proclus gives the Pythagorean proof, a Euclidean-style demonstration, but avoiding the preliminary assertion of the equality of the exterior angle ACD to the interior and opposite angles BAC, ABC (Figure 35.2). In Figure 35.5 FAG is parallel to BC, and the result is inferred in what amounts to two applications of I,29(a) from the equalities of ∠a to ∠a′ and ∠a* to ∠a*′.

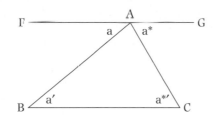

Figure 35.5

This proof is, of course, essentially equivalent to Euclid's, but it seems unlikely that early Pythagoreans would have proved I,29(a) and hence unlikely that that they enunciated the parallel postulate. Aristotle reports the existence of a *petitio principii* in the treatment of parallels when he says that some people who think they are drawing parallels assume, without being aware of it, things which cannot be proved unless there are parallel lines (*APr.* II.16, 65a4–7). It seems probable that Aristotle is referring to people taking for granted at least one of the parts of I,29, and the most likely one is the apparently most obvious one, I,29(b) which asserts the equality of angles like c′ and c in Figure 35.3. But even if I,29(b) and I,13 (or postulate 4) were taken for granted, a proof of I,32 would still seem to require I,15, and, although the argument for I,15 is simple, it does require the abstract step of subtracting ∠c′ from the two quantities consisting of angles b′, c′ and angles a′, c′. If we accept Proclus' claim about the Pythagorean origins of a proof of I,32, we are, I think, led to place the beginnings of such abstract geometrical reasoning in Greece back to at least 500. It is also significant that I,32, unlike, say, propositions about the area of figures, would seem to be a

693

theorem of "pure" geometry, of interest for its own sake rather than for its practical significance.

Of course, there remains a major difference between a geometry in which propositions like the common notions and postulates are taken for granted or made to rest on perception or intuition, and one in which they are explicitly formulated, as they are in the *Elements*. I am inclined to think that the codification of assumptions and permissible methods of argumentation and the formalization or, at least, stylization of the form of presentation of mathematics represent a more fundamental aspect of the fifth-century development of mathematics than does any move from more intuitive to more abstract reasoning.

Geometry and algebra

Although the Pythagoreans are not explicitly credited with the discovery of how to construct a parallelogram equal to a given rectilineal area (I,45), Proclus begins his discussion of the preceding proposition (I,44: to a given straight line to apply, in a given rectilineal angle, a parallelogram equal to a given triangle) by saying that "the application (*parabolē*) of areas, their exceeding (*huperbolē*), and their falling short (*elleipsis*) are ancient discoveries of the Pythagorean muse." Proclus goes on to explain these terms (see Figure 35.6):

> For when, given a straight line [AE], you make the given area [ABCD] extend along the whole of the line, they say you apply the area [case (a)]; when you make the length of the area greater than the straight line itself, then it exceeds [case (b)]; and when less, so that there is a part of the line extending beyond the area described, then it falls short [case (c)].
> (*In Euc.* 419.24–420.6)

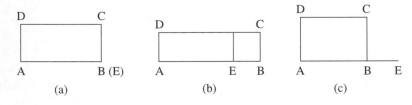

Figure 35.6

Commenting on I,45 Heath writes:

> We can now take stock of how far the propositions I,43–45 bring us in the matter of *transformation of areas*, which constitutes so important a part of what has fitly been called the *geometrical algebra* of the Greeks. We have now learnt how to represent any rectilineal area, which can of course be resolved into triangles, by a single parallelogram having one side equal to any given straight line and one angle equal to any given rectilineal angle. Most important of all such parallelograms is the rectangle, which is one of the simplest forms in which an area can be shown. (Heath, 1926, vol. 1, pp. 346–7; Heath's italics)

Here Heath makes two moves which are part of a highly influential interpretation of a central part of Greek mathematics, an interpretation summed up in the term "geometrical algebra": the replacement of Euclid's general term "parallelogram" with the more specific "rectangle" (and thereby the elimination of the phrase "in a given rectilineal angle"); and the introduction of the words "having one side equal to any given straight line," which have no correspondent in I,45 and that deliberately so, since Euclid could have added the words "on a given straight line" at the beginning of I,45 had he wished to do so.

With "rectangle" substituted for "parallelogram," propositions I,42–45 become:

I,42$_r$ To construct a rectangle equal to a given triangle.
I,43$_r$ In any rectangle the complements about the diagonal are equal.
I,44$_r$ To a given straight line [AB] to apply a rectangle [ABCD] equal to a given triangle.
I,45$_r$ To construct a rectangle equal to a given rectilineal figure.

As Heath indicates, I,45 follows from I,44 and the fact (see Figure 35.7) that any rectilineal figure can be divided into triangles (t,t′,t″, . . .). I,44 includes the words "to a given straight line" because each of the rectangles after r has to be applied to the side of the preceding rectangle.

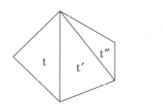

Figure 35.7

The proof of I,44$_r$ may be represented as follows (see Figure 35.8):

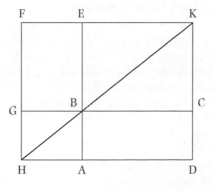

Figure 35.8

Construct (by I,42$_r$) the rectangle EBGF equal to the given triangle with BE in a straight line with BA. Complete the figure ABGH, and extend HB and FE to meet at K. (Euclid uses the parallel postulate to prove that they meet.) Complete Figure 35.8, which is a rectangle FHDK with diagonal HBK divided into four rectangles intersecting at B. In

695

the figure ABCD and BEFG are the complements about the diagonal, which are proved equal in I,43. This equality follows from I,34, which asserts that a diagonal of a parallelogram bisects it. As a result the following triangles are equal:

HKF to HKD, HBG to HBA, BKE to BKC.

Hence so is HKF − (HBG + BKE) equal to HKD − (HBA + BKC), that is, the two complements are equal.

It remains to establish I,42ᵣ. In Figure 35.9 the side GM of the given triangle GLM is bisected at B, FL is drawn parallel to GM, and the perpendiculars GF and BE are erected.

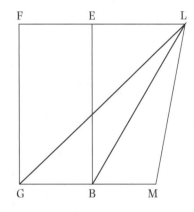

Figure 35.9

The result follows from the fact that a parallelogram (BEFG) with the same base and height as a triangle (GBL) has twice its area (I,41) and that triangles (GBL, BML) with equal bases and the same height are equal (I,38).

The previous quotation from Heath continues:

> Since a rectangle corresponds to the product of two magnitudes in algebra, we see that the *application* to a given straight line of a rectangle equal to a given area [as I have indicated, not something Euclid specifically shows how to do] is the geometrical equivalent of algebraical *division* of the product of two quantities by a third. Further than this, it enables us to add or subtract any rectilineal areas and to represent the sum or difference by *one* rectangle with one side of any given length, the process being the equivalent of obtaining a common factor. (Heath, 1926, vol. 1, p. 347; Heath's italics)

The idea lying behind Heath's representation here is that a given rectilineal figure corresponds to a quantity (which we might call a real number a), the given straight line represents another quantity (which we might call a real number b). The finding of a rectangle with side b and area a is the solution of the equation "bx = a" or the division of a by b (see Figure 35.10). Moreover, when we think of quantities as rectangles a, a′ with sides of length b and x, x′ then their sum is bx + bx′ = b(x + x′) and their difference is bx′ − bx = b(x − x′), where in both cases b is the common factor of which Heath speaks.

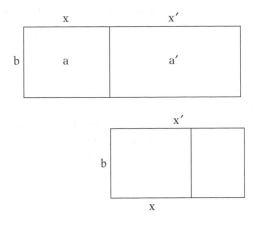

Figure 35.10

The "geometrical algebra," of which I,42–45 are only rudiments, goes well beyond any evidence we have about Greek mathematics and flies in the face of the Euclidean propositions themselves, which are formulated in terms of parallelograms, not rectangles, and have nothing corresponding to b in the essential I,45. All I,45 shows is how to construct a rectangle equal to a given rectilineal area. The only determinate solution to the problem of transforming areas comes in II,14 where Euclid shows how to construct a square equal to a given rectilineal area or, as we can now say, given rectangle.

Euclid's proof of II,14 is very clever, but is unlikely to have been the original proof of the proposition, which probably depended on ideas of proportionality, a concept which Euclid does not introduce until Book V and does not apply to geometry until Book VI. Here too Euclid usually speaks in terms of parallelograms, but it is easier to discuss what he says in terms of rectangles. The fundamental result is:

VI,14$_r$ (= VI,16) Rectangles ABCD and EFGH are equal if and only if their consecutive sides are reciprocally proportional, that is, e.g., if AB is to EF as FG is to BC.

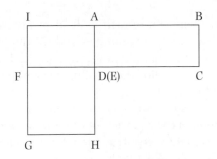

Figure 35.11

Proof. If the rectangles are placed as in Figure 35.11 and the rectangle ADFI is completed, then:

697

(i)   Rectangle ABCD is to rectangle ADFI as AB is to AI as AB is to EF;
(ii)   Rectangle EFGH is to rectangle ADFI as FG is to FI as FG is to BC;
(iii) therefore, rectangle ABCD = rectangle EFGH iff AB is to EF as FG is to BC.

(i) and (ii) are consequences of VI,1, which I discuss on pages 701–2. It says that parallelograms (and triangles) with the same height are to one another as their bases; (iii) follows from (i) and (ii) using elementary laws of proportion.

In VI,17 Euclid considers what for us is the special case of VI,16 in which EFGH is a square. In that case EF = FG, so that square EFGH = rectangle ABCD if and only if AB is to EF as EF is to AD. Hence, the task of finding a square equal to the rectangle ABCD is that of finding a mean proportional EF between AB and AD. If BA, AD are placed in a straight line BAD as in Figure 35.12, the problem is solved by finding a right triangle BDK with right angle at K and the perpendicular from K to BD intersecting BD at A (VI,13). For then BKD,BAK,KAD are similar triangles with BA to AK as AK to AD, so that AK is the required mean proportional (VI,8 with porism). The only problem is the construction of the triangle BDK, but that is solved by constructing a circle with diameter BD and erecting a perpendicular to BD at A and intersecting the circle at K. For the angle in a semicircle is always right (III,31).

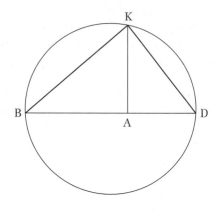

Figure 35.12

It will be seen that this whole argument really depends only on (1) the reciprocal proportionality of the sides of equal rectangles and (2) the fact that a perpendicular from the right angle of a right triangle to its base divides the triangle into triangles similar to it and to each other. With these things recognized the problem reduces to finding the relevant right triangle.

The point I wish to stress is that there is no reason to read the construction as "the equivalent of the extraction of the square root or of the solution of the pure quadratic equation '$x^2 = ab$'" (Heath, 1926, vol. 1, p. 410). It is in some sense the "equivalent," but not in a sense that should make us interpret what goes on in the *Elements* and elsewhere as an algebra in disguise. Implicit and often enough explicit in the algebraic representations of Greek geometry are numerical notions which we do not find in the mathematical texts. There is nothing necessarily illicit in transcribing geometrical propositions into algebraic formulas, but those who have done so have consistently used the formulas in connection with the importation of the foreign numerical ideas. For all we can tell, the Greeks were interested in the representation of areas as squares, possibly as a way of comparing them, although from a numerical point of view squares are not nearly so directly useful as Heath's representation of them as rectangles with a common length.

Euclid provides a full solution to the quadrature problem for rectilineal figures, and we know that the Greeks tried to solve the problem for circles and managed a number of non-elementary solutions.[6] I shall discuss certain aspects of the problem of quadrature on pages 712–15.

The "Pythagorean" theorem

We are not told how Pythagoras or the Pythagoreans proved the Pythagorean theorem, and in the nineteenth century Euclid's proof became a notorious example of a proof which gave the reader no understanding of the result. Heath (1921, vol. 1, pp. 148–9) gives three proportion-based proofs of the theorem which he indicates that Pythagoras himself might have used. I give the first, which depends on materials introduced in the preceding section, here because it is most closely related to Euclid's proof, which proceeds as follows (see Figure 35.13). According to VI,8, if BDK is a right triangle with the right angle at K and DKLM, BKJI, and BDFC are squares:

AB is to BK as BK is to BD, and AD is to DK as DK is to BD.

Hence by VI,17:

(a) Square BKJI = Rectangle ABCE, and
(b) Square DKLM = Rectangle AEFD; and
(c) Square BKJI + Square DKLM = Rectangle ABCE + Rectangle AEFD = Square BDFC.

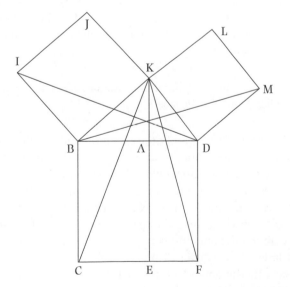

Figure 35.13

6. For a description of these results see Heath (1921, pp. 220–35).

In proving I,47 Euclid establishes (a) by drawing KC and DI and arguing that triangle BDI = triangle BCK because BD = BC, BI = BK and ∠IBD = ∠KBC (since each is a right angle plus ∠KBD). But triangle BDI is half of square BKJI because they have the same base and height, and for the same reason triangle BCK is half of rectangle ABCE. The proof for (b) uses triangles MDB and KDF in the same way.

It is possible that Euclid chose to reformulate proofs using proportionality as proofs avoiding it for pedagogical reasons. But it seems likely that the theory of proportion itself underwent changes in the fourth century, changes which may have been related to uncertainty about how to prove in a proper way quite ordinary laws of proportion, traditionally taken for granted in mathematics.

Proportionality

The definition of proportionality in Book V of the Elements

Proportion, which Euclid introduces in Book V, plays a fundamental role in the Greek mathematics of which we have direct knowledge, and, as we have just seen, there is good reason to think that proportion was always a fundamental part of Greek mathematical reasoning. The use of the theory of proportion is simply the application of laws of proportionality to manipulate proportions, e.g., to go from the fact that a is to b as c is to d to the fact that a + b is to b as c + d is to d. Euclid himself does not prove every law of proportion that he uses, and he does not use every law that he proves. It seems overwhelmingly likely that the laws of proportionality were part of a mathematician's stock in trade, things which the mathematician could use as freely as we use elementary logical laws or numerical calculations. However, to use laws of proportion is not the same as to have a theory of proportion. One way to produce such a theory is to assume some laws and prove the rest. This is not the way Euclid proceeds. Rather he gives a definition of proportionality and derives all the laws from that. His definition in Book V can be stated as follows:

> V, def. 5. a:b :: c:d if and only if for any multiples m·a, m·c, n·b, n·d, if m·a > n·b then m·c > n·d (and similarly for "=" and "<").

Here Euclid takes for granted notions of multiplication and comparison of size, which – like the notion of measurement and, to a lesser, but still significant, extent, addition and subtraction – are part of the unexplicated "logic" of the *Elements*.

Judged in terms of modern logic and foundations of mathematics, Book V is probably the high point of Greek mathematics. The definition of proportionality, which is thought to be due to Plato's contemporary, Eudoxus, contains the fundamental idea that Dedekind used in defining the real numbers as "cuts" in the rational numbers. And the derivation of the laws of proportion from the definition is in a class with Peano's reduction of classical mathematics to number theory or Frege's reduction of number theory to logic. But after Book V the definition is invoked only once, in the first proposition of Book VI; otherwise all that matters are the laws which are applied in the proof of particular propositions, as in the examples we saw on pages 694–700. There is no reason to doubt that many of those propositions were first used independently of anything like Book V and perhaps not proved on the basis of any *theory* of proportion at all.

A definition of proportionality in Aristotle

The first proposition of Book VI says:

> VI,1 Triangles and parallelograms which are under the same height are to one another as their bases.

Euclid derives the parallelogram case from the triangle case, using the fact (I,41) that a parallelogram with the same base and height as a triangle is twice its size. For the triangles Euclid imagines ACB and ACD arranged as in Figure 35.14 with BCD extended in either direction. One multiplies, e.g., CD by marking off segments DK, KL, etc. on the extension BDL of BD, and because triangles with equal bases and heights are equal (I,38) one multiplies triangle ACD by connecting KA, LA, etc. Euclid assumes what he could easily prove, namely that of triangles with the same height the one with the greater base is greater. From this and I,38 it follows that if the multiple of CD is greater than (equal to, less than) the multiple of BC, the multiple of triangle ACD is greater than (equal to, less than) the multiple of triangle ACB.

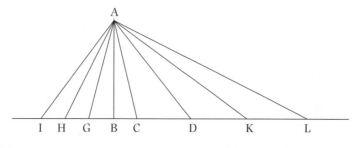

Figure 35.14

This theorem is of considerable interest because in the *Topics* (VIII.3, 158b24–35) Aristotle says that the version for parallelograms is immediately evident when the definition of same ratio is stated, the definition apparently being that a is to b as c is to d if and only if a,b and c,d have the same *antanairesis*. I shall translate this term as "alternate subtraction." It is easiest to illustrate alternate subtraction using numbers because it is equivalent to the method we use to find the greatest common divisor of two numbers. In the case of 27 and 87 alternate subtraction proceeds as follows. One subtracts 27 from 87 giving 60, and then 27 from 60 giving 33, and then 27 from 33 giving 6. One cannot subtract 33 from 6 so one "alternates" and subtracts 6 from 33. But before we do this one notes that three successive subtractions of 27 were performed, and one calls 3 the first alternate subtraction number for 27 and 87. Working with 6 and 33 one gets the successive results 27, 21, 15, 9, and 3 where subtraction stops with a second alternate subtraction number of 5. With 3 and 6 one gets a third alternate subtraction number of 2, and there is nothing more to do. Now to say that a,b and c,d have the same alternate subtraction is to say that the sequence of alternate subtraction numbers for a,b is the same as that for c,d. In the case of numbers the sequence always stops. In the case of geometric quantities the sequence might go on forever, but the definition would still apply.

There is no trace of the alternate subtraction definition of proportionality in the *Elements*, although Euclid does use alternate subtraction (which he refers to with the verb *anthuphairesthai*) to produce the greatest common measure of two numbers or magnitudes if it terminates, and he proves (in the case of magnitudes) that there is no common measure if it doesn't terminate. But the Aristotle passage shows that prior to Euclid there was another abstract and, in fact, more cumbersome definition of proportionality, which Aristotle could treat as *the* definition.[7] This fact suggests that the notion of proportionality was considered in some way problematic before the middle of the fifth century. Presumably the problem involved a felt need to prove certain laws of proportionality.

Proportionality in the arithmetic books of the Elements

Before discussing the character of that problem I want to mention that at the beginning of the arithmetic books VII–IX Euclid introduces and subsequently uses a separate definition of proportionality for numbers:

VII, def. 20. Numbers are proportional when the first is the same multiple or the same part or the same parts of the second that the third is of the fourth,

that is, ignoring certain formal difficulties,

$(m,n) = (i,j)$ if and only if, if $m = k \cdot n$, $i = k \cdot j$, and if $n = k \cdot m$, $j = k \cdot i$, and if m is k lths of n, i is k lths of j.

Here I use the notation "$(m,n) = (i,j)$" and not "$m{:}n :: i{:}j$" to indicate that the concept of proportionality introduced in Book VII is apparently different from the one introduced in Book V.

The Book VII definition makes clear that there is a real sense in which the foundation of Euclid's arithmetic is arithmetic itself, although in the foundation the arithmetic is hidden behind the words "multiple" or "part" (or equivalently "measure") or "parts." The issue which has been of much more concern to scholars is the relation of this definition of proportionality for numbers to the Book V definition of proportionality for magnitudes. One would suppose that magnitudes and numbers and proportionalities involving them are different kinds of things to be treated differently, but, then, there

7. The definition is standardly associated with Theaetetus, the title character of a Platonic dialogue.

would be no way to say, e.g., that one magnitude has to another the same ratio as a first number has to a second. However, in Book X Euclid does exactly that when he proves, e.g., that "commensurable magnitudes have to one another a ratio which a number has to a number" (X,5). The fact that Euclid proves this without explaining the relationship between the two definitions of proportionality is a major item in the case of scholars who view the *Elements* as a badly assembled patchwork of independent treatises resting on different ideas. Since, however, the patching needed here is not enormous, it is difficult to be sure how much evidentiary weight to assign to this alleged "gap" (see Mueller, 1996).

Incommensurability

It is now widely assumed that the Book VII definition of proportionality for numbers is an ancestor of a more general definition for geometric magnitudes and numbers and perhaps other quantities such as weights or time periods. This definition would not, of course, apply to incommensurable magnitudes, but a standard story supposes that earlier Pythagoreans assumed that all magnitudes of the same type were commensurable, so that their ratios were all expressible numerically, these ideas being somehow connected with a belief in the universality and cosmic power of number. The discovery of incommensurability would then be the downfall of this definition, which would be replaced first by the definition in terms of alternate subtraction and then by the less cumbersome definition we find in Euclid's *Elements*. Euclid's use of this definition in Book V and of the definition of proportionality for numbers in Book VII would then be explained by his reliance on disparate sources.

There has been much discussion of the question when and in what connection the Greeks discovered the fact of incommensurability. The tendency of more recent historiography has been to push the discovery into the later fifth century, although the suggestion of the earlier fifth century cannot be discounted. In any case it is to be expected that there would be a time lag between the discovery, the dissemination of the discovery, and the development of a mathematics capable of dealing with it in a formally satisfactory way, e.g., in terms of alternate subtraction. As to the question of how incommensurability was proved, it is possible to imagine a purely geometric proof of incommensurability in which it is shown that the alternate subtraction of two magnitudes never terminates. Von Fritz (1945) described what I think is the simplest "proof" of this kind based on the regular pentagon and the star or pentagram, a Pythagorean symbol formed by connecting alternating vertices of the pentagon. I describe the argument in terms of Figure 35.15.

The magnitudes for which one seeks the greatest common measure are the side AB and the diagonal AC of the regular pentagon. Now AB = AE′, so that AC − AB = CE′. But CE′ < AB, so that the first alternate subtraction number is 1. Moreover, CE′ = AD′, so that when CE′ is subtracted from AE′, it leaves D′E′ as remainder, and the second alternate subtraction number is again 1. However, D′E′ is the side of the regular pentagon A′E′D′C′B′ and CE′ = A′C = A′D′, the diagonal of that pentagon. Hence the third subtraction is just a repetition of the first, and clearly the alternate subtraction numbers for the side and diagonal of a regular pentagon are an unending series of 1s.

703

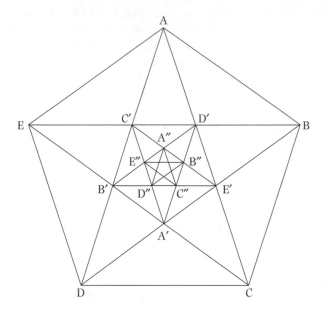

Figure 35.15

Von Fritz ascribed this proof and the discovery of incommensurability to Hippasus of Metapontum, a figure of the earlier fifth century, called by Burkert (1972, p. 206) "the earliest Pythagorean we know of who worked at mathematics and music theory." On pages 706–9 I will describe an arithmetic proof of incommensurability, which is closely related to the earliest proof that survives from antiquity and combines arithmetic and geometric ideas. At this point I wish only to remark that it seems extremely probable that the rigorous theory of proportion of Book V is the result of the desire to work out a way of dealing with incommensurable magnitudes. On the other hand, one could very well continue to do mathematics in the absence of such a theory, so long as one did not take incommensurability to cast doubt on the truth of the standard laws of proportionality.

Greek Arithmetic and its History

The arithmetic books of the Elements

It is not easy to give a general characterization of the content of the arithmetic books VII–IX of Euclid's *Elements*. Euclid starts Book VII by using alternate subtraction to find the greatest common measure of a set of numbers and giving a proof that if that measure is the unit (i.e., 1) the numbers are relatively prime (VII,1–3); in Book VII he also shows how to express numerical ratios in least terms (VII,33), and although he does not prove or use the so-called fundamental theorem of arithmetic (every integer has a unique factorization into primes), VII,30 and 31 provide all the materials needed to prove it.

In Book VIII Euclid takes up numbers in continued proportion in a given ratio (i,j), that is, numbers such that:

$$(m,m_1) = (m_1,m_2) = \ldots = (m_{n-1},m_n) = (i,j).$$

In the case where m is the unit m_1 is, in fact, m_1^n, although Euclid does not have any terminology for talking directly about powers greater than 3. The logical structure of Book VIII is not satisfactory. Perhaps the main result of the book is:

if i and j are the least numbers in their ratio, then the n + 1 least numbers in continued proportion in the ratio of i to j are:

$m = i^n$, $m_1 = i^{n-1} \cdot j$, $m_2 = i^{n-2} \cdot j^2$, ..., $m_{n-1} = i \cdot j^{n-1}$, $m_n = j^n$.[8]

Because Euclid proves (VIII,8) that the same number of mean proportionals fall between i and j and any other pair of numbers having the same ratio he is able to show (VIII,11) that, e.g., there is one mean proportional $(k \cdot l)$ between two square numbers k^2 and l^2.

The first part of Book IX mainly continues the topics of Book VIII, although only one of the propositions between IX,11 and the end of the book depends on Book VIII results. In IX,20 Euclid proves as an isolated proposition the infinity of the prime numbers. Immediately after this high point of the history of arithmetic, there follows one of the most rudimentary propositions of the arithmetic books:

IX,21 A sum of even numbers is even.

The proof of IX,21 rests entirely on the notion of an even number as divisible into two equal parts and intuitive ideas about addition. It amounts to pointing out that $(m_1 + m_1) + (m_2 + m_2) + \ldots + (m_n + m_n) = (m_1 + m_2 + \ldots + m_n) + (m_1 + m_2 + \ldots + m_n)$. There follows a string of similarly elementary propositions IX,22–34 about sums and products of odd and even numbers, differences between them, and some facts about powers of 2. Except for IX,32 the sequence is self-contained and only dependent on definitions and intuitive ideas. IX,35 and 36 make no use of this sequence and establish the important result that if a prime number p is equal to $2^0 + 2^1 + 2^2 + \ldots + 2^n$, then $p \cdot 2^n$ is a so-called perfect number, that is one which is equal to the sum of its factors other than itself.

Plato and arithmetic

It is easier to be confident about the general relationship between the geometry of Euclid's *Elements* and its predecessors in the later fifth and earlier fourth centuries than it is to be confident about the relation of the arithmetic books and their predecessors. The fact that both Herodotus and Aristophanes use the word "geometry" in the relevant sense indicates that the subject was a going concern in the later fifth century. However,

8. This result is not stated as a theorem, but is implied by the procedure Euclid uses to solve the problem of VIII,2: given a number (n + 1) and a ratio (i to j) to find the n + 1 least numbers in continued proportion in the ratio of i to j.

the word "arithmetic" does not show up until Plato, and it is not clear what Plato means by it. Most scholars assume that when Plato mentions arithmetic he is thinking about something very like what we find in Euclid. This is particularly true of the first subject of the curriculum of higher education in the *Republic*. However, Socrates introduces this subject as "the common thing which all art, thinking, and science uses and which is among the first things that everyone must learn." Asked what this is, he says, "the trivial business of distinguishing one, two, and three, that is, number and calculation (*logismos*)" (VII, 522b–c). At 525a Socrates refers to this subject as "arithmetic and calculating" (*logistikē*), and at 522e he speaks of calculating (*logizesthai*) and counting (*arithmein*). In the *Gorgias* at 451b–c Socrates distinguishes between arithmetic, which deals with "the odd and the even, however many each of them happens to be," and calculating, which deals with the same things but differs from arithmetic because "it also investigates how the odd and the even are related in quantity both to themselves and to one another," but then in the *Laws* at VII, 817e the Athenian says that calculations and what concerns numbers are one discipline. So, although there is a difference between arithmetic and calculating, they are sufficiently related to constitute one discipline, best called by a compound name. Klein (1968, pp. 17–25) has argued persuasively that arithmetic in Plato is simply counting, and calculating is adding, subtracting, multiplying, and dividing with whole numbers, and that it is first in Aristotle, in whom the word "calculating" in the relevant sense has disappeared, that we find the notion of arithmetic as a pure deductive science. The distinction between arithmetic and calculating is sometimes thought to be a distinction between a pure science which deals with numbers "which can only be thought and cannot be dealt with in any other way whatsoever" (*Rep.* VII, 526a), and an applied science which deals with the numbers of sensible things. Socrates does make a distinction of this kind at 56d–57a of the *Philebus*, but that is a distinction between two kinds of arithmetic, and it is said that there are parallel distinctions between calculating in commerce and measuring in carpentry, on the one hand, and calculating and geometry as practiced philosophically, on the other. So it may well be that Platonic arithmetic is simply counting and calculating, albeit counting and calculating with pure numbers.

The arithmetic of the Pythagoreans

Van der Waerden (1963) has argued that the arithmetic books were all derived from Pythagorean sources. According to him, the sequence of propositions at the end of Book IX is a self-contained "piece of archaic [apparently c. 500 BCE], and indeed typically Pythagorean mathematics" (p. 108), Book VIII "should be ascribed to Archytas" (p. 153), an approximate contemporary of Plato, and Book VII "was a textbook on the elements of the Theory of Numbers, in use in the Pythagorean School [prior to Archytas]" (p. 115). Thus, in van der Waerden's view, not only was something like the Euclidean deductive style already perfectly developed, at least in the case of number theory, by the time Plato was born, but there was a very early Pythagorean deductive theory, embodied for us at the end of Book IX, which could be said to satisfy Plato's characterization of arithmetic and calculating as concerned with the odd and the even.

However, van der Waerden's theory represents no more than a fascinating speculation on top of which many other speculations have been built. In interpreting Plato we have no right to take for granted that it is correct. On the other hand, there is no reason to doubt that Archytas did offer some kind of proof, very possibly a flawed one, of a quite sophisticated result fundamental to Pythagorean harmonics, which is mathematically related to material in Book VIII and in its simplest form might be stated as the assertion that there is no mean proportional between numbers in the ratio of m + 1 to m. This result shows that serious number theoretical reasoning was being carried on by a person in the Pythagorean tradition at the time of Plato. But even so, we do not have to suppose either that this reasoning was incorporated in or built upon an "elements of the Theory of Numbers."

Pythagoreans are also associated with another way of treating numbers, the representation of them as configurations of units or "pebbles" (psēphoi). The vast majority of our information about this aspect of Pythagoreanism comes from relatively late sources, the most important of which is Nicomachus of Gerasa (c. 100 CE). Aristotle (Met. N.5, 1092b10–13) tells us that a certain Eurytus, a Pythagorean of the late fifth century, determined what the number of something, for example, a human being or a horse, is by representing its shape with pebbles in the manner of those people who bring numbers into figures, the triangle and the square. We are not able to determine exactly how Eurytus proceeded, but clearly his procedure was nothing that we would now call mathematical and suggests that even in the later fifth century Pythagorean applications of numbers to the natural world were as whimsical and idiosyncratic as Aristotle's reports and criticisms suggest.

Aristotle compares Eurytus' procedure with that of those who bring numbers into geometric figures, and this is a subject to which Nicomachus pays a good deal of attention. Square numbers are the example best known to us, and the sequence of configurations in Figure 35.16 shows how Nicomachus presents them. In this figure and in all such generations of these so-called figurate numbers, the units added to a figure to get a new figure are called a gnomon.

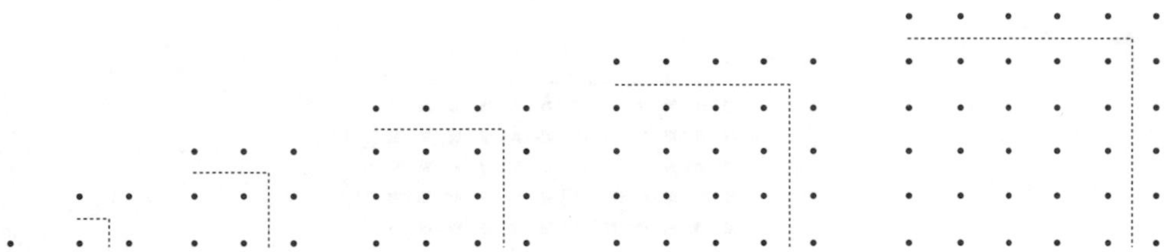

Figure 35.16

Figure 35.17, in which the last configuration is a central icon of Pythagorean numerical speculation, the *tetraktys*, shows that the nth triangular number is the sum

Figure 35.17

of the first n numbers. Nicomachus has something to say about the succeeding polygonal numbers up to the octagon, and makes clear that they go on indefinitely in the same vein.

Although our information about figurate numbers is primarily derived from later sources, most scholars believe that they and other topics discussed by Nicomachus can be assigned to "the theory of numbers of Pythagoras and his immediate followers" (van der Waerden, 1963, p. 97). I do not think the evidence is sufficient to justify this claim – ultimately one is forced to rely on the fact that the ideas seem "primitive." However, what is striking is that simple manipulations of geometrical arrays of units can yield relatively sophisticated arithmetic results without anything we would normally call proof. For example, it is easy to see from Figure 35.16 that the successive square numbers are 1, 1 + 3, 1 + 3 + 5, 1 + 3 + 5 + 7, and so on – in other words, the nth square number is the sum on the first n odd numbers. Other results can be obtained with the same kind of manipulation, e.g., rules for discovering Pythagorean triples <n,k,m>, that is, integers satisfying the "Pythagorean" formula "$n^2 + k^2 = m^2$."

When van der Waerden ascribed the last part of Book IX to early Pythagoreans he was following in the footsteps of Oskar Becker (1936), who argued that the whole of the sequence, including the result about perfect numbers, could be understood as an example of "pebble arithmetic." Later Becker (1954, p. 41 and 1957, pp. 51–2) offered an argument using these pebbles to establish – to use our terms – the irrationality of the square root of 2, that is to establish that there is no square number twice as big as another square number, that is no $n^2 = 2m^2$. Figure 35.18 makes clear that the square of an even number (a number divisible into two equal parts) is even and divisible into 4 equal square numbers. Suppose now $n^2 = 2m^2$, then the left and right halves of the figure are equal to m^2, and clearly $m^2 = 2 \cdot (n/2)^2$. So we now have two smaller numbers satisfying the original equation, and we can make the same argument with respect to them, getting two smaller numbers satisfying the equation, and so on indefinitely. But an infinite sequence of smaller and smaller numbers is not possible.

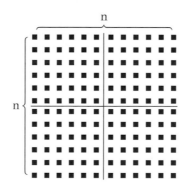

Figure 35.18

I have mentioned two passages in which Aristotle says something apparently related to the concrete representation of numbers as configurations of discrete units. Other Aristotelian passages about the Pythagoreans have been interpreted in the same way, and on their basis theories about early Pythagorean cosmology have been elaborated in conjunction with accounts of the early history of mathematics and philosophy. Whatever the status of these doctrines, it does not seem that the idea of figurate numbers had any influence on the way Plato or Aristotle thought about the subject of arithmetic. They both accept the notion that numbers are collections of units. However, Aristotle explicitly denies that these units have a position. And, although Plato does not do so explicitly, everything he says is compatible with Aristotle's view. In describing arithmetic in the *Republic* (VII, 522e–526b) Socrates stresses the fact that the conception of a unit is one of the ideas which lead the mind away from the sensible and to the intelligible world, since any sensible object is both one thing and many things and does not satisfy the condition of absolute indivisibility imposed on units by those who concern themselves with pure arithmetic.

The style of Euclid's arithmetic

The concept of figurate number is not present in Euclid's *Elements* either, although, in speaking of numbers, he does use terms like "square," "cube," "plane," "solid," and "similar," which presumably have geometric roots. Euclid's vocabulary in the arithmetic books is quite abstract. In the diagrams units and numbers are represented by straight lines, and, although it would, I suppose, be possible to argue that this representation shows that some kind of spatial thinking is involved in Euclid's arithmetic, the argument would quite miss the mark. Euclid's reasoning is purely combinatorial; the diagrams contribute nothing to the reasoning. As an example, I give his proof (VII,16) that multiplication is symmetric, i.e., that $m \cdot n = n \cdot m$:

> Let A,B be two numbers, and let A by multiplying B make C, and B by multiplying A make D. I say that C is equal to D.
> —— A
> ———B
> C ————————
> D————————
> ——E
>
> For since A by multiplying B has made C, therefore B measures C according to the units in A. But the unit E also measures the number A according to the units in it; therefore the unit E measures A the same number of times that B measures C. Therefore, alternately, the unit E measures the number B the same number of times that A measures C [by the preceding theorem]. Again since B by multiplying A has made D, therefore A measures D according to the units in B. But the unit E also measures B according to the units in it; therefore the unit E measures the number B the same number of times that A measures D. But the unit E measured the number B the same number of times that A measures C; therefore A measures each of the numbers C,D the same number of times. Therefore C is equal to D.

The diagram plays no role in the proof here, and one could not infer the character of the proof from it. One might use the diagram as a reminder of what A, B, C, D, and E are, but one could never call the diagram a representation of the proof in the way that a geometric diagram frequently is or can easily be seen as one. The reason for this difference between arithmetic and geometry is not clear to me. It would not exist if arithmetic argumentation was carried on by manipulation of configurations of monads, since such manipulations are quite of a piece with geometric constructions. The same would be true if multiplication were treated as the forming of a rectangle with the straight lines representing the numbers multiplied as sides. It appears that the turning of arithmetic into a deductive science also turned it into a more abstract science than deductive geometry, which retained its connection with intuitively grasped spatial configurations and their manipulation.

Incommensurability again

To complete this discussion of arithmetic I would like to say something about the other proof of incommensurability which I mentioned on page 704. I shall refer to it as the Aristotelian proof, since Aristotle refers to it at *APr.* I.23, 41a26–27 when he illustrates *reductio ad absurdum* by referring to the proof that "the diagonal of the square is incommensurable because odd numbers become equal to evens if it is supposed commensurable." Becker's arithmetic proof, given on page 708, might be thought of as arising from the search for Pythagorean triples <n,k,m>. It does not differ significantly from the Aristotelian proof, although that proof is most naturally thought of as an attempt to express the ratio of the side of a square to its diagonal numerically. A version of it occurs as what is universally thought to be an interpolation at the end of the main Greek manuscripts of Book X of the *Elements*. The proof requires a theory of proportionality which applies to both geometric magnitudes and numbers, and uses the fact that a square ACEF constructed on the diagonal of a given square ABCD is twice the size of ABCD (cf. Plato's *Meno* 82b–85b) (see Figure 35.19).

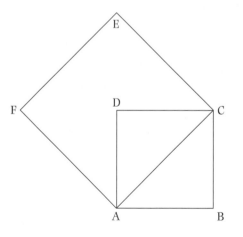

Figure 35.19

Suppose, then, that AC and AB are commensurable, i.e. (X,5), have the ratio of a number n to a number m. Then ACEF is to ABCD as n^2 to m^2, so that $n^2 = 2m^2$. At this point one could proceed as in the Becker proof, but in the proof in our manuscripts of the *Elements* reference to the impossibility of infinitely descending sequences of numbers is avoided by assuming that n and m are in least terms. Since n^2 is even by definition, so is n (IX,23), and m must be odd. Let n = 2k. But $(2k)^2 = 4k^2$, so $2m^2 = 4k^2$, $m^2 = 2k^2$, m^2 is even and so is m, contradicting the claim that m is odd.

Since Aristotle refers to this proof we can assume it is no later than the mid-fourth century. In Plato's *Theaetetus* at 147d someone named Theodorus, for whom we have no clearly independent evidence, is represented as describing on a case-by-case basis the incommensurability with a unit length of the sides of squares with areas of 3, 5, and so on up to 17. Theaetetus is thought to have been born no earlier than 420, so that the lesson which he attended, if it is anything like a historical occurrence, can be placed around 400. The fact that Theodorus started that lesson with the case of 3 rather than 2 suggests strongly that he took the latter as well understood, and because he dealt with the sides of squares there is reason to think that some version of proof we have just given was around at that time, and hence that the proof itself comes from the late fifth century. But we do not have to suppose that the proof involved reduction to least terms rather than the denial of infinitely descending numerical sequences. Moreover, we have no grounds for ruling out as earlier the proofs presented by von Fritz and Becker.

On the History of Greek Geometry

Thales

On page 693 I mentioned attributions of geometric results to Pythagoras or the Pythagoreans found in Proclus' commentary on Book I of the *Elements*, our major source for the history of Greek mathematics. The other early person who figures prominently in the commentary is Thales, standardly supposed to have flourished c. 585. Thales is first mentioned in a brief history of geometry usually thought to be importantly derived from Eudemus:

> Thales, who had traveled to Egypt [alleged to be the birthplace of geometry because of a need for accurate determinations of the areas of plots of land], was the first to introduce geometry into Greece. He made many discoveries himself and taught his successors the principles for many other discoveries, treating some things in a more universal way, others more in terms of perception. (Proclus, *In Euc.* 65.7–11)

Proclus' history is dominated by the idea that geometry was brought into the scientific form we find in the *Elements* mainly because of the work of people associated with Plato in one way or another, and he clearly wants to stress the somewhat rudimentary character of Thales' approach to the subject. However, it is very difficult to determine what Proclus or his source knew about Thales. In the course of the commentary Thales is credited with proving that the diameter of a circle bisects it, an assertion which Euclid includes in his definition of the diameter (I, def. 17) at *In Euc.* 157.10–11; with discovering the equality of the base angles of an isosceles triangle (*Elements* I,5) at *In Euc.* 250.20–251.2; with discovering but not proving scientifically the fact that the vertical angles made by two intersecting straight lines are equal (I,15; see pp. 691–2, this volume) at *In Euc.* 299.1–5; and with the theorem that pairs of triangles with two angles and one corresponding side equal are congruent (I,26) at *In Euc.*

352.14–18. In the passage on the last of these accomplishments it is pointed out that the theorem is presupposed by Thales' method for determining the distance of ships at sea. This has led some scholars to suppose that the ascriptions to Thales are inferences based on the idea that he must have justified his methods by proving the results that they presuppose. But all four of the results ascribed to Thales can be made plausible by simple operations such as "folding" a circle around its diameter or placing one triangle on top of another in an appropriate way. And it seems possible that Thales might have justified practical procedures by invoking geometrical assertions and justifying them by means of such simple operations. Such procedures would constitute a start toward a fully developed deductive geometry, but would certainly not constitute such a geometry. In this respect Thales' geometry might have been quite like the one we ascribed to the Pythagoreans on pages 691–700.

Oinopides of Chios

Thales was dead by the end of the sixth century, and Pythagoras did not live far into the fifth. The next figures in Proclus' history of geometry, Anaxagoras of Clazomenae, Oinopides and Hippocrates of Chios, and Theodorus of Cyrene, Theaetetus' teacher, are all from the later fifth century. Of these people we know most about the mathematical achievements of the two Chians. Oinopides did some work in astronomy, and according to Proclus (*In Euc.* 283.7–10) he investigated the problem of erecting a perpendicular to a given straight line (*Elements* I,12) "because he believed it was useful for astronomy." Proclus (*In Euc.* 333.5–9) also gives Oinopides credit for the discovery of another elementary construction, that of an angle equal to a given one (*Elements* I,23). It is difficult to believe that Oinopides' concern with these constructions was of a practical nature since there are simple instruments for copying angles and erecting perpendiculars. So it seems likely that Oinopides' concern was with justifying these constructions on the basis of simpler ones. But these constructions are themselves so simple as to make it quite likely that Oinopides was doing something very like the reduction to straightedge and compass which we find in the *Elements*. Because of the absence of historical evidence it is not possible to say how this came about, but if we are willing to attribute some notion of the justification of geometrical propositions to Thales and early Pythagoreans, the idea of a gradual evolution seems very plausible to me.

Hippocrates of Chios

The correctness of this description of Oinopides' concerns is to some extent confirmed by Proclus' statement (*In Euc.* 66.7–8) in the history that Oinopides' fellow Chian and approximate contemporary, Hippocrates, was the first to compose an elements of geometry. Moreover, Simplicius (*In Phys.* 60.22–69.34), writing in the sixth century CE, preserves for us what he characterizes as an expanded version of a report by Eudemus of arguments of Hippocrates showing how to square certain lunes, that is, plane figures contained by two circle arcs (see Figure 35.20). The doubly filtered presentation makes it impossible to say that we have here a fifth-century mathematical text, but some conclusions can be drawn with varying degrees of confidence from what we do have.

Figure 35.20

Aristotle refers in several places to Hippocrates' quadratures as if they were a fallacious attempt to square the circle. I have no doubt that Hippocrates was interested in squaring the circle because there is substantial evidence that this was a matter of great interest in the later fifth century. But the attempt to infer that the circle can be squared from the quadratures presented by Simplicius would be a gross logical fallacy, one which historians of mathematics are reluctant to ascribe to Hippocrates since his quadratures of the lunes themselves are quite fine pieces of mathematical reasoning.

The limitations of the evidence also makes it impossible to be certain about the exact nature of Hippocrates' style of argumentation. But there is no reason to doubt that he deduced his results in a way that is not substantively different from Euclid's. However, whatever Hippocrates' elements were like, there are serious problems in determining what the foundations of his quadratures were. Simplicius first says that Hippocrates took as a principle for his quadratures the assertion that:

(i) Similar segments of circles are to one another as the squares on their bases.

But he then implies that Hippocrates proved this as a consequence of something else he proved:

(ii) Circles are to one another as the squares on their diameters.

(ii) is proposition XII,2 of Euclid's *Elements*. It is proved by a sophisticated procedure of indefinite approximation thought to be due to Eudoxus, the grandfather of Book V. The procedure depends on a result now thought of as a principle, but which Euclid purports to prove as:

X,1 Let x_1 and y_1 be two magnitudes with x_1 greater than y_1; let $x_2 = x_1 - z_1$, $x_3 = x_2 - z_2$, etc. and let z_i always be greater than half of x_i; then some x_i will be less than y_1.

Euclid's proof of X,1 depends on an equivalent, apparently tacit, assumption that differs only slightly from the axiom of Archimedes, mentioned on page 691, that if x is greater than y, some multiple of y is greater than x.

Euclid proves as a lemma for XII,2 XII,1, which asserts that similar polygons P and P′ inscribed in circles C and C′ are to one another as the squares S and S′ on the diameters of the circles. He then argues indirectly for XII,2, assuming the case that C is to an area $C^* < C'$ as S is to S′. He inscribes in C′ a series of larger and larger polygons P_1', P_2', ..., as indicated in Figure 35.21. He shows that $P_{i+1}' - P_i'$ is greater than half of $C' - P_i'$, so that by X,1 some P_n' is greater than C^*. He inscribes in C a polygon P_n

713

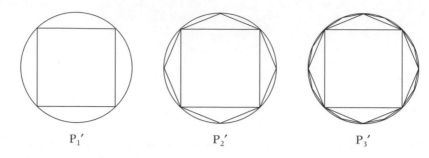

$$P_1' \qquad\qquad P_2' \qquad\qquad P_3'$$

Figure 35.21

similar to P_n'. According to XII,1, $P_n:P_n' :: S:S'$, so that $C:C^* :: P_n:P_n'$, and $C:P_n :: C^*:P_n'$. But this is impossible since C is greater than P_n and C^* is less than P_n'.

Evidence provided by Archimedes and Heron of Alexandria makes it clear that Eudoxus was the first person to prove (ii) in a way which measured up to the high standards of rigor of classical Greek mathematics. If Hippocrates "proved" it, he either argued fallaciously or relied on some kind of plausibility argument.

Simplicius gives a completely sketchy and unsatisfactory "derivation" of (i) from (ii) depending on the assertion that:

(iii) two segments of circles are similar if they are the same part of the circles of which they are segments,

a proposition which he illustrates in terms of semicircles and thirds of circles. (iii) would not be adequate as a characterization unless "are the same part of" were replaced by something like "have the same ratio to," but even in the simple case of (iii) Simplicius gives no indication of how one would establish that the squares on the bases of similar segments are to one another as the squares on the diameters of the circles of which they are segments. Finally Simplicius tries to connect (iii) with Euclid's characterization of similar segments (see Figure 35.22):

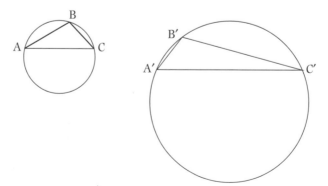

Figure 35.22

714

III, def. 23 If ABC and A'B'C' are segments of circles with bases AC and A'C', then they are similar if and only if ∠ABC = ∠A'B'C'.

Simplicius makes the connection with the weakest of plausibility considerations:

> Therefore, similar segments admit equal angles; at least the angles of all semicircles are right, and the angles of segments greater than semicircles are less than right angles and as much less as the segments are greater than semicircles, and the angles of segments less than semicircles are greater than right angles and as much greater as the segments are less than semicircles. (Simplicius, *In Phys.* 61.14–18)

Hippocrates is perhaps the pre-eminent mathematician of the late fifth century. If he reasoned in anything like the weak way we find in Simplicius, then we can presumably assume that around the time Plato was born standards of reasoning were still quite far from Euclidean, a situation which is, of course, quite compatible with there also being arguments which are fully rigorous by any standards, even in treatises where some of the argumentation is not rigorous. It also seems reasonable to assume that Hippocrates had no rigorous theory of proportion for dealing with the full generality of geometric magnitudes. But this in no way prevented him from reaching substantial geometrical results.

Before leaving Hippocrates I want to mention one other aspect of his quadratures, although I cannot describe it in detail here. In Figure 35.23 ABCDE is a semicircle with center B, EC is the perpendicular bisector of BD, and F'G' is a given straight line shorter than AD. In his argument Hippocrates determines point G on EC such that when DG is extended to meet the circle at F, FG is the same length as F'G'.

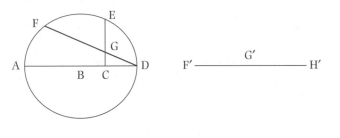

Figure 35.23

Simplicius does not tell us how Hippocrates found G. There is a quite elaborate elementary geometric argument for doing this in the particular case dealt with by Hippocrates, in which twice the square on F'G' is equal to three times the square on BD, but Simplicius' silence suggests that Hippocrates used what is called a *neusis* or verging construction in which F'G'H' is manipulated until it passes through D with G' on EC and F' on the circumference of the circle. In general such constructions cannot be carried out with just compass and straightedge, so that again we have a probable example of late fifth-century reasoning in which intuitively plausible but non-Euclidean methods are employed.

Conclusion

In this chapter on earlier Greek mathematics I have argued that the fully formal style of Euclid's *Elements* is the product of a gradual evolution which may well have substantive roots in the sixth and earlier fifth centuries. The issues I have raised do importantly concern style, and I have tried to make clear that the distinction between formal deduction from first principles and intuitive argument resting on "clearly perceived" truths is not a sharp one. Intuitive argument in elementary geometry and arithmetic can lead to surprisingly sophisticated results, as in the case of so-called pebble arithmetic; and argument without a clear sense of foundations can do the same, as in the case of Hippocrates' quadratures. Aristotle and more clearly Plato write at a time when mathematics is moving from being a variety of results justified in a variety of ways to a set of well demarcated disciplines with their own principles and methodologies. Our insight into this development is necessarily limited by the fact that extant Greek mathematical texts were produced at its end, and much of the evidence we have for what came before is colored by perceptions of its outcome.

Bibliography

Sources

Bekker, I. (ed.). (1831). *Aristoteles Graece.* Berlin: Reimer.

Burnet, J. (ed.). (1900–7). *Platonis Opera,* (5 vols.). Oxford: Clarendon Press.

Diels, H. (ed.). (1882). *Simplicii in Aristotelis Physicorum Libros Quattuor Priores Commentaria* (CAG 9). Berlin: George Reimer.

Friedlein, G. (ed.). (1873). *Procli Diadochi in Primum Euclidis Elementorum Librum Commentarii.* Leipzig: Teubner.

Heiberg, J. L. (ed.). (1910, 1913). *Archimidis Opera Omnia cum Commentariis Eutocii.* (vols. 1 and 2). 2nd edn. Leipzig: Teubner.

Heiberg, J. L. and Menge, H. (eds.). (1883–1916). *Euclidis Opera Omnia.* (9 vols.). Leipzig: Teubner.

Hoche, R. (ed.). (1866). *Nicomachi Geraseni Pythagorei Introductionis Arithmeticae Libri II.* Leipzig: Teubner.

Works Cited

Becker, O. (1936). "Die Lehre von Geraden und Ungeraden im neunten Buch der euklidischen Elemente." *Quellen und Studien zur Geschichte der Mathematik, Astronomie und Physik.* Abteilung B. 3, 533–53. Reprinted in O. Becker (1965). *Zur Geschichte der griechischen Mathematik* (pp. 125–45). Darmstadt: Wissenschaftliche Buchgesellschaft.

——. (1954). *Grundlagen der Mathematik in geschichtlicher Entwicklung.* Freiburg and Munich: Alber.

——. (1957). *Das mathematische Denken der Antike.* Göttingen: Vandenhoeck and Ruprecht.

Burkert, W. (1972). *Lore and Science in Ancient Pythagoreanism* (trans. Edwin L. Minar, Jr.). Cambridge, Mass.: Harvard University Press. (Original work published 1962.)

von Fritz, K. (1945). "The Discovery of Incommensurability by Hippasus of Metapontum." *Annals of Mathematics,* 46, 242–64. Repr. in R. E. Allen and D. J. Furley (eds.). (1970) *Studies in Presocratic Philosophy* (vol. 1, pp. 382–412). London: Routledge & Kegan Paul.

Heath, T. L. (1921). *A History of Greek Mathematics.* (2 vols.). Oxford: Clarendon Press.

——. (trans.). (1926). *The Thirteen Books of Euclid's Elements.* (3 vols.). 2nd edn. Cambridge: Cambridge University Press.

——. (1949). *Mathematics in Aristotle.* Oxford: Clarendon Press.

Hilbert, D. (1971). *Foundations of Geometry.* 10th edn. (trans. L. Unger). LaSalle: Open Court. (Original work published 1968.)

Klein, J. (1968). *Greek Mathematical Thought and the Origin of Algebra* (trans. Eva Brann). Cambridge, Mass.: MIT Press. (Original work published 1934 and 1936.)

Mueller, I. (1981). *Philosophy of Mathematics and Deductive Structure in Euclid's Elements.* Cambridge, Mass.: MIT Press.

——. (1996). "Euclid as Blundering Schoolmaster: A Problem of Proportion." In T. Berggren (ed.), *Proceedings of the Third International Conference on Ancient Mathematics* (pp. 145–52). Delphi: European Cultural Centre at Delphi.

——. (2003). "Remarks on Euclid's *Elements* I.32 and the parallel Postulate." In R. Netz (ed.), *New Questions and New Approaches in the History of Mathematics.* (Part I): *Ancient Mathematics* (= *Science in Context,* 16, 287–97).

van der Waerden, B. L. (1963). *Science Awakening* (trans. A. Dresden). New York: Wiley. (Original work published 1950.)

Vitrac, B. (trans.). (1990–2001). *Euclide d'Alexandrie, Les Eléments.* (4 vols.). Paris: Press Universitaires de France (vol. 1): Books I–IV, 1990; (vol. 2): Books V–IX, 1994; (vol. 3): Book X, 1998; (vol. 4): Books XI–XIII, 2001.

Further Reading

Artmann, B. (1999). *Euclid: The Creation of Mathematics.* New York: Springer.

Becker, O. (1933). "Eine voreudoxische Proportionenlehre und ihre Spuren bei Aristoteles und Euklid." *Quellen und Studien zur Geschichte der Mathematik, Astronomie und Physik,* Abteilung B. 2, 311–33.

Cherniss, H. (1951). "Plato as Mathematician." *Review of Metaphysics* 4, 395–405.

Dicks, D. R. (1959). "Thales." *Classical Quarterly* n.s., 9, 294–309.

Fowler, D. H. (1999). *The Mathematics of Plato's Academy: A New Reconstruction.* 2nd edn. Oxford: Clarendon Press.

von Fritz, K. (1971). *Grundprobleme der Geschichte der antiken Wissenschaft.* Berlin and New York: de Gruyter.

Høyrup, J. (1990). "Algebra and Naive Geometry. An Investigation of Some Basic Aspects of Old Babylonian Mathematical Thought." *Altorientalische Forschungen,* 17, 27–69, 262–354.

Knorr, W. R. (1975). *The Evolution of the Euclidean Elements.* Dordrecht and Boston: Reidel.

——. (1978). "Archimedes and the Pre-Euclidean Proportion Theory." *Archives internationales d'histoire des science,* 28, 183–244.

——. (1986). *The Ancient Tradition of Geometric Problems.* Boston, Basel, and Stuttgart: Birkhäuser.

——. (1990). "New Readings in Greek Mathematics: Sources, Problems, Publications." *Impact of Science on Society,* 40, 207–18.

Lan, C. E. (1985). "Eudemo y el 'catalogo de géometras' de Proclo." *Emerita,* 53, 127–57.

Mueller, I. (1982). "Aristotle and the Quadrature of the Circle." In N. Kretzmann (ed.), *The Infinite and the Continuous in Antiquity and the Middle Ages* (pp. 146–64). Ithaca, NY: Cornell University Press.

——. (ed.). (1991). *Essays on Greek Mathematics and its Later Development* (= *Apeiron* 14.4). South Edmonton: Academic Printing and Publishing.

——. (1991). "On the Notion of a Mathematical Starting Point in Plato, Aristotle, and Euclid." In A. C. Bowen (ed.), *Science and Philosophy in Classical Greece* (pp. 59–97). New York and London: Garland.

——. (1992). "Mathematical Method and Philosophical Truth." In R. Kraut (ed.), *The Cambridge Companion to Plato* (pp. 170–99). Cambridge: Cambridge University Press.

Netz, R. (1999). *The Shaping of Deduction in Greek Mathematics: A Study in Cognitive History.* Cambridge and New York: Cambridge University Press.

Neugebauer, O. (1957). *The Exact Sciences in Antiquity.* 2nd edn. Providence: Brown University Press.

Stein, H. (1990). "Eudoxus and Dedekind: On the Ancient Greek Theory of Ratios and its Relation to Modern Mathematics." *Synthese*, 84, 163–211.

Thomas, I. (ed. and trans.). (1939). *Selections Illustrating the History of Greek Mathematics.* (2 vols.). Cambridge, Mass.: Harvard University Press.

Unguru, S. (1975–6). "On the Need to Rewrite the History of Greek Mathematics." *Archive for History of Exact Sciences*, 15, 67–114.

——. (1979). "History of Ancient Mathematics: Some Reflections on the State of the Art." *Isis*, 70, 555–65.

Wedberg, A. (1955). *Plato's Philosophy of Mathematics.* Stockholm: Almqvist and Wiksell.

Zhmud, L. (1997). *Wissenschaft, Philosophie und Religion im frühen Pythagoreismus.* Berlin: Akademie Verlag.

Index Locorum

740

743

Index